W9-BUE-993

How to use your Connected Casebook

Step 1: Go to **www.CasebookConnect.com** and redeem your access code to get started.

Access Code: STXT92664859411

Step 2: Go to your **BOOKSHELF** and select your Connected Casebook to start reading, highlighting, and taking notes in the margins of your e-book.

Step 3: Select the **STUDY** tab in your toolbar to access a variety of practice materials designed to help you master the course material. These materials may include explanations, videos, multiple-choice questions, flashcards, short answer, essays, and issue spotting.

Step 4: Select the **OUTLINE** tab in your toolbar to access chapter outlines that automatically incorporate your highlights and annotations from the e-book. Use the My Notes area for copying, pasting, and editing your book notes or creating new notes.

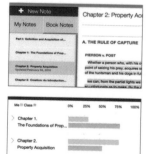

Step 5: If your professor has enrolled your class, you can select the **CLASS INSIGHTS** tab and compare your own study center results against the average of your classmates.

Is this a used casebook? Access code already scratched off?

You can purchase the Digital Version and still access all of the powerful tools listed above. Please visit CasebookConnect.com and select Catalog to learn more.

PLEASE NOTE: Each access code can only be used once. This access code will expire one year after the discontinuation of the corresponding print title and must be redeemed before then. CCH reserves the right to discontinue this program at any time for any business reason. For further details, please see the Casebook Connect End User Agreement.

PIN: 9111149716

06747

BASIC TORT LAW

EDITORIAL ADVISORS

Rachel E. Barkow
Segal Family Professor of Regulatory Law and Policy
Faculty Director, Center on the Administration of Criminal Law
New York University School of Law

Erwin Chemerinsky
Dean and Professor of Law
University of California, Berkeley School of Law

Richard A. Epstein
Laurence A. Tisch Professor of Law
New York University School of Law
Peter and Kirsten Bedford Senior Fellow
The Hoover Institution
Senior Lecturer in Law
The University of Chicago

Ronald J. Gilson
Charles J. Meyers Professor of Law and Business
Stanford University
Marc and Eva Stern Professor of Law and Business
Columbia Law School

James E. Krier
Earl Warren DeLano Professor of Law
The University of Michigan Law School

Tracey L. Meares
Walton Hale Hamilton Professor of Law
Director, The Justice Collaboratory
Yale Law School

Richard K. Neumann, Jr.
Professor of Law
Maurice A. Deane School of Law at Hofstra University

Robert H. Sitkoff
John L. Gray Professor of Law
Harvard Law School

David Alan Sklansky
Stanley Morrison Professor of Law
Faculty Co-Director, Stanford Criminal Justice Center
Stanford Law School

ASPEN CASEBOOK SERIES

Basic Tort Law

Cases, Statutes, and Problems

Fifth Edition

Arthur Best

Professor of Law
Sturm College of Law
University of Denver

David W. Barnes

Distinguished Research Professor of Law
Seton Hall University

Nicholas Kahn-Fogel

Associate Professor of Law
William H. Bowen School of Law
University of Arkansas at Little Rock

Wolters Kluwer

Copyright © 2018 CCH Incorporated. All Rights Reserved.

Published by Wolters Kluwer in New York.

Wolters Kluwer Legal & Regulatory U.S. serves customers worldwide with CCH, Aspen Publishers, and Kluwer Law International products. (www.WKLegaledu.com)

No part of this publication may be reproduced or transmitted in any form or by any means, electronic or mechanical, including photocopy, recording, or utilized by any information storage or retrieval system, without written permission from the publisher. For information about permissions or to request permissions online, visit us at www.WKLegaledu.com, or a written request may be faxed to our permissions department at 212-771-0803.

To contact Customer Service, e-mail customer.service@wolterskluwer.com, call 1-800-234-1660, fax 1-800-901-9075, or mail correspondence to:

> Wolters Kluwer
> Attn: Order Department
> PO Box 990
> Frederick, MD 21705

Printed in the United States of America.

1 2 3 4 5 6 7 8 9 0

ISBN 978-1-4548-9522-0

Library of Congress Cataloging-in-Publication Data

Names: Best, Arthur, author. | Barnes, David W., author. | Kahn-Fogel,
   Nicholas, author.
Title: Basic tort law : cases, statutes, and problems / Arthur Best,
   Professor of Law, Sturm College of Law, University of Denver; David W.
   Barnes, Distinguished Research Professor of Law, Seton Hall University;
   Nicholas Kahn-Fogel, Assistant Professor of Law, William H. Bowen School
   of Law, University of Arkansas at Little Rock.
Description: Fifth edition. | New York : Wolters Kluwer, [2018] | Series:
   Aspen casebook series | Includes bibliographical references and index.
Identifiers: LCCN 2017056080 | ISBN 9781454895220
Subjects: LCSH: Torts — United States. | LCGFT: Casebooks
Classification: LCC KF1250 .B427 2018 | DDC 346.7303 — dc23
LC record available at https://lccn.loc.gov/2017056080

SUSTAINABLE FORESTRY INITIATIVE

Certified Chain of Custody
Promoting Sustainable Forestry

www.sfiprogram.org
SFI-01681

SFI label applies to the text stock

About Wolters Kluwer Legal & Regulatory U.S.

Wolters Kluwer Legal & Regulatory U.S. delivers expert content and solutions in the areas of law, corporate compliance, health compliance, reimbursement, and legal education. Its practical solutions help customers successfully navigate the demands of a changing environment to drive their daily activities, enhance decision quality and inspire confident outcomes.

Serving customers worldwide, its legal and regulatory portfolio includes products under the Aspen Publishers, CCH Incorporated, Kluwer Law International, ftwilliam.com and MediRegs names. They are regarded as exceptional and trusted resources for general legal and practice-specific knowledge, compliance and risk management, dynamic workflow solutions, and expert commentary.

SUMMARY OF CONTENTS

CONTENTS

CHAPTER **4. PROVING BREACH**   153

CHAPTER 7. DEFENSES   321

CHAPTER 9. PROFESSIONALS   447

CHAPTER **11.** SPECIAL DUTY RULES   **547**

CHAPTER **12.** **DAMAGES**   619

CHAPTER **13.** **TRADITIONAL STRICT LIABILITY**   **681**

CHAPTER 15.   TRESPASS AND NUISANCE   789

CHAPTER **16.** **DEFAMATION** 833

CHAPTER **17.** ALTERNATIVES TO LITIGATION   **891**

TABLE OF PROBLEMS

CHAPTER **17.** **ALTERNATIVES TO LITIGATION**   **891**

PREFACE

This book takes a modern approach to teaching Torts. What makes its approach modern?

Without sacrificing the best of the classic cases, we frequently use *contemporary cases* with language, fact patterns, and issues that capture the interest of today's law school students. Our cases are edited to preserve and convey the language of the law, the factual context for judicial decisions, and the logic and precedents on which those decisions are based.

Although traditionally it has been thought that common law forms the foundation of tort law, increasingly we are coming to find that tort law is greatly influenced by legislative action, reflected in *statutory law*. Our book supplements judicial opinions with statutes, clearly delineated to support student understanding of salient topics.

Rather than inundating the student with a preponderance of undifferentiated exposition, we recognize that note material ought to be supplied judiciously with the aim of facilitating a deeper understanding of the cases and theory. We have gone one step further and organized our notes according to their function:

- *Introductory and transitional notes* promote close attention and deeper insight into doctrinal themes and issues

- *"Perspective Notes"* provide a window to seminal legal scholarship, critical analysis, and legal theory

Our students have responded with great enthusiasm to the *problem exercises* that we've created as a vehicle for analyzing the policy implications of doctrine. Increasingly, problem exercises are becoming a staple of pedagogy in newer course books. Ours are drawn for the greater part from actual cases, with citations provided. We have varied their difficulty, so students have the chance to work with both relatively easy and increasingly challenging examples. In this edition, we have changed the problems' formatting and added a Table of Problems, so that a problem covering a particular topic is easier to find. Most are essay problems focused on a single topic. We have also included at least one practice-related problem for each topic

When one looks at the interior of an older casebook, one often has difficulty discerning where a case ends and other material begins. We see no reason to add confusion to an amply challenging subject by obscuring the divisions between cases, notes, statutory material, and problem exercises. Generous use of heading levels and consistently clear design elements make it a pleasure to navigate through *Basic Tort Law*.

We have modeled our writing style for this book on the clarity and directness that have always been the hallmarks of fine legal analysis and writing. As with the appearance of our pages, we hope that our readers will find that a straightforward writing style helps set the stage for effective learning.

This edition reflects the results of a comprehensive survey of the adopters of earlier editions. It adds a new section on the intentional tort of false imprisonment and new cases including a straightforward introduction to joint and several liability, an abnormally dangerous activities case and a violation of custom case involving contemporary issues. We have reordered several cases and clarified the facts and discussion of others. We have, of course, updated all of the statutes.

We hope that our colleagues will find these materials as stimulating to teach from as we have in our own classes. Even more important, we hope that students will enjoy our modern style of teaching, which uses clarity as a springboard for a deeper and more nuanced understanding of the law.

Arthur Best
David W. Barnes
Nicholas Kahn-Fogel

January 2018

ACKNOWLEDGMENTS

For their generosity in commenting on various parts of earlier versions of the manuscript, we thank Professors John Jacobi, Ahmed Bulbulia, Timothy Glynn, Tristin Green, Denis McLaughlin, Thomas Russell, Joyce Saltalamachia, Alexander Tsesis, and Edward Hartnett. We also thank Douglas Lipsky, Shlomo Singer, and Cynthia Wilson for work as research assistants.

Deans at the University of Denver College of Law and Seton Hall University School of Law provided generous support for this project. It is a pleasure to offer thanks for that to Deans Kathleen Boozang, Patrick Hobbes, Martin Katz, Dennis O. Lynch, Nell Jessup Newton, and Mary Ricketson. We appreciate the contributions of Jessica Barmack, Susan Boulanger, Melody Davies, and Carol McGeehan at Aspen Publishers to many aspects of this book. In particular, we thank them for obtaining a large number of anonymous reviews of early drafts and for helping us to analyze and learn from those reviews.

We benefitted greatly this year from the advice and wisdom of torts colleagues at many law schools. Professor Jon Van Patten was particularly generous with his time and insight. Professors Patricia Bradford, Janie Kim, Larry Frolik, and Enrique Armijo also provided thoughtful comments on the previous edition. Professors Nancy Ehrenreich, Pat Chew, Ezra Friedman, Joi Monteil, Josh Weishart, and Peter Huang contributed to our understanding of what law professors value in teaching materials. We have tried to take all of their comments into account in the new edition. We finally express our appreciation to Professor Marianna Brown Bettman, whose comments and suggestions throughout the years have been very useful to us.

We are grateful for permission to include excerpts from the following articles:

Michael J. Saks, Do We Really Know Anything About the Behavior of the Tort Litigation System — And Why Not?, 140 U. Pa. L. Rev. 1147 (1992), copyright Michael J. Saks 1992. Reprinted by permission.

Steven D. Smith, The Critics and the "Crisis": A Reassessment of Current Conceptions of Tort Law, 72 Cornell L. Rev. 765 (1987), copyright Cornell University 1987. Reprinted by permission.

BASIC TORT LAW

CHAPTER 1

INTRODUCTION

I. In General

An honest introduction to this book would probably be "Jump in and see what happens." Your goal for the first year of law study is to learn how to learn and to begin to understand how lawyers analyze legal questions. You will do your best learning by observation, participation, and investigation. And as you immerse yourself in legal analysis, you will begin to develop ideas about the role of law in society and about how courts and legislatures create legal rules. You will also become familiar with typical solutions our legal system offers to various types of recurring problems.

Even though figuring things out for yourself is the essence of legal education, you might like to have some basic information about the legal world you are about to enter. This Introduction explains how this book is organized, gives you some basic background about the history of tort law, and offers excerpts from scholarly articles that will give you some points of reference as you begin your own work of finding out about tort law.

II. Categories of Tort Law

Tort law is a collection of principles describing the legal system's civil (non-criminal) response to injuries one person inflicts on another. When one person acts in a way that causes some injury to another person, tort law sometimes requires the injurer to pay money to the victim. A plaintiff (the injured person) may win damages from a defendant by proving that the defendant intentionally injured the plaintiff. These cases are called intentional tort cases. In other cases, a plaintiff can win damages by showing that even though the defendant did not mean to do anything that the law prohibits, the defendant failed to act as carefully as the law requires. These instances are negligence cases. Finally, in some circumstances a defendant will be liable to a plaintiff even if the defendant acted carefully and had no intent to injure the plaintiff. These cases are called strict liability cases.

Torts defined

1

III. Organization of This Book

This book begins with a discussion of intentional torts, such as assault, battery, and intentional infliction of emotional distress. These torts involve situations where one person intentionally contacts another in a harmful or offensive way, makes another fear that a harmful or offensive contact is impending, or causes another person severe emotional distress. In some circumstances, a person is entitled to (privileged to) harm another, such as when the person is acting in self-defense or with the consent of the other person. The book considers the defenses for each tort that may protect the person from liability.

Next, the book covers the basic aspects of the unintentional torts of negligent and reckless conduct, where one person's carelessness injures another. The injured person may recover damages if the careless person had an obligation of care to the injured person or failed to be reasonably careful, and the careless person's conduct caused the injured person's harm. The analysis of liability for careless conduct includes some policy limitations that define when one person owes a duty to another or when the causal connection between conduct and harm is close enough to support liability. The analysis also involves questions of how liability for damages is shared when more than one person has been careless. Finally, a defendant may avoid or reduce liability by proving a defense, such as the plaintiff's own negligence, or by showing that the defendant is entitled to immunity.

Some important elaborations of basic negligence doctrines are the book's next topics, including the special duties owed by professionals to their clients and by occupiers of land to people who enter the land. Other special issues involve the extent of a negligent person's liability to those who suffer economic or emotional harm in the absence of physical harm. A chapter on damages describes the categories of harms for which damages may be recovered and how those damages are proved and measured.

The book's remaining chapters treat strict liability in traditional contexts, strict liability for product-related injuries, negligence-based liability for product-related injuries, and the torts of trespass, nuisance, and defamation. The book concludes with a chapter on reform measures that provide substitutes for tort lawsuits.

Judicial decisions are the primary materials in this book. They show how courts have dealt with each of tort law's topics. Also, where legislatures have responded to the same topics, illustrative statutes are included. They describe how the law varies from state to state and how courts and legislatures may take different approaches to the same problems. Throughout the book, you will find problems that permit you to test your comprehension of the basic principles. In addition, special notes draw your attention to perspectives on the law to provoke thought or aid your understanding of the rationales for legal principles.

IV. Typical Stages of Tort Litigation

Most of the cases in this book are appellate court opinions. In each of them, a party who lost in the lower court has claimed that the judge in that lower court erred in some way and that the lower court judge's decision should be reversed. Understanding these appeals requires understanding the stages of a lawsuit, so a detailed study of civil procedure is essential. Nevertheless, it helps to understand the basics at this point.

Complaints and Initial Responses.   A lawsuit begins when a plaintiff files a complaint in a trial court. This document alleges that certain facts are true and that because these facts are true, the defendant should be required to pay damages to the plaintiff or give the plaintiff some other relief. A defendant has two options at this point. One is to ask the judge to dismiss the plaintiff's claim on the ground that even if the plaintiff's allegations are true, the plaintiff would have no legal right to recover damages from the defendant. The other is to file an answer to the complaint, admitting or denying the allegations. The answer may also describe defenses that the defendant believes protect the defendant from liability and facts relating to the plaintiff's conduct or the particular circumstances of the case that support a decision in favor of the defendant. After filing an answer, the defendant has another opportunity to ask that the case be dismissed. When a trial court considers a motion to dismiss made at any time, the court compares the parties' allegations and submissions with the legal principles the court believes apply to the type of case the plaintiff has described.

Summary Judgment.   Usually after discovery is completed, either a plaintiff or a defendant can move for summary judgment. (Discovery is the process in which parties may obtain information from each other and third parties and develop the evidence they plan to introduce to support their positions.) A court may enter judgment in favor of the moving party if, based on the evidence that the nonmoving party could produce at trial, the applicable legal doctrines would require a judgment against the non-moving party and for the moving party. Summary judgment eliminates the need for a trial when there are no genuine disputes about the facts.

Trial.   At a trial, parties present information in the form of testimony and physical things. The "trier of fact" is either a jury or, in what is called a bench trial, a judge. Once the trier of fact determines what it thinks is the truth about what happened, the trier of fact applies legal rules to those facts. The judge instructs the jury about the relevant legal rules. These jury instructions specify what result is required (judgment for the plaintiff or judgment for the defendant) according to what factual findings the trier of fact makes. If the trier of fact decides in the plaintiff's favor, ordinarily it also decides how much money the defendant should pay the plaintiff.

Judgments as a Matter of Law.   At several stages during the trial, each party may ask the judge to rule in its favor on the ground that, even if the opposing party's evidence is accepted as true, the opposing party should still lose. A court might enter judgment as a matter of law (sometimes called "directing a verdict") in favor of the defendant if the plaintiff fails to offer sufficient evidence to support an essential element of the plaintiff's case, such as the fact that the defendant's conduct was a cause of the plaintiff's injury. Or a judge might enter a judgment (direct a verdict) in favor of the plaintiff if no reasonable jury, viewing all of the evidence, could find against the plaintiff.

Judgment.   The trial court enters a judgment for the plaintiff, awarding damages or other relief, or for the defendant, depending on the verdict the jury has rendered. If the judge believes that no reasonable jury could have found in favor of a party, the judge may grant judgment as a matter of law (formerly called a judgment notwithstanding the verdict or judgment N.O.V.) to that party's opponent. Finally, a trial judge may decline to enter any judgment at all and may order that the case be tried again if the judge believes that there were errors in the administration of the trial, that the jury's deliberations seem to have been affected by consideration of improper factors, or that the verdict is against the weight of the evidence.

Appeal.   A party who loses at any stage of the litigation may be entitled to appeal. The appellate court will consider all of the trial judge's actions about which the parties have raised and preserved objections. With regard to facts, the appellate court will treat as true all the facts that the jury may have found to be true, as long as there was any reasonable basis in the evidence for the jury's conclusion. The appellate court may affirm the trial court's action, may reverse it, or may reverse it and remand for a new trial.

V. How Tort Law Works Now: An Empirical View

Compared with other law school courses, a torts course has the advantage or disadvantage of dealing with topics that people have already thought about a great deal before entering law school. Not too many of us have feelings about civil procedure prior to law study, but most people have lots of ideas about how the legal system treats events like automobile accidents and product-related injuries. It's helpful that tort law has an inherent interest, but it might be counterproductive to begin the study of tort law against a background of popular myths. The article below presents some basic empirical data about how tort law relates to injuries people suffer. It also compares that view of reality with a rival description composed of what the article calls anecdotal evidence.

MICHAEL J. SAKS, DO WE REALLY KNOW ANYTHING ABOUT THE
BEHAVIOR OF THE TORT LITIGATION SYSTEM — AND WHY NOT?*
140 U. Pa. L. Rev. 1147 (1992)

. . . The use of anecdotal evidence has been unusually popular in discussions about the nature of the litigation system.[30] Perhaps the use of anecdotes is not entirely inappropriate or unfair, given the central role cases play in law as the device for sampling social facts, the unit of accretion of judicial authority, and the principal tool for educating new lawyers. . . .

Nevertheless, anecdotal evidence is heavily discounted in most fields, and for a perfectly good reason: such evidence permits only the loosest and weakest of inferences about matters a field is trying to understand. Anecdotes do not permit one to determine

---

* Copyright Michael J. Saks 1992. Reprinted by permission.

[30] One example is the case of the burglar who fell through the skylight. According to this anecdote, the burglar sued and won damages of $206,000 plus $1,500 per month for life. Another case involved a plaintiff in a medical malpractice action who claimed that she lost her powers of extrasensory perception due to negligent treatment with a CAT scan. She won the case and was awarded $1 million in damages. A third example involved "[a]n overweight man with a history of coronary disease [who] suffered a heart attack trying to start a Sears lawnmower. He sued Sears, charging that too much force was required to yank the mower's pull rope. A jury in Pennsylvania awarded him $1.2 million, plus damages of $550,000 for delays in settling the claim."

either the frequency of occurrence of something or its causes and effects. They do no better in enlightening us about the behavior of the tort litigation system. . . .

Although the validity of the anecdotes themselves is the least important issue, their validity deserves mention. Some litigation system anecdotes are simply fabricated. Others are systematically distorted portrayals of the actual cases they claim to report.[34] More important than what we learn about these stories, perhaps, is what we learn about ourselves and our remarkable credulity. Even when true, anecdotes enjoy a persuasive power that far exceeds their evidentiary value.

. . . Anecdotes about undeserving plaintiffs are intriguing or outrageous and have been repeated often in the media. Consequently, people readily believe that the category of undeserving plaintiffs dominates the system. . . .

The first thing to determine is how many actionable injuries occur. . . .

The most interesting and legally useful studies of base rates have been done in relation to medical malpractice. In these studies, medical experts evaluate a large sample of hospital records to indentify iatrogenic injuries [harm caused by medical treatment] and determine which were negligently produced. Perhaps the best known study was conducted jointly by the California Hospital Association and the California Medical Association and published in 1977. This study found that 79 per 10,000 patients had suffered negligent injuries. The most recent such study, conducted in 1990 by researchers based at the Harvard School of Public Health, found that 100 of 10,000 New York hospital discharges suffered from negligent iatrogenic injuries. . . .

One of the most remarkable features of the tort system is how few plaintiffs there are. A great many potential plaintiffs are never heard from by the injurers or their insurers. The first and most dramatic step in this process of nonsuits is the failure of so many of the injury victims to take measures to obtain compensation from those who injured them.

By comparing the cases determined to be instances of negligent injury with insurance company records, the study of California medical malpractice found that at most only 10% of negligently injured patients sought compensation for their injuries. Even for those who suffered major, permanent injuries (the group with the highest probability of seeking compensation) only one in six filed. . . . The Harvard Medical Practice Study found that in New York State "eight times as many patients suffer an injury from medical negligence as there are malpractice claims. Because only about half

---

[34] Consider the three anecdotes presented supra note 30. The "burglar" who fell through the skylight was a teenager who climbed onto the roof of his former high school to get a floodlight. See Bodeine v. Enterprise High Sch., 73225, Shasta County Superior Court (1982), reported in Fred Strasser, *Tort Tales: Old Stories Never Die*, Nat'l L.J., Feb. 16, 1987, at 39. The fall rendered him a quadriplegic. See id. A similar accident at a neighboring school killed a student eight months earlier. See id. School officials already had contracted to have the skylights boarded over so as to "solve a . . . safety problem." Id. The payments were the result of a settlement; the case did not go to trial. See id. In the CAT scan/ESP case, the woman did claim economic loss due to her inability to perform her job as a psychic. But her claimed permanent injuries were due to a severe allergic reaction to a pre-scan drug injection. The judge instructed the jury not to consider the claim for loss of ESP and associated economic damages. The judge also set aside the million dollar award as either excessive or inconsistent with his instructions, and a new trial was ordered. See Haimes v. Hart, 81-4408, Philadelphia Court of Common Pleas, reported in Strasser, supra, at 39. In the third case, the man who suffered the heart attack was a 32-year-old doctor with no history of heart disease, and the lawnmower was shown to be defective. See Daniels & Martin, . . . at 325. Daniels and Martin also note that only the Time magazine version of the case gave accurate details. See id.; George J. Church, *Sorry, Your Policy Is Canceled,* Time, Mar. 24, 1986, at 20, 20.

the claimants receive compensation, there are about sixteen times as many patients who suffer an injury from negligence as there are persons who receive compensation through the tort system." . . .

Although trials are the legal system's iconographic center, they also are its chief aberration. Fewer than ten cases in one hundred proceed to trial. The great majority are resolved through negotiated settlements. . . . Out of 10,000 actionable negligent injuries, approximately 9600 disappeared when injury victims did not pursue a claim. Half of those that were presented to attorneys never became filed lawsuits. Of the 200 cases filed (2% of those negligently injured), 170 will be settled, paying most plaintiffs less than their actual losses. Trials will commence for about thirty of these cases. Of the 1,000,000 patients who were not negligently injured, an estimated 2400 will mistakenly regard their injuries as resulting from negligence, and about one third of those become filed lawsuits. . . .

Of the cases that finally arrive at trial for the judge or jury to take their turn at sorting, in which ones is liability found and why? Can we explain and predict trial outcomes? Or are they random and unpredictable? If patterns exist, have they changed over time? . . .

The best known research on juries, conducted by Kalven and Zeisel, found a rate of agreement of about 80% between the liability decisions of judges and juries in both criminal and civil trials.[310] Recall that these findings derived from the process of having hundreds of judges in thousands of jury trials provide their own assessment of the case while the jury was deliberating so the judges' views could be compared with those of the jury.

Of the basic level of agreement between judges and juries, Kalven observed that "the jury agrees with the judge often enough to be reassuring, yet disagrees often enough to keep it interesting." More refined analyses of the data strengthened the conclusion that the jury understood the evidence (as well as the judge did). . . .

A considerable body of research both on actual juries and in well controlled trial simulations supports the conclusion that juries make reasonable and rational decisions. . . .

. . . On average, awards undercompensate losses. A recent study of medical malpractice awards found that each one percent increase in loss resulted in an additional one-tenth to one-twentieth of a percent increase in award.

The benchmarks most often used to assess jury awards have been decisions of other decision-makers in comparable circumstances. We previously discussed the research of Kalven and Zeisel in regard to the rate of judge-jury agreement on liability verdicts. When judge and jury both decided for the plaintiff, juries awarded more damages than judges would have 52% of the time, while judges awarded more 39% of the time and they were in approximate agreement 9% of the time. Overall, juries awarded 20% more money than judges would have. Similarly, recent findings by the National Center for State Courts found that jury awards in tort trials were higher than judges' awards. Who came closer to the "correct" amount? We cannot say. . . .

At nearly every stage, the tort litigation system operates to diminish the likelihood that injurers will have to compensate their victims. . . . At the same time that it provides such infrequent and partial compensation, it succeeds in generating huge overestimates of its potency in the minds of potential defendants. . . .

---

[310] [Harry Kalven, Jr. & Hans Zeisel, The American Jury at 58 (1966). — EDS.]

The absence of empirically validated models of the behavior of the litigation system, incorporating data about both system and the environment which produces its cases, leads to a panoply of problems. Reform efforts must guess at which problems are real and which are mythical. Being the product of guesswork, some reforms will produce effects contrary to the intentions of their makers; indeed, some already have. We will fail to anticipate future changes in litigation activity caused by changes in the law or the legal system or the social, economic, or technological environment of the litigation system. Because they will arrive unexpectedly and their causes will be poorly understood, the effects of those changes will repeatedly arrive as new "crises." . . .

NOTES TO "DO WE REALLY KNOW ANYTHING ABOUT THE BEHAVIOR OF THE TORT LITIGATION SYSTEM — AND WHY NOT?"

1. *Another Famous Case: Hot Coffee.* A lawsuit involving McDonald's and its coffee has become very well known. The plaintiff bought a cup of coffee at a drive-thru window. She suffered serious burns when some of the coffee spilled in her lap. At trial, she showed that McDonald's served its coffee at temperatures significantly hotter than the temperatures used by other fast food outlets, and that the company had maintained that practice despite knowledge of many other serious burns over a ten-year period. A jury awarded the victim $160,000 in compensatory damages and $2.7 million in punitive damages. The trial court modified the award to a total of $640,000, and the parties later settled the case for an undisclosed amount. See *McDonald's Settles Lawsuit over Burn from Coffee,* Wall St. J., Dec. 2, 1994, at B6.

2. *Statistical Information About Possible Claims.* The Saks article states that many potential plaintiffs never seek compensation. One reason for this in the medical malpractice field may be that the victims know about an unwanted outcome but never learn that a medical mistake was made. The Harvard School of Public Health finding that one out of every hundred hospital cases involved harm produced by medical treatment was based on analysis of hospital records by researchers who had no connections with the hospitals or the patients. While the researchers identified cases that involved mistakes, the patients in those cases were not necessarily aware of those mistakes.

3. *Gaps Between Perception and Reality.* The article suggests that the tort system makes it unlikely that injurers will be required to compensate victims, that the victims who do receive compensation are usually undercompensated, and that many victims never seek compensation at all. The article also suggests that potential defendants overestimate the power of the tort system. Despite these facts, the tort system continues to be our society's main method of resolving disputes about injuries. Understanding the reasons for its continued prominence may be an underlying inquiry in the torts course.

VI. How Tort Law Serves Society

Tort law has developed over time through the adjudication of a huge number of cases. While courts seek to do justice in these individual cases, they usually do not attempt to describe the overall role of tort law in society. Scholars, on the other hand, often try to find patterns and broad rationales in the courts' output of articulated doctrines and decided cases. This section describes various goals tort law may serve, including compensating injured people, deterring risky behavior, punishing wrongdoers, and resolving disputes.

Compensation and Deterrence.

The classic tort law treatise describes compensation and deterrence as two primary factors that explain tort doctrines:

> A Recognized Need for Compensation. It is sometimes said that compensation for losses is the primary function of tort law and the primary factor influencing its development. It is perhaps more accurate to describe the primary function as one of determining when compensation is to be required. Courts leave a loss where it is unless they find a good reason to shift it. A recognized need for compensation is, however, a powerful factor influencing tort law. Even though, like other factors, it is not alone decisive, it nevertheless lends weight and cogency to an argument for liability that is supported also by an array of other factors. . . .
>
> Prevention and Punishment. The "prophylactic" factor of preventing future harm has been quite important in the field of torts. The courts are concerned not only with compensation of the victim, but with admonition of the wrongdoer. When the decisions of the courts become known and defendants realize that they may be held liable, there is of course a strong incentive to prevent the occurrence of the harm. Not infrequently one reason for imposing liability is the deliberate purpose of providing that incentive.

Prosser & Keeton on Torts §4 (5th ed.).

A Legal Realist Perspective.

Professor J. Clark Kelso, in an article titled "Sixty Years of Torts: Lessons for the Future," 29 Torts & Ins. L.J. 1 (1993), described the interest in how tort law serves society as having arisen from the legal realism movement in the first half of the twentieth century. Legal realism views law as a set of formal rules that provide little guidance as to what behavior would be tolerated by society. According to Professor Kelso, legal realism viewed law as being "conceptually empty" and as having "little predictive value." People subscribing to this point of view are called "realists" because they believe that legal rules are so easy to manipulate that courts can come to any results they want based on considerations such as their political viewpoints or, as is famously said, "what the judge had for breakfast." Lawyers have no trouble manipulating rules. You will find that part of a law school education is learning to interpret rules to favor a client's interests.

If legal rules are just a formality, then how should they be evaluated? Legal realists looked at the consequences of legal rules and court decisions applying those rules. For instance, did a federal law requiring all states to set a 55 mph speed limit on interstate highways really reduce speeds? Are laws prohibiting bigamy or extramarital sex really enforced? Do people who are harmed by the negligence of doctors usually sue, or do they just let it go? Do big corporations usually win or lose? Are juries more generous than judges?

Evaluating the consequences of legal rules caused legal scholars to ask what purposes we want legal rules to serve. What goals should tort law serve? Can tort law and the legal procedures used to apply it be refined to promote those goals? It is not easy to get people to agree on goals. Scholars, lawmakers, and judges have different political views and favor different interests. Plaintiffs and defendants argue for conflicting outcomes. When a defendant argues that he or she should not be obliged to pay for the harm suffered by the plaintiff, the defendant is implicitly arguing that his or her conduct was acceptable.

The different perspectives of plaintiffs and defendants illustrate two obvious consequences of a torts case. A court decides whether a defendant should pay money to an injured plaintiff, so one consequence is that the power of the state is used to compensate one party at the expense of another. Compensation of plaintiffs is usually viewed as one consequence and goal of tort law. From the point of view of the defendant and people like the defendant who create similar risks of harming others, the court's decision gives them notice that future acts like the defendant's may subject them to liability. Facing potential liability, those potential defendants may be discouraged from acting in ways that create risks for others. Prophylactic deterrence, or prevention, is usually viewed as a second consequence and goal of tort law. Compensation and deterrence are identified in the Prosser and Keaton treatise as key concepts for understanding tort law. Professor Kelso described them as the "twin pillars of tort law."

Conflicts Between Compensation and Deterrence. Compensation and deterrence seem like clear and acceptable goals, but they may conflict. For example, A might start to attack B and then B might act in self-defense and harm A. If our only interest were compensation, tort law could require someone like B to pay A for the costs of A's harm. But we probably want to encourage people to protect themselves from harm, so making someone like B pay for harm to an attacker like A is unappealing. And making every defendant pay would interfere with the goal of using tort law to discourage some types of behavior (such as careless conduct) and encourage other types (such as careful conduct).

While an exclusive focus on compensation would lead to too much compensation, an exclusive focus on deterrence could lead to other undesirable results. Deterrence focuses on discouraging only some kinds of conduct, such as unjustifiably risky conduct. Thus, people who are harmed by other kinds of conduct might not be compensated even though it might be nice to compensate everyone who suffers harm. And full-fledged deterrence might restrain even careful conduct that results in harm. If society wished to avoid all harms, it might have to outlaw automobiles — or at least surround every car with huge bumpers and line the highways with rubber padding. That would not be very sensible, and it is clearly not the choice our society has made.

The effects of compensation are easy to see: victorious tort plaintiffs get paid. But it is not so easy to see how or whether defendants may be deterred. To begin with, many defendants have liability insurance that pays for their damages. While this may result in higher future premiums and insurers insisting on changes in behavior, the deterrent effect is less obvious than the compensation effect of a judicial decision. Professor Kelso thought that this could cause courts typically to err on the side of giving too much compensation even it results in deterring desirable conduct, particularly if the defendant is a big corporation or is backed by a big insurance company.

One challenge of tort law is to find the right balance of compensation and deterrence. In most situations, to recover damages a plaintiff must show that the defendant's actions involved some degree of fault. In some unusual situations, a defendant whose conduct causes an injury must pay for the injury even if the defendant's conduct was free from fault. These are usually situations in which the business itself is inherently risky and cannot be made safe even with careful conduct.

Shifting Views of the Social Function of Tort Law.
Professor Kelso also argued that the balance between compensation and deterrence shifts in times of economic prosperity and hardship. He described the period from World War II to the early 1970s as a period of prosperity in which arguments in favor of greater compensation prevailed over arguments opposing increases in tort liability. Parties who were more likely to be tort defendants (corporations and insurance companies) complained that tort law was expanding in a way that increased the likelihood that they would be held liable for injuries they caused. Parties who were more likely to be or to represent individual tort plaintiffs argued that making businesses and insurance companies liable for more injuries was fair and beneficial to society. Making businesses liable was fair because businesses should bear the costs associated with their profit-making activities. Increased liability was also viewed as beneficial to society because it spread the risk. "Spreading the risk" means that instead of one person bearing the cost of an injury personally, businesses or insurance companies would pass on those costs to all of their consumers and policy holders in the form of higher prices. Professor Kelso argued that when times are good, tort law is more likely to increase compensation.

According to this view, there is pressure to protect business during tough economic times. Professor Kelso observed:

> In times of plenty it was somewhat easier for courts to ignore complaints from business that tort liability was too burdensome. After all, one additional lawsuit usually will not damage a company irreparably, especially when the theory is that tort liabilities ultimately will be distributed widely through the insurance industry and slight increases in prices. But when times are hard, expansive tort liability can drive companies over the edge. The insurance industry itself may be imperiled, and it may be impossible for a company to raise prices in light of world competition. These realities bring to the surface some of the negative consequences of expansive tort liability. Thus, during periods of recession or very slow growth, courts are more likely to focus their attention upon the deterrence goal of tort law (rather than the compensation goal), and are more likely to restrict tort liability in order to ensure that an optimal level of deterrence is attained (and a destructive over-deterrence is avoided).

A long period of slower economic growth in the United States began in the 1970s due in part to oil shortages and fear of inflation. Conservative Ronald Reagan was president during the 1980s and favored business interests. In the scholarly community the law and economics movement began to articulate arguments promoting concern for deterrence over compensation. Modern arguments for putting strict limits on recovery of damages for pain and suffering and making it harder for people to recover for harms resulting from defective products — in addition to many other tort doctrines you will study in this book — reflect this shift in focus from compensation to deterrence.

Criticism of Compensation and Deterrence as Goals.
Criticism of the compensation and deterrence goals focuses on the inability of courts to measure accurately the appropriate amount of money an injured person should receive and of tort law generally to establish incentives so that people creating risks will take

enough care without investing too much in accident prevention. The following excerpt describes common critiques of the goals of compensation and deterrence and introduces two additional functions of tort law: punishing wrongdoers and providing a process for resolving disputes and propounding social norms.

STEVEN D. SMITH, THE CRITICS AND THE "CRISIS": A REASSESSMENT OF CURRENT CONCEPTIONS OF TORT LAW

72 Cornell L. Rev. 765 (1987)

. . . Critics argue that tort law employs irrational criteria in deciding which injury victims should be compensated and which should not.* If tort law's function is to compensate persons who have suffered loss as a result of accidental injury, the critics argue, it makes little sense to compensate persons injured by another's negligence while denying compensation to those injured by non-negligent human activities, illnesses, natural catastrophes, or physical and mental disabilities. Such injuries may certainly be as severe as in the case of a negligently inflicted harm. Moreover, in each instance the injuries result from accidental or fortuitous causes. If a policy compensating for accidental injuries is justified, the critics assert, then the system should compensate all such victims. . . .

After deciding which claimants to compensate, tort law faces the daunting task of determining how much these claimants should receive. Critics argue that here too the system fails dismally. Compensation's cardinal principle prescribes that injured plaintiffs should receive an amount necessary to make them "whole," that is, to restore them to the position they would have occupied but for the defendant's tortious conduct. This "make whole" principle is difficult enough to apply to a plaintiff's purely monetary loss, such as medical expenses or future lost earnings. However, when we apply the standard to nonpecuniary intangible losses such as pain and suffering, psychic injury, or distress from the loss of a loved one, quantifying such losses in monetary terms becomes not merely difficult but conceptually impossible. . . .

Critics of the system respond to the deterrence rationale in two ways. Some broadly assert that tort law has no substantial deterrent effects. The deterrence view of tort law, these critics argue, rests upon wildly unrealistic assumptions about human knowledge, decision making, and conduct. To believe that tort law deters inefficient behavior, one must accept that (1) human beings know what the law is; (2) they have the information and ability to perform the sophisticated cost/benefit calculus upon which the deterrence rationale relies; and (3) humans are rational creatures who actually make and act upon such cost/benefit calculations. Critics claim that such assumptions contradict not only ordinary experience and observation, but psychological research as well.

The second objection to the deterrence rationale suggests that even if the psychological assumptions of the deterrence view were sound, tort law still would not produce optimal levels of safety investment. Optimal levels would be achieved only if all actual injury costs—and no more than actual costs—were allocated to the injury-causing activities. If injurers are liable for less than actual costs, their incentive to adopt safety

---

* Copyright Cornell University 1987. Reprinted by permission.

measures is insufficient; if they are liable for more than the actual costs of injuries, they overinvest in safety. . . .

A third objective often attributed to the tort law system is the punishment of wrongdoers. Critics of this ostensible function assert two principal objections. One holds simply that punishment is not a legitimate state function. This objection equates punishment with simple vengeance—a relic of the primitive need to "get even." . . .

A second objection to the punishment function asserts that even if punishment is an appropriate state function, tort law is a poor instrument for the task. Tort rules often impose liability upon persons or institutions for conduct that cannot be considered blameworthy. Strict liability doctrines expressly renounce "fault" as a requisite for liability. Even negligence principles employ an "objective" standard of reasonable conduct that may impose liability upon persons who lack the subjective ability to understand or conform to objective standards and who thus cannot be considered culpable. . . .

The criticisms considered [above] are powerful ones. In fact, they may be too powerful. The cogency of those criticisms rests, after all, upon the assumption that compensation, deterrence, and punishment are the objectives of tort law. If tort law is as ill-suited to accomplishing compensation, deterrence, and punishment as critics suggest, then we must question whether it is at all proper to attribute those goals to tort law. If tort law instead has a primary function different than compensation, deterrence, and punishment, then it is hardly pertinent to attack tort law for failing to achieve those ends. The very incompatibility of the tort law system with such objectives suggests that critics, as well as many proponents, have misconceived the proper function of that system. . . .

[This article proposes that tort law's primary function is simply to resolve disputes.] Dispute resolution's full significance becomes apparent only when viewed in the broader context of the social universe which human beings inhabit. That universe is composed, in large part, of a system of social norms—"shared expectations and guidelines for belief and behavior." In much the same way that gravitational and kinetic laws give order to the physical universe, social norms give order to the social universe: all of us rely constantly upon norms in deciding how we should think, speak, and behave and in anticipating how others in society will think, speak, and behave. Without such norms, social intercourse would be unpredictable and chaotic. Recognized norms are thus an essential condition of rational social life. . . .

In sum, society must enforce its norms, but it must not enforce them too rigorously or mechanically. Although no single test or criterion can wholly reconcile these competing needs, one factor which powerfully influences the response to norm violation is the resulting harm or lack of harm. A trivial norm violation, such as a breach of table etiquette, usually harms no one; such a violation therefore results at most in social disapproval. At the other extreme, criminal law enforces norms, such as the norm against taking human life, whose violation consistently results in serious harm. Between these extremes lies a set of norms that, although important, are not as imperative as those enacted into criminal law. Such middle level norms constitute the essence of tort law, which seeks to capture such norms with formulas that often amount to little more than open-ended, incorporative allusions to whatever pertinent social norms may exist. Thus, when people act in ways that affect others, tort law requires them to use the care expected of "the reasonable person." Similarly, manufacturers must produce goods that conform to "consumer expectation."

Tort law imposes sanctions for violations of these norms only when such violations result in injuries that in turn generate disputes among members of society. By limiting itself to dispute resolution, tort law avoids overly rigid enforcement of norms and directs its efforts to maintaining those norms which society most clearly wants reinforced. . . .

From a societal perspective, therefore, tort law's dispute resolution function is vital not merely because it prevents private violence, but more importantly because it reinforces the normative order upon which society depends. . . .

The narrow view of personal "injury" likely derives from the typical computation of tort damages, which generally enumerates the kinds of injuries for which the victim may recover damages in tort cases. The resulting list usually includes lost income, medical expenses, pain and suffering, and emotional distress or psychic injury. To be sure, a tort victim often suffers all of these kinds of injury, which this essay will refer to collectively as "actual loss." However, the list typically omits an important element of the tort victim's injury: it fails to recognize the victim's consciousness of having been wronged by the violation of a social norm. This aspect of injury — the sense of having been wronged — might be termed the "sense of injustice." . . .

Recognition of the full character of a tort injury leads to a deeper understanding of tort law's remedial function. Tort law's treatment of injury is not confined to payment of monetary damages. Although responsive to the victim's "actual loss," monetary damages do not specifically treat the victim's sense of injustice, an essential part of her injury. Rather, the tort process's response to injury includes the liability determination and the assessment of damages against the tortfeasor. A system of social insurance would go only halfway: although it would address the victim's "actual loss," it would lack the tort process's comprehensiveness and sensitivity to the full scope of the victim's injury. . . .

This essay does not pretend to make the case for preserving the tort law system. Its aim has been more modest. The essay simply claims that tort law should be understood — and hence evaluated — as a system for resolving disputes generated by the violation of social norms. Whether the system adequately performs its dispute resolution function remains an open question and is a question that can be answered not in the abstract, but only through experience and continuing practical evaluation. . . .

NOTES TO "THE CRITICS AND THE 'CRISIS': A REASSESSMENT OF CURRENT CONCEPTIONS OF TORT LAW"

1. *Observing Compensation and Deterrence.*   Professor Kelso pointed out that the compensation effects of tort doctrines are typically easier to observe than the deterrent effects of those doctrines. Compensation is easy to observe, because it consists of court orders that defendants pay money to plaintiffs. Changes in people's conduct may be difficult to link to deterrent effects of tort law, because changes in conduct may be the result of many influences.

It is easier to see the political pressures for expanding and contracting tort liability. As you study tort law, you will see how legal rules affect people who are likely to create risks and people who are likely to receive injuries. You will also see how changes in legal rules reflect different views of the appropriate amounts of compensation and deterrence.

2. *Additional Rationales for Tort Law.*   Professor Smith's article proposes that tort law may serve values in addition to compensation, deterrence, and punishment. He proposes that identifying injustice, even if it occurs only in a minority of instances of unjustly inflicted injuries, may be of great value to an individual who has felt wronged. He suggests that deterrence may come about indirectly through the institution of tort law, because the social norms that people learn are probably influenced by tort doctrines. Also, punishment through the tort system may be sensible if it is viewed as a type of restorative justice, because it can reinforce social norms to the victim and also to society as a whole.

CHAPTER 2

INTENTIONAL TORTS

I. Introduction

Functions of tort law. Tort law allows plaintiffs to obtain compensation for injuries inflicted on them by defendants or to obtain court orders that stop ongoing or anticipated injuries. As a whole, tort doctrines express society's standards for what types of conduct are acceptable and what kinds of effects one actor may impose on another. Tort law can direct compensation to victims of prohibited conduct and may also deter people from acting in those forbidden ways.

Categories of tort law. Tort law allows plaintiffs to recover for a wide variety of harms. For some types of harm, in order to recover damages a plaintiff must prove that the defendant intended to affect the plaintiff in some way that the law forbids — these are called *intentional tort* cases. For some other types of injury, a plaintiff may recover without proof that the defendant meant to cause a prohibited effect if the plaintiff proves that the defendant's conduct was less careful than the law requires — these are *unintentional tort* cases. *Negligence* and *recklessness* are the two main types of unintentional tort cases. Finally, a plaintiff may sometimes recover for an injury without proving either that the defendant meant to cause harm or that the defendant's conduct lacked some required degree of carefulness — these are *strict liability* cases.

Types of intentional torts. Tort law treats many types of conduct as intentional torts. This chapter covers *battery, assault, false imprisonment,* and *intentional infliction of emotional distress*. These tort actions represent one societal response to types of conduct that are highly reprehensible. They also illustrate a framework that applies to other types of intentional torts and to most other types of tort actions as well.

II. Battery

Intentional tort doctrines protect a person from having someone interfere with that person's recognized *legal interests*. A legal interest is a right or privilege that the law

Def. protects. The intentional tort of battery protects a person's bodily integrity, the right to be free from intentionally inflicted contact that is harmful or offensive.

A. Intent to Contact

Waters v. Blackshear introduces some important battery concepts. Be sure to note: (1) what the defendant did that interfered with the plaintiff's bodily integrity (the defendant's conduct); (2) what the law requires for the conduct to be characterized as a battery; and (3) why the court thought this defendant's conduct fit those requirements.

If someone picked you up and threw you at another person, thereby injuring that person, the law would not treat *you* as having committed an intentional tort. In a tort case, the plaintiff must satisfy an *act requirement* by showing that the defendant committed a voluntary act. Polmatier v. Russ examines this issue as well as the range of definitions of "intent" that may be used in intentional tort cases. The decision also elaborates on the rules for categorizing an intentional tort as a battery and illustrates some differences between tort and criminal law rules.

WATERS v. BLACKSHEAR

591 N.E.2d 184 (Mass. 1992)

WILKINS, J.

On June 6, 1987, the minor defendant placed a firecracker in the left sneaker of the unsuspecting minor plaintiff Maurice Waters and lit the firecracker. Maurice, who was then seven years old, sustained burn injuries. The defendant, also a minor, was somewhat older than Maurice. The defendant had been lighting firecrackers for about ten minutes before the incident, not holding them but tossing them on the ground and watching them ignite, jump, and spin.

Maurice and his mother now seek recovery in this action solely on the theory that the minor defendant was negligent. The judge instructed the jury, in terms that are not challenged on appeal, that the plaintiffs could recover only if the defendant's act was not intentional or purposeful and was negligent. The jury found for the plaintiffs, and judgment was entered accordingly. The trial judge then allowed the defendant's motion for judgment notwithstanding the verdict on the ground that the evidence showed intentional and not negligent conduct. We allowed the plaintiffs' application for direct appellate review and now affirm the judgment for the defendant.

We start with the established principle that intentional conduct cannot be negligent conduct and that negligent conduct cannot be intentional conduct. The only evidence of any conduct of the defendant on which liability could be based, on any theory, is that the defendant intentionally put a firecracker in one of Maurice's sneakers and lit the firecracker.

The defendant's conduct was a battery, an intentional tort. See Restatement (Second) of Torts §13 (1965) ("An actor is subject to liability to another for battery if [a] he acts intending to cause a harmful or offensive contact with the person of the other or a third person, or an imminent apprehension of such a contact, and [b] a harmful contact with the person of the other directly or indirectly results");

1 F.V. Harper, F. James, Jr., O.S. Gray, Torts §3.3, at 272-273 (2d ed. 1986) ("to constitute a battery, the actor must have intended to bring about a harmful or offensive contact or to put the other party in apprehension thereof[. A] result is intended if the act is done for the purpose of accomplishing the result or with knowledge that to a substantial certainty such a result will ensue") [footnote omitted]); W.L. Prosser & W.P. Keeton, Torts, §9, at 41 (5th ed. 1984) ("The act [of the defendant] must cause, and must be intended to cause, an unpermitted contact").

The intentional placing of the firecracker in Maurice's sneaker and the intentional lighting of the firecracker brought about a harmful contact that the defendant intended. The defendant may not have intended to cause the injuries that Maurice sustained. The defendant may not have understood the seriousness of his conduct and all the harm that might result from it. These facts are not significant, however, in determining whether the defendant committed a battery. See Horton v. Reaves, 186 Colo. 149, 155, 526 P.2d 304 (1974) ("the extent of the resulting harm need not be intended, nor even foreseen"). The only permissible conclusion on the uncontroverted facts is that the defendant intended an unpermitted contact. . . .

NOTES TO WATERS v. BLACKSHEAR

1. *Parties and Pleadings.* The person who brings an issue to a court's attention in a tort case is usually called the *plaintiff* or *petitioner* or *complainant*. The person whose conduct a plaintiff believes has caused or is about to cause an injury is usually called a *defendant* or *respondent*. A lawsuit begins with written documents called *pleadings*. A plaintiff files a formal written document called a *complaint*, stating that a defendant has done (or is doing) something for which tort law provides a remedy. The defendant responds to the complaint in a formal written *answer*. The answer may dispute the plaintiff's description of the defendant's actions. On the other hand, a defendant's answer may agree with the plaintiff's description of the defendant's actions but argue either that: (1) tort law allows those actions; or (2) tort law ordinarily forbids those actions but that something about the plaintiff's conduct or some other aspect of the case should prevent the court from ruling in the plaintiff's favor.

2. *Plaintiff's Characterizations of Facts and Legal Doctrines.* Every tort case must have a *legal theory* and a *factual theory*. A legal theory is a statement of the type of tort that the plaintiff claims the defendant committed. A legal theory determines what the plaintiff must prove to obtain the remedy he or she seeks. The plaintiff's choice of legal theory determines what facts are relevant. A factual theory is a statement of what caused the plaintiff's injury, including a statement of what the defendant did or did not do in the context of the significant circumstances related to the injury. A plaintiff will win a tort case if: (1) the plaintiff can persuade the trier of fact (the jury, or the judge in a case tried without a jury) that, as a matter of historical fact, some events occurred; and (2) the jurisdiction's legal doctrines support the conclusion that when events of the type the plaintiff described have occurred, a plaintiff is entitled to a remedy.

In *Waters*, the legal theory at stake on appeal involved the tort of battery. The plaintiff had sought recovery on another theory, negligence, probably because the defendant was covered by an insurance policy that would pay damages for negligent conduct but not for intentional torts. If the defendant's conduct satisfied the requirements for battery, then the plaintiff's negligence claim had to fail. What facts and/or events must a party prove to have occurred to support a finding that a battery occurred? What was the factual theory (presented by the defendant) to support a finding of battery? What facts did the defendant claim were true and sufficient to support a finding that the defendant's conduct was a battery?

3. *Variety of Legal Theories.*   A person may act without intending to invade the legally protected interests of another. If the defendant carelessly dropped the fire-cracker and it happened to fall into Waters's shoe, there would be no battery. There might, however, be a tort in these situations based on another legal theory such as recklessness or negligence. Learning tort law involves learning which legal theory fits the facts of a case.

4. *Variety of Sources of Law.*   The *Waters* court relied on several types of author-ity in reaching its conclusion: the Restatement (Second) of Torts, two treatises on tort law, and a decision from another court. Judges and lawyers (and law students) regu-larly rely on all of these resources to find accurate statements of the law. Statutes and regulations are additional sources of law discussed in this book.

5. *Restatements of Tort Law.*   The Restatement (Second) of Torts is a publication of a private organization called the American Law Institute (ALI). Members of the ALI are prominent judges, lawyers, and law professors. The ALI has prepared a large number of Restatements of the law for different fields of law. The Restatements are intended to codify common law doctrines as developed in state courts; where state court doctrines are not uniform, the authors of the Restatements either incorporate the doctrine they consider best or state that there are rival points of view on an issue. Restatement provisions are not binding authority in a state unless they have been adopted by that state's courts. The Restatements usually have had great persuasive power, though, because of the prestige of the members of the committees that have produced them and because of the quality of the analysis they have presented. A Restatement (Third) of Torts is currently being produced by the ALI.

POLMATIER v. RUSS
537 A.2d 468 (Conn. 1988)

GLASS, A.J. . . .

The plaintiff, Dorothy Polmatier, executrix of the estate of her deceased husband, Arthur R. Polmatier, brought this action against the defendant, Norman Russ, seeking to recover damages for wrongful death. The state trial referee, exercising the power of the Superior Court, rendered judgment for the plaintiff. The defendant has appealed from that judgment. We find no error.

The trial court's memorandum of decision and the record reveal the following undisputed facts. On the afternoon of November 20, 1976, the defendant and his two month old daughter visited the home of Arthur Polmatier, his father-in-law. Polmatier lived in East Windsor with his wife, Dorothy, the plaintiff, and their eleven year old son, Robert. During the early evening Robert noticed a disturbance in the living room where he saw the defendant astride Polmatier on a couch beating him on the head with a beer bottle. Robert heard Polmatier exclaim, "Norm, you're killing me!" and ran to get help. Thereafter, the defendant went into Polmatier's bedroom where he took a box of 30-30 caliber ammunition from the bottom drawer of a dresser and went to his brother-in-law's bedroom where he took a 30-30 caliber Winchester rifle from the closet. He then returned to the living room and shot Polmatier twice, causing his death.

About five hours later, the defendant was found sitting on a stump in a wooded area approximately one half mile from the Polmatier home. The defendant was naked and his daughter was in his arms wrapped in his clothes, and was crying. Blood was found on his clothes, and he had with him the Winchester rifle, later determined to be the murder weapon.

The defendant was taken to a local hospital and was later transferred to Norwich Hospital. While in custody he was confined in Norwich Hospital or the Whiting Forensic Institute. The defendant was charged with the crime of murder pursuant to General Statutes §53a-54a(a), but was found not guilty by reason of insanity pursuant to General Statutes §53a-13. Dr. Walter Borden, a psychiatrist, testified at both the criminal and this civil proceeding regarding the defendant's sanity. In the present civil case Borden testified that, at the time of the homicide, the defendant was suffering from a severe case of paranoid schizophrenia that involved delusions of persecution, grandeur, influence and reference, and also involved auditory hallucinations. He concluded that the defendant was legally insane and could not form a rational choice but that he could make a schizophrenic or crazy choice. He was not in a fugue state. The trial court found that at the time of the homicide the defendant was insane. . . .

After a trial to the court, the court found for the plaintiff . . . and awarded compensatory damages. On appeal the defendant claims that the trial court erred in failing to apply the following two-pronged analysis to his claim: first, whether the defendant intended the act which produced the injury; and second, whether he intended the resulting injury. . . .

. . . The first prong is whether the defendant intended the act that produced the injury. The defendant argues that for an act to be done with the requisite intent, the act must be an external manifestation of the actor's will. The defendant specifically relies on the Restatement (Second) of Torts §14, comment b, for the definition of what constitutes an "act," where it is stated that "a muscular movement which is purely reflexive or the convulsive movements of an epileptic are not acts in the sense in which that word is used in the Restatement. So too, movements of the body during sleep or while the will is otherwise in abeyance are not acts. An external manifestation of the will is necessary to constitute an act, and an act is necessary to make one liable [for a battery]. . . . The defendant argues that if his "activities were the external manifestations of irrational and uncontrollable thought disorders these activities cannot be acts for purposes of establishing liability for assault and battery." We disagree.

We note that we have not been referred to any evidence indicating that the defendant's acts were reflexive, convulsive or epileptic. Furthermore, under the Restatement (Second) of Torts §2, "act" is used "to denote an external manifestation of the actor's will and does not include any of its results, even the most direct, immediate, and intended." Comment b to this section provides in pertinent part: "A muscular reaction is always an act unless it is a purely reflexive reaction in which the mind and will have no share. Although the trial court found that the defendant could not form a rational choice, it did find that he could make a schizophrenic or crazy choice. Moreover, a rational choice is not required since "[a]n insane person may have an intent to invade the interests of another, even though his reasons and motives for forming that intention may be entirely irrational." 4 Restatement (Second), Torts §895J, comment c. The following example is given in the Restatement to illustrate the application of comment c: "A, who is insane, believes that he is Napoleon Bonaparte, and that B, his nurse, who confines him in his room, is an agent of the Duke of Wellington, who is endeavoring to prevent his arrival on the field of Waterloo in time to win the battle. Seeking to escape, he breaks off the leg of a chair, attacks B with it and fractures her skull. A is subject to liability to B for battery."

We recognize that the defendant made conflicting statements about the incident when discussing the homicide. At the hospital on the evening of the homicide the defendant told a police officer that his father-in-law was a heavy drinker and that he used the beer bottle for that reason. He stated he wanted to make his father-in-law suffer for his bad habits and so that he would realize the wrong that he had done. He also told the police officer that he was a supreme being and had the power to rule the destiny of the world and could make his bed fly out of the window. When interviewed by Dr. Borden, the defendant stated that he believed that his father-in-law was a spy for the red Chinese and that he believed his father-in-law was not only going to kill him, but going to harm his infant child so that he killed his father-in-law in self-defense. The explanations given by the defendant for committing the homicide are similar to the illustration of irrational reasons and motives given in comment c to §895J of the Restatement, set out above.

Under these circumstances we are persuaded that the defendant's behavior at the time of the beating and shooting of Polmatier constituted an "act" within the meaning of comment b, §2, of the Restatement. Following the majority rule in this case, we conclude that the trial court implicitly determined that the defendant committed an "act" in beating and shooting Polmatier. Accordingly, the trial court did not err as to the first prong of the defendant's claim.

The second prong of the defendant's claim is that the trial court erred in failing to determine whether the defendant intended the resulting injury to the decedent. The defendant argues in his brief that "[t]he trial court must satisfy the second prong of its intentional tort analysis with a finding that the defendant acted 'for the *purpose* of causing' [1 Restatement (Second) of Torts §13, comment d] or with a '*desire* to cause' [1 Restatement (Second) of Torts §8A] the resulting injury." (Emphasis added.) This argument is more persuasive in its application to proof of the elements of crimes than in its relation to civil liability.

In the criminal law the "act" and the "intent" of the actor are joined to determine the culpability of the offender. For example, the allegations of the essential elements of murder are as follows: "A person is guilty of murder when, with intent to cause the death of another person, he causes the death of such person." General Statutes §§53a-54a(a). The defendant claims that "[i]ntent need not involve ill will or malice, but must include a design, purpose and intent to do wrong and inflict the injury." Under the Restatement, "intent" is used "to denote that the actor desires to cause consequences of his act, or that he believes that the consequences are substantially certain to result from it." 1 Restatement (Second), Torts §8A. Comment b to §8A of the Restatement provides in pertinent part: "All consequences which the actor desires to bring about are intended, as the word is used in this Restatement. Intent is not, however, limited to consequences which are desired. If the actor knows that the consequences are certain, or substantially certain, to result from his act, and still goes ahead, he is treated by the law as if he had in fact desired to produce the result." We have stated that "[i]t is not essential that the precise injury which was done be the one intended." Alteiri v. Colasso, 168 Conn. 329, 334, 362 A.2d 798 (1975).

As discussed above, the defendant gave the police and Borden several reasons why he killed Polmatier. Under comment c to §895J of the Restatement, it is not necessary for a defendant's reasons and motives for forming his intention to be rational in order for him to have the intent to invade the interests of another. Considering his statements to the police and to Borden that he intended to punish Polmatier and to kill him, we are persuaded that the defendant intended to beat and shoot him. . . .

There is no error.

NOTES TO POLMATIER v. RUSS

1. The Act Requirement. The *Polmatier* court described a two-step process to determine if a defendant committed an intentional tort. The first question is whether the defendant "intended the act that produced the injury." This is the *act requirement*. Plaintiffs must satisfy the act requirement in all tort cases. The second question is whether the defendant "intended the resulting injury to the decedent." This is the *intent requirement*. Plaintiffs are obligated to satisfy the intent requirement only in intentional tort cases.

The act must be an *external manifestation* of the *actor's will*. This definition of "act" has two parts. First, an external manifestation is something that can be perceived. Even "standing still" or "doing nothing" can be perceived. What external manifestations were significant in establishing the plaintiff's case? Second, the movement or failure to move must result from the actor's will. A movement or failure to move when asleep ("or while the will is otherwise in abeyance") is not a manifestation of will. What reasons support the court's treatment of Russ's movements as manifestations of his will?

2. The Intent Requirement. The intent requirement for all intentional torts is described in Restatement (Second) of Torts §8A: "Intent . . . denotes that the actor desires to cause consequences of his act, or that he believes that the consequences are substantially certain to result from it."

The Restatement (Third) of Torts: Liability for Physical and Emotional Harm §1 defines "intent" as follows:

A person acts with the intent to produce a consequence if:

  (a) the person acts with the purpose of producing that consequence: or
  (b) the person acts knowing that the consequence is substantially certain to result.

For battery, the plaintiff must establish that the defendant intended to cause a contact that is harmful or offensive. Intent may be shown by demonstrating that the actor either (a) desired the harmful or offensive contact or (b) believed that the harmful or offensive contact was substantially certain to result. Other intentional torts protect different interests, and their intent requirements are modified accordingly.

What evidence supports a finding that Russ desired to invade Polmatier's interest in being free from harmful contact?

3. Intending the Precise Injury. As the *Polmatier* court stated, it is not essential that the precise injury that was done be the one intended. The tort of battery only requires that the actor intend a conduct that is harmful or offensive. Similarly, in Waters v. Blackshear, the court observed that for determining whether the defendant committed a battery it did not matter that the defendant may not have intended to cause the injuries that the plaintiff sustained, known the seriousness of the conduct, or desired all the harm that might result.

4. *Distinctions Between Tort Law and Criminal Law.* A person's conduct may be both a tort and a crime. For example, when one person shoots and kills another, the injury might be called a battery in tort law and murder in criminal law.

Different rules govern the treatment of torts and crimes. In criminal cases, the decision to initiate a case is made by a public official (a prosecutor); in tort cases it is made by a private individual (a plaintiff). The degree of persuasiveness the prosecutor must achieve in a criminal case is usually "beyond a reasonable doubt." The plaintiff in a tort case need only satisfy a "preponderance of the evidence" standard of persuasiveness. The sanctions usually imposed in criminal law are deprivation of a defendant's liberty by imprisonment (or by lesser requirements such as probation) or a fine that must be paid to the government. Tort law requires a defendant to pay money to a plaintiff and may also restrict a defendant's future conduct.

When a court orders a torts defendant to pay damages, it is said that the defendant *has been found liable.* In criminal law, when a court fines or jails a criminal defendant, it is said that the defendant *has been found guilty.* A torts case typically involves issues of liability rather than guilt.

Problems
Desire or Substantial Certainty

A. In a case involving the following facts, the court concluded that the defendant was substantially certain that he would injure the plaintiff. Which facts provide support for that conclusion?

> Regina Labadie was injured by a snowball thrown by William Semler, who was 17 years old. William testified that Regina Labadie pulled up in front of William's house and began yelling obscenities about his mother, Patricia Semler. William testified that he asked Labadie to leave many times but she refused. William further testified that because he wanted Labadie to "shut up and leave," he reached down to the side of the road and made a snowball. He then threw it at Labadie from a distance of 10 to 15 feet, hitting her in the face. William specifically testified that he did not intend to injure Labadie. William was an accomplished high school athlete in football and baseball. William admitted that he was aware that Labadie's car window was down. William took no precautions to avoid hitting Labadie in the face.

See Labadie v. Semler, 585 N.E.2d 862 (Ohio Ct. App. 1990).

B. You represent Larry Garley. He is interested in appealing the trial court's judgment, summarized below, that he battered the plaintiff. What do you advise him about his chances of success? Does the evidence support the trial court's conclusion that Garley intended a contact with the plaintiff, given tort law's definition of intent?

> Betty England was an employee at Dairy Queen who allegedly suffered humiliation and embarrassment as a result of an act of her manager, Larry Garley, though she suffered no physical harm. Betty testified that Larry used profane language when he told her to prepare the hamburgers correctly. She stated Larry, while looking straight at her, then threw the hamburger, which hit her on the leg, and that she argued with him about the matter and several patrons observed the incident, which caused her to cry and become emotionally upset. Larry testified he threw the hamburger toward a trash can because he was

disgusted with the way the hamburgers were being prepared. He stated he did not see where the hamburger hit, but noticed some of it splattered on Betty and another employee. He testified he did not intend to hit anyone with the hamburger. He stated he and Betty argued about the matter and he told Betty to go home. The other employee did not see Larry throw the hamburger, but observed a hamburger hit the floor and splatter mayonnaise and mustard on her and Betty. The court found that the intent requirement for battery was met.

See England v. S&M Foods, Inc., 511 So. 2d 1313 (La. Ct. App. 1987).

Perspective: Historical Developments

The distinction between intentional torts and nonintentional torts derives from legal theories used in the King's Court in England in the thirteenth century. Intentional torts were included in a theory called trespass *vi et armis,* which is an interference with a legally protected interest of another "by force and arms." Liability was imposed for harms caused by direct physical force, such as hitting another over the head with a log. Indirectly caused or *consequential* harms, such as leaving a log in the road, were included in a different theory, called "trespass on the case." In early English jurisprudence, trespass *vi et armis* did not require proof of intent to cause an injury and trespass on the case did not require proof of careless conduct, as intentional torts and the tort of negligence do now. The only available defense was proof that it was not the defendant's act that caused the harm, but rather the act of a third person or an act of God. The act requirement remains in modern law, but a fault requirement has been added: intent for the intentional torts and conduct falling short of some standard of carefulness for unintentional torts. See generally Elizabeth C. Price, *Toward a Unified Theory of Products Liability: Reviving the Causative Concept of Legal Fault,* 61 Tenn. L. Rev. 1277 (1994).

B. Intending Contact That Is Harmful

Nelson v. Carroll considers whether an actor who commits a battery may be liable for harms the actor did not intend and could not reasonably have foreseen. It also shows how a plaintiff's factual theory relates to the harm for which the plaintiff seeks damages.

NELSON v. CARROLL
735 A.2d 1096 (Md. 1999)

CHASANOW, J. . . .

We summarized the essential facts of this case [on a previous occasion when the case was before the court]:

Carroll shot Nelson in the stomach in the course of an altercation over a debt owed to Carroll by Nelson. The shooting occurred on the evening of July 25, 1992, in a private nightclub in Baltimore City that Nelson was patronizing. Carroll, who was described as being a "little tipsy," entered the club and demanded repayment by Nelson of the $3,800 balance of an $8,000 loan that Carroll had made to Nelson. Nelson immediately offered to make a payment on account but that was unsatisfactory to Carroll. At some point Carroll produced a handgun from his jacket.

Carroll did not testify. There were only two witnesses who described how the shooting came about, Nelson and Prestley Dukes (Dukes), a witness called by Carroll. Dukes testified that when Nelson did not give Carroll his money Carroll hit Nelson on the side of the head with the handgun and that, when Nelson did not "respond," Carroll "went to hit him again, and when [Carroll] drawed back, the gun went off." Nelson, in substance, testified that he tendered $2,300 to Carroll, that Carroll pulled out his pistol and said that he wanted all of his money, and that the next thing that Nelson knew, he heard a shot and saw that he was bleeding.

Nelson v. Carroll, 711 A.2d 228, 229 (Md. Ct. Sp. App. 1998). . . .

Nelson's sole contention before this Court is that he was entitled to a motion for judgment on the issue of liability for battery. He contends that the evidence that Carroll committed a battery is uncontested. Specifically, Nelson asserts that Carroll's primary defense on the issue of liability — that the discharge of the handgun was accidental — is unavailable under the circumstances of this case. . . .

A motion for judgment may be made at the close of evidence offered by an opposing party or after all the evidence has been presented. In considering a motion for judgment in a jury trial, "the court shall consider all evidence and inferences in the light most favorable to the party against whom the motion is made." Md. Rule 2-519(b). Our task, therefore, is to determine whether, considering the essential elements of a tort claim for battery, there is any dispute over material facts from which a jury could conclude that Carroll had not committed a battery when he shot Nelson. Since the only disputed fact relates to whether Carroll shot Nelson accidentally as he was striking him, we need only address the narrow question of whether, under the facts of this case, the defense that the shot was fired accidentally is capable of exonerating Carroll of liability.

A battery occurs when one intends a harmful or offensive contact with another without that person's consent. See Restatement (Second) of Torts §13 & cmt. d (1965). . . . A battery may occur through a defendant's direct or indirect contact with the plaintiff. In this case, Carroll unquestionably committed a battery when he struck Nelson on the side of his head with his handgun. Likewise, an indirect contact, such as occurs when a bullet strikes a victim, may constitute a battery. "[I]t is enough that the defendant sets a force in motion which ultimately produces the result. . . ." Prosser & Keeton, The Law of Torts §9, at 40 (5th ed. 1984). Thus, if we assume the element of intent was present, Carroll also committed a battery when he discharged his handgun, striking Nelson with a bullet. . . .

Carroll's defense that he accidentally discharged the handgun requires us to examine the "intent" requirement for the tort of battery. It is universally understood that some form of intent is required for battery. See Restatement (Second) of Torts §13 (1965) ("An actor is subject to liability to another for battery if . . . he acts *intending* to cause a harmful or offensive contact. . . ." (Emphasis added); Prosser & Keeton, The Law of Torts §9, at 39 (5th ed. 1984) (Battery requires "an act *intended* to cause the plaintiff . . . to suffer such a contact. . . ." (Emphasis added)); Harper, James & Gray, The Law of Torts §3.3, at 3:9 (3d ed. 1996) ("[T]o constitute a battery, the actor must have *intended* to bring about a harmful or offensive contact or to put the other party in apprehension thereof." (Emphasis added) (footnote omitted)). It is also clear, however, that the intent required is not a specific intent to cause the type of harm that occurred:

> The defendant's liability for the resulting harm extends, as in most other cases of intentional torts, to consequences which the defendant did not intend, and could not reasonably have foreseen, upon the obvious basis that it is better for unexpected losses to fall upon the intentional wrongdoer than upon the innocent victim.

Prosser & Keeton, The Law of Torts, §9, at 40 (5th ed. 1984).

On the other hand, a purely accidental touching, or one caused by mere inadvertence, is not enough to establish the intent requirement for battery. See, e.g., Steinman v. Laundry Co., 109 Md. 62, 66, 71 A. 517, 518 (1908) (finding a lack of intent for battery where "[t]here [was] no pretense here that this contact of his knee with hers was wilful, angry or insolent, and *the only inference from her testimony is that it was purely accidental,* as in the case of one stumbling, and, in his fall coming in contact with the person of another." (Emphasis added.)

The intent element of battery requires not a specific desire to bring about a certain result, but rather a general intent to unlawfully invade another's physical well-being through a harmful or offensive contact or an apprehension of such a contact. As Professors Harper, James, and Gray observe in their treatise, the intent element of battery must be carefully analyzed:

> It has been seen that to constitute a battery a defendant's conduct must be characterized by the factor of intent. But it is necessary to analyze the mental element more carefully. All that is necessary is (a) that the actor engage in volitional activity and (b) that he intend to violate the legally protected interest of another in his person. . . .

Harper, James & Gray, The Law of Torts §3.3, at 3:13-14 (3d ed. 1996).

Thus, innocent conduct that accidentally or inadvertently results in a harmful or offensive contact with another will not give rise to liability, but one will be liable for such contact if it comes about as a result of the actor's volitional conduct where there is an intent to invade the other person's legally protected interests. . . .

The only reasonable inference that can be drawn from the circumstances of this shooting, which in essence are uncontested, is that Carroll's actions evidenced an intent to commit a battery. Carroll presented no evidence disputing the fact that he carried a loaded handgun and that he struck Nelson on the head with the gun. The merely speculative evidence upon which Carroll claims the shot was an accident was Dukes' testimony that when Carroll "went to hit him again . . . the gun went off." In contrast, the evidence is undisputed that Carroll possessed a handgun which he openly carried into the nightclub, that Carroll struck Nelson with the handgun, and that the handgun discharged simultaneously as Carroll went to strike Nelson again. Indeed, taking every possible inference in favor of Carroll, the gunshot occurred as he attempted to strike Nelson with the gun. Under such circumstances, no reasonable inference can be drawn that Carroll lacked the required intent to commit the battery. . . .

The law imposes upon Carroll the responsibility for losses associated with his wrongful actions. It is of no import that he may not have intended to actually shoot Nelson since the uncontested facts demonstrate that he did intend to invade

Nelson's legally protected interests in not being physically harmed or assaulted. He violated those interests by committing a . . . battery when he threatened Nelson with the handgun and struck Nelson on the head. Even assuming as we must that Carroll did not intend to inflict the particular damages arising from the gunshot wound, it is more appropriate that those losses fall to Carroll as the wrongdoer than to Nelson as the innocent victim. Therefore, the motion for judgment as to liability should have been granted, with the only question remaining for the jury being the damages resulting from the discharge of the gun.

NOTES TO NELSON v. CARROLL

1. *Identifying Significant Facts.*   In Nelson v. Carroll, the defendant's actions included: (1) moving a gun toward the plaintiff and hitting him with it; and (2) moving a gun toward the plaintiff in a way that resulted in a bullet wound. Assuming that each of these actions could be characterized as a battery, from the plaintiff's point of view, which one provides the better basis for a lawsuit? From which action did the plaintiff suffer the greater harm?

2. *Defining "Injury" and "Harm."*   Even if the defendant in *Nelson* had no intention to hit the plaintiff with a bullet, the defendant was still subject to liability for battery. As the court stated, "the intent required is not a specific intent to cause the type of harm that occurred."

The Restatement (Second) of Torts distinguishes between an *injury* and a *harm*. Section 7 says that, to commit an intentional tort, an actor needs only to intend an injury. An *injury* "denotes the invasion of any legally protected interest of another."

A *harm* "denotes the existence of loss or detriment in fact of any kind to a person." An injury causes a harm if the injury actually has a detrimental effect on the plaintiff. According to the Restatement (Second) of Torts §7 comment b, harm is

> the detriment or loss to a person which occurs by virtue of, or as a result of, some alteration or change in his person, or in physical things, and also the detriment resulting to him from acts or conditions which impair his physical, emotional, or aesthetic well-being, his pecuniary advantage, his intangible rights, his reputation, or his other legally recognized interests.

The harm Carroll had in mind when he raised the gun was different from the harm Nelson suffered. In an intentional tort case, the plaintiff is required only to prove that the defendant inflicted a legally recognized injury. Damages are measured, however, by the amount of harm suffered.

3. *Direct and Indirect Contacts.*   The simplest battery cases involve direct contact between some part of the defendant's body and some part of the plaintiff's body (such as a contact between a defendant's fist and a plaintiff's chin). As *Nelson* shows, however, contact between the plaintiff's body and something put in motion by the defendant (e.g., a bullet) can also support a battery claim.

How should tort law respond if a defendant does not cause contact with the plaintiff's body but causes contact with something the plaintiff is holding or something the plaintiff is wearing? A treatise states:

> Thus, if all other requisites of a battery against the plaintiff are satisfied, contact with the plaintiff's clothing, or with a cane, a paper, or any other object held in the plaintiff's hand,

will be sufficient; and the same is true of the chair in which the plaintiff sits, the horse or the car the plaintiff rides or occupies, or the person against whom the plaintiff is leaning.

W. Page Keeton et al., Prosser & Keeton on the Law of Torts §9, at 39-40 (5th ed. 1984).

Problem
Factual Theories and Intent to Contact

In the following case, on what conduct does the plaintiff base a claim? Is battery an appropriate legal theory?

> Plaintiff, awaiting her husband's arrival, was sitting in a booth at Paul's Barbecue at 2:00 a.m. with her sister-in-law. After they had been there a short time, they were joined in the booth by a witness to the events, and a few minutes later the defendant came over. The plaintiff had a cup of coffee and a glass of water on the table in front of her when the defendant arrived; the defendant had a cup of coffee with him. The defendant told plaintiff he knew her from somewhere; she said that she did not know him and asked him to leave the table. Plaintiff stated she did not watch the defendant as he got up to leave; all she recalled was that he called her a name, and the next thing she knew was that she had been hit on the head, apparently by a water glass, and was covered by blood. She had a cup of coffee in her hand at the time and stated she threw it at defendant after she had been hit. The witness testified that defendant stood up, and after calling plaintiff a name, either threw the glass at her, or threw the water at her and the glass slipped out of his hand, and that after that plaintiff threw the coffee at defendant. The defendant testified that after standing up and calling plaintiff a name he was hit by hot coffee, and the glass then flew out of his hand. The defendant testified that he did not intentionally throw the water glass at plaintiff, but rather that it was an accident.

See Di Giorgio v. Indiveri, 10 Cal. Rptr. 3 (Cal. Dist. Ct. App. 1960).

Perspective: Judgments as a Matter of Law

In some situations, our legal system permits the judge to award victory to a party in a lawsuit before the presentation of evidence, after the presentation of evidence, and even after a jury has decided the case. In general, these judicial actions are called *judgments as a matter of law*. The specific varieties of judgments as a matter of law are sometimes called *summary judgment, directed verdict,* and *judgment notwithstanding the verdict* (also called a motion for judgment N.O.V., which abbreviates the Latin *non obstante veredicto*). In *Nelson*, the court considered all of the evidence in the light most favorable to Carroll. That hardly seems fair. Our general sense is that the jury is supposed to weigh the evidence offered by both parties before reaching a verdict. Under some circumstances, however, one party may request that the court end the trial and decide the case in favor of that party.

For example, a court will grant a defendant's motion for a judgment if the plaintiff has failed to show any facts that would entitle the plaintiff to win. A defendant could move for a directed verdict in a battery case if there was no evidence that the defendant intended to contact the plaintiff. A plaintiff could move for a directed verdict if the defendant offered no evidence to contradict the plaintiff's evidence. If the judge grants the motion, the judge enters judgment for the moving party, which means that the party making the motion wins the lawsuit without the case going to the jury.

Nelson's motion for judgment was based on the argument that Carroll had presented no acceptable defense. Carroll's only defense was that the gun went off accidently. The appellate court said that the motion should be granted because an unintended or accidental harm that accompanies an intended contact (Carroll did intend to hit Nelson with the pistol) is still a battery. The court concluded that, *even if everything Carroll said was true,* Carroll would still have to lose. The court will grant the motion only if there is no uncertainty about the facts involved — only if the case can be decided by looking at the law.

A motion for a *directed verdict* comes before the jury has decided the case. A motion for *judgment notwithstanding the verdict* comes after the jury has decided the case. In either case, the court will grant the motion only when there is just one legal conclusion that can reasonably be drawn from the facts. In many cases in this book, appellate courts analyze whether the facts were so clear that the trial court could decide the case without giving the case to the jury. Other cases are situations in which appellate courts are considering whether the juries' conclusions were adequately based on the evidence presented at trial.

C. Intending a Contact That Is Offensive

Battery actions are based on claims that a defendant intended to cause a contact that is harmful *or* offensive. Leichtman v. WLW Jacor Communications, Inc. and Andrews v. Peters both involve claims that the defendant intended a contact that was offensive. Consider whether the definitions the courts use and the ways the courts apply them seem sensible, and whether they provide a basis for predicting results when plaintiffs attempt to characterize other kinds of conduct as offensive. White v. Muniz considers whether the defendant must intend a contact that turns out to be harmful or offensive or whether the defendant must intend not only the contact but also to cause harm or offense.

LEICHTMAN v. WLW JACOR COMMUNICATIONS, INC.
634 N.E.2d 697 (Ohio Ct. App. 1994)

Per Curiam.

The plaintiff-appellant, Ahron Leichtman, appeals from the trial court's order dismissing his complaint against the defendants-appellees, WLW Jacor Communications ("WLW"), William Cunningham and Andy Furman, for battery . . .

In his complaint, Leichtman claims to be "a nationally known" antismoking advocate. Leichtman alleges that, on the date of the Great American Smokeout, he was invited to appear on the WLW Bill Cunningham radio talk show to discuss the harmful effects of smoking and breathing secondary smoke. He also alleges that, while he was in the studio, Furman, another WLW talk-show host, lit a cigar and repeatedly blew smoke in Leichtman's face "for the purpose of causing physical discomfort, humiliation and distress." . . .

Leichtman contends that Furman's intentional act constituted a battery. The Restatement of the Law 2d, Torts (1965), states:

An actor is subject to liability to another for battery if
    (a) he acts intending to cause a harmful or offensive contact with the person of the other . . . , and
    (b) a harmful contact with the person of the other directly or indirectly results[; or]
    (c) an offensive contact with the person of the other directly or indirectly results.

In determining if a person is liable for a battery, the Supreme Court has adopted the rule that "[c]ontact which is offensive to a reasonable sense of personal dignity is offensive contact." Love v. Port Clinton (1988), 524 N.E.2d 166, 167. It has defined "offensive" to mean "disagreeable or nauseating or painful because of outrage to taste and sensibilities or affronting insultingness." State v. Phipps (1979), 389 N.E.2d 1128, 1131. Furthermore, tobacco smoke, as "particulate matter," has the physical properties capable of making contact.

As alleged in Leichtman's complaint, when Furman intentionally blew cigar smoke in Leichtman's face, under Ohio common law, he committed a battery. No matter how trivial the incident, a battery is actionable, even if damages are only one dollar. The rationale is explained by Roscoe Pound in his essay "Liability": "[I]n civilized society men must be able to assume that others will do them no intentional injury — that others will commit no intentioned aggressions upon them." Pound, An Introduction to the Philosophy of Law (1922) 169. . . .

Judgment accordingly.

ANDREWS v. PETERS
330 S.E.2d 638 (N.C. Ct. App. 1985)

BECTON, J. . . .

The facts, briefly stated, are as follows. The plaintiff, Margaret H. Andrews, was injured on 27 September 1979 when her co-employee at Burroughs Wellcome Corporation, the defendant, August Richard Peters, III, walked up behind her at work and tapped the back of her right knee with the front of his right knee, causing her knee to buckle. Andrews lost her balance, fell to the floor, and dislocated her right kneecap. Andrews instituted this action against Peters for intentional assault and battery. She sought compensation for medical expenses, loss of income, pain and suffering, permanent disability, and punitive damages.

The trial judge submitted the case to the jury on the theory of battery. The jury entered a verdict in favor of Andrews on liability and awarded her $7,500 in damages. . . . Peters appeals. . . .

Peters contends that the trial court erred in denying his motions for a directed verdict at the close of Andrews' evidence and at the close of all the evidence. . . . Peters alleges that there is no evidence that he intended to injure Andrews. As summarized in Peters' brief:

[Peters] testified that he did not intend to be rude or offensive in tapping [Andrews] behind her knees. He stated that the same thing had only moments before been done to him by a co-worker and that it struck him as fun. He stated that he tried to catch [Andrews] to prevent her from striking the floor, that he was shocked by what had happened, and that he immediately apologized to [Andrews] and attempted to help her.

Peters' construction of the broad language in the . . . earlier case law ignores the nature of the intent required for an intentional tort action.

> The intent with which tort liability is concerned is not necessarily a hostile intent, or a desire to do any harm. Rather it is an intent to bring about a result which will invade the interests of another in a way that the law forbids. The defendant may be liable although intending nothing more than a good-natured practical joke, or honestly believing that the act would not injure the plaintiff, or even though seeking the plaintiff's own good.

W. Prosser & W. Keeton, The Law of Torts Sec. 8, at 36-7 (5th ed. 1984). . . .

Peters does not deny that he intended to tap Andrews behind the knee. Although tapping Andrews' knee was arguably not in and of itself a harmful contact, it easily qualifies as an offensive contact. "A bodily contact is offensive if it offends a reasonable sense of personal dignity." Restatement, supra, Sec. 19 and comments. . . .

The trial judge phrased the issue of liability succinctly: "Did the defendant commit a battery upon the plaintiff on September 27, 1979?" We note that the jury instructions are neither included in the record nor are they the subject of an assignment of error. We are therefore left to presume that the trial court instructed the jury correctly on the theory of battery. From the jury's verdict, we conclude that the jury found that Peters intended to cause a harmful or offensive contact, i.e., the tapping of Andrews' knee, and that he should therefore be liable for the unforeseen results of his intentional act.

Since there was evidence of the requisite intent to submit the case to the jury on the theory of battery, we hold that the trial court did not err in denying Peters' motions for a directed verdict. . . .

NOTES TO LEICHTMAN v. WLW JACOR COMMUNICATIONS, INC. AND ANDREWS v. PETERS

1. *Offensive Contact.*   According to the Restatement (Second) of Torts §19, "a bodily contact is offensive if it offends a reasonable sense of dignity." Comment a to that section says:

> In order that a contact be offensive to a reasonable sense of personal dignity, it must be one which would offend the ordinary person and as such one not unduly sensitive as to his personal dignity. It must, therefore, be a contact which is unwarranted by the social usages prevalent at the time and place at which it is inflicted.

Why were the contacts suffered by Leichtman and Andrews offensive?

2. *Subjective and Objective Tests.*

The intent test for any intentional tort requires the factfinder to determine what was going on in the defendant's mind—specifically, what the defendant desired or knew. For battery, the factfinder must conclude that the defendant desired to contact the plaintiff (or to cause the plaintiff to anticipate imminent contact) or was substantially certain that a contact (or anticipation of contact) would occur as a result of the defendant's act. This intent test is called a *subjective test* because it focuses on what the individual defendant desired or knew.

The test for offensiveness requires the factfinder to evaluate a defendant's conduct in terms of societal standards and a "reasonable sense of dignity." This offensiveness test is called an *objective test*, because it focuses on a general societal consensus rather than on what the individual defendant desired or knew. An act can be offensive regardless of what the defendant personally thought about its character.

To define "harmful" contact, the Restatement again uses an objective test. The Restatement (Third) of Torts §4 defines physical harm: "Physical harm" means the physical impairment of the human body ("bodily harm") or of real property or tangible personal property ("property damage"). Bodily harm includes physical injury, illness, disease, impairment of bodily function, and death." Comment c adds: "any level of physical impairment is sufficient for liability; no minimum amount of physical harm is required. Thus, any detrimental change in the physical condition of a person's body or property counts as a harmful impairment; there is no requirement that the detriment be major." The Restatement (Second) of Torts §15 comment b concluded, however, that "[t]he minute disturbance of the nerve centers caused by fear, shock or other emotions does not constitute bodily harm" unless some other effect on the body (such as an illness) results.

✸ Problems
Desire or Substantial Certainty

How would the Restatement's concept of "social usages prevalent at the time and place" apply in the following situations?

A. Defendant saw plaintiff, a stranger, stand up at a table in a fancy restaurant and cough loudly three times. Defendant rushed from another table behind the plaintiff and grabbed the plaintiff from behind to execute the Heimlich anti-choking maneuver.

B. Defendant saw plaintiff, a neighbor, receive a prize at a local art fair. Defendant rushed up to the plaintiff and gave the plaintiff a tight hug that lasted about one minute.

In either of these situations, would assigning a particular gender to any of the individuals affect your analysis?

Perspective: Motion for a Directed Verdict

In Andrews v. Peters, the defendant's motion for a directed verdict was based on his claim that Andrews presented no evidence that he had intended to injure her. Following the procedure described in the Perspective Note following Nelson v. Carroll, the trial court considered the facts in the light most favorable to Andrews and then denied Peters's motion. Did either the trial court or the appellate court believe that no reasonable juror could decide that the defendant's conduct was a harmful or offensive contact?

WHITE v. MUNIZ

999 P.2d 814 (Colo. 2000)

KOURLIS, J. . . .

In October of 1993, Barbara White placed her eighty-three year-old grandmother, Helen Everly, in an assisted living facility, the Beatrice Hover Personal Care Center. Within a few days of admission, Everly started exhibiting erratic behavior. She became agitated easily, and occasionally acted aggressively toward others.

On November 21, 1993, the caregiver in charge of Everly's wing asked Sherry Lynn Muniz, a shift supervisor at Hover, to change Everly's adult diaper. The caregiver informed Muniz that Everly was not cooperating in that effort. This did not surprise Muniz because she knew that Everly sometimes acted obstinately. Indeed, initially Everly refused to allow Muniz to change her diaper, but eventually Muniz thought that Everly relented. However, as Muniz reached toward the diaper, Everly struck Muniz on the jaw and ordered her out of the room.

The next day, Dr. Haven Howell, M.D. examined Everly at Longmont United Hospital. Dr. Howell deduced that "she [had] a progressive dementia with characteristic gradual loss of function, loss of higher cortical function including immediate and short term memory, impulse control and judgment." She diagnosed Everly with "[p]rimary degenerative dementia of the Alzheimer type, senile onset, with depression."

In November of 1994, Muniz filed suit alleging assault and battery[3] against Everly, and negligence against Barbara and Timothy White. The case proceeded to a jury trial on March 17, 1997. While arguing outside the presence of the jury for specific jury instructions, the parties took differing positions on the mental state required to commit the alleged intentional torts. Muniz requested the following instruction: "A person who has been found incompetent may intend to do an act even if he or she lacked control of reason and acted unreasonably." White tendered a different instruction:

> A person intends to make a contact with another person if he or she does an act for the purpose of bringing about such a contact, whether or not he or she also intends that the contact be harmful or offensive. The intent must include some awareness of the natural consequences of intentional acts, and the person must appreciate the consequences of intentional acts, and the person must appreciate the offensiveness or wrongfulness of her acts.

The trial court settled on a slightly modified version of White's instruction. It read:

> A person intends to make a contact with another person if she does an act for the purpose of bringing about such a contact, whether or not she also intends that the contact be harmful or offensive.
>
> The fact that a person may suffer from Dementia, Alzheimer type, does not prevent a finding that she acted intentionally. You may find that she acted intentionally if she intended to do what she did, even though her reasons and motives were entirely irrational. *However, she must have appreciated the offensiveness of her conduct.*

---

[3] For simplicity, we address the issues in this case in terms of the battery claim only. The same principles would apply in the assault context.

(Emphasis added.) In selecting the instruction on intent, the trial court determined that Everly's condition rendered her mental state comparable to that of a child.

Muniz's counsel objected to the last sentence of the instruction, claiming that it misstated the law. He argued that the instruction improperly broadened the holding in Horton v. Reaves, 186 Colo. 149, 526 P.2d 304 (1974), where the supreme court held that an infant must appreciate the offensiveness or wrongfulness of her conduct to be liable for an intentional tort. The jury rendered verdicts in favor of Everly and White.

The court of appeals reversed the decision of the trial court and remanded the case for a new trial. The court of appeals reasoned that most states continue to hold mentally deficient plaintiffs liable for their intentional acts regardless of their ability to understand the offensiveness of their actions. "[W]here one of two innocent persons must suffer a loss, it should be borne by the one who occasioned it." Muniz v. White, 979 P.2d 23, 25 (Colo. App. 1998). The court of appeals reasoned that insanity may not be asserted as a defense to an intentional tort, and thus concluded that the trial court erred in "instructing the jury that Everly must have appreciated the offensiveness of her conduct." Id. at 26.

The question we here address is whether an intentional tort requires some proof that the tortfeasor not only intended to contact another person, but also intended that the contact be harmful or offensive to the other person.

State courts and legal commentators generally agree that an intentional tort requires some proof that the tortfeasor intended harm or offense. See W. Page Keeton et al., Prosser and Keeton on the Law of Torts §8 (5th ed. 1984); Dan B. Dobbs, The Law of Torts §30 (2000). According to the Restatement (Second) of Torts,

> (1) An actor is subject to liability to another for battery if
>   (a) he acts *intending to cause a harmful or offensive contact* with the person of the other or a third person, or an imminent apprehension of such a contact, and
>   (b) an offensive [or harmful] contact with the person of the other directly or indirectly results.
> (2) An act which is not done with the intention stated in Subsection (1, a) does not make the actor liable to the other for a mere offensive contact with the other's person although the act involves an unreasonable risk of inflicting it and, therefore, would be negligent or reckless if the risk threatened bodily harm.

Restatement (Second) of Torts §18 (1965) (emphasis added).

Historically, the intentional tort of battery required a subjective desire on the part of the tortfeasor to inflict a harmful or offensive contact on another. Thus, it was not enough that a person intentionally contacted another *resulting* in a harmful or offensive contact. Instead, the actor had to understand that his contact would be harmful or offensive. The actor need not have intended, however, the harm that actually resulted from his action. Thus, if a slight punch to the victim resulted in traumatic injuries, the actor would be liable for all the damages resulting from the battery even if he only intended to knock the wind out of the victim.

Juries may find it difficult to determine the mental state of an actor, but they may rely on circumstantial evidence in reaching their conclusion. No person can pinpoint the thoughts in the mind of another, but a jury can examine the facts to conclude what another must have been thinking. For example, a person of reasonable intelligence knows with substantial certainty that a stone thrown into a crowd will strike someone and result in an offensive or harmful contact to that person. Hence, if an actor of average intelligence performs such an act, the jury can determine that the actor had the requisite intent to cause a harmful or offensive contact, even though the actor denies having such thoughts.

More recently, some courts around the nation have abandoned this dual intent requirement in an intentional tort setting, that being an intent to contact and an intent that the contact be harmful or offensive, and have required only that the tortfeasor intend a contact with another that *results* in a harmful or offensive touching. See Brzoska v. Olson, 668 A.2d 1355, 1360 (Del. 1995) (stating that battery is an intentional, unpermitted contact on another which is harmful or offensive; and that the intent necessary for battery is the intent to contact the person); White v. University of Idaho, 797 P.2d 108, 111 (1990) (determining that battery requires an intent to cause an unpermitted contact, not an intent to make a harmful or offensive contact). Under this view, a victim need only prove that a voluntary movement by the tortfeasor resulted in a contact which a reasonable person would find offensive or to which the victim did not consent. See *University of Idaho*, 797 P.2d at 111. These courts would find intent in contact to the back of a friend that results in a severe, unexpected injury even though the actor did not intend the contact to be harmful or offensive. The actor thus could be held liable for battery because a reasonable person would find an injury offensive or harmful, irrespective of the intent of the actor to harm or offend.

Courts occasionally have intertwined these two distinct understandings of the requisite intent. See *Brzoska*, 668 A.2d at 1360 (approving the Restatement view of the intent element of a battery, but summarizing the rule as "the intentional, unpermitted contact upon the person of another which *is* harmful or offensive") (emphasis added); Keeton, supra, §8 (noting that applying the element of intent frequently confuses authorities). In most instances when the defendant is a mentally alert adult, this commingling of definitions prejudices neither the plaintiff nor the defendant. However, when evaluating the culpability of particular classes of defendants, such as the very young and the mentally disabled, the intent required by a jurisdiction becomes critical.

In Horton v. Reaves, 186 Colo. 149, 526 P.2d 304 (1974), we examined the jury instructions used to determine if a four-year-old boy and a three-year-old boy intentionally battered an infant when they dropped a baby who suffered skull injuries as a result. We held that although a child need not intend the resulting harm, the child must understand that the contact may be harmful in order to be held liable. Our conclusion comported with the Restatement's definition of intent; it did not state a new special rule for children, but applied the general rule to the context of an intentional tort of battery committed by a child. Because a child made the contact, the jury had to examine the objective evidence to determine if the child actors intended their actions to be offensive or harmful. This result complied with both the Colorado jury instruction at the time, and the definition of battery in the Restatement.

In this case, we have the opportunity to examine intent in the context of an injury inflicted by a mentally deficient, Alzheimer's patient. White seeks an extension of *Horton* to the mentally ill, and Muniz argues that a mere voluntary movement by Everly can constitute the requisite intent. We find that the law of Colorado requires the jury to conclude that the defendant both intended the contact and intended it to be harmful or offensive.

Because Colorado law requires a dual intent, we apply here the Restatement's definition of the term. As a result, we reject the arguments of Muniz and find that the trial court delivered an adequate instruction to the jury.

Operating in accordance with this instruction, the jury had to find that Everly appreciated the offensiveness of her conduct in order to be liable for the intentional tort of battery. It necessarily had to consider her mental capabilities in making such a finding, including her age, infirmity, education, skill, or any other characteristic as to which the jury had evidence. We presume that the jury "looked into the mind of Everly," and reasoned that Everly did not possess the necessary intent to commit an assault or a battery.

A jury can, of course, find a mentally deficient person liable for an intentional tort, but in order to do so, the jury must find that the actor intended offensive or harmful consequences. As a result, insanity is not a defense to an intentional tort according to the ordinary use of that term, but is a characteristic, like infancy, that may make it more difficult to prove the intent element of battery. Our decision today does not create a special rule for the elderly, but applies Colorado's intent requirement in the context of a woman suffering the effects of Alzheimer's.

Contrary to Muniz's arguments, policy reasons do not compel a different result. Injured parties consistently have argued that even if the tortfeasor intended no harm or offense, "where one of two innocent persons must suffer a loss, it should be borne by the one who occasioned it." Keeton, supra, §135. Our decision may appear to erode that principle. Yet, our decision does not bar future injured persons from seeking compensation. Victims may still bring intentional tort actions against mentally disabled adults, but to prevail, they must prove all the elements of the alleged tort. Furthermore, because the mentally disabled are held to the reasonable person standard in negligence actions, victims may find relief more easily under a negligence cause of action.

With regard to the intent element of the intentional torts of assault and battery, we hold that regardless of the characteristics of the alleged tortfeasor, a plaintiff must prove that the actor desired to cause offensive or harmful consequences by his act. The plaintiff need not prove, however, that the actor intended the harm that actually results. Accordingly, we reverse the decision of the court of appeals, and remand the case to that court for reinstatement of the jury verdict in favor of White and consideration of any remaining issues.

NOTES TO WHITE v. MUNIZ

1. *Dual Intent.* Two typical rules for battery are (a) the defendant need not intend the specific harm that resulted from the defendant's intentional contact and (b) whether a contact is offensive is determined by reference to an objective test. For instance, a man intending to strike another on the head with a pistol will be liable for the harm associated with a bullet hitting the other in the chest. And, whether blowing smoke in another's eyes is offensive is not determined by reference to what the parties believe but by what societal standards reveal. Into that context White v. Muniz introduced what the court called a "dual intent" requirement for battery. The Colorado Supreme Court correctly stated that not all jurisdictions agree with its approach. Is the "dual intent" approach consistent with the two tort rules described above?

2. Dual Intent and Unintended Consequences. In White v. Muniz, the defendant hit the plaintiff in the jaw, causing severe injuries. Because the defendant was mentally ill, the question arose whether the defendant intended to cause harm when she struck the plaintiff. The issue in this case is closely related to an issue arising in cases when the actor touches another in a way that the actor believes is friendly (as opposed to harmful or offensive) but a harm or offense unexpectedly occurs. These cases are often described as "friendly unsolicited hug" cases, because of the apparent frequency with which one person puts his arm around the shoulders or neck of another person in a way he considers affectionate. In these cases, the contact causes an unexpected and severe injury to the other person's neck or back. The actor intended to contact the other, and a harmful contact resulted. Is that enough to make the actor liable for battery?

Problem
Bodily Harm from Offensive Contact

In the following case, was the intent element for battery met? The defendant argued that because he did not intend to cause harm, injury, or offensive contact, his act did not meet the intent requirement for battery. Does it matter whether the jurisdiction follows the "dual intent" approach described in White v. Muniz?

> The [defendant] professor and the plaintiff had long been acquainted because of their mutual interest in music, specifically, the piano. Professor Neher was a social guest at the Whites' home when the plaintiff was seated at a counter writing a resume for inclusion in the University's music department newsletter. Unanticipated by the plaintiff, the professor walked up behind her and touched her back with both of his hands in a movement later described as one a pianist would make in striking and lifting the fingers from a keyboard. The resulting contact generated unexpectedly harmful injuries. The plaintiff suffered thoracic outlet syndrome on the right side of her body, requiring the removal of the first rib on the right side and scarring of the brachial plexus nerve which necessitated the severing of the scalenus anterior muscles.
>
> The professor stated he intentionally touched the plaintiff's back, but his purpose was to demonstrate the sensation of this particular movement by a pianist, not to cause any harm. He explained that he has occasionally used this contact method in teaching his piano students. The plaintiff said that the professor's act took her by surprise and was non-consensual. She further remarked that she would not have consented to such contact and that she found it offensive.

See White v. University of Idaho, 768 P.2d 827 (Idaho. Ct. App. 1989), *aff'd*, 797 P.2d 108 (Idaho 1990).

D. Damages for Intentional Torts

In most tort cases, plaintiffs seek monetary damages. The plaintiff's desire to receive a monetary judgment is mentioned by the courts in Polmatier v. Russ, Nelson v. Carroll, and Andrews v. Peters. Awards for harms suffered are called *compensatory damages*. Methods for calculating damages are discussed in Chapter 12.

The opinion in Andrews v. Peters also mentions *punitive damages*, which are damages intended to punish the defendant rather than to compensate the plaintiff. While rules vary from state to state, punitive damages may be awarded when the defendant is malicious, or "oppressive, evil, wicked, guilty of wanton or morally cul-pable conduct, or shows flagrant indifference to the safety of others." See Dan B. Dobbs, Law of Remedies §3.11(2), p.319 (2d ed. 1993).

Taylor v. Barwick discusses a third type of damages, *nominal damages*, which may be awarded instead of compensatory damages when the plaintiff has suffered an injury but no harm. Nominal damages awards might also have been appropriate in Leichtman v. WLW Jacor Communications, Inc. Taylor v. Barwick also discusses a limitation of liability for intentional tort, the doctrine of *de minimis non curat lex*, which says that the law will not involve itself in trifling invasions of others' interests. To understand nominal damages, it is important to remember the distinction between *injury* and *harm*, discussed in Note 2 following Nelson v. Carroll.

TAYLOR v. BARWICK

1997 WL 527970 (Del. Super. Ct. 1997)

Quillen, A.J. . . .

On January 5, 1993, Plaintiff Moses Bernard Taylor ("Taylor"), then an inmate at the Delaware Correctional Center, filed a pro se action in this Court against Defendants George Barwick ("Barwick"), Richard Shockley, George Glascock, and Robert E. Snyder. Taylor alleged that Barwick, a Staff Lieutenant with the Department of Cor-rections, committed a battery against him on June 4, 1992 as he was entering the dining hall. Specifically, Taylor alleges that Barwick poked him on the back side with a tree branch. According to Taylor, Barwick then began to laugh at him and made some derogatory comments indicating his hairstyle was "for girls." . . .

For his part, Barwick admits to causing contact to Taylor with a tree branch, but he contends that the incident was an accident. Barwick testified in an affidavit that he observed a three foot stick on the floor and bent over to pick it up. As he was standing up, someone called his name, causing him to turn around, at which point the stick brushed against Taylor. Barwick states that he immediately apologized to Taylor and continued with his duties.

[The plaintiff and defendant both moved for summary judgment.]

Plaintiff's Motion clearly must be denied because issues of material fact remain for resolution by a trier of fact. Rather than engage in an extended colloquy of the disputed issues of fact, the Court will deny plaintiff's Motion because the existence of the intent to cause contact, one of the basic elements of a battery, remains disputed. Barwick asserts that his contact with Taylor was an accident. Plaintiff evidently has no eye-witnesses to contradict Barwick. The Court may rule as a matter of law only when the facts, as presented, allow only one possible inference as to what happened. Notwithstanding plaintiff's certainty, the record does not permit the Court to rule as a matter of law that defendant is liable for battery.

Although the issue is open to greater question, the record also does not permit the Court to rule as a matter of law that defendant is not liable for battery.

. . . The [defendant claims that he is entitled to judgment because] Taylor has failed to allege or establish any facts to sustain his burden of proving an actual injury. In this respect, defendant is correct. The record is void of any probative evidence of physical or mental injury. Defendant's interrogatories specifically asked plaintiff to set forth any injury or illness which Taylor claimed to have suffered from the alleged incident, and yet plaintiff has failed to set forth any evidence. . . . The Court concludes that there is no genuine issue of material fact regarding the existence of actual injury, physical or mental, and plaintiff is therefore unable to recover compensatory damages as a matter of law.

That being said, the Court is still hard pressed to grant the defendant summary judgment on the battery claim as a whole, as actual injury need not be shown to establish liability for battery. It is a long-settled principle of the common law that "the least touching of another in anger is a battery." Cole v. Turner, 6 Mod. 149, 87 Eng. Rep. 907, 90 Eng. Rep. 958 (K. B. 1704) (Holt, C.J.). . . . Technically, a battery has been alleged and actual damage is not necessary for a valid cause of action.

But this minor matter does raise in my mind the legal issue of *de minimis non curat lex,* the law cares not about trifles. It seems clear (from plaintiff's own statement indicating it was he, himself, who "became instantly furious" and "started arguing") that plaintiff is the one who made the battery mountain out of a seemingly de minimis poking or brushing mole hill. As this Court has said before:

> Courts are available for many purposes, and providing an outlet clothed with some sense of civility for minor emotional controversies is one service courts perform. . . . [T]here must be a "cultural sense of [a] community standard on de minimis. . . ." After all, we all suffer some inconvenience as the price of living. But *de minimis non curat lex.*

Read v. Carpenter, et al., Del. Super., C.A. No. 95C-03-171, Quillen, J. (June 8, 1995), letter op. at 7 n.3. . . . And the de minimis doctrine is important in determining whether a case for only nominal damages should proceed to trial or be dismissed.

> Thus, the allowance of nominal damages is generally based on the ground either that every injury from its very nature legally imports damage, or that the injury complained of would in the future be evidence in favor of the wrongdoer, [especially] where, if continued for a sufficient length of time, the invasion of the plaintiff's rights would ripen into a prescriptive right in favor of the defendant. The maxim "de minimis non curat lex" will not preclude the award of nominal damages in such cases. However, if there is no danger of prescription, no proof of substantial loss or injury, or willful wrongdoing by the defendant, it has been said that there is no purpose for allowing nominal damages, and judgment should be rendered for the defendant.

22 Am. Jur. 2d, Damages, §9, p.39.

As a matter of policy, the Court certainly does not want to preclude outright future dismissal of trumped-up claims in cases of incidental physical contact between prisoners and correctional personnel. On the other hand, the Court does not want to dismiss out-of-hand a complaint where it is alleged that a minor physical contact was deliberately used by supervisory correctional personnel as a form of humiliating the prisoner, even if the prisoner suffered no damage to be remedied by compensation.

In this case, there appear[] to be factual issues on the question of a battery which could result in nominal damages. In particular, genuine issues of material fact exist regarding the allegedly intentional nature of defendant's touching and whether the contact was offensive to a reasonable sense of personal dignity. For these reasons, plaintiff's Motion for Summary Judgment is denied. It is so ordered. Since plaintiff has failed to demonstrate that he has suffered any damage worthy of compensation as a result of the contact, plaintiff is restricted to the recovery of nominal damages in the event that this case goes to trial and plaintiff obtains a favorable verdict on liability. Due to the factual disputes, defendant's Motion for Summary Judgment is denied with respect to defendant's liability for battery but defendant's Motion is granted to the extent that it seeks to limit plaintiff's potential recovery to nominal damages. It is so ordered.

NOTES TO TAYLOR v. BARWICK

1. *Nominal Damages.* "Nominal damages are a trifling sum awarded to a plaintiff in an action, where there is no substantial loss or injury to be compensated, but still the law recognizes a technical invasion of his rights." Black's Law Dictionary at 392 (6th ed. 1990). Traditional awards for nominal damages in many states are six cents or one dollar. Money will not encourage a plaintiff to sue when only nominal damages can be expected. A plaintiff suing for nominal damages may be motivated by the desire to vindicate a right — that is, to have the court define the rights and privileges of each party. It is easy to see why this would be important to a prisoner and a prison guard, as in Taylor v. Barwick. That opinion also points out that, in addition to defining the rights of the parties, courts provide "an outlet clothed with some sense of civility for minor emotional controversies."

2. *De Minimis Non Curat Lex.* The doctrine of *de minimis non curat lex* contradicts some people's idea that our society is too litigious and that it is easy to sue and recover damages for any technical interference with a recognized legal interest. The doctrine frustrates lawsuits by people motivated by vengeance, as the plaintiff in Taylor v. Barwick might have been, or who complain about acts courts believe are of little social consequence. The court in Taylor v. Barwick recognized that, on the one hand, the plaintiff made a "battery mountain" out of a "poking or brushing mole hill." The court recognized that, on the other hand, prison guards ought not to be able to use minor physical contact as a form of humiliation. By allowing the trial to proceed, the court recognized that some social purpose would be furthered by the court's intervention in the dispute between the parties.

Perspective: Summary Judgment

In Taylor v. Barwick, both parties "moved for summary judgment." *Summary judgment* is a procedural device that will end the proceedings without a trial. A court will grant a party's motion for summary judgment only when the court concludes that there are no material factual questions to be decided and the law is so clearly in that party's favor that he or she is entitled to win without a trial. Taylor argued that Barwick's hitting him with a tree branch was unquestionably a battery because it was an intentional, offensive contact. Because the court was uncertain that the contact was intentional, Taylor's request for summary judgment was denied. The court concluded that there was an important factual question to be decided.

Barwick moved for summary judgment arguing that Taylor failed to prove that Taylor suffered any harm. Why did this argument fail to persuade the trial court to grant summary judgment in favor of Barwick?

III. Assault

The intentional tort of *assault* protects one's interest in being free from the *apprehension of imminent harmful or offensive contact.* A single act, like the firing of a gun in Polmatier v. Russ, may cause harmful or offensive contact and may also cause anticipation that such contact will imminently occur. Thus, a single act may be both an assault and a battery. A battery may occur without an assault if the victim does not perceive the impending contact. For example, on the facts of Waters v. Blackshear, an assault claim would be possible only if the plaintiff was aware of the lighted firecracker in his sneaker before it exploded. An assault may also occur without a battery.

Assault cases involve an *intent requirement.* They also require analysis of the meaning of *apprehension,* how *imminent* contact must appear to be to qualify as an assault, and the relationship between battery and assault.

A. Intending Apprehension of Imminent Contact

An assault plaintiff must satisfy an intent requirement by showing that the defendant desired or was substantially certain that an apprehension of imminent harmful or offensive contact would result from the defendant's act. Often a court or jury must infer intent from the acts of the defendant. Cullison v. Medley shows how this inference may be made. Brower v. Ackerley applies the definition of "assault" to conduct that was highly reprehensible but that might not have fit the precise definition of the tort.

CULLISON v. MEDLEY

570 N.E.2d 27 (Ind. 1991)

KRAHULIK, J. . . .

Dan R. Cullison (Appellant-Plaintiff below) petitions this Court to . . . to reverse the trial court's entry of summary judgment against him and in favor of the Appellees-Defendants below (collectively "the Medleys"). . . . According to Cullison's deposition testimony, on February 2, 1986, he encountered Sandy, the 16-year-old daughter of Ernest, in a Linton, Indiana, grocery store parking lot. They exchanged pleasantries and Cullison invited her to have a Coke with him and to come to his home to talk further. A few hours later, someone knocked on the door of his mobile home. Cullison got out of bed and answered the door. He testified that he saw a person standing in the darkness who said that she wanted to talk to him. Cullison answered that he would have to get dressed because he had been in bed. Cullison went back to his bedroom, dressed, and returned to the darkened living room of his trailer. When he entered the living room and turned the lights on, he was confronted by Sandy Medley, as well as by father Ernest, brother Ron, mother Doris, and brother-in-law Terry Simmons. Ernest was on crutches due to knee surgery and had a revolver in a holster strapped to his thigh. Cullison testified that Sandy called him a "pervert" and told him he was "sick," mother Doris berated him while keeping her hand in her pocket, convincing Cullison that she also was carrying a pistol. Ron and Terry said nothing to Cullison, but their presence in his trailer home further intimidated him. Primarily, however, Cullison's attention was riveted to the gun carried by Ernest. Cullison testified that, while Ernest never withdrew the gun from his holster, he "grabbed for the gun a few times and shook the gun" at plaintiff while threatening to "jump astraddle" of Cullison if he did not leave Sandy alone. Cullison testified that Ernest "kept grabbing at it with his hand, like he was going to take it out," and "took it to mean he was going to shoot me" when Ernest threatened to "jump astraddle" of Cullison. Although no one actually touched Cullison, his testimony was that he feared he was about to be shot throughout the episode because Ernest kept moving his hand toward the gun as if to draw the revolver from the holster while threatening Cullison to leave Sandy alone.

As the Medleys were leaving, Cullison suffered chest pains and feared that he was having a heart attack. Approximately two months later, Cullison testified that Ernest glared at him in a menacing manner while again armed with a handgun at a restaurant in Linton. On one of these occasions, Ernest stood next to the booth where Cullison was seated while wearing a pistol and a holster approximately one foot from Cullison's face. Shortly after the incident at his home, Cullison learned that Ernest had previously shot a man. This added greatly to his fear and apprehension of Ernest on the later occasions when Ernest glared at him and stood next to the booth at which he was seated while armed with a handgun in a holster. . . .

Cullison testified that as a result of the incident, he sought psychological counseling and therapy and continued to see a therapist for approximately 18 months. Additionally, Cullison sought psychiatric help and received prescription medication which prevented him from operating power tools or driving an automobile, thus injuring Cullison in his sole proprietorship construction business. Additionally, Cullison testified that he suffered from nervousness, depression, sleeplessness, inability to concentrate and impotency following his run-in with the Medleys. . . .

Cullison alleged an assault. The Court of Appeals decided that, because Ernest never removed his gun from the holster, his threat that he was going to "jump astraddle" of Cullison constituted conditional language which did not express any present intent to harm Cullison and, therefore, was not an assault. Further, the Court of Appeals decided that even if it were to find an assault, summary judgment was still appropriate because Cullison alleged only emotional distress and made no showing that the Medleys' actions were malicious, callous, or willful or that the alleged injuries he suffered were a foreseeable result of the Medleys' conduct. We disagree.

. . . It is the right to be free from the apprehension of a battery which is protected by the tort action which we call an assault. As this Court held approximately 90 years ago in Kline v. Kline (1901), 64 N.E. 9, an assault constitutes "a touching of the mind, if not of the body." Because it is a touching of the mind, as opposed to the body, the damages which are recoverable for an assault are damages for mental trauma and distress. "Any act of such a nature as to excite an apprehension of a battery may constitute an assault. It is an assault to shake a fist under another's nose, to aim or strike at him with a weapon, or to hold it in a threatening position, to rise or advance to strike another, to surround him with a display of force. . ." W. Prosser & J. Keaton, Prosser and Keaton on Torts §10 (5th ed. 1984). Additionally, the apprehension must be one which would normally be aroused in the mind of a reasonable person. Id. Finally, the tort is complete with the invasion of the plaintiff's mental peace.

The facts alleged and testified to by Cullison could, if believed, entitle him to recover for an assault against the Medleys. A jury could reasonably conclude that the Medleys intended to frighten Cullison by surrounding him in his trailer and threatening him with bodily harm while one of them was armed with a revolver, even if that revolver was not removed from [] its holster. Cullison testified that Ernest kept grabbing at the pistol as if he were going to take it out, and that Cullison thought Ernest was going to shoot him. It is for the jury to determine whether Cullison's apprehension of being shot or otherwise injured was one which would normally be aroused in the mind of a reasonable person. It was error for the trial court to enter summary judgment on the count two allegation of assault. . . .

BROWER v. ACKERLEY

943 P.2d 1141 (Wash. Ct. App. 1997)

BECKER, J.

Jordan Brower, who alleges that Christopher and Theodore Ackerley made anonymous threatening telephone calls to him, appeals from a summary judgment dismissal of his claims against them. . . . The plaintiff, Jordan Brower, is a Seattle resident active in civic affairs. Christopher and Theodore Ackerley, in their early twenties at the time of the alleged telephone calls, are two sons of the founder of Ackerley Communications, Inc., a company engaged in various activities in Seattle including billboard advertising. Brower perceived billboard advertising as a visual blight. Based on his own investigation, he concluded that Ackerley Communications had erected numerous billboards without obtaining permits from the City of Seattle; had not given the City an accurate accounting of its billboards; and was maintaining a number of billboards that were not on the tax rolls. In January, 1991, Brower presented his findings to the City. When the City did not respond, Brower filed suit in October of 1991 against the City and Ackerley Communications seeking enforcement of the City's billboard regulations.

Within two days an anonymous male caller began what Brower describes as "a campaign of harassing telephone calls" to Brower's home that continued over a period of 20 months. The first time, the caller shouted at Brower in an aggressive, mean-spirited voice to "get a life" and other words to that effect. Brower received at least one more harassing telephone call by January of 1992.

When the City agreed to pursue Brower's complaints about the billboard violations, Brower dropped his suit. In April of 1992, the City made a public announcement to the effect that Ackerley Communications had erected dozens of illegal billboards. Within a day of that announcement, Brower received an angry telephone call from a caller he identified as the same caller as the first call. In a loud, menacing voice, the caller told Brower that he should find a better way to spend his time. Two days later there was another call telling Brower to "give it up."

In July of 1992, shortly after the City Council passed a moratorium on billboard activity, Brower received another angry anonymous call. The male voice swore at him and said, "You think you're pretty smart, don't you?" Brower says he seriously wondered whether he was in any danger of physical harm from the caller. Over the following months Brower continued to receive calls from an unidentified male who he says "belittled me, told me what a rotten person I was, and who used offensive profanity."

On July 19, 1993, the City Council passed a new billboard ordinance. At about . . . 7:30 p.m. [an angry-voiced man] called and said, "I'm going to find out where you live and I'm going to kick your ass." At 9:43 p.m. Brower received another call from a voice disguised to sound, in Brower's words, "eerie and sinister." The caller said "Ooooo, Jordan, oooo, you're finished; cut you in your sleep. . . ." Brower recorded the last two calls on his telephone answering machine.

Brower made a complaint to the police, reporting that he was very frightened by these calls. Because Brower had activated a call trapping feature of his telephone service after the third telephone call, the police were able to learn that the call had originated in the residence of Christopher Ackerley. When contacted by the police, Christopher Ackerley denied making the calls. He said Brower's telephone number was in his apartment, and that his brother Ted Ackerley had been in the apartment at the time and perhaps had made the calls.

The City filed no criminal charges based on the police report. Brower then brought this civil suit against Christopher and Theodore Ackerley seeking compensation for the emotional distress he suffered as the result of the telephone calls. . . .

The elements of civil assault have not been frequently addressed in Washington cases. The gist of the cause of action is "the victim's apprehension of imminent physical violence caused by the perpetrator's action or threat." In the 1910 case of Howell v. Winters, [108 P. 1077 (quoting Cooley, Torts (3d ed.) p.278),] the Supreme Court relied on a definition [that] accords with the Restatement (Second) of Torts [§21], which defines assault, in relevant part, as follows:

> (1) An actor is subject to liability to another for assault if
>   (a) he acts intending to cause a harmful or offensive contact with the person of the other or a third person, or an imminent apprehension of such a contact, and
>   (b) the other is thereby put in such imminent apprehension.

According to section 31 of the Restatement, words alone are not enough to make an actor liable for assault "unless together with other acts or circumstances they put the other in reasonable apprehension of an imminent harmful or offensive contact with his person." The comments to section 31 indicate infliction of emotional distress is a better-suited cause of action when mere words cause injury, "even though the mental discomfort caused by a threat of serious future harm on the part of one who has the apparent intention and ability to carry out his threat may be far more emotionally disturbing than many of the attempts to inflict minor bodily contacts which are actionable as assaults." [Restatement (Second) of Torts §31 comment a.]

The Ackerleys argue that dismissal of Brower's assault claim was appropriate because the threatening words were unaccompanied by any physical acts or movements. Brower acknowledges that words alone cannot constitute an assault, but he contends the spoken threats became assaultive in view of the surrounding circumstances including the fact that the calls were made to his home, at night, creating the impression that the caller was stalking him.

Whether the repeated use of a telephone to make anonymous threats constitutes acts or circumstances sufficient to render the threats assaultive is an issue we need not resolve because we find another issue dispositive: the physical harm threatened in the telephone calls to Brower was not imminent.

To constitute civil assault, the threat must be of imminent harm. As one commentator observes, it is "the immediate physical threat which is important, rather than the manner in which it is conveyed." [Keeton, Prosser & Keeton on the Law of Torts §10, at 45 (5th ed. 1984).] The Restatement's comment is to similar effect: "The apprehension created must be one of imminent contact, as distinguished from any contact in the future." [Restatement Second of Torts §29 comment b.] The Restatement gives the following illustration: "A threatens to shoot B and leaves the room with the express purpose of getting his revolver. A is not liable to B" [Restatement (Second) of Torts §29 comment c, illus. 4.]

The telephone calls received by Brower on July 19 contained two explicit threats: "I'm going to find out where you live and I'm going to kick your ass"; and later, "you're finished; cut you in your sleep." The words threatened action in the near future, but not the imminent future. The immediacy of the threats was not greater than in the Restatement's illustration where A must leave the room to get his revolver. Because the threats, however frightening, were not accompanied by circumstances indicating that the caller was in a position to reach Brower and inflict physical violence "almost at once," we affirm the dismissal of the assault claim. . . .

NOTES TO CULLISON v. MEDLEY AND BROWER v. ACKERLEY

1. *Factual Theories.*   The two cases illustrate several types of factual theories a plaintiff might offer. The court in Brower v. Ackerley based its analysis on a series of phone calls made to Brower. By contrast, the court in Cullison v. Medley based its holding only on the acts of the Medleys at Cullison's trailer in February 1986. Among the specific acts of the Medleys that could form the basis for finding that there was an assault that night was Ernest Medley's grabbing and shaking of his gun in its holster. Several months later, Ernest stood next to the booth in a restaurant where Cullison was seated while Ernest was wearing a pistol and a holster approximately one foot from Cullison's face. Would this later act be sufficient to form the basis for finding that there was an assault at the restaurant? Are there other relevant facts provided in the opinion that make this more likely to be an assault? The Restatement recognizes that it is appropriate to consider the surrounding circumstances when deciding whether apprehension of imminent contact is reasonable. See Restatement (Second) of Torts §31.

2. *Injury and Harm.*   As for the tort of battery, the defendant need not intend or even foresee the specific consequence of an assault. The injury for assault is the invasion of the plaintiff's peace of mind by causing apprehension of an imminent harmful or offensive contact, without regard to whether the contact occurs. It is this injury that must be intended, not any other specific harm. The harms suffered by the plaintiff in Cullison v. Medley included chest pains, fear of a heart attack, and other physical and emotional consequences.

3. *Objective Test for Apprehension.*   The court in Cullison v. Medley applied an *objective test* to determine whether Cullison suffered apprehension. The court stated that the jury must find that the defendant's conduct would normally arouse apprehension in the mind of a reasonable person. This is an objective test because it refers to people in general, not to the specific assault plaintiff. The court in Brower v. Ackerley quoted Restatement (Second) of Torts §31, which says that words alone are not enough to make an actor liable for assault "unless together with other acts or circumstances they put the other *in reasonable apprehension* of an imminent harmful or offensive contact." (Emphasis added.)

4. *Should There Be a Subjective Test for Apprehension?*   There was no evidence in *Cullison* or *Brower* that either plaintiff was a particularly sensitive person who frightens easily. The Restatement (Second) of Torts §27 says that, even if a plaintiff

frightens easily, the defendant will be subject to liability if he intends to put the plaintiff in apprehension of an immediate bodily contact and succeeds in doing so. See comment a, "Actor's surprising success." The treatise cited in *Cullison* and *Brower*, W. Page Keeton, Prosser & Keeton on Torts at 44 (5th ed. 1984), states that no cases have applied this Restatement rule but that there might be liability if the defendant actually knew of the special sensitivity, but the treatise cites no cases.

Recall that in the context of battery, the test for whether a contact is offensive is an objective test. The Restatement (Second) of Torts §19 requires that the contact offend a *reasonable sense of dignity*. Section 19 comment a explains that "[i]n order that a contact be offensive to a reasonable sense of personal dignity, it must be one which would offend the ordinary person and as such one not unduly sensitive as to his personal dignity." The Restatement (Second) of Torts took no position on whether an actor would be subject to liability for battery if he or she knew that the contact would be offensive to the other's abnormally acute sense of personal dignity.

     5. *Conditional Language and Imminent Contact.*   The intermediate appellate court in *Cullison v. Medley* held that the Medleys' conduct constituted conditional language that did not express any present intent to harm Cullison. A *conditional threat* is one that threatens harm unless the plaintiff behaves in a certain way in the future. Because the harm depends on something that will happen in the future, any contact a plaintiff anticipates is future rather than imminent contact. While the *Cullison* court was correct that a conditional threat is not sufficient to justify an assault, the state's supreme court found that the Medleys threatened imminent contact as well as future contact. The interest protected by assault is the interest in freedom from *imminent* contact.

     By contrast, the court in Brower v. Ackerley found that there were no threats of imminent harmful or offensive contact, because the defendant did not threaten actions that would occur "almost at once." The *imminence* of the contact means that the contact will occur without significant delay. Injury threatened for the "near future" is not actionable under the legal theory of assault, while injury threatened for the immediate or imminent future is.

     Imminent apprehension sufficient to make an actor liable for assault is different from fear. It is more akin to the *anticipation* that a harmful or offensive contact may occur. Thus, even if the plaintiff's self-defensive action or the intervention of an outside force can prevent the contact, the apprehension or anticipation is still present. See Restatement (Second) of Torts §24.

     6. *Infliction of Emotional Distress.*   Even though the plaintiff in Brower v. Ackerley may have suffered serious emotional harm from the threats made by the defendants, the particular requirements of the assault and battery tort actions prevented recovery on either of those theories. Another tort, *infliction of emotional distress* provides an alternative theory on which such plaintiffs might rely. That tort, sometimes called *the tort of outrageous conduct*, is discussed later in this chapter.

Problem
Intent for Assault and Battery

Scott Gray began working for defendant Kevin Morley in the concrete business in the summer of 1991. On the morning of July 15, 1991, Morley picked up Gray for work. They worked through the morning and then adjourned to a local tavern for lunch. Gray testified that Morley was angry when they returned to the job site and left "cussing and bitching." At the end of the workday, another employee got into the front seat, and Gray jumped into the back open bed of Morley's truck. A short time later, Gray was thrown from the bed of the truck to the pavement. The impact caused him to suffer a skull fracture and closed head injuries.

Gray stated in a deposition that he did not recall anything unusual about Morley's driving in the moments preceding his injury, other than hearing the squeal of tires and a "sudden jerk." Gray stated that he had previously ridden in the back of Morley's truck, and that on most of those occasions Morley engaged in erratic driving, "swerving around and hitting the brakes and stuff like that, [and would] watch us roll around in the back of the truck, stuff like that." According to Gray, this conduct did not occur "every time, but the majority of the time. It was like fun for him, a game or something." At one point, Gray told Morley that he did not like being thrown around in the back of the truck. Gray could not recall exactly when he said this and conceded that he was not harmed during the previous episodes.

Defendant Morley has moved for summary judgment. You are clerking for the trial judge hearing the case, and she has asked for your opinion on whether the case should be allowed to proceed. Given the evidence, can Morley's conduct on July 15 be characterized as an assault or a battery? See Gray v. Morley, 596 N.W.2d 922 (Mich. 1999).

Perspective: Motion to Dismiss

A *motion to dismiss* is a procedural device that, like the motion for summary judgment discussed in Note 3 following Taylor v. Barwick, avoids a trial. A plaintiff may terminate an action by having the claim voluntarily dismissed before the defendant answers the complaint. An *involuntary dismissal* comes when the court grants a defendant's request that the court dismiss the plaintiff's claim. A court will grant a defendant's motion for dismissal when the plaintiff has failed to produce evidence to support each element of the claim. In Brower v. Ackerley, the defendants claimed that the plaintiff failed to produce any evidence of any threat of *imminent contact*. Because assault requires a threat of imminent harm, the appellate court affirmed the lower court's involuntary dismissal of Brower's claim.

B. Transfer of Intent Among People and Between Torts

Rules for *transfer of intent* facilitate a plaintiff's recovery in assault cases and battery cases. There are two kinds of transfer of intent. The first, *transfer of intent between torts*, allows a plaintiff who suffers a harmful or offensive contact to recover for a battery even if the defendant intended only an assault and allows a plaintiff who suffers apprehension of imminent harmful or offensive contact to recover for an assault even if the defendant intended only a battery. The second kind of transfer of intent is *transfer of intent among people*. If a defendant intends to assault or batter one person but ends up assaulting or battering another, the defendant will be liable to the other as if the other had been the intended target. The following case, Hall v. McBryde, illustrates both kinds of transfer of intent in a case where the defendant intends only to scare some boys passing in a car but ultimately shoots a neighbor.

HALL v. McBRYDE

919 P.2d 910 (Colo. Ct. App. 1996)

HUME, J.

. . . On January 14, 1993, Marcus was at his parents' home with another youth after school. Although, at that time, Marcus was, pursuant to his parents' wishes, actually living in a different neighborhood with a relative and attending a different high school in the hope of avoiding gang-related problems, he had sought and received permission from his father to come to the McBryde house that day to retrieve some clothing. Prior to that date, Marcus had discovered a loaded gun hidden under the mattress of his parents' bed. James McBryde had purchased the gun sometime earlier.

Soon after midday, Marcus noticed some other youths in a car approaching the McBryde house, and he retrieved the gun from its hiding place. After one of the other youths began shooting towards the McBryde house, Marcus fired four shots toward the car containing the other youths.

During the exchange of gunfire one bullet struck plaintiff, who lived next to the McBryde residence, causing an injury to his abdomen that required extensive medical treatment. . . .

. . . [P]laintiff contends that the trial court erred in entering judgment for Marcus on the claim of battery. We agree.

An actor is subject to liability to another for battery if he or she acts intending to cause a harmful or offensive contact with the person of the other or a third person, or an imminent apprehension of such a contact, and a harmful or offensive contact with the person of the other directly or indirectly results.

Here, the trial court found that there was no evidence indicating that Marcus intended to shoot at plaintiff. Furthermore, based upon statements by Marcus that he was not purposely trying to hit the other youths but, instead, was shooting at their car, the trial court also determined that plaintiff had failed to prove Marcus intended to make contact with any person other than plaintiff. Based upon this second finding, and relying on CJI-Civ.3d 20:5 and CJI-Civ.3d 20:8 (1989), the trial court concluded that the doctrine of transferred intent could not apply to create liability for battery upon plaintiff. We conclude that, in reaching its determination that no battery occurred, the trial court did not properly analyze the intent required for battery or the transferability of such intent.

As set forth above, the intent element for battery is satisfied if the actor either intends to cause a harmful or offensive contact or if the actor intends to cause an imminent apprehension of such contact. Moreover, with respect to the level of intent necessary for a battery and the transferability of such intent, Restatement (Second) of Torts §16 (1965) provides as follows:

> (1) If an act is done with the intention of inflicting upon another an offensive but not a harmful bodily contact, or of putting another in apprehension of either a harmful or offensive bodily contact, and such act causes a bodily contact to the other, the actor is liable to the other for a battery although the act was not done with the intention of bringing about the resulting bodily harm.

(2) If an act is done with the intention of affecting a third person in the manner stated in Subsection (1), but causes a harmful bodily contact to another, the actor is liable to such other as fully as though he intended so to affect him. (Emphasis added.)

See also Restatement (Second) of Torts §20 (1965); Alteiri v. Colasso, 362 A.2d 798 (Conn. 1975) (when one intends an assault, then, if bodily injury results to someone other than the person whom the actor intended to put in apprehension of harm, it is a battery actionable by the injured person).

Here, the trial court considered only whether Marcus intended to inflict a contact upon the other youths. It did not consider whether Marcus intended to put the other youths in apprehension of a harmful or offensive bodily contact.

However, we conclude, as a matter of law, that by aiming and firing a loaded weapon at the automobile for the stated purpose of protecting his house, Marcus did intend to put the youths who occupied the vehicle in apprehension of a harmful or offensive bodily contact. Hence, pursuant to the rule set forth in Restatement (Second) of Torts §16(2) (1965), Marcus' intent to place other persons in apprehension of a harmful or offensive contact was sufficient to satisfy the intent requirement for battery against plaintiff.

Accordingly, we conclude that the cause must be remanded for additional findings as to whether the bullet that struck plaintiff was fired by Marcus. If the trial court finds that the bullet was fired by Marcus, it shall find in favor of plaintiff on the battery claim and enter judgment for damages as proven by plaintiff on that claim.

NOTE TO HALL v. McBRYDE

Multiple Transfers of Intent.   The court in Hall v. McBryde held that if Marcus fired the bullet that struck the plaintiff, Marcus would be liable for the intentional tort of battery. This is surprising for two reasons: (1) Marcus did not intend to batter the plaintiff, who was his neighbor; and (2) Marcus did not even intend to assault the plaintiff. The evidence suggests that Marcus intended to assault the youths in the car. The court held that not only can the factfinder transfer the intent from assault to battery, it can transfer intent from intended victims to other people. The first of these transfers of intent is the transfer of intent between torts. The second is the transfer of intent among people. A Missouri court described the transfer of intent among people, saying, "The intention follows the bullet." State v. Batson, 96 S.W.2d 384, 389 (Mo. 1936). The court in Hall v. McBryde quotes the Restatement (Second) of Torts §16(1) to support the transfer of intent between assault and battery and §16(2) to support the transfer of intent among people. Would either of these subsections be applicable if Marcus had shot one of the occupants in the car?

Problem
Transfer of Intent

Tim was the son of Zeppo Marx, who starred in such famous comedic films as *Duck Soup, Horse Feathers, Monkey Business,* and *Animal Crackers.* When Tim was nine years old, he played with two friends, Denise and Barbara, both eight years old. At the time of the injury, Denise was standing four feet in front of Tim and Barbara was riding past on her bicycle 30 feet away. Tim said to Denise, "Watch Barbie," as he picked up a rock about the size of a small hen's egg. Barbara saw Tim raise his arm to throw at an angle toward her. Denise looked at Barbara, then back at Tim, and at that moment was hit in the eye by the rock. The line of throw toward Barbara would pass several feet in front of Denise. Deciding the case brought by Denise against Tim Marx, the court found that for the rock to strike Denise, "one of two things would have to occur, either (1) Tim changed the direction of throw without any warning, or (2) he held the rock too loosely, or let go of it too soon to control its flight, and inadvertently hit Denise. The evidence is susceptible of either of these inferences." Does Tim's liability to Denise for the tort of battery depend on which inference is more plausible? See Singer v. Marx, 301 P.2d 440 (Cal. Ct. App. 1956).

Perspective: Transferred Intent

The doctrine of *transferred intent* comes from criminal law, where the doctrine was recognized in England as early as 1553. Without regard to whether the defendant intended to cause injury to a specific victim, it seemed justified to hold the defendant liable for a violation of the criminal law, such as shooting at one person in a crowded restaurant and hitting another. Similarly, transferred intent seems appropriate where an actor acts with malice, an antisocial attitude. Also, where a number of persons are engaged in a brawl, it makes sense to hold all liable to a victim without regard to whether any particular brawler intended to injure another specific person. Finally, as the Restatement (Second) §13 states, a batterer is liable for any harm that "directly or indirectly results." This broad scope of liability logically encompasses the unintended victim. See generally Osborne M. Reynolds Jr., *Transferred Intent: Should Its "Curious Survival" Continue?*, 50 Okla. L. Rev. 529 (1997).

IV. Defenses to Assault and Battery

A defense protects a defendant from liability even if a plaintiff can prove that the defendant acted in a way that meets the definitions of "assault" or "battery." This Section considers the most common defenses to assault and battery: consent and defense of self, others, and property.

The *defense of consent* arises when a person voluntarily relinquishes the right to be free from harmful or offensive contact or imminent apprehension of such contact. The *defense of person or property* arises where tort law grants an individual the privilege to use threats or to contact others in ways that would ordinarily be treated as an assault or a battery. The defense that a threat or a contact was permissible as a defense of a person or property is different from the defense of consent, because it does not require a showing that the alleged victim had ever agreed to be threatened or touched.

A. Consent

Generally, an actor may give up the interests in freedom from harmful or offensive contact and from imminent apprehension of such contact. McQuiggan v. Boy Scouts of America focuses on the evidence from which consent and the withdrawal of consent may be inferred. It also describes whether injured parties may recover damages for harms suffered that were not anticipated when consent was given.

The law only allows people to give up their rights when the people know what they are doing and are acting willingly. Consent must be knowing, informed, and voluntary. Hogan v. Tavzel illustrates this idea in the context of sexual contact resulting in transmission of a disease.

Richard v. Mangion introduces the distinction between consent and self-defense in a case involving a fight between two boys. A fight may involve a battery, may involve conduct that would be a battery but is protected by a self-defense privilege, or may involve conduct to which both parties have agreed. Even when an actor has given consent to some types of conduct, that actor may claim that the other person exceeded the consent given. In Richard v. Mangion, the court considered whether the defendant used force that went beyond the type of force to which the plaintiff had consented.

McQUIGGAN v. BOY SCOUTS OF AMERICA
536 A.2d 137 (Md. Ct. Sp. App. 1987)

GILBERT, C.J.

The main question presented in this case is whether a twelve-year-old boy should be barred from recovery for an eye injury he sustained when he voluntarily participated in a paper clip shooting "game."

Nicholas Alexander McQuiggan, by and through his guardian, Jerome Keith Bradford, brought an action in tort against: the Boy Scouts of America . . . and Billy Hamm and Kevin McDonnell, fellow Boy Scouts. Nicholas alleged that . . . the minor defendants, Billy and Kevin, are liable for assault and battery. . . .

[A]t the conclusion of Nicholas's case, the court granted a motion for judgment in favor of all the defendants. Aggrieved by the trial court's action, Nicholas has appealed to this Court.

The events giving rise to this litigation date from April 8, 1981, when sometime between 7:10 and 7:15 p.m. Nicholas was dropped off by his mother at the Epworth Methodist Church in Montgomery County to attend a Boy Scout meeting. The meeting was scheduled to start at 7:30 p.m. When Nicholas arrived, he noticed several of the other scouts engaged in a game in which they shot paper clips at each other from rubber bands they held in their hands. The paper clips were pulled apart on one end and squeezed closed on the other. At trial, Nicholas demonstrated how the clip was shot by placing the closed end of the clip in a rubber band stretched between two upright fingers in the form of a "v" and pulling back on the open end of the paper clip and releasing it. Nicholas testified that when he arrived at the church, two Assistant Scoutmasters, William H. Hamm Sr. and Keith D. Rush, were present in the meeting room. Another Assistant Scoutmaster, Edmund Copeland, arrived after Nicholas but before the meeting actually started.

Upon arriving at the meeting room, Nicholas sat at a table and began to read his Boy Scout Handbook. Between four and eight other scouts had been playing the paper clip shooting game and running in and out of the hallway leading to the meeting room for about ten minutes before Nicholas decided to join them. Prior to his joining the game, no one had shot paper clips at him. When one of the boys asked Nicholas to join in the game, he did so freely, feeling no pressure to participate. Nicholas further related that he knew that the object of the game was to shoot paper clips; he knew that paper clips would be shot at him; he knew that there was a chance he would be hit with a paper clip.

When he decided to join in the game, Nicholas looked through some material on a shelf, and he located an elastic hair band with which he intended "to chase" the other boys. Nicholas and an unidentified Boy Scout then chased Billy Hamm Jr. and Kevin McDonnell up the hallway. Nicholas said he had no paper clips, but the boy with him was shooting them. Nicholas admitted at trial that his actions were such as to lead Kevin or Billy to believe that he had a paper clip in his possession. Nicholas further narrated that he was actively "participating" in the game.

After Nicholas had chased Billy and Kevin down the hallway for about ten feet, the two boys turned around and chased Nicholas back down the hall. Nicholas said that he dropped the hair band and entered the meeting room. He then stopped running, "split apart" from the unidentified boy, and started to walk toward a table. He told the court that at that point he "stopped playing," but he did not communicate that fact in any way to the other boys. Approximately five seconds later and five feet into the meeting room, Nicholas felt something in his right eye. When he brushed the eye, a paper clip dropped to the floor. According to Nicholas, his entire involvement in the game consumed approximately thirty seconds. . . .

The trial judge . . . found that Nicholas could not prevail on his assault and battery counts because by his actions "not only in participating in the game but pursuing . . . Billy Hamm [and Kevin McDonnell] down the hallway . . . as a matter of law he consented to the infliction of the injury upon him." We agree.

A battery consists of the unpermitted application of trauma by one person upon the body of another person. The gist of the action is not hostile intent but the absence of consent to the contact on plaintiff's part. When a plaintiff "manifests a willingness that the defendant engage in conduct and the defendant acts in response to such a manifestation," [W. Page Keeton, Prosser & Keeton on the Law of Torts (5th ed. 1984)] §18 at 113, "his consent negatives the wrongful element of the defendant's act, and prevents the existence of a tort." Id. at 112.

The circumstances leading to Nicholas's injury do not constitute an assault and battery. As stated in Prosser, §18 at 114:

> One who enters into a sport, game or contest may be taken to consent to physical contacts consistent with the understood rules of the game. *It is only when notice is given that all such conduct will no longer be tolerated that the defendant is no longer free to assume consent.* (Emphasis supplied.)

Nicholas's willful joining in the game, without any notice of his withdrawal from participation, bars recovery from either Billy or Kevin.

NOTES TO McQUIGGAN v. BOY SCOUTS OF AMERICA

1. *Express and Implied Consent.* Consent may be *express* ("Go ahead and hit me!") or *implied*. Nicholas found an elastic hair band and, despite his lack of ammunition, chased Billy and Kevin. He admitted "that his actions were such as to lead Kevin or Billy to believe that he had a paper clip in his possession." There was no express consent in this case. Rather, the defendant was able to establish that the plaintiff had implied by his conduct that he consented to participate in the risky game.

The same test for whether the plaintiff impliedly consented applies to the plaintiff's withdrawal from the game. Although Nicholas said that he "stopped playing" before being hit in the eye, he did not claim that he had communicated that fact to the other boys. As a result, they could reasonably assume that his consent was still operative and were entitled by the law to do so.

Whether consent may be inferred from any particular circumstances must be decided on a case-by-case basis. Because the law uses an objective test to determine whether another could "reasonably" assume that consent was given, the customs of the community are taken into account. The Restatement (Second) of Torts §892 comment c offers two illustrations.

> Illustration 2. *A*, a young man, is alone with *B*, a girl, in the moonlight. *A* proposes to kiss *B*. Although inwardly objecting, *B* says nothing and neither resists nor protests by any word or gesture. *A* kisses *B*.
>
> Illustration 3. In the course of a quarrel, *A* threatens to punch *B* in the nose. *B* says nothing but stands his ground. *A* punches *B* in the nose.

The Restatement (Second) concludes that it is reasonable to assume consent in one of these illustrations. Is it likely that contemporary analysts, living a generation later than the authors of the Restatement (Second), would consider these two examples different?

2. *Consent to Contact Rather than to Harm.* An actor will usually be treated as having consented to contact rather than to a particular harm. In McQuiggan v. Boy Scouts of America, Nicholas consented to relinquish his right to be free from harmful or offensive contacts. He certainly would not concede that he consented to the harm to his eye. Recall the distinction between injury and harm discussed in the notes following Nelson v. Carroll. To intend a battery, an actor must intend the injury, the invasion of another's interest, and, in dual intent states, to cause harm that would otherwise constitute a battery. But the actor need not intend the particular harm that occurred.

Consent is analyzed the same way. An actor consents to suffer the injury, the invasion of a right. Once the actor has consented to the invasion, the actor cannot recover for harms related to that invasion, even if they were unforeseeable.

An actor who consents to an invasion of an interest (to be free from harmful contact, for instance) does not thereby consent to all possible harmful conduct. If Nicholas consents to being hit with paper clips, Billy may not shoot him with a hand gun. Sometimes applying this idea is difficult, because the conduct to which an actor has consented may be defined only vaguely. The court in McQuiggan v. Boy Scouts of America quotes a treatise by Professor Keeton saying that the conduct to which one consents in a sport, game, or contest is "physical contacts consistent with the understood rules of the game." Thus, custom is relevant in determining the scope of conduct to which one has consented.

Perspective: Who Proves Consent?

There is a dispute in the common law over whether consent must be proved by the defendant as a defense or whether lack of consent must be proved by the plaintiff as an element of the plaintiff's case. This dispute matters only if the evidence of consent is "in equipoise," which means that consent and non-consent are equally likely. If the plaintiff must prove "no consent" as an element of the tort by a preponderance of the evidence, the plaintiff will lose if the evidence is in equipoise. If the defendant must prove consent as a defense, the plaintiff will win if the evidence is in equipoise. There have not been enough reported cases where the evidence of consent is in equipoise for the law of all the states to be clear and in agreement on this point. See generally Alan K. Chen, *The Burdens of Qualified Immunity: Summary Judgment and the Role of Facts in Constitutional Tort Law*, 47 Am. U. L. Rev. 1, 94 n.585 (1997).

HOGAN v. TAVZEL

660 So. 2d 350 (Fla. Ct. App. 1995)

W. Sharp, J. . . .

Hogan and Tavzel were married for fifteen years but encountered marital problems which caused them to separate. During a period of attempted reconciliation between October of 1989 and January 1990, Tavzel infected Hogan with genital warts. He knew of his condition but failed to warn Hogan or take any precaution against infecting her. The parties were divorced on May 8, 1990. Hogan brought this suit in 1993.

Tavzel moved to dismiss. . . .

We . . . turn our attention to dismissal of the battery count. Since this is a case of first impression in Florida, it is appropriate to look to other jurisdictions for guidance. A case similar to the one presented here is Kathleen K. v. Robert B., 198 Cal. Rptr. 273 (Cal. 2d Dist. 1984). There, a cause of action in battery was approved when one partner contracted genital herpes from the other partner. The facts indicated that the infecting partner had represented he was free from any sexually infectious disease, and the infected partner would not have engaged in sexual relations if she had been aware of the risk of infection. The court held that one party's consent to sexual intercourse is vitiated by the partner's fraudulent concealment of the risk of infection with venereal disease (whether or not the partners are married to each other). This is not a new theory.

The *Kathleen K.* court recognized that

> [a] certain amount of trust and confidence exists in any intimate relationship, at least to the extent that one sexual partner represents to the other that he or she is free from venereal or other dangerous contagious disease.

Kathleen K. at 198 Cal. Rptr. 273.

The Restatement of Torts Second (1977) also takes the view that consent to sexual intercourse is not the equivalent of consent to be infected with a venereal disease. Specifically, it provides the following example:

> A consents to sexual intercourse with B, who knows that A is ignorant of the fact that B has a venereal disease. B is subject to liability to A for battery.

Illus. 5 §892B. Other authorities also conclude that a cause of action in battery will lie, and consent will be ineffective, if the consenting person was mistaken about the nature and quality of the invasion intended.

We see no reason, should the facts support it, that a tortfeasor could not be held liable for battery for infecting another with a sexually transmissible disease in Florida.

In so holding, we align ourselves with the well established, majority view which permits lawsuits for sexually transmitted diseases. Hogan's consent, if without the knowledge that Tavzel was infected with a sexually transmitted disease, was the equivalent of no consent, and would not be a defense to the battery charge if successfully proven.

NOTES TO HOGAN v. TAVZEL

1. *Fraudulently Obtained or Mistaken Consent.* The *Hogan* court refers to two different situations in which a defendant will be barred from relying on a plaintiff's consent to avoid liability for battery: (1) where the plaintiff was mistaken about the nature and quality of the invasion intended; and (2) where the defendant concealed an important fact that would have affected the plaintiff's decision to consent. Which of these circumstances is most relevant to the facts in *Hogan*?

2. *Exceeding the Boundaries of Consent.* Another approach to the facts of *Hogan* would be to say that the contact exceeds the bounds of permitted contact. The notes following McQuiggan v. Boys Scouts of America stated that when Nicholas consented to be hit by paper clips, he did not consent to Billy shooting him with a handgun. The *McQuiggan* court said, "One who enters a sport, game or contest may be taken to consent to physical contacts consistent with the understood rules of the game." Could *Hogan* be analyzed in that way?

Problem
Scope of Consent

In Hellriegel v. Tholl, 417 P.2d 362 (Wash. 1966), 15-year-old Dikka and his friends were hanging out on a beach at Lake Washington. After throwing pillows and grass at one another, Dikka said to the other boys "Oh, you couldn't throw me in even if you tried." According to Dikka's testimony:

> And with that the three boys, Mike, Greg and John, jumped up and, well, tried to throw me into the water. I struggled for a while and I ended up in a sitting position parallel to the lake, facing, my head facing north, and Mike was behind me. Again, I was in a sitting position and John and Greg had my legs up in the air.
>
> I was trying to get them off, and I had my hands reaching toward my legs when Mike, trying to reach my hands, must have slipped or lost his balance, and he fell on the back of my head and pushed it forward. I heard two cracks like somebody snapping his knuckles, and right after that I lost all control, I couldn't move my legs, and it was kind of a numb sensation all over.

Dikka was permanently partially paralyzed. Would Dikka's words and the context support a consent defense offered by Mike?

RICHARD v. MANGION
535 So. 2d 414 (La. Ct. App. 1988)

Doucet, J.

Plaintiffs, James and Juanita Richard, in their individual capacity and as natural tutor and tutrix of their minor child, Shawn, appeal from a judgment dismissing their suit in favor of defendants, Mr. and Mrs. Joseph Mangion, and State Farm Fire & Casualty Insurance Company.

The issue presented on appeal is whether the trial judge erred in finding that Shawn voluntarily participated in an altercation with Jeremy Mangion, Mr. and Mrs. Mangion's son. The undisputed facts show that Jeremy and Shawn fought on the afternoon of May 8, 1985 at an outdoor hangout known as the "rope swing" located at the rear of some residential lots in their Lafayette neighborhood. During the fight Jeremy struck Shawn in his right eye causing later hemorrhaging in the eye. He underwent two operations and his parents incurred over $15,000 in related medical expenses.

Shawn was thirteen years old and Jeremy was fourteen at the time of the fight. Shawn had only recently moved into Jeremy's neighborhood. Both attended the same school, a grade apart, and rode on the same school bus each morning. Animosity between the boys developed after Jeremy made a derogatory comment to Shawn one morning regarding the trousers he was wearing. This incident occurred at a bus stop and, after Shawn retorted, "kiss my ass," Jeremy told him to move to another bus stop and kicked him in his buttocks.

Another incident occurred several days before the altercation in question. Two witnesses testified that the boys had been scheduled to fight one day but Shawn did not show up. The next day Jeremy and several boys and girls walked over to Shawn's bus stop to ask Shawn why he hadn't appeared. Shawn testified that Jeremy came up to him and asked him if he wanted to fight. Jeremy and Shawn apparently began squaring off but no actual blows were exchanged. When they saw the school bus coming, both boys stopped. But then Jeremy made a sudden move, Shawn raised his hands or fists in a defensive gesture, and Jeremy kicked Shawn in his groin. Shawn ran home while the others boarded the school bus. As the bus proceeded down the block, Shawn's father came running up, stopped the bus, and confronted Jeremy. Shawn then got back on the bus and walked up to Jeremy, who was seated, and glared at him. Shawn testified that he did not challenge Jeremy to fight as Jeremy claimed. Mark Comeaux, a friend of Jeremy's, stated that other children on the bus chided Shawn for not showing up for the fight. Mark recalled that Shawn said to Jeremy, "Well, let's fight this afternoon." No fight occurred that day, however.

On the afternoon of the fight in question there was much talk among the children that Jeremy and Shawn were going to fight. One witness, Kevin Alexander, stated that a time and place had been set for the fight. Laura Comeaux, Mark's sister, stated that Jeremy told Mark there was going to be a fight. Mark confirmed this and stated that the agreed-upon time for the fight was 4:30 p.m. Jeremy testified that Shawn had been telling people that he wanted to fight him but did not remember that he and Shawn agreed to fight at a certain time. However, he also said that he "somehow" understood the fight was supposed to be at 4:30 p.m. at the rope swing. When questioned if he clearly understood that there was to be a fight between [him] and Jeremy at a certain time and place, Shawn answered, "not really."

Jeremy testified that he did not intend to show up for the fight but Kevin Alexander came to his home and told him Shawn was waiting at the rope swing to fight. Jeremy and Mark Comeaux went to the rope swing but no one else was there. Other youths began arriving at the scene including Mark's sister, Laura, another girl, Amity Breaux, and Chad and Todd Pruitt, the latter a friend of Shawn's. After going to Jeremy's, Kevin Alexander went to Shawn's home and told him that Jeremy was waiting for him. Shawn said he decided to go ahead and "get it over with." He admitted he was fully aware there might be a fight but also thought he and Jeremy could "talk out" their differences.

Shawn first stated that when he arrived at the rope swing Jeremy came up to him and said, "Well, you want to fight," but Shawn didn't answer. Whereupon, Jeremy pushed him and shoved his knee into his stomach. However, Shawn later changed his story, testifying that there was a pushing match between the two before the fight. He said Jeremy pushed him, he backed off, Jeremy pushed him again and that's when the fight started. He also later stated that he didn't remember what Jeremy said to him before the fight. Soon after the fight began, Jeremy got Shawn in a headlock and hit him six to eight times in his face and head. It appears that at least some of these blows were prompted by Shawn's swinging his fists around to strike Jeremy even as he was in the headlock. Shawn said he was trying to strike Jeremy to get out of the headlock. Jeremy released Shawn from the headlock and threw him into a shallow ditch. Shawn jumped up, nose bleeding, and charged at Jeremy swinging wildly. Jeremy ducked and hit Shawn once in his eye. That was the end of the fight. Jeremy started to leave but was called back by Shawn and his friend, Todd Pruitt, who were yelling that Shawn wanted to fight some more. Shawn had offered Todd $5.00 to hit Jeremy. When Jeremy walked back over, Todd hit him once and Jeremy ran away as Shawn laughed.

Jeremy testified that he didn't remember who initially charged who that day, but he basically reiterated Shawn's testimony regarding the headlock and hitting. He said he wanted to stop when he bloodied Shawn's nose, so he pushed him away into the ditch. But Shawn got up and swung at him so he hit him once more, in the eye. That last punch appears to have been the one that caused the later hemorrhaging. As a result of the injury, Shawn has a greater than normal likelihood of developing glaucoma and/or a detached retina. His vision in the affected eye has improved to 20/25, near perfect vision, but it was a long recuperative period. Shawn's sports activities are limited due to the eye injury.

There was sketchy, conflicting, and dim recollection by witnesses to the fight as to who actually made the first move. Overall, the evidence seems to preponderate in favor of a finding that Jeremy made the first move. However, it appears that both went to the scene contemplating a fight. Todd Pruitt, Shawn's friend, testified that Jeremy pushed Shawn first, Shawn swung back, and then they both started swinging and hitting each other. Todd also stated that Shawn said he was going to be there to fight and that he appeared fully willing to fight.

The trial judge found that Jeremy Mangion was the initial instigator between the boys from the first meeting. He further found that the fight appeared to have been instigated by friends of the boys. However, he further found that both Jeremy and Shawn went to the scene expecting to engage in fisticuffs, neither was the aggressor, and neither used excessive force.

On appeal plaintiffs claim that Jeremy was the aggressor in the fight and that he attacked Shawn without justification or provocation. Defendants claim that Shawn voluntarily participated in the altercation, impliedly consenting to being struck in the eye by Jeremy.

We initially recognize that the trial court's finding that Shawn voluntarily participated in the altercation and that neither boy used excessive or unnecessary force are findings of fact which may not be disturbed unless, (1) the record evidence does not furnish a sufficient basis for the finding, or (2) that finding is clearly wrong.

The defense of consent to an intentional tort was examined in Andrepont v. Naquin, 345 So. 2d 1216 (La. App. 1st Cir. 1977). The court stated, "The defense of consent in Louisiana operates as a bar to recovery for the intentional infliction of harmful or offensive touchings of the victim. Consent may be expressed or implied; if implied, it must be determined on the basis of reasonable appearances. When a person voluntarily participates in an altercation, he may not recover for the injuries which he incurs, unless force in excess of that necessary is used and its use is not reasonably anticipated. The use of unnecessary and unanticipated force vitiates the consent. For example, when a party voluntarily engages in a fist fight and his adversary suddenly reveals a concealed or dangerous weapon, he does not necessarily consent to the use of such an instrument." (Citations omitted.)

The evidence shows that Jeremy was the instigator of bad feelings between the boys. In fact, he committed two batteries on Shawn before the fight in question. However, we agree with the finding by the trial judge that both Jeremy and Shawn went to the rope swing prepared to engage in fisticuffs and fully contemplating the altercation. There is evidence that Shawn, in anger, challenged Jeremy to a fight. The evidence shows the idea of a fight was actively advanced by classmates. The evidence also establishes that, when Shawn left the safety of his home to meet Jeremy at the rope swing, he understood or should have understood that his showing up would demonstrate his willingness to fight Jeremy. By showing up at the rope swing, knowing Jeremy was waiting to fight with him, Shawn implied to Jeremy that he was willing to engage in a fight and incur blows. When two parties expressly or impliedly agree to fight the consent of one is not vitiated merely because the other strikes the first blow. It is not necessary that simultaneous blows be struck. It is unfortunate that Shawn was so badly injured, but his alternative was to stay at home that afternoon. We recognize the tremendous peer pressure in these situations, but peer pressure does not vitiate consent.

We also find no error with the trial judge's finding that no unnecessary or excessive force was employed by either boy. It was a fistfight and no weapons were involved. Shawn was only a little smaller than Jeremy according to the testimony of most witnesses. Although Jeremy did hit Shawn in the face up to eight times while he had him in a headlock, we do not find that this was unnecessary or excessive force. It appears that Jeremy hit Shawn more than he would have while he had him in the headlock because he became angry when Shawn hit him. After Jeremy pushed Shawn into the ditch, Shawn charged back at Jeremy. Up until this point the only obvious injury to Shawn was a bloody nose. After Shawn charged back at him, Jeremy hit him one last time, in the eye. There is no indication at all that Jeremy intended to maim Shawn.

In conclusion, we find no error in the trial court judgment. For the reasons assigned, we affirm the judgment of the trial court. Costs of this appeal are assessed against plaintiffs-appellants.

NOTES TO RICHARD v. MANGION

1. Consent and Self-Defense.   The primary issue in Richard v. Mangion is whether Shawn voluntarily participated in the fight with Jeremy. Consent may be difficult to establish when the parties were engaged in a fight because the defenses of consent and self-defense may seem to overlap. As in McQuiggan v. Boy Scouts of America, the court looked at "reasonable appearances." On the one hand, Jeremy appeared to have provoked Shawn. On the other hand, there was testimony that Shawn went to the rope swing "fully willing to fight." The court observed that peer pressure does not vitiate consent.

In understanding the court's decision, is it helpful to look at the order of events and Shawn's options at each point — from arriving at the rope swing to getting up out of the ditch and swinging at Jeremy? Does it matter who swung first?

2. *Consent and Excessive Force.* The court in Richard v. Mangion states that consent is vitiated by unnecessary or excessive force. Excessive force is a contact that is not "consistent with the understood rules of the game." That is not the same as saying that consent is vitiated by unanticipated results. For example, in McQuiggan v. Boy Scouts of America, while the plaintiff had not consented to the particular harms he suffered, he was barred from recovering damages for them. Was the court's conclusion that there was no excessive force in Richard v. Mangion consistent with the fact that the plaintiff suffered hemorrhaging in his eye that required two operations and $15,000 in medical bills?

3. *Consent to a Breach of the Peace.* State laws differ as to whether the defense of consent is available to a defendant whose conduct is a crime. When abortion was criminalized in some states, for instance, a person performing an abortion could not use consent to contact as a defense if sued by an injured patient. Some fistfights and other activities leading to assaults and batteries are considered *breaches or disturbances of the peace*, which are crimes. In some states, perhaps the majority, consent is not an available defense if the fight is a breach of the peace.

Problem
Consent and Excessive Force

In Lane v. Holloway, 3 All Eng. Rep. 129 (Court of Appeal, 1967), there was a fight, of sorts, between Mr. Lane and Mr. Holloway. Mr. Lane, a somewhat infirm, 64-year-old retired gardener living in England, resided in a quiet courtyard onto which backed a noisy cafe run by 23-year-old Mr. Holloway. Returning from a bar at 11 o'clock one night, Mr. Lane was chatting in the courtyard. Holloway's wife, disturbed by the noise, called out to them, "You bloody lot." The court described the subsequent events as follows:

> Mr. Lane replied: "Shut up, you monkey-faced tart." Mr. Holloway sprang up and twice said: "What did you say to my wife?" He said it twice. Mr. Lane said: "I want to see you on your own," implying a challenge to fight. Whereupon Mr. Holloway came out in his pyjamas and dressing-gown. He walked up the courtyard to the place where Mr. Lane was standing at his door. He moved up close to Mr. Lane in a manner which made Mr. Lane think that he might himself be struck by Mr. Holloway. Whereupon Mr. Lane threw a punch at Mr. Holloway's shoulder. Then Mr. Holloway drew his right hand out of his pocket and punched Mr. Lane in the eye, a very severe blow.

Mr. Lane was taken to the hospital with a very serious eye injury requiring 16 stitches that worsened his chronic glaucoma. Did Mr. Lane consent to a battery? How much force was Mr. Holloway entitled to use? Did Mr. Holloway use excessive force?

Statute: DISTURBING THE PEACE
La. Rev. Stat. 14:103A(1)-(6) (2017)

A. Disturbing the peace is the doing of any of the following in such manner as would foreseeably disturb or alarm the public:
(1) Engaging in a fistic encounter; or

(2) Addressing any offensive, derisive, or annoying words to any other person who is lawfully in any street, or other public place; or call him by any offensive or derisive name, or make any noise or exclamation in his presence and hearing with the intent to deride, offend, or annoy him, or to prevent him from pursuing his lawful business, occupation, or duty; or

(3) Appearing in an intoxicated condition; or

(4) Engaging in any act in a violent and tumultuous manner by any three or more persons; or

(5) Holding of an unlawful assembly; or

(6) Interruption of any lawful assembly of people.

NOTE TO STATUTE

Defining "Disturbing the Peace."   Many states have statutes defining what constitutes disturbing the peace. These statutes may distinguish between when consent to a harmful contact is a defense and when it is not. The statute reproduced above applies in Louisiana, where the fight between Jeremy and Shawn in the Richard v. Mangion opinion occurred. Did Jeremy and Shawn's fight fit within this statute's definition of "disturbing the peace"?

B. Defense of Self and Others — The Proportionality Principle

Proportionality is central to the defenses to assault and battery. In defense of one's self, of another person, or of one's land or property, an actor may use force proportionate to: (1) the interest the actor is protecting; and (2) the injury or harm threatened by the other. The law values the interest in human life more highly than the interest in personal property. Accordingly, an actor is privileged to use greater force to protect a life than to protect an automobile. An actor is privileged to use greater force to prevent a stab than to prevent a slap. Appreciating how the law values different interests and weighs different kinds of injuries and harm makes it easier to understand how much force an actor may use in self-defense, defense of others, and defense of property.

In a case where a boy was followed home from school by another boy who threatened to beat him up, Slayton v. McDonald identifies factors relevant to determining how much force a person may use for self-defense. A general approach to this issue first requires establishing how much force may be used and then deciding whether the actual force used was greater than the allowable maximum. An actor who is entitled to use some force may still be liable for the consequences of using excessive force. Young v. Warren applies this principle to the privilege to use force to protect others.

SLAYTON v. McDONALD

690 So. 2d 914 (La. Ct. App. 1997)

WILLIAMS, J. . . .

On the afternoon of May 20, 1994, fourteen-year-old Daniel McDonald and fourteen-year-old James Slayton had a disagreement while riding the school bus to their neighboring Dubach homes. Slayton was the larger of the two boys and was attending high school. McDonald was attending junior high school. The disagreement began when Slayton threw a piece of paper at McDonald. After McDonald threw the paper back at Slayton, Slayton threatened to come to McDonald's house. McDonald told Slayton not to come to his house. When asked about Slayton's reputation as a fighter, McDonald testified he had heard that Slayton had won fights against people larger than himself, and that Slayton could "take care of himself pretty good."

Later that afternoon, after McDonald arrived at home, he went outside his house and saw Slayton walking up the long driveway toward him. Slayton testified that he went to McDonald's house because he wanted to talk to McDonald about "kicking and punching on little kids and about messing with me and stuff." There were no adults present at McDonald's home when Slayton arrived at the residence. McDonald yelled at Slayton to go home. However, Slayton kept walking up McDonald's driveway. Slayton testified that he did not hear McDonald's warning. After shouting the warning to Slayton, McDonald went into his house, got his twelve-gauge shotgun, came back outside and loaded the gun with #7½ shot shells. McDonald testified that Slayton saw him load the gun; Slayton said that he did not. Again, McDonald asked Slayton to leave and Slayton refused.

McDonald then retreated into his home and called 911 to request help. McDonald testified that he closed the front door of his house after retreating inside. Slayton testified that the door was open. However, it is undisputed that the front door of the McDonald home did not have a lock and anyone could open it from the outside.

As McDonald spoke to the 911 operator, Slayton came inside McDonald's house. The transcript of the 911 conversation reveals that McDonald told Slayton to leave several times, to no avail. McDonald can be heard to say: "I think he's like sixteen. He's a lot bigger than me and he's in my house"; "Don't take another step towards me"; and, "If he keeps coming toward me I'm going to shoot him."

McDonald testified that Slayton pointed at his own leg, dared McDonald to shoot, and said that McDonald "didn't have the guts" to shoot. McDonald also stated that Slayton told him he was going to teach him a lesson and "kick my [McDonald's] ass." Slayton testified that after McDonald threatened to shoot him, he told McDonald that if McDonald shot him, he would get up and beat McDonald.

When asked if he was afraid when Slayton came into his house, McDonald testified that Slayton frightened him because "he [Slayton] had a crazy look in his eye. I didn't know what he was going to do after he didn't stop for the gun, I thought he must have been crazy." McDonald also told the 911 operator that "he's kinda crazy, I think." McDonald testified that Slayton "asked me if I could get him before he got to me and got the gun first. I was afraid that if he came past the gun that he was crazy enough to kill me."

At some point during the encounter, Slayton's younger sister, Amanda, arrived at the McDonald home and asked Slayton to leave because McDonald was armed. According to McDonald, Slayton refused to leave by saying "he's too scared to shoot me. He's about to cry." The 911 operator told McDonald several times not to shoot Slayton; McDonald said "I ain't gonna shoot him but in the leg. But I have to defend myself." Slayton testified that McDonald never pointed the shotgun at his head or chest.

What happened next was a matter of some dispute. On the 911 transcript, McDonald tells Slayton that "I might just count to three." Slayton testified that he was kneeling down because he was "resting waiting for the cops to get there so I could tell my story." However, Amanda Slayton and McDonald testified that Slayton was standing. Both Amanda and James Slayton testified that Slayton did not make a move toward McDonald, and Slayton testified that at all times during the incident, he was never more than two feet inside the McDonald home. However, McDonald testified that Slayton then began to count and to move "eight feet at least" into the home. On the tape of the 911 conversation, most of what Slayton says is inaudible, but, at the point where McDonald states that he might count to three, Slayton can be heard to count "one — two — three." McDonald then shot Slayton once in the left knee. Slayton's grandmother arrived shortly thereafter, pulled Slayton out of the McDonald home and waited for the paramedics and law enforcement authorities to arrive.

McDonald testified that from his experience, a load of #7½ shot did not do a great deal of damage to animals at ordinary hunting distance, but he had never fired his shotgun at anything so close before. On the 911 tape, McDonald can be heard saying, "I ain't got but squirrel shot in here. . . ."

Nevertheless, according to one of Slayton's doctors, Dr. Richard I. Ballard, the shot charge caused Slayton a "devastating" and "severe" injury that will require knee fusion rendering his knee permanently stiff and the injured leg at least an inch shorter than the other leg. Slayton and his parents testified that the injury had caused Slayton tremendous pain and had drastically reduced or eliminated his ability to engage in activities he used to enjoy. Slayton is also unable to perform chores around the house. Moreover, plaintiff introduced evidence that his family had incurred $43,310.51 in medical costs and had lost $1,349.00 in wages due to doctor visits at the time of trial. Further, plaintiff anticipated at least one future operation on Slayton's knee. . . .

The plaintiff contends the trial court erred in finding that [Daniel McDonald] acted reasonably under the circumstances surrounding this incident, and thus, was justified in shooting [James Slayton] in the leg. We do not find that the trial court erred. . . .

[Generally, one is not justified in using a dangerous weapon in self-defense if the attacking party is not armed but only commits battery with his fists or in some manner not inherently dangerous to life. However, resort to dangerous weapons to repel an attack may be justifiable in certain cases when the fear of danger of the person attacked is genuine and founded on facts likely to produce similar emotions in reasonable men. Under this rule, it is only necessary that the actor have grounds which would lead a reasonable man to believe that the employment of a dangerous weapon is necessary, and that he actually so believes. All facts and circumstances must be taken into account to determine the reasonableness of the actor's belief, but detached reflections or a pause for consideration cannot be demanded under circumstances which by their nature require split second decisions. Various factors relied upon by the courts to determine the reasonableness of the actions of the party being attacked are the character and reputation of the attacker, the belligerence of the attacker, a large difference in size and strength between the parties, an overt act by the attacker, threats of serious bodily harm, and the impossibility of a peaceful retreat]

In the instant case, McDonald testified that he believed that Slayton had beaten up people larger than himself, and, in essence, was capable of giving McDonald a beating as well; Slayton admitted that he had been in two fights while attending junior high school but gave no details of those altercations. Moreover, Slayton exhibited marked belligerence by refusing to leave McDonald's home despite repeated demands by McDonald while the latter was on the telephone with law enforcement authorities and was armed with a loaded twelve-gauge shotgun. This combination of reputation and belligerence evidence provides support for the trial court's conclusion that "the presence of the shotgun and defendant's threats were insufficient to thwart plaintiff's advances." It is undisputed that Slayton was considerably physically larger than McDonald, and the trial court accepted McDonald's testimony that Slayton had threatened to harm him. Indeed, Slayton himself admitted that he told McDonald that if McDonald shot him, he was going to get up and beat McDonald.

The trial court's finding that McDonald shot Slayton "to stop the plaintiff's advance" is a decision based upon the court's judgment of the credibility of the witnesses. Although both Slayton and his sister contradicted McDonald's testimony that Slayton was advancing when he was shot, Slayton's testimony that he was kneeling down when he was shot is contradicted by that of his sister and McDonald. Additionally, Slayton's testimony that he never came more than two feet into the house is contradicted by McDonald's [father's] testimony that he found blood about ten feet inside his home. Finally, the 911 tape, on which Slayton's voice became clearly audible only seconds before McDonald shot him, is further support for the conclusion that Slayton was advancing upon McDonald when shot. From its reasons for judgment, it is apparent that the trial court chose to credit McDonald's version of events over Slayton's version. Because the record supports this decision, it will not be disturbed on appeal.

Finally, it is evident that McDonald was simply unable to retreat from the encounter. While retreat is not a condition precedent for a finding of self-defense using justifiable force, in our opinion, the retreat of a lawful occupant of a home into a position in his home from which he cannot escape an attacker except by the use of force is strong evidence that the occupant's use of force to prevent the attack is proper. Although a shotgun may be a deadly weapon, McDonald used the gun in a way that he calculated would stop the attack without fatally injuring Slayton. Further, as recited above, McDonald testified that he was "afraid that if he [Slayton] came past the gun that he was crazy enough to kill me." Under these circumstances, where McDonald was on the telephone with law enforcement authorities and had repeatedly demanded that Slayton leave, and Slayton continued to advance and threaten McDonald, we cannot disagree with the trial court's conclusion that McDonald used reasonable force to repel Slayton's attack. . . .

YOUNG v. WARREN

383 S.E.2d 381 (N.C. Ct. App. 1989)

GREENE, J.

In this civil action the plaintiff appeals from a final judgment entered by the trial court, pursuant to a jury verdict, denying any recovery on a wrongful death action.

The evidence introduced at trial showed that defendant shot and killed Lewis Reid Young ("Young") on 12 May 1986. The death occurred as a result of a 20-gauge shotgun blast fired at close range into the deceased's back. On 14 October 1986, the defendant pled guilty to involuntary manslaughter.

Prior to the shooting, in the early morning hours of 12 May 1986, Young, who had been dating defendant's daughter for several months, went to the home of defendant's daughter who lived with her two children within sight of the defendant's residence.

Upon arriving at the defendant's daughter's home, Young threw a large piece of wood through the glass in the front door. He then entered the home by reaching through the broken window and unlocking the door. Once inside the house Young argued with the defendant's daughter and "jerked" her arm. At that point, the defendant arrived with his loaded shotgun, having been awakened by a telephone call from a neighbor, his ex-wife, who had told him "something bad is going on" at his daughter's house. When the defendant arrived at his daughter's house, he heard screaming and saw Young standing inside the door. The defendant then testified:

A. I told him like, "Come on out. This doesn't make any sense," and he kind of came forward, you know, kind of had his hands up like that. (Indicating) I backed away from the door and I told him to get on out. "This can be taken care of tomorrow," or something to that effect.

Q. You told him to get the hell out, didn't you?

A. Well, okay; something like that.

Q. Okay. And then what happened?

A. Then he walked out the door and I just backed up like he came out the door and he walked over about six feet. There is a cement porch there, and he stepped right there, and I was behind him anywhere from a foot to eighteen inches, maybe even two foot, and he stopped. And in my opinion, he started to turn around. . . .

Q. What did he do?

A. He stopped and started to lower his hands and started to turn around.

Q. What did you do?

A. I prodded him with the gun and told him to get on out, and that's when it went off.

The trial judge submitted two issues to the jury, the second issue being submitted over the objection of the plaintiff: . . .

2. Did the defendant, William S. Warren, act in the lawful defense of his daughter, Autumn Stanley, and her children, his grandchildren?
Answer: Yes.

Pursuant to the jury's answers to the issues submitted by the judge, the trial court ordered "that the plaintiff, Lewis Rankin Young, Jr., have and recover nothing of the defendant, William S. Warren, and that the costs be taxed against the plaintiff."

The determinative issue is whether the trial court erred in submitting the defense of family issue to the jury.

We first determine whether a defendant in a civil action may assert defense of family to justify assault on a third party. While self-defense and defense of family are seen more often in the context of criminal law, these defenses are nonetheless appropriate in civil actions. . . .

An assault on a third party in defense of a family member is privileged only if the defendant had a well-grounded belief that an assault was about to be committed by another on the family member. . . ." State v. Hall, 366 S.E.2d 527, 529 (1988). However, in no event may defendant's action be in excess of the privilege of self-defense granted by law to the family member. The privilege protects the defendant from liability only to the extent that the defendant did not use more force than was necessary or reasonable. Finally, the necessity for the defense must "be immediate, and attacks made in the past, or threats for the future, will not justify" the privilege. . . .

[T]he record contains no evidence that the defendant reasonably believed his daughter was, at the time of the shooting of the plaintiff, in peril of death or serious bodily harm. At that time, the plaintiff stood outside the house with his back to the defendant. Defendant's daughter and children were inside the house, removed from any likely harm from plaintiff. Accordingly, ... the evidence in this trial did not support the submission of the issue to the jury, and the plaintiff is entitled to a new trial. ...

NOTES TO SLAYTON v. McDONALD AND YOUNG v. WARREN

1. ***Proportionality in Defense of Self and Others.*** Slayton v. McDonald and Young v. Warren illustrate the principle of proportionality as applied to defense of self and others. One may use *deadly force* only to prevent serious bodily harm. When an actor is faced with a battery or assault that does not involve serious bodily harm, he or she is entitled only to use *moderate* or *reasonable force.* In Restatement (Second) of Torts §63 comment b, "serious bodily harm" means

> a bodily harm the consequence of which is so grave or serious that it is regarded as differing in kind, and not merely in degree, from other bodily harm. A harm which creates a substantial risk of fatal consequences is a "serious bodily harm." ... The permanent or protracted loss of the function of any important member or organ is also a "serious bodily harm."

Compare the harm McDonald faced to the harm Warren's daughter faced *at the time of the shooting.* Note that Young was shot in the back, after he had left Warren's daughter's house. The privilege to use force to protect self and others is not a right to retaliate or seek revenge; it is a privilege to use force to protect. Are there any parts of Warren's testimony that, if believed, would support a privilege for Warren to use deadly force to protect himself?

Would Warren's daughter, Autumn, have been privileged to shoot Young after Young threw a large piece of wood through the glass, entered Autumn's house, and jerked Autumn's arm? If Young had been inside Autumn's house jerking Autumn's arm at the time Warren showed up with the shotgun, would Warren have been privileged to shoot Young?

2. ***Objective Test for Perception of Threat.*** Generally, one may not use deadly force to protect one's self or others from bodily harm that is not serious. If the actor actually fears serious bodily harm *and* a reasonable person in the actor's position would fear serious bodily harm, then the actor may defend him- or herself by using deadly force. This "reasonable person," according to the Restatement (Second) of Torts §63 comment i, must be a person of "ordinary firmness and courage." It does not matter what harm the attacker intends to inflict. The privilege arises from the reasonable perception of an impending battery.

Daniel McDonald testified that he thought James Slayton "was crazy enough to kill me." The court in Slayton v. McDonald identified six factors for determining the reasonableness of the actions of a party being attacked: (1) the character and reputation of the attacker, (2) the belligerence of the attacker, (3) differences in size and strength of the parties, (4) whether there was an overt act by the attacker, (5) whether serious bodily harm was threatened, and (6) whether a peaceful retreat was possible. A defendant need not show that all of these factors are present to be privileged to use deadly force. Which of these factors are present in Slayton v. McDonald?

Instead of the six-factor test used in Slayton v. McDonald, the Restatement (Second) of Torts focuses on the nature of the likely harm when determining the extent of force an actor may use to protect himself and others. Section 65 says that an actor may use deadly force if he reasonably believes he is "put in peril of death or serious bodily harm or ravishment." How does this test compare with the six-factor test?

3. *Extent of Force Used.* In addition to determining how much force an actor is entitled to use, the factfinder must determine how much force the actor actually did use. The extent of force used is not measured by the harm suffered but rather by the harm the defendant intended to cause or was likely to cause. Did Daniel McDonald and William Warren intend to use the same amount of force? Was it likely the force each used would cause the same amount of harm? Consider how they aimed their guns and the ammunition they used. What is the difference in the intent of McDonald and Warren?

4. *Assault in Criminal and Civil Law.* The court in Young v. Warren says that the question is "whether a defendant in a civil action may assert defense of family to justify assault on a third party." Frequently, courts use the word "assault" to indicate a harmful physical contact that tort law would describe as a "battery." In criminal law, an assault may occur even without the victim fearing an imminent contact. This difference between criminal law and the civil law action for assault will not cause confusion for readers who look carefully at the nature of the injury inflicted. Even though the court in Young v. Warren referred to the shotgun blast in the back as an assault, touching another person with shotgun pellets is certainly a harmful contact that tort law would describe as a battery.

Statute: USE OF DEADLY PHYSICAL FORCE AGAINST AN INTRUDER

Colo. Rev. St. §18-1-704.5 (2017)

(1) The general assembly hereby recognizes that the citizens of Colorado have a right to expect absolute safety within their own homes.

(2) Notwithstanding the provisions of §18-1-704 [adopting a proportionate force rule for other cases], any occupant of a dwelling is justified in using any degree of physical force, including deadly physical force, against another person when that other person has made an unlawful entry into the dwelling, and when the occupant has a reasonable belief that such other person has committed a crime in the dwelling in addition to the uninvited entry, or is committing or intends to commit a crime against a person or property in addition to the uninvited entry, and when the occupant reasonably believes that such other person might use any physical force, no matter how slight, against any occupant.

Statute: USE OF FORCE IN DEFENSE OF A PERSON

Fla. Stat. §776.012 (2017)

A person is justified in using force, except deadly force, against another when and to the extent that the person reasonably believes that such conduct is necessary to defend himself or herself or another against the other's imminent use of unlawful force. However, a person is justified in the use of deadly force and does not have a duty to retreat if:

(1) He or she reasonably believes that such force is necessary to prevent imminent death or great bodily harm to himself or herself or another or to prevent the imminent commission of a forcible felony; or

(2) Under those circumstances permitted pursuant to §776.013.

Statute: HOME PROTECTION; USE OF DEADLY FORCE; PRESUMPTION OF FEAR OF DEATH OR GREAT BODILY HARM

Fla. Stat. §776.013(1)(a), (b) (2017)

... (2) A person is presumed to have held a reasonable fear of imminent peril of death or great bodily harm to himself or herself or another when using defensive force that is intended or likely to cause death or great bodily harm to another if:

(a) The person against whom the defensive force was used was in the process of unlawfully and forcefully entering, or had unlawfully and forcibly entered, a dwelling, residence, or occupied vehicle, or if that person had removed or was attempting to remove another against that person's will from the dwelling, residence, or occupied vehicle; and

(b) The person who uses defensive force knew or had reason to believe that an unlawful and forcible entry or unlawful and forcible act was occurring or had occurred.

NOTES TO STATUTES

1. The "Make My Day" Myth?   Current street wisdom holds that a homeowner is entitled to shoot anyone who enters the home uninvited. Many state statutes make special mention of people's right to be secure in their dwellings. The Colorado statute, for instance, recognizes "that the citizens of Colorado have a right to expect *absolute safety* within their own homes," although, as the second paragraph of that section reveals, the right has substantial qualifications. The recently adopted Florida statute, which has been copied by some other states, has fewer qualifications. Does the Florida statute in effect allow individuals to kill others in defense of property?

2. The Obligation to Retreat.   Jurisdictions differ with respect to the obligation of a person to retreat. The court in Slayton v. McDonald considers the possibility of retreat as merely one factor to be considered in determining the amount of force one is privileged to use. The Restatement (Second) §65 denies the privilege to use deadly force in self-defense to one who "correctly or reasonably believes that he can safely avoid the necessity of so defending himself by ... retreating" unless he is attacked in a dwelling place. The dwelling place exception is sometimes called the "castle doctrine." When is a person obliged to retreat under the Florida statute?

C. Defense of Land and Personal Property

The privilege to use force to defend land and personal property is also based on the principle of proportionality. Because the law values human life more than land or other possessions, there is less justification for the use of deadly force in these cases than in cases involving defense of people. Woodard v. Turnipseed involves a farmer's use of force, allegedly to protect himself and his property. The majority opinion and the concurrence treat separate issues: One discusses the right to use force to prevent harm to one's self and one's property, and the other discusses the right to use force to prevent intruders from being on one's land without permission.

WOODARD v. TURNIPSEED

784 So. 2d 239 (Miss. Ct. App. 2000)

IRVING, J.

Kenwyon Woodard, a minor, by his father and next friend, filed a complaint against John Turnipseed in the Choctaw County Circuit Court seeking personal injury damages. The complaint arises from an assault and battery committed with a broom against him by Turnipseed, a large dairy farmer. . . .

The jury returned a verdict for Turnipseed. After the denial of his post-trial motion for judgment notwithstanding the verdict, or in the alternative, for a new trial, Kenwyon has appealed. . . .

On September 7, 1996, Kenwyon [Woodard] was employed as a minimum wage milker with Turnipseed Dairy Farms of Ackerman, Mississippi. He had been working for Turnipseed Dairy Farms approximately six months during his latest employment but had worked for the dairy once before. His first employment with the dairy ended when he, according to Turnipseed, was fired by Turnipseed for not cleaning the cows prior to attaching the milker. On September 7, he was fired again for the same reason. According to Kenwyon, he did not know why he was fired the first time.

On September 7, according to Turnipseed, Kenwyon, along with two other boys, were preparing cows to be milked. One boy was driving the cows into the stalls, another was dipping the cows' udders in disinfectant, and Kenwyon was using paper towels to clean the udders. Turnipseed observed that Kenwyon had passed over three filthy cows. Upon making this observation, Turnipseed told Kenwyon, "you are fired, and go punch out."

Turnipseed claims that when he fired Kenwyon the first time Kenwyon had threatened to get him. Specifically, Kenwyon had said at that time, "I will get you for this." Remembering the previous threat, Turnipseed "thought this boy may vandalize my time clock." Because of this, Turnipseed decided to escort Kenwyon to the time clock. According to Turnipseed, Kenwyon started with a verbal assault as they walked out of the barn. Turnipseed heard the same threat he had heard upon the first firing of Kenwyon. In any event, Turnipseed escorted Kenwyon to the time clock, and Kenwyon changed clothes and telephoned his father to get a ride home. . . .

Turnipseed gave this account of the physical assault:

And now listen to this. Shirley is my foreman. I told her Shirley, I don't care if the cows go dry, don't allow this boy back on the farm. I passed him off to her and went back to the barn and milked. . . . Ten minutes later I step out of the barn and there is Kenwyon. I said Kenwyon, didn't I tell you not to come back on my farm. Which wasn't quite the truth because I didn't address him. I addressed her in his presence. . . .

Kenwyon didn't say anything. I said Kenwyon I am telling you to get off my property. Kenwyon said I am not going anywhere. I stood there a minute. I looked down. There was a broom leaning against the barn. I picked the broom up. I said Kenwyon, you see this broom. I am telling you to get off my property. Kenwyon didn't respond in any way. I walked the eight steps to Kenwyon, and I hit him three times with the broom. The last lick I hit him, the broom handle cracked. Didn't break. Cracked. Kenwyon decided he wanted to leave my farm, and he did.

As a result of the attack, Kenwyon suffered a hematoma of the right flank, a contusion of the left forearm and some contusion to the kidney. . . .

Turnipseed contends that he attacked Kenwyon in defense of self and property. Turnipseed argues that because Kenwyon had threatened to get him on a previous occasion as well as on the occasion giving rise to this appeal, he reasonably feared for his safety and the safety of his property. He contends that this is particularly true in light of the fact that he told Kenwyon to leave, but Kenwyon refused to do so.

We first recognize that if the facts showed that Turnipseed or his property were imperiled by Kenwyon, he would have had a legitimate right to defend himself and his property, but using only such force as would have been reasonably necessary to accomplish the task. Did the facts show any such peril? The answer is an emphatic "no."

We look to the evidence in the light most favorable to Turnipseed. Turnipseed testified that, while he was escorting Kenwyon out of the barn to the time clock, Kenwyon repeated over and over again that Kenwyon was going to get Turnipseed. Kenwyon did nothing other than make this threat. Turnipseed went back into the barn and began to assist with the milking operation. Ten minutes later, Turnipseed sees Kenwyon sitting on a car parked on Turnipseed's property. Kenwyon has nothing in his hands and is doing nothing other than sitting on the car. Turnipseed says to Kenwyon, "didn't I tell you not to come back on my farm," and Kenwyon did not say anything. Turnipseed then tells Kenwyon to get off Turnipseed's property. Kenwyon says, "I am not going anywhere." Turnipseed picks up a broom and again tells Kenwyon to get off Turnipseed's property. Kenwyon does not respond. Turnipseed then walks eight steps to Kenwyon and hits him three times with the broom. This evidence clearly shows that neither Turnipseed nor his milking operation was in any danger of being attacked by Kenwyon, the ninety-five pound minor. Turnipseed knew that Kenwyon had not been able to reach anyone to get a ride off the property because Turnipseed was there when the unsuccessful calls were made. Further, Turnipseed knew that Kenwyon did not possess his own transportation and that Kenwyon's father or mother transported him to and from work at Turnipseed's Dairy Farm.

When Turnipseed approached Kenwyon just before the attack, Kenwyon was not near any of the milking operations. He had not come back into the barn or given any indications that he was attempting to do so. It had been at least ten minutes since he had been escorted out of the barn. Surely, that was enough time for him to return and launch any attack he wanted to make if indeed he had planned to do so.

The record is unclear as to how far Kenwyon lived from Turnipseed's dairy farm, but there is some indication that it was at least between five and ten miles. Having failed to reach anyone at his home or his grandmother's house, Kenwyon was left with the options of walking the distance, however far, or waiting until his friend got off work. Under these circumstances, it was not unreasonable for Kenwyon to wait for a ride home. Granted, when he was accosted by Turnipseed and told to leave, he should have left, but his failing to do so did not justify the brutal attack by Turnipseed, especially considering the fact that Kenwyon was a minor with no available means of leaving except on foot.

Moreover, the record is clear that Turnipseed really never viewed Kenwyon as a threat to either his person or his property. Consider this testimony:

Q. And when you struck him, did he get off your property?

A. The first two times he stood there and glared at me. After the third blow he started off my property.

Q. And he — did he run off the property?

A. I just observed the first few steps. I was satisfied that he was no longer an immediate threat, and I went back to work.

Surely, if Turnipseed had been concerned that Kenwyon had intentions of attacking him or sabotaging his milking operations, he would have observed Kenwyon for more than "the first few steps," and he certainly would not have gone immediately back to work. He would have stayed around to see just what Kenwyon was going to do.

The evidence leads us to the inevitable conclusion that the trial court erred in not granting Kenwyon's motion for a directed verdict. Viewing the evidence in the light most favorable to Turnipseed, as we are required to do and have done in the preceding discussion, we are convinced that reasonable and fairminded persons could not have concluded that Turnipseed, a fifty-seven year old mature man weighing one hundred forty-five pounds, believed himself or his property in danger of attack from 4'9", ninety-five pound Kenwyon. Accordingly, we reverse and render on the question of Turnipseed's liability but remand the case for a new trial on damages only. . . .

SOUTHWICK, P.J., concurring.

I agree that there was no evidence to support a defense of self or property from imminent harm. . . .

The final possible justification is a subset of what has just been described, but it is worth discussing as a separate matter. This justification does not require a threat of imminent harm, but it is the right of a person in possession of property to use reasonable force to evict a trespasser. The harm is just the presence of an obstinate trespasser. The rule permits a landowner whose demand upon a trespasser to leave has been ignored, to use the force reasonably perceived as necessary to remove the intruder. Cited for this proposition was a criminal case holding "that a person has the right to preserve the peace at his own home and to evict from his home and premises persons who are creating disturbances upon his premises." Cotton v. State, 100 So. 383 (Miss. 1924).

However, this rule goes beyond threatened or existing "disturbances." I find the following to be an apt statement of the elements:

An actor is privileged to use reasonable force, not intended or likely to cause death or serious bodily harm, to prevent or terminate another's intrusion upon the actor's land or chattels, if

(a) the intrusion is not privileged or the other intentionally or negligently causes the actor to believe that it is not privileged, and

(b) the actor reasonably believes that the intrusion can be prevented or terminated only by the force used, and

(c) the actor has first requested the other to desist and the other has disregarded the request, or the actor reasonably believes that a request will be useless or that substantial harm will be done before it can be made.

Restatement (Second) of Torts §77 (1965). This rule would not permit the use of deadly force, but it strikes a balance short of such severe measures by assuring that people without authorization to be on property can be physically removed without having to await the commission of an overtly menacing act.

[The concurring judge concluded that Turnipseed had not properly raised the specific defense of eviction of a trespasser, but it would have failed anyway because Turnipseed used unreasonable force.]

NOTES TO WOODARD v. TURNIPSEED

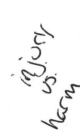

1. *Reasonable Force to Protect Land and Chattels.*   Farmer John Turnipseed claimed that he was privileged to beat Kenwyon Woodard with a broomstick because Turnipseed was protecting himself and his property. Moderate but not deadly force may be used to prevent harm to real or personal property. The time clock is an example of a *chattel*, the legal term for *personal property*, sometimes called "personalty," such as a car, a hat, or one's wallet. Interests in land, such as the right to possess land, are interests in *realty* or *real property*. Tort law analyzes defense of property the same way it analyzes defense of self or others. The amount of force one is entitled to use depends on what is threatened. Because property is valued less highly than human life, deadly force may not be used to protect property alone.

Turnipseed claimed that he was concerned about Woodard vandalizing the time clock and about the threat implicit in "I will get you for this." How does the force justified by these concerns compare to the force used?

2. *Reasonable Force to Eject Trespassers.*   Judge Southwick's concurring opinion in Woodard v. Turnipseed introduces a justification for the use of reasonable force even when harm to person or property is not threatened. Recall the distinction between injury and harm discussed in the notes following Nelson v. Carroll. An injury is an invasion of a legally protected interest, while a harm is an actual detriment. One interest related to land is the right to exclusive possession of the land. A person who intentionally enters another's land without permission or invitation is a trespasser and interferes with that right to exclusive possession. The person with the legal interest in land has the right to use reasonable force to prevent intrusions onto the land, as described by Judge Southwick in his quotation from Restatement (Second) of Torts §77. What actions would the law permit Turnipseed to take to defend his interest in exclusive possession of his property?

Problem
The Proportionality Principle and Defense to Assault and Battery

The proportionality principle helps to explain many privileges. The defense of arrest, for instance, creates a privilege for an actor to use reasonable force to arrest and detain someone who has or is committing a crime. In Mississippi, for instance, a private citizen may arrest any person without a warrant for an offense such as trespass on another's land or for a breach of the peace "attempted or threatened in his presence." See Whitten v. Cox, 799 So. 2d 1 (Miss. 2000). Police and private citizens alike are free from tort liability for the use of reasonable force when making a legal arrest. Applying the usual values the law assigns to life and property and the rules governing privileges to use force discussed in the cases in this section, consider the facts of Whitten v. Cox:

> On Sunday afternoon, March 19, 1995, Cox, Spinosa and Logan drove a pickup truck onto a tract of land which was being farmed and leased by Cox's brother. Cox claims he

Fires gun for truck Driving on Land

was inspecting the condition of the land at his brother's request to see whether it was ready to be worked. They attempted to access this land through a dirt road which crossed Whitten's land and then alongside an airstrip on property adjacent to Whitten's land. Whitten did not own the land that the airstrip was on, but he had built the airstrip with the permission of the owner of that land and was permitted to use it as such. Whitten also owned a camp and a firing range on his own land adjacent to the airstrip. The plaintiffs drove past the Whitten camp and drove the pickup down the center of the grass runway toward the field that Cox was going to inspect. Whitten saw the truck driving down the runway and ran after the truck, shouting for it to stop. When the truck did not stop Whitten drew his side arm, a .45 caliber semi-automatic pistol, and fired several shots. Whitten claims that he fired the shots into the air and at an angle away from the pickup in order to get the attention of the driver. Cox claims Whitten was shooting at the truck and that he heard a bullet pass by the open window. The truck then turned and came back towards the Whitten camp, this time along the side of the runway. Whitten placed himself in front of the truck and ordered the driver to stop the truck.

At this point, the facts become starkly disputed. Whitten claims that the driver of the truck refused to stop, forcing him to jump to one side, and hitting him with the side view mirror. The plaintiffs claim that the truck was slowing down, at idle speed, and that the driver was pumping the brakes, attempting to stop. The plaintiffs' recollection was that Whitten slipped in the mud and then grabbed onto the side mirror to support himself. It is undisputed that at this time Whitten shot out one of the back tires on the pickup. Whitten then ordered the plaintiffs out of the truck.

Again the facts are disputed. The plaintiffs claim that Whitten pointed the cocked pistol directly at them, waving it in their faces, shouting, cursing, and ordering them out of the truck and onto the ground. Cox claims that Whitten pressed the barrel of the gun to Cox's temple and told Cox he ought to kill him or "kick his face in" for being on the runway. Whitten denies pointing the gun at anyone, though it is undisputed that he was armed, that his friends standing around were armed with loaded assault rifles and that Whitten ordered the plaintiffs to kneel on the ground. Once they were out of the truck, Whitten informed all three that they were under arrest for trespass. One of Whitten's sons who was present brought some handcuffs from a nearby vehicle. It is undisputed that Whitten ordered one of the other men to handcuff Cox prior to taking him to a building at his camp. Cox claims that Whitten asked the other two plaintiffs whether they thought Cox could swim in the nearby Buzzard Bayou with those handcuffs on. Cox also claims that when he rose to his knees, Whitten pulled the bill of his cap down over his eyes and knocked his sunglasses off. Once the three plaintiffs were escorted back to Whitten's camp, Whitten unsuccessfully tried to telephone the Sheriff. Whitten then recognized Cox as the brother of the person who leased some farmland on the neighboring property where the airstrip was located. At this point Cox recalled that Whitten began to calm down and discuss how to resolve the situation. . . .

Did Whitten assault or batter Cox? Does the defense of arrest provide a privilege for Whitten? Consider first the extent of force justified and then the extent of force used.

Statute: FORCE IN DEFENSE OF PROPERTY

Utah Stat. §76-2-406 (2017)

A person is justified in using force, other than deadly force, against another when and to the extent he reasonably believes that force is necessary to prevent or terminate criminal interference with real property or personal property: (1) lawfully in his possession, (2) lawfully in the possession of a member of his immediate family, or (3) belonging to a person whose property he has a legal duty to protect.

Statute: USE OF FORCE IN DEFENSE OF PREMISES AND PROPERTY
N.D. Stat. §12.1-05-06 (2017)

Force is justified if it is used to prevent or terminate an unlawful entry or other trespass in or upon premises, or to prevent an unlawful carrying away or damaging of property, if the person using such force first requests the person against whom such force is to be used to desist from his interference with the premises or property, except that a request is not necessary if it would be useless or dangerous to make the request or substantial damage would be done to the property sought to be protected before the request could effectively be made.

Statute: USE OF FORCE IN DEFENSE OF PREMISES OR PERSONAL PROPERTY
N.J. Stat. §2C:3-6(b)(3) (2017)

Use of deadly force. The use of deadly force is not justifiable [in defense of premises] unless the actor reasonably believes that:

(a) The person against whom the force is used is attempting to dispossess him of his dwelling otherwise than under a claim of right to its possession; or

(b) The person against whom the force is used is attempting to commit or consummate arson, burglary, robbery or other criminal theft or property destruction; except that

(c) Deadly force does not become justifiable . . . unless the actor reasonably believes that:

(i) The person against whom it is employed has employed or threatened deadly force against or in the presence of the actor; or

(ii) The use of force other than deadly force to terminate or prevent the commission or the consummation of the crime would expose the actor or another in his presence to substantial danger of bodily harm. An actor within a dwelling shall be presumed to have a reasonable belief in the existence of the danger. . . .

NOTES TO STATUTES

1. *Limitations on the Use of Reasonable Force.* While some statutes privilege the use of reasonable force to protect property, as Utah's statute illustrates, others qualify the privilege. Requiring a request to desist is a common limitation, though a request is required only when it is reasonable, as the North Dakota statute indicates. Other statutes explicitly deny the privileged use of force when the actor knows that exclusion of the trespasser will expose the trespasser to a "substantial risk of serious bodily harm." See, e.g., N.J. Stat. §2C:3-6(b)(2) (2009).

2. *Limitations on the Use of Deadly Force.* While some states privilege use of deadly force to prevent serious crimes, others qualify the privilege. New Jersey's statute lists a number of crimes that justify the use of deadly force but qualifies the privilege by requiring that there also be threat of bodily harm to a person.

V. False Imprisonment

The tort of false imprisonment protects one's interest in being free from intentional confinement. As with assault and battery, a defendant who acts with the requisite intent will be liable for injury to the person confined regardless of whether harm results or whether the confinement is brief, subject to the principle of *de minimis non curat lex*.

A. Intent

"Intent" for false imprisonment has the usual meaning, including both purpose and substantial certainty. There is no liability for negligent or reckless imprisonment if the actor's conduct risks only a harmless confinement, so the courts carefully examine whether the intentionality requirement is met. Vumbaca v. Terminal One Group Ass'n L.P. examines the intent requirement in false imprisonment cases.

VUMBACA v. TERMINAL ONE GROUP ASS'N L.P.
859 F. Supp. 2d 343 (E.D.N.Y. 2012)

JACK B. WEINSTEIN, Senior District Judge.

. . . From December 26th to 27th, 2010, during the height of the holiday travel season, the New York metropolitan area was — somewhat unexpectedly — blanketed with over a foot of snow. John F. Kennedy International Airport (JFK) was closed to air traffic for the worst of the storm. When it reopened, there were continuing problems. Passengers on arriving flights were forced to endure substantial waits after landing before they were able to disembark. Difficulties appear to have been particularly severe at terminals serving international flights. The events sparked a federal investigation and new regulations that forbid foreign air carriers from permitting international flights to remain on the tarmac at a United States airport for more than four hours without allowing passengers to deplane.

Plaintiff Vivian Vumbaca was one of the stranded passengers. Trapped for most of the night aboard an Alitalia flight from Rome that had arrived at Terminal One, she was forced to endure, as she put it, "cramped, uncomfortable, malodorous conditions, without food, water and sanitation" for nearly seven hours. . . .

She sued Terminal One Group Association, L.P. (TOGA), which operates Terminal One, and seeks to represent similarly situated passengers claiming [among other theories] false imprisonment. . . .

Defendant moves to dismiss all of plaintiff's claims on the ground that plaintiff failed to state a claim under New York law. . . .

To establish a cause of action for false imprisonment under New York law, a plaintiff must show that: "(1) the defendant intended to confine him, (2) the plaintiff was conscious of the confinement, (3) the plaintiff did not consent to the confinement and (4) the confinement was not otherwise privileged." *Broughton v. State*, 335 N.E.2d 310, 314 (1975). When a legal duty exists to release plaintiff from confinement, an intentional refusal to release plaintiff constitutes false imprisonment. *E.g. Talcott v. National Exhibition Co.*, 128 N.Y.S. 1059 (2d Dep't 1911) (holding that, while staff of the defendant baseball park could prevent plaintiff visitor from exiting through the main exit, which was impassable due to a large crowd, it had a duty to inform him of another exit rather than detain him inside the stadium).

Under New York law, "mere knowledge and appreciation of a risk is not the same as the intent to cause injury. . . . A result is intended if the act is done with the purpose of accomplishing such a result or with knowledge that to a substantial certainty such a result will ensue. . . ." A defendant acting with intent must be more than merely negligent or reckless: "An act which is not done with [intent] does not make the actor liable to the other for a merely transitory or otherwise harmless confinement, although the act involves an unreasonable risk of imposing it and therefore would be negligent or reckless if the risk threatened bodily harm." Restatement (Second) of Torts §35(2) (1965). The Restatement illustrates the point as follows: "A, knowing that B, a customer, is in his shop, locks its only door in order to prevent a third person from entering. This is [an intentional] confinement of B, and A is subject to liability to him unless, under the circumstances, he is privileged." *Id.* cmt. d. Although A did not have the purpose of confining B — his purpose was to prevent a third person from entering — he was certain that his action would lead to the imprisonment of B.

Courts in other circuits, analyzing analogous circumstances under substantially similar common law rules, have dismissed claims for false imprisonment where plaintiffs were forced to remain inside a grounded aircraft for several hours.

In Abourezk v. New York Airline, Inc., 705 F. Supp. 656 (D.D.C. 1989), plaintiff booked a flight to New York in order to attend an event that same evening. When weather caused a three-hour delay that prevented him from actually reaching the event on time, he asked to deplane. The pilot refused, and flew on to New York. *Id.* at 658. The district court found that the plaintiff had consented to his initial confinement aboard the aircraft and thus framed the inquiry as whether he had "the right to revoke consent to a voluntary short term confinement." *Id.* at 664. It held that there could be no claim for false imprisonment, since there was no common law duty to release the plaintiff in the absence of exigent circumstances, "[n]or d[id] the facts indicate that [he] had the right to arrive in New York City at a specific time." *Id.* The court found dispositive the fact that "the airline's actions neither created nor lengthened the delay." *Id.* at 664. The D.C. Circuit affirmed. *Abourezk v. NY Airline*

Similarly, in Ray v. American Airlines, Inc., 609 F.3d 911 (2010), plaintiff's flight was held on a tarmac for nine hours due to bad weather conditions at its final destination. Despite being offered two opportunities to deplane, plaintiff chose to remain on the aircraft in the hopes that it would eventually take her to her final destination. The Court of Appeals for the Eighth Circuit held, on a motion for summary judgment, that defendants were entitled to judgment as a matter of law on plaintiff's false imprisonment claim because she "could not prove that her detention on the plane was without consent and without authority of law." *Id.* at 924. Because the plaintiff failed to present evidence of "any statute or regulation, federal or state, in existence on [the day of her confinement in the aircraft] that placed a limit on the number of hours [the air carrier] was permitted to keep passengers aboard one of its airplanes during a delay or that otherwise controlled the conduct [she] alleges forms the basis of her false imprisonment claim." *Id.*

In the instant case, plaintiff initially consented to her confinement in the aircraft for the purposes of her transportation from Rome to New York. Her consent was limited to that purpose; she did not consent to be detained indefinitely aboard the aircraft. . . . [D]efendant had a duty to provide a safe means of egress from the airplane it is assumed, for the purposes of this motion, that its failure to ensure that there were

[Margin note: ✻ Case law usually dismisses FI claims on planes]

adequate ground handling staff was the proximate cause of her confinement. The question remains, however, whether defendant's failure to provide a means of egress was intentional.

In general, courts are reluctant to decide issues of intent on a motion for summary judgment.

In this case, plaintiff has failed to create a genuine issue of material fact as to the defendant's intent to confine her. Nothing in the record demonstrates that the defendant was more than merely negligent in its handling of the events of late December 2010. While it was likely that passengers would be confined in the aircraft for some period of time after landing, this possibility fell far short of the high probability that is required for defendant's knowledge to rise to the level of intent. No reasonable juror could conclude otherwise.

The claim for false imprisonment is dismissed.

NOTES TO VUMBACA v. TERMINAL ONE GROUP ASS'N L.P.

1. *Intention and Negligence.*   Confinement may result from another's careless or negligent act, such as a defendant having insufficient ground crew to facilitate passengers' deplaning, or an intentional act, such as a defendant acting in a way that was substantially certain to result in confinement. As the court in *Vumbaca* observes, negligent confinement that does not result in harm is not actionable. Intentional false imprisonment, as for other intentional torts, may result in nominal damages even if there is no harm.

2. *Purpose or Substantial Certainty.*   The two options for proving intent are the same for false imprisonment as for other intentional torts. There is no suggestion in *Vumbaca* that the defendant desired or had an insufficient ground crew in order to falsely imprison the passengers. Reviewing previous discussions in this chapter of how certain a defendant must be to be classified as "substantially certain" that its act will injure someone helps explain why the court dismissed the passenger's claim.

B. Confinement and Consent

Liability for false imprisonment arises only when the actor intends to confine another within boundaries fixed by the actor and such confinement results. An actor must intend to confine, not merely to restrain movement in a particular direction. Additionally, if one is aware of a reasonable means of escape, one has not been confined. Barrett v. Watkins and Zavala v. Wal-Mart Stores, Inc. explore the concept of confinement. *Zavala* also examines when a person's conduct constitutes consent to confinement.

BARRETT v. WATKINS

82 A.D.3d 1569 (N.Y. App. Div. 2011)

PETERS, J.P.

. . . On April 25, 2005, plaintiffs drove to a remote, wooded public recreation area located at the southeast side of the Toronto Reservoir in Sullivan County. When they attempted to leave, they discovered that the access road was blocked by an unoccupied truck. After approximately 15 minutes, during which time plaintiffs honked the horn of their vehicle in an effort to get someone's attention, Wade Ebert emerged and, after speaking with plaintiffs, refused to move the truck. Ebert then called defendant Steven M. Dubrovsky, whose company, defendant Woodstone Lakes Development, LLC, owned the land adjacent to the recreational area. Dubrovsky arrived at the area about 40 minutes later, told plaintiffs that they did not belong there and stated that he did not care if they had to sit there all night. Dubrovsky then got into his vehicle with Ebert and left the area, leaving plaintiffs behind. The police, who were called earlier by both parties, eventually arrived with Dubrovsky and resolved the incident by instructing that the truck be moved. No charges were brought against any party as a result of this incident . . . .

Plaintiffs thereafter commenced this action alleging unlawful imprisonment against, among others, Dubrovsky and the Woodstone Companies based upon the April 2005 incident . . . . Supreme Court granted defendants' . . . motion . . . for summary judgment and dismissed the complaint, prompting this appeal.

We begin by addressing plaintiffs' claim of unlawful imprisonment. In order to establish such a claim, plaintiffs were required to show that (1) defendants intended to confine them, (2) they were conscious of the confinement, (3) they did not consent to the confinement and (4) the confinement was not otherwise privileged. Initially, we reject the assertion of Dubrovsky and the Woodstone Companies (hereinafter collectively referred to as the Woodstone defendants) that plaintiffs were not actually confined. Although Dubrovsky stated during his deposition that he believed there was another way out of the recreational area, there is no evidence that he informed plaintiffs of this, that plaintiffs were otherwise aware of any alternate means of egress, or that any such other means was reasonable (*see* Restatement [Second] of Torts §36a).

Furthermore, viewing the evidence in a light most favorable to plaintiffs and affording them the benefit of all reasonable inferences, we find a question of fact as to whether the Woodstone defendants intended to confine them. The Woodstone defendants contend that there is no evidence connecting them to Ebert and, therefore, no basis for attributing Ebert's conduct to them. However, plaintiffs testified during their examination before trial that Ebert informed them during the confrontation that he was employed by Dubrovsky, proceeded to call Dubrovsky to inform him of the situation and, following the conversation, continued to block the access road out of the recreation area. Furthermore, according to the constable who was called to investigate the incident, Ebert stated that he was ordered to block the road in order to prevent plaintiffs from leaving the area. Although Dubrovsky stated during his examination before trial that Ebert was not employed by one of the Woodland Companies at the time of the incident and that he never directed Ebert to prevent plaintiffs from leaving, this creates issues of credibility which cannot be resolved on this summary judgment motion. Moreover, even in the absence of an employment relationship, genuine issues of fact exist as to whether Dubrovsky actively encouraged, furthered or ratified the confinement when, upon his arrival at the scene, he acquiesced in the continued confinement of plaintiffs and then proceeded to remove the individual (Ebert) who could have ended it. . . .

Ordered that the order is modified, on the law, without costs, by reversing so much thereof as granted a motion for summary judgment dismissing the unlawful imprisonment claim. . . .

ZAVALA v. WAL-MART STORES, INC.
691 F.3d 527 (3rd Cir. 2012)

SMITH, Circuit Judge.

This suit was brought in the U.S. District Court for the District of New Jersey by Wal-Mart cleaning crew members who are seeking compensation for unpaid overtime [a claim the court rejected] and damages for false imprisonment. The workers — illegal immigrants who took jobs with contractors and subcontractors Wal-Mart engaged to clean its stores — allege [that] Wal-Mart's practice of locking some stores at night and on weekends — without always having a manager available with a key — constituted false imprisonment. . . .

Plaintiffs' false imprisonment claims survived Wal-Mart's initial motion to dismiss. Wal-Mart subsequently offered affidavits asserting that it locked its doors at night to provide security for its staff and merchandise, that managers were often available to open locked doors, and that Wal-Mart had accessible emergency exits, as required by state and federal law. Wal-Mart also argued that Plaintiffs' repeated return to stores where they were "imprisoned" constituted consent. In response, Plaintiffs: (1) cited specific instances where they wanted to leave and managers were unavailable or refused to let them leave; (2) noted that no one ever showed them the location of emergency exits and their minimal proficiency in English would make it difficult or impossible to find them on their own; and (3) argued that Wal-Mart had an interest in concealing emergency exits to prevent theft of merchandise and discovery of the illegal workers by federal agents. On summary judgment, the District Court found Wal-Mart's assertions regarding the presence of emergency exits dispositive, as false imprisonment cannot occur where there is a safe alternative exit. . . .

The majority of Plaintiffs' false imprisonment claims fail because Plaintiffs impliedly consented to their "imprisonment." Apparently from the very beginning of their employment, Plaintiffs were aware that Wal-Mart's policy was to close and lock the main doors of its stores when they are not open for business. Plaintiffs nevertheless chose to continue coming to work. They do not allege that they objected to the locked-door policy, nor do they allege that they requested a manager be available during their shift to open the doors. Continuing to come to work under these conditions is "conduct . . . reasonably understood by another to be intended as consent" and is therefore "as effective as consent in fact." Restatement (Second) of Torts §892. As such, Plaintiffs "cannot recover in an action of tort for the conduct or for harm resulting from it." Id. at §892A.

But consent can be withdrawn, and Plaintiffs allege two instances when they wanted to leave but were unable to do so. Teresa Jaros alleges that she was sick and wanted to leave, but no manager was available to open the door. Petr Zednek alleges that he had a toothache, asked to leave, and was told he could not. He also alleges that he believed his manager, a "muscular" "blond" man, would assault him if he attempted to leave.

Jaros' consent likely encompasses the incident she alleges. By the time of her illness, she knew that she must work in a locked store for the duration of the shift. She knew that a manager would often be absent and therefore unable to open the door should a problem arise. Her consent arguably includes that aspect of her work. Consent only terminates "when the actor knows or has reason to know that the other is no longer willing for him to continue the particular conduct." Restatement (Second) of Torts §892A cmt. h. Since Wal-Mart was unaware that Jaros wanted to leave (because no manager was there), Jaros could not terminate her consent.

Regardless, Jaros' complaint and Zednek's complaint are resolved by the availability of emergency exits. "To make the actor liable for false imprisonment, the other's confinement within the boundaries fixed by the actor must be complete. . . . The confinement is complete although there is a reasonable means of escape, unless the other knows of it." Restatement (Second) of Torts §36. While both Jaros and Zednek disclaim knowledge of the emergency exits, such knowledge is properly imputed to them, even over their proclaimed ignorance and even on summary judgment. Federal Rule of Evidence 201 permits judicial notice of facts "generally known within the trial court's territorial jurisdiction" and we have noted that this includes "matters of common knowledge." *See Gov't of Virgin Islands v. Gereau,* 523 F.2d 140, 147 (3d Cir.1975). Courts have used judicial notice to establish facts in similar situations.

Emergency exits are by regulation a common feature of commercial buildings in the United States. We agree with the District Court that "it appears . . . indisputable that these emergency exits are required by law to be clearly marked, easily accessible, and unobstructed." *Zavala,* No. 03-5309, 2011 WL 1337476, at *1. We conclude that Jaros and Zednek must have been aware of the existence of emergency exits as a general feature of buildings, and therefore they must have been aware that emergency exits were likely to exist in the stores in which they worked. A reasonable jury could not conclude otherwise.

The question remaining is whether emergency exits were in fact available and unobstructed at the Wal-Mart stores in question. Wal-Mart has offered evidence of the availability and unobstructed nature of emergency exits in its stores. Plaintiffs have not directly rebutted this evidence. They have merely offered speculation that Wal-Mart had motive to conceal any emergency exits. But Plaintiffs do not actually demonstrate that the exits were absent or obstructed in any way. Judgment in favor of Wal-Mart is appropriate.

Plaintiffs cannot succeed by advancing a defense that leaving through the emergency exit would trigger an alarm or potentially result in the loss of their jobs. Regarding the alarm, "it is unreasonable for one whom the actor intends to imprison to refuse to utilize a means of escape of which he is himself aware merely because it entails a slight inconvenience[.]" Restatement (Second) of Torts §36 cmt. a. Nor is potential loss of employment a sufficient threat to constitute false imprisonment.

The only remaining issue is Zednek's claim that when he approached his manager and was denied permission to leave, he "knew that [the manager] would assault [him] if [Zednek] tried to escape through any door that would let [him] out." Zednek asserts that the manager wanted the store clean for the impending visit of a Wal-Mart executive. But Zednek's sole evidence of the manager's supposed violent tendencies is that the manager "is a muscular man (with blond hair)[.]" We need not credit this statement in any way.

In an earlier declaration, Zednek relates the toothache story and the request made to and denied by his manager, but curiously omits any belief that his manager would assault him. It is only in his third supplemental declaration — filed only a few weeks after Wal-Mart moved for summary judgment — that Zednek mentions the prospect that his manager might randomly assault him. Even on summary judgment, we need not credit a declaration contradicting a witness' prior sworn statements. While not precisely contradictory, Zednek's omission of such a crucial fact is highly questionable.

But even absent these suspicious circumstances, we conclude that no reasonable jury could credit Zednek's speculative statement that his manager would assault him had he tried to leave. Zednek offers no evidence in support of the statement. He does not allege that the manager had a propensity for violence. And he does not allege that the manager overtly or impliedly threatened him. Thus, summary judgment was appropriate.

[T]he District Court . . . rejected the false imprisonment claim on the merits. We will affirm.

NOTES TO BARRETT v. WATKINS AND ZAVALA v. WAL-MART STORES, INC.:

1. Complete Confinement.   In order to impose liability on an actor for false imprisonment, the plaintiff's confinement must be complete. Often this means that blocking someone from proceeding in a particular direction does not give rise to a claim for false imprisonment. Thus, in Bird v. Jones, 115 Eng. Rep. 688 (K.B. 1845), defendant was not liable for false imprisonment after preventing plaintiff from entering an enclosed portion of a highway reserved for paying spectators of a boat race. Confinement may result from physical barriers, such as blocking the road in *Barrett* or locking the exits in *Zavala*, or physical force such as the alleged assault by the manager in *Zavala*. Submission to other forms of coercion such as threatening to keep someone's property or to use physical force unless they remain may also constitute confinement.

2. Escape from Confinement.   There is also a lack of complete confinement if there is a reasonable way for the plaintiff to escape. When discussing this alternative, both *Barrett* and *Zavala* refer to Restatement [Second] of Torts §36, comment (a):

> If the actor knows of an avenue of escape, he cannot intend to imprison the other by closing all the other exits unless he believes that the other is unaware of the available avenue of escape. Since the actor has intended to imprison the other, the other is not required to run any risk of harm to his person or to his chattels or of subjecting himself to any substantial liability to a third person in order to relieve the actor from a liability to which his intentional misconduct has subjected him. So too, even though there may be a perfectly safe avenue of escape, the other is not required to take it if the circumstances are such as to make it offensive to a reasonable sense of decency or personal dignity.

The court in *Barrett* considers whether Barrett and the other plaintiffs knew of other avenues of escape. The court in *Zavala* considers whether there were other means of escape, whether the plaintiffs knew about them, and whether using them was reasonable. If a defendant knows that a plaintiff was unaware of a reasonable avenue of escape, that may support a finding that the defendant intended to confine the plaintiff. Comment (a) also describes when an avenue of escape is unreasonable. Restatement §36 Illustrations 4 and 5 are illustrative:

> 4. A closes every exit except one, the use of which would involve material harm to B's clothing. A has confined B.

5. A is naked in a Turkish bath. B locks the door into the dressing room but leaves open the door to the general waiting room where persons of both sexes are congregated. B has confined A.

3. *Confinement to Limited Area.*   The plaintiff in *Vumbaca* was confined in a relatively small space, the cabin of an airplane. By contrast, the plaintiffs in *Barrett* claimed to have been confined in a public recreation area, which presumably was of significantly greater size. Courts have sometimes held that even confinement to a single state may be limited enough, though confinement to a country may not. The boundaries of one's confinement need not be stationary to support a claim for false imprisonment. Although most false imprisonment cases involve confinement within static, fixed boundaries, a defendant who transports a plaintiff against his will, what may loosely be described as kidnapping, may also be liable for false imprisonment because the plaintiff is confined to a limited area.

4. *Consent.*   In *Zavala,* the plaintiffs gave their consent by agreeing to work in the store knowing there was no manager present to unlock the doors, illustrating that consent may be given by word or conduct. They claimed to have withdrawn consent in two instances. Jaros alleged that she was sick and wanted to leave, but no manager was available to open the door. Zednek alleged that he had a toothache, asked to leave, and was told he could not. Jaros's withdrawal of consent was ineffective because Wal-Mart was unaware of it and had no reason to know of it. Zednek communicated his withdrawal of consent, but the court concluded that, in any case, neither he nor Jaros had been completely confined in the first place.

Withdrawal of consent, even when effectively communicated to the defendant, requires only that the defendant take reasonable measures to release the plaintiff from confinement. In Abourezk v. New York Airline, Inc., 705 F. Supp. 656 (D.D.C. 1989), discussed in *Vumbaca,* the plaintiff was confined in the cabin of an airplane on the runway during a flight delay. When Abourezk realized he would miss an appointment in his destination city, he decided he no longer wished to take the flight and requested that the pilot return to the gate and allow him to deplane. The pilot refused. The *Abourezk* court concluded that, given the lack of exigent circumstances (such as a health or safety emergency), the plaintiff could not withdraw his initial consent to be on the airplane, and the defendant had no duty to release the plaintiff until arrival at the agreed destination.

5. *False Imprisonment: Similarities to Assault and Battery.*   Under the Restatement approach, false imprisonment shares many of the same features as other intentional torts discussed in this chapter. There are few reported cases on many of these situations so it is difficult to generalize about how states would approach these issues if they arose.

Awareness of Invasion of Interest: Under the Restatement §35 a person who is unaware that he or she has been falsely imprisoned may recover damages only if that person suffered actual harm. Injury is not enough. One reported decision that did not require actual harm is Scofield v. Critical Air Medicine, Inc., 52 Cal. Rptr. 2d 915 (Ct. App. 1996). In that case, a California intermediate appellate court endorsed the view that contemporaneous awareness of confinement is not essential to the tort, even in the absence of more than nominal damages. In *Scofield*, the defendant, an air evacuation service, induced children injured in an accident in Mexico to board a flight through fraud. The children learned only later that the service was not the one their father had arranged for them. The court upheld an award of $120,000 to the children for emotional harm resulting from the false imprisonment. For assault, contemporary awareness is required because assault requires an apprehension of imminent contact. Contemporary awareness is not required for battery, which requires only that a harmful or offensive contact result from the defendant's act.

Transferred Intent: An actor who intends a false imprisonment, assault, or battery to another and injures a third party may be liable to the third party. And an actor who intends one of these torts may be liable for the injuries and harms associated with any of the others that result. Thus, intent may be transferred both between people and between these torts.

Defense of Self, Others, and Property: One is privileged intentionally to confine another in defense of self or others or exclusive possession of one's property under the same conditions that would create a privilege to assault or batter another. When might a person confine another in self-defense? Restatement §67 offers following illustration:

> 1. A enters B's office and attempts to attack him. B, to avoid the attack, leaves his office and, to prevent A from pursuing him, locks the door, thus imprisoning A. B is not liable to A unless B confines A for an unreasonable length of time or in a dangerous place.

As this example illustrates, the proportionality principle discussed earlier in this chapter applies to false imprisonment as well as the other intentional torts.

Although authorities in assault and battery cases generally treat self-defense and defense of property as affirmative defenses, for which the defendant bears the burden of proof, it is somewhat common for courts and commentators to describe lack of any privilege as an element of the tort of false imprisonment. The *Vumbaca* and *Barrett* courts each list the elements of false imprisonment in New York as including that "the confinement was not otherwise privileged." Thus, it seems, in some jurisdictions a plaintiff's recovery is dependent on the plaintiff's ability to prove the defendant had no privilege, including self-defense or defense of property, that would justify the intentional confinement.

Consent: Just as in cases of assault and battery, one who has given valid consent by word or conduct to confinement cannot recover for false imprisonment, though he or she may withdraw that consent. As discussed earlier in this chapter, courts are split on whether defendants in all intentional tort cases must prove consent as an affirmative defense or whether plaintiffs must prove absence of consent. The *Vumbaca* and *Barrett* courts describe a plaintiff's lack of consent as an element of the tort, a part of plaintiff's prima facie case.

Problem
Confinement for False Imprisonment

Mrs. Gavigan, who was 8-months pregnant at the time of the incident, worked as a clerk at defendant's 7-Eleven franchise in Croyden, Pennsylvania. On December 4, 1996, Denise Rodriguez, the assistant manager of this particular store, said to Mrs. Gavigan, "Jen, can you come back [to the franchise owner's office], these people want to talk to you[?]." Mrs. Gavigan complied, and when she entered the office, Ms. Rodriguez introduced her to two representatives of the defendant who handled security matters, James Dale and Marjorie LaSorsa.

Shortly thereafter, Ms. Rodriguez exited the office, leaving Mrs. Gavigan alone with the two security representatives. Mr. Dale and Ms. LaSorsa then began to question

Mrs. Gavigan about various shortages in the store. The interview, all taking place within the franchisee's small, windowless office, continued for approximately one and a quarter hours. The door to the office was closed during the entire incident. All three parties were seated during the interview, with Mr. Dale on one side of Mrs. Gavigan and Ms. LaSorsa on the other side. According to Mrs. Gavigan and undisputed by the defendant, Mr. Dale and Ms. LaSorsa took turns leaving the room. The path to the door was clear. At no point during the questioning did Mr. Dale or Ms. LaSorsa inform Mrs. Gavigan that she could leave the room. Neither did they tell her that she could not leave the room or physically prevent her from so doing.

In deposition, Mrs. Gavigan testified that despite her protestations, Mr. Dale continued to state that she had stolen the money and at one point stated that he would "see her in jail" if not for her advancing pregnancy. She also testified that she was afraid to leave because they closed the door, and spoke to her in a harsh tone of voice. In contrast, Mr. Dale testified that he never threatened Mrs. Gavigan with jail. Both Mr. Dale and Ms. LaSorsa stated that it is company policy not to block the exit during a security interview.

Your senior partner is considering whether to file a motion for judgment as a matter of law in favor of the defendant on the ground that there was no confinement. She asks you to read the deposition revealing the above facts and for your opinion on whether such a motion would be successful. What is your advice? See Gavigan v. Southland Corp., 1998 WL 103380 (E.D. Pa. 1998).

C. The Shopkeeper's Privilege

The privilege to imprison another in a reasonable manner to protect property discussed above may not sufficiently protect merchants against false arrest/imprisonment lawsuits by innocent shoppers who are temporarily detained because they are suspected of shoplifting. Some courts developed a privilege to protect merchants in this situation. The Restatement (Second) of Torts §120A endorses this position, allowing temporary detention on one's premises of a person the actor reasonably believes has tortiously taken goods on the premises. Padlo v. VG's Food Center, Inc. explores the elements of false imprisonment where the issue of a legal justification for the confinement arises. *Padlo* also illustrates how assault and battery claims may arise in the shoplifting context and the justification for using reasonable force.

PADLO v. VG'S FOOD CENTER, INC.
2005 WL 3556245 (E.D. Mich. 2005)

BORMAN, J.

. . . I. Background

On January 15, 2003, Cheryl Bigham ("Bigham"), a manager for VG's Food Center, Inc., doing business as VG's Food Center and Pharmacy ("VG") at its store in Howell, Michigan, reported that she was detaining two young females, Darla Padlo ("Plaintiff") and Cassandra Green ("Green"), at the store for attempted theft.

Defendant Michael Floeter ("Floeter"), an employee at VG's, heard merchandise being unwrapped as he walked by an aisle. He observed Plaintiff and Green "hanging around" the cosmetics' section, "looking suspiciously around them." According to Floeter, he saw "at least one of the two girls . . . place [ ] something in her pocket." Floeter stated that Plaintiff and Green stopped in another aisle and "began unwrapping the items." During this time, he contacted Employee Lisa Bay ("Bay") to assist him in observing the girls. Floeter stated that as the girls exited the aisle, he seized several wrappers that they had shoved behind displayed products. Both Bay and Floeter observed Plaintiff attempt to shield Green as Green unwrapped and concealed the items.

Floeter notified Bigham that he suspected that Plaintiff and Green committed theft. Bigham confronted Plaintiff and Green after Floeter observed them removing several cosmetic items from the shelves and place them into their pockets, and . . . she did not personally observe any items being stolen. Upon being confronted by Bigham, Plaintiff and Green began to cry. Green then took a couple of the items out of her pockets. All of the items recovered came from Green's clothing pockets. Plaintiff alleges that after she removed all of her personal items from her pockets, Bigham reached into Plaintiff's pockets to check again. Plaintiff and Green were then asked to accompany Bigham to an office in a different location of the store. Bigham called the police and Officer Deeann Oswald-DeBottis ("Officer DeBottis"), a trooper with the Michigan State Police, was dispatched to VG's store.

While waiting for the police, the blinds in the office were closed. Bigham and Bay were inside the office with Plaintiff and Green, and Floeter stood near the doorway. Plaintiff tried to phone her mother on her cell, but Bigham took the phone away. When Officer DeBottis arrived and began her investigation, Bay stood in the office doorway. After taking the employees' statements, Officer DeBottis arrested both Plaintiff and Green for retail fraud.[1] According to DeBottis, she arrested Plaintiff for aiding and abetting Green's retail fraud. . . .

The jury subsequently found Plaintiff not guilty of the charge.

On December 22, 2004, Plaintiff filed a . . . Complaint against VG, Bigham, Floeter, Bay, (collectively "Defendants") and Officer DeBottis based upon her detention, custodial arrest, and subsequent prosecution. Count I alleged that Defendants falsely arrested/imprisoned Plaintiff in violation of Michigan law by detaining, arresting, and imprisoning Plaintiff without the requisite legal basis. Count II alleged that Defendants assaulted and battered Plaintiff in violation of Michigan law by subjecting Plaintiff to "unwanted physical contact" or threatening Plaintiff with such contact without the requisite legal basis. . . . [The claim against Officer DeBottis was dismissed.]

On July 8, 2005, Defendants VG, Bigham, Bay, and Floeter filed the instant motion for summary judgment on all of Plaintiff's claims. . . .

II. Analysis

. . . 1. FALSE ARREST/IMPRISONMENT (COUNT I)

. . . False imprisonment is the unlawful restraining of a person's liberty or freedom of movement. "The [restraint] must be 'false,' i.e., without right or authority to do so." *Hess v. Wolverine Lake,* 189 N.W.2d 42 (1971). "The elements of false imprisonment are: (1) actually confining another; (2) intentionally performing the act of confining another; (3) the act of confining another was performed without legal

---

[1] [Shoplifting is a form of larceny, often called theft or, as here, "retail fraud." — EDS.]

justification; and (4) the victim was aware of the confinement." *Romanski v. Detroit Entertainment, LLC,* 265 F. Supp. 2d 835, 846 (E.D.Mich.2003). . . .

Plaintiff alleges the first element of false imprisonment/arrest when she claims that she was unjustly restrained and felt that she was not at liberty to leave. Defendants contend that they were legally justified. Indeed, "[i]n order to prevail on a claim of false arrest or false imprisonment, the plaintiff must show that the arrest was not legal, i.e., that it was made without probable cause." *Tope v. Howe,* 105, 445 N.W.2d 452 (1989). In an earlier ruling, this Court found that DeBottis had probable cause for arresting Plaintiff.

> [E]ven viewing the facts in the light most favorable to Plaintiff, no reasonable juror could conclude that Plaintiff's arrest for retail fraud lacked the requisite probable cause. Before Plaintiff's arrest, Floeter told DeBottis that he observed Plaintiff and Green 'hanging around' the cosmetics' section, 'looking suspiciously around them.' Upon interviewing Bay, DeBottis learned from Bay that, although Bay did not see Plaintiff or Green initially take any items, she later observed Plaintiff attempt to shield Green as Green unwrapped and concealed the items. Bigham advised DeBottis that, upon being confronted, Plaintiff and Green immediately began to cry, and Green took a couple of the items out of her pockets. Thus, as a matter of law, the facts and circumstances within DeBottis' knowledge would warrant a reasonable person in believing that Plaintiff knew that Green intended to commit retail fraud and that Plaintiff, nevertheless, aided and abetted Green in the commission of such fraud. (Docket No. 29, July 26, 2005, Opinion and Order 13).

Likewise, Defendants here were legally justified in suspecting that Plaintiff intended to commit retail fraud or, at the least, aided and abetted in the commission of such a crime. As stated above, Defendants' actions were the basis for Debottis' probable cause determination. Floeter heard packages being unwrapped when he walked by the aisle where Plaintiff and Green stood. He saw packages being opened by Green and Plaintiff, who were standing face to face with each other. It appeared to Floeter that Plaintiff was blocking Floeter's view of what was taking place. After Plaintiff and Green moved to a different part of the store, the opened packages and packaging were found in the area Plaintiff and Green vacated. When Bigham confronted Plaintiff and Green, Green removed the stolen items from her pockets and began to cry. These facts show reasonable grounds for suspicion, supported by circumstances that are sufficiently strong for a reasonable person to believe that a crime had been committed. Therefore, the Court finds that facts and circumstances within the Defendants' knowledge warrant a reasonable person in believing that Plaintiff knew that Green intended to commit retail fraud and that Plaintiff aided and abetted Green in the commission of such fraud.

Viewing the facts in a light most favorable to the Plaintiff, the result is a finding of probable cause for the detention. Plaintiff was not falsely arrested/imprisoned. Accordingly, the Court should deny Plaintiff's Motion for Summary Judgment on her False Arrest/Imprisonment claim.

2. ASSAULT AND BATTERY (COUNT II)

Defendants argue that they had probable cause for suspecting that Plaintiff was aiding or abetting a retail fraud. Defendants claim that no force was used against Plaintiff, nor was there any evidence that she was touched in a harmful or offensive manner. Further, Defendants assert that Mich. Comp. Law section 600.2917 applies to claims of assault and battery requiring that Plaintiff prove unreasonable force.

Plaintiff argues that Bigham's action was an intentional, offensive touching of Plaintiff's person without her consent.

"An assault is any 'intentional unlawful offer of corporal injury to another person by force . . . which create[s] a[n] . . . apprehension of imminent contact [with the] apparent ability to accomplish the contact.'" *Smith v. Stolberg*, 586 N.W.2d 103 (1998). A battery is a harmful or offensive touching of another person which is the result of an act intended to cause the contact. "An unwarranted 'touching' constituting assault and battery." *Shulman v. Lerner*, 2 Mich. App. 705, 707 (1966).

In the instant case, Plaintiff stated that she had nothing in her pockets. Bigham did not ask Plaintiff whether she could check Plaintiff's pocket and instead chose to forcibly search Plaintiff's pockets herself. Plaintiff stated in her deposition that she did not consent to the touching. Therefore, viewing the facts in a light most favorable to the Plaintiff, the Court finds that Bigham used force by searching Plaintiff's pockets without asking and that the search was non-consensual and offensive to Plaintiff.

Defendants respond that they had probable cause to detain Plaintiff. The Court understands this to mean that Defendants' claim they had probable cause to forcibly search Plaintiff under Mich. Comp. Law section 600.2917, the shopkeepers privilege. Defendants aver that the conduct did not rise to the level of unreasonable force under that section, and therefore there was no assault and battery. However, section 600.2917 does not completely bar liability of a shopkeeper. Section 600.2917 only bars damages resulting from mental anguish or punitive, exemplary, or aggravated damages.[2]

Accordingly, the Court finds that in a light most favorable to the Plaintiff, there is a genuine issue of material fact as to whether Defendants assaulted and battered Plaintiff. However, the Court permits Plaintiff to proceed to trial on her assault and battery claim and seek nominal damages solely against Defendant Bigham individually, and Defendant VG under *respondeat superior* liability. Summary Judgment is granted in favor of the Defendant for the remaining Defendants on this count.

NOTES TO PADLO v. VG'S FOOD CENTER, INC.

1. *Legal Justification/Probable Cause.* In *Padlo*, the opinion did not focus on whether the confinement was intentional or complete or whether the shoppers were aware of the confinement. An actionable imprisonment must be "false," in the sense that there is no legal justification for it. The defendants relied on their legal justification for the confinement arising from the shopkeeper's privilege. In this case, that amounted to whether the defendants were legally justified in suspecting that plaintiffs

---

[2] [600.2917. Suspected shoplifting; probable cause as defense in civil action Sec. 2917. (1) In a civil action against a library or merchant, an agent of the library or merchant, or an independent contractor providing security for the library or merchant for false imprisonment, unlawful arrest, assault, battery, libel, or slander, if the claim arises out of conduct involving a person suspected of removing or of attempting to remove, without right or permission, goods held for sale in a store from the store . . . and if the merchant, library, agent, or independent contractor had probable cause for believing and did believe that the plaintiff had committed or aided or abetted in the larceny of goods held for sale in the store . . . , damages for or resulting from mental anguish or punitive, exemplary, or aggravated damages shall not be allowed a plaintiff, unless it is proved that the merchant, library, agent, or independent contractor used unreasonable force, detained the plaintiff an unreasonable length of time, acted with unreasonable disregard of the plaintiff's rights or sensibilities, or acted with intent to injure the plaintiff. — Eds.]

intended to commit retail fraud or, at the least, aided and abetted in the commission of such a crime. Restatement (Second) of Torts §120A states the privilege as follows:

> One who reasonably believes that another has tortiously taken a chattel upon his premises, or has failed to make due cash payment for a chattel purchased or services rendered there, is privileged, without arresting the other, to detain him on the premises for the time necessary for a reasonable investigation of the facts.

Temporary confinement is different from arrest in that the permitted detention is only for "the time necessary for a reasonable investigation. Investigation does not mean discovery of all of the facts, but only such inquiry as may reasonably be made under the circumstances, promptly and without undue detention." Comment (f). An arrest, by contrast, is actually taking the other person into custody, not limited to the purpose of temporary investigative detention.

2. *Need for the Shopkeeper's Privilege.*   As discussed above, common law rules allow a property owner to impose a confinement on another to protect the actor's interest in exclusive possession of the property. However, the common law privilege to use force or to impose a confinement to retake property from another who had already taken possession of the property was limited to situations in which the other person had actually tortiously taken the property or had intentionally caused the actor to believe he had done so. Additionally, common law rules allowed a person other than a law enforcement officer to make an arrest only in limited circumstances, including a requirement that a crime had actually been committed. Together, these rules placed shopkeepers in a difficult position when they suspected someone of stealing their merchandise. Even when a shopkeeper reasonably believed someone was stealing, the shopkeeper who detained a suspect faced a likelihood of liability for false imprisonment or battery if the shopkeeper's reasonable belief turned out to be mistaken. In response to this perceived deficiency in the law, courts developed a so-called shopkeeper's privilege, reflected in the Restatement (Second) of Torts, which allows a property owner to detain a person who he reasonably believes has tortiously taken his property, even if that belief turns out to be mistaken.

3. *Reasonable Time and Manner of Confinement.*   What constitutes a reasonable amount of time for an investigative imprisonment depends on all of the circumstances, including the value of goods involved and whether the suspect is cooperative. In a famous, early case, the Supreme Court of California held the defendant's conduct reasonable when it detained a seventy-year-old man for twenty minutes after personnel saw him putting Christmas lights in his pocket. See Collyer v. S.H. Kress Co., 54 P.2d 20 (Cal. 1936). Often the reasonable time for detention will be short if all that the merchant needs to do is ask a clerk whether the shopper paid for the goods. In addition to the reasonable time limitation, several opinions (often based on statutory provisions) have conditioned the privilege on a general requirement that the property owner detain the suspect in a reasonable manner. Thus, for example, conducting a detention in a rude or humiliating manner can result in liability for false imprisonment, even if the actor had reasonable grounds to believe the plaintiff was stealing.

4. *Use of Force Against Shoplifters.*   As with other cases in this chapter involving protection of land and personal property, a shopkeeper may use only reasonable, as opposed to deadly, force to detain a suspected shoplifter. Restatement (Second) §120A comment h allows a property owner to use reasonable force if necessary to effectuate a

detention for investigation. However, Bigham reached into Padlo's pocket to search for store property, not in order to detain Padlo. Restatement (Second) §106 also permits a person to use reasonable force to recover his property from another, including from a shoplifter's pocket (see §106 cmt. c.), but Bigham was investigating rather than recovering property, and Padlo claimed her pockets were empty. Additionally, reflecting common law rules, the Restatement (Second) allows the use of force to retake property only when the other person actually tortiously took the property or intentionally caused the actor to believe she had done so. So the recovery of property privilege might not apply. If not, then the question is whether the search constituted an assault and battery. The court decided only that Padlo could go to trial against Bigham and VG on the assault and battery claim.

5. *Liability of Employers and Others for Third Party Actors.* The *respondeat superior* theory referred to by the court in *Padlo* is one that makes an employer liable for the tortious acts of its employees committed during the scope of their employment and is discussed in Chapter 8 of this book. The court in *Barrett* was also relying on this theory when considering whether the Woodstone defendants should be liable for false imprisonment initiated by Ebert. The court there decided that even if Ebert was not an employee, there were material issues of fact as to whether the Woodstone defendants acted in concert with Ebert by encouraging, furthering, and ratifying the confinement. Liability for concerted action is discussed in more detail in Chapter 5 this book.

Problem
The Shopkeeper's Privilege

Lyndon Silva went to a Dillard Department Store in Houston to exchange three shirts given to him as a gift. Silva attempted to exchange the shirts at the cosmetics/accessories counter, but was told to go to another department. Silva testified that on his way to exchange the shirts he was distracted by sale items and other merchandise in the store. Before exchanging his three shirts, Silva made three purchases: a back brush, a travel bag, and another shirt. While making these purchases and examining other merchandise, a Dillard sales associate reported him as a possible shoplifter to her supervisor who told her to call security. Kevin Rivera, an off-duty Houston police officer working security for Dillard, thereafter stopped Silva and asked to examine the contents of his bag. In the bag were the three items purchased by Silva that day with their receipts and the three shirts he had brought to exchange. There was no receipt in the bag for the three shirts although Silva maintained that he had one. He asked Rivera to go with him to his car to see if the receipt had fallen out there . . . . [Rivera then] accused him of theft, placed him on the floor, handcuffed him, emptied the contents of his bag on the floor, and questioned him while he lay handcuffed on the floor. Although Silva told Rivera that he had receipts for three of the shirts in his vehicle, Rivera declined to go look for them. Instead, Rivera escorted Silva in handcuffs up the escalator to an empty office. Silva . . . [felt] embarrassment and humiliation at being led through the store in handcuffs. Once in the office . . . Rivera and another Dillard employee verbally taunted him and refused him a glass of water he needed to take medication for a migraine headache . . . . Silva was thereafter charged with misdemeanor theft but was ultimately acquitted of the criminal charge.

Mr. Silva has sued your client Dillard Department Store for false imprisonment. What do you advise your client about its potential liability? Is Silva's acquittal in the criminal case dispositive? See Dillard Department Stores, Inc. v. Silva, 148 S.W.3d 370 (Tex. 2004).

Statute: DETENTION AND SEARCH IN THEFT OF
LIBRARY MATERIALS AND SHOPLIFTING

Iowa Code Ann. §808.12 (2017)

1. Persons concealing property . . . may be detained and searched by a peace officer, person employed in a facility containing library materials, merchant, or merchant's employee, provided that the detention is for a reasonable length of time and that the search is conducted in a reasonable manner by a person of the same sex and according to subsection 2 of this section.
2. No search of the person under this section shall be conducted by any person other than someone acting under the direction of a peace officer except where permission of the one to be searched has first been obtained.
3. The detention or search under this section by a peace officer, person employed in a facility containing library materials, merchant, or merchant's employee does not render the person liable, in a criminal or civil action, for false arrest or false imprisonment provided the person conducting the search or detention had reasonable grounds to believe the person detained or searched had concealed or was attempting to conceal property. . . .

NOTE TO STATUTE

Today, most states have codified versions of the shopkeeper's privilege. The Iowa statute makes clear that the privilege does not depend on a reasonable belief that the suspect has completed the tort of conversion (discussed in Chapter 15) or the crime of larceny. Rather, a reasonable belief that the suspect has concealed property is sufficient to trigger the privilege. The Restatement (Second) of Torts §120A is silent with regard to whether one conducting a detention in reliance on the privilege may search the suspect. Rather, under that standard, the reasonableness of the detention depends on the totality of the circumstances. What conditions does the Iowa statute place on searches of suspects detained subject to the shopkeeper's privilege? Some states entirely prohibit merchants from searching people they have detained.

VI. Infliction of Emotional Distress

The tort of *intentional infliction of emotional distress* protects a person's right to be free from serious emotional distress. This tort is also known as the *tort of outrageous conduct,* or, simply, the *tort of outrage.* Certain attributes of emotional distress have made it a complicated issue in tort law. Mental anguish occurs from time to time in everyone's life, it can be hard to measure, and a plaintiff can easily lie about it. For these reasons, courts have sought to limit the circumstances in which plaintiffs can recover damages from defendants whom they claim have caused them to suffer emotional distress. Nevertheless, tort doctrines sometimes permit plaintiffs to recover for emotional distress. For example, recovery of emotional distress damages is permitted when the distress is caused by an assault or a battery.

The development of the intentional infliction of emotional distress tort reflects the concerns about the universality of some mental suffering in human life and the problems of measurement and possible exaggeration. Plaintiffs are permitted to recover only if a defendant's conduct is "outrageous" and the resulting mental distress is "severe." These limitations may prevent plaintiffs from seeking damages when they suffer only the kind of sadness that is common in life, and may filter out cases in which lying or exaggerating about emotional impact would be likely.

A. Outrageousness

Liability for intentional infliction of emotional distress is based on proof of outrageous conduct. This leads to some basic questions: Just how outrageous must the conduct be in order to impose liability? Whose frame of reference counts in assessing outrageousness? Should the judge or the jury (if there is a jury) evaluate the defendant's conduct? Courts ordinarily use an *objective test* to determine whether conduct is outrageous, just as they use an objective test for offensiveness in battery cases. Zalnis v. Thoroughbred Datsun Car Company and Strauss v. Cilek introduce the outrageousness tort and deal with many of these issues.

ZALNIS v. THOROUGHBRED DATSUN CAR CO.
645 P.2d 292 (Colo. Ct. App. 1982)

KELLY, J.

Plaintiff, Christiane Zalnis, appeals the partial summary judgment dismissing her outrageous conduct claim against defendants. We reverse.

The following facts appear from viewing the record in a light most favorable to the plaintiff. In January 1978, Zalnis contracted with defendant Thoroughbred Datsun for the purchase of a 1978 Datsun automobile. She took possession of the car on that day, and paid the balance of the purchase price two days later. Zalnis dealt directly with Linnie Cade, a salesperson employed by Thoroughbred Datsun. Defendant Trosper, President of Thoroughbred Datsun, approved the transaction based on representations by Cade which were later determined to be based upon erroneous calculations. When Trosper discovered several days later that Cade had sold the car at a loss of approximately $1,000, he instructed Cade and the sales manager to make good the loss by either demanding more money from Zalnis, retrieving the car, or repaying the difference out of Cade's salary.

Cade refused to follow any of Trosper's alternative instructions, but another sales employee, defendant Anthony, telephoned Zalnis and told her to return her car to the dealership because it was being recalled. When Zalnis arrived at Thoroughbred Datsun, she refused to give up possession of her car without a work order explaining the need for the recall. Nevertheless, her car was taken from her. During the next few hours, Zalnis alleges that Anthony called her a "French whore," followed her throughout the showroom, told her they were keeping her automobile, yelled, screamed, used abusive language, grabbed her by the arm in a threatening manner, and continually threatened and intimidated her when she attempted to secure the return of her automobile by telling her to "shut up."

During this period, Zalnis telephoned her attorney, who then telephoned Trosper and eventually obtained the return of her car. During their conversation, Trosper told the attorney that Zalnis had "been sleeping with that salesman and that's the only reason she got the deal she got." Trosper had known Zalnis for many years, and had told Cade and the sales manager that she was crazy and she had watched her husband kill himself.

. . . Thoroughbred Datsun and Trosper moved for partial summary judgment on the outrageous conduct claim. The trial court granted the motion, determining that, although the conduct was "almost shocking to the conscience and person of anyone observing that behavior," it did not amount to outrageous conduct under Colorado precedent.

In Rugg v. McCarty, 476 P.2d 753 ([Colo.] 1970), the Supreme Court recognized the tort of outrageous conduct and adopted the definition set forth in the Restatement (Second) of Torts §46: "One who by extreme and outrageous conduct intentionally or recklessly causes severe emotional distress to another is subject to liability for such emotional distress, and if bodily harm to the other results from it, for such bodily harm." Although the question whether conduct is sufficiently outrageous is ordinarily a question for the jury, the court must determine in the first instance whether reasonable persons could differ on the outrageousness issue.

The defendants argue that their actions here were no more than "mere insults, indignities, threats, annoyances, petty oppressions, and other trivialities." Restatement (Second) of Torts §46, Comment d. However, the defendants did not merely threaten and insult Zalnis; they took away her car and repeatedly harassed her. Conduct, otherwise permissible, may become extreme and outrageous if it is an abuse by the actor of a position in which he has actual or apparent authority over the other, or the power to affect the other's interests. Restatement (Second) of Torts §46, Comment e.

The conduct here is not a mere insistence on rights in a permissible manner. See Restatement (Second) of Torts §46, Comment g. Rather, the defendants' recall of the car was to avoid a bad bargain, and accordingly, the conduct was not privileged.

Defendants assert that their actions must be judged by the impact they would have on an ordinary person with ordinary sensibilities. We disagree. The outrageous character of the conduct may arise from the actor's knowledge that the other is peculiarly susceptible to emotional distress by reason of some physical or mental condition or peculiarity. Restatement (Second) of Torts §46, Comment f. In Enright [v. Groves, 560 P.2d 851 (Colo. Ct. App. 1977)], outrageous conduct was found where a police officer effecting an illegal arrest grabbed and twisted the plaintiff's arm even after she told him her arm was easily dislocated. In the instant case, plaintiff was peculiarly susceptible to emotional distress because she had witnessed her husband's suicide, and Trosper and Anthony knew about her susceptibility. Here, as in Enright, the defendants' knowledge exacerbated the conduct.

. . . Zalnis has sufficiently alleged that Trosper and Anthony acted with the intent to bully her into giving up her car. In view of their knowledge of her emotional susceptibility, they could be considered to have acted intentionally or recklessly in causing her severe emotional distress.

The defendants argue that we should observe a distinction between a single outrageous occurrence and an outrageous course of conduct. While it is true that "the courts are more likely to find outrageous conduct in a series of incidents or a 'course of conduct' than in a single incident," it is the totality of conduct that must be evaluated to determine whether outrageous conduct has occurred. Our evaluation of the totality of the conduct leads to the conclusion that reasonable persons could differ on the question whether there was outrageous conduct, and thus, summary judgment was improper. . . .

NOTES TO ZALNIS v. THOROUGHBRED DATSUN CAR CO.

1. Intent. The intent element for the tort of outrageous conduct may be established by proof that the defendant either (a) intended to cause or (b) recklessly caused the plaintiff's severe emotional distress. Reckless infliction of emotional distress is discussed later in this chapter. "Intent" has the same meaning for this tort as for the torts of battery and assault. What evidence supports a conclusion that Trosper and Anthony intended to cause Zalnis severe emotional distress?

2. Particular Sensitivity. The test for outrageousness is an objective test, based on a typical community member's assessment of the challenged conduct. When deciding whether conduct is outrageous, an average member of the community would likely consider whether the defendant knew that the plaintiff was, for some idiosyncratic reason particular likely to suffer severe emotional distress. The Restatement (Second) of Torts §46 comment j states: "The distress must be reasonable and justified under the circumstances, and there is no liability where the plaintiff has suffered exaggerated and unreasonable emotional distress, *unless it results from a peculiar susceptibility to such distress of which the actor has knowledge.*" (Emphasis added.) What evidence permitted consideration of Ms. Zalnis's peculiar susceptibility? How did this evidence contribute to the court's conclusion that a reasonable person could find this conduct outrageous?

3. Person in Position of Authority or Power. Conduct that would otherwise not be outrageous might appear outrageous if one party has actual or apparent authority over the other or the power to affect the other's interests. The Restatement (Second) of Torts §46 comment e, illus. 5, provides an example of that principle:

> A, private detective, calls on B and represents himself to be a police officer. He threatens to arrest B on a charge of espionage unless B surrenders letters of a third person which are in her possession. B suffers severe emotional distress and resulting illness.

Would the intent and outrageous conduct elements be satisfied in this illustration?

STRAUSS v. CILEK

418 N.W.2d 378 (Iowa Ct. App. 1987)

SACKETT, Judge.

The sole issue in this interlocutory appeal is whether the trial court erred in denying defendant's motion for summary judgment on plaintiff's claim of intentional infliction of emotional distress arising from defendant's romantic and sexual relationship with plaintiff's wife.

Defendant's affair with plaintiff's wife lasted one year. Plaintiff did not learn about the affair until after it was over. Plaintiff and his wife were in the process of obtaining a divorce at the time plaintiff initiated the present action for actual and punitive damages. The issue whether plaintiff in this case can maintain a claim for intentional infliction of emotional distress that arises out of a failed marital relationship may be appropriately resolved upon presentation of evidence through summary judgment.

. . . The elements of the tort of intentional infliction of emotional distress are as follows:

(1) Outrageous conduct by the defendant;

(2) The defendant's intention of causing, or reckless disregard of the probability of causing emotional distress;

(3) The plaintiff's suffering severe or extreme emotional distress; and

(4) Actual and proximate causation of the emotional distress by the defendant's outrageous conduct.

In overruling defendant's motion for summary judgment, the trial court declined to rule as a matter of law that defendant's actions were not outrageous. We find the evidence in the summary judgment record insufficient to demonstrate a genuine issue of fact on the outrageous conduct element.

It is for the court to determine in the first instance whether the relevant conduct may reasonably be regarded as outrageous. To be outrageous the conduct must be so extreme in degree as to go beyond all possible bounds of decency to be regarded as atrocious and utterly intolerable in a civilized community.

In Roalson v. Chaney, 334 N.W.2d [754,] 755 [(Iowa 1983)], Chaney asked Roalson's wife to marry him while she and Roalson were still married. The Iowa Supreme Court held no trier of fact could reasonably find Chaney's conduct outrageous. More recently, in Kunau v. Pillers, Pillers & Pillers, 404 N.W.2d 573, 576 (Iowa App. 1987), we held the facts of a case in which Kunau's wife had a lengthy sexual and romantic affair with her dentist could not support a conclusion the dentist's conduct was outrageous.

Plaintiff claims defendant's conduct in the present case is outrageous because plaintiff and defendant had known each other since elementary school and were good friends. We do not say that sexual relations between a plaintiff's friend and spouse would never give rise to a finding of outrageous conduct. We find the facts in this case, however, do not support a conclusion defendant's conduct is outrageous.

Defendant and plaintiff's wife kept their relationship secret until after it was over. Personal letters written by defendant to plaintiff's wife reveal defendant's genuine intention to leave his wife and children and to create a permanent relationship with plaintiff's wife. Plaintiff did not discover these letters discussing defendant's plans for the future until after he knew the affair had occurred. The record also reveals plaintiff's wife was unhappy in her marriage. She had previously engaged in an extramarital affair that lasted for five years with another of plaintiff's good friends.

We do not condone promiscuous sexual conduct. However, we do not find defendant's conduct in participating in a sexual relationship with a married woman, his friend's wife, who willingly continued the affair over an extended period, is atrocious and utterly intolerable conduct so extreme in degree as to go beyond all possible bounds of decency. The parties are residents of Iowa City, a community of 50,000 and the home of the University of Iowa. A recitation of the facts of this case to an average member of the community would not lead him to exclaim, "Outrageous!"

The trial court erred in overruling defendant's motion for summary judgment. We **&** reverse and remand the case for entry of an order granting defendant's motion for summary judgment.

NOTES TO STRAUSS v. CILEK

1. *Exclaiming "Outrageous!"*   The court's use of the concept "lead him to exclaim, 'Outrageous!'" refers to Restatement (Second) of Torts §46 comment d. That comment, which has been highly influential, states,

> Generally, the case is one in which the recitation of the facts to an average member of the community would arouse his resentment against the actor, and lead him to exclaim, "Outrageous!"

How does the court characterize the community in which the defendant's conduct took place? Does that characterization support its conclusion?

2. *Interference with Spousal Relations.*   American tort law once recognized causes of action related to a defendant's conduct that could affect a plaintiff's relationship with the plaintiff's spouse. These were referred to as "heart balm" torts. Adultery could be the basis of civil liability in a tort action known as "criminal conversation." Depriving a plaintiff of the affection, love, and companionship of his or her spouse could make a defendant liable for "alienation of affections." By the midpoint of the twentieth century, these and other similar causes of action had been abolished in the vast majority of states. While the *Strauss* court does not refer to this history, it may have been affected by the possibility that allowing recovery for the plaintiff might contradict the public policy against allowing damages for alienation of affections.

Problem
Establishing Outrageous Conduct

Antonio Dominguez has come to your firm for advice about the feasibility of pursuing a suit against Equitable, an insurance company. A senior partner has asked you to write a memo evaluating the likelihood of success on a claim for intentional infliction of emotional distress. Do the following facts describe outrageous conduct on the part of the insurance agent?

> In 1973, Equitable issued Dominguez a disability income policy of insurance which provided for $500 per month income for accidental total disability for the insured's lifetime. Shortly after the policy issued, Dominguez was involved in an automobile accident which "caused severe injuries to his body and extremities, including both eyes being knocked out of their sockets, brain damage, multiple large scars, psychiatric problems, periodic incontinence, paralysis of nerve in eye and other physical and mental problems, and mental injuries as well, which resulted in his total disability." Equitable paid Dominguez the disability income through August 1979 and then stopped making payments.
>
> On April 21, 1980, Equitable sent an agent, Millie Dirube, to the home of Dominguez in Miami, Florida. Millie Dirube falsely represented to Dominguez that she had received a letter from the eye doctor saying that his eye(s) were OK now and that Dominguez was no longer disabled and falsely represented to Plaintiff that he was no longer totally disabled, that he was no longer covered under the policy, that the policy was no longer in force, that he had to sign a paper agreeing that no further payments

were due under the policy, that it no longer covered him, that he was no longer entitled to receive benefits under the policy and that he was giving up the policy voluntarily. At the time said Millie Dirube made said misrepresentation she knew them to be false and they were in fact false and she made them with the intention and expectation . . . that Dominguez be deceived and defrauded thereby and sign the paper and surrender the policy. A relative of Dominguez overheard and intervened at the last minute and prevented Dominguez from signing the paper and surrendering the policy.

See Dominguez v. Equitable Life Assurance Society, 438 So. 2d 58 (Fla. Dist. Ct. App. 1983).

B. Severe Emotional Distress

In addition to establishing outrageous conduct, the plaintiff in an intentional infliction of emotional distress or outrageousness tort action must also establish that he or she suffered severe emotional distress as a consequence of the defendant's conduct. Because of this requirement, some very reprehensible conduct may escape tort liability if its intended victim happens to tolerate it without suffering significant harm. This limitation on a plaintiff's ability to obtain redress may restrict the outrageousness action to circumstances where it is highly likely that the underlying conduct was outrageous and where the victim's suffering is genuine. Rogers v. Louisville Land Co. evaluates the severe emotional distress element and also considers how a plaintiff may prove the existence of that level of distress.

ROGERS v. LOUISVILLE LAND CO.

367 S.W.3d 196 (Tenn. 2012)

SHARON G. LEE, J.

In 2001, Betty Saint Rogers' son died in a motorcycle accident and was buried in a grave plot in the Fort Hill Cemetery ("the cemetery") in Cleveland, Tennessee. Following her son's death, Ms. Rogers purchased easements from Louisville Land Company to two adjacent burial plots in the cemetery. When she purchased the easements, she had some concerns about the maintenance of the cemetery. She asked a representative of Louisville Land Company if the cemetery was regularly mowed and maintained, and was assured that it was. This, however, was not the case. According to Ms. Rogers, grass was higher than the headstones in places, some of the headstones were overturned, the roads were not in good condition, and there was debris in the cemetery. Ms. Rogers became very emotional and tearful when she visited her son's grave and saw the lack of cemetery maintenance.

In April of 2004, she brought this action against Louisville Land Company and Joe V. Williams, III, its sole shareholder and owner, as owners of a portion of the cemetery, alleging that the defendants "knowingly, intentionally and recklessly allowed the [cemetery] properties to be grown up with weeds covering markers, accumulate trash and otherwise become a scene of disarray and disrespect for those whose bodies have been laid to rest in the cemetery."

. . . At the end of the trial, the trial court awarded Ms. Rogers a judgment of . . . $45,000 in compensatory ~~damages~~ for "outrageous conduct." . . . The defendants appealed. The Court of Appeals reversed the award of compensatory damages, holding that Ms. Rogers had failed to present sufficient proof establishing that she had suffered a "serious mental injury," which was a required element of her claim. . . .

At the outset, we note that Ms. Rogers' complaint incorrectly alleged a claim for both "intentional infliction of emotional distress" and "outrageous conduct." Intentional infliction of emotional distress and outrageous conduct are different names for the same cause of action — not two separate torts. . . . Although the term "outrageous conduct" has gained widespread use as a substitute or shorthand for intentional infliction of emotional distress, it is more accurately and correctly used as referring to an *element* of intentional infliction of emotional distress. . . .

Ms. Rogers' claim is based on the tort of intentional infliction of emotional distress. The elements of an intentional infliction of emotional distress claim are that the defendant's conduct was (1) intentional or reckless, (2) so outrageous that it is not tolerated by civilized society, and (3) resulted in serious mental injury to the plaintiff.

The issue presented in this case is whether Ms. Rogers proved the third required element of her claim, that the defendant's conduct caused her to suffer serious mental injury.

Although this case involves the tort of intentional infliction of emotional distress, our analysis would be the same if it were for negligent infliction of emotional distress because both torts require proof of serious or severe mental injury.

[An illustration] regarding what constitutes a "severe mental injury" is provided by Section 46 of the Restatement (Second) of Torts, often cited by our courts in a discussion of this area of the law:

> The rule stated in this Section applies only where the emotional distress has in fact resulted, and where it is severe. Emotional distress passes under various names, such as mental suffering, mental anguish, mental or nervous shock, or the like. It includes all highly unpleasant mental reactions, such as fright, horror, grief, shame, humiliation, embarrassment, anger, chagrin, disappointment, worry, and nausea. It is only where it is extreme that the liability arises. Complete emotional tranquillity is seldom attainable in this world, and some degree of transient and trivial emotional distress is a part of the price of living among people. The law intervenes only where the distress inflicted is so severe that no reasonable man could be expected to endure it. The intensity and the duration of the distress are factors to be considered in determining its severity. Severe distress must be proved; but in many cases the extreme and outrageous character of the defendant's conduct is in itself important evidence that the distress has existed.
>
> The reason for the rule imposing liability only when extreme and outrageous conduct causes serious or severe emotional distress is apparent — to avoid the judicial system being flooded with potentially fraudulent, manufactured, or overstated claims arising from the "transient and trivial" emotional distresses of daily life, recognizing that "[i]f the plaintiff is to recover every time that [his or] her feelings are hurt, we should all be in court twice a week." Note, Russell Fraker, *Reformulating Outrage: A Critical Analysis of the Problematic Tort of IIED*, 61 Vand. L. Rev. 983, 988 (2008) (quoting William L. Prosser, *Intentional Infliction of Mental Suffering: A New Tort*, 37 Mich. L. Rev. 874, 877 (1939)). The Restatement (Third) of Torts: Liability for Physical and Emotional Harm §45 (Tentative Draft No. 5, 2007) further explains the reasoning for "why recovery for emotional harm is more restrictive than recovery for physical harm"[13] by observing that

---

[13] Restatement (Third) of Torts: Liability for Physical and Emotional Harm §45 cmt. a (Tentative Draft No. 5, 2007).

[t]oo much trivial or modest emotional disturbance occurs in modern life for the law to attempt to provide universal peace of mind. . . . [S]ome degree of emotional disturbance, even significant disturbance, is part of the price of living in a complex and interactive society. Requiring proof that the emotional disturbance is severe (and the result of extreme and outrageous conduct) provides some assurance that the harm is genuine.

Id. at §45 cmt. i.

To summarize the . . . law in Tennessee regarding the "severe mental injury" element of the torts of intentional infliction of emotional distress and negligent infliction of emotional distress, the following nonexclusive factors inform the analysis and are pertinent to support a plaintiff's claim that he or she has suffered a serious mental injury:

(1) Evidence of physiological manifestations of emotional distress, including but not limited to nausea, vomiting, headaches, severe weight loss or gain, and the like;

(2) Evidence of psychological manifestations of emotional distress, including but not limited to sleeplessness, depression, anxiety, crying spells or emotional outbursts, nightmares, drug and/or alcohol abuse, and unpleasant mental reactions such as fright, horror, grief, shame, humiliation, embarrassment, anger, chagrin, disappointment, and worry;

(3) Evidence that the plaintiff sought medical treatment, was diagnosed with a medical or psychiatric disorder such as post-traumatic stress disorder, clinical depression, traumatically induced neurosis or psychosis, or phobia, and/or was prescribed medication;

(4) Evidence regarding the duration and intensity of the claimant's physiological symptoms, psychological symptoms, and medical treatment;

(5) Other evidence that the defendant's conduct caused the plaintiff to suffer significant impairment in his or her daily functioning; and

(6) In certain instances, the extreme and outrageous character of the defendant's conduct is itself important evidence of serious mental injury.

The plaintiff may present this evidence by his or her own testimony, the testimony of lay witnesses acquainted with the plaintiff such as family, friends, and colleagues, or by the testimony of medical experts.

The conclusion that a serious or severe mental injury occurs "where a reasonable person, normally constituted, would be unable to adequately cope with the mental stress engendered by the circumstances of the case" should be interpreted with the foregoing discussion and nonexclusive list of factors in mind. At least one knowledgeable commentator has criticized the "unable to adequately cope" standard, opining that "[t]his is an unfortunate definition. Over the long run, most people can 'cope' with almost anything. They may need therapy, they may need medication, they may need both, but they can 'cope.'" John A. Day, *A Primer on the Law of Negligent Infliction of Emotional Distress*, Tenn. B.J., May 2005, at 28 n. 5. We agree that the "unable to cope" language is somewhat hyperbolic. "Unable to cope with the mental stress engendered" means that the plaintiff has demonstrated, by means of the six enumerated factors above or other pertinent evidence, that he or she has suffered significant impairment in his or her daily life resulting from the defendant's extreme and outrageous conduct. . . .

We now apply the foregoing principles to Ms. Rogers' claim for intentional infliction of emotional distress. To recover damages, she was required to prove that the
defendant's conduct was: (1) intentional or reckless; (2) so outrageous that it is not
tolerated by civilized society; and (3) caused her to suffer serious mental injury.
The trial court in this case made findings of fact pertaining to only elements
(1) and (2), finding the conduct of Mr. Williams and Louisville Land Company to
be "reckless towards the dead and to the living who go to visit the dead" and to be
"outrageous" in several instances. The trial court made no finding of fact regarding
whether Ms. Rogers had suffered mental injury. Therefore, we review the record de
novo to determine where the preponderance of the evidence lies.

As the Court of Appeals correctly observed, the evidence regarding Ms. Rogers'
alleged mental injuries was "at best, sparse." The following is the entire proof in the
record regarding Ms. Rogers' injury or damages, consisting of her own testimony at
trial:

> Q. What impact did this have on you as you were going to your son's grave and taking
> care of the gravesite yourself? What — how did this affect you?
> A. You were already grieving because you have lost someone that's very precious to
> you. And when you go to the cemetery, you — this should be a time where you are
> reflecting on memories of that loved one, not a time of going to weed eat the
> cemetery, looking as if they didn't exist, that they didn't — they're not cared for.
> You're leaving someone — when you bury them, you're leaving them in the care of
> the people that you buy their lot from, and this was very degrading, it was disre-
> spectful, to say the least.
> Q. . . . What impact, in addition to feeling this sense of disrespect and those things —
> did it physically affect you? Did you cry? Did you — A: It was very, very emotional,
> very tearful. I knew that I had to do something to change this, and in 2004 I filed a
> suit with Mr. Logan; and since then I have seen some changes as a result of that; and
> I would like to see more.

Although we are not without sympathy for Ms. Rogers, who while mourning the
loss of her son was faced with an overgrown and ill-maintained cemetery where his
remains were interred, we agree with the intermediate court that the evidence preponderates against a finding of serious mental injury in this case. Ms. Rogers' testimony was insufficient to establish the requisite serious mental injury. Ms. Rogers
provided no evidence, by her own testimony or of anyone else, that she suffered
physiological or psychological symptoms, sought medical or professional treatment,
or incurred any significant impairment in her daily functioning resulting from the
defendants' conduct. We affirm the judgment of the Court of Appeals reversing the
trial court's judgment in the amount of $45,000 in compensatory damages for "out-
rageous conduct."

NOTES TO ROGERS v. LOUISVILLE LAND CO.

1. *Evidence of Severe Emotional Distress.* The element of severe emotional
distress involves two related issues. One is how serious a plaintiff's emotional distress
must be to allow recovery. The other is how a plaintiff proves that he or she suffered severe
emotional distress. *Rogers* considers both issues. The court offers a list of six nonexclusive
types of evidence plaintiffs may offer to prove the severity of their emotional harm. Some
may involve testimony by a medical professional. Creating a category of *severe* emotional

harm mirrors the Restatement (Second) of Torts characterization of some bodily harm as *serious* bodily harm. See Restatement (Second) of Torts §63 (permitting use of deadly force only in defense against a battery or assault that threatens serious bodily harm).

   2. *Outrageousness as Evidence of Severity of Emotional Distress and Expert Testimony.*   The outrageousness of the act may influence the factfinder's decisions about whether there was intent ("so outrageous that the defendant must have intended serious emotional harm") and whether the plaintiff actually suffered such harm ("so outrageous she must have suffered severe emotional distress"). Courts are often influenced by the nature of the outrageous conduct when deciding that the harm *must have been* severe because the conduct was so outrageous, even though outrageousness is properly interpreted as a separate element of the tort. In an earlier Tennessee case, Miller v. Willbanks, 8 S.W.3d 607 (Tenn. 1999), for instance, a doctor diagnosed a newborn baby as having drug withdrawal symptoms without testing the baby for the presence of drugs. The doctor contacted relatives of the parents and told the mother he did not believe her denials of drug abuse, while rumors spread through the hospital causing nurses to treat the parents rudely. The doctor also initiated an investigation of the parents and refused to give them information about tests performed on the baby. Another doctor's tests revealed no drug problems. The trial court held that the failure to offer expert testimony regarding the existence of severe emotional distress doomed the plaintiff's case. The Tennessee Supreme Court reversed, saying that the outrageousness of the conduct added weight to the plaintiff's claim of severe emotional distress and expert testimony was not required. This is the majority approach. A minority of courts require expert testimony regarding seriousness to prevent the tort from being reduced to a single element of outrageousness.

Problems
Evaluating Factual Showings of Severe Emotional Distress

   Severe emotional distress is required for recovery in a variety of areas of tort law. Can the types and intensities of emotional distress described in the following cases be ranked from most severe to least severe? Are there any in which a court could sensibly say the plaintiff had failed to provide evidence of severe emotional distress?

   A. In Katterhenrich v. Federal Hocking Local School District Board of Education, 700 N.E.2d 626, 633-634 (Ohio Ct. App. 1997), the plaintiff alleged "humiliation, serious emotional distress [and] loss of self-esteem." However, the plaintiff continued "to teach, to drive a car, and to be a father and husband. He now performs more household chores than before the incident of which he complains and, 'outwardly,' is operating normally. He is able to do the normal things that he would have done" before the incident. "In fact, appellant testified that he applied for, and was given, the position of junior high football coach for the 1994-1995 school year. Additionally, appellant testified that he has seen his family doctor and has spoken to his pastor, but that he has not sought treatment from a psychologist or psychiatrist."

   B. In Nadel v. Burger King Corporation, 695 N.E.2d 1185 (Ohio Ct. App. 1997), the only evidence of any emotional distress as a result of the incident is (1) one plaintiff's statement that she was "worried," though not enough to seek psychological treatment; and (2) the other's statement that while receiving psychological treatment for depression resulting from his divorce and stress, the incident "came up," although it was not a contributing reason for seeking or receiving counseling.

C. In Kurtz v. Harcourt Brace Jovanovich, Inc., 590 N.E.2d 772, 775-776 (Ohio Ct. App. 1990), the appellant claimed that he suffered emotional distress as a result of an employment termination. The appellant "explained that he worried about his future and caring for his family, that he was upset and 'just couldn't believe' he had been let go," while acknowledging "that he resolved these concerns without the aid of psychological or medical assistance."

D. In Escalante v. Koerner, 28 S.W.3d 641, 647 (Tex. Ct. App. 2000), after the incident in question, the plaintiff broke down for three hours and could not get up, and continued to have emotional distress until the day of trial some three years later.

E. In GTE Southwest, Inc. v. Bruce, 998 S.W.2d 605, 618 (Tex. 1999), as a result of the employer's behavior, employees experienced crying spells, emotional outbursts, nausea, stomach disorders, headaches, difficulty in sleeping and eating, stress, fear, anxiety, and depression, and sought medical treatment for these problems, and an expert testified that employees suffered from post-traumatic stress disorder.

F. In Stokes v. Puckett, 972 S.W.2d 921, 924-926 (Tex. Ct. App. 1998), the plaintiff suffered from anxiety with symptoms of arousal intrusion, humiliation, self-deprecation, inferiority, inadequacy, and significant symptoms of depression.

C. Intent and Recklessness

Although typical terminology refers to the tort of intentional infliction of emotional distress or to the intentional tort of outrage, most states permit recovery if the plaintiff can show either that the defendant's conduct was intentional or that it was reckless. Chapter 3 covers recklessness in more detail. In Dana v. Oak Park Marina, Inc., the court describes the essential distinguishing characteristic of recklessness, the defendant's disregard of a substantial probability of serious harm associated with his conduct.

DANA v. OAK PARK MARINA, INC.
660 N.Y.S.2d 906 (N.Y. App. Div. 1997)

BALIO, J.

Defendant Oak Park Marina, Inc. (corporation), owns and operates a marina on the shore of Lake Ontario in North Rose, New York. The individual defendants are officers of the corporation and operators of the marina. One of the buildings on the marina site includes an office area where employees, including lifeguards, are allowed to change. It also includes men's and ladies' rest rooms for use by marina patrons and their guests. The rest rooms include a changing area, shower facilities and toilets. In 1993 the corporation installed a video surveillance camera in each of the rest rooms purportedly for the purpose of detecting and curbing vandalism. The following year the corporation installed two video surveillance cameras in the office area purportedly for the purpose of detecting theft of marina property. Plaintiff, a marina patron who utilized the ladies' rest room, commenced this action by filing the summons and complaint with the Monroe County Clerk on February 26, 1996. The amended complaint, which seeks relief for plaintiff and all others similarly situated, alleges that defendants videotaped about 150 to 200 female patrons and guests in various stages of undress without their knowledge or consent; that the videotapes were viewed by defendants and others; and that the tapes were displayed to others for purposes of trade. The amended complaint asserts causes of action [including] reckless infliction of emotional distress. . . .

Defendants brought a pre-answer motion to dismiss the causes of action for reckless infliction of emotional distress. . . .

Supreme Court . . . denied the . . . motion. Defendants appeal.

Defendants contend that New York does not recognize a cause of action for the reckless infliction of emotional distress. We disagree. Although the Court of Appeals has not held that a cause of action exists in a case factually involving reckless, but not intentional, infliction of emotional distress, that Court, in a series of cases, has "adopted" the rule formulated in section 46(1) of the Restatement (Second) of Torts that "[o]ne who by extreme and outrageous conduct intentionally *or recklessly* causes severe emotional distress to another is subject to liability for such emotional distress [emphasis added]" (see, Howell v. New York Post Co., 81 N.Y.2d 115, 121). Moreover, the Court has stated that the tort has four elements: "(i) extreme and outrageous conduct; (ii) intent to cause, *or disregard of a substantial probability of causing*, severe emotional distress; (iii) a causal connection between the conduct and injury; and (iv) severe emotional distress" [emphasis added] (Howell v. New York Post Co., supra, at 121). The italicized phrase comports with general descriptions of recklessness in tort and is similar to the Restatement's description of recklessness (see, Restatement [Second] of Torts §46[1], comment i; §500). The Third Department similarly has considered reckless conduct to be encompassed within the tort that is commonly referred to as the intentional infliction of emotional distress and the Second Department has concluded that a complaint alleging reckless conduct states a cause of action for intentional infliction of emotional distress.

In our view, reckless conduct is encompassed within the tort denominated intentional infliction of emotional distress. We thus conclude that a complaint alleging that defendants acted "recklessly and with utter disregard that the Plaintiff and others would be harmed, humiliated and suffer extreme mental anguish and distress" alleges that defendants disregarded "a substantial probability of causing" severe emotional distress (Howell v. New York Post Co., supra, at 121). Further, the amended complaint alleges that defendants surreptitiously videotaped plaintiff without her consent, viewed videotapes of plaintiff and others in various stages of undress for personal and unjustifiable purposes and displayed those tapes to others for purposes of trade, thereby sufficiently alleging conduct that a jury could find to be extreme and outrageous (see, Liberti v. Walt Disney World Co., 912 F. Supp. 1494, 1505-1506). Thus, we conclude that the amended complaint states a cause of action for reckless infliction of emotional distress [and affirm the trial court's denial of the defendants' motion]. . . .

NOTES TO DANA v. OAK PARK MARINA, INC.

1. *Reckless and Intentional Infliction.* The court in *Dana* concludes that "reckless conduct is encompassed within the tort denominated intentional infliction of emotional distress." The result is that proof of either recklessness or intent will support recovery. Recklessness, an unintentional tort, has two distinguishing elements. First, while the defendant did not intend the harm in the sense of desiring it or being substantially certain it would occur, the defendant must have consciously disregarded the risk of harm. Second, the risk must have been very serious in terms of the substantial probability of causing serious emotional distress.

2. *Elements of Recklessness.*   The *Dana* court referred to the definition of "recklessness" in Restatement (Second) of Torts §500, which appears as follows:

> Reckless Disregard of Safety Defined: The actor's conduct is in reckless disregard of the safety of another if he does an act or intentionally fails to do an act which it is his duty to the other to do, [1] knowing or having reason to know of facts which would lead a reasonable man to realize, not only that his conduct creates an unreasonable risk of physical harm to another, but also [2] that such risk is substantially greater than that which is necessary to make his conduct negligent. (Numbering added.)

From what evidence is it reasonable to conclude that the defendant in *Dana* was aware of the substantial probability of harm? Why would the court conclude that the likely emotional harm would be severe?

Problem
Reckless Infliction of Emotional Distress

A parent of a school-age child made allegations of sexual misconduct against a school bus driver based on a complaint by the child after two independent investigators found no evidence of misconduct. Would the parent's conduct satisfy the required intent or reckless element even if there was no direct evidence that the parent desired to make the driver emotionally upset? See Kraemer v. Harding, 976 P.2d 1160 (Or. Ct. App. 1999).

Perspective: Frontiers of the Outrage Tort

Aaron Goldstein, *Intentional Infliction of Emotional Distress: Another Attempt at Eliminating Native American Mascots*, 3 J. Gender, Race & Just. 689, 710-711 (2000), argues that the tort of intentional infliction of emotional distress ought to be modified to recognize a cause of action for those who suffer emotional harm from sports teams' use of Native American mascots:

> First, these mascots cause serious emotional pain to people. Second, these mascots are part of a long history of Native American imagery used to socialize people to accept adverse policies against Native Americans. Speech and imagery can be quite harmful to individuals. No one enjoys being insulted, but to insult someone's race and culture has a much weightier impact. As explained in Bailey [v. Binyon, 583 F. Supp. 923 (W.D. Ill. 1984)], this type of language and imagery "generates a feeling of inferiority as to their status in the community that may affect their hearts and minds in a way unlikely ever to be undone." . . . Native American mascots are not "rough language" that merely hurts someone's feelings. These mascots are insults of the strongest proportion and have done a lot more than merely hurt people's feelings.
>
> Second, these mascots are part of a long line of Native American imagery used to justify and socialize people to accept adverse policies against Native Americans.

Put simply, Native American mascots and Native American racial imagery is a part of genocide. Native American racial imagery has been used to create images that justify genocide. But Native American racial imagery along with Native American mascots are also contributing to cultural genocide. It is because of this imagery's terrible impact that the law must allow for redress of these problems. . . .

What obstacles to recovery confront a Native American attempting to recover for emotional harm suffered from a particular baseball team's use of a Native American mascot?

D. Transferred Intent for Infliction of Emotional Distress

Intentional infliction of emotional distress doctrines recognize the *transfer of intent between people*, as do assault and battery doctrines. For both assault and battery, an actor who intends an act to cause a harmful or offensive contact or apprehension of such a contact to one person is potentially liable to another person who suffers the contact or apprehension. That transfer of intent among people can create a large class of potential plaintiffs. For intentional infliction of emotional distress, the class of people to whom intent may be transferred is more narrowly defined, as Green v. Chicago Tribune Co. illustrates.

GREEN v. CHICAGO TRIBUNE CO.
675 N.E.2d 249 (Ill. App. Ct. 1996)

O'BRIEN, J.

Plaintiff, Laura Green, filed an amended complaint against defendant, the Chicago Tribune Company (hereinafter Tribune), alleging . . . intentional infliction of emotional distress. . . .

The trial court dismissed plaintiff's amended complaint against the Tribune. . . . Plaintiff appeals.

. . . [P]laintiff pleaded the following allegations which must be assumed true for purposes of the motion: Tribune staffers photographed her son, Calvin Green, on December 30, 1992, while he was undergoing emergency treatment at Cook County Hospital for a bullet wound. The Tribune never asked plaintiff's permission to photograph Calvin. After attempts to resuscitate Calvin failed, medical personnel moved him to a private hospital room to await the coroner. The coroner pronounced Calvin dead at 12:10 a.m. on December 31, 1992. Around that time, a reporter for the Tribune asked plaintiff for a statement regarding her son's death. She refused to make a statement. Meanwhile, Tribune staffers entered the private hospital room and took further unauthorized photographs of Calvin. While photographing Calvin, they prevented plaintiff from entering the room. When plaintiff did enter the room, the Tribune staffers listened to her statements to Calvin.

On January 1, 1993, the Tribune published a front-page article, about Chicago's record homicide rate. The article included the following quotes from plaintiff's statements to Calvin on December 31: "I love you, Calvin. I have been telling you for the longest time about this street thing." "I love you, sweetheart. That is my baby. The Lord has taken him, and I don't have to worry about him anymore. I accept it." "They took him out of this troubled world. The boy has been troubled for a long time. Let the Lord have him." The Tribune also published one of the unauthorized photographs taken of Calvin after he died. In a January 3, 1993, article, the Tribune published one of the unauthorized photographs taken of Calvin while undergoing medical treatment.

. . . To state a cause of action for intentional infliction of emotional distress, plaintiff must allege facts establishing: (1) the Tribune's conduct was extreme and outrageous; (2) the Tribune either intended its conduct should inflict severe emotional distress, or knew a high probability existed its conduct would cause severe emotional distress; and (3) the Tribune's conduct in fact caused severe emotional distress.

. . . The trial court determined the Tribune's conduct was not extreme and outrageous as a matter of law, and it dismissed the complaint. Extreme and outrageous conduct sufficient to create liability for intentional infliction of emotional distress is defined as conduct going beyond all possible bounds of decency. Such conduct must extend beyond mere insults, indignities, threats, annoyances, petty oppressions or trivialities.

This case is similar to Miller v. National Broadcasting Co., 232 Cal. Rptr. 668 (1986). There, an NBC camera crew entered Dave and Brownie Miller's apartment without their consent to film the activities of paramedics called to the Miller home to administer life-saving techniques to Dave Miller, who had suffered a heart attack in his bedroom. NBC used the film on its nightly news without obtaining anyone's consent, and after Brownie Miller and her daughter complained to NBC, it used portions of the film in a commercial advertising an NBC mini-documentary about the paramedics' work.

The issue on appeal was whether Brownie had stated a cause of action for intentional infliction of emotional distress. The appellate court found that she had:

> With respect to [Brownie's] cause of action, we leave it to a reasonable jury whether the defendants' conduct was "outrageous." Not only was her home invaded without her consent, but the last moments of her dying husband's life were filmed and broadcast to the world without any regard for the subsequent protestations of [Brownie and her daughter] to the defendants. Again, the defendants' lack of response to these protestations suggests an alarming absence of sensitivity and civility. The record reflects that defendants appeared to imagine that they could show or not show Dave Miller in extremis at their pleasure, and with impunity. *Miller*, 187 Cal. App. 3d at 1488, 232 Cal. Rptr. 668.

Similarly, plaintiff pleaded that the Tribune entered Calvin's room on December 31 without plaintiff's consent in order to photograph him as he lay dying, and even prevented plaintiff from entering until they had finished. Although plaintiff told the Tribune reporter in the hospital that she wanted to make no public statement about Calvin's death, the Tribune published a story on January 1 co-authored by that same reporter featuring plaintiff's comments to Calvin and a photograph of his dead body. Reasonable people could find that like NBC's actions in *Miller*, the Tribune's actions on December 31 and January 1 suggest an alarming lack of sensitivity and civility, and reasonable people, in essence, a jury, could find the Tribune's behavior extended beyond mere indignities, annoyances, or petty oppressions and constituted extreme and outrageous conduct.

Further, reasonable people, a jury, could find that the Tribune knew a high probability existed its actions on December 31 and January 1 would cause plaintiff to suffer severe emotional distress. Plaintiff also adequately pleaded that she did in fact suffer severe emotional distress. . . .

We hold plaintiff stated a cause of action for intentional infliction of emotional distress caused by the Tribune when it barred her from seeing her dead son on December 31 while it photographed him, and when it published the January 1 article featuring her statements to her son and the photograph of him lying dead.

Plaintiff also pleaded intentional infliction of emotional distress for the January 3, 1993, article that included one of the December 30, 1992, photographs of her son undergoing medical treatment. The Tribune argues a cause of action based on the intentional infliction of emotional distress is a purely personal one. Therefore, because the January 3 publication never mentions plaintiff, her action must be dismissed.

The Restatement (Second) of Torts recognizes in some instances a plaintiff can bring an intentional infliction of emotional distress action based on conduct directed at a third person. Section 46(2) of the Restatement provides:

> Where [outrageous] conduct is directed at a third person, the actor is subject to liability if he intentionally or recklessly causes severe emotional distress
> > (a) to a member of such person's immediate family who is present at the time, whether or not such distress results in bodily harm, or
> > (b) to any other person who is present at the time, if such distress results in bodily harm.

Restatement (Second) of Torts Sec. 46(2), at 72 (1965).

The Tribune's publication of the January 3 article four days after plaintiff's son's death, which did not include any mention of plaintiff, does not fall under section 46(2)(a) or (b) of the Restatement. Accordingly, plaintiff cannot recover for intentional infliction of emotional distress based on the Tribune's January 3 publication.

Similarly, plaintiff's intentional infliction of emotional distress action based on the Tribune's conduct on December 30, 1992, when it photographed her son undergoing medical treatment, also must be dismissed. Plaintiff did not allege in her amended complaint that she was present when the Tribune photographed her son on December 30. Therefore, the Tribune's December 30 conduct does not fall under section 46(2)(a) or (b) of the Restatement. . . .

NOTES TO GREEN v. CHICAGO TRIBUNE CO.

1. *Factual Theories and Transferred Intent.*   In Green v. Chicago Tribune Co., the plaintiff claims that the defendant should be liable on three factual theories.

One description of the facts involves a course of conduct on December 31 and January 1 that included the Tribune reporter entering her son's hospital room without the plaintiff's consent to photograph the dying son, preventing the plaintiff from entering the room until the reporter was done, and publishing a story featuring the plaintiff's words to her son despite her statement that she wanted to make no public comments. Was the plaintiff successful in showing that she was personally involved in each of these acts and was thus a target of the Tribune's conduct?

The plaintiff's second description of relevant facts was based on the Tribune's publication of an article on January 3 including photographs of her son undergoing medical treatment. The court accepted the defendant's characterization of the article as *not* directed at the plaintiff. This led the court to consider Restatement (Second) of Torts §46(2) to see if a transferred intent theory was available to the plaintiff. In applying that section, who must the court have considered to have been a "third person," and how did the court apply the Restatement provision to the plaintiff's claim?

The plaintiff's third factual theory was based on the Tribune's photographing her son on December 30. For what reasons did the court analyze this conduct as similar to the publication of the January 3 article and photographs?

2. *Transfer of Intent and Guarantees of Genuineness.*   Under the rules followed in Green v. Chicago Tribune Co., intent may be transferred to a person who was not an intended target of the defendant's conduct *only* if that person was present. There is an additional obstacle for people who are not members of the target's immediate family. Restatement (Second) of Torts §46(2)(b) requires that a nonfamily member suffer bodily harm before being allowed to recover for severe emotional distress. The Restatement (Second) of Torts §46 comment l suggests that these limitations are more practical than principled:

> The limitation may be justified by the practical necessity of drawing the line somewhere, since the number of persons who may suffer emotional distress at the news of an assassination of the President is virtually unlimited, and the distress of a woman who is informed of her husband's murder ten years afterward may lack the guarantee of genuineness which her presence on the spot would afford.

The *guarantee of genuineness* to which the Restatement (Second) refers is the reliability or verifiability of the claim of emotional distress described in the materials introducing this tort. Because people are more likely to suffer harm from conduct directed at third parties if they are family members who are present at the time, their claims of emotional distress are more believable. For nonfamily members, the bodily harm they suffer from conduct directed at third parties provides another *indicator of reliability* for their claim of severe emotional distress.

3. *The "Directed at" Requirement in Reckless and Intentional Infliction of Emotional Distress.*   Some states distinguish between intentional and reckless infliction of emotional distress when applying transfer-of-intent rules. Following the language of Restatement (Second) §46, some states require that the reckless conduct be *directed at* the plaintiff or occur in the presence of a plaintiff of whom the defendant is aware. Others, by contrast, reject that requirement on the ground that the elements of recklessness, outlined in Dana v. Oak Park Marina, Inc., above, do not require any desire or substantial certainly that any particular person will be harmed. If directness is not required, then the limitations on liability to immediate family members and others who are present at the time are not relevant. The requirements of "outrageousness," of "severe" emotional distress, and of a high degree of fault in recklessness claims serve as a limitation on who can recover. Whether the marina patron in *Dana* could recover would thus depend on which kind of jurisdiction she was in and on whether the video cameras were always turned on or turned on only to capture particular individuals. Doe 1 v. Roman Catholic Diocese of Nashville, 154 S.W.3d 22 (Tenn. 2005), discussed this distinction in a case where victims of sexual abuse sued the church for recklessly inflicting emotional distress by failing to take steps to prevent a priest's abuse of young men.

NEGLIGENCE: THE DUTY OF REASONABLE CARE

CHAPTER 3

I. Introduction

Unintentional Harms. This chapter introduces the topic of accidental injuries. In modern life, injuries that happen by accident are much more common than intentional harms. For example, a patient may be harmed if a doctor makes a mistake in diagnosing an illness, or someone shopping in a store may slip and fall if a store employee cleans a floor in a way that makes it extremely slippery. A very large segment of modern tort law involves sorting out the consequences of accidental injuries. The legal system treats these cases with the doctrines known as *negligence* law.

A common analysis of negligence cases involves four elements. A plaintiff may recover damages if the defendant (1) *owed the plaintiff a duty* to act in a certain way, the defendant (2) *breached the duty* by failing to act as well as the duty required, and the defendant's conduct (3) *caused* some (4) *harm* to the plaintiff. These elements of a negligence case are usually summarized in the phrase "duty, breach, causation, and damages." Most of the time, a defendant's duty was to act as a reasonable person would act in the circumstances that led to an injury.

Illustration. A case involving a collision between a pedestrian and a car illustrates these concepts. If the injured pedestrian sought damages from the driver of the car, the pedestrian would have to establish that the law imposes a duty on drivers to act with some degree of care toward pedestrians. To show breach of duty, the pedestrian would have to show that the driver drove the car less well than the duty of care requires. To show causation and damages, the pedestrian would have to show that he or she had suffered some harm and that the collision had caused that harm.

This illustration is typical of the many cases in modern tort law where the defendants concede that they owed the plaintiff a duty to act reasonably. This chapter explores these kinds of cases to develop understanding of the reasonable care concept. Situations in which there is a dispute about whether any duty exists are treated in Chapters 6 and 11. In some situations, tort law evaluates conduct with standards other

Elements

than "reasonable care." A "reckless" standard is examined at the end of this chapter, and other substitutes for reasonable care are treated in Chapters 9, 10, and 11.

In cases where a duty exists, tort law identifies a *standard of care* for the jury to use in evaluating the conduct of any actor whose actions might be relevant to resolving the case. In this way, our legal system controls a fundamental societal issue. It tells us how careful some people are supposed to be to protect some other people from some types of injuries. This puts significant limits on the jury's discretion. In every tort case, the jury decides certain questions of historical fact: how the injury happened and whose actions or inaction contributed to it. As long as they act in a way that is consistent with legal standards, juries have freedom in reaching those conclusions. But once a jury has decided who did what, the next issue (the one that matters the most to the parties) is determining who should bear the financial cost of the injury. Our legal system *refuses* to allow the jury to select whatever it thinks is the wisest and fairest result based on whatever factors it might choose to consider. Instead, the trial judge instructs the jury to compare what it believes the actors did to a particular standard of care chosen by the legal system. The judge bases that instruction on the jurisdiction's tort doctrines established in appellate court decisions and in statutes.

Power of the Jury.   Even though the jury must apply the standard of care the judge tells it to use, if that standard is vague or subject to interpretation, members of a jury will apply it to the case by using their own ideas about safety and how people should act. A common standard of care requires that a person act "as a *reasonable person* would act." When a case involves that standard, the jury has considerable leeway in deciding exactly what conduct is reasonable in the specific circumstances that led to the injury. So, while the jury does not get to decide what standard to use (because the judge requires it to apply the reasonable person standard), the jury has significant control over the outcome of the case. It decides what the standard means in the specific factual context of the case.

Illustration.   In a car accident case, the jury might decide that a driver's eyes were very sensitive to light and that the driver had been driving on a sunny day without wearing sunglasses when a collision occurred. That conclusion would not, by itself, support a jury verdict in favor of someone the driver hit. To decide whether the driver should pay damages, the jury must decide whether the driver's conduct did or did not live up to the standard of care that the legal system requires. In this type of case, the reasonable person standard would apply. This means that the jury must decide in good faith how carefully it thinks a reasonable person would have driven under the circumstances. It then compares how the defendant drove with the way it concludes a reasonable person would have driven. The jury is forbidden to use other standards — for example, it cannot decide that the defendant should pay the victim because the defendant is rich. It cannot decide that the defendant should pay the victim because the defendant did not have a good reason for driving that day. Note, though, that even though the jury must use the reasonable person standard, it is usually allowed to decide what kind of specific conduct that standard requires.

II. The "Reasonable Person" Standard

When a duty does exist, people are usually required to act in accordance with the "reasonable person" standard. Sometimes courts add the word "prudent" and refer to the "reasonable prudent person" standard. The conduct of entities like corporations may also be judged by that standard, since they do their work through actions by individual employees whose conduct can be compared with what a reasonable person would do.

One explanation for the acceptance of this standard is that it simplifies life. We can assume that other people will be "reasonably" careful not to injure us, and we do not need to anticipate their particular personalities and capabilities. If they fail to act in a reasonable way and their conduct harms us, we can expect to be compensated with tort damages.

A. Defining and Justifying the "Reasonable Person" Standard

The reasonable person standard has dominated tort law since the early nineteenth century. Vaughan v. Menlove is the leading case articulating support for the standard: Should the conduct of someone who built a haystack that started a fire be compared with that person's best possible farm work or with the farm work that a reasonable person would do? Parrot v. Wells, Fargo & Co. shows that understanding the overall factual setting is crucial for applying the standard: Is opening a crate of nitroglycerine with a mallet reasonable conduct?

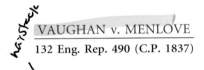

VAUGHAN v. MENLOVE

132 Eng. Rep. 490 (C.P. 1837)

[The defendant built a hayrick near his neighbor's land. The hayrick caught fire due to spontaneous combustion, and the fire spread to cottages on the neighbor's land and destroyed them. The neighbor sought damages, alleging that the defendant had built the hayrick badly in a way that facilitated the combustion. The trial court instructed the jury that the defendant was required to have acted as a prudent man would have acted under those circumstances. Following a verdict for the plaintiff, the defendant won an order ("rule nisi") requiring a new trial. That order was obtained] on the ground that the jury should have been directed to consider, not whether the Defendant had been guilty of gross negligence with reference to the standard of ordinary prudence, a standard too uncertain to afford any criterion, but whether he had acted bona fide to the best of his judgment; if he had, he ought not to be responsible for the misfortune of not possessing the highest order of intelligence. . . .

[Reviewing that grant of a new trial, the Court of Common Pleas stated:] It is contended . . . that the question ought to have been whether the Defendant had acted honestly and bona fide to the best of his own judgment. That, however, would leave so vague a line as to afford no rule at all, the degree of judgment belonging to each individual being infinitely various: and though it has been urged that the care which a prudent man would take, is not an intelligible proposition as a rule of law, yet such has always been the rule adopted in cases of bailment. . . . The care taken by a prudent man has always been the rule laid down; and as to the supposed difficulty of applying it, a jury has always been able to say, whether, taking that rule as their guide, there has been negligence on the occasion in question.

Instead, therefore, of saying that the liability for negligence should be co-extensive with the judgment of each individual, which would be as variable as the length of the foot of each individual, we ought rather to adhere to the rule which requires in all cases a regard to caution such as a man of ordinary prudence would observe. That was in substance the criterion presented to the jury in this case, and therefore the present rule must be discharged.

NOTES TO VAUGHAN v. MENLOVE

1. *Alternative Standards of Care.* The court compares two rules that might be used for evaluating a defendant's conduct. What are those rival standards? Which one did the court adopt?

2. *Evidence of Breach of the Standard of Care.* To decide a case under either of the standards examined in Vaughan v. Menlove, a jury would need information. Compare the types of information parties would present to the jury under the two rival standards.

3. *The Reasonable Person.* The Restatement (Second) of Torts provided the following description of the reasonable person (using the then-current term "reasonable man"), highlighting the idea that the reasonable person is not a typical person but a hypothetical person who is always reasonably prudent. Analyze whether this formulation is consistent with the one adopted in Vaughan v. Menlove.

> Sometimes this person is called a reasonable man of ordinary prudence, or an ordinarily prudent man, or a man of average prudence, or a man of reasonable sense exercising ordinary care. It is evident that all such phrases are intended to mean very much the same thing. The actor is required to do what this ideal individual would do in his place. The reasonable man is a fictitious person, who is never negligent, and whose conduct is always up to standard. He is not to be identified with the members of the jury, individually or collectively. It is therefore error to instruct the jury that the conduct of a reasonable man is to be determined by what they would themselves have done.

Restatement (Second) of Torts Section 283 comment c (1965).

Perspective: Law and Gender

Modern courts almost always use the expression "reasonable person" instead of the expression "reasonable man." An alternative approach would add "reasonable woman" to the law's terminology, to make both "reasonable man" and "reasonable woman" standards available to juries. Proponents of this view believe that using these gender-specific standards instead of the gender-neutral "reasonable person" standard can affect the outcomes of cases. Would analysis of this question depend on the type of case (for example, sexual harassment, bad driving, or substandard building of a hayrick)? See Nancy S. Ehrenreich, *Pluralist Myths and Powerless Men: The Ideology of Reasonableness in Sexual Harassment Law*, 99 Yale L.J. 1177 (1990).

PARROT v. WELLS, FARGO & CO. (THE NITRO-GLYCERINE CASE)
82 U.S. 524, 21 L. Ed. 206, 15 Wall. 524 (1872)

Parrot brought an action in the court below against certain defendants who composed the well-known firm of Wells, Fargo & Co., express carriers, to recover damages for injuries to certain large buildings owned by him in the city of San Francisco, caused in April, 1866, by the explosion of nitro-glycerine whilst in charge of the said defendants. . . .

[In 1866, the properties of nitroglycerine were not well known. It had only recently been invented, and some small initial efforts were being made to promote its use in mining. An individual paid the defendant to ship a 329-pound crate from New York City to San Francisco via the isthmus of Panama. When the crate] was taken from the steamer and placed upon the wharf, . . . it was discovered that the contents were leaking. These contents had the appearance of sweet oil. Another box of similar size had been stained by the contents leaking and appeared to be damaged. On the 16th of April, in accordance with the regular and ordinary course of the defendants' business, when express freight is found to be damaged, the two boxes were taken to the defendants' building, the premises in question, for examination. . . . A representative of the [steamship] company accordingly attended, and in his presence, and in the presence of an agent of the defendants, and of other persons, an employee of the defendants, by their direction, with a mallet and chisel, proceeded to open the case, and while thus engaged the substance contained in it exploded, instantly killing all the parties present, and causing the destruction of a large amount of property, and the injuries to the buildings occupied by the defendants, for which the present action was brought. Upon subsequent examination it was ascertained that the substance contained in the case was nitro-glycerine or glonoin oil. The other box contained silverware. . . .

[The court held that the defendant had no liability for damage to property other than property its lease required it to repair.] To review this judgment the plaintiff sued out a writ of error from this court.

Mr. Justice FIELD, after stating the facts of the case, delivered the opinion of the court, as follows: . . .

The question presented to us is, whether upon this state of facts the plaintiff is entitled to recover for the injuries caused by the explosion to his buildings, outside of that portion occupied by the defendants under their lease. . . .

To fasten a further liability on the defendants, and hold them for injuries to that portion of the buildings not covered by their lease, it was contended in the court below, and it is urged here, that, as matter of law, they were chargeable with notice of the character and properties of the merchandise in their possession, and of the proper mode of handling and dealing with it, and were consequently guilty of negligence in receiving, introducing, and handling the box containing the nitro-glycerine.

If express carriers are thus chargeable with notice of the contents of packages carried by them, they must have the right to refuse to receive packages offered for carriage without knowledge of their contents. It would, in that case, be unreasonable to require them to accept, as conclusive in every instance, the information given by the owner. They must be at liberty, whenever in doubt, to require, for their satisfaction, an inspection even of the contents as a condition of carrying the packages. This doctrine would be attended in practice with great inconvenience, and would seldom lead to any good. Fortunately the law is not so unreasonable. It does not exact any such knowledge on the part of the carrier, nor permit him, in cases free from suspicion, to require information as to the contents of the packages offered as a condition of carrying them. . . .

It not, then, being his duty to know the contents of any package offered to him for carriage, when there are no attendant circumstances awakening his suspicions as to their character, there can be no presumption of law that he had such knowledge in any particular case of that kind, and he cannot accordingly be charged as matter of law with notice of the properties and character of packages thus received. The first proposition of the plaintiff, therefore, falls, and the second, which depends upon the first, goes with it.

The defendants, being innocently ignorant of the contents of the case, received in the regular course of their business, were not guilty of negligence in introducing it into their place of business and handling it in the same manner as other packages of similar outward appearance were usually handled. "Negligence" has been defined to be "the omission to do something which a reasonable man, guided by those considerations which ordinarily regulate the conduct of human affairs, would do, or doing something which a prudent and reasonable man would not do." It must be determined in all cases by reference to the situation and knowledge of the parties and all the attendant circumstances. What would be extreme care under one condition of knowledge, and one state of circumstances, would be gross negligence with different knowledge and in changed circumstances. The law is reasonable in its judgments in this respect. It does not charge culpable negligence upon any one who takes the usual precautions against accident, which careful and prudent men are accustomed to take under similar circumstances. . . .

This action is . . . brought upon . . . the negligence of the defendants: unless that be established, they are not liable. The mere fact that injury has been caused is not sufficient to hold them. No one is responsible for injuries resulting from unavoidable accident, whilst engaged in a lawful business. A party charging negligence as a ground of action must prove it. He must show that the defendant, by his act or by his omission, has violated some duty incumbent upon him, which has caused the injury complained of. . . .

[This] case stands as one of unavoidable accident, for the consequences of which the defendants are not responsible. The consequences of all such accidents must be borne by the sufferer as his misfortune.

This principle is recognized and affirmed in a great variety of cases. . . . The rule deducible from them is, that the measure of care against accident, which one must take to avoid responsibility, is that which a person of ordinary prudence and caution would use if his own interests were to be affected, and the whole risk were his own. . . .

Judgment affirmed.

NOTE TO THE NITRO-GLYCERINE CASE

A Reasonable Person's Knowledge of Risks. The reasonableness of an actor's conduct will usually depend on the knowledge that the actor had about the riskiness of a situation. Tort law could treat an actor as possessing: (1) full knowledge of all the risks of his or her situation; (2) all of the knowledge a reasonable person would have had; or (3) only the knowledge the actor actually had. Which treatment of the defendant's knowledge did the plaintiff seek? Which treatment did the court apply, and how did the court justify that choice?

Problems
Reasonable Care

Would a jury be justified in finding the defendant negligent in the following cases?

A. The plaintiff's house was damaged by water that forced its way through the ground when a water main constructed and maintained by the defendant froze and broke. The winter frost that caused the break "penetrated to a greater depth than any which ordinarily occurs south of the Polar regions." See Blyth v. Birmingham Water Works, 156 Eng. Rep. 1047 (Ex. 1856).

B. The defendant suffered an epileptic seizure and became unconscious while driving his car. He collided with the plaintiff, injuring her. The defendant had been treated by his doctor for epilepsy for many years and had not suffered a seizure for 14 years prior to the one involved in the injury to the plaintiff. The defendant had a valid driver's license, issued under terms that required him to have his treating physician report his condition to the Department of Motor Vehicles once a year. See Hammontree v. Jenner, 97 Cal. Rptr. 739 (App. Ct. 1971).

Perspective: Social Costs and Benefits

The court refers to "inconvenience" that would be associated with a rule that required common carriers to know the contents of packages people asked them to ship. This is really an economic analysis. What the court refers to as "inconvenient" could certainly be accomplished, with a consequence of making shipping slower and more costly. Could considering whether there might be benefits that would make those costs worthwhile have altered the court's result?

B. Reasonable Conduct as a Balancing of Costs and Benefits

May reasonableness be defined in terms of costs and benefits? Many theorists and judges have sought to clarify the apparent vagueness of the reasonableness standard by proposing a systematic evaluation of costs and benefits. McCarty v. Pheasant Run illustrates an economic framework for defining reasonable conduct: Is it reasonable for a person to expose others to a costly risk that the person could have prevented with a small expenditure?

McCARTY v. PHEASANT RUN, INC.

826 F.2d 1554 (7th Cir. 1987)

POSNER, J.

. . . Dula McCarty, a guest at the Pheasant Run Lodge in St. Charles, Illinois, was assaulted by an intruder in her room, and brought suit against the owner of the resort. The suit charges negligence, and bases federal jurisdiction on diversity of citizenship. The parties agree that Illinois law governs the substantive issues. The jury brought in a verdict for the defendant, and Mrs. McCarty appeals. . . .

In 1981 Mrs. McCarty, then 58 years old and a merchandise manager for Sears Roebuck, checked into Pheasant Run — a large resort hotel on 160 acres outside Chicago — to attend a Sears business meeting. In one wall of her second-floor room was a sliding glass door equipped with a lock and a safety chain. The door opens onto a walkway that has stairs leading to a lighted courtyard to which there is public access. The drapes were drawn and the door covered by them. Mrs. McCarty left the room for dinner and a meeting. When she returned, she undressed and got ready for bed. As she was coming out of the bathroom, she was attacked by a man with a stocking mask. He beat and threatened to rape her. She fought him off, and he fled. He has never been caught. Although Mrs. McCarty's physical injuries were not serious, she claims that the incident caused prolonged emotional distress which, among other things, led her to take early retirement from Sears.

Investigation of the incident by the police revealed that the sliding glass door had been closed but not locked, that it had been pried open from the outside, and that the security chain had been broken. The intruder must have entered Mrs. McCarty's room by opening the door to the extent permitted by the chain, breaking the chain, and sliding the door open the rest of the way. Then he concealed himself somewhere in the room until she returned and entered the bathroom.

Mrs. McCarty argues that the judge should have granted her motion for judgment notwithstanding the jury's verdict for the defendant. . . .

As [a] ground for denying the motion for judgment n.o.v., the district judge correctly pointed out that the case was not so one-sided in the plaintiff's favor that the grant of a directed verdict or judgment n.o.v. in her favor would be proper. Her theories of negligence are that the defendant should have made sure the door was locked when she was first shown to her room; should have warned her to keep the sliding glass door locked; should have equipped the door with a better lock; should have had more security guards (only two were on duty, and the hotel has more than 500 rooms), . . . should have made the walkway on which the door opened inaccessible from ground level; should have adopted better procedures for preventing unauthorized persons from getting hold of keys to guests' rooms; or should have done some combination of these things. The suggestion that the defendant should have had better procedures for keeping keys away from unauthorized persons is irrelevant, for it is extremely unlikely that the intruder entered the room through the front door. . . . The other theories were for the jury to accept or reject, and its rejection of them was not unreasonable.

There are various ways in which courts formulate the negligence standard. The analytically (not necessarily the operationally) most precise is that it involves determining whether the burden of precaution is less than the magnitude of the accident, if it occurs, multiplied by the probability of occurrence. (The product of this multiplication, or "discounting," is what economists call an expected accident cost.) If the burden is less, the precaution should be taken. This is the famous "Hand Formula" announced in United States v. Carroll Towing Co., 159 F.2d 169, 173 (2d Cir. 1947) (L. Hand, J.), an admiralty case, and since applied in a variety of cases not limited to admiralty. . . .

We are not authorized to change the common law of Illinois, however, and Illinois courts do not cite the Hand Formula but instead define negligence as failure to use reasonable care, a term left undefined. . . . But as this is a distinction without a substantive difference, we have not hesitated to use the Hand Formula in cases governed by Illinois law. . . . The formula translates into economic terms the conventional legal test for negligence. This can be seen by considering the factors that the Illinois courts take into account in negligence cases: the same factors, and in the same relation, as in the Hand Formula. . . . Unreasonable conduct is merely the failure to take precautions that would generate greater benefits in avoiding accidents than the precautions would cost.

Ordinarily, and here, the parties do not give the jury the information required to quantify the variables that the Hand Formula picks out as relevant. That is why the formula has greater analytic than operational significance. Conceptual as well as practical difficulties in monetizing personal injuries may continue to frustrate efforts to measure expected accident costs with the precision that is possible, in principle at least, in measuring the other side of the equation—the cost or burden of precaution. . . . For many years to come juries may be forced to make rough judgments of reasonableness, intuiting rather than measuring the factors in the Hand Formula; and so long as their judgment is reasonable, the trial judge has no right to set it aside, let alone substitute his own judgment.

Having failed to make much effort to show that the mishap could have been prevented by precautions of reasonable cost and efficacy, Mrs. McCarty is in a weak position to complain about the jury verdict. No effort was made to inform the jury what it would have cost to equip every room in the Pheasant Run Lodge with a new lock, and whether the lock would have been jimmy-proof. . . . And since the door to Mrs. McCarty's room was unlocked, what good would a better lock have done? No effort was made, either, to specify an optimal security force for a resort the size of Pheasant Run. No one considered the fire or other hazards that a second-floor walkway not accessible from ground level would create. A notice in every room telling guests to lock all doors would be cheap, but since most people know better than to leave the door to a hotel room unlocked when they leave the room — and the sliding glass door gave on a walkway, not a balcony—the jury might have thought that the incremental benefits from the notice would be slight. . . .

Affirmed.

NOTES TO McCARTY v. PHEASANT RUN, INC.

1. *The Learned Hand Formula for Negligence.* The "Hand formula" (described by Judge Learned Hand in *Carroll Towing*) was expressed algebraically, stating that conduct would be negligent if $B < PL$. In that expression, B stands for the burden of prevention or avoidance, and an actor is negligent if that burden is less than P, which stands for the probability of loss, multiplied by L, which stands for the magnitude of loss that would be avoided with the possible prevention or avoidance. From whose perspective is it "reasonable" for one person to spend a small amount of money to protect another person from suffering a significant physical injury or a large financial loss? Would that make sense to the first person, the other person, or to society as a whole?

2. *Evidence of Reasonable Conduct.*   Judge Posner discounts the value of posting notices in the hotel's rooms by saying that people generally know that it is a good idea to lock doors. Would a notice have helped avoid the injury in this case if it had alerted the victim that there was a sliding glass door behind the room's closed curtains? That possibility apparently was presented weakly or not at all at the trial. It is important to notice, however, that once the jury has reached its decision, it is very difficult for a judge to rule that the jury has so severely misapplied the reasonable person standard that a new trial or judgment as a matter of law must be granted to reject the jury's verdict.

3. *Costs and Benefits in Non-Economic Terms.*   Some social values may be hard to quantify and therefore difficult to recognize in a cost-benefit analysis. Tort law, however, ordinarily recognizes a broad range of factors in defining *reasonable care*. For example, the definitions of *costs* and *benefits* contained in the Restatement (Second) of Torts definitions of *reasonable care* take societal values into account.

> Section 291. Unreasonableness; How Determined; Magnitude of Risk and Utility of Conduct
>
> Where an act is one which a reasonable man would recognize as involving a risk of harm to another, the risk is unreasonable and the act is negligent if the risk is of such magnitude as to outweigh what the law regards as the utility of the act or of the particular manner in which it is done.
>
> Section 292. Factors Considered in Determining Utility of Actor's Conduct
>
> In determining what the law regards as the utility of the actor's conduct for the purpose of determining whether the actor is negligent, the following factors are important:
>> (a) the social value which the law attaches to the interest which is to be advanced or protected by the conduct;
>> (b) the extent of the chance that this interest will be advanced or protected by the particular course of conduct;
>> (c) the extent of the chance that such interest can be adequately advanced or protected by another and less dangerous course of conduct.
>
> Section 293. Factors Considered in Determining Magnitude of Risk
>
> In determining the magnitude of the risk for the purpose of determining whether the actor is negligent, the following factors are important:
>> (a) the social value which the law attaches to the interests which are imperiled;
>> (b) the extent of the chance that the actor's conduct will cause an invasion of any interest of the other or of one of a class of which the other is a member;
>> (c) the extent of the harm likely to be caused to the interests imperiled;
>> (d) the number of persons whose interests are likely to be invaded if the risk takes effect in harm.

Problems
The Reasonable Person Standard

A. A large hospital operates several parking lots. One lot is used only by doctors, who in general have higher-than-average incomes and are thought of as performing work that is very important to everyone. The other lots are open to the general public. On average, the value of cars parked in the doctors' lot is greater than the value of cars parked in the other lots. In order to avoid tort liability, should the hospital allocate its resources for maintenance and snow removal evenly among all the parking lots, or should it spend more on the "doctors only" lot?

B. Plaintiff was injured one day while he was shopping in FoodPlace, a large supermarket. As he was walking down an aisle, a fairly heavy box of cake mix fell from the top of a large display. Someone brushed lightly against the display, causing the box to fall and hit plaintiff's face. The display was a pyramidal structure built about six feet high. It contained about 200 cake mix boxes. Plaintiff has sued FoodPlace, alleging that the display was set up negligently, both in terms of its location and its size, so that anyone brushing against it would cause some of its highest boxes to fall. See Cardina v. Kash N'Karry Food Stores, Inc., 663 So. 2d 642 (Fla. App. 1995).

(1) You are the plaintiff's lawyer. What kinds of information would you like to present at the trial to persuade the jury that FoodPlace's conduct related to the display fell below the reasonable person standard?

(2) Based on what you know about the reasonable person standard, analyze the following jury instructions. Does each one properly present the reasonable person standard to the jury? (These hypothetical instructions cover only part of what a jury would have to decide in the case. They don't cover causation or damages, for example.)

1. "Find in favor of the plaintiff if the evidence persuades you that FoodPlace set up its display in a way that created a risk of injury."

2. "Find in favor of the plaintiff if the evidence persuades you that the way FoodPlace set up its display was less safe than the way FoodPlace has set up other displays in the past."

3. "Find in favor of the plaintiff if the evidence persuades you that FoodPlace set up its display in a way that was less safe than the way a reasonable operator of a supermarket would have set up a display."

4. "Find in favor of the plaintiff if the evidence persuades you that FoodPlace set up its display in a way that was less safe than you would have done if you were the operator of a supermarket like FoodPlace."

Perspective: Law and Economics

Judge Posner is a leading scholar in the field known as "law and economics," so it is understandable that he would provide a detailed and persuasive description of the Hand formula, even though its direct application to the case is subject to the limits he described. Economic analysis may have great explanatory power for the analysis of tort doctrines and particular tort cases. It may also be a way of thinking that can develop and justify particular policy choices.

A controversial issue in law and economics involves the ways in which economic analysis does or does not reflect people's moral, spiritual, and irrational preferences. If the difficulty in quantifying those factors is large, it

> could be a reason to reject economic analysis of legal issues altogether or to understand that economic analysis can illuminate important aspects of a problem even if it cannot resolve all of its issues.

III. The Range of Application of the Reasonable Person Standard

The reasonable person standard can accommodate the evaluation of injuries involving many diverse factors. While there are some circumstances in which tort law replaces the reasonable person test with different standards, courts generally have shown great confidence in the ability of jurors to use the reasonable person test in many contexts.

A. Especially Dangerous Instrumentalities

Many injuries involve especially dangerous activities or things. Gasoline, for example, presents risks that are significantly greater than the risks presented by lots of other substances in common use. Stewart v. Motts presents an analysis of whether the reasonable person test can produce satisfactory results in cases where an injury involves something as dangerous as gasoline.

STEWART v. MOTTS

539 Pa. 596, 654 A.2d 535 (1995)

MONTEMURO, J.

Appellant, Jonathon Stewart, appeals from an order and memorandum opinion of the Superior Court affirming a judgment of the Court of Common Pleas of Monroe County following a verdict in favor of appellee, Martin Motts, in this action for personal injuries. . . .

The sole issue presented before us is whether there exists a higher standard of "extraordinary care" for the use of dangerous instrumentalities over and above the standard of "reasonable care" such that the trial court erred for failing to give an instruction to the jury that the Appellee should have used a "high degree of care" in handling gasoline. Because we believe that there is but one standard of care, the standard of "reasonable care," we affirm.

The pertinent facts of this case are simple and were ably stated by the trial court:

> On July 15, 1987, Plaintiff, Jonathon Stewart, stopped at Defendant, Martin Motts' auto repair shop and offered assistance to the Defendant in repairing an automobile fuel tank. . . . While the exact sequence of events was contested, the tragic result was that the car backfired, caused an explosion and resulted in Plaintiff suffering severe burns to his upper body. . . .

Stewart v. Motts, No. 52 Civil of 1988, slip op. at 1 (Court of Common Pleas of Monroe County, Dec. 18, 1992).

The only issue raised before this Court is the refusal of the trial court to read Stewart's requested point for charge No. 4. This point for charge reads:

> We are instructing you that gasoline due to its inflammability, is a very dangerous substance if not properly handled. . . . With an appreciation of such danger, and under conditions where its existence reasonably should have been known, there follows a high degree of care which circumscribes the conduct of everyone about the danger, and whether the parties, Motts, t/a Motts Radiator, and Stewart, acted as reasonable men under the circumstances is for you the jury to decide. See Konchar v. Cebular, 333 Pa. 499, 3 A.2d 913 (1939).

The trial court denied this point of charge finding that it was "cumulative with respect to the standard charge given by the Court. . . ." *Stewart*, slip op. at 3. In this appeal, Stewart argues that the trial court erred in failing to read point of charge No. 4 to the jury because Pennsylvania law applies an "extraordinary" or "heightened duty of care" to those employing a dangerous agency.

We begin our discussion by reaffirming the principle that there is but one standard of care to be applied to negligence actions involving dangerous instrumentalities in this Commonwealth. This standard of care is "reasonable care" as well stated in the Restatement (Second) of Torts:

> The care required is always reasonable care. The standard never varies, but the care which it is reasonable to require of the actor varies with the danger involved in his act and is proportionate to it. The greater the danger, the greater the care which must be exercised. . . .

Restatement (Second) of Torts §298 comment b (1965).

This comment goes on to say that where the reasonable character of an actor's conduct is in question "its utility is to be weighed against the magnitude of the risk which it involves." Id. Thus, if an act involves risk of death or bodily injury, "the highest attention and caution are required. . . ." Therefore, the comment concludes, "those who deal with firearms, explosives, poisonous drugs or high tension electricity are required to exercise the closest attention and the most careful precautions. . . ." Id.

Properly read, our cases involving dangerous agencies reaffirm these well accepted principles found in the Restatement. In Konchar v. Cebular, 333 Pa. 499, 3 A.2d 913 (1939), a case relied upon heavily by appellant in the case at bar, the plaintiff drove into a gas station and ordered a gallon of gasoline. The defendant began pumping gas into the motorcycle, but when three quarters of a gallon was placed in the tank, the gasoline overflowed and ran into the hot cylinders of the engine. The plaintiff, sitting on the motorcycle, was burned when the gasoline exploded. In the subsequent lawsuit for personal injuries, the jury returned a verdict to the defendant. The plaintiff claimed that the trial court erred in sending the question of his contributory negligence to the jury. In deciding the case, this Court noted that gasoline was a dangerous substance requiring a "high duty of care." *Konchar*, 333 Pa. at 501, 3 A.2d at 914. We affirmed, holding that, "[i]t was for the jury to decide whether, under all of the circumstances, [the plaintiff] had acted as a reasonably prudent man." Id. Thus, we recognized that the question of the plaintiff's contributory negligence was to be determined using the reasonable care standard in light of the particular circumstances of the case. One such circumstance, we acknowledged, was that gasoline, a dangerous substance, was involved requiring that the reasonably prudent person exercise a higher degree of care under these circumstances. Taken in context, our statement that the plaintiff was under a "high duty of care" did nothing more than reaffirm the general principle that the care employed by a reasonable man must be proportionate to the danger of the activity. . . .

Admittedly, this notion of a heightened level of "extraordinary care" for the handling of dangerous agencies has crept into our jurisprudence. In Kuhns v. Brugger, 390 Pa. 331, 135 A.2d 395 (1957), this Court considered the proper standard of care for negligence involving a handgun. The defendant in this case was a grandfather who had left a loaded handgun in an unlocked dresser drawer. While alone in the house, his grandchild found the gun and inadvertently shot another child. We affirmed the trial court's finding that the grandfather was negligent for permitting a highly dangerous instrumentality to be in the place where a child could come into contact with it. In so affirming, we found that the possession of a loaded handgun placed upon the defendant the duty of, "exercising not simply ordinary, but extraordinary care so that no harm might be visited upon others." *Kuhns*, 390 Pa. at 344, 135 A.2d at 403. This language in *Kuhns* on its face unfortunately suggests that this Commonwealth recognizes a separate standard of care, "extraordinary care," for dangerous instrumentalities above and beyond "ordinary care." We reject this suggestion. We note that the *Kuhns* Court adopted the above-quoted language without citation to or consideration of this Court's previous cases involving dangerous agencies or the Restatement (Second) of Torts. Since the *Kuhns* Court did not specifically overrule any of these previous cases, we choose to interpret *Kuhns* consistent with . . . *Konchar*. . . . We note that the *Kuhns* Court explained:

> We are not called upon to determine whether the possession of other instrumentalities or objects . . . would impose the same degree of care under similar circumstances; we are simply to determine the degree of care imposed upon the possessor of a loaded pistol, a weapon possessing lethal qualities, under the circumstances.

Kuhns, 390 Pa. at 344, 135 A.2d at 403.

This language strongly suggests that the *Kuhns* Court did not create a standard of "extraordinary care" for all dangerous instrumentalities as advocated by the appellant. Instead, we believe that the *Kuhns* Court considered the danger of an unattended hand gun under the circumstances of this case and fashioned a standard of care proportionate to that danger. . . .

In summation, this Commonwealth recognizes only one standard of care in negligence actions involving dangerous instrumentalities — the standard of reasonable care under the circumstances. It is well established by our case law that the reasonable man must exercise care in proportion to the danger involved in his act. See MacDougall [v. Pennsylvania Power and Light, 311 Pa. 387, 396, 166 A.2d 589, 592 (1933)] ("Vigilance must always be commensurate with danger. A high degree of danger always calls for a high degree of care."); Lineaweaver v. John Wanamaker Philadelphia, 299 Pa. 45, 49, 149 A. 91, 92 (1930) ("The care required increases with the danger."). Thus, when a reasonable man is presented with circumstances involving the use of dangerous instrumentalities, he must necessarily exercise a "higher" degree of care proportionate to the danger. Our case law has long recognized this common sense proposition that a reasonable man under the circumstances will exert a "higher" degree of care when handling dangerous agencies. . . .

With these principles in mind we must next examine the jury instructions in this case. In examining these instructions, our scope of review is to determine whether the trial court committed clear abuse of discretion or error of law controlling the outcome of the case. . . .

Reviewing the charge as a whole, we cannot conclude that it was inadequate. The trial judge explained to the jury that negligence is "the absence of ordinary care which a reasonably prudent person would exercise in the circumstances here presented." Transcript of Testimony 10/7/92 at 158. The trial judge further explained:

> It is for you to determine how a reasonably prudent person would act in those circumstances. Ordinary care is the care a reasonably prudent person would use under the circumstances presented in this case. It is the duty of every person to use ordinary care not only for his own safety and the protection of his property, but also to avoid serious injury to others. What constitutes ordinary care varies according to the particular circumstances and conditions existing then and there. The amount of care required by law must be in keeping with the degree of danger involved.

Id. at 158-59. . . .

We find that this charge, when read as a whole, adequately instructed the jury. The charge informed the jury that the proper standard of care was "reasonable" or "ordinary" care under the circumstances in accordance with the law of this Commonwealth. The charge properly instructed the jury that the level of care required changed with the circumstances. The charge also informed the jury that the level of care required increased proportionately with the level of danger in the activity. We find nothing in this charge that is confusing, misleading, or unclear. From these instructions, the jury had the tools to examine the circumstances of the case and determine that the defendant was required to exercise a "higher degree of care" in using the dangerous agency of gasoline. . . .

Appellant argues that the language in his point for charge was nearly identical to Pennsylvania Suggested Standard Civil Jury Instruction 3.16 which sets forth the standard of care to be employed on inherently dangerous instrumentalities. PSSCJI 3.16 provides that anyone using a dangerous instrumentality is "required by law to use the highest degree of care practicable."[2] Assuming the applicability of this instruction to the case at bar, we find nothing in it inconsistent with our holding today. The "highest degree of care practicable" is simply another way of phrasing reasonable or ordinary care under the circumstances. We note that this standard jury instruction and point of charge No. 4 are completely consistent with our law. In fact, the use of such an instruction may very well have made the issue clearer to the jury. However, our standard of review is not to determine whether the jury had the best or clearest instructions, but whether they had adequate instructions. We find the jury instructions given in this case to be adequate. The trial judge rejected the plaintiff's point for charge

---

[2]PSSCJI 3.16 states in full:

> Anyone who supplies or uses an inherently dangerous instrumentality, such as the high voltage current (acids, corrosives, explosives) provided (supplied) (used) by the defendant in this case is required by law to use the highest degree of care practicable to avoid injury to everyone who may be lawfully in the area of such activity.

No. 4 as "cumulative" of other jury instructions. We find no abuse of discretion or error of law on the part of the trial court in making this determination.

For the reasons set forth above, we affirm the order of the Superior Court.

NOTES TO STEWART v. MOTTS

1. Reasonable Care and Extraordinary Care. The court discusses its earlier *Konchar* opinion, which referred to a "high duty of care" and its *Kuhns* opinion, referring to "extraordinary care." The court also refers to "the standard of reasonable care under the circumstances." What is the status of each of these standards of care, following the *Stewart* decision?

2. Ordinary Care and the "Highest Degree of Care." Footnote 3 of the court's opinion includes the text of a jury instruction. The opinion states that "ordinary care under the circumstances" is the same as the instruction's phrase "highest degree of care practicable." What analysis would a jury have to adopt in order to give those phrases equivalent meaning?

3. Model or Pattern Jury Instructions. In *Stewart*, the court discusses a Pennsylvania Suggested Standard Civil Jury Instruction. In most states, *model* or *pattern* jury instructions are published to guide trial courts in creating instructions for the main issues that occur repeatedly in trials. In some states, these instructions are approved by the state's highest court or a committee appointed by the court. In other states they are created by bar committees. Model instructions are not statutes, and they have less force than a state's own decisional law. They do, however, represent authoritative interpretations of the current status of a state's law on most of the major issues in torts cases.

Perspective: Explicit and Implicit Overruling

On the way to stating that Pennsylvania recognizes only one standard of care, the court described its past opinions in ways that might not have been obvious to their authors. This allowed the court to reach its result without explicitly overruling those cases. Note, however, that the court failed to specify clear reasons for its doctrinal choice (rejecting a jury charge referring to a high degree of care). Would the court have been more likely to present clear reasons for its result if it had recognized a possible contradiction between that result and the results in the prior cases?

B. Emergencies

Sometimes injuries occur in situations that involve sudden emergencies. How should that context affect a jury's evaluation of an actor's conduct? Many jurisdictions have allowed a "sudden emergency" jury instruction to supplement the reasonable person test. As Myhaver v. Knutson shows, current tort law is divided on whether this type of instruction is a helpful addition to the reasonable person test.

MYHAVER v. KNUTSON
942 P.2d 445 (Ariz. 1997)

FELDMAN, J.

Plaintiffs Bruce and Barbara Myhaver sought review of a court of appeals' decision holding that the "sudden emergency" instruction was properly given in a case arising out of an automobile collision. We granted review to determine whether a sudden emergency instruction is ever appropriate. . . .

In November 1990, Elmo Knutson was driving north on 43rd Avenue near Bell Road in Phoenix when Theresa Magnusson entered 43rd Avenue from a shopping center driveway and headed south in Knutson's lane. Seeing Magnusson's car in his lane, Knutson accelerated and swerved left, avoiding what he perceived to be an impending head-on collision. In doing this, he crossed the double yellow line into oncoming traffic and collided with Bruce Myhaver's pickup. Magnusson continued south not realizing she was involved. A police officer who saw the accident stopped her a short distance away and asked her to return to the scene.

Myhaver was seriously injured as a result of the collision and brought a damage action against both Knutson and Magnusson. Magnusson settled and . . . the Myhavers proceeded to trial against Knutson. . . .

At trial, [the judge] ruled that the instruction was appropriate under the facts and instructed the jury as follows:

> In determining whether a person acted with reasonable care under the circumstances, you may consider whether such conduct was affected by an emergency.
>
> An "emergency" is defined as a sudden and unexpected encounter with a danger which is either real or reasonably seems to be real. If a person, without negligence on his or her part, encountered such an emergency and acted reasonably to avoid harm to self or others, you may find that the person was not negligent. This is so even though, in hindsight, you find that under normal conditions some other or better course of conduct could and should have been followed.

RAJI (Civil) 2d Negligence 6.

The jury found Knutson not liable. On appeal, the Myhavers argued that the sudden emergency doctrine . . . be abandoned. . . .

[T]he sudden emergency instruction tells the jury that in the absence of antecedent negligence, a person confronted with a sudden emergency that deprives him of time to contemplate the best reaction cannot be held to the same standard of care and accuracy of choice as one who has time to deliberate. Criticism of this doctrine has focused on its ability to confuse a jury as to . . . whether the reasonable person standard of care or some lower standard, applies in an emergency. . . .

Commentators on Arizona's negligence law have described the problem and the present state of our law as follows:

> Conceptually, the emergency doctrine is not an independent rule. It is merely an application of the general standard of reasonable care; the emergency is simply one of the circumstances faced. Arguably, giving a separate instruction on sudden emergency focuses the jury's attention unduly on that aspect of a case. The Arizona Supreme Court has expressly declined to decide the question of the propriety of a separate emergency instruction.

Jefferson L. Lankford & Douglas A. Blaze, The Law of Negligence in Arizona §3.5(1), at 43 (1992). . . .

[I]t is often the case that "despite the basic logic and simplicity of the sudden emergency instruction, it is all too frequently misapplied on the facts or misstated in jury instructions." W. Page Keeton et al., Prosser and Keeton on the Law of Torts §33, at 197. As a result, some states hold that the instruction should never be given. Other states do not require the instruction be given, leaving it to the trial judge's discretion. . . .

One of the more careful analyses of the subject was made in McKee v. Evans, 380 Pa. Super. 120, 551 A.2d 260 (Pa. Super. 1988). The Pennsylvania court found that the instruction had been improperly given in favor of a driver involved in a ten-mile pursuit. The court concluded that the instruction was not favored and should be given only in those cases in which evidence showed that (1) the party seeking the instruction had not been negligent prior to the emergency, (2) the emergency had come about suddenly and without warning, and (3) reaction to the emergency was spontaneous, without time for reflection. While these factors are certainly not all inclusive, we believe they help describe the situations to which the instruction should be confined.

Having noted that the instruction is but a factor to be considered in determining reasonable care, is subsumed within the general concept of negligence, is a matter of argument rather than a principle of law and can single out and unduly emphasize one factor and thus mislead a jury, we join those courts that have discouraged use of the instruction and urge our trial judges to give it only in the rare case. The instruction should be confined to the case in which the emergency is not of the routine sort produced by the impending accident but arises from events the driver could not be expected to anticipate.

We do not, however, join those courts that absolutely forbid use of the instruction. There are cases in which the instruction may be useful or may help to explain the need to consider a sudden emergency and the consequent reflexive actions of a party when determining reasonable care. We believe, however, that in those few cases in which the instruction is given, it would be important to explain that the existence of a sudden emergency and reaction to it are only some of the factors to be considered in determining what is reasonable conduct under the circumstances. Even though a judge may exercise his discretion and give a sudden emergency instruction in a particular case, it will rarely, if ever, be error to refuse to give it.

Applying these principles to the case at bench, we conclude that the trial judge did not abuse his discretion in giving the instruction. This is a case in which there was no evidence of antecedent negligence by Knutson, in whose favor the instruction was given. In light of the testimony of the various witnesses, there was no question about the existence of an emergency. Knutson was faced with a situation not ordinarily to be anticipated and one of imminent peril when Magnusson pulled out of the shopping center and suddenly turned toward him in the wrong lane of traffic. Finally, Knutson's reaction — swerving across the center line into the path of Myhaver's oncoming vehicle — was probably both reflexive in nature and the type of conduct that absent a sudden emergency would almost automatically be found as negligence. . . . Given these facts, the real and only issue was whether Knutson's conduct was reasonable under the circumstances of the emergency. We believe, therefore, the trial judge had discretion to instruct on the sudden emergency as a factor in the determination of negligence.

For the foregoing reasons, we approve the court of appeals' decision and affirm the judgment of the trial court.

Zlaket, C.J., specially concurring. . . .

[T]oday's resolution fails to address the essential flaw in the instruction — that it overemphasizes and tends to accord independent status to what is but one of many elements in every negligence analysis. If drivers cannot "be expected to anticipate" certain events, they are by definition free from negligence. Standard instructions, particularly when supplemented by oral argument of counsel, should be more than sufficient to convey this idea without having a trial judge specifically suggest that one party might be excused because he or she faced an "emergency." . . .

However, because the instruction in question has not yet been specifically disapproved in Arizona, and appears to have been harmless under the particular facts of this case, I am unwilling to say that the trial judge abused his discretion. I therefore concur in the result.

NOTES TO MYHAVER v. KNUTSON

1. *Significance of an Emergency.* Proof that a person acted in an emergency could be given several different effects in a negligence case. It could absolve the actor of liability, it could entitle the actor to be judged with a standard of care that is less demanding that a typical standard of care, or it could be treated as just one factor among many that a jury considers in applying the reasonable person test. What position did the *Myhaver* court take on this issue?

2. *The Learned Hand Test and Emergencies.* The presence of an emergency could affect all of the elements of the Learned Hand test for negligence. How, for example, would it affect the "burden" of prevention?

3. *Trial Court Discretion.* A common result among courts that have considered this issue is to express dissatisfaction with the sudden emergency doctrine while refusing to treat a trial court's use of it as reversible error. Why might that result be attractive to many jurisdictions?

C. An Actor's Knowledge and Skill

In comparing how a person acted with how a reasonable person would have acted, two important questions about knowledge sometimes arise. Should the jury treat that person as if he or she knew what typical people know about the possibility of accidents? Also, if the person has knowledge or skill that is greater than the knowledge or skill that a typical person has, how should the jury deal with that fact? Cervelli v. Graves reflects typical treatment of these issues.

CERVELLI v. GRAVES
661 P.2d 1032 (Wyo. 1983)

Raper, J.

This case arose when Larry B. Cervelli (appellant) filed a personal injury suit for injuries he sustained when a pickup truck driven by him collided with a cement truck owned by DeBernardi Brothers, Inc. (appellee). The cement truck was driven by

DeBernardi's employee, Kenneth H. Graves (appellee) while acting in the course of his employment. After trial, a jury found no negligence on the part of appellees. Appellant argues the jury was incorrectly instructed and, as a result, found as it did thereby prejudicing him. He raises the following [issue] on appeal:

> Did the court err in instructing the jury that it was not to consider a person's skills in determining whether that person is negligent?

We will reverse and remand.

Around 7:30 a.m., February 22, 1980, a collision occurred approximately nine miles west of Rock Springs, Wyoming in the westbound lane of Interstate Highway 80 involving a pickup driven by appellant and appellee's cement truck. At the time of the accident, the road was icy and very slick; witnesses described it as covered with "black ice." Just prior to the accident appellant had difficulty controlling his vehicle and began to "fishtail" on the ice. He eventually lost control of his vehicle and started to slide. Appellee Graves, who had been approaching appellant from behind at a speed of 35-40 m.p.h., attempted to pass appellant's swerving vehicle first on the left side, then the right. He too, thereafter, lost control of his cement truck and the two vehicles collided. It was from that accident that appellant brought suit to recover damages for the numerous injuries he suffered.

By his own admission, appellee Graves at the time of the accident was an experienced, professional truck driver with over ten years of truck driving experience. He possessed a class "A" driver's license which entitled him to drive most types of vehicles including heavy trucks. He had attended the Wyoming Highway Patrol's defensive driver course and had kept up-to-date with various driving safety literature. He was the senior driver employed by appellee DeBernardi Brothers, Inc.

The suit was tried to a jury on the issues of appellee's negligence as well as the degree, if any, of appellant's own negligence. After a four-day trial, the jury was instructed and received the case for their consideration. They found no negligence on the part of appellees. Judgment was entered on the jury verdict and appellant moved for a new trial claiming the jury was improperly instructed. The district court took no action on the motion; it was deemed denied in sixty days. Rule 59, W.R.C.P. This appeal followed.

Appellant calls our attention to and alleges as error the district court's jury instructions . . . that:

> Negligence is the lack of ordinary care. It is the failure of a person to do something a reasonable, careful person would do, or the act of a person in doing something a reasonable, careful person would not do, under circumstances the same or similar to those shown by the evidence. The law does not say how a reasonable, careful person would act under those circumstances, as that is for the Jury to decide.
>
> A reasonable, careful person, whose conduct is set up as a standard, is not the extraordinarily cautious person, nor the exceptionally skillful one, but rather a person of reasonable and ordinary prudence. . . .

. . . Appellant argues that the second paragraph of that instruction is an incorrect statement of the law. We agree.

. . . That language is an apparent attempt to enlarge upon the reasonable man standard. In that attempt to explain the reasonable man concept, however, the instruction goes too far. It contradicts the correct statement of the law contained in the first paragraph of the instruction. Simply put, the first paragraph of the instruction correctly states that negligence is the failure to exercise ordinary care where ordinary care is that degree of care which a reasonable person is expected to exercise under the same or similar circumstances. The trial court's instruction first allows the jury to consider the parties' acts as compared to how the reasonable person would act in similar circumstances and then limits the circumstances the jury can consider by taking out of their purview the circumstances of exceptional skill or knowledge which are a part of the totality of circumstances.

Our view that negligence should be determined in view of the circumstances is in accord with the general view. The Restatement, Torts 2d §283 (1965) defines the standard of conduct in negligence actions in terms of the reasonable man under like circumstances. Professor Prosser, discussing the reasonable man, likewise said that "negligence is a failure to do what the reasonable man would do 'under the same or similar circumstances.'" He contended a jury must be instructed to take the circumstances into account. Prosser, Law of Torts §32, p.151 (4th ed. 1971). Prosser also went on to note that under the latitude of the phrase "under the same or similar circumstances," courts have made allowance not only for external facts but for many of the characteristics of the actor himself.

It has been said that "circumstances are the index to the reasonable man's conduct. His degree of diligence varies not only with standard of ordinary care, but also with his ability to avoid injuries to others, as well as the consequences of his conduct." (Footnote omitted.) 1 Dooley, Modern Tort Law §3.08, p.27 (1982 Rev.). It was aptly put many years ago when it was said:

> It seems plain also that the degree of vigilance which the law will exact as implied by the requirement of ordinary care, must vary with the probable consequences of negligence and also with the command of means to avoid injuring others possessed by the person on whom the obligation is imposed. . . . Under some circumstances a very high degree of vigilance is demanded by the requirement of ordinary care. Where the consequence of negligence will probably be serious injury to others, and where the means of avoiding the infliction of injury upon others are completely within the party's power, ordinary care requires almost the utmost degree of human vigilance and foresight. (Footnote omitted.) Id., quoting from Kelsey v. Barney, 12 N.Y. 425 (1855).

At a minimum, as Justice Holmes once said, the reasonable man is required to know what every person in the community knows. Holmes, Common Law p.57 (1881). In a similar vein, Professor Prosser notes there is, at least, a minimum standard of knowledge attributable to the reasonable man based upon what is common to the community. Prosser, supra at pp.159-160. Prosser went on to say, however, that although the reasonable man standard provides a minimum standard below which an individual's conduct will not be permitted to fall, the existence of knowledge, skill, or even intelligence superior to that of an ordinary man will demand conduct consistent therewith. Along that same line, Restatement, Torts 2d §289 (1965) provides:

> The actor is required to recognize that his conduct involves a risk of causing an invasion of another's interest if a reasonable man would do so while exercising
>> (a) such attention, perception of the circumstances, memory, knowledge of other pertinent matters, intelligence, and judgment as a reasonable man would have; and
>> (b) such superior attention, perception, memory, knowledge, intelligence, and judgment as the actor himself has.

Section 289 comment m expands further on the effect of superior qualities of an individual when it states:

> m. Superior qualities of actor. The standard of the reasonable man requires only a minimum of attention, perception, memory, knowledge, intelligence, and judgment in order to recognize the existence of the risk. If the actor has in fact more than the minimum of these qualities, he is required to exercise the superior qualities that he has in a manner reasonable under the circumstances. The standard becomes, in other words, that of a reasonable man with such superior attributes.

The instruction given by the trial court could easily have been construed by the jury to preclude their consideration of exceptional skill or knowledge on the part of either party which the evidence may have shown. In determining negligence the jury must be allowed to consider all of the circumstances surrounding an occurrence, including the characteristics of the actors in reaching their decision. Where, as here, there was evidence from which the jury could have concluded appellee Graves was more skillful than others as a result of his experience as a driver, they should be allowed to consider that as one of the circumstances in reaching their decision. The second paragraph of [the instruction], as appellant points out, could easily have misled the jury into disregarding what they may have found from the evidence regarding appellee's skill and as such prejudiced appellant. The objectionable language of the instruction is surplus language which, rather than clarifying the fictional concept of the reasonable person, actually unduly limited it. Therefore, because [the instruction] was both an incorrect statement of the law and more importantly very probably misleading, we hold that the trial court committed reversible error in using it to instruct the jury.

NOTES TO CERVELLI v. GRAVES

1. *Knowledge Requirement.* The Restatement (Second) defines the background knowledge that it is fair to assume an actor would have as the "knowledge of . . . pertinent matters . . . a reasonable man would have." Is that standard consistent with the court's analysis in Parrot v. Wells, Fargo & Co. (the Nitro-Glycerine Case)?

2. *Below- and Above-Average Knowledge.* Vaughan v. Menlove required the conduct of the farmer to be evaluated against a standard of what a typical and reasonable farmer would do, regardless of whether the defendant possessed a reasonable person's knowledge or skill. In *Cervelli*, the court notes that in the evaluation of the conduct of a person who has superior knowledge or skill, that person's conduct should be evaluated against a standard that reflects the person's superior attributes. Why should tort law ignore an actor's below-average attributes but pay attention to an actor's above-average attributes?

Perspective: The Reasonable Person Test and Juror Discretion

Does the reasonable person test allow jurors to reach whatever decisions they think are fair, or does it control their discretion by applying an identifiable legal standard? In James A. Henderson, Jr., *Expanding the Negligence Concept: Retreat from the Rule of Law*, 51 Ind. L.J. 467 (1976), the author evaluates that test in the context of what he calls "polycentric" or "open-ended" and "many-centered" problems:

> [I]n cases involving the individual conduct of "the man in the street" in his arm's length relations with others in the society, courts have relied heavily upon two institutions which have, as a consequence, come to occupy a centrally important position in this area of the law: the reasonable man test and the lay jury. Given the nontechnical nature of the issues presented in these cases, the moralistic, flesh-and-blood qualities of the reasonable man have provided an adequate vehicle with which to bring a semblance of order to the task of addressing the polycentric question of what modes of conduct individual members of society have a right to expect from one another. And the collective jury verdict, reached in secret and rendered without explanation, is ideally suited to disguising and submerging the analytical difficulties encountered in applying so general a concept as "reasonableness" to the facts of particular cases. Admittedly, this combined technique of couching argument in terms of how a hypothetical reasonable person would or would not have acted, and then turning the ultimate question of liability over to a jury, depends for its success upon its ability to hide from view, rather than confront and solve, the polycentricity in these cases. Nevertheless, it must be conceded that in the negligence cases in which the content is given to the reciprocal duty of reasonable care owed generally by individuals in our society, the difficulties have not proven insurmountable.

D. Youth: Special Treatment for Minors

Tort cases sometimes require the evaluation of a *child's conduct*. A child may be a defendant who will be liable for having inflicted an injury if he or she did it negligently. More often, a child is a plaintiff seeking damages for an injury inflicted by the defendant. In those cases, the child's conduct must be characterized as negligent or non-negligent, because doctrines known as *contributory negligence* and *comparative negligence* prohibit or reduce recoveries when a plaintiff has been negligent in a way that contributed to his or her injury.

All jurisdictions use a *special standard of care* for children's conduct. Robinson v. Lindsay describes some of the history of that standard and also shows how modern courts apply it: Does a standard that makes sense for judging a child's conduct in traditional childhood activities work well for evaluating a child's use of a snowmobile? Peterson v. Taylor emphasizes the jury's ability to interpret the child's standard based on evidence it receives about the particular child whose conduct the jury must judge: Is there a reason to think that juries can estimate how carefully children of particular ages and particular levels of experience might reasonably act?

ROBINSON v. LINDSAY

598 P.2d 392 (Wash. 1979)

Utter, C.J.

An action seeking damages for personal injuries was brought on behalf of Kelly Robinson who lost full use of a thumb in a snowmobile accident when she was 11 years of age. The petitioner, Billy Anderson, 13 years of age at the time of the accident, was the driver of the snowmobile. After a jury verdict in favor of Anderson, the trial court ordered a new trial.

The single issue on appeal is whether a minor operating a snowmobile is to be held to an adult standard of care. The trial court failed to instruct the jury as to that standard and ordered a new trial because it believed the jury should have been so instructed. We agree and affirm the order granting a new trial.

The trial court instructed the jury under WPI 10.05 that:

> In considering the claimed negligence of a child, you are instructed that it is the duty of a child to exercise the same care that a reasonably careful child of the same age, intelligence, maturity, training and experience would exercise under the same or similar circumstances.

Respondent properly excepted to the giving of this instruction and to the court's failure to give an adult standard of care.

The question of what standard of care should apply to acts of children has a long historical background. Traditionally, a flexible standard of care has been used to determine if children's actions were negligent. Under some circumstances, however, courts have developed a rationale for applying an adult standard.

In the courts' search for a uniform standard of behavior to use in determining whether or not a person's conduct has fallen below minimal acceptable standards, the law has developed a fictitious person, the "reasonable man of ordinary prudence." That term was first used in Vaughan v. Menlove, 132 Eng. Rep. 490 (1837).

Exceptions to the reasonable person standard developed when the individual whose conduct was alleged to have been negligent suffered from some physical impairment, such as blindness, deafness, or lameness. Courts also found it necessary, as a practical matter, to depart considerably from the objective standard when dealing with children's behavior. Children are traditionally encouraged to pursue childhood activities without the same burdens and responsibilities with which adults must contend. See Bahr, *Tort Law and the Games Kids Play*, 23 S.D. L. Rev. 275 (1978). As a result, courts evolved a special standard of care to measure a child's negligence in a particular situation.

In Roth v. Union Depot Co., 13 Wash. 525, 43 P. 641 (1896), Washington joined "the overwhelming weight of authority" in distinguishing between the capacity of a child and that of an adult. As the court then stated, at page 544, 43 P. at page 647:

> [I]t would be a monstrous doctrine to hold that a child of inexperience — and experience can come only with years — should be held to the same degree of care in avoiding danger as a person of mature years and accumulated experience.

The court went on to hold, at page 545, 43 P. at page 647:

> The care or caution required is according to the capacity of the child, and this is to be determined, ordinarily, by the age of the child. . . .
>
> . . . a child is held . . . only to the exercise of such degree of care and discretion as is reasonably to be expected from children of his age.

The current law in this state is fairly reflected in WPI 10.05, given in this case. In the past we have always compared a child's conduct to that expected of a reasonably careful child of the same age, intelligence, maturity, training and experience. This case is the first to consider the question of a child's liability for injuries sustained as a result of his or her operation of a motorized vehicle or participation in an inherently dangerous activity.

Courts in other jurisdictions have created an exception to the special child standard because of the apparent injustice that would occur if a child who caused injury while engaged in certain dangerous activities were permitted to defend himself by saying that other children similarly situated would not have exercised a degree of care higher than his, and he is, therefore, not liable for his tort. Some courts have couched the exception in terms of children engaging in an activity which is normally one for adults only. See, e.g., Dellwo v. Pearson, 259 Minn. 452, 107 N.W.2d 859 (1961) (operation of a motorboat). We believe a better rationale is that when the activity a child engages in is inherently dangerous, as is the operation of powerful mechanized vehicles, the child should be held to an adult standard of care.

Such a rule protects the need of children to be children but at the same time discourages immature individuals from engaging in inherently dangerous activities. Children will still be free to enjoy traditional childhood activities without being held to an adult standard of care. Although accidents sometimes occur as the result of such activities, they are not activities generally considered capable of resulting in "grave danger to others and to the minor himself if the care used in the course of the activity drops below that care which the reasonable and prudent adult would use. . . ." Daniels v. Evans, 107 N.H. 407, 408, 224 A.2d 63, 64 (1966).

Other courts adopting the adult standard of care for children engaged in adult activities have emphasized the hazards to the public if the rule is otherwise. We agree with the Minnesota Supreme Court's language in its decision in Dellwo v. Pearson, supra, 259 Minn. at 457-58, 107 N.W.2d at 863:

> Certainly in the circumstances of modern life, where vehicles moved by powerful motors are readily available and frequently operated by immature individuals, we should be skeptical of a rule that would allow motor vehicles to be operated to the hazard of the public with less than the normal minimum degree of care and competence.

Dellwo applied the adult standard to a 12-year-old defendant operating a motor boat. Other jurisdictions have applied the adult standard to minors engaged in analogous activities. Goodfellow v. Coggburn, 98 Idaho 202, 203-04, 560 P.2d 873 (1977) (minor operating tractor); Williams v. Esaw, 214 Kan. 658, 668, 522 P.2d 950 (1974) (minor operating motorcycle); Perricone v. DiBartolo, 14 Ill. App. 3d 514, 520, 302 N.E.2d 637 (1973) (minor operating gasoline-powered minibike); Krahn v. LaMeres, 483 P.2d 522, 525-26 (Wyo. 1971) (minor operating automobile). The holding of minors to an adult standard of care when they operate motorized vehicles is gaining approval from an increasing number of courts and commentators.

The operation of a snowmobile likewise requires adult care and competence. Currently 2.2 million snowmobiles are in operation in the United States. 9 Envir. Rptr. (BNA) 876 [1978 Current Developments]. Studies show that collisions and other snowmobile accidents claim hundreds of casualties each year and that the incidence of accidents is particularly high among inexperienced operators. See Note, *Snowmobiles—A Legislative Program*, 1972 Wis. L. Rev. 477, 489 n.58.

At the time of the accident, the 13-year-old petitioner had operated snowmobiles for about 2 years. When the injury occurred, petitioner was operating a 30-horsepower snowmobile at speeds of 10-20 miles per hour. The record indicates that the machine itself was capable of 65 miles per hour. Because petitioner was operating a powerful motorized vehicle, he should be held to the standard of care and conduct expected of an adult.

The order granting a new trial is affirmed.

NOTES TO ROBINSON v. LINDSAY

1. *Basic Child Standard of Care.*   The court confirms the usual applicability of a special standard for children, approving the trial court's instruction that a child is required to exercise as "the same care that a reasonably careful child of the same age, intelligence, maturity, training and experience would exercise under the same or similar circumstances." The court quotes an earlier opinion saying it would be monstrous to require children to act as carefully as more experienced people act. The court also refers to "the need of children to be children." Consider how well this special standard for children relates to children's needs and society's needs for children to develop their abilities.

2. *Exception to the Basic Rule.*   The *Robinson* court rejects applying the basic rule to the conduct of a child who was operating a snowmobile. It notes the inherent danger in that activity and cites that as a reason to apply the adult standard rather than the child's standard. Other courts have withdrawn the child standard when an activity is one that is normally engaged in only by adults. Still another position would withdraw the child standard only for activities that are both dangerous and usually "adults only" activities. How would each of these approaches apply to the following activities?

A. Downhill skiing. See Goss v. Allen, 70 N.J. 442, 360 A.2d 388 (1976).

B. Hunting with a rifle in a state where minors are not required to have a license to hunt. See Purtle v. Shelton, 251 Ark. 519, 474 S.W.2d 123 (1971).

C. Playing golf. See Neumann v. Shlansky, 294 N.Y.S.2d 628 (1968).

D. Using a fire outdoors for cooking. See Farm Bureau Ins. Group v. Phillips, 323 N.W.2d 477 (Mich. App. 1982).

Perspective: Fairness to Victims?

The noted scholar Richard A. Epstein has written that the rule applying a child's standard of care to the conduct of a child who rides a bicycle "undercuts the protection offered innocent strangers rammed by children." Richard A. Epstein, Torts 119 (1999). Does that question suggest a frame of reference different from the orientation of those who favor the special standard for children? How would those proponents respond to Professor Epstein's observation?

PETERSON v. TAYLOR
316 N.W.2d 869 (Iowa 1982)

ALLBEE, J.

An unfortunate combination of gasoline, matches and a seven-year-old boy resulted in the lawsuit which underlies this appeal. Badly burned as a result of his experimentation with fire, the minor plaintiff David Peterson, by his mother as next friend, brought a negligence suit against his neighbors, the Taylors, from whose storage shed he obtained the gasoline. The jury returned a verdict for the defendants, and plaintiff appeals.

Evidence at trial showed that the Taylors and the Petersons lived on neighboring small acreages just outside the Des Moines city limits and that David Peterson frequently played with the Taylors' son Greg. On Sunday, August 7, 1977, David and his three-year-old sister Molly stopped at the Taylor place on their way home from another neighbor's house. Finding no one home, David decided to gather some twigs and build a fire on a concrete slab in the Taylors' back yard, using some matches he had taken from his uncle's car earlier that day. When the wind blew that fire out, David "got mad." He then went to the Taylors' storage shed, removed a can of gasoline, opened it, smelled it to confirm that it was gasoline, threw a lighted match into it and stood back to watch the fire come out of the can. When that fire appeared to have died out, he went to the shed, removed a second can of gasoline, and accidentally spilled some of it on his pants. Then he dropped the second can and either lit another match or knocked over the first can which was still flaming inside; in any event, David's gasoline-soaked pants somehow became ignited, and he rolled on the ground to put out the fire. As a result of the incident, David received serious burns. . . .

Plaintiff presented expert testimony to the effect that David was of average intelligence, that he was mildly hyperactive, and that hyperactive children tend to be somewhat more attracted to playing with fire than other children. The expert also testified that a child having David's characteristics probably would not realize the full extent of the danger involved in playing with matches and gasoline; for instance, he probably would not realize that a gasoline fire cannot be put out with water. The same expert did testify, however, that such a child "would certainly know that he'd get burned" if he played with gasoline and matches.

On appeal, plaintiff . . . questions . . . the sufficiency of the evidence of his contributory negligence. . . .

. . . The trend is to view the question of a child's capacity for negligence as an issue of fact. Comment, *Capacity of Minors to Be Chargeable with Negligence and Their Standard of Care*, 57 Neb. L. Rev. 763, 767 (1978). See, e.g., Mann [v. Fairbourn, 12 Utah 2d 342, 346, 366 P.2d 606, 606] ("The capacity or incapacity of a child [for contributory negligence] is a factual inquiry and the test to be applied is that applicable to any other question of fact."). Under this approach, a particular child's incapacity for negligence may be determined by the court as a matter of law only if the child is so young or the evidence of incapacity so overwhelming that reasonable minds could not differ on that issue. Id.; 57 Neb. L. Rev., supra, at 767; see W. Prosser [Handbook of the Law of Torts 156 (4th ed. 1971)]; Restatement (Second) of Torts §283A comment b (1965). If reasonable minds *could* differ, the question of the child's contributory negligence is submitted to the jury with instructions to apply a standard of care similar to that set forth in §283A of the Restatement, supra:

> If the actor is a child, the standard of conduct to which he must conform to avoid being negligent is that of a reasonable person of like age, intelligence, and experience under like circumstances.

In applying this standard, the jury must initially make a subjective determination of the particular child's capacity to perceive and avoid the specific risk involved, based on evidence of his age, intelligence and experience. . . .

We have articulated a standard of care for children similar to that in the Restatement, see, e.g., Ruby v. Easton, 207 N.W.2d 10, 20 (Iowa 1973) ("standard of reasonable behavior of children of similar age, intelligence and experience"). . . .

. . . Plaintiff argues that defendants had the burden of establishing the appropriate standard of care by which David's actions should be judged, and that they failed to meet that burden as a matter of law. Specifically, he asserts that evidence at trial showed David was generally a normal seven-year-old child, and that defendants presented no evidence that a normal seven-year-old child would have acted differently than David did. Therefore, it is argued, there was no evidence from which the jury could find that David did not exercise that degree of care which may be expected of a seven-year-old child. We believe this argument reflects a basic misunderstanding concerning the evidentiary showing which must be made in regard to the standard of care for children.

In applying the standard of care, as noted above, the jury's first inquiry is a subjective one: What was the capacity of this particular child — given what the evidence shows about his age, intelligence and experience — to perceive and avoid the particular risk involved in this case? Once this has been determined, the focus becomes objective: How would a reasonable child of like capacity have acted under similar circumstances? The particular child in question can be found negligent only if his actions fall short of what may reasonably be expected of children of similar capacity. . . .

Regarding the subjective inquiry, there must be evidence adduced at trial concerning the child's age, intelligence and experience so that the jury may determine the child's capacity, if any, to perceive and avoid the risk. Watts v. Erickson, 244 Minn. 264, 268-69, 69 N.W.2d 626, 629-30 (1955). We find there was ample evidence of that nature in this case, and the evidence was not such that David could be found incapable of contributory negligence as a matter of law. Plaintiff appears to complain, however, that no witness testified that a reasonable child of like capacity would not have acted as plaintiff did in this case. We hold that such testimony need not, and indeed may not, be presented. Determining how a reasonable person would have acted under the circumstances is clearly the function of the jury. The "reasonable child" inquiry differs from the "reasonable man" inquiry only in that the "circumstances" in the former case are broadened to include consideration of the child's age, intelligence and experience. In neither case should a witness, expert or otherwise, be permitted to express an opinion on what a reasonable person would have done in a similar situation, because such testimony would be tantamount to an opinion on whether the person in question was negligent. . . .

We conclude that there was sufficient evidence for trial court to submit the question of David's contributory negligence to the jury. . . .

Affirmed.

NOTES TO PETERSON v. TAYLOR

1. *Expert Testimony on Child's Abilities.*   The court rejected the idea that expert testimony should be required to enable a jury to determine what a typical child of a specific age, intelligence, and experience would do in a given situation. What experiences do typical jury members have that might enable them to decide that question in the absence of information from experts?

2. *Negligence of Very Young Children.* Some states hold that a child under seven is not capable of negligence as a matter of law. This is known as the "Illinois rule." See Toney v. Mazariegos, 166 Ill. App. 3d 399, 116 Ill. Dec. 820, 519 N.E.2d 1035 (1988). Most states follow the Restatement (Second) of Torts §283A (1964) and the comments to that section, taking the position that the variety of development and intelligence in children and the range of situations in which they may act make it preferable to allow the jury to interpret the standard in every case. See Honeycutt v. Phillips, 247 Kan. 250, 796 P.2d 549 (1990), for a discussion of this issue.

3. *Historical Pressures for Pro-Child Rules.* At the time when courts developed the child's standard of care, it was a nearly universal rule that a plaintiff who was negligent in any way in connection with his or her injury was completely barred from recovery. Adopting a pro-child standard at that time had the effect of allowing recovery for many children who otherwise would have recovered nothing if the defendant had been able to prove that their conduct was less careful than an adult's would have been. Since children are plaintiffs much more often than they are defendants, adopting the child's standard of care was probably seen as a step that could facilitate recoveries for relatively innocent children without causing a disadvantage to many other potential plaintiffs.

At present, almost every jurisdiction has rejected the "contributory negligence" doctrine that precluded recovery when a plaintiff was negligent. They have replaced it with "comparative negligence" doctrines that allow plaintiffs to recover in many situations even though a jury concludes they were negligent. This changes the importance of a special standard for children. When the standard was first developed, it protected children from total defeat. Now, when a jury uses the child's standard of care, the standard affects how severely a jury evaluates the child's conduct for the purpose of applying comparative negligence principles that often reduce and only sometimes preclude recovery by the child.

4. *Hypotheticals: Children's Activities in Modern Settings*

A. A 12-year-old walked across a street in a city and was hit by a car while in the street's crosswalk. The child was playing with a handheld electronic game and was listening to music with earphones — for these reasons, the youngster was not aware of the car's approach. When the jury evaluates the child's conduct, should it use a child's standard of care or the general reasonable person standard?

B. Two eight-year-olds, *A* and *B*, were playing together with a computer at *A*'s house. The computer stopped working, and *A* asked *B* to check to make sure its CD drive had a disk in it. As *B* did that, *A* clicked on a feature of the program that made the CD drive door close. The door cut one of *B*'s fingers badly. In a suit by *B* against *A*, should *A*'s conduct be judged by the child's standard of care or the reasonable person standard?

5. *Why Sue a Child?* As *Robinson* shows, children can be responsible under tort law for damages they inflict on others. Parents, though, are not obligated to pay for harms their children might cause. This leads to an obvious conclusion: It's not worth the effort to sue a child unless the child has his or her own wealth or the child is covered by an insurance policy that will pay a judgment entered against the child. A small number of children do have their own money, usually given to them by relatives or by their parents. Many children are covered by their parents' homeowner's insurance policies. These policies protect against damage to the insured's home, and they usually also provide coverage for personal injury liability incurred by anybody in the immediate family of the insured.

Some states have statutes that alter the common law position and make parents financially responsible for damage their children cause. These statutes generally cover only intentional misconduct and impose a ceiling on the amount of liability, such as $5,000 or $10,000.

Statute: LIABILITY OF PARENT OR GUARDIAN FOR WILLFUL
DESTRUCTION OF PROPERTY BY INFANT UNDER 18

N.J. Stat. Ann. §2A:53A-15 (2017)

A parent, guardian or other person having legal custody of an infant under 18 years of age who fails or neglects to exercise reasonable supervision and control of the conduct of such infant, shall be liable in a civil action for any willful, malicious or unlawful injury or destruction by such infant of the real or personal property of another.

Statute: LIABILITY OF PARENT FOR WILLFUL INJURY TO
PUBLIC TRANSPORTATION UTILITY BY MINOR

N.J. Stat. Ann. §2A:53A-16 (2017)

The parents of any minor who shall maliciously or willfully injure any property of a railroad, street railway, traction railway or autobus public utility shall be liable for damages in the amount of the injury to a limit of $5,000, to be collected by the property owner in the Superior Court, together with costs of suit.

Statute: PARENTAL LIABILITY FOR WILLFUL, MALICIOUS
OR CRIMINAL ACTS OF CHILDREN

W. Va. Code §55-7A-2 (2017)

The custodial parent or parents of any minor child shall be personally liable in an amount not to exceed five thousand dollars for damages which are the proximate result of any one or a combination of the following acts of the minor child:

(a) The malicious and willful injury to the person of another; or

(b) The malicious and willful injury or damage to the property of another, whether the property be real, personal or mixed; or

(c) The malicious and willful setting fire to a forest or wooded area belonging to another; or

(d) The willful taking, stealing and carrying away of the property of another, with the intent to permanently deprive the owner of possession.

For purposes of this section, "custodial parent or parents" shall mean the parent or parents with whom the minor child is living, or a divorced or separated parent who does not have legal custody but who is exercising supervisory control over the minor child at the time of the minor child's act. . . .

Recovery hereunder shall be limited to the actual damages based upon direct out-of-pocket loss, taxable court costs, and interest from date of judgment. The right of action and remedy granted herein shall be in addition to and not exclusive of any rights of action and remedies therefor against a parent or parents for the tortious acts of his or their children heretofore existing under the provisions of any law, statutory or otherwise, or now so existing independently of the provisions of this article.

Statute: NATURAL GUARDIAN; LIABILITY FOR TORTS OF CHILD

Haw. Rev. Stat. Ann. §577-3 (2017)

. . . The father and mother of unmarried minor children shall jointly and severally be liable in damages for tortious acts committed by their children, and shall be jointly and severally entitled to prosecute and defend all actions in which the children or their individual property may be concerned.

NOTES TO STATUTES

1. *Fault-Based and Vicarious Liability for Parents.* Parents are generally liable for their children's torts when the parents were themselves at fault. These statutes reveal variations on that general rule. In New Jersey, a parent will be liable for a harm inflicted by a child if the parent was also negligent and the child engaged in serious wrongdoing. However, New Jersey parents are vicariously liable (liable even if they were not themselves at fault) when some special interests are affected, such as transportation and public utilities. The West Virginia and Hawaii statutes impose vicarious liability and do not require a plaintiff to establish that parents were themselves at fault.

2. *Kinds of Children's Conduct Necessary to Trigger Vicarious Parental Liability.* The New Jersey and West Virginia statutes represent the majority view among states that have adopted statutes on this topic insofar as they impose vicarious liability on parents only when their children's conduct was malicious and willful. The Hawaii statute represents a minority position. If a young child rode a bicycle less carefully than a typical child of that age would usually ride and injured a pedestrian, under which of these four statutes could the child's parent be financially responsible for the injury?

3. *Alternative Statutory Approaches.* Under which of these statutes would a parent be responsible for the damage caused by his or her child's setting fire maliciously to a wooded area belonging to someone else despite the parent's reasonable supervision and control? What does the West Virginia statute accomplish by including an explicit reference to setting fires?

E. Physical and Mental Disabilities

When conduct by a person with a mental disability needs to be evaluated in a tort case, typical tort law evaluates that conduct by comparing it with how a reasonable person *without that mental disability* would act. For physical disabilities, the typical position is different. The physically disabled actor must act as well as a reasonable person *with that physical disability* would act. These two positions must reflect a belief that mental and physical disabilities are different in some important ways — a belief that may have had greater support in an earlier generation and that may be subject to criticism now.

Poyner v. Loftus applies a special standard to a legally blind plaintiff: When a person with limited vision goes to a public place, how careful does tort law require that person to be? In Creasy v. Rusk, involving an institutionalized person suffering from Alzheimer's disease, a court affirms the general rule that would compare that person's conduct with a reasonable person's conduct but withdraws the rule's application under the specific circumstances of the case.

<hr>

POYNER v. LOFTUS

694 A.2d 69 (D.C. Ct. App. 1997)

SCHWELB, Associate Judge.

This action for personal injuries was brought by William J. Poyner, who is legally blind, after he fell from an elevated walkway. The trial judge granted summary judgment in favor of the defendants, concluding that Mr. Poyner was contributorily negligent as a matter of law. On appeal, Mr. Poyner contends that, in light of his handicap, a genuine issue of material fact existed as to whether he exercised reasonable care, and that the entry of summary judgment was therefore erroneous. We affirm.

The essential evidentiary facts are undisputed. Mr. Poyner suffers from glaucoma and retrobulbar neuritis. He testified that he is able to see approximately six to eight feet in front of him. Notwithstanding his handicap, Mr. Poyner does not use a cane or a seeing eye dog in pursuing his daily activities.

On August 24, 1993, Mr. Poyner was proceeding from his home to Parklane Cleaners, a dry cleaning establishment. . . . The entrance to Parklane Cleaners is adjacent to an inclined platform which is located approximately four feet above street level. Mr. Poyner testified that he had walked by the area on three or four previous occasions, and that he was aware of the general layout. He stated that there were bushes along the edge of the platform, and that these bushes provided a natural barrier which would prevent him from falling if he attempted to walk too far. On the day of the accident, however, and unbeknownst to Mr. Poyner, one of the bushes was missing, and there was thus nothing to restrain him from falling off the platform.

Mr. Poyner testified that as he was walking along the elevated area, he heard someone call "Billy!" from Connecticut Avenue. He turned his head to the right, but continued to walk forward to the location at the end of the platform where he thought that a bush would be. There was no bush, however, and Mr. Poyner fell, suffering personal injuries.

Mr. Poyner brought suit against several defendants, including the owners of the building, the property manager in charge of its maintenance, and the proprietor of Parklane Cleaners. After the parties had conducted discovery, the defendants moved for summary judgment, contending, inter alia, that Mr. Poyner had been contributorily negligent as a matter of law. The trial judge granted the motion, and she stated her reasons, in pertinent part, as follows: . . .

Mr. Poyner's actions, in the court's judgment, clearly violate an objective reasonableness standard. . . . [N]o reasonable jurors could conclude that the plaintiff was not negligent when he continued to walk on an elevated surface with limited vision while his head was turned away from the direction of his travel in an area in which he was not very familiar.

In order to be entitled to summary judgment, the defendants were required to demonstrate that there was no genuine issue of material fact and that they were entitled to judgment as a matter of law. . . .

Ordinarily, questions of negligence and contributory negligence must be decided by the trier of fact. . . . The issue of contributory negligence should not be submitted to the jury, however, where the evidence, taken in the light most favorable to the plaintiff, establishes contributory negligence so clearly that no other inference can reasonably be drawn. . . .

The trial judge concluded that this was one of those rare cases in which contributory negligence — a defense with respect to which the defendants had the burden of proof — had been established as a matter of law. We agree. . . .

It is undisputed that, at the time of the accident, a shrub at the end of the elevated platform was missing. . . . In this case, Mr. Poyner acknowledged that his attention was distracted when someone called his name, and that he turned his head to the right, but continued to walk forward. At the critical moment, according to his own testimony, Mr. Poyner, who could see six to eight feet in front of him and was aware of his handicap, did not look where he was going. We agree with the trial judge that this constituted contributory negligence and that no impartial jury could reasonably find otherwise.

Mr. Poyner argues, however, that he is not a sighted person, and that "it is reasonable for a legally blind person . . . as a response to his name being called, [to] turn towards the direction of his caller, reach for the handle and continue his step towards the door." He claims that those actions "do not constitute contributory negligence." He contends, in other words, that on account of his visual impairment, his conduct should be tested against a different standard of care.

The parties have cited no authority on this issue, and we have found no applicable case law in the District of Columbia. The precedents in other jurisdictions, however, support affirmance of the trial court's order. "It seems to be the general rule that a blind or otherwise handicapped person, in using the public ways, must exercise for his own safety due care, or care commensurate with the known or reasonably foreseeable dangers. Due care is such care as an ordinarily prudent person with the same disability would exercise under the same or similar circumstances." Cook v. City of Winston-Salem, 85 S.E.2d 696, 700-01 (N.C. 1955). . . .

In Smith v. Sneller, 26 A.2d 452 (Pa. 1942), the Supreme Court of Pennsylvania considered a situation similar to the one before us, and its disposition is instructive. Sneller, a plumbing contractor, had removed a portion of the sidewalk and had dug a trench in order to make a sewer connection. On the north side of the trench, Sneller constructed a barricade. On the south side, however, Sneller simply left a pile of earth two feet high. The plaintiff, Smith, was walking north along the sidewalk towards the trench. As a result of defective eyesight, he failed to see the pile of earth. Mr. Smith fell into the trench, and sustained personal injuries. A jury returned a verdict in his favor.

The intermediate appellate court expressed sympathy for Mr. Smith "in his effort to make a living in spite of his physical handicap," but nevertheless felt constrained to reverse the decision and enter judgment n.o.v. in Sneller's favor. Smith appealed to the Pennsylvania Supreme Court, which affirmed the judgment. Noting that Mr. Smith's vision was so defective that he could not see a dangerous condition immediately in front of him, and that the accident could have been avoided if he had used "one of the common well-known compensatory devices for the blind, such as a cane, a 'seeing eye' dog, or a companion," the court concluded:

> Plaintiff's conduct was not equal to the degree of care required of him. The Superior Court very properly said: "A blind man may not rely wholly upon his other senses to warn him of danger but must use the devices usually employed, to compensate for his blindness. Only by so doing can he go about with comparative safety to himself." We are in accord with that learned court . . . and we must, therefore, affirm the judgment.

26 A.2d at 454.

The reasoning of the court in *Smith* applies equally to the present case. Here, as in *Smith*, the plaintiff was walking alone, and he did not use a guide dog or a cane. As a result, he fell from the walkway. Indeed, the evidence of contributory negligence is stronger here than in *Smith*, for Mr. Poyner, who could see six to eight feet in front of him, acknowledged that, at the moment that he fell, he was not looking where he was going.

In Coker v. McDonald's Corp., 537 A.2d 549 (Del. Super. 1987), the legally blind plaintiff was walking to the entrance of a McDonald's restaurant from the parking lot. Unlike the plaintiffs in *Smith* and in the present case, however, she was carrying a cane in her right hand, and she was holding on to a companion with her left hand. Ms. Coker lost her balance while attempting to navigate around an obstruction, and she sustained injuries. The defendant claimed that the obstruction was "open and obvious," and that the plaintiff was contributorily negligent as a matter of law. The court disagreed:

> A blind person is not bound to discover everything which a person of normal vision would. He is bound to use due care under the circumstances. Due care for a blind person includes a reasonable effort to compensate for his unfortunate affliction by use of artificial aids for discovery of obstacles in his path. When an effort in this direction is made, it will ordinarily be a jury question whether or not such effort was a reasonable one. . . .

Id. at 550-51 (citations and internal quotation marks omitted). Characterizing the issue presented as being whether Ms. Coker acted reasonably under the circumstances, the court concluded that . . . [b]ecause Ms. Coker was using two different aids, however — the cane and the companion — the question of contributory negligence was for the jury, and the defendant was not entitled to summary judgment. Id.

We agree with the analysis of the courts both in Smith v. Sneller and in *Coker*. Like the plaintiff in *Smith*, but unlike the plaintiff in *Coker*, Mr. Poyner was alone, and he used neither a cane nor a seeing eye dog. He also looked away at the critical moment. Under these circumstances, he was contributorily negligent as a matter of law, and summary judgment was properly granted.

Affirmed.

NOTES TO POYNER v. LOFTUS

1. *Basic Standard of Care for Persons with Physical Disabilities.* The reasonable person standard applies in a special way when an actor has a physical disability. The *Poyner* court approved the statement that for a person with a physical disability, due care "is such care as an ordinarily prudent person with the same disability would exercise under the same or similar circumstances." Using that test, on what basis did the court determine that the visually impaired plaintiff's conduct had been negligent?

2. *Intoxication.* Traditionally, the actions of a person who was intoxicated at the time he or she was injured or caused an injury have been evaluated with reference to the reasonable prudent person standard, completely ignoring the fact of intoxication. See, e.g., Hines v. Pollock, 229 Neb. 614, 428 N.W.2d 207 (1988) (intoxicated condition of plaintiff not relevant to whether the plaintiff used reasonable care when crossing street in the middle of the block and stumbling into the defendant's truck). There is no "reasonable intoxicated person" standard as there is a "reasonable visually-impaired person" in *Poyner*. In general, if the person's intoxication was involuntary, would it be consistent with *Poyner* to have the jury ignore the intoxication?

A contemporary approach to intoxication focuses on a person's decision to drink or to engage in a risky activity rather that the way in which the person engaged in the activity. According to the Restatement (Third), "actors can be found negligent precisely because they consume alcohol knowing that they will shortly be undertaking a dangerous task or because they undertake such a task knowing that they are under the influence of alcohol" Under this approach, excessive drinking can itself be negligent when a person becomes intoxicated knowing he will engage in dangerous conduct. Rather than asking whether a person used reasonable care when crossing a street in the middle of the block, one might ask whether a person used reasonable care when deciding to drink knowing that he would soon be crossing a street. Alternatively, a person may be negligent if he engages in a risky activity knowing he is intoxicated. It would thus be negligent for a person to work on the sloped roof of a building or to drive a motor vehicle knowing he is intoxicated.

Problem
Physical Disabilities

Wayne Hodges was partially paralyzed, but could walk using crutches and a leg brace. On his way to the defendant's insurance office, he attempted to walk up several steps that led to the office door. One of his feet caught on a small edge that projected from the front of a step, and he fell down and was injured. You represent Hodges in a negligence suit against the owner of the office, claiming that the step was poorly designed and poorly maintained. The defendant has claimed that Hodges was partly responsible for the fall because of the way he attempted to walk up the stairs. What jury instruction should you ask the court to give with regard to evaluating your client's conduct? See Hodges v. Jewel Cos., 390 N.E.2d 930 (Ill. App. 1979).

CREASY v. RUSK

730 N.E.2d 659 (Ind. 2000)

SULLIVAN, J.

Carol Creasy, a certified nursing assistant, sued Lloyd Rusk, an Alzheimer's patient, for injuries she suffered when he kicked her while she was trying to put him to bed. We hold that adults with mental disabilities have the same general duty of care toward others as those without. But we conclude that the relationship between the parties and public policy considerations here are such that Rusk had no such duty to Creasy.

In July, 1992, Lloyd Rusk's wife admitted Rusk to the Brethren Healthcare Center ("BHC") because he suffered from memory loss and confusion and Rusk's wife was unable to care for him. Rusk's primary diagnosis was Alzheimer's disease. Over the course of three years at BHC, Rusk experienced periods of anxiousness, confusion, depression, disorientation, and agitation. Rusk often resisted when staff members attempted to remove him from prohibited areas of the facility. On several occasions, Rusk was belligerent with both staff and other residents. In particular, Rusk was often combative, agitated, and aggressive and would hit staff members when they tried to care for him.

BHC had employed Creasy as a certified nursing assistant for nearly 20 months when the incident at issue occurred. Creasy's responsibilities included caring for Rusk and other patients with Alzheimer's disease. . . .

On May 16, 1995, Creasy and another certified nursing assistant, Linda Davis, were working through their routine of putting Rusk and other residents to bed. Creasy knew that Rusk had been "very agitated and combative that evening." By Creasy's account:

> [Davis] was helping me put Mr. Rusk to bed. She was holding his wrists to keep him from hitting us and I was trying to get his legs to put him to bed. He was hitting and kicking wildly. During this time, he kicked me several times in my left knee and hip area. My lower back popped and I yelled out with pain from my lower back and left knee.

Creasy filed a civil negligence suit against Rusk, seeking monetary damages for the injuries she suffered as a result of Rusk's conduct. Rusk moved for summary judgment and the trial court granted his motion. Creasy appealed. The Court of Appeals reversed, holding "that a person's mental capacity, whether that person is a child or an adult, must be factored [into] the determination of whether a legal duty exists," and that a genuine issue of material fact existed as to the level of Rusk's mental capacity.

This case requires us to decide two distinct questions of Indiana common law:

(1) Whether the general duty of care imposed upon adults with mental disabilities is the same as that for adults without mental disabilities?

(2) Whether the circumstances of Rusk's case are such that the general duty of care imposed upon adults with mental disabilities should be imposed upon him? . . .

. . . We believe that the Court of Appeals accurately stated Indiana law but that the law is in need of revision.

. . . [T]he generally accepted rule in jurisdictions other than Indiana is that mental disability does not excuse a person from liability for "conduct which does not conform to the standard of a reasonable man under like circumstances." Restatement (Second) of Torts §283B; accord Restatement (Third) of Torts §9(c) (Discussion Draft Apr. 5, 1999) ("Unless the actor is a child, the actor's mental or emotional disability is not considered in determining whether conduct is negligent."). People with mental disabilities are commonly held liable for their intentional and negligent torts. No allowance is made for lack of intelligence, ignorance, excitability, or proneness to accident. . . .

The public policy reasons most often cited for holding individuals with mental disabilities to a standard of reasonable care in negligence claims include the following.

(1) Allocates losses between two innocent parties to the one who caused or occasioned the loss. Under this rationale, the one who experienced the loss or injury as a result of the conduct of a person with a mental disability is presumed not to have assumed risks or to have been contributorily negligent with respect to the cause of the injury. This policy is also intended to protect even negligent third parties from bearing excessive liabilities.

(2) Provides incentive to those responsible for people with disabilities and interested in their estates to prevent harm and "restrain" those who are potentially dangerous.

(3) Removes inducements for alleged tort-feasors to fake a mental disability in order to escape liability. The Restatement mentions the ease with which mental disability can be feigned as one possible basis for this policy concern.

(4) Avoids administrative problems involved in courts and juries attempting to identify and assess the significance of an actor's disability. As a practical matter, it is arguably too difficult to account for or draw any "satisfactory line between mental deficiency and those variations of temperament, intellect, and emotional balance."

(5) Forces persons with disabilities to pay for the damage they do if they "are to live in the world." The Restatement adds that it is better that the assets, if any, of the one with the mental deficiency be used "to compensate innocent victims than that [the assets] remain in their hands." A discussion draft for the Restatement (Third) of Torts rephrases this policy rationale and concludes: "If a person is suffering from a mental disorder so serious as to make it likely that the person will engage in substandard conduct that threatens the safety of others, there can be doubts as to whether this person should be allowed to engage in the normal range of society's activities; given these doubts, there is nothing especially harsh in at least holding the person responsible for the harms the person may cause by substandard conduct."

To assist in deciding whether Indiana should adopt the generally accepted rule, we turn to an examination of contemporary public policy in Indiana as embodied in enactments of our state legislature.

Since the 1970's, Indiana law has strongly reflected policies to deinstitutionalize people with disabilities and integrate them into the least restrictive environment. National policy changes have led the way for some of Indiana's enactments in that several federal acts either guarantee the civil rights of people with disabilities or condition state aid upon state compliance with desegregation and integrationist practices.

These legislative developments reflect policies consistent with those supporting the Restatement rule generally accepted outside Indiana in that they reflect a determination that people with disabilities should be treated in the same way as non-disabled persons.

We pause for a moment to consider in greater detail the issue . . . that the Restatement rule may very well have been grounded in a policy determination that persons with mental disabilities should be institutionalized or otherwise confined rather than "live in the world." It is clear from our recitation of state and federal legislative and regulatory developments that contemporary public policy has rejected institutionalization and confinement for a "strong professional consensus in favor of . . . community treatment . . . and integration into the least restrictive . . . environment." Indeed, scholarly commentary has noted that "new statutes and case law . . . have transformed the areas of commitment, guardianship, confidentiality, consent to treatment, and institutional conditions." [Citing James W. Ellis, *Tort Responsibility of Mentally Disabled Persons*, 1981 Am. B. Found. Res. J. 1079, 1079-1080 (1981).] We observe that it is a matter of some irony that public policies favoring the opposite ends — institutionalization and confinement on the one hand and community treatment and integration into the least restrictive environment on the other — should nevertheless yield the same common law rule: that the general duty of care imposed on adults with mental disabilities is the same as that for adults without mental disabilities.

In balancing the considerations presented in the foregoing analysis, we reject the Court of Appeals's approach and adopt the Restatement rule. We hold that a person with mental disabilities is generally held to the same standard of care as that of a reasonable person under the same circumstances without regard to the alleged tortfeasor's capacity to control or understand the consequences of his or her actions.

We turn now to the question of whether the circumstances of Rusk's case are such that the general duty of care imposed upon adults with mental disabilities should be found to run from him to Creasy.

In asking this question, we recognize that exceptions to the general rule will arise where the factual circumstances negate the factors supporting imposition of a duty particularly with respect to the nature of the parties' relationship and public policy considerations. For example, courts in jurisdictions that apply the reasonable person standard to individuals with mental disabilities have uniformly held that Alzheimer's patients who have no capacity to control their conduct do not owe a duty to their caregivers to refrain from violent conduct because the factual circumstances negate the policy rationales behind the presumption of liability.

We find that the relationship between Rusk and Creasy and public policy concerns dictate that Rusk owed no duty of care to Creasy. See Webb v. Jarvis, 575 N.E.2d 992, 995 (Ind. 1991) (balancing three factors to determine whether an individual owes a duty to another: (1) the relationship between the parties; (2) the reasonable foreseeability of harm to the person injured; and (3) public policy concerns).

Unlike the typical victim supporting the Restatement rationale, Creasy was not a member of the public at large, unable to anticipate or safeguard against the harm she encountered. Creasy knew of Rusk's violent history. She could have changed her course of action or requested additional assistance when she recognized Rusk's state of mind on the evening when she received the alleged injury. Rusk's inability to comprehend the circumstances of his relationship with Creasy and others was the very reason Creasy was employed to support Rusk. The nursing home and Creasy, through the nursing home, were "employed to encounter, and knowingly did encounter, just the dangers which injured" Creasy. In fact, caregivers and their employers under these circumstances are better positioned to prevent caregiver injury and to protect against risks faced as a result of job responsibilities. In Indiana, the workers' compensation system, not the tort system, exists to cover such employment-related losses. To the extent that the workers' compensation system is inadequate as Creasy asserts, the inadequacy reflects defects in the workers' compensation system and is not a ground for alternative recovery under tort law. . . .

Public Policy Concerns. The first rationale behind the Restatement rule justifies imposing a duty on a defendant with a mental disability where it seems unfair to force a plaintiff who did not contribute to the cause of his or her injury to bear the cost of that injury. This policy concern overlaps with the relationship analysis set forth supra. The nature of Creasy and Rusk's relationship was such that Creasy cannot be "presumed not to have assumed risks . . . with respect to the cause of the injury." Therefore, imposing a duty on Rusk in this circumstance is not justified by the first Restatement policy rationale.

The second Restatement policy rationale creates an inducement for those responsible for a person with a mental disability to prevent harm to others. By placing Rusk in a nursing home, we presume Rusk's wife made a difficult decision based on her desire to prevent Rusk from being violent and harming himself, herself, or others. . . . Mrs. Rusk entrusted her husband's care, including prevention of the harm he might bring to others, to the nursing home staff and the nursing home. And as a business enterprise, the nursing home received compensation for its services.

With respect to the third policy rationale, "it is virtually impossible to imagine circumstances under which a person would feign the symptoms of mental disability and subject themselves to commitment to an institution in order to avoid some future civil liability." To the extent that such circumstances exist, there is no evidence whatsoever that they are present under the facts in this case.

Finally, there are no administrative difficulties in this case with respect to determining the degree and existence of Rusk's mental disability. Under the relationship analysis set forth above and the present policy analysis, it is unnecessary to determine the degree of Rusk's mental disability. We need only conclude that Rusk had a mental disability which served as the reason for his presence in the nursing home and the foundation of his relationship with Creasy.

. . . By May 1995, when Creasy was injured by Rusk, Rusk had been a resident of the nursing home for three years and his condition had deteriorated. He regularly displayed behaviors characteristic of a person with advanced Alzheimer's disease such as aggression, belligerence, and violence. . . .

In addition to the public policy concerns behind the Restatement rule, we find that it would be contrary to public policy to hold Rusk to a duty to Creasy when it would place "too great a burden on him because his disorientation and potential for violence is the very reason he was institutionalized and needed the aid of employed caretakers."

Rusk was entitled to summary judgment because public policy and the nature of the relationship between Rusk, Creasy, and the nursing home preclude holding that Rusk owed a duty of care to Creasy under these factual circumstances.

Having previously granted transfer, thereby vacating the opinion of the Court of Appeals pursuant to Ind. Appellate Rule 11(B)(3), we now affirm the trial court, finding that Rusk did not owe a duty to Creasy, and grant Rusk's motion for summary judgment.

[Concurring and dissenting opinion omitted.]

NOTES TO CREASY v. RUSK

1. *Basic Standard of Care for Persons with Mental Disabilities.* Supporting its decision by analyzing what it described as five social policy factors, the *Creasy* court adopted the majority rule defining the standard of care for people with mental disabilities. It held that tort law should ignore an actor's mental disability in evaluating the actor's conduct and should treat the actor as one with typical mental abilities. How would the reasons the court relied on for ignoring a mental condition such as Alzheimer's disease or developmental disabilities apply to physical conditions such as blindness?

2. *Avoiding Application of the Basic Rule.* The court adopted the majority rule that mental disabilities are ignored in judging an actor's conduct. The court avoided applying the rule, however, by holding that even if Rusk had been negligent, Rusk would not be liable because Rusk had no duty to Creasy.

The requirement that a defendant must owe a duty to a plaintiff in order to be liable is one way the law limits the liability of defendants. Chapters 6 and 11 explore duty in detail. The court found that Rusk owed no duty to Creasy under the circumstances of the case. How would the court's analysis be affected if the defendant had injured a stranger on a street near the nursing home (for example, by throwing something from a window)?

3. *Unanticipated Mental Illness.* Some cases have involved an actor who caused an injury while experiencing the sudden and unanticipated onset of mental impairment. In cases of this type, courts have sometimes been willing to take account of the impairment and protect the actor from liability. See Breunig v. American Family Insurance Co., 173 N.W.2d 619 (Wis. 1970).

Perspective: Scientific Knowledge and Judges' Knowledge

As medical and related fields develop, they identify more and more syndromes and diseases. Mental illness, for example, may become better understood. If greater scientific knowledge made it less likely that individuals could feign mental illness, how would the development of that knowledge have an effect on tort doctrines? What are the roles of trial judges, jurors, and appellate judges in accounting for changes in scientific knowledge?

IV. Recklessness

Tort law generally recognizes three theories of recovery: intentional torts, unintentional torts, and strict liability. Intentional torts, such as battery, which were covered in Chapter 2, require that the actor intend to invade a legally protected interest of the other person. Unintentional torts require that the actor create an unjustifiable risk of invading another's legally protected interest. Strict liability torts, covered in Chapters 13 through 16, impose liability without regard to whether the actor's conduct is blameworthy.

While negligence cases, introduced in this chapter, are the most common unintentional injury cases, tort law has also developed an additional concept of unintentional conduct known as "recklessness." In terms of fault or blameworthiness, recklessness falls in between intentional tort and negligence. Many courts and the Restatement (Second) of Torts use the term *recklessness* to embrace all unintentional torts other than negligence, including behavior described as "wanton misconduct" and "gross negligence."

At present, characterizing an actor's conduct as reckless is important in several contexts. Sometimes punitive damages will be available when a defendant's conduct was reckless but would be prohibited if the conduct was only negligent. Individuals sometimes sign waivers or releases of liability giving up the right to sue for negligence in connection with certain activities, but these agreements often preserve the right to recover for injuries inflicted due to recklessness. Also, for some activities common law doctrines or statutes expose an actor to tort responsibility for reckless conduct but protect an actor from liability for mere negligence.

Sandler v. Commonwealth introduces significant aspects of the recklessness doctrine in the context of a personal injury claim brought against the owner of land. An applicable statute protected the landowner from liability for negligence but exposed the landowner to responsibility for recklessly inflicted harms.

SANDLER v. COMMONWEALTH
644 N.E.2d 641 (Mass. 1995)

WILKINS, J.

In Molinaro v. Northbridge, 643 N.E.2d 1043 (1995), we reiterated our view that a governmental unit could be liable under G.L. c. 21, §17C (1992 ed.), for its wanton or reckless conduct that caused harm to a member of the public who used government land that was available for recreational purposes without charge. In this case we deal with the question whether the evidence, viewed most favorably to the plaintiff, justified the submission of the plaintiff's case to the jury. The Commonwealth appeals from a judgment for the plaintiff, arguing that the evidence was insufficient to warrant submission of the case to the jury and that, therefore, its motion for a directed verdict and its motion for judgment notwithstanding the verdict should have been allowed. . . .

The plaintiff was injured, not long after 5 p.m. on October 29, 1987, when he fell off his bicycle while attempting to pass through a tunnel under the Eliot Bridge in Cambridge. The tunnel is part of the Dr. Paul Dudley White Bikeway, along the Charles River, which is controlled by the Commonwealth through the Metropolitan District Commission [MDC]. The jury were warranted in concluding that the plaintiff's fall was caused by an uncovered, eight-inch wide, twelve-inch long drain in the unlit tunnel. The drain, which was about eight inches deep, had had a cover, and the tunnel was designed to be lit, but vandals had removed the drain cover and had made the lights inoperable. Before we discuss the evidence in detail, it is important that we define wanton or reckless conduct.

The judge used the words "wilful, wanton, or reckless" in instructing the jury but defined them by the standard this court has used for wanton or reckless conduct. This was appropriate because wilfulness in the sense of an intention to cause harm was not presented by the facts. "Indifferent or reckless wrongdoing is not deliberate or intentional wrongdoing." Andover Newton Theological Sch., Inc. v. Continental Casualty Co., 566 N.E.2d 1117 (1991). Wanton conduct may suggest arrogance, insolence, or heartlessness that reckless conduct lacks, but the difference is likely not to be significant in most cases. Our recent practice has been simply to refer to reckless conduct as constituting the conduct that produces liability for what the court has traditionally called wilful, wanton, or reckless conduct.

. . . Reckless conduct may consist of a failure to act, if there is a duty to act, as well as affirmative conduct. We are concerned here with an alleged breach of a duty to remedy or guard against a known or reasonably knowable dangerous condition.

Reckless failure to act involves an intentional or unreasonable disregard of a risk that presents a high degree of probability that substantial harm will result to another. The risk of death or grave bodily injury must be known or reasonably apparent, and the harm must be a probable consequence of the defendant's election to run that risk or of his failure reasonably to recognize it.) . .

There is no doubt that the MDC through its employees was aware that a risk of harm was created by a chronically unlit tunnel with missing drain covers. An MDC employee testified that he did not know when the lights last worked. Another witness testified that he had not seen them illuminated in at least thirteen years. There was evidence that the lights were frequently broken, that they once had had protective devices which were now broken, and that they were broken and not working on the day of the accident. The MDC used only unattached drain covers, held in place only by gravity. The covers loosened over the years, did not fit the drains, and were frequently stolen by vandals. The MDC knew that at least one drain in the tunnel was often without a cover from January 1 to October 30, 1987. The cover of the particular drain that caused the plaintiff's injury was frequently stolen and was not in place following the accident. The MDC knew that the lack of a drain cover posed a danger to individuals. The MDC also knew that the regularly used tunnel was often flooded with water because of inadequate drainage.

There was evidence that the MDC, knowing of the danger posed by absent drain covers in the dark tunnel, did not respond reasonably. It had no policy for bikeway inspection, had no record of the existence or replacement of drain covers from January 1 to October 30, 1987, and did not have drain cover replacements on hand, although they were frequently stolen and there was room to store replacement covers in the tunnel closet. There was expert testimony that the design of the lighting and drainage in the tunnel was deficient and that feasible alternatives were available at reasonable costs, including vandal-resistant lighting and drains capable of being fastened.

Nevertheless, the degree of the risk of injury in this case does not meet the standard that we have established for recklessness. While it is true that each case depends on its facts and that some cases are close to the line, this case, which involves a persistent failure to remedy defects in a tunnel on a traveled bikeway, simply does not present a level of dangerousness that warrants liability under G.L. c. 21, §17C, for the MDC's inaction. In the margin, we summarize several of our civil cases in which the degree of risk of injury was so great that a finding of recklessness justifying tort liability was warranted.[4] . . .

---

[4] Many of our cases involving reckless conduct justifying tort liability have involved the use of motor vehicles and the like. See, e.g., Sheehan v. Goriansky, 56 N.E.2d 883 (1944) (finding warranted that driver's conduct was reckless where driver knew that trespasser was on running board, increased speed, ran into pole, killing him); Baines v. Collins, 38 N.E.2d 626 (1942) (question for jury whether truck driver was reckless where he knew boy on bicycle was holding onto heavy truck, continued to drive thirty-five miles an hour on asphalt highway, and suddenly and unnecessarily veered onto shoulder of road, throwing boy from bicycle and injuring him); Isaacson v. Boston, Worcester & N.Y. St. Ry., 180 N.E. 118 (1932) (finding that bus driver was reckless warranted where brakes were not functioning and driver was speeding in a forbidden lane, in violation of three separate laws); Leonard v. Conquest, 174 N.E. 677 (1931) (evidence warranted finding of recklessness where driver drove thirty miles an hour in lane designated for oncoming traffic on crowded narrow road, forcing oncoming car off road and into pole and thereby injuring other driver, and noting that "[t]he jury could find that the driver rode with death and that no reasonable person would expect to be saved from great bodily harm"); Yancey v. Boston Elevated Ry., 91 N.E. 202 (1910) (jury

The level of fault in this case, measured by the degree of risk of serious injury, is more consistent with our cases in which we have held that the evidence did not warrant a finding of wanton or reckless conduct. See, e.g., Manning v. Nobile, 582 N.E.2d 942 (1991) (claim of recklessness based on hotel's failure to provide bartender for private party rejected); Hawco v. Massachusetts Bay Transp. Auth., 499 N.E.2d 295 (1986) (defendant not reckless in leaving bus passenger at station where it appeared to bus driver that burglary was in progress); Mounsey v. Ellard, 297 N.E.2d 43 (1973) (failure to repair drain resulting in accumulation of ice on defendant's premises, not wilful, wanton, or reckless conduct); Sawler v. Boston & Albany R.R., 157 N.E.2d 516 (1959) (long-standing failure to fulfil statutory duty to maintain fence along right of way, thus permitting child to cross railroad tracks, not wilful, wanton, or reckless misconduct); Siver v. Atlantic Union College, 154 N.E.2d 360 (1958) (where young child fell into pit and died because some third party removed pit's cover, landowner not liable for wilful, wanton, or reckless conduct); Carroll v. Hemenway, 51 N.E.2d 952 (1943) (where police officer investigating building fell into unguarded and unlit elevator well, lack of repair not wilful, wanton, or reckless conduct).

Judgment reversed.

NOTES TO SANDLER v. COMMONWEALTH

1. *Choosing a Recklessness Theory.* The plaintiff chose the legal theory of recklessness because a recreational use statute denied plaintiff the right to recover on a negligence theory. The Massachusetts recreational use statute reads as follows:

> (a) Any person having an interest in land including the structures, buildings, and equipment attached to the land, including without limitation, wetlands, rivers, streams, ponds, lakes, and other bodies of water, who lawfully permits the public to use such land for recreational, conservation, scientific, educational, environmental, ecological, research, religious, or charitable purposes without imposing a charge or fee therefor, or who leases such land for said purposes to the commonwealth or any political subdivision thereof or to any nonprofit corporation, trust or association, shall not be liable for personal injuries or property damage sustained by such members of the public, including without limitation a minor, while on said land in the absence of wilful, wanton, or reckless conduct by such person.

Mass. Gen. Laws ch. 21, §17C (2013).

2. *Elements of a Recklessness Theory.* The Restatement (Third) of Torts, Liability for Physical and Emotional Harm §2, defines "reckless conduct" as follows:

---

could have concluded that conductor acted recklessly when he deliberately and without warning started streetcar despite knowledge that disabled person stood on step and held onto car, so that plaintiff was dragged and fell onto street); Aiken v. Holyoke St. Ry., 68 N.E. 238 (1903) (proper question for jury whether motorman was reckless in quickly starting streetcar when he knew young boy, clinging to step of car and yelling for help, was in great peril, thereby throwing him under wheels of car). Other cases, not involving vehicles but warranting a finding of recklessness include Freeman v. United Fruit Co., 111 N.E. 789 (1916) (deliberately throwing large, heavy roll of canvas stiffened with ice off deck from great height, thereby breaking plaintiff's leg); Zink v. Foss, 108 N.E. 906 (1915) (setting dog on boy who had fallen into defendant's yard); Romana v. Boston Elevated Ry., 105 N.E. 598 (1914) (girl shocked and burned when she tripped into electrically charged pole on path commonly used by children with defendant's permission, where defendant had been warned of condition of pole, and had done nothing).

[handwritten margin note: Definition of recklessness]

A person acts with recklessness in engaging in conduct if:

    (a) the person knows of the risk of harm created by the conduct or knows facts that make that risk obvious to anyone in the person's situation, and

    (b) the precaution that would eliminate or reduce that risk involves burdens that are so slight relative to the magnitude of the risk as to render the person's failure to adopt the precaution a demonstration of the person's indifference to the risk.

The knowledge element in (a) has two options. The first, "knows of the risk," applies to a person who intentionally disregards the risk. The second, "knows facts that make that risk obvious," applies to a person who unreasonably disregards the risk. While one person ignores the risk and the other ignores the facts, both are considered reckless. The Restatement (Second) of Torts §500 described the knowledge requirement somewhat differently, stating that a reckless person is one who acts "knowing or having reason to know of facts which would lead a reasonable man to realize" that his conduct creates a serious risk. The court in *Sandler* states that recklessness requires a dangerous condition that is "known or reasonably knowable," reflecting the two options.

    3. *Serious Risk for Recklessness.* Sandler v. Commonwealth illustrates the degree of risk necessary to characterize conduct as reckless rather than negligent. The court says that reckless conduct "involves an intentional or unreasonable disregard of a risk that presents a high degree of probability that substantial harm will result." The plaintiff must prove the existence of this serious risk. The probability that harm will result from the conduct combined with the magnitude of the loss if the harm occurs make up the risk. Rather than describe the probability of harm or the magnitude of the loss in this case, the court cites to its previous decisions. In footnote 4, the court describes nine cases where the risk was serious enough to justify a finding of liability on a recklessness theory. Some of the cases involve a high probability of harm, while others involve serious losses. Most involve both. It is the combination of likelihood and seriousness that makes a risk a serious risk. In the last full paragraph of the *Sandler* case, the court refers to six cases in which the risk was not found to be serious enough to support a finding of recklessness. Consider how these fifteen cases could be ranked according to the degree of risk involved in the conduct they analyze.

    4. *Knowledge Requirements for Negligence, Recklessness, and Intentional Torts.* To show recklessness, the plaintiff must show that the actor either (a) knew of the risk or (b) knew of facts that made the risk obvious (Restatement (Third)) or "had reason to know of facts relating to the risk presented by the conduct" (Restatement (Second)). "Knowing" of risk or facts and "having reason to know of facts" refer to the actor's own experience. The Restatement (Second) of Torts §12(1) describes "having reason to know" as follows:

The words "reason to know" . . . denote the fact that the actor has information from which a person of reasonable intelligence or of the superior intelligence of the actor would infer that the fact in question exists.

The Restatement (Second) of Torts distinguishes "reason to know" from "should know," which is the standard used in negligence cases. To succeed with a recklessness claim, the plaintiff must prove some subjective knowledge by the defendant — that the defendant *actually knew of the risk* or *actually knew of facts or information* from which a reasonable, prudent person would recognize a risk. By contrast, in a negligence case, the plaintiff is required to show only that a defendant *should have known of the risk* or *should have known certain facts.* The Restatement (Second) of Torts §290 comment a offers an example of a man who was brought up on a small island where there are no automobiles and is ignorant about how fast automobiles go. When arriving in a community where automobiles are present, the man will be treated *in a negligence case* as if he knows of the risk of crossing the street in front of an approaching automobile. He should know of that risk even though he does not know of it and has no reason to know of it. Intentional torts require desire to harm or knowledge to a substantial certainty that the harm will occur, not just knowledge that there is a risk that the harm will occur.

   5. Willful, Wanton, and Reckless.   It is apparent that in 1995, the Supreme Judicial Court of Massachusetts in Sandler v. Commonwealth was still dealing with the distinctions among willfulness, wantonness, and recklessness. The court observed that willfulness sometimes carries with it a "sense of an intention to harm" and that wantonness suggests "arrogance, insolence, or heartlessness that reckless conduct lacks." Some courts use the term "willfulness" to refer to intentional conduct, like that required for battery or assault. Lawyers must be alert to this use of "willfulness" and judge whether the court means to refer to an intentional tort or to the tort of recklessness. As the Massachusetts Supreme Judicial Court reported, the general tendency of modern courts "has been simply to refer to reckless conduct as constituting the conduct that produces liability for what the court has traditionally called willful, wanton, or reckless conduct."

Problem
Recklessness

   Brock Van Gordon's parents have come to your law office with the following story about an accident that left their son with severe burns.

> Austin Hot Springs is a park located on the upper Clackamas River. The public is invited to use this facility without charge. There was evidence that as many as 6,000 people accept this invitation every year. PGE provides toilets, picnic tables, fire pits, garbage cans and parking. The hot springs themselves are the major attraction. Hot water percolates out of the riverbed and the banks. People move rocks to encircle the hot water coming up from the bed of the river in order to form small pools. This allows some control in the mixture of the hot water with the cold river water. The pools formed in this manner vary in temperature from comfortably warm to as hot as 190 degrees Fahrenheit. [W]ater at this temperature can cause severe burns in less than one second. At the time of the accident there were three signs saying "hot water" between the main parking lot and the principal bathing area of the river. There [is] evidence that PGE had knowledge of previous burns caused by the hot water.
>   On May 20, 1978, Brock Van Gordon, then two years old, went on a picnic with his grandparents and his four-year-old brother. The grandparents realized that the Austin Hot Springs were in this area, but had never been there before. They drove into the park by a secondary entrance to the west of the main entrance. This road had no sign indicating the name of the park. After they had their lunch in an area that had a picnic table and a fire pit, the grandmother took Brock and his brother for a walk. They came to the Clackamas River, evidently west of the main parking area. The children wanted

to wade, so after testing the water, their grandmother allowed them to do so. Brock climbed on a rock that was part of the rim of a warm pool in which he was wading. He slipped and fell backward into a neighboring pool. This pool was extremely hot, and Brock's legs and feet were scalded before his grandmother was able to lift him out of the water. He was burned severely enough to require hospitalization. The grand-mother testified that although she could see steam rising on the other side of the river, she did not know that the water on this side of the river was hot rather than warm. She [explained] that because of the route she followed from their picnic area to the river, the three warning signs were not visible.

The Van Gordons are considering a lawsuit against PGE. You've discovered that PGE is protected from negligence liability by a recreational use statute. Therefore, you can prevail in the case only if you can prove that PGE behaved recklessly. Because you will take the case on a contingency-fee basis if you decide to represent the Van Gordons, it is important for you to consider your likelihood of success before you accept the case. Do the facts suggest that PGE's failure to warn was reckless? What else might you want to know in order to answer that question? See Van Gordon v. Portland General Electric Co. [PGE], 662 P.2d 714 (Or. 1983).

Perspective: Recklessness in the Contexts of Neuroscience and Neuroeconomics

Professor Geoffrey Christopher Rapp, in *The Wreckage of Recklessness*, 68 Wash. U. L. Rev. 111, 120 (2008), suggests that modern research in the fields of neuroscience and neuroeconomics shows that current legal definitions of recklessness may fit poorly with the reality of how people think and act. For example, a person who miscalculates a risk may be negligent but cannot be described as acting with "conscious disregard" of the risk. A person who chooses to act despite knowing the risk may well satisfy the legal standard for intent. Thus negligence and intentional tort doctrines may apply to many actions that current courts would classify as reckless.

CHAPTER 4

PROVING BREACH

I. Introduction

To recover damages in a tort suit, a plaintiff must persuade the trier of fact that the opponent breached a duty. Cases in Chapter 3 illustrated some of the kinds of evidence and arguments parties can use to do this. To show that a party failed to behave as an ordinary, prudent person, the party's opponent typically offers evidence showing that the conduct created significant risks and that a reasonable person would have avoided those risks. For example, a party may introduce evidence about the risks involved in building a hayrick or providing hotel rooms with sliding glass doors behind curtains. Any information that sheds light on reasonableness can be presented to the jury.

Cases in this chapter show that for some recurring types of proof, tort law applies particular rules. First, if a statute applies to the factual circumstances in which the defendant acted, the statute may be considered as proof of how a reasonable person behaves. Second, a party may rely on custom to show what behavior is reasonable. Third, circumstantial evidence may be so strong in some cases that it can substitute for direct or eyewitness proof about how the defendant acted. When it is clear that the defendant must have been negligent in some way that caused the plaintiff's harm, the law excuses the plaintiff from identifying the specific negligent conduct of the defendant. The legal doctrine of *res ipsa loquitur*, which means "the thing speaks for itself," permits an inference of negligence from circumstantial evidence.

An important aspect of these methods of proof is their procedural effect. How much benefit will a jurisdiction give to a plaintiff who shows that a defendant violated a statute, failed to comply with a custom, or acted in a way that fits the *res ipsa loquitur* doctrine? These types of proof may: (a) require a finding that the defendant was negligent regardless of contradictory evidence; (b) require a finding that the defendant was negligent unless the defendant offers contradictory evidence; or (c) have no mandatory effect on the trial outcome.

II. Violation of a Statute

In many cases, a party may establish that the opponent's conduct violated a statute. If the statute's purpose was to protect the injured party from the type of harm that occurred, the proof of violation will have special evidentiary effect. Courts may treat proof of the statutory violation both as establishing a standard of care and as evidence that the opponent's conduct was negligent. Proof of violation of a statute may support a finding that either a plaintiff or a defendant was negligent.

Martin v. Herzog, a classic case, introduces the concept of using legislative standards to determine reasonable conduct. In Thomas v. McDonald, a modern court applies the basic rules concerning proof of violation of a statute. Wawanesa Mutual Insurance Co. v. Matlock illustrates the fundamental concept that the type of harm and type of plaintiff involved in the case must be related to the purposes of the statute in order for violation of the statute to be considered as evidence of negligence. Sikora v. Wenzel considers when justice might require recognizing a party's excuse for violating a statute.

MARTIN v. HERZOG

126 N.E. 814 (N.Y. 1920)

CARDOZO, J.

The action is one to recover damages for injuries resulting in death.

Plaintiff and her husband, while driving toward Tarrytown in a buggy on the night of August 21, 1915, were struck by the defendant's automobile coming in the opposite direction. They were thrown to the ground, and the man was killed. At the point of the collision the highway makes a curve. The car was rounding the curve when suddenly it came upon the buggy, emerging, the defendant tells us, from the gloom. Negligence is charged against the defendant, the driver of the car, in that he did not keep to the right of the center of the highway. . . . Negligence is charged against the plaintiff's intestate, the driver of the wagon, in that he was traveling without lights (Highway Law, sec. 329a, as amended by L. 1915, ch. 367). There is no evidence that the defendant was moving at an excessive speed. There is none of any defect in the equipment of his car. . . . The case against him must stand . . . upon the divergence of his course from the center of the highway. The jury found him delinquent and his victim blameless. The Appellate Division reversed, and ordered a new trial.

We agree with the Appellate Division that the charge to the jury was erroneous and misleading. The case was tried on the assumption that the hour had arrived when lights were due. . . . In the body of the charge the trial judge said that the jury could consider the absence of light "in determining whether the plaintiff's intestate was guilty of contributory negligence in failing to have a light upon the buggy as provided by law. I do not mean to say that the absence of light necessarily makes him negligent, but it is a fact for your consideration." . . . The plaintiff then requested a charge that "the fact that the plaintiff's intestate was driving without a light is not negligence in itself," and to this the court acceded. The defendant saved his rights by appropriate exceptions.

We think the unexcused omission of the statutory signals is more than some evidence of negligence. It *is* negligence in itself. Lights are intended for the guidance and protection of other travelers on the highway (Highway Law, sec. 329a). By the very terms of the hypothesis, to omit, willfully or heedlessly, the safeguards prescribed by law for the benefit of another that he may be preserved in life or limb, is to fall short of the standard of diligence to which those who live in organized society are under a duty to conform. That, we think, is now the established rule in this state. Whether the omission of an absolute duty, not willfully or heedlessly, but through unavoidable accident, is also to be characterized as negligence, is a question of nomenclature into which we need not enter, for it does not touch the case before us. There may be times, when if jural niceties are to be preserved, the two wrongs, negligence and breach of statutory duty, must be kept distinct in speech and thought. In the conditions here present they come together and coalesce. In the case at hand, we have an instance of the admitted violation of a statute intended for the protection of travelers on the highway, of whom the defendant at the time was one. Yet the jurors were instructed in effect that they were at liberty in their discretion to treat the omission of lights either as innocent or as culpable. They were allowed to "consider the default as lightly or gravely" as they would (Thomas, J., in the court below). They might as well have been told that they could use a like discretion in holding a master at fault for the omission of a safety appliance prescribed by positive law for the protection of a workman. Jurors have no dispensing power by which they may relax the duty that one traveler on the highway owes under the statute to another. It is error to tell them that they have. The omission of these lights was a wrong, and being wholly unexcused was also a negligent wrong. No license should have been conceded to the triers of the facts to find it anything else.

We must be on our guard, however, against confusing the question of negligence with that of the causal connection between the negligence and the injury. A defendant who travels without lights is not to pay damages for his fault unless the absence of lights is the cause of the disaster. A plaintiff who travels without them is not to forfeit the right to damages unless the absence of lights is at least a contributing cause of the disaster. To say that conduct is negligence is not to say that it is always contributory negligence. . . . We think, however, that evidence of a collision occurring more than an hour after sundown between a car and an unseen buggy, proceeding without lights, is evidence from which a causal connection may be inferred between the collision and the lack of signals. . . .

The order of the Appellate Division should be affirmed. . . .

NOTES TO MARTIN v. HERZOG

1. *Negligence Per Se.* While the Martin v. Herzog court stated that an *unexcused* statutory violation "*is* negligence in itself," other courts have used a famous phrase, "negligence per se," to characterize such a violation. An early use of that term came in Osborne v. McMasters, 41 N.W. 543 (Minn. 1889):

> Negligence is the breach of legal duty. It is immaterial whether the duty is one imposed by the rule of common law requiring the exercise of ordinary care not to injure another, or is imposed by a statute designed for the protection of others. In either case the failure to perform the duty constitutes negligence, and renders the party liable for injuries resulting from it. The only difference is that in the one case the measure of legal duty is to be determined upon common-law principles, while in the other the statute fixes it, so that the violation of the statute constitutes conclusive evidence of negligence, or, in other words, negligence per se.

2. *Effect of the Doctrine.* The doctrine adopted in Martin v. Herzog treats proof of an *unexcused* statutory violation as conclusive proof of the violator's breach of duty. Because the doctrine can have so much power, courts have given significant attention to defining *unexcused* and to considering how to treat excuses when they are offered.

3. *Role of the Jury.* The jury's role changes when a doctrine gives special effect to proof of a statutory violation. In a setting where this proof is treated as equivalent to proof of negligence, the jury's function is to determine whether a violation occurred. This is different from the usual jury function of analyzing whether an actor's conduct was reasonable.

4. *Rationale for Importing Statutory Standards.* Doctrines that give weight to proof of statutory violations represent the legal system's respect for the legislative process. In Chambers v. St. Mary's School, 697 N.E.2d 198, 202 (Ohio 1998), the Ohio Supreme Court analyzed reasons why the standards of care defined in statutes are appropriate for use in tort litigation. The court noted that "[t]he legislative process and accountability are the cornerstones of the democratic process which justify the General Assembly's role as lawmaker."

5. *Specificity Required for Negligence Per Se Treatment.* Some states refuse to recognize a statutory violation when it involves a statute that fails to provide a clear-cut statement of the conduct it requires. This aspect of negligence per se doctrine was explained in Supreme Beef Processors, Inc. v. Maddox, 67 S.W.3d 453 (Tex. Ct. App. 2002), as follows:

> [S]ome statutes do not define a mandatory standard of conduct, but merely create a standard of care, under which the duty of compliance may be conditional or less than absolute. Proving a violation of a statute imposing such a standard of care usually requires proof that the party charged with the violation has failed to exercise ordinary care. For example, when a statute requires a person to exercise his or her judgment, as when a driver should proceed only when it is safe to do so, the statute reflects a standard of care that is no different from the ordinarily prudent person standard. But if the statute requires all persons to stop in obedience to a red flashing light at an intersection, the statute clearly defines the prohibited conduct, leaving the driver no discretion or room for the exercise of judgment, and it is therefore a standard of conduct statute. Whether a statute describes a mandatory standard of conduct or incorporates the ordinarily prudent person standard of care must be determined on a case-by-case basis.
>
> Where a statute incorporates the ordinarily prudent person standard, negligence per se does not apply because the statute does not establish a specific standard of conduct different from the common-law standard of ordinary care. In those cases, "it is redundant to submit a question on the statutory standard or to instruct the jury regarding it, and the negligence per se standard is subsumed under the broad-form negligence question." . . .

6. *Proof of Causation.* The Martin v. Herzog court notes that even when violation of a statute may support a finding of unreasonable conduct, showing a causal connection between that conduct and a person's harm may be a separate question. For example, in Schwabe v. Custer's Inn Associates, LLP, 15 P.3d 903 (Mont. 2000), Schwabe drowned while swimming in Custer's Inn's indoor swimming pool and was later discovered by an Inn employee. Schwabe's estate sued alleging that the Inn was

negligent per se in violating a statute that required the Inn to have a CPR-trained employee on the premises. Because there was no evidence of how Schwabe got into distress in the pool, how he drowned, or how long he was at the bottom of the pool, there was no proof that a CPR-trained employee would have made any difference. Custer's Inn was awarded judgment as a matter of law. Violation of the statute did not support a finding that the violation was a cause of the injury. In Martin v. Herzog, in what way did proof of violation support a finding that the violation was a cause of the injury?

THOMAS v. McDONALD

667 So. 2d 594 (Miss. 1995)

McRae, J. . . .

Sam McCormick was injured on March 7, 1990, when his pick-up truck collided with an International "gang truck" owned by DAPSCO and operated by William McDonald. The DAPSCO truck had stalled on a hill, blocking the eastbound lane of Highway 528, near Heidelberg, Mississippi. Although it was about 6:30 p.m., the operator of the disabled vehicle had provided no warning to the other drivers on the road.

The DAPSCO truck had suffered mechanical problems throughout the week before the accident. It had failed to start on several occasions and a new battery had been installed. It remained idle at a job site until the evening of the accident. Sometime between 5:45 and 6:00 p.m., when it was "getting dark," the crew left the site to return to the DAPSCO yard in Heidelberg. McDonald drove the "gang truck" for the first time since it was last repaired. As he approached the intersection of Claiborne Road and Highway 528, the truck stalled. The engine stopped and the lights went off. After McDonald failed to arrive at the DAPSCO yard, the foreman went to look for him. Baker jump started the truck with booster cables. However, while going up a slight incline, the truck stalled again. McDonald attempted to "kick start" the truck, but it had already stopped. The disabled truck occupied the entire eastbound lane leading into town. Baker testified that he had turned around to warn oncoming cars of the stalled truck. Neither this truck, nor any of the other DAPSCO trucks, however, [was] equipped with warning devices in the event of vehicle breakdown.

McCormick filed a negligence action against McDonald and DAPSCO on May 14, 1990, in the First Judicial District of the Jasper County Circuit Court. . . . On August 12, 1991, the jury returned a verdict for McDonald and DAPSCO. Judgment was entered consistent with the verdict on August 19, 1991, and thereafter, Thomas [McCormick's administratrix—Sam McCormick having died of a heart attack due to a preexisting congestive heart condition after filing suit] perfected this appeal.

Thomas first asserts that the trial court erred in refusing to instruct the jury that the defendants' failure to place warning signals on the highway was negligence per se. The rejected Instruction P-10 stated as follows:

> This Court instructs the jury that at the time and place of the truck collision which occurred on March 7, 1990, William McDonald, Jr. was negligent as a matter of law in that he violated §63-7-71 of the Miss. Code by failing to place reflectors or other signals in an operating condition upon the highway. . . .

McDonald and DAPSCO . . . argued that drivers are only required to place signals with reasonable diligence. The refused instruction was based on Miss. Code Ann. §63-7-71 (1972) which, in relevant part, states:

> (1) Whenever any motor truck or bus is stopped upon the highway except for the purpose of picking up or discharging passengers . . . and such motor truck or bus cannot immediately be removed from the main traveled portion of a highway outside of a business or residence district, the driver or other person in charge of such *vehicle shall cause such flares, fuses [warning devices used by railroads and truckers], reflectors, or other signals to be lighted or otherwise placed in an operating condition and placed upon the highway,* one at a distance of approximately one hundred feet to the rear of the vehicle, one approximately one hundred feet in advance of the vehicle and the third upon the roadway side of the vehicle. . . . (Emphasis added.)

Generally, when two cars are traveling in the same direction, the primary duty of avoiding collision rests with the second driver, who, in the absence of an emergency or unusual condition, is negligent as a matter of law if he runs into the car ahead. Whether the circumstances rise to the level of an emergency or unusual condition is a matter for the jury to determine.

However, where there is a statute, the statute will be the controlling law for the parties' action or failure to act. Violations of statutes generally constitute negligence per se.

> The principle that violation of a statute constitutes negligence per se is so elementary that it does not require citation of authority. When a statute is violated, the injured party is entitled to an instruction that the party violating is guilty of negligence, and if that negligence proximately caused or contributed to the injury, then the injured party is entitled to recover.

Bryant v. Alpha Entertainment Corp., 508 So. 2d 1094, 1096 (Miss. 1987) (negligence per se to sell beer to person under the age of eighteen).

In order for the doctrine of negligence per se to apply, the plaintiff must show that he is a member of the class that the statute was designed to protect and that the harm he suffered was the type of harm which the statute was intended to prevent. McCormick, a traveler on a Mississippi highway, was within the class of individuals the statute was designed to protect. The accident that occurred on Highway 528 was the kind of harm that the statute was intended to prevent. "Sections 63-3-903 and 63-7-71 were enacted by our legislature to protect motorists on our highways." Golden Flake Snack Foods, Inc. v. Thornton, 548 So. 2d 382, 383 (Miss. 1989). . . .

Both Stong v. Freeman Truck Line, 456 So. 2d 698 (Miss. 1984), and Hankins v. Harvey, 160 So. 2d 63 (Miss. 1964), have imposed a reasonable time limit upon vehicle operators to set out reflectors or other warning devices. In *Hankins,* we stated that flares, reflectors, or other signals should be set out with "reasonable and proper diligence, or promptly under all the facts and circumstances of the case." 160 So. 2d at 63. In *Stong,* we applied the ten-minute time limit used in the federal regulations for interstate highways pursuant to 49 C.F.R. 392.22(b)(1), holding that "[w]here there is a conflict in the evidence and where more than one reasonable interpretation may be given the facts, *whether the driver acted with reasonable promptness under the circumstances or within a ten minute time limit* must be determined by the jury under proper instructions." *Stong,* 456 So. 2d at 710 (emphasis added).

When this Court interprets a statute, and the statute is retained in subsequent codes without amendment by the Legislature, our interpretation becomes, in effect, part of the statute. McDonald and DAPSCO contend that they did not have time to move the truck or to provide any warning that it was blocking the road. Because we have provided a "reasonable time" interpretation to the statute, McDonald and DAPSCO might have had a viable defense had the vehicle been equipped with the required warning devices. However, regardless of how we construe the statute, DAPSCO could not have complied. It is uncontroverted that the truck had no lights and was not equipped with reflectors or other warning devices. Thus, the circuit court erred in failing to grant Thomas the negligence per se instruction she sought) **Ʌ**

Thomas further contends that the circuit court erred in denying Instruction P-11, based on Miss. Code Ann. §63-7-69(1), which provides as follows:

> No person shall operate any truck or bus on any highway outside the limits of any municipality or residential adjacent thereto between the hours of one half hour after sunset and one half hour before sunrise unless there be carried in such vehicle, ready for use, certain warning and safety appliances such as flares, fuses, flags, reflectors, fire extinguishers, and the like.

STAT. VIOLATED

As Thomas recognized, it was her duty as the plaintiff to prove her case. While statutes furnish our standard of care, the facts must support the applicability of the statute. *Stong,* 456 So. 2d at 707-08. Courts may take issues from the jury only where "the facts are so clear that reasonable minds could not differ." Id. at 708. Although the fact that neither McDonald's vehicle nor any of the other DAPSCO trucks had safety devices in the event of truck failure as required by statute was admitted, Thomas failed to establish the requisite time component of the statute; that is, whether a half hour had passed since the sun set. Butler, the DAPSCO foreman, testified that the crew left the work site around 5:45 p.m. or 6:00 p.m. The investigating officer testified that he received a call for the wreck about 6:30 p.m. and described the light as "dusk dark." Although McDonald originally stated in his answer to interrogatories and in his Motion in Limine that it was dark at the time of the accident, he subsequently changed his testimony at trial to state that it was "getting dark." Whether it was dark at the approximate time of the accident is a fact that could easily have been determined and would have been a proper subject for the taking of judicial notice. Thomas could have offered into evidence *The Clarion Ledger* for that date, the *Farmer's Almanac,* or any other recognized publication documenting the time of the sunset on the day of the accident. Because Thomas failed to establish the requisite time component of §63-7-69(1), the circuit court cannot be held in error for denying this particular instruction. Therefore, her second assignment of error is without merit. . . .

The circuit court erred in refusing to grant a negligence per se jury instruction based on Miss. Code Ann. §§63-7-71(1) and (2). . . . Accordingly, we reverse the decision of the lower court and remand the case for a new trial.

NOTES TO THOMAS v. McDONALD

1. *Proof of Violation.*   To obtain the benefit of the negligence per se doctrine, a plaintiff must show that the defendant violated a statute. In *Thomas*, the plaintiff relied on two statutes. One requires the display of flares and other signal devices. The other requires the carrying of such signal devices. The trial court refused to give a negligence per se jury instruction based on either of the statutes. The Mississippi Supreme Court reversed with regard to only one. Why did the court base its reversal on the "display" statute and not on the "carry" statute?

2. *Statutory Interpretation.* The *Thomas* court refers to earlier decisions that had interpreted the "display" statute to include a grace period during which a failure to display warning devices would be excused. Without a grace period, a truck driver whose truck was equipped with warning equipment might have been treated as negligent if the truck had stopped and the driver had not yet used any warning devices, even if the driver had not had a reasonable amount of time to deploy them. Treating the statute as incorporating a grace period avoids a result in which reasonable conduct would be characterized as negligence.

3. *Variations in Treatment of Statutes.* States vary somewhat in the elements a plaintiff must prove to rely on a statute as evidence of breach. The *Thomas* court stated that "a plaintiff must show that he is a member of the class that the statute was designed to protect and that the harm he suffered was the type of harm which the statute was intended to prevent." What results would the following approaches have required on the facts of Thomas v. McDonald?

A. In Idaho, violation of a city ordinance may constitute negligence per se if several criteria are met:

> First, the ordinance must clearly define the required standard of conduct; second, the ordinance must have been intended to prevent the type of harm which occurred; and third, the plaintiff must be a member of the class of persons the ordinance was designed to protect.

See Nettleton v. Thompson, 787 P.2d 294 (Idaho Ct. App. 1990).

B. In VanLuchene v. State, 797 P.2d 932, 935 (Mont. 1990), the court recited five criteria that a plaintiff must prove in a negligence per se case in order to prevail:

> Those criteria are as follows: 1) the defendant violated the particular statute; 2) the statute was enacted to protect a specific class of persons; 3) the plaintiff is a member of that class; 4) the plaintiff's injury is of the sort the statute was enacted to prevent; and 5) the statute was intended to regulate members of defendant's class.

Problem
Statutory Interpretation and Proof of Violation

Fourteen-year-old Rob and a friend were walking across an open field leased by the Pleshas. The Pleshas were hosting a barbeque in their backyard and had taken their dog, Sampson, off his chain so he could play. As Rob and his friend walked by, Sampson began barking and ran toward them. The Pleshas yelled after Sampson to stop and told the boys, "Whatever you do, don't move. He won't hurt you if you don't move." Rob's friend ran, but Rob remained still, as he had been instructed. Sampson then bit Rob several times as Rob tried to protect himself by pushing the dog away. In a suit by Rob against the Pleshas, the plaintiff sought to obtain the benefit of the negligence per se doctrine in connection with the following ordinance:

> [A]ll dogs and cats shall be kept under restraint. It is an animal owner's responsibility to insure that animals on and off their real property be restrained. When off the real

property, animals shall be on a leash not to exceed six feet in length; or if without [a] leash, [the] animal must be under complete control of the owner and not more than three feet from the owner. Animals on real property must be within a fenced area sufficient in height to prevent the animal to escape; or if on a leash, the animal must be secured on a leash that is at least six feet in length and located where the animal cannot trespass beyond its owner's property line.

These facts are taken from Plesha v. Edmonds, 717 N.E.2d 981 (Ct. App. Ind. 1999). In its opinion, the court described the following generally accepted rules of statutory interpretation:

We note that the rules relating to statutory construction are equally applicable to construing ordinances. Every word in a statute must be given effect and meaning, and no part is to be held meaningless if it can be reconciled with the rest of the statute. A statute should be examined as a whole and a strict, literal, or selective reading of individual words should not be overemphasized. Moreover, this court endeavors to give statutory words their plain and ordinary meaning absent a clearly manifested purpose to do otherwise.

The defendants argued that the ordinance required only that owners prevent their dogs and cats from escaping beyond their property line. Because Sampson never left their property, the Pleshas maintain they could not have violated the ordinance. May the plaintiff rely on the statute?

WAWANESA MUTUAL INSURANCE CO. v. MATLOCK
60 Cal. App. 4th 583 (1997)

SILLS, P.J. . . .

Timothy Matlock, age seventeen, bought two packs of cigarettes from a gas station one day in April 1993. Tim gave one of the packs to his friend, Eric Erdley, age fifteen. Smoking as they walked, the two trespassed onto a private storage facility in Huntington Beach, where a couple of hundred telephone poles were stacked up high upon the ground, held in place by two vertical poles sticking out of the ground. The two had climbed on the logs many times before.

Timothy and Eric were joined by 2 younger boys, about 10 or 11 years old, who walked with them on the logs. Eric was smoking a cigarette held in his left hand. Timothy began to tease the younger boys, telling them the logs were going to fall. The boys started to run, though perhaps more out of laughter than of fear. One of the younger boys ran right into Eric's left arm. Eric dropped his cigarette down between the logs, where it landed on a bed of sand. For about 20 seconds Eric tried to retrieve the cigarette, but he couldn't reach it. He stood up and tried to extinguish it by spitting on it, and again was unsuccessful.

Then Eric caught up with Timothy, who was about 10 feet ahead. They went into some bunkers about 50 feet away; when they came out again after about 20 minutes, they saw flames at the base of the logs. They were seen running from the location.

The Woodman Pole Company suffered considerable property damage because of the fire. Eric was insured under a $100,000 policy with plaintiff Wawanesa Mutual Insurance Company. Wawanesa paid $89,000 to Woodman, $10,000 to the Orange County Fire Department, and $1,000 to the Huntington Beach Fire Department. Wawanesa, now subrogated to Eric's rights, filed this suit against Timothy and his father Paul E. Matlock for contribution.

After a bench trial, the court awarded the insurer $44,500 against Timothy and Paul, which included $25,000 against Paul based on a statute which fixes liability on a custodial parent for the willful misconduct of a minor. (See Civ. Code, §1714.1, subd. (a).) . . . The judge stated that the statute that makes it unlawful to give cigarettes to minors, Penal Code §308, had to have been enacted in 1891 with "more than health concerns" in mind, "since the health issues on tobacco are of considerably more recent concern."

Timothy and his father Paul now appeal, arguing that there is no basis on which to hold Timothy liable for the damage caused when Eric dropped the cigarette.

We agree. There is no valid basis on which to hold Timothy liable.

Just because a statute has been violated does not mean that the violator is necessarily liable for any damage that might be ultimately traced back to the violation. As the court stated in Olsen v. McGillicuddy (1971) 15 Cal. App. 3d 897, 902-903[, 93 Cal. Rptr. 530]: "The doctrine of negligence per se does not apply even though a statute has been violated if the plaintiff was not in the class of persons designed to be protected or the type of harm which occurred was not one which the statute was designed to prevent." Mere "but for" causation, as is urged in Wawanesa's brief, is simply not enough. The statute must be designed to protect against the kind of harm which occurred.

The statute that makes it illegal to furnish tobacco to minors, Penal Code §308, has nothing to do with fire suppression. As it now stands, it is intended to prevent early addiction to tobacco. It may be true, as the trial court opined, that when the first version of the statute was enacted in 1891 (see Stats. 1891, ch. 70, §1, p.64) it was not directed primarily at protecting minors' health.[3] But it is most certainly a health statute as it exists today. As our Supreme Court recently noted in Mangini v. R.J. Reynolds Tobacco Co. (1994) 7 Cal. 4th 1057, 1060[, 31 Cal. Rptr. 2d 358, 875 P.2d 73] (quoting from an affirmed decision of the Court of Appeal), §308 "reflects a statutory policy of protecting minors from addiction to cigarettes." The connection of §308 with health is emphasized by the court's specifically analogizing §308 to former Health and Safety Code §25967, which states that preventing children from "beginning to use tobacco products" is "among the highest priorities in disease prevention for the State of California." (Mangini, supra, 7 Cal. 4th at pp.1061-1062 [quoting from appellate opinion quoting statute].)

Nothing suggests that §308 is part of any scheme to prevent fires. Its placement in the general morals section of the Penal Code belies such an intent.

[Discussion of other recovery theories omitted.]

---

[3] Which raises the question — why was it originally enacted? The trial judge may have been a little hasty in concluding that health was not the reason behind the 1891 statute. The noxiousness of tobacco was known long before 1891. . . .

Assuming, for sake of argument, that the Legislature did not have minors' health at heart when it prohibited giving tobacco to them in 1891, the placement of section 308 in chapter 7 of title 9 of the Penal Code, dealing with crimes against religion, conscience and "good morals," furnishes another answer. While we do not have the legislative history from 1891, it appears the statute was most probably enacted to protect minors from the general licentiousness associated with the consumption of cigarettes in the 1890's. (These days — though we recognize that there is altogether too much teenage tobacco smoking — cigarettes tend to be associated more with the World War II generation than with cheesy dens of iniquity.) However, we have found nothing, and certainly Wawanesa has cited us to nothing, which would show that section 308 was ever enacted out of some concern that minors would pose a fire hazard.

Because there is no basis on which to hold Timothy liable we need not address the liability of his father. The judgment is reversed with directions to enter a new judgment in favor of Timothy and Paul Matlock. The Matlocks are to recover their costs on appeal.

NOTES TO WAWANESA MUTUAL INSURANCE CO. v. MATLOCK

1. *Sources of Statutory Interpretation.* To obtain the benefit of the negligence per se doctrine, in addition to showing that the defendant violated a statute, the plaintiff must prove that the harm that occurred was the type of harm the statute was designed to prevent. Sometimes it is obvious that the harm a statute was meant to prevent and the harm a plaintiff suffered are identical. In other cases, courts pay close attention to this aspect of the doctrine. On what sources did the *Wawanesa* court rely to determine whether the cigarette statute was designed to prevent fires?

2. *Subrogation.* Wawanesa Mutual was Eric's insurance company. It paid money to settle Eric's liabilities to the pole company and the fire departments. Having paid on Eric's behalf, Wawanesa was entitled to collect, on Eric's behalf, the portion of damages owed by Timothy, who bought the cigarettes. The court said that Wawanesa was "subrogated to Eric's rights," meaning that the rights Eric had to sue Timothy for reimbursement now belonged to the insurance company.

3. *Licensing Statutes.* In a number of cases, individuals who have failed to obtain a statutorily required license for an activity cause harm while engaging in that activity. Driving without a license is a primary example. Many courts decline to treat violation of a licensing statute by a driver as relevant to determining fault, sometimes on a theory that the lack of a license has no causal relationship with bad driving. See Duncan v. Hixon, 288 S.E.2d 494 (Va. 1982) (the majority of cases do not treat unlicensed driving as equivalent to negligent driving). In a decision that refused to apply negligence per se treatment to a defendant company's failure to obtain a Food and Drug Administration license for a medical device, a court wrote:

> . . . As Professors Prosser and Keeton have reasoned, "when a car is driven without a license, the act of driving the car certainly causes a collision; the absence of the license, or the existence of the statute, of course does not." W. Page Keeton et al., Prosser & Keeton on Torts §36, at 223-24 (5th ed. 1984).
>
> In summary, where a particular statutory requirement does not itself articulate a standard of care but rather requires only regulatory approval, or a license, or a report for the administration of a more general underlying standard, violation of that administrative requirement itself is not a breach of a standard of care. This violation rather indicates only a failure to comply with an administrative requirement, not the breach of a tort duty.

Talley v. Danek Medical, Inc., 179 F.3d 154 (4th Cir. 1999).

Where compliance with a licensing statute would prevent the occurrence of dangerous conduct, courts are likely to treat the violation as relevant. For example, in Bier v. Leanna Lakeside Property Association, 711 N.E.2d 773 (Ill. App. Ct. 1999), the defendant operated a beach without a required license, and the plaintiff was injured using a rope swing there. The licensing authority would have refused to grant a license unless the swing had been removed. The court held that this violation could serve as evidence of negligence.

Problems
Applicability of Statute

A. In Gorris v. Scott, L.R. 9 Ex. 125 (1874), sheep being carried as cargo on the deck of a ship were washed overboard during a severe storm. The plaintiff, seeking to recover damages for the lost sheep, attempted to rely on the provision of The Contagious Diseases (Animals) Act of 1869, which provided that animals onboard ship must be confined in pens no larger than 9 feet by 15 feet and that the pens must have strips of wood on the bottom that the animals can use as footholds. The pens in which the lost sheep were confined did not meet these specifications. May the plaintiff rely on this statute to prove breach?

B. In Kernan v. American Dredging Co., 355 U.S. 426 (1958), a kerosene lamp used as a navigation light on a scow, placed no more than three feet above the water, ignited petroleum fumes on the Schuylkill River in Philadelphia, Pennsylvania. The estate of a seaman who lost his life in the fire sought to rely on a Coast Guard navigation rule requiring that scows operating at night display a white navigation light not less than 8 feet from the water "so placed as to show an unbroken light all around the horizon, and . . . of such a character as to be visible on a dark night with a clear atmosphere at a distance of at least 5 miles." The court found that the river would not have caught fire if the light had been 8 feet or more above the river. May the seaman's estate rely on this statute to prove breach?

SIKORA v. WENZEL
727 N.E.2d 1277 (Ohio 2000)

[A deck attached to a condominium owned by Tom Wenzel collapsed during a party held by one of Wenzel's tenants. Aaron Sikora, a guest at the party, was injured as a result of the collapse. After the incident, an engineering firm hired by the city of Fairborn concluded that the deck's collapse resulted from improper construction and design in violation of the Ohio Basic Building Code ("OBBC").

A decade earlier, before the deck was built, Zink Road Manor Investment ("Zink") owned and was developing the property where the condominium was located. After Zink submitted plans for the condominiums to Fairborn, Zink decided to modify the units to include decks. Documents containing the deck design were given to the city for review at a meeting between the construction company and the city. The city, however, rejected these plans because they violated the OBBC and contained insufficient information. The city made no inspection of the decks during construction and received from Zink no modified plans or other documents sufficient for it to proceed with approval, but it nevertheless issued Zink a certificate of occupancy.

After the city issued the certificate, Wenzel purchased the property at issue from Zink. Wenzel had no knowledge of any defect in the deck that was attached to the condominium.

Following the deck's collapse, Sikora sued Wenzel, the contractor, and the design company, alleging that each was negligent and therefore jointly and severally liable. Sikora based his claim against Wenzel in part upon a violation of R.C. 5321.04(A)(1), which requires landlords to comply with all applicable provisions of the OBBC. The trial court granted summary judgment in Wenzel's favor on the basis that he lacked notice of the defect in the deck.

Sikora appealed the trial court's decision to the Second District Court of Appeals, which reversed and remanded the decision below.]

Cook, J.

With this decision we confirm that the doctrine of negligence *per se* countenances lack of notice of a defective condition as a legal excuse. We reverse the appellate court's determination that notice is irrelevant and strict liability applies, and instead hold that a violation of R.C. 5321.04(A)(1) (failing to comply with the Ohio Basic Building Code) constitutes negligence *per se*, but that such liability may be excused by a landlord's lack of actual or constructive notice of the defective condition.

In *Shroades v. Rental Homes, Inc.*[, 427 N.E.2d 774 (Ohio 1981)], this court set forth the broad principle that landlords are subject to tort liability for violations of R.C. 5321.04. Having decided that issue, the court concluded that a landlord's failure to make repairs as required by R.C. 5321.04(A)(2) constitutes negligence *per se*, but that a landlord's notice of the condition causing the violation is a prerequisite to liability. The court of appeals here declined to apply this conclusion from *Shroades* to the instant violation of R.C. 5321.04(A)(1). The appellate court reasoned that no justification exists for the imposition of a notice requirement in a negligence *per se* context, and therefore held Wenzel strictly liable without regard to his lack of notice of the defect.

Negligence *per se* and strict liability, however, are not synonymous. Courts view the evidentiary value of the violation of statutes imposed for public safety in three ways: as creating strict liability, as giving rise to negligence *per se*, or as simply evidence of negligence. These are three separate principles with unique effects upon a plaintiff's burden of proof and to which the concept of notice may or may not be relevant.

Strict liability is also termed "liability without fault." Black's Law Dictionary (7 Ed. 1999) 926. Thus, where a statute is interpreted as imposing strict liability, the defendant will be deemed liable *per se* — that is, no defenses or excuses, including lack of notice, are applicable. Areas where the law typically imposes strict liability include liability for injuries inflicted from a dangerous instrumentality, liability for violations of certain statutes, and liability for injuries caused by a manufacturer, distributor, or vendor of certain products.

Courts generally agree that violation of a statute will not preclude defenses and excuses — *i.e.*, [will not impose] strict liability — unless the statute clearly contemplates such a result. Notably, most courts refuse to impose strict liability in the context of landlord liability for defective conditions, recognizing the need for some kind of notice element prior to the imposition of liability.

More frequently, then, this sort of statutory violation either will be considered as evidence of negligence or will support a finding of negligence *per se*. As this court has consistently held, the distinction between the two depends upon the degree of specificity with which the particular duty is stated in the statute.

Where a statute contains a general, abstract description of a duty, a plaintiff proving that a defendant violated the statute must nevertheless prove each of the elements of negligence in order to prevail. Thus, proof will be necessary that the defendant failed to act as a reasonably prudent person under like circumstances, to which the defendant's lack of notice of a defective condition may be a relevant consideration.

But where a statute sets forth "'a positive and definite standard of care . . . whereby a jury may determine whether there has been a violation thereof by finding a single issue of fact,'" a violation of that statute constitutes negligence *per se*. In situations where a statutory violation constitutes negligence *per se*, the plaintiff will be considered to have "conclusively established that the defendant breached the duty that he or she owed to the plaintiff." In such instances, the statute "serves as a legislative declaration of the standard of care of a reasonably prudent person applicable in negligence actions." Thus the "reasonable person standard is supplanted by a standard of care established by the legislature." . . .

Furthermore, negligence *per se* and strict liability differ in that a negligence *per se* statutory violation may be "excused." As set forth in the Restatement of Torts 2d, *supra*, at 37, Section 288B(1): "The *unexcused* violation of a legislative enactment . . . which is adopted by the court as defining the standard of conduct of a reasonable man, is negligence in itself." (Emphasis added.) But "an *excused* violation of a legislative enactment . . . is not negligence." (Emphasis added.) Restatement of Torts 2d, *supra*, at 32, Section 288A(1).

Lack of notice is among the legal excuses recognized by other jurisdictions and set forth in the Restatement of Torts 2d. This excuse applies where "the actor neither knows nor should know of any occasion or necessity for action in compliance with the legislation or regulation." Restatement of Torts 2d, *supra*, at 35, Section 288A(2)(b), Comment *f*.

It follows, then, that a determination of liability and the relevance of notice under a statute imposed for safety depends first upon which of the above categories the statute occupies. Wenzel urges us to construe the violation of R.C. 5321.04(A)(1) only as evidence of his negligence and therefore to consider his lack of notice as crucial to a determination of the breach of his duty of care. Sikora, in contrast, would have us uphold the appellate court's determination that strict liability applies and that Wenzel's lack of notice is irrelevant.

We reject Sikora's argument that the statute imposes strict liability. R.C. 5321.04(A)(1) requires landlords to "comply with the requirements of all applicable building, housing, health, and safety codes that materially affect health and safety." Considering the general reluctance among courts to impose strict liability in this context, the wording of the statute fails to convince us that the General Assembly intended to create strict liability upon a violation of this statutory requirement. Absent language denoting that liability exists without possibility of excuses, we are unpersuaded that the intent behind this statute was to eliminate excuses and impose strict liability.

Nor do we agree with Wenzel that the language of that statute is so general or abstract as to constitute merely evidence of negligence. Rather, we believe the statutory requirement is stated with sufficient specificity to impose negligence *per se*. It is "fixed and absolute, the same under all circumstances and is imposed upon" all landlords. Accordingly, we conclude that the statute requires landlords to conform to a particular standard of care, the violation of which constitutes negligence *per se*.

Having determined that the statute's violation constitutes negligence *per se*, we turn now to the question of whether Wenzel's lack of notice of the defect in the deck excuses the violation. Both parties agree that Wenzel neither knew nor had any way of knowing of the defective condition. The City issued the necessary approval documents despite having failed to reinspect the situation. Because Wenzel was not involved at that point, however, he had no reason to question the validity of the City's certification. Thus, no factual circumstances existed that would have prompted or required Wenzel to investigate the process that occurred between the City and the developer prior to his involvement. Given that Wenzel neither knew nor should have known of the condition giving rise to the violation of R.C. 5321.04(A)(1), his violation is excused and he is not liable to Sikora for failing to comply with the OBBC.

We hold, therefore, that a landlord's violation of the duties imposed by R.C. 5321.04(A)(1) or 5321.04(A)(2) constitutes negligence *per se*, but a landlord will be excused from liability under either section if he neither knew nor should have known of the factual circumstances that caused the violation. . . .

For the foregoing reasons, the judgment of the court of appeals is reversed.

NOTES TO SIKORA v. WENZEL

1. *Terminology.* The *Sikora* court explains that proof of a statutory violation might establish strict liability, might establish negligence per se, or might simply be evidence of negligence. The court uses the term *strict liability* to mean that in some cases conduct that violates a statute will be treated as negligent conduct without regard to any excuse or justification an actor might assert.

A common alternative way to characterize the effect of a statute that allows no excuses is to describe its violation as creating a conclusive and irrebuttable presumption of negligence. If violation of a statute would constitute negligence per se and the statute allows excuses, violation either creates a *rebuttable* presumption of negligence or provides some evidence of negligence.

2. *Reasons for Recognizing Excuses.* Statutes may represent the product of careful study by a legislature, often aided by detailed expert presentations in many phases of the legislative process. In contrast to this strength, statutes suffer from the shortcoming of being insensitive to the detailed factual variations that real cases present. Most jurisdictions allow the violator of a statute to offer excuses for the violation. A 1928 opinion described why inflexible treatment of statutes could be unfair:

> We have held that a failure to obey an ordinance passed for the protection of the public is negligence per se. But this is not an inflexible rule, applicable to every conceivable situation. In some circumstances, it might be negligence, even gross negligence, for a passenger, upon alighting from a street car, to "proceed immediately to the sidewalk to the right," as the ordinance (sec. 1980) provides; for example, if automobiles between the street car and the sidewalk to the right are moving forward, and others are rapidly approaching; or if a runaway horse is approaching the space. Or, for other reasons, a compliance with the ordinance might be impracticable, or even impossible; for example, if there is a deep excavation in the space; or if street repairers are laying hot asphalt; or if the space is occupied by automobiles or other vehicles. Traffic ordinances are to be given a reasonable construction. They should not be so construed as to require a person to do the impossible, or to take a dangerous course when an apparently safe course is open. . . .

Crosby v. Canino, 84 Colo. 225, 268 P. 1021 (1928).

3. *Allowable Types of Excuses.* In *Sikora*, the reasonableness of the defendant's conduct protected the defendant from liability based on the statutory violation. Some courts have required excuses to fit narrowly defined categories different from general proof of reasonable conduct. For example, a 1963 Idaho decision adopted a summary of circumstances in which excuses for statutory violations related to operation of motor vehicles could be considered:

> Such circumstances may generally be classified in four categories: (1) Anything that would make compliance with the statute impossible; (2) Anything over which the driver has no control which places his car in a position violative of the statute; (3) An emergency not of the driver's own making by reason of which he fails to obey the statute; (4) An excuse specifically provided by statute.

Bale v. Perryman, 380 P.2d 510 (Idaho 1963). The *Sikora* opinion may exemplify a trend in general toward more acceptance of excuses for statutory violations. The Restatement (Second) of Torts offers a listing of types of excuses that a court should consider, but the list is explicitly nonexclusive. See §288A.

4. *Procedural Effect of Proof of Violation and Excuse.* When a jurisdiction seeks to give some effect to a statute violator's excuse, it cannot treat proof of violation as *requiring* a finding of breach of duty. Courts have responded to this dilemma in a variety of ways.

A. *"Some evidence": Excuse offered or no excuse offered.* Some courts treat a violation of a statute as merely "some evidence" that is admissible and that can be considered by the jury. The jury may find for or against the alleged violator on the basis of all the evidence in the case, including any excuse offered by the alleged violator.

B. *"Prima facie" evidence: No excuse offered.* Some courts treat violation of a statute as prima facie evidence of duty and breach. In some of these jurisdictions, a party who shows an opponent's violation is entitled to reach the jury on the issues of duty and breach. The jury may find for or against the alleged violator. In other prima facie jurisdictions, courts refer to proof of violation as creating a presumption of negligence. This usually means that if the alleged violator of a statute offers no evidence contradicting the existence of duty and breach, those issues must be decided against the alleged violator.

C. *"Negligence per se": No excuse offered.* In negligence per se jurisdictions, where violation of a statute is treated as negligence per se, proof of a statutory violation is conclusive on the issues of an actor's duty and breach. This is a difference between negligence per se and those prima facie jurisdictions where evidence of a statutory violation allows, but does not require, a finding in favor of the proponent of the evidence.

D. *"Prima facie" evidence and "negligence per se": Excuse offered.* Negligence per se and prima facie evidence jurisdictions would likely apply the same treatment when a violator offers evidence of an excuse. The case must go to the jury, and the jury is entitled to find for or against the violator.

5. *Judicial Ambiguity.* Clarifying the effect of proof of statutory violation has been difficult for courts. For example, a Utah court has written:

> The parties disagree about whether the violation of a statute or ordinance . . . constitutes "per se" or "prima facie" negligence in Utah. Their confusion is not surprising because Utah appellate courts have also occasionally confused these terms. However, though the terminology has been confused, the concept has remained the

same and was succinctly stated in Intermountain Farmers Ass'n v. Fitzgerald, 574 P.2d 1162 (Utah 1978).

> [T]he violation of a statute does not necessarily constitute negligence per se and may be considered *only as evidence of negligence*. . . . [The violation] may be regarded as "prima facie evidence of negligence, but is subject to justification or excuse. . . ."

Id. at 1164-65 (quoting Thompson v. Ford Motor Co., 16 Utah 2d 30, 395 P.2d 62, 64 (1964)) (emphasis added). "Prima facie" negligence is the correct standard and a trial court commits prejudicial error when it gives a jury instruction which provides that the violation of a statute *is* negligence without the possibility for justification or excuse. Id. at 1164.

Gaw v. State of Utah, 798 P.2d 1130 (Utah Ct. App. 1990). In this excerpt, the court referred to all three of the possible treatments of proof of statutory violation: "evidence of negligence," "prima facie evidence of negligence," and "negligence per se." What is the best interpretation of the court's position?

Problem
Violation of Statute Without Fault

A defendant drove his car into the plaintiff's car and injured her. The defendant had driven into an intersection against a red light, in violation of a statute. The defendant explained that the brakes on his car had failed suddenly and without warning. He had just purchased the car. The manager of the car dealership testified that the brakes were working properly at the time of sale. The defendant testified that the brakes were working up to the time of this incident. A highway patrol officer checked the brakes immediately after the accident and found they were not working. The manager inspected the brakes the morning after the accident and found that they were working. Evidence showed that this can happen due to dirt clogging a valve in a brake cylinder. At trial, the jury returned a verdict in favor of the defendant. The plaintiff moved for judgment notwithstanding the verdict, and the trial judge denied the motion. The plaintiff has now appealed the decision to the state's supreme court, arguing that the defendant's conduct constituted negligence as a matter of law. You are a judge of the supreme court. In your opinion, did the trial judge err in denying the plaintiff's motion? See Eddy v. McAninch, 347 P.2d 499 (Colo. 1959).

Statute: BREACH OF DUTY — EVIDENCE OF
NEGLIGENCE — NEGLIGENCE PER SE
Wash. Rev. Code §5.40.050 (2017)

A breach of a duty imposed by statute, ordinance, or administrative rule shall not be considered negligence per se, but may be considered by the trier of fact as evidence of negligence; however, any breach of duty as provided by statute, ordinance, or administrative rule relating to: (1) Electrical fire safety, (2) the use of smoke alarms, (3) sterilization of needles and instruments used by persons engaged in the practice of body art, body piercing, tattooing, or electrology . . . or (4) driving while under the influence of intoxicating liquor or any drug, shall be considered negligence per se.

Statute: DUE CARE; FAILURE TO EXERCISE

Cal. Evid. Code §669 (2017)

Failure to exercise due care

(a) The failure of a person to exercise due care is presumed if:

(1) He violated a statute, ordinance, or regulation of a public entity;

(2) The violation proximately caused death or injury to person or property;

(3) The death or injury resulted from an occurrence of the nature which the statute, ordinance, or regulation was designed to prevent; and

(4) The person suffering the death or the injury to his person or property was one of the class of persons for whose protection the statute, ordinance, or regulation was adopted.

(b) This presumption may be rebutted by proof that:

(1) The person violating the statute, ordinance, or regulation did what might reasonably be expected of a person of ordinary prudence, acting under similar circumstances, who desired to comply with the law; or

(2) The person violating the statute, ordinance, or regulation was a child and exercised the degree of care ordinarily exercised by persons of his maturity, intelligence, and capacity under similar circumstances, but the presumption may not be rebutted by such proof if the violation occurred in the course of an activity normally engaged in only by adults and requiring adult qualifications.

NOTES TO STATUTES

1. *Categorizing Violations.* The Washington state statute treats some violations of statutes, ordinances, and regulations as some evidence of negligence and others as negligence per se. It does not explicitly say that no excuses will be allowed for violations of rules relating to electrical fire safety, the use of smoke alarms, or driving while intoxicated, but what rationale would support that treatment? Are those likely to be enactments that prescribe standards of conduct in rigid terms?

2. *Presumption of Negligence.* The California evidence statute offers a typical definition of the elements necessary to make a statutory violation relevant in a torts case. With regard to the power given to proof of violation, it requires a finding of negligence unless the violator establishes ordinary prudence, under the usual rules defining reasonable care for adults and children.

III. Industry Custom

If a litigant can show that an industry as a whole has a customary way of doing something, that proof could support a number of conclusions. The customary way is probably affordable, well-known, safe, and consistent with the overall success of the activity. Courts acknowledge this, but typically give less power to proof of violation of an industry custom than they give to proof of violation of a statute. Compliance with a trade or industry custom is usually treated as relevant, but not conclusive. The T.J. Hooper case is a classic case about compliance with industry custom. Ludman v. Davenport Assumption High School is a modern case illustrating the weight given to evidence of custom, who may testify regarding custom, and limitations on the admissibility of custom evidence. Wal-Mart Stores, Inc. v. Wright examines the related question of an actor's violation of the actor's own established policies.

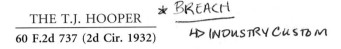

THE T.J. HOOPER   * BREACH

60 F.2d 737 (2d Cir. 1932)   *HD INDUSTRY CUSTOM*

L. HAND, J.

[The tugboat T.J. Hooper and another tugboat were tugging barges when they encountered a gale; the barges sank and their owners sought damages from the owners of the tugboats. The tugboats' captains would have sought shelter if they had received radio broadcasts from a weather bureau in Arlington forecasting that weather condition. The trial court imposed liability, holding that lack of a radio made a vessel unseaworthy.

The tugboats did not receive the broadcast storm warnings] because their private radio receiving sets, which were on board, were not in working order] These belonged to them personally, and were partly a toy, partly a part of the equipment, but neither furnished by the owner, nor supervised by it. It is not fair to say that there was a general custom among coastwise carriers so as to equip their tugs. One line alone did it; as for the rest, they relied upon their crews, so far as they can be said to have relied at all. An adequate receiving set suitable for a coastwise tug can now be got at small cost and is reasonably reliable if kept up; obviously it is a source of great protection to their tows. Twice every day they can receive these predictions, based upon the widest possible information, available to every vessel within two or three hundred miles and more. Such a set is the ears of the tug to catch the spoken word, just as the master's binoculars are her eyes to see a storm signal ashore. Whatever may be said as to other vessels, tugs towing heavy coal laden barges, strung out for half a mile, have little power to maneuvre, and do not, as this case proves, expose themselves to weather which would not turn back stauncher craft. They can have at hand protection against dangers of which they can learn in no other way.

Is it then a final answer that the business had not yet generally adopted receiving sets? There are yet, no doubt, cases where courts seem to make the general practice of the calling the standard of proper diligence; we have indeed given some currency to the notion ourselves. Indeed in most cases reasonable prudence is in fact common prudence; but strictly it is never its measure; a whole calling may have unduly lagged in the adoption of new and available devices. It may never set its own tests, however persuasive be its usages. Courts must in the end say what is required; there are precautions so imperative that even their universal disregard will not excuse their omission. But here there was no custom at all as to receiving sets; some had them, some did not; the most that can be urged is that they had not yet become general. Certainly in such a case we need not pause; when some have thought a device necessary, at least we may say that they were right, and the others too slack. The statute [46 U.S.C.A. §484] does not bear on this situation at all. It prescribes not a receiving, but a transmitting set, and for a very different purpose; to call for help, not to get news. We hold the tugs therefore

Cost/Ben

because had they been properly equipped, they would have got the Arlington reports. The injury was a direct consequence of this unseaworthiness.

Decree affirmed.

NOTES TO *THE T.J. HOOPER*

1. *Relevance of Custom Evidence.*   The *T.J. Hooper* is considered the classic case about the relevance of custom. Yet the practice among tugboat captains with respect to radios was mixed. Was it customary to have radios? Was it customary not to have radios? On what facts did the court ultimately base its decision that the tugboats were unseaworthy? How did the practice among tugboat captains affect the court's decision?

2. *Custom and the Learned Hand Test.*   Learned Hand, the author of this opinion, also wrote the opinion in Carroll Towing (discussed in McCarty v. Pheasant Run, in Chapter 3) proposing that a cost-benefit calculation could define reasonable care. If the custom of an industry might be characterized as representing the industry's consensus on an efficient balance between costs and benefits, is Hand's position rejecting custom in T.J. Hooper consistent with his position on a cost-benefit analysis of reasonable care?

LUDMAN v. DAVENPORT ASSUMPTION HIGH SCHOOL

2017 WL 2390645 (Iowa 2017)

WIGGINS, Justice.

A high school baseball player brought a[n] action against a high school for his injuries after a foul ball struck him while he was standing in an unprotected part of the visitor's dugout at the high school's baseball field. The high school appeals from the judgment entered on a jury verdict finding the high school's negligence was responsible for injuries sustained by the high school baseball player. . . .

I Background Facts and Proceedings.

In May 2011, Spencer Ludman graduated from Muscatine High School. During that summer, he was a member of the school's baseball team. On July 7, Ludman traveled with his team to play a baseball game against Davenport Assumption High School at the baseball field on their school grounds.

The visiting team's dugout was located on the first-base side of the field, thirty feet from the first-base foul line. The visitor's dugout was thirty-five feet and five inches long, seven feet wide, and two steps below the playing field. There was a fence in front of the majority of the visitor's dugout, twenty-five and a half feet in length, extending from the ground to the ceiling of the dugout. At each end of the visitor's dugout, there was a five-foot-wide opening in the fence to allow players access between the field and the dugout. There was a bench in the visitor's dugout positioned behind the fence, and it had two levels on which the players could sit.

At the top of the fifth inning, Muscatine was batting and Ludman was in the visitor's dugout with his teammates and coaches. There were two outs, and the current batter had two strikes. Ludman was due to bat after the current batter and the batter on deck. As it became unlikely he would bat that inning, Ludman grabbed his glove and hat in preparation to retake the field. After retrieving his glove and hat, he turned to watch the game and found room to stand in the south opening of the dugout, farthest from home plate.

Ludman watched the pitcher throw the ball to the batter. He heard the bat hit the ball and was looking to see where the ball went. He saw the ball in his peripheral vision before the line-drive foul ball entered the south opening of the dugout and struck him in the head. Assumption's coach saw Ludman react and try to defend himself from the ball. However, witnesses described the time from the moment the ball hit the bat until it hit Ludman as a split second.

The line-drive foul ball fractured Ludman's skull. An ambulance took him to Genesis Medical Center in Davenport, and thereafter, a helicopter transported him to the University of Iowa Hospitals and Clinics (UIHC) for treatment. Ludman's hospitalization at the UIHC lasted for twelve days before he was able to go home. After his discharge, Ludman received speech therapy, motor skills therapy, and treatment for depression and anxiety. In March of 2012, he began having seizures, requiring anti-seizure medication. He also continued to deal with posttraumatic stress symptoms, depression, and behavioral issues.

On April 5, 2013, Ludman filed a[n] action against Assumption, alleging negligence,

a) In building, maintaining, and using a baseball facility for high school baseball games, which failed to conform to accepted standards of protection for players[;]

b) In failing to erect a protective fence/screen between home plate and the dugout where players were expected to emerge from the dugout in preparation for going to bat;

c) Knowing the visitor's dugout was extremely close to home plate, failing to take reasonable steps to prevent foul balls from entering the dugout at high speed and causing injury.

Assumption denied the claims of negligence in its answer to the petition . . .

Before trial, . . . Ludman filed a motion in limine[3] to exclude Assumption's proffered evidence of other high school dugouts in the same conference as Assumption as proof of due care or as a standard of safety. The court sustained Ludman's motion in limine with regard to other high school dugouts. The court decided the parties were not to refer to other dugouts during the case, but to limit themselves to precise facts before the jury concerning Assumption's facility. . . .

III Issue[].

On appeal, Assumption argues [that] the district court erred in barring it from presenting evidence concerning the custom and standard practice in the design and construction of dugouts at schools throughout the Mississippi Athletic Conference, in which both Assumption and Muscatine High School were members. . . .

A. Law Generally.

"[E]vidence of what is usual and customary is generally admissible on the issue of negligence." *McCrady v. Sino,* 118 N.W.2d 592, 594–95 (1962). "An actor's compliance with the custom of the community, or of others in like circumstances, is evidence

---

[3] [A "motion in limine" is simply a motion made at the start of a trial requesting that the judge rule that certain evidence may not be introduced in trial. — Eds.]

that the actor's conduct is not negligent but does not preclude a finding of negligence." Restatement (Third) of Torts: Liab. for Physical & Emotional Harm §13, at 146. "A custom is a widespread and, for some courts, nearly universal practice." Kenneth S. Abraham, Custom, Noncustomary Practice, and Negligence, 109 Colum. L. Rev. 1784, 1788 (2009). In a footnote, Abraham further states,

> Although the courts rarely engage in an express headcount, discussions of the custom rule seem to me to presuppose that a practice must be followed by at least a majority of relevant actors in order to qualify as a custom. Id. at 1788 n.9.

A witness who is qualified by knowledge and experience can testify to a custom or usage's existence in a particular trade or business. The testimony does not have to call for the opinion of the witness as an expert. Instead, the record must establish the custom as a matter of fact, not as a matter of opinion. A witness may testify to the existence, as a fact, of a custom or usage, if he or she is qualified by knowledge and experience in any particular trade. To be qualified to testify as to custom and usage, the person testifying must have "adequate knowledge of the custom or usage as a fact" and "occup[y] such a position as to know of the existence of the custom as a fact." Gibson v. Shelby Cty. Fair Ass'n, 65 N.W.2d 433, 437 (1954). (quoting 32 C.J.S. Evidence §483). In other words if a person knows what a custom is, that person is qualified to testify to the custom.

However, we have developed some limitations on the admissibility of custom and usage testimony. One such exception is that a court should not admit a custom into evidence if the custom does not extend to the type of conduct at issue in the litigation. In Simon's Feed Store, Inc. v. Leslein, 478 N.W.2d 598, 602 (Iowa 1991), we concluded that a jury instruction on custom was reversible error because

> there was no showing made that the design criteria applicable to bridges on public highways constitute a custom that is generally followed in designing bridges on privately owned roadways. In the absence of proof of similar anticipated traffic patterns, the seemingly great difference in amounts and types of traffic negates any suggestion of comparability.

Another limitation is that we do not allow admission of custom or usage if the act itself is clearly careless or dangerous. In Iverson v. Vint, 54 N.W.2d 494, 495-96 (1952), we refused to admit evidence regarding the dumping of spoiled molasses. In reaching this conclusion, we stated,

> The evidence relied upon in the case at bar does not show a custom to exercise care in the disposal of large quantities of spoiled molasses. On the contrary, it shows the absence of any precautions. "It is common practice . . . to dump it wherever they can. We dumped it where it was most convenient." The failure to exercise any precautions in the disposal of this mass of molasses would indicate negligence rather than reasonable care.

Id. at 495-96.

B. Analysis.

Assumption attempted to introduce pictures of dugouts from nine other schools in the same high school conference as evidence of custom in the design of dugouts. The district court did not allow this testimony stating,

> Plaintiff is seeking to provide evidence of the alleged due care standard by expert testimony, not by custom. Therefore, what other schools do as to following the regulations

or agreeing to play on a non-regulated field is irrelevant to what Defendant did in this case or whether Defendant has no duty. To allow that comparison would be similar to allowing a motorist to argue that because they were in a line of cars that were all exceeding the speed limit that they did not violate the speeding law in effect for that portion of the roadway.

We find the district court's comparison to speed limit laws are [sic] like comparing apples to oranges. Generally, if there is a conflict between a statute and custom, the statute controls. Motorists are required to follow speed limit laws unless the motorist has a legal excuse. In this case, there are no mandatory statutes requiring Assumption to build its field in any specific manner. Second, parties can prove negligence by expert testimony or by custom. We cannot find any authority precluding a party from using a different method than that of the opposing party to prove or disprove negligence. See Parsons v. Nat'l Dairy Cattle Cong., 277 N.W.2d 620, 624 (Iowa 1979) (alluding to the fact that the jury weighs custom against expert testimony to determine negligence).

Assumption attempted to establish custom through the testimony of architect Greg Gowey. In its offer of proof and his testimony, Assumption established Gowey had designed baseball facilities and was familiar with nine dugouts from other schools in the conference. He testified concerning the design of those dugouts. One dugout at Bettendorf had openings at the sides of the visitor's dugout. All the other schools had openings in the front of the visitor's dugouts, although Pleasant Valley had only one opening in the front of the dugout nearest to home plate. The rest of the schools had two openings similar to Assumption's dugout for visitors.

Gowey, by his knowledge and experience, knew what the custom as to the design of the visitor's dugout was throughout the conference. This made him qualified to testify. Although one school only had one opening in the front of its visitor's dugout and another school had side entrances, we find the testimony was sufficient for the jury to consider if Assumption was not negligent due to the custom of the community.

Evidence of custom is not conclusive on Assumption's lack of negligence. It is still up to the jury to weigh the evidence of custom against the other evidence in the record and ultimately determine the issue of negligence based on the facts and circumstances of the case.

Accordingly, we find the district court abused its discretion by not allowing the evidence of custom. . . . Accordingly, we reverse the judgment of the district court and remand the case to the district court for a new trial.

NOTES TO LUDMAN v. DAVENPORT ASSUMPTION HIGH SCHOOL

1. *Uses of Custom Evidence.* Evidence of an industry custom might be introduced to show that an actor's failure to follow it amounts to negligence or might be introduced to show that conduct in conformity with custom meets a standard of reasonable care. The evidentiary weight given to custom evidence is the same in both contexts. Considering Judge Hand's treatment of evidence of custom and the *Ludman* court's discussion of how much weight is given to custom evidence, how does that weight compare to the weight given to evidence of a statutory violation?

2. *Custom as a Type of Fact.* The jury or judge (if there is no jury) weighs various facts to come to a conclusion about whether a party was negligent. Testimony about custom is like other testimony about facts. As *Ludman* observes, generally anyone who knows the facts may testify about the facts. And testimony about custom is given the same weight as testimony about other facts.

3. *Limitations on the Admissibility of Custom Evidence.*   The *Ludman* court discusses two limitations on custom evidence. The second reinforces the lesson from *T J. Hooper* that the general practice of the calling is not necessarily the standard of proper diligence. What is the logic of the first limitation?

Problem
Weight Given to Custom Evidence

In Franklin v. Toal, 19 P.3d 834 (Okla. 2000), the plaintiff was harmed when a "phrenic nerve pad" placed under her heart during surgery was left in her body at the conclusion of the operation. One defendant submitted evidence that other hospitals did not include phrenic nerve pads on their count lists. The jury returned a verdict for that defendant, and the plaintiff moved for judgment notwithstanding the verdict. The trial court denied the motion, and the intermediate appellate court affirmed. The plaintiff has now appealed the decision to the state supreme court. You are a judge of that court. Would it be possible for you to vote to find the defendant was negligent as a matter of law and, thus, that plaintiff was entitled to judgment notwithstanding the verdict, despite the evidence of a custom of not including phrenic nerve pads on count lists?

Perspective: Compliance with Custom as "Only Some Evidence"

A classic article on tort law's treatment of evidence of compliance with custom is Clarence Morris, *Custom and Negligence*, 42 Colum. L. Rev. 1147 (1942). Professor Steven Hetcher, in *Creating Safe Social Norms in a Dangerous World*, 73 S. Cal. L. Rev. 1, 19-22 (1999), summarized Professor Morris's arguments as follows:

> Morris argued that evidence of conformity to custom is relevant and should go to the jury because it tends to reduce natural jury prejudice against businesses that injure individuals. He contended, however, that there should be no per se rule protecting all injurers simply because they were conforming to an existent practice. Morris gave two main reasons in support of his view that evidence of conformity should go to the jury, beginning with the following: "Evidence of conformity induces objective thought; it counteracts sympathy for an injured plaintiff; it highlights the need for care in weighing the defendant's conduct; and inhibits the tendency to hold the defendant on the suspicion that he is able to absorb the loss better than the plaintiff." . . .

Morris's second point with respect to the evidentiary role of custom also concerns the connection between custom and jury prejudice rather than its connection to due care. Morris states this justification for preferring the evidentiary rule as follows:

> Evidence of conformity sharpens attention on the practicality of caution greater than the defendant used. It puts teeth in the requirement that the plaintiff establish negligence. Judges and jurymen seldom know much about the defendant's business. When the defendant's craft is palpably esoteric, the courts require the plaintiff to prove by experts that a feasible way of avoiding the

plaintiff's injury was open to the defendant. But unfortunately men do not always appreciate their ignorance. Those not in the know are prone to set impractical standards when they judge conduct that has caused injury. Evidence that the defendant has followed the ways of his calling checks hasty acceptance of suggestions for unfeasible change.

Professor Hetcher objected to the first point, that permitting custom evidence overcomes jurors' bias against businesses:

> These points have the ring of truth so far as they go, but their plausibility depends on the assumption that the defendant was following a reasonable or nearly reasonable custom. If the custom was flagrantly unreasonable, juries would be unlikely to worry that their verdict will make the defendant less competitive. It is more plausible to suppose that a jury would instead think that, as all industry participants in the practice were acting wrongfully, each should make changes in its behavior (and pay for failing to do so). In other words, the fact that the whole industry engages in an odious practice might well make a jury more sympathetic toward the victim of such a practice.

He also objected to the second point, that custom evidence focuses the juries' attention on the requirement that the plaintiff must prove that the defendant did not use reasonable care:

> Note that Morris' second point in defense of the evidentiary rule again speaks to the effect of the information on the jury's ability to arrive at a less prejudicial perspective on a situation, rather than to the intrinsic, epistemic value of the evidence. . . . We see then that just as with Morris' first rationale for the evidentiary rule, here too the argument, while of interest to the overall study of norms, does not increase our understanding as to why conformity to custom has independent, evidentiary value.

WAL-MART STORES, INC. v. WRIGHT
774 N.E.2d 891 (Ind. 2002)

BOEHM, J.

Ruth Ann Wright sued for injuries she sustained when she slipped on a puddle of water at the "Outdoor Lawn and Garden Corral" of the Carmel Wal-Mart. Wright alleged Wal-Mart was negligent in the maintenance, care and inspection of the premises, and Wal-Mart asserted contributory negligence. By stipulation of the parties, a number of Wal-Mart's employee documents assembled as a "Store Manual" were admitted into evidence at the jury trial that followed. Several of these detailed procedures for dealing with spills and other floor hazards. . . .

At the end of the trial, Wright tendered the following instruction:

> There was in effect at the time of the Plaintiff's injury a store manual and safety handbook prepared by the Defendant, Wal-Mart Stores, Inc., and issued to Wal-Mart Store, Inc. employees. You may consider the violation of any rules, policies, practices and procedures contained in these manuals and safety handbook along with all of the other evidence and the Court's instructions in deciding whether Wal-Mart was negligent.

The violation of its rules, policies, practices and procedures are a proper item of evidence tending to show the degree of care recognized by Wal-Mart as ordinary care under the conditions specified in its rules, policies, practices and procedures.

Wal-Mart objected on the ground that "you can set standards for yourself that exceed ordinary care and the fact that you've done that shouldn't be used, as this second paragraph says, as evidence tending to show the degree that you believe is ordinary. The jury decides what ordinary care is." The court overruled the objection and the tendered instruction became Final Instruction 17. The court also instructed the jury that . . . negligence is the failure to do what a reasonably careful and prudent person would do under the same or similar circumstances or the doing of something that a reasonably careful and prudent person would not do under the same or similar circumstances. . . .

The jury found Wal-Mart liable. . . . Wal-Mart appealed, contending that the second paragraph of Final Instruction 17 was an improper statement of law that incorrectly altered the standard of care from an objective one to a subjective one. The Court of Appeals affirmed, holding the challenged paragraph of the instruction was proper because it "did not require the jury to find that ordinary care, as recognized by Wal-Mart, was the standard to which Wal-Mart should be held," and because the trial court had not "instructed the jury that reasonable or ordinary care was anything other than that of a reasonably careful and ordinarily prudent person." This Court granted transfer.

. . . Wal-Mart argues that the second paragraph of Final Instruction 17 incorrectly stated the law because it invited jurors to apply Wal-Mart's subjective view of the standard of care as evidenced by the Manual, rather than an objective standard of ordinary care. Wright responds that the paragraph simply allows jurors to consider Wal-Mart's subjective view of ordinary care as some evidence of what was in fact ordinary care, and does not convert the objective standard to a subjective one. . . .

Initially, we note that implicit in each of these positions, and explicit in the second paragraph of the instruction, is the assumption that the Manual in fact "tend[s] to show the degree of care recognized by Wal-Mart as ordinary care under the conditions specified in [the Manual]." Wal-Mart also objected to this assumption, contending "you can set standards for yourself that exceed ordinary care and the fact that you've done that shouldn't be used, as this second paragraph says, as evidence tending to show the degree that you believe is ordinary." We agree. The second paragraph of the instruction told the jurors that because Wal-Mart has established certain rules and policies, those rules and policies are evidence of the degree of care recognized by Wal-Mart as ordinary care. But Wal-Mart is correct that its rules and policies may exceed its view of what is required by ordinary care in a given situation. Rules and policies in the Manual may have been established for any number of reasons having nothing to do with safety and ordinary care, including a desire to appear more clean and neat to attract customers, or a concern that spills may contaminate merchandise.

The law has long recognized that failure to follow a party's precautionary steps or procedures is not necessarily failure to exercise ordinary care. . . . We think this rule is salutary because it encourages following the best practices without necessarily establishing them as a legal norm.

There is a second problem with the instruction. Even if the Manual reflected Wal-Mart's subjective view of ordinary care, the second paragraph of the instruction incorrectly states the law because it invites jurors to apply Wal-Mart's subjective view — as evidenced by the Manual — rather than an objective standard of ordinary care. It is axiomatic that in a negligence action "[t]he standard of conduct which the community demands must be an external and objective one, rather than the individual judgment, good or bad, of the particular actor." W. Page Keeton et al., *Prosser & Keeton on the Law of Torts* §32, at 173-74 & n. 3 (5th ed. 1984). . . . A defendant's belief that it is acting reasonably is no defense if its conduct falls below reasonable care. Similarly, a defendant's belief that it should perform at a higher standard than objective reasonable care is equally irrelevant. . . .

Wright cites four cases in support of the instruction. . . . These authorities support the admissibility of the Manual, which Wal-Mart does not contest. They do not support an instruction to consider any "violation" of the Manual as "evidence tending to show the degree of care recognized by Wal-Mart as ordinary care under the conditions." We conclude that the second paragraph of Final Instruction 17 was an improper invitation to deviate from the accepted objective standard of ordinary care and therefore incorrectly stated the law.

The judgment of the trial court is reversed. This action is remanded for a new trial.

NOTES TO WAL-MART STORES, INC. v. WRIGHT

1. *Incentives for Internal Rules.* A trial court in a case similar to *Wright* stated:

> Let me tell you what I think public policy-wise. We want K-Mart and Publix and Burger King and all those places to have internal policies that assure the highest standard of public safety. And God forbid that there be jury instructions that, hey, if you fail to wash your hands or something like that the jury can consider it *in evidence* against you. In other words, these retail establishments being held to a higher standard than the reasonable man standard.

Mayo v. Publix Super Markets, Inc., 686 So. 2d 801, 802 (Fla. App. 1997). Do enterprises have incentives to adopt internal rules even if those rules might be brought to the attention of juries in negligence cases?

2. *Specific Relevance of Internal Rules.* The *Wright* court acknowledges the admissibility of Wal-Mart's rules, and there was no challenge to the first paragraph of the instruction. Apparently, a jury may learn about such rules but must not treat their violation as equivalent to unreasonable conduct. A jury could perhaps use information about a defendant's own rules to support a conclusion that the actions required by the rules were practical or were known to the defendant at the time of the plaintiff's injury.

IV. *Res Ipsa Loquitur*

Sometimes a litigant can introduce eyewitness testimony that totally explains what someone did or how something happened, but often litigants rely on circumstantial evidence. "Circumstantial" evidence is information a factfinder may use to make inferences about past events (for example, how a person acted or how an injury occurred). Tort law recognizes some uses of circumstantial evidence as proof of breach with the phrase "res ipsa loquitur," which is Latin for "the thing speaks for itself." When a plaintiff relies on the *res ipsa loquitur* doctrine, the jury will be allowed to conclude that the defendant was negligent even though the plaintiff may not have introduced detailed or direct evidence about the precise shortcomings of the defendant's actions.

The classic case introducing this concept to tort law is Byrne v. Boadle. Its facts are compelling: If someone walks on a sidewalk and gets hit by a barrel that comes out of a second-story window, should those facts alone be enough to entitle the pedestrian to damages in a lawsuit? As the *res ipsa* doctrine developed, courts tended to apply it only when four elements were present: (1) the type of injury was usually associated with negligence; (2) the defendant had exclusive control of whatever caused the injury; (3) the plaintiff had made no causal contribution to the harm; and (4) the defendant's access to information about the event was superior to the plaintiff's. Modern courts rarely refer to all four of these elements. Shull v. B.F. Goodrich focuses on the two most significant elements of the doctrine, the requirement that accidents like the one that occurred are usually the result of someone's negligence and the requirement that the instrumentality that caused the harm was in that actor's control at the time of the negligent act. In Dover Elevator Co. v. Swann, the court limits use of the doctrine in a circumstance where the plaintiff is able to provide fairly detailed proof about the events that caused injury.

BYRNE v. BOADLE

159 Eng. Rep. 299 (Ex. 1863)

[In a negligence action, the plaintiff introduced evidence showing that as he was walking on a street past the defendant's shop, a barrel fell from the shop's second-story window and hit him. The plaintiff was nonsuited at trial on the ground that there was no evidence of negligence. The plaintiff appealed.]

POLLOCK, C.B.

. . . We are all of opinion that the rule must be absolute to enter the verdict for the plaintiff. The learned counsel was quite right in saying that there are many accidents from which no presumption of negligence can arise, but I think it would be wrong to lay down as a rule that in no case can presumption of negligence arise from the fact of an accident. Suppose in this case the barrel had rolled out of the warehouse and fallen on the plaintiff, how could he possibly ascertain from what cause it occurred? It is the duty of persons who keep barrels in a warehouse to take care that they do not roll out, and I think that such a case would, beyond all doubt, afford prima facie evidence of negligence. A barrel could not roll out of a warehouse without some negligence, and to say that a plaintiff who is injured by it must call witnesses from the warehouse to prove negligence seems to me preposterous. So in the building or repairing a house, or putting pots on the chimneys, if a person passing along the road is injured by something falling upon him, I think the accident alone would be prima facie evidence of negligence. Or if an article calculated to cause damage is put in a wrong place and does mischief, I think that those whose duty it was to put it in the right place are prima facie responsible, and if there is any state of facts to rebut the presumption of negligence, they must prove them. The present case upon the evidence comes to this, a man is passing in front of the premises of a dealer in flour, and there falls down upon him a barrel of flour. I think it apparent that the barrel was in the custody of the defendant who occupied the premises, and who is responsible for the acts of his servants who had the control of it; and in my opinion the fact of its falling is prima facie evidence of negligence, and the plaintiff who was injured by it is not bound to shew that it could not fall without negligence, but if there are any facts inconsistent with negligence it is for the defendant to prove them.

NOTES TO BYRNE v. BOADLE

1. *Inference of Tortious Conduct.* Deciding whether a person used reasonable care usually requires comparing that person's conduct to the way a reasonable person would behave. In Byrne v. Boadle, the plaintiff could offer no explanation of what the defendant did that caused his injuries, so no comparison was possible. The court inferred from the circumstances, however, that the defendant (or its employees) more likely than not was negligent. Under these circumstances, it would be unfair to require the plaintiff to identify the defendant's specific tortious conduct. What was it about the circumstances that persuaded the court to permit this inference? What kind of evidence would have been direct evidence in a case of a barrel falling from an upstairs window?

2. *Circumstantial Evidence Generally.* The *res ipsa loquitur* doctrine is a label for the law's customary approach to circumstantial evidence. Circumstantial evidence is generally admissible in court on all kinds of issues. And factfinders are generally allowed to make inferences from evidence. So, despite its Latin label, the doctrine of *res ipsa loquitur* should not be interpreted as meaning that circumstantial evidence of negligence is admissible while other circumstantial evidence is not.

Circumstantial evidence of negligence is special because, when the elements of *res ipsa loquitur* are met, the party relying on the circumstantial evidence (usually the plaintiff) can avoid a directed verdict. In a case where the plaintiff had no direct evidence of what the defendant did wrong, the defendant might move for a directed verdict on the ground that the plaintiff has not introduced adequate proof of a negligent act. Where the *res ipsa loquitur* doctrine applies, the trial court will reject that motion. Furthermore, at the end of the trial, the doctrine will entitle the plaintiff to a special jury instruction. A *res ipsa* instruction informs the jury that, despite the plaintiff's failure to offer direct evidence of what the defendant did wrong, the jury may infer that the defendant was negligent.

SHULL v. B.F. GOODRICH CO.
477 N.E.2d 924 (Ind. Ct. App. 1985)

SULLIVAN, J.

A jury returned a defendant's verdict in a personal injury and loss of consortium case. Plaintiffs Everett D. Shull, Sr. and Lapaloma Shull, appeal the judgment entered thereon. They present one issue: Whether the trial court erred in refusing an instruction upon the doctrine of *res ipsa loquitur*.

In 1979 Mr. Shull, age 56, was a truck driver with a motor freight company. He was directed by his employer to the B.F. Goodrich plant in Woodburn, Indiana, to pick up a load of tires. While on Goodrich's loading dock Shull was injured when a dock-plate, a mechanical device which forms a bridge between the dock and the truck trailer and upon which Shull was standing, malfunctioned, throwing Shull to the floor of his trailer. The Shulls sued Goodrich for negligence. . . .

At the close of the evidence Shulls tendered and the court refused the following instruction:

> There is a doctrine in law called *res ipsa loquitor,* [sic] which doctrine may come into effect under certain conditions in a negligence case. In order for the doctrine to apply, you must find that the following facts existed on May 29, 1979, the time of the occurrence in question:
>
> First: That the plaintiff was injured as a proximate result of the occurrence;
>
> Second: That the instrumentality causing the injury was under the exclusive control of B.F. Goodrich;
>
> Third: That the occurrence was of a sort which usually does not occur in the absence of negligence on the part of the person in control.
>
> If you find that the plaintiffs have established each of the three elements as stated by a preponderance of the evidence then you may infer that the defendant, B.F. Goodrich was negligent and you may consider this inference together with all the other evidence in the case in arriving at your verdict. Record at 46. . . .

The words "*res ipsa loquitur*" literally mean "the thing speaks for itself." Black's Law Dictionary. The doctrine is a rule of evidence allowing an inference of negligence to be drawn under certain factual circumstances. . . .

The true question is whether the event was more probably occasioned by negligence of the defendant rather than some other cause. A plaintiff relying upon *res ipsa loquitur* may show that the event or occurrence was more probably the result of negligence by simply relying upon the basis of common sense and experience or he may present expert testimony to establish this proposition. [As] Dean Prosser [has observed]:

> In the usual case the basis of past experience from which the conclusion may be drawn that such events usually do not occur without negligence, is one common to the whole community, upon which the jury are simply permitted to rely. Even where such a basis of common knowledge is lacking, however, expert testimony may provide a sufficient foundation; and by the same token it may destroy an inference which would otherwise arise. In many cases the inference to be drawn is a double one, that the accident was caused in a particular manner, and that the defendant's conduct with reference to that cause was negligent. . . .
>
> The plaintiff is not required to eliminate with certainty all other possible causes or inferences, which would mean that he must prove a civil case beyond a reasonable doubt. All that is needed is evidence from which reasonable men can say that on the whole it is more likely that there was negligence associated with the cause of the event than that there was not. It is enough that the court cannot say that the jury could not reasonably come to that conclusion.

W. Prosser, Handbook of The Law of Torts, §39, p.217-218 (4th ed. 1971).

In Indiana the doctrine is invoked where (1) the injuring instrumentality is shown to have been under the exclusive control of the defendant, and (2) the accident is one which in the ordinary course of things does not happen if those who control the instrumentality use proper care.

The tendered instruction was derived from the Indiana Pattern Jury Instructions and was a correct statement of the law of *res ipsa loquitur* in Indiana. . . .

The precise issue thus becomes whether the Shulls presented evidence from which a reasonable jury could conclude that the dock-plate would not have malfunctioned in the absence of negligence on the part of the party in control and that Goodrich was the party in exclusive control. If so, then the Shulls were entitled to have the jurors instructed that if they did find those elements established by a preponderance of the evidence, they could infer that Goodrich was negligent.

When Shull arrived at Goodrich's plant he was directed to dock #7, one of Goodrich's eighteen loading docks. Each dock is equipped with a dock-plate. The dock-plate is a mechanical device consisting of a metal plate with a sixteen to eighteen inch metal lip, both operated by a torsion spring. The dock-plate is activated by pulling a ring which releases a spring raising the dock-plate to an angle of approximately 30°. Then the shipper walks the dock-plate down so that the lip is inside and rests upon the trailer bed. The plate is held in place by a ratchet device called a hold-down assembly consisting of a metal bar with serrated or grooved edges in it and into which a "pawl" or wedge fits. When in place the dock-plate serves as a bridge on which fork lift trucks and people walk back and forth between the loading area and the trailer bed.

The parties agree that the dock-plate on dock #7 was not operating properly on the day in question. Shull testified that upon arriving he went to the loading area and attempted to activate the dock-plate by pulling the metal ring but it would not respond. James Vogel, a Goodrich employee, then arrived at the scene and was successful in activating the dock-plate. Vogel and Shull testified they had problems getting the dock-plate to stay in a locked position. The first two times Vogel activated the dock-plate, it would spring up and the two men walked it down. On each of these first two attempts the dock-plate would not stay down but instead would "pop up" a couple of inches. The two men attempted the same process a third time and both testified that after they walked the dock-plate down it appeared locked. Vogel walked to his fork truck and Shull walked into the trailer. While Shull was on the lip of the dock-plate, the plate suddenly released to its fully elevated position throwing Shull to the floor of his trailer.

Neither party disputed that dock-plate failure is a rare event. There was evidence that after the accident Goodrich's maintenance department looked at the dock-plate but no specific cause of the malfunction was introduced into evidence. Shull argues that dock-plates don't normally fail without negligence on the part of the person responsible for maintaining them. In arguing for a directed verdict, Goodrich contended that the reason for this malfunction was not produced by Shull and that negligence could not be inferred from the mere fact of the malfunction. The Shulls argued *res ipsa loquitur,* and the judge, in denying the motion, held the evidence sufficient to avoid a directed verdict.

Generally, *res ipsa loquitur* would allow the jury to attribute Shull's injury under unexplained circumstances to Goodrich's negligence based upon evidence from which a reasonable person may conclude it is more likely than not that the accident was caused by Goodrich's negligence. This requirement necessitates a reasonable showing that the accident was indeed one which would not ordinarily occur in the absence [sic: presence?] of proper care on the part of those who manage or maintain the instrumentality causing injury.

This inference of negligence as a component of *res ipsa* may be based upon common knowledge and/or the testimony of experts or other witnesses. Jack Ringler,

Goodrich's engineer and head of maintenance, testified that under normal circumstances the dock-plates remained secured until the trailer pulled away or the ring was pulled down to release the hold-down assembly. On the occasion in question, however, the trailer was stationary and the ring had not been pulled. Nonetheless, according to the testimony of the Goodrich employee assisting Shull, the dock-plate raised as though the ring had been pulled.

The unexplained malfunction of machinery is ordinarily attributable to a defect and/or improper maintenance. Where responsibility for the defect may be attributed to the defendant, negligence may be inferred. In the instant case, Goodrich admitted that the dock-plates were serviced only after trouble arose. Ringler also specifically testified that Goodrich had experienced previous malfunctions with the dock-plates caused by a problem or defect in the ratchet device. He further testified, given Shull's report of the manner in which the malfunction occurred, that, in his opinion, the mechanism was faulty and should be replaced. This is evidence from which it might be reasonably concluded that it was more likely than not that the accident would not have ordinarily occurred in the absence of Goodrich's negligence. . . .

The evidence which tends to support the conclusion that Goodrich was in exclusive control of the dock-plate must be viewed in light of the definition of "exclusive control" in the law of *res ipsa loquitur*. As stated, the doctrine of *res ipsa loquitur* is an evidentiary rule.

It is not necessary that defendant be in control of the causative instrumentality at the moment of injury so long as defendant was the last person in control of the instrumentality under circumstances permitting an inference of negligence. Dean Prosser explained that:

> [exclusive control] of course does serve effectively to focus any negligence upon the defendant; but the strict and literal application of the formula has led some courts to ridiculous conclusions, requiring that the defendant be in possession at the time of the plaintiff's injury. . . . Of course this is wrong: it loses sight of the real purpose of the reasoning process in an attempt to reduce it to a fixed, mechanical and rigid rule. "Control," if it is not to be pernicious and misleading, must be a flexible term.

W. Prosser, Handbook of the Law of Torts, §39, p.220 (4th ed. 1971). In keeping with this concept courts must look to the defendant's right to control, and opportunity to exercise it. In some situations "control" is simply the wrong word and the courts should determine whether the evidence reasonably eliminates explanations other than the defendant's negligence. As noted by Prosser:

> The plaintiff is not required to eliminate *with certainty all* other possible causes and inferences, which would mean that he must prove a civil case beyond a reasonable doubt. . . . The injury must either be traced to a specific instrumentality or cause for which the defendant was responsible, *or it must be shown that he was responsible for all reasonably probable causes to which the accident could be attributed.*

Prosser, supra at 218. (Emphasis supplied.) . . .

The evidence which tends to support exclusive control in *Goodrich* is that Goodrich was the sole occupant of the factory since it was built in 1961. In 1968 the dock-plates were installed and, at all times thereafter, Goodrich performed all maintenance upon them. Goodrich employees were used for the purpose and no independent contractors were employed. Clearly if the jury were to believe that the dock-plate would not have malfunctioned but for an act or omission constituting negligence, there was sufficient evidence for them to conclude that Goodrich was in exclusive control of the dock-plates at the time the negligent acts would have occurred. . . .

Because Shull's tendered instruction on the doctrine of *res ipsa loquitur* correctly stated the law, was supported by sufficient evidence and was not covered by other instructions, it was error for the trial court to refuse it. We do not know what the jury's verdict would have been had they been properly instructed, therefore, we reverse the judgment and remand this case for a new trial.

NOTES TO SHULL v. B.F. GOODRICH

1. ***Elements of* Res Ipsa Loquitur.**   The court in Shull v. B.F. Goodrich describes the two basic elements a plaintiff must prove to be entitled to a *res ipsa loquitur* instruction. Would these elements have been met if required by the court in Bryne v. Boadle? What evidence demonstrated each element in *Shull*?

2. ***The Restatement (Third) and the Exclusive Control Requirement.***   The Restatement (Third) of Torts: Liability for Physical and Emotional Harm §17 proposes a one-sentence test for when the plaintiff is entitled to a *res ipsa loquitur* instruction: "The factfinder may infer that the defendant has been negligent when the accident causing the plaintiff's harm is a type of accident that ordinarily happens because of the negligence of the class of actors of which the defendant is the relevant member." The drafters objected to the exclusive control element that is so common in states' articulations of the standards for *res ipsa loquitur*:

> A number of courts adopt a two-step inquiry: step one asks whether the accident is of a type that usually happens because of negligence, while step two asks whether the "instrumentality" inflicting the harm was under the "exclusive control" of the defendant. This formulation, with its emphasis on exclusive control, is unsatisfactory for at least two reasons. One is that the test is sometimes indeterminate, since there may be several instruments that could be deemed the cause of the plaintiff's injury. Another objection is more basic. In one well-known early *res ipsa loquitur* case, a barrel fell out of the window of the defendant's business premises, injuring a pedestrian below. In such a case, exclusive control is an effective proxy for the underlying question of which party was probably negligent: the party with the exclusive control of the barrel at the time of the incident is in all likelihood the one whose negligence caused the barrel to fall. In fact, the exclusive-control criterion is often effective in identifying the negligent party, and in these cases exclusive control plays a vital role in *res ipsa loquitur* evaluations. Yet frequently exclusive control functions poorly as such a proxy. Consider, for example, the consumer who buys a new car; a day after the purchase, the car's brakes fail, and the car strikes a pedestrian who is in a crosswalk. Undeniably, the motorist has exclusive control of the car at the time of the accident. Yet there is no reason to believe that the consumer is the negligent party, and adequate reason to believe that the negligence belongs to the car manufacturer (or, more precisely, that the latter has manufactured a defective product). Accordingly, the injured pedestrian should not have a *res ipsa loquitur* claim against the consumer, despite the latter's exclusive control; furthermore, the pedestrian might have a *res-ipsa*-like claim against the manufacturer, despite the latter's lack of exclusive control.

Id., comment b. Does the flexible definition of "exclusive control" given by the court in Shull v. B.F. Goodrich overcome the drafters' objections?

3. *Plaintiff's Contributory Negligence.* In addition to the two basic elements, some jurisdictions have required the plaintiff to show that the occurrence was not due to any voluntary action or contribution by the plaintiff. The purpose of this element, like the element of exclusive control, is to eliminate the plaintiff as the responsible party. The court in Shull v. B.F. Goodrich, in a footnote omitted in this text, explained that Indiana law does not require this element because the exclusive control element is sufficient to eliminate the plaintiff as a responsible party.

Requiring the plaintiff to show that he or she was not responsible was related to another concept, the defense of contributory negligence. That defense precluded any recovery for a plaintiff whose own negligence had contributed to an injury. The vast majority of states have replaced the contributory negligence doctrine with rules that allow some negligent plaintiffs to recover damages. This change in the general treatment of a plaintiff's negligence has led many states to eliminate specific consideration of a plaintiff's negligence in the context of the *res ipsa loquitur* doctrine.

4. *Information Accessible Only to the Defendant.* Some states apply another variation in the elements of *res ipsa loquitur*. They require the plaintiff to show that evidence of the explanation for the harm's occurrence is more accessible to the defendant than to the plaintiff. This requirement was probably met in Bryne v. Boadle. It would be harder to establish in Shull v. B.F. Goodrich, particularly under modern discovery rules, which allow the plaintiff to find out, before trial, all information, such as maintenance logs and records of prior breakdowns that the defendant has about possible causes of the accident. The following case, Dover Elevator Co. v. Swann, applies this element.

5. *Procedural Role of* Res Ipsa Loquitur. Reviewing its *res ipsa loquitur* precedents, the New York Court of Appeals wrote:

> [There has been] confusion over the doctrine's procedural effects. Courts, including ours, used "prima facie case," "presumption of negligence" and "inference of negligence" interchangeably even though the phrases can carry different procedural consequences. One case went so far as to use all three interchangeably.

Morejon v. Rais Construction Co., 7 N.Y.3d 203 (2006). The court concluded:

> Res ipsa loquitur is a phrase that, perhaps because it is in Latin, has taken on its own mystique, although it is nothing more than a brand of circumstantial evidence. Viewed in that light, the summary judgment (or directed verdict) issue may also be properly approached by simply evaluating the circumstantial evidence. If that evidence presents a question of fact as to the defendant's liability under the . . . test for res ipsa loquitur, the case should go to trial. If the circumstantial evidence does not reach that level and present a question of fact, the defendant will prevail on the law. Alternatively, as we have said, the plaintiff should win summary judgment or a directed verdict in the exceptional case in which no facts are left for determination.

Id. at 211-212.

Problems
Application of *Res Ipsa Locquitur*

Should the doctrine of *res ipsa loquitur* be applied in the following circumstances? Is the common experience of humans sufficient to answer these questions or is expert testimony required to explain why such accidents occur?

A. A store customer sat down in a chair provided by the store, and the chair collapsed, throwing the customer to the floor and causing injuries. At trial, the court issued an instruction informing the jury that, in order for the exclusive control element of *res ipsa loquitur* to apply, the store's employees would have to have been the last to use the chair before the customer sat in it; if any other customers had sat in the chair in the interim, the exclusive control element would not be satisfied. The jury returned a verdict for the store. You represent the customer on appeal. What argument would you make in your attempt to convince the appellate court that the instruction was in error and that your client is entitled to a new trial? See Trujeque v. Service Merchandise Corp., 117 N.M. 388, 872 P.2d 361 (1994).

B. The handrail of an escalator stopped suddenly between floors, throwing a rider on that escalator to the floor and breaking her arm. Is such an accident likely to have occurred without negligence? Is the negligent party likely to have been the defendant (in this case, the airport insured by the defendant)? See Colmenares Vivas v. Sun Alliance Insurance Co., 807 F.2d 1102 (1st Cir. 1986).

C. A child was dropped off at a day care center in good health, but had a brain concussion at pickup time. Should the *res ipsa* doctrine apply? See Fowler v. Seaton, 394 P.2d 697 (Cal. 1964).

D. A twenty-five-pound box of tomatoes fell from the top of a large pallet while the pallet was being unloaded in a grocery store and hit a customer. The customer had her back to the pallet and did not observe the unloading process. There is no evidence that the plaintiff customer touched the pallet. Should *res ipsa* apply? See Cardina v. Kash N' Karry Food Stores, Inc., 663 So. 2d 642 (Fla. App. 1995).

E. A bottle of a carbonated drink exploded in a waitress's hand, cutting it severely. Is this accident likely to be the result of the negligence of the drink bottler? See Escola v. Coca Cola Bottling Co., 150 P.2d 436 (Cal. 1944).

F. A girl cut her foot while playing soccer on a school playground and sued the soccer club. There was no allegation of any specific negligent conduct on the part of the club in the complaint. The defendant moved for summary judgment, arguing that the plaintiff had failed to establish a factual issue with respect to whether the defendant was negligent. The plaintiff's lawyer suggested in his objection to the defendant's motion that it was a piece of glass or very sharp object on the field that caused the cut. Should the court grant the defendant's motion? See Rosenberg v. Rockville Center Soccer Club, Inc., 166 A.D.2d 570 (S. Ct. App. Div. 1990).

DOVER ELEVATOR CO. v. SWANN
334 Md. 231, 638 A.2d 762 (1994)

CHASANOW, J. . . .

The plaintiff, David Swann, was injured on February 2, 1987, while attempting to board an elevator that allegedly failed to level properly with the floor. . . .

. . . Swann filed a complaint against Prudential Insurance Company of America [owner of the building where the elevator was located] and Dover Elevator Company [which had manufactured, installed, and maintained the elevator]. The complaint alleged that Swann suffered $3,000,000.00 in damages as a result of the defendants' negligence and defects in the design, manufacture, installation and maintenance of elevator number two. . . .

At trial, Swann offered the expert testimony of Donald Moynihan, an elevator consultant and engineer. . . .

The specific negligence alleged by Moynihan's testimony was as follows: 1) Dover was negligent in filing and cleaning, as opposed to replacing, contacts 14 and 15 on elevator number two, resulting in a faulty current and the misleveling; 2) Dover was negligent by failing to spend adequate time servicing the elevator; 3) Dover's maintenance records were deficient; and 4) Dover failed to properly stock replacement parts in the elevator's machine room. Swann contends the elevator's misleveling was probably caused by an irregular current running between the number 14 and 15 contacts. The importance of this contention was explained by the Court of Special Appeals: "Although [Dover's Maintenance] Agreement specifically excludes several elevator components and associated systems, the component that Swann contends caused the misleveling, the '14 and 15 contacts,' was not excluded." . . .

Following a trial on the merits, the jury returned a verdict in favor of all the defendants. Swann appealed to the Court of Special Appeals, which affirmed the verdict as to Prudential . . . but reversed the verdict as to Dover [holding that the trial court had erred in refusing to instruct the jury on *res ipsa loquitur*]. . . . Dover petitioned this Court for a writ of certiorari, which was granted . . . to address the [following issue: May the plaintiff, who has proffered direct evidence of the specific cause of his injuries, also rely on the doctrine of *res ipsa loquitur* in order to establish the defendant's negligence?] . . .

The dilemma between the doctrine of *res ipsa loquitur* and offering direct evidence of negligence is best summarized by the oft-quoted discussion in Hickory Transfer Co. v. Nezbed, 202 Md. 253, 96 A.2d 241 (1953): "In this case the plaintiffs themselves proved the details of the happening, foregoing reliance on *res ipsa loquitur;* and, having undertaken to prove the details, they failed to show negligence on the part of the defendants. Indeed, they explained away the possible inference of negligence. Paradoxically, the plaintiffs proved too much and too little." . . . The question presented by the instant case is, therefore, whether the plaintiff attempted to prove the "details of the happening," thereby precluding his reliance on *res ipsa loquitur.* . . .

[T]he Court of Special Appeals in the instant case held that "Swann's attempt to prove specific acts of negligence did not prevent him from requesting that the jury be instructed on both negligence and *res ipsa loquitur.*" . . . In examining this evidence, the court declared the following:

> Swann did not, however, purport to furnish a complete explanation of the accident. Indeed, Swann offered evidence establishing that Dover responded to reports of mislevelings on two separate occasions following the January 7th repair [when contacts 14 and 15 were filed]. There was no evidence of what, if any, corrective measures Dover took on those dates. It may well be that Dover negligently repaired the elevator on one, or both, of those occasions and such negligent act or acts caused the February 2nd misleveling incident. Further, at the close of the evidence, there was a dispute as to what caused the accident. Bothell testified that it was proper to clean, rather than replace, the 14 and 15 contacts, and that the door clutch mechanism prevents the elevator doors from opening when the elevator cab is greater than an inch or two from floor level. Therefore, "reasonable men might [have] differ[ed] as to the effect of the evidence before the jury." . . .

We find that the plaintiff's expert witness, Donald Moynihan, did purport to furnish a sufficiently complete explanation of the specific causes of elevator number two's misleveling, which would preclude plaintiff's reliance on *res ipsa loquitur*. . . .

In arriving at its conclusion that this direct evidence of negligence did not preclude the plaintiff's reliance on *res ipsa loquitur,* the Court of Special Appeals extensively discussed two principal cases: Blankenship v. Wagner, 261 Md. 37, 273 A.2d 412 (1971), and Nalee, Inc. v. Jacobs, 228 Md. 525, 180 A.2d 677 (1962). We find these cases distinguishable from the instant case, however, because little or no direct evidence of negligence was offered in either of them. The only evidence offered by the plaintiff in *Blankenship* was that, as he and a coworker were carrying a refrigerator up a set of stairs behind the defendant's house, one of the steps collapsed underneath the coworker's feet. . . . The plaintiff was forced to support the entire weight of the refrigerator from above to prevent it from falling on his coworker, who was caught in the broken step. In doing so, the plaintiff injured his back. . . . *Blankenship* is distinguishable from the instant case because the plaintiff in *Blankenship* never sought to offer even a partial explanation of why the step collapsed beneath his coworker's feet. He only sought to prove *res ipsa loquitur*'s three basic elements. This Court therefore decided that the directed verdict in favor of the defendant was inappropriate and reversible error. . . .

In the course of its reasoning, the *Blankenship* Court also acknowledged the following principle which guides our reasoning in the instant case:

> The justice of the rule permitting proof of negligence by circumstantial evidence is found in the circumstance that the principal evidence of the true cause of the accident is accessible to the defendant, but inaccessible to the victim of the accident. The rule is not applied by the courts except where the facts and the demands of justice make its application essential, depending upon the facts and circumstances in each particular case.

261 Md. at 41, 273 A.2d at 414 (quoting Potts v. Armour & Co., 183 Md. 483, 488, 39 A.2d 552, 555 (1944)).

The Court recognized, however, in reference to the direct evidence standard established in *Nezbed,* that an offer of some "circumstantial evidence which tends to show the defendant's negligence" should not as a matter of policy preclude reliance on *res ipsa loquitur.* . . .

The instant case also does not present a situation where "the principal evidence of the true cause of the accident" was accessible only to the defendant and "inaccessible to the victim." . . . As stated herein, the plaintiff's expert witness testified to the specific cause of the accident within a reasonable degree of engineering probability. Mr. Moynihan did not merely provide some circumstantial evidence tending to show the defendant's negligence with regard to contacts 14 and 15 and the misleveling of elevator number two. He purported to offer a complete explanation of the precise cause and how the negligence of Dover's technician contributed to that cause. . . .

The other case relied upon by the Court of Special Appeals, Nalee, Inc. v. Jacobs, is equally distinguishable from the factual circumstances of the instant case. In *Nalee,* the plaintiff was injured in the defendant's hotel when a nearby bench fell over and struck him on the foot. The only arguably direct evidence offered by the plaintiff was testimony that the bench was not fastened to the floor or the wall. . . .

As in *Blankenship,* the *Nalee* Court also recognized that direct . . . evidence of negligence may preclude application of *res ipsa loquitur.* . . . The *Nalee* Court correctly concluded that, in cases where the plaintiff's evidence "did not stop at the point of showing the happening of the accident under circumstances in which negligence of the defendant was a permissible inference," the plaintiff was properly precluded from utilizing the *res ipsa loquitur* doctrine. . . . The Court concluded that "negligence on the part of the defendant could have properly been drawn by the jury from the evidence in this case without resort to the 'doctrine' of *res ipsa loquitur.* . . ." *Nalee,* 228 Md. at 533, 180 A.2d at 681.

This Court's reasoning in *Nalee* is equally applicable to the instant case. The plaintiff in this case did not stop at the inference of the defendant's negligence, drawn from the single misleveling of the elevator, but purported to establish more. In doing so, "all of the facts with regard to the actual happening of the accident had been developed, and when developed, they were held insufficient to establish negligence" on the part of Dover. . . .

In the instant action, Swann's primary complaint was not that a single misleveling created an inference of negligence, but that Dover's failure to properly correct the problem after prior mislevelings constituted negligence. More particularly, Swann contended Dover was negligent by cleaning, rather than replacing, contacts 14 and 15, failing to spend adequate time servicing the elevator, keeping deficient records, and failing to stock sufficient replacement parts. . . . The trial judge apparently concluded, and we agree, that a *res ipsa loquitur* instruction was not proper because the plaintiff's expert witness established that the most likely cause of the elevator's misleveling was an insufficient current running between contacts 14 and 15 and the defendant's negligence, if any, was the failure to correct the misleveling problem. In effect, the plaintiff's expert, Donald Moynihan, and the defendant's witness, Ronald Bothell, agreed that the probable cause of any possible misleveling was the contacts but they disagreed over whether cleaning rather than replacing these contacts constituted negligence.

Thus, the reasoning of *Nalee,* like that of *Blankenship,* leads us to the conclusion that *res ipsa loquitur* should not be applied to the facts and circumstances of the case before us. . . .

Judgment of the Court of Special Appeals reversed. . . .

NOTES TO DOVER ELEVATOR CO. v. SWANN

1. *Expert Testimony in* **Res Ipsa Loquitur** *Cases.* In many negligence cases, a defendant is entitled to have the judge instruct the jury that "the mere occurrence of an accident does not raise an inference of negligence." *Res ipsa loquitur* cases are those in which the mere occurrence of an accident under particular circumstances does raise such an inference. In *Dover Elevator Co.,* the plaintiff apparently did not need the usual benefit of the *res ipsa loquitur* doctrine — protection from a directed verdict for the defendant — because the plaintiff's expert testified as to what the defendant did that caused the accident. Is the plaintiff's use of an expert always fatal to the plaintiff's attempt to rely on *res ipsa loquitur* to prove breach? The plaintiff in Shull v. B.F. Goodrich was assisted by an expert. How was that testimony different from the expert's testimony in Dover Elevator Co. v. Swann?

2. *Expert Testimony in Medical* **Res Ipsa Loquitur** *Cases.* In some medical cases, experts testify that the plaintiff's injury was of a type usually associated with negligence.

This kind of testimony necessarily involves some detailed proof about the injurious event, but it does not identify specific acts of negligence in the plaintiff's case. Rather, it explains the general nature of the medical procedure and the risks associated with it. This testimony can give the jury the necessary background for deciding whether the accident was one that usually results from negligence and whether the defendant was more likely than not the negligent actor. Many courts allow both this type of expert testimony and the *res ipsa loquitur* inference. See, e.g., Connors v. University Associates in Obstetrics and Gynecology, 4 F.3d 123 (2d Cir. 1993).

Perspective: Counter-Intuitive Statistical Likelihood of Negligence

In a study with many respondents, federal magistrate judges reacted to a hypothetical problem in which it was stated that barrels fall from windows sometimes because of negligent conduct and sometimes in the absence of negligent conduct. The judges' analyses of the problem varied widely. Since one aspect of the *res ipsa loquitur* doctrine requires a belief that negligence was a highly likely cause of an injury, the wide range of the judges' responses suggests that application of the doctrine may sometimes be uneven or unfair. See Chris Guthrie, Jeffrey J. Rachlinski & Andrew J. Wistrich, *Inside the Judicial Mind*, 86 Cornell L. Rev. 777, 808-809 (2001):

> [W]e gave the judges in our study a *res ipsa loquitur* problem. In an item labeled "Evaluation of Probative Value of Evidence in a Torts Case," we presented all of the judges with a paragraph-long description of a case based loosely on the classic English case, Byrne v. Boadle:
>
> > The plaintiff was passing by a warehouse owned by the defendant when he was struck by a barrel, resulting in severe injuries. At the time, the barrel was in the final stages of being hoisted from the ground and loaded into the warehouse. The defendant's employees are not sure how the barrel broke loose and fell, but they agree that either the barrel was negligently secured or the rope was faulty. Government safety inspectors conducted an investigation of the warehouse and determined that in this warehouse: (1) when barrels are negligently secured, there is a 90% chance that they will break loose; (2) when barrels are safely secured, they break loose only 1% of the time; (3) workers negligently secure barrels only 1 in 1,000 times.
>
> > The materials then asked: "Given these facts, how likely is it that the barrel that hit the plaintiff fell due to the negligence of one of the workers?" The materials provided the judges with one of four probability ranges to select: 0-25%, 26-50%, 51-75%, or 76-100%.
>
> > [T]he actual probability that the defendant was negligent is only 8.3%. . . .
>
> > Of the 159 judges who responded to the question, 40.9% selected the right answer by choosing 0-25%; 8.8% indicated 26-50%; 10.1% indicated 51-75%; and 40.3% indicated 76-100%.

5

LEGAL CAUSE: CAUSE-IN-FACT

I. Introduction

Causation Doctrines Connect a Defendant's Conduct to a Plaintiff's Harm. Tort law limits the potential liability of individuals whose conduct is improper. Even when a plaintiff shows that a defendant's conduct was worse than the conduct required by an applicable standard of care, to win damages the plaintiff must also show that there was a causal connection between the defendant's conduct and the plaintiff's harm. This concept is known as *cause-in-fact*. The cause-in-fact part of a plaintiff's case requires proof that as a matter of historical and physical fact, it is more likely than not that the defendant's conduct was a cause of what happened to the plaintiff.

In addition to the cause-in-fact requirement, tort law provides some other limits to liability. These limits are based more on policy considerations than on an effort to determine historical or physical facts about the plaintiff's injury and the defendant's conduct. For example, proximate cause doctrines sometimes treat a defendant's conduct as too remote from a plaintiff's injury to justify holding the defendant liable. In certain cases, conduct by an actor other than the defendant will be treated as a *superseding cause*, which also insulates the defendant from responsibility. Also, the *duty* concept protects defendants from liability in cases where the law concludes that a person owes no obligation or only a limited obligation to another to protect another person from harm. These policy-based limits on liability are different from *cause-in-fact*. Limits on liability are treated in following chapters.

Terminology. Some courts and legal writers use legal cause to describe only cause-in-fact or only proximate cause. Others use *proximate cause* to describe cause-in-fact, proximate cause, and superseding cause. Still others include *superseding cause* under the category of *proximate cause*. This casebook uses *legal cause* as a term encompassing all aspects of causation. This usage is common but is certainly not universal. This casebook also attempts to treat each causation component separately and with a clear label (such as "cause-in-fact," "proximate cause," and "superseding cause").

II. Basic Cause-in-Fact: The But-for Test

In most situations, a defendant's action is defined as a "cause-in-fact" of a plaintiff's harm if the plaintiff's harm would not have occurred if the defendant had acted properly. Put another way, the question is whether the plaintiff would have been free from harm "but for" (in the absence of) the defendant's negligent conduct. This analysis of cause-in-fact is called the *but-for test.* It treats one occurrence as a cause of a second occurrence if the first occurrence was necessary or essential for the happening of the second occurrence.

In a negligence case, applying the but-for test requires the finder of fact to decide how the plaintiff's injury occurred and to compare that scenario with what the trier of fact thinks would have happened if the defendant's conduct had been free from negligence. If the finder of fact believes that without the defendant's negligent conduct the plaintiff's injury would not have happened, then the cause-in-fact element of the plaintiff's case is satisfied. The defendant's conduct will be treated as a cause-in-fact of the plaintiff's harm.

While *cause-in-fact* sounds like a straightforward historical inquiry, it actually can involve considerable speculation. It requires a comparison of some real past events with an alternative imagined set of past events (life as it would have been without the defendant's negligent conduct). Cay v. State of Louisiana illustrates this process, in a case where the "what if" question ("what if the defendant had acted reasonably?") involved the height of a bridge guardrail. Lyons v. Midnight Sun Transportation Services, Inc. applies a cause-in-fact analysis to a vehicular accident, showing the degree of deference an appellate court will ordinarily give to trial court findings about causation and highlighting the separate nature of causation and breach-of-duty inquiries.

CAY v. STATE OF LOUISIANA, DEPARTMENT OF
TRANSPORTATION AND DEVELOPMENT

631 So. 2d 393 (La. 1994)

Lemmon, J.

This is a wrongful death action filed by the parents of Keith Cay, who was killed in a fall from a bridge constructed and maintained by the Department of Transportation and Development (DOTD). The principal issue [is] whether plaintiffs proved that DOTD's construction of the bridge railing at a height lower than the minimum standard for pedestrian traffic was a cause-in-fact of Cay's fall from the bridge. . . .

Cay, a twenty-seven-year-old single offshore worker, returned to his home in Sandy Lake from a seven-day work shift on November 3, 1987. Later that afternoon his sister drove him to Jonesville, thirteen miles from his home, to obtain a hunting license and shotgun shells for a hunting trip the next day. Cay cashed a check for $60.00 and paid for the hunting items, but remained in Jonesville when his sister returned to Sandy Lake about 7:00 p.m. Around 10:00 p.m. Cay entered a barroom and stayed until about 11:00 p.m., when he left the barroom on foot after declining an offer for a ride to his home. He carried an opened beer with him.

Five days later, Cay's body was discovered on a rock bank of the Little River, thirty-five feet below the bridge across the river. Cay would have had to cross the bridge in order to travel from Jonesville to his home.

Cay's body was found in a thicket of brambles and brush. The broken brush above the body and the lack of a path through the brush at ground level indicated that Cay had fallen from the bridge. There was no evidence suggesting suicide or foul play.[1] There was evidence, however, that Cay, who was wearing dark clothes, was walking on the wrong side of the road for pedestrian traffic and was intoxicated.

The bridge, built in 1978, was forty feet wide, with two twelve-foot lanes of travel and an eight-foot shoulder on each side. The side railings were thirty-two inches high, the minimum height under existing standards for bridges designed for vehicular traffic. There were no curbs, sidewalks or separate railings for pedestrian traffic, although it was well known that many pedestrians had used the old bridge to cross the river to communities and recreation areas on the other side.

Cay's parents filed this action against DOTD, seeking recovery on the basis that the guard railings on the sides of the bridge were too low and therefore unsafe for pedestrians whom DOTD knew were using the bridge and that DOTD failed to provide pedestrian walkways or signs warning pedestrians about the hazardous conditions.

The trial court rendered judgment for plaintiffs, concluding that Cay accidently fell from the bridge. The court held that the fall was caused in part by the inadequate railing and in part by Cay's intoxicated condition. Pointing out that DOTD had closed the old bridge to both vehicular and pedestrian traffic and should have been aware that numerous pedestrians would use the new bridge to reach a recreational park, the Trinity community and other points across the river from Jonesville, the court found that DOTD breached its duty to pedestrians by failing to build the side railings to a height of thirty-six inches, as required by the American Association of State Highway and Transportation Officials (AASHTO) standards for pedestrian railings. The court concluded that this construction deficiency was a cause of the accident in that "a higher rail would have prevented the fall." Noting that there was no evidence establishing what actually caused the incident, the court surmised that Cay was "startled by oncoming traffic, moved quickly to avoid perceived danger, tripped over the low rail, lost his balance, and with nothing to prevent the fall, fell from the Little River Bridge." . . .

The court of appeal affirmed. The court concluded that the inadequate railing was a cause-in-fact of the accident, stating, "It is true that the accident might have occurred had the railing been higher. However, it is also true that the accident might not have happened had the railing been higher." The court further stated, "Had the railing been higher, the decedent might have been able to avoid the accident."

Because these statements are an incorrect articulation of the preponderance of the evidence standard for the plaintiffs' burden of proof in circumstantial evidence cases, we granted certiorari.

BURDEN OF PROOF

In a negligence action, the plaintiff has the burden of proving negligence and causation by a preponderance of the evidence. Proof is sufficient to constitute a preponderance

---

[1] The fact that Cay bought a hunting license and supplies militates against a conclusion that he planned to commit suicide.

when the entirety of the evidence, both direct and circumstantial, establishes that the fact or causation sought to be proved is more probable than not.

One critical issue in the present case is causation, and the entirety of the evidence bearing on that issue is circumstantial. For the plaintiff to prevail in this type of case, the inferences drawn from the circumstantial evidence must establish all the necessary elements of a negligence action, including causation, and the plaintiff must sustain the burden of proving that the injuries were more likely than not the result of the particular defendant's negligence. The plaintiff must present evidence of circumstances surrounding the incident from which the factfinder may reasonably conclude that the particular defendant's negligence caused the plaintiff's injuries.

CAUSE-IN-FACT

. . . Cause-in-fact is usually a "but for" inquiry which tests whether the injury would not have occurred but for the defendant's substandard conduct. The cause-in-fact issue is usually a jury question unless reasonable minds could not differ.

The principal negligence attributed to DOTD in the present case is the failure to build the bridge railings to the height required in the AASHTO standards. The causation inquiry is whether that failure caused Cay's fall or, conversely, whether the fall would have been prevented if DOTD had constructed the railing at least thirty-six inches high.

The determination of whether a higher railing would have prevented Cay's fall depends on how the accident occurred. Plaintiffs had the burden to prove that a higher railing would have prevented Cay's fall in the manner in which the accident occurred. . . .

The circumstantial evidence did not establish the exact cause of Cay's fall from the bridge, but it is more likely than not that Cay's going over the side was not intentional, either on his part or on the part of a third party. More probably than not, Cay did not commit suicide, as evidence of plans and preparation for a hunting trip minimize this possibility. More probably than not, he was not pushed, as he had little money or valuables on his person, and the evidence from barroom patrons does not suggest any hostility toward or by him during the evening. More likely than not, he was not struck by a vehicle and knocked over the railing. It is therefore most likely that he accidently fell over the railing.

The evidence suggests that Cay moved at a sharp angle toward the railing, for some unknown reason, and stumbled over. For purposes of the cause-in-fact analysis, it matters little whether his movement toward the railing was prompted by perceived danger of an approaching automobile or by staggering in an intoxicated condition or for some other reason. Whatever the cause of Cay's movement toward the railing at a sharp angle, the cause-in-fact inquiry is whether a higher railing would have prevented the accidental fall.

The trial judge's finding that a higher railing would have prevented the fall is supported by expert testimony that the very reason for the minimum height requirement for railing on bridges intended for pedestrian use is to have a railing above the center of gravity of most persons using the bridge so that the users will not fall over. . . .

A cause-in-fact determination is one of fact on which appellate courts must accord great deference to the trial court. We cannot say that the trial court erred manifestly in determining that a railing built to AASHTO minimum specifications would have prevented Cay's fall when he approached the railing at a sharp angle, although the exact cause of Cay's approaching the railing at a sharp angle is not known. While a higher rail would not have prevented Cay from jumping or a third party from throwing Cay over the rail, one could reasonably conclude that a rail above Cay's center of gravity would have prevented an accidental fall. . . .

NOTES TO CAY v. LOUISIANA

1. *Deciding Among Possible Causes.* The plaintiff's claims require the finder of fact to reach conclusions on two topics: (1) what happened to the decedent; and (2) whether the alleged negligent conduct by the defendant was a necessary element for what happened to the plaintiff. The lack of witnesses to Mr. Cay's death made the first of these two questions difficult; in some cases there will be no dispute about what actually happened, even if the parties do dispute whether a change in the defendant's conduct would have prevented the injurious event. What was the plaintiff's characterization of what occurred?

2. *Burden of Proof of Causation.*   The plaintiff must prove by a *preponderance of the evidence* that higher railings would have prevented the harm to Cay, that *more likely than not*, the railing height was a cause-in-fact. What supports the finding that the DOTD's negligence was more likely than not a but-for cause?

The appellate court held that the accident *might* have occurred and that the decedent *might* have been able to avoid the accident had the railing been higher. Bearing in mind that the preponderance of the evidence standard usually requires the proponent of a fact to show that the likelihood of that fact being true is greater than 50 percent, what probability was associated with concluding that the fall *might* have been prevented by higher railings?

3. *Multiple But-for Causes.*   There are an infinite number of but-for causes for any accident, even including the plaintiff's having been born. In Cay v. State of Louisiana, the trial court identified two occurrences that were each a cause-in-fact of the death: the height of the railing and Cay's intoxication. In a cause-in-fact analysis, the court asks whether, given all of the other factors present at the time, the defendant's act made a difference. How does that analysis support the conclusion that the intoxication *and* the railing height are each a cause-in-fact?

Perspective: But-for Cause and Toxic Substances

Proof that an actor's conduct is more likely than not a necessary event in the chain of causation is particularly difficult in cases involving exposure to allegedly toxic substances. Often, the best scientific evidence can establish only that exposure to a toxic substance generally increases the likelihood that a harm, such as cancer, will occur. Scientific evidence often cannot establish that the exposure caused the cancer in the specific case of a particular plaintiff because the plaintiff was exposed to many environmental carcinogens.

In such cases, scientists testify about the enhanced risk created by exposure to the substance. For example, they compare the background rate of cancers in populations where there is no exposure to the alleged toxin to the frequency of cancers in similar populations exposed to the toxin. Where there is credible proof that the frequency of cancers more than doubles, courts often hold that the but-for cause proof is met.

Why require a more than double increase in risk? Courts reason that if the number of cancers in populations exposed to the toxin is more than twice the number in the unexposed population, it is more likely than not that any particular plaintiff's cancer was due to the exposure. For example, if there are 30 cases of cancer in an unexposed population and 40 cases of cancer in an exposed population, then exposure to the toxin is a but-for cause of only 10 of the cancers. This would mean that more likely than not exposure to the toxin is not a necessary event in the development of any particular plaintiff's cancer.

LYONS v. MIDNIGHT SUN TRANSPORTATION SERVICES, INC.
928 P.2d 1202 (Alaska 1996)

PER CURIAM.

Esther Hunter-Lyons was killed when her Volkswagen van was struck broadside by a truck driven by David Jette and owned by Midnight Sun Transportation Services, Inc. When the accident occurred, Jette was driving south in the right-hand lane of Arctic Boulevard in Anchorage. Hunter-Lyons pulled out of a parking lot in front of him. Jette braked and steered to the left, but Hunter-Lyons continued to pull out further into the traffic lane. Jette's truck collided with Hunter-Lyons's vehicle. David Lyons, the deceased's husband, filed suit, asserting that Jette had been speeding and driving negligently.

At trial, conflicting testimony was introduced regarding Jette's speed before the collision. Lyons's expert witness testified that Jette may have been driving as fast as 53 miles per hour. Midnight Sun's expert testified that Jette probably had been driving significantly slower and that the collision could have occurred even if Jette had been driving at the speed limit, 35 miles per hour. Lyons's expert later testified that if Jette had stayed in his own lane, and had not steered to the left, there would have been no collision. Midnight Sun's expert contended that steering to the left when a vehicle pulls out onto the roadway from the right is a normal response and is generally the safest course of action to follow.

Over Lyons's objection, the jury was given an instruction on the sudden emergency doctrine. The jury found that Jette, in fact, had been negligent, but his negligence was not a legal cause of the accident. Lyons appeals, arguing that the court should not have given the jury the sudden emergency instruction. . . .

We find that Lyons has little cause to complain of the sudden emergency instruction because the jury decided the issue in his favor.

To the question "Was Midnight Sun's employee, David Jette, negligent?" the jury answered "YES." The jury finding of negligence indicates that the jury concluded David Jette was driving negligently or responded inappropriately when Ms. Hunter-Lyons entered the traffic lane and, thus, did not exercise the care and prudence a reasonable person would have exercised under the circumstances.

However, Lyons's claims were defeated on the basis of lack of causation. Although the jury found Jette to have been negligent, it also found that this negligence was not the legal cause of the accident. Duty, breach of duty, causation, and harm are the separate and distinct elements of a negligence claim, all of which must be proven before a defendant can be held liable for the plaintiff's injuries. . . .

. . . [W]e cannot say that the jury's finding of lack of causation was unreasonable. There was evidence presented at trial from which the jury could reasonably have drawn the conclusion that even though Jette was driving negligently, his negligence was not the proximate cause of the accident. Midnight Sun introduced expert testimony to the effect that the primary cause of the accident was Ms. Hunter-Lyons's action in pulling out of the parking lot in front of an oncoming truck. Terry Day, an accident reconstruction specialist testified that, depending on how fast Ms. Hunter-Lyons was moving, the accident could have happened even if Jette had been driving within the speed limit. Midnight Sun also introduced expert testimony to the effect that Jette responded properly to the unexpected introduction of an automobile in his traffic lane. Although all of this testimony was disputed by Lyons, a reasonable jury could have concluded that Ms. Hunter-Lyons caused the accident by abruptly pulling out in front of an oncoming truck, and that David Jette's negligence was not a contributing factor. With the element of causation lacking, even the most egregious negligence cannot result in liability. . . .

NOTES TO LYONS v. MIDNIGHT SUN TRANSPORTATION SERVICES, INC.

1. _Terminology._   The _Lyons_ court stated that there was evidence to support the jury's conclusion that the defendant's negligence was not a proximate cause, referring to testimony that the accident could have occurred even if Jette had been driving the speed limit. "Proximate cause" in this usage means the same thing as "cause-in-fact."

2. _Independence of Tort Elements._   How does the court justify victory for the defendant, when there is significant evidence showing that the defendant's truck driver acted negligently?

Problems
But-for Cause

A. A jockey was injured when the horse he was riding bolted from the race course and ran through a removable railing. The jockey sought damages from the operator of the race course. On the day of the accident, the railing was not painted. (The defendant's use of an unpainted railing was a violation of certain state regulations and was therefore negligent conduct.) The jockey introduced evidence that, because the railing was not painted white (and horses only distinguish between black and white), the fence may have visually blended with the gray infield. There was also evidence that horses are accustomed to leaving the racetrack at the precise location where the horse bolted. The defendant moved for a directed verdict, arguing that no reasonable jury could conclude its failure to paint the railing was a cause-in-fact of the plaintiff's harm, and the trial court denied the motion. The defendant has appealed the judgment to the state supreme court, of which you are a judge. Should you vote to affirm the trial court's ruling? See Martino v. Park Jefferson Racing Assn., 315 N.W.2d 309 (S.D. 1982).

B. Linda Musch was an experienced, careful horse rider. Her horse was trained to work with cattle, and she had worked with the horse many times without mishap. She was injured when she and her horse collided with an unmarked gray steel guy wire on a utility pole owned and maintained by a utility company. She claimed that the lack of markings was a cause-in-fact of her injury and sought damages from the utility. An opinion in the case stated:

> The evidence reflected that the horse was trained to pursue a calf and if "given its head" it would do that instinctively. Linda testified that she gave the horse some slack in the rein and said to the horse, "Let's go get him." The evidence reflected that Linda took off with her horse and the calf began darting in different directions. The horse followed the calf and when it darted under the guy wire the horse followed.

Was the utility's failure to provide a white cover on the guy wire a cause-in-fact of the plaintiff's injuries? See Musch v. H-D Cooperative, Inc., 487 N.W.2d 623 (S.D. 1992).

Perspective: Moral Role of Causation

A moral argument for imposing liability on an actor is that the actor caused harm to the other. Causation is not usually enough for liability, however, because there must also be a duty and fault on the part of the injurer. The combination of negligence and causation "particularizes" or singles out the injurer from other people who might be forced to pay:

> If A unreasonably puts B at risk, then this is a fact about A that is not true of everyone. Moreover, it is a fact about A that is morally relevant to B's claims against A's resources. For it is consistent with the value we place upon freedom of action that individuals are encouraged not *unjustifiably* to impose risks on others.

Causation also particularizes the victim. It is not enough that the actor's negligence created a risk:

> Causation particularizes the victim in the *analytic* sense that a victim, by definition, is someone who suffers harm. Thus, the fact that A causes B harm is normatively significant because it demonstrates that B, not someone else, was harmed by A. So if A must pay someone, it must be B, not C, D, or E, none of whom were harmed by A.

See Jules A. Coleman, *Property, Wrongfulness, and the Duty to Compensate*, 63 Chi.-Kent L. Rev. 451, 452 (1987).

III. Alternatives to the But-for Test

A. Reasons for Alternatives

A rigorous application of the but-for test would prevent a plaintiff from recovering in some cases where most people would believe that a defendant's actions actually did harm the plaintiff. These cases may involve multiple actors where the conduct of each actor might have been sufficient to cause the harm. In that circumstance, a plaintiff would probably not be able to prove that conduct by any one of the actors was a but-for cause of the plaintiff's entire harm. Courts may relieve the plaintiff of the obligation to prove who caused the harm.

Modern cases have also involved situations where conduct by only one or some, but not all, of a group of defendants could have caused a plaintiff's injury but the plaintiff cannot show who caused it. Variations on the but-for test known as *alternative liability* and *market share liability* may resolve these cases. Finally, courts have developed special causation rules for some medical malpractice cases where the likely effects of the normal risks inherent in a patient's condition make it difficult to evaluate whether a physician's substandard conduct actually made a difference in the outcome.

B. Multiple Sufficient Causes

The but-for test could prevent a plaintiff's recovery in a case where conduct by each of two or more actors was sufficient independently to have caused the plaintiff's harm. Asking whether the plaintiff would have been all right if a particular actor's conduct had been different would lead to the answer that the plaintiff would still have been injured. That result would prevent a finding of cause-in-fact under the but-for test. For these cases, most courts change the rules about who must prove cause. Once the plaintiff demonstrates that each of the defendant's acts would have been sufficient to cause the harm, the defendant must offer some type of evidence to show why it should not be considered a cause. Kingston v. Chicago & N.W. Ry. Co. is the classic case most often cited for situations where each actor's conduct was sufficient to produce the harm.

What must a defendant show to avoid being considered a legal cause of the harm? Some courts allow a defendant to show that its actions were not a substantial factor in causing the harm. Other courts require a defendant to rebut the plaintiff's evidence by showing that its actions were not sufficient. Ford Motor Company v. Boomer, a modern case, discusses both approaches.

KINGSTON v. CHICAGO & NORTHWESTERN RAILWAY CO.
211 N.W. 913 (Wis. 1927)

OWEN, J. . . . .

We, therefore, have this situation: The northeast fire was set by sparks emitted from defendant's locomotive. This fire, according to the finding of the jury, constituted a proximate cause of the destruction of plaintiff's property. This finding we find to be well supported by the evidence. We have the northwest fire, of unknown origin. This fire, according to the finding of the jury, also constituted a proximate cause of the destruction of the plaintiff's property. This finding we also find to be well supported by the evidence. We have a union of these two fires 940 feet north of plaintiff's property, from which point the united fire bore down upon and destroyed the property. We, therefore, have two separate, independent, and distinct agencies, each of which constituted the proximate cause of plaintiff's damage, and either of which, in the absence of the other, would have accomplished such result.

It is settled in the law of negligence that any one of two or more joint tort-feasors, or one of two or more wrongdoers whose concurring acts of negligence result in injury, are each individually responsible for the entire damage resulting from their joint or concurrent acts of negligence. This rule also obtains—

Rule

> where two causes, each attributable to the negligence of a responsible person, concur in producing an injury to another, either of which causes would produce it regardless of the other, . . . because, whether the concurrence be intentional, actual or constructive, each wrongdoer, in effect, adopts the conduct of his co-actor, and for the further reason that it is impossible to apportion the damage or to say that either perpetrated any distinct injury that can be separated from the whole. The whole loss must necessarily be considered and treated as an entirety.

Cook v. Minneapolis, St. Paul & Sault Ste. Marie R. Co., 98 Wis. 634, at page 642, 74 N.W. 561 (1898). That case presented a situation very similar to this. One fire, originating by sparks emitted from a locomotive, united with another fire of unknown origin and consumed plaintiff's property. There was nothing to indicate that the fire of unknown origin was not set by some human agency. The evidence in the case merely failed to identify the agency. In that case it was held that the railroad company which set one fire was not responsible for the damage committed by the united fires because the origin of the other fire was not identified. . . .

Emphasis is placed upon the fact, especially in the opinion, that one fire had "no responsible origin." At other times in the opinion the fact is emphasized that it had no "known responsible origin." The plain inference from the entire opinion is that, if both fires had been of responsible origin, or of known responsible origin, each wrongdoer would have been liable for the entire damage. The conclusion of the court exempting the railroad company from liability seems to be based upon the single fact that one fire had no responsible origin, or no known responsible origin. It is difficult to determine just what weight was accorded to the fact that the origin of the fire was unknown. If the conclusion of the court was founded upon the assumption that the fire of unknown origin had no responsible origin, the conclusion announced may be sound and in harmony with well-settled principles of negligence.

From our present consideration of the subject, we are not disposed to criticize the doctrine which exempts from liability a wrongdoer who sets a fire which unites with a fire originating from natural causes, such as lightning, not attributable to any human agency, resulting in damage. It is also conceivable that a fire so set might unite with a fire of so much greater proportions, such as a raging forest fire, so as to be enveloped or swallowed up by the greater holocaust and its identity destroyed, so that the greater fire could be said to be an intervening or superseding cause. But we have no such situation here. These fires were of comparatively equal rank. If there was any difference in their magnitude or threatening aspect the record indicates that the northeast fire was the larger fire and was really regarded as the menacing agency. At any rate, there is no intimation or suggestion that the northeast fire was enveloped and swallowed up by the northwest fire. We will err on the side of the defendant if we regard the two fires as of equal rank.

According to well-settled principles of negligence, it is undoubted that, if the proof disclosed the origin of the northwest fire, even though its origin be attributed to a third person, the railroad company, as the originator of the northwest [sic: northeast] fire, would be liable for the entire damage. There is no reason to believe that the northwest fire originated from any other than human agency. It was a small fire. It had traveled over a limited area. It had been in existence but for a day. For a time it was thought to have been extinguished. It was not in the nature of a raging forest fire. The record discloses nothing of natural phenomena which could have given rise to the fire. It is morally certain that it was set by some human agency.

Now the question is whether the railroad company, which is found to have been responsible for the origin of the northeast fire, escapes liability, because the origin of the northwest fire is not identified, although there is no reason to believe that it had any other than human origin. An affirmative answer to that question would certainly make a wrongdoer a favorite of the law at the expense of an innocent sufferer. The injustice of such a doctrine sufficiently impeaches the logic upon which it is founded. Where one who has suffered damage by fire proves the origin of a fire and the course of that fire up to the point of the destruction of his property, one has certainly established liability on the part of the originator of the fire. Granting that the union of that fire with another of natural origin, or with another of much greater proportions, is available as a defense the burden is on the defendant to show that, by reason of such union with a fire of such character, the fire set by him was not the proximate cause of the damage. No principle of justice requires that the plaintiff be placed under the burden of specifically identifying the origin of both fires in order to recover the damages for which either or both fires are responsible. . . .

. . . We are not disposed to apply the doctrine of the *Cook* Case to the instant situation. There being no attempt on the part of the defendant to prove that the northwest fire was due to an irresponsible origin — that is, an origin not attributable to a human being — and the evidence in the case affording no reason to believe that it had an origin not attributable to a human being, and it appearing that the northeast fire, for the origin of which the defendant is responsible, was a proximate cause of plaintiff's loss the defendant is responsible for the entire amount of that loss. While under some circumstances a wrongdoer is not responsible for damage which would have occurred in the absence of his wrongful act, even though such wrongful act was a proximate cause of the accident, that doctrine does not obtain "where two causes, each attributable to the negligence of a responsible person, concur in producing an injury to another, either of which causes would produce it regardless of the other." This is because "it is impossible to apportion the damages or to say that either perpetrated any distinct injury that can be separated from the whole," and to permit each of two wrongdoers to plead the wrong of the other as a defense to his own wrongdoing, would permit both wrongdoers to escape and penalize the innocent party who has been damaged by their wrongful acts.

The fact that the northeast fire was set by the railroad company, which fire was a proximate cause of plaintiff's damage, is sufficient to affirm the judgment. This conclusion renders it unnecessary to consider other grounds of liability stressed in respondent's brief.

Judgment affirmed.

NOTES TO KINGSTON v. CHICAGO & NORTHWESTERN RAILWAY CO.

1. *The Facts of* Kingston. Drawing a map of Kingston's property and that of his northern neighbor helps clarify the *Kingston* facts. The fire caused by the railroad came from the northeast. The fire caused by unknown but presumably human agency came from the northwest. The fires combined just north of Kingston's land and "bore down" (moved south) to damage Kingston's property. The holding in *Kingston* is based on the factual conclusions that it is "morally certain" that the northwest fire was set by some human agency and that the fires were of equal severity or "rank."

2. *Multiple Sufficient Causes.* The cause-in-fact rule usually places the burden on the plaintiff to show that the damage would not have occurred if the defendant had not acted as he or she did. Kingston v. Chicago & Northwestern Railway Co. illustrates the difficulty in proving cause-in-fact in cases involving more than one wrongdoer. If two fires would each have burned down the plaintiff's building without the other, neither one is a necessary event in the chain of causation. Without the northwest fire, the northeast fire would have destroyed the property, and vice versa. The doctrine of *multiple sufficient causes* prevents each of the two tortfeasors from escaping liability by blaming the other. This doctrine removes the obligation to prove that each defendant's act was a but-for cause.

3. *Shifting the Burden of Proof: Character of Actors' Conduct.* If each of several acts would be sufficient to produce the plaintiff's harm, the burden shifts to each defendant to avoid liability. A defendant will not be liable unless all defendants acted tortiously. There is no discussion in *Kingston* of why the railroad was at fault in setting fires by its locomotive, but state statutes commonly made railroads liable for damages caused by such fires without regard to whether they were at fault. It was not proved who the other tortious actor was, but the court concluded that it was some person engaging in tortious conduct. That is what the court means by the fire being "of responsible origin" as opposed to being set by natural forces.

In some jurisdictions, if a defendant's tortious act combines with a natural act, such as a lightning strike, because the other cause is not a human agency the multiple sufficient cause rule does not apply, and the plaintiff would be unable to meet his or her burden of proving that the defendant's act was a but-for cause. Other jurisdictions do not excuse a defendant from liability in this circumstance. See Moore v. Standard Paint & Glass Co., 358 P.2d 33, 36 (Colo. 1960):

> This court has on at least three occasions ruled that one whose wrongful acts cooperated with an act of God is liable for injuries which are the natural result thereof, the defense of an act of God being available only to defendants who can prove that the injury resulted *solely* from the act of God without any contributory negligence on the part of the defendant.

Under the *Kingston* rule, each of the acts that were independently sufficient to produce the harm must have been tortious for the plaintiff to avoid the harsh result of the but-for cause test. In contrast, some courts and the Restatements of Torts take the position that any defendant whose tortious act was independently sufficient to cause the plaintiff's harm may be liable even if other independently sufficient acts were innocent. See Restatement (Third) of Torts: Liability for Physical and Emotional Harm §27, comment d.

<u>FORD MOTOR CO. v. BOOMER</u>

736 S.E.2d 724 (Va. 2013)

Justice Leroy F. Millette, Jr.

These paired appeals arise out of a jury verdict against Honeywell International Incorporated [successor in interest to the Bendix Corporation] and Ford Motor Company for the wrongful death of James D. Lokey, caused by mesothelioma resulting from exposure to asbestos in dust from Bendix brakes installed in Ford and other vehicles.

On appeal, Ford [and Bendix] assign[] error to . . . the circuit court's jury instructions as to causation. . . .

Lokey was diagnosed with mesothelioma, a malignant cancer of the pleura of the lungs, in 2005. He passed away in 2007 due to complications related to his disease. Lokey testified at trial via a *de bene esse* deposition taken prior to his death. His son-in-law, Walter Boomer, is the Administrator of his estate. [Lokey testified that for eight years he served as a Virginia State trooper. His duties included observing vehicle inspections (including Ford vehicles using Bendix brakes) in which mechanics used compressed air to blow out brake dust. He recalled breathing that dust.]

Dr. John C. Maddox and Dr. Laura Welch, experts for Lokey's estate, testified that chrysotile asbestos, the type of asbestos found in brakes, can cause mesothelioma. They opined that the exposure to dust from Bendix brakes and brakes in new Ford cars were both substantial contributing factors to Lokey's mesothelioma. Maddox and Welch opined that the current medical evidence suggests that there is no safe level of chrysotile asbestos exposure above background levels in the ambient air.

Lokey also testified that he worked as a pipefitter at the Norfolk Naval Shipyard for slightly over a year in the early 1940s. Lokey testified that his own work and the work of those immediately around him involved packing sand into pipes so that the pipes could be bent to fit the ships. He had no personal knowledge of any exposure to asbestos in the shipyard. Lokey admitted, however, that he worked in a large warehouse and was unaware of all the work done and products used in the warehouse, whether asbestos products were present, or whether there was any ventilation.

Dr. David H. Garabrant, expert for the defense, testified that people who work around asbestos-containing brakes are at no higher risk of developing mesothelioma than those who do not, but noted documented evidence of increased risk of mesothelioma for those who worked around shipyards, both directly with asbestos material and also in its vicinity. Dr. Victor Roggli, a pathologist presented by the defense, testified that he found amosite asbestos fibers in Lokey's lung tissue. Following his analysis of Lokey's lung fibers, he opined that Lokey's profile was more consistent with a person who had exposure to amosite asbestos at a shipyard sixty years ago than a person exposed to chrysotile brake products. Dr. Roggli admitted, however, that his investigation did not include the pleura of the lungs and that he opined that each and every exposure to asbestos above background level experienced by an individual is a substantial contributing factor in the development of mesothelioma.

. . . The jury found in favor of the estate as to negligence and awarded damages in the amount of $282,685.69. . . . Bendix and Ford have timely appealed.

The circuit court instructed the jury on proximate cause but also on five occasions instructed the jury to determine whether Ford's or Bendix' negligence was a "substantial contributing factor" to Lokey's mesothelioma. Defendants challenge the use of the substantial contributing factor language as contrary to prevailing Virginia law as to causation. The determination of whether a jury instruction accurately states the relevant law is a question of law that we review de novo. . . .

We said in *Wells v. Whitaker,* 151 S.E.2d 422, 428 (Va. 1966), that the first element of proximate cause, causation in fact, is "often described as the 'but for' or *sine qua non* rule."[2] We explained that "[t]o impose liability upon one person for damages incurred by another, it must be shown that the negligent conduct was a necessary physical antecedent of the damages." *Id.*

The requirement of but-for causation came with a caveat, however: "The 'but for' test is a useful rule of exclusion in all but one situation: where two causes concur to bring about an event and either alone *would have been sufficient* to bring about an identical result." *Id.* at 428 n. 1 (emphasis added).

In such a scenario, our law provides a means of holding a defendant liable if his or her negligence is one of multiple concurrent causes which proximately caused an injury, when any of the multiple causes would . . . each have been a sufficient cause. . . .

Causation in a mesothelioma case, however, presents a challenge for the courts beyond even our standard concurring negligence instruction. Mesothelioma is a signature disease: it was uncontroverted at trial that the cause of mesothelioma is exposure to asbestos at some point during an individual's lifetime. The long latency period of the disease, however, makes it exceedingly difficult to pinpoint when the harmful asbestos exposure occurred and, in the presence of multiple exposures, equally difficult to distinguish the causative exposure(s). . . .

Despite this lack of certainty, we task juries with determining liability in multiple exposure mesothelioma cases. Virginia statutory and case law makes clear that the Commonwealth permits recovery for parties injured by asbestos exposure, including those with mesothelioma, even when a jury must draw inferences from indirect facts to determine whether an exposure was causal. . . .

Certainly, if the traditional but-for definition of proximate cause was invoked, the injured party would virtually never be able to recover for damages arising from mesothelioma in the context of multiple exposures, because injured parties would face the difficult if not impossible task of proving that any one single source of exposure, in light of other exposures, was the sole but-for cause of the disease.

The circuit court, in an admirable attempt to offer guidance to the jury as to this point, invoked a supplemental term in its jury instructions: "substantial contributing factor." . . .

In the last several decades, with the rise of asbestos-based lawsuits, the "substantial contributing factor" instruction has become prominent in some other jurisdictions. "Substantial factor" language was also utilized in the Restatement (First) and Restatement (Second) of Torts. The phrase "substantial contributing factor" is not grounded, however, in the jurisprudence of this Court: we have not, in the history of our case law, ever invoked this language. . . .

[W]e agree with the explicit rejection of substantial contributing factor language in the recent Restatement (Third) of Torts: Liability for Physical and Emotional Harm (2010). The Restatement (Second) of Torts used substantial factor language, stating that, absent an independent but-for cause, "[i]f two forces are actively operating . . . and each of itself is sufficient to bring about harm to another, [one]

---

[2] We note that there are inconsistencies in the national legal nomenclature as to whether cause-in-fact is considered to be a subset of proximate cause or whether cause-in-fact, in addition to proximate cause (defined as additional legal restrictions as to liability), together create legal cause. We opt for the former nomenclature as it is the more widely used terminology in Virginia as well as the terminology used by the circuit court in this case.

actor's negligence may be found to be a substantial factor in bringing it about." Restatement (Second) of Torts §432 (1965).

The latest revision of the Restatement, however, deliberately abandoned this language, explaining:

> [T]he substantial-factor rubric tends to obscure, rather than to assist, explanation and clarification of the basis of [causation] decisions. The element that must be established, by whatever standard of proof, is the but-for or necessary-condition standard of this Section. Section 27 provides a rule for finding each of two acts that are elements of sufficient competing causal sets to be factual causes without employing the substantial-factor language of the prior Torts Restatements. There is no question of degree for either of these concepts.

Restatement (Third) of Torts §26, cmt. j. . . . .

The Restatement (Third) of Torts relies instead on the combination of sections 26 and 27:

§26 Factual Cause

Tortious conduct must be a factual cause of harm for liability to be imposed. Conduct is a factual cause of harm when the harm would not have occurred absent the conduct. Tortious conduct may also be a factual cause of harm under §27.

§27 Multiple Sufficient Causes

If multiple acts occur, each of which under §26 alone would have been a factual cause of the physical harm at the same time in the absence of the other act(s), each is regarded as a factual cause of the harm.

This model, as explicated in the comments, is quite consistent with our statements in *Wells* regarding concurring causation. The rationale articulated in comment c of §27 echoes the logic behind our long history of recognizing concurring causes:

> A defendant whose tortious act was fully capable of causing the plaintiff's harm should not escape liability merely because of the fortuity of another sufficient cause. . . . When two tortious multiple sufficient causes exist, to deny liability would make the plaintiff worse off due to multiple tortfeasors than would have been the case if only one of the tortfeasors had existed. Perhaps most significant is the recognition that, while *the but-for standard provided in §26 is a helpful method for identifying causes, it is not the exclusive means for determining a factual cause. Multiple sufficient causes are also factual causes* because we recognize them as such in our common understanding of causation, even if the but-for standard does not. Thus, the standard for causation in this Section comports with deep-seated intuitions about causation and fairness in attributing responsibility.

Restatement (Third) of Torts §27, cmt. c. (emphasis added). . . .

The Reporters Note to §27, comment b, specifically observes that some jurisdictions use the term "concurrent causes" rather than multiple sufficient cause. Indeed, multiple-exposure mesothelioma cases fit quite squarely with our line of concurring cause cases, "where two causes concur to bring about an event and either alone *would have been sufficient* to bring about an identical result." *Wells,* 151 S.E.2d at 428 n. 1 (emphasis added).

Unfortunately, our model jury instruction for concurring negligence invokes only general language that each is a "proximate cause" of the harm, rather than more specifically articulating the standard indicated in *Wells*. The standard that, in this case, exposure to the defendant's product alone must have been *sufficient to have caused the harm* is both an accurate articulation of our concurring cause law and perfectly plain to the average juror. This standard constitutes the cause-in-fact portion of the proximate cause requirement in concurring cause cases. The factfinder is left, having heard the nature of the exposures to each of the products at issue, as well as the medical testimony as to the requisite exposure necessary to cause mesothelioma, to determine whether the exposure attributable to each defendant was more likely than not sufficient to have caused the harm.

While it might be clearly seen in a car accident or converging fires that both acts contributed in some degree to the harm, the nature of mesothelioma leaves greater uncertainty as to which exposure or exposures in fact constituted the triggering event. This is, however, a distinction without a difference: if the jurors, after hearing the testimony and evidence, believe that a negligent exposure was more likely than not *sufficient* to have triggered the harm, then the defendant can be found liable in the same way that a jury can conclude that a driver in a multiple-car collision or the negligent party in one of two converging fires is liable.

Established Virginia law indicates that in order for acts of negligence to constitute concurring causes, it is not necessary that concurring acts occur simultaneously. This appears at first glance to be contrary to the language in the latest Restatement:

> **§27 Multiple Sufficient Causes**
>   If multiple acts occur, each of which under §26 alone would have been a factual cause of the physical harm *at the same time* in the absence of the other act(s), each is regarded as a factual cause of the harm.

Restatement (Third) of Torts §27 (emphasis added). We note, however, that the phrase "at the same time" is placed so as to modify "factual cause of the physical harm" rather than "acts occur." We thus read this to be consistent with our precedent. The acts themselves do not have to be concurrent, so long as they are "operating and sufficient to cause the harm contemporaneously." Restatement (Third) of Torts §27, cmt. e. We have held, as to mesothelioma, that the "harm" occurs not at the time of exposure but at the time when competent medical evidence indicates that the cancer first exists and causes injury. Recognizing that this date, if possible to isolate, may be decades after an injured party's exposure(s) to asbestos, *id.,* it may often be the case that any exposure sufficient to cause harm that occurred prior to the development of the cancer may constitute one of multiple sufficient causes under the Restatement and a concurring cause in Virginia.

The exposure must have been "a" sufficient cause: if more than one party caused a sufficient exposure, each is responsible. Other sufficient causes, whether innocent or arising from negligence, do not provide a defense. Excluding other exposures from the pool of multiple sufficient causes will require competent medical testimony indicating whether the timing of exposure could possibly have caused the cancer. Defendants with sufficient exposures that occur after the cancer has already developed cannot be held liable. . . .

For the foregoing reasons, we reverse and remand for further proceedings.

NOTES TO FORD MOTOR CO. v. BOOMER

1. *Characterizing Causes.* The court discussed the plaintiff's exposure to asbestos at two different workplaces, the vehicle inspection locations and the shipyard, and medical testimony about the effects of asbestos exposure. For Ford and Bendix to be liable for the plaintiff's cancer, the plaintiff must demonstrate that the exposure to Bendix brakes in Ford cars was more likely than not independently sufficient to cause the cancer. What medical testimony supports the conclusion that this is a multiple-sufficient-causes case?

2. *Limitations on Liability for Multiple Sufficient Causes.* Many courts follow the liability-limiting approach of the Restatement (Second) of Torts §432(2), which states:

> If two forces are actively operating, one because of the actor's negligence, the other not because of any misconduct on his part, and each of itself is sufficient to bring about harm to another, the actor's negligence may be found to be a substantial factor in bringing it about.

The "substantial factor" test can limit an actor's liability, since the word *may* in the rule allows a court to find that some actors whose conduct was independently sufficient to cause the harm *may not be liable* for the harm caused.

Under Restatement (Second) §433, the first concept for the substantial factor test is "the number of other factors which contribute in producing the harm and the extent of the effect which they have in producing it." If there are many causes in addition to the particular actor's conduct, or if causes other than the actor's conduct have a much greater effect in producing the harm — and particularly if both are true — that actor is less likely to be liable. Here, there appear to be two factors, exposure to the asbestos in brakes and exposure at the shipyard. The substantial factor test would invite the jury to compare the relative importance of these two exposures in producing the plaintiff's cancer. The Restatement (Second) approach suggests that there may be more than one substantial factor, as where both exposures are important enough that neither can be said to be insubstantial in effect.

3. *The Restatement (Third) Approach.* Ford Motor Co. v. Boomer illustrates an approach to multiple sufficient causes reflecting the approach of the Restatement (Third) of Torts. The court rejects the substantial factor approach in favor of §27, which asks whether each act alone would have been a factual cause of the harm at the same time if the other act had not occurred, that is, whether each was sufficient. The court acknowledges that in multiple car collision cases or in converging fires cases it might be possible for a jury to assess the relative importance or substantiality of each contributing factor. The court does not believe the substantial factor approach would work in mesothelioma cases because of the underlying medical uncertainty. As the opinion in *Ford Motor Co.* notes, the Restatement (Third) rejects the substantial factor test in all of its applications to legal cause, which are explored in more detail in Chapter 6.

4. *Multi-Party Cases Where But-for Analysis Works Well.* In cases like *Kingston* or *Ford Motor Company*, the but-for test without the multiple sufficient cause exception would protect each defendant from liability because neither defendant's conduct alone was necessary to cause the harm. There are, however, many multi-actor situations where the but-for test can establish factual causation. These are cases where neither actor's conduct was independently sufficient to cause the harm. For example, in Glomb v. Glomb, 530 A.2d 1362 (Pa. Super. Ct. 1986), a babysitter intentionally hit and injured a child. The parents knew that the babysitter had hit the child in the past but continued to hire her. In this situation, injury to the child would not have occurred if the parents had not negligently continued to hire the babysitter. Also, injury to the child would not have occurred if the babysitter had not hit the child. The but-for test would treat the babysitter's conduct and the parents' conduct as each being a cause-in-fact of the child's injury. These are not multiple sufficient causes but rather "indivisible causes," causes that are both necessary and combine to produce a single indistinguishable harm. Actors whose tortious acts combine to produce such harms are both liable to the plaintiff as long as each one's conduct was a proximate cause. Indivisible causes are discussed in greater detail in Chapter 8.

Problem
Multiple Sufficient Causes

The bottom level of a parking garage shared a wall with the basement of a store. A cloudburst caused rain to flood the bottom level of the garage to a level of seven to eight feet along the common wall, and enough water seeped through the wall to cover the floor of the store's basement. There was so much rain that the city's sewer system was inadequate to carry it away. Thus, water in the store's basement might have come from backed-up sewers as well as from the parking structure.

The store owner sued the operator of the garage, seeking damages for the flooding. The defendant answered, claiming that even if it had been negligent, its negligence was not a legal cause of the harm, because the damage would have occurred anyway due to the city's negligently designed sewer system. If the city's sewer system was negligently designed, is the garage operator's argument correct? See *Moore v. Standard Paint & Glass Co.*, 358 P.2d 33 (Colo. 1960).

Perspective: Preemptive Causes

The Restatement approach to the multiple sufficient cause cases is described in §432(2), discussed in Note 2 following Ford Motor Company v. Boomer. Professor Richard W. Wright, *Extent of Legal Responsibility*, 54 Vand. L. Rev. 1071, 1098-1099 (2001), objects that this test "does not clearly distinguish cases of duplicative causation, . . . in which the different competing forces reinforced each other, from cases of preemptive causation, in which one competing force preempted the potential causal effect of the other." If the fire from the northeast reached and destroyed the plaintiff's property before the fire from the northwest could reach it, the northwest fire was potentially sufficient to destroy the property but "was not actually sufficient since it arrived too late." The plaintiff is entitled to recover from either defendant only if both fires were actually sufficient.

A classic multiple-causes hypothetical involves two enemies of a third person who is about to set out on a long trek across the desert. The first person mixes a deadly poison into the water in the intended victim's canteen. The second, ignorant of the first person's poisoning, dumps the water from the canteen so that the trekker will die of thirst. When the victim dies of thirst, is his estate entitled to recover from either of the two enemies under the multiple-sufficient-causes rule?

C. Concert of Action

Concert of action and *concerted action* are names for a theory that sometimes permits a plaintiff who is injured by a defendant's tortious conduct to impose liability on someone else in addition to that defendant. This additional defendant's relationship to the plaintiff's harm might not satisfy the but-for test of causation, but the concerted action theory makes the additional defendant liable to the plaintiff. As will be seen in detail in Chapter 8, a theory that increases the number of defendants against whom a plaintiff can state a cause of action is helpful to plaintiffs, because it increases the chance that the plaintiff will be able to collect damages if the plaintiff wins the case. Shinn v. Allen articulates a set of criteria for determining when "concert of action" applies to the conduct of two or more actors and applies them to an unfortunately common circumstance.

SHINN v. ALLEN
984 S.W.2d 308 (Tex. Ct. App. 1998)

WILSON, J. . . .

In December 1994, a vehicle driven by Jeremy Michael Faggard, in which Allen was a passenger, collided with a vehicle driven by Robert Wayne Shinn, Gail Shinn's husband. Robert Shinn was killed in the accident, and Gail Shinn was seriously injured.

Gail Shinn sued Allen for negligence, alleging Allen substantially assisted or encouraged an intoxicated person to drive an automobile on public roads that resulted in the collision which killed Robert Shinn and injured her. Allen . . . moved for summary judgment contending he owed no duty to Gail Shinn. The summary judgment was granted. In her sole point of error, Gail Shinn alleges the trial court erred in granting Allen's motion for summary judgment because the evidence established the existence of both a duty and a question of material fact under the concert-of-action theory of liability.

. . . The summary judgment evidence consists of Allen's affidavit, his deposition, his answers to interrogatories, and a copy of the judgment in Faggard's driving-while-intoxicated case.

On the day of the accident, Faggard picked Allen up from his parents' home at approximately 3:00 p.m. to go and "hang out." Allen and Faggard were acquaintances who had met playing volleyball. Allen stated that Faggard was not a "close buddy of mine." Both Allen and Faggard were under 21 years of age; however, about an hour before the accident Faggard decided to buy some beer. Faggard and Allen went to the convenience store where Faggard bought a twelve-pack of beer. Allen did not pay for the beer or arrange for the purchase of the beer. Allen stated he did not plan on drinking that day and did not know that Faggard drank. After buying the beer, Faggard and Allen went to Faggard's house and talked and drank the beer. Allen consumed four or five beers, and Faggard consumed six or seven. Allen and Faggard did not eat anything while drinking the beer, and the last time Allen ate was at "lunchtime."

Sometime before 7:00 p.m., Allen asked Faggard to take him home because his parents wanted him home by 7:00 p.m. to eat dinner. During the ride home, Allen did not think Faggard was speeding.

The summary judgment evidence indicates Allen did not exercise any control over the operation of Faggard's vehicle. Allen affirmatively stated that he did not know what Faggard's tolerance level to alcohol was. Allen did not observe anything indicating Faggard was intoxicated before the accident. Faggard did not slur his words and was not stumbling or walking in a way that would indicate he was intoxicated. Allen, however, did state that he (Allen) was drunk. Faggard was later convicted of driving while intoxicated. Gail Shinn asserts that the summary judgment should be reversed because there is a fact issue regarding whether Allen is liable under the concert-of-action theory. The Texas Supreme Court has stated that, "whether such a theory of liability is recognized in Texas is an open question." Juhl v. Airington, 936 S.W.2d 640, 643 (Tex. 1996). A version of the theory has been articulated by Professor Keeton as follows:

> All those who, in pursuance of a common plan or design to commit a tortious act, actively take part in it, or further it by cooperation or request, or who lend aid or encouragement to the wrongdoer, or ratify and adopt the wrongdoer's acts done for their benefit, are equally liable.

CoA Rule

W. Page Keeton et al., Prosser and Keeton on the Law of Torts §46, at 323 (5th ed. 1984).

The Restatement (Second) of Torts also incorporates this principle, imposing liability on a person for the conduct of another which causes harm. Section 876 states:

> **§876 Persons Acting in Concert**
> For harm resulting to a third person from the tortious conduct of another, one is subject to liability if he
>> (a) does a tortious act in concert with the other or pursuant to a common design with him, or
>> (b) knows that the other's conduct constitutes a breach of duty and gives substantial assistance or encouragement to the other so to conduct himself, or
>> (c) gives substantial assistance to the other in accomplishing a tortious result and his own conduct, separately considered, constitutes a breach of duty to the third person.

Restatement (Second) of Torts §876 (1977).

Gail Shinn argues that the facts of this case fall under section 876(b). Subsection (b) imposes liability not for an agreement, but for substantially assisting and encouraging a wrongdoer in a tortious act. This subsection requires that the defendant have "an unlawful intent, i.e., knowledge that the other party is breaching a duty and the intent to assist that party's actions." *Juhl*, 936 S.W.2d at 644. Comment d to section 876 lists five factors that can be relevant to whether the defendant substantially assisted the wrongdoer. These include: (1) the nature of the wrongful act; (2) the kind and amount of the assistance; (3) the relation of the defendant and the actor; (4) the presence or absence of the defendant at the occurrence of the wrongful act; and (5) the defendant's state of mind. Restatement (Second) of Torts §876 cmt. d (1977).

Sub. Assist. & Enc. 5 Fact.

1. Nature of the Wrongful Act

The purpose of the concert-of-action theory is to deter antisocial or dangerous behavior that is likely to cause serious injury or death to a person or certain harm to a large number of people. It is commonly recognized that driving while intoxicated is an antisocial and dangerous behavior, likely to cause serious injury or death to a person.

2. The Kind and Amount of the Assistance

Gail Shinn relies on Cooper v. Bondoni, 841 P.2d 608 (Okla. Ct. App. 1992), to support her position. The court in *Cooper* recognized that the non-acting person must give substantial assistance or encouragement to the tortfeasor in order to affix Section 876 liability. There is no evidence Allen purchased the beer, ordered the beer, paid for the beer, encouraged Faggard to consume the beer, or encouraged Faggard to drive recklessly. Allen asked for a ride home. Allen's request was gratuitous. There is no evidence that Faggard's decision to drive in an intoxicated condition was more than his alone.

3. Relation of the Parties

There is no special relationship between Allen and Faggard, such as an employee/employer relationship, that would place one party in a position of control over the other. Allen and Faggard were just acquaintances who decided to "hang out" one afternoon.

4. Presence or Absence of the Defendant

Although we are not bound by out-of-state decisions, we find Olson v. Ische, 343 N.W.2d 284 (Minn. 1984), informative on this issue. In *Olson*, the court held that "the mere presence of the particular defendant at the commission of the wrong, or his failure to object to it, is not enough to charge him with responsibility." Id. at 289 (citing Stock v. Fife, 430 N.E.2d 845, 849 n.10 (Mass. App. Ct. 1982) (quoting William Lloyd Prosser, Handbook of the Law of Torts §46, at 292 (4th ed. 1971))). It is uncontroverted that Allen was riding in Faggard's car as a passenger when the accident occurred.

5. Defendant's State of Mind

The summary judgment evidence shows Allen stated he did not think Faggard was intoxicated. While a fact issue exists as to whether Allen had knowledge that Faggard was intoxicated, that issue alone does not create a fact issue as to whether Allen substantially assisted or encouraged Faggard. Rather, Allen's state of mind is merely one of five factors that can be relevant to whether Allen substantially assisted Faggard.

In reviewing the summary judgment evidence in the context of the above five factors, we conclude Gail Shinn did not raise a material fact issue that Allen substantially assisted or encouraged Faggard in operating the vehicle.

Gail Shinn additionally relies on three out-of-state cases to support her position. All three of these cases, however, are factually distinguishable. In Price v. Halstead, 355 S.E.2d 380, 383 (W. Va. 1987), the complaint alleged that all of the passengers were actively engaged in providing alcohol and marijuana to the driver both before and during the trip and knew that the driver was intoxicated. In Cooper v. Bondoni, the driver and the passengers had all been drinking prior to getting into the car. 841 P.2d at 608-09. According to the driver, everybody in the car encouraged and urged him to violate the law and pass a pickup in a no passing zone. In Aebischer v. Reidt, 704 P.2d 531, 532 (Or. Ct. App. 1985), the passenger contributed equally to the purchase of additional marijuana and kept refilling the "bong" which the driver continued to grab from the passenger. All of these cases are distinguishable in that the assistance or encouragement to commit the wrongful act in these cases was more direct, ongoing, and apparent than the present case.

In reviewing the above factors in the context of the summary judgment standard of review, we conclude that the evidence conclusively disproves that Allen breached the concert-of-action theory of duty to Gail Shinn. . . .

The judgment is affirmed.

NOTES TO SHINN v. ALLEN

1. *Common Plan or Objective.*   The Restatement (Second) of Torts §876 describes three situations in which one person may be held liable for harm caused by another person. They all require proof that the second person's conduct was tortious.

The most obvious case of concerted action is described in subsection 876(a). In this situation, a defendant is liable for the harm caused by the tortious conduct of another if the defendant expressly or impliedly agrees to cooperate in a particular line of conduct or to accomplish a particular result. When *A* and *B* agree to beat up and rob *C*, *A* and *B* are committing a tortious act in concert, and each is liable for the acts of the other as well as his own acts. For this theory, the acts of all of the parties acting in concert must be tortious. The Restatement offers the following example:

> *A* is drunk and disorderly on the public street. *B*, *C*, and *D*, who are all police officers, attempt to arrest *A* for the misdemeanor committed in their presence. *A* resists arrest. *B* and *C* take hold of *A*, using no more force than is reasonable under the circumstances. *A* breaks away and attempts to escape. *D* draws a pistol and shoots *A* in the back [which is unreasonable force under the circumstances].

Will *B* and *C* be found to have acted in concert with *D*? Is this common design theory applicable to the facts of Shinn v. Allen?

2. *Substantial Assistance and Knowing Tortious Conduct.*   The plaintiff in Shinn v. Allen based her claim on the second type of concerted action. According to subsection 876(b), she must prove that (1) Allen knew Faggard's conduct was tortious ("constituted a breach of duty"), and (2) Allen substantially assisted or encouraged Faggard. What evidence supports or refutes each element?

3. *Substantial Assistance and Separate Tortious Conduct.*   According to subsection 876(c), concerted action will be found when (1) a person provides substantial assistance to the other person whose tortious conduct harms the plaintiff and (2) the person's conduct, separately considered, is tortious. While the second and third types of concerted action both involve a person who gives substantial assistance to the other, the third type requires that the person and the other both act tortiously.

Problem
Concerted Action

Would two drivers engaged in drag racing be acting in concert for the purposes of the Restatement (Second) of Torts §876? Carroll and Chapman were racing their cars on a public road, in violation of a state statute, when Carroll's car hit the car that Clausen, the plaintiff, was driving. Clausen and Carroll were killed. Clausen's estate sued Chapman (and Carroll's estate), even though Chapman's car was not physically involved in the collision.

Would a precedent involving a somewhat similar problem be helpful? In Sanke v. Bechina, 576 N.E.2d 1212 (Ill. App. Ct. 1991), the defendant and the plaintiff were both passengers in the driver's car. The defendant passenger "verbally encouraged the driver to exceed the posted speed limit and to disregard a stop sign," and "used physical gestures to encourage the driver's reckless operation of the vehicle." The driver subsequently lost control of the car, killing the plaintiff passenger. Citing Restatement (Second) of Torts §876, the court found that the defendant passenger and the driver were engaged in joint tortious concerted action.

Were Carroll and Chapman acting in concert according to any of the Restatement definitions? Were their activities the same type of concerted action as the activities of the parties in *Sanke*? See Clausen v. Carroll, 684 N.E.2d 167 (Ill. App. 1997).

D. Alternative Liability

In multiple sufficient-causes cases, it is possible that conduct by *each* of the defendants could have caused the plaintiff's harm. In concerted action cases, the conduct of *all* of the defendants combined to produce the plaintiff's harm. In contrast, there are some other multiple-actor situations where all the actors have acted unreasonably but *only one or some* of them (not all of them) caused the harm. The *alternative liability theory* exposes an actor to liability even where there is a possibility that the plaintiff's harm was entirely caused by someone else. Summers v. Tice is a classic two-wrongdoer case of alternative liability and is cited in many other cases discussing this treatment of cause-in-fact. Burke v. Schaffner is a modern case that identifies the critical elements of an alternative liability case and determines whether the theory might apply where there is only one wrongdoer but the identity of that wrongdoer is difficult to establish.

SUMMERS v. TICE

199 P.2d 1 (Cal. 1948)

CARTER, J.

Each of the two defendants appeals from a judgment against them in an action for personal injuries. Pursuant to stipulation the appeals have been consolidated.

Plaintiff's action was against both defendants for an injury to his right eye and face as the result of being struck by bird shot discharged from a shotgun. The case was tried by the court without a jury and the court found that on November 20, 1945, plaintiff and the two defendants were hunting quail on the open range. Each of the defendants was armed with a 12 gauge shotgun loaded with shells containing 7½ size shot. Prior to going hunting plaintiff discussed the hunting procedure with defendants, indicating that they were to exercise care when shooting and to "keep in line." In the course of hunting plaintiff proceeded up a hill, thus placing the hunters at the points of a triangle. The view of defendants with reference to plaintiff was unobstructed and they knew his location. Defendant Tice flushed a quail which rose in flight to a ten foot elevation and flew between plaintiff and defendants. Both defendants shot at the quail, shooting in plaintiff's direction. At that time defendants were 75 yards from plaintiff. One shot struck plaintiff in his eye and another in his upper lip. Finally it was found by the court that as the direct result of the shooting by defendants the shots struck plaintiff as above mentioned and that defendants were negligent in so shooting and plaintiff was not contributorily negligent.

First, on the subject of negligence, defendant Simonson contends that the evidence is insufficient to sustain the finding on that score, but he does not point out wherein it is lacking. There is evidence that both defendants, at about the same time or one immediately after the other, shot at a quail and in so doing shot toward plaintiff who was uphill from them, and that they knew his location. That is sufficient from which the trial court could conclude that they acted with respect to plaintiff other than as persons of ordinary prudence. The issue was one of fact for the trial court. . . .

The problem presented in this case is whether the judgment against both defendants may stand. It is argued by defendants that they are not joint tortfeasors, and thus jointly and severally liable, as they were not acting in concert, and that there is not sufficient evidence to show which defendant was guilty of the negligence which caused the injuries — the shooting by Tice or that by Simonson. Tice argues that there is evidence to show that the shot which struck plaintiff came from Simonson's gun because of admissions allegedly made by him to third persons and no evidence that they came from his gun. Further in connection with the latter contention, the court failed to find on plaintiff's allegation in his complaint that he did not know which one was at fault — did not find which defendant was guilty of the negligence which caused the injuries to plaintiff.

Considering the last argument first, we believe it is clear that the court sufficiently found on the issue that defendants were jointly liable and that thus the negligence of both was the cause of the injury or to that legal effect. It found that both defendants were negligent and "That as a direct and proximate result of the shots fired by defendants, and each of them, a birdshot pellet was caused to and did lodge in plaintiff's right eye and that another birdshot pellet was caused to and did lodge in plaintiff's upper lip." In so doing the court evidently did not give credence to the admissions of Simonson to third persons that he fired the shots, which it was justified in doing. It thus determined that the negligence of both defendants was the legal cause of the injury or that both were responsible. Implicit in such finding is the assumption that the court was unable to ascertain whether the shots were from the gun of one defendant or the other or one shot from each of them. The one shot that entered plaintiff's eye was the major factor in assessing damages and that shot could not have come from the gun of both defendants. It was from one or the other only.

It has been held that where a group of persons are on a hunting party, or otherwise engaged in the use of firearms, and two of them are negligent in firing in the direction of a third person who is injured thereby, both of those so firing are liable for the injury suffered by the third person, although the negligence of only one of them could have caused the injury. The same rule has been applied in criminal cases, and both drivers have been held liable for the negligence of one where they engaged in a racing contest causing an injury to a third person. These cases speak of the action of defendants as being in concert as the ground of decision, yet it would seem they are straining that concept and the more reasonable basis appears in Oliver v. Miles [110 So. 166 (Miss. 1926)]. There two persons were hunting together. Both shot at some partridges and in so doing shot across the highway injuring plaintiff who was travelling on it. The court stated they were acting in concert and thus both were liable. The court then stated (110 So. 668): "We think that . . . each is liable for the resulting injury to the boy, although no one can say definitely who actually shot him. *To hold otherwise would be to exonerate both from liability, although each was negligent, and the injury resulted from such negligence.*" (Emphasis added.) 110 So. p.668. It is said in the Restatement: "For harm resulting to a third person from the tortious conduct of another, a person is liable if he . . . (b) knows that the other's conduct constitutes a breach of duty and gives substantial assistance or encouragement to the other so to conduct himself, or (c) gives substantial assistance to the other in accomplishing a tortious result and his own conduct, separately considered, constitutes a breach of duty to the third person." (Rest., Torts, sec. 876(b)[-](c).) Under subsection (b) the example is given: "*A* and *B* are members of a hunting party. Each of them in the presence of the other shoots across a public road at an animal this being negligent as to persons on the road. *A* hits the animal. *B*'s bullet strikes *C*, a traveler on the road. *A* is liable to *C*." (Rest., Torts, Sec. 876(b), Com., Illus. 3.) An illustration given under subsection (c) is the same as above except the factor of both defendants shooting is missing and joint liability is not imposed. It is further said that: "If two forces are actively operating, one because of the actor's negligence, the other not because of any misconduct on his part, and each of itself sufficient to bring about harm to another, the actor's negligence may be held by the jury to be a substantial factor in bringing it about." (Rest., Torts, sec. 432.) Dean Wigmore has this to say: "When two or more persons by their acts are possibly the sole cause of a harm, or when two or more acts of the same person are possibly the sole cause, and the plaintiff has introduced evidence that the one of the two persons, or the one of the same person's two acts, is culpable, then the defendant has the burden of proving that the other person, or his other act, was the sole cause of the harm. (b) . . . The real reason for the rule that each joint tortfeasor is responsible for the whole damage is the practical unfairness of denying the injured person redress simply because he cannot prove how much damage each did, when it is certain that between them they did all; let them be the ones to apportion it among themselves. Since, then, the difficulty of proof is the reason, the rule should apply whenever the harm has plural causes, and not merely when they acted in conscious concert. . . ." (Wigmore, Select Cases on the Law of Torts, §153.) Similarly Professor Carpenter has said: "[Suppose] the case where A and B independently shoot at C and but one bullet touches C's body. In such case, such proof as is ordinarily required that either A or B shot C, of course, fails. It is suggested that there should be a relaxation of the proof required of the plaintiff . . . where the injury occurs as the result of one where more than one independent force is operating, and it is impossible to determine that the force set in operation by defendant did not in fact constitute a cause of the damage, and where it may have caused the damage, but the plaintiff is unable to establish that it was a cause." (20 Cal. L. Rev. 406.)

Rule

When we consider the relative position of the parties and the results that would flow if plaintiff was required to pin the injury on one of the defendants only, a requirement that the burden of proof on that subject be shifted to defendants becomes manifest. They are both wrongdoers both negligent toward plaintiff. They brought about a situation where the negligence of one of them injured the plaintiff, hence it should rest with them each to absolve himself if he can. The injured party has been placed by defendants in the unfair position of pointing to which defendant caused the harm. If one can escape the other may also and plaintiff is remediless. Ordinarily defendants are in a far better position to offer evidence to determine which one caused the injury. . . .

In addition to that, however, it should be pointed out that the same reasons of policy and justice shift the burden to each of defendants to absolve himself if he can — relieving the wronged person of the duty of apportioning the injury to a particular defendant, apply here where we are concerned with whether plaintiff is required to supply evidence for the apportionment of damages. If defendants are independent tort feasors and thus each liable for the damage caused by him alone, and, at least, where the matter of apportionment is incapable of proof, the innocent wronged party should not be deprived of his right to redress. The wrongdoers should be left to work out between themselves any apportionment. . . .

The judgment is affirmed.

NOTES TO SUMMERS v. TICE

1. *Fair Treatment of Gaps in Information.*   Usually, a plaintiff must bring information to a trial about all of the elements of the plaintiff's cause of action. If there is a gap with regard to some aspect of required information, the plaintiff will lose the case. Summers v. Tice reverses this standard procedure. Instead of having a plaintiff suffer because of a lack of information, one or both of the defendants will bear the financial cost of losing the case. This alternative liability doctrine is based on the notion that it is fairer under some circumstances to require the negligent defendants rather than the innocent plaintiff to prove who caused the harm. As the court said, "The one shot that entered plaintiff's eye was the major factor in assessing damages and that shot could not have come from the gun of both defendants. It was from one or the other only." The court concluded, "The injured party has been placed by defendants in the unfair position of pointing to which defendant caused the harm. If one can escape, the other may also and the plaintiff is remediless." One of the reasons the usual burden of proof would be unfair in these cases is that the defendants are likely to know better than the plaintiff which one caused the harm, but may strategically withhold that information. If crucial information were unavailable to the plaintiff and also unavailable to all the defendants, would that alter the fairness of the result in Summers v. Tice?

2. *Alternative Liability Compared with Concerted Action.*   The Summers v. Tice court referred to decisions that had applied the concerted action doctrine to cases like the one before the Summers v. Tice court. The court adopted alternative liability, a different doctrine. Would the concerted action theory fit the facts of Summers v. Tice? Was there sufficient evidence for the plaintiff to establish that there was an agreement to a course of conduct or to a common objective, or that a defendant gave substantial assistance or encouragement to another who caused the harm? If two different doctrines fit the facts of a case, a party may rely on either one.

Problem
Alternative Liability

Your firm represents Vivien Hood, who recently suffered injuries from a dog bite. A senior partner has asked you to draft a memo evaluating whether the rule from Summers v. Tice would help to resolve this case.

The incident occurred upon property belonging to Ernest Hagler, who allegedly owned a dog involved in the attack. The other dog belonged to the defendant, Charles Musick, who leased a portion of the Hagler premises. Approximately a year prior to the incident, the plaintiff, Ms. Hood, had gone to the Musick residence to purchase some homegrown tomatoes from the Haglers, and they regularly sold produce from their home. On the day in question, the plaintiff, being in the neighborhood, decided to stop by and see if the Haglers had any produce to sell. Upon arriving at the Haglers, the plaintiff parked in the common driveway between the Haglers' residence and that of their lessee, Mr. Musick. She got out of the car and proceeded up the driveway to the back door, where she was surprised to see two large dogs roaming free and unrestricted.

Ms. Hood [explained] that on her previous visit she saw no dogs or any evidence of dogs, and was not aware that dogs were on the premises. At this point, according to Ms. Hood, the dogs began weaving back and forth and snapping at her. She was gradually forced back because of the animals' advance. As she turned to enter her car, she was bitten in the leg by one of the dogs.

Unfortunately, because Ms. Hood had her back to the dogs when bitten, she was unable to identify which of the two dogs bit her. As a result of this bite and complications arising therefrom, Ms. Hood was hospitalized and underwent surgery. There is evidence that both dogs had behaved aggressively toward people on other occasions, but Mr. Hagler and Mr. Musick regularly allowed the dogs to roam freely.

Ms. Hood hired your firm to represent her in a lawsuit against both Mr. Hagler and Mr. Musick. Should the dog owners bear the burden of proof with respect to causation? See Hood v. Hagler, 606 P.2d 548 (Okla. 1979).

BURKE v. SCHAFFNER
683 N.E.2d 861 (Ohio Ct. App. 1996)

TYACK, J.

On October 4, 1994, Gary Burke and his wife, Tammy Burke, filed a complaint in the Franklin County Court of Common Pleas, naming Kerri Schaffner as the lone defendant. The lawsuit arose as a result of serious injuries sustained by Gary Burke on October 26, 1993, when he was struck by a pickup truck driven by Martin Malone, with whom the Burkes settled prior to commencing litigation. The incident occurred during a party held for officers of the City of Columbus Division of Police, Eighth Precinct.

There is no dispute between the parties that the pickup truck accelerated suddenly, causing Mr. Burke to be pinned between it and a parked car. The Burkes' complaint alleged that Schaffner, who was seated directly beside the driver, negligently stepped on the accelerator as she moved over on the front seat to make room for two other passengers getting into the truck.

Prior to trial, counsel for Schaffner filed a motion for summary judgment. Appended to the motion was an affidavit in which she stated, "At no time while I was in the vehicle did my foot hit the accelerator. . . ." In their memorandum contra, the Burkes relied upon deposition testimony of Malone, which included his denial of fault and resulting conclusion that Schaffner must have stepped on the accelerator. In a decision rendered August 24, 1995, the trial court denied the motion, holding that there existed a genuine issue of material fact as to who hit the accelerator.

The case proceeded to a trial by jury on March 11, 1996. Essentially, plaintiffs' theory, based in large part upon Malone's testimony, was that Schaffner stepped on the accelerator. To the evident surprise of plaintiffs' counsel, the defense rested without calling any witnesses, including Schaffner herself. Plaintiffs' counsel unsuccessfully attempted to reopen their case or, alternatively, to call the defendant as a "rebuttal" witness.

On March 14, 1996, the jury returned a verdict in favor of Schaffner. The jury's response to an interrogatory submitted with the verdict forms indicated the jury's express finding that Schaffner was not negligent.

Gary Burke and Tammy Burke ("appellants") have timely appealed. . . .

In their first assignment of error, appellants argue that the trial court erred in failing to grant their motion for a directed verdict. Specifically, appellants reason as follows. They "proved" that Schaffner was one of only two persons who could have negligently harmed Burke. The only other potentially responsible person, Martin Malone, called by appellants as a witness, testified that he did not step on the accelerator. Thus, since Schaffner failed to present any evidence to overcome her burden to demonstrate that she did not cause the harm, appellants should have been granted a directed verdict.

In addressing this specific contention, appellants necessarily incorporate issues pertaining to the doctrine of alternative liability, the subject of their second assignment of error. Thus, we address these arguments jointly. . . .

As discussed below, the evidence, construed most strongly in favor of the defendant, Schaffner, did not support a directed verdict, as reasonable minds could reach different conclusions as to whether or not defendant was negligent.

Appellants' argument relies heavily upon the testimony of Martin Malone, who, as indicated above, unequivocally denied stepping on the accelerator. Appellants contend that the doctrine of alternative liability mandates a finding that since Schaffner did not testify or otherwise present evidence, she failed to satisfy her burden to prove that she was not negligent. Appellees counter, and the trial court so held, that the doctrine of alternative liability is not applicable to this case.

The doctrine of alternative liability was adopted by a narrow majority of the Supreme Court of Ohio in Minnich v. Ashland Oil Co. 473 N.E.2d 1199 (Ohio 1984). . . .

In this case, the trial court found alternative liability (and thus, burden shifting) to be inappropriate based upon a narrow interpretation of *Minnich*, limiting its application to cases involving multiple defendants, each of whom acted tortiously. The trial court rejected the doctrine based upon appellants' theory that only one of two persons stepped on the accelerator — either the named defendant, Kerri Schaffner, or Martin Malone, the latter of whom denied fault.

Appellants acknowledge the current status of the doctrine in Ohio, citing pertinent case law; however, they construe the case law in a manner which broadens the scope of the doctrine to include situations involving a single negligent act committed by one potentially unidentifiable person, regardless of that person's status as a party or non-party. The trial court rejected this expansion of the doctrine. We too reject such a broad interpretation. We agree with the holding of the trial court and find its reasoning to be sound. Plain language in *Minnich* lends support to this narrow interpretation:

> It should be emphasized that under this alternative liability theory, plaintiff must still prove: (1) that two or more defendants committed tortious acts, and (2) that plaintiff was injured as a proximate result of the wrongdoing of one of the defendants. Only then will the burden shift to the defendants to prove that they were not the cause of plaintiff's injuries. *This doctrine does not apply in cases where there is no proof that the conduct of more than one defendant has been tortious.* (Emphasis added.)

473 N.E.2d at 1200.

The rationale for the doctrine of alternative liability, and the burden-shifting exception, is not applicable in circumstances where only one person has acted tortiously. The Supreme Court of Ohio has consistently reiterated the rationale justifying the seldom-employed burden shifting:

[T]he reason for the exception is the unfairness of permitting tortfeasors to escape liability simply because the nature of their conduct and of the resulting injury has made it difficult or impossible to prove which of them caused the harm. . . .

Huston v. Konieczny (1990), 556 N.E.2d 505, 510 (Ohio 1990).

Schaffner argues, and the trial court agreed, that the doctrine further requires that the multiple negligent persons be named as defendants in the litigation; if all negligent actors are brought before the court, then the burden shifts to each of them to disprove causation. We agree. In *Huston*, the court was careful to note:

> In order for the burden of proof to shift from the plaintiffs under 2 Restatement of the Law 2d, Torts, Section 433B(3), all tortfeasors should be before the court, if possible. . . .

The Supreme Court of Ohio has continued to limit the application of alternative liability to "unique situations," all of which have required a plaintiff to satisfy a threshold burden of proving that "*all the defendants* acted tortiously." (Emphasis added.) Horton v. Harwick Chem. Corp., 653 N.E.2d 1196, 1203 (Ohio 1995).

Only upon a plaintiff's showing that each of the multiple defendants acted tortiously should the causation burden shift to and among the defendants, who have each created a "substantially similar risk of harm." 653 N.E.2d at 1203. That rationale simply does not apply to these facts, since appellants attempted to prove that a single tortfeasor, Schaffner, committed a single tortious act, to the exclusion of the only other potentially responsible person, Martin Malone, whom appellants did not sue and, in fact, attempted to exculpate during trial. . . .

As Ms. Schaffner was the only defendant before the court, there was no other named defendant to whom the burden could or should have shifted. The trial court properly ruled that alternative liability was inappropriate under these circumstances and, thus, properly rejected the requested jury instruction. Further, since alternative liability was not applicable, the defendant had no burden to present evidence that she did not cause the harm. As a result, the trial court did not err in overruling appellants' motion for a directed verdict, since reasonable minds could differ in concluding who, if anyone, was negligent.

The first and second assignments of error were overruled. [Other assignments of error were also overruled and the judgment was affirmed.]

NOTE TO BURKE v. SCHAFFNER

Multiple Tortious Defendants. The Restatement (Third) of Torts: Liability for Physical and Emotional Harm §28 discusses which party has the burden of proof on the issue of cause-in-fact:

§28 Burden of Proof
    (a) Subject to Subsection (b), the plaintiff has the burden to prove that the defendant's tortious conduct was a factual cause of the plaintiff's harm.
    (b) When the plaintiff sues all of multiple actors and proves that each engaged in tortious conduct that exposed the plaintiff to a risk of harm and that the tortious conduct of one or more of them caused the plaintiff's harm but the plaintiff cannot reasonably be expected to prove which actor or actors caused the harm, the burden of proof, including both production and persuasion, on factual causation is shifted to the defendants.

The unusual facts of Burke v. Shaffner describe a failed attempt by the plaintiffs to shift the burden of proof on causation to a single defendant. The plaintiffs could not establish which of two possible people caused the sudden acceleration of the truck, but they were denied the advantage of the alternative liability theory. Why was the plaintiff unable to shift the burden of proof in Burke v. Shaffner? How was that requirement met in Summers v. Tice?

Problems
The Elements of Alternative Liability

A. Because of the use of forceps during his delivery, baby Adam received permanent brain injuries. The attending physician, Dr. Cohn, diagnosed the baby's position as face down, while in fact the baby was face up. When babies are face up, the use of forceps is inappropriate. The forceps slipped off the baby's head twice while Dr. Cohn attempted to deliver the baby. Dr. Brady was called, did not ascertain the baby's position, and, using the forceps, eventually delivered the baby. The parents claimed that both doctors negligently failed to determine the baby's position and negligently used forceps by applying too much compression pressure to the baby's head, causing brain injuries. The parents settled with Dr. Cohn, and only Dr. Brady was a defendant in the trial. Should the court grant the plaintiff parents their motion to shift the burden of proof with respect to causation to Dr. Brady based on the alternative liability theory? See Battocchi v. Washington Hospital Center, 581 A.2d 759 (D.C. 1990).

B. Two brothers hosted a party at which minors consumed alcohol. The brothers and some others at the party all bought alcoholic beverages and put them in a bathtub to which all the guests had access. It is negligent per se to serve alcohol to a minor because it is contrary to state law. One minor left the party while intoxicated and drove his car carelessly, injuring the plaintiff. The plaintiff sued the brothers and the others who had brought alcohol to the party. Is alternative liability a theory on which the plaintiff may rely to shift the burden of the proof on this issue to the defendants? See Huston v. Konieczny, 556 N.E.2d 505 (Ohio 1990).

Perspective: Alternative Liability

In alternative liability cases, both tortfeasors breached a duty to the plaintiff by creating a similar risk of harm to the plaintiff, and either could have caused the harm. Only one actually harmed the plaintiff, but the plaintiff cannot determine which one. The court's solution is to allow the plaintiff to collect the full amount of the damages from either defendant, to hold them "jointly" liable. Would it be fairer to hold each liable for 50 percent of the damages? That would match the share of liability to the probability each caused the harm.

Damage rules accomplish this 50/50 split in two ways. In states where joint liability is the rule, a defendant in a case like Summers v. Tice who pays more than his share (50 percent) may sue the other defendant in a legal action called a *contribution* action and recover any overpayment. The bottom line is that each will pay 50 percent (assuming that each has sufficient funds to pay). Other states arrive at this result more directly by holding each defendant "severally" liable for his share rather than "jointly" liable for the entire amount. This avoids the need for a contribution action.

E. Market Share Liability

In some cases where a victim has been harmed by a product that was produced by a number of manufacturers to identical specifications, courts have given plaintiffs the benefit of a modified alternative liability theory. In these cases, the plaintiff has no way of identifying the sources of the product that caused the injury and thus cannot be sure that he or she has sued the actor or actors who caused the injury. Hymowitz v. Eli Lilly and Company highlights the differences between alternative liability and modified alternative liability. It also treats apportionment of responsibility under the unusual circumstances of the case. Black v. Abex considers how similar the products of a number of manufacturers must be in order to subject them to modified alternative liability claims.

HYMOWITZ v. ELI LILLY & CO.

541 N.Y.S.2d 941 (1989)

WACHTLER, C.J.

Plaintiffs in these appeals allege that they were injured by the drug diethylstilbestrol (DES) ingested by their mothers during pregnancy. They seek relief against defendant DES manufacturers. . . .

The history of the development of DES and its marketing in this country has been repeatedly chronicled. Briefly, DES is a synthetic substance that mimics the effect of estrogen, the naturally formed female hormone. It was invented in 1937 by British researchers, but never patented.

In 1941, the Food and Drug Administration (FDA) approved the new drug applications (NDA) of 12 manufacturers to market DES for the treatment of various maladies, not directly involving pregnancy. In 1947, the FDA began approving the NDAs of manufacturers to market DES for the purpose of preventing human miscarriages; by 1951, the FDA had concluded that DES was generally safe for pregnancy use, and stopped requiring the filing of NDAs when new manufacturers sought to produce the drug for this purpose. In 1971, however, the FDA banned the use of DES as a miscarriage preventative, when studies established the harmful latent effects of DES upon the offspring of mothers who took the drug. Specifically, tests indicated that DES caused vaginal adenocarcinoma, a form of cancer, and adenosis, a precancerous vaginal or cervical growth.

Although strong evidence links prenatal DES exposure to later development of serious medical problems, plaintiffs seeking relief in court for their injuries faced two formidable and fundamental barriers to recovery in this State; not only is identification of the manufacturer of the DES ingested in a particular case generally impossible, but, due to the latent nature of DES injuries, many claims were barred by the Statute of Limitations before the injury was discovered. [The statute of limitations issue has now been resolved by a change in the relevant statute.]

The identification problem has many causes. All DES was of identical chemical composition. Druggists usually filled prescriptions from whatever was on hand. Approximately 300 manufacturers produced the drug, with companies entering and leaving the market continuously during the 24 years that DES was sold for pregnancy use. The long latency period of a DES injury compounds the identification problem;

memories fade, records are lost or destroyed, and witnesses die. Thus the pregnant women who took DES generally never knew who produced the drug they took, and there was no reason to attempt to discover this fact until many years after ingestion, at which time the information is not available. . . .

The present appeals are before the court in the context of summary judgment motions. In all of the appeals defendants moved for summary judgment dismissing the complaints because plaintiffs could not identify the manufacturer of the drug that allegedly injured them. . . . The trial court denied all of these motions. . . . The Appellate Division affirmed in all respects and certified to this court the questions of whether the orders of the trial court were properly made. We answer these questions in the affirmative.

In a products liability action, identification of the exact defendant whose product injured the plaintiff is, of course, generally required. In DES cases in which such identification is possible, actions may proceed under established principles of products liability. The record now before us, however, presents the question of whether a DES plaintiff may recover against a DES manufacturer when identification of the producer of the specific drug that caused the injury is impossible. . . .

[T]he accepted tort doctrines of alternative liability and concerted action are available in some personal injury cases to permit recovery where the precise identification of a wrongdoer is impossible. However, we agree with the near unanimous views of the high State courts that have considered the matter that these doctrines in their unaltered common-law forms do not permit recovery in DES cases.

The paradigm of alternative liability is found in the case of Summers v. Tice (33 Cal. 2d 80, 199 P.2d 1). In *Summers*, plaintiff and the two defendants were hunting, and defendants carried identical shotguns and ammunition. During the hunt, defendants shot simultaneously at the same bird, and plaintiff was struck by bird shot from one of the defendants' guns. The court held that where two defendants breach a duty to the plaintiff, but there is uncertainty regarding which one caused the injury, "the burden is upon each such actor to prove that he has not caused the harm" (Restatement [Second] of Torts §433B[3]). The central rationale for shifting the burden of proof in such a situation is that without this device both defendants will be silent, and plaintiff will not recover; with alternative liability, however, defendants will be forced to speak, and reveal the culpable party, or else be held jointly and severally liable themselves. Consequently, use of the alternative liability doctrine generally requires that the defendants have better access to information than does the plaintiff, and that all possible tortfeasors be before the court. It is also recognized that alternative liability rests on the notion that where there is a small number of possible wrongdoers, all of whom breached a duty to the plaintiff, the likelihood that any one of them injured the plaintiff is relatively high, so that forcing them to exonerate themselves, or be held liable, is not unfair.

In DES cases, however, there is a great number of possible wrongdoers, who entered and left the market at different times, and some of whom no longer exist. Additionally, in DES cases many years elapse between the ingestion of the drug and injury. Consequently, DES defendants are not in any better position than are plaintiffs to identify the manufacturer of the DES ingested in any given case, nor is there any real prospect of having all the possible producers before the court. Finally, while it may be fair to employ alternative liability in cases involving only a small number of potential wrongdoers, that fairness disappears with the decreasing probability that any one of the defendants actually caused the injury. This is particularly true when applied to DES where the chance that a particular producer caused the injury is often very remote. Alternative liability, therefore, provides DES plaintiffs no relief.

Nor does the theory of concerted action, in its pure form, supply a basis for recovery. This doctrine, seen in drag racing cases, provides for joint and several liability on the part of all defendants having an understanding, express or tacit, to participate in "a common plan or design to commit a tortious act" (Prosser and Keeton, Torts §46, at 323 [5th ed. 1984]). As . . . the present record reflects, drug companies were engaged in extensive parallel conduct in developing and marketing DES. There is nothing in the record, however, beyond this similar conduct to show any agreement, tacit or otherwise, to market DES for pregnancy use without taking proper steps to ensure the drug's safety. Parallel activity, without more, is insufficient to establish the agreement element necessary to maintain a concerted action claim. Thus this theory also fails in supporting an action by DES plaintiffs.

In short, extant common-law doctrines, unmodified, provide no relief for the DES plaintiff unable to identify the manufacturer of the drug that injured her. This is not a novel conclusion; in the last decade a number of courts in other jurisdictions also have concluded that present theories do not support a cause of action in DES cases. Some courts, upon reaching this conclusion, have declined to find any judicial remedy for the DES plaintiffs who cannot identify the particular manufacturer of the DES ingested by their mothers. Other courts, however, have found that some modification of existing doctrine is appropriate to allow for relief for those injured by DES of unknown manufacture.

We conclude that the present circumstances call for recognition of a realistic avenue of relief for plaintiffs injured by DES. . . .

Indeed, it would be inconsistent with the reasonable expectations of a modern society to say to these plaintiffs that because of the insidious nature of an injury that long remains dormant, and because so many manufacturers, each behind a curtain, contributed to the devastation, the cost of injury should be borne by the innocent and not the wrongdoers. This is particularly so where the Legislature consciously created these expectations by reviving hundreds of DES cases. Consequently, the ever-evolving dictates of justice and fairness, which are the heart of our common-law system, require formation of a remedy for injuries caused by DES.

We stress, however, that the DES situation is a singular case, with manufacturers acting in a parallel manner to produce an identical, generically marketed product, which causes injury many years later, and which has evoked a legislative response reviving previously barred actions. Given this unusual scenario, it is more appropriate that the loss be borne by those that produced the drug for use during pregnancy, rather than by those who were injured by the use, even where the precise manufacturer of the drug cannot be identified in a particular action. We turn then to the question of how to fairly and equitably apportion the loss occasioned by DES, in a case where the exact manufacturer of the drug that caused the injury is unknown.

The past decade of DES litigation has produced a number of alternative approaches to resolve this question. Thus, in a sense, we are now in an enviable position; the efforts of other courts provided examples for contending with this difficult issue, and enough time has passed so that the actual administration and real effects of these solutions now can be observed. With these useful guides in hand, a path may be struck for our own conclusion. . . .

A [narrow] basis for liability, tailored . . . closely to the varying culpableness of individual DES producers, is the market share concept. First judicially articulated by the California Supreme Court in Sindell v. Abbott Labs. [607 P.2d 924 (1980)], variations upon this theme have been adopted by other courts. In *Sindell*, the court synthesized the market share concept by modifying the Summers v. Tice alternative liability rationale in two ways. It first loosened the requirement that all possible wrongdoers be before the court, and instead made a "substantial share" sufficient. The court then held that each defendant who could not prove that it did not actually injure plaintiff would be liable according to that manufacturer's market share. The court's central justification for adopting this approach was its belief that limiting a defendant's liability to its market share will result, over the run of cases, in liability on the part of a defendant roughly equal to the injuries the defendant actually caused.

In the recent case of Brown v. Superior Ct., 44 Cal. 3d 1049, 245 Cal. Rptr. 412, 751 P.2d 470, the California Supreme Court resolved some apparent ambiguity in Sindell v. Abbott Labs., and held that a manufacturer's liability is several only, and, in cases in which all manufacturers in the market are not joined for any reason, liability will still be limited to market share, resulting in a less than 100% recovery for a plaintiff. Finally, it is noteworthy that determining market shares under Sindell v. Abbott Labs. proved difficult and engendered years of litigation. After attempts at using smaller geographical units, it was eventually determined that the national market provided the most feasible and fair solution, and this national market information was compiled. . . .

Turning to the structure to be adopted in New York, we heed both the lessons learned through experience in other jurisdictions and the realities of the mass litigation of DES claims in this State. Balancing these considerations, we are led to the conclusion that a market share theory, based upon a national market, provides the best solution. As California discovered, the reliable determination of any market smaller than the national one likely is not practicable. Moreover, even if it were possible, of the hundreds of cases in the New York courts, without a doubt there are many in which the DES that allegedly caused injury was ingested in another State. Among the thorny issues this could present, perhaps the most daunting is the spectre that the particular case could require the establishment of a separate market share matrix. We feel that this is an unfair, and perhaps impossible burden to routinely place upon the litigants in individual cases. . . .

Consequently, for essentially practical reasons, we adopt a market share theory using a national market. We are aware that the adoption of a national market will likely result in a disproportion between the liability of individual manufacturers and the actual injuries each manufacturer caused in this State. Thus our market share theory cannot be founded upon the belief that, over the run of cases, liability will approximate causation in this State. Nor does the use of a national market provide a reasonable link between liability and the risk created by a defendant to a particular plaintiff. Instead, we choose to apportion liability so as to correspond to the over-all culpability of each defendant, measured by the amount of risk of injury each defendant created to the public-at-large. Use of a national market is a fair method, we believe, of apportioning defendants' liabilities according to their total culpability in marketing DES for use during pregnancy. Under the circumstances, this is an equitable way to provide plaintiffs with the relief they deserve, while also rationally distributing the responsibility for plaintiffs' injuries among defendants.

To be sure, a defendant cannot be held liable if it did not participate in the marketing of DES for pregnancy use; if a DES producer satisfies its burden of proof of showing that it was not a member of the market of DES sold for pregnancy use, disallowing exculpation would be unfair and unjust. Nevertheless, because liability here is based on the over-all risk produced, and not causation in a single case, there should be no exculpation of a defendant who, although a member of the market producing DES for pregnancy use, appears not to have caused a particular plaintiff's injury. It is merely a windfall for a producer to escape liability solely because it manufactured a more identifiable pill, or sold only to certain drugstores. These fortuities in no way diminish the culpability of a defendant for marketing the product, which is the basis of liability here.

Finally, we hold that the liability of DES producers is several only, and should not be inflated when all participants in the market are not before the court in a particular case. We understand that, as a practical matter, this will prevent some plaintiffs from recovering 100% of their damages. However, we eschewed exculpation to prevent the fortuitous avoidance of liability, and thus, equitably, we decline to unleash the same forces to increase a defendant's liability beyond its fair share of responsibility. . . .

Accordingly, in each case the order of the Appellate Division should be affirmed.

NOTES TO HYMOWITZ v. ELI LILLY & CO.

1. *Identifying Defendants.* The causation problem in *Hymowitz* is similar to that in the alternative liability cases. In *Hymowitz*, each defendant was negligent, but some did not cause harm to the plaintiff (because the plaintiff's mother could not have taken pills made by every manufacturer). In Summers v. Tice, the classic alternative liability case, and in cases following that rule, only one negligent defendant harms the plaintiff, but the plaintiff does not know which one. Why are the plaintiffs unable to use the but-for test for causation to identify defendants whose conduct was related to their injuries? How do the DES cases and Summers v. Tice compare in this regard?

2. *Alternative Liability.* Because the identification problems are so similar, the court first considered the alternative liability theory, which shifts the burden of proof to the defendants when the plaintiff cannot identify which defendant caused the harm, all defendants engaged in tortious conduct, all defendants were included in the suit, and all defendants' conduct presented the same risk. Evaluating these requirements of the alternative liability doctrine, why does traditional alternative liability fail to provide a pro-plaintiff solution to the DES situation?

The *Hymowitz* court noted that in a case like Summers v. Tice, the likelihood of imposing responsibility on a defendant who actually did cause harm is "relatively high," but that in DES cases that likelihood is less. Does the court provide a quantitative explanation of how high the likelihood should be in order for alternative liability to be fair? Would being wrong about one out of two defendants be different from being wrong about ten out of twenty defendants?

3. *Concerted Action.* If the defendant drug manufacturers agreed to manufacture and market their products in the same negligent way, they might be held to have acted in concert. The *Hymowitz* court found no evidence of an agreement.

Would either of the other bases for the concerted action doctrine found in Restatement (Second) of Torts §876(b) or (c) apply in this case?

4. *Apportionment of Liability.* The *Hymowitz* court states that each defendant's liability will be "several only." In multiple-defendant cases, as will be seen in Chapter 8, some states make each liable defendant jointly responsible for the plaintiff's full damages. The plaintiff cannot collect more than the full amount but can choose which defendant will pay. This rule is called *joint and several liability*. Other states apply *several liability*, making each defendant responsible for only an individual share of the plaintiff's total damages. In a lawsuit to which *Hymowitz* applied, how would it affect the amount of damages a plaintiff could recover if she did not sue all of the defendants who might have caused her harm?

5. *Relevant Market.* The damages amount for which each defendant is individually liable is based on shares of the relevant market, so the definition of the market is highly important. Courts take different approaches to reflect the geographic scope of the market, whether the manufacturers sell to particular types of customers, and the defendants' ability to exclude themselves from the relevant market by proving that they did not sell in the geographic market or to customers like the plaintiff.

In Collins v. Eli Lilly & Co., 342 N.W.2d 37 (Wis. 1984), a defendant's liability was based on the amount of risk it created that a plaintiff would be harmed by DES, with market shares treated as relevant to determining shares of risk.

In Martin v. Abbott Labs., 689 P.2d 368 (Wash. 1984), defendants were permitted to exculpate themselves by showing that they did not manufacture the DES that harmed a plaintiff. Unexculpated defendants were treated as having equal market shares totaling 100 percent, but each defendant could rebut that presumption. If a defendant did exculpate itself, shares of remaining defendants were increased to provide a total recovery to the plaintiff.

How does the *Hymowitz* approach differ from these earlier efforts?

Statute: INFANCY, INSANITY

N.Y. C.P.L.R. 208 (2017)

If a person entitled to commence an action is under a disability because of infancy or insanity at the time the cause of action accrues, and the time otherwise limited for commencing the action is three years or more and expires no later than three years after the disability ceases, or the person under the disability dies, the time within which the action must be commenced shall be extended to three years after the disability ceases or the person under the disability dies, whichever event first occurs; if the time otherwise limited is less than three years, the time shall be extended by the period of disability. . . .

Statute: ACTIONS TO BE COMMENCED WITHIN THREE YEARS . . .

N.Y. C.P.L.R. 214(5) (2017)

The following actions must be commenced within three years: . . .

  5. an action to recover damages for a personal injury. . . .

Statute: CERTAIN ACTION TO BE COMMENCED WITHIN
THREE YEARS OF DISCOVERY

N.Y. C.P.L.R. 214-c(1), (2), (6) (2017)

1. In this section: "exposure" means direct or indirect exposure by absorption, contact, ingestion, inhalation, implantation or injection.

2. Notwithstanding the provisions of section 214, the three year period within which an action to recover damages for personal injury or injury to property caused by the latent effects of exposure to any substance or combination of substances, in any form, upon or within the body or upon or within property must be commenced shall be computed from the date of discovery of the injury by the plaintiff or from the date when through the exercise of reasonable diligence such injury should have been discovered by the plaintiff, whichever is earlier. . . .

6. This section shall be applicable to acts, omissions or failures occurring prior to, on or after July first, nineteen hundred eighty-six, except that this section shall not be applicable to any act, omission or failure:

(a) which occurred prior to July first, nineteen hundred eighty-six, and

(b) which caused or contributed to an injury that either was discovered or through the exercise of reasonable diligence should have been discovered prior to such date, and

(c) an action for which was or would have been barred because the applicable period of limitation had expired prior to such date.

NOTES TO STATUTES

1. *Statute of Limitations in* **Hymowitz.**   The defendants offered two defenses in *Hymowitz.* The first was that the plaintiff could not identify which defendant had caused the harm. This issue was resolved by adoption of the modified alternative liability rule and market share liability. The second defense was that the statute of limitations had run. According to the New York statute of limitations, N.Y. C.P.L.R. 214, personal injury actions must be brought within three years of the time "the cause of action accrues." In New York, the action generally accrues when the defendant breaches a duty to the plaintiff, causing harm to the plaintiff. New York C.P.L.R. 208 modified that rule for children, allowing them to bring actions up to three years from the time when they reach the age of 21.

Mindy Hymowitz was born on December 11, 1954, and reached the age of 21 in 1975. She alleged that she developed cancer as a result of prenatal exposure to DES taken by her mother in 1954. Mindy Hymowitz's cancer symptoms first appeared in 1979. She had been damaged by her mother's exposure to DES, but the symptoms did not appear until Ms. Hymowitz was 24 or 25. Under the rules in N.Y. C.P.L.R. 214 and 208, she could not sue after she reached the age of 24. Because she did not discover the injury in time to sue, she was barred from recovery.

In 1986, the New York Legislature passed specific "revival" legislation extending the statute of limitations for plaintiffs who had injuries resulting from exposures to DES, asbestos, tungsten-carbide, chlordane, and polyvinyl chloride and whose right to sue had expired because of the general statute of limitations. Mindy Hymowitz sued immediately after this revival statute was passed.

2. *Statutes of Limitations Based on Discovery.* Many states' statutes of limitations start the time clock after the time of discovery of the injury by the plaintiff rather than the time the injury occurs. See Chapter 7, Defenses, where statutes of limitations are discussed in detail. When the New York Legislature adopted the revival statute allowing Mindy Hymowitz to sue, it also adopted a "discovery rule" for some types of injuries, codified in N.Y. C.P.L.R. 214-c, above. The law governing the period of time in which one must bring suit in New York continues to evolve. In 2002, a New York trial court held that N.Y. C.P.L.R. 214-c was preempted, in part, by federal law. See Ruffing ex rel. Calton v. Union Carbide Corp., 746 N.Y.S.2d 798 (N.Y. Sup. 2002). Why does that New York statute not apply to Mindy Hymowitz's claim?

Perspective: Shifting Burden of Scientific Proof

Plaintiffs often have difficulty proving that a drug or other product has a dangerous side effect. The manufacturer is in a much better position than the plaintiff to organize and support the kind of epidemiological research necessary to demonstrate those side effects. In alternative liability cases and modified alternative liability cases, courts shift the burden of proof with respect to causation to the defendants, all of whom engaged in tortious conduct to someone, to prove they did not cause the harm to the particular plaintiff. A similar rule could apply to manufacturers of products. Courts could shift the burden of proof of causation in cases involving injuries from harmful products to the manufacturers, who can better conduct the research. Do the same equitable justifications that support shifting the burden of proof in alternative and modified alternative liability cases support this proposal? See generally Mark Geistfeld, *Scientific Uncertainty and Causation in Tort Law*, 54 Vand. L. Rev. 1011 (2001).

BLACK v. ABEX CORP.

603 N.W.2d 182 (N.D. 1999)

KAPSNER, J.

Rochelle Black appeals from a summary judgment dismissing her wrongful death and survival claims premised upon market share or alternative liability against numerous asbestos manufacturers. Concluding Black has failed to raise a genuine issue of material fact which would preclude summary judgment, we affirm.

Rochelle Black's husband, Markus, served in the Air Force as an auto mechanic from 1971 to 1986. He died of lung cancer in 1991. Black sued forty-eight asbestos manufacturers, alleging her husband's death had been caused by his occupational exposure to asbestos-containing products. Included in her complaint were claims based upon market share and alternative liability. . . .

Black asserts the district court erred in dismissing her claims based upon market share liability. She argues market share liability is a viable tort theory under North Dakota law and its application is appropriate under the facts of this case.

The genesis of market share liability lies in the California Supreme Court's decision in Sindell v. Abbott Laboratories, 26 Cal. 3d 588, 163 Cal. Rptr. 132, 607 P.2d 924 (1980). In *Sindell*, the court held that women who suffered injuries resulting from their mothers' ingestion of the drug DES during pregnancy could sue DES manufacturers, even though the plaintiffs could not identify the specific manufacturer of the DES each of their respective mothers had taken. The court fashioned a new form of liability which relaxed traditional causation requirements, allowing a plaintiff to recover upon showing that she could not identify the specific manufacturer of the DES which caused her injury, that the defendants produced DES from an identical formula, and that the defendants manufactured a "substantial share" of the DES the plaintiff's mother might have taken. The court held each defendant would be liable for a proportionate share of the judgment based upon its share of the relevant market, unless it demonstrated it could not have made the product which caused the plaintiff's injury.

The essential elements of market share liability are summarized in W. Page Keeton et al., Prosser and Keeton on the Law of Torts, §103, at 714 (5th ed. 1984):

> The requirements for market-share liability seem to be: (1) injury or illness occasioned by a fungible product (identical-type product) made by all of the defendants joined in the lawsuit; (2) injury or illness due to a design hazard, with each having been found to have sold the same type product in a manner that made it unreasonably dangerous; (3) inability to identify the specific manufacturer of the product or products that brought about the plaintiff's injury or illness; and (4) joinder of enough of the manufacturers of the fungible or identical product to represent a substantial share of the market.

The overwhelming majority of courts which have addressed the issue have held market share liability is inappropriate in cases alleging injury from exposure to asbestos. The most oft-cited rationale is that asbestos is not a fungible product, as evidenced by the wide variety of asbestos-containing products, the varying types and amounts of asbestos in those products, and the varying degrees of risk posed by those products. The leading treatise recognizes:

> [I]t can reasonably be argued that it would not be appropriate to apply this fungible product concept to asbestos-containing products because they are by no means identical since they contain widely varying amounts of asbestos.

Prosser, supra, §103, at 714.

Black essentially concedes market share liability is inappropriate in a "shotgun" asbestos case, where the plaintiff is alleging injury from exposure to many different types of asbestos products. Black asserts, however, market share liability may be appropriate when the plaintiff seeks to hold liable only manufacturers of one type of asbestos-containing product. Relying upon Wheeler v. Raybestos-Manhattan, 8 Cal. App. 4th 1152, 11 Cal. Rptr. 2d 109 (1992), Black asserts she should be allowed to proceed in her market share claims against the manufacturers of asbestos-containing "friction products," including brake and clutch products. In *Wheeler*, the California Court of Appeal held a plaintiff could proceed on a market share theory against manufacturers of asbestos-containing brake pads. The court overturned the trial court's order granting a nonsuit in favor of the manufacturers, concluding the plaintiff's offer of proof sufficiently alleged that the brake pads, although not identical, were "fungible" because they contained percentages of asbestos within a "restricted range" of between forty and sixty percent and posed nearly equivalent risks of harm.

Black requests that we recognize market share liability as a viable tort theory under North Dakota law. Black further requests that we follow *Wheeler* and hold that automotive "friction products," including asbestos-containing brake and clutch products, are sufficiently fungible to support a market share claim. . . .

This Court has never addressed whether market share liability is recognized under North Dakota tort law. Other courts faced with the question have reached varying conclusions on the general availability of this novel remedy. We find it unnecessary to resolve this general issue because we conclude, assuming market share liability were recognized in this state, summary judgment was still appropriate based upon the record in this case.

The dispositive question presented is whether Black has raised a genuine issue of material fact on the issue of fungibility. Market share liability is premised upon the fact that the defendants have produced identical (or virtually identical) defective products which carry equivalent risks of harm. Accordingly, under the market share theory, it is considered equitable to apportion liability based upon the percentage of products each defendant contributed to the entire relevant market.

This reasoning hinges, however, upon each defendant's product carrying an equal degree of risk. As the Supreme Court of Oklahoma explained in Case [v. Fiberboard Corp., 743 P.2d 1062, 1066 (Okla. 1987)]:

> In the *Sindell* case, and those following it, it was determined that public policy considerations supporting recovery in favor of an innocent plaintiff against negligent defendants would allow the application of a theory of liability which shifted the burden of proof of causation from plaintiff to defendants. However, as previously stated, that theory was crafted in a situation where each potential defendant shared responsibility for producing a product which carried with it a singular risk factor. The theory further provided that each potential defendant's liability would be proportional to that defendant's contribution of risk to the market in which the plaintiff was injured. This situation thus provided a balance between the rights of the defendants and the rights of the plaintiffs. A balance being achieved, public policy considerations were sufficient to justify the application of the market share theory of liability.

Similar reasoning was employed by the Supreme Court of Ohio in Goldman [v. Johns-Manville Sales Corp., 514 N.E.2d 691, 701 (1987)]:

> Crucial to the *Sindell* court's reasoning was this fact: there was no difference between the risks associated with the drug as marketed by one company or another, and as all DES sold presented the same risk of harm, there was no inherent unfairness in holding the companies accountable based on their share of the DES market.

Numerous other courts have stressed the importance of a singular risk factor in market share cases.

Unless the plaintiff can demonstrate that the defendants' products created a "singular risk factor," the balance between the rights of plaintiffs and defendants evaporates and it is no longer fair nor equitable to base liability upon each defendant's share of the relevant market. The rationale underlying market share liability, as developed in *Sindell*, is that it did not matter which manufacturer's product the plaintiff's mother actually ingested; because all DES was chemically identical, the same harm would have occurred. Thus, any individual manufacturer's product would have caused the identical injury, and it was through mere fortuity that any one manufacturer did not produce the actual product ingested. Under these circumstances, viewing the overall DES market and all injuries caused thereby, it may be presumed each manufacturer's products will produce a percentage of those injuries roughly equivalent to its percentage of the total DES market. As the *Sindell* court recognized, "[u]nder this approach, each manufacturer's liability would approximate its responsibility for the injuries caused by its own products." *Sindell*, 163 Cal. Rptr. 132, 607 P.2d at 937.

In order to prevail on its market share claims, Black would therefore have to demonstrate that the asbestos-containing "friction products" her husband was exposed to carried equivalent degrees of risk. Black asserts this problem has been "disposed of" by the holding in *Wheeler*. Although *Wheeler* recognized that non-identical products may give rise to market share liability if they contain roughly equivalent quantities of a single type of asbestos fiber, the court did not hold that all asbestos-containing friction brake products in all cases will be considered fungible. In fact, the court in *Wheeler* indicated that such products must carry a nearly equivalent risk of harm to support market share liability. Furthermore, *Wheeler* was a reversal of a nonsuit based upon an offer of proof made by the plaintiff. The court stressed its holding was narrow: the plaintiffs had not proven the elements of a market share case, but were merely being afforded the opportunity to prove it. Clearly, *Wheeler* does not serve as evidence of fungibility and equivalent risks of harm of the products in this case.

Black points to uncontroverted evidence in this record that the four remaining defendants produced friction products which contained between seven and seventy-five percent asbestos fibers. This is a far greater range than the forty to sixty percent the *Wheeler* court considered "roughly comparable" for purposes of fungibility under *Sindell*. It is closer to the fifteen to one-hundred percent range which the Supreme Court of Ohio held precluded market share liability as a matter of law. It seems obvious that a product which contains seventy-five percent asbestos would create a greater risk of harm than one which contains only seven percent. Absent introduction of expert evidence demonstrating that in spite of the differences the products would produce equivalent risks of harm, application of market share liability would be inappropriate.

Black failed to present competent, admissible evidence from which a fact finder could determine the "friction products" her husband was exposed to carried equivalent risks of harm and were fungible under *Sindell*. Accordingly, summary judgment was appropriate. . . .

NOTES TO BLACK v. ABEX CORP.

1. *Elements of Modified Alternative Liability.* The court in Black v. Abex Corp. refers to a treatise to identify the four elements of modified alternative liability, also called market share liability. Compare these to the four elements of regular alternative liability described in Summers v. Tice and Burke v. Schaffner. One difference is the area of activity to which this theory applies. While alternative liability is a general rule applying to a broad range of activities, modified alternative liability has been applied only to cases involving unreasonably dangerous products. Aside from that difference, how are the elements changed?

2. *Fungibility of Products and Market Share Liability.* The court in Black v. Abex Corp. declined to apply the modified alternative liability theory because the requirement that the products of the different manufacturers be fungible was not met. Even though all of the defendant manufacturers made friction brake products containing asbestos, the composition of the products was different. The different amounts of asbestos in the different manufacturers' products meant that the products created different risks for users. Compare this to the DES case, where all manufacturers used the same formula for the drug.

Problem
Modified Alternative Liability

In Shackil v. Lederle Laboratories, 561 A.2d 511 (N.J. 1989), the infant plaintiff developed brain damage from an injection of diphtheria-pertussis-tetanus vaccine, commonly known a DPT vaccine. The parents sued 13 years later, when they became aware of the link between the pertussis portion of the vaccine and the brain damage. After this lapse of time, the manufacturer of the vaccine, which was assumed to have been defective, could not be identified.

Each manufacturer of DPT made the vaccine by a different process that was protected by patent or trade secret law and was separately licensed by the Food and Drug Administration. Most used a "whole cell" manufacturing process for the pertussis portion, which causes serious adverse reactions once in every 110,000 cases. One used a "split cell" process that reduced those risks. Any one of the manufacturers might have been the source of the vaccine injected into the plaintiff.

Should modified alternative liability apply to this case? Should the doctrine apply just to the manufacturers of the whole-cell vaccine?

Perspective: Fungibility and Market Share Liability

One way in which modified alternative liability cases differ from alternative liability cases is that all of the defendants who could have caused the harm to the plaintiff are not included in the lawsuit in a modified liability case. A rule of joint liability, which made either defendant in Summers v. Tice liable for the entire amount of the plaintiff's damages, could be imposed in modified alternative liability cases, but it does not seem as fair. In an industry with 50 or 200 manufacturers, one small firm might have to foot the bill for all the rest. It seems that a larger producer, whose similar product injured more people, should pay more than the small producer. Contribution rules do not reallocate all of the losses in proportion to sales because all of the producers may not have been included in the suit and may be unavailable to sue. Even if they are available, an even division of the liability would not apportion damages in proportion to the probability that each caused the harm. Market share liability cleverly resolves this problem. How is the fungibility requirement, the rule that each defendant created similar risks, related to the fairness of the market share solution?

F. Liability for Lost Chance of Recovery or for Increased Risk of Eventual Harm

Because scientific knowledge is always increasing, plaintiffs have become able to present more and more detailed evidence about causation, particularly in medical malpractice cases. Experts can testify that a doctor's deviation from the professional standard deprived a patient of a small chance of recovery or placed the patient in some small peril of a future adverse consequence. The ability to prove this type of fact by a preponderance of the evidence has required tort law to confront issues that were unknown in an earlier time — when no expert was able to testify, for example, that proper intervention would have changed a very sick person's likelihood of death from, say, 100 percent to 80 percent.

Cases where a doctor acts negligently but the patient would likely have suffered some ultimate harm even with good medical treatment pose serious problems under typical causation doctrines. Under traditional principles, a plaintiff could recover only by proving that the adverse consequence (for example, death or disability) was caused by the doctor's error. This meant that where there was a more than 50 percent chance that the adverse consequence would have happened without the doctor's mistake, the doctor would be free from liability. If the patient's ultimate consequence was likely, by a preponderance of the evidence, to have happened regardless of the doctor's conduct, the doctor's conduct was not treated as a cause of that condition.

In Matsuyama v. Birnbaum, a patient's estate could prove only that the defendant's negligent conduct deprived the patient of a 37.5 percent chance of survival. The court adopts a common resolution that allows recovery for "loss of chance," even when the chance is less than 50 percent. Petriello v. Kalman allows recovery for a predicted consequence of the defendant's conduct, even though the likelihood of the occurrence is small.

MATSUYAMA v. BIRNBAUM
890 N.E.2d 819 (Mass. 2008)

MARSHALL, C.J.

We are asked to determine whether Massachusetts law permits recovery for a "loss of chance" in a medical malpractice wrongful death action, where a jury found that the defendant physician's negligence deprived the plaintiff's decedent of a less than even chance of surviving cancer. We answer in the affirmative. . . .

[I]n response to a special jury question . . . the jury awarded damages for loss of chance, which they calculated as follows: they awarded $875,000 as "full" wrongful death damages, and found that Matsuyama was suffering from stage 2 adenocarcinoma at the time of [the defendant's] initial negligence and had a 37.5% chance of survival at that time. They awarded the plaintiff "final" loss of chance damages of $328,125 ($875,000 multiplied by .375).

[The defendant appealed, asserting, among other things, that loss of chance was not cognizable under Massachusetts law.] Although we address the issue for the first time today, a substantial and growing majority of the States that have considered the question have indorsed the loss of chance doctrine, in one form or another, in medical malpractice actions. We join that majority to ensure that the fundamental aims and principles of our tort law remain fully applicable to the modern world of sophisticated medical diagnosis and treatment.

The development of the loss of chance doctrine offers a window into why it is needed. The doctrine originated in dissatisfaction with the prevailing "all or nothing" rule of tort recovery. Under the all or nothing rule, a plaintiff may recover damages only by showing that the defendant's negligence more likely than not caused the ultimate outcome, in this case the patient's death; if the plaintiff meets this burden, the plaintiff then recovers 100% of her damages. Thus, if a patient had a 51% chance of survival, and the negligent misdiagnosis or treatment caused that chance to drop to zero, the estate is awarded *full* wrongful death damages. On the other hand, if a patient had a 49% chance of survival, and the negligent misdiagnosis or treatment caused that chance to drop to zero, the plaintiff receives nothing. So long as the patient's chance of survival before the physician's negligence was less than even, it is logically impossible for her to show that the physician's negligence was the but-for cause of her death, so she can recover nothing. Thus, the all or nothing rule provides a "blanket release from liability for doctors and hospitals any time there was less than a 50 percent chance of survival, regardless of how flagrant the negligence."

As many courts and commentators have noted, the all or nothing rule is inadequate to advance the fundamental aims of tort law. . . . The all or nothing rule "fails to deter" medical negligence because it immunizes "whole areas of medical practice from liability." . . . It fails to provide the proper incentives to ensure that the care patients receive does not slip below the "standard of care and skill of the average member of the profession practising the specialty." And the all or nothing rule fails to ensure that victims, who incur the real harm of losing their opportunity for a better outcome, are fairly compensated for their loss. . . .

Courts adopting the loss of chance doctrine also have noted that, because a defendant's negligence effectively made it impossible to know whether the person would have achieved a more favorable outcome had he received the appropriate standard of care, it is particularly unjust to deny the person recovery for being unable "to demonstrate to an absolute certainty what would have happened in circumstances that the wrongdoer did not allow to come to pass."

. . . The defendants argue that the loss of chance doctrine "lowers the threshold of proof of causation" by diluting the preponderance of the evidence standard that "has been the bedrock of the Massachusetts civil justice system." . . . [I]n a case involving loss of chance, as in any other negligence context, a plaintiff must establish by a preponderance of the evidence that the defendant caused his injury.

However, "injury" need not mean a patient's death. Although there are few certainties in medicine or in life, progress in medical science now makes it possible, at least with regard to certain medical conditions, to estimate a patient's probability of survival to a reasonable degree of medical certainty. That probability of survival is part of the patient's condition. When a physician's negligence diminishes or destroys a patient's chance of survival, the patient has suffered real injury. The patient has lost something of great value: a chance to survive, to be cured, or otherwise to achieve a more favorable medical outcome.

Recognizing loss of chance as a theory of injury is consistent with our law of causation, which requires that plaintiffs establish causation by a preponderance of the evidence. In order to prove loss of chance, a plaintiff must prove by a preponderance of the evidence that the physician's negligence caused the plaintiff's likelihood of achieving a more favorable outcome to be diminished. That is, the plaintiff must prove by a preponderance of the evidence that the physician's negligence caused the plaintiff's injury, where the injury consists of the diminished likelihood of achieving a more favorable medical outcome. The loss of chance doctrine, so delineated, makes no amendment or exception to the burdens of proof applicable in all negligence claims. . . .

The key is the reliability of the evidence available to the fact finder. In earlier periods, Massachusetts courts grappling with what we would now call loss of chance claims often lacked reliable expert evidence of what the patient's chances of survival or recovery would have been absent the alleged negligence. More recently . . . at least for certain conditions, medical science has progressed to the point that physicians can gauge a patient's chances of survival to a reasonable degree of medical certainty, and indeed routinely use such statistics as a tool of medicine. Reliable modern techniques of gathering and analyzing medical data have made it possible for fact finders to determine based on expert testimony — rather than speculate based on insufficient evidence — whether a negligent failure to diagnose a disease injured a patient by preventing the disease from being treated at an earlier stage, when prospects were more favorable. The availability of such expert evidence on probabilities of survival makes it appropriate to recognize loss of chance as a form of injury. Through appropriate expert evidence, a plaintiff in a medical malpractice case may be able to sustain her burden of showing that, as a result of defendant's negligence, a decedent suffered a diminished likelihood of achieving a more favorable medical outcome.

We are unmoved by the defendants' argument that "the ramifications of adoption of loss of chance are immense" across "all areas of tort." We emphasize that our decision today is limited to loss of chance in medical malpractice actions. Such cases are particularly well suited to application of the loss of chance doctrine. First, as we noted above, reliable expert evidence establishing loss of chance is more likely to be available in a medical malpractice case than in some other domains of tort law. Second, medical negligence that harms the patient's chances of a more favorable outcome contravenes the expectation at the heart of the doctor-patient relationship that "the physician will take every reasonable measure to obtain an optimal outcome for the patient." Third, it is not uncommon for patients to have a less than even chance of survival or of achieving a better outcome when they present themselves for diagnosis, so the shortcomings of the all or nothing rule are particularly widespread. Finally, failure to recognize loss of chance in medical malpractice actions forces the party who is the least capable of preventing the harm to bear the consequences of the more capable party's negligence.

In sum, whatever difficulties may attend recognizing loss of chance as an item of damages in a medical malpractice action, these difficulties are far outweighed by the strong reasons to adopt the doctrine. . . .

A . . . challenging issue is how to calculate the monetary value for the lost chance. Courts adopting the loss of chance doctrine have arrived at different methods for calculating such damages. The most widely adopted of these methods of valuation is the "proportional damages" approach. Under the proportional damages approach, loss of chance damages are measured as "the percentage probability by which the defendant's tortious conduct diminished the likelihood of achieving some more favorable outcome." The formula aims to ensure that a defendant is liable in damages only for the monetary value of the *portion* of the decedent's prospects that the defendant's negligence destroyed. In applying the proportional damages method, the court must first measure the monetary value of the patient's full life expectancy and, if relevant, work life expectancy as it would in any wrongful death case. But the defendant must then be held liable only for the portion of that value that the defendant's negligence destroyed.

Deriving the damages for which the physician is liable will require the fact finder to undertake the following calculations:

(1) The fact finder must first calculate the total amount of damages allowable for the death under the wrongful death statute . . . or, in the case of medical malpractice not resulting in death, the full amount of damages allowable for the injury. This is the amount to which the decedent would be entitled if the case were *not* a loss of chance case: the full amount of compensation for the decedent's death or injury.

(2) The fact finder must next calculate the patient's chance of survival or cure immediately preceding ("but for") the medical malpractice.

(3) The fact finder must then calculate the chance of survival or cure that the patient had as a result of the medical malpractice.

(4) The fact finder must then subtract the amount derived in step 3 from the amount derived in step 2.

(5) The fact finder must then multiply the amount determined in step 1 by the percentage calculated in step 4 to derive the proportional damages award for loss of chance.

To illustrate, suppose in a wrongful death case that a jury found, based on expert testimony and the facts of the case, that full wrongful death damages would be $600,000 (step 1), that the patient had a 45% chance of survival prior to the medical malpractice (step 2), and that the physician's tortious acts reduced the chances of survival to 15% (step 3). The patient's chances of survival were reduced 30% (i.e., 45% minus 15%) due to the physician's malpractice (step 4), and the patient's loss of chance damages would be $600,000 multiplied by 30%, for a total of $180,000 (step 5).

We are . . . in accord with those courts that have determined that the proportional damages method is the most appropriate way to quantify the value of the loss of chance for a more favorable outcome, because it is an easily applied calculation that fairly ensures that a defendant is not assessed damages for harm that he did not cause. . . .

Judgment affirmed.

NOTES TO MATSUYAMA v. BIRNBAUM

1. *Burden of Proof: Legal Cause of Plaintiff's Death.* The court in *Matsuyama* discusses two concepts critical to its loss of chance theory. First the court discusses the preponderance of evidence standard for causation. A plaintiff must prove that there is a greater than 50% likelihood that something is true, that something is true to "a reasonable medical certainty." The other idea involves a reconceptualization of the definition of the injury a plaintiff must prove in a typical negligence case. The question in *Matsuyama* is not "How much proof must a plaintiff offer?" but rather "What is the nature of the injury the plaintiff must prove?"

Does the loss of chance doctrine adopted in Matsuyama v. Birnbaum require the plaintiff to prove that the defendant's negligence more likely than not caused the decedent's death? To what factual proposition does the court apply the more likely than not (preponderance of the evidence) standard?

2. *Alternative Approaches to the Plaintiff's Causation Problems in Loss of Chance Cases.* Allowing or rejecting recovery for loss of chance involves three factors: (1) identifying a compensable harm; (2) specifying what the plaintiff must prove; and (3) calculating damages. Consider how the following approaches treat each of these factors.

A. Some courts reject all "loss of chance" doctrines and prohibit recovery of any damages unless a preponderance of evidence shows that the defendant's negligence caused a particular identifiable physical outcome, such as death.

B. Other courts allow full recovery for a particular outcome even if the plaintiff cannot prove by a preponderance of evidence that the defendant's negligence caused it so long as the plaintiff can show by a preponderance of the evidence that the defendant's conduct "increased the harm" or "destroyed a substantial possibility of a more favorable outcome."

C. The *Matsuyama* court's holding.

3. *What Chance Did a Defendant Impair?* The *Matsuyama* court relies on the availability of expert testimony about survival chances for patients with various health problems as a basis for stating that its loss of chance doctrine applies only to medical malpractice cases. "Survival" is a concept that may require careful definition. For example, for many kinds of cancer doctors refer to "five-year survival," meaning that they can predict what percentage of patients with particular diagnoses will survive for at least five years after diagnosis if they receive typical treatment. But it is likely that *no* patients live for *100 years* after diagnosis, and that *all* patients live at least a *few days* after diagnosis. In loss of chance cases courts typically adopt the medical profession's consensus about what period of years constitutes "survival."

4. *Limiting Loss of Chance to the Medical Context.* Recognizing recovery for loss of chance could complicate treatment of cases involving failures to warn, to have rescue and safety equipment, or to take other precautions. Courts have generally limited the loss of chance doctrine to medical malpractice cases. The medical context may be different from these other areas because of the preexisting contractual relationship between the parties and because good empirical evidence may be available to show the probability of adverse results in many circumstances. The *Matsuyama* court considers the distinctions between medical malpractice cases and other situations in which the victim suffered a loss of chance of a better outcome.

PETRIELLO v. KALMAN

576 A.2d 474 (Conn. 1990)

SHEA, A.J.

In this medical malpractice action, . . . the jury . . . returned a verdict for the plaintiff, Ann Petriello, in her action against the named defendant, Roy E. Kalman, a physician. . . . The . . . defendant . . . has appealed. . . . The principal issue in that appeal is whether the trial court correctly instructed the jury that the plaintiff could be awarded compensation for an increased risk of future injury. We conclude that the trial court was correct in giving such an instruction.

The jury could reasonably have found the following facts from the evidence. [Because the defendant was negligent in his performance of a procedure on the plaintiff, corrective surgery was required, leaving the plaintiff with an 8 to 16 percent increased risk of future bowel adhesions and obstructions.]

In *Healy* [v. White, 173 Conn. 438, 378 A.2d 540 (1977)], we affirmed our adherence to the prevailing all or nothing standard for compensating those who have either suffered present harm and seek compensation as if the harm will be permanent, or have suffered present harm and seek compensation for possible future consequences of that harm. In essence, if a plaintiff can prove that there exists a 51 percent chance that his injury is permanent or that future injury will result, he may receive full compensation for that injury as if it were a certainty. If, however, the plaintiff establishes only a 49 percent chance of such a consequence, he may recover nothing for the risk to which he is presently exposed. Although this all or nothing view has been adopted by a majority of courts faced with the issue,[8] the concept has been severely criticized by numerous commentators. By denying any compensation unless a plaintiff proves that a future consequence is more likely to occur than not, courts have created a system in which a significant number of persons receive compensation for future consequences that never occur and, conversely, a significant number of persons receive no compensation at all for consequences that later ensue from risks not rising to the level of probability. This system is inconsistent with the goal of compensating tort victims fairly for all the consequences of the injuries they have sustained, while avoiding, so far as possible, windfall awards for consequences that never happen.

In seeking to enforce their right to individualized compensation, plaintiffs in negligence cases are confronted by the requirements that they must claim all applicable damages in a single cause of action and must bring their actions no "more than three years from the date of the act or omission complained of." General Statutes §52-584. Under these circumstances, no recovery may be had for future consequences of an injury when the evidence at trial does not satisfy the more probable than not criterion approved in *Healy,* despite a substantial risk of such consequences. Conversely, a defendant cannot seek reimbursement from a plaintiff who may have recovered for a future consequence, which appeared likely at the time of trial, on the ground that subsequent events have made that consequence remote or impossible. Our legal system provides no opportunity for a second look at a damage award so that it may be revised with the benefit of hindsight. In cases presenting similar problems, some courts "have liberalized the rules for causal proof so that any substantial chance of future harm might be sufficient to permit a recovery." D. Dobbs, R. Keeton, D. Owen & W. Keeton, Torts (5th ed. sup. 1988) §30, p.26. Further, some courts have counteracted the strict application of the rule of probability in proving damages "where the *fact* of damage has been established and the question to be decided is the *extent* of that damage." 4 F. Harper, F. James & O. Gray, Torts (2d ed.) §25.3, p.509.

If the plaintiff in this case had claimed that she was entitled to compensation to the extent that a future bowel obstruction was a certainty, she would have been foreclosed from such compensation solely on the basis of her experts' testimony that the likelihood of the occurrence of a bowel obstruction was either very remote or only 8 to 16 percent probable. Her claim, however, was for compensation for the increased risk that she would suffer such an obstruction sometime in the future. If this increased risk was more likely than not the result of the bowel resection necessitated by the defendant's actions, we conclude that there is no legitimate reason why she should not

---

[8] "The traditional American rule . . . is that recovery of damages based on future consequences may be had only if such consequences are 'reasonably certain.' . . . To meet the 'reasonably certain' standard, courts have generally required plaintiffs to prove that it is more likely than not (a greater than 50% chance) that the projected consequence will occur. If such proof is made, the alleged future effect may be treated as certain to happen and the injured party may be awarded full compensation for it; if the proof does not establish a greater than 50% chance, the injured party's award must be limited to damages for harm already manifest." Wilson v. Johns-Manville Sales Corporation, 684 F.2d 111, 119 (D.C. Cir. 1982).

receive present compensation based upon the likelihood of the risk becoming a reality. When viewed in this manner, the plaintiff was attempting merely to establish the extent of her present injuries. She should not be burdened with proving that the occurrence of a future event is more likely than not, when it is a present risk, rather than a future event for which she claims damages. In our judgment, it was fairer to instruct the jury to compensate the plaintiff for the increased risk of a bowel obstruction based upon the likelihood of its occurrence rather than to ignore that risk entirely. The medical evidence in this case concerning the probability of such a future consequence provided a sufficient basis for estimating that likelihood and compensating the plaintiff for it.

This view is consistent with the Second Restatement of the Law of Torts, which states, in §912, that "[o]ne to whom another has tortiously caused harm is entitled to compensatory damages for the harm if, but only if, he establishes by proof the extent of the harm and the amount of money representing adequate compensation with as much certainty as the nature of the tort and the circumstances permit." Damages for the future consequences of an injury can never be forecast with certainty. With respect to awards for permanent injuries, actuarial tables of average life expectancy are commonly used to assist the trier in measuring the loss a plaintiff is likely to sustain from the future effects of an injury. Such statistical evidence does, of course, satisfy the more likely than not standard as to the duration of a permanent injury. Similar evidence, based upon medical statistics of the average incidence of a particular future consequence from an injury, such as that produced by the plaintiff in this case, may be said to establish with the same degree of certitude the likelihood of the occurrence of the future harm to which a tort victim is exposed as a result of a present injury. Such evidence provides an adequate basis for measuring damages for the risk to which the victim has been exposed because of a wrongful act.

The probability percentage for the occurrence of a particular harm, the risk of which has been created by the tortfeasor, can be applied to the damages that would be justified if that harm should be realized. We regard this system of compensation as preferable to our present practice of denying any recovery for substantial risks of future harm not satisfying the more likely than not standard. We also believe that such a system is fairer to a defendant, who should be required to pay damages for a future loss based upon the statistical probability that such a loss will be sustained rather than upon the assumption that the loss is a certainty because it is more likely than not. We hold, therefore, that in a tort action, a plaintiff who has established a breach of duty that was a substantial factor in causing a present injury which has resulted in an increased risk of future harm is entitled to compensation to the extent that the future harm is likely to occur.

Applying this holding to the facts of this case, we conclude that the trial court correctly instructed the jury that the plaintiff could be awarded compensation for the increased likelihood that she will suffer a bowel obstruction some time in the future. The court's instruction was fully in accord with our holding today. The court first set forth the defendant's duty toward the plaintiff and then instructed the jury that: "If you find the defendant negligent and that such negligence was a substantial factor in increasing the plaintiff's risk of an intestinal blockage then the plaintiff is entitled to compensation for this element of damage." This instruction was a correct statement of the applicable law of causation and advised the jurors to award damages only if they were satisfied that there existed a causal relationship between the defendant's actions, the plaintiff's present injury and the increased risk to which she was exposed. Under these circumstances, we conclude that the trial court's instructions correctly allowed this issue to be considered by the jury.

The judgment of the trial court is affirmed.

NOTES TO PETRIELLO v. KALMAN

1. *Burden of Proof and Increased Risk of Harm.* In Petriello v. Kalman, the plaintiff seeks recovery for an increased chance of a bad result in the future. Traditional doctrines have allowed recovery only if a plaintiff shows that the probability of the harm occurring is greater than 50 percent. What probability of future harm did the plaintiff allege?

2. *Statute of Limitations and Single Cause of Action Rule.* The Petriello v. Kalman court referred to the statute of limitations and the single cause of action rule. Statutes of limitations control how long a plaintiff is permitted to wait to sue, either after the occurrence of an injurious event or after the plaintiff's discovery of the injury. In the *Petriello* case, a three-year period (beginning with the date of the injury) applied. The single cause of action rule requires that a plaintiff seek damages for all the consequences of a defendant's conduct in one lawsuit. This rule is justified by the societal interest in efficiency and finality, that is, dealing with all of the implications of a tortious act in one lawsuit.

3. *Accuracy of Compensation.* *Petriello* adopts an approach to damages that addresses the fairness of compensation. If the plaintiff actually does suffer the possible future consequence, will tort law have provided her with enough money to deal with it? If the plaintiff never suffers that consequence, what justification can there be for tort law having awarded her money on the chance that it would occur?

The *Petriello* approach to damages also has implications for deterrence. In theory, the total amount of compensation paid to victims properly deters actors if it is equal to the total value of the harm suffered. If victims who suffer the possible future harm are undercompensated and those who do not are overcompensated, does the *Petriello* approach create proper deterrence?

4. *Discovery Rule and Future Injury.* For some cases in some states, a "discovery" rule prevents the statute of limitations period from beginning to run until a victim knows or reasonably should know of the injury. This possibility of suing for actually incurred damages at a future time would make the *Petriello* approach less persuasive. See, e.g., Mauro v. Raymark Industries, Inc., 561 A.2d 257 (N.J. 1989) (victims with greater than 50 percent likelihood of future harm may recover full damages; victims with a lower likelihood are barred at present but may sue in the future if injury occurs).

6

LIMITS ON LIABILITY: DUTY AND PROXIMATE CAUSE

I. Introduction

The Role of Duty and Proximate Cause. A defendant's negligent act can be a cause in fact of infinite harmful consequences. For example, an electrician might install a light fixture negligently. The fixture might give someone a shock. That person might be knocked out and suffer a broken bone and therefore fail to go to a friend's house to give the friend a promised ride to a library. The friend might therefore fail a medical school test and lose a job as a graduate assistant in a research lab. The lab's work might be slowed up, and so on. Some other person might see the immediate victim get the shock and might suffer an emotionally debilitating response to it. Tort law devotes considerable attention to separating the many harms a defendant's conduct causes into two categories: (1) harms the defendant should be required to pay for and (2) harms whose costs the victims should bear themselves.

It is commonly said that to recover damages a tort plaintiff must prove duty, breach, cause, and damages. Tort law limits the liability of defendants with policy-based doctrines related to both the duty and the cause elements. Even if a defendant has acted tortiously and was the cause-in-fact of a plaintiff's harm, the defendant will not be liable if a court rules that the defendant did not owe a duty to the plaintiff or that the defendant's act was not a proximate cause of the plaintiff's harm.

Because proximate cause doctrines and certain duty doctrines represent responses to the same problem—putting some limits on actors' tort liability—this chapter discusses both types of doctrines. They are introduced in Palsgraf v. Long Island Railway Co., probably tort law's most famous case. The circumstances of the plaintiff's injury were highly unusual, so deciding whether the defendant railroad might be responsible was difficult. The majority opinion, by Justice Cardozo, decided that regardless of causation issues, a lack of duty owed by the defendant to the plaintiff should resolve the case. The dissenting opinion by Justice Andrews rejected this duty analysis and proposed a range of approaches to proximate cause. The dissent explores the main dilemmas of proximate cause doctrine. An analysis of the majority and dissenting opinions highlights the fact that limiting the range of a defendant's liability can be accomplished through doctrines related to either duty or causation.

PALSGRAF v. LONG ISLAND RAILWAY CO.
162 N.E. 99 (N.Y. 1928)

CARDOZO, C.J.

[Appeal from a judgment of the Appellate Division of the Supreme Court . . . affirming a judgment in favor of plaintiff entered upon a verdict.]

Plaintiff was standing on a platform of defendant's railroad after buying a ticket to go to Rockaway Beach. A train stopped at the station, bound for another place. Two men ran forward to catch it. One of the men reached the platform of the car without mishap, though the train was already moving. The other man, carrying a package, jumped aboard the car, but seemed unsteady as if about to fall. A guard on the car, who had held the door open, reached forward to help him in, and another guard on the platform pushed him from behind. In this act, the package was dislodged, and fell upon the rails. It was a package of small size, about fifteen inches long, and was covered by a newspaper. In fact it contained fireworks, but there was nothing in its appearance to give notice of its contents. The fireworks when they fell exploded. The shock of the explosion threw down some scales at the other end of the platform many feet away. The scales struck the plaintiff, causing injuries for which she sues.

The conduct of the defendant's guard, if a wrong in its relation to the holder of the package, was not a wrong in its relation to the plaintiff, standing far away. Relatively to her it was not negligence at all. Nothing in the situation gave notice that the falling package had in it the potency of peril to persons thus removed. Negligence is not actionable unless it involves the invasion of a legally protected interest, the violation of a right. "Proof of negligence in the air, so to speak, will not do." Pollock, Torts (11th ed.) p.455. The plaintiff, as she stood upon the platform of the station, might claim to be protected against intentional invasion of her bodily security. Such invasion is not charged. She might claim to be protected against unintentional invasion by conduct involving in the thought of reasonable men an unreasonable hazard that such invasion would ensue. These, from the point of view of the law, were the bounds of her immunity, with perhaps some rare exceptions. . . . If no hazard was apparent to the eye of ordinary vigilance, an act innocent and harmless, at least to outward seeming, with reference to her, did not take to itself the quality of a tort because it happened to be a wrong, though apparently not one involving the risk of bodily insecurity, with reference to some one else. "In every instance, before negligence can be predicated of a given act, back of the act must be sought and found a duty to the individual complaining, the observance of which would have averted or avoided the injury." McSherry, C.J., in West Virginia Central & P.R. Co. v. State, 96 Md. 652, 666, 54 A. 669, 671 (61 L.R.A. 574). . . . The plaintiff sues in her own right for a wrong personal to her, and not as the vicarious beneficiary of a breach of duty to another.

A different conclusion will involve us, and swiftly too, in a maze of contradictions. A guard stumbles over a package which has been left upon a platform. It seems to be a bundle of newspapers. It turns out to be a can of dynamite. To the eye of ordinary vigilance, the bundle is abandoned waste, which may be kicked or trod on with impunity. Is a passenger at the other end of the platform protected by the law against the unsuspected hazard concealed beneath the waste? If not, is the result to be any different, so far as the distant passenger is concerned, when the guard stumbles over a valise which a truckman or a porter has left upon the walk? The passenger far away, if the victim of a wrong at all, has a cause of action, not derivative, but original and primary. His claim to be protected against invasion of his bodily security is neither greater nor less because the act resulting in the invasion is a wrong to another far removed. In this case, the rights that are said to have been violated, are not even of the same order. The man was not injured in his person nor even put in danger. The purpose of the act, as well as its effect, was to make his person safe. If there was a wrong to him at all, which may very well be doubted, it was a wrong to a property interest only, the safety of his package. Out of this wrong to property, which threatened injury to nothing else, there has passed, we are told, to the plaintiff by derivation or succession a right of action for the invasion of an interest of another order, the right to bodily security. The diversity of interests emphasizes the futility of the effort to build the plaintiff's right upon the basis of a wrong to some one else. The gain is one of emphasis, for a like result would follow if the interests were the same. Even then, the orbit of the danger as disclosed to the eye of reasonable vigilance would be the orbit of the duty. One who jostles one's neighbor in a crowd does not invade the rights of others standing at the outer fringe when the unintended contact casts a bomb upon the ground. The wrongdoer as to them is the man who carries the bomb, not the one who explodes it without suspicion of the danger. Life will have to be made over, and human nature transformed, before prevision so extravagant can be accepted as the norm of conduct, the customary standard to which behavior must conform.

The argument for the plaintiff is built upon the shifting meanings of such words as "wrong" and "wrongful," and shares their instability. What the plaintiff must show is "a wrong" to herself; i.e., a violation of her own right, and not merely a wrong to some one else, nor conduct "wrongful" because unsocial, but not "a wrong" to any one. We are told that one who drives at reckless speed through a crowded city street is guilty of a negligent act and therefore of a wrongful one, irrespective of the consequences. Negligent the act is, and wrongful in the sense that it is unsocial, but wrongful and unsocial in relation to other travelers, only because the eye of vigilance perceives the risk of damage. If the same act were to be committed on a speedway or a race course, it would lose its wrongful quality. The risk reasonably to be perceived defines the duty to be obeyed, and risk imports relation; it is risk to another or to others within the range of apprehension. This does not mean, of course, that one who launches a destructive force is always relieved of liability, if the force, though known to be destructive, pursues an unexpected path. "It was not necessary that the defendant should have had notice of the particular method in which an accident would occur, if the possibility of an accident was clear to the ordinarily prudent eye." Munsey v. Webb, 231 U.S. 150, 156. Some acts, such as shooting, are so imminently dangerous to any one who may come within reach of the missile however unexpectedly, as to impose a duty of prevision not far from that of an insurer. Even today, and much oftener in earlier stages of the law, one acts sometimes at one's peril. Under this head, it may be, fall certain cases of what is known as transferred intent, an act willfully dangerous to *A* resulting by misadventure in injury to *B*. These cases aside, wrong is defined in terms of the natural or probable, at least when unintentional. The range of reasonable apprehension is at times a question for the court, and at times, if varying inferences are possible, a question for the jury. Here, by concession, there was nothing in the situation to suggest to the most cautious mind that the parcel wrapped in newspaper would spread wreckage through the station. If the guard had thrown it down knowingly and willfully, he would not have threatened the plaintiff's safety, so far as appearances could warn him. His conduct would not have involved, even then, an unreasonable probability of invasion of her bodily security. Liability can be no greater where the act is inadvertent. . . .

The law of causation, remote or proximate, is thus foreign to the case before us. The question of liability is always anterior to the question of the measure of the consequences that go with liability. If there is no tort to be redressed, there is no occasion to consider what damage might be recovered if there were a finding of a tort. We may assume, without deciding, that negligence, not at large or in the abstract, but in relation to the plaintiff, would entail liability for any and all consequences, however novel or extraordinary. There is room for argument that a distinction is to be drawn according to the diversity of interests invaded by the act, as where conduct negligent in that it threatens an insignificant invasion of an interest in property results in an unforeseeable invasion of an interest of another order, as, e.g., one of bodily security. Perhaps other distinctions may be necessary. We do not go into the question now. The consequences to be followed must first be rooted in a wrong.

The judgment of the Appellate Division and that of the Trial Term should be reversed, and the complaint dismissed, with costs in all courts.

Andrews, J. (dissenting). . . .

. . . The result we shall reach depends upon our theory as to the nature of negligence. Is it a relative concept — the breach of some duty owing to a particular person or to particular persons? Or, where there is an act which unreasonably threatens the safety of others, is the doer liable for all its proximate consequences, even where they result in injury to one who would generally be thought to be outside the radius of danger? This is not a mere dispute as to words. We might not believe that to the average mind the dropping of the bundle would seem to involve the probability of harm to the plaintiff standing many feet away whatever might be the case as to the owner or to one so near as to be likely to be struck by its fall. If, however, we adopt the second hypothesis, we have to inquire only as to the relation between cause and effect. We deal in terms of proximate cause, not of negligence. . . .

But we are told that "there is no negligence unless there is in the particular case a legal duty to take care, and this duty must be one which is owed to the plaintiff himself and not merely to others." Salmond, Torts (6th ed.) 24. This I think too narrow a conception. Where there is the unreasonable act, and some right that may be affected there is negligence whether damage does or does not result. That is immaterial. Should we drive down Broadway at a reckless speed, we are negligent whether we strike an approaching car or miss it by an inch. The act itself is wrongful. It is a wrong not only to those who happen to be within the radius of danger, but to all who might have been there — a wrong to the public at large. Such [is] the language of the street. Such [is] the language of the courts when speaking of contributory negligence. Such again and again their language in speaking of the duty of some defendant and discussing proximate cause in cases where such a discussion is wholly irrelevant on any other theory. As was said by Mr. Justice Holmes many years ago: "The measure of the defendant's duty in determining whether a wrong has been committed is one thing, the measure of liability when a wrong has been committed is another." Spade v. Lynn & Boston R.R. Co., 52 N.E. 747, 748. Due care is a duty imposed on each one of us to protect society from unnecessary danger, not to protect A, B, or C alone.

It may well be that there is no such thing as negligence in the abstract. "Proof of negligence in the air, so to speak, will not do." In an empty world negligence would not exist. It does involve a relationship between man and his fellows, but not merely a relationship between man and those whom he might reasonably expect his act would injure; rather, a relationship between him and those whom he does in fact injure. If his act has a tendency to harm some one, it harms him a mile away as surely as it does those on the scene. . . .

In the well-known *Polhemis* Case, Scrutton, L.J., said that the dropping of a plank was negligent, for it might injure "workman or cargo or ship." Because of either possibility, the owner of the vessel was to be made good for his loss. The act being wrongful, the doer was liable for its proximate results. Criticized and explained as this statement may have been, I think it states the law as it should be and as it is.

The proposition is this: Every one owes to the world at large the duty of refraining from those acts that may unreasonably threaten the safety of others. Such an act occurs. Not only is he wronged to whom harm might reasonably be expected to result, but he also who is in fact injured, even if he be outside what would generally be thought the danger zone. There needs be duty due the one complaining, but this is not a duty to a particular individual because as to him harm might be expected. Harm to some one being the natural result of the act, not only that one alone, but all those in fact injured may complain. We have never, I think, held otherwise. . . . Unreasonable risk being taken, its consequences are not confined to those who might probably be hurt.

If this be so, we do not have a plaintiff suing by "derivation or succession." Her action is original and primary. Her claim is for a breach of duty to herself — not that she is subrogated to any right of action of the owner of the parcel or of a passenger standing at the scene of the explosion.

The right to recover damages rests on additional considerations. The plaintiff's rights must be injured, and this injury must be caused by the negligence. We build a dam, but are negligent as to its foundations. Breaking, it injures property down stream. We are not liable if all this happened because of some reason other than the insecure foundation. But, when injuries do result from our unlawful act, we are liable for the consequences. It does not matter that they are unusual, unexpected, unforeseen, and unforeseeable. But there is one limitation. The damages must be so connected with the negligence that the latter may be said to be the proximate cause of the former.

These two words have never been given an inclusive definition. What is a cause in a legal sense, still more what is a proximate cause, depend in each case upon many considerations, as does the existence of negligence itself. Any philosophical doctrine of causation does not help us. A boy throws a stone into a pond. The ripples spread. The water level rises. The history of that pond is altered to all eternity. It will be altered by other causes also. Yet it will be forever the resultant of all causes combined. Each one will have an influence. How great only omniscience can say. You may speak of a chain, or, if you please, a net. An analogy is of little aid. Each cause brings about future events. Without each the future would not be the same. Each is proximate in the sense it is essential. But that is not what we mean by the word. Nor on the other hand do we mean sole cause. There is no such thing.

Should analogy be thought helpful, however, I prefer that of a stream. The spring, starting on its journey, is joined by tributary after tributary. The river, reaching the ocean, comes from a hundred sources. No man may say whence any drop of water is

• REASONABLE DUTY OWED •
— SOCIETY

• CAUSATION •

Does not make sense

• CAUS. → NEG.

derived. Yet for a time distinction may be possible. Into the clear creek, brown swamp water flows from the left. Later, from the right comes water stained by its clay bed. The three may remain for a space, sharply divided. But at last inevitably no trace of separation remains. They are so commingled that all distinction is lost.

As we have said, we cannot trace the effect of an act to the end, if end there is. Again, however, we may trace it part of the way. A murder at Serajevo may be the necessary antecedent to an assassination in London twenty years hence. An overturned lantern may burn all Chicago. We may follow the fire from the shed to the last building. We rightly say the fire started by the lantern caused its destruction.

A cause, but not the proximate cause. What we do mean by the word "proximate" is that, because of convenience, of public policy, of a rough sense of justice, the law arbitrarily declines to trace a series of events beyond a certain point. This is not logic. It is practical politics. Take our rule as to fires. Sparks from my burning haystack set on fire my house and my neighbor's. I may recover from a negligent railroad. He may not. Yet the wrongful act as directly harmed the one as the other. We may regret that the line was drawn just where it was, but drawn somewhere it had to be. We said the act of the railroad was not the proximate cause of our neighbor's fire. Cause it surely was. The words we used were simply indicative of our notions of public policy. Other courts think differently. But somewhere they reach the point where they cannot say the stream comes from any one source. . . .

Prox. Cause Analysis

There are some hints that may help us. The proximate cause, involved as it may be with many other causes, must be, at the least, something without which the event would not happen. The court must ask itself whether there was a natural and continuous sequence between cause and effect. Was the one a substantial factor in producing the other? Was there a direct connection between them, without too many intervening causes? Is the effect of cause on result not too attenuated? Is the cause likely, in the usual judgment of mankind, to produce the result? Or, by the exercise of prudent foresight, could the result be foreseen? Is the result too remote from the cause, and here we consider remoteness in time and space. Clearly we must so consider, for the greater the distance either in time or space, the more surely do other causes intervene to affect the result. When a lantern is overturned, the firing of a shed is a fairly direct consequence. Many things contribute to the spread of the conflagration — the force of the wind, the direction and width of streets, the character of intervening structures, other factors. We draw an uncertain and wavering line, but draw it we must as best we can.

Once again, it is all a question of fair judgment, always keeping in mind the fact that we endeavor to make a rule in each case that will be practical and in keeping with the general understanding of mankind. . . .

This last suggestion is the factor which must determine the case before us. The act upon which defendant's liability rests is knocking an apparently harmless package onto the platform. The act was negligent. For its proximate consequences the defendant is liable. If its contents were broken, to the owner; if it fell upon and crushed a passenger's foot, then to him; if it exploded and injured one in the immediate vicinity, to him. . . . Mrs. Palsgraf was standing some distance away. How far cannot be told from the record — apparently 25 or 30 feet, perhaps less. Except for the explosion, she would not have been injured. We are told by the appellant in his brief, "It cannot be denied that the explosion was the direct cause of the plaintiff's injuries." So it was a substantial factor in producing the result — there was here a natural and continuous sequence — direct connection. The only intervening cause was that, instead of blowing her to the ground, the concussion smashed the weighing machine which in turn fell upon her. There was no remoteness in time, little in space. And surely, given such an explosion as here, it needed no great foresight to predict that the natural result would be to injure one on the platform at no greater distance from its scene than was the plaintiff. Just how no one might be able to predict. Whether by flying fragments, by broken glass, by wreckage of machines or structures no one could say. But injury in some form was most probable.

Under these circumstances I cannot say as a matter of law that the plaintiff's injuries were not the proximate result of the negligence. That is all we have before us. The court refused to so charge. No request was made to submit the matter to the jury as a question of fact, even would that have been proper upon the record before us.

The judgment appealed from should be affirmed, with costs.

NOTES TO PALSGRAF v. LONG ISLAND RAILWAY CO.

1. *Duty and Proximate Cause as Liability-Limiting Elements.* Justice Cardozo based his decision against Ms. Palsgraf on an analysis of duty. Even if there is negligence ("in the air"), that is not enough to support liability. For Justice Cardozo, proximate cause was irrelevant, because if there is no duty to the plaintiff, there can never be any liability to the plaintiff regardless of causation. Justice Andrews would have used a proximate cause analysis to limit liability because he concluded that the defendant did owe a duty to Ms. Palsgraf. What is the difference between the two judges' rules for when one actor has a duty to another?

2. *Factors Relevant to Legal Cause.* Justice Andrews identified as many as nine factors to be considered in legal causation (the exact number is hard to say because many overlap): (1) but-for cause, (2) natural and continuous sequence between cause and effect, (3) substantial factor, (4) directness without too many intervening events, (5) attenuation, (6) likelihood of injury, (7) foreseeability, (8) remoteness in time, and (9) remoteness in space. He considered the explosion to be a but-for cause of the harm to Mrs. Palsgraf, to be a direct cause, with only one intervening event (the falling of the scales), occurring in a natural and continuing sequence, and a substantial factor. The harm was foreseeable and not too remote in time or space.

Generally courts consider selected factors when analyzing causation but not all of them together. Cases in this chapter show the usual practice of focusing on only one or two factors. Consider, however, that many of these factors are related. Is an act likely to be a direct cause, for instance, if it is unlikely to produce the harm and is remote in time or space? The answer depends on the particular facts of each case.

3. *Foreseeability and Hindsight.* In Justice Andrews's analysis, the foreseeability of injury would be evaluated on the basis of information available after the defendant has acted. Specifically, he wrote that "given such an explosion as here, it needed no great foresight to predict that the natural result would be to injure one on the plat-form." This use of hindsight has not usually been followed. The Restatement (Second) of Torts, in §435 comment d, took the position that if the result of a defendant's conduct seems highly extraordinary in hindsight, the conduct should not be considered a proximate cause of the result.

Perspective: Duty as a Question of Law

Following the approach suggested by Justice Cardozo, the existence of a duty is based on whether the plaintiff was a foreseeable victim of the defendant's conduct and, in some jurisdictions, the foreseeability of the type of harm that occurred. Duty is a question of law, which means that the judge rather than the jury decides whether a duty exists. Professor Patrick J. Kelley, *Restating Duty, Breach, and Proximate Cause in Negligence Law; Descriptive Theory and the Rule of Law,* 54 Vand. L. Rev. 1039, 1062 (2001), suggests looking at duties not as creations of judges but as "social obligations derived from the community's accepted ways of doing things":

> Community standards of coordinating behavior may be developed so that certain goods can be achieved by some, or certain evils can be avoided by others, if everyone follows the practice. For example, if everyone drives on the left, collisions can be avoided and everyone can get where they are going more quickly and safely. Everyone engaged in the practice understands what those purposes are. For the practice to give rise to a claim of wrong, therefore, the plaintiff must be within the group of those whose interests the practice was developed to protect, and the hazard by which he was harmed must be one that the practice was developed to avoid.

> The judge's role is to recognize the "community's coordinating conventions or practices." The "[p]laintiff is wronged if she is harmed when the defendant breaches a social convention whose purpose is to protect people like the plaintiff from that kind of harm." Id.

> Applying community standards to complex questions in particular cases may be the type of function best assigned to a jury. Since the issue of proximate cause is almost always treated as a question for the jury, an alternative to Justice Cardozo's rule would assume that an actor owes a duty to the whole world and treat the question of whether the plaintiff and harm were foreseeable as part of the jury's consideration of proximate cause.

II. Duty

Identifying Duties.   Justice Cardozo's *Palsgraf* opinion is consistent with recognizing a duty to all whom one's conduct might foreseeably injure. The Andrews opinion articulates a duty owed to everyone, with foreseeability treated as one of many components of a causation analysis once a defendant's negligence has been established. Modern courts use a number of techniques to identify duties. Hegyes v. Unjian Enterprises, Inc. is based on foreseeability where a defendant's conduct has created a risk. Dykema v. Gus Macker Enterprises, Inc. links duty to the relationship between a plaintiff and defendant, where someone other than the defendant has created a risk. Graff v. Beard and Kubert v. Best examine multiple factors to decide whether to recognize a duty in circumstances where precedents had not required an actor like the defendant to exercise reasonable care with respect to the type of risk and type of plaintiff present in each case. Chapter 11 offers a fuller treatment of special duty rules, but *Hegyes, Dykema, Graff,* and *Kubert* are presented here to highlight the way a duty analysis can accomplish some of the same purposes served by the proximate cause inquiry.

HEGYES v. UNJIAN ENTERPRISES, INC.
286 Cal. Rptr. 85 (Cal. Ct. App. 1992)

FRED WOODS, Associate Justice.

. . . On January 24, 1989, plaintiff Cassondra Hegyes (hereinafter "Hegyes" or "plaintiff") filed her complaint [alleging] that the corporate defendant, Unjian Enterprises, Inc., dba Office Supply Company (hereafter "defendant"), was the owner of a passenger vehicle involved in an automobile accident on July 4, 1985, while it was being operated by defendant's employee, Donald George. Lynn O'Hare Hegyes (hereinafter "O'Hare") was allegedly injured in that accident. It is claimed that, as a result of that accident, O'Hare was fitted with a lumbo-peritoneal shunt.

In 1987, O'Hare became pregnant with plaintiff. During that pregnancy, the fetus compressed the lumbo-peritoneal shunt and, in order to avoid further injury to O'Hare, plaintiff was delivered 51 days premature, by Cesarean section on October 31, 1987. Plaintiff alleged that the personal injuries she sustained were a proximate result of the negligence of defendants.

On or about November 1, 1989, defendant served its demurrer to plaintiff's complaint. . . .

Defendant's demurrer challenged the sufficiency of plaintiff's complaint on several grounds, one of which was the absence of any legal duty of care. Defendant contended that no legal duty was owed by defendant to plaintiff under the facts presented since claims for preconception negligence involve a special "physician-patient" relationship which gives rise to a duty to the subsequently conceived "foreseeable" fetus. In the absence of such a special relationship, defendant contended that a legal duty had never been found under California law. . . .

After considering the arguments of counsel, the trial court sustained the demurrer without leave to amend on the ground that recognition of such a cause of action would "be an unwarranted extension of a duty of care." [The plaintiff appealed.]

This appeal presents a single issue, which may be framed as follows: Does a negligent motorist owe a legal duty of care to the subsequently conceived child of a woman who is injured in an automobile accident? . . .

While the question of whether one owes a duty to another must be decided on a case by case basis, every case is governed by the rule of general application that persons are required to use ordinary care for the protection of those to whom harm can be reasonably foreseen. This rule not only establishes, but limits, the principle of negligence liability. The court's task in determining duty is to evaluate "whether the category of negligent conduct at issue is sufficiently likely to result in the kind of harm experienced" such that liability may appropriately be imposed upon the negligent party. *Ballard v. Uribe,* 715 P.2d 624 (1986).

Applying that standard to the aforementioned "special relationship" cases where a duty was found to exist, the birth of a handicapped child was arguably a "likely result" of the defendant's professionally negligent conduct. In this case, however, that standard leads to a different result. Defendant's conduct was not "likely to result" in plaintiff's conception or birth, let alone her alleged injuries nearly three years after the car accident. Unlike a medical professional's conduct which is directly and intentionally related to whether a child is conceived or born, such conception or birth is not a reasonably foreseeable result of the operation of a car.

This doctrine was fully expounded in the landmark case of *Palsgraf v. Long Island R. Co.* (1928) 162 N.E. 99. . . .

In narrowing the area of actionable causation, Chief Justice Cardozo drew the line at foreseeability. Negligence must be a matter of some relation between the parties, some duty, which could be founded only on the foreseeability of some harm to the plaintiff in fact injured. . . .

Thus, despite the broad maxim that for every wrong there is a remedy, the courts and legislature of this state have decided that *not* all injuries are compensable at law. Plaintiff's alleged injuries must necessarily fall within that category. A motorist cannot reasonably foresee that his or her negligent conduct might injure a child subsequently conceived by a woman several years after a car accident.

Even accepting, arguendo, that it is foreseeable that a woman of child bearing years may some day have a child, there are areas of foreseeable harm where legal obligation still does not arise. It must be admitted that there existed the bare *possibility* that the injury complained of in this case could result from the acts of defendant. However, the creation of a legal duty requires more than a mere possibility of occurrence since, through hindsight, everything is foreseeable.

Judicial discretion is an integral part of the duty concept in evaluating foreseeability of harm. That sentiment is best evidenced by the following comment by Dean Prosser: "In the end the court will decide whether there is a duty on the basis of the mores of the community, 'always keeping in mind the fact that we endeavor to make a rule in each case that will be practical and in keeping with the general understanding of mankind.'" Prosser, *Palsgraf* Revisited (1953) 52 Mich. L. Rev. 1, 15.

Thus, the concept of legal duty necessarily includes and expresses considerations of social policy. The trial court's determination with respect to those considerations have merit and rationality, and we so find. [The judgment is affirmed.]

NOTES TO HEGYES v. UNJIAN ENTERPRISES, INC.

1. *Foreseeability as a Limit on Duty.* Following the *Palsgraf* approach, the court in *Hegyes* found that a person in the position of the negligent driver could not reasonably anticipate that his bad driving would cause an injury to a child born more than two years later, even though the driver's conduct was a cause-in-fact of that injury. The entire chain of causation (bad driving, need for a shunt, danger to O'Hare's health during pregnancy, early delivery of the plaintiff) is irrelevant. The jury has no opportunity to decide whether the car driver's negligence was a proximate cause of the baby's injuries once the court decides that the baby's injuries were not foreseeable.

2. *Prenatal Negligence and Foreseeable Harm.* When negligent conduct that harms a child occurs before a child's conception or birth, recovery against the negligent actor is sometimes allowed. For example, if the harm is caused by negligent genetic counseling of the child's parents or by negligent treatment of the child's mother while she is pregnant, harm to the child is treated as foreseeable. See the discussion of "wrongful birth" and "wrongful life" claims in Chapter 11.

DYKEMA v. GUS MACKER ENTERPRISES, INC.
492 N.W.2d 472 (Mich. Ct. App. 1992)

KELLY, J.

Plaintiffs, Lee Dykema and Linda Dykema, appeal as of right from the trial court's order granting defendants' motion for summary disposition pursuant to MCR 2.116(C)(8). We affirm.

In July 1988, defendant Gus Macker Enterprises, Inc., organized and conducted the Gus Macker basketball tournament. . . . The tournament was held outdoors on the public streets of Belding, Michigan. Spectators were charged no admission fee and were free to move about and watch the various basketball games in progress. On July 10, 1988, Lee Dykema attended the tournament as a nonpaying spectator. . . . At approximately 4:30 p.m., a thunderstorm struck the area. During the storm, the winds were blowing in excess of forty miles an hour. Plaintiff, while running for shelter, was struck by a falling tree limb and paralyzed.

Plaintiff argues that because of the special relationship that existed between Gus Macker Enterprises, Inc. (hereafter defendant), the organizer of the outdoor basketball tournament, and himself, a spectator at the tournament, defendant was under a duty to warn plaintiff of the approaching thunderstorm. We acknowledge that this is an issue of first impression in Michigan, and hold that defendant was under no duty to warn plaintiff of the approaching thunderstorm.

In order to assert negligence, a plaintiff must establish the existence of a duty owed by the defendant to the plaintiff. The term "duty" has been defined as "essentially a question of whether the relationship between the actor and the injured person gives rise to any legal obligation on the actor's part for the benefit of the injured person." Moning v. Alfono, 400 Mich. 425, 438-439; 254 N.W.2d 759 (1977). The general rule is that there is no duty to aid or protect another. However, there is a limited exception to this rule. A duty may be found if there is a special relationship between the plaintiff and the defendant. Some generally recognized "special relationships" include common carrier-passenger, innkeeper-guest, employer-employee, landlord-tenant, and invitor-invitee. The rationale behind imposing a legal duty to act in these special relationships is based on the element of control. In a special relationship, one person entrusts himself to the control and protection of another, with a consequent loss of control to protect himself. The duty to protect is imposed upon the person in control because he is in the best position to provide a place of safety. Thus, the determination whether a duty-imposing special relationship exists in a particular case involves the determination whether the plaintiff entrusted himself to the control and protection of the defendant, with a consequent loss of control to protect himself.

In order to determine whether a "special relationship" giving rise to a legal duty to act does exist in a particular case, this Court has held that it is necessary to

> balance the societal interests involved, the severity of the risk, the burden upon the defendant, the likelihood of occurrence, and the relationship between the parties. . . . Other factors which may give rise to a duty include the foreseeability of the [harm], the defendant's ability to comply with the proposed duty, the victim's inability to protect himself from the [harm], the costs of providing protection, and whether the plaintiff had bestowed some economic benefit on the defendant.

[Roberts v. Pinkins, 171 Mich. App. 648, 652-653; 430 N.W.2d 808 (1988).] If a trial court determines that, as a matter of law, the defendant owed no duty to the plaintiff, summary disposition is properly granted in the defendant's favor under MCR 2.116(C)(8).

Our review of the record indicates that no special relationship existed between plaintiff and defendant. Contrary to plaintiff's argument, plaintiff and defendant were not engaged in a business invitee-invitor relationship at the time of plaintiff's accident. Plaintiff was not on the land where the basketball tournament was being held in connection "with business dealings" of defendant. In support of this conclusion, we note that plaintiff paid no admission fee to observe the tournament, and no contractual or business relationship was shown to exist between plaintiff and defendant. Nor do we perceive any other type of special relationship from which a duty to warn could arise with regard to inclement weather. There is no indication in the record that plaintiff entrusted himself to the control and protection of defendant. Further, there is no indication that, pursuant to his relationship with defendant, plaintiff lost the ability to protect himself. Plaintiff was free to leave the tournament at any time, and his movements were not restricted by defendant. He was able to see the changing weather conditions by looking at the sky and was able to seek shelter as the storm approached. Clearly, plaintiff did not entrust himself to the control and protection of defendant, with a consequent loss of control to protect himself. Because no special relationship existed between plaintiff and defendant, defendant was under no duty to warn plaintiff of the approaching thunderstorm. . . .

Affirmed.

NOTES TO DYKEMA v. GUS MACKER ENTERPRISES, INC.

1. *Special Relationships as Sources of Duty.*   The *Dykema* court contrasted the facts of its case with a number of types of relationships that are typically treated as creating duties. Those cases, involving common carriers and their passengers, innkeepers and their guests, employers and their employees, landlords and their tenants, and businesses and their customers, have all been recognized as giving rise to duties in many common law decisions.

2. *Attributes of Special Relationships That Support Recognition of Duty.*   Even if the *Dykema* court had decided that the plaintiff and defendant did have some type of special relationship, that would not be enough to support finding that a duty existed. The court noted that an analysis of many societal considerations would have to be made in order to see whether, even in the case of a special relationship, imposing a duty would be sensible. For instance, those relationships supporting the finding of a duty also involve plaintiffs who have given themselves over to (or have been placed in) the care of defendants.

The Restatement (Third) of Torts: Liability for Physical and Emotional Harm §40 (2012) offers examples of relationships that may support a finding of duty:

§40 Duty Based on Special Relationship with Another
(a) An actor in a special relationship with another owes the other a duty of reasonable care with regard to risks that arise within the scope of the relationship.
(b) Special relationships giving rise to the duty provided in Subsection (a) include:
(1) a common carrier with its passengers,
(2) an innkeeper with its guests,
(3) a business or other possessor of land that holds its premises open to the public with those who are lawfully on the premises,

(4) an employer with its employees who, while at work, are:
  (a) in imminent danger; or
  (b) injured or ill and thereby rendered helpless,
(5) a school with its students,
(6) a landlord with its tenants, and
(7) a custodian with those in its custody, if:
  (a) the custodian is required by law to take custody or voluntarily takes custody of the other; and
  (b) the custodian has a superior ability to protect the other.

Problem
Duty and Special Relationship

The plaintiffs attended a showing of a movie at a movie theater in a shopping mall. At the conclusion of the movie, the plaintiffs left the theater using a door that opened directly into the parking area. They drove a short distance and then encountered flash floods, which a severe rainstorm had caused near the theater. Consequently, the plaintiffs' daughter drowned, and the plaintiffs suffered severe injuries. The manager of the theater had learned about the dangerous weather during the showing of the movie but had taken no steps to warn patrons. Plaintiffs have sued the theater operator on the theory that it negligently failed to warn them of the weather, and the defendant has moved for summary judgment on the basis that it owed no duty to warn. You are the judge. What factors will you take into account in deciding whether to impose a duty? What do you conclude? See Mostert v. CBL & Associates, 741 P.2d 1090 (Wyo. 1987).

GRAFF v. BEARD
858 S.W.2d 918 (Tex. 1993)

CORNYN, J.

We are asked in this case to impose a common-law duty on a social host who makes alcohol available to an intoxicated adult guest who the host knows will be driving. For the reasons given below, we decline to do so. Accordingly, we reverse the judgment of the court of appeals and render a take-nothing judgment. Houston Moos consumed alcohol at a party hosted by the Graffs and Hausmons, and allegedly left in his vehicle in an intoxicated condition. En route from the party, Moos collided with a motorcycle, injuring Brett Beard. Beard sued both Moos and his hosts for his injuries. The trial court ultimately dismissed Beard's claims against the hosts for failure to state a cause of action. An en banc divided court of appeals reversed the trial court's judgment and remanded the case, holding for the first time in Texas jurisprudence that social hosts may be liable to third parties for the acts of their intoxicated adult guests.

Under the court of appeals' standard, a social host violates a legal duty to third parties when the host makes an alcoholic beverage available to an adult guest who the host knows is intoxicated and will be driving. In practical effect, this duty is twofold. The first aspect of the host's duty is to prevent guests who will be driving from becoming intoxicated. If the host fails to do so, however, a second aspect of the duty comes into play—the host must prevent the intoxicated guest from driving.

The legislatures in most states, including Texas, have enacted dram shop laws that impose a statutory duty to third parties on commercial providers under specified circumstances. . . . Because the dram shop statute applies only to commercial providers, however, it does not govern the duty asserted in this case. . . .

Deciding whether to impose a new common-law duty involves complex considerations of public policy. We have said that these considerations include "'social, economic, and political questions,' and their application to the particular facts at hand." Among other factors, we consider the extent of the risk involved, "the foreseeability and likelihood of injury weighed against the social utility of the actor's conduct, the magnitude of the burden of guarding against the injury, and the consequences of placing the burden on the defendant." We have also emphasized other factors. For example, questions of duty have turned on whether one party has superior knowledge of the risk, and whether a right to control the actor whose conduct precipitated the harm exists. See, e.g., Seagram v. McGuire, 814 S.W.2d 385 (Tex. 1991) (declining to recognize a legal duty of an alcohol manufacturer to warn consumers against danger of alcoholism because the risk is common knowledge); *Greater Houston Transp. Co.*, 801 S.W.2d at 525 (citing Otis Engineering Corp. v. Clark, 658 S.W.2d 307, 309 (Tex. 1984); Restatement (Second) of Torts §315 (1965) (noting that no general duty exists to control the conduct of others)).

Following our decisions in *Seagram* and *Otis Engineering Corp.*, we deem it appropriate to focus on two tacit assumptions underlying the holding of the court of appeals: that the social host can reasonably know of the guest's alcohol consumption and possible intoxication, and possesses the right to control the conduct of the guest. Under Texas law, in the absence of a relationship between the parties giving rise to the right of control, one person is under no legal duty to control the conduct of another, even if there exists the practical ability to do so. For example, in *Otis Engineering Corp.* we held that an employer breached a duty of care to the public when he directed an intoxicated employee to drive home and the employee caused a fatal car crash. While we noted that there is no general duty to control the conduct of another, we recognized a duty in that instance because of the employer's authority over the employee. 668 S.W.2d at 309. As we later explained in *Greater Houston Transportation Co.*, our decision in *Otis* was premised on "the employer's *negligent exercise of control* over the employee," rather than on a general duty to prevent intoxicated individuals from driving. 801 S.W.2d at 526 (emphasis in original).

Instead of focusing on the host's right of control over the guest, the court of appeals conditioned a social host's duty on the host's "exclusive control" of the alcohol supply. The court defined "exclusive control," however, as nothing more than a degree of control "greater than that of the guest user." Under the court's definition, at a barbecue, a wedding reception, a back-yard picnic, a pachanga, a Bar Mitzvah — or a variety of other common social settings — the host would always have exclusive control over the alcohol supply because the host chooses whether alcohol will be provided and the manner in which it will be provided. The duty imposed by the court of appeals would apparently attach in any social setting in which alcohol is available regardless of the host's right to control the guest. Thus, as a practical matter, the host has but one choice — whether to make alcohol available to guests at all.

But should the host venture to make alcohol available to adult guests, the court of appeals' standard would allow the host to avoid liability by cutting off the guest's access to alcohol at some point before the guest becomes intoxicated. Implicit in that standard is the assumption that the reasonably careful host can accurately determine how much alcohol guests have consumed and when they have approached their limit. We believe, though, that it is far from clear that a social host can reliably recognize a guest's level of intoxication. First, it is unlikely that a host can be expected to know how much alcohol, if any, a guest has consumed before the guest arrives on the host's premises. Second, in many social settings, the total number of guests present may practically inhibit the host from discovering a guest's approaching intoxication. Third, the condition may be apparent in some people but certainly not in all. . . .

This brings us to the second aspect of the duty implicit in the court of appeals' standard: that should the guest become intoxicated, the host must prevent the guest from driving. Unlike the court of appeals, however, we cannot assume that guests will respond to a host's attempts, verbal or physical, to prevent the guests from driving. . . .

Ideally, guests will drink responsibly, and hosts will monitor their social functions to reduce the likelihood of intoxication. Once a guest becomes impaired by alcohol to the point at which he becomes a threat to himself and others, we would hope that the host can persuade the guest to take public transportation, stay on the premises, or be transported home by an unimpaired driver. But we know that too often reality conflicts with ideal behavior. And, given the ultimate power of guests to control their own alcohol consumption and the absence of any legal right of the host to control the guest, we find the arguments for shifting legal responsibility from the guest to the host, who merely makes alcohol available at social gatherings, unconvincing. As the common law has long recognized, the imbiber maintains the ultimate power and thus the obligation to control his own behavior: to decide to drink or not to drink, to drive or not to drive. We therefore conclude that the common law's focus should remain on the drinker as the person primarily responsible for his own behavior and best able to avoid the foreseeable risks of that behavior.

We accordingly reverse the judgment of the court of appeals and render judgment that Beard take nothing.

[Dissenting opinion omitted.]

NOTES TO GRAFF v. BEARD

1. *Specificity of Duties.*   A court may recognize a general standard of care, such as a duty to act reasonably, or it may provide a more precise description of one's obligations in a particular setting. The degree of specificity may affect a court's analysis of the consequences of recognizing a duty.

In *Graff*, the Texas Court of Appeals recognized a "duty to third parties when the host makes an alcoholic beverage available to an adult guest who the host knows is intoxicated and will be driving." The Texas Supreme Court elaborated on that general description, stating that such a duty would require a host to prevent guests from becoming intoxicated and would require a host to prevent an intoxicated guest from driving. The court of appeals' version of this duty would have been applied by juries using a reasonable person test and might or might not have required the types of conduct the Texas Supreme Court described. The supreme court's vision of how hosts would be required to act to satisfy a duty apparently contributed to that court's assessment of the impracticality of such a duty.

2. *Social Factor Analysis.*   When courts consider development of new duties, they often evaluate the possible duty in terms of various social factors. The *Graff* court noted, among others, foreseeability of injury, the utility of an actor's conduct, and the burden of prevention. Of the factors presented by the court, which most strongly support its conclusion?

Statute: CIVIL LIABILITY FOR SOCIAL HOSTS

N.J. Stat. Ann. 2A:15-5.6 (2017)

a. This act shall be the exclusive civil remedy for personal injury or property damage resulting from the negligent provision of alcoholic beverages by a social host to a person who has attained the legal age to purchase and consume alcoholic beverages.

b. A person who sustains bodily injury or injury to real or personal property as a result of the negligent provision of alcoholic beverages by a social host to a person who has attained the legal age to purchase and consume alcoholic beverages may recover damages from a social host only if:

(1) The social host willfully and knowingly provided alcoholic beverages either:

(a) To a person who was visibly intoxicated in the social host's presence; or

(b) To a person who was visibly intoxicated under circumstances manifesting reckless disregard of the consequences as affecting the life or property of another; and

(2) The social host provided alcoholic beverages to the visibly intoxicated person under circumstances which created an unreasonable risk of foreseeable harm to the life or property of another, and the social host failed to exercise reasonable care and diligence to avoid the foreseeable risk; and

(3) The injury arose out of an accident caused by the negligent operation of a vehicle by the visibly intoxicated person who was provided alcoholic beverages by a social host.

Statute: CIVIL LIABILITY OF PERSONS PROVIDING ALCOHOLIC BEVERAGES

Alaska Stat. §04.21.020(a) (2017)

(a) A person who provides alcoholic beverages to another person may not be held civilly liable for injuries resulting from the intoxication of that person unless the person who provides the alcoholic beverages holds a license authorized under [Alaska statutes] or is an agent or employee of such a licensee and

(1) the alcoholic beverages are provided to a person under the age of 21 years . . . unless the licensee, agent, or employee secures in good faith from the person a signed statement, liquor identification card, or driver's license . . . that indicates that the person is 21 years of age or older; or

(2) the alcoholic beverages are provided to a drunken person . . .

NOTES TO STATUTES

1. *Duty of Care for Social Hosts Who Provide Alcohol.*   Graff v. Beard represents the strong majority view on this issue. An early opinion imposing a duty of care on social hosts in the alcohol-serving context was Kelly v. Grinnell, 476 A.2d 1219 (N.J. 1984). The New Jersey statute limits that duty in a variety of ways.

2. Dramshop Acts.   The Alaska statute applies to persons with licenses to sell alcohol. It establishes that they owe a duty to people who are injured by intoxicated patrons. Statutes of this kind are known as dramshop acts. They apply only when a server continues to provide alcohol to a person who is drunk. Many states have adopted dramshop acts to overcome arguments by victims that liability should rest only on the intoxicated person. These statutes do not excuse the intoxicated person from liability. Instead, they make both the licensee *and* the intoxicated person potentially liable for the injuries.

3. Knowledge of Drunkenness.   While this Alaska statute may appear to create liability whenever the person to whom alcohol is served is drunk, state statutes (including Alaska's) require proof of some knowledge on the part of the server. Common approaches require proof that the server knew or should have known that the person was intoxicated or that the server sold to or served a person who the server knew or should have known would become intoxicated.

KUBERT v. BEST

75 A.3d 1214 (N.J. Super. 2013)

ASHRAFI, J.A.D.

Plaintiffs Linda and David Kubert were grievously injured by an eighteen-year-old driver who was texting while driving and crossed the center-line of the road. Their claims for compensation from the young driver have been settled and are no longer part of this lawsuit. Plaintiffs appeal the trial court's dismissal of their claims against the driver's seventeen-year-old friend who was texting the driver much of the day and sent a text message to him immediately before the accident.

New Jersey prohibits texting while driving. A statute under our motor vehicle laws makes it illegal to use a cell phone that is not "hands-free" while driving, except in certain specifically-described emergency situations. N.J.S.A. 39:4-97.3. . . .

The issue before us is not directly addressed by these statutes or any case law that has been brought to our attention. We must determine as a matter of civil common law whether one who is texting from a location remote from the driver of a motor vehicle can be liable to persons injured because the driver was distracted by the text. . . .

. . . On the afternoon of September 21, 2009, David Kubert was riding his motorcycle, with his wife, Linda Kubert, riding as a passenger. As they came south around a curve on Hurd Street in Mine Hill Township, a pick-up truck being driven north by eighteen-year-old Kyle Best crossed the double center line of the roadway into their lane of travel. David Kubert attempted to evade the pick-up truck but could not. The front driver's side of the truck struck the Kuberts and their motorcycle. The collision severed, or nearly severed, David's left leg. It shattered Linda's left leg, leaving her fractured thighbone protruding out of the skin as she lay injured in the road.

Best stopped his truck, saw the severity of the injuries, and called 911. The time of the 911 call was 17:49:15, that is, fifteen seconds after 5:49 p.m. Best, a volunteer fireman, aided the Kuberts to the best of his ability until the police and emergency medical responders arrived. Medical treatment could not save either victim's leg. Both lost their left legs as a result of the accident.

During the day of the accident, a Monday, Best and Colonna exchanged many text messages in the morning, had lunch together at his house, and watched television until he had to go to his part-time job at a YMCA in Randolph Township. The time record from the YMCA showed that Best punched in on a time clock at 3:35 p.m. At 3:49 p.m., Colonna texted him, but he did not respond at that time. He punched out of work at 5:41. A minute later, at 5:42, Best sent a text to Colonna. He then exchanged three text messages with his father, testifying at his deposition that he did so while in the parking lot of the YMCA and that the purpose was to notify his parents he was coming home to eat dinner with them.

The accident occurred about four or five minutes after Best began driving home from the YMCA. . . .

The sequence of texts between Best and Colonna . . . indicates the precise time of the accident — within seconds of 5:48:58. Seventeen seconds elapsed from Best's sending a text to Colonna and the time of the 911 call after the accident. Those seconds had to include Best's stopping his vehicle, observing the injuries to the Kuberts, and dialing 911. It appears, therefore, that Best collided with the Kuberts' motorcycle immediately after sending a text at 5:48:58. It can be inferred that he sent that text in response to Colonna's text to him that he received twenty-five seconds earlier. Finally, it appears that Best initiated the texting with Colonna as he was about to and after he began to drive home.

Missing from the evidence is the content of the text messages. Plaintiffs were not able to obtain the messages Best and Colonna actually exchanged, and Best and Colonna did not provide that information in their depositions. . . .

After plaintiffs learned of Colonna's involvement and added her to their lawsuit, she moved for summary judgment. Her attorney argued to the trial court that Colonna had no liability for the accident because she was not present at the scene, had no legal duty to avoid sending a text to Best when he was driving, and further, that she did not know he was driving. The trial judge reviewed the evidence and the arguments of the attorneys, conducted independent research on the law, and ultimately concluded that Colonna did not have a legal duty to avoid sending a text message to Best, even if she knew he was driving. The judge dismissed plaintiffs' claims against Colonna.

. . . We first address generally the nature of a duty imposed by the common law. . . .

The New Jersey Supreme Court recently analyzed the common law process by which a court decides whether a legal duty of care exists to prevent injury to another. *Estate of Desir ex rel. Estiverne v. Vertus*, 214 N.J. 303, 69 A.3d 1247 (2013). The Court reviewed precedents developed over the years in our courts and restated the "most cogent explanation of the principles that guide [the courts] in determining whether to recognize the existence of a duty of care":

> [w]hether a person owes a duty of reasonable care toward another turns on whether the imposition of such a duty satisfies an abiding sense of basic fairness under all of the circumstances in light of considerations of public policy. That inquiry involves identifying, weighing, and balancing several factors — the relationship of the parties, the nature of the attendant risk, the opportunity and ability to exercise care, and the public interest in the proposed solution. . . . The analysis is both very fact-specific and principled; it must lead to solutions that properly and fairly resolve the specific case and generate intelligible and sensible rules to govern future conduct.

(*Id.* at 322). . . .

Plaintiffs argue . . . that Colonna independently had a duty not to send texts to a person who she knew was driving a vehicle. They have not cited a case in New Jersey or any other jurisdiction that so holds, and we have not found one in our own research. . . .

We have recognized that a passenger who distracts a driver can be held liable for the passenger's own negligence in causing an accident. In other words, a passenger in a motor vehicle has a duty "not to interfere with the driver's operations." *Champion ex rel. Ezzo v. Dunfee*, 398 N.J. Super. 112, 118 (App. Div.).

One form of interference with a driver might be obstructing his view or otherwise diverting his attention from the tasks of driving. It would be reasonable to hold a passenger liable for causing an accident if the passenger obstructed the driver's view of the road, for example, by suddenly holding a piece of paper in front of the driver's face and urging the driver to look at what is written or depicted on the paper. The same can be said if a passenger were to hold a cell phone with a text message or a picture in front of the driver's eyes. Such distracting conduct would be direct, independent negligence of the passenger, not aiding and abetting of the driver's negligent conduct. Here, of course, Colonna did not hold Best's cell phone in front of his eyes and physically distract his view of the road.

The more relevant question is whether a passenger can be liable not for actually obstructing the driver's view but only for urging the driver to take his eyes off the road and to look at a distracting object. We think the answer is yes, but only if the passenger's conduct is unreasonably risky because the passenger knows, or has special reason to know, that the driver will in fact be distracted and drive negligently as a result of the passenger's actions.

It is the primary responsibility of the driver to obey the law and to avoid distractions. Imposing a duty on a passenger to avoid any conduct that might theoretically distract the driver would open too broad a swath of potential liability in ordinary and innocent circumstances. As the Supreme Court stated in *Desir*, supra, 214 N.J. at 323 courts must be careful not to "create a broadly worded duty and . . . run the risk of unintentionally imposing liability in situations far beyond the parameters we now face." "The scope of a duty is determined under 'the totality of the circumstances,' and must be 'reasonable' under those circumstances." *J.S. v. R.T.H.*, 155 N.J. 330, 339 (1998).

"Foreseeability of the risk of harm is the foundational element in the determination of whether a duty exists." *Id.* at 337, "Foreseeability, in turn, is based on the defendant's knowledge of the risk of injury." *Podias*, supra, 394 N.J. Super. at 350.

It is foreseeable that a driver who is actually distracted by a text message might cause an accident and serious injuries or death, but it is not generally foreseeable that every recipient of a text message who is driving will neglect his obligation to obey the law and will be distracted by the text. Like a call to voicemail or an answering machine, the sending of a text message by itself does not demand that the recipient take any action. The sender should be able to assume that the recipient will read a text message only when it is safe and legal to do so, that is, when not operating a vehicle. However, if the sender knows that the recipient is both driving and will read the text immediately, then the sender has taken a foreseeable risk in sending a text at that time. The sender has knowingly engaged in distracting conduct, and it is not unfair also to hold the sender responsible for the distraction.

"When the risk of harm is that posed by third persons, a plaintiff may be required to prove that defendant was in a position to 'know or have reason to know, from past experience, that there [was] a likelihood of conduct on the part of [a] third person]' that was 'likely to endanger the safety' of another." *J.S.*, supra, 155 N.J. at 338. In *J S.*, the Court used the phrase "special reason to know" in reference to a personal relationship or prior experience that put a defendant "in a position" to "discover the risk of harm." *Ibid.* Consequently, when the sender "has actual knowledge or special reason to know," *id.* at 352, from prior texting experience or otherwise, that the recipient will view the text while driving, the sender has breached a duty of care to the public by distracting the driver.

Our conclusion that a limited duty should be imposed on the sender is supported by the "full duty analysis" described by the Supreme Court—identifying, weighing, and balancing "the relationship of the parties, the nature of the attendant risk, the opportunity and ability to exercise care, and the public interest in the proposed solution." *Desir*, supra, 214 N.J. at 332. When the sender knows that the text will reach the driver while operating a vehicle, the sender has a relationship to the public who use the roadways similar to that of a passenger physically present in the vehicle. As we have stated, a passenger must avoid distracting the driver. The remote sender of a text who knows the recipient is then driving must do the same.

When the sender texts a person who is then driving, knowing that the driver will immediately view the text, the sender has disregarded the attendant and foreseeable risk of harm to the public. The risk is substantial, as evidenced by the dire consequences in this and similar cases where texting drivers have caused severe injuries or death.

With respect to the sender's opportunity to exercise care, "[a] corresponding consideration is the practicality of preventing [the risk]." *Podias*, supra, 394 N.J. Super. at 350. We must take into account "how establishing this duty will work in practice." *Desir*, supra, 214 N.J. at 328. In imposing an independent duty of the passengers in *Podias*, we noted the "relative ease" with which they could have used their cell phones to summon help for the injured motorcyclist. It is just as easy for the sender of a text message to avoid texting to a driver who the sender knows will immediately view the text and thus be distracted from driving safely. "When the defendant's actions are 'relatively easily corrected' and the harm sought to be presented is 'serious,' it is fair to impose a duty." *Id.* at 350.

At the same time, "[c]onsiderations of fairness implicate the scope as well as the existence of a duty." *J.S.*, supra, 155 N.J. at 349. Limiting the duty to persons who have such knowledge will not require that the sender of a text predict in every instance how a recipient will act. It will not interfere with use of text messaging to a driver that one expects will obey the law. The limited duty we impose will not hold texters liable for the unlawful conduct of others, but it will hold them liable for their own negligence when they have knowingly disregarded a foreseeable risk of serious injury to others.

Finally, the public interest requires fair measures to deter dangerous texting while driving. Just as the public has learned the dangers of drinking and driving through a sustained campaign and enhanced criminal penalties and civil liability, the hazards of texting when on the road, or to someone who is on the road, may become part of the public consciousness when the liability of those involved matches the seriousness of the harm. . . .

. . . As our recitation of the facts shows, Colonna sent only one text while Best was driving. The contents of that text are unknown. No testimony established that she was aware Best would violate the law and read her text as he was driving, or that he would respond immediately. The evidence of multiple texting at other times when Best was not driving did not prove that Colonna breached the limited duty we have described.

Because the necessary evidence to prove breach of the remote texter's duty is absent on this record, summary judgment was properly granted dismissing plaintiffs' claims against Colonna.

Affirmed.

NOTES TO KUBERT v. BEST

1. *Duty as a Limit on Liability.* The trial court dismissed the plaintiffs' claims against Colonna, holding that a person has no duty to avoid texting another even if she knows the other is driving. If there is no duty, the defendant has no obligation to act reasonably in any of its actions that might have had a causal connection to the injuries resulting from the accident. The appellate court disagreed with the trial court's reasoning in a *limited-duty* analysis that considered a range of factors to determine when and whether this type of defendant owes a duty to act reasonably. This limited-duty rule is a general rule applicable to all cases with similar facts and based on general policy considerations. Why did the appellate court affirm the trial court's ruling?

2. *Policy Factors in Duty Analysis.* When one party questions whether the defendant had a duty to the plaintiff, many courts consider whether the type of harm that occurred and the type of person that was harmed were reasonably foreseeable to the defendant, consistent with the approach in *Palsgraf.* Even though it was not specifically listed among the policy elements considered by the court in *Kubert*, the court stated, as many courts do, that "foreseeability of the risk of harm is the foundational element in the determination of whether a duty exists." Often, foreseeability is the sole test of whether there is a duty. When addressing novel questions of fact, however, such as the liability of texters, courts usually consider foreseeability as the first among a number of policy factors. The court in *Kubert* weighed and balanced four additional factors. All of the cases in this section illustrate situations where novel questions of fact are presented and the connection between the actor's conduct and the harm is somewhat tenuous. In each case, the court considered whether there should be a duty from a policy perspective.

3. *The Restatement (Third) Approach to Duty Analysis.* The Restatement (Third) of Torts Liability for Physical and Emotional Harms §7 takes a different view of duty analysis generally and foreseeability in particular. Section 7 states that actors ordinarily have a duty to exercise reasonable care when their conduct creates a risk of physical harm, so courts generally do not need to consider duty in individual cases. Section 7 recognizes that sometimes novel questions of fact do raise policy considerations that may justify denying or limiting liability in some categories of cases. When this happens, a court may decide that there is no duty as a general rule for those categories of cases. Foreseeability is, however, emphatically not among the factors to be considered:

> Comment j. Foreseeable risk is an element in the determination of negligence. In order to determine whether appropriate care was exercised, the factfinder must assess the foreseeable risk at the time of the defendant's alleged negligence. The extent of foreseeable risk depends on the specific facts of the case and cannot be usefully assessed for a category of cases; small changes in the facts may make a dramatic change in how much

risk is foreseeable. Thus, for reasons explained in Comment *i*, courts should leave such determinations to juries unless no reasonable person could differ on the matter.

4. *Burdens a Duty Would Impose.* Courts generally consider how difficult it would be for potential defendants to avoid the risks to potential plaintiffs. The *Kubert* court noted that it is easy to refrain from sending a text to someone known to be driving. That observation, along with consideration of dire consequences of texting while driving, the fairness of imposing liability on those who knowingly disregard a foreseeable risk, and the public policy against texting while driving, led the court to acknowledge a limited duty.

5. *Implications of Adopting Limited-Duty Rules.* A concurrence in *Kubert* argued that a new limited-duty rule was unnecessary because existing rules governing liability based on concerted action and giving substantial assistance to the tortfeasor and liability for the acts of third parties based on special relationships were sufficient to protect Colonna from liability: "I see no reason to establish a new standard for such conduct, particularly when the record before us does not support the imposition of liability upon the remote texter." The implication of adopting a limited-duty rule is that it creates potential for liability (here for the remote texter who knows the recipient will violate the law and read the text or respond to it while driving) without resort to the details of the other tort doctrines.

Problem
Is There a Duty?

The plaintiff was riding a horse on a bridle path in a suburban area. Part of the bridle path was alongside a street. The driver of a garbage truck drove down the street, stopped the truck, and operated its noisy machinery to collect some garbage. The noise of the truck made the horse bolt, and the plaintiff was injured.

The plaintiff sought damages from the operator of the garbage truck. The defendant argued that the operator of a socially beneficial machine or apparatus who uses it for its intended purpose should have no duty to protect horses from fright and no duty for any consequences related to fright suffered by horses. Could the factors that the *Kubert* court enumerated support a court's adoption of the no-duty position suggested by the defendant? See Parsons v. Crown Disposal Co., 936 P.2d 70 (Cal. 1997).

III. Proximate Cause

A. Introduction

A torts plaintiff must do more than show that a defendant's conduct was a cause-in-fact of the plaintiff's harm. The plaintiff must also satisfy the requirement of *proximate cause*. This requirement expresses the law's policy judgment that in some cases it would be unfair to make defendants pay for all of the harms associated with their conduct. Proximate cause doctrines reflect the idea that the defendant's conduct and the plaintiff's harm must have a connection that is reasonably close in order to justify imposing liability on the defendant.

Complex Doctrines.   While "proximate" literally means "near," "close," or "imminent," these definitions do not help in understanding proximate cause. In legal causation, "proximate" means that a defendant's act satisfies whatever policy criteria a jurisdiction uses to treat a harm a person causes as one the person must pay for, instead of as one that the person may inflict for free.

Courts have developed a variety of approaches to proximate cause. The *directness* test treats a defendant's conduct that is a cause-in-fact of a plaintiff's harm as a proximate cause if there are no intervening forces between the defendant's act and the plaintiff's harm. The *substantial factor* test treats a defendant's conduct as a proximate cause of a plaintiff's harm if the conduct is important enough, compared to other causes of the harm, to justify liability. The *foreseeability* test treats a cause-in-fact as a proximate cause if the type of accident that occurred was reasonably foreseeable. The recently adopted Restatement (Third) of Torts: Liability for Physical and Emotional Harm adopts a *risk standard* that imposes liability only for injuries within the scope of the risk that supported an initial finding of an actor's negligence. This section considers each of these approaches.

Simple Applications.   In almost all cases, courts treat proximate cause as a question of fact for the jury. This limits appellate review. Courts will reject appeals on proximate cause grounds if the jury received proper instructions and some evidence supports the jury's verdict.

Further insulating proximate cause issues from judicial review is the practice of using fairly general jury instructions about proximate cause. In a great many states, the jury will be instructed that "a proximate cause is one which in natural and continuous sequence, unbroken by any efficient intervening cause produces the injury and without which the result would not have occurred." See, e.g., Russell v. K-Mart Corp., 761 A.2d 1 (Del. 2000); Cruz-Mendez v. ISU/Insurance Servs., 156 N.J. 556 (1999); Torres v. El Paso Elec. Co., 172 N.M. 729 (1999). Note that this instruction is consistent, to varying extents, with the directness, substantial factor, foreseeability, and risk standard approaches.

Understanding Proximate Cause in Practice.   In each jurisdiction, the accepted doctrines of proximate cause are the background against which litigants attempt to structure their cases and attempt to persuade juries. The doctrines are also the context in which an occasional jury decision may be subject to reversal. For these reasons, developing an understanding of the rival views is important.

B. Directness

Under the direct cause test, an act that is a cause-in-fact of an injury will be treated as a proximate cause of the injury if there is a direct connection between the act and the injury. Note that under this doctrine, even if the defendant's act is a but-for cause of the plaintiff's harm, the plaintiff may sometimes fail to establish proximate cause. In the language of some courts, an additional act subsequent to the defendant's can "break the chain of causation" or "divert" the force created by the defendant's negligence and "make the injury its own." *In re Polemis* is a classic British case applying a direct cause test. The opinions also consider whether another test, the foreseeability test, should be used. *Laureano v. Louzoun* is a modern American application of the directness test.

IN RE AN ARBITRATION BETWEEN POLEMIS AND FURNESS, WITHY & CO., LTD.

3 K.B. 560 (Ct. App. 1921)

[The owners of a Greek steamship, the Thrasyvoulos, sought damages for the total loss of the ship due to fire. The ship carried a cargo of cement and general cargo as well as benzine and petrol and iron to Casablanca. After arrival in Casablanca in July of 1917, a portion of the Thrasyvoulos's cargo was removed by stevedores sent on board by the people who had chartered the boat. On July 21, the stevedores placed heavy wooden planks across one of the ship's holds to serve as a platform while moving some of the cases of cargo. The cargo was raised using slings, which held the cases, and a winch, which raised and lowered the slings. There had been leakage of benzine or petrol into that hold, and there was a considerable amount of petrol vapor present.] In the course of heaving a sling of the cases from the hold, the rope by which the sling was being raised or the sling itself came into contact with the boards placed across the forward end of the hatch, causing one of the boards to fall into the lower hold, and the fall was instantaneously followed by a rush of flames from the lower hold, and this resulted eventually in the total destruction of the ship.

The owners contended (so far as material) that the charterers were liable for the loss of the ship; that fire caused by negligence [was a type of loss for which the charterers could be found liable under the terms of the charter], and that the ship was in fact lost by the negligence of the stevedores, who were the charterers' servants, in letting the sling strike the board, knocking it into the hold, and thereby causing a spark which set fire to the petrol vapour and destroyed the ship.

The charterers contended that fire however caused was [not the type of loss for which the charterers could be found liable]; that there was no negligence for which the charterers were responsible, inasmuch as to let a board fall into the hold of the ship could do no harm to the ship and therefore was not negligence towards the owners; and that the danger and/or damage were too remote — i.e., no reasonable man would have foreseen danger and/or damage of this kind resulting from the fall of the board.

[Arbitrators found that (1) the stevedores negligently caused the board to fall, which created a spark that ignited the petrol in the hold; (2) causing the spark could not reasonably have been anticipated from the falling of the board, though some damage to the ship might reasonably have been anticipated; and (3) damages suffered by the owners amounted to £196,165. Sankey, J., affirmed the award, and the charterers appealed.]

BANKES L.J. . . .

In the present case the arbitrators have found as a fact that the falling of the plank was due to the negligence of the defendants' servants. The fire appears to me to have been directly caused by the falling of the plank. Under these circumstances I consider that it is immaterial that the causing of the spark by the falling of the plank could not have been reasonably anticipated. . . . Given the breach of duty which constitutes the negligence, and given the damages as a direct result of that negligence, the anticipations of the person whose negligent act has produced the damage appear to me to be irrelevant. I consider that the damages claimed are not too remote.

SCRUTTON L.J. . . .

The . . . defence is that the damage is too remote from the negligence, as it could not be reasonably foreseen as a consequence. On this head we were referred to a number of well known cases in which vague language, which I cannot think to be really helpful, has been used in an attempt to define the point at which damage becomes too remote from, or not sufficiently directly caused by, the breach of duty, which is the original cause of action, to be recoverable. For instance, I cannot think it useful to say the damage must be the natural and probable result. This suggests that there are results which are natural but not probable, and other results which are probable but not natural. I am not sure what either adjective means in this connection; if they mean the same thing, two need not be used; if they mean different things, the difference between them should be defined. . . . To determine whether an act is negligent, it is relevant to determine whether any reasonable person would foresee that the act would cause damage; if he would not, the act is not negligent. But if the act would or might probably cause damage, the fact that the damage it in fact causes is not the exact kind of damage one would expect is immaterial, so long as the damage is in fact directly traceable to the negligent act, and not due to the operation of independent causes having no connection with the negligent act, except that they could not avoid its results. Once the act is negligent, the fact that its exact operation was not foreseen is immaterial. . . . In the present case it was negligent in discharging cargo to knock down the planks of the temporary staging, for they might easily cause some damages either to workmen, or cargo, or the ship. The fact that they did directly produce an unexpected result, a spark in an atmosphere of petrol vapour which caused a fire, does not relieve the person who was negligent from the damage which his negligent act directly caused. . . .

LAUREANO v. LOUZOUN

560 N.Y.S.2d 337 (N.Y. App. Div. 1990)

Memorandum by The Court. . . .

On January 21, 1985, the plaintiff, a tenant in the defendants' premises, arose from bed at approximately 5 a.m. and put two large pots of water on her stove to boil. While in the process of pouring the boiling water from one pot into the other, the plaintiff banged the pots against each other, causing the boiling water to spill onto her knee and feet. The plaintiff commenced the instant action, alleging, inter alia, that the defendants' negligence in failing to provide heat and hot water to the premises and in failing to maintain the boiler in proper working condition caused the incident and her resulting injuries. The plaintiff further alleged that the defendants had constructive notice of the defective condition at least two weeks prior to the incident, as well as actual notice. The defendants moved for summary judgment on the ground that their conduct was not, as a matter of law, the proximate cause of the plaintiff's injuries. The trial court granted the motion holding that "[t]here was no connection of proximate cause between the lack of heat and the accident." We affirm.

The defendants' failure to provide heat and hot water to the premises was not the proximate cause, as a matter of law, of the injuries sustained by the plaintiff. While the defendants' conduct gave rise to the plaintiff's attempt to provide a substitute supply of heat, the act of boiling water was not the direct cause of the injuries. Rather, the intervening act of banging one pot against the other brought about the injuries sustained by the plaintiff. Those injuries would not have resulted from the failure to supply hot water alone, and cannot be classified as injuries normally to have been expected to ensue from the landlord's conduct.

NOTES TO *IN RE POLEMIS* AND LAUREANO v. LOUZOUN

1. *Simplicity of the Direct Cause Test.*   Judicial opinions finding that an act is a *direct cause* of a plaintiff's harm usually involve situations where all would agree that the connection between the defendant's act and the plaintiff's harm was so close that the defendant should be liable. The direct cause test is, however, not limited to clear-cut cases. Laureano v. Louzoun demonstrates that the directness test can limit liability without any complicated analysis. In Laureano v. Louzoun, the court describes three acts: the landlord's inadequate operation of the apartment's heating system, the tenant's boiling of water, and the tenant's banging pots together. Was the landlord's act a direct cause of either one of the tenant's acts? Does the court make clear how it decides what effects are directly related to an actor's conduct and what effects are not directly related to it?

2. *Liability for Unforeseen Harms.*   The directness approach may lead to liability for unexpected consequences, as *In re Polemis* illustrates. Dropping a wooden board into the hull of a ship might foreseeably cause a dent in the ship, but is a fire foreseeable? Arguing that other tests are unclear, an opinion in *Polemis* states that a negligent defendant must pay for damage related to negligent conduct "so long as the damage is in fact directly traceable" to that conduct. Does the opinion define "directly traceable"? How do the *Polemis* opinions justify placing the cost of the fire on an actor whose negligent conduct could have been expected to cause only a dent in the ship?

3. *Directness and Foreseeability.*   The foreseeability concept shows up at the end of the court's discussion of direct cause in Laureano v. Louzoun. It is not unusual for a court to combine various tests for proximate cause, either intentionally or without apparent recognition that it has happened.

Problem
The Direct Cause Test

A ten-year-old boy picked up a metal box that contained some blasting caps while he was walking to school on a path near a mining company's facilities. A foreman employed by the mining company had thrown the box away, thinking that the caps inside it were empty. The boy's mother and father saw him play with the caps. After a few days, the boy traded the caps to another boy in exchange for writing paper. The other boy was seriously wounded when the caps exploded as he played with them. How would the direct cause test treat the relationship between the foreman's conduct and the victim's injury? See Pittsburg Reduction Co. v. Horton, 113 S.W. 647 (Ark. 1903).

Statute: OCCUPATIONAL DISEASES; PROXIMATE CAUSATION
N.M. Stat. §52-3-32 (2017)

The occupational diseases defined in Section 52-3-33 NMSA 1978 shall be deemed to arise out of the employment only if there is a direct causal connection between the conditions under which the work is performed and the occupational disease and which can be seen to have followed as a natural incident of the work as a result of the exposure occasioned by the nature of the employment and which can be fairly traced to the employment as the proximate cause. The disease must be incidental to the character of the business and not independent of the relation of employer and employee. The disease need not have been foreseen or expected but after its contraction must appear to have had its origin in a risk connected with the employment and to have flowed from that source as a natural consequence. In all cases where the defendant denies that an alleged occupational disease is the material and direct result of the conditions under which work was performed, the worker must establish that causal connection as a medical probability by medical expert testimony. No award of compensation benefits shall be based on speculation or on expert testimony that as a medical possibility the causal connection exists.

Statute: GOVERNMENTAL IMMUNITY FROM TORT LIABILITY

Michigan Compiled Laws §691.1407(2)(c) (2017)

(2) [E]ach officer and employee of a governmental agency . . . is immune from tort liability for an injury to a person or damage to property caused by the officer, employee, or member while in the course of employment or service or caused by the volunteer while acting on behalf of a governmental agency if all of the following are met:

> (c) The officer's, employee's, member's, or volunteer's conduct does not amount to gross negligence that is the proximate cause of the injury or damage.

NOTES TO STATUTES

1. *Special Rules for Special Circumstances.* States sometimes adopt different cause rules for different purposes. New Mexico has adopted the following rule for proximate cause in routine cases: "[A]ny harm which is in itself foreseeable, as to which the actor has created or increased the recognizable risk, is always "proximate," no matter how it is brought about." Torres v. El Paso Electric Co., 987 P.2d 386, 396 (1999). Like many other states, New Mexico has adopted a different rule for workers' compensation cases — cases involving injuries arising out of employment. How is the New Mexico proximate cause rule for workers' compensation cases different from its proximate cause rule for routine cases?

2. *Interpreting Proximate Cause Language.* The Michigan statute permits suits against grossly negligent government employees if their conduct is a "proximate cause" of injury or damage to another. Defining "proximate cause" is crucial for understanding the effect of this statute. Michigan courts have defined it as the one most immediate and efficient cause preceding the injury or damage. By this rule, even if police officers were grossly negligent in choosing a roadside location for a sobriety checkpoint, they would be immune from liability when a speeding car killed an arrestee at that location. George v. Michigan, 136 F. Supp. 2d 695 (E.D. Mich. 2001).

Perspective: The Necessity of a Proximate Cause Doctrine

Because a multitude of antecedent events are logically and physically necessary to produce any tort victim's harm, the cause-in-fact test is a very blunt tool for deciding who should be liable to the victim:

> The "but for" test does not provide a satisfactory account of the concept of causation if the words "in fact" are taken seriously. *A* carelessly sets his alarm one hour early. When he wakes up the next morning he has ample time before work and decides to take an early morning drive in the country. While on the road he is spotted by *B*, an old college roommate, who becomes so excited that he runs off the road and hurts *C*. But for the negligence of *A*, *C* would never have been injured, because *B* doubtless would have continued along his uneventful way. Nonetheless, it is common ground that *A*, even if negligent, is in no way responsible for the injury to *C*, caused by *B*.
>
> Its affinity for absurd hypotheticals should suggest that the "but for" test should be abandoned as even a tentative account of the concept of causation. But there has been no such abandonment. Instead, it has been argued that the "but for" test provides a "philosophical" test for the concept of causation which shows that the "consequences" of any act (or at least any negligent act) extend indefinitely into the future. But there is no merit, philosophic or otherwise, to an account of any concept which cannot handle the simplest of cases, and only a mistaken view of philosophic inquiry demands an acceptance of an account of causation that conflicts so utterly with ordinary usage.
>
> Once the "philosophical" account of causation was accepted, it could not be applied in legal contexts without modification because of the unacceptable results that it required. The concept of "cause in law" or "proximate" cause became necessary to confine the concept within acceptable limits.

See Richard A. Epstein, *A Theory of Strict Liability*, 2 J. Legal Stud. 151, 160 (1973).

C. Substantial Factor

The *substantial factor test* for proximate cause considers whether the contribution of a party's act was relatively important compared with other but-for causes in producing the harm suffered by the plaintiff. The opinion in American Truck Leasing, Inc. v. Thorne Equipment Company relies on the considerations identified in the Restatement (Second) of Torts §431 to analyze whether the defendant's act was a substantial factor. Just as "direct" and "foreseeable" are subject to interpretation, the Restatement factors are similarly malleable. Chelcher v. Spider Staging Corp. focuses on how the number of factors contributing to a plaintiff's harm affects the substantial factor analysis. Taylor v. Jackson considers the relevance of the lapse of time between a defendant's conduct and a plaintiff's harm.

AMERICAN TRUCK LEASING, INC. v. THORNE EQUIPMENT CO.

583 A.2d 1242 (Pa. Super. Ct. 1991)

WIELAND, J.

. . . Dorothy Gross was the owner of a vacant building at Nos. 1758-1762 North Front Street, Philadelphia. On June 27, 1988, between 1:30 and 2:30 a.m., a fire started in combustible trash and debris which had been allowed to accumulate on the premises. The fire spread across a narrow street and damaged premises at Nos. 105-109 West Palmer Street, which premises were owned by Joseph A. Tartaglia and occupied for business purposes by JATCO, Inc. The fire burned for more than eight hours before being extinguished. Pursuant to a determination made by the City of Philadelphia, Thorne Equipment was engaged thereafter to demolish a six story elevator shaft on Tartaglia's land. This elevator shaft, although still standing, had been damaged by the fire. Thorne Equipment began its demolition work on June 28, 1988, but during the course thereof a portion of the elevator shaft fell upon and damaged buildings and vehicles owned by the plaintiffs, American Truck Lines, Inc. and American Truck Leasing, Inc. (American). American thereafter filed a civil action against Thorne Equipment, the City of Philadelphia, Tartaglia, JATCO, Inc. and Dorothy Gross. All claims remain undetermined in the trial court except the claim against Dorothy Gross, which has been summarily dismissed.

American alleged in its complaint that Gross had been negligent by allowing combustible trash and debris to accumulate on her property and in otherwise failing to exercise care to prevent the occurrence of a fire. That negligence, if it existed, would be a legal cause of American's harm only if it could be shown to be a substantial factor in bringing about such harm. Restatement (Second) of Torts §431. Factors to be considered in determining whether an act is a substantial factor in bringing about harm to another are enumerated in Restatement (Second) of Torts §433 as follows:

> The following considerations are in themselves or in combination with one another important in determining whether the actor's conduct is a substantial factor in bringing about harm to another:
>> (a) the number of other factors which contribute in producing the harm and the extent of the effect which they have in producing it;
>> (b) whether the actor's conduct has created a force or series of forces which are in continuous and active operation up to the time of the harm, or has created a situation harmless unless acted upon by other forces for which the actor is not responsible;
>> (c) lapse of time.

When these considerations are applied to the facts of the instant case, they demonstrate that even if Dorothy Gross had been negligent in allowing combustible trash to accumulate on her property, such accumulation was too far removed factually and chronologically from American's harm to be a legal cause thereof. Gross's negligence was passive and harmless until acted upon by an independent force. Moreover, the fire which erupted on her property was extinguished before any harm had occurred to American. The negligence for which she was responsible, if any, was not in active operation at the time when damages were caused to American's property. Those damages were caused on the day following the fire because of the manner in which the fire weakened elevator shaft was demolished by Thorne Equipment. Because the negligent accumulation of combustible trash was too far removed from the damages to American's property and because those damages were caused by the intervening act of the demolition contractor, it cannot be said legally or factually that the alleged negligence of Dorothy Gross was a substantial factor in causing harm to American.

In Ford v. Jeffries, 474 Pa. 588, 379 A.2d 111 (1977), the Supreme Court held that it was for the jury to determine whether a property owner's negligence in maintaining his property in a state of disrepair was a substantial factor in causing the harm to a neighbor's property damaged by fire originating on the original owner's property. In the instant case, however, American's property damage was not caused by a spreading fire. It was caused, rather, by the demolition of a fire damaged grain elevator after the fire had been extinguished. This demolition constituted an independent agency. We conclude, therefore, that the trial court correctly determined that Dorothy Gross, as a matter of law, was not legally responsible for appellant's harm.

Affirmed.

NOTES TO AMERICAN TRUCK LEASING, INC. v. THORNE EQUIPMENT CO.

1. Substantial Factor Test. The court describes its earlier decision in Ford v. Jeffries, where a defendant who had maintained property in disrepair was liable, when a fire started on the defendant's property, for fire damage to a neighbor's property. Why was a finding of liability proper there but rejected as a matter of law in *American Truck Leasing*? How would the court have decided *American Truck Leasing* if the elevator shaft had collapsed onto the plaintiff's property while the fire was still burning?

2. Foreseeability and the Restatement (Second)'s Substantial Factor Test. The Restatement (Second) of Torts §435(1) states that the foreseeability of the harm or the manner in which it occurred to someone in the defendant's position is irrelevant to the determination of whether the defendant's act is a substantial factor. Section 435(2) qualifies this rule by saying that "if, looking back from the harm to the actor's negligent conduct, it appears to the court highly extraordinary that it should have brought about the harm," the actor's conduct should not be considered a legal cause.

Problem
"Continuous Forces" and the Substantial Factor Test

How should a court apply the Restatement's "continuous" forces factor to the following facts? A manufacturer failed to warn about the dangers associated with its pipeline valve. A distributor of the valve supplied a bracket that was unsafe to hold the valve. Workers, who were injured while trying to repair the valve, neglected to check diagrams that would have enabled them to repair the valve safely and failed to wear safety equipment. Could the Restatement provision justify treating the failure to warn as a substantial factor in the worker's injuries? See Torres v. Xomox Corporation, 49 Cal. App. 4th 1, 18 (1996).

CHELCHER v. SPIDER STAGING CORP.
892 F. Supp. 710 (D.V.I. 1995)

MOORE, District Judge.

This matter is before the Court on the plaintiffs' motion for partial summary judgment, filed June 5, 1995, and the defendant's motion for summary judgment, filed May 19, 1995. Having carefully reviewed the parties' submissions, the Court will deny plaintiffs' motion and grant the defendant's motion for the following reasons.

On May 17, 1989, plaintiff Lennox Chelcher worked at sandblasting the top hemisphere of a spherical propane tank belonging to Hess Oil Virgin Islands ("HOVIC") while employed by Industrial Maintenance Corporation ("IMC"). Working from [a] movable, cage-like scaffold or "spider" allegedly manufactured by defendant Spider Staging Corporation ("Spider"), plaintiff Lennox Chelcher ("Chelcher") allegedly sustained permanently disabling damage to his lower back from approximately five hours of sandblasting in an uncomfortable position. The spider scaffold had been mis-rigged on the day in question by HOVIC and/or Chelcher's employer, IMC, such that it did not hang plumb from its suspension wires, but rather dragged along the side of the spherical tank. This mis-rigging caused the floor-platform of the spider to tilt increasingly away from the horizontal as it progressed up the side of the tank. Having become fully aware of this situation, Chelcher nonetheless boarded the spider cage and sandblasted from its increasingly tilted platform for about five hours. . . . The instant summary judgment motion[] concern[s] causes of action against Spider in the nature of . . . negligent failure to warn. . . .

The first prong of causation plaintiffs must prove is whether the alleged product defect, a [negligent] failure to affix an instruction manual to the scaffold, was a cause-in-fact of Chelcher's injuries. . . .

Chelcher had worked on similar, if not identical scaffolds, for approximately three years before he proceeded to sandblast the tank from the spider on the morning May 17, 1989. In these circumstances, the Court can find no credible evidence that Spider's alleged failure to warn could have caused Chelcher's injury. First, plaintiffs' claim that a pictogram depicting a man falling from a scaffold would have caused him to request access to information in the owner's manual is highly speculative. Second, the assertion that Chelcher would have acted differently that morning, upon seeing a pictogram, is belied by the fact that he proceeded to sandblast on the day of his injury despite the absence of the job-site safety inspector and despite the obvious mis-rigging of the spider. Third, plaintiffs have presented no credible evidence from which reasonable jurors could conclude that information in the safety manual would have prevented Chelcher's injury; although the manual admonishes users to keep the spider vertical to avoid accidents, it does not warn that back strain is a likely consequence of prolonged use of a leaning spider.

The second prong of the causation element is whether the alleged defect, Spider's failure to warn or affix an instruction manual to the spider cage, was the proximate or legal cause of Chelcher's injuries. Spider's conduct is a proximate, or legal, "cause of harm to another if . . . [its] conduct is a substantial factor in bringing about the harm." Restatement (Second) of Torts §431(a). Even if we had found Spider's conduct to have been a factual (but for) cause of the harm, we would find that plaintiffs failed to show it was a proximate cause of Chelcher's injuries. The use of the phrase "substantial" in the Restatement and the case law demonstrates that there is no litmus test for causation; rather, proximate causation, and hence liability, "hinges on principles of responsibility, not physics." *Van Buskirk v. Carey Canadian Mines, Ltd.,* 760 F.2d 481, 492 (3d Cir. 1985); Restatement (Second) of Torts §431, cmt. a.

Section 433(a) of the Restatement directs a court to consider "the number of other factors which contribute in producing the harm and the extent of the effect which they have in producing it." Section 434 notes that a determination of proximate causation properly lies within the province of the court when, as here, reasonable minds cannot differ. Weighing all the evidence put forth by both parties and accepting *arguendo* plaintiffs' factual allegations regarding Spider's failure to warn, the Court finds that said failure could not have been a substantial factor in bringing about Chelcher's injuries. HOVIC's and IMC's mis-rigging of the scaffold, their failure to supervise the worksite, and their request that Chelcher proceed in his sandblasting, and his ready acquiescence despite the absence of the safety inspector, were all substantial contributing factors in causing his injury. The combined effect of these contributing factors had such a predominant impact and so diluted Spider's contribution, if any, as to prevent it from being a substantial factor in producing the harm to Chelcher. As no reasonable jury could conclude that Spider's alleged failure to warn was the proximate cause of Chelcher's back pain, Spider is not liable in tort to plaintiffs. . . .

For the foregoing reasons, neither Chelcher nor his wife may succeed in an action against the manufacturer of the spider scaffold. An order granting summary judgment in favor of Spider is attached.

NOTES TO CHELCHER v. SPIDER STAGING CORP.

1. *Cause-in-Fact and Proximate Cause.* The *Chelcher* court analyzed cause-in-fact and proximate cause individually. For proximate cause, the court focused on the first consideration identified in Restatement (Second) §433(a), the number of other causes and the extent of their effect. The court evaluated whether, considering the other factors that influenced the course of events, the defendant's conduct *was significant enough* to justify imposing liability. For cause-in-fact, the court considered whether a warning by the defendant would have *made any difference* to the course of events. Thus, the cause-in-fact question is factual ("Would it have made any difference?") while the proximate cause question involves policy judgment ("Is imposing liability justifiable?").

2. *The Potential for Numerous Proximate Causes.* The court recognized that there may be many substantial factors contributing to an accident, so there need not be just one proximate cause. The court's opinion lists four factors that were all substantial and whose combined effect was great enough to make Spider's contribution relatively insignificant. Does it make sense that there can be more than one proximate cause? Does the Restatement (Second) language quoted in *American Truck Leasing* allow for more than one proximate cause?

TAYLOR v. JACKSON
643 A.2d 771 (Commw. Ct. Pa. 1994)

NEWMAN, J.

In these consolidated actions, Valerie Taylor (Taylor) and her parents, Robert and Peggy Taylor, and Joan D. Lindow and her husband, Myron G. Lindow (Lindows), appeal from orders of the Court of Common Pleas of Northumberland County (trial court) granting appellees' motions for summary judgment. . . . We reverse and remand. . . .

On the evening of July 30, 1988, at approximately 6:15 p.m., Diane L. Klopp (Klopp) was driving her motor vehicle in one of the two westbound lanes of Interstate 80, when she either slowed down or stopped on the roadway due to a sudden, heavy rainstorm. Consequently, Jackson, who was following Klopp in his tractor-trailer, jackknifed his vehicle in an attempt to stop so that he would not collide with her vehicle; this incident occurred at mile post number 227.1 of the highway. As a result, the jackknifed vehicle blocked both westbound lanes of the highway.

Traffic immediately began to accumulate behind the disabled vehicle. Two tractor-trailers, driven by John Barrett (Barrett) and Carol Porter (Porter), respectively, were the first vehicles to queue behind Jackson's jackknifed tractor-trailer. Minutes after the accident, an electric utility line owned by Pennsylvania Power and Light Company (PPL), which had been strung across Interstate Route 80, sagged or fell for unknown reasons. The line came to rest on the ground across the eastbound lanes of traffic and on top of Barrett's and Porter's vehicles in the westbound lanes.

At approximately 6:20 p.m. a second motor vehicle accident occurred as vehicles were coming to a stop behind Jackson's tractor-trailer. At mile post number 227.6, one-half mile from the initial accident, the tractor-trailer of Chester Ray Watley, Jr. (Watley) struck the rear of a car operated by Mirita Shroff (Shroff) in the right-hand westbound lane of the highway. After impacting with Shroff's vehicle, Watley's tractor-trailer jackknifed and came to rest against a guard rail at the north side of the right-hand berm.

At 7:05 p.m., State Police Trooper William Nice arrived to detour traffic at Exit 34 of the highway, which was approximately 4.5 miles east of the second accident site. Trooper Nice set up flares across the westbound lanes of the highway and remained at the westbound exit ramp directing traffic until approximately 12:30 a.m. At approximately 7:20 p.m., two PPL employees . . . were at the scene of the first accident and attempted to remove the electrical wire from the road.

It was about 8:15 p.m. when the Lindows came to a stop near mile post number 228.1, one half mile from the second accident scene. Following the Lindows' vehicle was the vehicle of Gerald A. Franz (Franz) along with his passenger, Taylor. A third motor vehicle accident occurred when Joseph J. Questore (Questore) drove his delivery truck into the rear of the Franz vehicle, propelling it eighty-seven feet. Questore's truck also struck, *inter alia,* the rear of the Lindows' vehicle. Because of these collisions, Taylor and the Lindows suffered serious injuries [and sued the appellees, Klopp, Jackson, Watley, PPL, and the Pennsylvania State Police]. . . .

After briefing and oral argument, the trial court granted the motions for summary judgment of appellees [from which the Taylors and Lindows filed this appeal].

Taylor and the Lindows contend that the trial court improperly invaded the province of the jury in determining that the conduct of the various appellees was not a substantial factor in causing their injuries. . . .

In the instant matter, the trial court listed the factors which contributed to the third accident. These factors were:

1. Klopp coming to a stop during the sudden thunderstorm;
2. Jackson jackknifing his tractor-trailer;
3. the initial back-up of traffic behind the first accident;
4. the downed PPL power line;
5. the efforts of the Pennsylvania State Police [PSP];
6. Watley's jackknifing his tractor-trailer in the second accident;
7. the traffic continuing to back up behind the second accident for approximately two (2) hours; and
8. Questore's negligent conduct.

The trial court then concluded that the fact that two hours elapsed between the conduct of Klopp, Jackson, Watley, PPL, and the PSP and the injuries complained of, rendered any negligent conduct on their part not continuous and not active up to the time of the harm. The court thus held that no reasonable jury could find proximate cause between the appellees' conduct and the harm complained of, and accordingly entered summary judgment on their behalf. After a thorough review of the record, we conclude that the trial court's determination in this matter was in error.

Comment (f) of Restatement (Second) of Torts §433(c) provides that "where it is evident that the influence of the actor's negligence is still a substantial factor, mere lapse of time, no matter how long it is, is not sufficient to prevent it from being the legal cause of the other harm." Moreover, our supreme court in *Ford v. Jeffries*, 474 Pa. 588, 379 A.2d 111 (1977), observed that the determination of whether an actor's conduct was a substantial cause of the injuries complained of should not be taken from the jury if the jury may reasonably differ about whether the conduct of the actor has been a substantial factor in causing the harm. Since we believe that reasonable individuals can differ regarding the question of whether a two hour period should insulate a negligent actor from suit given the particular and unique facts of the instant matter, we hold that the trial court erred in granting summary judgment. . . . [Judgment reversed and remanded.]

NOTE TO TAYLOR v. JACKSON

Lapse of Time.   As the length of time between an act and an injury increases, more time is available for other independent acts to contribute significantly to the harm. If more acts contribute significantly to the harm, then the original act is less likely to be a substantial factor. The Restatement (Second) of Torts §433 comment f treats this issue:

> Experience has shown that where a great length of time has elapsed between the actor's negligence and harm to another, a great number of contributing factors may have operated, many of which may be difficult or impossible of actual proof. Where the time has been long, the effect of the actor's conduct may thus become so attenuated as to be insignificant and unsubstantial as compared to the aggregate of other factors which have contributed. However, where it is evident that the influence of the actor's negligence is still a substantial factor, mere lapse of time, no matter how long, is not sufficient to prevent it from being the legal cause of another's harm.

Evidence of lapse of time may reinforce a conclusion, also supported by other factors, that a defendant's act was not a substantial factor. In Brown v. Philadelphia College of Osteopathic Medicine, 760 A.2d 863 (Pa. Super. 2000), the lapse of time confirmed the analysis of other considerations:

> In the present case, the child was born August 29, 1991 and was tested for syphilis shortly thereafter. The erroneous test results [that are the factual basis for the Browns' suit against the hospital] were delivered to the Browns, and Mr. Brown confessed his adultery while Mrs. Brown was still hospitalized recovering from the birth. By some time in October, they had learned that the diagnosis had been made in error. The primary physical altercation between the couple that resulted in Mrs. Brown's physical injury, the arrest of both parties, the filing of a protection from abuse order against Mr. Brown and the couple's separation, occurred more than two months after the receipt of the erroneous diagnosis and in the month after they learned that the diagnosis had been in error. Thus, the lapse of more than two months, between the erroneous diagnosis and the initial break up of their marriage, point to a finding that

[the hospital's] negligence was not a substantial factor in bringing about this harm. Accordingly, under all three factors set forth in the Restatement analysis, the [hospital's] negligence was not a substantial factor in bringing about the breakdown of the Browns' marriage and, thus, was not a proximate cause of this harm.

The relevance of lapse of time may depend on the mechanism by which the act produces the harm. If the construction materials used in a building, for instance, cause ill effects only after an occupant's long exposure, the lapse of time will not prevent the act from being a substantial factor. But if the consequences of defective materials usually manifest themselves immediately, the significance of the causal contribution of the construction materials may be suspect. See Bahura v. S.E.W. Investors, 754 A.2d 928 (D.C. Ct. App. 1999).

Problems
Applying the Restatement Substantial Factor Test

Which Restatement factors would be particularly relevant when deciding whether the defendant's act in each of the following cases was a substantial factor in causing the plaintiff's harm?

A. A tractor-trailer operator drove off the road and parked on the shoulder so that he could sleep, in violation of a statute prohibiting parking on the shoulder of an interstate highway in a non-emergency situation. An automobile driver on the same road fell asleep at the wheel, lost control of his car, and collided with the parked tractor-trailer. The car driver's widow sued the tractor-trailer driver for negligently parking on the shoulder. Tennyson v. Brower, 823 F. Supp. 421 (E.D. Ky. 1993).

B. A driver carelessly drove her automobile on a paved road that was 20 feet wide and had a 15-foot-wide right-of-way on either side. Her car veered to the left, crossed the eastbound lane, and struck an electric pole. The pole was newly installed by the power company and was located in the right-of-way, 8 feet from the edge of the paved road, which was contrary to statute. The driver sued the power company for negligently locating its pole in the right-of-way. See Talarico v. Bonham, 650 A.2d 1192 (Pa. Commw. 1994).

C. Employees at a hospital negligently disposed of used needles contaminated with hepatitis B in a trash receptacle. A custodial worker emptying the trash was pricked by a needle, which should have been placed in a needle breaker box. The worker became contaminated with hepatitis B, and her family sued the hospital based on their fear of contracting the disease from her, claiming that the fear was caused by the hospital's negligence. See Raney v. Walter O. Moss Regional Hospital, 629 So. 2d 485, 493 (La. Ct. App. 1993).

D. Foreseeability

1. Linking Liability to Foreseeability

Foreseeability is ignored in the directness test and given only a small function in the Restatement (Second)'s substantial factor test. However, for a large number of states foreseeability has central importance in their proximate cause jurisprudence. For those states, under the foreseeability test a defendant's conduct is a proximate cause of a plaintiff's harm if (1) the conduct is a cause-in-fact of the accident and (2) the general type of accident was a reasonably foreseeable consequence of the defendant's conduct. Tieder v. Little presents a typical application of the foreseeability test, showing that the test is not self-applying but that it involves descriptions of the type of harm the defendant risked and the type of harm that the plaintiff suffered.

TIEDER v. LITTLE
502 So. 2d 923 (Fla. Dist. Ct. App. 1987)

HUBBART, J. . . .

On January 7, 1983, at approximately 9:00 p.m., the plaintiffs' decedent, Trudi Beth Tieder, was struck by an automobile, pinned up against a brick wall, and killed when the wall collapsed on her—as she walked out the front door of Eaton Hall dormitory on the University of Miami campus. At the time, two students were attempting to clutch-start an automobile in the circular drive in front of Eaton Hall—one student was pushing the car while the other student was in the car behind the wheel—when, suddenly, the student behind the wheel lost control of the car. The automobile left the circular driveway, lurched over a three-inch curb onto a grassy area, and traveled some thirty-three feet across the front lawn parallel to Eaton Hall. The automobile collided with an elevated walkway leading out of the front door of Eaton Hall, jumped onto the walkway, and struck the plaintiffs' decedent as she walked out the front door of the dormitory. The automobile continued forward, pinning the decedent against a high brick wall that supported a concrete canopy at the entrance to the dormitory. Because the wall was negligently designed and constructed without adequate supports required by the applicable building code, the entire wall came off intact from its foundation and crushed her to death. Dr. Joseph Davis, the Dade County Medical Examiner, averred by affidavit that in his opinion the decedent would not have died merely from the automobile impact; in his opinion, she died as a result of the brick wall falling intact and in one piece upon her. Two affidavits of professional engineers were also filed below detailing the negligent design and construction of the subject brick wall.

The plaintiffs Sheila M. Tieder and Richard J. Tieder, administrators of the estate of Trudi Beth Tieder, brought a wrongful death action against: (1) the owner and the operator of the automobile (not parties to this appeal), (2) Robert M. Little, the architect who designed the allegedly defective brick wall, and (3) the University of Miami, which caused the said brick wall to be erected and maintained. The amended complaint charged the defendant Little and the University of Miami with various acts of negligent conduct including negligence in the design and construction of the brick wall. The defendant Little moved to dismiss the complaint against him and urged that his alleged negligence was not, as a matter of law, the proximate cause of the decedent's death because the entire accident was so bizarre as to be entirely unforeseeable; the University of Miami moved for a summary judgment in its favor and made the same argument. The trial court agreed and granted both motions. . . . The plaintiffs appeal. . . .

At the outset, the "proximate cause" element of a negligence action embraces, as a sine qua non ingredient, a causation-in-fact test, that is, the defendant's negligence must be a cause-in-fact of the plaintiff's injuries. Generally speaking, Florida courts have followed a "but for" causation-in-fact test, that is, "to constitute proximate cause there must be such a natural, direct and continuous sequence between the negligent act [or omission] and the [plaintiff's] injury that it can be reasonably said that but for the [negligent] act [or omission] the injury would not have occurred." Pope v. Pinkerton-Hays Lumber Co., 120 So. 2d 227, 230 (Fla. 1st DCA 1960). . . .

In addition to the causation-in-fact test, the "proximate cause" element of a negligence action includes a second indispensable showing. This showing is designed to protect defendants from tort liability for results which, although caused-in-fact by the defendant's negligent act or omission, seem to the judicial mind highly unusual, extraordinary, or bizarre, or, stated differently, seem beyond the scope of any fair assessment of the danger created by the defendant's negligence. The courts here have required a common sense, fairness showing that the accident in which the plaintiff suffered his injuries was within the scope of the danger created by the defendant's negligence or stated differently, that the said accident was a reasonably foreseeable consequence of the defendant's negligence.

It is not necessary, however, that the defendant foresee the exact sequence of events which led to the accident sued upon; it is only necessary that the general type of accident which has occurred was within the scope of the danger created by the defendant's negligence, or, stated differently, it must be shown that the said general-type accident was a reasonably foreseeable consequence of the defendant's negligence. For example, it has been held that injuries sustained by business patrons while attempting to escape from a fire in a cafeteria or a hotel were within the scope of the danger and a reasonably foreseeable consequence of the cafeteria or hotel's negligence in failing to have adequate fire exits — even though the exact sequence of events which led to the fire, namely, a mad arsonist setting the building aflame, was entirely unforeseeable. Concord Florida, Inc. v. Lewin, 341 So. 2d 242 (Fla. 3d DCA 1976). Moreover, it has long been held that "proximate cause" issues are generally for juries to decide using their common sense upon appropriate instructions, although occasionally when reasonable people cannot differ, the issue has been said to be one of law for the court.

Turning now to the instant case, we have no difficulty in concluding that the trial court erred in dismissing the complaint against the defendant Little and in entering a final summary judgment in favor of the University of Miami. This is so because the complaint sufficiently alleges the proximate cause element herein as to the defendant Little, and the record raises genuine issues of material fact with reference to the same element as to the defendant University of Miami.

Plainly, the alleged negligence in designing and constructing the brick wall adjoining the entrance way to Eaton Hall in this case was a cause-in-fact of the accident which led to the death of the plaintiffs' decedent. It is alleged that the said wall was designed and built with insufficient supports as required by the applicable building code so that, when it was impacted in this case, it fell over intact, and in one piece, on the decedent. Dr. Joseph Davis, the Dade County Medical Examiner, avers that in his opinion the decedent died as a result of the brick wall falling intact upon her. "But for" the negligent design and construction of the brick wall which led to its collapse in one piece, then, the decedent would not have died. A jury question is therefore presented on this aspect of the proximate cause element.

The foreseeability aspect of the proximate cause element is also satisfied in this case for the complaint dismissal and summary judgment purposes. The collapse of a brick wall resulting in the death of a person near such wall is plainly a reasonably foreseeable consequence of negligently designing and constructing such a wall without adequate supports in violation of applicable building codes — even though the exact sequence of events leading to the collapse of the wall — as in this case, the bizarre incident involving the clutch-started automobile leaving the circular driveway and striking the wall — may have been entirely unforeseeable. The general-type accident which occurred in this case — namely, the collapse of the brick wall resulting in the decedent's death — was entirely within the scope of the danger created by the defendants' negligence in designing and constructing the wall without adequate supports, and was a reasonably foreseeable consequence of such negligence. Just as injuries sustained by business patrons in attempting to escape a fire in a cafeteria or hotel was a reasonably foreseeable consequence of the cafeteria or hotel's negligence in failing to have adequate fire exits, even though the act of the arsonist in setting the building aflame was entirely unforeseeable — so too the death of the plaintiffs' decedent was entirely foreseeable in this case even though the exact sequence of events leading to the collapse of the wall may have been unforeseeable. This being so, a jury issue is presented on the proximate cause element as pled in the complaint and revealed by this record. . . .

The final order of dismissal and the final summary judgment under review are both reversed and the cause is remanded to the trial court for further proceedings.

Reversed and remanded.

NOTES TO TIEDER v. LITTLE

1. *Foreseeability Test for Proximate Cause.* The *Tieder* court states that whether an injury "was a reasonably foreseeable consequence of the defendant's negligence" is the same as whether the injury "was within the scope of the danger created by the defendant's negligence." Note the similarity to Justice Cardozo's test for when there is a duty. What was the "scope of the danger" caused by the defendant's conduct in *Tieder*?

2. *Degree of Generality in Describing Foreseeable Risks and Plaintiffs' Injuries.* The plaintiff in *Tieder* had also alleged that the university was negligent in building the circular drive with an inadequate barrier around it. The lack of a barrier was a but-for cause because if there had been a barrier, the out-of-control car would not have pinned Tieder to the wall. How does the foreseeability analysis for proximate cause apply to the lack of a barrier and the injury caused by a falling wall? A highly precise and specific description of the risks related to an inadequate barrier would not involve physical injury due to a falling wall. A very general description, something like "injury to a human being," might find proximate causation in all cases. In the context of the inadequate barrier claim, how would lawyers for the plaintiff and defendant each characterize the risk the defendant created and the harm the plaintiff suffered?

3. *Foreseeability in Both Duty and Proximate Cause.* Judges, lawyers, law professors, and law students have all struggled with the apparent redundancy of including the foreseeability of harm in both the duty and proximate cause analysis. One court dealt with this by identifying a difference between general and specific foreseeability. For duty, one considers whether, in general, conduct like the defendant's creates a foreseeable risk of harm, a zone of risk. For proximate cause, foreseeability is concerned with the specific, narrow factual details of the case rather than the broader zone of risk. In McCain v. Florida Power Corporation, 593 So. 2d 500 (Fla. 1992), a power company negligently marked as "safe to dig" an area with buried high-power cables. That conduct created a duty because, in general, it is foreseeable that running energized power cables under the ground creates risks. A person using a mechanical trencher was electrocuted when the trencher's blade struck the power cable. The power company argued that a finding of proximate cause was wrong, because the power cable was equipped with safety devices and no such accident had previously occurred. Treating the proximate cause issue as involving specific foreseeability, the court held that it was legitimate to find that the power company's conduct was a proximate cause of the death, because it is foreseeable that safety equipment can fail and that severing an energized cable is likely to cause a shock.

Problem
Unusual Foreseeable Accident

One afternoon, telephone company workers were repairing cables located under a road that was fairly far away from residences. The workers removed the cover of a manhole and entered a chamber nine feet deep under the road. They put up a canvas tent over the manhole and placed four red oil-burning lamps around the tent and their equipment. After dark, they left the worksite. They removed a ladder from the manhole and put it on the ground next to the tent. Two young boys then came to the tent and attempted to explore the manhole and underground chamber. One of the lamps was either knocked or dropped into the manhole and a violent explosion occurred. One of the boys suffered severe burning injuries, the most disabling of which were to his fingers, which were probably caused by his trying to hold on to and climb up the metal rungs of the ladder out of the manhole after the metal became intensely hot as a result of the explosion. The injured boy claimed that he had stumbled over the lamp and knocked it into the hole when a violent explosion occurred, and he himself fell in. When the lamp was recovered from the manhole, its tank was half empty and its wick-holder was completely out of the lamp. The explanation of the accident that was accepted was that when the lamp fell down the hole and was broken, some fuel escaped, and enough was vaporized to create an explosive mixture, which was detonated by the lamp's flame.

Your firm represents the defendant telephone company. A partner has asked you to draft a memo evaluating proximate cause under the foreseeability test. If the defendant's employees were negligent either in leaving the work site unattended or in locating the warning lamps, would the unusual sequence of events leading to the accident preclude liability under the foreseeability test? In litigating the case, how should your firm characterize the type of harm that must have been foreseeable in order for the plaintiff to prevail? How is the plaintiff's characterization of the issue likely to differ from yours? See Hughes v. Lord Advocate, 1 All E.R. 705 (1963).

Perspective: Who Decides Whether a New Cause of Action Is Valid?

In his dissent in *Palsgraf*, Justice Andrews promoted a rule that "every one owes to the world at large the duty of refraining from those acts that may unreasonably threaten the safety of others." Jurisdictions following this expansive duty rule can come under pressure from lawyers arguing that there should be liability for a wide array of types of acts and omissions. Adopting a proximate cause rule requiring that the general type of accident that occurred be reasonably foreseeable is an attempt to limit liability in nontraditional cases. Adopting a duty rule requiring that the type of plaintiff and type of harm be reasonably foreseeable is another way to accomplish this result. Because the existence of a duty is generally a question of law for the judge to decide, and the issue of proximate cause is a question of fact for the factfinder to decide, the choice of whether to put the foreseeability question in the duty or proximate cause analysis depends in part on whether one prefers to have liability limited by judges or by juries.

2. Relating the "Eggshell Plaintiff" Rule to a Foreseeability Analysis

Sometimes conduct that would ordinarily be negligent because it creates a certain risk turns out to create unforeseeably large damages because the victim has an unusual weakness. In these situations, tort law must decide whether the unpredictable extent of the injury represents a cost that the defendant should bear, even though it is difficult to call that loss foreseeable. Schafer v. Hoffman applies the colorfully named "eggshell" or "thin skull" plaintiff rule in the context of the foreseeability approach to proximate cause. The eggshell plaintiff rule applies to the *extent* of harm, while the foreseeability rule in the proximate cause context applies to the *type* of harm.

SCHAFER v. HOFFMAN

831 P.2d 897 (Colo. 1992)

VOLLACK, J.

Petitioner, Larry Schafer (Schafer), petitions from a court of appeals decision. . . . The court of appeals affirmed the judgment entered on a jury verdict in favor of Shirley Hoffman (Hoffman) in the amount of $715,000. We affirm.

On January 15, 1988, Schafer struck Hoffman, a pedestrian, with his vehicle. Schafer was under the influence of alcohol and drugs at the time of the collision. As a result of the collision, Hoffman sustained numerous injuries, including a compression fracture in a spinal vertebra, a concussion with intracranial bleeding, a fractured femur in her left leg, and torn cartilage in her left knee. Hoffman also sustained other injuries to her left leg, left hand, and right elbow.

Hoffman filed an action against Schafer which proceeded to trial on January 3, 1989. Schafer admitted negligence in the operation of his vehicle but denied that his conduct was willful and wanton, and disputed the nature and extent of Hoffman's injuries. Schafer contended that Hoffman had pre-existing injuries for which he was not liable because they were not caused by his conduct.

Hoffman produced numerous witnesses at trial, including Dr. Rupp, her orthopedic surgeon. Dr. Rupp testified that he treated Hoffman shortly after the January 15, 1988, accident. Dr. Rupp was aware that Hoffman had developed thrombophlebitis (blood clots) in her left leg, around her knee, as a result of the accident. Hoffman took anticoagulant drugs in order to reduce clotting. As a result, Dr. Rupp could not perform surgery on Hoffman's knee until the clotting had sufficiently dissipated. Dr. Rupp referred Hoffman to a physical therapist, but determined early in the fall of 1988 that surgery was necessary based on the lack of improvement in her condition through the course of her therapy. . . .

On cross-examination, Schafer elicited testimony that Dr. Rupp had treated Hoffman two months prior to the accident, in November 1987, for pain in her right knee. She could not fully extend her knee at that time and was taking Motrin (a drug designed to decrease swelling of arthritic joints) on an as-needed basis. Dr. Rupp prescribed Darvocet, a mild pain killer, and Chlorinol, an anti-inflammatory drug, during November 1987. . . .

In summary, the jury heard evidence introduced by Schafer that Hoffman had complained of knee pain and lower back problems prior to the accident, and that the vertebra fracture might have occurred prior to the January 15, 1988, accident. The jury also was aware that Hoffman's knee had some degeneration as a result of the normal aging process, that Hoffman might be predisposed to causalgia, and that Hoffman's knee surgery was delayed longer than the average person's because of her blood clotting condition. At the close of trial, Hoffman submitted a "thin skull" instruction which read as follows:

> In determining the amount(s) of plaintiff's actual damages in each of the various categories set forth in Instruction No. 16, you may not refuse to award nor reduce the amount of any such damages because of any physical frailties of the plaintiff that may have made her more susceptible to injury, disability or impairment.

Schafer objected to the giving of this instruction on the grounds that the instruction told the jury that they may not refuse or reduce the amount of damages because of Hoffman's pre-existing physical ailments. Schafer contended that there was no evidence of aggravation of Hoffman's condition and thus Schafer could not be held liable for her pre-existing conditions. The district court, however, gave the challenged instruction to the jury.

The jury found for Hoffman, and Schafer appealed. The court of appeals concluded that the instruction was a proper statement of the law and that it was supported by the evidence in this case. Schafer petitions this court for a determination that the thin skull instruction is not a correct statement of law and that the court of appeals erred in holding that Hoffman was entitled to the instruction as her theory of the case. We disagree.

The term "thin skull," or "eggshell skull," is derived from illustrations appearing in English cases wherein a plaintiff with an "eggshell skull" suffers death as a result of a defendant's negligence where a normal person would only suffer a bump on the head. Dulieu v. White & Sons, 2 K.B. 669, 679 (1901); W. Page Keeton et al., Prosser and Keaton on the Law of Torts §43, at 292 (5th ed. 1984) [hereinafter "Prosser"] (citing Glanville Williams, *The Risk Principle,* 77 L.Q. Rev. 179, 193-97 (1961)). The negligent defendant is liable for the resulting harm even though the harm is increased by the particular plaintiff's condition at the time of the negligent conduct. Prosser §43, at 291; see also Restatement (Second) of Torts §461 cmt. a (1965) ("A negligent actor must bear the risk that his liability will be increased by reason of the actual physical condition of the other toward whom his act is negligent.").

As Prosser notes, there is almost universal agreement on this rule. Prosser §43, at 291 ("There is almost universal agreement upon liability beyond the risk, for quite unforeseeable consequences, when they follow an impact upon the person of the plaintiff."). Liability "beyond the risk," however, is not solely premised on the existence of ascertainable pre-existing physical conditions:

> The defendant is held liable when the defendant's negligence operates upon a concealed physical condition, such as pregnancy, or latent disease, or *susceptibility* to disease, to produce consequences which the defendant could not reasonably anticipate. The defendant is held liable for unusual results of personal injuries which are

regarded as unforeseeable, such as tuberculosis, paralysis, pneumonia, heart or kidney disease, blood poisoning, cancer, or the loss of hair from fright.

Prosser §43, at 291-92 (emphasis added). Some scholars have interpreted the thin skull doctrine to encompass the plaintiff's physical, mental, or financial condition. 4 Fowler Harper et al., The Law of Torts §20.3 (2d ed. 1986). "And these preexisting conditions may have the greatest bearing on the extent of the injury actually suffered by any particular plaintiff in a given case. Thus the same slight blow in the abdomen might cause only fleeting discomfort to a man but a miscarriage to a pregnant woman." Id.

Under Colorado law, it is fundamental that a tortfeasor must accept his or her victim as the victim is found. Stephens and Kraftco Corp. v. Koch, 192 Colo. 531, 533, 561 P.2d 333, 334 (1977) ("As this court has made clear, a defendant must take his 'victim' as he finds him."); Fischer v. Moore, 183 Colo. 392, 394, 517 P.2d 458, 459 (1973) ("Under the common-law principles of tort law, it is axiomatic that the tortfeasor must accept the plaintiff as he finds him. . . .").

Accordingly, under the thin skull doctrine, a tortfeasor "may not seek to reduce the amount of damages [owed to the victim] by spotlighting the physical frailties of the injured party at the time the tortious force was applied to him." Id. A thin skull instruction is appropriately given when the defendant seeks to avoid liability by asserting that the victim's injuries would have been less severe had the victim been an average person. See Priel v. R.E.D., Inc., 392 N.W.2d 65, 69 (N.D. 1986) (citing *Dulieu,* 2 K.B. at 679) (holding that the defendant could not escape liability where plaintiff had a prior fragile condition making her more susceptible to certain injuries than the average person). . . .[7]

The thin skull doctrine has not been limited to pre-existing bodily conditions. See Prosser §43, at 291-92 and discussion supra. The doctrine appropriately applies where a plaintiff may be predisposed or more susceptible to ill effects than a normal person. See City of Scottsdale v. Kokaska, 17 Ariz. App. 120, 495 P.2d 1327, 1335 (1972) (plaintiff had no pre-existing injury but rather an anatomically different spine); Walton v. William Wolf Baking Co., 406 So. 2d 168, 175 (La. 1981) (holding that tortfeasor was required to take plaintiff as found, with predisposition to neurosis); Reck v. Stevens, 373 So. 2d 498, 502 (La. 1979) (plaintiff had an underlying emotional instability); Freyermuth v. Lutfy, 376 Mass. 612, 382 N.E.2d 1059, 1064 n.5 (1978) ("The established rule is that where the result of an accident is to activate a dormant or incipient disease, or one to which the person is predisposed, the negligence which caused the accident is the proximate cause of the disability.").

The challenged instruction encapsulates the fundamental thin skull doctrine. A party "is entitled to an instruction embodying his theory of the case, if there is evidence in the record to support it." Newbury v. Vogel, 151 Colo. 520, 524, 379 P.2d 811, 813 (1963).

During trial, Schafer . . . attempted to establish that Hoffman had longstanding complaints with regard to her knees. Schafer sought to prove that Hoffman's recovery

---

[7] In Dulieu v. White & Sons, 2 K.B. 669, 679 (1901), the court stated:

If a man is negligently run over or otherwise negligently injured in his body, it is no answer to the sufferer's claim for damages that he would have suffered less injury, or no injury at all, if he had not had an unusually thin skull or an unusually weak heart.

process was longer than the average person's because arthroscopic surgery expedites recovery but was delayed in Hoffman's case as a result of her blood clotting condition.

Schafer also attempted to establish . . . that chondromalacia can develop over the course of the normal aging process. Schafer elicited, through cross-examination of Hoffman's physical therapist, that Hoffman had some degeneration in her knee as a result of her age.

The testimony elicited by Schafer in this case could lead the jury to believe that Hoffman suffered frailties or was more susceptible to certain medical infirmities than the average person. The challenged instruction merely informed the jury that Schafer could not escape liability because of Hoffman's condition at the time of the accident. The trial court did not err by giving the thin skull instruction in this case.

Schafer contends that the court of appeals erred in holding that Hoffman was entitled to a thin skull instruction as her theory of the case. Schafer specifically argues that the court of appeals determination was based on Ms. Woodward's testimony, and that her testimony supported analysis of "true value" issues and not the thin skull instruction. We disagree.

The true value or "shabby millionaire" rule complements the thin skull doctrine. Gary Bahr & Bruce Graham, *The Thin Skull Plaintiff Concept: Evasive or Persuasive?*, 15 Loy. L.A. L. Rev. 409, 410 (1982). The thin skull doctrine declares that foreseeability of plaintiff's injuries is not an issue in determining *the extent of injury* suffered, while the true value or shabby millionaire rule declares that foreseeability is not an issue in determining *the extent of damages* that the injuries cause.[9] Id. (citing Rowe, *The Demise of the Thin Skull Rule*, 40 Mod. L. Rev. 377 (1977)).

The court of appeals discussed the testimony of the orthopedic surgeons regarding Hoffman's particular condition at the time of the accident. In the context of this discussion, the court of appeals noted that Ms. Woodward, a vocational rehabilitation counselor, testified that Hoffman would be disadvantaged in the job market. The record amply supports the court of appeals determination that the thin skull instruction was proper in this case. We thus find Schafer's contention to be without merit, and affirm the judgment of the court of appeals.

NOTES TO SCHAFER v. HOFFMAN

1. *Take the Plaintiff as You Find Him or Her.* The eggshell plaintiff principle is sometimes expressed as a statement to defendants: "You must take the plaintiff as you find him or her." If a plaintiff happens to have an unusual weakness, the eggshell plaintiff rule requires the defendant to pay damages for an injury that could not have been foreseen. How does that fit with the foreseeability approach to proximate causation?

---

[9] The shabby millionaire rule is illustrated as follows:

> If a person fires across a road when it is dangerous to do so and kills a man who is in receipt of a large income, he will be liable for the whole damage, however great, that may have resulted to his family, and cannot set up that he could not have reasonably expected to have injured any one but a labourer.

Gary Bahr & William Graham, *The Thin Skull Plaintiff Concept: Evasive or Persuasive?*, 15 Loy. L.A. L. Rev. 409, 410-11 (1982) (citing Smith v. London & S.W. Ry., L.R. 6 C.P. 14, 22-23 (1870)); Glanville Williams, *The Risk Principle*, 77 L.Q. Rev. 179 (1961).

2. *Who Should Bear the Risk of Unusual Susceptibility?* In a case where a defendant does something that could harm a typical person but happens to do it to a person with an unusual weakness, the consequences of the defendant's act will likely be more severe than the defendant could have anticipated. Compare the fairness of the eggshell plaintiff rule and an alternative approach (rejected by typical tort law) that would make the plaintiff bear the unusual costs related to the plaintiff's unusual condition. Should it affect your analysis if negligent defendants sometimes injure people who are abnormally robust and healthy and therefore defendants will be liable for unusually small damages? On average, would the damages paid even out and be equal to the expected amount of damages that typical people would suffer from the negligent conduct?

3. *Unusual Weakness and Damages.* Even though a defendant may be liable for more severe harm than would have been suffered by a normally healthy person, the calculation of damages can mitigate the severity of the eggshell plaintiff rule. Consider how the rule would apply in a case where the plaintiff died even though a typical person would have suffered a lesser injury. If the decedent's life expectancy was already short-ened by his or her preexisting condition, the jury would take that into account. The jury would be required to place a dollar amount on the loss of living for the number of years projected for that abnormally short life expectancy. Contrast this approach to a typical case in which the life expectancy the jury uses is a typical or average one.

3. Difficulty in Applying Foreseeability Analysis

To proponents of foreseeability analysis, the directness test seems primitive because it imposes virtually unlimited liability on some defendants. They criticize the substantial factor test because imposing liability for unforeseeable consequences fails to provide clearly limited deterrence. The foreseeability approach, on the other hand, tailors liability to the risks a defendant should have comprehended. This limitation may direct tort law's deterrent power properly. The fear of tort liability for foreseeable harms can cause an actor to avoid conduct that could cause those foreseeable harms. In contrast, an actor who fears unlimited tort liability or tort liability for unforeseeable harms cannot make any change in behavior other than a general decrease in his or her level of activity.

The theoretical appeal of the foreseeability approach is tempered by difficulty in applying it. In Petition of Kinsman Transit Co., that complication is confronted. The opinion also describes the continuing vitality of the directness test in some circumstances.

PETITION OF KINSMAN TRANSIT CO.
338 F.2d 708 (2d Cir. 1964)

[Jams of ice were floating downstream in the Buffalo River. The crew of Kinsman's barge, Shiras, acted negligently, and the barge was torn from its moorings at a dock operated by Continental. Continental had been negligent in construction and inspection of some of its equipment. The Shiras floated downstream and crashed into a moored ship, the Tewksbury. Both vessels moved toward a bridge. Due to negligence on the part of city employees, the bridge was not raised in time to let the vessels and ice pass under it, and the bridge was destroyed. The wreckage dammed up the river, and property damage was sustained as far upstream as the Continental dock. Claims were made for property damage. An admiralty decree adjudicated liability, and several parties appealed.]

FRIENDLY, J.

... We see little similarity between the *Palsgraf* case and the situation before us. The point of *Palsgraf* was that the appearance of the newspaper-wrapped package gave no notice that its dislodgement could do any harm save to itself and those nearby, and this by impact, perhaps with consequent breakage, and not by explosion. In contrast, a ship insecurely moored in a fast flowing river is a known danger not only to herself but to the owners of all other ships and structures down-river, and to persons upon them. No one would dream of saying that a shipowner who "knowingly and wilfully" failed to secure his ship at a pier on such a river "would not have threatened" persons and owners of property downstream in some manner.[6] The shipowner and the wharfinger in this case having thus owed a duty of care to all within the reach of the ship's known destructive power, the impossibility of advance identification of the particular person who would be hurt is without legal consequence. ... Similarly the foreseeable consequences of the City's failure to raise the bridge were not limited to the Shiras and the Tewksbury. Collision plainly created a danger that the bridge towers might fall onto adjoining property, and the crash of two uncontrolled lake vessels, one 425 feet and the other 525 feet long, into a bridge over a swift ice-ridden stream, with a channel only 177 feet wide, could well result in a partial damming that would flood property upstream. As to the City also, it is useful to consider, by way of contrast, Chief Judge Cardozo's statement that the Long Island would not have been liable to Mrs. Palsgraf had the guard wilfully thrown the package down. If the City had deliberately kept the bridge closed in the face of the onrushing vessels, taking the risk that they might not come so far, no one would give house-room to a claim that it "owed no duty" to those who later suffered from the flooding. Unlike Mrs. Palsgraf, they were within the area of hazard. ...

Since all the claimants here met the *Palsgraf* requirement of being persons to whom the actors owed a "duty of care," we are not obliged to reconsider whether that case furnishes as useful a standard for determining the boundaries of liability in admiralty for negligent conduct as was thought in *Sinram* [v. Pennsylvania R. Co., 61 F.2d 767 (2d Cir. 1932)], when *Palsgraf* was still in its infancy. But this does not dispose of the alternative argument that the manner in which several of the claimants were harmed, particularly by flood damage, was unforeseeable and that recovery for this may not be had — whether the argument is put in the forthright form that unforeseeable damages are not recoverable or is concealed under a formula of lack of "proximate cause."[8]

---

[6] The facts here do not oblige us to decide whether the Shiras and Continental could successfully invoke *Palsgraf* against claims of owners of shore-side property upstream from the Concrete Elevator or of non-riparian property other than the real and personal property which was sufficiently close to the bridge to have been damaged by the fall of the towers.

[8] It is worth underscoring that the *ratio decidendi* in *Palsgraf* was that the Long Island was not required to use *any* care with respect to the package vis-à-vis Mrs. Palsgraf; Chief Judge Cardozo did not reach the issue of "proximate cause" for which the case is often cited. 248 N.Y. at 346-347, 162 N.E. 99.

So far as concerns the City, the argument lacks factual support. Although the obvious risks from not raising the bridge were damage to itself and to the vessels, the danger of a fall of the bridge and of flooding would not have been unforeseeable under the circumstances to anyone who gave them thought. And the same can be said as to the failure of Kinsman's shipkeeper to ready the anchors after the danger had become apparent. The exhibits indicate that the width of the channel between the Concrete Elevator and the bridge is at most points less than two hundred fifty feet. If the Shiras caught up on a dock or vessel moored along the shore, the current might well swing her bow across the channel so as to block the ice floes, as indeed could easily have occurred at the Standard Elevator dock where the stern of the Shiras struck the Tewksbury's bow. At this point the channel scarcely exceeds two hundred feet, and this was further narrowed by the presence of the Druckenmiller moored on the opposite bank. Had the Tewksbury's mooring held, it is thus by no means unlikely that these three ships would have dammed the river. Nor was it unforeseeable that the drawbridge would not be raised since, apart from any other reason, there was no assurance of timely warning. What may have been less foreseeable was that the Shiras would get that far down the twisting river, but this is somewhat negated both by the known speed of the current when freshets developed and by the evidence that, on learning of the Shiras' departure, Continental's employees and those they informed foresaw precisely that.

Continental's position on the facts is stronger. It was indeed foreseeable that the improper construction and lack of inspection of the "deadman" might cause a ship to break loose and damage persons and property on or near the river — that was what made Continental's conduct negligent. With the aid of hindsight one can also say that a prudent man, carefully pondering the problem, would have realized that the danger of this would be greatest under such water conditions as developed during the night of January 21, 1959, and that if a vessel should break loose under those circumstances, events might transpire as they did. But such post hoc step by step analysis would render "foreseeable" almost anything that has in fact occurred; if the argument relied upon has legal validity, it ought not be circumvented by characterizing as foreseeable what almost no one would in fact have foreseen at the time.

The effect of unforeseeability of damage upon liability for negligence has recently been considered by the Judicial Committee of the Privy Council, Overseas Tankship (U.K.) Ltd. v. Morts Dock & Engineering Co. (*The Wagon Mound*), (1961) 1 All E.R. 404. The Committee there disapproved the proposition, thought to be supported by Re Polemis and Furness, Withy & Co. Ltd. (1921) 3 K.B. 560 (C.A.), "that unforeseeability is irrelevant if damage is 'direct.'" We have no difficulty with the result of *The Wagon Mound*, in view of the finding, 1 All E.R. at 407, that the appellant had no reason to believe that the floating furnace oil would burn. . . . On that view the decision simply applies the principle which excludes liability where the injury sprang from a hazard different from that which was improperly risked. . . . Although some language in the judgment goes beyond this, we would find it difficult to understand why one who had failed to use the care required to protect others in the light of expectable forces should be exonerated when the very risks that rendered his conduct negligent produced other and more serious consequences to such persons than were fairly foreseeable when he fell short of what the law demanded. Foreseeability of danger is necessary to render conduct negligent; where as here the damage was caused by just those forces whose existence required the exercise of greater care than was taken — the current, the ice, and the physical mass of the Shiras, the incurring of consequences other and greater than foreseen does not make the conduct less culpable or provide a reasoned basis for insulation.[9] The oft encountered argument that failure to limit liability to foreseeable consequences may subject the defendant to a loss wholly out of proportion to his fault seems scarcely consistent with the universally accepted rule that the defendant takes the plaintiff as he finds him and will be responsible for the full extent of the injury even though a latent susceptibility of the plaintiff renders this far more serious than could reasonably have been anticipated. . . .

The weight of authority in this country rejects the limitation of damages to consequences foreseeable at the time of the negligent conduct when the consequences are "direct," and the damage, although other and greater than expectable, is of the same general sort that was risked. . . . Other American courts, purporting to apply a test of foreseeability to damages, extend that concept to such unforeseen lengths as to raise serious doubt whether the concept is meaningful;[10] indeed, we wonder whether the British courts are not finding it necessary to limit the language of *The Wagon Mound* as we have indicated.

We see no reason why an actor engaging in conduct which entails a large risk of small damage and a small risk of other and greater damage, of the same general sort, from the same forces, and to the same class of persons, should be relieved of responsibility for the latter simply because the chance of its occurrence, if viewed alone, may not have been large enough to require the exercise of care. By hypothesis, the risk of the

---

[9] The contrasting situation is illustrated by the familiar instances of the running down of a pedestrian by a safely driven but carelessly loaded car, or of the explosion of unlabeled rat poison, inflammable but not known to be, placed near a coffee burner. Larrimore v. American Nat. Ins. Co., 184 Okla. 614, 89 P.2d 340 (1939). Exoneration of the defendant in such cases rests on the basis that a negligent actor is responsible only for harm the risk of which was increased by the negligent aspect of his conduct. See Keeton, Legal Cause in the Law of Torts, 1-10 (1963); Hart & Honore, Causation in the Law, 157-58 (1959). Compare Berry v. Borough of Sugar Notch, 191 Pa. 345, 43 A. 240 (1899). This principle supports the judgment for the defendant in the recent case of Doughty v. Turner Mfg. Co., (1964) 2 W.L.R. 240 (C.A.). The company maintained a bath of molten cyanide protected by an asbestos cover, reasonably believed to be incapable of causing an explosion if immersed. An employee inadvertently knocked the cover into the bath, but there was no damage from splashing. A minute or two later an explosion occurred as a result of chemical changes in the cover and the plaintiff, who was standing near the bath, was injured by the molten drops. The risk against which defendant was required to use care — splashing of the molten liquid from dropping the supposedly explosion proof cover — did not materialize, and the defendant was found not to have lacked proper care against the risk that did. As said by Lord Justice Diplock, (1964) 2 W.L.R. at 247, "The former risk was well known (that was foreseeable) at the time of the accident; but it did not happen. It was the second risk which happened and caused the plaintiff damage by burning." Moreover, if, as indicated in Lord Pearce's judgment, (1964) 2 W.L.R. at 244, the plaintiff was not within the area of potential splashing, the case parallels *Palsgraf*; Lord Justice Diplock's statement, (1964) 2 W.L.R. at 248, that defendants "would have been under no liability to the plaintiff if they had intentionally immersed the cover in the liquid" is reminiscent of Chief Judge Cardozo's quoted above. . . .

[10] An instance is In re Guardian Casualty Co., 253 App. Div. 360, 2 N.Y.S.2d 232 (1st Dept.), *aff'd*, 278 N.Y. 674, 16 N.E.2d 397 (1938), where the majority gravely asserted that a foreseeable consequence of driving a taxicab too fast was that a collision with another car would project the cab against a building with such force as to cause a portion of the building to collapse twenty minutes later, when the cab was being removed, and injure a spectator twenty feet away. Surely this is "straining the idea of foreseeability past the breaking point," Bohlen, *Book Review*, 47 Harv. L. Rev. 556, 557 (1934), at least if the matter be viewed as of the time of the negligent act, as the supposedly symmetrical test of *The Wagon Mound* demands, (1961) 1 All Eng. R. at 415. On the other hand, if the issue of foreseeability is viewed as of the moment of impact, see Seavey, *Mr. Justice Cardozo and the Law of Torts*, 52 Harv. L. Rev. 372, 385 (1939), the test loses functional significance since at that time the defendant is no longer able to amend his conduct so as to avert the consequences.

lesser harm was sufficient to render his disregard of it actionable; the existence of a less likely additional risk that the very forces against whose action he was required to guard would produce other and greater damage than could have been reasonably anticipated should inculpate him further rather than limit his liability. This does not mean that the careless actor will always be held for all damages for which the forces that he risked were a cause in fact. Somewhere a point will be reached when courts will agree that the link has become too tenuous — that what is claimed to be consequence is only fortuity. Thus, if the destruction of the Michigan Avenue Bridge had delayed the arrival of a doctor, with consequent loss of a patient's life, few judges would impose liability on any of the parties here, although the agreement in result might not be paralleled by similar unanimity in reasoning; perhaps in the long run one returns to Judge Andrews' statement in *Palsgraf* . . . "It is all a question of expediency, . . . of fair judgment, always keeping in mind the fact that we endeavor to make a rule in each case that will be practical and in keeping with the general understanding of mankind." It would be pleasant if greater certainty were possible . . . but the many efforts that have been made at defining the locus of the "uncertain and wavering line," 248 N.Y. at 354, 162 N.E. 99, are not very promising; what courts do in such cases makes better sense than what they, or others, say. Where the line will be drawn will vary from age to age; as society has come to rely increasingly on insurance and other methods of loss-sharing, the point may lie further off than a century ago. Here it is surely more equitable that the losses from the operators' negligent failure to raise the Michigan Avenue Bridge should be ratably borne by Buffalo's taxpayers than left with the innocent victims of the flooding; yet the mind is also repelled by a solution that would impose liability solely on the City and exonerate the persons whose negligent acts of commission and omission were the precipitating force of the collision with the bridge and its sequelae. We go only so far as to hold that where, as here, the damages resulted from the same physical forces whose existence required the exercise of greater care than was displayed and were of the same general sort that was expectable, unforeseeability of the exact developments and of the extent of the loss will not limit liability. Other fact situations can be dealt with when they arise. . . .

NOTES TO PETITION OF KINSMAN TRANSIT CO.

1. *The* Wagon Mound. The *Wagon Mound* case discussed in *Kinsman Transit* involved the destruction of a dock by fire. The defendant spilled a large quantity of oil into a harbor. That oil floated on the surface of the water, and a third party's employees allowed sparks to come into contact with it. The oil ignited and caused the fire that harmed the plaintiff's dock. The plaintiff and defendant agreed that no one could foresee that the floating oil could be ignited by the conduct of the workers. Liability was rejected on the theory that the defendant's conduct was negligent only because of the risk that its oil could smudge or otherwise foul equipment at the plaintiff's dock and that liability for unforeseeable risks should not be imposed.

2. *General Type of Damage.* Judge Friendly wrote:

We see no reason why an actor engaging in conduct which entails a large risk of small damage and a small risk of other and greater damage, of the same general sort, from the same forces, and to the same class of persons, should be relieved of responsibility for the latter simply because the chance of its occurrence, if viewed alone, may not have been large enough to require the exercise of care.

What degree of foreseeability is required by this formulation? How does it relate to the "thin skull" rule?

E. The Restatement (Third) Approach to Duty and Proximate Cause

1. Duty

After years of debate, the Restatement (Third) of Torts approach to duty and proximate cause, published in 2010, simplified the analysis of both elements. Behrendt v. Gulf Underwriters illustrates how the analysis of duty under the Restatement (Third) comes close to adopting the position of Judge Andrews in *Palsgraf*: a negligent person generally has a duty to the whole world. Instead of considering whether a plaintiff or a type of harm was foreseeable in the duty analysis, the Restatement (Third) addresses those questions in the context of breach.

The Restatement (Third) approach requires a careful analysis of the breach element. When analyzing breach, a lawyer must carefully identify the likelihood and severity of the potential risks created by a party's conduct and consider how difficult it would be to avoid those risks. Once those risks are identified in the breach analysis, they provide the foundation for the scope of liability analysis. *Behrendt* illustrates how the foreseeability analysis is shifted from duty to breach and how the breach analysis then may limit liability.

BEHRENDT v. GULF UNDERWRITERS INSURANCE CO.
768 N.W.2d 568 (Wis. 2009)

N. PATRICK CROOKS, J.

This is a review of an unpublished court of appeals decision affirming an order granting summary judgment to Silvan Industries, Inc. (Silvan) and its insurer, Gulf Underwriters Insurance Co. (Gulf). Silvan and Gulf were among those sued by Kenneth Behrendt (Behrendt) after he was injured when a tank exploded while he was using it at his job in an oil change business. The tank had been fabricated as a favor to Behrendt's employer; it was made as a side job by someone who worked at Silvan at the time, and it was subsequently customized for use in the oil change business. Behrendt claimed that Silvan was negligent in permitting the tank to be made as a side job ... but Silvan won dismissal of the claims, and the court of appeals affirmed. Behrendt sought review here of the court of appeals' decision.

Behrendt's claims arise from the explosion of a tank, and the tank, to which fixtures were later added, was originally built as a side job by a Silvan employee. The questions raised in this appeal thus concern Silvan's policy of permitting employees to use company equipment and scrap materials to make items for personal use. Silvan manufactures tanks to be used under pressure, such as air receivers and water tanks. Pressurized vessels are subject to strict manufacturing codes and third-party inspection; after each tank is tested, inspected and certified, it is labeled and registered with the National Board of Boilers and Pressure Vessel Inspectors. Silvan's policy permitting side jobs prohibited employees from making pressurized tanks, and a system was in place to prevent employees' personal use of any tanks that were scrapped by the company: holes were cut in any scrapped tanks to make them worthless as pressurized vessels.

As noted above, one of the side jobs made by a Silvan employee is at the center of this case. When Daniel Linczeski (Linczeski) decided to open an oil change business, he needed a piece of equipment to collect oil drained from vehicles, and he went to his father-in-law, James Fisher (Fisher), who worked at Silvan. Fisher and a co-worker at Silvan, Rex Sommers (Sommers), welded pieces of scrap metal to create a large flat-bottomed cylinder with a domed top. The tank, which was several feet high and held about 55 gallons of oil, was delivered to Linczeski. Testimony in the record indicates that after the tank was fabricated, the system for collecting and disposing of oil was modified over a period of weeks. Linczeski got Peter Harding (Harding), a plumber, to plug several holes in the side of the tank. The plumber also fitted the tank with valves — one for the top that allowed oil to be drained into the tank but could be closed to keep oil from splashing out when the tank was moved, and one at the bottom of the tank to allow oil to be drained out of the tank. Other changes were made to make the tank more convenient to use; for example, wheels were added to the bottom to make it easy to move around, and studs were added to the side so that wrenches could be hung on the tank. Linczeski's modifications ultimately included having one of the plugs that had originally plugged a hole taken off the tank and substituting instead a fitting that could be hooked up to an air hose. Air pressure could then be used to empty the tank.

The tank was apparently used without incident until June 15, 2004, when Behrendt, an employee of Linczeski's, was using the tank with air pressure. It exploded, and he was injured. Behrendt sued Silvan, alleging [that] Silvan was liable in its own right for having a policy permitting side jobs. . . . [The circuit court granted Silvan's summary judgment motion on the negligence claim and Behrendt appealed.]

The court of appeals . . . affirmed the grant of summary judgment on the grounds that the first element, a duty of care on the part of the defendant, was not present here. The court focused on the issue of foreseeability, ruling that it was unforeseeable as a matter of law that a non-pressurized tank made as a side job by an employee would later be pressurized and, after years of use, explode and cause injury. The court said "[d]uty is established 'when it can be said that [an act's potential to harm] was foreseeable. . . .'" quoting *Rolph v. EBI Companies*, 464 N.W.2d 667 (1991). The court of appeals held that in this case no duty was established as to Silvan because it cannot be said that it was foreseeable that Silvan's alleged act, permitting employees to do side jobs, would lead to injury.

We agree with the court of appeals that the question of foreseeability is the proper one on which to focus. However, we disagree that the consideration of foreseeability necessarily leads to a finding of no duty in this case. . . .

As has been often stated, "Wisconsin has long followed the minority view of duty set forth in the dissent of *Palsgraf v. Long Island Railroad*, [248 N.Y. 339, 162 N.E. 99 (1928)]. In that dissent, Judge Andrews explained that '[e]veryone owes to the world at large the duty of refraining from those acts that may unreasonably threaten the safety of others.'" *Alvarado v. Sersch*, 662 N.W.2d 350.

[W]e find . . . language in Section 7 of the Third Restatement of Torts helpful in clarifying the role foreseeability plays in the analysis. The Restatement says, "An actor ordinarily has a duty to exercise reasonable care when the actor's conduct creates a risk of physical harm." Restatement (Third) of Torts: Liability for Physical Harm §7(a) (Proposed Final Draft No. 1, 2005). The comments accompanying this stated principle are helpful because they make a clear distinction between the determinations required for duty and for breach. . . .

> Courts do appropriately rule that the defendant has not breached a duty of reasonable care when reasonable minds cannot differ on that question. These determinations are based on the specific facts of the case, are applicable only to that case, and are appropriately cognizant of the role of the jury in factual determinations. *A lack of foreseeable risk in a specific case may be a basis for a no-breach determination, but such a ruling is not a no-duty determination.* Rather it is a determination that no reasonable person could find that the defendant has breached the duty of reasonable care.

Id., cmt. j (emphasis added).

[T]he approach set forth in Section 7 . . . is consistent with the approach we have taken on the issue of duty in the vast majority of our cases.

Occasionally, there are cases where a negligence claim fails because the duty of care does not encompass the acts or omissions that caused the harm, but this is not one of them. The allegations are that the tank involved here was built at Silvan with its materials under a policy that permitted workers to fabricate personal projects at work. Under Wisconsin law and our *Palsgraf* minority approach, Silvan had a duty to exercise ordinary care under the circumstances so that its policy permitting side jobs did not create "an unreasonable risk of injury" to Behrendt. . . .

Here the lack of foreseeable risk is the basis for the determination that there was no breach, and, therefore, the granting of summary judgment as to the negligence claim was proper. . . .

We reach the same result as the court of appeals though we arrive at that result via a somewhat different analysis. We agree with both the circuit court and the court of appeals that the focus here is properly on whether Silvan could have foreseen the effects of its policy. We also agree that, as a matter of law, it was not foreseeable that under Silvan's policy of allowing employees to do side projects, a non-pressurized tank built as a side job would later be modified and pressurized and, years later, explode and cause injury. However, while the court of appeals affirmed the grant of summary judgment on the grounds that the lack of foreseeability meant that Silvan had no duty to Behrendt, we reiterate our prior holdings in the vast majority of cases that every person is subject to a duty to exercise ordinary care in all of his or her activities. Silvan was subject to such a duty with regard to its policies on side jobs, and under these circumstances, that duty required Silvan to exercise care that its policy on side jobs did not create an unreasonable risk of injury to Behrendt.

However, we then look at whether Silvan breached that duty by failing to exercise the care a reasonable person would use in similar circumstances. In most cases, whether a defendant breached a duty is a question of fact that is submitted to the jury and thus is not appropriate for summary judgment. In this case, however, it is the lack of foreseeable risk that convinces us, as a matter of law, that Silvan cannot be said to have failed to exercise ordinary care with regard to its policy on side jobs. Further, there is no material fact in dispute as to Silvan's policies about side jobs and its prohibition on employees making pressurized vessels as side jobs for personal use. There is in addition uncontroverted evidence in the record that Silvan took steps such as having holes cut into any tanks that were considered as scrap — as well as testimony of the tank's owner that this tank itself originally had holes in it — and that the point of cutting holes into the tanks was to keep them from being used with air pressure.

Summary judgment is appropriate on the negligence claim because under these circumstances Silvan did not breach its duty to act with ordinary care.

The decision of the court of appeals is affirmed.

NOTES TO BEHRENDT v. GULF UNDERWRITERS INSURANCE CO.

1. *Judge Andrews's and the Restatement (Third)'s Approach to Duty.* The Restatement (Third) of Torts: Liability for Physical and Emotional Harm resurrects Judge Andrews's approach to duty seen in Palsgraf v. Long Island Railway Co., at the beginning of this chapter. Andrews said everyone owes a duty to the world at large, so liability depends on whether the defendant's negligence proximately caused the plaintiff's harm. The Restatement (Third) §6 says that ordinarily there is a duty and courts may proceed directly to the question of whether the defendant was negligent, whether the negligence was a factual cause of the plaintiff's harm, and whether the harm was within the scope of the defendant's liability.

2. *No Duty in Exceptional Cases.* The Restatement (Third) recognizes that in exceptional cases a court may rely on public policies to find there is no duty. Section 7(b) says:

> In exceptional cases, when an articulated countervailing principle or policy warrants denying or limiting liability in a particular class of cases, a court may decide that the defendant has no duty or that the ordinary duty of reasonable care requires modification.

This provision rejects the idea that a "no-duty" ruling can be based on the facts of an individual case. It adopts the idea that a no-duty rule should apply to an entire class of cases when a court can articulate policies supporting a no-duty rule. See the discussion following Kubert v. Best, earlier in this chapter.

3. *New Duty Rule/Old Proximate Cause Rule.* The adoption of the Restatement (Third) approach to duty does not require adoption of the Restatement (Third) approach to proximate cause. *Behrendt* is a Wisconsin case. Wisconsin courts apply the substantial factor approach to analyzing proximate cause.

4. *Foreseeability in the Breach Element.* The Restatement (Third) eliminates explicit consideration of foreseeability in the duty and cause elements of a negligence claim and leaves questions of foreseeability to the element of breach: "*A lack of foreseeable risk in a specific case may be the basis for a no-breach determination, but such a ruling is not a no-duty determination.*" In *Behrendt*, the court found that it was improbable that an explosion injury would occur as a result of permitting employees to do side jobs, given the precautions the employer had taken.

5. *Proximate Cause/Scope of Liability.* The Restatement (Third) uses a "risk standard" to define the scope of a defendant's liability and substitutes "scope of liability" for the term "proximate cause." A defendant is liable only for those types of accidents that made the defendant's conduct negligent in the first place. Because a careful breach analysis will consider what types of risks the defendant's conduct created, the scope of liability analysis may be straightforward. Thompson v. Kaczinski illustrates how this standard is applied and discusses how it compares to the foreseeability test for proximate cause.

THOMPSON v. KACZINSKI
774 N.W.2d 829 (Iowa 2009)

HECHT, Justice.

... James Kaczinski and Michelle Lockwood resided in rural Madison County, near Earlham, on property abutting a gravel road. During the late summer of 2006, they disassembled a trampoline and placed its component parts on their yard approximately thirty-eight feet from the road. Intending to dispose of them at a later time, Kaczinski and Lockwood did not secure the parts in place. A few weeks later, on the night of September 16 and morning of September 17, 2006, a severe thunderstorm moved through the Earlham area. Wind gusts from the storm displaced the top of the trampoline from the yard to the surface of the road.

Later that morning, while driving from one church to another where he served as a pastor, Charles Thompson approached the defendants' property. When he swerved to avoid the obstruction on the road, Thompson lost control of his vehicle. His car entered the ditch and rolled several times. Kaczinski and Lockwood were awakened by Thompson's screams at about 9:40 a.m., shortly after the accident. When they went outside to investigate, they discovered the top of their trampoline lying on the roadway. Lockwood dragged the object back into the yard while Kaczinski assisted Thompson.

Thompson and his wife filed suit, alleging Kaczinski and Lockwood ... negligently allow[ed] the trampoline to obstruct the roadway. Kaczinski and Lockwood moved for summary judgment, contending they owed no duty under the circumstances because the risk of the trampoline's displacement from their yard to the surface of the road was not foreseeable. The district court granted the motion, concluding Kaczinski and Lockwood breached no duty and the damages claimed by the plaintiffs were not proximately caused by the defendants' negligence. The Thompsons appealed. We transferred the case to the court of appeals, which affirmed the district court's ruling. We granted the Thompsons' application for further review. ...

An actionable claim of negligence requires "the existence of a duty to conform to a standard of conduct to protect others, a failure to conform to that standard, proximate cause, and damages." *Stotts v. Eveleth,* 688 N.W.2d 803, 807 (Iowa 2004). Plaintiffs contend Kaczinski and Lockwood owed a common law duty to exercise reasonable care to prevent their personal property from obstructing the roadway and to remove their property from the roadway within a reasonable time after it became an obstruction. Whether a duty arises out of a given relationship is a matter of law for the court's determination.

Our cases have suggested three factors should be considered in determining whether a duty to exercise reasonable care exists: " '(1) the relationship between the parties, (2) reasonable foreseeability of harm to the person who is injured, and (3) public policy considerations.' " *Stotts,* 688 N.W.2d at 810 (quoting *J.A.H. ex rel. R.M.H. v. Wadle & Assocs., P.C.,* 589 N.W.2d 256, 258 (Iowa 1999)). Our previous decisions have characterized the proposition that the relationship giving rise to a duty of care must be premised on the foreseeability of harm to the injured person as "a fundamental rule of negligence law." *Sankey v. Richenberger,* 456 N.W.2d 206, 209-10 (Iowa 1990). The factors have not been viewed as three distinct and necessary elements, but rather as considerations employed in a balancing process. "In the end, whether a duty exists is a policy decision based upon all relevant considerations that guide us to conclude a particular person is entitled to be protected from a particular type of harm." *J.A.H.*, 589 N.W.2d at 258.

The role of foreseeability of risk in the assessment of duty in negligence actions has recently been revisited by drafters of the Restatement (Third) of Torts. "An actor ordinarily has a duty to exercise reasonable care when the actor's conduct creates a risk of physical harm." Restatement (Third) of Torts: Liab. for Physical Harm §7(a), at 90 (Proposed Final Draft No. 1, 2005) [hereinafter Restatement (Third)]. Thus, in most cases involving physical harm, courts "need not concern themselves with the existence or content of this ordinary duty," but instead may proceed directly to the elements of liability set forth in section 6.* *Id.* §6 cmt. *f*, at 81. The general duty of reasonable care will apply in most cases, and thus courts "can rely directly on §6 and need not refer to duty on a case-by-case basis." *Id.* §7 cmt. *a*, at 90. . . .

The drafters acknowledge that courts have frequently used foreseeability in no-duty determinations, but have now explicitly disapproved the practice in the Restatement (Third) and limited no-duty rulings to "articulated policy or principle in order to facilitate more transparent explanations of the reasons for a no-duty ruling and to protect the traditional function of the jury as factfinder." *Id.* at 98-99. We find the drafters' clarification of the duty analysis in the Restatement (Third) compelling, and we now, therefore, adopt it.

The district court clearly considered foreseeability in concluding the defendants owed no duty in this case. When the consideration of foreseeability is removed from the determination of duty, as we now hold it should be, there remains the question of whether a principle or strong policy consideration justifies the exemption of Kaczinski and Lockwood — as part of a class of defendants — from the duty to exercise reasonable care. We conclude no such principle or policy consideration exempts property owners from a duty to exercise reasonable care to avoid the placement of obstructions on a roadway. In fact, we have previously noted the public's interest in ensuring roadways are safe and clear of dangerous obstructions for travelers. . . . Accordingly, we conclude the district court erred in determining Kaczinski and Lockwood owed no common law duty under the circumstances presented here.

Although the memorandum filed by Kaczinski and Lockwood in support of their motion for summary judgment raised only the questions of whether a duty was owed and whether a duty was breached, the district court concluded the plaintiffs' claims must fail for the further reason that they did not establish a causal connection between their claimed injuries and damages and the acts and omissions of Kaczinski and Lockwood. Again relying on its determination that the risk of the trampoline's displacement from the yard to the roadway was not foreseeable, the court resolved the causation issue against the Thompsons as a matter of law.

[T]he drafters of the Restatement (Third) have clarified the essential role of policy considerations in the determination of the scope of liability. "An actor's liability is limited to those physical harms that result from the risks that made the actor's conduct tortious." *Id.* §29, at 575. This principle, referred to as the "risk standard," is intended

---

* Restatement (Third) of Torts: Liability for Physical and Emotional Harm §6 reads as follows:

§6. Liability for Negligence Causing Physical Harm
An actor whose negligence is a factual cause of physical harm is subject to liability for any such harm within the scope of liability, unless the court determines that the ordinary duty of reasonable care is inapplicable.

to prevent the unjustified imposition of liability by "confining liability's scope to the reasons for holding the actor liable in the first place." *Id.* §29 cmt. *d,* at 579-80. As an example of the standard's application, the drafters provide an illustration of a hunter returning from the field and handing his loaded shotgun to a child as he enters the house. The child drops the gun (an object assumed for the purposes of the illustration to be neither too heavy nor unwieldy for a child of that age and size to handle) which lands on her foot and breaks her toe. *Id.* Applying the risk standard described above, the hunter would not be liable for the broken toe because the risk that made his action negligent was the risk that the child would shoot someone, not that she would drop the gun and sustain an injury to her foot.

The scope-of-liability issue is fact-intensive as it requires consideration of the risks that made the actor's conduct tortious and a determination of whether the harm at issue is a result of any of those risks. When, as in this case, the court considers in advance of trial whether

> the plaintiff's harm is beyond the scope of liability as a matter of law, courts must initially consider all of the range of harms risked by the defendant's conduct that the jury *could* find as the basis for determining [the defendant's] conduct tortious. Then, the court can compare the plaintiff's harm with the range of harms risked by the defendant to determine whether a reasonable jury might find the former among the latter.

Id. at 580.

The drafters advance several advantages of limiting liability in this way. First, the application of the risk standard is comparatively simple. *Id.* cmt. *e,* at 585. The standard "appeals to intuitive notions of fairness and proportionality by limiting liability to harms that result from risks created by the actor's wrongful conduct, but for no others." *Id.* It also is flexible enough to "accommodate fairness concerns raised by the specific facts of a case." *Id.* . . .

The drafters of the Restatement (Third) explain that foreseeability is still relevant in scope-of-liability determinations. "In a negligence action, prior incidents or other facts evidencing risks may make certain risks foreseeable that otherwise were not, thereby changing the scope-of-liability analysis." Restatement (Third) §29 cmt. *d,* at 584-85. In fact, they acknowledge the similarity between the risk standard they articulate and the foreseeability tests applied by most jurisdictions in making causation determinations in negligence cases.

> Properly understood, both the risk standard and a foreseeability test exclude liability for harms that were sufficiently unforeseeable at the time of the actor's tortious conduct that they were not among the risks — potential harms — that made the actor negligent. . . . [W]hen scope of liability arises in a negligence case, the risks that make an actor negligent are limited to foreseeable ones, and the factfinder must determine whether the type of harm that occurred is among those reasonably foreseeable potential harms that made the actor's conduct negligent.

Id. §29 cmt. *j,* at 594. Although the risk standard and the foreseeability test are comparable in negligence actions, the drafters favor the risk standard because it "provides greater clarity, facilitates clearer analysis in a given case, and better reveals the reason for its existence." *Id.* They explain that a foreseeability test "risks being misunderstood because of uncertainty about what must be foreseen, by whom, and at what time." *Id.* at 595.

We find the drafters' clarification of scope of liability sound and are persuaded by their explanation of the advantages of applying the risk standard as articulated in the Restatement (Third), and, accordingly, adopt it.

Our next task, then, is to consider whether the district court erred in concluding the harm suffered by the Thompsons was, a matter of law, outside the scope of the risk of Kaczinski and Lockwood's conduct. We conclude the question of whether a serious injury to a motorist was within the range of harms risked by disassembling the trampoline and leaving it untethered for a few weeks on the yard less than forty feet from the road is not so clear in this case as to justify the district court's resolution of the issue as a matter of law at the summary judgment stage. A reasonable fact finder could determine Kaczinski and Lockwood should have known high winds occasionally occur in Iowa in September and a strong gust of wind could displace the unsecured trampoline parts the short distance from the yard to the roadway and endanger motorists. Although they were in their home for several hours after the storm passed and approximately two-and-a-half hours after daybreak, Kaczinski and Lockwood did not discover their property on the nearby roadway, remove it, or warn approaching motorists of it. On this record, viewed in the light most favorable to the Thompsons, we conclude a reasonable fact finder could find the harm suffered by the Thompsons resulted from the risks that made the defendants' conduct negligent. Accordingly, the district court erred in deciding the scope-of-liability question as a matter of law in this case.

[T]he district court erred in concluding Kaczinski and Lockwood owed the Thompsons no common law duty. As a reasonable fact finder could conclude the Thompsons' injuries and damages were within the scope of the risk of Kaczinski and Lockwood's acts or omissions, the district court erred in resolving the scope of liability question as a matter of law. Accordingly, we reverse the district court's dismissal of this claim and remand this case for trial.

NOTE TO THOMPSON v. KACZINSKI

The Risk Standard Approach to Causation.   Rather than treating proximate cause as a distinct issue, the Restatement (Third) considers whether the scope of an actor's liability should extend to the harm that resulted in a particular case. The factfinder considers all of the harms risked by the actor's conduct and whether the harm that occurred was one of them. If not, the harm is beyond the actor's scope of liability and the actor is not liable. The *Thompson* court acknowledged that the risk standard approach is similar to the foreseeability approach, but was persuaded that focusing on whether the type of harm was one of the risks created by the defendant's conduct would lead to "greater clarity" and "clearer analysis." The courts in Tieder v. Little and Petition of Kinsman Transit Co., in the opinions in Part III, Section D of this chapter, used foreseeability language but may have acted consistently with the risk standard approach articulated in Restatement (Third) of Torts: Liability for Physical and Emotional Harm §29:

> §29. Limitations on Liability for Tortious Conduct
>   An actor's liability is limited to those harms that result from the risks that made the actor's conduct tortious.

Section 30 states this rule slightly differently:

§30. Risk of Harm Not Generally Increased by Tortious Conduct

An actor is not liable for harm when the tortious aspect of the actor's conduct was of a type that does not generally increase the risk of that harm.

Problem
Scope of Liability

A drug dealer sold marijuana to a person who, not wanting to be seen smoking it, took it into his bathroom. While he was there smoking, the bathroom ceiling collapsed due to its negligent construction and killed him. Had the person not smoked the marijuana in the bathroom, he would not have been killed. Would the death of the smoker be within the drug dealer's scope of liability? Is the risk that occurred one of the types of risk that would make the drug dealer's conduct tortious? Did the tortious aspect of the drug dealer's behavior increase the risk of the type of harm that occurred? See United States v. Hatfield, 591 F.3d 945 (7th Cir. 2010) (discussing this hypothetical).

F. Combining Approaches

The directness, substantial factor, and foreseeability tests are sometimes combined. References to foreseeability occur in opinions that otherwise focus on direct causation, as in Laureano v. Louzoun, in Part III, Section B of this chapter. Some states have applied rules requiring that the defendant's conduct be a substantial factor in producing the harm *and* that the harm be foreseeable. Before adopting the Restatement (Third) of Torts approach in *Thompson*, the Iowa Supreme Court had authorized a trial judge to give the jury instructions on proximate cause that included both a substantial factor test and a foreseeability test. That court identified the purpose of the substantial factor test as being to impose liability only on defendants whose conduct "has such an effect in producing the harm as to lead reasonable minds to regard it as a cause." The foreseeability test, according to the court, "goes beyond the substantial factor analysis," "reflects a legal judgment, and is rooted in social policy." The foreseeability test imposes liability "to those causes that are so closely connected with the result that our legal system is justified in imposing liability." Because the foreseeability analysis comes into play after the substantial factor test, it must exclude from the category of proximate causes some acts that would otherwise be treated as a basis for liability. See Sumpter v. Moulton, 519 N.W.2d 427 (Iowa 1994).

Alternatively, states may have one proximate cause rule for some cases and another rule for other cases. The Tennessee Supreme Court outlined a three-pronged test for proximate cause:

> (1) the tortfeasor's conduct must have been a "substantial factor" in bringing about the harm being complained of; and (2) there is no rule or policy that should relieve the wrongdoer from liability because of the manner in which the negligence has resulted in the harm; and (3) the harm giving rise to the action could have reasonably been foreseen or anticipated by a person of ordinary intelligence and prudence.

Haynes v. Hamilton County, 883 S.W.2d 606, 612 (Tenn. 1994).

In contrast, the Tennessee legislature adopted a different test *for special circumstances.*

Statute: LEGISLATIVE FINDINGS; PROXIMATE CAUSE
Tenn. Stat. §57-10-101 (2017)

The general assembly hereby finds and declares that the consumption of any alcoholic beverage or beer rather than the furnishing of any alcoholic beverage or beer is the proximate cause of injuries inflicted upon another by an intoxicated person.

Statute: PROXIMATE CAUSE; STANDARD OF PROOF
Tenn. Stat. §57-10-102 (2017)

Notwithstanding the provisions of §57-10-101, no judge or jury may pronounce a judgment awarding damages to or on behalf of any party who has suffered personal injury or death against any person who has sold any alcoholic beverage or beer, unless such jury of twelve (12) persons has first ascertained beyond a reasonable doubt that the sale by such person of the alcoholic beverage or beer was the proximate cause of the personal injury or death sustained and that such person:

(1) Sold the alcoholic beverage or beer to a person known to be under the age of twenty-one (21) years and such person caused the personal injury or death as the direct result of the consumption of the alcoholic beverage or beer so sold; or

(2) Sold the alcoholic beverage or beer to an obviously intoxicated person and such person caused the personal injury or death as the direct result of the consumption of the alcoholic beverage or beer so sold.

NOTES TO STATUTES

1. *Coping with the Variety of Proximate Cause Rules.* What proximate cause test applies in Tennessee (a) if the defendant sold an alcoholic beverage to a person known to be under the age of twenty-one and not obviously intoxicated, and (b) if the defendant sold to a person over the age of twenty-one and not obviously intoxicated? The only way to cope with the variety of tests applied by various jurisdictions or within a single jurisdiction is to understand each of the tests independently.

2. *Burden of Proof on Proximate Cause.* Whatever the test for proximate cause, a party obliged to prove that another's conduct was a proximate cause must ordinarily do so by a preponderance of the evidence. Legislatures may change this burden of proof for policy reasons, as the Tennessee legislature did. Must evidence of proximate cause be more persuasive in a case where the defendant sold an alcoholic beverage to a person known to be under the age of twenty-one but not obviously intoxicated, or one where the defendant sold to a person over the age of twenty-one who was not obviously intoxicated?

G. Intervening and Superseding Forces

1. In General

All approaches to proximate cause take account of "intervening" or "superseding" events. When a third party's conduct comes after the defendant's act in the chain of events leading to the plaintiff's injury, that conduct is referred to as an intervening act.

When an intervening third-party act prevents the defendant from being liable, that intervening act is labeled a "superseding act" or "superseding cause." Courts generally agree on the test for determining when an intervening act will be superseding, but may articulate it in various ways.

Many courts ask whether the intervening *act* was foreseeable. This contrasts with the traditional duty analysis, which focuses on the foreseeability of the *plaintiff* or the *harm.* It also contrasts with the foreseeability test for proximate cause, which focuses on the foreseeability of the *general type of accident* that occurred.

A similar approach is to ask whether the risk that materialized was among the risks that made the defendant's conduct tortious. Using this approach, courts ask whether the type of intervening act and its consequences were foreseeable when the defendant acted. Foreseeable acts and consequences define the scope of the risk created by the defendant's conduct. Unforeseeable risks that do not support a finding of defendant negligence are outside the scope of the risk. This approach differs from the traditional duty and proximate cause analysis, although it reflects the "scope of liability" analysis of the Restatement (Third) of Torts.

Terminology. This discussion of intervening causes begins by following the common practice of describing cause-in-fact, proximate cause, and superseding cause as three separate elements of legal cause to be considered individually. Some courts and writers include treatment of superseding cause issues under the heading of "proximate cause." In either analysis, consideration of superseding cause comes after and in addition to the analysis of whatever other proximate cause or scope of liability test the court uses. Price v. Blaine Kern Artisa, Inc. and McClenahan v. Cooley illustrate this three-element approach. Recently, a few courts have completely eliminated the analysis of intervening forces in a distinct and separate superseding cause analysis. These courts analyze the effect of intervening forces in the proximate cause analysis. Barry v. Quality Steel Products Inc. illustrates the two-element approach.

2. When Is an Intervening Force Treated as Superseding?

Price v. Blaine Kern Artista, Inc. shows that there can sometimes be a close relationship between a plaintiff's characterization of a defendant's conduct and the issue of whether a subsequent act is or is not foreseeable. McClenahan v. Cooley demonstrates how a court may decide what facts are relevant to deciding whether an intervening act is superseding in the context of a car owner's negligent act of leaving keys in a car and a thief's conduct after stealing the car.

PRICE v. BLAINE KERN ARTISTA, INC.

893 P.2d 367 (Nev. 1995)

Per Curiam. . . .

Appellant Thomas Price filed an action . . . against Blaine Kern Artista, Inc. ("BKA"), a Louisiana corporation that manufactures oversized masks in the form of caricatures resembling various celebrities and characters (hereafter "caricature mask"). The caricature mask covers the entire head of the wearer. Price alleged in his complaint that the caricature mask of George Bush which he wore during employment as an entertainer at Harrah's Club in Reno was defective due to the absence of a safety harness to support his head and neck under the heavy weight. He also alleged that his injury occurred when a Harrah's patron pushed him from behind, causing the weight of the caricature mask to strain and injure his neck as he fell to the ground.

On BKA's motion for summary judgment, the district court determined that the patron's push that precipitated Price's fall constituted an unforeseeable superseding cause absolving BKA of liability. . . .

Price argues that legal causation is a question of fact to be decided by the trier of fact and that an intervening criminal or tortious act by a third party does not necessarily preclude liability as a matter of law. In so arguing, however, he concedes (rather improvidently, we suggest) that BKA, a Louisiana corporation, could not reasonably be expected to have foreseen an attack on a user of one of its products by a third-party assailant in Reno, Nevada, and relies exclusively on the prospect that a jury might reasonably infer that a performer wearing a top-heavy, oversized caricature mask may stumble, trip, be pushed, or become imbalanced for numerous reasons. That same jury, according to Price, may find that BKA proximately caused Price's injury due to its failure to equip the caricature mask of our former President with a safety harness.

BKA first counters that legal causation, although normally a jury issue, may nevertheless be resolved summarily in appropriate cases when there is no genuine issue of material fact on the issue of foreseeability. BKA next argues that this is an appropriate case for summary judgment because, by Price's own admission, the third-party attack forming the basis of his complaint was not foreseeable to BKA, and is thus a superseding cause of Price's injuries.

Contrary to BKA's assertions, we conclude . . . that genuine issues of material fact remain with respect to the issue of legal causation.

While it is true that criminal or tortious third-party conduct typically severs the chain of proximate causation between a plaintiff and a defendant, the chain remains unbroken when the third party's intervening intentional act is reasonably foreseeable. Under the circumstances of this case, the trier of fact could reasonably find that BKA should have foreseen the possibility or probability of some sort of violent reaction, such as pushing, by intoxicated or politically volatile persons, ignited by the sight of an oversized caricature of a prominent political figure. We certainly cannot preclude such an inference as a matter of law and decline to penalize Price for his attorney's lack of acuity in conceding this issue. Indeed, while the precise force that caused Price's fall is uncertain, shortly before the fall, an irate and perhaps somewhat confused patron of Harrah's took issue with the bedecked Price over Bush's policy on abortion rights. . . .

For the reasons discussed above, we conclude that a genuine issue of material fact remains with respect to the issue of the legal and proximate cause of Price's injuries. Accordingly, we reverse the district court's entry of summary judgment and remand for trial.

McCLENAHAN v. COOLEY

806 S.W.2d 767 (Tenn. 1991)

DROWOTA, J.

In this action for the wrongful death of his wife and two children and personal injuries to another child, William McClenahan, Plaintiff-Appellant, appeals the dismissal of his lawsuit against Glenn Cooley, Defendant-Appellee, by the Circuit Court of Bradley County. The central issue presented in this litigation is whether a jury should be permitted to determine the issue of proximate causation in cases where the keys are left in the ignition of a parked automobile that is subsequently stolen and thereafter involved in an accident. For the reasons that follow, we reverse and remand. . . .

The facts to be taken as true in this case reveal that on May 20, 1988, at approximately 11 a.m., the Defendant, Glenn Cooley, drove his 1981 Pontiac Bonneville automobile to a bank located in the public parking lot of a shopping center in Athens. The Defendant left the keys in the ignition to his parked automobile while he went inside of the bank to transact business. While the Defendant was in the bank, a thief spotted the keys in the ignition of the vehicle, started the engine, and began driving down the interstate where he was spotted by a state trooper. When the thief exited the interstate a short time later, a high speed chase ensued on the busiest stretch of highway in Cleveland at the lunchtime hour. The thief was pursued by police officers approximately 80 miles per hour approaching the most dangerous intersection in the city. When the vehicles reached the intersection, the thief ran a red light traveling in excess of 80 miles per hour and slammed into another vehicle broadside. That vehicle was being driven by the Plaintiff's thirty-one year old wife who was six to eight months pregnant. She died approximately fourteen hours later in a nearby hospital. The viable fetus was delivered before Mrs. McClenahan's untimely death but likewise perished as a result of injuries arising out of the accident. The Plaintiff's four year old son, a passenger in the vehicle, also died. Another young child who was also riding in the vehicle sustained substantial injuries but survived. The Defendant's vehicle was reported stolen at 11:13 a.m. and the collision between the stolen car and the one owned by the Plaintiff occurred at 11:33 a.m. It should be noted that the Defendant was employed as a law enforcement officer and had formerly been a high ranking officer with various law enforcement agencies in McMinn County. . . .

. . . The question of a vehicle owner's liability for the consequences of an accident caused by a thief, enabled to misappropriate the vehicle through the presence of a key left in the ignition switch by the owner, is a frequently litigated question upon which there is considerable disagreement among the states. . . . An accurate summary of the jurisprudence nationwide concerning the topic at hand was recently provided by the Supreme Court of New Mexico:

> [A] substantial number of courts have not held owners liable for leaving the keys in their unattended vehicles and for the injuries to third persons as a result of the thefts and subsequent negligent operation of those vehicles. Those courts have concluded either that an owner owes no duty to the general public to guard against the risk of a thief's negligent operation of a vehicle in which the owner left his keys; that the theft and subsequent negligence of the thief could not reasonably be foreseen by the owner as a natural or probable consequence of leaving the keys in the ignition of the car; or have concluded that even if the owner was negligent, his actions were not the proximate cause of the injury because the thief's actions constituted an independent, intervening cause.
>
> An emerging group of jurisdictions, on the other hand, have rejected the contention that an intervening criminal act automatically breaks the chain of causation as a matter of law, concluding instead that a reasonable person could foresee a theft of an automobile left unattended with the keys in the ignition and reasonably could foresee

the increased risk to the public should the theft occur. In addition, a few courts, including some of those that earlier denied liability, have indicated a willingness to impose liability upon the owner under special circumstances. Courts looking at special circumstances seek to determine whether an owner's conduct enhanced the probability that his car would be stolen and thus increased the hazard to third persons. Considering special circumstances, then, is just another way of examining the degree of foreseeability of injury and whether the owner is subject to a duty to exercise reasonable care.

This Court is of the opinion that the approach taken by the substantial (and growing) number of jurisdictions representing the minority view is the approach that should be taken in Tennessee, in part, because principles of common law negligence long established in this state provide a sufficient analytical framework to dispose of cases with fact patterns similar to the one presented in this appeal. First, it is axiomatic that in order for there to be a cause of action for common law negligence, the following elements must be established: (1) a duty of care owed by the defendant to the plaintiff; (2) conduct falling below the applicable standard of care amounting to a breach of that duty; (3) an injury or loss; (4) causation in fact; and (5) proximate, or legal, cause. Our opinions have recognized that proximate causation is the "ultimate issue" in negligence cases. This is particularly true in cases involving the situation where keys are left in the ignition of an unattended vehicle that is subsequently stolen as a result. . . .

With respect to superseding intervening causes that might break the chain of proximate causation, the rule is established that it is not necessary that tortfeasors or concurrent forces act in concert, or that there be a joint operation or a union of act or intent, in order for the negligence of each to be regarded as the proximate cause of the injuries, thereby rendering all tortfeasors liable. There is no requirement that a cause, to be regarded as the proximate cause of an injury, be the sole cause, the last act, or the one nearest to the injury, provided it is a substantial factor in producing the end result. An intervening act, which is a normal response created by negligence, is not a superseding, intervening cause so as to relieve the original wrongdoer of liability, provided the intervening act could have reasonably been foreseen and the conduct was a substantial factor in bringing about the harm. "An intervening act will not exculpate the original wrongdoer unless it appears that the negligent intervening act could not have been reasonably anticipated." Evridge v. American Honda Motor Co., 685 S.W.2d 632, 635 (Tenn. 1985). See also Restatement (Second) of Torts, Section 447 (1965). "It is only where misconduct was to be anticipated, and taking the risk of it was unreasonable, that liability will be imposed for consequences to which such intervening acts contributed." Prosser [& Keeton, The Law of Torts, §44, p.314 (5th ed. 1984)]. Just as in the case of proximate causation, the question of superseding intervening cause is a matter peculiarly for the jury because of foreseeability considerations.

. . . The basic issue is foreseeability, both as to proximate causation and superseding intervening cause, and that is a question of fact rather than of law upon which reasonable minds can and do differ, at least where the accident has occurred during the flight of the thief relatively close thereto in time and distance.[8] . . . We thus expressly

---

[8] A study conducted by the United States Department of Justice reveals that 42.3 percent of all automobiles stolen during the period covered by the study were left unattended with the keys in the ignition and that the rate of accidents involving such stolen vehicles was 200 times the normal accident rate. See 45 A.L.R.3d at 797.

reject the contention that an intervening criminal act under the circumstances presented here automatically breaks the chain of causation as a matter of law, concluding
instead that reasonable minds can differ as to whether a person of ordinary prudence
and intelligence through the exercise of reasonable diligence could foresee, or should
have foreseen, the theft of an unattended automobile with the keys in the ignition left in
an area where the public has access, and could likewise foresee the increased risk to the
public should a theft occur. . . . In sum, a jury might conclude in this case that a
reasonable person would not have left the keys in the ignition of his unattended car
parked in a lot where the public had ready access. As a result, the decisions with regard
to foreseeability as it relates to proximate cause and intervening cause should properly
be submitted to a jury.

Nothing, however, stated hereinabove is intended to imply that a fact-finder could
not reasonably return a verdict for the car owner in this case, or that the evidence in
some comparable situation might not possibly justify even a judgment for the vehicle
owner as a matter of law. Determinations in this regard must necessarily depend on the
entire circumstantial spectrum, such as the position of the vehicle and the nature of the
locality in which the vehicle is left, the extent of access thereto, operational condition of
the vehicle, its proximity to surveillance, the time of day or night the vehicle is left
unattended, and the length of time (and distance) elapsing from the theft to the
accident. . . .

NOTES TO PRICE v. BLAINE KERN ARTISTA, INC. AND McCLENAHAN v. COOLEY

1. *Superseding Cause: Alternative Formulations.*   The court in McClenahan v.
Cooley describes three ways intervening acts are not superseding causes that prevent
the defendant from being liable. An intervening act is not superseding if (1) it is a
normal response to the negligent act that is reasonably foreseeable, and the original
actor's conduct was a substantial factor in bringing about the harm; (2) it could
reasonably have been anticipated; or (3) the intervening conduct could have been
anticipated and taking the risk of it was unreasonable. The third of these formulations
is sometimes referred to as the scope of the risk test. The scope of the risk test asks
whether the intervening act was among the foreseeable circumstances that made the
defendant's conduct blameworthy. Which approach was used by the court in Price v.
Blaine Kern Artista, Inc.?

2. *Liability of the Intervening Actor.*   If the intervening actor and the original actor
both breached a duty to the plaintiff, and the intervening act is not a superseding cause,
then the two actors will share liability. How their shares are determined is the subject of
Chapter 8, Apportionment of Damages. If the intervening actor breached a duty to the
plaintiff and his or her act supersedes that of the first actor, only the intervening actor
will be liable to the plaintiff.

3. *Factual Considerations Relevant to Superseding Cause.*   The foreseeability test
for superseding cause asks whether the intervening act that contributed to the plaintiff's injury was foreseeable. The court in McClenahan v. Cooley stated that a jury
should decide whether theft was foreseeable *and* whether an increased risk to the public
in the event of a theft was also foreseeable. The court listed a number of factors the jury

should consider in answering those questions. How do those factors compare with the factors analyzed by the court in Price v. Blaine Kern Artista, Inc.?

   4. *Foreseeability of the Intervening Act That Occurred.*   In Price v. Blaine Kern Artista, Inc., the plaintiff's lawyer conceded that BKA, a Louisiana corporation, could not have reasonably foreseen the specific intervening act that occurred, someone attacking a performer wearing a George Bush caricature mask in Reno, Nevada. The lawyer argued, however, that foreseeability of a less specific event, which the court characterizes as "falling for a variety of reasons," was sufficient. That argument fails because the plaintiff's "falling" is not a third-party act; it is the result of a third-party act. But the court helped the plaintiff by explaining that the intervening act need not be specifically identified. The court held that a jury could find that the intervening act, a "violent reaction, such as pushing" stimulated by someone's seeing a caricature of a controversial political figure, was foreseeable. Thus, the superseding cause analysis considers the reasonable foreseeability of the type of intervening act, here a violent reaction to the mask, rather than the precise act or its consequence. In McClenahan v. Cooley, what intervening act is analyzed?

Problem
Superseding Cause

   A defendant operates an automobile dealership and service facility. About 10 a.m. on the day involved, a customer's automobile was delivered to the dealership for repairs. The defendant's employees allowed the automobile to remain outside the building, double-parked in the street with the key in the ignition. About three hours later, it was stolen by an adult stranger who then drove it around the block in such a careless manner that it mounted a sidewalk and struck the plaintiff, a pedestrian thereon, causing her serious injury. The defendant's garage was located in an urban area that had experienced a high and increasing number of automobile thefts in the immediately preceding months. See Liney v. Chestnut Motors, Inc., 218 A.2d 336 (Pa. 1966). Would your analysis be changed if the dealership was located near a high school? See Anderson v. Bushong Pontiac Co., 404 Pa. 382, 171 A.2d 771 (1961).

3. Analyzing Intervening Forces Under the Proximate Cause Analysis

   Several courts have concluded either that the superseding cause analysis is redundant or inappropriate given modern legal developments. Historically, a plaintiff whose own negligence was causally related to his harm was totally barred from recovery. This policy favored defendants in cases where both plaintiffs and defendants were negligent. Currently, most states favor a modern policy of comparing the degrees of negligence of all parties whose conduct was casually related to the harm and apportioning damages among them. This policy sometimes allows a negligent plaintiff to collect a portion of his damages. These topics are covered in the next two chapters, Chapter 7: Defenses and Chapter 8: Apportionment of Damages. Barry v. Quality Steel Products Inc. considers the implications of this modern policy for the superseding cause doctrine.

BARRY v. QUALITY STEEL PRODUCTS, INC.

820 A.2d 258 (Conn. 2003)

NORCOTT, J.

The dispositive issue in this appeal involves the viability of the doctrine of super-seding cause. The plaintiffs, Neil Barry, Diana Barry, Bernard Cohade and Lynn Cohade, appeal from the judgment of the trial court in favor of the named defendant, Quality Steel Products, Inc. (Quality Steel), and the defendant Ring's End, Inc. (Ring's End). On appeal, the plaintiffs claim that the trial court improperly instructed the jury on the doctrine of superseding cause. . . .

This appeal followed.

The jury reasonably could have found the following facts. The plaintiffs were employed as carpenters by DeLuca. On February 26, 1998, the plaintiffs were putting shingles on the roof of the New Canaan Nature Center when the platform staging on which they were working collapsed, causing the plaintiffs to fall to the ground and sustain severe injuries. Immediately prior to the collapse, the plaintiffs were working on a wooden plank attached to the roof by roof brackets designed and manufactured by Quality Steel and purchased from Ring's End.

The roof brackets were used as part of a structure that created a platform on which the plaintiffs could work. To install the brackets, the plaintiffs nailed them to the roof through three slots on the bracket. After the brackets were attached to the roof, a plank was placed on top of the brackets, which then provided a surface on which the plaintiffs could stand in order to shingle the roof. . . .

After working on the planks for several hours in the morning, the plaintiffs returned to the planking after lunch and began shingling the roof on the right side of the building. Shortly after the plaintiffs returned to work on the roof, the planking suddenly fell out from under them and they fell to the ground. Almost immediately after the plaintiffs fell, Gene Marini, the general superintendent at DeLuca, discovered one of the roof brackets used by the plaintiffs in a distorted condition on the ground near where they fell.

Quality Steel's instruction label on the roof brackets suggests that the user attach the brackets to the roof using sixteenpenny nails.[1] The defendants introduced evidence that some of the brackets were installed by another DeLuca employee, Nate Manizza, using eightpenny nails. The plaintiffs both testified that when they installed roof brackets they used larger, twelvepenny nails. Neither the plaintiffs nor Manizza could remember if they had installed the specific brackets that had collapsed causing the plaintiffs to fall. Cohade testified, however, that he saw Manizza installing the brackets in the general area where the plaintiffs fell. There was also testimony from both the plaintiffs' and the defendants' experts that the use of a twelvepenny nail would be sufficient to hold the bracket to the roof and would not be causative of the collapse of the planking that occurred in this case.

The defendants also introduced evidence, through expert testimony, that DeLuca had violated the federal Occupational Safety and Health Administration (OSHA) regulations by failing to provide additional fall protection for the plaintiffs while they were working on the New Canaan Nature Center roof. The plaintiffs offered,

---

[1] The penny reference indicates the size of a nail. The plaintiffs' expert witness, Karl Puttlitz, a metallurgist, explained during his testimony: "As you increase in penny size, the dimensions [of the shaft and the nail itself] increase incrementally. . . ."

and the jury reasonably could have found, however, that OSHA, in its investigation of the plaintiffs' accident, did not find any violations of roofing standards at the project site and that the roof brackets were an acceptable method of providing fall protection.

The jury also reasonably could have found that the roof bracket designed and manufactured by Quality Steel and used by the plaintiffs before the platform collapsed was undersized in comparison to the manufacturing specifications. Specifically, both the plaintiffs' and the defendants' experts testified that the platform arm of the roof bracket was thinner than required by Quality Steel's own specifications. Additionally, the jury, through their special interrogatories, found that Quality Steel's product was defective and unreasonably dangerous at the time it was manufactured and sold by the defendants, and that the defective condition of the product was a proximate cause of the plaintiffs' accident. . . .

In the present case, the jury's interrogatories reveal two possible sources of a superseding cause. The first possible superseding cause of the plaintiffs' injuries was DeLuca's failure to provide additional fall protection for the plaintiffs. The second possible superseding cause was Manizza's use of eightpenny nails to attach the roof brackets to the roof.

We take this opportunity to clarify our approach to the doctrine of superseding cause and its continuing validity in our tort jurisprudence. As will be discussed in further detail later in this opinion, we conclude that the doctrine of superseding cause no longer serves a useful purpose in our jurisprudence when a defendant claims that a subsequent negligent act by a third party cuts off its own liability for the plaintiff's injuries. We conclude that under those circumstances, superseding cause instructions serve to complicate what is fundamentally a proximate cause analysis. Specifically, we conclude that, because our statutes allow for apportionment among negligent defendants; and because Connecticut is a comparative negligence jurisdiction; the simpler and less confusing approach to cases, such as the present one, where the jury must determine which, among many, causes contributed to the plaintiffs' injury, is to couch the analysis in proximate cause rather than allowing the defendants to raise a defense of superseding cause.

Our conclusion that the doctrine of superseding cause no longer serves a useful purpose is limited to the situation in cases, such as the one presently before us, wherein a defendant claims that its tortious conduct is superseded by a subsequent negligent act or there are multiple acts of negligence. Our conclusion does not necessarily affect those cases where the defendant claims that an unforeseeable intentional tort, force of nature, or criminal event supersedes its tortious conduct. We leave those questions to cases that squarely present them. . . .[2]

At least two other states also have addressed the issue of whether the doctrine of superseding cause continues to play a useful role in their negligence jurisprudence after the advent of comparative fault and apportionment regimes. Because these cases illustrate aspects of the approach we adopt here today, we discuss them in detail.

In *Torres v. El Paso Electric Co.*, 127 N.M. 729, 732, 987 P.2d 386 (1999), the plaintiff was injured when he came into contact with a power line while replacing the roof of his employer's building. In the negligence action brought by the plaintiff against the electric company, the defendant claimed that the actions of the plaintiff, the plaintiff's employer and various other electrical contractors, constituted a superseding cause of the plaintiff's injuries that relieved the defendant of any liability. The jury ultimately determined that, although the defendant was negligent, its negligence was not the proximate cause of the plaintiff's injuries.

The New Mexico Supreme Court, in *Torres,* began its analysis of the plaintiff's appeal by explaining that New Mexico previously had adopted a pure comparative negligence system and, as a natural corollary, subsequently had abolished joint and several liability. The court went on to explain that, prior to the adoption of comparative negligence, courts had used the doctrine of superseding cause to avoid the contributory negligence bar that some deemed to be unfair. The court determined that this application of the doctrine of superseding cause was inconsistent with New Mexico's comparative fault laws. Moreover, when analyzing the doctrine, the court appropriately stated: "A finding of an independent [superseding] cause represents a finding against the plaintiff on proximate cause or, in other words, a finding that the defendant's act or omission did not, in a natural and continuous sequence, produce the injury." Id., at 736, 987 P.2d 386. Thus, the court determined that, the doctrine was no longer appropriate in cases where the defendant alleged that the plaintiff's negligence superseded its own liability, because the use of the doctrine created an unacceptable risk that the jury would inadvertently apply the common-law rule of contributory negligence.

Additionally, with respect to cases in which the superseding cause doctrine is used by defendants to attempt to shift their fault to other intervening tortfeasors, the New Mexico Supreme Court concluded that a jury instruction based on superseding cause would "unduly emphasize the conduct of one tortfeasor over another and would potentially conflict with the jury's duty to apportion fault." Id., at 737, 987 P.2d 386. The court explained that there were cases in which the unforeseeable negligence of a third party could break the chain of causation. In such a case, however, the defendant's act or omission simply would not be a proximate cause of the plaintiff's injury. Because, as the New Mexico Supreme Court determined, the issue of superseding cause adds a complex layer of analysis to the jury's determination of proximate cause, the appropriate analysis is merely that of proximate cause. Finally, the court concluded that, "consistent with our prior cases discussing the effect of comparative negligence on traditional negligence principles, we believe that the instruction on [superseding] cause is sufficiently repetitive of the instruction on proximate cause and the task of apportioning fault that any potential for jury confusion and misdirection outweighs its usefulness." Id. Ultimately, based on the foregoing analysis, the court determined that the doctrine of superseding cause could not apply to the defendant's acts, therefore resulting in a new trial.

In *Control Techniques, Inc. v. Johnson,* 762 N.E.2d 104 (Ind.2002), the Indiana Supreme Court analyzed the relationship between that state's comparative fault act and the doctrine of superseding cause. In *Control Techniques, Inc.,* the plaintiff sustained serious injuries while measuring the voltage of a circuit breaker. The jury allocated 5 percent of the fault to the defendant. On appeal, the defendant contended that the negligence of another company that had installed the circuit breaker constituted a superseding cause of the accident and foreclosed any liability on its part for defective design and manufacture.

After an analysis of that state's common-law doctrine of superseding cause, the court in *Control Techniques, Inc.,* concluded that the doctrines of causation and foreseeability impose the same limitations on liability as the superseding cause doctrine. As the court aptly noted: "Causation limits a negligent actor's liability to foreseeable consequences. A superseding cause is, by definition, one that is not reasonably foreseeable. As a result, the doctrine in today's world adds nothing to the requirement of foreseeability that is not already inherent in the requirement of causation." Id., at 108. Ultimately, the Indiana Supreme Court concluded that it was proper for the trial court to instruct only on proximate causation because the substance of the doctrine of superseding cause was fully explained in the instruction on proximate cause.

We find these two cases persuasive and conclude that the rationale supporting the abandonment of the doctrine of superseding cause outweighs any of the doctrine's remaining usefulness in our modern system of torts. Specifically, as the New Mexico Supreme Court determined, we believe that the instruction on superseding cause complicates what is essentially a proximate cause analysis and risks jury confusion. The doctrine also no longer serves a useful purpose in our tort jurisprudence, especially considering our system of comparative negligence and apportionment, where defendants are responsible solely for their proportionate share of the injury suffered by the plaintiff. Thus, it is no longer appropriate to give an instruction of the doctrine of superseding cause in cases involving multiple acts of negligence. Instead, under the approach we adopt herein, if the defendant was both the cause in fact and a proximate cause of the plaintiff's injury, the defendant will be liable for his or her proportionate share of the damages, notwithstanding other acts of negligence that also may have contributed to the plaintiff's injury.

This analysis leads to the conclusion that the doctrine of superseding cause should not have been presented to the jury in the present case. Upon retrial, therefore, the fact finder must determine if the defendants' manufacture and sale of a defective product was a cause in fact and a proximate cause of the plaintiffs' injuries, without reference to the doctrine of superseding cause.

The judgment for the defendants is reversed and the case is remanded for a new trial. . . .

NOTES TO BARRY v. QUALITY STEEL PRODUCTS INC.

1. *Abandoning Superseding Cause Analysis.*   The *Barry* court abandons superseding cause analysis in part because it is inconsistent with modern rules of comparative negligence and apportionment, which are briefly explained in the introduction preceding the case. Comparing the degree of negligence of all parties whose conduct was casually related to the harm and apportioning damages among them can result in a dramatically different allocation of financial responsibility than the superseding cause approach. The superseding cause analysis may result in one negligent defendant being entirely absolved of liability and another being responsible for all of the damages. The current rules dividing damages among the defendants make the superseding cause rule less necessary.

2. *When Proximate and Superseding Cause Overlap.*   According to the court in *Control Techniques*, discussed in *Barry*, whether or not proximate cause exists in Indiana is primarily a question of foreseeability of the injury given the specific facts of the case. (By contrast, in Indiana, foreseeability in the duty context is a general threshold determination that involves the foreseeability of (1) the broad type of plaintiff and, (2) the broad type of harm, without addressing the specific facts of the occurrence. *See* Rodgers v. Martin Eyeglasses, 63 N.E.3d 316 (Ind. 2016).) In a state like Indiana with a foreseeability test for proximate cause, if the defendant can foresee the injury coming about through the intervention of a third party, both the proximate cause and superseding cause test lead to liability for that defendant. If the injury coming about through

the intervening force is unforeseeable, both tests lead to no liability. Having both tests is redundant as long as what it is that must be foreseeable is the same in both tests.

3. *Abandoning Superseding Cause Where the Substantial Factor Test Is Used.* The *Barry* jurisdiction's test for proximate cause is whether a party's conduct was a substantial factor in producing the plaintiff's injuries. Foreseeability of the harm or the manner in which it occurred to someone in the defendant's position is generally irrelevant to whether the defendant's act is a substantial factor. The substantial factor test does not overlap with the superseding cause test, which focuses on foreseeability, so the redundancy rationale for abandoning superseding cause analysis does not apply as well. The rationale for abandoning superseding cause in a substantial factor jurisdiction rests on the policy underlying adoption of modern comparative negligence and apportionment rules.

Torres, discussed in *Barry,* is a New Mexico case. In New Mexico, the courts follow the modern comparative negligence rules and proximate cause encompasses "whether and to what extent the defendant's conduct foreseeably and substantially caused the specific injury that actually occurred." Lujan v. N.M. Dept. of Transportation, 341 P.3d 1, 10 (Ct. App. N.M. 2014). Given these New Mexico rules, could the New Mexico court rely on the redundancy argument from Indiana, the policy argument related to comparative negligence and apportionment, or both in considering whether to abandon superseding cause?

4. *Restatement (Third) and Superseding Cause.* Most states have not abandoned the superseding cause analysis. The Restatement (Third) recognizes this even though it has effectively abandoned the doctrine. For both proximate cause, (which the Restatement (Third) characterizes as "limitations on liability") and superseding cause, the rule is that "an actor's liability is limited to those harms that result from the risks that made the actor's conduct tortious." Compare §29 Limitations on Liability for Tortious Conduct and §34 Intervening Acts and Superseding Causes, both containing that language. The Restatement (Third) §34 cmt. c observes:

> The rule stated in this Section [34] is functionally the same as §29, but it recognizes that other human acts and forces of nature may concur with tortious conduct to cause harm. Were it not for the long history of intervening and superseding causes playing a significant role in limiting the scope of liability, this Section would not be necessary. However, to address the substantial body of law on this subject and to explain the bases for its declining importance, this Section is necessary.

<hr>

Statute: PROXIMATE CAUSE

Colo. Stat. §13-21-504(2) and (3) (2017)

(2) The manufacturer's, importer's, or distributor's placement of a firearm or ammunition in the stream of commerce, even if such placement is found to be foreseeable, shall not be conduct sufficient to constitute the proximate cause of injury, damage, or death resulting from a third party's use of the product.

(3) In a product liability action concerning the accidental discharge of a firearm, the manufacturer's, importer's, or distributor's placement of the product in the stream of commerce shall not be conduct deemed sufficient to constitute proximate cause, even if accidental discharge is found to be foreseeable.

NOTE TO STATUTE

Legislation Directed at Recurring Issues.   The statute related to firearms and ammunition may be viewed as a legislative response to a recurring problem facing courts or as special interest legislation. Does the statute appear to resolve the issue of proximate cause or of superseding cause? Does it help to know that Colorado applies the substantial factor test for proximate cause?

Perspective: Superseding Causes and the Direct Cause Test

A superseding cause prevents an actor whose conduct was a proximate cause of the plaintiff's injury from being liable for damages. When the test for proximate cause is the foreseeability or substantial factor test, the test makes sense because the existence of an intervening cause does not, *by itself,* prevent the conduct from being a proximate cause. But the direct cause test for proximate cause seems to imply that there may be no significant intervening causes. In *In re Polemis,* Lord Justice Banks said that a harm is proximately caused by an actor's conduct if the harm "is directly traceable to the negligent act, and not due to the operation of independent causes having no connection with the negligent act." What is the role of superseding cause when a direct cause test is applied?

At least one jurisdiction with a direct cause test also applies a superseding cause test to see whether the "independent cause" has a "connection with the negligent act." Delaware's proximate cause test, which they call a "but-for" test, asks whether the actor's conduct is a direct cause without which the accident would not have occurred:

> The mere occurrence of an intervening cause, however, does not automatically break the chain of causation stemming from the original tortious conduct. This Court has long recognized that there may be more than one proximate cause of an injury. In order to break the causal chain, the intervening cause must also be a superseding cause, that is, the intervening act or event itself must have been neither anticipated nor reasonably foreseeable by the original tortfeasor.

See Duphily v. Delaware Elec. Co-op., Inc., 662 A.2d 821, 828 (Del. 1995).

---

4. Negligent Treatment of a Plaintiff's Injury: Intervening or Superseding?

Many cases involve medical malpractice taking place after a plaintiff has suffered an injury due to a defendant's negligence. Weems v. Hy-Vee Food Stores, Inc. involves an unpredictable complication from medical care required by the consequences of the defendant's negligence. In Corbett v. Weisband, the plaintiff's initial injury resulted from medical care, but the problem treated in the case involves the role of subsequent medical treatment.

WEEMS v. HY-VEE FOOD STORES, INC.

526 N.W.2d 571 (Iowa App. 1994)

CADY, J.

This is a single issue appeal in a premise liability/slip-and-fall case. The premise owner claims the trial court erred in failing to allow the jury to consider whether the harmful side effects of medical treatment rendered eighteen months after the fall constituted an intervening superseding cause of the subsequent damages. We conclude the trial court properly denied the superseding cause instruction and affirm.

Leonard Weems slipped and fell on a wet floor at a Drug Town Store in Cedar Rapids. Weems was a customer in the store at the time. The store is owned by Hy-Vee Stores, Inc. Weems experienced lower-back pain following the fall. Approximately eighteen months later, Weems visited Dr. Arnold Delbridge, an orthopedic surgeon, in response to his lingering lower-back pain. Dr. Delbridge administered an epidural block in an effort to relieve the pain. The procedure involved a spinal steroid injection. As a result of the epidural block, Weems developed an infection which led to spinal meningitis. He eventually recovered from the disease.

Weems and his wife brought suit against Hy-Vee seeking damages associated with the injuries he received as a result of his fall. The damage claim included the spinal meningitis. The matter proceeded to a jury trial.

At trial, the court refused to submit Hy-Vee's requested instruction concerning whether Dr. Delbridge's administration of the epidural block was a superseding cause of any damages associated with Weems' spinal meningitis. Hy-Vee would be relieved from responsibility for the resulting damages under the proposed instruction if the jury determined the treatment was a superseding cause. . . .

The rule that a tortfeasor is responsible for injuries which result from his or her negligence is not absolute. An exception exists when an intervening act turns into a superseding cause. If an independent force intervenes after the original negligent conduct and plays a substantial role in creating a particular injury to the plaintiff, the original tortfeasor will be relieved from responsibility for the later injury under narrowly-defined circumstances. If these circumstances are met, the intervening act becomes the superseding cause of the injury. In order for an intervening act to become a superseding cause, it must not have been a normal consequence of the original tortfeasor's acts or must not have been reasonably foreseeable.

Hy-Vee argues the spinal meningitis which occurred some eighteen months after the fall was not a reasonably foreseeable consequence of maintaining a wet floor in its drug store. They point out the uncontradicted evidence revealing it is extremely rare for a patient to contract the disease from a spinal injection, possibly as rare as one in ten thousand cases. At the very least, Hy-Vee insists this evidence presented a jury question whether the later intervening medical treatment was a superseding cause of the spinal meningitis.

An intervening act is reasonably foreseeable, and will not break the causal connection between the original negligence and the later injury, if the subsequent force or conduct is within the scope of the original risk. It is unnecessary, however, that the original tortfeasor foresee the specific conduct which makes up the intervening force. It is sufficient if the risk of harm attributable to the intervening act is foreseeable. If the conduct of the original tortfeasor has created or increased the risk of a particular harm to the plaintiff, and has been a substantial factor in causing the harm, it is immaterial to the imposition of liability that the harm results in a manner which no person could have possibly foreseen or anticipated.

An intervening act is a normal consequence of the original tortfeasor's negligence if it is normal to the situation which the tortfeasor created. This means the intervention of the act was not so extraordinary as to fall outside the class of normal events in light of the ultimate situation.

Generally, medical treatment sought by an injured person is considered a normal consequence of the tortfeasor's conduct. The general rule is framed as follows:

> If the negligent actor is liable for another's bodily injury, he is also subject to liability for any additional bodily harm resulting from normal efforts of third persons in rendering aid which the other's injury reasonably requires, irrespective of whether such acts are done in a proper or negligent manner.

Restatement (Second) of Torts §457. A defendant will be liable for the adverse results of medical treatment unless the treatment is extraordinary or the harm is outside the risks incident to the medical treatment.

It is immaterial in our analysis that the later injury in this case, spinal meningitis, was a rare side effect of the medical treatment. The important evidence was the undisputed testimony that an epidural block was an accepted and common treatment for chronic back pain and that spinal meningitis was a known risk of the procedure. These facts establish the lack of superseding cause. . . .

We conclude the trial court correctly rejected Hy-Vee's requested jury instruction on superseding cause. It was not supported by substantial evidence. The undisputed evidence revealed that medical treatment rendered to Weems was not an extraordinary or unforeseeable act. It was within the scope of the original risk of harm of Hy-Vee's negligence. Hy-Vee exposed Weems to the risk of harm and under the superseding cause analysis, it is immaterial that the precise harm to Weems was rare or even unforeseeable. The instructions by the court properly allowed the jury to consider whether the negligence of Hy-Vee was a proximate cause of the subsequent spinal meningitis, but under the record in this case it was not possible to conclude that the epidural block treatment was a superseding cause.

Affirmed.

CORBETT v. WEISBAND

551 A.2d 1059 (Pa. Super. Ct. 1988)

Rowley, J.

. . . The plaintiff, Lucille Corbett, alleged in both actions that the defendants had been negligent in the care and treatment of a post-operative infection in her left knee, which ultimately led to the amputation of her leg in July of 1983. . . .

The events giving rise to these lawsuits commenced in July 1978 with the operation by Dr. DeMoura on Ms. Corbett's left knee. Following the operation, Dr. DeMoura continued to treat Ms. Corbett through October 1978. In December 1978, she came under the care of Dr. Weisband, for treatment of a knee infection. He treated her through August 1981. During that time, in October 1980, she had a left knee fusion performed by Dr. Weisband at Metropolitan Hospital. According to Dr. Greene, who began treating her in September 1981, the left knee fusion was not successful. Ms. Corbett was hospitalized in December 1981, at which time Dr. Greene performed a total knee replacement on her left knee. From January 5 through 30, 1982, Ms. Corbett was readmitted to the hospital under Dr. Greene's care because the wound in front of her left knee joint had opened. She was discharged once the wound began to heal. In March, Ms. Corbett again was admitted to the hospital under Dr. Greene's care because the wound had not yet healed.

Ms. Corbett was not hospitalized again until November 1982, when she broke her left leg as she was climbing out of bed. She remained in the hospital for nine months following this admission. During this time period, in April 1983, the knee implant was removed because it had become infected. Several months later, in July 1983, Ms. Corbett's leg was amputated above the knee because it was Dr. Greene's belief that the infection would never clear. [The plaintiff alleged that Dr. Weisband was negligent in performing the left knee fusion and in a separate suit alleged that Dr. Greene was negligent in performing a total knee replacement.] . . .

At the trial on damages, Dr. Weisband and ROPA [the Regional Orthopedic Professional Association, a group of doctors with whom Dr. Weisband was associated] argued, and the trial court agreed, that Dr. Weisband is not responsible, as a matter of law, for the damages suffered by Ms. Corbett after she came under the care of Dr. Greene because Dr. Greene's conduct was so "highly extraordinary" as to constitute a superseding cause of her subsequent injuries, i.e., aggravation and prolongation of her pain and the ultimate amputation of her leg. On appeal, Ms. Corbett essentially responds that although Dr. Weisband cannot, as a matter of law, be held responsible for damages flowing from a highly extraordinary act, i.e., a superseding cause, the question of whether an intervening act is "highly extraordinary" should properly be left to the jury, and the trial judge erred in making that determination and taking it from the jury under the facts of this case. The trial court held that the opinion testimony from every physician who commented on Dr. Greene's subsequent conduct — that a total knee replacement in a patient of Ms. Corbett's condition was highly unusual and constituted extraordinary negligence — was sufficient to remove the issue from the province of the jury. For the reasons which follow, we disagree with the trial court and award Ms. Corbett a new trial limited to the issue of damages.

An exception to the general rule that a tortfeasor is responsible for injuries arising from his or her negligence may be provided by an intervening act, however, if it constitutes a superseding cause. "A superseding cause is an act of a third person or other force which by its intervention prevents the actor from being liable for harm to another which his antecedent negligence is a substantial factor in bringing about." Restatement (Second) of Torts §440. As Professors Prosser and Keeton have stated, "the problem is one of whether the defendant is to be held liable for an injury to which the defendant has in fact made a substantial contribution, when it is brought about by a later cause of independent origin, for which the defendant is not responsible." Prosser & Keeton on Torts §44 (5th ed. 1984), at 301. The law as to negligent intervening acts is set forth in Restatement (Second) of Torts §447, which has been adopted in Pennsylvania. The section outlines the circumstances under which a negligent intervening act is not a superseding cause:

The fact that an intervening act of a third person is negligent in itself or is done in a negligent manner does not make it a superseding cause of harm to another which the actor's negligent conduct is a substantial factor in bringing about, if

(a) the actor at the time of his negligent conduct should have realized that a third person might so act, or

(b) a reasonable man knowing the situation existing when the act of the third person was done would not regard it as highly extraordinary that the third person had so acted, or

(c) the intervening act is a normal consequence of a situation created by the actor's conduct and the manner in which it is done is not extraordinarily negligent.

Whether or not the intervening act of a third person is so highly extraordinary as to constitute a superseding cause is a jury question, as held by our Supreme Court in Estate of Flickinger v. Ritsky, 452 Pa. 69, 305 A.2d 40 (1973). There the Court adopted Comment b to §453 of the Restatement (Second) of Torts:

If . . . the negligent character of the third person's intervening act or the reasonable foreseeability of its being done is a factor in determining whether the intervening act relieves the actor from liability for his antecedent negligence, and under the undisputed facts there is room for reasonable difference of opinion as to whether such act was negligent or foreseeable, the question should be left to the jury.

This concept has been continuously reaffirmed in subsequent cases. See Ross v. Vereb, 481 Pa. 446, 392 A.2d 1376 (1978) (whether victim's intervening act of running away from school children and into path of skidding car constituted a superseding cause of harm was a matter for the jury's determination); Thompson v. City of Philadelphia, 320 Pa. Super. 124, 466 A.2d 1349 (1983) (whether City of Philadelphia, as first actor who installed guardrails, could have reasonably foreseen negligent operation by second actor truck driver who drove his rig through guardrail resulting in death to motorist, was a fact question for the jury); Harvey v. Hansen, 299 Pa. Super. 474, 445 A.2d 1228 (1982) (whether a reasonable person would find injured driver's conduct to have been highly extraordinary within the meaning of §447 was a question for the jury); Amabile v. Auto Kleen Car Wash, 249 Pa. Super. 240, 376 A.2d 247 (1977) (whether vacuum pumps at car wash were negligently placed so as to expose injured party to unreasonable dangers was a question for the factfinder).

In each of the above-cited cases, the recurring concept is that "where reasonable minds could differ, resolution of such questions is properly left to the jury." Estate of Flickinger v. Ritsky, 452 Pa. 69, 76, 305 A.2d 40, 44 (1973). Thus, our task in the case at bar is to determine whether reasonable minds could differ on the question of whether Dr. Greene's decision to perform a total knee replacement in the absence of taking an adequate history was so highly extraordinary as to constitute a superseding cause which insulates Dr. Weisband and ROPA from liability for the harm resulting from Dr. Greene's care.

Dr. Weisband and ROPA argue that all of the testimony elicited at trial regarding Dr. Greene's conduct establishes that Dr. Greene acted in a highly extraordinary manner. They point to the following: First, responding to a hypothetical fact situation in which the questioner postulated that Dr. Greene knew of the existence of the chronic osteomyelitis (which he did not, due to his failure to take an adequate history) Dr. Meinhard testified that "it borders on insanity to go ahead and do a total knee [replacement]." He added that such a procedure "would not be good medical practice," and agreed that it could be characterized as gross negligence.

Second, Dr. John Sbarbaro, an expert witness for Dr. Weisband, testified, "I cannot conceive of how [Dr. Greene] could have missed the diagnosis of osteomyelitis." He added that the total knee replacement "was doomed to failure the day it was done because it was a totally and poorly conceived procedure." Third, Dr. Weisband testified that he would not have considered doing a total knee replacement on a patient with chronic osteomyelitis:

> That would be the most inhumane thing you could do to a patient with this condition. . . . [A]s soon as you put a foreign substance into a knee joint that has chronic osteomyelitis, it's going to flare up the chronic osteomyelitis, if not the day of the surgery, within a period of time. No sane orthopedic surgeon would ever do this without planning to amputate soon afterwards.

Finally, Dr. Weisband and ROPA point to deposition testimony of Dr. Greene, admitted at trial, in which he admits that he was completely unaware of any infection in Ms. Corbett's left knee prior to performing the total knee replacement.

The trial court held that the cumulative effect of the foregoing testimony was to establish as a matter of law that Dr. Greene had been grossly negligent in his treatment of Ms. Corbett and that reasonable minds could not differ. "This lack of skill or want of care," said the trial court, "is so obvious as to be within the range of ordinary experience and comprehension of even non-professional persons." We agree that the record establishes that, without question, Dr. Greene was negligent and that expert testimony is not necessary to establish that proposition as a fact. In fact, no one contends that Dr. Greene was not negligent. Whether or not he was negligent is not, however, the issue. The issue is whether his negligence was "highly extraordinary." About that question, reasonable minds could differ.

We hold, therefore, that the trial court erred, under the circumstances of this case, in reaching such a conclusion as a matter of law. . . . Whether or not such conduct was so extreme as to constitute a superseding cause was a question that should properly have been left to the jury. . . .

NOTES TO WEEMS v. HY-VEE FOOD STORES, INC. AND CORBETT v. WEISBAND

1. *Keeping Track of All the Doctors*.   In many cases involving intervening causes, it is hard to keep track of all of the actors. Weems is not too hard to follow but the opinion in *Weisband* mentions five different doctors. To help keep them straight, here are the *dramatis personae* in *Weisband*:

> Dr. DeMoura — first treated Ms. Corbett, had been a party to this suit but the trial court issued a judgment in his favor ending her case against him.
> Dr. Weisband — performed a left-knee fusion on Ms. Corbett.
> Dr. Greene — performed a total-knee replacement on Ms. Corbett.
> Dr. Meinhard — a witness, not a party in this case.
> Dr. Sbarbaro — a witness, not a party in this case.

2. *Foreseeability of the Intervening Act*.   When a defendant's conduct requires a plaintiff to seek medical care, courts are reluctant to treat the medical care as a superseding act. In Weems v. Hy-Vee Food Stores, Inc., on what basis did the court treat the highly unusual occurrence of spinal meningitis as intervening but not superseding?

In Corbett v. Weisband, how did the court analyze the poor performance of knee replacement surgery?

3. *Is Medical Malpractice Foreseeable?* The Restatement (Second) of Torts imposes liability on an original tortfeasor for additional harm from negligent medical care. Section 457 comment b says that the human fallibility of health care providers means that the risks associated with receiving medical attention are within the scope of the risk created by the defendant's negligence:

> It would be stretching the idea of probability too far to regard it as within the foresight of a negligent actor that his negligence might result in harm so severe as to require such services and therefore that he should foresee that such services might be improperly rendered. However, there is a risk involved in the human fallibility of physicians, surgeons, nurses, and hospital staffs which is inherent in the necessity of seeking their services. If the actor knows that his negligence may result in harm sufficiently severe to require such services, he should also recognize this as a risk involved in the other's forced submission to such services, and having put the other in a position to require them, the actor is responsible for any additional injury resulting from the other's exposure to this risk.

Does this comment reflect a belief that medical malpractice is always foreseeable?

4. *Harm Outside the Scope of the Risk.* If, during the course of treatment, the medical professional created risks not inherent in the defendant's negligent conduct, the defendant will ordinarily not be liable for the enhanced injuries that result from that conduct. Infection is a risk of any surgery, so if the defendant's conduct foreseeably leads to injuries requiring surgery, the defendant will usually be liable for infections resulting from the surgery. But if the infection results from a different risk, such as the risk created by two hospital orderlies playing catch with a container of infectious hospital waste, the defendant will not usually be liable. The Restatement (Third) of Torts: Liability for Physical and Emotional Harm expresses this rule as follows:

> **§35 Enhanced Harm Due to Efforts to Render Medical or Other Aid**
> An actor whose tortious conduct is a factual cause of harm to another is subject to liability for any enhanced harm the other suffers due to the efforts of third persons to render aid reasonably required by the other's injury, so long as the enhanced harm arises from a risk that inheres in the effort to render aid.

How would the Restatement (Third) treat Dr. Weisband's claim that Dr. Greene's conduct was a superseding cause?

5. *Intervening Contributory Conduct by Plaintiffs.* Usually, a superseding cause is an unforeseeable intervening act by a third party (the plaintiff and defendant being the first and second parties). Chapter 7 deals with issues presented by the negligent or otherwise blameworthy conduct of the plaintiff. Typically, when a plaintiff is negligent, the plaintiff's recovery of damages is either reduced or eliminated entirely. As the court in Sumpter v. Moulton, 519 N.W.2d 427 (Iowa 1994), observed, however, courts have, under limited circumstances, considered plaintiff's intervening acts in their superseding cause analysis:

> Generally, the doctrine of intervening cause embraces the intervention of the acts of a third-party or an outside force, not the actions of the injured plaintiff. We recognize, however, that some jurisdictions have applied the doctrine to conduct of the injured plaintiff. In addition to requiring the plaintiff's conduct to be wholly unforeseeable,

these cases often involve acts of the plaintiff that rise above mere negligence. On the other hand, "if the acts of the plaintiff are within the ambit of the hazards covered by the duty imposed upon the defendant, they are foreseeable and do not supersede the defendant's negligence." 57A Am. Jur. 2d Negligence §652. Moreover, if the negligent act of the defendant establishes the stimulus for the plaintiff's act, there is ordinarily no break in the chain of events to relieve the defendant from liability, and the subsequent acts of the plaintiff cannot constitute the superseding cause of the injury. Because of our preference for addressing the conduct of parties under the concept of comparative fault, and under the circumstances of this case, we believe the intervening cause of instruction was improperly given.

Statute: EFFECT UPON CHAIN OF PROXIMATE CAUSE
Ind. Stat. §16-36-5-26 (2017)

The act of withholding or withdrawing CPR, when done under:

> (1) an out of hospital DNR [do not resuscitate] declaration and order issued under this chapter;
> (2) a court order or decision of a court appointed guardian; or
> (3) a good faith medical decision by the attending physician that the patient has a terminal illness;

is not an intervening force and does not affect the chain of proximate cause between the conduct of a person that placed the patient in a terminal condition and the patient's death.

Statute: INTERVENING FORCES; PROXIMATE CAUSATION
Ind. Stat §16-36-4-20 (2017)

The act of withholding or withdrawing life prolonging procedures, when done under:

> (1) a living will declaration made under this chapter;
> (2) a court order or decision of a court appointed guardian; or
> (3) a good faith medical decision by the attending physician that the patient has a terminal condition;

is not an intervening force and does not affect the chain of proximate cause between the conduct of any person that placed the patient in a terminal condition and the patient's death.

NOTES TO STATUTES

1. *Statutory Modifications of Proximate Cause Rules.* States occasionally modify legal cause rules for policy reasons. Indiana courts have adopted the following rule for proximate cause:

> We point out that as an element of a negligence cause of action, the test for proximate cause is whether the injury is a natural and probable consequence which, in light of the circumstances, should reasonably have been foreseen or anticipated.

Reynolds v. Strauss Veal, Inc. (1988), Ind. Ct. App., 519 N.E.2d 226, 229, *trans. denied.* What policy reasons support the legislative action reflected in the Indiana statutes?

2. *Statutory Modifications of Superseding Cause Rules.* The Indiana statute describes the effect on legal cause of withholding or withdrawing CPR or life-prolonging procedures. How does this statute affect the proximate cause determination in Indiana? Can either of these acts be a superseding cause that would relieve an actor who negligently put the patient's life in danger from liability?

7

Defenses

I. Introduction

Tort law recognizes a number of defenses that protect a defendant from liability for negligence even though a plaintiff might be able to establish duty, breach, causation, and damages. Negligent conduct by a plaintiff can bar or limit recovery. A plaintiff's agreement to accept risks created by the defendant's conduct may also prevent recovery. A plaintiff's failure to minimize the consequences of a defendant's conduct or a failure to protect against it may also reduce or eliminate damages.

Governmental entities are sometimes immune from suit, and immunity principles also apply to some claims brought by family members against one another. Finally, statutes of limitation and repose apply time limits to the filing of claims. Cases begun after the expiration of these statutory time periods are subject to dismissal.

II. Plaintiff's Contributory Fault

Some injuries are caused by the combined effect of the negligent conduct by the plaintiff and the negligent conduct of one or more defendants. Common law treated a plaintiff's negligence under the doctrine known as *contributory negligence*, making it a complete bar to a plaintiff's recovery no matter how small a contribution that negligence had made to the plaintiff's injury.

Modern approaches require a jury to assign a percentage to the plaintiff's share of responsibility for the injury. Under a system known as *modified comparative negligence* or *modified comparative fault*, a plaintiff is barred from recovering only if the plaintiff's percentage of responsibility is greater than 49 percent or 50 percent (depending on the jurisdiction). Under a system known as *pure comparative negligence* or *pure comparative fault*, a plaintiff is barred from recovering only if the plaintiff's percentage of responsibility is 100 percent. In these comparative systems, when a plaintiff's negligence does not bar recovery, the total damages awarded to the plaintiff are reduced to reflect the percentage of the plaintiff's responsibility.

A. Traditional Common Law Treatment of a Plaintiff's Negligence

Under traditional tort law, a plaintiff's negligent conduct was a total bar to recovery if it was one of the legal causes of the plaintiff's injury. A "total bar" means that the plaintiff's contributory negligence shielded a negligent defendant from all liability. Wright v. Norfolk and Western Railway Company illustrates the power of this doctrine in the context of a railroad crossing accident where the evidence supported findings that the plaintiff was negligent in his driving and that the defendant railroad was negligent in its design of the crossing. The only jurisdictions that currently apply the contributory negligence doctrine are Alabama, Maryland, North Carolina, Virginia, and the District of Columbia.

WRIGHT v. NORFOLK AND WESTERN RAILWAY CO.
427 S.E.2d 724 (Va. 1993)

A. CHRISTIAN COMPTON, J.

On May 12, 1988, Riley E. Wright was severely injured in a collision between the dump truck he was operating and a Norfolk and Western Railway Company [N & W] train at a public crossing. Wright's guardians filed this negligence action against N & W seeking damages on behalf of their ward, a disabled person. A jury returned a verdict in favor of the plaintiffs for $4 million.

Sustaining a post-trial motion, the court below set the verdict aside and entered judgment for the defendant. We awarded the plaintiffs an appeal. . . . The principal issue on appeal . . . is whether the trial court correctly ruled that Wright was guilty of contributory negligence as a matter of law. Although the trial court set the verdict aside, we shall accord the plaintiffs, the recipients of the jury verdict, the benefit of any substantial conflicts in the evidence and of all reasonable inferences that may be drawn from the facts. The evidence is virtually undisputed.

The accident occurred in the town of Brookneal where Maddox Street crosses N & W's main line. The track runs north and south, and the two-way street runs generally east and west. U.S. Highway 501, a north-south roadway, closely parallels the track to the east. At the crossing, Maddox Street intersects Route 501 about 20 feet east of the track and ends there. . . .

The crossing was marked by crossbucks (signal boards) and an advance railroad warning sign ("a yellow sign that had RR on it"). There were no other signals, warning devices, or traffic controls in place at or near the crossing.

The collision took place on a Thursday about 12:45 p.m. The weather was clear, hot, and humid. The roadways were dry.

At the time, the train, composed of 17 cars loaded with wood chips and pulpwood, was moving southbound through Brookneal. Travelling approximately 34 miles per hour, the train approached the crossing with the headlight burning on the engine. Also, an air-operated bell was ringing continuously. In addition, an air-operated whistle was sounding "two longs, a short and a long."

At the same time, Wright, who was operating his employer's truck alone, was proceeding southbound on Route 501 approaching the crossing. Wright's destination was a lumber yard located just west of the crossing on Maddox Street.

The vehicle was a tandem dump truck with "front axles and . . . a dual axle at the back." Its overall length was "around 25 feet." The unit included a solid metal dump body that "sits approximately two inches behind the cab" preventing the operator from seeing "out of" the rear cab window. The vehicle had "regular West Coast" rear view mirrors "set to show what's behind the truck." The truck, in good operating condition, was equipped with an air conditioner, an AM/FM stereo radio, and a CB radio. It had a capacity of 53,500 pounds and was loaded with gravel.

Wright, age 36 and an experienced dump truck operator, had lived less than a mile from the crossing for ten years. On the day of the accident, he "had hauled . . . four loads of gravel" over the crossing to the lumber yard prior to the incident; the previous day, he had delivered five loads to the same destination. Eyewitness testimony revealed that Wright approached the crossing behind another south-bound dump truck. The first truck turned from Route 501 and stopped on Maddox Street east of the crossing. Wright stopped his truck behind the first vehicle. After the first truck moved over the crossing, clearing the track, Wright drove his truck onto the track in front of the train when the train's engine was less than ten feet from the truck. The truck traveled at a slow, steady speed, less than five miles per hour, to a point where the train engine struck the truck in the center of its right side, demolishing it and injuring Wright.

One eyewitness pointed out that there was "a slight incline from 501 up to the crossing." He stated that "as the truck was coming off of 501 onto Maddox the front end of the truck sort of shifted downward as if he were [braking] or changing gears." The witness said, "I had the thought he was going to stop and then the truck, the front end, raised up as he accelerated onto the tracks." The train engineer testified that "just before hitting the edge of the crossing, like six feet, the truck whipped in front of me. It was no time to do anything."

The witnesses did not see any brake lights "come on" on the truck before the impact. The window on the right side of the truck's cab was closed at the time of the collision. Although Wright did not testify due to his disability, his employer testified that Wright, whose hobby was country music, normally operated the truck's air conditioner on hot days and normally "kept his radio on and CB on."

Expert testimony offered by the plaintiffs established that the crossing was not "reasonably safe" and that it was "ultradangerous, or an ultrahazardous crossing." This opinion was based upon "the sight distance available to the motorist, the geometry of the crossing, the type and mix of the traffic that uses the crossing, the speed of the trains, the condition of the tracks and crossing." According to the expert, "All of those in conjunction with the type of protection afforded at the crossing, which is essentially the cross bucks, made it an ultrahazardous crossing." . . .

During trial, the defendant moved the court to strike the plaintiffs' evidence at the conclusion of the plaintiffs' case-in-chief. The grounds of the motion were that the plaintiffs failed to establish, prima facie, the defendant's primary negligence, and that the plaintiffs' own evidence established Wright was guilty of contributory negligence as a matter of law. This motion was overruled. The trial court, after stating, "I'm very troubled, very troubled by Mr. Wright's conduct," decided to allow the contributory negligence issue to go to the jury. . . .

After verdict, the court considered memoranda of law and oral argument on defendant's motion to set aside. . . . [T]he trial court, in a letter opinion, sustained the defendant's motion. The court ruled that . . . Wright was guilty of contributory negligence as a matter of law. . . .

On appeal, the plaintiffs contend that the trial court erred in its ruling on the contributory negligence issue. . . .

We turn now to the merits of the contributory negligence issue, the jury having settled the issue of primary negligence against the defendant. At trial, a defendant has the burden to prove by the greater weight of the evidence that the plaintiff was negligent and that such negligence was a proximate cause of the plaintiff's injuries. Contributory negligence, however, may be shown by the defendant's evidence or by the plaintiff's own evidence. . . .

There is no conflict in the evidence on the issue of contributory negligence. And, there are no direct and reasonable inferences to be drawn from the whole evidence to sustain a conclusion that Wright was free of contributory negligence. Rather, when the evidence is viewed in the light most favorable to the plaintiffs, reasonable persons could not differ in concluding that Wright was guilty of negligence as a matter of law that proximately contributed to the accident and his injuries.

Wright was thoroughly familiar with the crossing, both as the result of living near it and from having traversed it in his truck on nine occasions during a two-day period before the accident. He was aware of the fact that he would have to rely on his senses of sight and hearing to be aware of an approaching train, because of the absence of automatically operated warning devices to remind him. He was aware of the limitations to sight and hearing posed by the configuration of the cab of his truck and by the angle at which Maddox Street ran southwest from Route 501. Yet, despite all these hazards confronting him, Wright drove his truck from a stopped position of safety onto the crossing directly in front of the train when its engine was less than ten feet away.

The expert testified that it was "impossible" for Wright to have heard or seen the train. But, he was not forced to approach the crossing with his right window closed, and presumably with his air conditioner and radio operating. He could have opened his window after his truck had been loaded and before he left the quarry, knowing the dangers to be encountered at the crossing. He could have moved onto Maddox Street and the crossing by making a wider right turn, thus bringing his truck to an attitude with relation to the crossing that he could see clearly north along the track. Obviously, Wright did none of these things, and caused this unfortunate accident.

The only conclusion to be drawn from the whole evidence is that Wright either failed to look and listen with reasonable care, or if he did so look and listen, he failed to discover the immediate presence of the train. In either event, he was the architect of his own misfortune. Thus, we hold that the trial court properly set the verdict aside on the ground that Wright was guilty of contributory negligence as a matter of law. . . .

Accordingly, we hold that the trial court committed no error, and the judgment below will be *Affirmed.*

NOTES TO WRIGHT v. NORFOLK AND WESTERN RAILWAY CO.

1. *The Traditional Effect of a Contributory Negligence Finding.* *Wright* illustrates the effect of a finding of plaintiff's negligence in a contributory negligence jurisdiction. Considering the evidence of both plaintiffs' and defendant's negligence, why did the trial judge refuse to enter a judgment based on the jury verdict?

2. *Characterization of Plaintiff's Conduct as Negligent.*   Contributory negligence and comparative negligence jurisdictions use the same rules to determine whether a plaintiff or a defendant was negligent. The two systems differ only in the *effect* they give to a plaintiff's negligence.

3. *The Scene of the Accident.*   You can view satellite imagery of the site of the accident in *Wright* by searching <<maps.google.com>> for the intersection of Mattox and Lynchburg in Brookneal, Virginia and looking at the satellite view to reveal the railroad tracks. Given the geometry of the crossing, would you conclude that Wright was contributorily negligent as a matter of law? Or does the geometry suggest that there is factual question with respect to contributory negligence?

Perspective: Contributory Negligence and Incentives to Avoid Accidents

From an economic perspective, it is sensible to encourage parties who can avoid accidents at the least cost to do so. Even if either the plaintiff or the defendant could have avoided an accident acting alone, it might have been easier (less costly) for one to do so than the other. If the defendant is always the best accident-avoider, perhaps a system where a negligent plaintiff can recover provides superior incentives. If the plaintiff is always the best accident-avoider, perhaps a system where a negligent plaintiff can never recover provides superior incentives. If neither is always true, then neither system would always encourage the best cost-avoiders to take precautions to avoid accidents.

B. Modern Comparative Treatment of a Plaintiff's Negligence

Criticism of the contributory negligence system has led courts and legislatures to replace it with an alternative system, comparative negligence. Two main varieties of comparative negligence have been developed: pure and modified. All comparative negligence systems reject the idea that negligence by a plaintiff is an absolute bar to recovery.

"Pure" comparative negligence allows a contributorily negligent plaintiff to recover some portion of his or her total damages as long as the defendant's negligence was also a proximate cause of the accident. The damages will be reduced by whatever percentage the jury assigns to the plaintiff's negligence.

"Modified" comparative negligence has been adopted in two forms. In one system, a negligent plaintiff is allowed to recover damages only if his or her negligence is *less than* that of the defendant or defendants. In other words, a 49 percent share of responsibility will allow recovery, but a 50 percent share will not (because the fault of a plaintiff who is 50 percent responsible is equal to, not less than, the fault of the defendant or defendants). This is usually called the 49 percent form of comparative negligence.

The other form of modified comparative negligence allows a negligent plaintiff to recover damages only if his or her negligence is *less than or equal to* that of the defendant or defendants. In this system, a plaintiff whom the jury finds to have been as much as 50 percent responsible for his or her injury will be entitled to recover damages. This is usually called the 50 percent form of comparative negligence. The two types of modified comparative negligence reach different results only in cases where a jury finds the plaintiff to be exactly 50 percent responsible for his or her injury.

McIntyre v. Balentine is a state supreme court decision adopting comparative negligence. It provides a survey and analysis of the doctrine. Dobson v. Louisiana Power and Light Company illustrates one court's examination of how to determine parties' precise degrees of fault. Jensen v. Intermountain Health Care, Inc. describes how modified comparative negligence may apply in a case with more than one defendant.

Examples.   If a jury finds that a plaintiff's damages equal $10,000, that the plaintiff was 40 percent responsible, and that a single defendant was 60 percent responsible, the plaintiff would be entitled to a judgment of $6,000 under all forms of comparative negligence.

If a jury finds that a plaintiff's damages equal $10,000, that the plaintiff was 50 percent responsible, and that a single defendant was 50 percent responsible, the plaintiff would be entitled to a judgment of $5,000 under the 50 percent form and under the pure form of comparative negligence but would receive no damages at all under the 49 percent form.

If a jury finds that a plaintiff's damages equal $10,000, that the plaintiff was 51 percent responsible, and that a single defendant was 49 percent responsible, the plaintiff would be entitled to a judgment of $4,900 under the pure form of comparative negligence and would receive nothing under the two types of modified comparative negligence.

McINTYRE v. BALENTINE
833 S.W.2d 52 (Tenn. 1992)

DROWOTA, J.

In this personal injury action, we granted Plaintiff's application for permission to appeal in order to decide whether to adopt a system of comparative fault in Tennessee. . . . We now replace the common law defense of contributory negligence with a system of comparative fault. . . .

In the early morning darkness of November 2, 1986, Plaintiff Harry Douglas McIntyre and Defendant Clifford Balentine were involved in a motor vehicle accident resulting in severe injuries to Plaintiff. The accident occurred in the vicinity of Smith's Truck Stop in Savannah, Tennessee. As Defendant Balentine was traveling south on Highway 69, Plaintiff entered the highway (also traveling south) from the truck stop parking lot. Shortly after Plaintiff entered the highway, his pickup truck was struck by Defendant's Peterbilt tractor. At trial, the parties disputed the exact chronology of events immediately preceding the accident.

Both men had consumed alcohol the evening of the accident. After the accident Plaintiff's blood alcohol level was measured at .17 percent by weight. Testimony suggested that Defendant was traveling in excess of the posted speed limit.

Plaintiff brought a negligence action against Defendant Balentine and Defendant East-West Motor Freight, Inc. Defendants answered that Plaintiff was contributorally negligent, in part due to operating his vehicle while intoxicated. After trial, the jury returned a verdict stating: "We, the jury, find the plaintiff and the defendant equally at fault in this accident; therefore, we rule in favor of the defendant."

After judgment was entered for Defendants, Plaintiff brought an appeal alleging the trial court erred by refusing to instruct the jury regarding the doctrine of comparative negligence. . . . The Court of Appeals affirmed, holding that comparative negligence is not the law in Tennessee. . . .

The common law contributory negligence doctrine has traditionally been traced to Lord Ellenborough's opinion in Butterfield v. Forrester, 11 East 60, 103 Eng. Rep. 926 (1809). There, plaintiff, "riding as fast as his horse would go," was injured after running into an obstruction defendant had placed in the road. Stating as the rule that "[o]ne person being in fault will not dispense with another's using ordinary care," plaintiff was denied recovery on the basis that he did not use ordinary care to avoid the obstruction. . . .

The contributory negligence bar was soon brought to America as part of the common law, see Smith v. Smith, 19 Mass. 621, 624 (1824), and proceeded to spread throughout the states. . . . This strict bar may have been a direct outgrowth of the common law system of issue pleading; issue pleading posed questions to be answered "yes" or "no," leaving common law courts, the theory goes, no choice but to award all or nothing. . . . A number of other rationalizations have been advanced in the attempt to justify the harshness of the "all-or-nothing" bar. Among these: the plaintiff should be penalized for his misconduct; the plaintiff should be deterred from injuring himself; and the plaintiff's negligence supersedes the defendant's so as to render defendant's negligence no longer proximate. . . .

In Tennessee, the rule as initially stated was that "if a party, by his own gross negligence, brings an injury upon himself, or contributes to such injury, he cannot recover"; for, in such cases, the party "must be regarded as the author of his own misfortune." Whirley v. Whiteman, 38 Tenn. 610, 619 (1858). In subsequent decisions, we have continued to follow the general rule that a plaintiff's contributory negligence completely bars recovery. . . .

In contrast, comparative fault has long been the federal rule in cases involving injured employees of interstate railroad carriers, see Federal Employers' Liability Act, ch. 149, §3, 35 Stat. 66 (1908) (codified at 45 U.S.C. §53 (1988)), and injured seamen. See Death On The High Seas Act, ch. 111, §6, 41 Stat. 537 (1920) (codified at 46 U.S.C. §766 (1988)). . . .

Similarly, by the early 1900s, many states, including Tennessee, had statutes providing for the apportionment of damages in railroad injury cases. . . . While Tennessee's railroad statute did not expressly sanction damage apportionment, it was soon given that judicial construction. In 1856, the statute was passed in an effort to prevent railroad accidents; it imposed certain obligations and liabilities on railroads "for all damages accruing or resulting from a failure to perform said dut[ies]." . . .

Between 1920 and 1969, a few states began utilizing the principles of comparative fault in all tort litigation. . . . Then, between 1969 and 1984, comparative fault replaced contributory negligence in 37 additional states. . . . In 1991, South Carolina became the 45th state to adopt comparative fault . . . leaving Alabama, Maryland, North Carolina, Virginia, and Tennessee as the only remaining common law contributory negligence jurisdictions.

Eleven states have judicially adopted comparative fault.[3] Thirty-four states have legislatively adopted comparative fault.[4]

. . . After exhaustive deliberation that was facilitated by extensive briefing and argument by the parties, amicus curiae, and Tennessee's scholastic community, we conclude that it is time to abandon the outmoded and unjust common law doctrine of contributory negligence and adopt in its place a system of comparative fault. Justice simply will not permit our continued adherence to a rule that, in the face of a judicial determination that others bear primary responsibility, nevertheless completely denies injured litigants recompense for their damages.

We recognize that this action could be taken by our General Assembly. However, legislative inaction has never prevented judicial abolition of obsolete common law doctrines, especially those, such as contributory negligence, conceived in the judicial womb. . . .

Two basic forms of comparative fault are utilized by 45 of our sister jurisdictions, these variants being commonly referred to as either "pure" or "modified." In the "pure" form a plaintiff's damages are reduced in proportion to the percentage negligence attributed to him; for example, a plaintiff responsible for 90 percent of the negligence that caused his injuries nevertheless may recover 10 percent of his damages. In the "modified" form plaintiffs recover as in pure jurisdictions, but only if the plaintiff's negligence either (1) does not exceed ("50 percent" jurisdictions) or (2) is less than ("49 percent" jurisdictions) the defendant's negligence. . . .

Although we conclude that the all-or-nothing rule of contributory negligence must be replaced, we nevertheless decline to abandon totally our fault-based tort system. We do not agree that a party should necessarily be able to recover in tort even though he may be 80, 90, or 95 percent at fault. We therefore reject the pure form of comparative fault.

We recognize that modified comparative fault systems have been criticized as merely shifting the arbitrary contributory negligence bar to a new ground. . . . However, we feel the "49 percent rule" ameliorates the harshness of the common law rule while remaining compatible with a fault-based tort system. . . . We therefore hold that so long as a plaintiff's negligence remains less than the defendant's negligence the plaintiff may recover; in such a case, plaintiff's damages are to be reduced in proportion to the percentage of the total negligence attributable to the plaintiff.

In all trials where the issue of comparative fault is before a jury, the trial court shall instruct the jury on the effect of the jury's finding as to the percentage of negligence as

---

[3] In the order of their adoption, these states are Florida, California, Alaska, Michigan, West Virginia, New Mexico, Illinois, Iowa, Missouri, Kentucky, and South Carolina. Nine courts adopted pure comparative fault. . . . In two of these states, legislatures subsequently enacted a modified form. . . . Two courts adopted a modified form of comparative fault. . . .

[4] Six states have legislatively adopted pure comparative fault: Mississippi, Rhode Island, Washington, New York, Louisiana, and Arizona; eight legislatures have enacted the modified "49 percent" rule (plaintiff may recover if plaintiff's negligence is less than defendant's): Georgia, Arkansas, Maine, Colorado, Idaho, North Dakota, Utah, and Kansas; eighteen legislatures have enacted the modified "50 percent" rule (plaintiff may recover so long as plaintiff's negligence is not greater than defendant's): Wisconsin, Hawaii, Massachusetts, Minnesota, New Hampshire, Vermont, Oregon, Connecticut, Nevada, New Jersey, Oklahoma, Texas, Wyoming, Montana, Pennsylvania, Ohio, Indiana, and Delaware; two legislatures have enacted statutes that allow a plaintiff to recover if plaintiff's negligence is slight when compared to defendant's gross negligence: Nebraska and South Dakota. . . . [Nebraska now uses the 49 percent form of modified comparative negligence. — Eds.]

between the plaintiff or plaintiffs and the defendant or defendants. . . . The attorneys for each party shall be allowed to argue how this instruction affects a plaintiff's ability to recover.

Turning to the case at bar, the jury found that "the plaintiff and defendant [were] equally at fault." Because the jury, without the benefit of proper instructions by the trial court, made a gratuitous apportionment of fault, we find that their "equal" apportionment is not sufficiently trustworthy to form the basis of a final determination between these parties. . . .

For the foregoing reasons, the judgment of the Court of Appeals is reversed . . . and the case is remanded to the trial court for a new trial in accordance with the dictates of this opinion.

DOBSON v. LOUISIANA POWER & LIGHT CO.
567 So. 2d 569 (La. 1990)

DENNIS, J.

This is a wrongful death action . . . by the surviving spouse and five minor children of a tree trimmer, Dwane L. Dobson, who was electrocuted on April 24, 1985 when his metallically reinforced safety rope contacted an uninsulated 8,000 volt electric power distribution line. The trial court awarded the widow and her children $1,034,054.50 in damages, after finding the deceased free from fault and holding the Louisiana Power & Light Company liable in negligence for failure to maintain its right of way, insulate its high voltage distribution line, or give adequate warnings of the line's dangerous nature. The Court of Appeal affirmed the decree as to the power company's negligence, but reversed in part, reducing the plaintiff's recovery by 70% based on a finding that the deceased had been guilty of fault to that degree. . . .

We see no error in the Court of Appeal's conclusion that LP & L was guilty of negligence that caused Dobson's death and should be held at least partially responsible for the damages occasioned by the accident [and that Dobson was contributorily negligent for using a metal reinforced safety rope near power lines]. But we granted certiorari because . . . we felt called upon to further elaborate a method for determining the degree or percentage of negligence attributable to a person for purposes of reducing recovery due to comparative fault. . . .

It assists us to concentrate here on the costs of the precautions necessary to avoid the accident because the magnitude of the danger caused by the conduct of either Dobson or LP & L was extreme. If the risk that a person might come into contact with the bare high voltage distribution line were to take effect, the anticipated gravity of the loss was of the highest degree. Dobson's conduct in lowering himself down the tree trunk with a metallically reinforced safety line dangling below near the electric wires substantially increased the possibility of such an accident. But so did LP & L's conduct. . . .

Confining ourselves to the factor of the cost of taking an effective precaution to avoid the risk, it appears to us that the cost or burden of eliminating the danger would have been greater for Dobson than for LP & L. As we have indicated, the power company had a number of relatively inexpensive, efficacious precautions available to it, e.g., inspection, maintenance, partial insulation, public education, and visible warnings. . . . On the other hand, the cost to Dobson, who was ignorant of the characteristics of the uninsulated distribution lines and therefore unaware of their special danger, exceeded the cost to a person with superior capacity and knowledge. An actor with "inferior" capacity to avoid harm must expend more effort to avoid a danger than need a person with "superior" ability. A person about to cause injury inadvertently must expend much more effort to avoid the danger than need one who is at least aware of the danger involved. For this reason courts have traditionally cited "awareness of danger" as a factor distinguishing mere negligence from the higher state of culpability commonly known as "recklessness" or "willful and wanton conduct."

In conclusion we believe that, while the magnitude of the risk of harm created by either Dobson or LP & L was great, under the circumstances of the present case, the cost of taking effective precautions to avoid the risk was greater for the tree trimmer than for the power company. This disparity is heightened by the fact that LP & L was clearly in a superior position to avoid the danger. Because the cost of taking effective precautions was significantly less for LP & L than for Dobson, the fault of LP & L was the greater of the two. We do not think that the unreasonable nature of LP & L's conduct was so great as to be double the fault of Dobson. But we conclude that a palpable majority of the fault should be attributed to the power company in order to achieve substantial justice in this case. Accordingly, we attribute 60% of the negligence herein to LP & L and 40% to Dobson. Consequently, the recovery of the plaintiffs, the surviving spouse and five minor children, will be reduced by 40%. . . .

NOTES TO McINTYRE v. BALENTINE AND DOBSON v. LOUISIANA POWER & LIGHT CO.

1. *Effect of Comparative Negligence.* The court in *McIntyre* chose the 49 percent form of comparative negligence. Despite the fact that Tennessee was a contributory negligence jurisdiction and did not require apportionment of fault between the parties, the jury made a factual finding that the plaintiff and defendant were equally at fault. If the court had stayed with the traditional contributory negligence rule, would the plaintiff have recovered any damages? Under the 49 percent form of comparative negligence the court adopted, would the plaintiff recover any damages?

2. *Asymmetry of Modified Comparative Negligence Systems.* Modified comparative negligence retains some aspects of the "all or nothing" contributory negligence system, because recovering nothing is still a possible outcome for a negligent plaintiff who is harmed by a negligent defendant. For example, in a case where the plaintiff's degree of fault is 75 percent, what percentage of the total financial responsibility falls on the plaintiff? In a case where the defendant's degree of fault is 75 percent, what percentage of financial responsibility falls on the defendant?

3. *Apportionment According to Relative Degrees of Fault.* The comparative negligence rule requires factfinders to determine shares of liability. Court opinions and statutes refer to this finding by different names, such as "percentage of fault," "percentage of responsibility," "degree of fault," "relative degree of fault," or "degree of culpable conduct." It is never completely clear, however, how the factfinder is to calculate the percentages necessary to apportion damages, although the percentages of all the people who contributed to the harm must total 100 percent. In *Dobson*, the court used the Learned Hand approach to negligence, reasoning that since it can be used to determine *whether* a person was negligent, it can also be used to determine *how* negligent one person was compared to another.

Knowing the logic of apportionment helps lawyers strategize about what evidence to present and how to structure their opening and closing arguments. *Dobson* offers an unusual glimpse into determining shares of liability. In most states, appellate courts would remand the issue of proper apportionment to the trial court and the factfinder. For this reason, the logic of apportionment is hidden in a jury's deliberations or the mind of a trial judge (who does the apportionment if there is no jury). In *Dobson*, because Louisiana appellate courts are permitted to make such determinations, the court focused on the relative cost of precautions the two parties could have taken and found that the power company could have avoided the accident more easily.

The cost to avoid the accident is only one of the Hand factors (burden of avoiding the harm, or *B*, probability of the occurrence of the harm, or *P*, and extent of likely loss, or *L*). This approach works only if the parties have similar risks, measured in terms of the severity of the likely harms and the probability of the harms occurring if precautions were not taken. In *Dobson*, the court found that *P* and *L* were the same for the two parties. Similar logic would support giving a higher percentage to the party that created the greater risk. If one person created risks ten times as great as another, his or her share of liability should be ten times as great. See David W. Barnes & Mark Baeverstad, *Social Choices and Comparative Negligence*, 31 DePaul L. Rev. 273 (1982) (demonstrating that degrees of fault can be determined by reference to each party's ratio of *B* to *PL*).

Another approach would be to identify a large range of factors. The court in Watson v. State Farm Fire & Cas. Ins. Co., 469 So. 2d 967 (La. 1985), said:

> In determining the percentages of fault, the trier of fact shall consider both the nature of the conduct of each party at fault and the extent of the causal relation between the conduct and the damages claimed. In assessing the nature of the conduct of the parties, various factors may influence the degree of fault assigned, including: (1) whether the conduct resulted from inadvertence or involved an awareness of the danger, (2) how great a risk was created by the conduct, (3) the significance of what was sought by the conduct, (4) the capacities of the actor, whether superior or inferior, and (5) any extenuating circumstances which might require the actor to proceed in haste, without proper thought.

4. *Apportionment Reflecting Relative Degrees of Causation.* States and commentators are divided on whether the relative causal contribution of the parties ought to be considered along with the relative negligence of the parties. William L. Prosser, *Comparative Negligence*, 51 Mich. L. Rev. 465, 481 (1953), for instance, argues that "once causation is found, the apportionment must be made on the basis of comparative fault, rather than comparative contribution" to the accident or injury. One state case that agrees with this view is Sandford v. Chevrolet Division of General Motors, 642 P.2d 624 (Or. 1982):

> There is no reference to causation, or any question how much the fault of each contributed to the injury [in the Oregon statute definition of "proportionate fault"]. Indeed, the reference to negligence "contributing to the injury" in former [Oregon Revised Statutes] 18.470 was removed in the 1975 amendment. We do not mean that the allegedly faulty conduct or condition need not have affected the event for which recovery is sought; as we have said, it must have been a cause in fact. But the statute does not call for apportioning damages by quantifying the contribution of several causes that had to coincide to produce the injury.

If relative degree of causal contribution is to be considered, the factfinder might examine the relative substantiality of each party's conduct as a factor in producing the harm, the relative foreseeability of the harm to the actor, or the relative directness of the connection between the actor's conduct and the harm.

Suppose a bicycle rider was hit by a truck on a dark night and was injured. How would these various approaches help you, if you were a juror, to apportion negligence if the truck driver had been driving at 45 miles per hour in a 35 mile per hour zone, and the cyclist ignored a stop sign, was wearing dark clothing, and was talking on a cell phone at the time of the collision?

Statute: COMPARATIVE FAULT
Fla. Stat. §768.81 (2017)

(2) Effect of contributory fault. — In an action to which this section applies, any contributory fault chargeable to the claimant diminishes proportionately the amount awarded as economic and noneconomic damages for an injury attributable to the claimant's contributory fault, but does not bar recovery.

Statute: COMPARATIVE FAULT; EFFECT
Minn. Stat. §604.01 (2017)

Subdivision 1. Scope of application. Contributory fault does not bar recovery in an action by any person or the person's legal representative to recover damages for fault resulting in death, in injury to person or property, or in economic loss, if the contributory fault was not greater than the fault of the person against whom recovery is sought, but any damages allowed must be diminished in proportion to the amount of fault attributable to the person recovering. The court may, and when requested by any party shall, direct the jury to find separate special verdicts determining the amount of damages and the percentage of fault attributable to each party and the court shall then reduce the amount of damages in proportion to the amount of fault attributable to the person recovering.

Perspective: Jury Nullification of Modified Comparative Negligence?

Two scholars studied how juries assigned responsibility in modified and pure comparative negligence states by looking at 1,000 jury findings. The table below shows how often juries found plaintiffs more than 50 percent responsible:

Distribution of Jury Findings

Percentage of Negligence Assigned to Plaintiff	Frequency in Pure Jurisdictions	Frequency in Modified Jurisdictions
0-39	50.0%	52.0%
40-49	12.1%	19.5%
50	16.0%	20.9%
51-100	21.9%	7.6%

Juries found plaintiffs to be more than 50 percent at fault in 22 percent of cases in pure jurisdictions and in only 8 percent of cases in modified jurisdictions. Perhaps plaintiffs in the modified states actually are, overall, less culpable than plaintiffs in pure states. Perhaps cases with very culpable plaintiffs are less likely to go to trial in modified states. The authors of this study argue that juries in modified states may disagree with the consequences of the modified system and may avoid outcomes that completely bar plaintiffs' recoveries by skewing the percentages of negligence they apportion. See Eli K. Best & John J. Donohue III, *Jury Nullification in Modified Comparative Negligence Regimes*, 79 U. Chi. L. Rev. 945, 962 (2012).

Statute: NEGLIGENCE CASES — COMPARATIVE NEGLIGENCE AS A MEASURE OF DAMAGES

Colo. Rev. Stat. §13-21-111 (2017)

(1) Contributory negligence shall not bar recovery in any action by any person or his legal representative to recover damages for negligence resulting in death or in injury to person or property, if such negligence was not as great as the negligence of the person against whom recovery is sought, but any damages allowed shall be diminished in proportion to the amount of negligence attributable to the person for whose injury, damage, or death recovery is made.

NOTE TO STATUTE

Comparative Negligence.   Many states' statutes establish systems of comparative negligence. In analyzing the preceding examples of these statutes, identify the form of comparative negligence (or comparative fault) adopted by each one. Determine how each statute would treat a two-party case in which the shares of responsibility were the following:

	Plaintiff's Share of Responsibility	*Defendant's Share of Responsibility*
Case A	75%	25%
Case B	51%	49%
Case C	50%	50%
Case D	49%	51%
Case E	25%	75%

Perspective: Incentive Effects of Comparative Negligence

From an economic perspective, it is sensible to give to the party who can most easily avoid an accident the incentive to do so. Where both a negligent defendant and a negligent plaintiff contribute to an accident, contributory negligence creates an incentive for the plaintiff by imposing all of the liability on that party.

> Comparative negligence gives incentives to both parties. The party paying the larger share of the damages is the party who had the greater degree of fault. If "degree of fault" corresponds to the ease with which the party could avoid the accident, a comparative negligence system gives a greater incentive to the party who could avoid the accident more easily. See David W. Barnes & Mark Baeverstad, *Social Choices and Comparative Negligence: Resurrecting* Galena, 31 DePaul L. Rev. 273 (1982).

JENSEN v. INTERMOUNTAIN HEALTH CARE, INC.
679 P.2d 903 (Utah 1984)

Stewart, J.

This is an appeal from the dismissal of a medical malpractice action in which the plaintiffs' decedent Dale Jensen died as a result of negligence on the part of an emergency room physician and the hospital. The plaintiffs settled with the defendant doctor and went to trial against the hospital. The jury returned a special verdict, finding plaintiffs' decedent 46 percent negligent in causing his own death; Intermountain Health Care, Inc., 36 percent negligent; and the doctor, 18 percent negligent. Judgment was entered in favor of plaintiff Shirley J. Jensen and against the defendant hospital. The trial court then set aside the original award and entered a judgment of no cause of action. We reverse.

The issue in this case is one of first impression. It is whether the Utah Comparative Negligence Act requires the negligence of each defendant in a multi-defendant case to be compared individually against the negligence of the plaintiff or whether the total negligence of all the defendants should be compared to that of the plaintiff to determine whether a particular defendant is liable. Under the latter approach, or the "unit" rule, the negligence of all defendants is taken together in making the comparison; under the "Wisconsin" rule, the negligence of each defendant is compared against the plaintiff's negligence to determine whether a particular defendant is liable.

Thus, under the "unit" rule, the plaintiffs' decedent's 46 percent negligence in this case is compared with the combined 54 percent negligence of the defendants, and the plaintiffs would therefore be entitled to recover against the defendant. Under the "Wisconsin" rule, which was applied by the trial court, the negligence attributed to plaintiffs is greater than that of Intermountain's negligence by itself, and plaintiffs would not recover. . . .

The Utah Comparative Negligence Act . . . provides . . .

> Section 1. Actions based on negligence or gross negligence — Contributory negligence.
>
> Contributory negligence shall not bar recovery in an action by any person or his legal representative to recover damages for negligence or gross negligence resulting in death or in injury to person or property if such negligence was not as great as the negligence or gross negligence of the person against whom recovery is sought, but any damages allowed shall be diminished in the proportion to the amount of negligence attributable to the person recovering. As used in this act, "contributory negligence" includes "assumption of the risk."

. . . [T]he language of Section 1, as such, is not necessarily inconsistent with the unit rule. That section only refers to a plaintiff's negligence not being "as great as the negligence or gross negligence of *the person* against whom recovery is sought. . . ." (Emphasis added.) The statutory language is not the "negligence of *any* person against whom recovery is sought"; rather the language used was intended to mean "the person or persons" so as to include both single-defendant and multi-defendant cases. That construction is suggested by the text and is in full harmony with U.C.A., 1953, §68-3-12, which provides rules for construction of Utah statutes. Subparagraph (6) states, "The singular number includes the plural, and the plural the singular." Application of §68-3-12 makes Section 1 of the Utah Comparative Negligence Act harmonious with the rest of the Act. Graci v. Damon, 374 N.E.2d 311, 317 (1978), applied a comparable Massachusetts statutory provision to the precise word at issue here, thereby requiring that the statute be read to mean "persons" in a multi-defendant case so that the plaintiff's negligence was compared against the aggregate of all the defendants.

The meaning that emerges from Section 1 by applying §68-3-12(6) is consistent with the rulings of a number of courts which have held that the singular term *defendant* (or other synonymous nouns) also means the plural.

The Wisconsin rule is the minority position in this country. . . .

The refusal of the majority of the states that have dealt with the subject to adopt the Wisconsin rule indicates a widespread perception that that rule is not sound. Almost without variation, those states that have adopted the Wisconsin rule have done so on the rather wooden analysis that the Legislature must have intended to adopt the court decisions construing the Wisconsin statute as a part of that state's law.

Even apart from the evident meaning and effect of the sections which were added to the first section of the act to provide a comprehensive treatment of the subject matter, we would be reluctant to construe the Act to enact a policy that is so inequitable that even the Wisconsin Supreme Court, based on much experience with that policy, has severely criticized it.

The defects of the Wisconsin rule suggest why the Legislature undertook to remedy the defects of that rule. First, it is axiomatic that there can be no more than 100 percent negligence when the negligence of all defendants and the plaintiff is added up. But that would never be the case in multi-defendant cases in which a defendant is excused from liability under the Wisconsin rule. Thus, for example, if a plaintiff is 20 percent negligent in stopping on a highway and each of four defendants who rear-end the plaintiff is 20 percent negligent, the plaintiff under the Wisconsin rule will recover nothing because the plaintiff's 20 percent negligence is not measured against the total negligence of the defendants. If it were, there would be a total of 100 percent negligence when plaintiff's and defendants' negligence are combined. [U]nder the Wisconsin rule, plaintiff's negligence is used four different times to cancel out each of the defendants' negligence. By the magic of the formula employed, his 20 percent becomes an effective 80 percent of negligence, and the total percentage of negligence in the case, combining that attributable to the plaintiff and that attributable to the defendants, totals 160 percent!

The unfairness of the Wisconsin rule is also apparent in a situation where a plaintiff is 33⅓ percent negligent and each of two defendants is also 33⅓ percent. Under those circumstances, the plaintiff could recover nothing. However, if the same injury were inflicted by the same cause but only one defendant were responsible for producing the injury, the plaintiff would recover 66⅔ percent of the damages inflicted.

In short, one of the anomalous consequences of the Wisconsin rule is that the more defendants who inflict an injury, the less likely a plaintiff will be to recover. Thus, if 50 riparian landowners are responsible for polluting a stream and are negligent in equal percentages for causing 98 percent of the damage to the property of a downstream owner who is only 2 percent contributorily responsible, the plaintiff recovers nothing! The Utah Act was not intended to adopt a rule that would permit such extraordinary consequences.[3]

It may be that Wisconsin has reason to live with such a rule, but Utah does not, and the Legislature in effect has said so.

Reversed and remanded for entry of judgment on the verdict. Costs to appellants.

NOTES TO JENSEN v. INTERMOUNTAIN HEATH CARE, INC.

1. *Unit Rule in Modified Comparative Negligence Jurisdiction Only.* In a modified comparative negligence jurisdiction, the plaintiff's degree of fault is compared to the defendant's degree of fault. A plaintiff can recover some damages only if the plaintiff's fault is less than (or, in some states, not greater than) the single defendant's. If there are multiple defendants, a state may chose to compare the plaintiff's fault to each defendant separately, applying its modified rule to each pair of parties. Under this approach, a defendant may escape liability altogether. Alternatively, a state may treat the defendants as a unit, comparing the plaintiff's relative degree of fault to the total of the defendants' fault. No defendant escapes liability under this approach. This problem never arises in a pure comparative negligence jurisdiction because in pure systems no defendant escapes liability on the basis of having a lesser (or equal) degree of fault.

2. *Applying the Unit Rule.* The opinion in *Jensen* reported the relative degrees of fault of the plaintiff and each defendant. If damages in that case totaled $100,000, what is the total amount the plaintiff could collect from the defendants if there were no unit rule? If there were a unit rule? Does it matter what form of modified comparative

---

[3] There are three situations sometimes asserted to demonstrate that the unit rule leads to unfair results. The first is the situation presented by the instant case; the plaintiff's negligence is less than the cumulative negligence of all the tortfeasors but is more than a particular defendant's. That is said to be unfair because a plaintiff should not be able to recover from a defendant who is less negligent than the plaintiff. See Bd. of County Comm'rs v. Ridenour, Wyo., 623 P.2d 1174 (1981). The second situation is where there are two defendants and one plaintiff; all parties are 33⅓ percent at fault. Under the unit rule, the plaintiff recovers 66⅔ percent of his or her total damages. That is said to be unfair because if there were only one defendant who is 50 percent liable, the plaintiff would recover nothing. However, the plaintiff is not the primary cause of the injuries in either of the two situations discussed and therefore should be entitled to recover. The defendants, meanwhile, are required to do nothing more than compensate the plaintiff for the injury in proportion to their fault, with the plaintiff absorbing his own proportion of fault. The third alleged inequitable result under the unit rule arises when one defendant is judgment proof. For example, suppose plaintiff is 15 percent negligent, defendant A is 10 percent negligent, and defendant B is 75 percent negligent; B, however, is judgment proof. Under the Utah statute, A might be liable for 85 percent of plaintiff's damages. That situation, however, is a product of the rule of joint and several liability — not comparative fault. Prior to adoption of the comparative negligence statute, a plaintiff free from contributory negligence could recover the entire amount of damages from a defendant whose negligence was slight. And the problem of the judgment-proof defendant exists under the Wisconsin rule as well. Suppose plaintiff is 10 percent at fault, defendant A is 15 percent at fault, and defendant B is 75 percent at fault; B is judgment proof. Under the Wisconsin rule, defendant A is liable for 90 percent of plaintiff's damages, a result no less inequitable than that reached by the unit rule.

negligence the state has adopted? What result if the state were a pure comparative negligence jurisdiction?

3. Is the Unit Rule Fair?   A motivation for switching from contributory negligence to comparative negligence was eliminating the harsh bar to recovery under contributory negligence. Another was the belief that parties should pay damages in proportion to their degree of fault. Is the unit rule consistent with these justifications for switching to comparative fault?

C. Reckless Conduct

Contributory negligence jurisdictions developed a number of rules that moderated the impact of that doctrine. When a negligent plaintiff sought damages from a reckless defendant, the negligent plaintiff was protected from the ordinary recovery-barring effect of his or her negligence. Another doctrine, the "last clear chance" doctrine, allowed a negligent plaintiff to recover if injured in circumstances where the defendant's failure to act carefully was especially egregious. Comparative negligence jurisdictions have had to decide whether to preserve special treatment for cases involving these types of conduct. These issues are treated in Coleman v. Hines (in a contributory negligence jurisdiction) and Downing v. United Auto Racing Association (in a comparative negligence jurisdiction).

COLEMAN v. HINES

515 S.E.2d 57 (N.C. Ct. App. 1999)

HORTON, J.

Although plaintiff and Mr. Hines raise a variety of issues in their briefs, the central question before this Court is whether Ms. Musso contributed by her own actions to her own death so that plaintiff's claim for wrongful death is barred. . . . Plaintiff contends that there were material questions of fact as to Ms. Musso's knowledge of Wirt's being under the influence of intoxicating liquor, so that the trial court erred in granting summary judgment on the issue of contributory negligence. . . .

Evidence forecast by defendants included the following undisputed facts: (1) defendant Wirt Hines was drinking early on the afternoon of the accident when he stopped by to see Ms. Musso at her place of employment at Domino's Pizza; (2) according to Ms. Hansma, Ms. Musso's employer, Ms. Musso knew Wirt was drinking when he stopped by Domino's, and Ms. Musso also stated that they planned to drink that evening on their way to an engagement party, during the party, and following the party; (3) Ms. Hansma begged Ms. Musso not to ride with Wirt that night, and repeatedly offered to pick them up at the party and drive them home, no matter how late they stayed at the party; (4) when Wirt picked up Ms. Musso later that evening, they went to a convenience store and purchased a 12-pack of beer, which they drank in each other's presence over the evening; (5) the only alcohol Wirt drank that evening was consumed in Ms. Musso's presence; (6) at the time of the accident, Wirt's blood-alcohol content was at least .184, more than twice the legal limit, according to the treating physician, Dr. Anderson; and (7) it was obvious to the officer investigating the accident, Officer Melee, who arrived about three minutes after the accident, that Wirt was under the influence of alcohol at the time of the accident.

Although plaintiff argues that there is a question of material fact as to whether Ms. Musso knew or should have known that Wirt was under the influence, that argument does not refute the clear evidence of Ms. Hansma, Officer Melee, and Dr. Anderson. As a result, we conclude that there is no question of material fact about either Wirt's condition at the time of the accident, nor Ms. Musso's knowledge of his condition. The trial court properly entered summary judgment on the issues of Wirt's negligence and Ms. Musso's contributory negligence.

Plaintiff further contends, however, that even if Ms. Musso was found to be contributorily negligent, Wirt was willfully and wantonly negligent as evidenced by his plea to manslaughter in the death of Ms. Musso, so that contributory negligence on the part of Ms. Musso would not bar plaintiff's claim. "It is well settled that contributory negligence, even if admitted by the plaintiff, is no defense to willful and wanton injury." Pearce v. Barham, 156 S.E.2d 290, 294 (1967) (quoting Brendle v. R.R., 34 S.E. 634, 635 (1899)). We agree with plaintiff that under the facts of this case Wirt was willfully and wantonly negligent in operating a motor vehicle while under the influence of intoxicating liquor. Defendants contend, however, that Ms. Musso's own negligence in riding with a person whom she knew to be under the influence of intoxicating liquor rose at least to the same level as that of Wirt, so that a claim for her death is barred as a result. See Coble v. Knight, 130 N.C. App. 652, 655-56, 503 S.E.2d 703, 706 (1998), and Sorrells v. M.Y.B. Hospitality Ventures of Asheville, 332 N.C. 645, 648, 423 S.E.2d 72, 74 (1992).

In *Sorrells*, our Supreme Court reinstated the trial court's dismissal of a Rule 12(b)(5) claim in an action against a dram shop and stated that while they recognized

> the viability of the rule [that the defendant's willful or wanton negligence would avoid the bar of ordinary contributory negligence], we do not find it applicable in this case. Instead, we hold that plaintiff's claim is barred as a result of decedent's own actions, as alleged in the complaint, which rise to the same level of negligence as that of defendant. . . . In fact, to the extent the allegations in the complaint establish more than ordinary negligence on the part of defendant, they also establish a similarly high degree of contributory negligence on the part of the decedent. Thus, we conclude that plaintiff cannot prevail.

Sorrells, 332 N.C. at 648, 423 S.E.2d at 74.

Likewise, in the present case (heard in the context of a motion for summary judgment), to the extent that the evidence establishes willful and wanton negligence on the part of Wirt, it also establishes a "similarly high degree of contributory negligence on the part of" Ms. Musso. The same point is made in *Coble*, where the decedent and the driver of an automobile had been drinking together for several hours. At one point, the driver locked the keys inside the car and called his father to bring an extra set of keys. The father did so and the young men unlocked the car and drove off, and a tragic accident followed, resulting in the passenger's death. The estate of the passenger sought to recover from the driver's father for negligently entrusting the car keys to the driver. In affirming summary judgment for the father, we held in part:

> Indeed, if, as [decedent's] estate argues, the intoxicated condition of the son was, or at least should have been apparent to his father when he handed the spare keys to his son, then under the facts of this case, the only conclusion to be drawn is that the son's

intoxicated state was equally obvious to [decedent] when he got into the vehicle with the son. The record shows that [decedent] and the [son] drank alcoholic beverages for hours prior to stopping at the gas station. Thereafter, they waited together until [the son's] father arrived. These facts show conclusively that [decedent's] negligence in riding with the intoxicated son rose at least to the level of the father's alleged negligence in entrusting the automobile to his son. Such negligence on [decedent's] part, of course, acts as a bar to any claim his estate has against the father's negligence.

Coble, 130 N.C. App. at 656-57, 503 S.E.2d at 706. . . .

Applying the logic of the cases cited above, we hold as a matter of law that under the facts of this case, the actions of the decedent, Ms. Musso, rose to the same level of negligence as that of Wirt. Tragically, Ms. Musso consciously assumed the risk of entering a vehicle, and riding as a passenger in that vehicle while it was being driven by a person under the influence of alcohol. She was with the driver, Wirt, when they purchased alcohol and she consumed alcohol along with him at a party. She knew in advance that they planned to consume alcohol and that Wirt intended to drive the vehicle home after drinking alcohol, and yet did not accept her employer's offer to drive them home regardless of the hour of the morning. We know of no principle of logic nor any overriding social policy which would militate in favor of allowing a recovery of damages under these facts.

Finally, we have carefully considered plaintiff's argument that the doctrine of last clear chance would operate to preserve her claim, but find that the doctrine would not apply under the facts of this case. In order to show last clear chance a plaintiff must allege and prove that

> (1) [p]laintiff, by [her] own negligence, placed [herself] in a position of peril from which [she] could not escape; (2) defendant saw, or by the exercise of reasonable care should have seen and understood, the perilous position of plaintiff; (3) defendant had the time and the means to avoid the accident if defendant had seen or discovered plaintiff's perilous position; (4) . . . defendant failed or refused to use every reasonable means at his command to avoid impending injury to plaintiff; and (5) plaintiff was injured as a result of defendant's failure or refusal to avoid impending injury.

Williams v. Lee Brick and Tile, 88 N.C. App. 725, 728, 364 S.E.2d 720, 721 (1988). In reviewing the complaint, plaintiff presented no allegations that Ms. Musso had placed herself in a position of peril from which she could not escape. Indeed, evidence from the depositions tends to show that Ms. Musso had opportunities to avoid riding with Wirt, but declined to follow through with them and, instead, chose to ride with him. . . .

We reverse the action of the trial court and find that no issues of material fact exist as to whether Wirt was grossly negligent and whether Ms. Musso was grossly contributorily negligent. In all other respects, we affirm the order of the trial court.

Affirmed in part and reversed in part.

DOWNING v. UNITED AUTO RACING ASSOCIATION
570 N.E.2d 828 (Ill. App. Ct. 1991)

McMorrow, J.

Plaintiff was injured on August 12, 1978, during a midget car race at Joliet Memorial Stadium. Defendant Willis leased the track to promote, organize and supervise such races. Under the agreement, defendant Willis was to provide a safe, adequate, and properly prepared track for the races, including personnel to supervise activities near the track and in the pit area. Defendant UARA agreed to sanction races held by defendant Willis at the stadium.

At the time of his injury, plaintiff was a member of a pit crew for Richard Pole (Pole), a midget car driver. Plaintiff helped others in the crew to prepare the car and push it onto the track. As plaintiff waited on the track for the car to be pushed into a warm-up race, he noticed that the car being driven by Guess bicycled in the turns nearer to plaintiff. "Bicycling" occurs when the car's inner wheels lose contact with the track surface.

According to plaintiff's trial testimony, Guess' car bicycled approximately two feet off the asphalt in these turns. After Guess' car passed through the turns, plaintiff and other members of the crew pushed Pole's car onto the track to participate in the warm-up race. Thereafter, plaintiff began to walk off the track toward the pit area. He was accompanied by George Boban (Boban), who was also a pit crew member for Pole. Both plaintiff and Boban noted that Guess' car again bicycled a few feet in the air when the car made the two turns at the far end of the track. Plaintiff testified that he mentioned to Boban, and to David Valentino (Valentino), a pit crew member for another driver who was nearby, that Guess' car should be blackflagged off the track. "Blackflag" occurs when the racing steward waves a black flag to a driver to signal to the driver that his car should leave the track. Valentino also testified at trial that he noticed that Guess' car bicycled when making turns around the track. . . .

Boban and Valentino testified that as Guess' car reached the turns nearer to the pit area, the car again bicycled. It then flipped over and began skidding toward the area where plaintiff, Boban, and Valentino were located. Although Boban and Valentino avoided injury, plaintiff was struck by the car and pinned against the fence next to the track straightaway. He sustained injuries requiring extensive surgery and lengthy post-operative care.

Plaintiff contended that defendants UARA and Willis were guilty of willful and wanton conduct because they (1) failed to extend the guardrail near the pit area and (2) failed to provide a pit steward to ensure that persons did not remain in the exposed area near the pit. In addition, plaintiff claimed that defendant UARA was guilty of willful and wanton misconduct because it failed to blackflag Guess' car off the track once it began to bicycle. . . .

Defendants presented evidence to show that none of the alternatives suggested by plaintiff was reasonably necessary, and that none would have prevented plaintiff's injuries. Testimony from experts detailed these points. Defendants also presented testimony to establish that they had warned pit crew members, including plaintiff, not to stand in the area where the plaintiff's injuries occurred.

Based upon this evidence, the jury returned a verdict against defendants UARA and Willis. It awarded plaintiff $1.5 million in damages, reduced to $615,000 for plaintiff's comparative fault, which the jury assessed at 59%. The trial court entered judgment in conformity with this verdict. Defendants UARA and Willis appeal, and plaintiff cross-appeals.

Defendants argue that the jury's finding of willful and wanton misconduct was not supported by the evidence of record. They contend that the trial court should have granted their motion for judgment notwithstanding the verdict or in the alternative for a new trial. . . .

A review of the record reveals sufficient basis to justify the jury's verdict that defendants UARA and Willis were willful and wanton. Plaintiff produced evidence that showed defendants were aware that the exposed area near the pit presented a substantial risk of serious injury to persons who stood there, and that defendants knew pit crew members were often located in the vicinity during warm-up and hot laps. . . . We cannot say, as a matter of law, that this evidence was insufficient to prove that defendants' omissions constituted willful and wanton conduct. . . .

. . . In addition, the plaintiff's understanding of the scope of harm associated with remaining in the exposed area near the pit was considered by the jury with respect to plaintiff's comparative fault, and we cannot say upon review that the jury's apportionment of comparative fault between the parties was erroneous as a matter of law. . . .

In a cross-appeal, plaintiff challenges the apportionment of damages between the parties. Specifically, plaintiff argues that his ordinary negligence could not be considered by the jury as an offset in the assessment of compensatory damages for the defendants' willful and wanton misconduct.

Illinois precedent is in conflict with respect to this question. In State Farm Mutual Automobile Insurance Co. v. Mendenhall (1987), 517 N.E.2d 341, the court determined that a plaintiff's ordinary negligence could be considered by the jury to reduce the compensatory damages assessed for the defendant's willful and wanton conduct. The court's ruling in *Mendenhall* was expressly reaffirmed in Yates v. Brock (1989), 547 N.E.2d 1031, *appeal denied* (1990), 553 N.E.2d 403. Relying on *Mendenhall,* the trial court judge in the instant cause permitted the jury to consider the plaintiff's ordinary negligence in reducing the damages assessed for the defendants' willful and wanton conduct.

However, the decisions of *Mendenhall* and *Yates* were subsequently rejected in Burke v. 12 Rothschild's Liquor Mart, Inc. (1991), 568 N.E.2d 80, wherein the court determined that the plaintiff's ordinary negligence could not reduce the damages recovered for the defendant's willful and wanton acts. Cases from other jurisdictions also represent a split of authority on this question.

The decisions of *Mendenhall* and *Burke* founded much of their analysis on the Illinois Supreme Court's adoption of comparative fault in Alvis v. Ribar (1981), 421 N.E.2d 886. The courts noted that prior to Alvis, Illinois adhered to the contributory negligence rule. Under this rule, a plaintiff was prevented from any recovery for compensatory damages from a negligent defendant, if the plaintiff's ordinary negligence also contributed to his injuries. However, the plaintiff was permitted full recovery of compensatory damages, irrespective of the plaintiff's ordinary negligence, if the defendant's acts amounted to willful and wanton conduct. The advent of comparative fault in *Alvis* eliminated the harsh effect of the contributory negligence rule upon a negligent plaintiff's recovery of compensatory damages from a negligent defendant. Under *Alvis*, compensatory damages are assessed according to an apportionment of the parties' respective negligence in proximately causing the plaintiff's injuries. The supreme court in *Alvis* did not resolve the collateral issue of whether the jury should be permitted to apportion damages between the negligent plaintiff and the willful and wanton defendant.

The courts in *Mendenhall* and *Burke* adopted divergent views with respect to the significance that should be accorded to the equitable principles underlying comparative fault. The *Mendenhall* court concluded that equitable principles of comparative fault outweigh the social opprobrium associated with willful and wanton acts, because of the "thin line" between ordinary negligence and willful and wanton conduct. The *Burke* court determined that the social stigma attached to willful and wanton conduct overrides the equitable principles of comparative fault, because of the significant difference in the degree of culpability associated with ordinary negligence as compared to willful and wanton acts. Thus, the divergent views expressed in *Mendenhall* and *Burke* reflect the hybrid nature of willful and wanton conduct, which under the facts of one case may be only degrees more than ordinary negligence, while under the facts of another case may be only degrees less than intentional wrongdoing. . . .

Under the facts of the instant cause, we conclude that the trial court properly permitted the jury to consider the plaintiff's comparative fault, based upon principles of ordinary negligence, as an offset to the compensatory damages awarded for the defendants' willful and wanton conduct. In light of the hybrid nature of the concept of willful and wanton conduct, and the circumstance that such behavior may not amount to an intentional tort per se, we agree with the court in *Mendenhall* that "the fact finder's ability to prorate the damages between plaintiff and defendant best serves justice and is most consistent with the reasons for comparative negligence. . . ." (164 Ill. App. 3d at 61, 115 Ill. Dec. 139, 517 N.E.2d 341.) Although we agree with the court's observation in *Burke* that there is a distinction in the degrees of culpability associated with ordinary negligence and willful and wanton conduct, we are unable to conclude that this distinction should preclude an equitable apportionment of compensatory damages between the plaintiff and defendants in the case at bar. . . .

For the reasons stated, the judgment of the circuit court of Cook County is affirmed.

NOTES TO COLEMAN v. HINES AND DOWNING v. UNITED AUTO RACING ASSOCIATION

1. ***The Effect on Damage Recovery of Reckless Conduct.*** Four years after Downing v. United Auto Racing Association was decided, the Illinois Supreme Court reaffirmed that apportioning fault was appropriate between a negligent plaintiff and a reckless defendant but not between a negligent plaintiff and a defendant who had committed an intentional tort. See Poole v. City of Rolling Meadows, 656 N.E.2d 768 (Ill. 1995). Nonetheless, it is useful to note that Coleman v. Hines, Downing v. United Auto Racing Association, and Burke v. 12 Rothschild's Liquor Mart, Inc. (discussed in *Downing*) describe three alternative methods for determining the damages a defendant must pay when one or more parties has been reckless. How are damages calculated under each rule if the plaintiff is negligent and the defendant is reckless? How are damages calculated under each rule if both parties are reckless?

2. ***Last Clear Chance as a Rebuttal to Contributory Negligence.*** The North Carolina Appellate Court in Coleman v. Hines described the *last clear chance doctrine*. The plaintiff may recover full damages upon showing that the defendant had the last clear chance to avoid the injury to the plaintiff but failed to take that chance. The court in *Coleman* found that the last clear chance doctrine did not apply because the plaintiff could have extricated herself from the perilous situation.

3. ***Last Clear Chance Concept Under Comparative Negligence.*** The last clear chance doctrine is an "all or nothing" doctrine because, if the plaintiff asserts it successfully, the plaintiff is allowed full recovery despite any contributory negligence. If the plaintiff fails, the plaintiff is denied any recovery. Comparative negligence balances

the plaintiff's and defendant's fault, allowing only a reduction in recovery under the pure version, and under the modified versions only when the plaintiff's negligence is relatively small. Upon adoption of comparative negligence rules, many courts have formally abandoned the last clear chance doctrine because comparative negligence is not an "all or nothing" doctrine and does not need special rules designed to ameliorate the harshness of contributory negligence.

Problem
Recklessness as a Defense

The plaintiff was crossing trolley tracks when he noticed a trolley approaching from his left and a fire engine approaching from the direction he was facing. He stood on the tracks and waved his arms at the trolley to get it to stop. The trolley driver sounded the trolley's horn, but the plaintiff did not move. When the trolley finally stopped after hitting the plaintiff, the driver got down from his seat and said, "Why didn't that man get off of my tracks?" How would these cases be decided in a contributory negligence state? In a modified comparative negligence state? In a pure comparative negligence state? See Elliott v. Philadelphia Transp. Co., 53 A.2d 81 (Pa. 1947).

Problem
Last Clear Chance

Your firm represents the defendant in the following case. The events took place in a contributory negligence jurisdiction. A partner in your firm is assessing potential settlement offers and would like you to evaluate the defendant's potential liability if the case goes to trial. Please write a memo assessing whether the last clear chance doctrine is likely to insulate the plaintiff against the application of the contributory negligence bar to recovery against your client.

Moreno, the victim, and Bass, the defendant, were picking cotton. Bass was driving the cotton picker, which moved forward as it dumped cotton into an adjacent metal trailer. Moreno walked along the top of the cotton in the trailer to tamp down the cotton as the trailer filled. Bass negligently drove the cotton picker into a power line, electrocuting Moreno. Moreno was contributorily negligent for failing to notice the power line, which was in front of the trailer and picker when Moreno jumped into the back of the trailer. Bass admitted that there was no way Moreno could have seen how close the power line was once he was in the back of the trailer. Should the plaintiff's recovery be completely barred? Should the last clear chance doctrine negate the plaintiff's contributory negligence? See Kenan v. Bass, 511 S.E.2d 6 (N.C. Ct. App. 1999).

Perspective: Last Clear Chance in Modern Practice

The doctrine is still useful to tort lawyers as a way of comparing the fault of plaintiffs and defendants. The facts related to when each party could have avoided the injury may affect the relative shares of fault assigned to each party:

> As with any other evidence, either party may argue the temporal factors important to the application of the last clear chance doctrine (e.g., plaintiff's

helplessness which led to predicament, defendant's subsequent discovery and negligent failure to avoid accident) to the trier of fact, and it may properly consider those factors in apportioning fault. In addition, either party may attempt to persuade the trier of fact that the other party should bear a greater percentage of liability for an accident because he or she had the last clear chance to avoid injury. However, "last clear chance" becomes only one of many factors to be weighed by the trier of fact in assessing and comparing the parties' relative fault, instead of an inflexible "all or nothing" doctrine of liability.

Laws v. Webb, 658 A.2d 1000 (Del. 1995). In some comparative negligence states, the plaintiff may request the court to give a special instruction to the jury identifying the elements that make up a last clear chance situation, but telling the jury that these elements are only factors to be considered, among others, when evaluating the parties' relative degrees of fault. See, e.g., Spahn v. Town of Port Royal, 499 S.E.2d 205 (S.C. 1998).

Statute: EFFECT OF CONTRIBUTORY FAULT; DEFINITION

Alaska Stat. §§09.17.060; 09.17.900 (2017)

Sec. 09.17.060. In an action based on fault seeking to recover damages for injury or death to a person or harm to property, contributory fault chargeable to the claimant diminishes proportionately the amount awarded as compensatory damages for the injury attributable to the claimant's contributory fault, but does not bar recovery.

Sec. 09.17.900. Definition. In this chapter, "fault" includes acts or omissions that are in any measure negligent, reckless, or intentional toward the person or property of the actor or others, or that subject a person to strict tort liability. The term also includes breach of warranty, unreasonable assumption of risk not constituting an enforceable express consent, misuse of a product for which the defendant otherwise would be liable, and unreasonable failure to avoid an injury or to mitigate damages. . . .

Statute: JOINT TORTFEASORS, LIABILITY

Miss. Stat. §85-5-7(1) (2017)

(1) As used in this section "fault" means an act or omission of a person which is a proximate cause of injury or death to another person or persons, damages to property, tangible or intangible, or economic injury, including but not limited to negligence, malpractice, strict liability, absolute liability or failure to warn. "Fault" shall not include any tort which results from an act or omission committed with a specific wrongful intent.

Statute: COMPARATIVE FAULT

Wyo. St. §1-1-109 (2017)

(iv) "Fault" includes acts or omissions, determined to be a proximate cause of death or injury to person or property, that are in any measure negligent, or that subject an actor to strict tort or strict products liability, and includes breach of warranty, assumption of risk and misuse or alteration of a product.

NOTES TO STATUTES

    1. *Legislative Responses to the Problem in* **Downing.**   States have taken various positions on this issue. How do the Alaska, Mississippi, and Wyoming statutes resolve the issue raised in *Downing*?

    2. *Negligence and Recklessness Compared.*   In Danculovich v. Brown, 593 P.2d 187, 193-194 (Wyo. 1979), the Wyoming Supreme Court distinguished between negligence and recklessness to explain the rationale of the Wyoming statute. Negligence is based on acts done while one is unaware of risks, on inadvertence, on lack of attention to risks. Recklessness is based on acts done while one is aware of serious risks, on the conscious ignoring of serious risks, on ignoring the reasonable conclusion from known facts that there is a serious risk associated with one's conduct. Under traditional rules, contributory negligence was not a defense if the defendant was reckless. The Wyoming Supreme Court concluded that in the comparative negligence context, where a defendant has been reckless, a plaintiff's contributory negligence should continue to be ignored, since comparative negligence was designed to ameliorate the harsh effects of traditional contributory negligence as a complete bar.

Perspective: Balancing Reckless and Negligent Conduct

Can the problem of how to treat reckless conduct in a comparative system be resolved by considering the characteristics a jurisdiction associates with recklessness and the purposes for which a jurisdiction adopted comparative fault?

> After considering the reasons underlying the adoption of comparative fault in the jurisdiction, the court should balance these against the policies underlying the jurisdiction's recklessness doctrine. . . .
>
>   On the recklessness side of the equation, the element militating in favor of the comparison of recklessness with ordinary negligence is the extent to which the jurisdiction's recklessness doctrine exists to mitigate the harshness of contributory negligence and has been rendered obsolete by the adoption of comparative fault. The element militating against comparison is the extent to which the recklessness doctrine carries with it a judgment that the reckless party's state of mind so closely approximates intent that he should bear the totality of the loss. On the comparative fault side of the equation, the element militating in favor of comparisons between recklessness and ordinary negligence is the extent to which the jurisdiction's comparative fault system exists to assess liability equitably in proportion to the contributing fault. The element militating against comparison on this side is the extent to which the jurisdiction's comparative fault system may have been created for some other inconsistent purpose.

See Jim Hasenfus, *Comment: The Role of Recklessness in American Systems of Comparative Fault*, 43 Ohio St. L.J. 399, 423 (1982). How does this balancing compare to the analysis of the Illinois Supreme Court in *Downing*?

III. Assumption of Risk

Can a person give up the right to sue a defendant for harms that might be caused in the future by that defendant's negligence? The concept of *assumption of risk* provides tort law's answer to this question. Sometimes an express agreement to forgo a right to sue will bar a plaintiff from recovery for harm caused by a defendant's negligent conduct.

In some cases, a plaintiff has not made an explicit agreement to excuse the defendant's negligence, but the plaintiff has acted as if he or she was willing to encounter the risks presented by that negligence. These cases, involving *implied assumption of risk*, have presented a number of analytical difficulties. The adoption of comparative negligence has worked significant changes on this part of assumption of risk doctrine.

A. Express Assumption of Risk

Express assumption of risk cases involve agreements by plaintiffs to accept risks created by defendants' activities. They almost always involve written releases in which a plaintiff agrees not to sue a defendant if certain risks cause harm. In exchange, the defendant provides a service or product to the plaintiff. Enforceability of a release involves two questions: (1) Does public policy permit releases in connection with the activity? (2) If public policy allows assumption of risk for that activity, does the particular release provided by the plaintiff merit enforcement?

Wagenblast v. Odessa School District examines categories of activities for which releases are generally unenforceable. The court considers the legality of agreements by parents not to sue schools for risks associated with school-related activities. The court applies six factors to determine whether *any* release would be enforceable in this context. Turnbough v. Ladner examines the enforceability of an agreement not to sue a scuba diving instructor and the yacht club that employed her if decompression sickness resulted from using compressed air. In this case, the activity is one for which a release might be appropriate. The court considers both the terms of the release and the negotiations underlying its signing to determine whether the release is enforceable.

WAGENBLAST v. ODESSA SCHOOL DISTRICT

758 P.2d 968 (Wash. 1988)

ANDERSON, J.

In these consolidated cases we consider an issue of first impression — the legality of public school districts requiring students and their parents to sign a release of all potential future claims as a condition to student participation in certain school-related activities. [Lower courts treated the release as legal in one of the consolidated cases and as illegal in the other of the consolidated cases.]

The plaintiffs in these cases are public school children and their parents. . . .

The courts have generally recognized that, subject to certain exceptions, parties may contract that one shall not be liable for his or her own negligence to another. As Prosser and Keeton explain:

> It is quite possible for the parties expressly to agree in advance that the defendant is under no obligation of care for the benefit of the plaintiff, and shall not be liable for the

consequences of conduct which would otherwise be negligent. There is in the ordinary case no public policy which prevents the parties from contracting as they see fit, as to whether the plaintiff will undertake the responsibility of looking out for himself.

(Footnotes omitted.)

In accordance with the foregoing general rule, appellate decisions in this state have upheld exculpatory agreements where the subject was a toboggan slide, a scuba diving class, mountain climbing instruction, an automobile demolition derby, and ski jumping.

As Prosser and Keeton further observe, however, there are instances where public policy reasons for preserving an obligation of care owed by one person to another outweigh our traditional regard for the freedom to contract. Courts in this century are generally agreed on several such categories of cases.

Courts, for example, are usually reluctant to allow those charged with a public duty, which includes the obligation to use reasonable care, to rid themselves of that obligation by contract.

Thus, where the defendant is a common carrier, an innkeeper, a professional bailee, a public utility, or the like, an agreement discharging the defendant's performance will not ordinarily be given effect. Implicit in such decisions is the notion that the service performed is one of importance to the public, and that a certain standard of performance is therefore required.

Courts generally also hold that an employer cannot require an employee to sign a contract releasing the employer from liability for job-related injuries caused by the employer's negligence. Such decisions are grounded on the recognition that the disparity of bargaining power between employer and employee forces the employee to accept such agreements.

Consistent with these general views, this court has held that a bank which rents out safety deposit boxes cannot, by contract, exempt itself from liability for its own negligence, and that if the circumstances of a particular case suggest that a gas company has a duty to inspect the pipes and fittings belonging to the owner of the building, any contractual limitation on that duty would be against public policy.

This court has also gone beyond these usually accepted categories to hold future releases invalid in other circumstances as well. It has struck down a lease provision exculpating a public housing authority from liability for injuries caused by the authority's negligence and has also struck down a landlord's exculpatory clause relating to common areas in a multi-family dwelling complex.

In reaching these decisions, this court has focused at times on disparity of bargaining power, at times on the importance of the service provided, and at other times on other factors. In reviewing these decisions, it is apparent that the court has not always been particularly clear on what rationale it used to decide what type of release was and was not violative of "public policy." Undoubtedly, it has been much easier for courts to simply declare releases violative of public policy in a given situation than to state a principled basis for so holding.

Probably the best exposition of the test to be applied in determining whether exculpatory agreements violate public policy is that stated by the California Supreme Court. In writing for a unanimous court, the late Justice Tobriner outlined the factors in Tunkl v. Regents of Univ. of Cal., 383 P.2d 441 (Cal. 1963):

> Thus the attempted but invalid exemption involves a transaction which exhibits some or
> all of the following characteristics. It concerns a business of a type generally thought

suitable for public regulation. The party seeking exculpation is engaged in performing a service of great importance to the public, which is often a matter of practical necessity for some members of the public. The party holds himself out as willing to perform this service for any member of the public who seeks it, or at least for any member coming within certain established standards. As a result of the essential nature of the service, in the economic setting of the transaction, the party invoking exculpation possesses a decisive advantage of bargaining strength against any member of the public who seeks his services. In exercising a superior bargaining power the party confronts the public with a standardized adhesion contract of exculpation, and makes no provision whereby a purchaser may pay additional reasonable fees and obtain protection against negligence. Finally, as a result of the transaction, the person or property of the purchaser is placed under the control of the seller, subject to the risk of carelessness by the seller or his agents.

(Footnotes omitted.) *Tunkl*, 60 Cal. 2d at 98-101, 383 P.2d 441, 32 Cal. Rptr. 33. We agree.

Obviously, the more of the foregoing six characteristics that appear in a given exculpatory agreement case, the more likely the agreement is to be declared invalid on public policy grounds.

In the consolidated cases before us, *all* of the characteristics are present in *each* case. We separately, then, examine each of these six characteristics as applied to the cases before us.

1. The agreement concerns an endeavor of a type generally thought suitable for public regulation.

Regulation of governmental entities usually means self-regulation. Thus, the Legislature has by statute granted to each school board the authority to control, supervise, and regulate the conduct of interscholastic athletics. In some situations, a school board is permitted, in turn, to delegate this authority to the Washington Interscholastic Activities Association (WIAA) or to another voluntary nonprofit entity. In the cases before us, both school boards look to the WIAA for regulation of interscholastic sports. The WIAA handbook contains an extensive constitution with rules for such athletic endeavors. These rules cover numerous topics, including student eligibility standards, athletic awards, insurance, coaches, officials, tournaments and state championships. Special regulations for each sport cover such topics as turnout schedules, regular season game or meet limitations, and various areas of regulation peculiar to the sport, including the rule book governing the sport.

Clearly then, interscholastic sports in Washington are extensively regulated, and are a fit subject for such regulation.

2. The party seeking exculpation is engaged in performing a service of great importance to the public, which is often a matter of practical necessity for some members of the public.

This court has held that public school students have no fundamental right to participate in interscholastic athletics. Nonetheless, the court also has observed that the justification advanced for interscholastic athletics is their educational and cultural value. As the testimony of then Seattle School Superintendent Robert Nelson and others amply demonstrate, interscholastic athletics is part and parcel of the overall educational scheme in Washington. The total expenditure of time, effort and money on these endeavors makes this clear. The importance of these programs to the public is substantive; they represent a significant tie of the public at large to our system of public education. Nor can the importance of these programs to certain students be denied; as Superintendent Nelson agreed, some students undoubtedly remain in school and maintain their academic standing only because they can participate in these programs. Given this emphasis on sports by the public and the school system, it would be unrealistic to expect students to view athletics as an activity entirely separate and apart from the remainder of their schooling.

This court observed in McCutcheon v. United Homes Corp., 486 P.2d 1093 (1971), that it makes little sense to insist that a worker have a safe place to work but at the same time to deny that worker a safe place to live. There is likewise little logic in insisting that one who entrusts personal property to a bank for safekeeping in a deposit box must be protected from the bank's negligence while denying such protection to a student who entrusts his or her person to the coaches, trainers, bus drivers and other agents of a school sports program.

In sum, under any rational view of the subject, interscholastic sports in public schools are a matter of public importance in this jurisdiction.

3. Such party holds itself out as willing to perform this service for any member of the public who seeks it, or at least for any member coming within certain established standards.

Implicit in the nature of interscholastic sports is the notion that such programs are open to all students who meet certain skill and eligibility standards. This conclusion finds direct support in the testimony of former Superintendent Nelson and the WIAA eligibility and nondiscrimination policies set forth in the WIAA handbook.

4. Because of the essential nature of the service, in the economic setting of the transaction, the party invoking exculpation possesses a decisive advantage of bargaining strength against any member of the public who seeks the services.

Not only have interscholastic sports become of considerable importance to students and the general public alike, but in most instances there exists no alternative program of organized competition. For instance, former Superintendent Nelson knew of no alternative to the Seattle School District's wrestling program. While outside alternatives exist for some activities, they possess little of the inherent allure of interscholastic competition. Many students cannot afford private programs or the private schools where such releases might not be employed. In this regard, school districts have near-monopoly power. And, because such programs have become important to student participants, school districts possess a clear and disparate bargaining strength when they insist that students and their parents sign these releases.

5. In exercising a superior bargaining power, the party confronts the public with a standardized adhesion contract of exculpation, and makes no provision whereby a purchaser may pay additional reasonable fees and obtain protection against negligence.

Both school districts admit to an unwavering policy regarding these releases; no student athlete will be allowed to participate in any program without first signing the release form as written by the school district. In both of these cases, students and their parents unsuccessfully attempted to modify the forms by deleting the release language. In both cases, the school district rejected the attempted modifications. Student athletes and their parents or guardians have no alternative but to sign the standard release forms provided to them or have the student barred from the program.

    6. The person or property of members of the public seeking such services must be placed under the control of the furnisher of the services, subject to the risk of carelessness on the part of the furnisher, its employees or agents.

    A school district owes a duty to its students to employ ordinary care and to anticipate reasonably foreseeable dangers so as to take precautions for protecting the children in its custody from such dangers. This duty extends to students engaged in interscholastic sports. As a natural incident to the relationship of a student athlete and his or her coach, the student athlete is usually placed under the coach's considerable degree of control. The student is thus subject to the risk that the school district or its agent will breach this duty of care.

    In sum, the attempted releases in the cases before us exhibit all six of the characteristics denominated in Tunkl v. Regents of Univ. of Cal., 60 Cal. 2d 92, 98-101, 383 P.2d 441, 32 Cal. Rptr. 33, 6 A.L.R.3d 693 (1963). Because of this, and for the aforesaid reasons, we hold that the releases in these consolidated cases are invalid as against public policy.

    Having decided the case on this basis, [the relationship of this decision to the doctrine of assumption of risk] requires discussion. . . .

    . . . Another name for a release of the sort presented here is an express assumption of risk. If a plaintiff has released a defendant from liability for a future occurrence, the plaintiff may also be said to have assumed the risk of the occurrence. If the release is against public policy, however, it is also against public policy to say that the plaintiff has assumed that particular risk. This court has implicitly recognized that an express assumption of risk which relieves the defendant's duty to the plaintiff may violate public policy. Accordingly, to the extent that the release portions of these forms represent a consent to relieve the school districts of their duty of care, they are invalid whether they are termed releases or express assumptions of risk. . . .

    [In the case where the release was invalidated, the decision was affirmed. Where it was upheld, the decision was reversed.]

TURNBOUGH v. LADNER
754 So. 2d 467 (Miss. 1999)

McRae, J. . . .

    Michael Turnbough decided in 1994 that he wanted to obtain his open-water certification as a scuba diver. He had previously been certified as a scuba diver, but his certification had expired back in the 1980's. Turnbough enrolled in a scuba diving class offered by Gulfport Yacht Club and taught by Janet Ladner. Upon learning from Ladner that all of the participants would be required to execute a release in favor of her and the Gulfport Yacht Club in order to participate in the class, Turnbough questioned a fellow student who also happened to be an attorney. After Turnbough's classmate informed him that such releases were unenforceable, Turnbough then executed the document entitled "Liability Release and Express Assumption of Risk." The release, in pertinent part, stated

> Further, I understand that diving with compressed air involves certain inherent risks: decompression sickness [and others]. . . .

At the conclusion of the six-week course, the class convened in Panama City, Florida to perform the first of their "check-out dives" in order to receive certification. On Saturday, July 23, 1994, the class performed two dives from the beach. However, Turnbough's participation in the first dive was cut short by a leaking tank. He completed the second dive with no apparent problems. The next morning, Sunday, July 24, 1994, the class performed two dives from a dive boat. Two dives of sixty feet each were scheduled, but because the dive boat had engine problems, the first dive site was only forty-six to forty-eight feet deep. The second dive descended to sixty feet, and Ladner calculated the maximum time allowable for the second dive as thirty-eight minutes.

Turnbough began to feel the first effects of decompression sickness, commonly known as "the bends," on his way back to Gulfport that evening. The next day Turnbough began experiencing a pain that he described as "arthritic" in his joints. On Tuesday, Turnbough began attempting to contact Ladner to inform her of his symptoms. He continued to make attempts to contact her throughout the week, finally reaching her on Friday. Ladner advised Turnbough to call a diver's hotline, which in turn instructed him to seek medical attention at a dive hospital. Turnbough received treatment for decompression sickness at the Jo Ellen Smith Hospital in New Orleans. Turnbough states that he was told by the doctors at the hospital who ran the dive profile that the dive was too long, and there should have been a decompression stop before the divers surfaced. He further states that he was told that he could never dive again. Tom Ebro, an expert in water safety and scuba diving, opined that Ladner was negligent in planning the depths of the dives as well as in failing to make safety stops and that these errors significantly increased the risk that her students might suffer decompression illness.

On February 10, 1995, Turnbough filed suit against Ladner. In his complaint, Turnbough alleged that Ladner was negligent in her supervision of the dive and in exposing him to decompression injury. Ladner filed a motion for summary judgment on October 27, 1995, based on the release Turnbough had signed. The circuit court granted the motion, and dismissed the case.

Turnbough appealed, asserting that the release should be declared void as against public policy, and the case was assigned to the Court of Appeals. The Court of Appeals found that the release was a contract of a purely personal nature and did not violate Mississippi public policy because scuba diving does not implicate a public concern. We subsequently granted certiorari.

The law does not look with favor on contracts intended to exculpate a party from the liability of his or her own negligence although, with some exceptions, they are enforceable. However, such agreements are subject to close judicial scrutiny and are not upheld unless the intention of the parties is expressed in clear and unmistakable language.

The wording of an exculpatory agreement should express as clearly and precisely as possible the *extent* to which a party intends to be absolved from liability. Failing that, we do not sanction broad, general "waiver of negligence" provisions, and strictly construe them against the party asserting them as a defense.

In further determining the extent of exemption from liability in releases, this Court has looked to the intention of the parties in light of the circumstances existing at the time of the instrument's execution. The affidavit of Tom Ebro, an expert in water safety and scuba diving, shows that the alleged negligent acts on which Turnbough's claim is based could not have been contemplated by the parties. Ebro stated that Ladner's instruction fell "woefully short" of minimally acceptable standards of scuba instruction. Specifically, he averred that Ladner negligently planned the depths of the dives and failed to make safety stops which significantly increased the risk of decompression illness, especially with a student class. Assuming Turnbough was aware of the inherent risks in scuba diving, it does not reasonably follow that he, a student, intended to waive his right to recover from Ladner for failing to follow even the most basic industry safety standards. This is especially true since Ladner, who held herself out as an expert scuba instructor and is presumed to have superior knowledge, is the very one on whom Turnbough depended for safety. In this case it appears that Ladner may have miscalculated the amount of time for the dive or may have failed to take into account previous dives. This is important because nitrogen builds up in the body while underwater and, with too much nitrogen, the "bends" and permanent damage including loss of life may occur. Surely it cannot be said from the language of the agreement that Turnbough intended to accept any heightened exposure to injury caused by the malfeasance of an expert instructor. Turnbough, by executing the release, did not knowingly waive his right to seek recovery for injuries caused by Ladner's failure to follow basic safety guidelines that should be common knowledge to any instructor of novice students.

We have held in *Quinn* that contracts attempting to limit the liabilities of one of the parties would not "be enforced unless the limitation is fairly and honestly negotiated and understood by both parties." Quinn v. Mississippi State Univ., 720 So. 2d 843, 851 (Miss. 1998). In this case, Turnbough signed a pre-printed contract, the terms of which were not negotiated. Since the contract was not negotiated and contained a broad waiver of negligence provision, the terms of the contract should be strictly construed against the party seeking to enforce such a provision.

Although waivers are commonly used and necessary for some activities and the attendant risks and hazards associated with them, those who wish to relieve themselves from responsibility associated with a lack of due care or negligence should do so in specific and unmistakable terms. The agreement in this case fails to do that.

We therefore reverse the judgment of the Court of Appeals and the trial court's summary judgment and we remand this case to the trial court for further proceedings consistent with this opinion.

NOTES TO WAGENBLAST v. ODESSA SCHOOL DISTRICT AND TURNBOUGH v. LADNER

1. *Express Assumption of Risk in Torts and Contracts.* Express assumptions of risk raise two questions also raised in contract law: Will the court enforce agreements in the factual setting involved in the case? And, is the particular contract enforceable? Contracts contrary to public policy, such as a promise to pay money for another to commit murder, are unenforceable. *Wagenblast* identifies factors used to determine whether releases, also called exculpatory clauses when found in contracts, are contrary to public policy for some activities. Releases signed under conditions that do not provide the potential plaintiff with an informed, voluntary choice or that contain oppressive terms are unenforceable even if a proper agreement would be acceptable under the public policy analysis. *Turnbough* is such a case.

2. *Injuries to Children.* In Scott v. Pacific West Mountain Resort, 834 P.2d 6 (Wash. 1992), the Washington Supreme Court held that a parent has no right to waive a child's right to sue. A small number of other states have also taken this position. Since a child's own contract not to sue would be unenforceable, what options remain for a business that would like to have children participate in a risky activity?

Problems
Express Assumption of Risk

In the following cases, how would a court likely treat the validity of the assumption of risk agreements, in terms of general public policy and the specific details of each release?

A. The adult plaintiff brought suit alleging malpractice on the part of two physicians employed by the charitable hospital to which the plaintiff had been admitted. The plaintiff at the time of signing the release was in great pain, under sedation, and probably unable to read. The release stated:

> RELEASE: The hospital is a nonprofit, charitable institution. In consideration of the hospital and allied services to be rendered and the rates charged therefor, the patient or his legal representative agrees to and hereby releases. The Regents of the University of California, and the hospital from any and all liability for the negligent or wrongful acts or omissions of its employees, if the hospital has used due care in selecting its employees.

See Tunkl v. Regents of Univ. of Cal., 383 P.2d 441 (Cal. 1963).

B. The adult victim was injured while snowtubing at a ski resort. His right foot became caught between his snow tube and the man-made bank of the snowtubing run, resulting in serious injuries that required multiple surgeries to repair. He signed the following release before participating in the activity:

> SNOWTUBING RELEASE FROM LIABILITY PLEASE READ CAREFULLY BEFORE SIGNING . . . .
>
> "1. I understand that there are inherent risks involved in snowtubing, including the risk of serious physical injury or death and I fully assume all risks associated with [s]nowtubing, even if due to the NEGLIGENCE of White Water Mountain Resorts of Connecticut, Inc., d/b/a Powder Ridge Ski Area and its Affiliates, Officers, Directors, Agents, Servants and/or Employees, including but not limited to: variations in the snow conditions; steepness and terrain; the presence of ice, moguls, bare spots and objects beneath the snowtubing surface such as rocks, debris and tree stumps; collisions with objects both on and off the snowtubing chutes such as hay bales, trees, rocks, snowmaking equipment, barriers, lift cables and equipment, lift towers, lift attendants, employees, volunteers, other patrons and spectators or their property; equipment or lift condition or failure; lack of safety devices or inadequate safety devices; lack of warnings or inadequate warnings; lack of instructions or inadequate instructions; use of any lift; and the like.

The victim has come into your law office for advice about a possible lawsuit against the ski resort. From his story, it seems possible the resort behaved negligently by failing to groom the snow tubing run so as to direct patrons away from the sidewalls. What do you advise the victim about the likely enforceability of the release he signed? See Hanks v. Powder Ridge Restaurant Corporation, 885 A.2d 734 (Conn. 2005).

C. Plaintiff Larry Cornell slipped and fell on a patch of ice in the parking lot of the Royal Hawaiian Condominium in Ocean City, Maryland, on December 31, 1993. Plaintiff owned a unit at the Royal Hawaiian that he used as a vacation home. Plaintiff has now sued the condominium's governing body and various individuals and corporations involved in the design, construction, and maintenance of the condominium, alleging that the defendants were negligent in the maintenance and design of the Royal Hawaiian, resulting in faulty drainage leading to the ice formation that caused his injuries. The condominium council alleges plaintiff waived his right to sue it for failure to maintain the premises when he became a unit owner, which automatically enrolled him in the council and subjected him to its bylaws, which limit the council's liability for personal injuries. The release was contained in the bylaws of the condominium association, of which Cornell was a member:

> Limitation of Liability. The Council shall not be liable . . . for injury or damage to persons or property caused by the elements, or by the Unit Owner of any unit, or any other person, or resulting from electricity, water, snow, or ice, which may leak or flow from any portion of the general or limited common elements, or from any pipe, drain, conduit, appliance, or equipment.

See Cornell v. Council of Unit Owners Hawaiian Village Condominiums, Inc, 983 F. Supp. 640 (D. Md. 1997).

Statute: EXPRESS ASSUMPTION OF RISK
Ohio Stat. §4171.09 (2017)

The general assembly recognizes that roller skating as a recreational sport can be hazardous to roller skaters regardless of all feasible safety measures that can be taken. Therefore, roller skaters are deemed to have knowledge of and to expressly assume the risks of and legal responsibility for any losses, damages, or injuries that result from contact with other roller skaters or spectators, injuries that result from falls caused by loss of balance, and injuries that involve objects or artificial structures properly within the intended path of travel of the roller skater, which are not otherwise attributable to an operator's breach of his duties pursuant to sections 4171.06 and 4171.07 of the Revised Code [describing safety measures the operator is obliged to take].

Statute: WAIVER OF LIABILITY
Haw. Stat. §663-10.95(a) (2017)

(a) Any waiver and release, waiver of liability, or indemnity agreement in favor of an owner, lessor, lessee, operator, or promoter of a motorsports facility, which releases or waives any claim by a participant or anyone claiming on behalf of the participant which is signed by the participant in any motor sports or sports event involving motorsports in the State, shall be valid and enforceable against any negligence claim for personal injury of the participant or anyone claiming on behalf of and for the participant against the motorsports facility, or the owner, operator, or promoter of a motorsports facility. The waiver and release shall be valid notwithstanding any claim that the participant did not read, understand, or comprehend the waiver and release, waiver of liability, or indemnity agreement if the waiver or release is signed by both the participant and a witness; provided that a waiver and release, waiver of liability, or indemnity agreement executed pursuant to this section shall not be enforceable against the rights of any minor, unless executed in writing by a parent or legal guardian.

NOTES TO STATUTES

1. *Legislative Solutions to Judicial Invalidation of Waivers.* Legislatures have responded in various ways to claims by operators of public facilities that they could not reasonably operate their facilities without enforceable waivers of liability. How does the Ohio approach to protecting operators of roller skating arenas differ from Hawaii's approach to protecting operators of motorsports facilities? Which provides greater protection?

2. *Judicial Enforceability of Waivers.* Would a waiver signed under the conditions described in the Hawaii statute be enforceable under the rules described in *Wagenblast* and *Turnbough*?

B. Implied Assumption of Risk

Tort law recognizes two kinds of implied assumption of risk. One is *primary implied assumption of risk.* This doctrine has nothing to do with an individual's knowledge of risks or interest in giving up the ability to sue for injuries. It describes situations in which a court concludes or a statute states that the defendant has no duty to the plaintiff or has not breached a duty to the plaintiff. This doctrine is treated in more detail in Chapter 11.

Secondary implied assumption of risk requires a subjective test of whether the plaintiff actually knew and appreciated the risk created by the defendant's wrongful conduct and voluntarily accepted the risk. This doctrine serves as a defense for a defendant who would otherwise be liable for tortious conduct. Primary implied assumption of risk, by contrast, is an argument that the defendant did not breach a duty to the plaintiff. While secondary implied assumption of risk is a defense, primary implied assumption of risk is a rebuttal to the plaintiff's arguments for duty and breach.

Traditionally, contributory negligence and secondary implied assumption of risk were complete bars to recovery. Schroyer v. McNeal distinguishes between the contributory negligence and the secondary implied assumption of risk defenses, in a traditional contributory negligence jurisdiction. Davenport v. Cotton Hope Plantation Horizontal Property Regime discusses how express assumption of risk, primary implied assumption of risk, and secondary implied assumption of risk should be treated in comparative negligence jurisdictions.

SCHROYER v. McNEAL

592 A.2d 1119 (Md. 1991)

ROBERT M. BELL, J.

The genesis of this case was a slip and fall accident which occurred on the parking lot of the Grantsville Holiday Inn in Garrett County, Maryland. Frances C. McNeal (McNeal), the respondent, sustained a broken ankle in the accident and, as a result, sued Thomas Edward Schroyer and his wife, Patricia A. Schroyer (the Schroyers), the petitioners, in the Circuit Court for Garrett County, alleging both that they negligently maintained the parking lot and negligently failed to warn her of its condition. The jury having returned a verdict in favor of McNeal for $50,000.00 and their motion for judgment notwithstanding the verdict or for new trial having been denied, the Schroyers appealed to the Court of Special Appeals, which affirmed. In its opinion, the intermediate appellate court directly addressed the Schroyers's primary negligence and McNeal's contributory negligence; however, although it was properly presented, that court did not specifically address whether McNeal had assumed the risk of her injury. We issued the writ of certiorari at the request of the Schroyers and now reverse. We hold that, as a matter of law, McNeal assumed the risk of the injury. . . .

The events surrounding McNeal's accident and her subsequent complaint against the Schroyers are largely not in dispute. McNeal arrived at the Grantsville Holiday Inn at approximately 5:30 p.m. on January 9, 1985. At that time, although approximately four inches of sleet and ice had accumulated, she observed that the area in front of, and surrounding, the main lobby area, where hotel guests registered, had been shoveled and, thus, was reasonably clear of ice and snow. She also noticed, however, that the rest of the parking lot had neither been shoveled nor otherwise cleared of the ice and snow. McNeal parked her car in front of the hotel while she registered. While registering, she requested a room closest to an exit due to her need to "cart" boxes and paperwork back and forth to her room. She was assigned a room close to the west side entrance, which was at the far end of the hall, away from the lobby. This was done notwithstanding the hotel's policy of not assigning such rooms during inclement weather. Also, contrary to policy, McNeal was not advised that she should not use the west entrance and, of course, no warnings to that effect were posted near that entrance.

Having registered, McNeal drove her car from the main entrance to within ten to fifteen feet of the west side entrance. She parked on packed ice and snow. Moreover, as she got out of her car, she noticed that the sidewalk near the entrance had not been shoveled and, furthermore, that the area was slippery. Nevertheless, she removed her cat from the car and crossed the ice and snow carefully, and without mishap. On the return trip to her car to retrieve the remainder of her belongings, she slipped and fell, sustaining the injury previously described.

Concerning her knowledge of the parking lot's condition, McNeal testified that, in the immediate vicinity of where she parked her car, the "packed ice and snow" was slippery and that, as a result, she entered the building "carefully." She denied, however, that it was unreasonable for her, under the circumstances, to try to traverse the parking lot; she "didn't think it was that slippery. I didn't slip the first time in."

The Schroyers moved for judgment, both at the end of McNeal's case in chief and at the conclusion of all the evidence. That McNeal had assumed the risk of her injury was one of the grounds advanced in support of those motions. Both motions were denied. The jury having returned its verdict in favor of McNeal, the Schroyers filed a motion for judgment notwithstanding the verdict or a new trial. As in the case of the motions for judgment, they argued, *inter alia*, that respondent was barred from recovery by the doctrine of assumption of the risk. The trial court denied that motion.

. . . [T]he Court of Special Appeals did not directly address whether McNeal assumed the risk of injury. Although it recognized that she "knew of the dangerous condition" and, presumably, acted voluntarily when she started to cross the ice and snow covered parking lot and sidewalk, the court perceived the question to be "whether she acted reasonably under the circumstances." It concluded that whether McNeal was contributorily negligent, *i.e.*, acted reasonably in light of the known risk, was a question appropriately left to the jury for decision.

Assumption of the risk and contributory negligence are closely related and often overlapping defenses. They may arise from the same facts and, in a given case, a decision as to one may necessarily include the other.

The relationship between the defenses has also been addressed in the Restatement (Second) of Torts:

> The same conduct on the part of the plaintiff may . . . amount to both assumption of risk and contributory negligence, and may subject him to both defenses. His conduct in accepting the risk may be unreasonable and thus negligent, because the danger is out of all proportion to the interest he is seeking to advance, as where he consents to ride with a drunken driver in an unlighted car on a dark night, or dashes into a burning building to save his hat. Likewise, even after accepting an entirely reasonable risk, he may fail to exercise reasonable care for his own protection against that risk.

§496A, comment d, at 562. The overlap between assumption of the risk and contributory negligence is a complete one where "the plaintiff's conduct in voluntarily encountering a known risk is itself unreasonable. . . ." §496A, comment c4. When that occurs, the bar to recovery is two-pronged: 1) because the plaintiff assumed the risk of injury and 2) because the plaintiff was contributorily negligent.

There is, however, a distinction, and an important one, between the defenses of assumption of the risk and contributory negligence. That distinction was stated in *Warner v. Markoe*, 189 A. 260, 264 (Md. 1937), thusly:

> The distinction between contributory negligence and voluntary assumption of the risk is often difficult to draw in concrete cases, and under the law of this state usually without importance, but it may be well to keep it in mind. Contributory negligence, of course, means negligence which contributes to cause a particular accident which occurs, while assumption of risk of accident means voluntary incurring that of an accident which may not occur, and which the person assuming the risk may be careful to avoid after starting. Contributory negligence defeats recovery because it is a proximate cause of the accident which happens, but assumption of the risk defeats recovery because it is a previous abandonment of the right to complain if an accident occurs.

The distinction is no less clearly made by reference to the rationale underlying the doctrine of assumption of the risk. We explicated that rationale in *Gibson v. Beaver*, 226 A.2d 273, 275 (1967) (quoting W. Prosser, *Handbook of the Law of Torts* §55 at 303 (2nd ed. 1955)):

> The defense of assumption of risk rests upon the plaintiff's consent to relieve the defendant of an obligation of conduct toward him, and to take his chances of harm from a particular risk. Such consent may be found: . . . by implication from the conduct of the parties. When the plaintiff enters voluntarily into a relation or situation involving obvious danger, he may be taken to assume the risk, and to relieve the defendant of responsibility. Such implied assumption of risk requires knowledge and appreciation of the risk, and a voluntary choice to encounter it.

. . . While, ordinarily, application of either defense will produce the same result, that is not always the case. Especially is that so in the instant case. The record reflects, and the Court of Special Appeals held, a matter not in dispute on this appeal, that McNeal was fully aware of the dangerous condition of the premises. She knew that the area was ice and snow covered and that the ice and snow were slippery. Nevertheless, she parked in the area and, notwithstanding, according to her testimony, that she proceeded carefully, she took a chance and walked over the ice and snow covered parking lot and sidewalk because she did not think it was "that" slippery.

It is clear, on this record, that McNeal took an informed chance. Fully aware of the danger posed by an ice and snow covered parking lot and sidewalk, she voluntarily chose to park and traverse it, *albeit* carefully, for her own purposes, *i.e.,* her convenience in unloading her belongings. Assuming that the decision to park on the ice and snow covered parking lot and to cross it and the sidewalk was not, itself, contributory negligence, McNeal's testimony as to how she proceeded may well have generated a jury question as to the reasonableness of her actions. On the other hand it cannot be gainsaid that she intentionally exposed herself to a known risk. With full knowledge that the parking lot and sidewalk were ice and snow covered and aware that the ice and snow were slippery, McNeal voluntarily chose to park on the parking lot and to walk across it and the sidewalk, thus indicating her willingness to accept the risk and relieving the Schroyers of responsibility for her safety. Consequently, while the issue of her contributory negligence may well have been for the jury, the opposite is true with respect to her assumption of the risk. We hold, as a matter of law, that McNeal assumed the risk of her own injuries.

Judgment of the Court of Special Appeals Reversed and case remanded to that court with directions to reverse the judgment of the Circuit Court for Garrett County. . . .

NOTES TO SCHROYER v. McNEAL

1. *Comparing Contributory Negligence and Assumption of Risk.* The defense of secondary implied assumption of risk requires that the defendant prove that the plaintiff had subjective actual knowledge of the risk, had subjective actual appreciation of its nature and extent, and voluntarily accepted it. The defense of contributory negligence is objective; it requires the defendant to prove only that the plaintiff *should have* known of the risk and that a reasonable person would not have behaved as the plaintiff behaved.

2. *Overlap Between Contributory Negligence and Assumption of Risk.* The opinion in *Schroyer* points out that both defenses may apply in cases where (1) the plaintiff knew and appreciated and voluntarily accepted the risk and (2) a reasonable person either would not have accepted the risk or, having done so, would not have behaved as the plaintiff behaved. If a person drives just at the posted speed limit on an icy, snowy road to get to a video rental store before it closes, knowing of road conditions and appreciating the risk losing control on the ice and crashing, she might be assuming a risk that a reasonable person would not assume. Both defenses would apply. But if that person drove the same way while rushing to a hospital in a life-or-death emergency, she might not be found to be contributorily negligent. Nevertheless, in a traditional contributory negligence jurisdiction like *Schroyer*, her recovery would be barred by secondary implied assumption of risk even though her conduct was reasonable.

3. *Reasonable and Unreasonable Assumption of Risk.* The type of assumption of risk illustrated in *Schroyer* is often called *secondary unqualified implied assumption of risk*. It bars or reduces a plaintiff's recovery even if the plaintiff acted reasonably. Even before the advent of comparative negligence, some jurisdictions, unlike Maryland (the jurisdiction in *Schroyer*), added a fourth requirement to the defense of secondary implied

assumption of risk. In addition to showing that the plaintiff (1) knew of the risk, (2) appreciated the nature of extent of the risk, and (3) voluntarily exposed herself to the risk, the defendant was also required to show that (4) it was objectively unreasonable for the plaintiff to expose herself to the risk. Assumption of risk with this fourth element added is sometimes called *secondary qualified assumption of risk.* The "qualification" is that the assumption of risk must be unreasonable for plaintiff's recovery to be barred.

The secondary qualified assumption of risk defense is very similar to the defense of contributory negligence. Although differences remain (i.e., the first three elements), every case in which the defense of secondary qualified assumption of risk applies is also a case in which the defense of contributory negligence applies. This complete overlap has led some jurisdictions to abandon the secondary implied assumption of risk terminology. See, e.g., Meistrich v. Casino Arena Attractions, Inc., 155 A.2d 90, 96 (N.J. 1959) ("We are satisfied there is no reason to charge assumption of risk in its secondary sense as something distinct from contributory negligence and hence . . . the terminology should not be used.").

DAVENPORT v. COTTON HOPE PLANTATION HORIZONTAL PROPERTY REGIME

508 S.E.2d 565 (S.C. 1998)

TOAL, J. . . .

Alvin Davenport is a resident of Cotton Hope Plantation located on Hilton Head Island. The plantation is organized under state law as Cotton Hope Plantation Horizontal Regime ("Cotton Hope"). Cotton Hope is composed of ninety-six condominium units located in multiple buildings. Each building consists of three levels. The buildings have three stairways each, one in the middle and two on either side. Davenport's unit is on the top level, approximately five feet from a stairway. Davenport leases his unit from the owner.

Cotton Hope employed Property Administrators, Incorporated ("PAI") to maintain the grounds at Cotton Hope Plantation. In April 1991, PAI, as Cotton Hope's agent, hired Carson Landscaping Company, Inc., ("Carson") to perform landscaping and general maintenance work at the condominiums. Carson's duties included checking the outdoor lights and changing light bulbs as needed. . . .

In June 1991, Davenport began reporting that the floodlights at the bottom of the stairway he used were not working. Davenport testified he made several phone calls to PAI complaining about the problem. Davenport nevertheless continued to use the stairway during this time. On the evening of August 12, 1991, Davenport fell while descending the stairway closest to his apartment. Davenport testified he fell after attempting to place his foot on what appeared to be a step but was really a shadow caused by the broken floodlights. He admitted not using the handrail in the stairway.

Davenport sued Cotton Hope for his injuries. . . . At the close of all the evidence, the trial court directed a verdict against Davenport, finding he had assumed the risk of injury. The trial court also held that even if assumption of risk were abrogated by the adoption of comparative negligence, Davenport was more than fifty-percent negligent. [Davenport appealed.]

[T]he Court of Appeals held that assumption of risk had been subsumed by South Carolina's adoption of comparative negligence. As such, assumption of risk was no longer a complete defense to a negligence claim but, instead, was simply another factor to consider in comparing the parties' negligence. The court ruled that the relative negligence of Davenport and Cotton Hope turned on factual considerations which should have been submitted to the jury. . . .

This Court granted Cotton Hope's petition for a writ of certiorari. . . .

The threshold question we must answer is whether assumption of risk survives as a complete bar to recovery under South Carolina's comparative negligence system. In Nelson v. Concrete Supply Company, 303 S.C. 243, 399 S.E.2d 783 (1991), we adopted a modified version of comparative negligence. Under this system, "for all causes of action arising on or after July 1, 1991, a plaintiff in a negligence action may recover damages if his or her negligence is not greater than that of the defendant." *Nelson* made clear that a plaintiff's contributory negligence would no longer bar recovery unless such negligence exceeded that of the defendant. Not so clear was what would become of the defense of assumption of risk. . . .

Currently in South Carolina, there are four requirements to establishing the defense of assumption of risk: (1) the plaintiff must have knowledge of the facts constituting a dangerous condition; (2) the plaintiff must know the condition is dangerous; (3) the plaintiff must appreciate the nature and extent of the danger; and (4) the plaintiff must voluntarily expose himself to the danger. Senn v. Sun Printing Co., 295 S.C. 169, 367 S.E.2d 456 (Ct. App. 1988). "The doctrine is predicated on the factual situation of a defendant's acts alone creating the danger and causing the accident, with the plaintiff's act being that of voluntarily exposing himself to such an obvious danger with appreciation thereof which resulted in the injury."

Assumption of risk may be implied from the plaintiff's conduct.

[A]n overwhelming majority of jurisdictions that have adopted some form of comparative negligence have essentially abolished assumption of risk as an absolute bar to recovery. In analyzing the continuing viability of assumption of risk in a comparative negligence system, many courts distinguish between "express" assumption of risk and "implied" assumption of risk. See W. Page Keeton et al., Prosser and Keeton on the Law of Torts, §68 at 496 (5th ed. 1984). Implied assumption of risk is further divided into the categories of "primary" and "secondary" implied assumption of risk. We will discuss each of these concepts below.

Express assumption of risk applies when the parties expressly agree in advance, either in writing or orally, that the plaintiff will relieve the defendant of his or her legal duty toward the plaintiff. Thus, being under no legal duty, the defendant cannot be charged with negligence. Even in those comparative fault jurisdictions that have abrogated assumption of risk, the rule remains that express assumption of risk continues as an absolute defense in an action for negligence. The reason for this is that express assumption of risk sounds in contract, not tort, and is based upon an express manifestation of consent. . . .

Express assumption of risk is contrasted with implied assumption of risk which arises when the plaintiff implicitly, rather than expressly, assumes known risks. As noted above, implied assumption of risk is characterized as either primary or secondary. Primary implied assumption of risk arises when the plaintiff impliedly assumes those risks that are *inherent* in a particular activity. See, e.g., Fortier v. Los Rios Community College Dist., 45 Cal. App. 4th 430 (1996) (student injured in a collision during football drill); Swagger v. City of Crystal, 379 N.W.2d 183 (Minn. App. 1985) (injured while watching softball game). Primary implied assumption of risk is not a true affirmative defense, but instead goes to the initial determination of whether the defendant's legal duty encompasses the risk encountered by the plaintiff. E.g., Perez v. McConkey, 872 S.W.2d 897 (Tenn. 1994). In *Perez*, the Tennessee Supreme Court summarized the doctrine in the following way:

> In its primary sense, implied assumption of risk focuses not on the plaintiff's conduct in assuming the risk, but on the defendant's general duty of care. . . . Clearly, primary implied assumption of risk is but another way of stating the conclusion that a plaintiff has failed to establish a prima facie case [of negligence] by failing to establish that a duty exists.

In this sense, primary implied assumption of risk is simply a part of the initial negligence analysis.

Secondary implied assumption of risk, on the other hand, arises when the plaintiff knowingly encounters a risk created by the defendant's negligence. It is a true defense because it is asserted only after the plaintiff establishes a prima facie case of negligence against the defendant. Secondary implied assumption of risk may involve either reasonable or unreasonable conduct on the part of the plaintiff. In Litchfield Company of South Carolina, Inc. v. Sur-Tech, Inc., 289 S.C. 247, 249, 345 S.E.2d 765, 766 (Ct. App. 1986), the Court of Appeals illustrated secondary "unreasonable" implied assumption of risk:

> The conduct of a plaintiff in assuming a risk may itself be unreasonable and thus negligent because the risk he assumes is out of all proportion to the advantage which he is seeking to gain. For example, if a plaintiff dashed into a fire in order to save his hat, it might well be argued that he both assumed the risk of being injured and that he acted unreasonably. *In such cases, a defendant can maintain both defenses.*[4]

Since express and primary implied assumption of risk are compatible with comparative negligence, we will refer to secondary implied assumption of risk simply as "assumption of risk."

[A]ssumption of risk and contributory negligence have historically been recognized as separate defenses in South Carolina. However, other courts have found assumption of risk functionally indistinguishable from contributory negligence and consequently abolished assumption of risk as a complete defense.

To date, the only comparative fault jurisdictions that have retained assumption of risk as an absolute defense are Georgia, Mississippi, Nebraska, Rhode Island, and South Dakota. Only the Rhode Island Supreme Court has provided a detailed discussion of why it believes the common law form of assumption of risk should survive under comparative negligence. In Kennedy v. Providence Hockey Club, Inc., 119 R.I. 70, 376 A.2d 329 (R.I. 1977), the Rhode Island Supreme Court distinguished between assumption of risk and contributory negligence, emphasizing the former was measured by a subjective standard while the latter was based on an objective, reasonable person standard. The court further noted that it had in the past limited the application of assumption of risk to those situations where the plaintiff had actual knowledge of the hazard. The court then rejected the premise that assumption of risk and contributory negligence overlap:

> Contributory negligence and assumption of the risk do not overlap; the key difference is, of course, the exercise of one's free will in encountering the risk. Negligence

---

[4] Reasonable implied assumption of risk exists when the plaintiff is aware of a risk negligently created by the defendant but, nonetheless, voluntarily proceeds to encounter the risk; when weighed against the risk of injury, the plaintiff's action is reasonable.

analysis, couched in reasonable hypotheses, has no place in the assumption of the risk framework. When one acts knowingly, it is immaterial whether he acts reasonably.

Rhode Island's conclusions are in sharp contrast with the West Virginia Supreme Court's opinion in King v. Kayak Manufacturing Corp., 182 W. Va. 276, 387 S.E.2d 511 (W. Va. 1989). Like Rhode Island, the West Virginia Supreme Court in *King* recognized that assumption of risk was conceptually distinct from contributory negligence. The court specifically noted that West Virginia's doctrine of assumption of risk required actual knowledge of the dangerous condition, which conformed with the general rule elsewhere in the country. In fact, the court cited Rhode Island's decision in *Kennedy* as evidence of this general rule. Nevertheless, the West Virginia court concluded that the absolute defense of assumption of risk was incompatible with its comparative fault system. The court therefore adopted a *comparative assumption of risk* rule, stating, "a plaintiff is not barred from recovery by the doctrine of assumption of risk unless his degree of fault arising therefrom equals or exceeds the combined fault or negligence of the other parties to the accident." The court explained that the absolute defense of assumption of risk was as repugnant to its fault system as the common law rule of contributory negligence.

A comparison between the approaches in West Virginia and Rhode Island is informative. Both jurisdictions recognize that assumption of risk is conceptually distinct from contributory negligence. However, Rhode Island focuses on the objective/ subjective distinction between the two defenses and, therefore, retains assumption of risk as a complete bar to recovery. On the other hand, West Virginia emphasizes that the main purpose of its comparative negligence system is to apportion fault. Thus, West Virginia rejects assumption of risk as a total bar to recovery and only allows a jury to consider the plaintiff's negligence in assuming the risk. If the plaintiff's total negligence exceeds or equals that of the defendant, only then is the plaintiff completely barred from recovery.

Like Rhode Island and West Virginia, South Carolina has historically maintained a distinction between assumption of risk and contributory negligence, even when the two doctrines appear to overlap. Thus, the pertinent question is whether a plaintiff should be completely barred from recovery when he voluntarily assumes a known risk, regardless of whether his assumption of that risk was reasonable or unreasonable. Upon considering the purpose of our comparative fault system, we conclude that West Virginia's approach is the most persuasive model.

In *Nelson*, we adopted . . . the following justification for adopting a comparative negligence system: "It is contrary to the basic premise of our fault system to allow a defendant, who is at fault in causing an accident, to escape bearing any of its cost, while requiring a plaintiff, who is no more than equally at fault or even less at fault, to bear all of its costs." By contrast, the main reason for having the defense of assumption of risk is not to determine fault, but to prevent a person who knowingly and voluntarily incurs a risk of harm from holding another person liable. Cotton Hope argues that the justification behind assumption of risk is not in conflict with South Carolina's comparative fault system. We disagree.

[I]t is contrary to the premise of our comparative fault system to require a plaintiff, who is fifty-percent or less at fault, to bear all of the costs of the injury. In accord with this logic, the defendant's fault in causing an accident is not diminished solely because the plaintiff knowingly assumes a risk. If assumption of risk is retained in its current common law form, a plaintiff would be completely barred from recovery even if his conduct is reasonable or only slightly unreasonable. In our comparative fault system, it would be incongruous to absolve the defendant of all liability based only on whether the plaintiff assumed the risk of injury. Comparative negligence by definition seeks to assess and compare the negligence of both the plaintiff and defendant. This goal would clearly be thwarted by adhering to the common law defense of assumption of risk. . . .

We therefore hold that a plaintiff is not barred from recovery by the doctrine of assumption of risk unless the degree of fault arising therefrom is greater than the negligence of the defendant. To the extent that any prior South Carolina cases are inconsistent with this approach, they are overruled. Express and primary implied assumption of risk remain unaffected by our decision. . . .

Based on the foregoing, the Court of Appeals' decision is affirmed as modified.

NOTES TO DAVENPORT v. COTTON HOPE PLANTATION HORIZONTAL PROPERTY REGIME

1. *Secondary Implied Distinguished from Primary Implied Assumption of Risk.* The doctrine of primary assumption of risk is discussed in Chapter 11. Under the doctrine of primary implied assumption of risk, a defendant has no duty to take precautions to prevent a risk that is inherent in its activity. "Inherent" means that the risks are obvious (in the objective sense that reasonable people know about them) and necessary (in the sense that the cost of avoiding the risk outweighs the benefit of doing so). The doctrine of secondary implied assumption of risk applies to those risks created by the defendant that are not necessary — in fact, it was negligent (or reckless) for the defendant to create those risks.

2. *Treatment of Careful and Careless Victims.* Suppose a plaintiff *saw a dangerous condition* on a defendant's property, understood the risk, voluntarily encountered it, and was hurt. In the small number of comparative negligence jurisdictions that recognize implied secondary assumption of risk, if the plaintiff established that the defendant had been negligent in creating that condition, could the plaintiff recover damages? Could the plaintiff recover in a jurisdiction like South Carolina or other comparative negligence jurisdictions that adopt the majority approach?

Suppose a plaintiff *carelessly failed to see a dangerous condition* on a defendant's property and then was hurt by the condition. In the small number of comparative negligence jurisdictions that recognize implied secondary assumption of risk, if the plaintiff established that the defendant had been negligent in creating that condition, could the plaintiff recover damages? Could the plaintiff recover in a jurisdiction like South Carolina or other comparative negligence jurisdictions that adopt the majority approach?

Giving a careless victim better treatment than a careful victim is the result in the minority jurisdictions, criticized in *Davenport.*

Problems
Implied Assumption of Risk

A. In Kirk v. Washington State University, 746 P.2d 285 (Wash. 1987), the Washington Supreme Court considered whether primary or secondary assumption of risk applied to the claims of a cheerleader who had sued her university to recover for injuries sustained while she was practicing cheerleading on an allegedly dangerous surface and without adequate supervision. Does this appear to be a case where the doctrines of primary or secondary implied assumption of risk would apply? What are the inherent risks in the sport of cheerleading? Are these the risks that the plaintiff encountered?

B. In Scott v. Pacific West Mountain Resort, 834 P.2d 6, 13 (Wash. 1992), the plaintiff, a 12-year-old boy, was injured while he was attending a ski school at a ski resort. As he was practicing a slalom race, he veered off the race course and ran into an unused tow-rope shack that was allegedly positioned too close to the slalom course. The plaintiff sued the ski area, alleging that his injuries were caused by negligent provision of dangerous facilities. Is this a case where primary or secondary implied assumption of risk applies?

IV. Mitigation and Avoidable Consequences

A plaintiff who is hurt can seek medical attention to mitigate the extent of the harm after an accident. Wearing a seatbelt is something a plaintiff can do *before* encountering a defendant's injurious conduct that can protect against some of the harm that conduct might otherwise have inflicted. Miller v. Eichhorn and Klanseck v. Anderson Sales and Service, Inc. illustrate contrasting ways courts reduce damages to reflect a plaintiff's post-accident failure to mitigate harm. Law v. Superior Court confronts the issue of whether a vehicular accident plaintiff's failure to use a seatbelt should affect the plaintiff's recovery of damages.

MILLER v. EICHHORN

426 N.W.2d 641 (Iowa Ct. App. 1988)

Sackett, J. . . .

A car driven by Plaintiff-Appellant Connie M. Miller collided with a car driven by Defendant-Appellee Harold Eichhorn. Defendant Gloria Eichhorn was not involved in the collision. The collision occurred when defendant backed his car from his driveway into the street. Plaintiffs sued defendants for injuries Connie allegedly received in the accident. Plaintiff Keith Miller is Connie's husband. His claim was for loss of consortium. The case was tried to a jury which found Connie's damages to be $3,569.70. The jury found no damages for Keith. The jury determined Connie's fault to be fifteen percent and Harold's fault to be eighty-five percent. . . .

Plaintiff . . . challenges the trial court's submission of an instruction on mitigation of damages. Plaintiff objected to the mitigation of damage instruction claiming the failure to mitigate damages is not fault. We disagree. Iowa Comparative Fault Act, Iowa Code section 668.1, provides: "As used in this chapter, . . . the term ["fault"] also includes . . . unreasonable failure to avoid an injury or to mitigate damages." Section 668.3 provides: "In determining the percentages of fault, the trier of fact shall consider both the nature of the conduct of each party and the extent of the causal relation between the conduct and the damages claimed."

The statute clearly provides the unreasonable failure to mitigate damages means fault as used in the statute.

Defendant argues it was not error to give the instruction because there is substantial evidence plaintiff failed to mitigate damages. Defendant also argues there is substantial evidence because plaintiff claimed medical problems and the need to employ substitute labor in her business from the time of the accident to the time of trial. There were periods of time when Connie did not see a doctor regularly. We reject defendant's argument on these grounds. For the failure to consult a doctor on a regular basis to be evidence of failure to mitigate damages there must be a showing consultations on a regular basis would have mitigated damages. Connie's duty is to use ordinary care in consulting a physician. There is, however, testimony by one of Connie's doctors that additional chiropractic treatments would have helped Connie's condition. This evidence supports the submission of the mitigation of damage issue and is evidence from which the jury could find she did not use due care in following her doctor's advice. . . .

We affirm.

KLANSECK v. ANDERSON SALES & SERVICE, INC.
393 N.W.2d 356 (Mich. 1986)

WILLIAMS, J. . . .

Plaintiff, Stephen Klanseck, brought this action, seeking damages for injuries suffered in a motorcycle accident which occurred May 27, 1976. Mr. Klanseck had that day purchased a Honda GL 1000 motorcycle from defendant Anderson Sales & Service, Inc., and was heading for home with his new cycle when the machine began to "fishtail." Plaintiff applied the brakes and the motorcycle slid sideways and went down, resulting in plaintiff's injuries.

Following the accident, plaintiff received sutures in his left arm, was x-rayed and released. Twelve days later, a fracture of plaintiff's right wrist was diagnosed and treated. Plaintiff, who was employed as an auto mechanic, claimed that his injuries resulted in chronic pain and numbness in his left arm and hand, which interfered with his work and eventually resulted in a serious mental disorder. . . .

With regard to plaintiff's alleged failure to mitigate damages, the court gave the following instruction:

> Now, a person has a duty to use ordinary care to minimize his own damages after he has been injured, and it is for you to decide whether the Plaintiff failed to use such ordinary care and, if so, whether any damages resulted from such failure.
>
> You may not compensate the Plaintiff for any portion of his damages which resulted from his failure to use ordinary care.

Plaintiff contends that this instruction was erroneous because no evidence was presented that would create an issue as to plaintiff's failure to mitigate his damages. Defendant points to the testimony of Dr. Gary W. Roat, and claims that it creates an issue on the question of mitigation. Dr. Roat, a neurologist, testified that the plaintiff had come to him on referral from another physician about a year after the accident and that he had treated the plaintiff a number of times for numbness and tingling in his hand as well as back and leg pain. After trying several medications, Dr. Roat recommended that plaintiff undergo additional diagnostic tests, including nerve conduction studies, an electromyelographic examination, and a myelogram to determine whether he had a herniated disk. According to Dr. Roat's testimony, plaintiff decided against taking these tests unless his symptoms worsened.

It is well-settled that an injured party has a duty to exercise reasonable care to minimize damages, including obtaining proper medical or surgical treatment. It is also settled that the charge of the court must be based upon the evidence and should be confined to the issues presented by the evidence.

Although the evidence of plaintiff's alleged failure to mitigate damages was weak, there was evidence that plaintiff had not followed the recommendation of Dr. Roat. Even scant evidence may support an instruction where it raises an issue for the jury's decision. The trial court's instruction on failure to mitigate damages was proper.

Affirmed.

NOTE TO MILLER v. EICHORN AND KLANSECK v. ANDERSON SALES & SERVICE, INC.

Effect on Damage Recovery of Failure to Mitigate. The courts in *Miller* and *Klanseck* adopted different approaches to reducing damages to reflect the failure of the plaintiff to seek proper medical attention. If the plaintiffs in *Miller* and *Klanseck* each had $10,000 total damages, with $3,000 being due to failure to seek proper medical treatment, how much would each collect under each of the rules?

LAW v. SUPERIOR COURT
755 P.2d 1135 (Ariz. 1988)

FELDMAN, J. . . .

On the evening of November 8, 1985, Cindy Law was driving her parents' car in Tempe, Arizona. She apparently pulled in front of an automobile operated by James Harder, who swerved violently to avoid a collision. Unfortunately, his evasive maneuver overturned the Harder vehicle. Harder and his wife were not wearing their seat belts and were thrown from their car — James through a closed sunroof. The Harders suffered severe orthopedic injuries as a result of the accident.

The Harders (plaintiffs) brought a negligence action against Cindy Law and her parents (defendants). During the course of discovery, defendants sought information concerning plaintiffs' use and experience with seat belts and shoulder restraints. Plaintiffs objected to these discovery requests on the grounds that the subject was irrelevant under the holding of Nash v. Kamrath, 521 P.2d 161 (1974). In that case, division two of our court of appeals held that evidence of a passenger's failure to wear a seat belt was inadmissible either to show breach of a duty to minimize damages or to prove contributory negligence. [The trial court ruled that there was no duty to wear seatbelts. In an interlocutory appeal the court of appeals held that evidence of seatbelt non-use could be admissible.]

Given modern-day conditions, we conclude as a matter of public policy that the law must recognize the responsibility of every person to anticipate and take reasonable measures to guard against the danger of motor vehicle accidents that are not only foreseeable but virtually certain to occur sooner or later. Rejection of the seat belt defense can no longer be based on the antediluvian doctrine that one need not anticipate the negligence of others. There is nothing to anticipate; the negligence of motorists is omnipresent. . . .

Nash held there was no duty to wear seat belts. We acknowledge that "duty" to use restraints is generally considered the prime question in cases such as this. . . .

[W]e believe that injuries sustained by the plaintiff as a result of his nonuse of an available seat belt are not so much a failure to use care to avoid endangering others but part of the related obligation to conduct oneself reasonably to minimize damages and avoid foreseeable harm to oneself.

Thus, the seat belt defense would ordinarily raise issues concerning the doctrine of avoidable consequences — a theory that denies recovery for those injuries plaintiff could reasonably have avoided. Plaintiffs argue that this doctrine is applied only to post-accident conduct and is inapplicable to events preceding the accident — a time when plaintiffs supposedly had a right to assume that others would not act negligently. Assuming this is ordinarily true, we believe the common law conceptualization of the doctrine of avoidable consequences has been modified by our comparative negligence statute, which applies that doctrine to pre-accident conduct.

When the Arizona legislature enacted the Uniform Contribution Among Tortfeasors Act in 1984, it added several important provisions to the model law delineated in 12 U.L.A. 63-107 (1975). These new sections constituted the statutory adoption of comparative negligence for our state. In any given case, the relevance of comparative negligence principles is normally a question for the jury. If the jury does apply comparative negligence standards, the plaintiff's action is not barred, "but the full damages shall be reduced in proportion to the relative degree of *fault which is a proximate cause of the injury or death,* if any." A.R.S. §12-2505(A) (emphasis added).

The essential question is whether a plaintiff who does not wear an automobile seat belt is at "fault" for injuries enhanced or caused by the failure to use the seat belt. Neither the Arizona comparative negligence statute nor its progenitor uniform law contains any definition of "fault." We do note the instructive definition of this term given in §1(b) of the Uniform Comparative Fault Act (UCFA), 12 U.L.A. 39-40 (Cum. Supp. 1987).

> "Fault" includes acts or omissions that are in any measure negligent or reckless toward the person or property of the actor or others, or that subject a person to strict tort liability. *The term also includes . . . unreasonable failure to avoid an injury or to mitigate damages.* Legal requirements of causal relation apply both to fault as the basis for liability and to contributory fault.

(Emphasis added.) As stated in the official comment to the UCFA, negligent failure to use a seat belt would reduce damages solely for those injuries directly attributable to the lack of seat belt restraint. Thus, as far as the calculation of damages is concerned, the comparative negligence statutes apply the doctrine of avoidable consequences to pre-accident conduct. . . .

Our examination of the applicable caselaw and our analysis of the concept of "duty" lead us to the conclusion that the seat belt defense is not a question of duty at all. We reject those cases . . . that rely on the absence of "duty" to reject the seat belt defense. We also disapprove the *Nash* analysis. At least under the comparative fault statute, each person is under an obligation to act reasonably to minimize foreseeable injuries and damages. Thus, if a person chooses not to use an available, simple safety device, that person may be at "fault." . . .

Plaintiffs claim that by recognizing the seat belt defense, we would confer a windfall on tortfeasors. As noted ante, the crux of comparative negligence is a proper apportionment of damages based upon the fault of the respective parties. If a victim unreasonably failed to use an available, simple prophylactic device, then he will not be able to recover for damages created or enhanced by the nonuse. Thus, although some tortfeasors may pay less than they otherwise *would*, they will not pay less than they *should*. We do not believe this rule creates a windfall to the tortfeasor; it is an unavoidable consequence of our comparative negligence system.

Petitioners maintain that allowing apportionment of damages based on failure to use seat belts will unnecessarily complicate and protract litigation. The defendant must establish several factual predicates before seat belt nonuse may be presented to the jury. To prove these factors, the defendant may utilize qualified experts in the medical, scientific, and accident reconstruction fields. It is then up to the factfinder to evaluate the evidence and quantify the results under comparative negligence principles.

Of course, this process will take time and create new issues for the jury to decide. These problems are hardly insurmountable. Juries perform this type of operation on a regular basis in many types of civil and criminal cases. The very idea of comparative negligence requires that juries apportion fault. The same is true when juries apportion fault between joint tortfeasors. . . .

There is no doubt that the seat belt defense will complicate and lengthen litigation in some cases. While this certainly does not militate in favor of its acceptance, we believe the problem is no different in principle from that posed by any legal, technological or scientific advance. Neither law nor society can ignore technological change simply because it makes decision more complex.

As the final argument, plaintiffs assert that introducing evidence of seat belt nonuse would propel our courts into a morass of unforeseen consequences. If seat belt nonuse is relevant, why not introduce evidence of failure to install air bags? Why not hold the plaintiff responsible for failure to buy a large car which is normally much safer in a crash than a small car?

We are faced with a concrete application of comparative negligence principles. . . . The exact bounds of fault in other fact situations is a matter for the common law to address in its customary evolutionary fashion. . . .

Within the analytical framework of this opinion, we recognize the seat belt defense as a matter which the jury may consider in apportioning damages due to the "fault" of the plaintiff. Accordingly, in appropriate cases discovery will be available on the issue of nonuse.

We approve the portions of the opinion by the court of appeals that conform to this opinion. This case is remanded to the trial court for further proceedings consistent with our holding.

NOTES TO LAW v. SUPERIOR COURT

1. *Mitigation and Seatbelt Use.* The majority of decisions since *Law* have rejected its position. A South Dakota opinion reflects this trend:

Drivers and other persons in the front seat of passenger vehicles must use seat belts in South Dakota. SDCL 32-38-1 (effective July 1, 1994). However, by statute, proof of failure to wear a seat belt may not be introduced as evidence in any civil litigation on the issue of mitigation of damages. SDCL 32-38-4. As the accident occurred in August 1993, these enactments are inapplicable to this case.

[T]he trial court instructed the jury that it may consider plaintiff's "failure to use a seatbelt as evidence that the plaintiff had failed to avoid or minimize" his injuries.

. . . Accordingly, despite the existence of statutes controlling the issue for future cases, we must decide whether the mitigation doctrine applied to injured plaintiffs not wearing seatbelts before the effective date of these enactments. Whether the doctrine applies to the use of seatbelts is a question of law. On legal questions, this Court is obligated to reach its decision independent of the conclusion reached by the trial court.

A clear majority of states have judicially refused to admit evidence of a plaintiff's nonuse of an available seatbelt as proof of failure to mitigate damages likely to occur in an automobile accident. A few jurisdictions reason a plaintiff's failure to use an available seatbelt can be considered a substantial factor in increasing the harm, but we conclude the better approach rejects this theory.

A duty to mitigate ordinarily arises only after a tortfeasor's negligent act. A plaintiff's "preaccident" failure to fasten an available seat belt contributes nothing to the transpiring of the accident itself. Such omission occurs before a tortfeasor's negligent act and is, therefore, inconsistent with a plaintiff's later burden to minimize damages. . . . The trial court erred when it instructed the jury it may consider Davis's failure to use a seatbelt as evidence he failed to avoid or minimize his injuries.

Davis v. Knippling, 576 N.W.2d 525 (S.D. 1998).

2. *Statutory Treatment of Non-Use of Seatbelt.* Statutory responses to this problem have been varied. South Dakota, for example, prohibits introduction of seatbelt non-use for any purpose. Other states have imposed precise limits on the percentage of responsibility a jury is permitted to assign to a plaintiff's failure to use a seatbelt. See Mo. Rev. Stat. §307.178(4), imposing a 1 percent limit on that responsibility.

Statute: FAULT

Ind. Code §34-6-2-45 (2017)

(a) "Fault," for purposes of IC 34-20 [referring to injuries caused by products], means an act or omission that is negligent, willful, wanton, reckless, or intentional toward the person or property of others. The term includes the following:

(1) Unreasonable failure to avoid an injury or to mitigate damages. . . .

(b) "Fault," for purposes of IC 34-51-2 [referring to comparative negligence], includes any act or omission that is negligent, willful, wanton, reckless, or intentional toward the person or property of others. The term also includes unreasonable assumption of risk not constituting an enforceable express consent, incurred risk, and unreasonable failure to avoid an injury or to mitigate damages.

Statute: FAILURE TO COMPLY; FAULT; LIABILITY OF INSURER; MITIGATION OF DAMAGES

Ind. Code §9-19-10-7 (2017)

(a) Failure to comply with section 1, 2, 3.1(a) [requiring front seat occupants of passenger motor vehicles to wear safety belts] of this chapter does not constitute fault under IC 34-51-2 and does not limit the liability of an insurer.

(b) Except as provided in subsection (c), evidence of the failure to comply with section 1, 2, or 3.1(a) of this chapter may not be admitted in a civil action to mitigate damages.

(c) Evidence of a failure to comply with this chapter may be admitted in a civil action as to mitigation of damages in a product liability action involving a motor vehicle restraint or supplemental restraint system. The defendant in such an action has the burden of proving noncompliance with this chapter and that compliance with this chapter would have reduced injuries, and the extent of the reduction.

NOTES TO STATUTES

1. *Mitigation and Fault.* The statutory option illustrated by the Indiana Code is to consider that failure to wear a seatbelt is not fault and can be used as evidence of mitigation in a products liability action only. What is the implication for the plaintiff of allowing failure to use a seatbelt as evidence of mitigation but not fault?

2. *Statutes and Judicial Interpretation.* Indiana courts have applied its seatbelt and mitigation statutes very narrowly. In Morgen v. Ford Motor Co., 762 N.E.2d 137 (Ind. App. 2002), the court held that it was not misuse of a vehicle not to wear seatbelts because there is no statutory or common law duty to wear a seatbelt in the backseat of a vehicle. In Hopper v. Carey, 716 N.E.2d 566 (Ind. App. 1999), the court held that there was no common law or statutory duty to wear a seatbelt in a fire truck and, while there is a statutory duty to wear a seatbelt in a passenger vehicle, a failure to do so cannot be used as evidence of fault.

V. Immunities

A. Sovereign Immunity

Because "the king can do no wrong," at one time federal and state governments were all immune from suit. At present, that immunity has been modified in various ways for all levels of government. The historical basis for this "sovereign immunity" is deference to the monarchy. In the United States, some have justified this immunity by arguing that it is absurd to think of a wrong committed by an entire people (a government "of the people" and "by the people"), that it is wasteful to use public funds to compensate private parties, or that government should be protected from the inconvenience and embarrassment of litigation.

All levels of government now allow themselves to be sued for some categories of activities. The statute permitting suits for wrongful acts of the federal government is the Federal Torts Claims Act, 28 U.S.C. §1346(b)(1), discussed in Coulthurst v. United States. Most states have similar statutes. Municipalities traditionally have been immune from tort liability in connection with "governmental" activities and subject to tort liability in connection with their "proprietary" activities. Even when the government is not immune, it may still avoid liability if the plaintiff fails to establish the elements of the tort (such as duty, breach, cause, and damages).

The most notable exception to the Federal Tort Claims Act's authorization of suits against the government precludes suits based on *discretionary functions*, as set out in 28 U.S.C. §2680(a). State torts claims statutes usually have similar provisions. Courts are reluctant to decide whether policy decisions were properly made because of concern that too much judicial supervision would contradict the separation of powers constitutionally required among the legislative, executive, and judicial branches of government.

Coulthurst v. United States illustrates the modern two-part test for whether the discretionary function exemption applies to conduct of part of the federal government, the U.S. Bureau of Prisons. In re World Trade Center Bombing Litigation examines the governmental/proprietary distinction for immunity under state law.

Statute: UNITED STATES AS A DEFENDANT
28 U.S.C. §1346(b)(1) (2017)

Subject to the provisions of chapter 171 of this title, the district courts, together with the United States District Court for the District of the Canal Zone and the District Court of the Virgin Islands, shall have exclusive jurisdiction of civil actions on claims against the United States, for money damages, accruing on and after January 1, 1945, for injury or loss of property, or personal injury or death caused by the negligent or wrongful act or omission of any employee of the Government while acting within the scope of his office or employment, under circumstances where the United States, if a private person, would be liable to the claimant in accordance with the law of the place where the act or omission occurred.

Statute: LIABILITY OF THE UNITED STATES
28 U.S.C. §2674 (2017)

The United States shall be liable, respecting the provisions of this title relating to tort claims, in the same manner and to the same extent as a private individual under like circumstances, but shall not be liable for interest prior to judgment or for punitive damages. . . .

Statute: EXCEPTIONS
28 U.S.C. §2680 (2017)

The provisions of this chapter and section 1346(b) of this title shall not apply to —
   (a) Any claim based upon an act or omission of an employee of the Government, exercising due care, in the execution of a statute or regulation, whether

or not such statute or regulation be valid, or based upon the exercise or performance or the failure to exercise or perform a discretionary function or duty on the part of a federal agency or an employee of the Government, whether or not the discretion involved be abused.

(b) Any claim arising out of the loss, miscarriage, or negligent transmission of letters or postal matter.

(c) Any claim arising in respect of the assessment or collection of any tax or customs duty, or the detention of any goods, merchandise, or other property by any officer of customs or excise or any other law enforcement officer. . . .

(d) Any claim for which a remedy is provided by sections 741-752, 781-790 of Title 46, relating to claims or suits in admiralty against the United States.

(e) Any claim arising out of an act or omission of any employee of the Government in administering the provisions of sections 1-31 of Title 50, Appendix.

(f) Any claim for damages caused by the imposition or establishment of a quarantine by the United States.

[(g) Repealed. Sept. 26, 1950, ch. 1049, §13(5), 64 Stat. 1043.]

(h) Any claim arising out of assault, battery, false imprisonment, false arrest, malicious prosecution, abuse of process, libel, slander, misrepresentation, deceit, or interference with contract rights: Provided, That, with regard to acts or omissions of investigative or law enforcement officers of the United States Government, the provisions of this chapter and section 1346(b) of this title shall apply to any claim arising, on or after the date of the enactment of this proviso, out of assault, battery, false imprisonment, false arrest, abuse of process, or malicious prosecution. For the purpose of this subsection, "investigative or law enforcement officer" means any officer of the United States who is empowered by law to execute searches, to seize evidence, or to make arrests for violations of Federal law.

(i) Any claim for damages caused by the fiscal operations of the Treasury or by the regulation of the monetary system.

(j) Any claim arising out of the combatant activities of the military or naval forces, or the Coast Guard, during time of war.

(k) Any claim arising in a foreign country.

(l) Any claim arising from the activities of the Tennessee Valley Authority.

(m) Any claim arising from the activities of the Panama Canal Company.

(n) Any claim arising from the activities of a Federal land bank, a Federal intermediate credit bank, or a bank for cooperatives.

NOTES TO STATUTES

1. *Negligent or Wrongful Acts.* Because §1346 waives sovereign immunity only for a "negligent or wrongful act or omission," the U.S. government cannot be held liable under strict liability theories — theories that do not require proof of fault. For this reason, the Supreme Court in Laird v. Nelms, 406 U.S. 797 (1972), held that a property owner could not sue on a theory of strict liability for ultrahazardous activities for damage allegedly caused by sonic booms caused by military planes flying over North Carolina on a training mission.

2. *Discretionary Function Exemption.* The Supreme Court found, in §2680, an alternative basis for denying recovery on a strict liability theory in Laird v. Nelms.

Section 2680(a) exempts the U.S. government from liability for acts based on the performance of a discretionary function. While the manner in which an activity is carried out may subject the government to liability, the decision to engage in an activity may not, even if the activity is ultrahazardous.

COULTHURST v. UNITED STATES
214 F.3d 106 (2d Cir. 2000)

Leval, J. . . .

In October 1992, plaintiff was a federal prisoner, serving a felony sentence at FCI-Danbury. According to the allegations of his complaint, at approximately 7 p.m. on October 9, he was lifting weights in the prison exercise room, performing "pull downs" on a lateral pull-down machine. The cable connecting the steel pull-down bar to the weights snapped, bringing the bar down onto his shoulders and neck with approximately 270 pounds of force. As a result of the incident, he suffered a torn rotator cuff in his left shoulder and various injuries to his back and neck.

Guidelines promulgated by the Bureau of Prisons require prison officials to "visit the inmate wellness area (if there is one) and determine if the equipment is arranged in a safe manner and if participants use the equipment properly." The pertinent Guidelines contain no instructions as to the method to be followed in inspecting the machine that caused the injury or the frequency of inspections. The evidence placed before the court on the government's motion to dismiss included no information whether the person assigned to conduct the inspection received any instructions as to what procedures should be followed in conducting the inspection or as to frequency of inspection. Records introduced by the defendant included an inspection log bearing initials purporting to indicate that an inspection of the exercise room had been conducted two days prior to Coulthurst's injury.

The complaint seeks damages, alleging that Coulthurst's injuries were caused by the defendant's "negligence and carelessness" in that the defendant "failed to diligently and periodically inspect the weight equipment, and the cable" and "failed to replace the cable after undue wear and tear." Plaintiff's right to recover was premised on the Federal Tort Claims Act (FTCA), 28 U.S.C. §§1346(b), 2671 et seq. The defendant moved to dismiss for lack of subject matter jurisdiction on the ground that the [discretionary function exception (DFE)] barred recovery for the alleged conduct, even if government negligence could be established. The district court granted the defendant's motion and dismissed the case. . . .

Plaintiff appealed the dismissal to this court.

Under traditional principles of sovereign immunity, the United States is immune from suit except to the extent the government has waived its immunity. In 1946, Congress adopted the FTCA which, subject to numerous exceptions, waives the sovereign immunity of the federal government for claims based on the negligence of its employees. In relevant part, the FTCA, 28 U.S.C. §1346(b)(1), authorizes suits against the government to recover damages

> for injury or loss of property, or personal injury or death caused by the negligent or wrongful act or omission of any employee of the Government while acting within the scope of his office or employment, under circumstances where the United States, if a

private person, would be liable to the claimant in accordance with the law of the place where the act or omission occurred.

A significant limitation on the waiver of immunity provided by the Act is the exception known as the DFE, 28 U.S.C. §2680(a), which provides that Congress's authorization to sue the United States for damages

> shall not apply to . . . any claim . . . based upon the exercise or performance or the failure to exercise or perform a discretionary function or duty on the part of . . . an employee of the Government, whether or not the discretion involved be abused.

Over the last two decades, the Supreme Court has handed down a series of decisions clarifying the scope of the DFE. The Court's decisions in Berkovitz v. United States, 486 U.S. 531, 100 L. Ed. 2d 531, 108 S. Ct. 1954 (1988), and United States v. Gaubert, 499 U.S. 315, 113 L. Ed. 2d 335, 111 S. Ct. 1267 (1991), establish the framework for evaluating whether particular governmental conduct falls under the DFE. According to the *Berkovitz-Gaubert* test, the DFE bars suit only if two conditions are met: (1) the acts alleged to be negligent must be discretionary, in that they involve an "element of judgment or choice" and are not compelled by statute or regulation and (2) the judgment or choice in question must be grounded in "considerations of public policy" or susceptible to policy analysis.

In this case, the district court read the complaint to allege a deficiency in the scheduling and procedures for the inspection of the gym equipment. According to the district court's analysis, the acts alleged as negligent involved decisions establishing the procedures and frequency of inspection — decisions themselves involving elements of judgment or choice and a balancing of policy considerations (including inmate safety, providing sufficient recreational opportunities to inmates, and efficient resource allocation). The court therefore concluded that the government is shielded from liability for any negligence arising out of these decisions. As noted above, the relevant regulations do not mandate any particular course of inspection or the frequency of such inspections, and, thus, the officials at each prison are charged with making decisions about maintenance procedures and frequencies of inspection, balancing the relevant policy considerations in the process. The court thus concluded that both prongs of the *Gaubert* test were met as to these claims, and the court therefore lacked jurisdiction.

However, the complaint is susceptible to various readings. There are numerous potential ways in which an inspector's "carelessness" may have triggered the accident. The operative words of the complaint — "negligence and carelessness" in the "failure to diligently and periodically inspect the weight equipment and cable" — encompass the possibility of various different types of careless and negligent conduct. On the one hand, the person charged with designing inspection procedures might have designed procedures that were deficient in that an inspector following those procedures would be likely to overlook, or fail to appreciate, a latent danger resulting from a frayed or strained cable. Similarly, the person deciding how frequently the inspection should be conducted might be negligent in that reasonable precaution might require more frequent inspections than provided in the schedule. We assume that if the negligence or carelessness involved in the case were of those sorts, the United States would be shielded from suit by the DFE. These types of negligently made decisions would involve elements of judgment or choice, would not be compelled by statute or regulation, and would be grounded in considerations of public policy since they would involve choices motivated by considerations of economy, efficiency, and safety.

On the other hand, the complaint's allegations of negligence and carelessness in the failure to diligently and periodically inspect might also refer to a very different type of negligence. For example, the official assigned to inspect the machine may in laziness or haste have failed to do the inspection he claimed (by his initials in the log) to have performed; the official may have been distracted or inattentive, and thus failed to notice the frayed cable; or he may have seen the frayed cable but been too lazy to make the repairs or deal with the paperwork involved in reporting the damage. Such negligent acts neither involve an element of judgment or choice within the meaning of *Gaubert* nor are grounded in considerations of governmental policy.

All of the foregoing possibilities are fairly alleged by the complaint's allegations that the responsible officers "failed to diligently and periodically inspect the weight equipment" and "failed to replace the cable after undue wear and tear." The complaint was broad enough to cover both the types of negligence that are covered by the DFE and thus cannot be the basis of suit, and the types of negligence that fall outside the DFE. We therefore think the district court erred in assuming that the negligence alleged in the complaint involved only discretionary functions. For the reasons further developed below, we believe that if the inspector failed to perform a diligent inspection out of laziness or was carelessly inattentive, the DFE does not shield the United States from liability.

We acknowledge that the text of the DFE is somewhat ambiguous, and conceivably could be interpreted to bar damage suits based on any actions or decisions that are not directly controlled by statute or regulation. In particular, it is unclear what weight to give to the concluding phrase of the DFE, which asserts that the exception is applicable "whether or not the discretion involved be abused." 28 U.S.C. §2680(a). Reading the words out of context, one might characterize an official's lazy or careless failure to perform his or her discretionary duties with due care as an "abuse of discretion." Reading the statute in this fashion, however, would lead to absurd results. For example, the driver of a mail truck undoubtedly exercises discretion in the manner of driving and makes innumerable judgment calls in the course of making his or her deliveries. In some manner of speaking, therefore, one might characterize it as an "abuse of discretion" for that driver to fail to step on the brake when a pedestrian steps in front of the car, to fail to signal before turning, or to drive 80 miles per hour in a 35 mile per hour zone. Such a characterization, however, would effectively shield almost all government negligence from suit, because almost every act involves some modicum of discretion regarding the manner in which one carries it out. Such a result is not required by the language of the DFE and would undercut the policy aims at the heart of the FTCA. We therefore would be reluctant to adopt that reading of the statute if that question had never before been considered.

In our view, furthermore, such a reading of the statute is foreclosed by a half-century of caselaw interpreting the DFE. As *Gaubert* and *Berkovitz* make clear, the prevailing test for the application of the DFE is two-pronged. It is not enough to establish that an activity is not mandated by statute and involves some element of judgment or choice; to obtain dismissal of the suit, the United States must also establish that the decision in question was grounded in considerations of public policy.

As the Court noted in *Gaubert*, "There are obviously discretionary acts performed by a Government agent that are within the scope of his employment but not within the discretionary function exception because these acts cannot be said to be based on the purposes that the regulatory regime seeks to accomplish." The *Gaubert* court explicitly offered the example of a government official negligently driving a car while on official business as a discretionary act that clearly falls outside the DFE because the negligence in question cannot be said to be based on policy considerations. Supreme Court and Second Circuit caselaw provide other examples. See, e.g., Indian Towing Co. v. United States, 350 U.S. 61, 68-69, 100 L. Ed. 48, 76 S. Ct. 122 (1955) (careless maintenance of a lighthouse triggers liability); Andrulonis v. United States, 952 F.2d 652, 655 (2d Cir. 1991) (careless failure of government scientist to maintain proper safety procedures and warn others of potential dangers); Caraballo v. United States, 830 F.2d 19, 22 (2d Cir. 1987) (negligent patrol of a beach).

Under various fair readings of the complaint, this case similarly involves negligence unrelated to any plausible policy objectives. An inspector's decision (motivated simply by laziness) to take a smoke break rather than inspect the machines, or an absent-minded or lazy failure to notify the appropriate authorities upon noticing the damaged cable, are examples of negligence fairly encompassed by the allegations of the complaint that do not involve "considerations of public policy." *Gaubert*, 499 U.S. at 323. Such actions do not reflect the kind of considered judgment "grounded in social, economic, and political policy" which the DFE is intended to shield from "judicial 'second-guessing.'" United States v. Varig Airlines, 467 U.S. 797, 814, 104 S. Ct. 2755, 81 L. Ed. 2d 660 (1984). If the plaintiff can establish that negligence of this sort occurred, his claims are not barred by the DFE, and he is entitled to recover under the FTCA.

The district court dismissed Coulthurst's suit based on its interpretation of the complaint. For the reasons outlined above, we believe that the complaint fairly alleges negligence outside the scope of the DFE and that dismissal on the basis of the allegations of the complaint was inappropriate. We accordingly vacate the district court's dismissal and remand the case for further proceedings.

This does not necessarily mean that plaintiff is entitled to trial on the basis of an ambiguous complaint. The government may compel plaintiff, by interrogatories or otherwise, to declare what is the negligent conduct he alleges occurred and to reveal whatever evidence he relies on to show such negligence. If the plaintiff is unable to offer sufficient evidence to establish a triable issue of fact on any theory of negligence outside the scope of the DFE, then the United States will be entitled to judgment. Such a dismissal, however, cannot be justified given the ambiguous allegations of Coulthurst's complaint.

For the foregoing reasons, the judgment of the district court is vacated and the case is remanded for further proceedings.

NOTES TO COULTHURST v. UNITED STATES

1. *Development of the Federal Tort Claims Act.* Prior to the adoption of the FTCA, "private bills" passed by Congress allowed particular individuals to seek tort damages from the federal government for specific injuries. The demand for such bills increased over time. Finally, in 1946, the FTCA was adopted, eliminating the need for individual legislation favoring selected tort plaintiffs.

2. *Procedural Protections.* The discretionary function exemption represents a choice to prohibit recovery for injuries related to certain types of governmental conduct. For cases where the FTCA does allow recovery, the statute includes a variety of provisions to discourage excessive litigation or excessive damages. Cases must be tried in federal, not state, court. Cases are tried to a judge, not a jury. Contingent fees for the

plaintiff's lawyer are limited, with federal criminal sanctions for collection of fees that exceed the limits. See 28 U.S.C. §§1402, 2402, and 2678.

Problem
Discretionary Functions

On June 7, 1984, Musick was cutting timber in a wooded, mountainous area of Scott County, Virginia. The trees in this area were approximately 50 to 60 feet tall. As he stood under a hickory tree, a U.S. Air Force RF-4 reconnaissance plane flew over him at such a low altitude that the turbulence from its wake caused a large limb from the tree to fall on and severely injure him. The trees over which the plane flew swayed from its passing, and the plane was banking at an approximate 90 degree angle at an altitude of 200 feet when it passed over Musick. The jet that caused the limb to fall on Musick was engaged in a training mission as part of a reconnaissance squadron stationed at Shaw Air Force Base in South Carolina. On the date of the accident, a Department of Defense flight information publication (Flip) was in effect that required pilots to fly at least 100 feet above ground level. A squadron policy in effect at the time of the accident required pilots to fly at an altitude of at least 300 feet. Musick has sued the U.S. government for his injuries. You are an Assistant United States Attorney, and the United States Attorney for the Western District of Virginia has asked you to examine the government's chances of success if it moves to dismiss because the court lacks subject matter jurisdiction based on the discretionary function exception. Please write a memo explaining your conclusion. See Musick v. United States of America, 768 F. Supp. 183 (W.D. Va. 1991).

Perspective: Competencies of Branches of Government

The doctrine of separation of powers may provide principled guidance for deciding what acts of the executive branch of the government are subject to judicial scrutiny. The following excerpt focuses on the relative competencies of the judicial, executive, and legislative branches:

> Courts are ill-equipped to balance the various concerns necessary in formulating governmental policy or to make decisions about the most efficient allocation of resources. The courtroom processes are better suited to the application of a principle to a given set of facts rather than to the formulation of policy for major governmental undertakings that affect a multitude of people in a wide variety of situations across the country. Such decisions frequently require technical expertise in a variety of disciplines. The judiciary usually cannot consistently attain the desired depth of knowledge in any field because of the wide variety of cases that must be heard. . . .
>
> Scarce manpower and financial resources accentuate the judiciary's inability to make the best policy decisions. Because a court is constrained by the facts of the case before it, it may too easily render a decision without full appreciation of the consequences. An apparently just result in one case may have an adverse impact on a larger scale. . . . A court simply does not have the depth of expertise and sufficient data before it to evaluate effectively all of the countervailing considerations. For example, consideration of the other regulatory functions that an agency must perform, may not be properly before a court when it applies

> a principle of law to the facts of the case. To avoid the danger that far-reaching policy decisions will be made by courts, discretionary-policy decisions should be immune from scrutiny in the courtroom.
>
> Donald S. Ingraham, *The Suits in Admiralty Act and the Implied Discretionary Function*, 1982 Duke L.J. 146, 163-164 (1982).
>
> To what extent do judicial decisions reflect concern about the balance of powers between the branches of government and to what extent do they reflect the relative competencies of those branches?

IN RE WORLD TRADE CENTER BOMBING LITIGATION
957 N.E.2d 733 (N.Y. 2011)

JONES, J.

This appeal, involving litigation arising from the 1993 terrorist bombing incident in the parking garage of the World Trade Center complex (WTC), raises critical issues regarding the interplay of the proprietary and governmental functions of a public entity and the provision of security, particularly against the risk of terrorist attack. . . .

The Port Authority is a public entity jointly created by a 1921 compact between New York and New Jersey to oversee and operate critical centers of commerce and trade, as well as transportation hubs such as ports, airports, bridges, and tunnels. The Port Authority is a financially self-reliant public entity that draws its revenue and income from fees generated by its various properties, and not from the tax revenue of either New York or New Jersey.

Among its properties, the WTC was a key facility developed, constructed, and operated by the Port Authority . . . .

On February 26, 1993, terrorists Ramzi Yousef and Eyad Ismoil drove a rented van containing a fertilizer bomb into the B–2 level of the WTC parking garage. Without entering an actual parking lot, they parked the van on the side of one of the garage access ramps and lit the fuse on the bomb for a timed detonation to occur approximately 10 minutes later. Both men were able to enter and exit the parking garage area undetected. The resulting explosion, occurring at 12:18 p.m., created a blast crater six stories deep and killed six people, including four Port Authority employees.

Six hundred and forty-eight plaintiffs commenced 174 actions against the Port Authority for injuries sustained as a result of the bombing . . . .

Following the completion of discovery, the Port Authority moved for summary judgment on grounds that it was entitled to the protection of governmental immunity and that the terrorist attack was not foreseeable as a matter of law. Supreme Court denied the motion, concluding that the negligent acts at issue stemmed from the Port Authority's proprietary capacity as a landowner, and not any exercise of a governmental function. The Appellate Division affirmed without opinion. . . .

We granted the Port Authority leave to appeal. . . .

[W]e now turn to the crux of this appeal — whether the Port Authority's provision of security at the WTC was the performance of a governmental function or was that of a landlord. . . .

The difficulty in a case such as this — where a governmental entity performs dual proprietary and governmental functions — is in ascertaining the proper capacity in which the Port Authority's actions should be assessed. In *Miller v. State of New York*, 62 N.Y.2d 506, 511-512 (1984), this Court explained that the functions of a governmental entity can be viewed along a "continuum of responsibility" ranging from the most basic proprietary obligation, like that of a private landlord, to the most complex governmental function, such as the provision of police protection.

Generally, when a governmental agency

> acts in a proprietary capacity as a landlord, it is subject to the same principles of tort law as is a private landlord . . . . A governmental entity's conduct may fall along a *continuum of responsibility* to individuals and society deriving from its governmental and proprietary functions. This begins with the simplest matters directly concerning a piece of property for which the entity acting as landlord has a certain duty of care, for example, the repair of steps or the maintenance of doors in an apartment building. *The spectrum extends gradually out to more complex measures of safety and security for a greater area and populace, whereupon the actions increasingly, and at a certain point only, involve governmental functions, for example, the maintenance of general police and fire protection.* Consequently, any issue relating to the safety or security of an individual claimant must be carefully scrutinized to determine the point along the continuum that the State's alleged negligent action falls into, either a proprietary or governmental category (62 N.Y.2d at 511-512 [emphasis added]).

The relevant inquiry in determining whether a governmental agency is acting within a governmental or proprietary capacity is to examine

> the specific act or omission out of which the injury is claimed to have arisen and the capacity in which that act or failure to act occurred . . . , not whether the agency involved is engaged generally in proprietary activity or is in control of the location in which the injury occurred (*id.* at 513).

As such, in light of the fact that the varied functions of a governmental entity can be interspersed with both governmental and proprietary elements, the determination of the primary capacity under which a governmental agency was acting turns solely on the acts or omissions claimed to have caused the injury. That is, we must now consider whether the precise failures for which the Port Authority was found liable were governmental or proprietary in nature.

The gravamen of plaintiffs' complaint alleges a failure to provide adequate security for the WTC. Specifically, Supreme Court summarized the plaintiffs' claims as:

> [B]ased on . . . allegations that the Port Authority was negligent with respect to security: in failing to adopt, implement, and follow the recommendations in the security reports; in failing to restrict public access to the parking levels; in failing to have an adequate security plan; in failing to provide an electronic security system; in failing to institute a manned checkpoint at the garage; in failing to subject vehicles to inspection and to have security signs; in failing to have adequate security personnel; in failing to employ recording devices concerning vehicles, operators, occupants, and pedestrians; and in failing to conduct studies of the possible results of a bombing of the complex (*Matter of World Trade Ctr. Bombing Litig.*, 3 Misc. 3d at 453).

While some of plaintiffs' claims may touch upon the proprietary obligations of a landlord, when scrutinizing the purported injury-causing acts or omissions, they allude to lapses in adequately examining the risk and nature of terrorist attack and adopting specifically recommended security protocols to deter terrorist intrusion.

These actions are not separable from the Port Authority's provision of security at the WTC . . . rather, they were a consequence of the Port Authority's mobilization of police resources for the exhaustive study of the risk of terrorist attack, the policy-based planning of effective counterterrorist strategy, and the consequent allocation of such resources. Thus, the ostensible acts or omissions for which plaintiffs seek to hold the Port Authority liable stem directly from its failure to allocate police resources as these failures lie, not within the safety measures that a reasonable landowner would implement, but within security operations featuring extensive counterterrorism planning and investigation that required discretionary decisionmaking with respect to the strategic allocation of police resources . . . .

Here, the Port Authority's general operating responsibilities at the WTC, like at its other facilities, necessarily included the provision of security for the premises as it was tasked with administering security measures to counter criminal activity. This obligation was not limited to the benefit of commercial tenants and their customers, but extended to all who would avail themselves of the WTC facility. More significantly, the security planning was broad in scope as it also concentrated on the risk of terrorist attack, not just within the parking garage, but the entire premises. To guard against terrorism, police resources were deployed in the investigation of threats and the implementation of security measures. But, unlike the safety precautions required of every reasonable landowner, the Port Authority's security operations featured policy-based decisionmaking involving due consideration of pertinent factors such as the risk of harm, and the costs and benefits of pursuing a particular allocation of resources. As a result, the Port Authority placed police resources in priority areas deemed more susceptible to attack — i.e., the high-risk plaza and concourse rather than the low-risk parking garage . . . .

These responsibilities were more expansive and discretionary in nature than the "repair of steps or the maintenance of doors in an apartment building" deemed proprietary in *Miller*, 62 N.Y.2d at 511-512. To equate the broad scope of the Port Authority's security operations at the WTC with a proprietary responsibility belies the record. Our conclusion is also consistent with *Miller* which recognizes that "complex measures of safety and security for a greater area and populace" is more indicative of the performance of a governmental function. Accordingly, the breadth and nature of the Port Authority's responsibilities places its security-related conduct squarely within the ambit of governmental function. . . .

. . . Governmental entities cannot be expected to be absolute, infallible guarantors of public safety, but in order to encourage them to engage in the affirmative conduct of diligently investigating security vulnerabilities and implementing appropriate safeguards, they must be provided with the latitude to render those critical decisions without threat of legal repercussion.

The judgment appealed from and the order of the Appellate Division brought up for review should be reversed, with costs, and the complaint of plaintiff Antonio Ruiz dismissed.

NOTES TO IN RE WORLD TRADE CENTER BOMBING LITIGATION

1. *Difficulty in Applying the Governmental/Proprietary Distinction.* Many states distinguish between governmental and proprietary acts to define the range of state immunity from tort lawsuits. The *World Trade Center* opinion illustrates the challenge associated with using this distinction when the defendant is engaged in both proprietary and governmental functions. The court looked at whether "proprietary" acts and omissions alleged to have caused the injuries were separable from the policy-based decisions confronting the defendant. In many sovereign immunity cases, courts focus on the underlying policy to guide their decisions. One objective is to preserve the separation of powers between the judicial and executive branches of government. Here, the Port Authority is part of the executive branch of the states. This reasoning would not apply to judicial scrutiny of the conduct of private actors. Other objectives, emphasized in *World Trade Center*, are to encourage entities to investigate and address the potential for harm, and to allow public entities to operate without fear of legal reprisal. Reasons for distinguishing between public and private actors on these grounds are less obvious.

2. *State Tort Claims Acts.* Most states have statutes defining state immunity from tort liability. The Federal Tort Claims Act generally allows plaintiffs to assert tort causes of action against the federal government but provides a number of exceptions to that permission. Some state statutes take an opposite approach: They describe sovereign immunity as the general rule but define particular circumstances in which that immunity will be waived. For state statutes of this type, common circumstances in which tort liability is allowed include injuries associated with the operation of motor vehicles or the maintenance of buildings or of equipment.

3. *Municipal Tort Liability.* Local government entities are also immune from tort liability, to the extent dictated by state law, often along the same lines distinguishing governmental from proprietary (or discretionary from operational) functions. Restatement (Second) of Torts §895C(2) provides that local government entities are immune from tort liability only for their acts or omissions "constituting (a) the exercise of a legislative or judicial function, and (b) the exercise of an administrative function involving the determination of fundamental governmental policy."

Supporting this position, a justice of the Vermont Supreme Court wrote: "The goal should be to place municipalities on an equal footing with private corporate entities with respect to responsibility for injuries caused by the common torts of their employees, but to shield them from liability for acts and omissions that are policy-based or that are adjudicative, legislative, or regulatory in nature." Hillerby v. Town of Colchester, 706 A.2d 446, 458 (Vt. 1997) (dissenting opinion).

Problems
State Immunity Provisions

New Mexico's Tort Claims Act provides that there is no immunity from "liability for damages resulting from bodily injury, wrongful death or property damage caused by the negligence of public employees while acting within the scope of their duties in the operation or maintenance of any building, public park, machinery, equipment or furnishings." N.M. Stat. §41-4-6. Should the statute be interpreted to allow liability based on the following claims?

 A. Swimming pool injury that could have been avoided if more trained lifeguards had been on duty. See Leithead v. City of Santa Fe, 940 P.2d 459 (N.M. App. 1997).

 B. A resident of Valle Vista Housing Project, a residential community run by the County of Santa Fe, was injured by a dog running loose in a park within the community. See Castillo v. Santa Fe County, 204 P.2d 48 (N.M. 1988).

C. Injury to a prison inmate that could have been avoided if prison officials had segregated prisoners who were known to be dangerous gang members. See Callaway v. New Mexico Dept. of Corrections, 875 P.2d 393 (N.M. App. 1994).

B. Intrafamilial Immunity

Common law rules traditionally prevented suits by one family member against another. This bar was meant to preserve family harmony, to protect insurance companies from false claims, and to avoid using judicial resources just to transfer wealth from one family member to another. Protecting parental discretion, authority, and control has been another concern. Modern perspectives on these issues have changed, and the common law immunities have been widely modified.

Jurisdictions have made a wide variety of changes in these doctrines. Boone v. Boone considers reasons underlying the nearly total abolition of interspousal immunity while Broadwell v. Holmes compares various approaches states take to parent-child immunity.

BOONE v. BOONE

546 S.E.2d 191 (S.C. 2001)

Burnett, J.

The question presented by this appeal is whether interspousal immunity from personal injury actions violates the public policy of South Carolina. We conclude it does.

Appellant Juanita Boone (Wife) was injured in a car accident in Georgia. At the time of the accident, Wife was a passenger in a vehicle driven by her husband Respondent Freddie Boone (Husband). Wife and Husband reside in South Carolina.

Wife brought this tort action against Husband in South Carolina. Concluding Georgia law which provides interspousal immunity in personal injury actions was applicable, the trial judge granted Husband's motion to dismiss. Wife appeals. We reverse.

Issue. Does Georgia law providing interspousal immunity in personal injury actions violate the public policy of South Carolina? Interspousal immunity is a common law doctrine based on the legal fiction that husband and wife share the same identity in law, namely that of the husband. 92 A.L.R.3d 901 (1979). Accordingly, at common law, it was "both morally and conceptually objectionable to permit a tort suit between two spouses."

With the passage of Married Women's Property Acts in the mid-nineteenth century, married women were given a legal estate in their own property and the capacity to sue and be sued. Under this legislation, a married woman could maintain an action against her husband for any tort against her property interest such as trespass to land or conversion. Since the legislation destroyed the "unity of persons," a husband could also maintain an action against his wife for torts to his property. See 1 Dan B. Dobbs, The Law of Torts §279 (2001).

For a long time, however, the majority of courts held Married Women's Property Acts did not destroy interspousal immunity for personal torts. Courts adopted two inconsistent arguments in favor of continued immunity. First, they theorized suits between spouses would be fictitious and fraudulent, particularly against insurance companies. Second, they claimed interspousal suits would destroy domestic harmony.

In the twentieth century, most courts either abrogated or provided exceptions to interspousal immunity. South Carolina has abolished the doctrine of interspousal immunity from tort liability for personal injury. S.C. Code Ann. §15-5-170 (1976) ("[a] married woman may sue and be sued as if she were unmarried.").

Very few jurisdictions now recognize interspousal tort immunity.

Georgia continues to recognize the common law doctrine of interspousal immunity. Under Georgia law, interspousal tort immunity bars personal injury actions between spouses, except where the traditional policy reasons for applying the doctrine are absent, i.e., where there is no marital harmony to be preserved and where there exists no possibility of collusion between the spouses.

Under traditional South Carolina choice of law principles, the substantive law governing a tort action is determined by the *lex loci delicti*, the law of the state in which the injury occurred. However,

> foreign law may not be given effect in this State if 'it is against good morals or natural justice . . . .' . . .

Although South Carolina had abolished the doctrine of interspousal immunity from tort liability for personal injury thirty years before, this Court held it would apply the law of the foreign state even if it recognized interspousal immunity. Oshiek v. Oshiek, 244 S.C. 249, 136 S.E.2d 303 (1964). If a spouse had no right of action against her spouse where the tort occurred, the action would not be enforced in South Carolina.

In Algie v. Algie, 261 S.C. 103, 198 S.E.2d 529 (1973), the Court expressly declined to overrule Oshiek v. Oshiek, supra. In *Algie*, the parties lived in Florida. The wife was injured in an airplane accident in South Carolina. Her husband had piloted the airplane. The husband urged the Court to apply Florida law which, at that time, recognized interspousal immunity. The Court declined, noting "[w]e are not persuaded that this result would be in furtherance of justice." Id., 261 S.C. at 106, 198 S.E.2d at 530.

It is the public policy of our State to provide married persons with the same legal rights and remedies possessed by unmarried persons. Had the parties to this action not been married to each other, Wife could have maintained a personal injury action against Husband. We find it contrary to "natural justice," see Rauton v. Pullman Co., supra, to hold that because of their marital status, Wife is precluded from maintaining this action against Husband. Accordingly, we conclude application of the doctrine of interspousal immunity violates the public policy of South Carolina.

Moreover, the reasons given in support of interspousal immunity are simply not justified in the twenty-first century. There is no reason to presume married couples are more likely than others to engage in a collusive action. Whether or not parties are married, if fraudulent conduct is suspected, insurers can examine and investigate the claim and, at trial, cross-examine the parties as to their financial stakes in the outcome of the suit. Fraudulent claims would be subject to the trial court's contempt powers and to criminal prosecution for perjury and other crimes. It is unjustified to prohibit all personal injury tort suits between spouses simply because some suits may be fraudulent.

Additionally, we do not agree that precluding spouses from maintaining a personal injury action against each other fosters domestic harmony. Instead, we find marital harmony is promoted by allowing the negligent spouse, who has most likely purchased liability insurance, to provide for his injured spouse.

Furthermore, in Georgia, spouses may maintain an action against each other for torts committed against their property. If suits encompassing one type of tort are permitted between spouses, we fail to see how suits encompassing a different tort should be prohibited under the guise of protecting domestic tranquility. In our opinion, marital disharmony will not increase because married persons are permitted to maintain a personal injury action against each other. . . .

Because interspousal immunity violates the public policy of South Carolina, we will no longer apply the *lex loci delicti* when the law of the foreign state recognizes the doctrine. Oshiek v. Oshiek, supra, is overruled.

Reversed.

BROADWELL v. HOLMES
871 S.W.2d 471 (Tenn. 1994)

REID, J.

This case presents for review the judgment of the Court of Appeals dismissing a suit on behalf of two unemancipated minor children against their mother for personal injuries to one child and for the wrongful death of the other child. The children were injured while riding as passengers in an automobile operated by the mother. The trial court found that the complaint did not state a cause of action, and the Court of Appeals affirmed.

This Court granted permission to appeal in order to re-examine the parental immunity doctrine, first adopted in this state in McKelvey v. McKelvey, 77 S.W. 664 (1903), and most recently reaffirmed in Barranco v. Jackson, 690 S.W.2d 221 (Tenn. 1985), a case in which the dissent advocated that parental immunity be abolished in "automobile tort" cases.

In the case before the Court, Mindy Elaine Broadwell, age 8, and Justin L. Broadwell, age 6, were passengers in a pickup truck driven by their mother, the defendant, when the vehicle was involved in an accident. The complaint alleges that the defendant negligently lost control of the vehicle and that her negligence proximately caused the death of Mindy and serious bodily injuries to Justin. The suit was brought on behalf of the children by their father as next friend. At the time of the accident, the parents were divorced, and the mother had custody of the children.

The majority in *Barranco* declined to discuss the substantive issue of whether the parental immunity doctrine should be modified, observing only that the doctrine "has continuing vitality and should be adhered to unless modified or changed by action of the General Assembly." Id. at 222. Therefore, the first matter for consideration is whether the court will persist in the view expressed by the majority in *Barranco*, that it has no role in the development of the law in this area. . . .

The dissent in *Barranco* reviewed the development of parental immunity beginning with the doctrine's initial adoption by the Mississippi Supreme Court in Hewellette v. George, 9 So. 885 (Miss. 1891), and noted that the doctrine had been subjected to criticism and modification in recent decisions. The dissent concluded:

> [T]he sole policy consideration which justifies its application [is] a parent's right to discipline and use discretion in the care and rearing of children.

Since the decision in *Barranco*, the trend to modify the parental immunity doctrine has continued. Although state courts have continued to modify parental immunity, the decisions have established no uniform standard for imposing parental liability. However, the cases uniformly exempt from liability, expressly or implicitly, conduct, whether acts or omissions, incident to the exercise of parental authority and supervision.

In the first case in which the parent-child immunity doctrine was modified, the Supreme Court of Wisconsin expressed the concern that total abrogation of the doctrine would unduly interfere with parental authority and discipline. Goller v. White, 122 N.W.2d 193 (1963). In an effort to prevent such interference, the court abrogated immunity in all cases except those involving the exercise of parental authority over the child and/or the exercise of ordinary parental discretion with respect to the provision of food, clothing, housing, medical and dental services and other care. Id. 122 N.W.2d at 198. This approach reflects a recognition that the parent-child relationship is unique and that traditional negligence concepts cannot be applied in situations where the relationship is involved.

Several courts have adopted the *Goller* approach with minor variations of the standard. In Sandoval v. Sandoval, 623 P.2d 800, 803 (Ariz. 1981), the court stated that the immunity applies only if "the parent breached a duty owed to a child within the family sphere" rather than to the world at large. In Rigdon v. Rigdon, 465 S.W.2d 921 (Ky. 1971), the court further varied the *Goller* standard. Instead of listing specific activities as to which a parent is immune in the use of ordinary parental discretion, the court narrowed the applicability of the immunity to parental acts of ordinary discretion used "with respect to provisions for the care and necessities of the child." Id. at 923. The Supreme Court of Michigan adopted the *Goller* approach but varied it by substituting the term "reasonable" for "ordinary." Plumley v. Klein, 199 N.W.2d 169, 173 (1972). In Cates v. Cates, the Illinois Supreme Court modified the *Goller* approach by limiting immunity to "conduct inherent to the parent-child relationship." Cates v. Cates, 619 N.E.2d [715, 729 (Ill. 1993)].

Other courts have created their own standards regarding the immunity applicable in parent-child tort actions. In Gibson v. Gibson, 3 Cal. 3d 914, 92 Cal. Rptr. 288, 293, 479 P.2d 648, 653 (1971), the California Supreme Court held that the proper test of a parent's conduct is: "What would an ordinary, reasonable and prudent *parent* have done in similar circumstances?" One of the states originally following the *Goller* approach has rejected it in favor of the reasonable parent standard. In Anderson v. Stream, 295 N.W.2d 595 (Minn. 1980), the Minnesota Supreme Court rejected the *Goller* approach it had adopted earlier in Silesky v. Kelman, 161 N.W.2d 631 (1968). In *Anderson*, the court reasoned that the *Goller* standard was not very helpful because it still required a case-by-case analysis to determine whether the conduct at issue was within one of the exemptions. The court also was concerned that the standard added "to the potential for arbitrary decision-making in the area." 295 N.W.2d at 598. The determinative consideration for the court's holding was "that the areas of parental authority and discretion, for which the *Silesky* exceptions were designed to provide safeguards, can be effectively protected by use of a 'reasonable parent standard.'" Id.

Another approach to modifying the parental immunity doctrine was articulated by the New York Court of Appeals in Holodook v. Spencer, 36 N.Y.2d 35, 364 N.Y.S.2d 859, 324 N.E.2d 338 (1974), in which it was alleged that the minor child's mother had negligently supervised her child when, as a result of being left untended, the child wandered into the street where she was struck by a passing automobile. Though noting the parents' obligations to support, guide, protect, and supervise their children, the court held that negligent supervision was not a tort actionable by the child, reasoning that there are very few accidental injuries to children that could not have been prevented by more intense parental supervision. Id. 364 N.Y.S.2d at 865-67, at 342-43. That court stated that imposing a parental duty of "constant surveillance and instruction" would place an overwhelming burden on parents since it is virtually impossible to supervise a child 24 hours a day. Nevertheless, the *Holodook* court went on to say that when there is a breach of a recognized duty ordinarily owed apart from the family relationship, the law will not withhold liability merely because the parties are parent and child. Id. at 870-71, 324 N.E.2d at 346. The *Holodook* court criticized the reasonable parent standard for its attempt to apply a uniform standard of parental conduct across the spectrum of different economic, educational, cultural, ethnic, and religious backgrounds. The court stated that to apply the reasonable parent standard "would be to circumscribe the wide range of discretion a parent ought to have in permitting his child to undertake responsibility and gain independence." Id. at 871, 324 N.E.2d at 346.

The exemption from liability recognized in these cases is not based on the absence of a duty of care. Obviously, parents owe a high duty of care to their children. However, the rights, responsibilities, and privileges of parents in relation to their children are so unique that the ordinary standards of care which regulate conduct between others are not applicable to conduct incident to the particular relationship of parent and child. That relationship includes responsibilities not owed by parents to any persons other than their children; these responsibilities are inseparable from the privileges that parents have in rearing their children which are not recognized in any other relationship.

> Each parent has unique and inimitable methods and attitudes on how children should be supervised. Likewise, each child requires individualized guidance depending on intuitive concerns which only a parent can understand. . . . Consequently, [a]llowing a cause of action for negligent supervision would enable others, ignorant of a case's peculiar familial distinctions and bereft of any standards, to second-guess a parent's management of family affairs. . . .

Paige v. Bing Construction Co., 61 Mich. App. 480, 233 N.W.2d 46, 49 (1975). Even though the courts routinely and successfully intervene in order to protect a child when the parent's conduct towards the child is criminal or where the child's physical or mental health is seriously endangered, the court system is not an appropriate or effective forum for resolving controversies between parent and child, when such controversies necessarily involve ethical, religious, moral, or cultural values.

The parental right to govern the rearing of a child has been afforded protection under both the federal and state constitutions. This Court has stated, "Tennessee's historically strong protection of parental rights and the reasoning of federal constitutional cases convince us that parental rights constitute a fundamental liberty interest under Article I, Section 8 of the Tennessee Constitution." Hawk v. Hawk, 855 S.W.2d 573, 579 (Tenn. 1973).

Courts have expressed a concern that without the imposition of parent-child immunity, juries would feel free to express their disapproval of what they consider to be unusual or inappropriate child rearing practices by awarding damages to children whose parents' conduct was only unconventional. Courts also properly have found that parents whose "[p]hysical, mental or financial weakness [causes them] to provide what many a reasonable man would consider substandard maintenance, guidance, education and recreation for their children, and in many instances to provide a family home which is not reasonably safe as a place of abode," should not be liable to the child for these "unintended injuries." Chaffin v. Chaffin, 239 Or. 374, 397 P.2d 771, 774 (1964) (*en banc*), overruled by Heino v. Harper, 306 Or. 347, 759 P.2d 253 (1988) (abolishing interspousal immunity). Such imposition of liability could effectively curtail the exercise of constitutionally guaranteed parental discretion in matters of child rearing. Consequently, it reasonably can be argued that parental immunity that relates to the right and duty to rear children implements a constitutional right.

However, the relationship between parents and their children is not exclusively that of parent-child. A parent's conduct that injures a child may be outside the scope of their relationship as parent-child, and a child may be injured by a parent's conduct that is not in the exercise of parental authority, supervision, care, or custody. Consequently, the scope of the exemption from liability should be limited or defined by the purpose for granting the immunity, and the definition of the duty alleged to have been breached will disclose whether there is immunity. See Cates v. Cates, 619 N.E.2d at 729.

The Court's essential task is to craft an objective standard, recognized in the above cases, that defines the conduct that should be protected by a parental immunity. The principle is perhaps most precisely stated in Cates v. Cates. In *Cates*, as in the case before the Court, the plaintiff was injured while riding in an automobile operated by her parent. The court declined to limit the modification of parental immunity to automobile negligence cases, finding that "there is no fundamental distinction between automobile negligence situations and other negligence scenarios." 619 N.E.2d at 720. The Illinois court, instead, limited immunity to "conduct [that] concerns parental discretion in discipline, supervision and care of the child." 619 N.E.2d at 729. The court stated:

[I]mmunity should afford protection to conduct inherent to the parent-child relationship; such conduct constitutes an exercise of parental authority and supervision over the child or an exercise of discretion in the provision of care to the child. These limited areas of conduct require the skills, knowledge, intuition, affection, wisdom, faith, humor, perspective, background, experience, and culture which only a parent and his or her child can bring to the situation; our legal system is ill-equipped to decide the reasonableness of such matters.

Parental immunity in Tennessee is limited to conduct that constitutes the exercise of parental authority, the performance of parental supervision, and the provision of parental care and custody. The operation of an automobile under the circumstances alleged in this case is not protected conduct under this standard.

This decision applies to all cases tried or retried after the date of this opinion and all cases on appeal on the date of this opinion in which a claim challenging the parental immunity doctrine was asserted in the trial court and preserved for appeal. Those cases in conflict with this decision, including McKelvey v. McKelvey and Barranco v. Jackson, are overruled.

The judgments of the trial court and the Court of Appeals are reversed, and the case is remanded for further proceedings consistent with this opinion.

NOTES TO BOONE v. BOONE AND BROADWELL v. HOLMES

1. *Policy Approaches to Intrafamilial Immunity.* Interspousal immunity was totally abolished in South Carolina, but parental immunity was retained in a limited form in Tennessee. How are the policy arguments in favor of and opposed to interspousal immunity different from those in favor of and opposed to parental immunity?

2. *Alternative Approaches to Parent-Child Suits.* Currently, a small number of states have no parent-child immunity doctrine, either because they have abrogated it completely or because they had never adopted it. Some other states have abolished the doctrine only with respect to particular activities, such as automobile accidents.

Jurisdictions partially abrogating the immunity have adopted different approaches to accommodating a child's right to sue with parental rights to discipline and use discretion in child care. The California approach in Gibson v. Gibson and the New York approach in Holodook v. Spencer, both discussed in *Broadwell,* and the Tennessee rule adopted in *Broadwell* represent the range of variations. For the following activities, which of the three approaches would provide parents with immunity from a suit brought by a child?

A. Child passenger injured when automobile negligently driven by her parent hits a tree while going to the grocery store.

B. Child burned when his parent lets campfire get out of control and burn 100 acres of national forest during vacation trip.

C. Child injured when her parent punishes child by hitting repeatedly with a baseball bat.

D. Child's hand mangled when using snowblower as negligently instructed by his father.

VI. Statutes of Limitation and Repose

Tort law imposes two types of limits on the length of time that may elapse between an injury and the filing of a lawsuit about the injury. A *statute of limitations* relates to the time a plaintiff should reasonably have known that he or she had a legal claim and bars a claim unless it is filed within a certain period after that time. A *statute of repose* relates to the time when a defendant committed the act or omission that is the basis for a plaintiff's claim and bars a claim unless it is filed within a certain period after that time, even if the statute of limitations would not bar the claim. These statutes are designed to ensure that cases are tried when memories are fresh and evidence is relatively easy to obtain. Some suggest that the court system should be relieved of the burden of trying "stale" claims where a plaintiff has "slept on" his or her rights.

Hanley v. Citizens Bank of Massachusetts presents the *discovery rule,* which governs when the time period for a statute of limitations begins — that is, when the time "begins to run." Kern v. St. Joseph's Hospital demonstrates the effect of a defendant's *fraudulent concealment* that keeps a plaintiff from knowing that he or she had a legal claim. Fraudulent concealment *tolls* a statute of limitations, stopping the clock during the concealment period. Sedar v. Knowlton Construction Company involves a statute of repose applicable to construction and real property.

HANLEY v. CITIZENS BANK OF MASSACHUSETTS
2001 WL 717106 (Mass. Super.)

BURNES, J.

This case arises out of a negligence claim filed by Plaintiff, James M. Hanley ("Hanley") against Defendant, Citizens Bank of Massachusetts ("Citizens"). Hanley alleges that as a result of Citizens' negligence, he sustained personal injuries during a bank robbery. Hanley has asserted only one count for negligence (Count I) as to the bank. Citizens now moves to dismiss Hanley's complaint on the grounds that . . . Hanley's complaint is barred by the statute of limitations . . .

On or about February 10, 1990, Hanley was employed as a security guard by Metropolitan Security Service ("Metropolitan"). Metropolitan assigned Hanley to a branch of the Somerset Savings Bank ("Somerset") [which later merged into Citizens Bank], located at 40 Union Square, Somerville, Massachusetts ("Union Branch").

On the night of February 9, 1990, an alarm sounded at the Union Branch and the police responded by arriving on the scene at the bank. However, the police did not enter the bank since no one from the bank was present to allow the police to gain entry into the building.

On the morning of February 10, 1990, Hanley entered the Union Branch and robbers "disarmed him, kicked him repeatedly, held a gun to his head and threatened to execute him." The robbery was committed by the "Hole-in-the-Roof Gang." This gang has been known to rob numerous greater Boston banks by cutting a hole in the roof of the target bank at night, entering the bank and waiting for bank employees to arrive in the morning. In the morning, the gang forces the bank employees to open the vault at gun point.

On or about March 17, 1997, the first jury trial of the "Hole-in-the-Roof Gang" began in federal court. Hanley first discovered that the Somerville police responded to an alarm at the Union Branch on February 9, 1990, and could not enter the bank to inspect the interior because nobody from the bank responded to the alarm to enable the police to gain entry.

Specifically, Hanley alleges that the bank was negligent in hiring, training, and supervising the bank personnel in charge of the security of the Union Branch on February 9, 1990 and February 10, 1990. In addition, Hanley asserts that the bank was negligent in failing to investigate and failing to allow the Somerville Police to enter the Union Branch on February 9, 1990.

General Laws chapter 260, §2A provides, "Except as otherwise provided, actions of tort, actions of contract to recover for personal injuries and actions of replevin, shall be commenced only within three years next after the cause of action accrues." This incident occurred on February 10, 1990 and this suit was commenced on March 14, 2000. Therefore, Citizens argues that the three-year statute of limitations has expired.

Hanley argues that his claim is not barred by the statute of limitations since the discovery rule is applicable to this case. The discovery rule provides that "the statute of limitations does not run against a claim until 'an event or events have occurred that were reasonably likely to put the plaintiff on notice that someone may have caused her injury.'" Bernier v. Upjohn Co., 144 F.3d 178, 180 (1st Cir. 1998), citing Bowen v. Eli Lilly & Co., 408 Mass. 204 (1990).

In *Bernier*, the First Circuit also stated that "[p]ut another way, the statute runs from the point at which a reasonably prudent person in the plaintiff's position, 'reacting to any suspicious circumstances of which he might have been aware,' would have discovered that another party might be liable for her injury." Bernier v. Upjohn Co., 144 F.3d 178, 180 (1st Cir. 1998), citing Malapanis v. Shirazi, 21 Mass. App. Ct. 378 (1986).

In this case, it is clear that Hanley failed to take steps to ascertain that he might have been injured by the bank's negligence. It is obvious that Hanley knew of the robbers' presence in the bank at the time he arrived and acting in a reasonably prudent manner, he could have investigated the lack of response by the bank to the alarm, and thus discovered whether he had a cause of action against the bank. Instead, Hanley argues that he only discovered the lack of response by the bank at the criminal trial in federal court. Hanley's failure to investigate facts that could have been known to him immediately after the robbery bars this claim under the discovery rule and ultimately under the statute of limitations. See Bowen v. Eli Lilly & Co., 409 Mass. 204, 211 (1990) (holding that "reasonable notice that a particular product or a particular act of another person may have been a cause of harm to a plaintiff creates a duty of inquiry and starts the running of the statute of limitations"). Accordingly, Citizens' Motion to Dismiss is allowed.

KERN v. ST. JOSEPH'S HOSPITAL
697 P.2d 135 (N.M. 1985)

FEDERICI, C.J. . . .

Petitioner's decedent, Dale Kern, received external beam radiation therapy for cancer of the bladder at St. Joseph Hospital in Albuquerque, New Mexico. The treatments were administered by defendant-respondent Dr. Simmons, an employee of defendant-respondent, X-Ray Associates, from August 16, 1977, through September 22, 1977. Kern and his wife were told by Dr. Simmons that Kern's therapy would consist of 30 treatments of radiation. After Kern had received 25 treatments, however, the therapy was discontinued without explanation. When Kern and his wife asked Dr. Simmons the reason for the early termination of the therapy, Dr. Simmons did not respond and appeared to stare off in the other direction. After the radiation treatments, Kern experienced problems with frequency of urination and the passing of blood in his bowel movements and urine. Kern died on August 30, 1982. The cause of death listed on the death certificate was sepsis-urinary tract infection due to or as a consequence of irradiation cystitis and proctitis and/or urinary bladder cancer.

Both Kern and his wife believed that the problems Kern experienced after the radiation therapy were acceptable complications of the treatments. They were never informed that Kern had received an excessive amount of radiation. However, after reading a newspaper article in 1981 regarding excessive radiation having allegedly been administered at St. Joseph Hospital, they began to suspect the propriety of Kern's treatment. Kern and his wife employed a lawyer to investigate whether Kern's radiation therapy had been administered properly.

This lawsuit was filed on March 21, 1983, by Kern's widow in her capacity as personal representative of her husband's estate. She alleged that her husband's death was due to the negligent administration and calculation of external beam radiation therapy. Dr. Simmons and X-Ray Associates filed a motion for summary judgment contending that petitioner's lawsuit was barred by [New Mexico Statutes §41-5-13 (Repl. Pamp. 1982):

> No claim for malpractice arising out of an act of malpractice which occurred subsequent to the effective date of the Medical Malpractice Act [ch. 41, art. 5 N.M. Stat. Ann. 1978] may be brought against a health care provider unless filed within three years after the date that the act of malpractice occurred except that a minor under the full age of six years shall have until his ninth birthday in which to file. This subsection [section] applies to all persons regardless of minority or other legal disability.]

The trial court and the Court of Appeals agreed. . . .

We recognize that this statute may be harsh when applied to latent injury cases. Although the "wrongful act rule," as our type of statute has become known, was once the general rule, it is now generally disfavored and many states have enacted some form of discovery provision which typically provides for the cause of action not to accrue until the patient discovers or should have discovered the injury. Any changes to our statute, however, should be made by the Legislature and not by the courts.

In the present case, petitioner's lawsuit was filed more than three years after Kern's last radiation treatment and is barred by Section 41-5-13 unless the statute was tolled by the doctrine of fraudulent concealment. New Mexico recognizes the doctrine of fraudulent concealment in medical malpractice actions. The doctrine is based not upon a construction of the statute, but rather upon the principle of equitable estoppel. The theory is premised on the notion that the one who has prevented the plaintiff from bringing suit within the statutory period should be estopped from asserting the statute of limitations as a defense.

In *Hardin*, the court recognized the estoppel nature of fraudulent concealment and stated:

> We therefore conclude that where a party against whom a cause of action accrues prevents the one entitled to bring the cause from obtaining knowledge thereof by fraudulent concealment, or where the cause is known to the injuring party, but is of such character as to conceal itself from the injured party, the statutory limitation on the time for bringing the action will not begin to run until the right of action is discovered, or, by the exercise of ordinary diligence, could have been discovered.

Hardin v. Farris, 87 N.M. at 146, 530 P.2d at 410 (citations omitted). Silence may sometimes constitute fraudulent concealment where a physician breaches his fiduciary duty to disclose material information concerning a patient's treatment. Hardin v. Farris. The statute of limitations, however, is not tolled if the patient knew, or through the exercise of reasonable diligence should have known, of his cause of action within the statutory period. If tolled by fraudulent concealment, the statute commences to run again when the patient discovers, or through the exercise of reasonable diligence should have discovered, the malpractice.

To toll the statute of limitations under the doctrine of fraudulent concealment, a patient has the burden, therefore, of showing (1) that the physician knew of the alleged wrongful act and concealed it from the patient or had material information pertinent to its discovery which he failed to disclose, and (2) that the patient did not know, or could not have known through the exercise of reasonable diligence, of his cause of action within the statutory period. . . .

When we consider the record, we find that petitioner did present sufficient evidence to raise an issue of material fact regarding Dr. Simmons' knowledge of excessive radiation having been administered to Kern. The record reveals that in opposition to respondent's motion for summary judgment, petitioner presented the affidavit of a doctor knowledgeable in the field of therapeutic radiology who stated that although the intended treatment plan for Kern conformed with the customary standards at that time, the dose levels given did not follow the plan and were greatly excessive and that such dose levels "will cause unacceptable complications such as those recorded in the medical records as being suffered by Dale Kern, deceased." In addition, the affidavit of a radiation physicist stated, "Whoever calculated the treatment times needed to implement this treatment plan performed a *gross calculation error*." (Emphasis added.) Petitioner also presented her own affidavit which contained the facts set forth at the beginning of this opinion.

In support of his motion for summary judgment, Dr. Simmons filed an affidavit denying knowledge of any malpractice and denying concealment of any material facts. Resolving, however, all doubts in favor of petitioner, we find the evidence sufficient to create a fact issue. The early termination of the treatments without explanation, Dr. Simmons' failure to answer the Kerns' question concerning the early termination, and the statements in the affidavits filed by petitioner lend possible support to petitioner's claims of excessive radiation having been given to Kern, and of "a gross calculation error" having been made in implementing Kern's treatment plan.

Summary judgment was improperly granted. The trial court and the Court of Appeals are reversed. The case is remanded to the trial court for proceedings consistent with this opinion.

SEDAR v. KNOWLTON CONSTRUCTION CO.
551 N.E.2d 938 (Ohio 1990)

Syllabus by the Court. . . .

Appellant, Michael R. Sedar, was a nineteen-year-old student at Kent State University when, on September 11, 1985, he was severely injured by passing his right hand and arm through a panel of wire-reinforced glass in one of the doors of his dormitory, Clark Hall. Clark Hall had been designed between 1961 and 1963 by appellee Larson & Nassau, architectural engineers (formerly known as Fulton, DelaMotte, Larson & Nassau). Appellee Knowlton Construction Company (now known as Arga Company) of Bellefontaine, Ohio, was the general contractor throughout the construction of Clark Hall, which construction was completed by December 31, 1966.

On April 8, 1987, appellant filed this action, alleging that appellees had been negligent and careless in the design and/or construction of Clark Hall including the door containing the glass panel on which he was injured. Appellees moved for summary judgment on the basis that appellant's claim was barred by the ten-year statute of repose provided in R.C. 2305.131. On November 18, 1987, the trial court granted summary judgment in favor of appellees.

The court of appeals affirmed. . . .

HOLMES, J.

We are asked in this case to decide whether R.C. 2305.131 may constitutionally prevent the accrual of actions sounding in tort against architects, construction contractors and others who perform services related to the design and construction of improvements to real property, where such action arises more than ten years following the completion of such services. For the reasons which follow, and as applied to bar the claims of appellant herein, we answer such query in the affirmative.

R.C. 2305.131 provides:

> No action to recover damages for any injury to property, real or personal, or for bodily injury or wrongful death, arising out of the defective and unsafe condition of an improvement to real property nor any action for contribution or indemnity for damages sustained as a result of said injury, shall be brought against any person performing services for or furnishing the design, planning, supervision of construction, or construction of such improvement to real property, more than ten years after the performance or furnishing of such services and construction. This limitation does not apply to actions against any person in actual possession and control as owner, tenant, or otherwise of the improvement at the time the defective and unsafe condition of such improvement constitutes the proximate cause of the injury or damage for which the action is brought.

This ten-year statute of repose applies to architects, construction contractors and others who supply services in the design, planning, supervision of construction or construction of buildings and other improvements to real property. Unlike a true statute of limitations, which limits the time in which a plaintiff may bring suit *after* the cause of action accrues, a statute of repose, such as R.C. 2305.131, potentially bars a plaintiff's suit *before* the cause of action arises. . . .

All legislative enactments enjoy a presumption of constitutionality. . . .

The legislature's choice of ten years to achieve its valid goal of limiting liability here was neither unreasonable nor arbitrary. An oft-quoted study presented to a committee of the United States House of Representatives studying a similar statute of repose for the District of Columbia revealed that 89.7 percent of all claims against architects were brought within five years of completion of the building, *99.6 percent* of all such claims were brought within ten years, and 100 percent of all such claims were brought within fourteen years. See Comment, Limitation of Action Statutes for Architects and Builders, supra, at 367. Indeed, a substantial majority of states have found no due process violations in similar statutes, some of which afford periods as brief as four years.

We realize that faded memories, lost evidence, unavailable witnesses and intervening negligence hinders plaintiffs, who bear the burden of proving negligence, as well as defendants. We also recognize that R.C. 2305.131 bars *all* claims after ten years, whether meritorious or frivolous. However, we do not sit in judgment of the wisdom of legislative enactments. ". . . [A] court has nothing to do with the policy or wisdom of a statute. That is the exclusive concern of the legislative branch of the government. When the validity of a statute is challenged on constitutional grounds, the sole function of the court is to determine whether it transcends the limits of legislative power." State, ex rel. Bishop, v. Bd. of Edn. (1942), 40 N.E.2d 913, 919. We agree that "[t]he Legislature could reasonably conclude that the statistical improbability of meritorious claims after a certain length of time, . . . and the inability of the courts to adjudicate stale claims weigh more heavily than allowing the adjudication of a few meritorious claims. . . ." *Klein* [v. Catalano, 437 N.E.2d 514, 521, fn. 11 (Mass. 1982)]. Thus, we hold that R.C. 2305.131 does not violate the due course of law provision of Section 16, Article I of the Ohio Constitution.

... [T]he differences in work conditions provide a rational basis for limiting the liability of architects and builders, but not materialmen:

> ... Suppliers and manufacturers, who typically supply and produce components in large quantities, make standard goods and develop standard processes. They can thus maintain high quality control standards in the controlled environment of the factory. On the other hand, the architect or contractor can pre-test and standardize construction designs and plans only in a limited fashion. In addition, the inspection, supervision and observation of construction by architects and contractors involv[e] individual expertise not susceptible of the quality control standards of the factory. ... Burmaster v. Gravity Drainage Dist. No. 2 (La. 1978), 366 So. 2d 1381, 1386.

Moreover, some courts have upheld these distinctions as "necessary to encourage ... [architects and builders] to experiment with new designs and materials. ..." *Klein*, supra, 437 N.E.2d at 524. "... Design creativity might be stifled if architects and engineers labored under the fear that every untried configuration might have unsuspected flaws that could lead to liability decades later." O'Brien v. Hazelet & Erdal (1980), 299 N.W.2d 336, 342. ...

We hold that R.C. 2305.131 does not violate the equal protection guarantees of the Ohio and United States Constitutions by limiting the liability of architects and builders without corresponding limits on the liability of occupiers of improvements to real property and materialmen supplying materials used in the construction of such improvements. Because we also have held that the statute does not violate either the due process or right-to-a-remedy provisions of Section 16, Article I of the Ohio Constitution, we thus affirm the court of appeals.

NOTES TO HANLEY v. CITIZENS BANK OF MASSACHUSETTS, KERN v. ST. JOSEPH'S HOSPITAL, AND SEDAR v. KNOWLTON CONSTRUCTION CO.

1. *Differences Between Statutes of Repose and Limitation.* Statutes of limitation generally begin to run from the time a person could have discovered that he or she had a legal claim, as discussed in *Hanley*. Statutes of repose generally begin to run from the time of the tortious conduct, as in *Kern* and *Sedar*. What social policies support the differences in these two types of statutes? Why should some claims be accepted even if they are brought long after the time of the defendant's conduct, so long as they are brought fairly soon after the plaintiff discovers the conduct? If this scenario is acceptable for some kinds of claims, why should statutes of repose identify particular types of harmful conduct and give it a different type of protection?

2. *Fraudulent Concealment.* A defendant's fraudulent concealment of information that would enable an individual to suspect the defendant's tortious conduct will toll any type of statute of limitations. This doctrine was particularly significant for the plaintiff in *Kern*, because the statute in that case would have continued to protect the defendant if the plaintiff's only basis for avoiding the statute had been a showing that the plaintiff could not have known through the exercise of reasonable diligence about the cause of action within the statutory period.

Statute: EFFECT OF DISABILITY

Tex. Civ. Prac. & Rem. Code §16.001 (2017)

(a) For the purposes of this subchapter, a person is under a legal disability if the person is:

(1) younger than 18 years of age, regardless of whether the person is married; or

(2) of unsound mind.

(b) If a person entitled to bring a personal action is under a legal disability when the cause of action accrues, the time of the disability is not included in a limitations period.

(c) A person may not tack one legal disability to another to extend a limitations period.

(d) A disability that arises after a limitations period starts does not suspend the running of the period.

Statute: CLAIM BY MINOR AGAINST PROVIDER OF HEALTH CARE; LIMITATIONS

Mass. Gen. Laws ch. 231 §60D (2017)

Notwithstanding the provisions of section seven of chapter two hundred and sixty, any claim by a minor against a health care provider stemming from professional services or health care rendered, whether in contract or tort, based on an alleged act, omission or neglect shall be commenced within three years from the date the cause of action accrues, except that a minor under the full age of six years shall have until his ninth birthday in which the action may be commenced, but in no event shall any such action be commenced more than seven years after occurrence of the act or omission which is the alleged cause of the injury upon which such action is based except where the action is based upon the leaving of a foreign object in the body.

Statute: TEN YEARS; DEVELOPER, CONTRACTOR, ARCHITECT, ETC.

Cal. Civ. Proc. Code §337.15 (2017)

(a) No action may be brought to recover damages from any person, or the surety of a person, who develops real property or performs or furnishes the design, specifications, surveying, planning, supervision, testing, or observation of construction or construction of an improvement to real property more than 10 years after the substantial completion of the development or improvement for any of the following:

(1) Any latent deficiency in the design, specification, surveying, planning, supervision, or observation of construction or construction of an improvement to, or survey of, real property.

(2) Injury to property, real or personal, arising out of any such latent deficiency.

Statute: LIMITATION OF ACTIONS

Tenn. Stat. §29-28-103 (2017)

(a) Any action against a manufacturer or seller of a product for injury to person or property caused by its defective or unreasonably dangerous condition must be brought within the period fixed by [statutes of limitations in other sections] but notwithstanding any exceptions to these provisions, it must be brought within six (6) years of the date of injury, in any event, the action must be brought within ten (10) years from the date on which the product was first purchased for use or consumption, or within one (1) year after the expiration of the anticipated life of the product, whichever is the shorter, except in the case of injury to minors whose action must be brought within a period of one (1) year after attaining the age of majority, whichever occurs sooner.

NOTES TO STATUTES

1. *Tolling of Statutes of Limitation for Children and Certain Disabled People.* Another circumstance suspends the running of the statute of limitations to protect children and others who are not able to care for their own property or protect their own rights. A disability exception ensures that those individuals' rights to bring suit will not be precluded by the running of the statute of limitations. An example of a statutory provision that tolls the statute until a child reaches the age of majority appears in §16.001(b) of the Texas Civil Practice and Remedies Code.

2. *Combining Statutes of Repose and Limitation.* A lawyer must be alert to the combined effect of statutes of limitation and statutes of repose. Statutes of repose may limit the application of the discovery rule and bar recovery even though the plaintiff had insufficient time to discover that he or she had a claim. States differ about whether fraudulent concealment tolls statutes of repose. Statutes of repose may also reduce the effect of the disability exception, as the Massachusetts statute does. Even though the disability exception to the statute of limitations may generally toll the statute of limitations until a child reaches his or her majority, the statute of repose for health care providers in Massachusetts creates a maximum time from the occurrence of the tortious act.

3. *Other Contexts for Statutes of Repose.* In addition to activity related to "improvements to land," illustrated in *Sedar* and the medical malpractice context of the Massachusetts statute, statutes of repose are important in products liability cases. Note how limitation periods and repose periods are combined in the Massachusetts and California statutes. Finally, compare the Tennessee statute of limitation and repose for construction claims, which combines the two limits with §2305.131 of the Ohio statute, discussed in *Sedar*.

8

APPORTIONMENT OF DAMAGES

I. Introduction

When tortious actions by multiple individuals are legal causes of a plaintiff's injury, tort law allocates responsibility for damages among those individuals. This apportionment used to be accomplished with a few clear rules that were based on an "all or nothing" approach to responsibility for injuries. They allocated all of the responsibility to either the plaintiff or the defendants. In contrast, modern tort law increasingly recognizes proportional and shared responsibility among plaintiffs and defendants.

The Defenses chapter examined multiple-cause cases in which one of the causes was the plaintiff's own negligence. As that chapter shows, when a plaintiff's injury is caused by a combination of negligent conduct by the plaintiff and one or more defendants, a small minority of jurisdictions allocate *all* of the responsibility to the *plaintiff*. Most jurisdictions now use doctrines that spread the responsibility among the *plaintiff* and the *defendant* or *defendants* in many of these cases. Contributory negligence and comparative negligence doctrines answer the question "When the plaintiff's conduct is one of the legal causes of the plaintiff's injury, does tort law allocate entire responsibility to the plaintiff, or will the plaintiff be entitled to receive some damages?"

This chapter deals with multiple-cause cases in which a jurisdiction does allow a plaintiff to recover damages. In some of these cases the plaintiff's own negligent conduct was a cause, but the jurisdiction's rules still allow the plaintiff some recovery. In other cases, the multiple causes are all negligent conduct by defendants, and the plaintiff's conduct was not tortious. For all of these cases, the primary question is "How much should each defendant pay?" If there are two or more defendants, tort law must determine the share of the damages for which each defendant is liable.

II. Apportioning Damages Among Liable Defendants

When more than one defendant's conduct is a legal cause of a plaintiff's injury and the plaintiff is entitled to recover damages, there are two solutions to the question of how much each defendant should pay. Common law recognized a system known as *joint and several liability*, with related doctrines of *contribution* and *indemnity*. Modern comparative fault systems sometimes apply joint and several liability and sometimes apply another doctrine, *several liability*.

At common law, when all plaintiffs who were entitled to damages were free from negligent conduct, there was a strong emphasis on maximizing the likelihood that the plaintiff would be able to collect the full amount of his or her judgment. Under the common law doctrine of joint and several liability, a plaintiff was entitled to enforce his or her entire judgment against each one of the defendants. This meant that the plaintiff could collect the entire sum from one of them or could collect part from one and part from another. However, the plaintiff was not allowed to collect a total amount greater than the judgment.

Because joint and several liability can lead to a situation in which a single defendant has paid all or most of a judgment, the common law developed procedures for redistributing that burden. One defendant may sue a second defendant for contribution if the first defendant pays more than his or her proper share. States have adopted a variety of rules for determining each defendant's proper share.

Several liability is a system in which each defendant is assigned an individual obligation to the plaintiff. The plaintiff may collect only that amount from each defendant. There are no procedures to redistribute the costs of the judgment among the defendants, because no defendant can have paid an amount in excess of his or her assigned share.

A. Joint and Several Liability

Joint and several liability treats each defendant as responsible for the entire judgment awarded to the plaintiff. When this doctrine developed under the contributory negligence system, cases did not involve findings about percentages of any parties' responsibility for injuries. Successful plaintiffs were always free from blame and liable defendants were always involved in *tortious* conduct. The adoption of comparative fault systems has led jurisdictions to question whether joint and several liability should be continued. Should each defendant be potentially responsible for paying the entire damages to which the plaintiff is entitled?

Carolina C. & O. Ry. et al. v. Hill introduces the traditional doctrine of joint and several liability, its application, and its implications. Lacy v. CSX Transportation, Inc. demonstrates the practical significance of the joint and several liability doctrine. Sitzes v. Anchor Motor Freight, Inc. reviews the common law development of joint and several liability and its related doctrine of contribution.

CAROLINA, C.& O. RY. ET AL. v. HILL

119 Va. 416 (1916)

HARRISON, J.

This action was brought by the plaintiff, Elkanah Hill, against Carolina, Clinchfield & Ohio Railway and certain contractors, the defendants, to recover damages for injuries alleged to have been done the plaintiff's real estate.

It appears that the plaintiff owned a farm in Dickenson County, on the bank of Russell Fork River, a nonnavigable stream, where he had resided for many years, containing 103 acres, upon which he had a mill which had for many years done the grinding for the people of the mountainous section in which it was located. In 1912 the defendants commenced the construction of a railroad down Russell Fork River on the opposite bank from the plaintiff, which resulted in the injuries to the plaintiff which are herein complained of.

The evidence tends to sustain the following allegations of the declaration: That the defendants, while constructing the railroad along Russell Fork river opposite the plaintiff's land, by blasting, excavating, and the careless use of explosives, hurled rocks, dirt, stumps, trees and other material upon his land, destroying his vegetation, timber, brush, shrubbery, grass and orchards; tore down and destroyed his fences, walls, and barns, damaged his fields, bottom lands, milldam and water power, filled up his milldam, choked his water wheel, millrace, mill appendages, and destroyed his mill site. The declaration further alleges that in constructing the railroad down the right bank, said embankment was so carelessly constructed out of loose material, and so impinged upon the bed of the river, that it diverted rainwater, natural floods and freshets towards the left bank, so that a portion of plaintiff's bottom land was washed away and the loose material, gravel, and stones from the embankment and banks and bottom land were washed in around the mill, and below the waterfall, so as to fill up the millrace, choke up the mill wheel, destroy the water power at that place, and divert the natural flow of the water away from the mill. By virtue of all which the plaintiff alleges that he is greatly damaged. The evidence further tends to show that the Yellow Poplar Lumber Company was engaged in removing from this section large quantities of lumber, which was done by floating or splashing the same down the river. This was accomplished by building in the river large splash dams which floated the logs out and down the river; that in March, 1913, an unusual freshet occurred in which great numbers of logs floated by the plaintiff's mill, thereby, as contended, contributing to the injuries complained of.

The trial resulted in a verdict and judgment in favor of the plaintiff for $2,000, which we are asked to review.

The objections taken to the action of the court in giving, refusing, and modifying instructions all involve the contention of the defendants that the splashes of the Yellow Poplar Lumber Company largely contributed to the damage sustained by the plaintiff, and that there could be no recovery in this action for that part of the damage properly chargeable to the Yellow Poplar Lumber Company; that where there are several concurrent causes due to independent authors, neither being sufficient to produce the entire loss, then each of the several parties concerned is liable only for the injuries due to his negligence. . . .

It does not satisfactorily appear from the evidence what, if any, part the Yellow Poplar Lumber Company had in bringing about the injuries sustained by the plaintiff. If the lumber company caused any part of the damage, it is manifest from the evidence that it would be impossible to separate the effects and ascertain, what part of the injury was attributable to its negligence. It is further clear from the evidence in the present case that the acts of the defendants alone were sufficient to have produced the entire damage complained of. Under the circumstances disclosed by the record, it is immaterial how many others may have been in fault, if the defendants' act was an efficient cause of the injury.

The doctrine is thoroughly established that where there are several concurrent negligent causes, the effects of which are not separable, though due to independent authors, either of which is sufficient to produce the entire loss, all are jointly or severally liable for the entire loss.

In Carlton v. Boudar, 118 Va. 521, 88 S. E. 174, 11 Va. App. 579, quoting from Shear. & Red. on Neg. §31, it is said:

> "If the injuries caused by the concurrent acts of two persons are plainly separable, so that the damage caused by each can be distinguished, each would be liable only for the damage which he caused, but if this is not the case, all persons who contribute to the injury by their negligence are liable jointly and severally for the whole damage." . . .

In Walton, Witten & Graham v. Miller, 109 Va. 210, 63 S. E. 458, 2 Va. App. 875, 132 Am. St. Rep. 908, it is said:

> "The weight of authority will, we think, support the more general proposition that when the negligence of two or more persons concurs in producing a single indivisible injury, then such persons are jointly and severally liable, although there was no common duty, common design or concert of action."

In Arminius Chemical Co. v. Landrum, 113 Va. 7, 73 S. E. 459, 6 Va. App. 111, 38 L. R. A. (N. S.) 272, Ann. Cas. 1913D, 1075, Judge Buchanan, in commenting upon an instruction, says:

> "It seems to have been based upon the principle announced in Grand Trunk Co. v. Cummings, 106 U. S. 700, 1 Sup. Ct. 493, 27 L. Ed. 266, in which it was held that, where separate and independent acts of negligence of two parties are the direct cause of a single injury to a third person, and it is impossible to determine in what proportion each contributed to the injury, either is responsible for the whole injury; and this although his act alone might not have caused the entire injury, and although, without fault on his part, the same damage would have resulted from the act of another."

In 21 Am. & Eng. Enc. of Law, 496, . . . it is further said:

> "Where the negligence of two or more persons, acting independently, concurrently results in an injury to a third, the latter may maintain his action for the entire loss against any one or all of the negligent parties, it not being essential to the maintenance of a joint action against several for negligence that they should be engaged in a common enterprise or sustain any relation whatever between themselves."

We are of opinion that, under the evidence of record, and in the light of the authorities cited, the plaintiff had the right to sue for and recover from the defendants alone the entire damages sustained by him, and therefore the action of the circuit court in giving, refusing, and modifying instructions was without prejudice to their rights. . . .

For these reasons the judgment complained of must be affirmed.

NOTES TO CAROLINA C. AND O. RY. v. HILL.

1. *Joint and Several Liability as a Damage Rule.* The joint and several rule described in *Carolina C. and O. Ry* is a damages rule applicable in cases where it is difficult or impossible to identify distinct injuries for which each of multiple defendants is a but-for cause. If the damage caused by each can be separated, liability is several—each defendant would be liable only for the damage he caused. If the damage cannot be separated, liability is joint and several—either defendant is responsible for all the damages. It does not matter whether the parties are acting in concert or whether each alone was sufficient to cause the entire harm, although there would also be joint and several liability in these cases. Joint and several liability has also been applied in cases where an employer and its employee are both sued for harm caused by the employee (see *respondeat superior* discussed later in this chapter).

2. Effect of Joint and Several Liability. Under joint and several liability, a plaintiff can sue any of two or more tortfeasors and recover his full damages. The rule supports the policy of compensating plaintiffs and deterring parties at fault, though it may put a burden on a defendant disproportionate to its fault. If the plaintiff recovers full damages from one party, the plaintiff cannot then seek recovery from any of the others. This encouraged plaintiffs to sue first the defendant with the best ability to pay. If the plaintiff recovered full compensation, she need not proceed further. If she did not, that might lead to new trials with the same basic facts against other defendants, which is not efficient from an administrative viewpoint. Courts have developed various rules permitting or requiring that all defendants be joined in the first trial.

LACY v. CSX TRANSPORTATION, INC.
520 S.E.2d 418 (W. Va. 1999)

McGRAW, J. . . .

Shortly after 11:00 p.m. on January 11, 1995, a car driven by Cacoe Sullivan left the Kroger parking lot in St. Albans, heading west on Third Avenue. Sullivan's fiancee, Richard Brooks, was riding in the front passenger's seat, while her mother, Tanya Lacy, was in the back seat with Sullivan's and Brooks's infant son. CSX's railroad tracks, comprised of two main-line and two side tracks, run parallel to Third Avenue immediately to the south.

While traveling on Third Avenue, Sullivan's car encountered a stop sign from where the occupants could see that the flashing lights and gates of the still-distant Fifth Street crossing were activated. Sullivan's vehicle proceeded to the intersection of Third Avenue and Fifth Street (adjacent to the crossing), slowed but did not stop at a stop sign, made a left turn onto Fifth Street, went around one of the lowered gate arms onto the tracks, and was struck broadside by a westbound train traveling at 50 miles per hour. Brooks was apparently rendered paraplegic by the accident. . . .

The central issue at trial with respect to CSX was whether it was negligent in permitting both fast- and slow-moving locomotives to approach the Fifth Street crossing simultaneously on its main-line tracks. The crossing had an active warning system consisting of flashing-light signals and automatic gates. Plaintiffs asserted at trial that the ability of the crossing warning system to provide a "positive warning" of an approaching train was effectively neutralized by CSX's practice of allowing slow-moving switching locomotives to use the main-line tracks. . . .

After hearing the evidence, the jury . . . rendered a special verdict regarding liability, finding CSX and Sullivan, as well as plaintiffs Tanya Lacy and Richard Brooks, negligent, but determining that Sullivan's negligence was the sole proximate cause of the accident. The jury ascribed one percent negligence each to CSX, Lacy and Brooks, and ninety-seven percent to defendant Sullivan. The circuit court entered judgment in favor of CSX based upon the jury's special verdict. Plaintiffs' subsequent Motion for a New Trial and Judgment Notwithstanding the Verdict was denied by the trial court.

Plaintiffs first contend that the trial court erred in permitting counsel for CSX to argue the potential post-judgment effects of joint and several liability to the jury.[8] We reverse on this issue, finding that the trial court abused its discretion by permitting counsel for CSX to speculate and otherwise mislead the jury regarding whether the railroad would ultimately be charged with paying the entire judgment if both CSX and defendant Sullivan were found at fault.

Prior to trial, plaintiffs filed a motion in limine "to exclude any questions, suggestions, comments, allegations, testimony or argument by the defendant, [CSX], as to the effect that West Virginia's joint and several liability law may have upon [CSX]." . . .

The trial court . . . ruled that CSX could argue joint and several liability and "point out the intrigue." . . .

Counsel for CSX stated the following during closing argument:

> Let's just stop for a minute and let's talk about what this case is really about, what has been going on here for two weeks in this trial. Tanya Lacy, Richard Brooks, and Cacoe Sullivan are family. This is not a case where we have two plaintiffs suing two defendants. This is a case in which the family is trying to get money from the railroad. Tanya Lacy doesn't want anything from her daughter.
>
> They spent two weeks trying to convince you that CSX was at fault. They didn't spend two weeks trying to convince you that Cacoe Sullivan was at fault. Why not? I'll tell why not. If you go back into that jury room and return this verdict of shared responsibility that [plaintiffs' counsel] wants, if you go back into that jury room and return a verdict that says . . . 99 percent Cacoe Sullivan's fault, 1 percent CSX's fault, guess what? Tanya Lacy and Richard Brooks can collect the entire judgment from CSX. They can also collect it from Cacoe Sullivan, if they wanted, but what are the odds a mother is going to actually ask her daughter.
>
> So when you go back into that jury room and fill out this verdict form, any finding on the part of CSX, 1 percent, 10 percent, 50 percent, 100 percent, it's the same thing. One percent is, in essence, telling CSX, you are completely and totally responsible for this accident. . . .

Counsel for Cacoe Sullivan objected to this argument at the time it was delivered, but was overruled by the trial court. . . .

There are divergent views concerning the appropriateness of informing the jury of the effects of joint and several liability. Some jurisdictions, employing the same rationale used to permit instruction and argument on the workings of modified comparative negligence, sanction informing juries about joint and several liability because, in their estimation, juries are likely to respond to such information by being more conscientious about assigning responsibility to defendants. For example, in *Luna* [v. Shockey Sheet Metal & Welding Co., 113 Idaho 193, 195-197, 743 P.2d 61, 64 (1987)], the Idaho Supreme Court stated that the doctrine of joint and several liability, under which a defendant assessed a mere 1% negligence may be

---

[8] Under the doctrine of joint and several liability, "[a] plaintiff may elect to sue any and all of those responsible for his [or her] injuries and collect his [or her] damages from whomever is able to pay, irrespective of their percentage of fault." Syl. pt. 2, in part, Sitzes v. Anchor Motor Freight, Inc., 169 W. Va. 698, 289 S.E.2d 679 (1982).

required to pay 100% of plaintiff's damages if, for some reason, the joint tortfeasor is unreachable through the judicial process, "poses a trap for the uninformed jury." An informed jury will be much more likely to carefully examine the facts prior to reaching a verdict holding a defendant even 1% at fault, no matter how cosmetically appealing a partial allocation of fault might be.

Other courts stress that consideration of joint and several liability is not relevant to determining any issue of fact. The Court of Appeals of South Carolina recently took this approach, where it held that it was not error for a trial court to refuse an instruction on joint and several liability "because the doctrine has no bearing on the jury's ultimate fact-finding role in determining the relative negligence of joint tortfeasors." Fernanders v. Marks Constr. of S.C., Inc., 330 S.C. 470, 475, 499 S.E.2d 509, 510-11 (S.C. Ct. App. 1998).

Courts on both sides of the debate take credible positions; however, we perceive that resolution of this issue turns on practical considerations that have only been lightly touched upon.

. . . Any conclusion about how joint and several liability will ultimately affect a particular defendant is largely speculative. As the Superior Court of Pennsylvania pointed out in holding that it was proper for a trial court to refuse a jury instruction on joint and several liability, "neither the court nor the jury can say with assurance how much of the verdict rendered, if any, any one tortfeasor will in fact pay." *Dranzo* [v. Winterhalter, 395 Pa. Super. 578, 592, 577 A.2d 1349, 1356 (1990)]. . . .

The line of argument pursued by CSX in the present case demonstrates how any consideration of the potential post-judgment effects of joint and several liability is likely to degenerate into conjecture about whether a particular defendant will ultimately bear a greater portion of the plaintiff's loss than is attributable to its fault. Counsel for CSX speculated that plaintiffs would be unwilling to collect any judgment against Cacoe Sullivan, and would instead resort to forcing CSX to pay the entire judgment. While such an outcome is perhaps a plausible inference given the unique familial relationship of these parties, there was nothing in evidence that otherwise directly supported such a contention.

CSX's argument was, in any event, misleading to the extent that it implied that plaintiffs could ultimately control who would pay. This obviously ignores the fact that CSX would, if it were called upon by plaintiffs to satisfy the entire judgment, have a right of comparative contribution against Sullivan. . . .

We are not inclined to sanction forays into matters that invite speculation and conjecture on the part of the jury, and which do not suggest an easy stopping point with respect to the disclosures necessary to avoid misleading the trier of fact. Nor in the case of joint and several liability do we discern, as we did in [a prior decision authorizing instructions about the effects of comparative negligence] that juries are likely to harbor or otherwise act upon misconceptions regarding this doctrine. Accordingly, we hold that in a civil trial it is generally an abuse of discretion for the trial court to instruct the jury or permit argument by counsel regarding the operation of the doctrine of joint and several liability, where the purpose thereof is to communicate to the jury the potential post-judgment effect of their assignment of fault.

. . . If, as we have repeatedly declared, "this jurisdiction is committed to the concept of joint and several liability among tortfeasors," a defendant cannot be permitted to argue against a finding of fault based upon misleading speculation about the possible ramifications of the doctrine's application. . . .

For the reasons stated, the judgment of the Circuit Court of Kanawha County is hereby reversed and remanded for a new trial consistent with this opinion.

[Dissenting opinion omitted.]

NOTES TO LACY v. CSX TRANSPORTATION, INC.

1. *The Plaintiff's Options Under Joint and Several Liability.* Under the doctrine of joint and several liability, the plaintiff may collect the entire amount of damages from any defendant whose negligence was a proximate cause of her harms. Cacoe Sullivan negligently drove around the lowered gates. The railroad was negligent for permitting both fast- and slow-moving trains to approach the crossing simultaneously. The other plaintiffs were apparently also negligent, in some way that is not clear from the case, but that negligence was not a proximate cause of the harm, so their contributions were ignored. If Cacoe Sullivan's conduct and CSX's conduct were both proximate causes of the accident and Richard Brooks's damages were $100,000, how much would he be entitled to collect from each defendant? How did the jury's special verdict affect that plaintiff's option?

2. *Plaintiff's Choice Among Defendants.* In *Lacy*, one defendant, Cacoe Sullivan, was relatively poor and the other, CSX, was relatively wealthy. How might this affect Richard Brooks's choice of how to collect his damages in a joint and several liability jurisdiction? How would the family relationship affect the choice? What supports the court's conclusion that the amount any one tortfeasor will pay is "conjecture"?

3. *Jury Comprehension of Legal Doctrines.* The *Lacy* court notes that jurisdictions are split on the issue of informing the jury about the joint and several liability doctrine. On a related question, informing the jury about the operation of the general system of comparative negligence, almost all states approve letting the jury know the consequences of various allocations of fault. The *Lacy* court distinguishes that body of law, saying that while juries might harbor misconceptions about comparative fault, they are not likely to have similar misconceptions about joint and several liability. Do differences between those two rules support the court's supposition about juries?

SITZES v. ANCHOR MOTOR FREIGHT, INC.
289 S.E.2d 679 (W. Va. 1982)

MILLER, J.

We have accepted certain certified questions from the United States District Court for the Southern District of West Virginia. . . . Generally, we are asked to state . . . what effect our adoption of comparative negligence as announced in Bradley v. Appalachian Power Co., 163 W. Va. 332, 256 S.E.2d 879 (1979), has upon the rules of contribution among joint tortfeasors. . . .

The facts of the case have been presented to us as follows:

Plaintiffs in this action, Arnold L. Sitzes and Edward L. Rucks, are administrators of the estate of Patricia Ann Roberson. Mrs. Roberson was killed in an automobile accident on January 19, 1977. At the time, she was a passenger in a pick-up truck driven by her husband, James R. Roberson, which collided with a motor truck driven by Oswald R. Carter, an agent and employee of the defendant Anchor

Motor Freight, Inc. Mrs. Roberson is survived by her husband and her son, Joseph Eugene Roberson.

Plaintiffs commenced this action against the defendant on November 23, 1977. With leave of court, defendant filed a third-party complaint for contribution against Mr. Roberson on February 12, 1980. This court, perceiving a potential conflict between West Virginia's normal rules of contribution (which would apportion damages equally among joint tortfeasors) and the state's newly-adopted rule of comparative negligence (which requires a jury to "assign the proportion or degree of this total negligence among the various parties," Bradley v. Appalachian Power, 163 W. Va. 332, 256 S.E. 2d 879, 885 (1979), and which denies recovery to a plaintiff whose negligence equals or exceeds 50% of the combined negligence of the parties to the accident), instructed the jury to assign percentages of fault to the third-party plaintiff [Anchor Motor Freight] and third-party defendant [James R. Roberson] if it found that both had been negligent. Plaintiffs' decedent was not negligent, and was therefore excluded from the apportioning.

On March 31, 1981, the jury returned a verdict for the plaintiffs and against the defendants and assessed plaintiffs' damages in the amount of $100,000. . . .

In the present case, the trial court permitted the jury to apportion the degree of primary negligence (as opposed to contributory negligence) between the two joint tortfeasors. The jury concluded that the defendant, Anchor Motor Freight, Inc., [hereinafter Anchor], was 70% at fault while the third-party defendant, Mr. Roberson, was found to be 30% at fault. The certified question inherently demands consideration of whether we recognized that primary fault or negligence should be apportioned among joint tortfeasors in accordance with their degrees of fault.

The basic purpose of the joint and several liability rule is to permit the injured plaintiff to select and collect the full amount of his damages against one or more joint tortfeasors. This rule however need not preclude a right of comparative contribution between the joint tortfeasors inter se. The purpose of this latter rule is to require the joint tortfeasors to share in contribution based upon the degree of fault that each has contributed to the accident. There is a definite trend in the field of tort law toward allocation of judgmental liability between the joint tortfeasors inter se. It is thought to be fairer to require them to respond in damages based on their degrees of fault.

Historically, at common law, there was no right of contribution between joint tortfeasors on the theory that the law should not aid wrongdoers. The historic development of this point is contained in Northwest Airlines, Inc. v. Transport Workers Union of America, AFL-CIO, et al., 451 U.S. 77, 101 S. Ct. 1571, 67 L. Ed. 2d 750 (1981), where Justice Stevens states in note 17:

> Thirty-nine States and the District of Columbia recognize to some extent a right to contribution among joint tortfeasors. In 10 jurisdictions, the common-law rule was initially changed by judicial action.

The right of contribution developed because it was thought unfair to have one of several joint tortfeasors pay the entire judgment and not be able to obtain contribution from any of his fellow wrongdoers. It would seem proper social policy that a wrongdoer should not escape his liability on the fortuitous event that another paid the entire joint judgment. . . .

In this State since 1872, by virtue of W. Va. Code, 55-7-13, we have permitted a right of contribution between joint tortfeasors after judgment. . . . Thus, our cases in both contract and tort have utilized the phrases "joint and several liability" and the "right of contribution" if the judgment debtor pays more than his pro tanto share of the liability. The traditional method of assigning pro tanto liability was to divide the judgment by the number of debtors who were liable on the judgment.

Once a right of contribution was recognized between joint tortfeasors, courts and commentators began to realize that a more equitable method of handling the right of contribution inter se would be to allocate it according to the degrees of fault attributable to each tortfeasor. This concept arose from the fact that in many cases involving joint tortfeasors, the tortfeasors were vastly unequal in their degrees of fault or negligence.

One of the catalysts for adopting a system of comparative contribution was the relaxation of the common law rule that a plaintiff's contributory negligence completely barred his recovery. With the adoption of comparative negligence statutes and case decisions allowing allocation of negligence between plaintiffs and defendants, the allocation of fault among joint tortfeasors seemed the next logical step.

Comparative contribution makes the right of contribution equitable to the degree of fault between each tortfeasor. This is in keeping with the trend toward reducing substantial artificiality or unfairness in tort law. A number of states by statute now base contribution on relative fault. Several courts have independent of any legislation adopted a form of comparative contribution.

Over the last twenty years there has been a noticeable trend in our tort decisions to ameliorate the rigidity of many common law rules. In the earlier portions of this opinion, we cited our cases which have lifted the bar of various common law immunity doctrines. In *Bradley* we alleviated the harshness of the doctrine of contributory negligence. . . .

. . . *Bradley* did [not] discuss the question of whether the primary fault of the defendant joint tortfeasors should be allocated in accordance with their respective degrees of fault. However, the fundamental concepts of . . . *Bradley* lead ineluctably to this conclusion as they are . . . premised on making a more equitable adjustment of tort liability based on a party's degree of fault. . . . We, therefore, conclude that as between joint tortfeasors a right of comparative contribution exists inter se based upon their relative degrees of primary fault or negligence. By moderating the bar of contributory negligence for the plaintiff and permitting comparative contribution between joint tortfeasors, we have provided a reasonable balance of fairness for both plaintiffs and defendants. . . .

The certified [question] having been answered, this case is dismissed from the docket.

NOTES TO SITZES v. ANCHOR MOTOR FREIGHT, INC.

1. *Terminology: Third-Party Plaintiffs and Defendants.* *Sitzes* involved a tort claim and a contribution claim. The administrators of the estate of Patricia Ann Roberson sued the defendant, Anchor Motor Freight, for damages due to her death in a motor vehicle accident. In the contribution claim, Anchor Motor Freight, described as a "third party plaintiff," sued James R. Roberson, the plaintiff's husband, who became the "third party defendant." Anchor Motor Freight alleged that James Roberson's negligence also contributed to the death of the original plaintiff and that he should therefore contribute to the damages. Factual issues arising from both claims — most significantly, the defendants' relative degrees of fault — were decided in the same trial.

2. Contribution Under Joint and Several Liability. After adopting modified comparative negligence, West Virginia retained its joint and several liability rule but modified its contribution rule. Under joint and several liability, how much of the $100,000 damages could the estate collect from either Anchor Motor Freight or James R. Roberson?

Sitzes substituted contribution based on degree of fault for contribution based on an equal division of liability. After the plaintiff's estate had recovered from one or the other of the defendants (or perhaps some part of the total from each), any defendant who has paid more than its share is entitled to collect the overage from the other defendant. Imagine that the plaintiff's estate collected the $100,000 from Anchor Motor Freight. How much would Anchor Motor Freight collect from James R. Roberson under the equal division rule or under the degree-of-fault rule?

B. Several Liability

In recent years, many state legislatures have eliminated or modified the joint and several liability doctrine. Several liability is often the general rule, with joint and several liability retained as an exception for specifically identified types of cases. Piner v. Superior Court illustrates how several liability works when multiple defendants have contributed to a single "indivisible" injury. The statutes following *Piner* show various ways of defining special circumstances in which joint and several liability will apply. Roderick v. Lake examines apportionment where the liability of multiple defendants arises for reasons other than a plaintiff's having suffered an indivisible harm.

PINER v. SUPERIOR COURT
962 P.2d 909 (Ariz. 1998)

FELDMAN, J.

On his way to work on Friday, October 12, 1990, William Piner stopped his truck to let a pedestrian cross the street. While he was stopped, a car driven by Billy Jones hit Piner's truck from behind. Police were called to investigate the incident. Piner waited for the police to finish their investigation before calling his physician to complain of pain in his neck, upper back, left arm, and head. The doctor's staff told Piner that the doctor was unavailable but would call him back later that day. Piner then fixed the broken tail lights on his truck and went to work.

Later that day, Piner was driving to lunch when the car ahead of him stopped to let some pedestrians cross the street. Piner stopped and was again hit from the rear, this time by a vehicle driven by Cynthia Richardson. Feeling similar pain symptoms after this accident, Piner called his doctor's office and was again told that the doctor was occupied and would contact him later.

Piner was unable to see his physician until Monday. After examination, the doctor concluded that Piner suffered a number of injuries as a result of the collisions. Due to the nature of the injuries, however, neither she nor any other physician has been able to attribute any particular part of Piner's total injuries to one accident or the other.

Piner filed an action against Jones and Richardson (together "Defendants") alleging indivisible injuries resulting from the successive impacts. Neither defendant has asserted that he or she could apportion the particular physical harm Piner suffered between the separate accidents. Apparently, all parties agree that both collisions contributed to Piner's total physical injuries.

Piner moved for partial summary judgment, arguing that because his injuries are indivisible, defendants should be held jointly and severally liable. According to Piner, in a successive accident, indivisible injury case, defendants have the burden of proving apportionment; if neither defendant can demonstrate what portion of the total damage he or she caused, they should be held jointly and severally liable for the entire amount.

Richardson responded that A.R.S. §12-2506 abolished the system of joint and several liability, leaving only two exceptions in which the doctrine can still be invoked. Richardson concluded that because neither exception applied to Piner's claim, "the trier of fact must be directed to either apportion, or deny damages in this case." After hearing oral argument on the motion, the trial judge, in a June 4, 1996 order, denied Piner's motion for "the reasons stated [by] Defendant Richardson. . . ."

. . . We granted review to determine which rule of liability applies to cases in which successive acts of negligence combine to produce separate but indivisible injuries. . . .

The Arizona Legislature enacted its first version of [the Uniform Contribution Among Tortfeasors Act] (UCATA) in 1984. . . . Under this new regime, the factfinder allocated a percentage of fault to each culpable actor. Even though the culpable defendants were still jointly and severally liable for all damages, the legislature established a right of contribution that allowed a defendant held liable for more than his share of fault to recover from the other tortfeasors in proportion to their several contributions of fault. This change was intended to bring about a system in which each tortfeasor would eventually contribute only a portion of damage equal to the percentage of fault attributed to that tortfeasor by the factfinder. But Arizona's negligence law still produced harsh results when one defendant was insolvent, thus leaving the others unable to obtain contribution. See, e.g., *Gehres* [v. City of Phoenix, 753 P.2d 174 (Ariz. App. 1987)] (defendants assigned five percent of fault held jointly and severally liable for one hundred percent of damages).

In response, the Arizona Legislature amended UCATA, abolishing joint liability and replacing it with a system that requires the court to allocate responsibility among all parties who caused the injury, whether or not they are present in the action. §12-2506. Under the present version of UCATA, "the liability of each defendant is several only and not joint." §12-2506(D). Taken in isolation, this wording tends to support Defendants' argument, but several factors militate against such an interpretation. First, the legislative intent was to cure the *Gehres* "deep pocket" problem of a defendant only minimally at fault yet liable for the full amount of damages.

A second factor is that the old rule conditioned the plaintiff's recovery on the impossible: if unable to divide the indivisible, the plaintiff was denied relief and the culpable parties were relieved of all responsibility. The injustice inherent in this policy has been repeatedly recognized by our courts. We do not believe that when the legislature attempted to eliminate the injustice it perceived in the deep pocket problem, it also intended to reestablish an unfair regime under which an innocent victim is denied any relief because the damages caused by independent wrongdoers result in an indivisible, unapportionable injury.

Most important, the clear text of UCATA does not require that a defendant's liability be limited by apportioning damages, but only by apportioning fault:

A. In an action for personal injury, property damage or wrongful death, the liability of each defendant for damages is several only and is not joint. . . . Each defendant is liable only for the amount of damages allocated to that defendant in direct proportion to that defendant's percentage of fault. . . . [T]he trier of fact shall multiply the total amount of damages recoverable by the plaintiff by the percentage of each defendant's fault, and that amount is the maximum recoverable against the defendant. . . .

B. In assessing percentages of fault the trier of fact shall consider the fault of all persons who contributed to the alleged injury. . . .

F. (2) "Fault" means an actionable breach of legal duty, act or omission proximately causing or contributing to injury or damages sustained by a person seeking recovery, including negligence in all of its degrees. . . .

§12-2506(A), (B), & (F)(2).

Thus, while UCATA requires the plaintiff to prove that a defendant's conduct was a cause of injury, it does not instruct us to limit liability by apportioning damages. Instead, each tortfeasor whose conduct caused injury is severally liable only for a percentage of the total damages recoverable by the plaintiff, the percentage based on each actor's allocated share of fault.

We conclude, therefore, that the present version of UCATA has left intact the rule of indivisible injury, relieving the plaintiff of apportioning damage according to causal contribution. When the tortious conduct of more than one defendant contributes to one indivisible injury, the entire amount of damage resulting from all contributing causes is the total amount "of damages recoverable by the plaintiff," as that term is used in §12-2506(A). . . . Contrary to the common law and cases such as *Gehres*, the fault of all actors is compared and each defendant is severally liable for damages allocated "in direct proportion to that defendant's percentage of fault." §12-2506(A). To determine each defendant's liability "the trier of fact shall multiply the total amount of damages recoverable by the plaintiff by the percentage of each defendant's fault, and that amount is the maximum recoverable against the defendant." Id.

Thus in an indivisible injury case, the factfinder is to compute the total amount of damage sustained by the plaintiff and the percentage of fault of each tortfeasor. Multiplying the first figure by the second gives the maximum recoverable against each tortfeasor. This result conforms not only with the intent of the legislature and the text of the statute but also with common sense. When damages cannot be apportioned between multiple tortfeasors, there is no reason why those whose conduct produced successive but indivisible injuries should be treated differently from those whose independent conduct caused injury in a single accident. . . . [W]e see no reason to employ a different rule if the injuries occur at once, five minutes apart or, as in the present case, several hours apart. The operative fact is simply that the conduct of each defendant was a cause and the result is indivisible damage. . . .

In the present case, the trial judge erred in placing the burden of proof on apportionment on Piner. Assuming Piner proves that the conduct of both Jones and Richardson contributed to the final result, the burden of proof on apportionment is on them. If the judge concludes there is no evidence that would permit apportionment, then the case should be treated as one involving indivisible injuries. If the judge further concludes there is no evidence on which to base a jury finding of inability to apportion, then the jurors must be instructed to apportion. If the evidence on the question of apportionment is conflicting, the jurors should be instructed that if they are able to apportion damages, they should do so, allocating fault and damages for each accident separately. They should also be instructed that if they are unable to apportion damages, then they are to determine Piner's total damages resulting from both accidents. In such case, the indivisible injury rule will apply. In all cases in which the indivisible injury rule applies as either a matter of law or on a jury finding of inability to apportion, the plaintiff's recovery will be the total damage sustained. But in all such indivisible injury cases, the jurors must be instructed to allocate fault in accordance with §12-2506. The judge is then to multiply each tortfeasor's percentage of fault by the amount recoverable by the plaintiff. Each tortfeasor in an indivisible injury case is then severally liable for the product of that calculation. . . .

The trial court's June 4, 1996 order denying Piner's motion for partial summary judgment and July 31, 1996 ruling regarding jury instruction content are vacated. The trial court may proceed in accordance with this opinion.

NOTES TO PINER v. SUPERIOR COURT

1. *Divisible and Indivisible Injuries.* Multi-actor cases can involve divisible or indivisible injuries. When injuries are divisible, it is possible to establish which actor caused which harm. For divisible injuries, the but-for test for causation could assign responsibility for each injury to the particular defendant without whose act the injury would not have occurred. So if Defendant One acted negligently in a way that broke a plaintiff's arm and Defendant Two acted negligently in a way that broke that plaintiff's leg, the but-for test would treat Defendant One as a cause-in-fact of the broken arm and would treat Defendant Two as a cause-in-fact of the broken leg. Each actor would pay for the injury that he or she caused.

If the victim who suffered a broken arm and a broken leg suffered a further problem that could have been caused by either the broken leg or broken arm, such as an allergic reaction to materials used to make casts for the broken limbs, that allergic reaction would be called an indivisible injury. There would be no way to identify whether it had been caused by the defendant who broke the victim's arm or the defendant who broke the victim's leg. Death can also be an indivisible injury. If death occurs after a victim has suffered a number of separate injuries, there will often be no way to determine whether any single injury was a but-for cause of the death.

The lack of precise information about whose conduct caused what part of an indivisible injury requires a decision about who should suffer due to the lack of information: the plaintiff or the defendants. Where injuries are divisible, the plaintiff must establish which defendant caused which harm or recover nothing. Where injuries are indivisible, the traditional rule is that defendants must establish which defendant caused which harm or share the liability between them. The Restatement (Second) of Torts §433B comment d provides the rationale for this rule, stating that it would be unjust to allow "a proved wrongdoer who has in fact caused harm to the plaintiff to escape liability merely because the harm which he has inflicted has combined with similar harm inflicted by other wrongdoers, and the nature of the harm itself has made it necessary that evidence be produced before it can be apportioned."

The defendants in *Piner* claimed that abolishing joint and several liability meant that defendants' joint responsibility for indivisible harms was also abolished. If joint responsibility for indivisible harm is abolished and several liability based on who caused what is impossible, the court must either award nothing or find some new way to determine defendants' respective shares of liability. How does the court reconcile the abolition of joint and several liability with requiring defendants who cause indivisible harm to share the liability?

2. Practical and Conceptual Indivisibility. If the plaintiff in *Piner* had been examined by doctors after each of the two vehicular accidents, perhaps the effects of each one might have been identifiable. The lack of such an examination presents a practical reason why the plaintiff's injuries came to be treated as indivisible. In some cases, there is no possibility that more information could assign particular harms to particular actors. For example, in Lacy v. CSX Transportation, Inc., the negligence of the car driver putting the plaintiff on the railroad tracks in front of a train combined with the negligence of the railroad to produce a single impact with indivisible consequences. Because there was just one impact, conceptualizing separate causal contributions is impossible as a matter of logic. Tort doctrines treat apportionment the same way in cases involving practically indivisible and conceptually indivisible harms.

Problem
Effect of Applying Several Liability

In Glomb v. Glomb, 530 A.2d 1362 (Pa. Super. Ct. 1986), the child-plaintiff's parents were negligent in their hiring and supervision of the child's babysitter, Sherry Ginosky. Even after noticing that the child was often bruised after being left with the sitter, the parents continued to employ Ms. Ginosky. Eventually, the child suffered severe injuries while under the babysitter's care, due to the babysitter's tortious conduct. A guardian for the child sued the parents for the severe injuries resulting from parents continuing to hire Ginosky. The parents joined the babysitter in the suit as a co-defendant.

Imagine that this jurisdiction has been a joint and several liability jurisdiction and only recently adopted comparative negligence. If the jurisdiction has not yet decided whether to abandon joint and several liability and you are representing the plaintiff, should you argue for adoption of the rule in *Piner* or the rule in *Lacy*? If the babysitter has no money to satisfy a judgment, will that affect your decision?

Statute: RECOVERY OF DAMAGES BASED ON PARTY'S RESPONSIBILITY
N.J. Stat. §2A:15-5.3(a), (c) (2017)

Except as provided in subsection d. of this section [covering environmental tort actions], the party so recovering may recover as follows:

a. The full amount of the damages from any party determined by the trier of fact to be 60% or more responsible for the total damages. . . .

c. Only that percentage of the damages directly attributable to that party's negligence or fault from any party determined by the trier of fact to be less than 60% responsible for the total damages.

Statute: JOINT TORT-FEASORS; NATURE OF LIABILITY

Miss. Stat. Ann. §85-5-7(1), (2), (4) (2017)

(1) As used in this section, "fault" means an act or omission of a person which is a proximate cause of injury or death to another person or persons, damages to property, tangible or intangible, or economic injury, including, but not limited to, negligence, malpractice, strict liability, absolute liability or failure to warn. "Fault" shall not include any tort which results from an act or omission committed with a specific wrongful intent.

(2) Except as otherwise provided in subsection (4) of this section, in any civil action based on fault, the liability for damages caused by two (2) or more persons shall be several only, and not joint and several and a joint tort-feasor shall be liable only for the amount of damages allocated to him in direct proportion to his percentage of fault. . . .

(4) Joint and several liability shall be imposed on all who consciously and deliberately pursue a common plan or design to commit a tortious act, or actively take part in it. Any person held jointly and severally liable under this section shall have a right of contribution from his fellow defendants acting in concert.

Statute: ABOLITION OF JOINT AND SEVERAL LIABILITY; EXCEPTIONS

Haw. Rev. Stat. Ann. §663-10.9 (2017)

Joint and several liability for joint tortfeasors as defined in section 663-11 is abolished except in the following circumstances:

(1) For the recovery of economic damages against joint tortfeasors in actions involving injury or death to persons;

(2) For the recovery of economic and noneconomic damages against joint tortfeasors in actions involving:

(A) Intentional torts;

(B) Torts relating to environmental pollution;

(C) Toxic and asbestos-related torts;

(D) Torts relating to aircraft accidents;

(E) Strict and products liability torts. . . .

NOTES TO STATUTES

1. *Fault Threshold and Damage Threshold Several Liability.*   The New Jersey statute illustrates one way of serving two competing goals: providing full compensation to plaintiffs and apportioning liability according to fault. The statute retains joint liability to some extent. Imagine a case with defendants *A, B,* and *C* whose shares of fault are 65 percent, 20 percent, and 10 percent, respectively, and a plaintiff with a 5 percent share of fault whose damages total $100,000. Under New Jersey's fault threshold approach, what is the maximum the plaintiff would be entitled to collect from each defendant?

An alternative approach retained joint liability up to a percentage of damages threshold. Until 1996 and 2004, respectively, Mississippi and Louisiana statutes provided that liability for damages caused by two or more persons was joint only to the extent necessary for the person suffering injury, death, or loss to recover 50 percent of his damages. As a result, a defendant could be assessed up to 50 percent of the damages even if the person's fault amounted to less than 50 percent. This approach seems to have died out after those statutes were amended. As the statute reproduced above illustrates, Mississippi has abolished joint and several liability except in concerted action cases. Louisiana now takes that approach as well.

2. *Harm-Based Retention of Joint and Several Liability.* The Hawaii statute illustrates a third approach taken by state legislatures concerning the switch from joint to several liability: retaining joint and several liability for certain types of conduct and harms.

RODERICK v. LAKE
778 P.2d 443 (N.M. Ct. App. 1989)

BIVINS, C.J.

Plaintiff sued to recover damages for personal injuries sustained when the car he was driving struck two thoroughbred horses on Christmas Eve 1985. Following a bench trial, the court found no negligence on the part of defendant Robert W. Lake, the owner of the fenced property on which the horses were kept, and dismissed plaintiff's complaint against him with prejudice. Plaintiff does not appeal that dismissal. The trial court found the remaining defendants, Edgar L. Lake and Roland Hohenberg, the owners of the two horses, . . . jointly and severally liable to plaintiff for the damages awarded. It predicated liability on the doctrine of *res ipsa loquitur* as well as negligent violation of applicable statutes and San Juan County, N.M., Ordinance 10 (July 20, 1982) [which provides that "Any person owning or having charge, custody, care or control of any animal shall keep such animal on his premises."]. The trial court assessed no negligence against plaintiff. From a judgment on the findings, Edgar and Roland appeal. . . .

Summarizing the trial court's findings of fact, plaintiff was traveling west on County Road 6700 in San Juan County at approximately 6:00 p.m. on December 24, 1985, in a safe and lawful manner, when two horses darted onto the highway in front of him. "It was dark at the time . . . and the horses were dark colored." Plaintiff did not have time to brake and recalled no details of the accident. He suffered serious injuries.

Robert owned the land adjacent to the county road. His brother, Edgar, kept several of his horses there, including one of the horses involved in the accident. Roland, an associate and trainer for Edgar, owned the other horse and also kept it on Robert's property.

Edgar had brought the two horses from the racetrack around 3:30 p.m. the day of the accident and fed them at 5:00 p.m., after which Edgar left. Roland remained there. Since Roland did not testify, we are not told if he left subsequent to Edgar and before the accident or remained there until the accident occurred.

There was testimony that the horses could not escape except through the gate. After the accident the gate was found "sprung open." The latch on the gate confining the horses had been left open.

[The court affirmed the trial court's finding that defendants' conduct constituted negligence for which they were liable.]

Except to the extent modified by statute, NMSA 1978, Section 41-3A-1 (Cum. Supp. 1988), which the parties agree does not apply to this case, joint and several liability among concurrent tortfeasors no longer exists in New Mexico. Each concurrent tortfeasor is liable only for his apportioned fault or negligence. . . .

We agree that the trial court must apportion fault in this case, and remand for that purpose. Because of the rather unusual circumstances, we offer guidance to the trial court.

The question presented is, How does the trier of fact apportion fault or negligence when there is no direct evidence as to which concurrent tortfeasor caused the harm? Ancillary to that question is the further question of which party bears the burden of proving apportionment under these circumstances.

Normally, of course, the plaintiff bears the burden of proving that a defendant's negligence caused his injury. In cases such as this, however, we hold that, where defendants are independent but concurrent tortfeasors and thus each liable for the damage caused by him alone, but the matter of apportionment is incapable of proof, the innocent wronged party should not be deprived of redress. Rather, the wrongdoers should be left to work out between themselves any apportionment. Under the circumstances present in this case, the burden shifts to each defendant to absolve himself, if he can, thereby relieving the wronged party of the duty of apportioning fault as between defendants. . . .

We adopt this rule in New Mexico as the fairest and most logical way to determine the amount of fault of two or more tortfeasors in the unusual circumstances of cases such as this one, where plaintiff can prove defendants were negligent, but cannot prove which defendant's negligence caused the injury, or which defendant was more at fault.

On remand the trial court should consider apportionment between defendants, based upon this burden which rests with them, not plaintiff. While this task is difficult, we do not believe it impossible. As we have previously discussed, there is evidence from which the court could infer that Edgar was the last one to leave the gate before the horses escaped, and that Roland remained on the property but was somewhere else at the time Edgar left. If the trial court infers that Roland did not leave before the accident, then his negligence would be for not observing the improperly secured gate or the fact that the horses had escaped. We express no opinion as to how such apportionment should be made based on these and other relevant facts before the court. . . .

NOTES TO RODERICK v. LAKE

1. *Alternative Liability and Indivisible Harms.* Both horse owners were negligent per se because each violated the statute obliging them to keep the horses on their premises. Under joint and several liability, both horse owners would have been liable to the car driver for the full amount of damages. A New Mexico statute had, however, replaced joint and several liability with several liability. Because this was a bench trial, the judge was obliged to determine the defendants' respective liability, and, therefore, their relative degrees of fault. The appellate court acknowledged the difficulty in apportioning fault in alternative liability cases where the plaintiff cannot show which of two concurrent tortfeasors caused an indivisible harm, but it required the trial court to examine each defendant's conduct.

Each party's degree of negligence depends on the trial court's factual findings. Both violated the statute, but the court, as factfinder, was obliged to find some way to distinguish between the conduct of the horse owners. The appellate court found that there was at least some evidence about the horse owners' conduct. Perhaps the trial court could find that one defendant came through the gate last and left it open. Or perhaps Edgar was the last one to leave the gate open before the horses escaped and Roland later failed to observe that the gate was improperly secured or that the horses had escaped. In that situation, would the case involve alternative liability or concurrent tortfeasors creating an indivisible harm? Based on its conclusions about the facts, the trial court could find that one was more at fault than the other or that their degrees of fault were equal.

2. *Concerted Action and Apportionment of Liability.* Courts and legislatures have taken different positions on whether defendants who act in concert will be held jointly and severally liable or only severally liable. Concerted action cases are those in which an actor

> (a) does a tortious act in concert with the other or pursuant to a common design with him, or (b) knows that the other's conduct constitutes a breach of duty and gives substantial assistance or encouragement to the other so to conduct himself, or (c) gives substantial assistance to the other in accomplishing a tortious result and his own conduct, separately considered, constitutes a breach of duty to the third person.

See Restatement (Second) of Torts §876.

In Woods v. Cole, 675 N.E.2d 132, 133 (Ill. App. 1996), the court considered whether the state statute abolishing joint and several liability for some defendants applied to defendants acting in concert. The majority of the court said that it did not. Referring to each of the three types of concerted action, Justice McCullough stated:

> In our view, each of these scenarios depicts a single and indivisible course of tortious conduct for which each is an equal participant and equally liable. The conduct of one actor cannot be compared to the conduct of another for purposes of apportioning liability because each agreed to cooperate in the tortious conduct or tortious result and each is liable for the entirety of the damages as if there were but one actor.

The dissent disagreed, in part because the judge thought that it was up to the legislature to create exceptions to legislatively created statutes and in part because he thought the conduct of the actors could be compared and one's fault might be found to be greater than others.

Other states have dealt with this problem by statute. See, e.g., Colo. Rev. Stat. §13-21-111.5:

> (1) In an action brought as a result of a death or an injury to person or property, no defendant shall be liable for an amount greater than that represented by the degree or percentage of the negligence or fault attributable to such defendant that produced the claimed injury, death, damage, or loss, except as provided in subsection (4) of this section. . . .
>
> (4) Joint liability shall be imposed on two or more persons who consciously conspire and deliberately pursue a common plan or design to commit a tortious act. Any person held jointly liable under this subsection (4) shall have a right of contribution from his fellow defendants acting in concert. A defendant shall be held responsible under this subsection (4) only for the degree or percentage of fault assessed to those persons who are held jointly liable pursuant to this subsection (4).

Problem
Apportionment of Liability for Concerted Acts

The claim in Woods v. Cole, 675 N.E.2d 132, 133 (Ill. App. Ct. 1996), was based on the shooting of Eric Woods by Jason Hill, who was convicted of involuntary manslaughter. Jason Hill, Laurencio Carrera, and Todd Cole were alleged to have acted in concert. These three had embarked on a shooting expedition with Eric Woods at a farm belonging to Todd Cole's grandfather:

> When decedent [Eric Woods] fell asleep during the drive to the farm, defendant [Todd Cole] hatched a plan to scare him. At the farm, the group woke decedent as planned by simultaneously firing their weapons into the ground. Defendant and Carrera then pointed their weapons at decedent, said "it's time to die," and pulled their triggers on an empty chamber, producing a click. Hill then pulled the trigger of his revolver and it discharged, killing decedent.

In order to maximize the likelihood of obtaining full recovery for Eric's damages, his lawyer must argue that Hill, Carrera, and Cole should all be liable even though only Hill pulled the trigger. For which type of concerted action should Eric's lawyer argue? If the jurisdiction has adopted a several liability rule or joint and several liability with comparative contribution, the factfinder under the rule of Roderick v. Lake must compare the three defendants' degrees of negligence. If you are the judge in this case and there is no jury, what facts would help you distinguish the conduct of the defendants? If damages total $100,000, how much would you, as judge, apportion to each defendant under several liability? If the jurisdiction has adopted a joint and several liability rule and apportions according to relative degrees of negligence, how much would you, as judge, apportion to each defendant?

Perspective: Fairness and Several Liability

In Guido Calabresi & Jeffrey O. Cooper, *New Directions in Tort Law*, 30 Val. U. L. Rev. 859 (1996), the authors suggest that one explanation for judicial and legislative adoption of restrictions on joint and several liability is the comfort courts and legislatures have experienced in assigning percentages of responsibility to the conduct of individuals.

> One powerful aspect of today's so-called tort reform movement comes from not understanding the effect that moving from all-or-nothing rules to splitting rules has had on joint and several liability. The notion of joint and several liability is as old as tort law. It has always been the case that if one defendant is ten percent negligent, and another defendant is ninety percent negligent, and together they combine to injure Marshall, they are both liable to him. Marshall can recover a hundred percent of his damages from either one. How they might choose to apportion the damages between themselves later is of no interest to Marshall. . . .
>
> Comparative negligence introduced important new wrinkles into these situations. Suppose now that one defendant is sixty percent responsible — not negligent, but responsible, because that is what we compare under comparative negligence — and another defendant is ten percent responsible, while the plaintiff is thirty percent responsible. Suppose also that the sixty percent responsible

defendant is judgment-proof and cannot pay. Is it appropriate to put seventy percent of the loss on the ten percent responsible defendant and thirty percent of the loss on the thirty percent responsible plaintiff?

Fairness now depends on what the jury intended to do when it assessed responsibility. Did the jury mean, in allocating responsibility, that the plaintiff was three times as responsible as the ten percent responsible defendant? If so, requiring the ten percent responsible defendant to bear seventy percent of the loss seems both unfair and contrary to what the jury found. Or did the jury mean, instead, that the defendants as a whole were to be held seventy percent responsible — that the ten percent/sixty percent division between the defendants was no more than an equitable split as to them, a split that did not concern their individual responsibility to the plaintiff at all? Did the jury intend, in other words, that the plaintiff, in fact, deserved to recover seventy percent of his or her damages, regardless of who would ultimately pay? If this is the case, then the old rule, perhaps slightly modified, might be as fair as the previous hypothetical made it seem unfair.

C. Allocating Responsibility to Absent or Immune Actors

When injuries are caused by more than one actor, sometimes all of the actors can be identified and sued. Sometimes, however, it is impossible to impose liability on an actor, either because that actor's identity is unknown or because that actor is immune from liability. This leads to the question of how to treat the missing actor's conduct in allocating responsibility for the plaintiff's injury.

At common law, with joint and several liability, any defendant could be liable to pay the entire damages awarded to the plaintiff. If another tortfeasor was immune or unknown, the defendant who paid the damages would never be able to be reimbursed through a contribution action. This is a pro-plaintiff result that is supported by a variety of rationales, including the fact that under the contributory negligence system the only plaintiffs who were ever entitled to recover were plaintiffs who were entirely free from blame. That factor may have supported the choice of a system that maximized the chance for the plaintiff to be fully compensated.

Some states now allow the conduct of an absent or immune tortfeasor to be evaluated, even though that actor will never pay any damages. Examples would be harms caused by: (1) a criminal and a landowner who failed to provide adequate security; (2) the employer of an injured worker and the manufacturer of a machine that hurt the worker; or (3) a child's parent and someone else who harmed a poorly supervised child. In these cases, the criminal's identity might be unknown, the employer might be immune under state workers' compensation law, and the parent might be protected by a parental immunity rule. If the jury assigns a share of responsibility to conduct by the unknown or immune actor, this will place the cost of that actor's conduct on the plaintiff, in contrast to the common law's choice of placing it on any solvent defendant.

Sullivan v. Scoular Grain Co. of Utah explores one state's statutory approach to this issue, in the context of an injury allegedly caused both by an employer, a grain company that was immune under the state's workers' compensation law, and others who were not immune.

SULLIVAN v. SCOULAR GRAIN CO. OF UTAH
853 P.2d 877 (Utah 1993)

DURHAM, Justice.

This case comes to us pursuant to rule 41 of the Utah Rules of Appellate Procedure as a question certified from the United States District Court for the District of Utah[:]

> 1. Under the Utah Comparative Fault Act, can a jury apportion the fault of the plaintiff's employers that caused or contributed to the accident although said employers are immune from suit under Utah Workers' Compensation Act. . . .

The following facts are taken from the federal district court's certification order. In October 1986, plaintiff Kenneth Sullivan lost his left arm and left leg in an accident on the railroad tracks at the Freeport Center in Clearfield, Utah. At the time of his injury, Sullivan was assigned to unload grain from rail cars into warehouses. He was employed by Scoular Grain Company, Freeport Center Associates, and Scoular Grain Company of Utah ("the Scoular parties").

Sullivan filed this action against the Scoular parties, Union Pacific Railroad Company, Denver & Rio Grande Western Railroad Company, Oregon Short Line Railroad Company, Utah Power & Light Company, Trackmobile, Inc., and G.W. Van Keppel Company. In 1989, the federal district court found the Scoular parties immune from plaintiff's claim under the exclusive remedy provision of Utah's Workers' Compensation Law and dismissed them from the action. That court also found that defendant Denver & Rio Grande Western Railroad had no legal duty to Sullivan and dismissed it from the lawsuit. The remaining defendants in the case are Utah Power & Light, Trackmobile, G.W. Van Keppel, Union Pacific Railroad, and Oregon Short Line Railroad. A motion to dismiss Utah Power & Light for lack of jurisdiction is pending at this time.

Defendant Trackmobile moved to have the jury apportion and compare the fault of all the originally named defendants, whether dismissed or present at trial. Plaintiff opposed this motion, claiming that only the fault of parties who are defendants at trial may be compared.

The court's principal duty in interpreting statutes is to determine legislative intent, and the best evidence of legislative intent is the plain language of the statute.

Plaintiff argues that his former employers must be excluded from the apportionment process because they are not "defendants" under the Liability Reform Act's definition. Section 68-3-11 of the Utah Code states that "words and phrases . . . [which] are defined by statute, are to be construed according to such peculiar and appropriate meaning or definition." Under section 78-27-39 of the Liability Reform Act, a jury may be instructed "to find separate special verdicts determining the total amount of damages sustained and the percentage or proportion of fault attributable to each person seeking recovery and to each defendant." Section 78-27-37(1) defines "defendant" as "any person *not immune from suit* who is claimed to be liable because of fault to any person seeking recovery." (Emphasis added.) Therefore, plaintiff argues, because the district court found the Scoular parties to be "immune from suit" under the exclusive remedy provision of Utah Workers' Compensation Act, Utah Code Ann. §35-1-60, they are not defendants and are excluded from apportionment under the plain language of the Act.

Excluding plaintiff's employers from the apportionment process, however, would directly conflict with the language of other sections of the Act which require that no defendant be held liable for damages in excess of its proportion of fault. The relevant portions of sections 78-27-38 and -40 read as follows:

> **78-27-38. Comparative negligence.** The fault of a person seeking recovery shall not alone bar recovery by that person. He may recover from any defendant or group of defendants whose fault exceeds his own. However, *no defendant is liable to any person seeking recovery for any amount in excess of the proportion of fault attributable to that defendant.*
>
> **78-27-40. Amount of liability limited to proportion of fault — No contribution.** Subject to Section 78-27-38, *the maximum amount for which a defendant may be liable to any person seeking recovery is that percentage or proportion of the damages equivalent to the percentage or proportion of fault attributed to that defendant.* No defendant is entitled to contribution from any other person.

(Emphasis added.) If the Scoular parties, who allegedly contributed to the accident, are not included on the special verdict form, the remaining defendants will be potentially liable to plaintiff for an amount in excess of their proportion of fault. For example, if the Scoular parties were 90% at fault and the defendants remaining in the action were 10% at fault, the remaining defendants would be apportioned 100% of any damages awarded even though they were only 10% at fault. Such a result would violate the plain language of sections 78-27-38 and -40.

Thus, we are faced with two arguably contradictory statutes within the same article. Section 78-27-37 defines "defendant" in a way that appears to preclude the inclusion of an employer from apportionment. But excluding employers from apportionment would violate the mandate of section 78-27-40 that no defendant be held liable for damages greater than its proportion of fault. This conflict creates an ambiguity that requires the court to make a policy inference as to the overall purpose and intent of the Act.

"When interpreting an ambiguous statute, we first try to discover the underlying intent of the legislature, guided by the purpose of the statute as a whole and the legislative history." Hansen v. Salt Lake County, 794 P.2d 838, 841 (Utah 1990) (citations omitted). We then try to harmonize ambiguous provisions accordingly.

In the 1986 session of the Utah Legislature, Substitute Senate Bill No. 64 proposed that a jury may determine the "total amount of damages sustained and a percentage or proportion of fault attributable to each person seeking recovery, to each defendant, *and to each other person whose fault contributed to the injury or damages.*" (Emphasis added.) Before being enacted, the bill was amended by deleting the part emphasized above and inserting the word "and" before "to each defendant." The result is codified at Utah Code Ann. §78-27-39:

> The trial court may, and when requested by any party shall, direct the jury, if any, to find separate special verdicts determining the total amount of damages sustained and the percentage or proportion of fault attributable to each person seeking recovery and to each defendant.

Sullivan argues that this amendment shows that the legislature did not intend to include nonparties in the apportionment process.

Trackmobile counters that the *reason* for the amendment is not clear and argues that, by contrast, the intent of the comparative negligence statute to limit a defendant's liability to his or her proportion of fault *is* clear. That purpose is to ensure that "no defendant is liable to any person seeking recovery for any amount in excess of the proportion of fault attributable to that defendant." Utah Code Ann. §78-27-38.

"The primary rule of statutory interpretation is to give effect to the intent of the legislature in light of the purpose the statute was meant to achieve." Reeves v. Gentile, 813 P.2d 111, 115 (Utah 1991) (footnote omitted). Thus, failing to include immune employers in the apportionment violates the main purpose of the Act by improperly subjecting the remaining defendants to liability in excess of their proportion of fault.

Other portions of the Act's history support this conclusion. First, during a floor debate prior to the adoption of the bill, one senator observed that "it is the basic fairness concept we're driving at. The defendant ought to be on the hook only for its own percentage of damages, but ought not be the guarantor for everyone else's damages." Floor Debate, Utah Senate, 46th Leg. 1986, General Sess., Senate Day 31, Records No. 63 (Feb. 12, 1986). Second, each preliminary draft of Senate Bill 64 states in the title that the purpose of the Act was, among other things, "abolishing joint and several liability." If the jury is prevented in this case from considering the relative fault of the Scoular parties in the apportionment process, Trackmobile and the other defendants will be held liable in the event of a verdict for plaintiff, not only for their own proportionate share of fault, but also for the proportionate share of fault attributable to the Scoular parties. Thus, one of the major evils of joint and several liability would result, and the stated purpose of the legislature in abolishing it would be frustrated. . . .

Any judicial or legislative decision concerning tort liability requires a balancing of competing interests and a policy decision as to which party should bear the risks of an immune or insolvent tort-feasor. Prior to 1986, under joint and several liability, a tort-feasor bore the risk of paying not only his or her share of the plaintiff's damages, but also the shares of other tort-feasors who were impecunious or immune from suit. The 1986 Utah Liability Reform Act shifted the risks caused by impecunious or immune tort-feasors to the plaintiffs by abolishing joint and several liability and contribution among tort-feasors.

Plaintiff correctly asserts that if his employer's actions are included in apportionment, his recovery may be significantly reduced. Plaintiff's recovery from nonemployer defendants would be reduced directly in proportion to the percentage of fault, if any, the jury attributes to the employer.

On the other hand, in Trackmobile's view, fairness to the defendants requires that each defendant pay only its proportionate share of the plaintiff's damages. If the Scoular parties are not included in apportionment, Trackmobile and the other defendants would be liable for damages in excess of their proportion of fault. "There is nothing inherently fair about a defendant who is[, for example,] 10% at fault paying 100% of the loss. . . ." Brown v. Keill, 580 P.2d 867, 874 (Kansas 1978).

General comparative negligence theory also supports the inclusion of nonparty employers in apportionment. For example, according to Heft and Heft:

> It is accepted practice to include all tortfeasors in the apportionment question. This includes nonparties who may be unknown tortfeasors, phantom drivers, and persons alleged to be negligent but not liable in damages to the injured party such as in the third party cases arising in the workmen's compensation area. . . .
>
> The reason for such rules is that true apportionment cannot be achieved unless that apportionment includes all tortfeasors guilty of causal negligence either causing or contributing to the occurrence in question, whether or not they are parties to the case.

Carroll R. Heft & C. James Heft, *Comparative Negligence Manual*, §8.100, at 14 (John J. Palmer & Stephen M. Flanagan eds., rev. ed. 1992) (footnote omitted). Thus, it is accepted practice for the jury to apportion the comparative fault of all tort-feasors when comparative negligence is at issue. . . .

Based on the foregoing analysis, [we answer the question] certified from the federal court[] as follows:

> 1. A jury may apportion the fault of employers under Utah Code Ann. §78-27-38 to -43 notwithstanding their immunity under Utah Code Ann. §35-1-60. . . .

NOTES TO SULLIVAN v. SCOULAR GRAIN CO. OF UTAH

1. *Apportionment to Immune Parties.* Both the plaintiff and defendant in *Sullivan* cited statutory language supporting conflicting interpretations of whether the liability of non-immune defendants should be reduced to reflect the contributory fault of immune parties. How did the court resolve the conflict in statutory language?

2. *Apportionment to Non-Tortious Defendants.* One of the defendants in *Sullivan* argued that liability of each defendant should be reduced to reflect the causal contribution of defendants who were found to be non-negligent. The defendant relied on two statutory definitions in Utah Code Ann. §78-27-37(1), (2) (1986):

> (1) "Defendant" means any person not immune from suit who is claimed to be liable *because of fault* to any person seeking recovery.
> (2) "Fault" means any *actionable* breach of legal duty, act, or omission proximately causing or contributing to injury or damages. . . .

(Emphasis added.)

The defendant argued that non-negligent defendants are not immune from suit under the definition of "Defendant" in (1) and they are claimed to be liable because of an "actionable breach" of duty under (2). The defendant argued that "actionable" means only that there are grounds to sue the defendant, not that the plaintiff will necessarily win. Given the statutory language discussed in *Sullivan*, should the contribution of non-negligent defendants be included in the apportionment?

3. *Diversity of State Approaches to Apportionment to Immune Parties.* In an appendix to *Sullivan*, the court categorized the approaches states in its region had taken to this problem. In five states the legislature had adopted a similar practice by statute: Arizona, Colorado, Kansas, New Mexico, and Washington. In five states courts have interpreted general comparative negligence statutes to require apportionment of nonparty fault: California, Hawaii, Idaho, Oklahoma, and Wyoming. Two states retain joint and several liability but allow the consideration of nonparty negligence for the limited purpose of determining whether all or none of the total fault can be attributed to the nonparty: Alaska and Montana. Finally, two states refuse to allow a jury to consider the fault of nonparties in apportionment: Nevada and Oregon.

4. *Procedural Note: Joinder of Missing Defendants.* A plaintiff may choose not to sue all of the potential defendants. The traditional rule is that plaintiffs are not required to join all potential defendants in a single action; the plaintiffs may bring successive suits against defendants. Some states, however, do require that all responsible parties be combined in a single claim on the ground that it is easier to resolve issues of causation and to apportion liability among the parties if all parties are included in the case. Eliminating successive suits with different factfinders eliminates inconsistent verdicts. A plaintiff may *join* a previously omitted defendant with whom a defendant seeks to share liability. A defendant may also move to join that omitted defendant for the purposes of apportionment in the hope of spreading the liability more widely. See Federal Rules of Civil Procedure 14(a) and Restatement (Third) of Torts: Apportionment of Liability §B19, comment g and Reporter's notes to comment c, p.177. In Field v. The Boyer Co., discussed in the problem above, the court justified its conclusion that apportionment between an unknown and unsued criminal was inappropriate because the mall owners could have joined the criminal in the trial but failed to do so.

**Problem
Apportionment to Absent Parties**

In Field v. The Boyer Co., 952 P.2d 1078 (Utah 1998), the same court that decided *Sullivan* considered whether the fault of an unidentified criminal assailant should be considered in an apportionment of fault that would reduce the liability of owners and operators who negligently failed to provide security at a shopping mall. The criminal was not sued. Under the Utah statutory definition of "defendant" discussed in *Sullivan*, would the criminal be a defendant for the purpose of apportionment? If so, the plaintiff's damage recovery from the mall owners would be reduced and thus would be unrecoverable, because the criminal is unidentified. The court referred to Utah Code §78-27-38(4), which stated, "the court may allocate fault to each person seeking recovery, to each defendant, and to any person immune from suit who contributed to the alleged injury." Does this language help the plaintiff recover more damages from the owner?

D. Intentional Conduct in a Comparative Setting

In some cases, a plaintiff's harm is caused by one actor's negligence and another actor's intentional tort. For example, a retailer might negligently fail to provide security in a store's parking lot, and an intentional tortfeasor might harm a customer there. Under traditional contributory negligence doctrines, even though a plaintiff's contributory negligence was a complete defense to a negligence action, it was ignored if the defendant had committed an intentional tort. Some comparative negligence jurisdictions continue this practice of ignoring a plaintiff's negligent conduct if the defendant was an intentional tortfeasor. Others permit a comparison of negligent and intentional tortious conduct. Slack v. Farmers Insurance Exchange considers these issues where a plaintiff's harm was caused by a negligent insurance company and an intentionally tortious chiropractor.

SLACK v. FARMERS INSURANCE EXCHANGE

5 P.3d 280 (Colo. 2000)

Kourlis, J.

The question in this case is whether section 13-21-111.5, 5 C.R.S. (1999) requires the pro rata distribution of civil liability among intentional and negligent tortfeasors who jointly cause indivisible injuries. Section 13-21-111.5 states that a tortfeasor shall only be liable for damages to the extent of her negligence or fault. . . .

On September 8, 1992, Juliette Diane Slack suffered injuries in an automobile accident. Slack, driving a minivan, was stopped at a stoplight waiting to make a right turn. When she began to make the turn, a young man in a small, green car ran the stoplight and forced Slack to slam on the brakes. The abrupt stop caused Slack to strike her chin on the steering wheel and then to hit the back of her head on the headrest.

The following day, Slack visited her chiropractor, Dr. Steven Lee Schuster, for treatment of her neck and back pain caused by the accident. Dr. Schuster submitted all charges for treatment to Slack's insurer, Farmers Insurance. . . . Farmers Insurance elected to obtain a second opinion regarding the nature of Slack's injuries from an independent medical examiner (an IME).

Farmers Insurance scheduled an appointment for Slack with Dr. Lloyd Lachow, a chiropractor. At that time, another one of Farmers' insureds, Jodi Lynn Harvey, had claimed that Lachow sexually assaulted her during an examination. Slack testified that during her exam, Lachow touched her clothed breast and pushed his pelvis into her back. In addition, she testified that he pulled hard on her neck and shook her head violently from side-to-side, putting her in additional pain. . . .

Following an investigation, the Colorado Department of Regulatory Agencies (the Agency) suspended Lachow's license effective March 31, 1993. Lachow admitted in a Stipulation and Final Agency Order that the State Board of Chiropractic Examiners, a Board contained within the Agency, would be able to establish a prima facie case of unprofessional conduct during the examinations of Slack and Harvey.

Slack filed suit against Lachow claiming assault, battery, negligence, extreme and outrageous conduct/intentional infliction of emotional distress, negligent infliction of emotional distress, and malpractice. In the same suit, she claimed negligence, breach of contract, bad faith breach of contract, and outrageous conduct against Farmers Insurance. Slack claimed that Farmers Insurance acted improperly by sending her to a chiropractor it knew or should have known would injure her. Brett Slack, her husband, brought a loss of consortium claim.

Before trial, the Slacks settled their claims with Lachow. Farmers Insurance, however, designated Lachow a nonparty [whose fault should be considered in apportioning liability] pursuant to section 13-21-111.5(3), 5 C.R.S. (1999). Following a trial, the jury returned a verdict in favor of the Slacks and against Farmers Insurance on the negligence claim, bad faith breach of contract claim, and on Brett's loss of consortium claim. The jury also found that Farmers Insurance acted [recklessly]. The jury awarded Slack $40,000 for her injuries and $16,000 in exemplary damages. It awarded Brett $6000 for his loss and $2400 in exemplary damages. The jury apportioned sixty percent of the fault for Slack's injuries to Lachow and forty percent to Farmers Insurance. In accordance with section 13-21-111.5(1), the trial court reduced Slack's award to $16,000 in compensatory damages and $16,000 in exemplary damages. The trial court did not reduce the compensatory portion of Brett's damage award.

Slack appealed the reduction of her award to the court of appeals. Farmers Insurance cross-appealed the trial court's refusal to apportion the damages awarded to Brett. The court of appeals held in favor of Farmers Insurance on both issues. This appeal followed. . . .

We move . . . to the question of whether the jury could properly apportion Slack's damages between Lachow and Farmers Insurance. As part of the tort reform movement in Colorado, the General Assembly eliminated joint and several liability wherein one tortfeasor might be liable in damages for the acts of another tortfeasor, and adopted a several liability scheme, wherein a tortfeasor is responsible only for the portion of the damages that he or she caused. Section 13-21-111.5 states

> In an action brought as a result of a death or an injury to person or property, no defendant shall be liable for an amount greater than that represented by the degree or percentage of the negligence or fault attributable to such defendant that produced the claimed injury, death, damage, or loss. . . .

The General Assembly also provided that the negligence or fault of a nonparty who settled with the plaintiff could be considered in the apportionment of damages.

We are called upon to determine whether the General Assembly intended that liability may be apportioned only between negligent tortfeasors, or also between a negligent and an intentional tortfeasor. In other words, may a jury apportion fault among tortfeasors who were merely negligent and others who intended to do wrong?

. . . For analytical purposes, the statute can be separated into two parts. The first explains that the statute applies to "an action brought as a result of a death or an injury to person or property." §13-21-111.5(1). The language of this part clearly applies to a wide variety of situations, and includes intentional torts. Undoubtedly, a sexual assault can result in an action for an injury to a person. Therefore, on its face, the language would cover the intentional torts of assault and battery.

The second part of the statute states "no defendant shall be liable for an amount greater than that represented by the degree or percentage of the *negligence or fault* attributable to such defendant that produced the claimed injury, death, damage, or loss." §13-21-111.5(1) (emphasis added). The critical portion of this section is the phrase "negligence or fault." If this second part of the statute does not limit the first part, then intentional torts must fall within its reach. . . .

Black's Law Dictionary defines fault as "[a]n error or defect of judgment or of conduct; any deviation from prudence or duty resulting from inattention, incapacity, perversity, bad faith, or mismanagement." Black's Law Dictionary 623 (7th ed. 1999). . . .

. . . Black's offers this definition of negligence:

> The failure to exercise the standard of care that a reasonably prudent person would have exercised in a similar situation; any conduct that falls below the legal standard established to protect others against unreasonable risk of harm, except for conduct that is intentionally, wantonly, or willfully disregardful of others' rights. . . .

These definitions suggest that the General Assembly used the word "fault" purposefully in section 13-21-111.5(1) and that the common understanding of that term controls our interpretation. Fault contemplates more than mere negligence, and includes intentional acts. . . .

In short, we can find nothing in the statutes or in our cases interpreting the statutes to suggest that the General Assembly intended to expose a negligent tortfeasor to greater liability when his conduct was coupled with that of an intentional tortfeasor, than when his conduct combined with that of another negligent tortfeasor. Accordingly, we conclude that section 13-21-111.5(1) applies even when one of several tortfeasors commits an intentional tort that contributes to an indivisible injury.

The General Assembly abolished joint and several liability in Colorado "to reduce unfair burdens placed on defendants." General Elec. Co. v. Niemet, 866 P.2d 1361, 1364 (Colo. 1994). "The adoption of [the pro rata division of liability based on degree of fault] was intended to cure the perceived inequity under the common law concept of joint and several liability whereby wrongdoers could be held fully responsible for a plaintiff's entire loss, despite the fact that another wrongdoer, who was not held accountable, contributed to the result." Barton v. Adams Rental, Inc., 938 P.2d 532, 535 (Colo. 1997). In our view, neither the reasoning nor the result differ when an intentional wrongdoer contributes to the loss.

Other courts facing this issue have adopted a similar construction. In Bhinder v. Sun Co., 246 Conn. 223, 717 A.2d 202 (1998), the Supreme Court of Connecticut held that the apportionment statute did not apply to situations where one defendant committed an intentional act and another committed a negligent act, because unlike Colorado's law, the Connecticut statute was limited to "negligence actions." However, the court extended the statute to such situations as a matter of common law. The court noted that failure to apportion "would have the incongruous effect of rendering a negligent party solely responsible for the conduct of an intentional actor, whose deviation from the standard of reasonable care is clearly greater." Id. at 210; see also Roman Catholic Diocese of Covington v. Secter, 966 S.W.2d 286 (Ky. Ct. App. 1998) (interpreting an apportionment statute covering tort actions involving "fault" to allow apportionment between a church operated school that negligently hired and retained an employee that sexually abused a student and the intentional tortfeasor).

Slack acknowledges that the pro-rata liability statute would apply were Lachow a mere negligent actor, and that Farmers Insurance would bear only their portion of the liability. She argues, however, that since Lachow was an intentional actor, Farmers Insurance (not Lachow) should bear a greater proportion of the loss. In our estimation, the public policy rationale for apportioning the loss commensurate with wrongdoing is even more compelling when an intentional tortfeasor contributes to the injury. Under the terms of the statute, a negligent actor is only responsible for his contribution to an injury, irrespective of whether the other tortfeasor accidentally or purposefully injured the victim. To hold otherwise would lead to the anomaly that a negligent tortfeasor would bear the full risk of the injury if the other tortfeasor purposefully injured the victim, but only his portion of the risk if the other actor were negligent. If any disproportionate responsibility were to be assessed, it would more logically fall upon the intentional tortfeasor — not the negligent one. Nonetheless, section 13-21-111.5 demonstrates the General Assembly's intent that a tortfeasor should pay only for the portion of the injury he caused. . . .

The Colorado several liability statute does not differentiate between intentional acts and negligent acts in its mandate to apportion liability among tortfeasors. Accordingly, the trial court properly apportioned liability in this case based upon the jury's decision as to relative fault between Farmers Insurance and Lachow for Slack's injuries, but erred in failing to apportion liability for Brett's loss of consortium. Therefore, we affirm the court of appeals, and remand the case with directions to return it to the district court with instructions to reduce Brett's award of compensatory damages to $2400 in accordance with this opinion and otherwise to reinstate the trial court judgment.

Rice, J., dissenting.

... Other jurisdictions that have addressed this issue have ... concluded that a negligent tortfeasor should not be permitted to reduce his liability by comparing his negligence to the actions of an intentional tortfeasor. As I find the reasoning and rationale underlying these cases persuasive on the issue before us, I proceed to review them here.

In a negligence suit brought by a customer of a convenience store against the store owner for personal injuries he sustained when he was robbed by an unknown assailant while leaving the store, the Washington Supreme Court interpreted the term "fault," as defined in their state's liability statutes, as not including intentional conduct. See Welch v. Southland Corp., 134 Wash. 2d 629, 952 P.2d 162, 163-165 (1998). The court first noted that the applicable statute "makes clear that ... several liability is now intended to be the general rule and that the statute now evidences legislative intent that fault be apportioned and that generally an entity be required to pay that entity's proportionate share of damages only." Id. at 164 (internal quotation marks omitted). The court then noted that the statute defines "fault" as:

> acts or omissions, including misuse of a product, that are in any measure negligent or reckless toward the person or property of the actor or others, or that subject a person to strict tort liability or liability on a product liability claim. ... Legal requirements of causal relation apply both to fault as the basis for liability and to contributory fault.

Id. (quoting Wash. Rev. Code §4.22.015) (internal quotation marks omitted).

From this broad definition of fault, and despite its recognition that the legislature intended that liability should be apportioned only to the extent of each defendant's fault, the *Welch* court held that the intentional conduct of a tortfeasor could not reduce the liability of a negligent tortfeasor.

The Tennessee Supreme Court addressed this issue in Turner v. Jordan and held that the conduct of a negligent defendant could not be compared with the intentional conduct of another in determining comparative fault where the intentional conduct is the foreseeable risk created by the negligent tortfeasor. See 957 S.W.2d 815, 823 (Tenn. 1997). In *Turner,* a hospital nurse brought a medical malpractice action against a patient's treating psychiatrist after she was assaulted by the mentally ill patient. The nurse offered evidence at trial in the form of expert testimony that the defendant psychiatrist's failure to medicate, restrain, seclude, or transfer the patient fell below the standard of care and that, as a result of this negligence, she was assaulted by the patient. The trial court instructed the jury that it could allocate the liability for the nurse's injuries between the negligent doctor and the patient's intentional conduct. The jury returned a verdict for the nurse and allocated 100% of the liability for her injuries to the negligent psychiatrist.

On appeal, the Tennessee Supreme Court determined first that the psychiatrist owed a duty of care to the nurse and breached this duty because the psychiatrist was aware of the patient's violent tendencies, including a previous assault on another hospital staff member, and took no reasonable steps to avoid this type of assault from occurring again. The court then held that it was error for the trial court to allow the jury to apportion liability between the psychiatrist and the mental patient, but concluded that this error was harmless in this case because the jury allocated 100% of the liability to the psychiatrist. In reaching its holding, the court first noted that "comparison presents practical difficulties in allocating fault between negligent and intentional acts, because negligent and intentional torts are different in degree, in kind, and in society's view of the relative culpability of such act." Id. The court then observed that this type of comparison "reduces the negligent person's incentive to comply with the applicable duty of care." Id. Finally, the court addressed the policy rationale for the holding and noted that the principle of "'holding the tortfeasor liable for only his own percentage of fault is *not* abrogated by nonapportionment when the nature of the tortfeasor's breach is that *he created the risk of the second tortfeasor's [intentional] act.*'" Id. (brackets in original) (emphasis added).

I find the Tennessee Supreme Court's rationale underlying its holding particularly persuasive on this issue with respect to the facts of the case before us. As the *Turner* court noted, a tortfeasor should not be allowed to reduce his liability by shifting some or all of the blame to an intentional tortfeasor whose actions constitute the precise risk for which the negligent tortfeasor has been found liable for not preventing. In *Turner,* the psychiatrist breached the duty by not taking steps to prevent the assault. In the instant case, Farmers not only did not take steps to remove Dr. Lachow from its list of approved independent medical examiners after learning of the earlier sexual assault, but they instructed Mrs. Slack that she must be examined by Dr. Lachow before they would process her claim. As such, the rationale expressed by the *Turner* court applies with even greater force to the facts of the instant case. . . .

In my view, precluding a negligent tortfeasor from reducing his liability by pointing to the actions of an intentional tortfeasor in no way undermines the General Assembly's goal of reducing the unfair burdens placed on defendants. This case is an ideal example of a "burden" that should not be considered "unfair," and a result that was likely not contemplated by the General Assembly when it passed the statute. Under my construction of the statute, Farmers would not be allowed to reduce its liability by pointing to Dr. Lachow's conduct. Farmers' negligence in referring Mrs. Slack to Dr. Lachow, when it knew he had just recently sexually assaulted another insured, created the exact risk of harm that occurred. Precluding Farmers from reducing its liability in this manner does not impose any unfair burden on Farmers in contravention of the General Assembly's purpose. Accordingly, I believe that this interpretation of the statute is consistent with the General Assembly's purpose in enacting section 13-21-111.5. . . .

NOTES TO SLACK v. FARMERS INSURANCE EXCHANGE

1. *Apportionment Between Negligent and Intentional Defendants.* The majority and dissenting opinions in *Slack* relied on their perceptions of fairness in deciding whether liability should be apportioned among negligent and intentional defendants. How did the different perceptions of fairness result in different outcomes? Under the dissenting justice's view, should there never be apportionment between such defendants or should apportionment be denied only in certain cases?

2. *Apportioning Compensatory and Exemplary Damages.* In a portion of the opinion not included here, the *Slack* court discussed apportionment of punitive damages. The defendant insurance company had been reckless in referring Juliet Slack to Dr. Lachow, about whom prior complaints of unprofessional conduct had been made. Both Juliet Slack and her husband were awarded *exemplary or punitive damages* in addition to compensatory damages. Exemplary or punitive damages are added to compensatory damages to punish the defendant. According to the court in *Slack*, most states do not allow the apportionment of exemplary damages. Instead,

courts require juries to determine separate amounts of appropriate exemplary damages for each defendant and make each defendant liable for the full amount of its own exemplary damages. A logical reason for this treatment is that compensatory damages are designed to make up for indivisible harm caused by several defendants, while exemplary or punitive damages are designed to punish a particular defendant's reprehensible conduct.

Perspective: Restatement (Third) and Responsibility for Intentional Actors' Wrongdoing

In a symposium on the Restatement (Third) of Torts, one of the Reporters for Apportionment of Liability section of that project explained its position on assigning financial responsibility when one defendant is negligent and another has committed an intentional tort. See comments by Dean Michael Green in *Third Annual Judges and Lawyers Symposium: The Restatement (Third) of Torts and the Future of Tort Law: Overview by the ALI Reporters: Apportionment of Liability,* 10 Kan. J.L. & Pub. Pol'y 30 (2000):

> Finally, let me just close out with what I think is the most cutting edge, least law to support it, [provision in the Restatement (Third) on Apportionment of Liability]. . . . [T]his was actually the *Howard Johnson* case, and it involved Connie Francis. It was when Connie Francis was sexually assaulted in a *Howard Johnson's* motel and sued Howard Johnson's, not the assaulter, for inadequate security. Well, with several liability, and this is where it becomes particularly a problem, if we are going to include intentional tortfeasors, all of a sudden we are apportioning comparative responsibility to an intentional tortfeasor and to Howard Johnson's. As a factfinder compares their culpability, surely the intentional tortfeasor ends up with a whole bunch, and Howard Johnson's may end up with some, but it is going to be relatively minimal. Yet, if we are going to hold Howard Johnson's liable for negligent security in that situation, if there is a tort duty that was breached we intended that Howard Johnson's protect the plaintiff from the intentional tortfeasor. Section Fourteen says, no matter what form of joint and several or several liability adopted in the jurisdiction, a negligent tortfeasor who fails to protect the plaintiff, who breaches a duty to protect a plaintiff from an intentional tort, is liable not only for its share of comparative responsibility, but also for any share assigned to the intentional tortfeasor. The negligent tortfeasor, of course, would have a contribution claim against the intentional tortfeasor, but I leave it to you to try to figure out how the negligent defendant is going to collect on that contribution judgment.

E. Allocating the Risk of Insolvency

Under joint and several liability, the plaintiff may collect his or her damages from any subset of the jointly and severally liable defendants because each is liable for the entire amount. Under several liability, however, each defendant is only liable for a share of the damages. Without some special rules relating to insolvent defendants, if one defendant is insolvent, the plaintiff will be unable to collect that share. Some courts refer to these uncollectible shares as *orphan shares*. See Martignetti v. Haigh-Farr, Inc., 680 N.E.2d 1131, 1145 and n.39 (Mass. 1997) (defining "orphan share" as "the amount for which a liable party should be responsible under an equitable allocation procedure, but which cannot be collected because the party is insolvent, unidentifiable, or otherwise unreachable").

To prevent the risk of insolvency from resting on plaintiffs, a few states use real-location rules that spread the insolvent defendant's share either among the solvent defendants or among the plaintiff and any solvent defendants. The following Connecticut and Minnesota statutes illustrate these approaches.

Statute: LIABILITY OF MULTIPLE TORTFEASORS FOR DAMAGES
Conn. Gen. Stat. Ann. §52-572h(g)(3) (2017)

The court shall order that the portion of such uncollectible amount which represents recoverable economic damages be reallocated among the other defendants. The court shall reallocate to any such other defendant an amount equal to such uncollectible amount of . . . economic damages multiplied by a fraction in which the numerator is such defendant's percentage of negligence and the denominator is the total of the percentages of negligence of all defendants, excluding any defendant whose liability is being reallocated.

Statute: APPORTIONMENT OF DAMAGES
Minn. Stat. Ann. §604.02 (2017)

Subd. 2. Upon motion made not later than one year after judgment is entered, the court shall determine whether all or part of a party's equitable share of the obligation is uncollectible from that party and shall reallocate any uncollectible amount among the other parties, including a claimant at fault, according to their respective percentages of fault. A party whose liability is reallocated is nonetheless subject to contribution and to any continuing liability to the claimant on the judgment.

Subd. 3. In the case of a claim arising from the manufacture, sale, use or consumption of a product, an amount uncollectible from any person in the chain of manufacture and distribution shall be reallocated among all other persons in the chain of manufacture and distribution but not among the claimant or others at fault who are not in the chain of manufacture or distribution of the product. Provided, however, that a person whose fault is less than that of a claimant is liable to the claimant only for that portion of the judgment which represents the percentage of fault attributable to the person whose fault is less.

NOTE TO STATUTES

Suppose that a plaintiff has suffered economic damages of $70,000 arising from the sale of a negligently manufactured power saw. The plaintiff was negligent for failing to wear protective eyewear. The manufacturer was negligent for failing to secure the saw's safety guard during manufacture. A retailer was negligent for failing to provide written or oral safety instructions to the plaintiff. A jury allocated the following shares of responsibility for the plaintiff's injuries:

Plaintiff	30% responsible
Defendant Manufacturer	60% responsible
Defendant Retailer	10% responsible

In a jurisdiction that applies comparative fault principles and several liability, the plaintiff would receive a judgment for $42,000 against the manufacturer and a judgment for $7,000 against the retailer. If the manufacturer was insolvent, how would the Connecticut and Minnesota statutes treat the $42,000 judgment that the manufacturer would otherwise have paid? If the retailer was insolvent, how would these statutes treat the $7,000 the retailer would otherwise have paid? Which statute is more favorable to plaintiffs?

III. Vicarious Liability

A special variety of joint liability is the doctrine known as *vicarious liability*. Under this doctrine, an actor is liable for someone else's tortious conduct. The primary instance of vicarious liability is an employer's obligation to pay for an employee's tortious conduct, known as the doctrine of *respondeat superior*. Even if an employer has been totally free from negligence, tort law subjects the employer to liability for negligent acts by an employee committed within the scope of employment. Vicarious liability is also applied to vehicle owners, allowing people injured by the negligent use of an automobile or other vehicle to recover from the owner even if the owner was not negligent in any way.

A. Respondeat Superior

Trahan-Laroche v. Lockheed Sanders, Inc. introduces the basic elements of the *respondeat superior* doctrine. It shows that a plaintiff injured by an employee may seek damages from the employer with two separate causes of action. One cause of action is based on vicarious liability *for the employee's tortious act*. The other is based on a claim that the employer is responsible for some other negligent act, such as negligent supervision or negligent hiring.

Holding an employer responsible for an employee's torts raises the question of whether the negligent person was acting as an employee at the time of the tortious conduct. *McDonald's Restaurants of California* analyzes whether a person who was admittedly an employee was acting within the scope of that employment when his car collided with the plaintiff's motorcycle. In Santiago v. Phoenix Newspapers, Inc., a newspaper company denied that a driver was an employee and argued that the court should classify the driver as an *independent contractor* for whose conduct the newspaper would be free from vicarious liability.

TRAHAN-LAROCHE v. LOCKHEED SANDERS, INC.
657 A.2d 417 (N.H. 1995)

HORTON, J.

The plaintiffs, Rita Trahan-Laroche and Lucien Laroche, appeal a decision of the Superior Court granting the motion of the defendant, Lockheed Sanders, Inc., for summary judgment on their *respondeat superior* and negligent supervision claims. We reverse and remand.

On October 24, 1990, a flatbed trailer separated from the pickup truck towing it and collided with the plaintiffs' vehicle. Patrick J. Maimone, employed by the defendant as a maintenance mechanic, was the driver as well as the owner of both the truck and the trailer. One of his tasks was to hay the fields at the defendant's facilities in Hudson and Litchfield. Maimone provided most of the haying equipment, most of which he towed to the defendant's premises with his truck and trailer. The defendant did not compensate Maimone for the use of the equipment or the time spent transporting it, but did pay him his normal wages while haying the fields and permitted him to keep any hay he removed. Prior to the day of the accident, Maimone had completed haying the fields at the defendant's Litchfield facility, but had not removed his trailer or all of the farming equipment. After work on October 24, 1990, but before leaving the defendant's premises, Maimone hitched his trailer to his truck for use in transporting hay from his farm to the Agway store to sell that evening. He planned to return the trailer to remove the remaining farm machinery. The trailer separated from the truck during the drive from the defendant's Litchfield facility to Maimone's farm.

The plaintiffs sued the defendant under theories of *respondeat superior* and negligent supervision. They argued that Maimone was acting within the scope of his employment at the time of the accident. Alternatively, they argued that while on the defendant's property and under the defendant's supervision and control, Maimone negligently attached his trailer and used inadequate safety chains in violation of the common law and RSA 266:63 (1993). The defendants moved for summary judgment, arguing that no disputed issues of material fact existed and that the plaintiffs failed to state a claim upon which relief may be granted because Maimone was not acting within the scope of his employment. . . .

The trial court ruled as a matter of law that Maimone acted outside the scope of his employment. Treating the defendant's motion as a motion to dismiss, the court concluded that "even taking the facts and reasonable inferences drawn therefrom in the light most favorable to them, the plaintiffs have failed to state a claim that would permit them to recover." . . . The plaintiffs appealed. . . .

Under the doctrine of *respondeat superior*, an employer may be held vicariously responsible for the tortious acts of an employee committed incidental to or during the scope of employment. Here, the plaintiff has alleged that the movement of Maimone's trailer for temporary personal use was understood to be part of the agreement between Maimone and the defendant regarding Maimone's provision of the farming equipment and removal of the hay, and therefore incidental to Maimone's employment. This allegation could lead to a finding that would support recovery based on the doctrine of *respondeat superior* if found to be true by a jury.

An employer may be directly liable for damages resulting from the negligent supervision of its employee's activities. The employer's duty to exercise reasonable care to control its employee may extend to activities performed outside the scope of employment. The plaintiffs alleged that although Maimone was involved in several accidents involving vehicles and equipment while in the defendant's employ, his activities were not closely supervised, and his equipment and vehicles were not regularly inspected. This allegation and the reasonable inferences therefrom raise a jury issue as to whether the defendant negligently supervised Maimone. We therefore hold that it was error to dismiss the plaintiffs' claims.

. . . A review of the record, including the depositions, reveals evidence from which conflicting inferences could be drawn both as to whether Maimone was acting incidental to or within the scope of his employment when he moved his trailer for temporary personal use and whether the defendant was independently negligent in supervising Maimone and in inspecting his truck and his trailer. We conclude that neither party is entitled to judgment as a matter of law on either the plaintiff's *respondeat superior* or negligent supervision claims. We reverse the trial court's granting of the defendant's motion for summary judgment and remand.

NOTES TO TRAHAN-LAROCHE v. LOCKHEED SANDERS, INC.

1. *Elements of* Respondeat Superior. The basic definition of the *respondeat superior* doctrine is straightforward. An employer will be liable for the torts of an employee committed within the scope of employment. What allegations did the plaintiff make to establish those elements?

2. *Negligent Supervision.* To obtain a judgment against an employer under the *respondeat superior* doctrine, the plaintiff must show that the employee acted negligently. There is no requirement that the plaintiff show anything about the employer's conduct other than the employer's participation in the employer-employee relationship. In contrast, in the tort action for negligent supervision, a plaintiff seeks damages from an employer on the theory that the employer was negligent in supervising an employee. To win a judgment on that theory, a plaintiff must show that the employer's supervision was worse than the supervision a reasonable employer would have provided.

3. *Practical Effect of* Respondeat Superior. A plaintiff who wins a judgment in a *respondeat superior* case can enforce the judgment against the employer. The plaintiff is also entitled to a judgment against the employee. The doctrine's practical effect is to supply a "deep pocket" to the injured plaintiff. In general, employers are more capable than employees of paying tort judgments.

4. *Contribution and Indemnification.* The obvious difference between vicarious liability and other cases of apportioned liability discussed in this chapter is that in those other cases, each of the multiple liable defendants acted tortiously. Vicarious liability is imposed on a defendant, the employer, who did not act tortiously. A defendant in a joint tortfeasor case who pays more than his or her share of the damages for which the defendant was jointly and severally liable is usually allowed to sue other defendants for contribution. Under vicarious liability for an employee's negligence, most states hold that there can be no right to contribution between employer and employee:

> The rules of vicarious liability respond to a specific need in the law of torts: how to fully compensate an injury caused by the act of a *single* tortfeasor. . . . [A] principal whose liability rests solely upon the doctrine of *respondeat superior* and not upon any

independent act of the principal is not a joint tortfeasor with the agent from whose conduct the principal's liability is derived. . . . [T]he principal is not a tortfeasor in the true sense of the word because he is not [necessarily] independently liable based upon his own independent actionable fault. . . . Consequently, there is no right of contribution, only indemnification.

See Alvarez v. New Haven Register Inc., 249 Conn. 709, 720-721, 735 A.2d 306 (1999).

Indemnification is a defendant's right to full compensation for all damages paid due to the tortious conduct of some other actor. In some states, an employer may sue the employee to recover all of the damages the employer paid because of the relationship between them. This rule shifts liability from a passive employer who was not proved to have acted negligently to the active employee who acted tortiously. In other states, an employer is entitled to indemnification from an employee only if the employee's conduct was characterized as reckless or intentional.

Perspective: Rationale for Respondeat Superior

A number of theories justify the *respondeat superior* doctrine. The *deep pocket theory*, which ensures that a plaintiff can sue someone who is likely to have assets or insurance, is the most commonly cited justification. A second is the *risk spreading theory*. According to this theory, the employer is better situated than either the employee or the plaintiff to cover the loss by reimbursing itself through higher prices to its customers or by accumulating reserves in advance of an accident (perhaps through insurance). A third theory is the *enterprise risk theory*. This theory reflects the view that even though an employer was not at fault for the way in which it engaged in a particular activity, the activity ought, nevertheless, pay its own way by paying for the risks it creates. If tortious employee conduct is one of the foreseeable risks, the enterprise should pay for those risks that are characteristic of its activity. A fourth perspective is the *risk avoidance theory*, which argues that if an employer is required to pay for the tortious acts of its employees (or the resulting higher insurance premiums), it will have an incentive to discover ways to minimize those acts and thereby minimize harm. Understanding the theoretical foundations of vicarious liability (and other legal doctrines) helps lawyers argue cases for their clients. By recognizing these justifications for imposing vicarious liability, lawyers may argue that no persuasive justification exists for liability in a particular case where the employment status of the tortfeasor is not obvious.

O'CONNOR v. McDONALD'S RESTAURANTS OF CALIFORNIA, INC.

269 Cal. Rptr. 101 (Cal. Ct. App. 1990)

KREMER, P.J.

Plaintiff Martin O'Connor appeals summary judgment favoring defendants McDonald's Restaurants of California, Inc., and McDonald's Corporation (together

McDonald's) on his complaint for damages for personal injuries on a theory of McDonald's vicarious liability for the negligence of its employee Evans. O'Connor, injured when his motorcycle collided with an automobile driven by Evans, contends the superior court erred in determining Evans had completely departed from a special errand on behalf of McDonald's and was not acting within the scope of his employment at the time of the accident. . . .

In reviewing the propriety of the summary judgment, we state the facts in the light most favorable to O'Connor.

From about 8 p.m. on August 12, 1982, until between 1 a.m. and 2 a.m. the next day, Evans and several McDonald's co-workers scoured the children's playground area of McDonald's San Ysidro restaurant. The special cleaning prepared the restaurant for inspection as part of McDonald's "spring-blitz" competition. Evans — who aspired to a managerial position — worked without pay in the cleanup party at McDonald's request. Evans's voluntary contribution of work and time is the type of extra effort leading to advancement in McDonald's organization.

After completing the cleanup, Evans and four fellow workers went to the house of McDonald's employee Duffer. Duffer had also participated in the evening's work. At Duffer's house, Evans and the others talked shop and socialized into the early hours of the morning. About 6:30 a.m., as Evans drove from Duffer's house toward his own home, his automobile collided with O'Connor's motorcycle.

O'Connor filed a lawsuit for negligence against Evans, McDonald's and others. O'Connor complained of serious injuries resulting in permanent disability and the loss of his left leg below the knee. The suit claimed McDonald's was liable for negligence on a theory of *respondeat superior.*

Essentially, O'Connor claimed Evans was on a "special errand" for his employer McDonald's when he worked on the spring-blitz clean-up on his own time. According to O'Connor, if Evans were on a special errand, then his driving would be exempt from the "going and coming" rule by which an employer ordinarily is not liable for an employee's negligence while commuting.[2] Under O'Connor's theory, the special errand began when Evans left his own home and continued until he returned home.

McDonald's sought summary judgment, contending as a matter of law Evans was acting outside the scope of his employment at the time of the accident.

The superior court found Evans was on a special errand for McDonald's when he voluntarily reported for cleanup duties at the San Ysidro restaurant. However, the superior court further found Evans's stop at Duffer's house was a "complete departure" from his special errand. Thus, the court concluded any responsibility of McDonald's for Evans's driving terminated before the accident. The court granted summary judgment for McDonald's. O'Connor appeals.

---

[2] "Generally, an employee is outside the scope of his employment while engaged in his ordinary commute to and from his place of work. [Citation.] This principle is known as the going-and-coming rule and is based on the theory that the employment relationship is suspended from the time the employee leaves his job until he returns and on the theory that during the normal everyday commute, the employee is not rendering services directly or indirectly to his employer. [Citation.]" (Felix v. Asai, [192 Cal. App. 3d 926, 931, 237 Cal. Rptr. 718 (1987)].)

However, when "the employee is traveling from his residence or returning to it as part of his usual duties or at the specific request or order of his employer, he is considered to be on a special errand for his employer and thus acting within the scope of his employment. [Citations.]" (Robbins v. Hewlett-Packard Corp. (1972) 26 Cal. App. 3d 489, 494, 103 Cal. Rptr. 184.)

The central issue before us is of some antiquity. In 1834 Baron Parke addressed the issue:

> The master is only liable where the servant is acting in the course of his employment. If he was going out of his way, against his master's implied commands, when driving on his master's business, he will make his master liable; but if he was going on a frolic of his own, without being at all on his master's business, the master will not be liable. (Joel v. Morison (1834) 6 Car. & P. 501, 503, 172 Eng. Rep. 1338, 1339.)

Unfortunately, as an academic commentator observed in 1923, "It is relatively simple to state that the master is responsible for his servant's torts only when the latter is engaged in the master's business, or doing the master's work, or acting within the scope of his employment; but to determine in a particular case whether the servant's act falls within or without the operation of the rule presents a more difficult task." (Smith, *Frolic and Detour* (1923) 23 Colum. L. Rev. 444, 463.)

Here we must determine whether the superior court properly concluded as a matter of law that Evans's activity in attending the gathering at Duffer's house constituted a complete departure from a special errand for McDonald's (a frolic of his own) rather than a mere deviation (a detour).

Whether there has been a deviation so material as to constitute a complete departure by an employee from the course of his employment so as to release employer from liability for employee's negligence, is usually a question of fact.

"In determining whether an employee has completely abandoned pursuit of a business errand for pursuit of a personal objective, a variety of relevant circumstances should be considered and weighed. Such factors may include the intent of the employee, the nature, time and place of the employee's conduct, the work the employee was hired to do, the incidental acts the employer should reasonably have expected the employee to do, the amount of freedom allowed the employee in performing his duties, and the amount of time consumed in the personal activity. [Citations.] While the question of whether an employee has departed from his special errand is normally one of fact for the jury, where the evidence clearly shows a complete abandonment, the court may make the determination that the employee is outside the scope of his employment as a matter of law. [Citations.]" (Felix v. Asai, supra, 192 Cal. App. 3d at pp.932-933, 237 Cal. Rptr. 718.)

Here the evidence does not clearly show complete abandonment. Instead, the evidence raises triable issues on the factors bearing on whether Evans completely abandoned the special errand in favor of pursuing a personal objective.

A. Evans's Intent. In its motion for summary judgment, McDonald's did not identify any evidence Evans intended to abandon his special errand when he decided to join his co-workers in the gathering at Duffer's house. However, in opposing McDonald's motion, O'Connor presented evidence bearing on Evans's intent from which a jury might reasonably infer Evans did not completely abandon his special errand when he went to Duffer's house.

The record contains evidence McDonald's encourages its employees and aspiring managers to show greater dedication than simply working a shift and going home. O'Connor presented McDonald's operations and training manual and employee handbook to demonstrate McDonald's fosters employee initiative and involvement in problem solving. Such evidence could reasonably support a finding of "a direct and specific connection" between McDonald's business and the gathering at Duffer's because the gathering was consistent with the "family" spirit and teamwork emphasized by McDonald's in its communications with employees. Such evidence could also reasonably support a finding McDonald's emphasis on teamwork made a group discussion of McDonald's business at Duffer's house a foreseeable continuation of Evans's special errand. The record also contains evidence supporting a reasonable inference Evans went to Duffer's house intending to continue his work on the spring blitz for McDonald's. Much of the conversation during the gathering centered on McDonald's business or concerned employee-manager relations. A "main inspection" was scheduled for the day after the spring-blitz cleanup of the playground area. The persons at Duffer's house continued their mental inventory of last minute things they could do to improve their chances in the spring-blitz competition. According to Evans, the group was concerned about whether "we were going to win [the spring blitz], and we did." The group discussed the cleaning activities of the spring blitz to determine whether they might return to the restaurant to correct any deficiencies. According to Duffer, the activity during the gathering at his house consisted of "sitting around talking about the blitz and relaxing." The group also "talked about other stores, how they had been doing [and] about passing the quality checks that we had or spot checks that we had."

Thus, evidence and reasonable inferences bearing on Evans's intent raises triable factual issues about whether he completely abandoned the special errand.

B. Nature, Time and Place of Evans's Conduct. McDonald's contends the gathering at Duffer's house after normal business hours was an informal social function unconnected to Evans's special errand for his employer. However, O'Connor submitted evidence suggesting the gathering benefitted McDonald's, occurred at Evans's fellow employee's house immediately after McDonald's place of business closed, consisted of continuation of employees' discussion about the spring blitz, and was inspired by the spirit of competition engendered by McDonald's. That evidence and reasonable inferences bearing on the nature, time and place of Evans's conduct raise triable factual issues about whether he completely abandoned the special errand.

C. Work Evans Was Hired to Do. McDonald's contends the asserted managerial discussions at Duffer's house went beyond the scope of work Evans was hired to do. However, O'Connor introduced evidence suggesting Evans was in training to become a manager and was expected to show initiative in his work to be worthy of future promotion. Such evidence raises an inference Evans's participation in discussions at Duffer's house did not exceed the scope of his assigned work.

D. McDonald's Reasonable Expectations. In a declaration supporting McDonald's motion for summary judgment, Evans's direct supervisor Cardenas asserted Evans "was under no instruction from me, or any other authorized employee of McDonald's, with respect to his activities after he left the restaurant. . . . I had no knowledge that other co-employees would go to Joe Duffer's house after the final clean-up." McDonald's also presented evidence it required official employee conferences be attended by a salaried manager and no such salaried manager attended the Duffer gathering. However, these facts do not compel a finding as a matter of law contrary to O'Connor's claim McDonald's implicitly encouraged Evans to continue his special errand by conferring with co-employees on what they might do to win the spring-blitz competition.

E. Evans's Freedom in Performing Duties. O'Connor presented evidence Evans had considerable latitude in performing his duties. Evans was not paid for his performance of the special errand. His work was voluntary and consistent with other occasions where he and fellow workers were expected to pitch in to help the team effort without punching in on the time clock.

F. Amount of Time Consumed in Personal Activity. McDonald's contends Evans stopped at Duffer's home for four hours on his own volition, for his own enjoyment and without McDonald's explicit direction or suggestion. However, O'Connor presented evidence showing much of the discussion at Duffer's home was related to Evans's employment at McDonald's. Such evidence raises a triable factual issue about the combination of personal entertainment and company business at Duffer's house. "Where the employee may be deemed to be pursuing a business errand and a personal objective simultaneously, he will still be acting within the scope of his employment." (Felix v. Asai, supra, 192 Cal. App. 3d at p.932, 237 Cal. Rptr. 718.)

G. Conclusion. The superior court found—and the parties here do not challenge—Evans's voluntary participation in the spring blitz until after midnight constituted a special errand on McDonald's behalf. The question here is whether the gathering at Duffer's to discuss the spring blitz and socialize constituted a complete departure from the special errand.

Because disputed factual questions and reasonable inferences preclude determination as a matter of law of the issue whether Evans completely abandoned his special errand, the court should have denied McDonald's motion for summary judgment. . . .

NOTES TO O'CONNOR v. McDONALD'S RESTAURANTS OF CALIFORNIA, INC.

1. *Scope of Employment.* Courts use many terms in analyzing whether an employee acted within the scope of employment at the time of tortious conduct. Terminology includes references to "frolics," "detours," "comings and goings," "special errands," and "complete abandonment of special errands." In which of these circumstances is the employer potentially vicariously liable? What evidence supported vicarious liability in *McDonald's*?

2. *Alternative Tests for Scope of Employment.* Jurisdictions consider a variety of factors relevant to whether an employee is acting within the scope of employment. Some follow the test from §228 of the Restatement (Second) of Agency, which provides:

(1) Conduct of a servant is within the scope of employment if, but only if:
    (a) it is of the kind he is employed to perform;
    (b) it occurs substantially within the authorized time and space limits;
    (c) it is actuated, at least in part, by a purpose to serve the master, and
    (d) if force is intentionally used by the servant against another, the use of
force is not unexpected by the master.
(2) Conduct of a servant is not within the scope of employment if it is different in kind from that authorized, far beyond the authorized time or space limits, or too little actuated by a purpose to serve the master.

Another approach emphasizes whether the employee's tortious conduct was foreseeable in light of the duties the employee was hired to perform. Foreseeability in this context means

> that in the context of the particular enterprise an employee's conduct is not so unusual or startling that it would seem unfair to include the loss resulting from it among other costs of the employer's business. In other words, where the question is one of vicarious liability, the inquiry should be whether the risk was one "that may fairly be regarded as typical of or broadly incidental" to the enterprise undertaken by the employer.

Rodgers v. Kemper Constr. Co., 50 Cal. App. 3d 608, 619 (1975).

3. *Misconduct Prohibited by Employer.* An employee who violates an employer's rules might still be treated as having acted within the scope of employment. If all employee violations of workplace rules were treated as acts outside the scope of employment, employers could avoid the impact of the *respondeat superior* doctrine by adopting rules that prohibited all risky conduct or potentially harmful conduct.

4. *Intentional Torts.* Courts use a variety of approaches for determining when an employee's intentional tort may be treated as the responsibility of the employer. California, for example, has held that a sexual tort will not be treated as within the scope of employment unless its motivating emotions were attributable to work-related events or conditions. See Lisa M. v. Henry Mayo Newhall Memorial Hospital, 907 P.2d 358 (Cal. 1995). In some cases, courts have held that the circumstances of employment create a special risk of intentional tort and for that reason will impose *respondeat superior* liability. See, e.g., Costos v. Coconut Island Corp., 137 F.3d 46 (1st Cir. 1998), where the manager of an inn raped a guest. See also Fearing v. Bucher, 977 P.2d 1163 (Or. 1999), in which a young person who allegedly was the victim of sexual abuse by a member of the clergy was permitted to seek damages against the church. The court stated that "a jury reasonably could infer that . . . performance of his pastoral duties with respect to plaintiff and his family were a necessary precursor to the sexual abuse and that the assaults thus were a direct outgrowth of and were engendered by conduct that was within the scope of . . . employment."

***Perspective: Relating "Deep Pocket" to Enterprise
and Risk Avoidance Theories***

A court or a jurisdiction may choose a test that reflects its theory for why vicarious liability is imposed. The foreseeability approach, for instance, focuses on making a business pay its own way by internalizing the risks it creates and is consistent with the *enterprise risk theory*. Some elements of the Restatement (Second) of Agency test and the *McDonald's* test are relevant to whether the employer could have taken precautions to minimize the risks created, reflecting the *risk avoidance theory*. Do any of the factors seem to relate directly to the most frequently stated justification, the desire to ensure that victims are compensated by a defendant who is likely to have assets or insurance?

SANTIAGO v. PHOENIX NEWSPAPERS, INC.

794 P.2d 138 (Ariz. 1990)

GRANT, C.J.

... On April 20, 1986, a car driven by Frank Frausto (Frausto) collided with a motorcycle driven by Santiago. At the time Frausto was delivering the Sunday edition of the Arizona Republic on his route for PNI. Santiago filed a negligence action against Frausto and PNI, alleging that Frausto was PNI's agent. Both parties moved for summary judgment. The court, finding no genuine issues of material fact, concluded that Frausto was an independent contractor. The court of appeals agreed, stating that "[p]arties have a perfect right, in their dealings with each other, to establish the independent contractor status in order to avoid the relationship of employer-employee, and it is clear from the undisputed facts that there was no employer-employee relationship created between PNI and Frausto." Santiago seeks review of this ruling.

We view the facts most favorably to Santiago, as the party opposing the summary judgment.

Frausto began delivering papers for PNI in August 1984 under a "Delivery Agent Agreement," prepared by PNI. The agreement provided that Frausto was an "independent contractor," retained to provide prompt delivery of its newspapers by the times specified in the contract. . . .

In ruling on the summary judgment motion, the court considered the affidavits of Frausto and David L. Miller, a delivery agent and former employee driver. Frausto stated in his affidavit that, despite the contractual nomenclature, he considered himself an employee and delivered the papers any way his supervisor directed him to. This included placing the paper in a particular spot if requested by a customer. If he did not comply with these requests, his supervisor would speak to him and he could be fired. Miller stated in his affidavit that he had been a service driver, later switched to being a delivery agent, and that, in his view, there was no significant difference between the level of supervision provided to those holding the two positions. . . .

Section 220 of the Restatement (Second) of Agency, adopted by Arizona, defines a servant as "a person employed to perform services in the affairs of another and who with respect to the physical conduct in the performance of the services is subject to the other's control or right to control." The Restatement lists several additional factors, none of which is dispositive, in determining whether one acting for another is a servant or an independent contractor. We now review those factors, along with the cases considering them, for evidence of an employer-employee relationship which could preclude the entry of summary judgment.

As a prefatory note, we reject PNI's argument that the language of the employment contract is determinative. Contract language does not determine the relationship of the parties, rather the "objective nature of the relationship, [is] determined upon an analysis of the totality of the facts and circumstances of each case." Anton v. Industrial Commission, 688 P.2d 192, 194 (App. 1984). . . .

In determining whether an employer-employee relationship exists, the fact finder must evaluate a number of criteria. They include: 1. The extent of control exercised by the master over details of the work and the degree of supervision; 2. The distinct nature of the worker's business; 3. Specialization or skilled occupation; 4. Materials and place of work; 5. Duration of employment; 6. Method of payment; 7. Relationship of work done to the regular business of the employer; 8. Belief of the parties.

1. *The extent of control exercised by the master over the details of the work.* Such control may be manifested in a variety of ways. A worker who must comply with another's instructions about when, where, and how to work is an employee. . . .

. . . For example, an appellate court overturned the trial court's finding of no employer-employee relationship in Gallaher v. Ricketts, 187 So. 351, 355 (La. Ct. App. 1939). The newspaper carrier in *Gallaher* provided his own transportation and was paid a commission for every dollar worth of papers delivered on his assigned route. The company conducted training programs, including tips on how to distribute the paper and stimulate sales, reimbursed him for some transportation expenses, and retained the right to terminate him at any time. The court concluded that these indices of control demonstrated that the carrier "was merely a cog in the wheel of the defendant's enterprise," and held that Ricketts was an employee. . . .

In this case, PNI designated the time for pick-up and delivery, the area covered, the manner in which the papers were delivered, i.e., bagged and banded, and the persons to whom delivery was made. Although PNI did little actual supervising, it had the authority under the contract to send a supervisor with Frausto on his route. Frausto claimed he did the job as he was told, without renegotiating the contract terms, adding customers and following specific customer requests relayed by PNI.

2. *The distinct nature of the worker's business.* Whether the worker's tasks are efforts to promote his own independent enterprise or to further his employer's business will aid the fact finder in ascertaining the existence of an employer-employee relationship. Tanner v. USA Today, 179 Ga. App. 722, 347 S.E.2d 690 (1986). The agent in *Tanner* contracted with USA Today to distribute papers. The agent in turn hired carriers to deliver the papers using his trucks. USA Today had no control over the choice of drivers, the trucks used, or the route taken. Under these circumstances, and despite USA Today's imposition of time parameters for delivery, the court found insufficient evidence to raise the issue of an employer-employee relationship. . . .

As far as the nature of the worker's business, Frausto had no delivery business distinct from that of his responsibilities to PNI. Unlike the drivers in *Tanner,* Frausto had an individual relationship and contract with the newspaper company. Furthermore, he did not purchase the papers and then sell them at a profit or loss. Payments were made directly to PNI and any complaints or requests for delivery changes went through PNI. If Frausto missed a customer, a PNI employee would deliver a paper.

3. *Specialization or skilled occupation.* The jury is more likely to find a master-servant relationship where the work does not require the services of one highly educated or skilled. PNI argues that its agents must drive, follow directions, and be diligent in order to perform the job for which they are paid. However, these skills are required in differing degrees for virtually any job. Frausto's services were not specialized and required no particular training. In addition, an agreement that work cannot be delegated indicates a master-servant relationship. In this case, Frausto could delegate work but only up to twenty-five percent of the days.

4. *Materials and place of work.* If an employer supplies tools, and employment is over a specific area or over a fixed route, a master-servant relationship is indicated. In this case, PNI supplied the product but did not supply the bags, rubber bands, or

transportation necessary to complete the deliveries satisfactorily. However, PNI did designate the route to be covered.

5. *Duration of employment.* Whether the employer seeks a worker's services as a one-time, discrete job or as part of a continuous working relationship may indicate that the employer-employee relationship exists. The shorter in time the relationship, the less likely the worker will subject himself to control over job details. In addition, the employer's right to terminate may indicate control and therefore an employer-employee relationship. The "right to fire" is considered one of the most effective methods of control. In this case, the contract provided for a six-month term, renewable as long as the carrier performed satisfactorily. Frausto could be terminated without cause in 28 days and with cause immediately. The definition of cause in the contract was defined only as a failure to provide "satisfactory" service. A jury could reasonably infer that an employer-employee relationship existed since PNI retained significant latitude to fire Frausto inasmuch as the "satisfactory service" provision provides no effective standards. In addition, the jury could also infer that PNI provided health insurance to encourage a long-term relationship and disability insurance to protect itself in case of injury to the carrier, both of which support the existence of an employer-employee relationship.

6. *Method of payment.* PNI paid Frausto each week, but argues that because Frausto was not paid by the hour, he was an independent contractor. Santiago responds that payment was not made by the "job" because Frausto's responsibilities changed without any adjustment to his pay or contract.

7. *Relation of work done to the employer's regular business.* A court is more likely to find a worker an employee if the work is part of the employer's regular business. . . .

Home delivery is critical to the survival of a local daily paper; it may be its essential core. As one court explained:

> The delivery of newspapers within a reasonable time after publication is essential to the success of the newspaper business. For the greater portion of its income the paper depends on advertising, and the rates for advertising are governed by the paper's circulation. Circulation is a necessity for success. The delivery boys are just as much an integral part of the newspaper industry as are the typesetters and pressmen or the editorial staff.

Cooper v. Asheville Citizen-Times Publishing Co., 129 S.E.2d 107, 114 (1963). PNI is hard-pressed to detach the business of delivering news from that of reporting and printing it, especially when it retains an individual relationship with each carrier.

8. *Belief of the parties.* As stated above, Frausto believed that he was an employee, despite contract language to the contrary. Even if he believed he was an independent contractor, that would not preclude a finding of vicarious liability. As the Restatement explains: "It is not determinative that the parties believe or disbelieve that the relation of master and servant exists, except insofar as such belief indicates an assumption of control by the one and submission of control by the other." Restatement §220 comment m. In addition to the parties' belief, the finder of fact should look to the community's belief. "Community custom in thinking that a kind of service is rendered by servants . . . is of importance." Restatement §220 comment h. The fact that the community regards those doing such work as servants indicates the relation of master

and servant. The newspaper's customers did not have individual contact or contracts with Frausto. All payments, complaints, and changes were made directly to PNI. From these facts, a jury could infer that the community regarded Frausto as PNI's employee.

Again, analyzing these factors in relation to the facts of this case a jury could determine that an employer-employee relationship existed between PNI and Frausto.

Whether an employer-employee relationship exists may not be determined as a matter of law in either side's favor, because reasonable minds may disagree on the nature of the employment relationship. A jury could infer from these facts that Frausto was an employee because PNI involved itself with the details of delivery, received directly all customer complaints and changes so as to remove much of Frausto's independence, retained broad discretion to terminate, and relied heavily on Frausto's services for the survival of its business. The jury could also infer that Frausto was an independent contractor because he used his own car, was subject to little supervision, provided some of his own supplies, and could have someone else deliver for him within limits. Therefore, the trial court erred in finding as a matter of law that Frausto was an independent contractor. Summary judgment on the vicarious liability claim was inappropriate. The opinion of the court of appeals is vacated and the case is remanded to the superior court for proceedings consistent with this opinion.

NOTES TO SANTIAGO v. PHOENIX NEWSPAPERS, INC.

1. *Multifactor Test for Independent Contractor.* The court's examination of the multiple factors for determining independent contractor status does not explain how much weight each factor should receive. Nor does the court say what each factor indicates in this particular case. Apparently a jury would be entitled to find either that Frausto was or was not an employee of PNI. The court does say how, in general, each factor is relevant to the issue of whether the worker is an employee or an independent contractor. Reviewing the court's discussion of each factor, to what conclusion does the evidence in *Santiago* point?

2. *Inherently Dangerous Activities.* An exception to the rule precluding vicarious liability for the acts of independent contractors applies to situations where an employer hires an independent contractor to perform an inherently dangerous task. The exception applies to work that is dangerous even when done with reasonable care, such as demolition and excavation. It applies to dangers that are naturally understood to be present in the endeavor. Construction work, for instance, may not be inherently dangerous because building a deck on the back of a house is not dangerous if done carefully. Construction work may be inherently dangerous, however, if it involves blowing up an office building in order to clear the work site. Such tasks are said to give rise to "nondelegable duties" to use reasonable care to protect third parties against injuries from those activities. Courts have denied employers the insulation of the independent contractor exception to *respondeat superior* in connection with the following activities: transporting large logs on highways (Risley v. Lenwell, 27 P.2d 897 (1954)); marking lines on the pavement of a busy street (Van Arsdale v. Hollinger, 437 P.2d 508 (Cal. 1968)); crop-dusting (Boroughs v. Joiner, 337 So. 2d 340 (Ala. 1976)); using a scaffold to carry out work on a high floor of a building located on a busy street (Lockowitz v. Melnyk, 148 N.Y.S.2d 232 (1956)).

B. *Vicarious Liability for Vehicle Owners*

To increase the likelihood that people injured by the use and operation of automobiles will recover damages, state statutes make vehicle owners vicariously liable for the tortious conduct of all users of their vehicles. Levitt v. Peluso illustrates that this rule applies even when vehicle's owner is not driving it and the tortfeasor is a passenger rather than a driver. The case also discusses the limits on this source of vicarious liability.

LEVITT v. PELUSO

638 N.Y.S.2d 878 (N.Y. Sup. Ct. 1995)

McCaffrey, J.

This is a negligence action arising out of a May 20, 1994 accident wherein the plaintiff, a pedestrian, was blinded in one eye by an egg thrown from a moving automobile owned by defendant Eugene Peluso and permissively operated by defendant Patrick Peluso in which defendant Russell DiBenedetto was a passenger. The sole basis of liability alleged against defendant Eugene Peluso is Vehicle and Traffic Law (VTL) §388 which imposes vicarious liability against the owner of a motor vehicle for injury resulting from negligence in its permissive use or operation. . . .

Under certain circumstances, Vehicle and Traffic Law §388 imposes civil liability on the absent owner of a negligently used or operated vehicle when such use or operation results in death or injury. Specifically the statute provides, in part:

> Every owner of a vehicle used or operated in this state shall be liable and responsible for death or injuries to person or property resulting from negligence in the use or operation of such vehicle, in the business of such owner or otherwise, by any person using or operating the same with the permission, express or implied, of such owner. . . .

VTL §388 imposes liability upon an absent owner when four prerequisites are met: 1) death or injury to person or property, 2) the harm is the result of the operator's negligence, 3) the negligence arose from the use or operation of the vehicle, and 4) the operator was using the vehicle with the owner's permission.

The imposition of civil liability upon an absent owner is an expression of policy that one injured by the negligent use or operation of a motor vehicle should have recourse to a financially responsible defendant, i.e., the owner.

Plaintiff alleges he was injured by the permissive but negligent "use and operation" of an automobile owned by Eugene Peluso. Thus, plaintiff contends, pursuant to VTL §388, defendant Eugene Peluso is civilly liable for his injuries. . . .

Plaintiff's contention is that employment of the car as a means of transportation to and from the situs of the injury and as the place from which the eggs were thrown (i.e., "use" of the vehicle), plus the effect of the car's speed and forward momentum (i.e., "operation" of the vehicle) on the velocity of the thrown egg, makes such use and operation a substantial factor in the production of the injury. . . .

Among the jurisdictions which have determined that an accident or injury caused by objects thrown from a moving vehicle arose out of the "use or operation" of a vehicle are: a) a remarkably similar case from California involving the use of an automobile by four teenage boys and the throwing of an egg from a moving car which resulted in a severe eye injury to a pedestrian (National Am. Ins. Co. v. Insurance Co. of

N. America, 74 Cal. App. 3d 565, 140 Cal. Rptr. 828 [1977]); b) a Florida incident (Valdes v. Smalley, 303 So. 2d 342 [Fla. App. 3d Dist. 1974], *cert. den.,* 341 So. 2d 975 [Fla. 1977]) involving the death of a pedestrian from a beer mug thrown from a moving vehicle; and c) a New Jersey case involving a bicyclist who was struck by a stick with a nail in it tossed from a moving vehicle (Westchester Fire Ins. Co. v. Continental Ins. Co., 126 N.J. Super. 29, 312 A.2d 664, *affd.,* 65 N.J. 152, 319 A.2d 732). Those decisions all . . . appear to be premised upon the general principle that insurance policies should be construed liberally in favor of the insured in order to afford purchasers a broad measure of protection. For example, the New Jersey Appellate Division in *Westchester Fire Ins. Co.,* supra, stated in part:

> We agree with the automobile carriers' contention that the phrase "arising out of the . . . use" is not synonymous with "while riding." As one court commented, such a construction would write from the contract the words "arising out of." See Speziale v. Kohnke, 194 So. 2d 485 (La. App. 1967).
>
> But we do not agree that the words "arising out of the . . . use" require or justify the interpretation that before coverage exists it must appear that the injury is a direct and proximate result, in a strict legal sense, of the use of the automobile.
>
> We consider that the phrase "arising out of" must be interpreted in a broad and comprehensive sense to mean "originating from" or "growing out of" the use of the automobile. So interpreted, there need be shown only a substantial nexus between the injury and the use of the vehicle in order for the obligation to provide coverage to arise. The inquiry should be whether the negligent act which caused the injury, although not foreseen or expected, was in the contemplation of the parties to the insurance contract a natural and reasonable incident or consequence of the use of the automobile, and thus a risk against which they might reasonably expect those insured under the policy would be protected. (126 N.J. Super., at 37-38, 312 A.2d, at 668-669, *supra.*)

Under similar fact patterns, numerous other foreign courts have found an insufficient causal relationship between the use or operation of the vehicle and the incident. In Government Employees Ins. Co. v. Melton, 357 F. Supp. 416 (D.C.S.C. 1972), *aff'd,* 473 F.2d 909 (4th Cir. 1973), applying South Carolina law,

> The court noted that the complaint alleged that one or more of the occupants in the rear of a pickup truck threw a bottle or bottles out of the rear of the truck and struck the injured parties. The court stated that a causal relation or connection has to exist between an accident or the injury and the use of the vehicle in order for the accident or injury to come within the meaning of the phrase "arising out of the use" of a vehicle. The court pointed out that the vehicle in question was not used for the purpose for which it was designed, for there could be no realistic conclusion that it was designed for the purpose of allowing, permitting, or encouraging bottles or other injurious matter to be thrown therefrom. The court thus concluded that the causal relationship between the use of the vehicle and the incident in question simply did not exist. (Schaefer, *Automobile Liability Insurance: What Are Accidents or Injuries Arising Out of Ownership, Maintenance, or Use of Insured Vehicle,* 15 ALR 4th 10, §9[b].)

A variety of additional determinations from other jurisdictions holding that no causal relationship was present in the throwing of objects from a moving vehicle exist.

A review of the aforementioned determinations from other jurisdictions reveals that the prevailing opinion of our sister states concerning *insurance coverage* for injuries from objects thrown from a moving vehicle in that an element of causality, though not necessarily the proximate cause, is required.

Such as in *Westchester Fire Ins. Co.,* supra, the New Jersey Appellate Division opined that:

> In our mobile society the act of throwing or dropping objects from moving vehicles is not such an uncommon phenomenon that such occurrence may not be anticipated, nor so inconsequential that members of the public need no financial protection from the consequences thereof. (126 N.J. Super., at 38-39, 312 A.2d, at 669, supra.)

However, any such broadening of statutorily imposed vicarious *liability* in New York should be accomplished legislatively and not by judicial fiat.

In *Manhattan and Bronx Surface Transit Operating Authority (Gholson),* 71 A.D.2d 1004, 1005, 420 N.Y.S.2d 298, 299 (2d Dept. 1979), the Appellate Division, Second Department enunciated a definition of "use or operation" for purposes of determining an insurer's liability under standard automobile liability policies which is instructive for purposes of determining defendant Eugene Peluso's potential vicarious liability pursuant to VTL §388.

In *Gholson,* a bus driver was stabbed after refusing to allow a passenger to disembark at an unmarked stop. The court held that the bus driver was not injured as a result of the use or operation of a motor vehicle. More specifically, the court set forth the following test which must be met before finding "use and operation": (1) The accident must have arisen out of the inherent nature of the automobile, as such; (2) [t]he accident must have arisen within the natural territorial limits of an automobile and the actual use, loading or unloading must not have terminated; and (3) [t]he automobile must not have merely contributed to the cause and the condition but itself must produce or be a proximate cause of the injury.

The second element of the *Gholson* test, which deals with territorial limits, seems to be satisfied by the facts of this case. The first and third elements, however, are not met. First of all, the inherent nature of an automobile is to serve as a means of transportation to and from a certain location, and not to serve as a "launching pad" to project foreign matter such as eggs. The term "inherent," as defined by the Living Webster's Dictionary of the English Language means "innate, existing inseparably within an object." To say that the inherent nature of an automobile is to serve as a "launching pad" for eggs mischaracterizes the innate nature of a car. The injury here did not arise from the inherent nature of a car; rather, the injury arose incident to an intentional act, i.e., the throwing of an egg.

With respect to element number three in the *Gholson* test dealing with causation, the car itself did not produce the injury in question. Rather, the injury resulted from the occupant or driver intentionally throwing an egg out of the automobile. That is, the driving of the automobile was merely incidental. The car indirectly contributed to the injury which was brought about by the intentional assault of throwing the egg. *Gholson* states mere contribution to the incident does not constitute "use or operation."

Furthermore, "where the operation of driving function of an automobile or the condition of the vehicle itself is not the proximate cause of the injury, the occurrence does not arise out of its use or operation." United Servs. Automobile Assn. v. Aetna Cas. & Sur. Co., 75 A.D.2d 1022, 429 N.Y.S.2d 508 (4th Dept. 1980). In that case, the injured party was a passenger in a vehicle hit in the eye by a wadded tinfoil gum wrapper thrown by another passenger while the vehicle was moving. The court held that "use or operation" of vehicle was not shown to be a proximate cause of the injury. In Olin v. Moore, 178 A.D.2d 517, 577 N.Y.S.2d 446 (2d Dept. 1991), it was held that where a passenger in a moving bus was bitten by a fellow passenger the injury did not arise from the use or operation of the vehicle. . . .

Therefore, in order to impose vicarious liability under Vehicle and Traffic Law §388 the "operation of driving function of an automobile or the condition of the vehicle itself" must be the proximate cause of injury (*United Services Automobile Association,* supra at 510). While the use of Mr. Peluso's vehicle may have contributed to the severity of plaintiff's injury and the infant defendants' temporary escape, the proximate cause of plaintiff's injury was the independent act of throwing the egg. Plaintiff's injury did not therefore arise out of the "use or operation" of the vehicle pursuant to §388 and defendant Eugene Peluso, individually, is not vicariously liable for co-defendants' acts. . . .

NOTES TO LEVITT v. PELUSO

1. *Use and Operation of a Motor Vehicle.* Imposing vicarious liability on a vehicle's owner requires more than the mere presence of an auto at the scene of an injury and more than the fact that the tortfeasor was *in* the auto. How much more is required? The court in *Levitt* used the "use and operation" language from the statute to create limits on the owner's vicarious liability. Why was the egg throwing not a "use" of the motor vehicle?

2. *Rationale for Vicarious Liability.* The *Levitt* court cites the desire to compensate victims as the justification for imposing vicarious liability on automobile owners, who are likely to have accident insurance. If compensation is the goal, why would the law limit vicarious liability to only some victims of negligence associated with the car? Limits on the scope of coverage of automobile insurance suggested to this court that similar limits on vicarious liability might be appropriate.

Perspective: Use and Operation of a Motor Vehicle

In *Levitt,* the court's analysis of whether the accident resulted from "use or operation" of the vehicle reflected three different perspectives. The first is whether the vehicle was involved in an important enough way to justify vicarious liability. From this perspective the court was concerned about whether there was a "substantial nexus" between the injury and the use of the vehicle and whether use and operation of the vehicle was "a substantial factor in producing the injury." A second perspective focuses on whether the accident is an expected consequence of the use of the vehicle. The accident is less foreseeably related to use if it is a consequence that was not "in the contemplation of the parties" to an insurance contract protecting the owner. The third perspective is whether the accident is "a natural and reasonable incident or consequence of the use of the automobile." These perspectives overlap with one another and are reminiscent of the three major approaches to the analysis of proximate cause: the substantial factor, foreseeability, and directness tests.

9

PROFESSIONALS

I. Introduction

Tort cases involving *professionals*, like other cases, require proof of duty, breach, causation, and damages. A number of doctrines have developed to clarify the role of those elements for professional malpractice cases. This chapter examines issues in defining the standard of care for professionals, in selecting a local or national context for evaluating their conduct, and in determining when these cases should require the use of expert testimony.

II. Professional Standard's Basic Definition and Rationale

Courts differ on whether the standard of care for professionals requires a jury to compare a professional's conduct to his or her profession's position on proper conduct or to the jury's own conclusion about what conduct is reasonable. Osborn v. Irwin Memorial Blood Bank presents a typical description of the professional standard and highlights the differences between determinations of the negligence of a professional and a nonprofessional. Nowatske v. Osterloh articulates an alternative standard that incorporates the reasonable person standard. Another facet of the professional standard involves identifying the activities to which it should apply. Rossell v. Volkswagen of America considers whether that standard should govern an activity that is complex and technologically advanced but that might not fit a traditional definition of "professional."

OSBORN v. IRWIN MEMORIAL BLOOD BANK
7 Cal. Rptr. 2d 101 (Ct. App. Cal. 1992)

PERLEY, A.J. . . .

In February of 1983, at the age of three weeks, Michael Osborn contracted the AIDS virus from a blood transfusion in the course of surgery on his heart at the University of

California at San Francisco Medical Center. The blood used in the operation was supplied by the Irwin Memorial Blood Bank. Michael and his parents, Paul and Mary Osborn, sued Irwin and the University for damages on various theories. . . .

The most significant issue on appeal is whether Irwin was entitled to judgment notwithstanding the verdict on the issue of negligence. Qualified experts opined for plaintiffs that Irwin's blood testing and donor screening practices prior to Michael's surgery were negligent in light of concerns about AIDS at the time [because they did not include anti-HBc tests]. On matters such as these that are outside common knowledge, expert opinion is ordinarily sufficient to create a prima facie case. Here, however, there was uncontradicted evidence that Irwin was doing as much if not more in the areas of testing and screening than any other blood bank in the country, and there is no question that it followed accepted practices within the profession. We hold that Irwin cannot be found negligent in these circumstances. . . .

The form of [the plaintiffs'] experts' testimony suggests that plaintiffs assumed their case against Irwin was one of ordinary negligence. Plaintiffs' experts did not couch their opinions in terms of the standard of care for blood banks in early 1983. They simply said what Irwin "should" have done, or what a "reasonable person" would have done, in light of what was known about AIDS at the time. We ultimately conclude that this distinction is one of substance as well as form, but the threshold question is whether Irwin should be held to a professional standard of care.

We note that this appears to be a point of first impression in California. The precedents indicating that blood banks are not subject to strict liability for providing contaminated blood have observed that blood banks may be sued for negligence but have not undertaken to define the standard of care. We have determined that Irwin is a "health care provider" within the meaning of MICRA [the Medical Injury Compensation Reform Act], and there is no question that donor screening and blood testing are "professional services" for purposes of MICRA (see Civ. Code, §3333.1, subd. (c)(2), 3333.2, subd. (c)(2); and Code Civ. Proc., §667.7, subd. (e)(4) [defining "professional negligence" in pertinent part as "a negligent act or omission to act by a health care provider in the rendering of professional services"].) However, MICRA's damage limitations do not purport to define the standard of care.

We conclude that the adequacy of a blood bank's actions to prevent the contamination of blood is a question of professional negligence and fulfillment of a professional standard of care. . . .

Plaintiffs contend that custom and practice are relevant, but not conclusive, on the standard of care. This is the general rule in cases of ordinary negligence. (See Keeton, *Medical Negligence — The Standard of Care* (1979) 10 Tex. Tech L. Rev. 351, 354 [hereafter Keeton].) The leading case for this rule is *The T.J. Hooper* (2d Cir. 1932) 60 F.2d 737, 740, where Learned Hand wrote that "in most cases reasonable prudence is in fact common prudence; but strictly it is never its measure; a whole calling may have unduly lagged in the adoption of new and available devices. It never may set its own tests, however persuasive be its usages. Courts must in the end say what is required; there are precautions so imperative that even their universal disregard will not excuse their omission." There is no question that California follows this rule in ordinary negligence cases.

This is a case of professional negligence, however, and we must assess the role of custom and practice in that context. The question presented here is whether California law permits an expert to second-guess an entire profession. We have found no definitive precedent on this issue and it is not one that is likely to arise.

Custom and practice are not controlling in cases, unlike ours, where a layperson can infer negligence by a professional without any expert testimony. . . .

On the other hand, in cases like ours where experts are needed to show negligence, their testimony sets the standard of care and is said to be "conclusive." . . .

Here it is undisputed that no blood bank in the country was doing what the plaintiffs' experts' standard of care would require of Irwin, and we have an unusual situation where we are called upon to address the significance of a universal practice.

This issue was certified to the South Carolina Supreme Court in Doe v. American Red Cross Blood Services, S.C. Region, supra, 125 F.R.D. 637, in the context of a claim that the Red Cross was negligent for failing to perform anti-HBc surrogate tests for AIDS before January of 1985. The federal court asked whether "professionals are always absolved from negligence liability where their conduct is consistent with generally recognized and accepted professional practices," and stated that "courts and commentators across the country are sharply split on this question."

While it may be true that "[a]n increasing number of courts are rejecting the customary practice standard in favor of a reasonable care or reasonably prudent doctor standard" (Prosser & Keeton, *The Law of Torts* (5th ed., 1988 pocket supp.) p.30, fn. 53 [citing cases outside California]), numerous commentaries have noted that custom generally sets the standard of care. (See, e.g., King, *In Search of a Standard of Care for the Medical Profession: The "Accepted Practice" Formula* (1975) 28 Vand. L. Rev. 1213, 1235, 1245-1246 [hereafter King].)

Most commentators have urged that a customary or accepted practice standard is preferable to one that allows for the disregard of professional judgment. . . .

The basic reason why professionals are usually held only to a standard of custom and practice is that their informed approach to matters outside common knowledge should not be "evaluated by the ad hoc judgments of a lay judge or lay jurors aided by hindsight." (King, supra, 28 Vand. L. Rev. at p.1249.) In the words of a leading authority, "When it can be said that the collective wisdom of the profession is that a particular course of action is the desirable course, then it would seem that the collective wisdom should be followed by the courts." (Keeton, supra, 10 Tex. Tech L. Rev. at pp.364-365.) . . .

[I]n Landeros v. Flood, 17 Cal. 3d 399 [1976], the [California Supreme Court] considered whether a cause of action for malpractice could be stated for failure to diagnose the battered child syndrome. The trial court had sustained the defendants' demurrers and dismissed the case. The Supreme Court reversed, observing that battered child syndrome had been widely reported in the medical literature prior to the plaintiff's treatment, and thus it could not be said as a matter of law that the defendants were not negligent in failing to recognize the syndrome. Justice Mosk's opinion for a unanimous court, however, also noted that proof of the standard of care would require expert testimony on whether the procedures recommended in the literature had actually become the norm within the profession: "The question is whether a reasonably prudent physician examining this plaintiff in 1971 would have been led to suspect she was a victim of the battered child syndrome from the particular injuries and circumstances presented to him, would have confirmed that diagnosis by ordering X-rays of her entire skeleton, and would have promptly reported his findings to appropriate authorities to prevent a recurrence of the injuries. There are numerous recommendations to follow each of these diagnostic and treatment procedures in the medical literature cited above.

"Despite these published admonitions to the profession, however, neither this nor any other court possesses the specialized knowledge necessary to resolve the issue as a matter of law. We simply do not know whether the views espoused in the literature *had been generally adopted in the medical profession by the year 1971, and whether the ordinarily prudent physician was conducting his practice in accordance therewith.* The question remains one of fact, to be decided on the basis of expert testimony. . . ." (Landeros v. Flood, supra, 17 Cal. 3d at pp.409-410 [footnote omitted, italics added].) . . .

The [*Landeros*] court does not refer to custom, and its discussion suggests that the lack of an established custom for diagnosing and treating battered child syndrome would not preclude a finding of negligence if it could be said that professional admonitions on the subject had been "generally adopted." The court may thus have moved beyond a customary practice standard to one of "accepted" practice, based on "reasonable expectations that the profession collectively holds for its members" rather than "tradition and habit." (King, supra, 28 Vand. L. Rev. at p.1241; see also at p.1243 [proof of accepted practice may be based inter alia on "the best of available medical literature"].)

Like . . . earlier cases, however, Landeros v. Flood confirms that professional prudence is defined by actual or accepted practice within a profession, rather than theories about what "should" have been done. The issue was not the existence of recommendations with respect to battered child syndrome, but whether physicians were "conducting [their] practice in accordance therewith." This is implicit in the definition of the standard of care as skill and knowledge "ordinarily possessed *and exercised*" in a profession. (Landeros v. Flood, supra, 17 Cal. 3d at pp.408, 410 [italics supplied].)

It follows that Irwin cannot be found negligent for failing to perform tests that no other blood bank in the nation was using. Judgment notwithstanding the verdict was properly granted to Irwin on the issue of anti-HBc testing because there was no substantial evidence that failure to conduct the tests was not accepted *practice* for blood banks in January and February of 1983. . . .

NOTES TO OSBORN v. IRWIN MEMORIAL BLOOD BANK

1. *Rationale for the Directed Verdict.* A defendant is entitled to judgment as a matter of law if the plaintiff's evidence, construed most favorably to the plaintiff, cannot rationally support a verdict for the plaintiff under applicable legal doctrines. In *Osborn*, what shortcoming in the plaintiff's evidence required a verdict in favor of the defendant? Would the defendant have been entitled to a directed verdict if the professional standard had not been applied?

2. *Majority View.* The court in *Osborn* states that "professional prudence is defined by actual or accepted practice with a profession, rather than theories about what 'should' have been done." The Restatement (Second) of Torts states that a physician must "exercise the skill and knowledge normally possessed" by other physicians (§299A). The *Osborn* court observes that implicit in the "skill and knowledge" language is reference to the skill and knowledge "ordinarily possessed *and exercised*" by the profession. A number of writers have contended that the traditional approach to professional malpractice allows the profession to establish its own standard. See, e.g., Clarence Morris & C. Robert Morris, Jr., *Morris on Torts* 55 (2d ed. 1980) (custom controls medical malpractice cases); Prosser & Keeton, *The Law of Torts* 189 (5th ed. 1984) ("the standard becomes one of 'good medical practice,' which is to say, what is customary and usual in the profession").

3. *Power of the Professional Standard.* The *Osborn* court discusses a California Supreme Court decision, Landeros v. Flood, which distinguished between the actual conduct of physicians and published admonitions about how physicians should act in certain circumstances. Under the standards adopted in *Osborn* and *Landeros*, may a plaintiff win a medical malpractice case by showing that a physician acted in accordance with customary practices but that those practices were being criticized at the time by some members of the profession?

Problem
Evidence of Professional Standard

In a state where a malpractice plaintiff is required to introduce evidence of the professional standard of care, the defendant moves for judgment as a matter of law. If you represent the plaintiff, what argument would you make to oppose this motion? Based on the following expert testimony, is your argument likely to be successful?

> Q. Are you familiar with the appropriate standard of care and skill that reasonably competent physicians and surgeons in the national medical community would ordinarily exercise when acting under the same or similar circumstances for the treatment and care given to the plaintiff by the defendant doctor?
> A. My main objection was the breakdown or the absence of or the deterrence of any communication between the various caretakers.
> Q. Doctor, then, is it your opinion that the defendant doctor deviated from the national medical community standards in the care and treatment of the plaintiff in that regard in this case?
> A. Well, I don't want to point fingers. But I do think that there was some reduced care below the standards.

See Pruitt v. Zeiger, 590 So. 2d 236 (Ala. 1991).

> ### *Perspective: Class Allegiance*
>
> In his famous treatise, William L. Prosser suggested that the legal system developed the professional standard of care because of "the healthy respect which the courts have had for the learning of a fellow profession, and their reluctance to overburden it with liability." Prosser and Keeton, *The Law of Torts* 189 (5th ed. 1984). Most physicians nowadays would not agree that the law has worked to protect them from liability, but assuming Prosser's historical intuition is correct, does it reveal a class bias in appellate courts?

NOWATSKE v. OSTERLOH
198 Wis. 2d 419, 543 N.W.2d 265 (1996)

ABRAHAMSON, J.

This is an appeal by Kim and Julie Nowatske from a judgment of the circuit court for Winnebago County, Thomas S. Williams, judge. The circuit court dismissed the complaint upon a jury finding that Mark D. Osterloh, M.D. (the defendant), did not negligently cause the Nowatskes' injuries. Upon certification of the court of appeals pursuant to Wis. Stat. (Rule) §809.61 (1993-94), this court accepted the case but limited its review to the following issue: "Whether standard jury instruction Wis JI-Civil 1023 accurately states the law of negligence for medical malpractice cases?" We conclude that the jury instruction read as a whole was not erroneous. . . .

We briefly summarize the facts giving rise to this case, recognizing that the parties dispute whether certain events occurred, whether the surgery and care provided by the defendant were negligent and whether the defendant's alleged negligence caused the plaintiff's injury.[2]

One morning the plaintiff noticed an area of blurred vision in his right eye. He was referred to the defendant, a retina specialist in Oshkosh, who diagnosed him as having a retinal detachment.

Prior to surgery to repair his retina, the plaintiff signed a consent form explaining the risks and possible complications involved in the proposed treatment. . . .

On the morning following surgery, the defendant conducted a post-operative visit to assess the success of his surgery. The parties dispute whether the defendant measured the IOP [internal pressure in the eye]. The defendant tested the plaintiff's vision with an ophthalmoscope, shining a light into the eye to check its response. . . .

By the next morning, the swelling around the plaintiff's eye had subsided. Because the defendant had not indicated when the plaintiff's vision would return, the plaintiff remained unconcerned about his continuing inability to see out of his right eye. At the plaintiff's scheduled follow-up appointment, however, the defendant informed the plaintiff that he would be permanently blind in the right eye. The parties dispute whether the blindness was caused by increased anterior IOP resulting from the surgery or by a discrete vascular event such as an occlusion of the central retinal artery posteriorly.

On April 22, 1991, the plaintiff filed a complaint alleging that the defendant negligently treated him. During a five-day jury trial in January 1993, the plaintiff introduced expert testimony suggesting that if the defendant had utilized reasonable care, the plaintiff would not have lost his eyesight. The defendant, in turn, introduced expert testimony suggesting that the defendant had exercised ordinary care and that a high IOP was not the cause of the plaintiff's blindness.

At the defendant's request and over the plaintiff's objection, the circuit court used various paragraphs from the standard jury instruction pertaining to medical malpractice, Wis JI-Civil 1023, to instruct the jury. In response to the verdict question asking whether the defendant was negligent, the jury answered "no," thus returning a verdict in his favor. The circuit court entered a judgment dismissing the complaint. . . .

The plaintiff's claim that Wis JI-Civil 1023 is erroneous and prejudicial focuses on the first three paragraphs of the instruction. As presented to the jury in this case, those paragraphs, virtually unmodified from the pattern instruction, read as follows:

> In treating Kim Nowatske, Dr. Osterloh was required to use the degree of care, skill, and judgment which is usually exercised in the same or similar circumstances by the average specialist who practices the specialty which Dr. Osterloh practices, having due regard for the state of medical science at the time Kim Nowatske was treated.

---

[2] Both Kim Nowatske and his wife Julie Nowatske are plaintiffs in this case. In the interest of clarity, we refer only to Kim Nowatske as the plaintiff.

The burden in this case is on the plaintiffs to prove that Dr. Osterloh failed to conform to this standard.

A physician does not guarantee the results of his care and treatment. A physician must use reasonable care and is not liable for failing to use the highest degree of care, skill, and judgment. Dr. Osterloh cannot be found negligent simply because there was a bad result. Medicine is not an exact science. Therefore, the issue you must decide in determining whether Dr. Osterloh was negligent is not whether there was a bad result but whether he failed to use the degree of care, skill, and judgment which is exercised by the average physician practicing the sub-specialty of retinal surgery.

If you find that more than one method of treatment for Kim Nowatske's injuries is recognized, then Dr. Osterloh was at liberty to select any of the recognized methods. Dr. Osterloh was not negligent merely because he made a choice of a recognized alternative method of treatment if he used the required care, skill, and judgment in administering the method. This is true even though other medical witnesses may not agree with him on the choice that was made. . . .

The plaintiff's principal objection to [the first] paragraph is that it defines the standard of care as that care usually exercised by the average physician practicing within the same specialty. According to the plaintiff the instruction thus equates the reasonable care required by law with customary medical care as defined by the medical profession, regardless of whether what is customary in the profession reflects what is reasonable in the wake of current medical science.

Because the medical profession is allowed to set its own definition of reasonable behavior in accordance with the customs of the profession, argues the plaintiff, what counts as an exercise of due care is established as a matter of law by doctors rather than as an issue to be resolved by the jury. Under Wis JI-Civil 1023, the plaintiff continues, all a defendant doctor need do is demonstrate that the methods used in treating the patient were customary in the medical profession. Even if the challenged custom is unreasonable and outdated, claims the plaintiff, the fact that it is "usually exercised in the same or similar circumstances by the average physician" is sufficient to shield clearly negligent conduct and negligent practitioners from liability.

The plaintiff is correct in suggesting that physicians, like all others in this state, are bound by a duty to exercise due care. Every person in Wisconsin must conform to the standard of a reasonable person under like circumstances; so too, then, "[t]he duty of a physician or surgeon is to exercise ordinary care." Scaria v. St. Paul Fire & Marine Ins. Co., 68 Wis. 2d 1, 11, 227 N.W.2d 647 (1975). As the amicus brief of the State Medical Society of Wisconsin correctly states, "the basic standard — ordinary care — does not change when the defendant is a physician. The only thing that changes is the makeup of the group to which the defendant's conduct is compared."

The Medical Society's characterization of how the law gauges whether physicians have met their duty of ordinary care is correct. Generally a determination of negligence involves comparing an alleged tortfeasor's standard of care with "the degree of care which the great mass of mankind exercises under the same or similar circumstances." Wis JI-Civil 1005. When a claim arises out of highly specialized conduct requiring professional training, however, the alleged tortfeasor's conduct is compared with the conduct of others who are similarly situated and who have had similar professional training.

Thus physicians are required to exercise ordinary care, a standard to which they have been held since early Wisconsin case law. In Reynolds v. Graves, 3 Wis. 371 [416],

375-76 [421-22] (1854), a physician's duty of care was alternately expressed as the obligation "to use reasonable professional skill and attention" and "to use due and reasonable skill and diligence" in an effort to cure the patient. . . .

Both the amicus brief of the State Medical Society of Wisconsin and the defendant have acknowledged that the first paragraph of Wis JI-Civil 1023 requires that custom must be dynamic to be reasonable. As interpreted by the Medical Society, the portion of Wis JI-Civil 1023 which instructs the jury to judge the defendant's conduct with "due regard for the state of medical science at the time the plaintiff was treated" means that "[p]laintiffs can always, if appropriate, present evidence regarding the 'state of medical science' to show that a professional custom is obsolete or unreasonable." Brief for the State Medical Society of Wisconsin as Amicus Curiae at 3.

The defendant interprets the same jury instruction language as applying "a dynamic standard" to professionals because the standard "changes as the state of knowledge of the profession changes." Brief for Defendant at 17. "Absent a dynamic standard," the defendant continues, "the law could not adjust to changes and improvement in medical science." At oral argument before this court, counsel for the defendant stated that if a particular custom in the medical profession failed to keep pace with what developments in medical science had rendered reasonable, the plaintiff could introduce evidence demonstrating that the custom in question constituted negligent conduct.

We agree with the parties and the Medical Society that while evidence of the usual and customary conduct of others under similar circumstances is ordinarily relevant and admissible as an indication of what is reasonably prudent, customary conduct is not dispositive and cannot overcome the requirement that physicians exercise ordinary care. . . .

We recognize that in most situations there will be no significant difference between customary and reasonable practices. In most situations physicians, like other professionals, will revise their customary practices so that the care they offer reflects a due regard for advances in the profession. An emphasis on reasonable rather than customary practices, however, insures that custom will not shelter physicians who fail to adopt advances in their respective fields and who consequently fail to conform to the standard of care which both the profession and its patients have a right to expect.

The issue then is whether the first paragraph of the instruction conveys the correct legal message that the defendant is held to a standard of reasonable care, skill and judgment and that reasonable care, skill and judgment are not necessarily embodied by the customary practice of the profession but rather represent the practice of physicians who keep abreast of advances in medical knowledge.

We conclude that the first paragraph of Wis JI-Civil 1023, read in conjunction with the remainder of the instructions given, conveys this message. The first paragraph speaks of the degree of care, skill, and judgment usually exercised in the same or similar circumstances by the average specialist. The second paragraph expressly states that a physician must use reasonable care. The third paragraph cautions that even a physician who has chosen a recognized method of treatment can nevertheless be found negligent for failing to exercise "the required care, skill, and judgment in administering the method" chosen. And much like the first paragraph of the plaintiff's proposed instruction, the first paragraph of the instruction given requires that in determining the degree of care, skill and judgment required of a physician, "due regard" should be given to "the state of medical science." The phrase "due regard for the state of medical science" tells the jury that a reasonably competent practitioner is one who keeps up with advances in medical knowledge. . . .

To sum up, we conclude that these three paragraphs of Wis JI-Civil 1023, read as a whole and in conjunction with the other instructions given in this case, were not erroneous. . . .

For the reasons set forth we remand the cause to the court of appeals for further proceedings consistent with this opinion.

NOTES TO NOWATSKE v. OSTERLOH

1. *Juror Freedom Under the Approved Jury Instruction.* The court states that custom should not shelter physicians who fail to adopt advances in their fields. How would the quoted jury charge enable a juror to find such a physician liable if failure to adopt an advance injured a patient?

2. *Clarity of Standard.* Describing the *Nowatske* holding is difficult, because the opinion offers a variety of statements about the proper standard for physicians' conduct:

> customary conduct is not dispositive and cannot overcome the requirement that physicians exercise ordinary care.

> defendant is held to a standard of reasonable care, skill and judgment . . . .

> a reasonably competent practitioner is one who keeps up with advances in medical knowledge.

> reasonable care, skill and judgment . . . represent the practice of physicians who keep abreast of advances in medical knowledge.

Does the *Nowatske* court approve the jury instruction because it defines "reasonable physician" as one who keeps up with advances in medical knowledge, or because it defines "reasonable care" as the practice of physicians who keep abreast of advances in medical knowledge? To establish unreasonable conduct, must a plaintiff show that a physician's conduct differed from the conduct of "physicians who keep abreast of advances"?

3. *Compliance with Custom as a Complete Defense.* How does *Nowatske* compare with *Osborn* (the previous case) on whether compliance with custom is a complete defense in a professional malpractice case? In Philip P. Peters, Jr., *The Role of the Jury in Modern Malpractice Law*, 87 Iowa L. Rev. 909 (2002), the author reports that eleven states and the District of Columbia have expressly rejected the traditional view of compliance with custom as a complete defense, and that nine other states have adopted a reasonable physician standard while not addressing the effect of proof of compliance with custom.

4. *Schools of Thought.* The jury charge discussed in *Nowatske* indicates that a physician is at liberty to select any "recognized alternative method" even if some medical witnesses disagree with that choice. Some jurisdictions refer to this idea with the expression "schools of thought," holding that compliance with any recognized school of thought satisfies the professional standard. Does the language of the charge with respect to alternative methods support the claim that the professional standard allows the medical profession to set its own standards?

5. *Judicial Standard Setting.* In a well-known case, a plaintiff sought to show that had the defendant doctor included a simple test in a routine eye examination, the plaintiff would have had an early warning of a serious disease. The defendant physician did not include the test because it was the professional custom to perform it only for patients significantly older than the plaintiff. In Helling v. Carey, 519 P.2d 981 (Wash. 1974), the court reversed a directed verdict won by the defendant in the trial court. The court noted that the risks the test could avert were grave, and the costs of the test were low. See also Gates v. Jensen, 595 P.2d 919 (Wash. 1979), in which the Washington court interpreted a statute enacted in response to its decision in *Helling*. The court concluded that the statute permitted a holding that reasonable prudence by a professional might require greater care than the care typically exercised by a relevant professional group.

Perspective: Custom-Based Standards

As one article claims,

> The prospect of a widespread retreat from the custom-based standard of care has obvious policy implications. On the one hand, abandonment of the custom-based standard will enable judges and juries to police the practices of physicians facing intense pressure to cut costs. On the other hand, it may demand more of lay jurors than we can reasonably expect of them. And if, as some suspect, juries are unwilling to allow physicians and managed care organizations to be cost-conscious, then jury standard-setting could threaten efforts to keep health care affordable. The choice between these two rival standards is made more difficult by the fact that each has serious shortcomings. Juries may misuse statistical proof evidence, may be susceptible to hindsight bias, and may penalize responsible efforts to keep health care costs under control. Sadly, the evidence regarding medical customs is no less disappointing. Research on physician behavior has revealed that physicians, like the rest of us, are vulnerable to self-interest, habit, and other competing influences. Customs vary inexplicably from one location to another. In addition, market imperfections so permeate health care delivery that competition cannot be trusted to discipline medical customs.

Phillip G. Peters Jr., *The Role of the Jury in Modern Malpractice Law*, 87 Iowa L. Rev. 909 (2002).

ROSSELL v. VOLKSWAGEN OF AMERICA
147 Ariz. 160, 709 P.2d 517 (1985)

FELDMAN, J.

This is a product liability action brought by Phyllis A. Rossell, as guardian ad litem on behalf of her daughter, Julie Ann Kennon (plaintiff), against the manufacturer and the North American distributor of Volkswagen automobiles. The defendants will be referred to collectively as "Volkswagen." The case involves the design of the battery system in the model of the Volkswagen automobile popularly known as the "Beetle" or "Bug." The jury found for the plaintiff and awarded damages in the sum of $1,500,000. The court of appeals held that the plaintiff had failed to establish a prima facie case of . . . negligence . . . and that the trial judge had erred in denying Volkswagen's motion for judgment n.o.v. Believing that the court of appeals had incorrectly stated the applicable law with respect to both issues, we granted review. . . .

We view the facts in the light most favorable to the party who prevailed at trial . . . This action arises from a 1970, one-vehicle accident. At the time of the accident Julie, then eleven months old, was sleeping in the front passenger seat of a 1958 Volkswagen driven by her mother. At approximately 11:00 p.m., on State Route 93, Ms. Rossell fell asleep and the vehicle drifted to the right, off the paved roadway. The sound of the car hitting a sign awakened Rossell, and she attempted to correct the path of the car, but oversteered. The car flipped over, skidded off the road and landed on its roof at the bottom of a cement culvert. The force of the accident dislodged and fractured the battery which was located inside the passenger compartment. In the seven hours it took Rossell to regain full consciousness and then extract herself and her daughter from the car, the broken battery slowly dripped sulfuric acid on Julie. The acid severely burned her. . . .

Plaintiff filed the complaint in May, 1978. She alleged . . . negligent design of the battery system. . . .

Plaintiff argued at trial that battery placement within the passenger compartment created an unreasonable risk of harm and that alternative designs were available and practicable. In their trial motions and later motion for judgment n.o.v., Volkswagen argued that plaintiff had failed to make a prima facie case. First, it claimed that in a negligent design case the defendant must comply with the standard of a reasonably prudent designer of automobiles and that

> knowledge of automobile design principles and engineering practices often is beyond the knowledge of laymen, [so that] plaintiff in a case such as this must produce expert testimony establishing the minimum standard of care and deviation therefrom in designing the automobile. . . .

Concluding its argument, Volkswagen pointed out that plaintiff produced no testimony

> expert or otherwise, [to] describe what was expected of [or done by] a reasonable automobile designer or manufacturer in 1958 or . . . that defendants failed to meet [that] standard of care. . . .

The trial judge characterized Volkswagen's position as a contention that plaintiff could not prevail

> in the absence of testimony . . . from a qualified expert as opposed to simply permitting the jury to infer it, . . . that the standard of care required of a prudent manufacturer would require that the battery be placed elsewhere [or that] it was negligent . . . not to have placed it outside of the passenger compartment. . . .

The trial judge disagreed with Volkswagen and denied the motion for judgment n.o.v. However, a majority of the court of appeals held that such evidence was required for a prima facie case. . . .

We turn, then, to the central issue presented. What type of proof must plaintiff produce in order to make a prima facie case of negligent design against a product manufacturer? What is the standard of care? In the ordinary negligence case, tried under the familiar rubric of "reasonable care," plaintiff's proof must provide facts from which the jury may conclude that defendant's behavior fell below the "reasonable man" standard. . . .

Volkswagen claims that negligent design cases are an exception. They contend that product manufacturers are held to an expert's standard of care, as are professionals such as lawyers, doctors and accountants. In professional malpractice cases the reasonable man standard has been replaced with the standard of "what is customary and usual in the profession." [W. Prosser & W. Keeton, *The Law of Torts* §32 at 189 (5th ed. 1984).] This, of course, requires plaintiff to establish by expert testimony the usual conduct of other practitioners of defendant's profession and to prove, further, that defendant deviated from that standard.

It has been pointed out often enough that this gives the

medical profession, and also the [other professions], the privilege, *which is usually emphatically denied to other groups*, of setting their own legal standards of conduct, merely by adopting their own practices.

Id. (emphasis supplied) (citations omitted).

Should we adopt for manufacturers in negligent design cases a rule "emphatically denied to other groups" but similar to those applied to defendants in professional malpractice cases? Such a rule, of course, would require — not just permit — plaintiff to present explicit evidence of the usual conduct of other persons in the field of design by offering expert evidence of what constitutes "good design practice." Plaintiff would also be required to establish that the design adopted by the defendant deviated from such "good practice." We believe that such a rule is inappropriate.

The malpractice requirement that plaintiff show the details of conduct practiced by others in defendant's profession is not some special favor which the law gives to professionals who may be sued by their clients. It is, instead, a method of holding such defendants to an even higher standard of care than that of an ordinary, prudent person. . . . Such a technique has not been applied in commercial settings, probably because the danger of allowing a commercial group to set its own standard of what is reasonable is not offset by professional obligations which tend to prevent the group from setting standards at a low level in order to accommodate other interests. Thus, it is the general law that industries are not permitted to establish their own standard of conduct because they may be influenced by motives of saving "time, effort or money." Prosser, supra §33 at 194. . . .

In view of public policy and existing law, we decline to transform defective design cases into malpractice cases. We believe the law is best left as it is in this field. Special groups will be allowed to create their own standards of reasonably prudent conduct only when the nature of the group and its special relationship with its clients assure society that those standards will be set with primary regard to protection of the public rather than to such considerations as increased profitability. We do not believe that automobile manufacturers fit into this category. This is no reflection upon automobile manufacturers, but merely a recognition that the necessities of the marketplace permit manufacturers neither the working relationship nor the concern about the welfare of their customers that the professions generally permit and require from their practitioners.

Therefore, in Arizona the rule in negligence cases shall continue to be that evidence of industry custom and practice is generally admissible as evidence relevant to whether defendant's conduct was reasonable under the circumstances. In determining what is reasonable care for manufacturers, the plaintiff need only prove the defendant's conduct presented a foreseeable, unreasonable risk of harm. As in all other negligence cases, the jury is permitted to decide what is reasonable from the common experience of mankind. We do not disturb the rule that in determining what is "reasonable care," expert evidence may be required in those cases in which factual issues are outside the common understanding of jurors. . . . However, unlike most malpractice cases, there need not be explicit expert testimony establishing the standard of care and the manner in which defendant deviated from that standard. . . . With these principles in mind, we now turn to a consideration of the evidence in order to determine whether plaintiff did prove a prima facie case.

Plaintiff presented two experts, Jon McKibben, an automotive engineer, and Charles Turnbow, a safety engineer. Their testimony established that the great majority of cars on the road at the time the Beetle in question was designed had batteries located outside the passenger compartment, usually in the engine compartment and occasionally in the luggage compartment. There was evidence from which the jury could find that from both an engineering and practical standpoint the 1958 Volkswagen could have been designed with the battery outside the passenger compartment, as was the Karmann Ghia, an upscale model which used the same chassis as the Beetle. There was further testimony that placement of the battery inside the passenger compartment was unreasonably dangerous because "batteries do fracture in crashes, not infrequently." . . .

We conclude that the plaintiff did present expert evidence that the battery design location presented a foreseeable, unreasonable risk of harm, that alternative designs were available and that they were feasible from a technological and practical standpoint. We reject Volkswagen's contention that in addition to the evidence outlined above, plaintiff was compelled to produce expert opinion evidence that the standard of "good design practice" required Volkswagen to design the car so that the battery system was located outside the passenger compartment. Unlike a malpractice case, the jury was free to reach or reject this conclusion on the basis of its own experience and knowledge of what is "reasonable," with the assistance of expert opinion describing only the dangers, hazards and factors of design involved. . . .

We hold that plaintiff did make a prima facie case of negligence. . . . The trial court did not err in failing to direct a verdict or grant judgment n.o.v. . . .

The opinion of the court of appeals is vacated. The judgment is affirmed.

NOTES TO ROSSELL v. VOLKSWAGEN OF AMERICA

1. *Eligibility for Professional Standard.*   The *Rossell* court states that the professional standard should be used when "the nature of the group and its special relationship with its clients assure society that those standards will be set with primary regard to protection of the public rather than to such considerations as increased profitability."

An alternative approach to determining whether a person should be judged by the professional standard of care applies standards from federal statutes such as the National Labor Relations Act and the Fair Labor Standards Act. See Lewis v. Rodriguez, 759 P.2d 1012, 1014-1015 (N.M. App. 1988). The National Labor Relations Act defines work as professional if four requirements are met: the work must be predominantly intellectual and nonroutine, must involve the consistent exercise of discretion and judgment, must not be standardized in terms of time, and must require knowledge customarily acquired by specialized study in an institution of higher learning.

How do the factors used in these two approaches relate to engineers in the field of automobile design?

2. *Professionals Other Than Doctors, Lawyers, and Accountants.* Many courts have applied the professional standard to work in a wide range of fields. For example, Montana courts use that standard for cases involving doctors, dentists, and orthodontists; manufacturers and distributors of pharmaceuticals; abstractors of title; veterinarians; and "professional counselors." See Newville v. Department of Family Services, 267 Mont. 237, 883 P.2d 793 (1993).

Problem
Attributes of a Profession

Plaintiff underwent a polygraph examination in connection with his employment. The polygraph examiner gave a report to Plaintiff's employer that led to Plaintiff being fired from his job. If Plaintiff claims that the polygraph examiner was careless in administering a polygraph exam, would the *Rossell* guidelines call for evaluating the polygraph examiner's conduct with a professional standard or a reasonable prudent person standard? See Lewis v. Rodriguez, 107 N.M. 430, 759 P.2d 1012 (1988).

Problem
Non-"Professional" Work in a Professional Setting

Plaintiff was injured in a traffic accident and taken to HealthCenter Hospital, a private for-profit hospital. Emergency room personnel determined that he might have injuries that could be diagnosed with a CAT-scan. Plaintiff was taken to the CAT-scan department, but had to wait almost two hours to be examined, because other patients with similarly serious conditions were being examined first. The CAT-scan showed that Plaintiff had a serious injury. Proper treatment was begun for the injury as soon as it was diagnosed, but Plaintiff suffered permanent debilitating consequences from that injury.

Plaintiff has discovered the following facts:

1. If treatment for his injury had begun about an hour sooner, its permanent effects would likely have been much less severe.
2. HealthCenter's CAT-scan machine was about ten years old. Newer models work more rapidly than the one HealthCenter used but are more expensive to buy and maintain.
3. At HealthCenter Hospital, decisions about what types of equipment to buy and how often to replace equipment are made by executives trained in the management of large enterprises and experienced in the management of hospitals. These executives do not have medical degrees (each of them has an M.B.A.), but they consult with physicians when they plan the hospital's budget.
4. Many hospitals that are similar to HealthCenter Hospital in terms of size and types of patients typically treated use CAT-scan machines that are newer than HealthCenter's, although some use machines similar to HealthCenter's.

What issues would be raised if Plaintiff sought damages from HealthCenter, claiming that it had been negligent in failing to buy and operate a newer CAT-scan machine? In particular, should that decision be evaluated in the context of a professional standard, a standard that was drawn from practices of similar hospitals, or a reasonable person standard?

III. Applying the Professional Standard in Medical Cases

A. Geographic Scope of Professional Standard

In its earliest forms, the professional standard referred to practice by professionals in the same community as the defendant professional. Vergara v. Doan and the statutes that follow it show that jurisdictions currently take a range of positions on the basic question: Should a doctor be required to act as well as other doctors in his or her *locality*, or should a doctor's conduct be measured against a *national standard of care*?

VERGARA v. DOAN

593 N.E.2d 185 (Ind. 1992)

SHEPARD, C.J.

Javier Vergara was born on May 31, 1979, at the Adams Memorial Hospital in Decatur, Indiana. His parents, Jose and Concepcion, claimed that negligence on the part of Dr. John Doan during Javier's delivery caused him severe and permanent injuries. A jury returned a verdict for Dr. Doan and the plaintiffs appealed. The Court of Appeals affirmed. Plaintiffs seek transfer, asking us to abandon Indiana's modified locality rule. We grant transfer to examine the standard of care appropriate for medical malpractice cases.

In most negligence cases, the defendant's conduct is tested against the hypothetical reasonable and prudent person acting under the same or similar circumstances. In medical malpractice cases, however, Indiana has applied a more specific articulation of this standard. It has become known as the modified locality rule: "The standard of care . . . is that degree of care, skill, and proficiency which is commonly exercised by ordinarily careful, skillful, and prudent [physicians], at the time of the operation and in similar localities." Appellants have urged us to abandon this standard, arguing that the reasons for the modified locality rule are no longer applicable in today's society. We agree.

The modified locality rule is a less stringent version of the strict locality rule, which measured the defendant's conduct against that of other doctors in the same community. When the strict locality rule originated in the late 19th century, there was great disparity between the medical opportunities, equipment, facilities, and training in rural and urban communities. Travel and communication between rural and urban communities were difficult. The locality rule was intended to prevent the inequity that would result from holding rural doctors to the same standards as doctors in large cities.

With advances in communication, travel, and medical education, the disparity between rural and urban health care diminished and justification for the locality rule waned. The strict locality rule also had two major drawbacks, especially as applied to smaller communities. First, there was a scarcity of local doctors to serve as expert witnesses against other local doctors. Second, there was the possibility that practices among a small group of doctors would establish a local standard of care below that which the law required. In response to these changes and criticisms, many courts adopted a modified locality rule, expanding the area of comparison to similar localities. This is the standard applied in Indiana.

Use of a modified locality rule has not quelled the criticism. See Brent R. Cohen, *The Locality Rule in Colorado: Updating the Standard of Care*, 51 U. Colo. L. Rev. 537 (1980) (urging a standard based on medical resources available to the doctor under the circumstances in which patient was treated). Many of the common criticisms seem valid. The modified locality rule still permits a lower standard of care to be exercised in smaller communities because other similar communities are likely to have the same care. We also spend time and money on the difficulty of defining what is a similar community. . . . The rule also seems inconsistent with the reality of modern medical practice. The disparity between small town and urban medicine continues to lessen with advances in communication, transportation, and education. In addition, widespread insurance coverage has provided patients with more choice of doctors and hospitals by reducing the financial constraints on the consumer in selecting caregivers. These reasons and others have led our Court of Appeals to observe that the modified locality rule has fallen into disfavor. . . . Many states describe the care a physician owes without emphasizing the locality of practice. Today we join these states and adopt the following: a physician must exercise that degree of care, skill, and proficiency exercised by reasonably careful, skillful, and prudent practitioners in the same class to which he belongs, acting under the same or similar circumstances. Rather than focusing on different standards for different communities, this standard uses locality as but one of the factors to be considered in determining whether the doctor acted reasonably. Other relevant considerations would include advances in the profession, availability of facilities, and whether the doctor is a specialist or general practitioner. . . .

We now turn to whether the instruction given at trial, legally correct at the time, requires a reversal in light of our decision today. . . .

We regard our new formulation of a doctor's duty as a relatively modest alteration of existing law. It is unlikely to have changed the way this case was tried. We are satisfied that an instruction without the locality language would not lead a new jury to a different conclusion.

Therefore, we hold that giving [a modified locality rule instruction] was harmless and does not require reversal. In a different factual situation, however, an erroneous instruction with the locality language present might well constitute reversible error. The standard that we set out today, without the locality language, should be used from today forward.

NOTES TO VERGARA v. DOAN

1. Comparing Standards. The *Vergara* court describes three standards: the strict locality rule, the modified locality rule, and a national standard. How does the court say that they differ?

2. Local Conditions and the National Standard. Courts that apply a national standard of care do not require a physician in a rural area to use diagnostic equipment that is available in urban centers but unavailable in the rural locale. How does the *Vergara* court attempt to integrate the attributes of local circumstances into the national standard it adopts?

3. Availability of Expert Witnesses. The *Vergara* court refers to the availability of witnesses as one reason for adopting the national standard. The national standard allows testimony, for example, by a medical school professor from one state in a trial involving a physician who practiced in another state. That professor would likely be barred from testifying about the standard of care in a state other than his or her own if that state applied the strict locality rule.

4. Cost of the Locality Rule. Among its reasons for abrogating the modified locality rule, the *Vergara* court stated that defining "similar community" had cost time and money in the past. How does that idea relate to the court's other reasons for changing the rule? If high cost were the only drawback to a rule, would that be a reason for eliminating it?

Statute: STANDARD OF ACCEPTABLE PROFESSIONAL PRACTICE

Mich. Comp. Laws §600.2912a(1) (2017)

Action Alleging Malpractice; Burden of Proof, Standard of Acceptable Professional Practice and Standard of Care

Sec. 2912a. (1) Subject to subsection (2), in an action alleging malpractice, the plaintiff has the burden of proving that in light of the state of the art existing at the time of the alleged malpractice:

(a) The defendant, if a general practitioner, failed to provide the plaintiff the recognized standard of acceptable professional practice or care in the community in which the defendant practices or in a similar community, and that as a proximate result of the defendant failing to provide that standard, the plaintiff suffered an injury.

(b) The defendant, if a specialist, failed to provide the recognized standard of practice or care within that specialty as reasonably applied in light of the facilities available in the community or other facilities reasonably available under the circumstances, and as a proximate result of the defendant failing to provide that standard, the plaintiff suffered an injury.

Statute: COMMUNITY STANDARD

Idaho Code §6-1012 (2017)

Proof of Community Standard of Health Care Practice in Malpractice Case

In any case, claim or action for damages due to injury to or death of any person, brought against any physician and surgeon or other provider of health care, including, without limitation, any dentist, physicians' assistant, nurse practitioner, registered nurse, licensed practical nurse, nurse anesthetist, medical technologist, physical therapist, hospital or nursing home, or any person vicariously liable for the negligence of them or any of them, on account of the provision of or failure to provide health care or on account of any matter incidental or related thereto, such claimant or plaintiff must, as an essential part of his or her case in chief, affirmatively prove by direct expert testimony and by a preponderance of all the competent evidence, that such defendant then and there negligently failed to meet the applicable standard of health care practice of the community in which such care allegedly was or should have been provided, as such standard existed at the time and place of the alleged negligence of such physician and surgeon, hospital or other such health care provider and as such standard then and there existed with respect to the class of health care provider that such defendant then and there belonged to and in which capacity he, she or it was functioning. Such individual providers of health care shall be judged in such cases in comparison with similarly trained and qualified providers of the same class in the same community, taking into account his or her training, experience, and fields of medical specialization, if any. If there be no other like provider in the community and the standard of practice is therefore indeterminable, evidence of such standard in similar Idaho communities at said time may be considered. As used in this act, the term "community" refers to that geographical area ordinarily served by the licensed general hospital at or nearest to which such care was or allegedly should have been provided.

NOTE TO STATUTES

Universe of Available Witnesses. The choice between a strict locality rule, a similar locality rule, and a national standard affects the ability of parties to find physicians to provide expert testimony. How do the requirements of the Michigan and Idaho statutes affect the number of expert witnesses who might be available for plaintiffs or defendants?

Perspective: Legislative and Judicial Roles

Why should legislatures set rules for expert testimony in medical malpractice cases when issues of the qualifications of expert witnesses in other types of cases are typically left to the discretion of trial judges (controlled by appellate precedents or evidence rules of general application)? Malpractice cases are easy to identify. They represent a significant component of tort litigation. Health care is an important topic in the minds of voters and legislators. Do any of those aspects of this issue make it desirable for legislatures to act on it?

B. Common Knowledge

In some medical malpractice cases, the alleged substandard care is nontechnical in nature. Cases within the range of *laypeople's knowledge* may go to the jury in the absence of expert testimony about the professional standard. McGraw v. St. Joseph's Hospital applies the general rule: Is the deployment of nursing staff something lay people can understand, or is it so related to the practice of medicine and scientific judgments that the jury must be informed about professional standards for it?

McGRAW v. ST. JOSEPH'S HOSPITAL

488 S.E.2d 389 (W. Va. 1997)

Davis, J.

This is an appeal by Robert S. McGraw, plaintiff below, from a summary judgment order of the Circuit Court of Wood County dismissing his complaint against the defendant below, St. Joseph's Hospital. On appeal the plaintiff argues that the circuit court committed error in granting summary judgment on the grounds that medical expert testimony was required to show the defendant violated the standard of care in its treatment of him. . . .

The facts of this case are straightforward, though some critical points remain in dispute. On May 10, 1991 the plaintiff walked into the defendant's emergency room complaining of shortness of breath. After several hours of waiting to be seen by medical personnel, the plaintiff was admitted into the hospital. On the morning of May 11, four female hospital personnel attempted to assist the plaintiff back into bed. The plaintiff testified during his deposition that he informed the four women that he did not believe they could put him in bed because he weighed too much.[3] The plaintiff's memory of what happened immediately after making that statement is minimal. He testified that all he could remember is that he "had a sensation of falling." During the early morning hours of May 12 the plaintiff was discovered on the floor near his bed. The plaintiff indicated in his deposition that he fell out of bed. The plaintiff further testified that on the afternoon of May 21, four female nurses and nurse's aides dropped him while attempting to place him in bed. He stated that "they had to get men to put me — get me up and put me in bed after they had dropped me[.]" The plaintiff was eventually discharged from the hospital on June 28, 1991.

[T]he plaintiff filed the instant action against the defendant. The complaint charged the defendant with dropping or permitting him to fall on two occasions. It was also alleged that he sustained "a fractured neck and other injuries in, about and upon his arms, knees and other parts of his body" as a result of both incidents. After discovery in the case, the defendant moved for summary judgment "premised upon the failure of McGraw to produce expert testimony demonstrating that the hospital deviated from the standard of care and that any deviation caused injury or damage to McGraw."

[T]he circuit court granted the defendant's motion for summary judgment on the grounds that "West Virginia law requires that a violation of the standard of care by a health care provider be proven by expert testimony," but that the plaintiff "is unable to produce expert testimony as to any violation of the standard of care by the Hospital[.]" This appeal followed. We reverse. . . .

We pointed out in Neary v. Charleston Area Medical Center, Inc., 194 W. Va. 329, 334, 460 S.E.2d 464, 469 (1995) that "[w]hen the principles of summary judgment are applied in a medical malpractice case, one of the threshold questions is the existence of expert witnesses opining the alleged negligence." Defendant takes the position that medical expert testimony was mandatory in this case pursuant to W. Va. Code §55-7B-7 (1986), which provides in relevant part:

---

[3] The record is not clear as to the exact weight of the plaintiff. It appears that he weighed somewhere between 280 to 306 pounds.

The applicable standard of care and a defendant's failure to meet said standard, if at issue, shall be established in medical professional liability cases by the plaintiff by testimony of one or more knowledgeable, competent expert witnesses if required by the court.

In granting the defendant summary judgment in this case, the circuit court did not cite the above statute. The circuit court held that our law required "a violation of the standard of care by a health care provider be proven by expert testimony[.]" We address the meaning of the above quoted passage from W. Va. Code §55-7B-7.

Our traditional rule of statutory construction is set out in syllabus point 2 of Keen v. Maxey, 193 W. Va. 423, 456 S.E.2d 550 (1995) as follows:

When a statute is clear and unambiguous and the legislative intent is plain the statute should not be interpreted by the courts, and in such a case it is the duty of the courts not to construe but to apply the statute. Point 1, syllabus, State ex rel. Fox v. Board of Trustees of the Policemen's Pension or Relief Fund of the City of Bluefield, et al., 148 W. Va. 369 [135 S.E.2d 262 (1964)]. . . .

We hold that W. Va. Code §55-7B-7 provides that circuit courts have discretion to require expert testimony in medical professional liability cases. . . .

We note some general principles that our prior cases have developed in this area. In syllabus point 1 of *Farley* [v. Meadows, 185 W. Va. 48, 404 S.E.2d 537 (1991),] we stated that " '[i]t is the general rule that in medical malpractice cases negligence or want of professional skill can be proved only by expert witnesses.' Syl. pt. 2, Roberts v. Gale, 149 W. Va. 166, 139 S.E.2d 272 (1964)."

In Totten v. Adongay, 175 W. Va. 634, 638, 337 S.E.2d 2, 6 (1985), the Court stated that "cases may arise where there is such want of skill as to dispense with expert testimony." Quoting, in part, Syl., Buskirk v. Bucklew, 115 W. Va. 424, 176 S.E. 603 (1934); Syl. pt. 2, Howell v. Biggart, 108 W. Va. 560, 152 S.E. 323 (1930). We held in syllabus point 4 of *Totten* that:

In medical malpractice cases where lack of care or want of skill is so gross, so as to be apparent, or the alleged breach relates to noncomplex matters of diagnosis and treatment within the understanding of lay jurors by resort to common knowledge and experience, failure to present expert testimony on the accepted standard of care and degree of skill under such circumstances is not fatal to a plaintiff's prima facie showing of negligence.

Totten recognizes what is known as the "common knowledge" exception to expert testimony.

Was expert testimony necessary in this case? The defendant takes the position that the common knowledge exception is not applicable here, because "liability is premised upon complex medical management issues involving professional management." We have reviewed cases addressing hospital fall incidents and found that a majority of jurisdictions do not require expert testimony in such cases. . . .

In Cramer v. Theda Clerk Memorial Hospital, 45 Wis. 2d 147, 172 N.W.2d 427, 428 (1969) the Wisconsin Supreme Court articulated the rationale used by jurisdictions that generally do not require expert testimony in hospital fall cases:

Courts generally make a distinction between medical care and custodial care or routine hospital care. The general rule is that a hospital must in the care of its patients exercise such ordinary care and attention for their safety as their mental and physical condition, known or should have been known, may require. . . . If the patient requires professional nursing or professional hospital care, then expert testimony as to the standard of that type of care is necessary. . . . But it does not follow that the standard of all care and attention rendered by nurses or by a hospital to its patients necessarily require proof by expert testimony. The standard of nonmedical, administrative, ministerial or routine care in a hospital need not be established by expert testimony because the jury is competent from its own experience to determine and apply such a reasonable-care standard.

(Citations omitted).

We find the reasoning of *Cramer* persuasive and consistent with the direction of our law in this area. . . . Although the defendant has contended on appeal that complex management issues are involved in this case, the defendant has not articulated such issues. Because the circuit court erroneously assumed that our law makes it mandatory that expert testimony be proffered in all medical professional liability cases, the court did not make a finding on whether complex management issues existed in this case which would necessitate expert testimony. On remand the circuit court is directed to determine, before the trial of this case, whether complex management issues are involved in the May 21 incident only. As we explain below, the May 12 incident where Mr. McGraw fell out of his hospital bed is ripe for trial on the merits. . . .

[With regard to the May 12 incident, the circuit court concluded that the plaintiff had failed to provide expert testimony. That conclusion was wrong because a deposition by an expert witness for the plaintiff did describe a standard of care for that incident and did state that the defendant violated that standard.] This case is reversed and remanded for a determination by the trial court consistent with this opinion.

NOTE TO McGRAW v. ST. JOSEPH'S HOSPITAL

Common Knowledge.   The trial court was influenced by the erroneous idea that all medical cases require expert testimony. How does the West Virginia Supreme Court instruct the trial court to determine if this plaintiff's claim is the type of medical claim for which expert testimony is needed?

Problem
Common Knowledge and Patient Care

Employees of a nursing home were aware that one of its residents was unable to feed herself properly and that she had suffered serious choking incidents when she tried to do so. The resident choked to death on food after a nurse brought her a tray of food and neglected to assist her in eating it. In a malpractice claim, would the plaintiff be required to introduce expert testimony about nursing home staffing practices or proper care for individuals who are subject to choking? See Beverly Enterprises-Virginia v. Nichols, 441 S.E.2d 1 (Va. 1994).

Problem
Common Knowledge and Hospital Negligence

A patient's hip replacement surgery had to be stopped after the surgeon had made the incision because the artificial hip ordered by the surgeon had not been received prior to the start of the operation. The plaintiff sued for the harms associated with having to begin the surgery again the next day, contending that hospital personnel had been negligent in failing to be sure that the proper item had been delivered. As you prepare this case for trial representing the patient, you must consider whether expert testimony on hospital procedures would be required. Because the ultimate hip surgery was successful, the damages might be relatively small. Expert witnesses are expensive. Would it be safe to avoid hiring the expert if the consequence of failing to do so could be a summary judgment for the defendant? See Dalton v. Kalispell Regional Hospital, 846 P.2d 960 (Mont. 1993).

Statute: PRESUMPTION OF NEGLIGENCE
Nev. Rev. Stat. §41A.100 (2017)

Expert Testimony Required; Exceptions; Rebuttable Presumption of Negligence

1. Liability for personal injury or death is not imposed upon any provider of medical care based on alleged negligence in the performance of that care unless evidence consisting of expert medical testimony, material from recognized medical texts or treatises or the regulations of the licensed medical facility wherein the alleged negligence occurred is presented to demonstrate the alleged deviation from the accepted standard of care in the specific circumstances of the case and to prove causation of the alleged personal injury or death, except that such evidence is not required and a rebuttable presumption that the personal injury or death was caused by negligence arises where evidence is presented that the personal injury or death occurred in any one or more of the following circumstances:

(a) A foreign substance other than medication or a prosthetic device was unintentionally left within the body of a patient following surgery;

(b) An explosion or fire originating in a substance used in treatment occurred in the course of treatment;

(c) An unintended burn caused by heat, radiation or chemicals was suffered in the course of medical care;

(d) An injury was suffered during the course of treatment to a part of the body not directly involved in the treatment or proximate thereto; or

(e) A surgical procedure was performed on the wrong patient or the wrong organ, limb or part of a patient's body.

2. Expert medical testimony provided pursuant to subsection 1 may only be given by a provider of medical care who practices or has practiced in an area that is substantially similar to the type of practice engaged in at the time of the alleged negligence.

3. As used in this section, "provider of medical care" means a physician, dentist, registered nurse or a licensed hospital as the employer of any such person.

NOTES TO STATUTE

1. *Effect of Detailed Provisions.* This Nevada statute adopts the similar locality standard and provides a list of detailed provisions governing the need for expert

medical testimony. What is the consequence of those provisions for a case involving something not specified, such as the dropping of a patient in *McGraw*?

2. *Hypothetical: Application of Statute.* A patient recovering from hand surgery suffered an electric shock and consequential burn from a defective push button on a device provided by the hospital to call for nursing assistance. Would the statute require expert medical testimony in a suit against a hospital based on this claim?

Perspective: Malpractice Litigation and the Quality of Medical Care

Some question whether malpractice litigation can improve the quality of medical care. Some people believe that the interest in helping people is a much stronger incentive for most doctors than the interest in avoiding financial liability. It is also likely that most medical mistakes never become the subject of litigation, and that when litigation does occur, the specific financial impact on a defendant doctor is likely to be small, because of insurance. These factors may weaken the ability of the tort system as a force for improving quality. A related question is whether the possibility of litigation impairs quality improvement efforts. Do doctors avoid discussing errors with their peers because of fear of litigation? For a review of these issues, and a proposal for nonlitigation treatment of medical injuries, see P. Weiler, *Medical Malpractice on Trial* (1991).

C. Informed Consent

All courts agree that doctors must obtain *informed consent* from their patients before performing procedures on them. They disagree about the standard for judging whether a doctor has provided enough information to a patient to satisfy the informed consent process. Largey v. Rothman compares two rules on whether doctors should disclose the risks that doctors consider important or the risks that patients consider important.

LARGEY v. ROTHMAN
110 N.J. 204, 540 A.2d 504 (1988)

PER CURIAM.

This medical malpractice case raises an issue of a patient's informed consent to treatment. The jury found that plaintiff Janice Largey had consented to an operative procedure performed by the defendant physician. The single question presented goes to the correctness of the standard by which the jury was instructed to determine whether the defendant, Dr. Rothman, had adequately informed his patient of the risks of that operation.

The trial court told the jury that when informing the plaintiff Janice Largey of the risks of undergoing a certain biopsy procedure, . . . defendant was required to tell her "what reasonable medical practitioners in the same or similar circumstances would have told their patients undertaking the same type of operation." [The defendant surgeon performed a breast biopsy on the plaintiff. There was a sharp dispute at trial over whether he stated that the biopsy would include the lymph nodes as well as the breast tissue. About six weeks after the operation, plaintiff developed a right arm and hand lymphedema, a swelling caused by inadequate drainage in the lymphatic system. The condition resulted from the excision of the lymph nodes. Defendant did not advise plaintiff of this risk. Plaintiff's experts testified that defendant should have informed plaintiff that lymphedema was a risk of the operation. Defendant's experts testified that it was too rare to be discussed with a patient.] By answer to a specific interrogatory on this point, the jurors responded that defendant had not "fail[ed] to provide Janice Largey with sufficient information so that she could give informed consent" for the operative procedure. On plaintiffs' appeal the Appellate Division affirmed in an unreported opinion, noting that the trial court's charge on informed consent followed the holding in Kaplan v. Haines, 96 N.J. Super. 242, 257, 232 A.2d 840 (App. Div. 1967), which this Court affirmed. . . .

Plaintiffs argued below, and repeat the contention here, that the proper standard is one that focuses not on what information a reasonable doctor should impart to the patient (the "professional" standard) but rather on what the physician should disclose to a reasonable patient in order that the patient might make an informed decision (the "prudent patient" or "materiality of risk" standard). The latter is the standard announced in Canterbury v. Spence, 464 F.2d 772 (D.C. Cir.), *cert. den.*, 409 U.S. 1064, 93 S. Ct. 560, 34 L. Ed. 2d 518 (1972). . . .

An early statement of the "informed consent" rule is found in Salgo v. Leland Stanford, Jr. Univ. Bd. of Trustees, 154 Cal. App. 2d 560, 317 P.2d 170 (Dist. Ct. App. 1957), in which the court declared that "[a] physician violates his duty to his patient and subjects himself to liability if he withholds any facts which are necessary to form the basis of an intelligent consent by the patient to the proposed treatment." . . .

Further development of the doctrine came shortly thereafter, in Natanson v. Kline, 186 Kan. 393, 350 P.2d 1093, modified on other grounds, 187 Kan. 186, 354 P.2d 670 (1960), which represented one of the leading cases on informed consent at that time. . . . The *Natanson* court established the standard of care to be exercised by a physician in an informed consent case as "limited to those disclosures which a reasonable medical practitioner would make under the same or similar circumstances." At bottom the decision turned on the principle of a patient's right of self-determination:

> Anglo-American law starts with the premise of thorough self-determination. It follows that each man is considered to be master of his own body, and he may, if he be of sound mind, expressly prohibit the performance of life-saving surgery, or other medical treatment. . . .

After *Salgo* and *Natanson* the doctrine of informed consent came to be adopted and developed in other jurisdictions, which, until 1972, followed the "traditional" or "professional" standard formulation of the rule. Under that standard, as applied by the majority of the jurisdictions that adopted it, a physician is required to make such disclosure as comports with the prevailing medical standard in the community — that is, the disclosure of those risks that a reasonable physician in the community, of like training, would customarily make in similar circumstances. 2 D. Louisell and H. Williams, Medical Malpractice §22.08 at 22-23 (1987) (hereinafter Louisell and Williams). . . .

[T]he "professional" standard rests on the belief that a physician, and only a physician, can effectively estimate both the psychological and physical consequences that a risk inherent in a medical procedure might produce in a patient. The burden imposed on the physician under this standard is to "consider the state of the patient's health, and whether the risks involved are mere remote possibilities or real hazards which occur with appreciable regularity. . . ." Louisell and Williams, supra, §22.08 at 22-34. A second basic justification offered in support of the "professional" standard is that "a general standard of care, as required under the prudent patient rule, would require a physician to waste unnecessary time in reviewing with the patient every possible risk, thereby interfering with the flexibility a physician needs in deciding what form of treatment is best for the patient." Ibid. (footnotes omitted). . . .

In 1972 a new standard of disclosure for "informed consent" was established in Canterbury v. Spence, supra, 464 F.2d 772. The case raised a question of the defendant physician's duty to warn the patient beforehand of the risk involved in a laminectomy, a surgical procedure the purpose of which was to relieve pain in plaintiff's lower back, and particularly the risk attendant on a myelogram, the diagnostic procedure preceding the surgery. . . .

The *Canterbury* court announced a duty on the part of a physician to "warn of the dangers lurking in the proposed treatment" and to "impart information [that] the patient has every right to expect," as well as a duty of "reasonable disclosure of the choices with respect to proposed therapy and the dangers inherently and potentially involved." Id. at 782. The court held that the scope of the duty to disclose

> must be measured by the patient's need, and that need is the information material to the decision. Thus the test for determining whether a particular peril must be divulged is its materiality to the patient's decision: all risks potentially affecting the decision must be unmasked. And to safeguard the patient's interest in achieving his own determination on treatment, the law must itself set the standard for adequate disclosure. [Id. at 786-787 (footnotes omitted).]

The breadth of the disclosure of the risks legally to be required is measured, under *Canterbury*, by a standard whose scope is "not subjective as to either the physician or the patient," id. at 787; rather, "it remains *objective* with due regard for the patient's informational needs and with suitable leeway for the physician's situation." Ibid. (emphasis added). A risk would be deemed "material" when a reasonable patient, in what the physician knows or should know to be the patient's position, would be "likely to attach significance to the risk or cluster of risks" in deciding whether to forgo the proposed therapy or to submit to it.

The foregoing standard for adequate disclosure, known as the "prudent patient" or "materiality of risk" standard, has been adopted in a number of jurisdictions. . . .

The jurisdictions that have rejected the "professional" standard in favor of the "prudent patient" rule have given a number of reasons in support of their preference. Those include:

(1) The existence of a discernible custom reflecting a medical consensus is open to serious doubt. . . .

(2) Since a physician in obtaining a patient's informed consent to proposed treatment is often obligated to consider non-medical factors, such as a patient's

emotional condition, professional custom should not furnish the legal criterion for measuring the physician's obligation to disclose. . . .

(3) Closely related to both (1) and (2) is the notion that a professional standard is totally subject to the whim of the physicians in the particular community. Under this view a physician is vested with virtually unlimited discretion in establishing the proper scope of disclosure; this is inconsistent with the patient's right of self-determination. . . .

(4) The requirement that the patient present expert testimony to establish the professional standard has created problems for patients trying to find physicians willing to breach the "community of silence" by testifying against fellow colleagues. [Louisell and Williams, supra, §22.12 at 22-45 to 22-47 (footnotes omitted).]

Taken together, the reasons supporting adoption of the "prudent patient" standard persuade us that the time has come for us to abandon so much of the decision by which this Court embraced the doctrine of informed consent as accepts the "professional" standard. To that extent Kaplan v. Haines, 51 N.J. 404, 241 A.2d 235, *aff'g* 96 N.J. Super. 242, 232 A.2d 840, is overruled. . . .

Perhaps the strongest consideration that influences our decision in favor of the "prudent patient" standard lies in the notion that the physician's duty of disclosure "arises from phenomena apart from medical custom and practice": the patient's right of self-determination. *Canterbury*, supra, 464 F.2d at 786-87. The foundation for the physician's duty to disclose in the first place is found in the idea that "it is the prerogative of the patient, not the physician, to determine for himself the direction in which his interests seem to lie." Id. at 781. In contrast the arguments for the "professional" standard smack of an anachronistic paternalism that is at odds with any strong conception of a patient's right of self-determination. Id. at 781, 784, 789. . . .

. . . We therefore align ourselves with those jurisdictions that have adopted *Canterbury*'s "prudent patient" standard.

Finally, we address the issue of proximate cause. As with other medical malpractice actions, informed-consent cases require that plaintiff prove not only that the physician failed to comply with the applicable standard for disclosure but also that such failure was the proximate cause of plaintiff's injuries. . . .

Under the "prudent patient" standard "causation must also be shown: i.e., that the prudent person in the patient's position would have decided differently if adequately informed." . . . As *Canterbury* observes,

> [t]he patient obviously has no complaint if he would have submitted to the therapy notwithstanding awareness that the risk was one of its perils. On the other hand, the very purpose of the disclosure rule is to protect the patient against consequences which, if known, he would have avoided by foregoing the treatment. The more difficult question is whether the factual issue on causality calls for an objective or a subjective determination.

Canterbury decided its own question in favor of an objective determination. The subjective approach, which the court rejected, inquires whether, if the patient had been informed of the risks that in fact materialized, he or she would have consented to the treatment. The shortcoming of this approach, according to *Canterbury*, is that it places the physician in jeopardy of the patient's hindsight and bitterness. It places the factfinder in the position of deciding whether a speculative answer to a hypothetical question is to be credited. It calls for a subjective determination solely on testimony of a patient-witness shadowed by the occurrence of the undisclosed risk.

The court therefore elected to adopt an objective test, as do we. Because we would not presume to attempt an improvement in its articulation of the reasons, we quote once again the *Canterbury* court:

> Better it is, we believe, to resolve the causality issue on an objective basis: in terms of what a prudent person in the patient's position would have decided if suitably informed of all perils bearing significance. . . . The patient's testimony is relevant on that score of course but it would not threaten to dominate the findings. And since that testimony would probably be appraised congruently with the factfinder's belief in its reasonableness, the case for a wholly objective standard for passing on causation is strengthened. Such a standard would in any event ease the fact-finding process and better assure the truth as its product. . . .

The judgment of the Appellate Division is reversed. The cause is remanded for a new trial consistent with this opinion.

NOTES TO LARGEY v. ROTHMAN

1. *Basic Analysis.* In all jurisdictions, to recover damages on an informed consent theory, the plaintiff must show that the defendant provided less information than the jurisdiction's standards required the defendant to provide, that there was a causal link between that lack of information and the patient's consent to treatment, and that the patient suffered an injury. *Largey* describes the range of positions jurisdictions have taken about defining what information should be given and about what proof of causation a plaintiff must provide.

2. *Reasonable Physician or Reasonable Patient.* What are the differences between the reasonable physician and reasonable patient standards for defining the information a physician must provide to a patient prior to treatment?

3. *Application of the Reasonable Patient Test.* The *Largey* court adopts the reasonable patient test, stating that it is supported by a number of factors, including doubt about whether customs really exist with regard to disclosures, the consideration of nonmedical factors in providing information, and the need for the law to support a patient's right of self-determination. How would those factors apply if a defendant physician in an informed consent case did not tell a patient about a particular risk because the physician did not realize it could occur in the proposed procedure? In that type of case, what standard of care should the jury use in evaluating whether that lack of knowledge was negligent?

4. *Causation.* The *Largey* court points out that to recover damages, a plaintiff must do more than show the defendant's failure to make a required communication: The plaintiff must also show that he or she would have declined to undergo the procedure if the defendant had provided fuller information about its risks. How will using an objective standard for this part of the case "ease the fact-finding process"?

Statute: PLAINTIFF'S BURDEN OF PROOF FOR
INFORMED CONSENT CLAIMS

N.H. Rev. Stat. §507-E:2 (2017)

I. In any action for medical injury, the plaintiff shall have the burden of proving by affirmative evidence which must include expert testimony of a competent witness or witnesses:

(a) The standard of reasonable professional practice in the medical care provider's profession or specialty thereof, if any, at the time the medical care in question was rendered; and

(b) That the medical care provider failed to act in accordance with such standard; and

(c) That as a proximate result thereof, the injured person suffered injuries which would not otherwise have occurred.

II. Without limiting the applicability of paragraph I of this section, where the plaintiff claims that a medical care provider failed to supply adequate information to obtain the informed consent of the injured person:

(a) The plaintiff shall have the burden of proving by affirmative evidence, which must include expert testimony of a competent witness or witnesses, that the treatment, procedure or surgery was performed in other than an emergency situation and that the medical care provider did not supply that type of information regarding the treatment, procedure or surgery as should reasonably have been given to a patient in the position of the injured person or other persons authorized to give consent for such a patient by other competent medical care providers with similar training and experience at the time of the treatment, procedure or surgery.

(b) In determining whether the plaintiff has satisfied the requirements of subparagraph (a) of this paragraph, the following matters shall also be considered as material issues:

(1) Whether the injured person or person giving consent on his behalf could reasonably be expected to know of the risks or hazards inherent in such treatment, procedure, or surgery;

(2) Whether the injured person or the person giving consent on his behalf knew of the risks or hazards inherent in such treatment, procedure, or surgery;

(3) Whether the injured party would have undergone the treatment, procedure, or surgery regardless of the risk involved or whether he declined to be informed thereof;

(4) Whether it was reasonable for the medical care provider to limit disclosure of information because such disclosure could be expected to adversely and substantially affect the injured person's condition.

NOTE TO STATUTE

Description of Standard.   Does this statute apply a professional standard of care to informed consent cases?

Problem
Informed Consent and Silence for Patient's Own Good

Assume that a doctor believed that a particular medical procedure would benefit a patient and also believed that the patient would have rejected the procedure if the patient had known its risks. If the doctor performed the procedure without giving the patient information about the risks, should the doctor be treated as having failed to obtain informed consent under this statute?

Perspective: Informed Consent

Informed consent based on a reasonable patient rule requires a delicate balancing act between the patient's interest in autonomy and the physician's interest in expeditious treatment.

> [T]he law has forgotten about a physician's duty to get to know his or her patients as a prerequisite to adequate informed consent. Courts take for granted that this duty is met in the course of a medical history and exam. But in order to meet the goal of autonomous medical decision-making, informed consent law must extend the physician's duty to require that he or she makes a reasonable inquiry into the treatment goals of each patient. Only then can physicians adequately sort material from immaterial treatment information and present material information to patients in ways that truly enable patients to make choices that reflect their preferences.
>
> At the same time, the law must not interpret the duty of physician inquiry too broadly. As important as the principle of patient autonomy may be, it must be balanced against other competing interests, such as maintaining an efficient health care delivery system that does not unnecessarily spend valuable clinical time on learning a patient's every idiosyncrasy. In other words, while current law enforces a standard of inquiry that is too depersonalized, the law can also overcompensate by enforcing a standard that is so personalized as to be inefficient.

Robert Gatter, *Informed Consent Law and the Forgotten Duty of Physician Inquiry*, 31 Loy. U. Chi. L.J. 557, 559 (2000).

D. Identifying the Defendant

Identifying the proper defendant can be problematic for a plaintiff injured in the course of treatment by numerous medical professionals, especially if some of the professionals treat the plaintiff simultaneously. One pro-plaintiff approach to solving that problem was devised in the famous case Ybarra v. Spangard. The case also tests the boundaries of the *res ipsa loquitur* doctrine.

YBARRA v. SPANGARD

25 Cal. 2d 486, 154 P.2d 687 (1945)

GIBSON, C.J.

This is an action for damages for personal injuries alleged to have been inflicted on plaintiff by defendants during the course of a surgical operation. The trial court entered judgments of nonsuit as to all defendants and plaintiff appealed.

On October 28, 1939, plaintiff consulted defendant Dr. Tilley, who diagnosed his ailment as appendicitis, and made arrangements for an appendectomy to be performed by defendant Dr. Spangard at a hospital owned and managed by defendant Dr. Swift. Plaintiff entered the hospital, was given a hypodermic injection, slept, and later was awakened by Drs. Tilley and Spangard and wheeled into the operating room by a nurse whom he believed to be defendant Gisler, an employee of Dr. Swift. Defendant Dr. Reser, the anesthetist, also an employee of Dr. Swift, adjusted plaintiff for the operation, pulling his body to the head of the operating table and, according to plaintiff's testimony, laying him back against two hard objects at the top of his shoulders, about an inch below his neck. Dr. Reser then administered the anesthetic and plaintiff lost consciousness. When he awoke early the following morning he was in his hospital room attended by defendant Thompson, the special nurse, and another nurse who was not made a defendant.

Plaintiff testified that prior to the operation he had never had any pain in, or injury to, his right arm or shoulder, but that when he awakened he felt a sharp pain about half way between the neck and the point of the right shoulder. He complained to the nurse, and then to Dr. Tilley, who gave him diathermy treatments while he remained in the hospital. The pain did not cease but spread down to the lower part of his arm, and after his release from the hospital the condition grew worse. He was unable to rotate or lift his arm, and developed paralysis and atrophy of the muscles around the shoulder. He received further treatments from Dr. Tilley until March, 1940, and then returned to work, wearing his arm in a splint on the advice of Dr. Spangard.

Plaintiff also consulted Dr. Wilfred Sterling Clark, who had X-ray pictures taken which showed an area of diminished sensation below the shoulder and atrophy and wasting away of the muscles around the shoulder. In the opinion of Dr. Clark, plaintiff's condition was due to trauma or injury by pressure or strain applied between his right shoulder and neck.

Plaintiff was also examined by Dr. Fernando Garduno, who expressed the opinion that plaintiff's injury was a paralysis of traumatic origin, not arising from pathological causes, and not systemic. . . .

Plaintiff's theory is that the foregoing evidence presents a proper case for the application of the doctrine of *res ipsa loquitur,* and that the inference of negligence arising therefrom makes the granting of a nonsuit improper. Defendants take the position that, assuming that plaintiff's condition was in fact the result of an injury, there is no showing that the act of any particular defendant, nor any particular instrumentality, was the cause thereof. They attack plaintiff's action as an attempt to fix liability "en masse" on various defendants, some of whom were not responsible for the acts of others; and they further point to the failure to show which defendants had control of the instrumentalities that may have been involved. Their main defense may be briefly stated in two propositions: (1) that where there are several defendants, and there is a division of responsibility in the use of an instrumentality causing the injury, and the injury might have resulted from the separate act of either one of two or more persons, the rule of *res ipsa loquitur* cannot be invoked against any one of them; and (2) that where there are several instrumentalities, and no showing is made as to which caused the injury or as to the particular defendant in control of it, the doctrine cannot apply. We are satisfied, however, that these objections are not well taken in the circumstances of this case.

The doctrine of *res ipsa loquitur* has three conditions: "(1) the accident must be of a kind which ordinarily does not occur in the absence of someone's negligence; (2) it must be caused by an agency or instrumentality within the exclusive control of the defendant; (3) it must not have been due to any voluntary action or contribution on the part of the plaintiff." Prosser, Torts, p.295. It is applied in a wide variety of situations, including cases of medical or dental treatment and hospital care. . . .

There is, however, some uncertainty as to the extent to which *res ipsa loquitur* may be invoked in cases of injury from medical treatment. This is in part due to the tendency, in some decisions, to lay undue emphasis on the limitations of the doctrine, and to give too little attention to its basic underlying purpose. The result has been that a simple, understandable rule of circumstantial evidence, with a sound background of common sense and human experience, has occasionally been transformed into a rigid legal formula, which arbitrarily precludes its application in many cases where it is most important that it should be applied. If the doctrine is to continue to serve a useful purpose, we should not forget that "the particular force and justice of the rule, regarded as a presumption throwing upon the party charged the duty of producing evidence, consists in the circumstance that the chief evidence of the true cause, whether culpable or innocent, is practically accessible to him but inaccessible to the injured person." 9 Wigmore, Evidence, 3d ed., §2509, p.382 . . . Maki v. Murray Hospital, 91 Mont. 251, 7 P.2d 228, 231. In the last-named case, where an unconscious patient in a hospital received injuries from a fall, the court declared that without the doctrine the maxim that for every wrong there is a remedy would be rendered nugatory, "by denying one, patently entitled to damages, satisfaction merely because he is ignorant of facts peculiarly within the knowledge of the party who should, in all justice, pay them."

The present case is of a type which comes within the reason and spirit of the doctrine more fully perhaps than any other. The passenger sitting awake in a railroad car at the time of a collision, the pedestrian walking along the street and struck by a falling object or the debris of an explosion, are surely not more entitled to an explanation than the unconscious patient on the operating table. Viewed from this aspect, it is difficult to see how the doctrine can, with any justification, be so restricted in its statement as to become inapplicable to a patient who submits himself to the care and custody of doctors and nurses, is rendered unconscious, and receives some injury from instrumentalities used in his treatment. Without the aid of the doctrine a patient who received permanent injuries of a serious character, obviously the result of some one's negligence, would be entirely unable to recover unless the doctors and nurses in attendance voluntarily chose to disclose the identity of the negligent person and the facts establishing liability. . . . If this were the state of the law of negligence, the courts, to avoid gross injustice, would be forced to invoke the principles of absolute liability, irrespective of negligence, in actions by persons suffering injuries during the course of treatment under anesthesia. But we think this juncture has not yet been reached, and that the doctrine of *res ipsa loquitur* is properly applicable to the case before us.

The condition that the injury must not have been due to the plaintiff's voluntary action is of course fully satisfied under the evidence produced herein; and the same is true of the condition that the accident must be one which ordinarily does not occur unless some one was negligent. We have here no problem of negligence in treatment, but of distinct injury to a healthy part of the body not the subject of treatment, nor within the area covered by the operation. The decisions in this state make it clear that such circumstances raise the inference of negligence and call upon the defendant to explain the unusual result. . . .

The argument of defendants is simply that plaintiff has not shown an injury caused by an instrumentality under a defendant's control, because he has not shown which of the several instrumentalities that he came in contact with while in the hospital caused the injury; and he has not shown that any one defendant or his servants had exclusive control over any particular instrumentality. Defendants assert that some of them were not the employees of other defendants, that some did not stand in any permanent relationship from which liability in tort would follow, and that in view of the nature of the injury, the number of defendants and the different functions performed by each, they could not all be liable for the wrong, if any.

We have no doubt that in a modern hospital a patient is quite likely to come under the care of a number of persons in different types of contractual and other relationships with each other. For example, in the present case it appears that Drs. Smith, Spangard and Tilley were physicians or surgeons commonly placed in the legal category of independent contractors; and Dr. Reser, the anesthetist, and defendant Thompson, the special nurse, were employees of Dr. Swift and not of the other doctors. But we do not believe that either the number or relationship of the defendants alone determines whether the doctrine of *res ipsa loquitur* applies. Every defendant in whose custody the plaintiff was placed for any period was bound to exercise ordinary care to see that no unnecessary harm came to him and each would be liable for failure in this regard. Any defendant who negligently injured him, and any defendant charged with his care who so neglected him as to allow injury to occur, would be liable. The defendant employers would be liable for the neglect of their employees; and the doctor in charge of the operation would be liable for the negligence of those who became his temporary servants for the purpose of assisting in the operation.

In this connection, it should be noted that while the assisting physicians and nurses may be employed by the hospital, or engaged by the patient, they normally become the temporary servants or agents of the surgeon in charge while the operation is in progress, and liability may be imposed upon him for their negligent acts under the doctrine of *respondeat superior*. Thus a surgeon has been held liable for the negligence of an assisting nurse who leaves a sponge or other object inside a patient, and the fact that the duty of seeing that such mistakes do not occur is delegated to others does not absolve the doctor from responsibility for their negligence. . . .

It may appear at the trial that, consistent with the principles outlined above, one or more defendants will be found liable and others absolved, but this should not preclude the application of the rule of *res ipsa loquitur*. The control at one time or another, of one or more of the various agencies or instrumentalities which might have harmed the plaintiff was in the hands of every defendant or of his employees or temporary servants. This, we think, places upon them the burden of initial explanation. Plaintiff was rendered unconscious for the purpose of undergoing surgical treatment by the defendants; it is manifestly unreasonable for them to insist that he identify any one of them as the person who did the alleged negligent act.

The other aspect of the case which defendants so strongly emphasize is that plaintiff has not identified the instrumentality any more than he has the particular guilty defendant. Here, again, there is a misconception which, if carried to the extreme for which defendants contend, would unreasonably limit the application of the *res ipsa loquitur* rule. It should be enough that the plaintiff can show an injury resulting from an external force applied while he lay unconscious in the hospital; this is as clear a case of identification of the instrumentality as the plaintiff may ever be able to make.

An examination of the recent cases, particularly in this state, discloses that the test of actual exclusive control of an instrumentality has not been strictly followed, but exceptions have been recognized where the purpose of the doctrine of *res ipsa loquitur* would otherwise be defeated. Thus, the test has become one of right of control rather than actual control. . . . In the bursting bottle cases where the bottler has delivered the instrumentality to a retailer and thus has given up actual control, he will nevertheless be subject to the doctrine where it is shown that no change in the condition of the bottle occurred after it left the bottler's possession, and it can accordingly be said that he was in constructive control. . . . Moreover, this court departed from the single instrumentality theory in the colliding vehicle cases, where two defendants were involved, each in control of a separate vehicle. . . . Finally, it has been suggested that the hospital cases may properly be considered exceptional, and that the doctrine of *res ipsa loquitur* "should apply with equal force in cases wherein medical and nursing staffs take the place of machinery and may, through carelessness or lack of skill, inflict, or permit the infliction of injury upon a patient who is thereafter in no position to say how he received his injuries." Maki v. Murray Hospital, 91 Mont. 251, 7 P.2d 228, 231; see, also, Whetstine v. Moravec, 228 Iowa 352, 291 N.W. 425, 435, where the court refers to the "instrumentalities" as including "the unconscious body of the plaintiff."

In the face of these examples of liberalization of the tests for *res ipsa loquitur,* there can be no justification for the rejection of the doctrine in the instant case. As pointed out above, if we accept the contention of defendants herein, there will rarely be any compensation for patients injured while unconscious. A hospital today conducts a highly integrated system of activities, with many persons contributing their efforts. There may be, e.g., preparation for surgery by nurses and interns who are employees of the hospital; administering of an anesthetic by a doctor who may be an employee of the hospital, an employee of the operating surgeon, or an independent contractor; performance of an operation by a surgeon and assistants who may be his employees, employees of the hospital, or independent contractors; and post surgical care by the surgeon, a hospital physician, and nurses. The number of those in whose care the patient is placed is not a good reason for denying him all reasonable opportunity to recover for negligent harm. It is rather a good reason for re-examination of the statement of legal theories which supposedly compel such a shocking result.

We do not at this time undertake to state the extent to which the reasoning of this case may be applied to other situations in which the doctrine of *res ipsa loquitur* is invoked. We merely hold that where a plaintiff receives unusual injuries while unconscious and in the course of medical treatment, all those defendants who had any control over his body or the instrumentalities which might have caused the injuries may properly be called upon to meet the inference of negligence by giving an explanation of their conduct.

The judgment is reversed.

NOTE TO YBARRA v. SPANGARD

Factual Setting. The court refers to three elements of the *res ipsa loquitur* doctrine. Which defendants would most likely be successful in controverting the application of which elements? Were all the defendants likely to have had access to information about the conduct of each of them that might have caused the plaintiff's injury?

Problem
Informed Consent and Partial Information

A medical team operated on the plaintiff's decedent

> using a cauterizing machine, referred to as a "bovie." The bovie machine is a heat producing device used to make an incision in the patient's trachea. During the operation, a flame of fire approximately six inches in length emanated from the patient's throat which flame was extinguished by the nurse anesthetist and nurses.

See Schmidt v. Gibbs, 305 Ark. 383, 807 S.W.2d 928 (1991). The plaintiff sought damages from members of the medical team, including the anesthesiologist, the nurse anesthetist, and the surgical nurses. There was testimony that an accident like this could only occur if someone on the medical team was negligent. There was "clear and unequivocal evidence" that the conduct of the anesthesiologist and the nurse anesthetist conformed to the standard of reasonable care. The only testimony with respect to the surgical nurses was from an expert who said that he was not "in any way critical of the nurses in the care they provided during the tracheostomy procedure." The hospital, employer of the surgical nurses, moves for summary judgment, arguing that the plaintiff has not offered any evidence that the surgical nurses breached their duty of care. If you represent the plaintiff, would it be advisable to rely on the doctrine of *res ipsa loquitur* to satisfy the plaintiff's burden of showing breach by the nurses?

Perspective: Using Res Ipsa *to Identify Defendants*

It seems to make sense for an unconscious plaintiff to be able to require the caretakers to prove that they were not individually responsible for the plaintiff's harm. Difficulties may follow from extending this rule to other situations. Imagine that a pedestrian was injured by someone's negligence driving in a large airport parking garage, but that the pedestrian had no memory of the incident. If the operator of the lot maintained records of the license plates of all cars that used the garage, would it be consistent with *Ybarra* to permit the pedestrian to seek damages from all the drivers whose cars had used the garage on the day of the injury? Is it desirable to extend the *Ybarra* rule to this context? If not, how is the medical situation different?

IV. Legal Malpractice

Attorneys are sometimes defendants in professional malpractice suits. The professional standard of care governs these suits. Russo v. Griffin considers whether to apply a locality, state, or national version of the standard. Bevan v. Fix treats the issue of the role of the Rules of Professional Conduct in assessing malpractice liability.

The legal malpractice setting involves some unique issues for measuring damages. In Fishman v. Brooks, the court describes the "trial within a trial" that is sometimes used to determine damages caused by a lawyer's malpractice. Carbone v. Tierney explores whether a malpractice plaintiff should have to prove that proper work by the defendant lawyer would have led to a collectible judgment, and whether the judgment awarded to a victorious malpractice plaintiff should be reduced to reflect the fee the plaintiff would have paid the defendant lawyer for proper legal work.

RUSSO v. GRIFFIN

510 A.2d 436 (Vt. 1986)

HILL, J.

This is a legal malpractice action. The trial court found for defendants, H. Vaughn Griffin, Jr. and Griffin & Griffin, Ltd., and entered judgment on their behalf. Plaintiff, J.A. Russo Paving, Inc., appealed. We reverse.

Sometime during the 1930's Joseph Russo established a paving business in Rutland, Vermont. In 1975, Mr. Russo decided to turn the business over to his two sons, Anthony (Tony) and Francis (Frank). They approached defendant Griffin, a lawyer in the Rutland area, to help them with the process of incorporation. As their attorney, defendant Griffin drew up the corporate charter, filed it with the Secretary of State and arranged the necessary transfer of assets. Between 1975 and 1978 the corporation held its annual meetings at Mr. Griffin's office.

In early 1978, Frank entertained thoughts of purchasing a laundromat in Rutland, and he entered into discussions with his brother concerning the sale of his interest in the corporation. The father, who was not happy with the proposed arrangements, eventually got involved in the negotiations, which culminated in a meeting at Mr. Griffin's office.

According to defendant Griffin, the main purpose of the meeting, and the documents he prepared pursuant thereto, was to protect Frank. In this regard, a $6,000 promissory note from the corporation to Frank Russo was personally guaranteed by Tony Russo and his wife, and it was secured by a chattel mortgage. In return, Frank resigned as president and transferred his stock to the corporation.

At no time during the meeting did defendant Griffin inform the corporation or Tony Russo, the sole remaining shareholder, of the desirability of obtaining a covenant not to compete or explain the implications thereof. Three months after the stock transfer, Frank went back into the paving business in Rutland in direct competition with the plaintiff corporation. A properly drafted noncompetition covenant would have prevented this from occurring.

At trial, plaintiff introduced two expert witnesses, both well-respected practicing attorneys from the Burlington area, who testified that defendant Griffin's failure to advise the corporation to exact a covenant not to compete deviated from the standard of care required of attorneys practicing in Vermont at that time. Defendants introduced two similarly qualified Rutland attorneys who testified that defendant Griffin's conduct comported with the standard of care then expected of Rutland attorneys.

The question for determination was clearly whether defendant Griffin's conduct violated the attorney standard of care as it existed at the time of the alleged breach. In answering this question, the trial court focused on the long-standing professional relationship between defendant Griffin and the Russo family and the fact that this was not an arms-length transaction. It did not, however, find these facts to be dispositive. The court ultimately chose to accept the testimony of defendants', rather than plaintiff's, expert witnesses on the premise that "those attorneys whose practice primarily was conducted in the Rutland area prior to and during 1978 are more familiar with the standard of care then required of lawyers."

Defendants claim that the trial court was more concerned with the time frame of the alleged act of malpractice then [sic] the locale in which it occurred. We cannot agree. In ruling for the defendants, the court found the relevant standard of care to be limited to what a careful and prudent practitioner in the Rutland area would do under the circumstances. The court concluded:

> The *standard of care in the Rutland area* in 1978 required of an attorney did not require him to suggest or recommend to a purchasing client that a noncompete agreement be obtained from a seller who is a relative and who has been a business associate for several years, the transaction not being one at arms length. (Emphasis added.)

In Hughes v. Klein, 139 Vt. 232, 233, 427 A.2d 353, 354 (1981), this Court held that the standard of care within the legal profession required lawyers to exercise "the customary skill and knowledge which normally prevails at the time and place." We are now asked to reexamine the underlying rationale and continued vitality of the so-called locality rule.

The locality rule is an exclusive product of the United States. It was first applied to the medical profession approximately a century ago when there existed a great disparity between standards of practice in large urban centers and remote rural areas. . . .

The shortcomings of the locality rule are well recognized. It immunizes persons who are sole practitioners in their community from malpractice liability and it promotes a "conspiracy of silence" in the plaintiffs' locality which, in many cases, effectively precludes plaintiffs from retaining qualified experts to testify on their behalf. Recent developments in technology and the trend toward standardization have further undermined support for the rule.

According to defendants, the reasoning of the courts which have rejected the locality rule in medical malpractice decisions is inapposite to legal malpractice. We disagree.

> The ability of the practitioner and the minimum knowledge required should not vary with geography. The rural practitioner should not be less careful, less able or less skillful than the urban attorney. The fact that a lower degree of care or less able practice may be prevalent in a particular local community should not dictate the standard of care.

Mallen & Levit, Legal Malpractice §254, at 334 (2d ed. 1981). Defendants correctly note that "knowledge of local practices, rules, or customs may be determinative of, and essential to, the exercise of adequate care and skill." Id. To argue this fact in support of continued application of the locality rule, however, is to confuse "the *degree* of 'skill and knowledge' and the relevance of local factors which constitute the *knowledge* required by the standard of care." Id. at 337. Although attorneys throughout this state may be required to familiarize themselves with local practices, rules or customs peculiar to their area, the crucial inquiry for malpractice purposes turns not on the substance of the underlying practice, rule, or custom but on whether a reasonable and prudent attorney can be expected to know of its existence and practical applications.

In selecting a territorial limitation on the standard of care, we believe that the most logical is that of the state. See Restatement (Second) of Torts §299A comment g (1965) (allowance for variations in type of community or degree of skill and knowledge possessed by practitioners therein has seldom been made in legal profession as such variations either do not exist or are not worthy of recognition). In Vermont, the rules governing the practice of law do not vary from community to community but are the same throughout the state. Moreover, in order to practice law in Vermont attorneys must successfully complete the requirements for admission established by this Court and administered by the Vermont Board of Bar Examiners. Among these prerequisites is the requirement that all candidates for admission complete a study of law in the office of a judge or practicing attorney in this state.

The relevant geographic area then is not the community in which the attorney's office is located or the nation as a whole, but the jurisdiction in which the attorney is licensed to practice. Accordingly, we hold that the appropriate standard of care to which a lawyer is held in the performance of professional services is "that degree of care, skill, diligence and knowledge commonly possessed and exercised by a reasonable, careful and prudent lawyer in the practice of law in this jurisdiction." Cook, Flanagan & Berst v. Clausing, 73 Wash. 2d 393, 395, 438 P.2d 865, 867 (1968); see also Ramp v. St. Paul Fire & Marine Insurance Co., 254 So. 2d 79, 82 (La. App. 1971) (attorney liable for failure to exercise that degree of care, skill and diligence which is commonly possessed and exercised by practicing attorneys in his or her jurisdiction). . . .

In this case, defendant Griffin, in advising a family-held business on how to structure a buy-out and drafting the documents necessary to the transaction, failed to inform his clients of the possible need for, and implications of, a covenant not to compete. Both sides presented expert testimony addressing whether this failure constituted attorney malpractice. In answering this question, the trial court erroneously applied the locality rule in defining the applicable standard of care. This ruling clearly prejudiced the plaintiffs as the court chose to accept the testimony of defendants', rather than plaintiff's, expert witnesses on the rationale that they were from the Rutland area, and therefore were more familiar with the applicable standard of care. Accordingly, the decision of the superior court is reversed and the cause is remanded for a new trial.

NOTES TO RUSSO v. GRIFFIN

1. *Elements of Malpractice Claim.*   In order to establish a claim of legal malpractice, a plaintiff client must demonstrate three basic elements: employment of the attorney or some other basis for a duty; the failure of the attorney to act as well as the standard of care required; and a causal connection between the negligence and the plaintiff's damage.

2. *Standard of Care.* The court adopts a standard of care from a Washington case that requires the "care, skill, diligence and knowledge commonly possessed and exercised by a reasonable, careful and prudent lawyer," but cites as support of that standard a Louisiana holding that refers to "care, skill and diligence which is commonly possessed and exercised by practicing attorneys." One of these standards explicitly calls for "reasonable" conduct, and the other does not, but the court apparently considered them equivalent.

3. *Geographic Scope.* In selecting a statewide scope for its standard of care, the court rejected a suggestion in a concurring opinion (not reproduced here) that because the state's bar exam incorporates multistate questions and because law schools are truly national, a national standard ought to be used.

4. *Common Knowledge Exception to Requirement of Expert Testimony.* As is true in medical malpractice cases, courts in legal malpractice cases require expert testimony when the challenged conduct is outside the knowledge of jurors, but they withdraw that requirement for conduct that can be evaluated with common knowledge. Allowing a statute of limitations period to elapse without filing a suit on behalf of a client is typical of conduct that can be held to violate the standard of care in the absence of expert testimony. See O'Neil v. Bergan, 452 A.2d 337 (D.C. App. 1982).

BEVAN v. FIX

42 P.3d 1013 (Wyo. 2002)

Lehman, C.J.

... Defendant William Fix is an attorney licensed to practice law in the state of Wyoming with an office in Jackson. In July of 1992, Bevan hired Fix to represent him as defense counsel on a charge of criminal battery for family violence against his then girlfriend Jenni Jones (Jones). Fix represented Bevan throughout the course of those proceedings, which ultimately ended in a plea agreement. In December of 1994, Bevan and Jones married. ...

In January of 1997, Jones, represented by Fix, filed a complaint for divorce from Bevan. Bevan was not consulted in regard to Fix's representation of his wife Jones nor did he consent to the representation. Subsequently, in June of 1997, Fix withdrew from representation of his client Jones because he had begun a sexual relationship with her. ... Bevan and Jones' divorce was finalized in December of 1997.

... Bevan contends that the district court committed error by granting summary judgment to Fix on Bevan's claim of legal malpractice, which he argues arose when Fix represented Jones against Bevan, his former client, in the couple's divorce proceeding. After analysis of this claim in its procedural posture, we affirm the district court's grant of summary judgment in favor of Fix. ...

The district court ... found that Fix owed no duty of care to Bevan because their attorney/client relationship had terminated. [It also] found that ... Bevan had presented no evidence on the issue of his damages or legal injury. ...

"Whether a legal duty exists is a question of law, and absent a duty, there is no liability." We agree with the district court's finding that Bevan was not a "current client" of Fix's at the time Fix undertook to represent Jones against Bevan in the divorce proceeding. ...

It is true that this court has consistently rejected legal malpractice claims by "nonclient" plaintiffs of the alleged negligent attorney on the basis of several important policy considerations discussed within those decisions. Notwithstanding that line of precedent, the instant case cannot be pigeonholed into those analyses for the simple reason that Bevan is not a "nonclient" in relation to attorney Fix. Rather, he is, in fact, a "former client." These parties at one point in time had an attorney/client relationship.

This court has not had previous occasion to squarely address the presence or scope of the duty an attorney owes to a former client and whether a breach of that duty may give rise to tort liability as legal malpractice. However, courts from other jurisdictions have consistently recognized that an attorney continues to owe a legal duty of confidentiality and loyalty to former clients, although the latter duty is more limited in nature. These duties are considered fiduciary obligations. Moreover, the continuing duties of confidentiality and loyalty are reflected in the Wyoming Rules of Professional Conduct §§1.6 and 1.9 and comments thereto.

Appellee argues that paragraph [6] of the "Scope" section of the Rules of Professional Conduct prevents this court from recognizing those duties embodied within them when it proclaims:

> Violation of a Rule should not give rise to a cause of action nor should it create any presumption that a legal duty has been breached. The Rules are designed to give guidance to lawyers and to provide a structure for regulating conduct through disciplinary agencies. They are not designed to be a basis for civil liability. . . . Accordingly, nothing in the Rules should be deemed to augment any substantive legal duty of lawyers or the extra-disciplinary consequences of violating such a duty.

We respond to this argument simply, by stressing "it is important to remember that attorneys' fiduciary obligations substantially pre-date the ethical codes." In fact, preservation of a client's confidences has been described as the "bedrock principle of the Anglo-American legal system." As the Pennsylvania Supreme Court noted in its well reasoned opinion Maritrans GP Inc. v. Pepper, Hamilton, & Scheetz, 529 Pa. 241, 602 A.2d 1277, 1284-85 (Pa. 1992): . . . "The Superior Court seems to have the idea that because conduct is not a tort simply because it is a disciplinary violation, then conduct ceases to be a tort when it is at the same time a disciplinary violation. This is an inversion of logic and legal policy and misunderstands the history of the disciplinary rules." . . .

[I]n recognizing the fiduciary duties owed to former clients in relation to conflicts of interest, courts regularly recite the following language from 7 Am. Jur. 2d Attorneys at Law §200 (1997):

> **Representation of Interest Adverse to That of Former Client**
> An attorney cannot, on termination of employment by a client, represent one whose interest in the transaction is adverse to that of the former client, or in a matter that is substantially related to the former representation. Underlying the rule that an attorney is prohibited from representing a party in a lawsuit where an opposing party is the lawyer's former client is the notion that an attorney, as part of his or her fiduciary obligation, owes a continuing duty to a former client not to reveal confidences learned in the course of the professional relationship.

Accordingly, this court herein expressly recognizes the fiduciary duties of confidentiality and loyalty an attorney owes to a former client embodied in Wyoming Rules of Professional Conduct §§1.6 and 1.9 as a codification of the common law. Specifi-cally, we think Rule 1.9 sets the proper limited parameters of the duty of loyalty owed to former clients:

> (a) A lawyer who has formally represented a client in a matter shall not thereafter represent another person in the same or a substantially related matter in which that person's interests are materially adverse to the interests of the former client unless the former client consents after consultation except that when the former client is a governmental entity, consent is not permitted.

Absent a showing of actual disclosure of confidences in breach of the duty reflected in Rule 1.6, we think it is only those cases of adverse representation falling within Rule 1.9 which potentially meet the following test set forth in 7 Am. Jur. 2d Attorneys at Law §200:

> The test of whether the attorney's employment is inconsistent with his or her duty to a former client is whether acceptance of the new retainer will require the attorney, in forwarding the interest of the new client, to do anything that will injuriously affect a former client in any matter in which the attorney formerly represented the client, and also whether the attorney will be called on, in the new relation, to use against a former client any knowledge or information acquired in the former relationship.

Having established that Rules 1.6 and 1.9 accurately reflect the parameters of the fiduciary duties owed to former clients, we think it is obvious that a breach of those standards by the attorney gives rise to potential civil liability to the former client. Furthermore, we hold that a breach of the attorney's duties of confidentiality and loyalty will be analyzed within the framework of a legal malpractice action. . . .

The district court in granting summary judgment to Fix found "there is no evidence in the record which demonstrates how Fix's conduct as an attorney caused [Bevan] harm. Simply asserting that Fix's conduct was improper or even immoral is insufficient to support a claim for malpractice." We agree with the district court's conclusion and affirm the grant of summary judgment to Fix on this basis. . . .

NOTES TO BEVAN v. FIX

1. *Damages.*   The Bevan v. Fix court affirmed the trial court's grant of summary judgment because the plaintiff failed to present evidence of damages. What kinds of damage claims, if supported by facts, might have precluded summary judgment? The defendant might have used private information to affect the outcome of the divorce proceeding, causing the original client to suffer economic loss. Alternatively, the former client might have spent money to investigate whether the former lawyer had wrongly used private information.

2. *Role of Rules of Professional Conduct in Legal Malpractice Litigation.* Although the American Bar Association Model Rules (adopted in many states) assert that they are not intended as a basis for civil liability, states have adopted a range of positions regarding their role in malpractice litigation.

> Courts have been mixed in how they apply the Model Rules in malpractice actions. The majority of courts have presented a compromise position: the Model Rules cannot stand in as the duty of care, a violation of the Model Rules is not negligence per se, but they can be considered as evidence of a breach. A few courts have allowed the Model Rules to

inform the duty of care question more directly, some by creating a rebuttable presumption of a breach of duty if the Model Rules are violated. On the other hand, some courts have held that the Model Rules are flatly inadmissible in a legal malpractice action.

Benjamin H. Barton, *Do Judges Systematically Favor the Interests of the Legal Profession?*, 59 Ala. L. Rev. 453, 502 (2008).

3. Presumption of Disclosure of Confidences. In the contexts of attorney discipline and disqualification, courts usually apply an irrebuttable presumption that a former client's private information has been disclosed when that former client's interests are adverse to those of a client whom the attorney later represents. The *Bevan* court (in a part of its opinion not reproduced above) rejected that position for legal malpractice claims, suggesting that a plaintiff should be required to prove a breach of confidentiality. The *Bevan* court noted that a plaintiff could have the benefit of an inference of disclosure, if the defendant lawyer's represented a new client with interests adverse to the former client's interests.

FISHMAN v. BROOKS

487 N.E.2d 1377 (Mass. 1986)

WILKINS, J.

This appeal principally concerns the propriety of certain evidentiary rulings in the trial of a counterclaim for malpractice filed by Larimore S. Brooks against Irving Fishman, a member of the bar of the Commonwealth. Brooks persuaded the jury that (a) Fishman was negligent in representing Brooks in an action for personal injuries Brooks sustained when a negligently operated motor vehicle collided with the bicycle he was riding; (b) as a result of Fishman's negligence, Brooks was obliged to settle the personal injury action; and (c) the damages which Brooks should have recovered in that action were substantially greater than the amount of the settlement.

Fishman commenced this action by filing a complaint for declaratory relief against Brooks, who, after the settlement, had notified his health care providers that the case had been settled and they would be paid. Fishman alleged that Brooks had violated the terms of an agreement between them which would have given Fishman, as an additional fee, any amount he saved in negotiating settlements of Brooks's medical bills. Fishman voluntarily abandoned this claim shortly before Brooks filed his counterclaim. . . . On our own motion, we transferred Fishman's appeal to this court, and we now affirm the judgment in favor of Brooks.

We need recite the facts only in general terms in order to present the legal issues raised in Fishman's appeal. On the night of September 25, 1975, Brooks suffered serious injuries when a motor vehicle traveling in the same direction struck him as he rode his bicycle in the breakdown lane of Route Nine in Newton. Brooks wore dark clothing, and his bicycle may have lacked proper light reflectors. Shortly after the accident Brooks retained Fishman to represent him.

The jury would have been warranted in finding various facts bearing on Fishman's negligence. Fishman had not tried a case of any sort since 1961. His part-time solo practice mainly involved real estate conveyancing. He did not commence suit until sixteen months after the accident and, for no apparent reason, did not obtain service on the driver defendant for more than ten months after filing the complaint, a delay which, by his own admission, interfered with his handling of the case. Fishman made no effort to examine the motor vehicle or to investigate in any detail what the driver had been doing immediately prior to the accident. He engaged in no useful pretrial discovery. Instead, he relied on information the driver's insurer volunteered. He did not learn, for example, that shortly after the accident the driver had stated that she neither saw Brooks nor the bicycle before her vehicle struck them.

In April, 1978, a Federal District Court judge assigned the case for trial on June fifth. Fishman thereupon consulted an able attorney experienced in personal injury litigation about referring the case to him, but the negotiations failed because Fishman would not agree to an even division of his one-third contingent fee.

In April, 1978, Fishman made a settlement demand of $250,000 on the driver's insurer. At various times the driver's insurer made offers of settlement. Fishman did not know what the available insurance coverage was. He told Brooks that only $250,000 was available when, in fact, $1,000,000 was available. Brooks rejected several offers of settlement, although Fishman had recommended that Brooks accept them. Finally, shortly before trial, after Fishman had told Brooks that he could not win if he went to trial, Brooks agreed to settle his personal injury claim for $160,000, knowing that Fishman was not prepared to try the case.

In the trial of this case, the jury answered special questions concerning the malpractice action. They found that Fishman was negligent in his handling of the personal injury action and that Brooks was damaged thereby in the amount of $525,000. The driver's negligence was 90% and Brooks's negligence was 10% of the contributing cause of his injuries. . . .

The judge entered judgment on the malpractice count by reducing Brooks's damages ($525,000) to reflect (a) his contributory fault (10% or $52,500), (b) the amount of medical expenses paid from the settlement ($32,000), and (c) the amount Brooks received personally from the settlement ($90,000) and by allowing interest on the balance. No reduction was allowed for Fishman's counsel fees collected in the earlier action.

An attorney who has not held himself out as a specialist owes his client a duty to exercise the degree of care and skill of the average qualified practitioner. An attorney who violates this duty is liable to his client for any reasonably foreseeable loss caused by his negligence. Thus an attorney is liable for negligently causing a client to settle a claim for an amount below what a properly represented client would have accepted. Although properly informed of all the relevant law and facts, an attorney may nevertheless cause a client to settle a case for an amount below that which competent counsel would approve. . . . The typical case of malpractice liability for an inadequate settlement involves an attorney who, having failed to prepare his case properly or lacking the ability to handle the case through trial (or both), causes his client to accept a settlement not reasonable in the circumstances.

A plaintiff who claims that his attorney was negligent in the prosecution of a tort claim will prevail if he proves that he probably would have obtained a better result had the attorney exercised adequate skill and care. Brooks's case was tried on this theory, and thus first involved the question of Fishman's negligence in the settlement of Brooks's claim and, second, if that were established, the question whether, if the claim had not been settled, Brooks would probably have recovered more than he received in the settlement. This is the traditional approach in the trial of such a case. The original or underlying action is presented to the trier of fact as a trial within a trial. If the trier of fact concludes that the attorney was negligent, a matter on which expert testimony is usually required, the consequences of that negligence are determined by the result of the trial within the trial. Thus, in the trial within the trial in this case, the jury had to determine whether the driver negligently caused Brooks's injury and, if so, the damages Brooks suffered and the comparative fault of Brooks and the driver. On this approach to the trial of a legal malpractice action, except as to reasonable settlement values, no expert testimony from an attorney is required to establish the cause and the extent of the plaintiff's damages.

Over Fishman's objection, the judge properly admitted expert testimony from an experienced tort lawyer and an experienced claims adjuster as to the reasonable settlement value of the underlying claim at the time it was settled. The attorney testified that such a case normally would have settled for $450,000 to $500,000. The claims adjuster estimated that such a case would have settled for $400,000 to $450,000.

Fishman argues that the settlement value of the underlying action was not a proper measure of damages. Brooks does not assert that it was; rather, he argues that proof of the fair settlement value of the underlying action was an important element of his case against Fishman. If, in spite of Fishman's negligent preparation of the personal injury case, settlement was made in an amount that properly prepared counsel reasonably could have recommended, Brooks would have suffered no loss from Fishman's negligence. Consequently, evidence of the fair settlement value of the underlying claim was admissible to prove not only Fishman's negligence but also that his negligence caused a loss to Brooks. In precisely these terms and without objection from Fishman, the judge submitted a special question to the jury as to whether $160,000 was a fair settlement. The reasonableness of the $160,000 settlement was relevant, therefore, and on that question expert testimony was appropriate.

Fishman also contends that admission of evidence concerning the fairness of the settlement was improper because it allowed the jury to impose liability by second-guessing the attorney's judgment. The answer is that no liability would have been imposed for a settlement made within the range of settlement values that an attorney exercising due care would have recommended. Like a member of any other profession, an attorney is not immune from liability for the consequences of a negligent exercise of professional judgment. The absence of any evidence that the insurer of the defendant in the underlying action would have settled for more than $160,000 is immaterial on the theory on which Brooks presented his case. If $160,000 did not equal or exceed the amount that a nonnegligent attorney would have recommended for settlement, the case should not have been settled.

If Fishman had wished the jury to understand that the experts' testimony was not to be considered on the issue of the damages that would have been recovered in the underlying action, he could have asked for a limiting instruction both at the time the evidence was admitted and in the judge's final charge. He did neither. In fact, the judge instructed the jury on damages as in the typical personal injury tort action without reference to the settlement value of the underlying action. . . .

Judgment affirmed.

NOTES TO FISHMAN v. BROOKS

1. Trial Within a Trial. In most negligence cases, a jury must try to imagine what would have happened in the absence of the defendant's negligent conduct. In legal malpractice cases, the jury has a slightly different ability. Instead of deducing how a past jury would have responded to a case if it had been tried correctly, the current malpractice jury assumes the role of the past jury and decides the issues of the under-lying claim by itself.

The "case within a case" requires a switch in what otherwise would have been the position of one of the parties. The malpractice plaintiff's original lawyer (now the malpractice defendant) would have sought to establish the validity of the plaintiff's claim if he or she had filed the case on time. In the malpractice case, the original lawyer must seek to refute the validity of the plaintiff's original claim.

2. *Damages for Transactional Malpractice.* When a lawyer acts negligently in transactional work, instead of using the "trial within a trial" method for assessing damages, courts require juries to determine what kind of deal the malpractice plaintiff might have achieved if proper legal service had been provided. This may be highly speculative. One commentator has suggested that it is easy to blame lawyers for many kinds of misjudgments business people make, and that in many instances "the unfavorable outcome was likely to occur anyway, the client already knew the problems with the deal, or . . . the client's own misconduct or misjudgment caused the problems." See John H. Bauman, *Damages for Legal Malpractice: An Appraisal of the Crumbling Dike and Threatening Flood,* 61 Temp. L. Rev. 1127, 1154-1155 (1988).

3. *Judgmental Immunity.* A lawyer is ordinarily protected from liability for an error in judgment about an unsettled point of law. See, e.g., Baker v. Fabian, Thielen & Thielen, 578 N.W.2d 446 (Neb. 1998) (involving a claim that a lawyer had negligently failed to introduce evidence that an envelope had been placed in an authorized U.S. postal depository). If a lawyer is aware of an unsettled issue that could be of conse-quence to a client, the lawyer would be required to disclose the nature of the issue to the client. Failure to do so could be treated as malpractice, even though making a wrong prediction about the outcome of the issue would be protected by judgmental immu-nity. See, e.g., Wood v. McGrath, North, Mullin & Kratz, P.C., 589 N.W.2d 103 (Neb. 1999) (involving alleged negligence of lawyer in failing to properly advise divorc-ing client about unsettled nature of the law regarding stock options and their valuation).

CARBONE v. TIERNEY

864 A.2d 308 (N.H. 2004)

Duggan, J.

The defendant, Nancy S. Tierney, appeals a jury verdict . . . finding her liable for legal malpractice in her representation of the plaintiff, Alfred Carbone. We affirm in part, reverse in part and remand.

Tierney's representation of Carbone arose out of a dispute between Carbone and his son, Daniel. [In the performance of her duty as Carbone's counsel, Tierney: (1) failed to allege in the complaint she filed for him in the United States District Court for the District of New Hampshire an amount in controversy sufficient to establish subject matter jurisdiction, as a result of which the complaint was dismissed; (2) failed to appeal the dismissal, leading to the dismissal of a second complaint she filed in the district court alleging a sufficient amount, as a result of which a subsequent complaint filed in the United States District Court for the District of Massachusetts was also dismissed; (3) after filing a complaint in the Massachusetts Superior Court, failed to inquire why it was dismissed; (4) having failed to make this inquiry, did not appeal the unjustified dismissal; (5) then, while representing the plaintiff in a bankruptcy proceeding initiated by a party against whom he had been making the dismissed claims, failed to appear at the first meeting of creditors; and (6) failed to oppose the homestead exemption asserted in the bankruptcy, as a result of which the responsible party was discharged.]

In September 2000, Carbone filed the instant action claiming that Tierney committed legal malpractice when she represented him. . . .

A jury trial was held in January 2003. The jury returned a verdict in Carbone's favor. . . . This appeal followed. . . .

Tierney first argues that expert testimony is required to prove proximate causation in a legal malpractice action. Because Carbone failed to provide any expert testimony in the present case, Tierney contends that the trial court erred when it granted Carbone's motion for summary judgment on liability. We agree. . . .

In legal malpractice cases, "[e]xpert testimony may be essential for the plaintiff to establish causation. The trier of fact must be able to determine what . . . result should have occurred if the lawyer had not been negligent." 5 R. Mallen & J. Smith, *Legal Malpractice* §33.16, at 116 (5th ed. 2000). "[U]nless the causal link is obvious or can be established by other evidence, expert testimony may be essential to prove what the lawyer should have done." *Id.* We thus hold that expert testimony on proximate cause is required "in cases where determination of that issue is not one that lay people would ordinarily be competent to make."

In the present case, the trial court characterized Tierney's lack of knowledge about the Federal Rules of Civil Procedure and her failure to contest the dismissal of Carbone's case in the Essex County Superior Court as "obvious breach[es] of . . . equally obvious professional norm[s]." The court further characterized Tierney's failure to oppose both [his son's wife's] bankruptcy and the homestead exemption that she was seeking as complete inaction that resulted in "a blatant breach of the standard of care an attorney owes to her client." The trial court thus ruled that Carbone was not required to offer expert testimony and granted summary judgment in his favor on the legal malpractice claim.

Even assuming that no expert testimony was required to establish the appropriate standard of care and Tierney's breach of that standard, Carbone was nonetheless required to provide expert testimony to establish that Tierney's breach was the legal cause of his injuries. [T]he trier of fact must be able to determine what result would have occurred if the attorney had not been negligent. An analysis of what Tierney should have done and whether her negligence was the legal cause of Carbone's injuries is so distinctly related to the practice of law as to be beyond the ken of the average layperson.

We disagree that this is one of those exceptional cases where Tierney's breach of the standard of care was so obviously the legal cause of Carbone's injuries that expert testimony was not required. The trial court was correct in characterizing Tierney's conduct as egregious. . . . Nonetheless, it is unclear which egregious conduct, if any, was the legal cause of Carbone's injuries. Accordingly, expert testimony was required to explain whether, if the underlying case had not been dismissed in federal or state court, Carbone would have prevailed in the cause of action against his son. Expert testimony was also required to explain whether Tierney's failure to represent Carbone's interests in [his son's wife's] bankruptcy proceeding actually resulted in harm to Carbone. The facts of this case are thus sufficiently complicated to require expert testimony with respect to causation.

We thus conclude that the trial court erred when it ruled that expert testimony was not required and granted summary judgment in favor of Carbone. Accordingly, we reverse the trial court's ruling with respect to its grant of summary judgment on liability and remand for further proceedings consistent with this opinion. . . .

Tierney next argues that the trial court erred when it ruled that she had the burden of proving that the judgment in the underlying action would not have been collectible. We disagree.

. . . As we have previously stated, a plaintiff who alleges that an attorney's negligence caused the loss of a legal action can succeed only by proving that the action would have been successful but for the attorney's misconduct. . . . The plaintiff's actual loss is thus "measured by the judgment the plaintiff lost in the underlying action." It would, however, "be inequitable for the plaintiff to be able to obtain a judgment against the attorney which is greater than the judgment that the plaintiff could have collected from the third party; the plaintiff would be receiving a windfall at the attorney's expense." We therefore hold that the collectibility of damages in the underlying case is a matter which should be considered in a legal malpractice action.

Given our holding that collectibility of damages in the underlying case is a proper consideration in a legal malpractice action, we must now determine the proper allocation of the burden of proof. A majority of courts that have considered this issue view collectibility as being closely related to proximate cause, a burden which the plaintiff bears as part of his or her prima facie case. Consequently, these courts have concluded that the plaintiff must demonstrate that if the defendant had performed adequately, "the plaintiff would have succeeded on the merits in the underlying case *and* would have succeeded in collecting on the resulting judgment, because only then would [the] plaintiff have proven that the lawyer's malfeasance was the proximate cause of [the] plaintiff's loss." As the Washington Court of Appeals noted, this approach avoids "awarding the aggrieved more than he or she would have recovered had the attorney not been negligent." *Lavigne v. Chase, Haskell, Hayes & Kalamon,* 112 Wash. App. 677, 50 P.3d 306, 310 (2002).

On the other hand, "a growing minority of jurisdictions holds uncollectibility to be an affirmative defense that must be pleaded and proved by the negligent attorney." These jurisdictions have advanced a number of reasons for rejecting the majority rule.

First, these jurisdictions reject the proposition that the plaintiff should bear the burden of proving collectibility because collectibility is closely related to proximate causation, which is an element of the plaintiff's prima facie case. Rather, these jurisdictions contend that although the plaintiff has the burden of proving that he or she would have been successful in the underlying claim, "it does not logically follow that [the plaintiff] must also prove that if [the plaintiff] had obtained a judgment it would have been collectible."

Second, these jurisdictions maintain: "To require the plaintiff to . . . prove collectibility of damages would result in placing an unfair burden on the plaintiff." This is particularly true "when a legal malpractice suit is . . . brought years after the underlying events and when the delay by the plaintiff in bringing such a suit is because of the defendant-lawyer's failure to act in a timely manner in the first place."

We find the reasoning advanced by the minority of jurisdictions that have considered this issue to be persuasive. Accordingly, we hold that, in a legal malpractice action, noncollectibility of the underlying judgment is an affirmative defense that must be proved by the defendant.

In the present case, the trial court ruled that Tierney "would have the burden of proving noncollectibility of any verdict amount that the jury determined [Carbone] was entitled to." For the reasons set forth above, we agree with the trial court's determination and conclude that the trial court did not err when it ruled that Tierney had the burden of proving that the judgment against Carbone's son, Daniel, would not have been collectible.

Tierney next argues that the trial court erred when it denied her motion to reduce the jury verdict "to reflect the amount that [Carbone] would have paid [her] in accordance with the contingency fee agreement." . . .

To begin, we recognize that whether a plaintiff's legal malpractice recovery should be reduced by the amount of attorney's fees the plaintiff would have paid for the defendant's competent performance is "still [an] unsettled issue." 3 Mallen & Smith, *supra* §20.18, at 161. Indeed, it is a question of first impression for this court.

In addressing the issue of collectibility above, we enunciated the well-established principle that in a legal malpractice action, a plaintiff is entitled to recover damages for his actual loss, which is "measured by the judgment the plaintiff lost in the underlying action." This principle is the foundation of our analysis.

Some jurisdictions that have addressed this issue have held that the verdict should be reduced by the amount of the contingency fee because only then would the verdict reflect what the plaintiff would have recovered had the defendant performed competently in the underlying action.

We disagree that reducing the verdict by the amount of the contingency fee puts the plaintiff in the same position that he or she would have been in if the defendant had performed competently in the underlying action. If we were to hold that the verdict must be reduced by the amount of the contingency fee, at the conclusion of the malpractice action, the verdict would be reduced by the amount of the contingency fee, *and* the plaintiff would have to pay his or her new attorney for the services that the new attorney provided in the prosecution of the malpractice action. We think this is an inequitable result.

On the other hand, if the defendant is barred from reducing the verdict to reflect the contingency fee, the plaintiff is in the same position he would have been in if the defendant had performed competently in the underlying action. The plaintiff will still be required to compensate his or her new attorney for the services the attorney provided in pursuit of the malpractice action. The plaintiff, however, will not be penalized for having to employ two attorneys to get the result the plaintiff should have obtained in the original action. Accordingly, we hold that, in a legal malpractice action, the verdict should not be reduced to reflect the amount of a contingency fee agreement. Our holding is consistent with a number of other jurisdictions that have addressed this issue. . . .

Affirmed in part; reversed in part; and remanded.

NOTES TO CARBONE v. TIERNEY

1. *Burdens of Proof.* The *Carbone* court stated that a legal malpractice plaintiff must prove that his or her underlying action would have been successful but for the misconduct by the defendant attorney. But with regard to the collectibility of damages, it allocated the burden of proof to the defendant, so that to avoid liability the defendant would be required to prove that damages in the underlying action would have been uncollectible. Does the court explain why proving collectibility of damages would ordinarily be more difficult than proving success on the merits of the underlying claim?

2. *Attorney's Fees and Damages.* In concluding that the plaintiff's judgment should be for the full amount that would have been awarded in the underlying action, the *Carbone* court rejected the idea that the malpractice judgment should be reduced by the amount the plaintiff would have had to pay in attorney's fees in that underlying action. The court stated that the plaintiff should not be treated as though he or she had been required to hire two lawyers. This logic may conflict with the usual rule in tort cases that each party bears the costs of its own lawyers.

Problem
Analyzing the Quality of a Lawyer's Conduct

A client told his lawyer that in connection with a planned land purchase, he wanted to limit his liability to $5,000 for cleaning up environmental contamination that might be there. He instructed his lawyer to prepare an indemnity agreement to accomplish that goal. The lawyer understood that a limit on the client's liability for cleaning up the site was a critical condition. The prospective seller rejected the indemnity agreement the lawyer had drafted and submitted another indemnity agreement at the closing meeting. Although the lawyer knew that the new indemnity agreement did not limit his client's liability to $5,000, he instructed the client to sign that agreement nonetheless. Costs of environmental work were more than $500,000. If the client seeks damages from the lawyer for the amount of expense over $5,000, should a court require the client to introduce expert testimony about the lawyer's work? See Vandermay v. Clayton, 984 P.2d 272 (Or. 1999).

CHAPTER 10

OWNERS AND OCCUPIERS OF LAND

I. Introduction

The traditional approach to liability of landowners and occupiers categorizes the injured person as a trespasser, a licensee, or an invitee, and a different standard of care is applied for the protection of each kind. Modern doctrines in a number of jurisdictions abandon some or all of these classifications or change the standard of care for evaluating land possessors' conduct.

Under common law, landlords have responsibility for certain narrowly defined types of hazards on the land. Tenants have significant burdens for providing safe conditions. In a development parallel to modern changes for general landowner law, some jurisdictions have changed the standard of care for landlords' conduct as well.

II. Traditional Rules

In jurisdictions applying the traditional rules for land possessors' liability to land entrants, important issues concern identifying the status of the plaintiff-entrant and defining the degree of care the landowner must provide. To analyze the liability of a land possessor, a lawyer must determine the status of the person and then must identify the nature of the obligation to that person. The cases in this section illustrate the traditional approaches to these tasks. Additional doctrines supplement the basic status-related rules, for recurring situations such as trespasses by children, or entrants' encounters with open and obvious hazards.

A. Trespassers

Ryals v. United States Steel Corp. examines the traditional duty owed to trespassers and considers whether the traditional rules should apply when a trespasser has entered land to commit a crime. In Merrill v. Central Maine Power Co. and Hill v. National Grid, the courts explain and apply the *attractive nuisance* doctrine, an exception to the usual treatment of trespassers that applies under certain conditions when the trespasser is a child.

RYALS v. UNITED STATES STEEL CORP.
562 So. 2d 192 (Ala. 1990)

Jones, J.

Wilson Ryals, Jr., as administrator of the estate of his brother, David Ryals, appeals from a summary judgment in favor of the defendant, United States Steel Corporation ("U.S. Steel"). The plaintiff alleged that the defendant caused the decedent's death by negligently or wantonly failing to maintain and secure a "switch rack."[1] Ryals later voluntarily dismissed the negligence claim, and the trial court entered summary judgment in favor of U.S. Steel on the wantonness claim.

Because this Court, by this opinion, recognizes two distinct classes of trespassers to land — (1) mere trespassers, to whom the landowner owes the duty not to wantonly injure them; and (2) trespassers who enter upon the land of another with the manifest intent to commit a criminal act and to whom the landowner owes only the duty not to intentionally injure them — we affirm the judgment.

On March 31, 1984, Wilson and David Ryals, as trespassers, went to U.S. Steel's Muscoda Mines switch rack for the purpose of "stripping out" copper, brass, and other salvageable metals. Wilson Ryals testified at his deposition that, when they arrived at the site, they found the base of the structure to be partially stripped; that they found one rusty warning sign, detached metals lying on the ground, dangling wires, garbage in and around the fenced area and wild vegetation growing around the fence; and that they found the gate leading into the switch rack to be "wide open." David Ryals contacted a 44,000-volt copper line; he suffered third degree burns over 95% of his body and died several days later as a result.

The only issue presented here is whether U.S. Steel was entitled to a summary judgment under the appropriate standard of care owed by U.S. Steel to David Ryals, as a trespasser, who, at the time of his injury, was engaged in the crime of theft of U.S. Steel's property. Rule 56, A.R. Civ. P., sets forth a two-tiered standard for granting summary judgment. That rule requires the trial court to determine 1) that there is no genuine issue of material fact, and 2) that the moving party is entitled to a judgment as a matter of law.

Necessarily antecedent to any evaluation of the facts, however, is a determination of the legal duty owed by a landowner to a trespasser. David Ryals was, without question, a trespasser. The standard of care that a landowner owes to a trespasser is generally recognized as the lowest standard of care owed to one who enters upon another's land. The landowner is bound only to refrain from reckless, willful, or wanton conduct toward the trespasser. . . .

It is noteworthy that the highest degree of care imposed upon a landowner by this traditional common law rule toward a *mere* trespasser, i.e., one who wrongfully comes upon the land of another but without any motive, design, or intent to engage in further wrongful conduct, is not to recklessly or wantonly injure that person. Ryals does not

---

[1] A "switch rack" is somewhat similar in function and appearance to an electrical substation.

contend otherwise; rather, he argues that the facts, when construed most favorably to him, support a finding of wantonness on the part of U.S. Steel, and, thus, that summary judgment was inappropriate. Admittedly, if all trespassers are to be treated equally, and if we agree that the conduct of U.S. Steel amounted to wantonness, then the summary judgment is due to be reversed.

"Wantonness" has been defined by this Court as follows:

> [Wantonness is] the conscious doing of some act or the omission of some duty under the knowledge of the existing conditions, and conscious that from the doing of such act or omission of such duty injury will likely or probably result. Wantonness may arise [when one has] knowledge that persons, though not seen, are likely to be in a position of danger, and[,] with conscious disregard of known conditions of danger and in violation of law[,] brings on the disaster. Wantonness may arise after discovery of actual peril, by conscious failure to use preventive means at hand. Knowledge need not be shown by direct proof, but may be shown by adducing facts from which knowledge is a legitimate inference.

Ryals contends that a genuine issue of material fact was presented on the question whether U.S. Steel wantonly caused the death of David Ryals. Ryals bases his wantonness argument primarily on his claim that when he and his brother arrived at the site they found it in the condition hereinabove set out. He also points out that agents of U.S. Steel acknowledged in deposition and in answers to interrogatories that there had been two prior deaths at the same switch rack under similar circumstances. He maintains, in light of those alleged and admitted facts, that the factfinder could reasonably infer that U.S. Steel had actual or constructive notice that persons might come into contact with the electrical lines at the switch rack.

We agree; if reckless or wanton conduct is the appropriate standard of care applicable to these facts, then a jury question has been presented as to U.S. Steel's conduct. We believe, however, that these facts strongly demonstrate a public policy justification for lowering the requisite degree of care due from a landowner to one who, as here, wrongfully enters upon the land of another to commit a crime. For public policy reasons, therefore, we hold that the duty owed by a landowner to an adult trespasser who comes upon the land and is injured while committing a crime is the duty not to *intentionally* injure such trespasser.

Applying this standard to the full context of the instant case, we conclude that a fact question was not presented on the issue whether U.S. Steel intentionally caused the death of David Ryals. The switch rack was surrounded by a chain link fence topped with barbed wire. On the fence surrounding the switch rack there was at least one sign warning of the electrical danger within. Given these conspicuous indications of danger, an unlocked gate would not imperil a person unless that person elected to disregard the obvious danger presented by the electricity. In summary, the evidence, as a matter of law, fails to suggest that U.S. Steel breached its duty not to intentionally injure David Ryals, who undisputedly, at the time of his injury, was an adult illegally upon U.S. Steel's property for the purpose of stealing copper wire. . . .

Accordingly, the judgment of the trial court is due to be, and it hereby is, affirmed.

NOTES TO RYALS v. UNITED STATES STEEL CORP.

1. Basic Rules. In most jurisdictions, all trespassers receive the treatment the *Ryals* court described as the general rule in its state: a landowner can be liable to a trespasser only for intentional torts or for reckless or wanton conduct. In some jurisdictions, all trespassers receive the treatment the *Ryals* court developed for individuals who trespass for the purpose of committing a crime. No landowner will be liable to a trespasser under these rules for mere negligence (a failure to use reasonable care).

2. Rationale for Basic Rules. These rules maximize a land occupier's freedom of choice regarding how to use and maintain land. They facilitate a decision to ignore dangerous conditions that might be costly to remedy. Since trespassers may be difficult to anticipate, these rules may also be seen as a standardized application of the reasonable person test. If trespassers as a class are very difficult to anticipate, then protecting them from harm would be very expensive, and failing to protect them from harm could be reasonable.

3. Discovered, Frequent, or Tolerated Trespassers. Where trespassers are either discovered or are frequent or tolerated, many states require a landowner to use reasonable care in order to protect the trespasser from injuries caused either by the landowner's activities or by artificial conditions on the land. Under these rules, a possessor of land has a higher duty of care when engaged in "active conduct" than for just being the owner of land with "passive conditions." For example, operating a machine would be active conduct, while the presence of a cliff would be a passive condition. Jurisdictions that change their position on duty to trespassers when active conduct is involved and a trespasser's presence is known or easily anticipated may be reflecting the fact that it might be easier and cheaper to protect identified or identifiable trespassers from active conduct than to protect unidentified and unknown persons from passive conditions.

4. Exception for Criminal Trespassers. Most states have not confronted the question of a special rule for trespassers who commit crimes. For that circumstance, the *Ryals* court adopted an exception to its state's ordinary rules regarding trespassers to increase a landowner's protection from liability in cases where a trespasser enters the land to commit a crime. The court refers to "public policy" as the basis for its new rule but does not define that term. What policy arguments might support the decision?

MERRILL v. CENTRAL MAINE POWER CO.
628 A.2d 1062 (Me. 1993)

RUDMAN, J.

Douglas Merrill appeals from the summary judgment entered in the Superior Court . . . in favor of Central Maine Power Company (CMP), in Merrill's action seeking damages for personal injuries allegedly caused by an attractive nuisance located on CMP's property. We affirm the judgment of the Superior Court.

On June 13, 1976, Merrill, then nine years of age, entered CMP's property in South Berwick to fish in the Salmon Falls River. After catching an eel in the river, Merrill walked to the nearby CMP electrical sub-station, climbed the surrounding fence, and attempted to cook the eel by leaning over the top of the fence and placing the eel on a live electrical wire. Merrill received an electric shock and suffered severe burns.

Merrill's complaint alleges, inter alia, a cause of action under the theory of attractive nuisance. The court granted a summary judgment in favor of CMP, finding that

(1) Merrill appreciated the risk at the time of the accident; [and] (2) electrical sub-stations are not, as a matter of law, attractive nuisances . . . . This timely appeal followed.

In Jones v. Billings, 289 A.2d 39 (Me. 1972), we incorporated the attractive nuisance doctrine into Maine law by adopting the definition provided in the Restatement (Second) of Torts §339 (1965):

> A possessor of land is subject to liability for physical harm to children trespassing thereon caused by an artificial condition upon the land if
>
>   (a) the place where the condition exists is one upon which the possessor knows or has reason to know that children are likely to trespass, and
>   (b) the condition is one of which the possessor knows or has reason to know and which he realizes or should realize will involve an unreasonable risk of death or serious bodily harm to such children, and
>   (c) the children because of their youth do not discover the condition or realize the risk involved in intermeddling with it or in coming within the area made dangerous by it, and
>   (d) the utility to the possessor of maintaining the condition and the burden of eliminating the danger are slight as compared with the risk to children involved, and
>   (e) the possessor fails to exercise reasonable care to eliminate the danger or otherwise to protect the children.

Jones, 289 A.2d at 42 (quoting Restatement). We will apply a strict interpretation of the Restatement criteria in determining whether a plaintiff has satisfied its burden of establishing the existence of an attractive nuisance. . . .

The present controversy surrounds the third element of the Restatement rule, namely, whether the child appreciated the risk at the time of the accident. A landowner is not required "to keep his land free from conditions which even young children are likely to observe and the full extent of the risk involved in which they are likely to realize." Restatement (Second) of Torts §339 comment m (1965). As one prominent commentator has recognized,

> [t]he child, because of his immaturity, either must not discover the condition or must not in fact appreciate the danger involved. Since the principal reason for the rule distinguishing trespassing children from trespassing adults is the inability of the child to protect himself, the courts have been quite firm in their insistence that if the child is fully aware of the condition, understands the risk which it carries, and is quite able to avoid it, he stands in no better position than an adult with similar knowledge and understanding.

W. Keeton, Prosser and Keeton on the Law of Torts §59 at 408 (5th ed. 1984) (foot-notes & citations omitted). . . .

It is undisputed that Merrill appreciated the risk inherent in placing an eel on a live electrical wire. In deposition testimony, Merrill admitted that, at the time of the accident, he knew (1) that the purpose of the fence surrounding the sub-station was to keep people out; (2) that electricity could both burn and hurt him; (3) that he was careful not to touch the wire himself; and (4) that what he did was a "dumb idea." Thus, since Merrill was unable to generate a factual issue concerning an indispensable element of the attractive nuisance doctrine, and, therefore, was conclusively precluded from recovery, a summary judgment was properly granted. . . . See Lister v. Campbell, 371 So. 2d 133,

136 (Fla. Dist. Ct. App. 1979) ("[o]ften the child's own testimony is the best evidence of whether he possessed sufficient intelligence and knowledge to understand or avoid the danger").

Finally, because our finding that Merrill appreciated the risk posed by the substation disposes of the case, we need not reach the other [issue] raised by the parties on appeal.

The entry is: Judgment affirmed.

NOTES TO MERRILL v. CENTRAL MAINE POWER CO.

1. *History of the Attractive Nuisance Doctrine.*   The attractive nuisance doctrine began at a time when many children trespassed onto the property of railroad companies and many were injured playing on large turntables, which railroads used to change the direction of locomotives. An engineer would drive onto the turntable, and the turntable could be turned to allow the locomotive to drive off onto another track or return to the first track headed in the opposite direction. The so-called *turntable doctrine* evolved into the common law rule of attractive nuisance. In Sioux City & Pacific RR. Co. v. Stout, 84 U.S. (17 Wall.) 657, 21 L. Ed. 745 (1873), the Supreme Court permitted recovery where a minor was attracted to the danger of an unlocked turntable.

2. *Basic Rule.*   The traditional attractive nuisance doctrine created an exception to the usual rule that landowners owe trespassers only a duty to refrain from willful and wanton misconduct. A child trespasser could recover by proving (1) that the child was attracted onto the land by an artificial, rather than natural, condition on the land; and (2) the possessor of the land failed to use reasonable care. Some states, such as the jurisdiction in which *Merrill* was decided, have adopted §339 of the Restatement (Second) of Torts, representing a further evolution of the turntable doctrine, by requiring consideration of additional elements (a) though (d). How would *Merrill* have been decided under the traditional attractive nuisance rule?

3. *Policy Justification.*   The attractive nuisance doctrine was supported by the Ohio Supreme Court as necessary because "[d]espite our societal changes, children are still children. They still learn through their curiosity. They still have developing senses of judgment. They still do not always appreciate danger. They still need protection by adults." See Bennett, Admr. v. Stanley, 748 N.E.2d 41 (Ohio 2001).

HILL v. NATIONAL GRID
11 A.3d 110 (R.I. 2011)

Justice FLAHERTY.

On an idyllic fall afternoon, a group of youngsters was engaged in the classic American pastime of touch football. Their play was abruptly interrupted when twelve-year-old Austin Hill stumbled and cut himself on a protruding metal post. The plaintiffs filed a complaint for negligence in Providence County Superior Court, alleging that Austin was injured by a dangerous condition on property owned by the defendant, National Grid. The plaintiffs now appeal from a grant of summary judgment in favor of the defendant.

This case came before the Supreme Court on December 7, 2010, pursuant to an order directing the parties to appear and show cause why the issues raised in this appeal should not summarily be decided. After hearing the arguments of counsel and reviewing the memoranda of the parties, we are satisfied that cause has not been shown. Accordingly, we shall decide the appeal at this time without further briefing or argument. For the reasons set forth in this opinion, we vacate the judgment of the Superior Court.

On the afternoon of October 4, 2006, Austin Hill accompanied several friends to a grass-covered vacant lot at the corner of Monticello Road and Williston Way in Pawtucket for a game of touch football. While he was running, he suddenly tripped over an unseen metal pole that was protruding from the ground. Austin fell on the ground and struck a second metal pole, lacerating his left thigh. Because he was bleeding profusely, Austin hopped on his bike and went home. Austin's mother, Rebecca, brought the boy to a local emergency room, where he received treatment for the laceration. The wound eventually healed, but a permanent scar remains.

Harry and Rebecca Hill filed suit in Superior Court individually and as parents and next-of-kin to Austin and his siblings, Aydan and Jake. In their complaint, the Hills alleged that National Grid negligently maintained its property and that, as a result, Austin suffered injuries. The defendant, a public utility that owned the lot, asserted that it owed no duty to Austin under the circumstances because he was a trespasser on its property. The plaintiffs contended that defendant had a duty under the attractive nuisance doctrine. After hearing arguments about the applicability of that doctrine, a justice of the Superior Court granted defendant's motion for summary judgment. She determined that plaintiffs had failed to make any showing that defendant knew or had reason to know that children were trespassing. It is from that decision that plaintiffs have sought review in this Court. . . .

It is a well-established principle of law that property owners owe no duty of care to trespassers but to refrain from wanton or willful conduct; and even then, only upon discovering a trespasser in a position of danger. An exception to this principle is the so-called "attractive nuisance" doctrine, which, in some instances, imposes a duty of care on landowners to trespassing children. At the core of this doctrine is the policy that

> [t]here must and should be an accommodation between the landowner's unrestricted right to use of his land and society's interest in the protection of the life and limb of its young. When these respective social-economic interests are placed on the scale, the public's concern for a youth's safety far outweighs the owner's desire to utilize his land as he sees fit. *Haddad v. First National Stores, Inc.,* 280 A.2d 93, 96 (1971).

Rhode Island adopted the Restatement (Second) *Torts'* [§339] articulation of the attractive nuisance doctrine in its 1971 decision in *Haddad.* . . .

Since deciding *Haddad* in 1971, we have had but a few opportunities to consider the attractive nuisance doctrine. In applying the doctrine to the situation at issue here, it is useful to consider the cases that have come before this Court recently. In 1992, we affirmed the Superior Court's grant of a directed verdict in favor of the landowner in *Bateman v. Mello,* 617 A.2d 877, 881 (R.I. 1992) (child injured when he fell from a natural gas pipe upon which he was climbing while on defendant landowner's property). There we concluded that "[the] defendant had no reason to foresee that the gas pipe might be dangerous or involve an unreasonable risk of serious injury to [trespassing children]. The pipe and the spotlight are not, in and of themselves, inherently dangerous objects." *Id.* at 880. We further noted that the gas pipe served a useful purpose and, because it was not only the gas pipe, but also a spotlight activated by a preset timer that caused the plaintiff to fall, "that such a coincidental string of happenings could not, under any test of reasonable foreseeability, have been anticipated by [the] defendant." *Id.*

We next considered the doctrine in *Wolf v. National Railroad Passenger Corp.,* 697 A.2d 1082, 1086-87 (R.I. 1997). There we affirmed summary judgment in favor of the defendant railroad after a twelve-year-old boy was killed tragically while trying to outrun a train on a trestle that extended over the water. In *Wolf,* we embraced the view of the overwhelming majority of jurisdictions that train trestles, as a matter of law, are not attractive nuisances. That rule rests on the notion that train trestles are an "obvious danger" to even young prospective trespassers.

. . . As it did in the Superior Court, defendant argues before us that plaintiffs raised no material facts from which a jury could conclude (1) that defendant knew or had reason to know children were likely to trespass on the property or (2) that there was any dangerous condition on its land of which it knew or had reason to know. The Superior Court agreed with that argument, but we do not.

In our opinion, plaintiffs have raised sufficient facts from which a reasonable jury could conclude that defendant knew or had reason to know trespass was likely.[5] First, defendant suggests in its argument that it must know or have reason to know that children *are* trespassing on the property. This, however, is not the teaching of §339(a) of the *Restatement (Second) Torts;* that section does not require the defendant to know or have reason to know that children *are* trespassing on the property, but rather that children are *likely* to trespass on the premises. Indeed, comment *e* in the Reporter's Notes in the Restatement highlight this distinction by noting that §339(a) applies "whether children *are* trespassing, or are *likely* to trespass." (Emphases added.)

In the deposition of Eric Gemborys, a National Grid employee, it was disclosed that he looks at the property five or six times a year. He further indicated that he was familiar with the area surrounding the lot, that it was between School Street and Route 1A, and that it was situated in the midst of "quite a few" residential homes. He conceded that National Grid had a policy in place to address trespassers, noting that in the event children were playing on the property, the employee who observed that activity was supposed to call the police. Collectively, these facts give rise to a genuine factual dispute about whether the defendant knew or had reason to know that children were likely to trespass on the lot. Questions of fact must be resolved by a fact-finder and are not appropriate for summary judgment.

Also, defendant argues that the condition causing the injury, two protruding metal posts, was not one of which it knew or had reason to know. However, Mr. Gemborys testified at his deposition that he personally had visited the property five or six times over two years. He also described monthly maintenance by a grounds-keeping crew that mowed the grass and removed debris. Based on these activities by a variety of National Grid agents, a reasonable jury could conclude that defendant knew or had reason to know of the metal stakes protruding from the ground.

---

[5] "The words 'reason to know' . . . denote the fact that the actor has information from which a person of reasonable intelligence or of the superior intelligence of the actor would infer that the fact in question exists, or that such person would govern his conduct upon the assumption that such fact exists." Restatement (Second) *Torts* §12 at 19 (1965).

In summary, because there are disputed material facts from which a reasonable jury could find that the defendant knew or had reason to know that children were likely to trespass and knew or had reason to know of the potentially dangerous condition, the entry of summary judgment was improper.

For the reasons set forth in this opinion, we vacate the judgment of the Superior Court. This file is remanded to that court.

NOTES TO HILL v. NATIONAL GRID

1. *Heightened Knowledge Requirement.* *Hill* illustrates the Restatement §339 attractive nuisance requirement that the landowner knew *or had reason to know* of the risk (element (a)). *Hill* considered evidence that National Grid knew or had reason to know of the presence of children and the danger presented by the protruding metal posts. In contrast, liability for negligence under the traditional attractive nuisance doctrine is based on failure to use reasonable care. This includes the requirement that the landowner knew or *should have known* of the risk presented by the condition on the land. Liability to adult trespassers requires intent to harm another or willful or wanton misconduct.

2. *Restatement §339 and Recklessness.* The §339 requirement that the landowner knew or had reason to know of the risk to children reflects the same knowledge requirement as required to establish recklessness. In addition, element (d) also reflects the recklessness standard, which requires a "serious risk." (See the discussion of recklessness in Chapter 3.) Another requirement of §339 reflects negligence principles: element (e) requires the possessor to exercise reasonable care to eliminate the danger or otherwise protect the children.

3. *Water as an Attractive Nuisance.* Courts usually reject application of the attractive nuisance doctrine to swimming pools and ponds or other bodies of water. Comment j of the Restatement (Second) of Torts §339 states:

> there are many dangers, such [as] those of fire and water, . . . which under ordinary conditions may reasonably be expected to be fully understood and appreciated by any child of an age to be allowed at large. To such conditions the rule stated in this Section ordinarily has no application, in the absence of some other factor creating a special risk that the child will not avoid the danger, such as the fact that the condition is so hidden as not to be readily visible, or a distracting influence which makes it likely that the child will not discover or appreciate it.

Courts in some western states have taken conflicting views on whether irrigation ditches, which distribute water in arid areas, can be attractive nuisances. In Salladay v. Old Dominion Copper Mining & Smelting Co., 100 P. 441 (Ariz. 1909), the court held that because distribution of water for farming is so important, the attractive nuisance doctrine should not be extended to irrigation ditches and flumes. Another western state, Utah, also exempts irrigation ditches from coverage under the attractive nuisance doctrine. See Kessler v. Mortenson, 16 P.3d 1225 (Utah 2000). In contrast, the court in Carmona v. Hagerman Irrigation Company, 957 P.2d 44 (N.M. 1998), refused to find that such ditches, as a matter of law, are always outside the coverage of the doctrine.

4. *Artificial versus Natural Conditions.* Restatement (Second) §339 applies only to "physical harm to children trespassing thereon caused by an artificial condition

upon the land." The Restatement (Second) §339 refers to artificial conditions such as "structures" while the Restatement (Third) §51(e) describes artificial conditions on the premises as "those that the possessor has personally constructed or had constructed by an agent and those that the possessor inherited from a former possessor." A landowner would not normally be liable for harm caused by natural conditions because children are likely to appreciate inherent dangers and because it may be may generally be more expensive to alter them.

Statute: LIABILITY FOR CERTAIN INJURIES

Ky. Rev. Stat. §381.232 (2017)

The owner of real estate shall not be liable to any trespasser for injuries sustained by the trespasser on the real estate of the owner, except for injuries which are intentionally inflicted by the owner or someone acting for the owner.

Statute: TITLE TO PROPERTY AND RESTRICTIONS ON USE, OWNERSHIP, AND ALIENATION: DEFINITIONS

Ky. Rev. Stat. §381.231 (2017)

(1) A "trespasser" means any person who enters or goes upon the real estate of another without any right, lawful authority or invitation, either expressed or implied, but does not include persons who come within the scope of the "attractive nuisance" doctrine.

Statute: LIABILITY OF OWNERS OR OCCUPIERS OF LAND FOR INJURY TO GUESTS OR TRESPASSERS

Del. Stat. tit. 25 §1501 (2017)

No person who enters onto private residential or farm premises owned or occupied by another person, either as a guest without payment or as a trespasser, shall have a cause of action against the owner or occupier of such premises for any injuries or damages sustained by such person while on the premises unless such accident was intentional on the part of the owner or occupier or was caused by the willful or wanton disregard of the rights of others.

NOTE TO STATUTES

Statutes Related to Attractive Nuisance.   The Kentucky statutes limit responsibility of landowners to trespassers in §381.232 after preserving the application of the attractive nuisance doctrine in §381.231. Unlike the rule illustrated in *Ryals*, recognizing different standards of care owed to different categories of trespassers, the Kentucky statute adopts the common rule that possessors of land are liable to all trespassers only for intentionally inflicted harms. The Delaware statute does not refer to attractive nuisance and no companion statute preserves the attractive nuisance doctrine. Could a court hold that child trespassers in Delaware are still entitled to special protections? In Porter v. Delmarva Power & Light Co., 547 A.2d 124 (Del. 1988), the Delaware Supreme Court held that the word "trespasser" in the statute should not be read to include child trespassers, since the legislature would have been explicit if it had intended to abrogate the attractive nuisance doctrine, which had been part of the state's jurisprudence for a long period prior to adoption of the statute.

Perspective: Deterrence and Corrective Justice Rationales for Limited Liability to Trespassers

Can limited liability to trespassers be understood in terms of general societal notions of fairness? See Gary T. Schwartz, *Mixed Theories of Tort Law: Affirming Both Deterrence and Corrective Justice*, 75 Tex. L. Rev. 1801 (1997):

> Currently there are two major camps of tort scholars. One understands tort liability as an instrument aimed largely at the goal of deterrence, commonly explained within the framework of economics. The other looks at tort law as a way of achieving corrective justice between the parties. If these are alternative camps, they are also to a large measure unfriendly camps: much of the time each treats the other with neglect or even derision. . . .
>
> Consider . . . the liability of landowners to trespassers. While landowners owe a full duty of non-negligence to their invitees, under the traditional rules that most jurisdictions still accept landowners' liability to trespassers is sharply limited. Landes and Posner have explained the limited liability rules by suggesting that "the cost of avoiding" the injury-producing activity of trespassing "normally is very low," much lower than "the landowner's cost" of adopting precautions. This explanation, however, seems unsatisfactory, because in many cases the trespasser neither knows nor has reason to know of the particular hazard on the landowner's property. Much more satisfactory is the ethical perception that when the plaintiff's encounter with the defendant's danger has been a consequence of the plaintiff's flouting of the defendant's rights as landowner, the plaintiff cannot claim that the injury he ends up suffering is a result of any injustice imposed on him by the possibly negligent defendant.

Professor Schwartz considers the trespasser's ability to avoid the harm as limited by lack of awareness of the risk. Does the trespasser's ability to avoid trespassing altogether change Professor Schwartz's conclusion?

B. Licensees and Invitees

For entrants who are not trespassers, classification as either a licensee or an invitee can be outcome-determinative. In many cases, plaintiffs have difficulty in showing that the defendant failed to provide the level of care owed to a licensee. In contrast, landowners owe a level of care to invitees that is often described simply as "reasonable care" and is significantly higher than the care owed to a licensee. Knorpp v. Hale discusses the implications of characterizing an entrant as a licensee rather than an invitee. In Richardson v. The Commodore, Inc., the entrant was clearly an invitee, but the dispute involved whether the plaintiff's proof could support a finding that the defendant failed to provide the required level of care.

KNORPP v. HALE
<hr>

981 S.W.2d 469 (Tex. App. 1998)

GRANT, J.

Bonita Knorpp appeals from a directed verdict in a premises liability case. Knorpp contends that the trial court erred by finding her son, Todd Erwin, to be a licensee rather than an invitee at the time of his death and by rendering a directed verdict against her claim for damages.

The decedent, Todd Erwin, was killed while cutting down a tree at the Hales' house. The evidence shows that he had moved to Texarkana to be near the Hales' daughter Autumn, who he had been dating for about a year, and that he spent a great deal of time at their house. The Hales were planning a New Year's Eve bonfire at a location in a pasture near their house around the base of a dead pine tree. They decided to cut down the tree. Erwin went to the house on December 6, 1994, took the Hales' chain saw, and began to cut down the tree. After about forty-five minutes, the tree fell in an unexpected direction and landed on Erwin, killing him. . . .

When Knorpp completed the presentation of her evidence, the trial court granted the landowner's motion for a directed verdict and ruled as a matter of law that Hale [sic Erwin] was a licensee and that there was no evidence that the landowners were negligent under applicable standards for a licensee.

Knorpp contends that the trial court erred in determining that there was no evidence that Erwin was an invitee and that the court therefore erred by rendering a directed verdict. Knorpp further contends that there was evidence that Erwin was an invitee on this particular day when he came onto the property. . . .

A landowner owes an invitee a duty to exercise ordinary care to protect him from risks of which the owner is actually aware and those risks of which the owner should be aware after reasonable inspection. To recover, a plaintiff must plead and prove that the landowner (1) had actual or constructive knowledge of some condition on the premises; (2) that the condition posed an unreasonable risk of harm; (3) that the landowner did not exercise reasonable care to reduce or eliminate the risk; and (4) that the landowner's failure to use such care proximately caused the plaintiff's injuries.

The duty that an owner owes to a licensee is to not injure him by "willful, wanton or grossly negligent conduct, and that the owner use ordinary care to either warn a licensee of, or to make reasonably safe, a dangerous condition of which the owner is aware and the licensee is not." In order to establish liability, a licensee must prove (1) that a condition of the premises created an unreasonable risk of harm to him; (2) that the owner actually knew of the condition; (3) that the licensee did not actually know of the condition; (4) that the owner failed to exercise ordinary care to protect the licensee from danger; and (5) that the owner's failure was a proximate cause of injury to the licensee.

In the present case, it is admitted by all that Erwin was a regular visitor to the Hales' house, that he had his own key to the house and came and went unsupervised, and that he was looked on as a likely son-in-law. He was clearly invited onto the property. Thus, it would appear that he should be defined as an "invitee."[3]

This is not, however, the case. In Texas, a "social guest" is classified as a licensee. As set out above, a host owes a social guest a duty not to injure him by willful, wanton or gross negligence.

All of the evidence in the present case shows that the decedent was invited onto the premises, but also shows that he falls into the category of a "social guest." In Texas, as a matter of law, he was a licensee. The trial court did not err by finding him to be a licensee.

Knorpp also contends that this conclusion is erroneous and that the trial court erred by rendering a directed verdict in the Hales' favor, because regardless of the decedent's usual status, a different one existed in this particular situation. She argues that because there was a discussion, at which the decedent was present, about cutting down the tree, because Reeda Hale had asked Erwin if he was going to help her husband cut down the tree, and because Erwin was going to be present at the bonfire, then the cutting of the tree was done for the mutual advantage (or benefit) of the decedent and the landowner. This, Knorpp argues, constitutes some evidence that the decedent was an invitee and that the trial court therefore erred by finding him to be a licensee as a matter of law.

In determining whether an individual is an invitee or a licensee, the cases typically use the language "mutual benefit" or "mutual advantage." Knorpp argues that this term stretches so far as to include an intangible benefit, such as having the opportunity to attend or conduct the New Year's Eve bonfire.

The concept behind this language was originally brought into Texas cases as a paraphrase of the predecessor of Restatement (Second) of Torts §332 (1965). *Carlisle v. J. Weingarten, Inc.*, 137 Tex. 220, 152 S.W.2d 1073, 1076 (1941). In *Carlisle*, the Court discussed an invitee in terms of business-related ventures exclusively, as discussed in the Restatement. Later cases discussed the necessity of determining who qualified as an invitee and cited to the Restatement and cases applying the Restatement concepts. However, instead of using the more explicit terminology contained in Section 332[6] to determine whether a person was an invitee, the courts instead looked to see whether an entry was one by a person invited and to the "mutual advantage" of both parties. . . .

---

[3] The difficulty in applying this area of law to social guests is addressed by the Restatement as follows:

Some confusion has resulted from the fact that, although a social guest normally is invited, and even urged to come, he is not an "invitee," within the legal meaning of that term, as stated in §332. He does not come as a member of the public upon premises held open to the public for that purpose, and he does not enter for a purpose directly or indirectly connected with business dealings with the possessor. The use of the premises is extended to him merely as a personal favor to him. The explanation usually given by the courts for the classification of social guests as licensees is that there is a common understanding that the guest is expected to take the premises as the possessor himself uses them, and does not expect and is not entitled to expect that they will be prepared for his reception, or that precautions will be taken for his safety in any manner in which the possessor does not prepare or take precautions for his own safety, or that of the members of his family.

[6] Restatement (Second) of Torts §332 (1965) defines invitee:

(1) An invitee is either a public invitee or a business visitor.

(2) A public invitee is a person who is invited to enter or remain on land as a member of the public for a purpose for which the land is held open to the public.

(3) A business visitor is a person who is invited to enter or remain on land for a purpose directly or indirectly connected with business dealings with the possessor of the land.

It appears that the formula set out by the Restatement for analysis of invitee/licensee/trespasser status was adopted for use in Texas by *Carlisle* ... and that it remains the proper analysis to apply.

The decedent was a social guest of the landowners. He was not expecting payment for cutting down the tree, and the evidence is that no one asked him personally to do so, but that he volunteered to do so. There was no business relationship or dealing in existence or contemplated between the decedent and the landowner, and it is unquestioned that the land was not open to the public. Accordingly, as a matter of law, the decedent was not an invitee, but was a licensee on this particular occasion, and the trial court did not err by so holding.

Knorpp also argues that, in the alternative, there was evidence that the dead tree presented an unreasonable risk of harm and that there is at least some evidence that the landowners were negligent in failing to warn of the danger involved in cutting down the tree. This contention is based upon Knorpp's contention that the landowners were aware of the risk of harm and failed to use reasonable care to reduce the risk. This analysis is applied when the claimant is in the status of an invitee. We have concluded that the decedent was a licensee; thus, the analysis does not apply to the present case. Even if we analyze this argument as an attempt to show liability for a licensee, the attempt fails on several grounds.

In the present case, the undisputed evidence is that the decedent had worked with his father trimming and felling trees and that he had at least a passing acquaintance with the dangers involved. The undisputed evidence also shows that the landowners were unaware of any special dangers involved in cutting down a dead tree. Thus, the evidence shows that the licensee was aware of the danger involved in the action that he intentionally undertook.

The evidence also shows that the tree itself was not a dangerous condition. The worry stated by the landowners was that if they burned it in the bonfire, it would fall on someone. Cutting the tree was the act that caused the danger. . . .

In summary, the condition did not exist until Erwin began cutting the tree, thus, it was not a "condition of the premises"; the owner did not know that the licensee was creating a dangerous condition; and the licensee was the one creating the condition. In light of those facts, there was nothing for the landowner to warn the licensee about, because no dangerous condition existed until it was created by the licensee and, therefore, no duty to warn was shown by the evidence.

The judgment is affirmed.

NOTES TO KNORPP v. HALE

1. *Degree of Care.* In *Knorpp*, the court describes the duty owed to a licensee by stating that a landowner must not injure the licensee by willful, wanton, or grossly negligent conduct and must use reasonable care to warn about or to make reasonably safe a dangerous condition that the owner knows and the licensee did not know. This formulation does not require a landowner to make reasonable inspections of the land for the licensee, and it protects a landowner from liability even in a situation where the landowner's ignorance of a danger was unreasonable.

2. *Active Conduct on the Land.* Some states modify the duty owed to licensees by holding that landowners owe licensees a duty of reasonable care when they conduct activities on their land. For example, in Hoffman v. Planters Gin Co., 358 So. 2d 1008

(Miss. 1978), the court held that the defendant was required to exercise reasonable care to protect non-employees who were allowed to come into the vicinity of machinery that loaded cotton seeds into trucks.

3. *Public Invitees.* In addition to the category of business invitees discussed in *Knorpp*, many courts recognize the category of public invitees. See Restatement (Second) §332, cited in footnote 6 of *Knorpp*: "A public invitee is a person who is invited to enter or remain on the land as a member of the public for a purpose for which the land is held open to the public." A person need not pay any benefit to the landowner to be a public invitee. The landowner owes the same standard of care to public and business invitees.

Problem
Cooperation and Invitee Status

In a region where farmers produced fruit and needed to pack the fruit in boxes, farmers customarily sold boxes to each other when one farmer had more fruit than anticipated and another farmer had more boxes than that farmer needed. Would a farmer who was injured while picking up boxes in this arrangement be a licensee or an invitee? Is one characterization so clearly correct that a jury would have to adopt it, or would these facts present a case close enough so that either conclusion, if reached by a jury, could be the basis for a judgment? See Holzheimer v. Johannesen, 871 P.2d 814 (Idaho 1994).

Problem
Status of People at Church Services and Home Tours

Would you treat a person who attends a church service as the church's licensee or invitee? Would it matter if the person was a member of the choir? See Hambright v. First Baptist Church, 638 So. 2d 865 (Ala. 1994). Should a person who tours a private home as a participant in a garden club tour of homes, and who pays $25 to the garden club but nothing to the homeowner, be characterized as a licensee or an invitee? See Post v. Lunney, 261 So. 2d 146 (Fla. 1972).

Statute: ACTIONS AGAINST LANDOWNERS
Colo. Rev. Stat. §13-21-115(2), (3)(b), (5)(b) (2017)

(2) In any civil action brought against a landowner by a person who alleges injury occurring while on the real property of another and by reason of the condition of such property, or activities conducted or circumstances existing on such property, the landowner shall be liable only as provided in subsection (3) of this section. . . .

(3) . . . (b) A licensee may recover only for damages caused:

(I) By the landowner's unreasonable failure to exercise reasonable care with respect to dangers created by the landowner of which the landowner actually knew; or

(II) By the landowner's unreasonable failure to warn of dangers not created by the landowner which are not ordinarily present on property of the type involved and of which the landowner actually knew. . . .

(5) As used in this section: . . . (b) "Licensee" means a person who enters or remains on the land of another for the licensee's own convenience or to advance his own interests, pursuant to the landowner's permission or consent. "Licensee" includes a social guest. . . .

Statute: DUTY OF OWNER OF PREMISES TO LICENSEE

Ga. Code Ann. §51-3-2 (2017)

(a) A licensee is a person who:

(1) Is neither a customer, a servant, nor a trespasser;

(2) Does not stand in any contractual relation with the owner of the premises; and

(3) Is permitted, expressly or impliedly, to go on the premises merely for his own interests, convenience, or gratification.

(b) The owner of the premises is liable to a licensee only for willful or wanton injury.

Statute: STANDARD OF CARE OWED SOCIAL INVITEE

Conn. Stat. §52-557a (2017)

The standard of care owed to a social invitee shall be the same as the standard of care owed to a business invitee.

NOTES TO STATUTES

1. ***Alternative Definitions.*** The Colorado and Georgia statutes take different approaches to defining the term "licensee." Would the entrants specifically excluded in the Georgia statute fit within the Colorado statute's definition? How do these two definitions promote resolution of difficult cases, such as those concerning churchgoers or participants in social club meetings?

2. ***Classifying Social Guests.*** As indicated in footnote 3 of *Knorpp*, social guests usually meet the definition of "licensee." In a few states, however, modern decisions define social guests as invitees or classify them as licensees but hold that they are entitled to the same care as an invitee. See, e.g., Burrell v. Meads, 569 N.E.2d 637 (Ind. 1991) (treating social guests as invitees), and Wood v. Camp, 284 So. 2d 691 (Fla. 1973) (calling social guests "licensees by invitation" and applying a duty is to use reasonable care). The Connecticut statute is an example of this approach.

RICHARDSON v. THE COMMODORE, INC.

599 N.W.2d 693 (Iowa 1999)

Ternus, J.

Appellant, Russell Richardson, was injured at a bar owned and operated by the defendants/appellees when a portion of the ceiling fell on him. His suit against the defendants was dismissed on their motion for summary judgment. The court of appeals affirmed. On further review, we find sufficient evidence to create a jury question on Richardson's premises liability claim. Therefore, we vacate the court of appeals decision and reverse the judgment of the district court, remanding for further proceedings. . . .

The accident giving rise to this action occurred on September 12, 1994. While shooting pool at the bar on that date, Richardson was suddenly struck by falling plaster. Richardson thereafter brought this action against the defendants to recover damages for his physical injuries. Richardson's claim was based on a theory of premises liability. He alleged that he was a business invitee and the collapse of the ceiling and his resulting injuries were caused by the defendants' negligence in failing to maintain the premises in a reasonably safe condition.

The record shows that the building that housed The Commodore Tap was built in 1913. Ralph and Betty Hauerwas acquired the building in 1982, and subsequently moved their tavern business into it. The tavern was on the first floor of this two-story building. Prior to opening for business, the Hauerwases contracted with Wayne Blumer to repair portions of the plaster ceiling of the first floor where the wood lath had been exposed by the removal of some partition walls. Blumer did not notice any signs of damage to or other problems with the plaster ceiling at the time of his repairs.

In 1985, the Hauerwases installed a drop ceiling on the first floor of the building to improve the efficiency of heating and cooling the premises. They did not notice any problems with the plaster ceiling at that time. Between 1985 and the date of the accident in 1994, the Hauerwases did not inspect the plaster ceiling, were unaware of any problems in that ceiling, and made no repairs to it.

It is undisputed that Richardson was struck by a portion of the original (1913) plaster ceiling when the plaster separated from the lath and fell through the drop ceiling. Blumer repaired the plaster ceiling after its collapse in 1994. He estimated that a piece of ceiling measuring two feet by five feet fell. This piece was not close to the areas he had repaired in 1982. Blumer testified that the ceiling collapsed due to its age and the effect, over time, of vibration from heavy traffic on the adjoining street. He thought this particular area of the ceiling may have fallen off because it was thicker than the rest of the plaster ceiling. While making the repairs in 1994, Blumer inspected the remainder of the plaster ceiling by looking through the drop ceiling where the tiles had been pushed off by falling plaster, and using a spotlight to view whether the plaster was sagging in any other areas.

As noted above, Richardson's suit is based on a theory of premises liability. The district court granted the defendants' motion for summary judgment, holding there was no evidence they knew or should have known of the dangerous condition of the plaster ceiling. Richardson's appeal was transferred to the court of appeals. That court affirmed, and we granted Richardson's application for further review. . . .

The general rule applicable to the liability of possessors of land [to invitees] for injuries caused by conditions on the land is found in the Restatement (Second) of Torts:

A possessor of land is subject to liability for physical harm caused to his invitees by a condition on the land if, but only if, he

(a) knows or by the exercise of reasonable care would discover the condition, and should realize that it involves an unreasonable risk of harm to such invitees, and

(b) should expect that they will not discover or realize the danger, or will fail to protect themselves against it, and

(c) fails to exercise reasonable care to protect them against the danger.

Restatement (Second) of Torts §343, at 215-16 (1965). The parties do not dispute Richardson's status as an invitee nor the defendants' status as possessors of the land. The dispute in this case centers on the requirement that the defendants know of the dangerous condition or by the exercise of reasonable care should have known of the condition.

Although Richardson does not contend that the defendants had actual knowledge of the condition of the plaster ceiling, he argues that this knowledge should be imputed to them because the defendants created the dangerous condition by installing the drop ceiling. Alternatively, he claims that if the defendants had exercised reasonable care in inspecting the plaster ceiling, they would have discovered the condition of the ceiling. We discuss these issues separately.

Knowledge of a dangerous condition is imputed to a possessor of land who has created the condition that causes the plaintiff's injury. See Smith v. Cedar Rapids Country Club, 255 Iowa 1199, 1210, 124 N.W.2d 557, 564 (1963). For example, in *Smith*, the plaintiff was injured when she slipped and fell on a floor that had been waxed to an uneven and extremely slippery finish. There was no dispute that the defendant had applied the finish to the floor. We stated that when "the condition has been created by the owner[,] . . . he will not be heard to deny he had notice of it."

This rule does not, however, help the plaintiff here. There is no evidence that the defendants created the condition in the plaster ceiling *that caused it to fall*. The defendants merely installed a drop ceiling over the plaster ceiling, and there is nothing in the record to indicate that the drop ceiling contributed in any way to the collapse of the plaster ceiling. Therefore, knowledge of the dangerous condition in the plaster ceiling cannot be imputed to the defendants.

The defendants' duty of reasonable care as possessors of the premises extends to an inspection of the premises to discover any dangerous conditions or latent defects, "followed by such repair, safeguards, or warning as may be reasonably necessary for [the invitee's] protection under the circumstances." Wieseler v. Sisters of Mercy Health Corp., 540 N.W.2d 445, 450 (Iowa 1995) (quoting Restatement (Second) of Torts §343 cmt. b, at 216). The action necessary to satisfy this duty of reasonable care depends upon "the nature of the land and the purposes for which it is used." Restatement (Second) of Torts §343 cmt. e, at 217. "The duty of one who operates a place of entertainment or amusement is higher than that of the owner of private property generally." Grall v. Meyer, 173 N.W.2d 61, 63 (Iowa 1969). . . .

[T]he facts here could support a jury finding that reasonable care warranted an inspection. Although the plaster ceiling had not collapsed in the past, the defendants were aware of the age of the ceiling (it was built in 1913), and they should have realized that a falling ceiling posed a serious danger to their patrons. Even more important, an inspection was not an onerous and impractical burden. . . . [W]ith a ladder and a flashlight, the defendants could have conducted periodic inspections by simply lifting a ceiling tile in the drop ceiling and viewing the original ceiling, as Blumer did after the accident in 1994. . . . We think these facts . . . provide an evidentiary basis for a jury finding that the defendants' duty of reasonable care included inspection for hidden defects in the plaster ceiling.

Of course, a failure to inspect is relevant only to the extent such an inspection would have revealed the defect in the ceiling. See Restatement (Second) of Torts §343, at 215 (imposing liability only if the possessor knew or *would have discovered* the defect in the exercise of reasonable care). The record in this case shows that the plaster ceiling fell because the plaster separated from the wood lath. In addition, the record reveals that the cause of this separation was vibration of the ceiling over many years caused by traffic outside the building. We think the jury could make a common-sense inference from this evidence that the separation would not occur instantly, but that the plaster would gradually separate over time and begin to sag, thereby resulting in an appearance observable to someone looking at the ceiling. In fact, the repairman, Blumer, testified that was exactly what he was looking for when he inspected the ceiling after Richardson's accident — signs of sagging that would indicate the need for additional repairs. Therefore, we conclude that the plaintiff generated a jury question on whether the defect in the ceiling would have been discoverable upon inspection.

We think material issues of disputed fact exist as to whether reasonable care warranted an inspection of the plaster ceiling and whether such an inspection would have alerted the defendants to the dangerous condition of the ceiling. Therefore, the district court erred in ruling that the defendants were entitled to judgment as a matter of law. Accordingly, we vacate the court of appeals decision affirming the district court, reverse the decision of the district court, and remand the case for further proceedings.

NOTE TO RICHARDSON v. THE COMMODORE, INC.

Duty to Invitee.   The *Richardson* court adopts the Restatement's description of the duty owed by a landowner to an invitee. Unlike the duty owed to a licensee, the duty owed to an invitee covers a reasonable response to hazards that the landowner would discover by the exercise of reasonable care. Duty to licensees is usually limited to hazards that the landowner actually knows about, regardless of whether reasonable actions would have given the landowner more knowledge. If Russell Richardson had been a licensee, would the district court have been justified in awarding the defendant a summary judgment?

Problem
Duty to Invitee

Emily Hopkins, her son, and her daughter-in-law went to see a house that was for sale. The party had been invited by a salesperson employed by a real estate broker. The broker left them free to inspect the house unaccompanied. The kitchen of the house led up to a family room that was slightly elevated from the front portion of the house. On the same level as the family room were a powder room and laundry room. Ms. Hopkins waited on the upper level in the family room while her family viewed the patio and grounds. When Ms. Hopkins heard her son and daughter-in-law reenter, she attempted to join them in the foyer, where the staircase to the second floor was located. She proceeded down the hallway from the laundry room toward the foyer, unaware that a step led down from the hallway into the foyer. The floors on both levels and the step were covered with the same pattern of vinyl. According to Ms. Hopkins, the use of the same floor covering on both levels camouflaged the presence of a step. Not anticipating the step, she lost her footing and fell, fracturing her right ankle. What was Ms. Hopkins' status on the land? What standard of care applies? See Hopkins v. Fox & Lazo Realtors, 625 A.2d 1110 (N.J. 1992).

C. Specific Rules for Particular Hazards to Legal Entrants

For some recurring situations, specific doctrines supplement the general rules for duties owed to legal entrants on land. This section considers special rules for

(1) "slip and fall" cases where a plaintiff seeks damages for injuries suffered in a fall at a defendant's premises, (2) injuries due to natural or "open and obvious" conditions on land, and (3) instances in which a landowner may be obligated to protect an entrant from criminal conduct by a third party.

Nisivoccia v. Glass Gardens, Inc. examines certain pro-plaintiff rules for slip-and-fall cases. From the plaintiff's point of view in that type of case, ideal proof would be evidence that the defendant had known about a hazard and failed to remove it. This kind of *actual knowledge* of a danger might be established, for example, with testimony showing that the defendant or an employee of the defendant dropped something slippery on the floor. In most cases, however, plaintiffs are unable to produce testimony showing a defendant's actual knowledge of debris or objects on the defendant's floor. Tort law has responded by developing two doctrines. In one, a plaintiff may establish *constructive notice* of a hazard. A defendant will be treated as if he or she had actual knowledge of a hazardous condition if there is proof supporting the conclusion that the condition was present for a significant period of time prior to the plaintiff's injury. Another approach, focused on the *mode of operation*, treats a defendant as having actual knowledge of a hazardous condition if the defendant has chosen to operate an enterprise in a way that makes it likely that dangerous conditions will occur often. *Nisivoccia* describes one state's transition from the constructive notice to the mode of operation approach and considers how broadly to characterize a food store's "mode of operation."

For injuries caused by a hazard that was open and obvious or was the result of a natural accumulation (usually of water, snow, or ice), common law doctrines have moderated the obligations of landowners to licensees and invitees. Valance v. VI-Doug, Inc. examines whether wind, which caused an injury because it blew open a restaurant's door, could be treated as an *open and obvious* danger. It also describes connections between a natural accumulation and open and obvious danger doctrines.

Finally, the victim of a crime can rarely recover damages from the criminal, because the criminal's identity is sometimes unknown, and the criminal is unlikely to have resources adequate to pay a tort judgment. For this reason, crime victims sometimes seek to impose liability on others who are associated with the crime. Owners and occupiers of land have increasingly become subject to liability to invitees for conduct that contributed to an attack on an invitee. Seibert v. Vic Regnier Builders, Inc. is representative of modern cases treating this problem.

NISIVOCCIA v. GLASS GARDENS, INC.

818 A.2d 314 (N.J. 2003)

LaVecchia, J.

. . . The facts are straightforward. Approximately three feet from the entry of a supermarket checkout aisle, plaintiff slipped when she stepped on a grape with the heel of her right shoe. After she had fallen, she observed at least five other grapes within a three-foot diameter around her. No other grape had been squashed. She and her husband reported the incident to the employee at the checkout register and to the store manager.

Plaintiff filed this complaint in negligence against defendant Glass Gardens, Inc. doing business as Shop-Rite of Rockaway (the store). At trial, plaintiff and her husband testified to the circumstances involved in the slip and fall. The defense presented two store employees who were working on the day of the accident, a customer service clerk and the assistant manager. The customer service clerk recounted that he completed an incident report that day. However, the report failed to include any description of the accident area or what the post-accident inspection revealed. The store's assistant manager described the store's method of selling grapes and its floor maintenance program. The grapes arrive at the store from the wholesaler already packaged in clear plastic bags that are open at the top and have slits for air vents on the sides. Those bags are then placed in the produce area for display to customers. The manager acknowledged that grapes may fall onto the store floor during the process of being handled by either customers or store employees and that that tended to happen at the two locations where the grapes were handled most frequently, in the produce aisle and at the checkout area. . . .

At the close of testimony, plaintiff requested and was denied an inference of negligence. The trial court distinguished *Wollerman* [*v. Grand Union Stores, Inc.*, 47 N.J. 426 (1966)], reasoning that the accident here did not occur, as in *Wollerman*, in the supermarket's produce aisle, nor did it occur close enough to the checkout cashier to have constituted part of the self-service operation. The court concluded that a reasonable juror could not find that any specific mode of store operation created a significant risk of harm, and it refused to make the store a general insurer of customer safety.

Defendant was granted a directed no-cause verdict because plaintiff had not produced any evidence of the store's actual or constructive notice of a dangerous condition. The Appellate Division affirmed in an unpublished opinion, and we granted certification.

Business owners owe to invitees a duty of reasonable or due care to provide a safe environment for doing that which is within the scope of the invitation. . . . Ordinarily an injured plaintiff asserting a breach of that duty must prove, as an element of the cause of action, that the defendant had actual or constructive knowledge of the dangerous condition that caused the accident. Equitable considerations have, however, motivated this Court to relieve the plaintiff of proof of that element in circumstances in which, as a matter of probability, a dangerous condition is likely to occur as the result of the nature of the business, the property's condition, or a demonstrable pattern of conduct or incidents. In those circumstances, we have accorded the plaintiff an inference of negligence, imposing on the defendant the obligation to come forward with rebutting proof that it had taken prudent and reasonable steps to avoid the potential hazard.

We first articulated that modification of the cause of action in *Bozza v. Vornado, Inc.*, 42 N.J. 355, 359-60 (1964). . . . In *Bozza*, the plaintiff, when leaving the counter of a self-service cafeteria, claimed to have slipped on a sticky, slimy substance on the littered and dirty floor. We pointed out that spillage by customers was a hazard inherent in that type of business operation from which the owner is obliged to protect its patrons, and we held that when it is the nature of the business that creates the hazard, the inference of negligence thus raised shifts the burden to the defendant to "negate the inference by submitting evidence of due care." We further addressed the mode-of-operation rule in *Wollerman*, in which the plaintiff had slipped on a string bean in the produce aisle of a supermarket. We explained in *Wollerman* that the defendant's self-service method of operation required it to anticipate the hazard of produce falling to the ground from open bins because of the carelessness of either customers or employees, imposing upon the defendant the obligation to use reasonable measures promptly to detect and remove such hazards in order to avoid the inference that it was at fault.

Our courts have adhered to the mode-of-operation rule since *Wollerman* . . . and it has been incorporated as well into the *Model Jury Charges (Civil)*, §5.24B-11 Duty Owed as to Condition of Premises (1970). The Model Charge correctly states the rule that when a substantial risk of injury is inherent in a business operator's method of doing business, the plaintiff is relieved of showing actual or constructive notice of the dangerous condition. The plaintiff is entitled to an inference of negligence, shifting the burden of production to the defendant, who may avoid liability if it shows that it did "all that a reasonably prudent man would do in the light of the risk of injury [the] operation entailed." . . . The ultimate burden of persuasion remains, of course, with the plaintiff.

Applying the foregoing principles to the matter before us, we conclude that plaintiff was entitled to a mode-of-operation instruction to the jury.

A location within a store where a customer handles loose items during the process of selection and bagging from an open display obviously is a self-service area. A mode-of-operation charge is appropriate when loose items that are reasonably likely to fall to the ground during customer or employee handling would create a dangerous condition. In *Wollerman*, the location was the produce area. But the same considerations apply to the checkout area of a supermarket. Customers typically unload their carts onto the checkout counter. Droppage and spillage during that process are foreseeable. Indeed, because of the way the grapes were packaged, they could easily have fallen out when accidentally tipped or upended in a shopping cart anywhere in the store. The open and air-vented bags invited spillage. It was foreseeable then that loose grapes would fall to the ground near the checkout area, creating a dangerous condition for an unsuspecting customer walking in that area.

The trial court took a restrictive view of what constituted the "checkout area," concluding that the location of the wayward grapes was too far removed from the actual cashier counter to be attributable to a mode of operation involving the handling of goods by customers and employees during checkout. The grape on which plaintiff slipped was approximately three feet from the entry to the checkout lanes. The trial court's analysis, however, failed to take into account the fact that grapes can be expected to roll if they fall to the ground. Thus, the dangerous condition caused by stray grapes in the entry area of the checkout lanes was a foreseeable risk posed by the store's mode of operation. "Mode of operation" here includes the customer's necessary handling of goods when checking out, an employee's handling of goods during checkout, and the characteristics of the goods themselves and the way in which they are packaged.

Given the combination of factors, negligence shall be inferred requiring the store to come forward and produce evidence of its due care. The question of the adequacy of the store's efforts to exercise due care was one for the jury. It was error for the court to have entered a directed verdict for defendant. Plaintiff was entitled to have the jury decide the issue of negligence.

The judgment of the Appellate Division is reversed and the matter remanded for further proceedings.

NOTES TO NISIVOCCIA v. GLASS GARDENS, INC.

1. *Comparing Constructive Notice and Mode of Operation Theories.* The plaintiff in *Nisivoccia* sought to establish the defendant's obligation to act reasonably with respect to the fallen grape by relying on the mode of operation rule. That effort required proof that the store operator had chosen a style of business that made the presence of debris on the floor reasonably likely. The prior New Jersey approach, the constructive notice doctrine, would have required proof that the particular grape on which the plaintiff slipped had been present on the floor for a significant period of time prior to the accident.

2. *Time Lapse for Constructive Notice.* In establishing constructive notice, plaintiffs typically introduce evidence describing the condition of the thing that caused the accident. For judicial treatment of bananas, the paradigm of slippery objects, see Anjou v. Boston Elevated Railway Co., 208 Mass. 273, 94 N.E. 386 (1911) (dry, gritty, black, flattened banana peel could have been found by jury to have been on ground long enough to establish constructive notice); Joye v. Great Atlantic & Pacific Tea Co., 405 F.2d 464 (4th Cir. 1968) (dark banana with dirt and sand on it could not support finding of constructive notice, because it could have been on the defendant's floor for "30 seconds or 3 days").

The following Florida cases indicate other types of proof plaintiffs typically use in the effort to establish constructive notice: Ramey v. Winn-Dixie Montgomery, Inc., 710 So. 2d 191, 192-193 (Fla. Dist. App. 1998) (partially melted butter with lumps in it); Woods v. Winn-Dixie Stores, Inc., 621 So. 2d 710, 711 (Fla. Dist. App. 1993) (unidentified substance described as "very dirty," "trampled," "containing skid marks, scuff marks," and "chewed up"); Ress v. X-tra Super Food Ctrs., Inc., 616 So. 2d 110, 110-111 (Fla. Dist. App. 1993) (substance that appeared to be sauerkraut was "gunky, dirty and wet and black"); Hodges v. Walsh, 553 So. 2d 221, 222 (Fla. Dist. App. 1989) (sticky substance in bowling alley had dried); Washington v. Pic-N-Pay Supermarket, Inc., 453 So. 2d 508, 509 (Fla. Dist. App. 1984) (collard green leaves were "old, nasty" and "looked like they had been there for quite a while"); Camina v. Parliament Ins. Co., 417 So. 2d 1093, 1094 (Fla. Dist. App. 1982) (ice cream was thawed, dirty, and splattered).

3. *Required Proof of Unreasonable Conduct?* Under the Restatement's formulation, to be entitled to damages from a land occupier in a slip-and-fall case, an invitee must establish that the defendant knew or should have known about a risk, that the defendant should have expected that an invitee would not protect himself or herself from it, and that the defendant failed to exercise reasonable care to protect the invitee from the danger. See Restatement (Second) of Torts §343. This last element might call for proof about the defendant's response to a hazard. In constructive notice cases, courts generally treat proof that a hazard was present long enough to have been noticed as equivalent to proof that the defendant's non-response to the hazard was unreasonable. In theory, a full description of the circumstances surrounding the non-response could support a jury finding in favor of a defendant. See J.C. Penney Co. v. Sumrall, 318 So. 2d 829 (Miss. 1975) (even when a defendant store operator had actual notice of a dangerous condition, an employee's choice to call for help rather than to attend to it personally was reasonable as a matter of law).

4. *Shifting the Burden of Proof in Slip-and-Fall Cases.* Some jurisdictions have incorporated a shift in the burden of proof while adopting the mode of operation doctrine. For example, the Colorado Supreme Court has held that

> the plaintiff establishes a prima facie case of negligence when he presents evidence that the nature of the defendant's business gives rise to a substantial risk of injury to customers from slip-and-fall accident, and that the plaintiff's injury was proximately caused by such an accident within the zone of risk. It is then incumbent upon the defendant to produce evidence that it exercised reasonable care under the circumstances. The ultimate decision whether the defendant exercised such care is to be made by the finder of fact.

Safeway Stores, Inc. v. Smith, 658 P.2d 255, 258 (Colo. 1983).

5. *Public Policy Basis for Pro-Plaintiff Slip-and-Fall Doctrines.* The Florida Supreme Court has adopted a burden-shifting approach for slip-and-fall cases. It supported this with the following ideas:

> [M]odern-day supermarkets, self-service marts, cafeterias, fast-food restaurants and other business premises should be aware of the potentially hazardous conditions that arise from the way in which they conduct their business. Indeed, the very operation of many of these types of establishments requires that the customers select merchandise directly from the store's displays, which are arranged to invite customers to focus on the displays and not on the floors. In addition, the premises owners are in a superior position to establish that they did or did not regularly maintain the premises in a safe condition and they are generally in a superior position to ascertain what occurred by making an immediate investigation, interviewing witnesses and taking photographs. In each of these cases, the nature of the defendant's business gives rise to a substantial risk of injury to customers from slip-and-fall accidents and that the plaintiff's injury was caused by such an accident within the zone of risk.

Owens v. Publix Supermarkets, Inc., 802 So. 2d 3165 (Fla. 2001). Most of these ideas would support either adoption of the mode of operation rule or of the version of the mode of operation rule that additionally incorporates a shift in the burden of proof.

Problem
Limits of the Mode of Operation Rule

A leaky roof in a supermarket caused water to collect on the floor, and a plaintiff slipped on the water. In a jurisdiction that has adopted the mode of operation rule, could a plaintiff's negligence claim be based on that doctrine? What evidence would be required in a traditional constructive notice jurisdiction? See *Wiltse v. Albertson's Inc.,* 805 P.2d 793 (Wash. 1991).

Problem
Proof Required for Constructive Notice of Mode of Operation Theories

In a case where you could prove the following facts, what additional information would you want to have? Would the plaintiff's chance of recovery be the same in a jurisdiction that requires proof of constructive notice as in a jurisdiction that has adopted the mode of operation rule?

The plaintiff entered a K-Mart department store as a business invitee for the purpose of shopping for children's clothing. While walking down an aisle in the children's clothing department, she slipped and fell near a round clothing rack. In the middle of the tile floor near the rack, there was an accumulation of a green liquid substance that was apparently avocado juice. She did not see the spilled juice, did not know how it got there, and did not know how long it had been there. After her fall, an unidentified K-Mart employee found a partially full can of avocado juice near the spill and told the plaintiff that she apparently had slipped on the substance. Later, the plaintiff overheard an unidentified K-Mart customer say a woman had passed through the children's clothing department accompanied by a small child who was carrying a can of avocado juice. The customer surmised the child disposed of the can by placing it on the floor underneath the clothing rack. K-Mart operates an in-store cafeteria and allows cafeteria patrons to remove food and drink from the cafeteria area and consume it on the shopping floor. K-Mart sells small cans of avocado juice in the cafeteria.

See Jackson v. K-Mart Corporation, 251 Kan. 700, 840 P.2d 463 (1992).

VALANCE v. VI-DOUG, INC.
50 P.3d 697 (Wyo. 2002)

KITE, J. . . .

On March 5, 1999, Mrs. Miles went to the Village Inn Restaurant in Douglas [VI-Doug] with her grandson. She recalled that it was a terribly windy day. Her grandson let her off in front of the entrance to the restaurant, and he parked the car. . . . Mrs. Miles claimed that, as she opened the door, a strong gust of wind caught it and caused her to fall to the ground. As a result of her fall, she suffered a broken hip that required surgery. The owner of VI-Doug testified that, three or four months prior to Mrs. Miles' accident, another woman was slightly injured under very similar circumstances. . . .

Mrs. Miles alleged VI-Doug was negligent in failing to provide a reasonably safe entry for its patrons and claimed damages for her resulting severe physical injuries. On October 16, 2000, the district court granted VI-Doug's motion for summary judgment concluding the same policy reasons that support the open-and-obvious-danger exception and the natural-accumulation-of-ice-and-snow rule, which immunize defendants from liability, applied equally to wind. . . . This appeal followed.

The elements a plaintiff must establish to maintain a negligence action are: (1) The defendant owed the plaintiff a duty to conform to a specified standard of care, (2) the defendant breached the duty of care, (3) the defendant's breach of the duty of care proximately caused injury to the plaintiff, and (4) the injury sustained by the plaintiff is compensable by money damages. In this case, we are required to address the first element: whether a duty exists. The application of the natural accumulation rule and the open-and-obvious-danger exception determines whether the defendant has a duty. This is a question of law that the courts normally determine. We have, however, recognized that in certain instances the question of the existence of a duty hinges upon the initial determination of certain basic facts and, in those circumstances, the initial determination of those basic facts is properly placed before the trier of fact.

"As a general rule, a possessor of land owes a duty to his business invitees to maintain his premises in a reasonably safe condition." Eiselein v. K-Mart, Inc., 868

P.2d 893, 895 (Wyo. 1994). VI-Doug, as the possessor of land in this case, relies on the recognized open-and-obvious-danger exception and posits that wind is like a natural accumulation of ice or snow in that it is a force of nature, an element of weather, and a naturally occurring phenomenon which a business invitee encounters off the business premises as well as when entering the business premises. The issues in this appeal are whether the natural accumulation rule and the open-and-obvious-danger exception are applicable to injuries resulting from naturally occurring wind. . . .

It is important to note that one of the underlying principles of the natural accumulation rule is that the dangers of natural accumulations are obvious; thus, the open-and-obvious-danger exception is contained within, and is part and parcel of, the natural accumulation rule. . . .

In this case, the district court concluded the same policy reasons exist for the element of wind as exist for the elements of ice and snow.

> The justification for the natural-accumulation rule comports with the factors to be considered in determining the existence of a duty. The magnitude of the burden on defendant to prevent injuries from snow or ice is great. . . . Natural winter conditions make it impossible to prevent all accidents. The plaintiff is in a much better position to prevent injuries from ice or snow because the plaintiff can take precautions at the very moment the conditions are encountered. Even if the plaintiff is unaware of the ice or snow he happens to slip on, he may be charged with knowledge that ice or snow is a common hazard in winter, one which he must consistently guard against.

Eiselein, 868 P.2d at 897-98. Therefore, the rules should naturally be extended to include the natural effect of the wind:

> "[A] proprietor is not considered negligent for allowing the natural accumulation of ice due to weather conditions where he has not created the condition. The conditions created by the elements, such as the forming of ice and falling of snow, are universally known and there is no liability where the danger is obvious or is as well known to the plaintiff as the property owner." Bluejacket [v. Carney, 550 P.2d 494], at 497 [(Wyo. 1976)]. The rationale underlying this rule is that "in a climate where there are frequent snowstorms and sudden changes of temperature, these dangerous conditions appear with a frequency and suddenness which defy prevention and, usually, correction; consequently, the danger from ice and snow in such locations is an obvious one, and the occupier of the premises may expect that an invitee on his premises will discover and realize the danger and protect himself against it." 62A Am. Jur. 2d *Premises Liability* §699 (1990).

Paulson v. Andicoechea, 926 P.2d 955, 957 (Wyo. 1996).

We agree with the district court's statement:

> Anyone who has ever lived anywhere in Wyoming knows that the wind and its potential severity are just as natural as the accumulation of ice and snow. The wind is an open and obvious danger. Probably the most common manifestation of that danger is in the opening of doors. The same policy reasons for the existence of the obvious danger rule and the natural accumulation rule apply equally to wind[.]

We conclude the terms of naturally occurring forces such as ice, snow, and wind can be used interchangeably in this court's social policy analysis. In general, the possibility of a sudden gust of wind, particularly in Wyoming, is an obvious danger foreseeable to anyone. A plaintiff is in a superior position to protect against hazards caused by wind at the moment it is encountered. A proprietor does not owe a duty of care to invitees to prevent the natural consequences of wind on his premises where he has not created or aggravated the naturally existing condition. . . .

Affirmed in part [and reversed and remanded based on issues omitted].

NOTES TO VALANCE v. VI-DOUG, INC.

1. *Variations on the "Open and Obvious Danger" Rule.*   In some jurisdictions, the open and obvious danger rule applies to all hazards that are open and obvious, whether natural or made by a person. A jurisdiction applying this version of the doctrine, for example, would reject liability to an invitee who slipped and fell over spilled milk in a grocery store if evidence showed that the milk was obvious to the victim. See Moore v. Albertson's Inc., 7 P.3d 506 (Okla. 2000). As described in *Valance*, Wyoming applies the doctrine only to conditions that arise from natural causes.

2. *Non-Natural Accumulations.*   As its name suggests, the "natural accumulations" rule protects landowners from responsibility for hazards such as ice, drifts of snow, and puddles of water. If a landowner's conduct intensifies risks related to these conditions, such as by directing a flow of water from one place to another, the landowner will ordinarily lose the benefit of the rule. See, e.g., Moore v. Standard Paint & Glass Co. of Pueblo, 358 P.2d 33 (Colo. 1960).

Problem
Liability for Invisible Natural Accumulation

Linda Brown was injured when she slipped and fell on a patch of ice outside the door of a real estate office. She filed suit against the premises' owners alleging that they were negligent in that they failed to clear the path of ingress and egress to their place of business and failed to protect the plaintiff from the slick condition of the path of ingress and egress. On summary judgment, the defendants asserted that the ice was the result of a natural accumulation; the defendants had done nothing to enhance the accumulation of the ice, and the plaintiff's injury was caused by her own negligence. The plaintiff responded with evidence tending to establish that the patch of ice was not visible upon due care. That evidence showed that on the day of the accident, the weather was cold and clear but there was no indication of any ice in the vicinity; the sidewalk appeared to be dry but there was a patch of clear and virtually invisible ice, which is known as "black ice"; and another person had slipped and fallen on the same patch of black ice earlier the same day and had informed an employee in the real estate office of the dangerous invisible patch of ice. Black ice is not an ordinarily perceptible hazard, nor is it within ordinary knowledge, such as an ordinary accumulation of ice and snow. Is the defendant entitled to summary judgment? See Brown v. Alliance Real Estate Group, 976 P.2d 1043 (Okla. 1999).

SEIBERT v. VIC REGNIER BUILDERS, INC.

253 Kan. 540, 856 P.2d 1332 (1993)

McFARLAND, J.

This is a premises liability action brought by a woman who was shot in the parking lot of a shopping center in an armed robbery by an unknown assailant. Liability is sought to be imposed upon the owner of the shopping center on the basis of negligence in not providing security for the area. The district court, utilizing the "prior similar incidents" rule of foreseeability, entered summary judgment in favor of the defendant. The plaintiff appeals therefrom. . . .

There are controverted facts relative to whether plaintiff Betsy Seibert had the legal status of a licensee or business invitee at the time she was injured. For purposes of ruling on the defendant's summary judgment motion, the district court, appropriately, held Ms. Seibert to be a business invitee. We shall do the same.

On April 2, 1989, Ms. Seibert was a passenger in an automobile owned and driven by her friend Michelle Brandes. At about 3:00 p.m., they drove to the Ranch Mart Shopping Center and parked in the subterranean parking garage. They got out of the automobile and reached into the back to retrieve their purses from the "cubby" area of the Corvette. Suddenly, each had an assailant. Where the two robbers had been prior to assaulting the women is unknown. Ms. Seibert had her handbag and a cola can in her hands. When confronted, Ms. Seibert screamed and either dropped or threw the can of cola at her assailant, who then shot her in the head. The robbers fled.

Ms. Seibert brought this action against Vic Regnier Builders, Inc., the owner of Ranch Mart, Inc., alleging it was negligent in not providing security for its patrons when the assault upon her was foreseeable. Specifically, she alleged that by virtue of past criminal activity in the shopping center's parking areas plus the nature of the underground parking area, including dim lighting by virtue of numerous burned-out fluorescent tubes, the defendant owed a duty to her as a business invitee to provide security. The shopping center had no security for its patrons — no warning signs, video surveillance, or security guards. The plaintiff offered expert testimony that the security, including the lighting, was inadequate and had appropriate security measures been in place, the attack upon her would probably not have occurred.

No evidence of prior crimes in the underground parking area was offered or suggested. There was sketchy evidence of crimes occurring in above-ground areas of the parking lot, as follows: (1) Prior to 1986, a car window was broken and personal property taken from the vehicle; (2) in 1986, an armed robbery occurred (details unknown); (3) in 1988, a strong-armed robbery attempt was interrupted when witnesses intervened, and a second armed robbery was thwarted when the victim resisted.

In granting summary judgment to the defendant premises owner, the district court stated:

> Maybe you can get the guys up in the appellate courts to tell me I'm wrong, but in this case, factually, there are a total of four crimes in the preceding two years upon which to base a conclusion that there would be a criminal act taking place in the future . . . .
>
> [B]ut I just don't know where to draw the line here.
>
> So, I'm going to find in this case that the criminal act was not foreseeable. . . .
>
> The effect of my ruling is, basically, even if there was no lighting, the criminal act was still not foreseeable. . . .

The plaintiff contends that under the "prior similar incidents" rule utilized by the district court, the court erred in holding that such prior incidents were insufficient to establish a duty owed. Alternatively, plaintiff contends the court erred in not applying the broader "totality of the circumstances" rule. The two rules are different methods for determining the foreseeability requirement of whether or not there is a duty owed by the premises owner to the customer injured by the criminal conduct of a third party.

In 62A Am. Jur. 2d, Premises Liability §513, p.69, it is stated:

> In accordance with the general rule (subject to some major exceptions) that an owner of premises has no duty to protect another from criminal attack, a storekeeper or proprietor of other commercial premises will not generally be held responsible for the willful criminal act of a third person which could not be foreseen or anticipated.

The difference between the two methods of determining foreseeability is stated in 62A Am. Jur. 2d, Premises Liability §520, p.77, as follows:

> Where the courts apply the "prior similar incidents" test of foreseeability, the occurrence of prior offenses on the premises is a key element of proof, and the proffered offenses apparently must be not only of the same type and nature as the offense complained of, but also must have occurred with some frequency. . . . Some courts have abrogated the "prior similar incidents" test in favor of the "totality of circumstances" test on the ground that application of such test contravened the policy of preventing future harm by forestalling a duty to safeguard until someone was injured; invaded the province of the jury to determine foreseeability from all of the facts and circumstances, and erroneously equated foreseeability of a particular act with previous occurrences of similar acts. Under such a rule, . . . foreseeability of criminal conduct may be established by the place and character of the business.
>
> Comment: This is in accord with the comment to the Restatement that a possessor of land has a duty to take precautions against criminal conduct on the part of third persons if "the place or character of his business, or his past experience, is such that he should reasonably anticipate careless or criminal conduct on the part of third persons."

The above reference to the Restatement is to Restatement (Second) of Torts §344 (1965), which states:

> A possessor of land who holds it open to the public for entry for his business purposes is subject to liability to members of the public while they are upon the land for such a purpose, for physical harm caused by the accidental, negligent, or intentionally harmful acts of third persons or animals, and by the failure of the possessor to exercise reasonable care to (a) discover that such acts are being done or are likely to be done, or (b) give a warning adequate to enable the visitors to avoid the harm, or otherwise to protect them against it.

Comment f to §344 explains that although the owner of the property is not an insurer of the land, there are certain circumstances in which liability is warranted:

> Since the possessor is not an insurer of the visitor's safety, he is ordinarily under no duty to exercise any care until he knows or has reason to know that the acts of the third person are occurring, or are about to occur. He may, however, know or have reason to know, from past experience, that there is a likelihood of conduct on the part of third persons in general which is likely to endanger the safety of the visitor, even though he has no reason to expect it on the part of any particular individual. If the place or character of his business, or his past experience, is such that he should reasonably anticipate careless or criminal conduct on the part of third persons, either generally or at some particular time, he may be under a duty to take precautions against it, and to provide a reasonably sufficient number of servants to afford a reasonable protection.

The plaintiff acknowledges there are no Kansas cases precisely on point. She likens the situation herein to those in Gould v. Taco Bell, 239 Kan. 564, 722 P.2d 511 (1986), and the earlier *Kimple v. Foster*, 205 Kan. 415, 469 P.2d 281 (1970). There are some significant distinctions between the *Gould/Kimple* cases and the factual situation before us. In both *Gould* and *Kimple* the criminal assaults occurred among fellow patrons of a restaurant and tavern, respectively. Explosive confrontational situations developed inside the business premises. The proprietors neither intervened nor called the police. . . .

In the case before us, the attack upon the plaintiff did not occur inside the business premises under the noses, so to speak, of the proprietors. The attack occurred in a parking lot. Neither the premises owner nor any of its employees were aware of the presence of the plaintiff or her attackers or that an attack was occurring. Neither failure to intervene nor to summon police is the basis of liability asserted herein, as was true in the *Gould* and *Kimple* cases. Rather, the liability sought to be imposed herein is predicated upon the frequency and severity of prior attacks against different patrons by presumably different attackers at different times and in different areas of the parking lot, plus the totality of the circumstances making the attack upon the plaintiff or some other business invitee foreseeable to the defendant, who then had a duty to take appropriate security action to prevent or make less likely the same from occurring.

Negligence exists where there is a duty owed by one person to another and a breach of that duty occurs. Further, if recovery is to be had for such negligence, the injured party must show: (1) a causal connection between the duty breached and the injury received; and (2) he or she was damaged by the negligence. Whether a duty exists is a question of law. Whether the duty has been breached is a question of fact. . . .

In determining whether there is a duty owed, we start with two general rules. The owner of a business is not the insurer of the safety of its patrons or customers. The owner ordinarily has no liability for injuries inflicted upon patrons or customers by the criminal acts of third parties in the business' parking lot, as the owner has no duty to provide security. Such a duty may arise, however, where circumstances exist from which the owner could reasonably foresee that its customers have a risk of peril above and beyond the ordinary and that appropriate security measures should be taken. In determining foreseeability, should the rule be limited to prior similar acts or include the totality of the circumstances? . . .

Perhaps the most commonly cited case accepting the totality of circumstances rule of foreseeability is Isaacs v. Huntington Memorial Hospital, 38 Cal. 3d 112, 211 Cal. Rptr. 356, 695 P.2d 653 (1985). The scene of the crime was the physicians' parking lot at a major hospital located in what was stated to be a high crime area. At the nearby emergency room parking area, numerous crimes had occurred, and security guards were employed therein. The emergency department was open 24 hours a day and attracted large numbers of drunks, drug addicts, and assorted violent criminal types. Dr. Isaacs was an anesthesiologist who was shot by an assailant near his car in the physicians' parking lot. There had been no prior criminal incidents in this parking lot. The California Supreme Court rejected the prior similar incidents rule and embraced the totality of the circumstances test for foreseeability. In essence, the California court held that this particular parking lot could not be isolated and foreseeability based just upon events therein. The lot was in a high crime area and adjacent to the emergency room parking lot where violent behavior was known to be a common occurrence requiring security. . . .

We believe that totality of the circumstances is the better reasoned basis for determining foreseeability. The circumstances to be considered must, however, have a direct relationship to the harm incurred in regard to foreseeability. Prior incidents remain perhaps the most significant factor, but the precise area of the parking lot is not the only area which must be considered. If the parking lot is located in a known high crime area, that factor should be considered. For instance, one should not be able to open an all-night, poorly lit parking lot in a dangerous high crime area of an inner city with no security and have no legal foreseeability until after a substantial number of one's own patrons have fallen victim to violent crimes. Criminal activity in such circumstances is not only foreseeable but virtually inevitable.

It is a sad commentary on our times that there is probably no shopping center parking lot that is likely to be crime free. Thefts of vehicles and from vehicles do occur, as well as purse snatches, etc. It is only where the frequency and severity of criminal conduct substantially exceed the norm or where the totality of the circumstances indicates the risk is foreseeably high that a duty should be placed upon the owner of the premises to provide security. The duty to provide security is determined under the reasonable person standard. Thus, the duty to provide security and the level of such security must be reasonable — that includes the economic feasibility of the level of security. In some instances, the installation of better lighting or a fence or cutting down shrubbery might be cost effective and yet greatly reduce the risk to customers. We note with concern the plaintiff's expert's references to the security not being adequate or being inadequate. This is a poor choice of terms. Presumably, the fact that the attack on the plaintiff occurred shows that the security was "inadequate." Had it been "adequate" the attack would not have occurred. The shopping center owner is not under a duty to provide such security as will prevent attacks on the patrons — such a duty would make the owner the insurer of his patrons' safety. Rather, if because of the totality of the circumstances the owner has a duty to take security precautions by virtue of the foreseeability of criminal conduct, such security measures must also be reasonable under the totality of the circumstances. Such an approach is consistent with the Restatement (Second) of Torts §344 (1965).

. . . We must reverse and remand the case for reconsideration under the totality of the circumstances test for foreseeability. The circumstances to be considered must relate specifically to the foreseeability of the attack on the plaintiff. We note that under the facts presented, it is unknown where plaintiff's and her friend's assailants were immediately prior to the attack. Thus, the district court will have to consider the claims of deficient lighting in the context of whether this factor played any role in increasing the risk of this attack upon the plaintiff.

The summary judgment is reversed, and the case is remanded for reconsideration under the totality of the circumstances test of foreseeability.

NOTES TO SEIBERT v. VIC REGNIER BUILDERS, INC.

1. *Required Showing of Foreseeability.* The court describes and chooses between the "prior similar incidents" rule and the "totality of circumstances" rule, which each deal with the foreseeability of crime. How do the rules differ?

2. *Degree of Required Foreseeability.* The court states that a duty to protect invitees from third-party criminal conduct arises where "the frequency and severity of criminal conduct" around the defendant's location "substantially exceed the norm,"

and when the risk of crime is "above and beyond the ordinary." Other courts have recognized a duty to act reasonably in response to possible third-party crime in instances when that crime is foreseeable. The test adopted in *Seibert* would make summary judgment available to defendants more often than a test based only on "foreseeability" because foreseeability or lack of foreseeability is rarely clear enough to preclude consideration by a jury.

Problem
Aberrant Conduct and Foreseeability of Crime

In Maysonet v. KFC, National Management Co., 906 F.2d 929 (2d Cir. 1990), the victim of an attack at a fast food restaurant sought damages from its operator:

> Late one May night appellant Jose Maysonet entered a Kentucky Fried Chicken restaurant in the South Bronx, New York. He had been there before and had often seen loiterers panhandling patrons. This night was no different. When Maysonet entered there were 20-25 customers present, including a panhandler who was bothering and harassing customers, asking them for money and attracting attention by "crazy laughing." After Maysonet had waited on line for 15 minutes, the panhandler approached him and asked for money. When Maysonet refused, the man stabbed him in the abdomen. The police and ambulance came and took him to the hospital where he eventually recovered, but the assailant was never found.

The trial court granted summary judgment to the defendant, on the ground that the plaintiff's evidence could not support a finding of foreseeable violent crime. With respect to that issue, the appellate court majority wrote:

> The panhandler's conduct up to the time he stabbed appellant was of the sort regularly seen nowadays in the streets and spaces where the public congregates in New York City and elsewhere. It may have been bothersome and annoying, but bothersome or annoying actions unaccompanied by assaultive or abusive conduct are simply too common an occurrence to alert a property owner that such person may commit a violent act.

What arguments would have supported reversal of the summary judgment? Would these arguments depend on the state's choice between the prior similar incidents rule and the totality of circumstances rule?

Perspective: Allocating Crime Prevention Resources

The goal of protecting people from crime is served by decisions that lead businesses to devote resources to safety measures. It would also be served by greater allocations of public funds to public police work. One way to decide which allocation method is superior would be to consider why the security measures are needed. If crime is widespread throughout the area of the defendant's business, perhaps that is best addressed by public resources rather than the business's security measures. On the other hand, if criminals are drawn to the specific location of the business or are in that general locale because of the business, perhaps the business should pay for security as part of its cost of doing business.

Another way to look at the problem is to consider how crime prevention resources are most effectively spent. If businesses are in a better position than the police to know what security measures are needed and when, perhaps they can most efficaciously reduce crime on a business-by-business basis. On the other hand, if increased public expenditures on police can reduce everyone's crime problem simultaneously, that might be the best way to allocate resources.

D. Liability to Tenants and Their Guests

A tenant is permitted to enter a landlord's land because of a commercial agreement between the tenant and the landlord for the mutual benefit of those two parties. Looked at this way, it might seem that tenants and their guests could be classified as invitees. The common law rejected that analysis. The common law's primary position has been that landlords ordinarily do not owe any duty of care to tenants with regard to the safety of leased premises. This general immunity has been limited somewhat with doctrines that identify specific circumstances in which a landlord might be liable to a tenant or tenant's guest for injuries related to the condition of leased premises. Borders v. Roseberry applies the common law doctrines in a case where a tenant's social guest was injured because gutters that would have kept rain from creating hazardous ice had been removed.

BORDERS v. ROSEBERRY
532 P.2d 1366 (Kan. 1975)

PRAGER, J.

This case involves the liability of a landlord for personal injuries suffered by the social guest of the tenant as the result of a slip and fall on the leased premises. The facts in this case are undisputed and are as follows: The defendant-appellee, Agnes Roseberry, is the owner of a single-family, one-story residence located at 827 Brown Avenue, Osawatomie, Kansas. Several months prior to January 9, 1971, the defendant leased the property on a month to month basis to a tenant, Rienecker. Just prior to the time the tenant took occupancy of the house the defendant landlord had work performed on the house. The remodeling of the house included a new roof. In repairing the house the repairmen removed the roof guttering from the front of the house but failed to reinstall it. The landlord knew the guttering had been removed by the workmen, intended to have it reinstalled, and knew that it had not been reinstalled. The roof line on the house was such that without the guttering the rain drained off the entire north side of the house onto the front porch steps. In freezing weather water from the roof would accumulate and freeze on the steps. The landlord as well as the tenant knew that the guttering had not been reinstalled and knew that without the guttering, water from the roof would drain onto the front porch steps and in freezing weather would accumulate and freeze. The tenant had complained to the landlord about the absence of guttering and the resulting icy steps.

On January 9, 1971, there was ice and snow on the street and ice on the front steps. During the afternoon the tenant worked on the front steps, removing the ice accumulation with a hammer. The plaintiff-appellant, Gary D. Borders, arrived on the premises at approximately 4:00 p.m. in response to an invitation of the tenant for dinner. . . . At 9:00 p.m. as plaintiff Borders was leaving the house he slipped and fell on an accumulation of ice on the steps and received personal injuries. There is no contention that the plaintiff Borders was negligent in a way which contributed to cause his injuries. After a pretrial conference the case was tried to the court without a jury. Following submission of the case the trial court entered judgment for the defendant, making findings of fact which are essentially those set forth above. The trial court based its judgment upon a conclusion of law which stated that a landlord of a single-family house is under no obligation or duty to a social guest, a licensee of his tenant to repair or remedy a known condition whereby water dripped onto the front steps of a house fronting north froze and caused plaintiff to slip and fall. The plaintiff has appealed to this court.

The sole point raised on this appeal by the plaintiff, Gary D. Borders, is that the trial court committed reversible error in concluding as a matter of law that a landlord of a single-family house is under no obligation or duty to a social guest of his tenant to repair or remedy a known condition whereby water dripped from the roof onto the front steps of a house fronting north, froze and caused the social guest to slip and fall.

At the outset it should be emphasized that we do not have involved here an action brought by a social guest to recover damages for personal injuries from his host, a possessor of real property. The issue raised involves the liability of a lessor who has leased his property to a tenant for a period of time. Furthermore, it should be pointed out that the plaintiff, a social guest of the tenant, has based his claim of liability against the landlord upon the existence of a defective condition which existed on the leased property *at the time the tenant took possession.*

Traditionally the law in this country has placed upon the lessee as the person in possession of the land the burden of maintaining the premises in a reasonably safe condition to protect persons who come upon the land. It is the tenant as possessor who, at least initially, has the burden of maintaining the premises in good repair. The relationship of landlord and tenant is not in itself sufficient to make the landlord liable for the tortious acts of the tenant. When land is leased to a tenant, the law of property regards the lease as equivalent to a sale of the premises for the term. The lessee acquires an estate in the land, and becomes for the time being the owner and occupier, subject to all of the responsibilities of one in possession, both to those who enter onto the land and to those outside of its boundaries. Professor William L. Prosser in his Law of Torts, 4th ed. §63, points out that in the absence of agreement to the contrary, the lessor surrenders both possession and control of the land to the lessee, retaining only a reversionary interest; and he has no right even to enter without the permission of the lessee. There is therefore, as a general rule, no liability upon the landlord, either to the tenant or to others entering the land, for defective conditions existing at the time of the lease.

The general rule of non-liability has been modified, however, by a number of exceptions which have been created as a matter of social policy. Modern case law on the subject today usually limits the liability of a landlord for injuries arising from a defective condition existing at the time of the lease to six recognized exceptions. These exceptions are as follows:

1. Undisclosed Dangerous Conditions Known to Lessor and Unknown to the Lessee . . .

. . . It should be pointed out that this exception applies only to latent conditions and not to conditions which are patent or reasonably discernible to the tenant.

2. Conditions Dangerous to Persons Outside of the Premises

The theory of liability under such circumstances is that where a nuisance dangerous to persons outside the leased premises (such as the traveling public or persons on adjoining property) exists on the premises at the time of the lease, the lessor should not be permitted to escape liability by leasing the premises to another. . . .

3. Premises Leased for Admission of the Public

The third exception arises where land is leased for a purpose involving the admission of the public. The cases usually agree that in that situation the lessor is under an affirmative duty to exercise reasonable care to inspect and repair the premises before possession is transferred, to prevent any unreasonable risk or harm to the public who may enter. . . .

4. Parts of Land Retained in Lessor's Control Which Lessee Is Entitled to Use

When different parts of a building, such as an office building or an apartment house, are leased to several tenants, the approaches and common passageways normally do not pass to the tenant, but remain in the possession and control of the landlord. Hence the lessor is under an affirmative obligation to exercise reasonable care to inspect and repair those parts of the premises for the protection of the lessee, members of his family, his employees, invitees, guests, and others on the land in the right of the tenant. . . .

5. Where Lessor Contracts to Repair

At one time the law in most jurisdictions and in Kansas was that if a landlord breached his contract to keep the premises in good repair, the only remedy of the tenant was an action in contract in which damages were limited to the cost of repair or loss of rental value of the property. Neither the tenant nor members of his family nor his guests were permitted to recover for personal injuries suffered as a result of the breach of the agreement. In most jurisdictions this rule has been modified and a cause of action given in tort to the injured person to enable him recovery for his personal injuries. . . .

6. Negligence by Lessor in Making Repairs

When the lessor does in fact attempt to make repairs, whether he is bound by a covenant to do so or not, and fails to exercise reasonable care, he is held liable for injuries to the tenant or others on the premises in his right, if the tenant neither knows nor should know that the repairs have been negligently made. . . .

[Section] d of [Restatement (Second) of Torts] Section 362 declares that the lessor is subject to liability if, but only if, the lessee neither knows nor should know that the purported repairs have not been made or have been negligently made and so, relying upon the deceptive appearance of safety, subjects himself to the dangers or invites or permits his licensees to encounter them. Conversely it would follow that if the lessee knows or should know that the purported repairs have not been made or have been negligently made, then the lessor is not liable under this exception. . . .

With the general rule and its exceptions in mind we shall now examine the undisputed facts in this case to determine whether or not the landlord can be held liable to the plaintiff here. It is clear that the exceptions pertaining to undisclosed dangerous conditions known to the lessor (exception 1), conditions dangerous to persons outside of the premises (exception 2), premises leased for admission of the public (exception 3), and parts of land retained in the lessor's control (exception 4) have no application in this case. Nor do we believe that exception 5, which comes into play when the lessor has contracted to repair, has been established by the court's findings of fact. It does not appear that the plaintiff takes the position that the lessor contracted to keep the premises in repair; nor has any consideration for such an agreement been shown. As to exception 6, although it is obvious that the repairs to the roof were not completed by installation of the guttering and although the landlord expressed his intention to replace the guttering, we do not believe that the factual circumstances bring the plaintiff within the application of exception 6 where the lessor has been negligent in making repairs. As pointed out above, that exception comes into play only when the lessee lacks knowledge that the purported repairs have not been made or have been negligently made. Here it is undisputed that the tenant had full knowledge of the icy condition on the steps created by the absence of guttering. It seems to us that the landlord could reasonably assume that the tenant would inform his guest about the icy condition on the front steps. We have concluded that the factual circumstances do not establish liability on the landlord on the basis of negligent repairs made by him.

In his brief counsel for the plaintiff vigorously argues that the law should be changed to make the landlord liable for injuries resulting from a defective condition on the leased premises where the landlord has knowledge of that condition. He has not cited any authority in support of his position, nor does he state with particularity how the existing law pertaining to a landlord's liability should be modified. We do not believe that the facts and circumstances of this case justify a departure from the established rules of law discussed above.

The judgment of the district court is affirmed.

NOTES TO BORDERS v. ROSEBERRY

1. *Landlord Immunity.*   The plaintiff in *Borders* was a social guest of a lessee. States that follow the doctrines described in the decision apply the immunity (with exceptions) to suits by tenants and members of tenants' families as well.

2. *Access to Information.*   Some of the common law exceptions to landlord immunity may be based on the ability of landlords and tenants to know about hazards. The exception for dangerous conditions known to the landlord and unknown to the tenant fits this analysis. Similarly, the exceptions for conditions that cause injury outside the land or that harm a member of the public also involve a landlord whose opportunity to know about the risk is greater than the opportunity possessed by the injured individual.

3. *Incentives to Inspect and Repair.* The exception to immunity for common areas (or areas under control of the landlord) can be justified on two grounds. First, the landlord is able to inspect those places easily and therefore to discover dangerous conditions. Second, if the law did not provide an incentive to landlords to maintain those areas, it is unclear how multiple tenants might organize themselves to maintain or repair those places. If landlords were immune and individual tenants had no incentive to take action, dangerous conditions would likely remain unremedied.

4. *Third-Party Crime.* As is true for land occupier cases in general, landlord-tenant cases have seen an increase in recognition of landlords' liability for crimes committed on their premises by third parties. The court in Walls v. Oxford Management, Inc., 633 A.2d. 103 (N.H. 1993), provided a typical statement of current law:

> We hold that while landlords have no general duty to protect tenants from criminal attack, such a duty may arise when a landlord has created, or is responsible for, a known defective condition on a premises that foreseeably enhanced the risk of criminal attack. Moreover, a landlord who undertakes, either gratuitously or by contract, to provide security will thereafter have a duty to act with reasonable care. Where, however, a landlord has made no affirmative attempt to provide security, and is not responsible for a physical defect that enhances the risk of crime, we will not find such a duty.

Problem
Availability and Application of Traditional Rules in a Non-Lease Setting

Pauline Burch, a 67-year-old grandmother, was hurt in a fall in an unlighted stairwell located in a University of Kansas dormitory. The stairwell connected the main lobby with a lounge used by residents and visitors. When Ms. Burch fell, she was attempting to visit her granddaughter, who lived in the dormitory. Ms. Burch sought damages from the university. The agreement between the granddaughter and the University of Kansas was set out in a "Residence Hall Contract." Under the contract, the university guaranteed space, meals, and other services in a residence hall, but did not guarantee a specific room in a specific hall. Payments under the contract were denominated installments, not rent. Assuming that the jurisdiction's treatment of licensees would not provide recovery for Ms. Burch, could she base a claim under any aspects of the duties owed by landlords to their tenants and tenants' guests? See Burch v. University of Kansas, 756 P.2d 431 (Kan. 1988).

III. Modern Approaches

Dissatisfaction with the process of resolving land entrant cases according to the three-category system of trespasser, licensee, and invitee has led many states to modify that common law doctrine. Landlord-tenant law has evolved in some states in a similar fashion, moving away from the doctrinal framework of a general no-duty rule accompanied by specifically enumerated exceptions.

A. Rejection of the Three-Category System

In some states, landowners now owe all entrants a duty of reasonable care. Other states have combined the licensee and invitee category to develop a system with two categories: lawful entrants to whom a duty of reasonable care is owed, and trespassers to whom a lesser duty is owed. Nelson v. Freeland discusses the advantages and disadvantages of these positions. Foster v. Costco Wholesale Corporation considers how adopting a general reasonable care duty may affect special rules, such as the open and obvious danger rule, that have been associated with the traditional three-category treatment of landowner cases.

NELSON v. FREELAND
507 S.E.2d 882 (N.C. 1998)

Wynn, J.

The sole issue arising out of the case sub judice is whether defendant Dean Freeland's ("Freeland") act of leaving a stick on his porch constituted negligence. Indeed, this case presents us with the simplest of factual scenarios — Freeland requested that plaintiff John Harvey Nelson ("Nelson") pick him up at his house for a business meeting the two were attending, and Nelson, while doing so, tripped over a stick that Freeland had inadvertently left lying on his porch. Nelson brought this action against Freeland and his wife seeking damages for the injuries he sustained in the fall. The trial court granted summary judgment for the defendants, and the Court of Appeals affirmed.

Although the most basic principles of tort law should provide an easy answer to this case, our current premises liability trichotomy — that is, the invitee, licensee, and trespasser classifications — provides no clear solution and has created dissension and confusion amongst the attorneys and judges involved. Thus, once again, this Court confronts the problem of clarifying our enigmatic premises-liability scheme — a problem that we have addressed over fourteen times.

. . . [W]e have repeatedly waded through the mire of North Carolina premises-liability law. Nonetheless, despite our numerous attempts to clarify this liability scheme and transform it into a system capable of guiding North Carolina landowners toward appropriate conduct, this case and its similarly situated predecessors convincingly demonstrate that our current premises-liability scheme has failed to establish a stable and predictable system of laws. Significantly, despite over one hundred years of utilizing the common-law trichotomy, we still are unable to determine unquestionably whether a man who trips over a stick at a friend/business partner's house is entitled to a jury trial — a question ostensibly answerable by the most basic tenet and duty under tort law: the reasonable-person standard of care. . . .

Although the common-law trichotomy has been entrenched in this country's tort-liability jurisprudence since our nation's inception, over the past fifty years, many states have questioned, modified, and even abolished it after analyzing its utility in modern times. At first, states believed that although the policies underlying the trichotomy — specifically those involving the supremacy of land ownership rights — were no longer viable, they nonetheless could find means to salvage it. In particular, states attempted to salvage the trichotomy by engrafting into it certain exceptions and subclassifications which would allow it to better congeal with our present-day policy of balancing land-ownership rights with the right of entrants to receive adequate protection from harm. . . .

Additionally, courts were often confronted with situations where none of the exceptions or subclassifications applied, yet if they utilized the basic trichotomy, unjust and unfair results would emerge. Therefore, these courts were forced to define terms such as "invitee" and "active conduct" in a broad or strained manner to avoid leaving an injured plaintiff deserving of compensation without redress. Although these broad or strained definitions may have led to just and fair results, they often involved rationales teetering on the edge of absurdity. For example, in Hansen v. Richey, 237 Cal. App. 2d 475, 480-81, 46 Cal. Rptr. 909, 913 (1965), under the trichotomy the court would not have been able to compensate the plaintiffs for their licensee son's drowning because the defendant did not maintain his pool in a manner which wantonly or recklessly exposed the decedent to danger. Therefore, to reach a just result, the court in *Hansen* read the phrase "active conduct" broadly to include the general "active" act of having a party. Under this strained reading, however, "active conduct" could plausibly exist whenever a landowner "actively" invites someone to his home. . . .

The first significant move toward abolishing the common-law trichotomy occurred in 1957 when England—the jurisdiction giving rise to the trichotomy—passed the Occupier's Liability Act which abolished the distinction between invitees, licensees and so-called contractual visitors. . . .

[In 1968], the Supreme Court of California decided the seminal case of Rowland v. Christian, 69 Cal. 2d 108, 443 P.2d 561, 70 Cal. Rptr. 97, which abolished the common-law trichotomy in California in favor of modern negligence principles. Specifically, the court in *Rowland* held that the proper question to be asked in premises-liability actions is whether "in the management of his property [the landowner] has acted as a reasonable man in view of the probability of injury to others." Moreover, the court [noted] that "whatever may have been the historical justifications for the common law distinctions, it is clear that those distinctions are not justified in the light of our modern society." The court continued by stating that the trichotomy was "contrary to our modern social mores and humanitarian values . . . [, and it] obscures rather than illuminates the proper considerations which should govern determination of the question of duty."

The *Rowland* decision ultimately served as a catalyst for similar judicial decisions across the country. Indeed, since *Rowland*, twenty-five jurisdictions have either modified or abolished their common-law trichotomy scheme—seven within the last five years.

Specifically, eleven jurisdictions have completely eliminated the common-law distinctions between licensee, invitee, and trespasser.

Further, fourteen jurisdictions have repudiated the licensee-invitee distinction while maintaining the limited-duty rule for trespassers.

In summation, nearly half of all jurisdictions in this country have judicially abandoned or modified the common-law trichotomy in favor of the modern "reasonable-person" approach that is the norm in all areas of tort law.

To assess the advantages and disadvantages of abolishing the common-law trichotomy, we first consider the purposes and policies behind its creation and current use. The common-law trichotomy traces its roots to nineteenth-century England. Indeed, it emanated from an English culture deeply rooted to the land; tied with feudal heritage; and wrought with lords whose land ownership represented power, wealth, and dominance. Even though nineteenth-century courts were aware of the threat that unlimited landowner freedom and its accompanying immunity placed upon the community, they nevertheless refused to provide juries with unbounded authority to determine premises-liability cases. Rather, these courts restricted the jury's power because juries were comprised mainly of potential land entrants who most likely would act to protect the community at large and thereby reign (sic) in the landowner's sovereign power over his land. Thus, the trichotomy was created to disgorge the jury of some of its power by either allowing the judge to take the case from the jury based on legal rulings or by forcing the jury to apply the mechanical rules of the trichotomy instead of considering the pertinent issue of whether the landowner acted reasonably in maintaining his land. . . .

Although the modern trend of premises-liability law in this country has been toward abolishing the trichotomy in favor of a reasonable-person standard, there are some jurisdictions that have refused to modify or abolish it. One of the primary reasons that some jurisdictions have retained the trichotomy is fear of jury abuse — a fear similar to the reason it was created in the first place. Specifically, jurisdictions retaining the trichotomy fear that plaintiff-oriented juries — like feudal juries composed mostly of land entrants — will impose unreasonable burdens upon defendant-landowners. This argument, however, fails to take into account that juries have properly applied negligence principles in all other areas of tort law, and there has been no indication that defendants in other areas have had unreasonable burdens placed upon them. Moreover, given that modern jurors are more likely than feudal jurors to be landowners themselves, it is unlikely that they would be willing to place a burden upon a defendant that they would be unwilling to accept upon themselves.

Another fear held by jurisdictions retaining the trichotomy is that by substituting the negligence standard of care for the common-law categories, landowners will be forced to bear the burden of taking precautions such as the expensive cost associated with maintaining adequate insurance policies. This argument, however, ignores the fact that every court which has abolished the trichotomy has explicitly stated that its holding was not intended to make the landowner an absolute insurer against all injuries suffered on his property. Rather, they require landowners only to exercise reasonable care in the maintenance of their premises. . . .

On a more practical level, the trichotomy has been criticized for creating a complex, confusing, and unpredictable state of law. . . .

The complexity and confusion associated with the trichotomy is twofold. First, the trichotomy itself often leads to irrational results not only because the entrant's status can change on a whim, but also because the nuances which alter an entrant's status are undefinable. Consider, for example, the following scenario: A real-estate agent trespasses onto another's land to determine the value of property adjoining that which he is trying to sell; the real-estate agent is discovered by the landowner, and the two men engage in a business conversation with respect to the landowner's willingness to sell his property; after completing the business conversation, the two men realize that they went to the same college and have a nostalgic conversation about school while the landowner walks with the man for one acre until they get to the edge of the property; lastly, the two men stand on the property's edge and speak for another ten minutes about school. If the real-estate agent was injured while they were walking off the property, what is his classification? Surely, he is no longer a trespasser, but did his status change from invitee to licensee once the business conversation ended? What if he was hurt while the two men were talking at the property's edge? Does it matter how long they were talking? . . .

The preceding [illustration demonstrates] that the trichotomy often forces the trier of fact to focus upon irrelevant factual gradations instead of the pertinent question of whether the landowner acted reasonably toward the injured entrant. For instance, in the real-estate agent hypothetical . . . the trier of fact would be focused on determining the agent's purpose for being on the land at the time of injury instead of addressing the pertinent question of whether the landowner acted as a reasonable person would under the circumstances.

Corresponding to this argument is the fact that "in many instances, recovery by an entrant has become largely a matter of chance, dependent upon the pigeonhole in which the law has put him, e.g., 'trespasser,' 'licensee,' or 'invitee' — each of which has radically different consequences in law." . . .

Lastly, we note that the trichotomy has been criticized because its underlying landowner-immunity principles force many courts to reach unfair and unjust results disjunctive to the modern fault-based tenets of tort law. For example, . . . the California Supreme Court noted that using the trichotomy to determine whether a landowner owed the injured plaintiff a duty of care "is contrary to our modern social mores and humanitarian values." *Rowland*, 69 Cal. 2d at 118, 443 P.2d at 567, 70 Cal. Rptr. at 104. Indeed, modern thought dictates that "[a] man's life or limb does not become less worthy of protection by the law nor a loss less worthy of compensation . . . because he has come upon the land of another without permission or with permission but without a business purpose." Id. . . .

Given the numerous advantages associated with abolishing the trichotomy, this Court concludes that we should eliminate the distinction between licensees and invitees by requiring a standard of reasonable care toward all lawful visitors. Adoption of a true negligence standard eliminates the complex, confusing, and unpredictable state of premises-liability law and replaces it with a rule which focuses the jury's attention upon the pertinent issue of whether the landowner acted as a reasonable person would under the circumstances.

In so holding, we note that we do not hold that owners and occupiers of land are now insurers of their premises. Moreover, we do not intend for owners and occupiers of land to undergo unwarranted burdens in maintaining their premises. Rather, we impose upon them only the duty to exercise reasonable care in the maintenance of their premises for the protection of lawful visitors.

Further, we emphasize that we will retain a separate classification for trespassers. We believe that the status of trespasser still maintains viability in modern society, and more importantly, we believe that abandoning the status of trespasser may place an unfair burden on a landowner who has no reason to expect a trespasser's presence. Indeed, whereas both invitees and licensees enter another's land under color of right, a trespasser has no basis for claiming protection beyond refraining from willful injury. . . .

Accordingly, plaintiff Nelson is entitled to a trial at which the jury shall be instructed under the new rule adopted by this opinion. Specifically, the jury must determine whether defendant Freeland fulfilled his duty of reasonable care under the circumstances. This case is therefore remanded . . . for proceedings consistent with this opinion.

NOTES TO NELSON v. FREELAND

1. ***Complexity of the Three-Category System.*** The court describes the three-category system as having been difficult to apply, as leading to irrational results, and leading to unfair outcomes. Considering two examples, the facts of *Nelson* and the hypothetical about the real estate agent discussed in *Nelson*, would a two-category system (trespassers and legal entrants) resolve these difficulties in those cases?

2. ***Effect of Combining Licensee and Invitee Categories.*** The court states that landowners will not be insurers of the safety of entrants, even under its newly adopted rules. Being an "insurer" in this context means paying for all harms suffered by legal entrants. What must injured land entrants prove to win cases that keeps landowners from being "insurers"?

3. ***Recreational Uses.*** Almost all states have statutes that limit the liability of landowners to people they allow to enter their land for recreational purposes without charge. The impetus for these statutes has been a desire to insulate these landowners from the effect of pro-plaintiff changes in their states' underlying landowner–land entrant doctrines. Typically under these statutes, landowners are liable only for intentionally or wantonly caused injuries regardless of any changes a state might make in its general definition of duties owed to licensees. A statute of this type is quoted in Note 1 to Sandler v. Commonwealth in Chapter 3.

4. ***Moral Rationale for Rejecting the Three-Category System.*** The court noted that the two-category system would be better than the three-category system because the three-category system led to lots of confusion. It also quoted a California opinion's statement that "a man's life or limb does not become less worthy of protection . . . because he has come upon the land of another without permission. . . ." Each of these ideas logically supports the court's decision to treat licensees and invitees equally. Do they each support the court's decision to continue to use separate rules for trespassers?

5. ***Effect on Outcomes.*** The same facts that lead to classifying a plaintiff as a trespasser or licensee or invitee might affect a jury's evaluation of whether a landowner had been reasonable in jurisdictions adopting a rule applying a single standard to people who would formerly have had different status classifications. A clear example of this would be jury evaluation of what care is reasonable on the part of a landowner toward a trespasser. Where a trespasser was unforeseeable, the reasonable care standard would probably demand very little care from a landowner. And there is less that a landowner can reasonably do to protect a licensee who merely has permission of the landowner to be on the land (to hunt, for instance). The outcomes of cases under modern approaches may be similar to the outcomes that the traditional rules would have produced.

FOSTER v. COSTCO WHOLESALE CORP.
291 P.3d 150 (Nev. 2012)

CHERRY, C.J.:

. . . In October 2005, Foster visited a Costco store in Henderson, Nevada, with the intent of purchasing paper goods and general groceries. While searching for trash bags in the paper goods aisle, Foster's left toe caught the corner of a wooden pallet, which was covered by a slightly turned box. Foster fell and sustained injuries. He subsequently sued Costco in district court, alleging that Costco was negligent in creating a dangerous condition and in failing to warn him of the existence of the dangerous condition. Foster claimed that Costco owed him a duty to maintain an establishment free of dangerous conditions, including exposed pallets throughout the aisles.

Foster's deposition was taken, and Costco then filed a motion for summary judgment, contending that the presence of the pallets was open and obvious and that it was not liable for injuries arising from an open and obvious hazard. According to Costco's summary judgment motion, it is undisputed that Foster was in the paper goods section of the warehouse shopping for, among other things, trash bags, when the incident occurred. Foster testified in his deposition that, as he entered the aisle, he saw approximately three pallets on the right side and two pallets on the left side. Each of the pallets had boxes on them. Foster observed a Costco employee moving boxes from the pallets onto the shelves. There were no barricades placed to warn customers or to prevent them from entering the aisle while the Costco employee was restocking the shelves.

Foster also testified that a slightly turned box was hanging over the edge of the pallet that caused his fall. Foster further stated that he was able to see some of the wood comprising the pallet in question and that he was aware that the subject pallet was obscured by a box. However, Foster claimed that he did not see the corner of the pallet. Foster then testified that he looked at the Costco employee moving the boxes, looked up at the displayed products on the shelves, and when he walked around the employee and the pallet, stepped around the slightly turned box thinking that he had bypassed the pallet. But "somehow [his] left toe caught on the corner of the pallet," and he fell. As a result of the accident, Foster sustained injuries to his left knee, right shoulder, and right-hand ring finger.

In opposing Costco's summary judgment motion, Foster argued that there were material questions of fact as to whether the dangerous condition was obvious, because even though he could see some of the pallet underneath the boxes, he could not see the corner of the pallet due to the way the box was positioned. Foster also asserted that even if the condition was obvious, there were further material questions of fact as to whether Costco was liable in creating or subjecting him to the peril.

The district court granted Costco's motion for summary judgment, finding that the peril created by the pallet was open and obvious to Foster, that the boxes partially concealing the pallet created notice to Foster of the potential hazard, and that Foster's testimony demonstrated his comprehension of the dangerous condition. Citing *Gunlock v. New Frontier Hotel,* 370 P.2d 682, 684 (Nev. 1962), the district court concluded that Costco did not breach its duty of care because under the circumstances, it had no duty to warn Foster or to remedy the open and obvious condition. Therefore, the court concluded that Costco's actions were not negligent. This appeal followed.

. . . With roots in English and early American common law, and most likely derived from the political power of landowners prior to the twentieth century, the open and obvious doctrine eliminates landowner liability to business visitors resulting from open and obvious dangers. . . . This court adopted this position in the case relied on by the district court.

The open and obvious doctrine was widely criticized by legal scholars and courts as being too harsh, however, and courts began to depart from it in the mid-twentieth century.

In 1965, the Restatement (Second) of Torts was published, recognizing this trend and modifying its assessment of the open and obvious doctrine so that "[a] possessor of land is not liable to his invitees for physical harm caused to them by any activity or condition on the land whose danger is known or obvious to them, unless the possessor should anticipate the harm despite such knowledge or obviousness." Restatement (Second) of Torts §343A(1) (1965). As a result, jurisdictions throughout the country have retreated from strict application of the open and obvious doctrine, departing "from the traditional rule absolving, *ipso facto,* owners and occupiers of land from liability for injuries resulting from known or obvious conditions, and [moving] toward the standard expressed in section 343A(1) of the Restatement (Second) of Torts (1965)." *Ward v. K Mart Corp.,* 554 N.E.2d 223, 231 (Ill. 1990) (listing cases from state supreme courts that have adopted the Second Restatement approach). . . .

Under the Second Restatement, a landowner should anticipate, and is liable for failing to remedy, the risk of harm from obvious hazards when an invitee could be distracted from observing or avoiding the dangerous condition, or may forget what he or she has discovered, and the landowner has "reason to expect that the invitee will nevertheless suffer physical harm." Restatement (Second) of Torts §343A cm. f (1965). This principle is known as the distraction exception to the open and obvious rule. For example, a landowner should anticipate that, in certain circumstances, store displays will distract customers and potentially prevent them from discovering and avoiding even conspicuous dangers. . . .

The general duty of reasonable care is the focus of the newly adopted Restatement (Third) of Torts: Physical and Emotional Harm section 51 (2012):

> [A] land possessor owes a duty of reasonable care to entrants on the land with regard to:
>> (a) conduct by the land possessor that creates risks to entrants on the land;
>> (b) artificial conditions on the land that pose risks to entrants on the land;
>> (c) natural conditions on the land that pose risks to entrants on the land; and
>> (d) other risks to entrants on the land when any of the affirmative
> duties . . . is applicable.

The duty espoused in the newest iteration is similar to, and includes, both the general landowner's duty imposed with regard to invitees in the Restatement (Second) of Torts section 343, and the "distraction exception" to the open and obvious rule reflected in the Restatement (Second) of Torts section 343A. However, the duty imposed in the Third Restatement is amplified, as it is extended to all entrants on the land (except for flagrant trespassers, *see* Restatement (Third) of Torts: Phys. & Emot. Harm §52 (2012)), not just invitees.[1] Thus, under the Restatement (Third), landowners bear a general duty of reasonable care to all entrants, regardless of the open and obvious nature of dangerous conditions. . . .

While the open and obvious nature of the conditions does not automatically preclude liability, it instead is part of assessing whether reasonable care was employed. In considering whether reasonable care was taken, the fact-finder must also take into account the surrounding circumstances, such as whether nearby displays were

---

[1] This court has already "abandon[ed] former principles of landowner liability based upon the status of the person injured on the premises, such as whether that person is a trespasser, licensee, or invitee." *Moody v. Manny's Auto Repair,* 110 Nev. 320, 331, 871 P.2d 935, 942 (1994).

distracting and whether the landowner had reason to suspect that the entrant would proceed despite a known or obvious danger.[2] . . .

. . . Costco is not free from liability under Nevada law solely because the danger of the pallet in its aisle may have been open and obvious to Foster. A jury could reasonably believe that Foster walked down the paper goods aisle without observing the corner of the subject pallet because the corner was obscured by a slightly turned box, which blocked it from his sight. Even if a jury finds the risk to be open and obvious, it must also decide whether Costco nevertheless breached its duty of care to Foster by allowing the conditions to exist and by permitting Foster to encounter those existing conditions; if so, the jury must further determine whether Foster was partially at fault under comparative negligence theories. Accordingly, viewing the evidence in the light most favorable to Foster, we conclude that genuine issues of material fact precluded summary judgment, as material facts remain as to whether Costco exercised reasonable care. . . .

NOTES TO FOSTER v. COSTCO WHOLESALE CORP.

1. *Abolition of Rules Arising from Status-Based Distinctions.* *Foster* illustrates the implications of abolishing status-based distinctions for land entrants. When negligence is the standard of care for all entrants and a jurisdiction has adopted comparative negligence, some prior rules related to the status-based distinctions may be anachronistic. This understanding has led some states to reject or limit the open and obvious danger rule. The New Mexico Supreme Court has stated:

> Simply by making hazards obvious to reasonably prudent persons, the occupier of premises cannot avoid liability to a business visitor for injuries caused by dangers that otherwise may be made safe through reasonable means. A risk is not made reasonable simply because it is made open and obvious to persons exercising normal care. Klopp v. The Wackenhut Corp., 824 P.2d 293 (N.M. 1992).

As the court in *Foster* explains, the obviousness of the danger is simply part of assessing whether reasonable care was employed.

2. *Flagrant Trespassers.* As the court in *Foster* noted, the Restatement (Third) of Torts §51 abolishes all classifications of entrants onto land, except for "flagrant trespassers." Section 52 creates a special class of trespassers to whom a lesser duty is owed:

> **§52 Duty of Land Possessors to Flagrant Trespassers**
> (a) The only duty a land possessor owes to flagrant trespassers is the duty not to act in an intentional, willful, or wanton manner to cause physical harm.
> (b) Notwithstanding Subsection (a), a land possessor has a duty to flagrant trespassers to exercise reasonable care if the trespasser reasonably appears to be imperiled and
> > (1) helpless; or
> > (2) unable to protect him- or herself.

Section 52 does not define "flagrant trespasser" but rather leaves the definition up to individual states. The Restatement does say "'Flagrant' is used here in the sense of

---

[2] "Known or obvious dangers pose a reduced risk compared to comparable latent dangers because those exposed can take precautions to protect themselves. Nevertheless, in some circumstances, a residual risk will remain despite the opportunity of entrants to avoid an open and obvious risk." Restatement (Third) of Torts: Phys. & Emot. Harm §51 cmt. k (2012).

egregious or atrocious rather than in its alternative meaning of conspicuous" and offers as examples the late night liquor store burglar who slips and falls on a wet floor and a late night trespasser who assaults a guest at a B&B, snatches her purse, and is electrocuted by an uninsulated wire.

Statute: IMMUNITY FROM LIABILITY; INJURIES OR DEATH OCCURRING
ON PROPERTY DURING OR AFTER THE
COMMISSION OF CERTAIN FELONIES

Cal. Civ. Code §847 (2017)

(a) An owner . . . of any estate or any other interest in real property, whether possessory or nonpossessory, shall not be liable to any person for any injury or death that occurs upon that property during the course of or after the commission of any of the felonies set forth in subdivision (b) by the injured or deceased person.

(b) The felonies to which the provisions of this section apply [include, among others,] the following: (1) Murder or voluntary manslaughter; . . . (7) any felony punishable by death or imprisonment in the state prison for life; (8) any other felony in which the defendant inflicts great bodily injury on any person, other than an accomplice, or any felony in which the defendant uses a firearm; . . . (18) burglary; (19) robbery; (20) kidnapping; . . . and (25) any attempt to commit a crime listed in this subdivision other than an assault. . . .

(f) This section does not limit the liability of an owner or an owner's agent which otherwise exists for willful, wanton, or criminal conduct, or for willful or malicious failure to guard or warn against a dangerous condition, use, structure, or activity. . . .

NOTE TO STATUTE

Abolition and Rehabilitation of Status-Based Categories.   As *Nelson* explained, in 1968, California eliminated all of the status-based classifications between trespassers, licensees, and invitees in the *Rowland* case. In 1985, the California legislature resurrected the distinction for some types of trespassers, reflecting an approach similar to that in *Ryals*. California Civil Code §847(b) details specific types of criminal trespassers to whom the standard of care described in §847(f) applies. Is the standard of care adopted in §847 identical to the standard of care described in *Ryals*?

Perspective: Efficiency of Common Law Rules

Courts that have abolished the three-category approach to landowner liability have usually believed that the traditional categorical distinctions were artificial and failed to reflect the genuine circumstances of real cases. In Jason Scott Johnston, *Uncertainty, Chaos, and the Torts Process: An Economic Analysis of Legal Form*, 76 Cornell L. Rev. 341 (1991), the author contends that the common law approach offers substantial efficiencies, arguing:

> My model suggests that a categorical rule will generate proper incentives when circumstances are either typical or extreme. In typical circumstances, the rule is correct. In extreme circumstances, actors will essentially ignore the rule and do

what is socially optimal. Moreover, because it is easy for a judge to accurately determine whether circumstances were extreme, exceptions to the categorical rule for extreme circumstances may be self-enforcing. At the very least such an exception does not significantly worsen the incentives. . . .

In some circumstances, such as when risk to a trespasser will be very likely and risk to an invitee will not, the rule's distinctions will not make sense. But the common-law approach makes several explicit exceptions to the no duty to trespasser rule in those cases. These exceptions are not only theoretically correct but also probably self-enforcing. One such exception imposes a full duty to use reasonable care toward an adult trespasser once she is discovered on the land. Another such exception treats a child as an invitee under the attractive nuisance doctrine when the trespasser is a child drawn to trespass on the land by something attractive upon it. Neither of these exceptions is easy to fabricate. Only children can invoke the attractive nuisance doctrine. Only a known trespasser is owed a duty of reasonable care. There may be some blurring around the edges of these exceptions, as in determining an upper age limit for the attractive nuisance doctrine or defining when a trespasser is known. But generally the exceptions are narrowly drawn, cover circumstances distinctly different from the usual case, and likely send substantially correct signals.

The *Rowland* court was apparently concerned not only about the tendency of the no duty to trespasser rule to inadequately deter, but also about the rule's tendency to make landowners behave too cautiously towards invitees. . . . One may argue that landowners may be too careful toward invitees because invitees are owed a full duty of care. With a full duty of care, the landowner's liability to an invitee is determined under case-by-case balancing. It is the uncertainty inherent in balancing, rather than the status distinction, that is most likely to cause landowners to be too careful toward invitees. And in this lies the great irony of *Rowland*, for if balancing is likely to overdeter in the case of invitees, it is likely to do so also with respect to trespassers and licensees.

B. Changes in Landlord-Tenant Doctrines

Landlord-tenant tort law has been affected in some states by the same trends that have influenced the evolution of landowner–land entrant law in general. Just as some states have abrogated the three-category approach to landowner–land entrant cases, some have rejected the detailed structure of the common law's landlord immunity system. Newton v. Magill is representative of cases implementing this change.

NEWTON v. MAGILL
872 P.2d 1213 (Alaska 1994)

MATTHEWS, J.

This is a slip and fall case brought by a tenant against her landlord. The superior court granted summary judgment in favor of the landlord based on the traditional common law rule that a landlord is generally not liable for dangerous conditions in leased premises. We hold that this rule no longer applies in view of the legislature's enactment of the Uniform Residential Landlord and Tenant Act, and therefore reverse.

In the summer of 1988, Darline Newton moved from Idaho to Petersburg to join her husband, Stan, who had moved to Alaska a few months earlier. In Petersburg, Stan Newton had leased a house in a trailer park owned by Enid and Fred Magill.

The front door of the house opened onto a wooden walkway about six feet long and five feet wide. This walkway served the Newtons' house. It was partly covered by an overhanging roof, had no hand railing, and no "anti-slip" material on its surface.

On November 20, 1988, Darline Newton slipped and fell on the walkway, breaking her ankle. The Newtons filed suit against the Magills claiming that the walkway had been slippery and hazardous for a considerable period of time prior to the accident, that the Magills had a duty to remedy its condition, and that they negligently failed to do so.

The Magills moved for summary judgment on the ground that the tenants were responsible for "any slippery conditions resulting from rain" under both the common law and the Uniform Residential Landlord and Tenant Act (URLTA) as adopted in Alaska, AS 34.03.010-380. The Magills argued, further, that they could not be liable under a latent defect theory because the walkway was not defective; further, even assuming that it had a tendency to become dangerously slippery when wet, this hazard should have been obvious to the tenants. The superior court granted the motion. The court ruled:

> Plaintiff's . . . claim is barred by Alaska's interpretation of the Uniform Residential Landlord [and] Tenant Act; AS 34.03.010-380. In Coburn v. Burton, 790 P.2d 1355, 1357 (Alaska 1990), the Supreme Court held that the landlord had the duty to keep common areas in a safe and clean condition, while at the same time, the tenant had a correlative duty to keep areas occupied and used solely by the tenant in a clean and safe condition. Here, the injury did not occur in a common area. The plaintiff states that she slipped and fell on the entryway, which was for the sole use of the plaintiff to enter the single-family residence. Pursuant to *Coburn*, the plaintiff had the duty to keep the entryway in a clean and safe condition. The defendant could not have breached the plaintiff's duty.
>
> Additionally, there is no evidence that the entryway was latently defective. The plaintiff even admits that no complaints were made to the defendant about the entryway.

The Newtons moved to reconsider. The court denied the motion in a written order which stated, after noting that the accident occurred in an area which the Newtons had a duty to maintain:

> Nevertheless, the Newtons argue that other circumstances involved here should require the burden to remain with the Magills. They argue that the entryway had latent or design defects. The fact that the entryway did not have a handrail, a gutter on the roof, or anti-slip material on the boards are not latent defects. These conditions existed in plain view and the Newtons knew these conditions existed. This is not a case involving a guest unfamiliar with the house or entryway. Mrs. Newton lived in the house for nearly five months before the fall. The Newtons used the entryway daily and it rained on numerous days before [the accident].

Even if the lack of a gutter and a handrail could be considered design defects, given the width of the entryway and its outside location, it is difficult to see, and the Newtons have offered no evidence to suggest, how these fixtures would have played any role in preventing the accident. Furthermore, the parties have not argued that the handrail or the rain gutters are required by any building code, ordinance or statute.

The anti-slip material is not a design problem, but is a maintenance problem. As noted above, the duty to maintain the entryway rests with the Newtons.

(Footnote omitted.)

From this order the Newtons have appealed. . . .

This court will uphold a summary judgment only if the record presents no genuine issues of material fact and "the moving party was entitled to judgment on the law applicable to the established facts." Wassink v. Hawkins, 763 P.2d 971, 973 (Alaska 1988). . . .

The Newtons describe Petersburg as a city where "constant drizzle" is "prevalent" except in the summer "when the rainfall is broken by periods of sun." They contend that the wet climate fosters the growth of a plant organism on exposed wooden boards, causing them to become dangerously slippery when wet. To guard against this tendency, the Newtons contend that permanent installation of some sort of anti-slip device is necessary. They argue that the general community standard in Petersburg is to install such devices.

Under the traditional common law rule governing the liability of a landlord, failure by the Magills to meet the community standard, assuming it exists, would be irrelevant. The traditional rule is that real property lessors are not liable to their tenants for injuries caused by dangerous conditions on the property. . . . There are exceptions to this rule of non-liability. If the dangerous condition is not reasonably apparent or disclosed, if it exists on a part of the premises which remains subject to the landlord's control, if the landlord has undertaken to repair the condition, or if the property is leased for a purpose which involves admission of the public, the landlord is subject to liability for negligence. None of these exceptions applies to this case.

The general rule of landlord immunity follows from the conception of a lease as a conveyance of an estate in land under which the lessee becomes, in effect, the owner for the term of the lease. As such, the lease was subject to the principle of *caveat emptor*. The tenant had to "inspect the land for himself and take it as he finds it, for better or for worse." William L. Prosser, Law of Torts §63 at 400 (4th ed. 1971).

The courts of a number of jurisdictions have begun to discard this common law rule, however, in favor of the principle that landlords are liable for injuries caused by their failure to exercise reasonable care to discover or remedy dangerous conditions. These courts have relied in part on statutory or common law warranties of habitability and in part on a belief that the rule of landlord immunity is inconsistent with modern needs and conditions. . . .

With the 1974 adoption in Alaska of the URLTA, the theoretical foundation of the traditional rule of *caveat emptor* has been undermined in this state as well. Landlords subject to the act have a continuing duty to "make all repairs and do whatever is necessary to put and keep the premises in a fit and habitable condition." AS 34.03.100(a)(1). This means that landlords retain responsibility for dangerous conditions on leased property.

The duty of a tenant is to "keep that part of the premises occupied and used by the tenant as clean and safe as the condition of the premises permit[s]." AS 34.03.120(1). This obligation exists as part of the same statute which defines the landlord's obligation to "make all repairs and do whatever is necessary to put and keep the premises in a fit and habitable condition." AS 34.03.100(a)(1). It follows that the legislature intended these obligations to be reconcilable. Reconciliation can be accomplished by interpreting the tenant's duty to pertain to activities such as cleaning, ice and snow removal, and other light maintenance activities pertaining to the safety of the premises which do not involve an alteration of the premises, whereas the landlord's duty relates to the physical state of the premises. This distinction is suggested by the phrase "as the condition of the premises permit[s]" in section 120(1). In context this must refer to the inherent physical qualities of the premises.

Our case law has also reflected the trend toward a more general duty of care for landlords. In Webb v. City & Borough of Sitka, 561 P.2d 731 (Alaska 1977), we rejected the prevailing common law view that a landlord's [sic landowner's] duty was controlled by the rigid classification of the person seeking compensation as a trespasser, licensee or invitee. Instead, we adopted a rule based on general tort law that an owner "must act as a reasonable person in maintaining his property in a reasonably safe condition in view of all the circumstances, including the likelihood of injury to others, the seriousness of the injury, and the burden on the respective parties of avoiding the risk." Id. at 733.

We now further expand the landlord's duty of care in aligning Alaska with the jurisdictions following Sargent v. Ross, 308 A.2d 528 (N.H. 1973), and thus reject the traditional rule of landlord immunity. . . . We do this because it would be inconsistent with a landlord's continuing duty to repair premises imposed under the URLTA to exempt from tort liability a landlord who fails in this duty. The legislature by adopting the URLTA has accepted the policy reasons on which the warranty of habitability is based. These are the need for safe and adequate housing, recognition of the inability of many tenants to make repairs, and of their financial disincentives for doing so, since the value of permanent repairs will not be fully realized by a short-term occupant. The traditional rule of landlord tort immunity cannot be squared with these policies. . . .

Our rejection of the general rule of landlord immunity does not make landlords liable as insurers. Their duty is to use reasonable care to discover and remedy conditions which present an unreasonable risk of harm under the circumstances. Nor does our ruling mean that questions as to whether a dangerous condition existed in an area occupied solely by the tenant or in a common area, or whether the condition was apparent or hidden, are irrelevant. These are circumstances which must be accounted for in customary negligence analysis. They may pertain to the reasonableness of the landlord's or the tenant's conduct and to the foreseeability and magnitude of the risk. In particular, a landlord ordinarily gives up the right to enter premises under the exclusive control of the tenant without the tenant's permission. The landlord's ability to inspect or repair tenant areas is therefore limited. In such cases "a landlord should not be liable in negligence unless he knew or reasonably should have known of the defect and had a reasonable opportunity to repair it." Young v. Garwacki, 380 Mass. 162, 402 N.E.2d 1045, 1050 (1980).

The trial court observed in this case that slipperiness can be regarded as a hazard which comes within the tenant's maintenance duties rather than the duties of the landlord to keep the premises safe. A tenant can throw sand onto wet and slippery boards. On the other hand, this method has limitations, especially in an area of near constant rainfall. A jury could find that a landlord in such an area should take any one of a number of steps relating to the physical condition of the premises which would prevent a board walkway from becoming dangerously slippery when wet.

In our view genuine issues of material fact exist as to whether the appellees breached their duty to Darline Newton to exercise reasonable care in light of all the circumstances with respect to the condition of the walkway. Determination of whether that duty was breached should be left for the trier of fact. We therefore reverse the trial court's grant of summary judgment in favor of the Magills and remand this case for further proceedings.

NOTE TO NEWTON v. MAGILL

Landlords as Insurers.   The *Newton* court raised the question of whether its holding would make landlords insurers — that is, liable to compensate tenants for all their injuries. The facts of the *Newton* case represent one circumstance in which the traditional rules would bar liability, but a reasonable care test might permit it. This could increase the liability of landlords. What proof required of the plaintiff under the new rule limits this liability?

Perspective: Best Cost Avoider

The respective obligations of landlords and tenants to take reasonable care to avoid harms illustrate a wide range of cases where two parties might each have been in a good position to recognize the risks presented by some activity, to evaluate whether there are reasonable precautions available to minimize those risks, and to take action to avoid the risks if reasonable precautions are available. The traditional rules take a categorical approach, listing situations in which the landlord rather than the tenant would generally be the best cost avoider. For instance, when the landlord but not the tenant knows of a danger, the landlord better appreciates the risk. When an area of the property is a common area like a shared stairwell, the landlord is in a better position than any single tenant to remedy unsafe conditions. When the landlord undertakes to make repairs, the landlord is in the best position to do so carefully. The evaluation of whether a landlord used reasonable care under the modern rules described in Newton v. Magill might also involve consideration of which party was in the best position to appreciate, evaluate, and avoid those risks. Under the modern rule, the "best cost-avoider" analysis is done by the jury on a case-by-case basis rather than by the categorical approach of the old rule. This raises the general question of whether the jury (using a case-by-case approach) or the court (using a categorical approach) is in a better position to do this analysis.

SPECIAL DUTY RULES

I. Introduction

For a number of recurring circumstances, special rules control the application of the general principle that one has a duty to use reasonable care to protect foreseeable victims from foreseeable harms. "No-duty" or "limited-duty" rules limit application of the foreseeability test. Examples of this type of duty rule are found in tort law's treatment of negligent infliction of emotional distress. Other special duty rules are routinized applications of the general principles for establishing a duty. *Primary assumption of risk* rules are an important instance of this type of rule. This chapter considers the most important special duty rules.

II. Duty to Rescue or Protect

Tort law does not generally require one person to rescue another from harm, despite the foreseeability of harm to that other person. A classic example involves a person who sees a heavy object about to hit someone on the head. From the point of view of tort doctrine, there is no obligation to act to avert the impending calamity, even if the action would be easy and the harm it might avert is enormous. To many, tort law's refusal to require helpful actions sometimes seems immoral. Perhaps in response to this feeling, exceptions to the no-duty rule have developed. In addition, tort law has special rules defining the obligations of those who choose to become rescuers.

A. General No-Duty-to-Rescue Rule and Its Exceptions

Lundy v. Adamar of New Jersey, Inc. applies doctrines originally developed for common carriers and innkeepers to an invitee's claim that a casino was obligated to provide emergency medical treatment. The opinion also deals with the issue of the degree of care a rescuer is obligated to provide. *Good Samaritan* statutes affect this issue. The *Lundy* opinion highlights the significance of these statutes.

LUNDY v. ADAMAR OF NEW JERSEY, INC.
34 F.3d 1173 (3d Cir. 1994)

STAPLETON, J.

Appellant Sidney Lundy suffered a heart attack while a patron at appellee's casino, TropWorld Casino ("TropWorld"), in Atlantic City, New Jersey. While he survived, Lundy was left with permanent disabilities. Lundy and his wife here appeal on a summary judgment entered against them by the district court. . . .

The district court held that TropWorld's duty is, at most, to provide basic first aid to the patron when the need becomes apparent and to take reasonable steps to procure appropriate medical care. Because the court found no evidence that TropWorld was negligent in carrying out this duty to Lundy, it granted TropWorld's motion for summary judgment. . . . We will affirm.

On August 3, 1989, Lundy, a 66 year old man with a history of coronary artery disease, was patronizing TropWorld Casino. While Lundy was gambling at a blackjack table, he suffered cardiac arrest and fell to the ground unconscious. Three other patrons quickly ran to Lundy and began to assist him. The first to reach him was Essie Greenberg ("Ms. Greenberg"), a critical care nurse. Ms. Greenberg was soon joined by her husband, Dr. Martin Greenberg ("Dr. Greenberg"), who is a pulmonary specialist. The third individual who aided Lundy did not disclose his identity, but he indicated to Dr. Greenberg that he was a surgeon. . . .

Meanwhile, the blackjack dealer at the table where Lundy had been gambling pushed an emergency "call" button at his table which alerted TropWorld's Security Command Post that a problem existed. . . .

A sergeant in TropWorld's security force and a TropWorld security guard arrived at the blackjack table apparently within fifteen seconds of their receiving the radio message from the Security Command Post. . . . Upon arriving, the security guard called the Security Command Post on her hand-held radio and requested that someone contact the casino medical station, which was located one floor above the casino. Several witnesses agree that Nurse Margaret Slusher ("Nurse Slusher"), the nurse who was on-duty at the casino medical station at the time, arrived on the scene within a minute or two of being summoned. . . .

Nurse Slusher brought with her an ambu-bag, oxygen, and an airway. She did not, however, bring an intubation kit to the scene. Dr. Greenberg testified that he asked Nurse Slusher for one and she told him that it was TropWorld's "policy" not to have an intubation kit on the premises. . . . Nurse Slusher testified at her deposition that some of the equipment normally found in an intubation kit was stocked in TropWorld's medical center, but that she did not bring this equipment with her because she was not qualified to use it.

Nurse Slusher proceeded to assist the three patrons in performing CPR on Lundy. Specifically, Nurse Slusher placed the ambu-bag over Lundy's face while the others took turns doing chest compressions. The ambu-bag was connected to an oxygen source. Dr. Greenberg testified that he was sure that air was entering Lundy's respiratory system and that Lundy was being adequately oxygenated during the period when he was receiving both CPR treatment and air through the ambu-bag. Dr. Greenberg went on to say that the only reason he had requested an intubation kit was "to establish an airway and subsequently provide oxygen in a more efficient manner."

The TropWorld Security Command Post radio log reflects that an Emergency Medical Technician ("EMT") unit arrived at TropWorld by ambulance at approximately 11:03 p.m. . . .

Upon the arrival of the EMT unit, a technician, with the help of the two doctor patrons, attempted to intubate Lundy using an intubation kit brought by the EMT unit. Dr. Greenberg claimed that, due to Lundy's stout physique and rigid muscle tone, it was a very difficult intubation, and that there were at least a half dozen failed attempts before the procedure was successfully completed. After intubation, Lundy regained a pulse and his color improved. . . .

The district court held that TropWorld had fulfilled its duty to Lundy under New Jersey law. The court found that TropWorld had "immediately summoned medical attention for Mr. Lundy once it became aware of his need for it." Additionally, the court stated that ". . . TropWorld . . . fulfilled its duty to aid injured patrons by having at least a registered nurse available, trained in emergency care, who could immediately size up a patron's medical situation and summon appropriate emergency medical personnel and equipment by ambulance to respond to the patrons's (sic) emergency needs." . . .

Additionally, the court held that New Jersey's Good Samaritan Statute, N.J. Stat. Ann. §2A:62A-1 (West 1993), shielded TropWorld and its employees from liability for any acts or omissions they took while rendering care in good faith to Lundy. . . .

Generally, a bystander has no duty to provide affirmative aid to an injured person, even if the bystander has the ability to help. See W. Page Keeton et al., Prosser and Keeton on the Law of Torts §56, at 375 (5th ed. 1984). New Jersey courts have recognized, however, that the existence of a relationship between the victim and one in a position to render aid may create a duty to render assistance. In Szabo v. Pennsylvania R.R. Co., 132 N.J.L. 331, 40 A.2d 562 (N.J. Err. & App. 1945), for example, New Jersey's highest court held that, in the absence of a contract or statute, an employer generally has no duty to provide medical service to treat an ill or injured employee, even if the illness or injury was the result of the employer's negligence. However, if the employee, while engaged in the work of his or her employer, sustains an injury rendering him or her helpless to provide for his or her own care, the employer must secure medical care for the employee. If a casino owner in New Jersey owes no greater duty to its patrons than an employer owes its employees while they are engaged in the employer's business, we think it clear that TropWorld did not fail in its duty to render assistance.

The Lundys insist, however, that TropWorld had a duty beyond that recognized in *Szabo*. They urge specifically that the Supreme Court of New Jersey would adopt the rule set forth in the Restatement (Second) of Torts §314A (1965). Section 314A states in pertinent part:

> (1) A common carrier is under a duty to its passengers to take reasonable action
>> (a) to protect them against unreasonable risk of physical harm, and
>> (b) to give them first aid after it knows or has reason to know that they are
> ill or injured, and to care for them until they can be cared for by others.
> (2) An innkeeper is under a similar duty to its guests.
> (3) A possessor of land who holds it open to the public is under a similar duty to
> members of the public who enter in response to his invitation.

We think it likely that the Supreme Court of New Jersey would accept the principles enunciated in §314A and would apply them in a case involving a casino and one of its patrons. We need not so hold, however. The pertinent commentary following §314A indicates that the duty "to take reasonable action . . . to give . . . first aid" in times of emergency requires only that carriers, innkeepers and landowners procure appropriate medical care as soon as the need for such care becomes apparent and provide such first aid prior to the arrival of qualified assistance as the carrier's, innkeeper's or landowner's employees are reasonably capable of giving. Clearly, the duty recognized in §314A does not extend to providing all medical care that the carrier or innkeeper could reasonably foresee might be needed by a patron. . . .

Nurse Slusher was a registered, licensed nurse who had been trained in emergency care and who had fifteen years of nursing experience. The uncontradicted evidence was that, despite this training and experience, she was not competent to perform an intubation. It necessarily follows that the duty which the Lundys insist the New Jersey Supreme Court would recognize in this case would require casinos to provide a full-time on-site staff physician. Certainly, maintaining on a full-time basis the capability of performing an intubation goes far beyond any "first aid" contemplated by §314A. We are confident the New Jersey Supreme Court would decline to impose liability on TropWorld for failing to maintain that full-time capability.

The Lundys further claim that, even if there would otherwise be no duty to provide a level of care encompassing intubation, TropWorld voluntarily assumed a duty to provide such care and breached that duty by negligently failing to provide it. As we understand the argument, TropWorld voluntarily assumed this duty in two ways. First, by [having] a laryngoscope with intubation tube on the premises, TropWorld voluntarily assumed the duty of having it available for use on request. Second, by voluntarily undertaking to assist Mr. Lundy, TropWorld assumed a duty to use due care in providing that assistance and breached this duty when Nurse Slusher failed to bring the laryngoscope with intubation tube to Dr. Greenberg. In connection with this second argument, the Lundys rely upon the principles outlined in §324 of the Restatement (Second) of Torts which provides:

> One who, being under no duty to do so, takes charge of another who is helpless adequately to aid or protect himself is subject to liability to the other for any bodily harm caused to him by
>
> > (a) the failure of the actor to exercise reasonable care to secure the safety of the other while within the actor's charge, or
> >
> > (b) the actor's discontinuing his aid or protection, if by so doing he leaves the other in a worse position than when the actor took charge of him.

As we have indicated, TropWorld's medical center . . . did have a laryngoscope with intubation tube as part of its inventory of equipment. Nurse Slusher did not bring this equipment with her when she was summoned . . . , however. She brought only that equipment that she was qualified to use: the ambu-bag, oxygen, and an airway. At some point after her arrival on the scene, Dr. Greenberg asked for an intubation kit. While the Lundys do not expressly so state, we understand their contention to be that Nurse Slusher should have returned to the medical center at this point and retrieved the intubation tube for Dr. Greenberg's use and TropWorld is liable for her failure to do so. They suggest that her failure to do so was the result of an ill-considered TropWorld policy that she was not permitted to use intubation equipment.

We reject the notion that TropWorld, by [having intubation equipment on its premises], voluntarily assumed a duty to Mr. Lundy it would not otherwise have had.

The Lundys have referred us to no New Jersey case law supporting this proposition and we have found none.

The Lundys' argument based on §324 of the Restatement, ignores the fact that the principles restated therein have been materially altered by New Jersey's Good Samaritan Act, §2A:62A-1 N.J. Stat. Ann. That Act provides that anyone "who in good faith renders emergency aid at the scene of an . . . emergency to the victim . . . shall not be liable for any civil damages as a result of acts or omissions by such person in rendering the emergency care." We believe the Supreme Court of New Jersey would hold that this mandate protects TropWorld from liability in the situation before us.

The Lundys do not, and cannot, assert that there was bad faith here. Rather, they seek to avoid the effect of New Jersey's Good Samaritan Act by relying on what is known as the "preexisting duty" exception to the Act. Under this exception, the Act provides no immunity from liability if the duty allegedly breached by the volunteer was a duty that existed prior to the voluntary activity. We do not believe the preexisting duty exception is applicable under New Jersey law in a situation, like the present one, where the preexisting duty is a limited one and the alleged negligence is the failure to provide a level of assistance beyond that required by the preexisting duty.

We think this becomes apparent when one focuses on the purposes of the Good Samaritan Act and the preexisting duty exception and on the nature of the preexisting duty in this case. The purpose of the Good Samaritan Act is to encourage the rendering of assistance to victims by providing that the voluntary rendering of aid will not give rise to any liability that would not otherwise exist. The preexisting duty exception recognizes that fulfillment of this objective of the statute can be accomplished without the eradication of preexisting duties.

Nurse Slusher had no preexisting duty to Lundy apart from her role as an employee of TropWorld. . . . Nurse Slusher, if she had been a fellow patron, for example, would have had no preexisting duty obligation and she would have been fully protected by the Good Samaritan Act. Thus, the only relevant preexisting duty for purposes of applying the Act under New Jersey law is the preexisting duty owed by TropWorld to Mr. Lundy. That preexisting duty, as we have seen, was a duty limited to summoning aid and, in the interim, taking reasonable first aid measures. It did not include the duty to provide the medical equipment and personnel necessary to perform an intubation. It follows, we believe, that Nurse Slusher's conduct with respect to the providing or withholding of the intubation equipment on the premises was not conduct with respect to which she or TropWorld owed a preexisting duty to Lundy. It further follows that, if TropWorld is responsible for the assistance voluntarily provided by Nurse Slusher, it is protected by the Act from liability arising from her alleged negligence in failing to provide that intubation equipment. Accordingly, we conclude that TropWorld's motion for summary judgment was properly granted.

NOTES TO LUNDY v. ADAMAR OF NEW JERSEY, INC.

1. *No Duty to Rescue.* Understanding the *Lundy* opinion begins with recognizing the general rule that no person has a duty to rescue another from peril, even if that rescue could be accomplished easily. In one famous case, the defendant challenged his neighbor to jump into a pit that was filled with water. The neighbor jumped into the water and drowned, and the defendant was protected from liability for having declined to rescue him. See Yania v. Bigan, 155 A.2d 343 (Pa. 1959). The rule is sometimes justified on the grounds that individual freedom of choice is a paramount good—autonomy triumphs over obligations to others with whom there is no special relationship. Another justification is that a requirement of altruism would have no logical stopping point—a victim who was not rescued could sue a huge number of people who failed to assist.

The *Lundy* plaintiffs tried to rely on the exceptions to the general rule. The first exception applies to common carriers, innkeepers, and possessors of land held open to the public. Anticipating difficulties with that exception, the plaintiffs also tried to rely on the exception applying to people who, although under no duty to help another in peril, attempt to help. How did the court in *Lundy* respond to each of these asserted exceptions to the general rule?

2. ***Duty to Rescue in Special Relationships.***   The *Lundy* court refers to the Restatement's position that imposes a duty to rescue in certain situations on innkeepers, common carriers, and possessors of land held open to the public. Perhaps responding to the harshness of the general rule, the law first recognized an obligation for common carriers and innkeepers to use reasonable care to aid their patrons. These businesses are sometimes required to be licensed to serve the public, and the duty to rescue may be viewed as an obligation that accompanies that license. The extension to possessors of land open to the public logically imposes obligations on others who seek the public's patronage. Limiting the obligation to these types of enterprises may be a logical way to prevent everyone from being obliged to rescue everyone else. How do these rationales apply to a casino operator?

3. ***Voluntary Rescues.***   An individual who decides to attempt to rescue another person must do so with some degree of care, even if he or she would have been free to ignore the person's need for help. It seems obvious that unreasonable conduct in assisting another person would be a basis for liability. The Restatement provision quoted in *Lundy* also recognizes liability for stopping assistance if the person being assisted would then be in a worse position than he or she was in prior to the effort to help. Good Samaritan statutes modify the application of a reasonable care duty to volunteer rescuers.

Statute: GOOD SAMARITANS
Ala. Code §6-5-332(a) (2017)

(a) When any doctor of medicine or dentistry, nurse, member of any organized rescue squad, member of any police or fire department, member of any organized volunteer fire department, Alabama-licensed emergency medical technician, intern or resident practicing in an Alabama hospital with training programs approved by the American Medical Association, Alabama state trooper, medical aidman functioning as a part of the military assistance to safety and traffic program, chiropractor, or public education employee gratuitously and in good faith, renders first aid or emergency care at the scene of an accident, casualty, or disaster to a person injured therein, he or she shall not be liable for any civil damages as a result of his or her acts or omissions in rendering first aid or emergency care, nor shall he or she be liable for any civil damages as a result of any act or failure to act to provide or arrange for further medical treatment or care for the injured person.

Statute: LIABILITY OF PHYSICIAN, DENTIST, NURSE,
OR EMERGENCY MEDICAL TECHNICIAN FOR
RENDERING EMERGENCY CARE

Miss. Code §73-25-37(1) (2017)

(1) No duly licensed, practicing physician, physician's assistant, dentist, registered nurse, licensed practical nurse, certified registered emergency medical technician, or any other person who, in good faith and in the exercise of reasonable care, renders emergency care to any injured person at the scene of an emergency, or in transporting said injured person to a point where medical assistance can be reasonably expected, shall be liable for any civil damages to said injured person as a result of any acts committed in good faith and in the exercise of reasonable care or omissions in good faith and in the exercise of reasonable care by such persons in rendering the emergency care to said injured person.

NOTES TO GOOD SAMARITAN STATUTES

1. *Purpose.*   Statutes of this type are designed to encourage individuals to offer assistance to others in emergencies. They may strike a balance between protecting defendants and assuring injured people that those who aid them will act with some care. Which of these statutes provides greater protection for rescuers?

The Mississippi Supreme Court stated that the state's Good Samaritan statute "fails miserably" and invited the legislature to amend it, but applied it as written in Willard v. Mayor and Aldermen of the City of Vicksburg, 571 So. 2d 972, 975 (Miss. 1990).

2. *Persons Protected.*   These statutes differ in how they identify those whom their provisions will protect. How does the phrase "or any other person" in the Mississippi statute affect its coverage in comparison with the coverage provided in the Alabama statute?

3. *Prior Duty.*   The statute described in *Lundy* withdraws immunity if the duty allegedly breached by the volunteer existed prior to the voluntary activity. What would justify that limitation? Do the Alabama and Mississippi statutes incorporate it?

Statute: EMERGENCY MEDICAL CARE

12 Vt. Stat. §519(a) (2017)

A person who knows that another is exposed to grave physical harm shall, to the extent that the same can be rendered without danger or peril to himself or without interference with important duties owed to others, give reasonable assistance to the exposed person unless that assistance or care is being provided by others.

Statute: GOOD SAMARITAN LAW DUTY TO ASSIST

Minn. Stat. §604A.01 Sub. 1 (2017)

A person at the scene of an emergency who knows that another person is exposed to or has suffered grave physical harm shall, to the extent that the person can do so without danger or peril to self or others, give reasonable assistance to the exposed person. Reasonable assistance may include obtaining or attempting to obtain aid from law enforcement or medical personnel. A person who violates this subdivision is guilty of a petty misdemeanor.

Statute: DUTY TO RENDER ASSISTANCE

R.I. Gen. Laws §11-56-1 (2017)

Any person at the scene of an emergency who knows that another person is exposed to, or has suffered, grave physical harm shall, to the extent that he or she can do so without danger or peril to himself or herself or to others, give reasonable assistance to the exposed person. Any person violating the provisions of this section is guilty of a petty misdemeanor and shall be subject to imprisonment for not more than six (6) months or by a fine of not more than five hundred dollars ($500), or both.

Statute: DUTY TO AID VICTIM OR REPORT CRIME

Wis. Stat. §940.34(2)(a), (d)1 (2017)

Aff. duty to help

(a) Any person who knows that a crime is being committed and that a victim is exposed to bodily harm shall summon law enforcement officers or other assistance or shall provide assistance to the victim. . . .

(d) A person need not comply with this subsection if any of the following apply:
    1. Compliance would place him or her in danger. . . .

NOTES TO DUTY TO AID STATUTES

1. *Statutory Duty to Rescue.* The above statutes are from the only states that appear to recognize a duty to rescue (though there are additional statutes requiring the reporting of crimes). These statutes create immunity from liability similar to the immunity described in the Good Samaritan laws. While England does not have a general duty to rescue, all civil law countries in Europe (except Sweden) apparently do, as well as most Latin American countries. See Edward Tomlinson, *The French Experience with Duty to Rescue: A Dubious Case for Criminal Enforcement*, 20 N.Y.L. Sch. J. Int'l & Comp. L. 451 (2000) (comparing treatment of failure to rescue under American and French statutes).

2. *Differences Among Statutes.* While the Vermont and Minnesota statutes impose fines of $100 and $200, respectively, Wisconsin and Rhode Island impose fines up to $500 and also authorize jail terms of up to 30 days and six months, respectively. On whom is the duty imposed under the different states' statutes? What is a person on whom a duty is imposed obliged to do under the various statutes?

Perspective: Individualism, Altruism, and Duty to Rescue

Torts students are often shocked to learn that there is no duty of one person to take even easy steps to rescue another. This "no-duty" rule has been the subject of a great deal of scholarly commentary, as the following two extracts illustrate.

> The first task of the law of torts is to define the boundaries of individual liberty. . . . [T]he liberty of one person ends when he causes harm to another. Until that point he is free to act as he chooses, and need not take into account the welfare of others.

Richard A. Epstein, *A Theory of Strict Liability*, 2 J. Legal Stud. 151, 203-204 (1973).

> The individual receives two kinds of benefits from a law requiring easy rescue. First, pertaining to actual rescues, such a law increases the likelihood of his being rescued should he need to be. In exchange for this the individual suffers only minor inconvenience would he ever be required to rescue someone else. Second, even if a person is never in need of rescue himself, the individual still benefits from a law requiring easy rescue. In this case, the existence of such a law gives the individualist reason to believe that, should he be in need of rescue, the law requires action on his behalf. This knowledge makes him better able to plan his activities and, therefore, enhances his freedom. It is arbitrary and irrational for an individualist not to accept as a general legal duty the principle of easy rescue.

Robert Justin Lipkin, Comment, *Beyond Good Samaritans and Moral Monsters: An Individualistic Justification of the General Legal Duty to Rescue*, 31 UCLA L. Rev. 252, 290 (1983).

Perspective: Feminism and the Duty to Rescue

> I argue that "the recognition that we are all interdependent and connected and that we are by nature social beings who must interact with one another should lead us to judge conduct as tortious when it does not evidence responsible care or concern for another's safety, welfare, or health." Utilizing this analysis, the "no-duty" doctrine might be transformed into a duty to exercise the "conscious care and concern of a responsible neighbor or social acquaintance," which would impose a duty to aid or rescue within one's capacity under the circumstances. Tort law would no longer condone the inhumane response of doing absolutely nothing to aid or rescue when one could save another from dying.

Leslie Bender, *An Overview of Feminist Torts Scholarship*, 78 Cornell L. Rev. 575, 580-581 (1993).

B. *Obligations to Rescuers*

One of tort law's most famous phrases is "danger invites rescue." Those words are quoted in McCoy v. American Suzuki Motor Corp. as part of the court's analysis of the duty owed to a rescuer by one whose conduct places a person in peril. Moody v. Delta Western, Inc. examines the scope of the "firefighter's rule," an important doctrine that limits liability to rescuers.

McCOY v. AMERICAN SUZUKI MOTOR CORP.
961 P.2d 952 (Wash. 1998)

SANDERS, J. . . .

At 5:00 p.m. on a cold November evening James McCoy drove eastbound on Interstate 90 outside Spokane as the car which preceded him, a Suzuki Samurai, swerved off the roadway and rolled. McCoy stopped to render assistance, finding the driver seriously injured. Shortly thereafter a Washington State Patrol trooper arrived on the scene and asked McCoy to place flares on the roadway to warn approaching vehicles. McCoy did so, but concerned the flares were insufficient, continued further and positioned himself a quarter-mile from the accident scene with a lit flare in each hand, manually directing traffic to the inside lane.

By 6:50 p.m., almost two hours after the accident, the injured driver and passenger of the Suzuki were removed and the scene was cleared, leaving only the trooper and McCoy on the roadway. McCoy walked back on the shoulder of the roadway to his car with a lit flare in his roadside hand. When McCoy was within three or four car-lengths of the trooper, the trooper pulled away without comment. Moments later McCoy was struck from behind while still walking on the roadway's shoulder by a hit-and-run vehicle.

McCoy and his wife filed a . . . complaint against . . . American Suzuki Motor Corporation and its parent corporation, Suzuki Motor Company, Ltd., for its allegedly defective Samurai which allegedly caused the wreck in the first place. . . .

This claim against Suzuki was brought under the Washington product liability act (PLA), RCW 7.72. McCoy alleged the Suzuki Samurai was defectively designed and manufactured, was not reasonably safe by virtue of its tendency to roll, and lacked proper warnings. McCoy also alleged these defects caused the principal accident, that he was injured while a rescuer within the purview of the "rescue doctrine," and Suzuki should therefore be held liable for his injuries.

Suzuki moved for summary judgment asserting: (1) the rescue doctrine does not apply to product liability actions; and (2) even if it does, McCoy must still, but cannot, prove Suzuki proximately caused his injuries. The trial court found the rescue doctrine applies to product liability actions but concluded any alleged defect in the Suzuki was not the proximate cause of McCoy's injuries and, accordingly, granted summary judgment of dismissal.

McCoy appealed the dismissal to the Court of Appeals which reversed in a published, split decision. The appellate court found the rescue doctrine applies in product liability actions just as it does in negligence actions. The court agreed with the trial court that McCoy's injuries were not proximately caused by Suzuki, however, held under the rescue doctrine an injured rescuer need not prove the defendant proximately caused his injuries. . . .

The Court of Appeals thus concluded McCoy alleged sufficient facts to avoid summary judgment of dismissal and, accordingly, remanded for trial. We granted review. . . .

The rescue doctrine is invoked in tort cases for a variety of purposes in a variety of scenarios. The doctrine, as here asserted, allows an injured rescuer to sue the party which caused the danger requiring the rescue in the first place. As Justice Cardozo succinctly summarized, the heart of this doctrine is the notion that "danger invites rescue." Wagner v. International Ry. Co., 232 N.Y. 176, 133 N.E. 437, 437, 19 A.L.R.1 (1921). This doctrine serves two functions. First, it informs a tort-feasor it is foreseeable a rescuer will come to the aid of the person imperiled by the tort-feasor's actions, and, therefore, the tort-feasor owes the rescuer a duty similar to the duty he owes the person he imperils. Second, the rescue doctrine negates the presumption that the rescuer assumed the risk of injury when he knowingly undertook the dangerous rescue, so long as he does not act rashly or recklessly.

To achieve rescuer status one must demonstrate: (1) the defendant was negligent to the person rescued and such negligence caused the peril or appearance of peril to the person rescued; (2) the peril or appearance of peril was imminent; (3) a reasonably prudent person would have concluded such peril or appearance of peril existed; and (4) the rescuer acted with reasonable care in effectuating the rescue. The Court of Appeals found McCoy demonstrated sufficient facts of rescuer status to put the issue of whether he met [those] four requirements . . . to the jury. Suzuki does not question this finding. Nor will we.

Suzuki argues the rescue doctrine may not be invoked in product liability actions. Suzuki contends the PLA supplants all common law remedies and contends the rescue doctrine is nothing more than a common law remedy. We disagree. The rescue doctrine is not a common law remedy. Rather, it is shorthand for the idea that rescuers are to be anticipated and is a reflection of a societal value judgment that rescuers should not be barred from bringing suit for knowingly placing themselves in danger to undertake a rescue. We can conceive of no reason why this doctrine should not apply with equal force when a product manufacturer causes the danger. . . .

McCoy argues the rescue doctrine relieves the rescuer-plaintiff of proving the defendant's wrongdoing proximately caused his injuries. McCoy asserts a rescuer may prevail in a suit by showing the defendant proximately caused the danger and that, while serving as rescuer, the plaintiff was injured. The Court of Appeals agreed stating the rescue doctrine "varies the ordinary rules of negligence."

The Court of Appeals erred on this point. [T]he rescuer, like any other plaintiff, must still show the defendant proximately caused his injuries. . . .

Here, we do not find the alleged fault of Suzuki, if proved, to be so remote from these injuries that its liability should be cut off as a matter of law. . . . Accordingly, we will not dismiss this case for lack of legal causation. Instead we remand the case for trial consistent with this opinion.

The Court of Appeals is therefore affirmed and McCoy is awarded his costs on appeal.

NOTE TO McCOY v. AMERICAN SUZUKI MOTOR CORP.

Significance of Rescue Doctrine.   The rescue doctrine facilitates recovery by a rescuer against a defendant whose conduct created the need for a rescue by recognizing the foreseeability of a rescuer and harm to that rescuer. These elements are usually associated with finding that there is a duty to a plaintiff. With respect to proximate cause, the doctrine's utility depends on each jurisdiction's treatment of that issue. Demonstrating foreseeability of the type of harm that resulted might be easier than proving that the defendant's negligence directly caused the harm or was a substantial factor in producing it.

Problem
Anticipated Peril

An individual who was watching someone pilot a hot air balloon noticed that wind was directing the balloon toward some high voltage power lines. As the balloon skimmed across the ground toward the lines, the observer seized the basket of the balloon, hoping to protect the pilot. The observer was badly injured when he came into contact with the power lines himself. He sought damages from the pilot, claiming that the pilot should have used a device on the balloon that could make it stop immediately, relying on the rescue doctrine to establish a duty between the pilot and the observer. The pilot argues that he has no duty to the observer. You are the judge. Decide whether the rescue doctrine applies here. See Thompson v. Summers, 567 N.W.2d 387 (S.D. 1997).

MOODY v. DELTA WESTERN, INC.
38 P.3d 1139 (Alaska 2002)

MATTHEWS, J.

The question in this case is whether the so-called Firefighter's Rule applies in Alaska. The Firefighter's Rule holds that firefighters and police officers who are injured may not recover based on the negligent conduct that required their presence. For public policy reasons we join the overwhelming majority of states that have adopted the rule.

The facts of this case are undisputed. On or around July 25, 1996, a Delta Western employee left a fuel truck owned by Delta Western in a driveway in Dillingham. The keys were in the ignition, the door was unlocked, and the truck contained fuel and weighed over 10,000 pounds. Delta Western had a policy of removing the keys from the ignitions of its trucks. Delta Western enacted this policy because of past incidents involving the theft and unauthorized entry of its trucks.

Joseph Coolidge, who was highly intoxicated, entered the unlocked truck and proceeded to drive around Dillingham. He ran cars off the road, nearly collided with several vehicles, and drove at speeds exceeding seventy miles per hour. Brent Moody, the chief of the Dillingham Police Department, was one of the officers who responded to the reports of the recklessly driven fuel truck. The driver of the van in which Moody was a passenger attempted to stop the truck after moving in front of it but Coolidge rammed the van, throwing Moody against the dashboard and windshield. Moody suffered permanent injuries.

Moody filed suit against Delta Western, alleging that the company (through its employee) negligently failed to remove the truck's keys from the ignition. In its amended answer, Delta Western argued that the "Firefighter's Rule" barred Moody's cause of action. Delta Western moved for summary judgment based on its Firefighter's Rule defense. The superior court granted Delta Western's motion, holding that the Firefighter's Rule bars police officers from recovering for injuries caused by the "negligence which creates the very occasion for their engagement."

Moody now appeals.

Nearly all of the courts that have considered whether or not to adopt the Firefighter's Rule have in fact adopted it. Only one court has rejected it. . . .

Modern courts stress interrelated reasons, based on public policy, for the rule. The negligent party is said to have no duty to the public safety officer to act without negligence in creating the condition that necessitates the officer's intervention because the officer is employed by the public to respond to such conditions and receives compensation and benefits for the risks inherent in such responses. Requiring members of the public to pay for injuries resulting from such responses effectively imposes a double payment obligation on them. Further, because negligence is at the root of many calls for public safety officers, allowing recovery would compound the growth of litigation.

Courts find an analogy in cases in which a contractor is injured while repairing the condition that necessitated his employment. In these cases, the owner is under no duty to protect the contractor against risks arising from the condition the contractor is hired to repair, and thus is not liable even if the condition was the product of the owner's negligence. This "contractor for repairs" exception to the general duty of reasonable care is grounded in necessity and fairness. Property owners should not be deterred by the threat of liability to the contractor from summoning experts to repair their property, regardless of why repairs are needed. Further, owners have paid for the contractor's expertise at confronting the very danger that injured him and should not have to pay again if the contractor is then injured. The same factors are found to apply with respect to the public's need to call for the services of public safety officers.

We agree with the reasoning of the modern courts and with the analogy to contractor cases. The Firefighter's Rule reflects sound public policy. The public pays for emergency responses of public safety officials in the form of salaries and enhanced benefits. Requiring members of the public to pay for injuries incurred by officers in such responses asks an individual to pay again for services the community has collectively purchased. Further, negligence is a common factor in emergencies that require the intervention of public safety officers. Allowing recovery would cause a proliferation of litigation aimed at shifting to individuals or their insurers costs that have already been widely shared. . . .

We thus conclude that the Firefighter's Rule applies in Alaska. We reach this conclusion based on the merits of the rule as accepted by the overwhelming majority of the courts of our sister states. It follows that summary judgment was properly granted.

NOTES TO MOODY v. DELTA WESTERN, INC.

1. *Public Safety Workers in General.*   The firefighter's rule obviously applies to firefighters as well as to police officers. Where a landowner's negligence requires the presence of firefighters, the rule bars recovery by firefighters for injuries they suffer. See Zanghi v. Niagara Frontier Transp. Comm'n, 649 N.E.2d 1167 (N.Y. 1995). Sanitation

workers, not paid to anticipate hazardous conditions, are not covered by the rule. See Ciervo v. City of New York, 715 N.E.2d 91 (N.Y. 1999).

2. ***Volunteers.*** In *Moody*, the court described the policy reasons for a related rule that protects homeowners from liability to contractors who are hired to repair the results of the homeowner's negligence. The court extends that reasoning to firefighters and police officers. Under the reasoning in *Moody*, should the firefighter's rule be applied to a person injured while fighting a fire as an unpaid member of a volunteer fire department? See Roberts v. Vaughn, 587 N.W.2d 249 (Mich. 1998).

3. ***Limitations on Application.*** Jurisdictions typically withdraw the effect of the firefighter's rule in cases where a firefighter or police officer is injured while doing a routine inspection of a negligent defendant's premises. See Gray v. Russell, 853 S.W.2d 928 (Mo. 1993). Also, the rule does not protect defendants for harms associated with dangers different from the dangers that are typical of police or firefighting work. Concealing dangers or lying about them are examples of conduct for which a land-owner will be liable to a firefighter when that conduct causes an injury. See Hack v. Gillespie, 658 N.E.2d 1046 (Ohio 1996). Do the reasons that support the rule in general also support limiting its application to emergency situations and the dangers normally associated with the profession?

Statute: PROFESSIONAL RESCUERS' CAUSE OF ACTION

N.J. Stat. §2A:62A-21 (2017)

In addition to any other right of action or recovery otherwise available under law, whenever any law enforcement officer, firefighter, or member of a duly incorporated first aid, emergency, ambulance or rescue squad association suffers any injury, disease or death while in the lawful discharge of his official duties and that injury, disease or death is directly or indirectly the result of the neglect, willful omission, or willful or culpable conduct of any person or entity, other than that law enforcement officer, firefighter or first aid, emergency, ambulance or rescue squad member's employer or co-employee, the law enforcement officer, firefighter, or first aid, emergency, ambulance or rescue squad member suffering that injury or disease, or, in the case of death, a representative of that law enforcement officer, firefighter or first aid, emergency, ambulance or rescue squad member's estate, may seek recovery and damages from the person or entity whose neglect, willful omission, or willful or culpable conduct resulted in that injury, disease or death.

NOTE TO STATUTE

Statutory Purpose. Does this statute abrogate the firefighter's rule partially or completely?

Problem
Firefighter Rule and Effect of Statute

In a New Jersey case that predates this statute, a police officer slipped on powdered sugar that had spilled on the floor of a donut shop. The officer was barred from recovery against the shop because he was carrying an injured person out of the shop when he was hurt, even though he would have been entitled to a cause of action if he had been in the shop as a customer. See Rosa v. Dunkin' Donuts, 583 A.2d 1129 (N.J. 1991). Would the statute have affected that result?

C. Protecting Third Parties from Criminal Attacks or Disease

In the medical context, some courts have taken positions that require affirmative acts by health care professionals who have an opportunity to protect strangers from danger. Emerich v. Philadelphia Center for Human Development, Inc. describes the obligations of a physician who becomes aware that a patient might cause harm to others. Bradshaw v. Daniel resolves a claim that individuals other than the defendant doctor's patient were entitled to have the doctor warn them about possible harm they might suffer if information derived from treating the doctor's patient could have indicated to the doctor that they were in peril.

EMERICH v. PHILADELPHIA CENTER
FOR HUMAN DEVELOPMENT, INC.

720 A.2d 1032 (Pa. 1998)

Cappy, J.

We granted allocatur limited to the issues of one, whether a mental health professional has a duty to warn a third party of a patient's threat to harm the third party; two, if there is a duty to warn, the scope thereof; and finally, whether in this case a judgment on the pleadings was proper.

This admittedly tragic matter arises from the murder of Appellant's decedent, Teresa Hausler, by her former boyfriend, Gad Joseph ("Joseph"). At the time of the murder, Joseph was being treated for mental illness and drug problems. Appellant brought wrongful death and survival actions against Appellees. Judgment on the pleadings was granted in favor of Appellees by the trial court and was affirmed on appeal by the Superior Court.

A detailed recitation of the facts is necessary to analyze the complex and important issues before us. The factual allegations raised in Appellant's complaint, which we must accept as true, are as follows.

Ms. Hausler and Joseph, girlfriend and boyfriend, were cohabitating in Philadelphia. For a substantial period of time, both Ms. Hausler and Joseph had been receiving mental health treatment at Appellee Philadelphia Center for Human Development (the "Center" or "PCHD"). . . . Appellee Anthony Scuderi was a counselor at the Center. . . .

Joseph was diagnosed as suffering from, among other illnesses, post-traumatic stress disorder, drug and alcohol problems, and explosive and schizo-affective personality disorders. He also had a history of physically and verbally abusing Ms. Hausler, as well as his former wife, and a history of other violent propensities. Joseph often threatened to murder Ms. Hausler and suffered from homicidal ideations.

Several weeks prior to June 27, 1991, Ms. Hausler ended her relationship with Joseph, moved from their Philadelphia residence, and relocated to Reading,

Pennsylvania. Angered by Ms. Hausler's decision to terminate their relationship, Joseph had indicated during several therapy sessions at the Center that he wanted to harm Ms. Hausler.

On the morning of June 27, 1991, at or about 9:25 a.m., Joseph telephoned his counselor, Mr. Scuderi, and advised him that he was going to kill Ms. Hausler. Mr. Scuderi immediately scheduled and carried out a therapy session with Joseph at 11:00 that morning. During the therapy session, Joseph told Mr. Scuderi that his irritation with Ms. Hausler was becoming worse because that day she was returning to their apartment to get her clothing, that he was under great stress, and that he was going to kill her if he found her removing her clothing from their residence.

Mr. Scuderi recommended that Joseph voluntarily commit himself to a psychiatric hospital. Joseph refused; however, he stated that he was in control and would not hurt Ms. Hausler. At 12:00 p.m., the therapy session ended, and, as stated in the complaint, Joseph was permitted to leave the Center "based solely upon his assurances that he would not harm" Ms. Hausler.

At 12:15 p.m., Mr. Scuderi received a telephone call from Ms. Hausler informing him that she was in Philadelphia en route to retrieve her clothing from their apartment, located at 6924 Large Street. Ms. Hausler inquired as to Joseph's whereabouts. Mr. Scuderi instructed Ms. Hausler not to go to the apartment and to return to Reading.

In what ultimately became a fatal decision, Ms. Hausler ignored Mr. Scuderi's instructions and went to the residence where she was fatally shot by Joseph at or about 12:30 p.m. Five minutes later, Joseph telephoned Mr. Scuderi who in turn called the police at the instruction of Director Friedrich.

Joseph was subsequently arrested and convicted of the murder of Ms. Hausler. Based upon these facts, Appellant filed two wrongful death and survival actions, alleging, inter alia, that Appellees negligently failed to properly warn Ms. Hausler, and others including her family, friends and the police, that Joseph presented a clear and present danger of harm to her.

The trial court granted judgment on the pleadings in favor of Appellees finding, inter alia, that the duty of a mental health professional to warn a third party had not yet been adopted in Pennsylvania, but that even if such a legal duty existed, Mr. Scuderi's personal warning discharged that duty. The Superior Court affirmed, reiterating that mental health care providers currently have no duty to warn a third party of a patient's violent propensities, and that even if such a duty existed, Appellant failed to establish a cause of action as his decedent was killed when she ignored Mr. Scuderi's warning not to go to Joseph's apartment.

Initially, we must determine if in this Commonwealth, a mental health care professional owes a duty to warn a third party of a patient's threat of harm to that third party, and if so, the scope of such a duty. While this precise issue is one of first impression for this court, it is an issue which has been considered by a number of state and federal courts and has been the subject of much commentary. [W]e determine that a mental health care professional, under certain limited circumstances, owes a duty to warn a third party of threats of harm against that third party. Nevertheless, we find that in this case, judgment on the pleadings was proper, and thus, we affirm the decision of the learned Superior Court, albeit, for different reasons.

Under common law, as a general rule, there is no duty to control the conduct of a third party to protect another from harm. However, a judicial exception to the general rule has been recognized where a defendant stands in some special relationship with either the person whose conduct needs to be controlled or in a relationship with the intended victim of the conduct, which gives to the intended victim a right to protection. See Restatement (Second) of Torts §315 (1965). Appellant argues that this exception, and thus, a duty, should be recognized in Pennsylvania.

Our analysis must begin with the California Supreme Court's landmark decision in Tarasoff v. Regents of Univ. of California, 17 Cal. 3d 425, 131 Cal. Rptr. 14, 551 P.2d 334 (1976), which was the first case to find that a mental health professional may have a duty to protect others from possible harm by their patients. In *Tarasoff*, a lawsuit was filed against, among others, psychotherapists employed by the Regents of the University of California to recover for the death of the plaintiffs' daughter, Tatiana Tarasoff, who was killed by a psychiatric outpatient.

Two months prior to the killing, the patient had expressly informed his therapist that he was going to kill an unnamed girl (who was readily identifiable as the plaintiffs' daughter) when she returned home from spending the summer in Brazil. The therapist, with the concurrence of two colleagues, decided to commit the patient for observation. The campus police detained the patient at the oral and written request of the therapist, but released him after satisfying themselves that he was rational and exacting his promise to stay away from Ms. Tarasoff. The therapist's superior directed that no further action be taken to confine or otherwise restrain the patient. No one warned either Ms. Tarasoff or her parents of the patient's dangerousness.

After the patient murdered Ms. Tarasoff, her parents filed suit alleging, among other things, that the therapists involved had failed either to warn them of the threat to their daughter or to confine the patient.

The California Supreme Court, while recognizing the general rule that a person owes no duty to control the conduct of another, determined that there is an exception to this general rule where the defendant stands in a special relationship to either the person whose conduct needs to be controlled or in a relationship to the foreseeable victim of that conduct, citing Restatement (Second) of Torts §315-320. Applying that exception, the court found that the special relationship between the defendant therapists and the patient could support affirmative duties for the benefit of third persons.

The court made an analogy to cases which have imposed a duty upon physicians to diagnose and warn about a patient's contagious disease and concluded that "by entering into a doctor-patient relationship the therapist becomes sufficiently involved to assume some responsibility for the safety, not only of the patient himself, but also of any third person whom the doctor knows to be threatened by the patient."

The court also considered various public policy interests determining that the public interest in safety from violent assault outweighed countervailing interests of the confidentiality of patient-therapist communications and the difficulty in predicting dangerousness.

The California Supreme Court ultimately held:

> When a therapist determines, or pursuant to the standards of his profession should determine, that his patient presents a serious danger of violence to another, he incurs an obligation to use reasonable care to protect the intended victim against such danger.

Following *Tarasoff*, the vast majority of courts that have considered the issue have concluded that the relationship between a mental health care professional and his patient constitutes a special relationship which imposes upon the professional an affirmative duty to protect a third party against harm. Thus, the concept of a duty to protect by warning, albeit limited in certain circumstances, has met with virtually universal approval.

. . . [W]e find that the special relationship between a mental health professional and his patient may, in certain circumstances, give rise to an affirmative duty to warn for the benefit of an intended victim. We find, in accord with *Tarasoff*, that a mental health professional who determines, or under the standards of the mental health professional, should have determined, that this patient presents a serious danger to another bears a duty to exercise reasonable care to protect by warning the intended victim against such danger.

Mindful that the treatment of mental illness is not an exact science, we emphasize that we hold a mental health professional only to the standard of care of his profession, which takes into account the uncertainty of such treatment. Thus, we will not require a mental health professional to be liable for a patient's violent behavior because he fails to predict such behavior accurately.

Moreover, recognizing the importance of the therapist-patient relationship, the warning to the intended victim should be the least expansive based upon the circumstances. . . .

Having determined that a mental health professional has a duty to protect by warning a third party of potential harm, we must further consider under what circumstances such a duty arises. We are extremely sensitive to the conundrum a mental health care professional faces regarding the competing concerns of productive therapy, confidentiality and other aspects of the patient's well being, as well as an interest in public safety. In light of these valid concerns and the fact that the duty being recognized is an exception to the general rule that there is no duty to warn those endangered by another, we find that the circumstances in which a duty to warn a third party arises are extremely limited.

First, the predicate for a duty to warn is the existence of a specific and immediate threat of serious bodily injury that has been communicated to the professional. . .

Moreover, the duty to warn will only arise where the threat is made against a specifically identified or readily identifiable victim. Strong reasons support the determination that the duty to warn must have some limits. We are cognizant of the fact that the nature of therapy encourages patients to profess threats of violence, few of which are acted upon. Public disclosure of every generalized threat would vitiate the therapist's efforts to build a trusting relationship necessary for progress. Moreover, as a practical matter, a mental health care professional would have great difficulty in warning the public at large of a threat against an unidentified person. Even if possible, warnings to the general public would "produce a cacophony of warnings that by reason of their sheer volume would add little to the effective protection of the public." . . .

Appellees offer two primary arguments as to why this court should not recognize any duty to warn a third party of a patient's threats of harm. First, Appellees argue that a duty to warn should not be imposed on a mental health professional because such a professional is no better able than anyone else to predict violent behavior. Appellees offer various studies in support of its argument that purport to prove that dangerousness cannot be predicted.

While this court is cognizant of the difficulties predicting whether a patient may truly pose a danger to others, this argument rings hollow for a number of reasons. First, . . . the legislature has determined, and this court has already found, that liability may attach for negligently discharging a dangerous patient. Subsumed in finding such liability is a failure to recognize that the patient was dangerous. . . .

Moreover, we are unpersuaded that difficulty in predicting violent conduct alone should justify barring recovery in all situations. The standard of care for mental health professionals adequately takes into account the difficult nature of the problem facing them. . . .

Appellees also argue that the strong policies underlying the protection of the therapist-patient privilege prohibit disclosure of confidential information, and, thus, preclude the finding of a duty to warn. This court is aware of the critical role that confidentiality plays in the relationship between therapist and patient, constituting, as one author has described, the "sine qua non of successful psychiatric treatment." Nevertheless, we believe that the protection against disclosure of confidential information gained in the therapist-patient relationship does not bar the finding of a duty to warn. . . .

Indeed, the existence of a duty to warn is in accord with the limits on patient-therapist confidentiality recognized by the American Psychiatric Association and the American Medical Association. "When in the clinical judgment of the treating psychiatrist the risk of danger is deemed to be significant, the psychiatrist may reveal confidential information disclosed by the patient." American Psychiatric Association, The Principles of Medical Ethics with Annotations Especially Applicable to Psychiatry (1995 ed.). . . .

Based upon the above, it is clear that the law regarding privileged communications between patient and mental health care professional is not violated by, and does not prohibit, a finding of a duty on the part of a mental health professional to warn an intended victim of a patient's threats of serious bodily harm. As succinctly stated by the court in *Tarasoff*, "The protective privilege ends where the public peril begins."

In summary, we find that in Pennsylvania, based upon the special relationship between a mental health professional and his patient, when the patient has communicated to the professional a specific and immediate threat of serious bodily injury against a specifically identified or readily identifiable third party and when the professional, determines, or should determine under the standards of the mental health profession that his patient presents a serious danger of violence to the third party, then the professional bears a duty to exercise reasonable care to protect by warning the third party against such danger.

Finally we must decide whether judgment on the pleadings was proper in this case. . . .

After consideration of the facts as pled regarding the circumstances surrounding the events of June 27, 1991, and after consideration of Mr. Scuderi's specific instructions designed to prevent the threatened harm, including the reasonable inferences that Ms. Hausler knew of Joseph's violent propensities and that she telephoned Mr. Scuderi in concern for her safety, we find that Mr. Scuderi's warning was reasonable as a matter of law. The warning was discreet and in accord with preserving the privacy of his patient to the maximum extent possible consistent with preventing the threatened harm to Ms. Hausler. Thus, Mr. Scuderi discharged any duty to warn.

While this matter evokes great sympathy, we agree with the lower courts that after examining the complaint in this case, it is clear that on the facts averred, as a matter of law, recovery by Appellant is not possible. Thus, judgment on the pleadings was proper.

For the foregoing reasons, we affirm the judgment of the Superior Court.

[Concurring and concurring and dissenting opinions omitted.]

NOTES TO EMERICH v. PHILADELPHIA CENTER FOR HUMAN DEVELOPMENT, INC.

1. *Origin of Rule.* The Restatement (Second) recognizes a person's duty to control his or her minor children, employees, dangerous persons in his or her custody, and those on the person's land or using the person's chattels. See §§316-318. What are the similarities and differences between those circumstances and the relationship between a patient and a therapist?

2. *Standard of Care.* The *Emerich* court held that there would be a duty owed by the psychiatrist to the victim "under certain limited circumstances," which included the specificity of the threats. The court also considered the possibility that the psychiatrist did not, but should have, discovered the threat. Under the *Emerich* holding, could a psychiatrist be liable to the victim of a patient on a claim that, although the patient did not make an explicit threat, a psychiatrist whose treatment of the patient had conformed to the applicable standard of care would have understood that the patient was planning to harm the victim?

3. *Required Response.* The *Emerich* court held that as a matter of law, the defendant's response to the perceived risk was adequate. Following *Tarasoff,* the California legislature adopted a statute specifying that in cases where a psychotherapist's duty to warn and protect arises, that duty "shall be discharged by the psychotherapist making reasonable efforts to communicate the threat to the victim or victims and to a law enforcement agency." Cal. Civil Code §43.92.

4. *Practicality of Warnings.* Where a potentially violent person makes a general threat, a duty to warn may not arise. In Thompson v. County of Alameda, 614 P.2d 728 (Cal. 1980), the court that decided *Tarasoff* rejected imposition of a duty to warn where a county released on furlough a young person who had been in custody in connection with his history of violence and sexual abuse. Despite his threat to kill an unnamed child, the county made no effort to provide warnings. The court concluded that generalized warnings would be difficult to give and would not likely be helpful.

Perspective: Reliability of Predictions of Dangerousness

The defendant in *Emerich* argued that there should not be any duty to warn because dangerousness cannot be predicted with any reliability. Barefoot v. Estelle, 463 U.S. 880, 921 (1983), involved psychiatric predictions of dangerousness relevant to whether the defendant should be executed. Justice Blackmun, dissenting, stated that "psychiatric predictions of long-term future violence are wrong more often than they are right." The American Psychological Association concluded at one time that "the validity of psychological prediction of violent behavior . . . is extremely poor, so poor that one could oppose their use on the strictly empirical grounds that psychologists are not professionally competent to make such judgments." *Report of the Task Force on the Role of Psychology in the Criminal Justice System,* 33 Am. Psychol. 1099, 1110 (1978). How reliable such predictions should be depends on the purpose for such predictions. The reliability appropriate for giving the death penalty might be different from the reliability required to give a warning. One expert, having reviewed the literature, found that psychiatrists and psychologists were accurate one-third of the time in their predictions of future violence among institutionalized patients who had been diagnosed as mentally ill and had previously been violent. See generally David L. Faigman et al., 1 *Modern Scientific Evidence: The Law and Science of Expert Testimony* §9.2.1 (2d ed. 2002).

BRADSHAW v. DANIEL
854 S.W.2d 865 (Tenn. 1993)

ANDERSON, J.

We granted this appeal to determine whether a physician has a legal duty to warn a non-patient of the risk of exposure to the source of his patient's non-contagious disease—Rocky Mountain Spotted Fever. The trial court denied the defendant physician's motion for summary judgment, but granted an interlocutory appeal on the issue of the physician's legal duty. The Court of Appeals limited the record and held that the facts were insufficient to show that the risk to the non-patient of contracting Rocky Mountain Spotted Fever was such that a legal duty arose on the part of the physician. We disagree and conclude, for the reasons stated herein, that the physician had a legal duty to warn the non-patient of the risk of exposure to the source of the patient's non-contagious disease.

On July 19, 1986, Elmer Johns went to the emergency room at Methodist Hospital South in Memphis, Tennessee, complaining of headaches, muscle aches, fever, and chills. He was admitted to the hospital under the care and treatment of the defendant, Dr. Chalmers B. Daniel, Jr. Dr. Daniel first saw Johns on July 22, 1986, at which time he ordered the drug Chloramphenicol, which is the drug of choice for a person in the latter stages of Rocky Mountain Spotted Fever. Johns' condition rapidly deteriorated, and he died the next day, July 23, 1986. An autopsy was performed, and the Center for Disease Control in Atlanta conclusively confirmed, in late September 1986, that the cause of death was Rocky Mountain Spotted Fever. Although Dr. Daniel communicated with Elmer Johns' wife, Genevieve, during Johns' treatment, he never advised her of the risks of exposure to Rocky Mountain Spotted Fever, or that the disease could have been the cause of Johns' death.

A week after her husband's death, on August 1, 1986, Genevieve Johns came to the emergency room of Baptist Memorial Hospital in Memphis, Tennessee, with similar symptoms of chills, fever, mental disorientation, nausea, lung congestion, myalgia, and swelling of the hands. She was admitted to the hospital and treated for Rocky Mountain Spotted Fever, but she died three days later, on August 4, 1986, of that disease. It is undisputed that no patient-physician relationship existed between Genevieve Johns and Dr. Daniel.

The plaintiff, William Jerome Bradshaw, is Genevieve Johns' son. He filed this suit alleging that the defendant's negligence in failing to advise Genevieve Johns that her husband died of Rocky Mountain Spotted Fever, and in failing to warn her of the risk of exposure, proximately caused her death. . . .

Here, we are asked to determine whether a physician has an affirmative duty to warn a patient's family member about the symptoms and risks of exposure to Rocky

Mountain Spotted Fever, a non-contagious disease. Insofar as we are able to determine, there is no reported decision from this or any other jurisdiction involving circumstances exactly similar to those presented in this case.

We begin by observing that all persons have a duty to use reasonable care to refrain from conduct that will foreseeably cause injury to others. . . .

In determining the existence of a duty, courts have distinguished between action and inaction. Professor Prosser has commented that "the reason for the distinction may be said to lie in the fact that by 'misfeasance' the defendant has created a new risk of harm to the plaintiff, while by 'nonfeasance' he has at least made his situation no worse, and has merely failed to benefit him by interfering in his affairs." Prosser, §56 at 373. . . .

Because of this reluctance to countenance nonfeasance as a basis of liability, as a general rule, under the common law, one person owed no affirmative duty to warn those endangered by the conduct of another. . . .

To mitigate the harshness of this rule, courts have carved out exceptions for cases in which the defendant stands in some special relationship to either the person who is the source of the danger, or to the person who is foreseeably at risk from the danger. . . . Accordingly,

> while an actor is always bound to prevent his acts from creating an unreasonable risk to others, he is under the affirmative duty to act to prevent another from sustaining harm only when certain socially recognized relations exist which constitute the basis for such legal duty. . . .

Decisions of other jurisdictions have . . . held that the relationship of a physician to his patient is sufficient to support the duty to exercise reasonable care to protect third persons against foreseeable risks emanating from a patient's physical illness. Specifically, other courts have recognized that physicians may be liable to persons infected by a patient, if the physician negligently fails to diagnose a contagious disease, or having diagnosed the illness, fails to warn family members or others who are foreseeably at risk of exposure to the disease. See Gammill v. United States, 727 F.2d 950, 954 (10th Cir. 1984) (physician may be found liable for failing to warn a patient's family, treating attendants, or other persons likely to be exposed to the patient of the nature of the disease and the danger of exposure); Hofmann v. Blackmon, 241 So. 2d 752, 753 (Fla. Dist. Ct. App. 1970), *cert. denied*, 245 So. 2d 257 (Fla. 1971) (physician has a duty to use reasonable care to advise a patient's family members of the existence and dangers of a disease). . . .

For example, in *Hofmann*, supra, an action was brought against a physician by a child who had contracted tuberculosis as a result of the physician's negligent failure to diagnose the disease in his patient, the child's father. Reversing a summary judgment for the physician, the Florida District Court of Appeals held

> that a physician owes a duty to a minor child who is a member of the immediate family and living with a patient suffering from a contagious disease to inform those charged with the minor's well being of the nature of the contagious disease and the precautionary steps to be taken to prevent the child from contracting such disease and that the duty is not negated by the physician negligently failing to become aware of the presence of such a contagious disease. . . .

Returning to the facts of this case, first, it is undisputed that there was a physician-patient relationship between Dr. Daniel and Elmer Johns. Second, here, as in the contagious disease context, it is also undisputed that Elmer Johns' wife, who was residing with him, was at risk of contracting the disease. This is so even though the disease is not contagious in the narrow sense that it can be transmitted from one person to another. Both Dr. Daniel and Dr. Prater, the plaintiff's expert, testified that family members of patients suffering from Rocky Mountain Spotted Fever are at risk of contracting the disease due to a phenomenon called clustering, which is related to the activity of infected ticks who transmit the disease to humans. Dr. Prater also testified that Dr. Daniel negligently failed to diagnose the disease and negligently failed to warn his patient's wife, Genevieve Johns, of her risk of exposure to the source of disease. Dr. Daniel's expert disputed these conclusions, but Dr. Daniel conceded there is a medical duty to inform the family when there is a diagnosis of the disease. Thus, this case is analogous to the *Tarasoff* line of cases adopting a duty to warn of danger and the contagious disease cases adopting a comparable duty to warn. Here, as in those cases, there was a foreseeable risk of harm to an identifiable third party, and the reasons supporting the recognition of the duty to warn are equally compelling here.

We, therefore, conclude that the existence of the physician-patient relationship is sufficient to impose upon a physician an affirmative duty to warn identifiable third persons in the patient's immediate family against foreseeable risks emanating from a patient's illness. Accordingly, we hold that under the factual circumstances of this case, viewing the evidence in a light most favorable to the plaintiff, the defendant physician had a duty to warn his patient's wife of the risk to her of contracting Rocky Mountain Spotted Fever, when he knew, or in the exercise of reasonable care, should have known, that his patient was suffering from the disease. Our holding here is necessarily limited to the conclusion that the defendant physician owed Genevieve Johns a legal duty. We express no opinion on the other elements which would be required to establish a cause of action for common-law negligence in this case.

Accordingly, the judgment of the Court of Appeals granting the defendant's motion for summary judgment is reversed, and this cause is remanded to the trial court for proceedings consistent with this opinion. . . .

NOTE TO BRADSHAW v. DANIEL

Beneficiaries of Duty.   The duty recognized in *Bradshaw* is owed to family members of the physician's patient. A physician who was aware that a patient suffered from a contagious disease would have an obligation to warn members of that patient's family or individuals who might treat the patient, but would have no obligation to extend a warning to members of the public in general. See Gammill v. United States, 727 F.2d 950 (9th Cir. 1984). The disease in *Bradshaw* was not contagious. Why did the court conclude that there was a duty to the family in this case?

Problem
Duty to Protect and Range of Risks

Would the analysis in *Bradshaw* support imposition of liability in the following situations?

A. After an infant receives a dose of oral polio vaccine, some amounts of live polio virus may grow in the infant's digestive tract. This can be dangerous to adults who come into contact with the infant if the adults are not immune to polio. A physician did not explain this risk to the parents of an immunized baby, and one of the parents contracted polio from the baby in this manner. See Tenuto v. Lederle Laboratories, 687 N.E.2d 1300 (N.Y. 1997).

B. A taxi driver was called to a place of business to pick up one of its customers. The customer murdered him shortly after getting into the taxi. The driver's estate claimed that the business operator was aware that the murderer had just committed other crimes and sought to impose liability on the business for its failure to warn the driver about the customer's likely conduct. Would the analysis in Bradshaw v. Daniel support this claim? See Mangeris v. Gordon (DBA Velvet Touch Massage Salon), 580 P.2d 481 (Nev. 1978).

C. A physician concluded that a patient faced significant health risks because of eating a diet extraordinarily heavy in saturated fats but did not warn members of the patient's family that they, too, faced those health risks. Would the physician be liable to the family members if those health risks materialized?

III. Duty Limited by Type of Harm

For two types of damages, the causal link between the defendant's act and the plaintiff's harm has traditionally been thought of as too tenuous to allow recovery. One of these is emotional distress caused by a defendant's negligent conduct that did not simultaneously involve some physical harm or impact to the plaintiff. The other is "mere economic harm," a claim of financial loss related to conduct by the defendant that did not involve any physical harm to the plaintiff or the plaintiff's property. The difficulties in proof and courts' fear of fraud led courts to refuse to impose liability in these situations.

In another situation, the birth of a child, courts have dealt with the fundamental question of whether to recognize any harm at all when the child was unwanted. These cases involve claims related to the birth of children whom their parents did not want, either because a sterilization procedure failed or because of errors in genetic counseling or other prenatal work that would have led the mother to abort the pregnancy had the prenatal tests been done correctly. Courts recognized policy problems with allowing recovery in these cases as well.

A. Negligently Inflicted Emotional Distress

In cases where a defendant's negligent conduct causes the plaintiff to suffer a physical injury at the time of the defendant's conduct, all courts allow the plaintiff to recover damages for the immediate physical harm and also for emotional harm associated with that initial physical harm. On the other hand, courts have had difficulty with cases where a plaintiff suffers no initial physical injury due to a defendant's negligent conduct but claims that the defendant's conduct caused an emotional injury. Robb v. The Pennsylvania Railroad Co. traces the history of legal developments in cases involving negligent conduct that inflicts emotional harm directly on a plaintiff. Among individuals who suffer emotional distress as a consequence of a defendant's negligence, should recovery be permitted for (1) all of them, (2) only those who were in a "zone of danger" in which they might have suffered an initial physical impact, or (3) only those who did suffer an initial physical impact?

For the situation where a plaintiff suffers emotional harm as a result of observing another person being physically harmed by a defendant's negligent conduct, courts have developed "bystander recovery" doctrines. James v. Lieb explains the development of that concept and applies it in a case involving a brother's reaction to his sister's fatal injury. Grotts v. Zahner treats the question of how close the relationship must be between the bystander and the defendant's initial victim in order to support recovery. Rabideau v. City of Racine continues that inquiry and addresses the issue of emotional distress damages in cases of harm to property.

ROBB v. THE PENNSYLVANIA RAILROAD CO.
210 A.2d 709 (Del. 1965)

HERRMANN, J.

The question before us for decision is this: May the plaintiff recover for the physical consequences of fright caused by the negligence of the defendant, the plaintiff being within the immediate zone of physical danger created by such negligence, although there was no contemporaneous bodily impact?

Considering the record in the light most favorable to the plaintiff, the facts may be thus summarized:

A private lane leading to the home of the plaintiff, Dixie B. Robb, was intersected by a railroad right-of-way leased to the defendant, The Pennsylvania Railroad Company. On March 11, 1961, the plaintiff was driving an automobile up the lane toward her home when the vehicle stalled at the railroad grade crossing. A rut about a foot deep had been negligently permitted by the defendant to form at the crossing. The rear wheels of the automobile lodged in the rut and, although the plaintiff tried to move the vehicle for several minutes, she was unable to do so. While thus engaged in attempting to move the vehicle, the plaintiff saw the defendant's train bearing down upon her. With only seconds to spare, she jumped from the stalled vehicle and fled for her life. Immediately thereafter, the locomotive collided with the vehicle, hurled it into the air and demolished it. The plaintiff was standing within a few feet of the track when the collision occurred and her face was covered with train soot and dirt. However—and this is the nub of the problem—she was not touched by the train; there was no bodily impact; and she suffered no contemporaneous physical injury. Nevertheless, the plaintiff was greatly frightened and emotionally disturbed by the accident as the result of which she sustained shock to her nervous system. The fright and nervous shock resulted in physical injuries. . . .

The defendant moved for summary judgment taking the position that, assuming the defendant's negligence and its proximate causation of the plaintiff's fright and nervous shock, she may not recover because there was no "impact" and contemporaneous physical injury. The trial judge agreed and granted summary judgment in the defendant's favor, stating: "In spite of a modern trend to the contrary in other jurisdictions, I feel compelled to follow the 'impact theory' in this matter by reason of well established precedents in this State." The plaintiff appeals. . . .

There is sharp diversity of judicial opinion as to the right to recover for the physical consequences of fright in the absence of an impact and contemporaneous physical injury. . . .

The two schools of thought in the matter at hand evolved from two lines of cases originating about the turn of the century. The impact rule was established in America by the leading cases of Ewing v. Pittsburgh, etc. R. Co., 147 Pa. 40, 23 A. 340, 14 L.R.A. 666 (1892); Mitchell v. Rochester R. Co., 151 N.Y. 107, 45 N.E. 354, 34 L.R.A. 731 (1896); and Spade v. Lynn & Boston R. Co., 168 Mass. 285, 47 N.E. 88, 38 L.R.A. 512 (1897). These cases reflected the influence of the earlier English case of Victorian Railways Commissioners v. Coultas, 13 App. Cas. 222 (1888), recognized generally as the first notable case to espouse the impact rule. . . .

The impact rule is based, generally speaking, upon three propositions expounded in the *Mitchell* and *Spade* cases:

1) It is stated that since fright alone does not give rise to a cause of action, the consequences of fright will not give rise to a cause of action. This is now generally recognized to be a non-sequitur, want of damage being recognized as the reason that negligence causing mere fright is not actionable. It is now generally agreed, even in jurisdictions which have adopted the impact rule, that the gist of the action is the injury flowing from the negligence, whether operating through the medium of physical impact or nervous shock.

2) It is stated that the physical consequences of fright are too remote and that the requisite causal connection is unprovable. The fallacies of this ground of the impact rule, viewed in the light of growing medical knowledge, were well stated by Chief Justice Maltbie in Orlo v. Connecticut Co., 128 Conn. 231, 21 A.2d 402 (1941). It was there pointed out that the early difficulty in tracing a resulting injury back through fright or nervous shock has been minimized by the advance of medical science; and that the line of cases permitting recovery for serious injuries resulting from fright, where there has been but a trivial impact in itself causing little or no injury, demonstrate that there is no insuperable difficulty in tracing causal connection between the wrongdoing and the injury via the fright.

3) It is stated that public policy and expediency demand that there be no recovery for the physical consequences of fright in the absence of a contemporaneous physical injury. In recent years, this has become the principal reason for denying recovery on the basis of the impact rule. In support of this argument, it is said that fright is a subjective state of mind, difficult to evaluate, and of such nature that proof by the claimant is too easy and disproof by the party charged too difficult, thus making it unsafe as a practical matter for the law to deal with such claims. This school of thought concludes that to permit recovery in such cases would open a "Pandora's Box" of fictitious and fraudulent claims involving speculative and conjectural damages with which the law and medical science cannot justly cope. . . .

In considering the expediency ground, the Supreme Court of Connecticut said in the *Orlo* case, supra:

". . . There is hardly more risk to the accomplishment of justice because of disparity in possibilities of proof in such situations than in those where mental suffering is allowed as an element of damage following a physical injury or recovery is permitted for the results of nervous shock provided there be some contemporaneous slight battery or physical injury. Certainly it is a very questionable position for a court to take, that because of the possibility of encouraging fictitious claims compensation should be denied those who have actually suffered serious injury through the negligence of another." . . .

It is our opinion that the reasons for rejecting the impact rule far outweigh the reasons which have been advanced in its support.

The cause of action and proximate cause grounds for the rule have been discredited in the very jurisdictions which first gave them credence. As stated by Holmes, C.J., for the Supreme Judicial Court of Massachusetts, the *Spade* decision did not result from "a logical deduction from the general principles of liability in tort, but as a limitation of those principles upon purely practical grounds." Smith v. Postal Telegraph Cable Co., 174 Mass. 576, 55 N.E. 380, 47 L.R.A. 323 (1899). . . .

If more were needed to warrant a declination to follow the cause of action and the proximate cause arguments, reference to the fictional and mechanical ends to which the impact rule has been carried would suffice for the purpose. The most trivial bodily contact, itself causing little or no injury, has been considered sufficient to take a case out of the rule and permit recovery for serious physical injuries resulting from the accompanying fright. Token impact sufficient to satisfy the rule has been held to be a slight bump against the seat, dust in the eyes, inhalation of smoke, a trifling burn, jostling in an automobile; indeed any degree of physical impact, however slight. . . .

This leaves the public policy or expediency ground to support the impact rule. We think that ground untenable.

It is the duty of the courts to afford a remedy and redress for every substantial wrong. . . . Neither volume of cases, nor danger of fraudulent claims, nor difficulty of proof, will relieve the courts of their obligation in this regard. None of these problems are insuperable. Statistics fail to show that there has been a "flood" of such cases in those jurisdictions in which recovery is allowed; but if there be increased litigation, the courts must willingly cope with the task. As to the danger of illusory and fictional claims, this is not a new problem; our courts deal constantly with claims for pain and suffering based upon subjective symptoms only; and the courts and the medical profession have been found equal to the danger. Fraudulent claims may be feigned in a slight-impact case as well as in a no-impact case. Likewise, the problems of adequacy of proof, for the avoidance of speculative and conjectural damages, are common to personal injury cases generally and are surmountable, being satisfactorily solved by our courts in case after case.

We are unwilling to accept a rule, or an expediency argument in support thereof, which results in the denial of a logical legal right and remedy in all cases because in some a fictitious injury may be urged or a difficult problem of the proof or disproof of speculative damage may be presented. Justice is not best served, we think, when compensation is denied to one who has suffered injury through the negligence of another merely because of the possibility of encouraging fictitious claims or speculative damages in other cases. Public policy requires the courts, with the aid of the legal and medical professions, to find ways and means to solve satisfactorily the problems thus presented — not expedient ways to avoid them.

Accordingly, we decline to adopt the impact rule, as urged by the defendant in this cause. . . .

We hold, therefore, that where negligence proximately caused fright, in one within the immediate area of physical danger from that negligence, which in turn produced physical consequences such as would be elements of damage if a bodily injury had been suffered, the injured party is entitled to recover under an application of the prevailing principles of law as to negligence and proximate causation. Otherwise stated, where results, which are regarded as proper elements of recovery as a consequence of physical injury, are proximately caused by fright due to negligence, recovery by one in the immediate zone of physical risk should be permitted.

This view has the general approval of the writers on the subject and is now distinctly the majority rule. We are satisfied that it is the better rule, supported by reason, logic and fairness.

We conclude, therefore, that the Superior Court erred in the instant case in holding that the plaintiff's right to recover is barred by the impact rule. The plaintiff claims physical injuries resulting from fright proximately caused by the negligence of the defendant. She should have the opportunity to prove such injuries and to recover therefor if she succeeds. The summary judgment granted in favor of the defendant must be reversed and the cause remanded for further proceedings.

NOTES TO ROBB v. THE PENNSYLVANIA RAILROAD CO.

1. *Distinguishing Emotional Consequences of Physical Harms.* In all jurisdictions, a defendant who causes physical harm to a plaintiff will be liable in damages for both that physical harm and any emotional consequences of that harm. *Robb* and other negligent infliction of emotional distress cases present a different problem. In these cases, a plaintiff does not claim that sustaining a physical harm has led to emotional consequences. Rather, the plaintiff claims that an emotional response to the defendant's conduct led to harmful consequences to the plaintiff. In *Robb*, the court permitted recovery for harmful physical consequences of emotional trauma, holding that if a result would be recoverable as a consequence of physical injury, it is recoverable as a result of emotional trauma, as long as the plaintiff was in the zone of danger.

2. *Shortcomings of the Impact Rule.* The *Robb* opinion describes the types of minimal impact that impact rule jurisdictions were willing to treat as satisfying the impact requirement and therefore authorizing the plaintiff to recover for the consequences of emotional harm. Why does their relative insignificance ("slight bump," "jostling") contradict the purposes for which the impact rule was developed?

3. *Definition of "Zone of Danger."* The rule ultimately adopted by the court in *Robb* is called the *zone of danger* rule. The rule does not allow everyone who suffers an adverse emotional result from a defendant's conduct to attempt to prove causation. How does the *Robb* court's opinion determine which individuals, out of all the individuals who might suffer emotional reactions to a defendant's conduct, are eligible to seek damages? How was the plaintiff in *Robb* within a zone of danger created by the defendant's negligent conduct?

4. *Justification of Zone of Danger Test.* The *Robb* court rejects the position that requiring impact can weed out false claims of harmful emotional reactions to defendants' negligent conduct. Tort law, the court states, can use other methods to avoid "fictitious claims or speculative damages." How might the zone of danger requirement work to avoid the risks of false or imaginary claims?

5. *Restatement (Third) of Torts Approach.* The Restatement (Third) of Torts: Liability for Physical and Emotional Harm §47 treats directly inflicted emotional distress as follows:

§47 Negligent Conduct Directly Inflicting Emotional Harm on Another
An actor whose negligent conduct causes serious emotional harm to another is subject to liability to the other if the conduct:

> (a) places the other in danger of immediate bodily harm and the emotional harm results from the danger; or
> (b) occurs in the course of specified categories of activities, undertakings, or relationships in which negligent conduct is especially likely to cause serious emotional harm.

Section 47(a) indicates that the rule applies to people, like Robb, who were themselves in imminent danger of bodily harm. Section 47(b) refers to special circumstances in which a plaintiff was not in imminent danger of bodily harm. Comment f to §47 describes some of those circumstances:

> Under the rule stated in Subsection (b), an actor who negligently performs specified undertakings or activities is subject to liability for emotional harm caused by negligence in conducting the undertaking or activity. Unlike Subsection (a), recovery under this Subsection does not require that the defendant have created a risk of bodily harm to the plaintiff. Early cases were of two types: (1) delivering a telegram or other communication erroneously announcing death or illness; and (2) mishandling a corpse or bodily remains. More recently, courts have recognized the awkwardness of relying on "impact" or "zone of danger" in cases involving consumption of a food that is then found to have been contaminated with a repulsive foreign object, such as a condom or a rodent, and instead have recognized these cases as falling within the rule of Subsection (b).

JAMES v. LIEB
375 N.W.2d 109 (Neb. 1985)

WHITE, J. . . .

The following facts were alleged in the petition. On August 10, 1983, plaintiffs' son, Gregory Duwayne James, and their daughter, Demetria, were riding their bicycles north on 50th Street in Omaha, Nebraska. A garbage truck owned by the defendant Watts Trucking Service, Inc., and driven by its employee, John Milton Lieb, was backing west on Spaulding Street. The truck backed into the intersection of 50th and Spaulding Streets, through a stop sign, and hit and ran over Demetria, killing her. Gregory helplessly watched the entire incident. As a result of witnessing his sister's peril, Gregory became physically ill and suffered, and will continue to suffer, mental anguish and emotional distress. . . .

The defendants demurred, contending that since plaintiffs' petition failed to allege that Gregory was within the "zone of danger" or in fear for his own safety, no cause of action for emotional distress had been asserted under Nebraska law. Based upon our prior holding in Fournell v. Usher Pest Control Co., 208 Neb. 684, 305 N.W.2d 605 (1981), the trial court dismissed the petition. . . .

. . . The majority in [*Fournell*] held that, under Nebraska law, to state a claim for negligent infliction of emotional distress or trauma, a plaintiff must first show that some type of physical injury resulted from the emotional trauma and, secondly, that he or she was within the "zone of danger or actually put in fear for his [or her] own safety." . . .

The "zone of danger" rule in general has been defended as a more rational means of determining liability than the "impact" rule which it replaced. . . .

However, in 1968 the California Supreme Court became the first jurisdiction to abolish the "zone of danger" rule and allow a bystander to recover for negligently inflicted emotional distress in its now landmark decision of Dillon v. Legg, 68 Cal. 2d 728, 441 P.2d 912, 69 Cal. Rptr. 72 (1968). . . .

In *Dillon* the plaintiffs, a mother and daughter, both witnessed an accident in which another daughter was struck and killed by a negligent driver. Arguably, the sister of the victim was within the zone of danger; her mother was not. In the view of the California Supreme Court, the facts of *Dillon* illustrated the fallacy of the "zone of danger" rule, which would deny recovery to one plaintiff, the mother, and allow recovery to the daughter. In the court's view, relief for the trauma equally suffered by both plaintiffs upon the apprehension of the child's death should not be based on the happenstance of a few yards. . . .

The interest worthy of legal protection presented by bystander cases such as the one before us was best described by the New Jersey Supreme Court when it adopted *Dillon*:

> [T]he interest assertedly injured is more than a general interest in emotional tranquility. It is the profound and abiding sentiment of parental love. The knowledge that loved ones are safe and whole is the deepest wellspring of emotional welfare. Against that reassuring background, the flashes of anxiety and disappointment that mar our lives take on safer hues. No loss is greater than the loss of a loved one, and no tragedy is more wrenching than the helpless apprehension of the death or serious injury of one whose very existence is a precious treasure.

Portee v. Jaffee, 84 N.J. 88, 97, 417 A.2d 521, 526 (1980). We find the profound and abiding love for one's sibling to be no less significant.

In its analysis the *Dillon* court reversed its position on the concept of a limited duty precluding liability to a plaintiff outside the zone of physical danger. According to the court, "the chief element in determining whether defendant owes a duty or an obligation to plaintiff is the foreseeability of the risk, that factor will be of prime concern in every case." . . .

While recognizing that "no immutable rule" could establish the defendant's duty for every future case, the court suggested the following "guidelines" as aids in resolution of bystander claims:

> (1) Whether plaintiff was located near the scene of the accident as contrasted with one who was a distance away from it. (2) Whether the shock resulted from a direct emotional impact upon plaintiff from the sensory and contemporaneous observance of the accident, as contrasted with learning of the accident from others after its occurrence. (3) Whether plaintiff and the victim were closely related, as contrasted with an absence of any relationship or the presence of only a distant relationship. . . .

We adopt the foreseeability approach of *Dillon*, with the following comments and modifications.

First, of the three *Dillon* factors the relationship between the plaintiff and victim is the most valuable in determining foreseeability, and therefore the most crucial.

[M]edical authorities are generally in agreement that a mere bystander who has no significant relationship with the victim will not suffer the profound, systematic mental and emotional reaction likely to befall a close relative as a result of witnessing or learning of the victim's death.

To satisfy this factor we choose not to require a relationship within a certain degree of consanguinity. . . . Rather, we will require that there be a marital or intimate familial relationship between the plaintiff and the victim. . . .

Our holding would not eliminate aunts, uncles, and grandparents from the class of potential plaintiffs, but would place upon them a heavier burden of proving a significant attachment.

Second, we address the factor that plaintiff's shock result from a "sensory and contemporaneous observance of the accident." No other aspect of the *Dillon* decision has drawn more attention than this factor. We agree with the observation of the Montana Supreme Court that if a "plaintiff is required to experience actual sensory perception of the accident, the requirement of proximity is necessarily satisfied." Versland v. Caron Transport, 671 P.2d 583, 586 (1983). It has been suggested that the requirements of physical proximity and "contemporaneous observation" impugn the integrity of the *Dillon* approach and that *Dillon* has merely replaced the arbitrary spatial boundary of the "zone of danger" rule with an arbitrary temporal boundary.

It is true in cases such as the one before us that the contemporaneous observation guideline would serve to assure the minds of a jury that the emotional injury is serious. However, if a sufficiently close relationship exists, the psychological reaction of the plaintiff in many cases could be the same or perhaps worse upon the hearing of the loss.

Rather, this guideline is, in effect, a policy consideration concerning the extent of the defendant's liability. As one court has stated, "Without such perception, the threat of emotional injury is lessened and the justification for liability is fatally weakened. The law of negligence, while it redresses suffering wrongfully caused by others, must not itself inflict undue harm by imposing an unreasonably excessive measure of liability." Portee v. Jaffee, 84 N.J. 88, 99, 417 A.2d 521, 527 (1980).

We believe that the Massachusetts Supreme Court has a better perspective on this criterion. . . .

> A plaintiff who rushes onto the accident scene and finds a loved one injured has no greater entitlement to compensation for that shock than a plaintiff who rushes instead to the hospital. So long as the shock follows closely on the heels of the accident, the two types of injury are equally foreseeable.

Ferriter v. Daniel O'Connell's Sons, Inc., 381 Mass. 507, 518, 413 N.E.2d 690, 697 (1980).

In addition to proving a sufficiently close relationship, we hold that the emotional trauma, the foreseeable harm to be redressed, must result from either death or serious injury to the victim. While minor injuries to a loved one may trigger emotions of sorrow and anxiety, these emotions pale in comparison to the profound grief, fright, and shock experienced following an accidental death or serious injury.

Before concluding, we must also address the further requirement of a cause of action for emotional distress in *Fournell*, that plaintiff must evidence some concurrent physical injury resulting from the emotional trauma. Other courts adopting the *Dillon* approach, to a certain degree, have retained this feature of the "zone of danger" rule. We now reject this requirement for many of the reasons stated in the Chief Justice's dissent in *Fournell*, supra at 697, 305 N.W.2d at 611: "To . . . require that, before one who is mentally injured may recover, he must at least regurgitate once seems . . . to be imposing upon the law a requirement that makes little or no sense."

Ostensibly, the problem in this area is of proving to a jury that a reasonable person in the position of the bystander plaintiff has suffered a compensable injury. While physical manifestation of the psychological injury may be highly persuasive, such proof is not necessary given the current state of medical science and advances in psychology. There are primarily three problems with this requirement: (1) It is overinclusive, since it could possibly lead to recovery for trivial claims of mental distress accompanied by physical symptoms; (2) It is underinclusive, since serious distress is arbitrarily deemed not compensable if not accompanied by physical symptoms; and (3) It encourages extravagant pleadings and distorted testimony.

In reaching our decision we are not unmindful of the several policy arguments advanced against the cause of action we have adopted. Typically, opponents of expanding liability in this area contend that (1) bystander recovery will inundate the courts with fictitious injuries and fraudulent claims; (2) courts will be deluged with a flood of litigation; (3) bystander recovery will unduly burden defendants with undue liability; and (4) once recognized, liability cannot reasonably be restrained. Each of these arguments have been adequately reflected by other courts. We add the following comments.

First, even courts opposed to recognizing this cause of action have acknowledged that the fear of fraudulent claims alone is an insufficient reason to deny all such claims. Furthermore, the "zone of danger" rule also carries with it the risk of fraudulent claims. "It is not hard to imagine plaintiffs and their attorneys falsely alleging that the claimant was in some small way injured by the defendant's negligence, or was within the zone of danger in order to present a valid cause of action." Leibson, *Recovery of Damages for Emotional Distress Caused by Physical Injury to Another*, 15 J. Fam. L. 163, 174 (1977). Also, it is not unlikely that under a "zone of danger" rule plaintiffs would carefully draft pleadings so as to vaguely present a factual question that the plaintiff was also in peril.

Second, taking California as an example, experience shows that its courts have not been overwhelmed with litigation in this area.

Third, the "dollars and cents" argument that society cannot afford the costs that will ensue from recognizing liability for the demonstrable injury of emotional distress naturally resulting from defendant's negligent act has been aptly dispelled. The possibility of increased insurance costs alone should not deny recovery for an otherwise valid claim.

Finally, we are not delayed by the specter that recognizing a cause of action for bystander recovery will naturally entail liability to every acquaintance of the victim. As we have emphasized, the class of bystanders limited to those with a marital or intimate familial status will sufficiently circumscribe the defendant's liability.

In summary, we hold that a plaintiff bystander has a cause of action for negligently inflicted foreseeable emotional distress upon a showing of marital or intimate familial relationship with a victim who was seriously injured or killed as a result of the proven negligence of a defendant. We thus find error in the district court's order sustaining the defendants' demurrer.

Reversed and remanded for further proceedings.

[Dissenting opinion omitted.]

NOTES TO JAMES v. LIEB

1. *Bystander Recovery.*   In bystander recovery cases, the plaintiff suffers emotional distress in reaction to someone else's injury, rather than in reaction to being personally in peril.

2. *Significance of Dillon v. Legg Guidelines.*   The *Dillon* court stated that three factors, or "guidelines," can establish the foreseeability to the defendant of the plaintiff's emotional distress. Those guidelines are the plaintiff's physical proximity to the injurious event, the plaintiff's contemporaneous observance of the event, and the relationship between the plaintiff and the direct victim of the defendant's conduct. Twenty-one years after deciding *Dillon*, the California Supreme Court held, in Thing v. La Chusa, 771 P.2d 814 (Cal. 1989), that those guidelines are required factors. Courts apply the *Dillon* factors with varying degrees of strictness. Focusing on what factual circumstances made the bystander's harm foreseeable, the *Lieb* court was more flexible than some courts. For instance, with respect to the closeness of the relationship between the victim and the plaintiff, the *Lieb* court chose not to require a close degree of consanguinity (such as parents, siblings, and offspring), but rather a "significant attachment" through a "marital or intimate familial relationship," which would not exclude aunts, uncles, and grandparents. The *Lieb* court also adopted the more flexible Massachusetts application of the contemporaneous observation requirement, requiring only that "the shock follows closely on the heels of the accident" and abandoned any requirement of physical injury resulting from the emotional trauma. On the other hand, the *Lieb* court would not permit bystander recovery when the loved one suffers only minor injuries, requiring that the direct victim of the negligence suffer serious injury or death. This requirement is absent from the *Dillon* factors. What policy reasons does the *Lieb* court give for each of these choices?

3. *Plaintiff's Awareness of Direct Victim's Injury.*   Following *Dillon*, decisions in California interpreted the contemporaneous observance criterion with varied degrees of strictness. In Archibald v. Braverman, 275 Cal. App. 2d 253, 79 Cal. Rptr. 723 (1969), the plaintiff mother was allowed to recover when she immediately arrived on the scene after the injury caused by an explosion that she had heard. In Arauz v. Gerhardt, 68 Cal. App. 3d 937, 137 Cal. Rptr. 619 (1977), the plaintiff mother was denied recovery where she had arrived at the scene of an accident after its occurrence.

Numerous decisions have rejected negligent infliction of emotional distress claims where the plaintiff learned of the direct victim's injury in a telephone call. See, e.g., Cohen v. McDonnell Douglas Corp., 450 N.E.2d 581 (Mass. 1983), where the plaintiff learned of her son's death seven hours after an airplane crash and did not observe the crash or her son's injury. Denying a cause of action, the court noted that the plaintiff was informed by means of a telephone conversation at her home in Massachusetts and that "at all pertinent times, Nellie Cohen was more than 1,000 miles from the scene of the crash." Should the physical distance affect the court's analysis of the fact that the plaintiff received the information in a phone call?

4. *Physical Manifestation of Emotional Distress.*   Many courts continue to require physical manifestation of emotional distress as an element of this cause of action, although they sometimes have difficulty in defining "physical." Temporary physical responses, such as loss of bladder control, may suffice. See Armstrong v. Paoli Memorial Hospital, 633 A.2d 605 (Pa. Super. Ct. 1993). Post-traumatic stress disorder, including weight loss and poor appetite, has been rejected as inadequate by one

court in a jurisdiction that requires physical manifestations. See Wilson v. Sears, Roebuck & Co., 757 F.2d 948 (8th Cir. 1985). The rival point of view treats the existence of emotional distress as a fact question that the plaintiff may attempt to prove with any relevant evidence. A justice of the Nebraska Supreme Court supported this position, stating, "To . . . require that, before one who is mentally injured may recover, he must at least regurgitate once seems . . . to be imposing upon the law a requirement that makes little or no sense." Fournell v. Usher Pest Control Co., 305 N.W.2d 605, 611 (Neb. 1981) (dissenting opinion).

The Restatement of Torts (Third): Liability for Physical and Emotional Harms §48 requires contemporary perception of the event (unlike *Lieb*):

> **§48 Negligent Infliction of Emotional Harm Resulting from Bodily Harm to a Third Person**
> An actor who negligently causes sudden serious bodily injury to a third person is subject to liability for serious emotional harm caused thereby to a person who:
> > (a) perceives the event contemporaneously, and
> > (b) is a close family member of the person suffering the bodily injury.

Consistent with *Lieb*, Restatement (Third) §48 does not require a physical manifestation of the emotional distress:

> This Section applies to a person who suffers emotional harm from contemporaneously perceiving bodily injury to a close family member even though the actor's negligent conduct does not cause direct physical impact to the person or cause that person to have fear or apprehension for his or her own safety.

See §48, comment j. According to the Restatement (published in 2012), 29 states follow the rule-based approach from *Dillon*, which *Lieb* followed in a very flexible way. Eleven states permit emotional distress recovery only if the plaintiff was in the zone of danger (applying the rule from *Robb*) and four follow the old impact rule that requires a plaintiff to have suffered some impact to recover for emotional harms.

Problem
Foreseeability of Non-Relative's Distress

While walking down a street, the plaintiff came upon Joanne Perkins, who had been negligently struck by a van operated by Airborne Freight Corporation. The plaintiff immediately went to Perkins's aid. On discovering that Perkins had no pulse, the plaintiff began to administer CPR and managed to restore Perkins's heartbeat on two brief occasions. Perkins was bleeding from her eyes, ears, nose, and mouth, as well as from other injured areas of her body, and the plaintiff became drenched in blood in the course of administering CPR. Public safety personnel soon responded to the accident, and the plaintiff watched as they placed Perkins in an ambulance and drove away. Perkins was taken to Massachusetts General Hospital and was soon pronounced dead. As a result of the failed rescue attempt, the plaintiff developed various symptoms of emotional distress that led to physical problems. The plaintiff apparently blamed himself for Perkins's death and was of the opinion that he had failed at the most important thing in his life. At the time of the accident, Perkins and the plaintiff were strangers. Should the "danger invites rescue" rule be of help to the plaintiff seeking damages for negligent infliction of emotional distress? See Migliori v. Airborne Freight Corp., 690 N.E.2d 413 (Mass. 1998).

Perspective: Negligent Infliction of Emotional Distress

A wide array of arguments can support treating negligently inflicted emotional distress like other negligently caused harms. If defendants do not pay for the emotional harm they cause, they will not have a proper incentive to take desirable precautions or to cut back their activities to an appropriate level. Also, emotional harms are no less speculative in terms of their existence and amount than other injuries for which recovery is allowed, such as pain and suffering accompanying immediate physical harm. See Peter A. Bell, *The Bell Tolls: Towards Full Tort Recovery for Psychic Injury*, 36 Fla. L. Rev. 333 (1992). If the existence and severity of emotional harm could be evaluated accurately by modern technology, would these arguments be sufficient to justify equal treatment of negligently inflicted emotional and physical harms?

GROTTS v. ZAHNER
989 P.2d 415 (Nev. 1999)

Mupin, J.

Appellant, Kellie Grotts ("Grotts"), and her fiance were involved in an accident with respondent Gertrude Zahner ("Zahner"). Grotts commenced her action below against Zahner seeking "bystander" emotional distress damages in connection with fatal injuries sustained by her fiance in the accident. The district court dismissed her claim of bystander emotional distress on the ground that she was not, as a matter of law, "closely related" to her fiancé for these purposes. Grotts appeals.

A bystander who witnesses an accident may recover for emotional distress in certain limited situations. See State v. Eaton, 101 Nev. 705, 716, 710 P.2d 1370, 1377-78 (1985) (citing Dillon v. Legg, 68 Cal. 2d 728, 441 P.2d 912, 916, 69 Cal. Rptr. 72 (Cal. 1968)). To recover, the witness-plaintiff must prove that he or she (1) was located near the scene; (2) was emotionally injured by the contemporaneous sensory observance of the accident; and (3) was closely related to the victim.

In State Department of Transportation v. Hill, 114 Nev. 810, 816, 963 P.2d 480, 483 (1998), a plurality of this court determined that "whether a plaintiff can recover [damages] for NIED [negligent infliction of emotional distress] after witnessing injury to another based on the plaintiff's relationship to the victim is generally a question of fact." Acknowledging that obvious cases will exist where the issue of "closeness" can be determined as a matter of law, the plurality concluded that the fact finder in most cases should be left with the task of assessing the nature and quality of the claimant's relationship to the victim for these purposes.

We now conclude, contrary to the plurality holding in *Hill*, that standing issues concerning "closeness of relationship" between a victim and a bystander should, as a general proposition, be determined based upon family membership, either by blood or marriage. Immediate family members of the victim qualify for standing to bring NIED claims as a matter of law. When the family relationship between the victim and the bystander is beyond the immediate family,[1] the fact finder should assess the nature and quality of the relationship and, therefrom, determine as a factual matter whether the relationship is close enough to confer standing. This latter category represents the "few close cases" where standing will be determined as an issue of fact, either by a jury or the trial court sitting without a jury. We therefore hold that any non-family "relationship" fails, as a matter of law, to qualify for NIED standing.

In this case, Grotts claims standing to lodge a "bystander" NIED claim because of her affianced relationship to the victim. Because she was not a member of his "family" by blood or marriage, we hold that she does not enjoy the type of "close relationship" required under *Eaton*.

For the above reasons, we affirm the trial court.

Rose, C.J., dissenting.

Just a year ago, in State, Department of Transportation v. Hill, 114 Nev. 810, 953 P.2d 480 (1998), we drafted a less rigid and more equitable framework for deciding negligent infliction of emotional distress issues. The majority's departure from the framework set forth in *Hill* prevents that procedure from being tested in our district courts to determine its validity. I believe we are discarding this precedent prematurely. . . .

The rule adopted by the majority requires a relationship by blood or marriage before one can claim to have a close relationship for purposes of pursuing damages for negligent infliction of emotional distress. While this rule will be predictable, it will permit some people to pursue this claim who have no close relationship, and yet prohibit others who have a loving, close relationship with someone injured or killed from pursuing these claims merely because they are not related by blood or marriage.

The case at issue provides a good example. Kellie Grotts and John Colwell were very much in love and expected to marry in the near future. They were at the zenith of love and commitment. Numerous plays and novels have been written about the great loss suffered when this type of relationship ends with the death of one party. Yet the majority denies Kellie Grotts' claim for emotional distress caused as a result of witnessing the death of the love of her life and constant companion simply because their wedding date was a few months off. This same scenario could happen to an older man and woman who, for a variety of reasons, had lived together for years but were not formally married.

And the unfairness of the rule adopted today does not stop there. Anyone living in a non-traditional relationship will be denied the chance to recover emotional distress damages, while those living together with benefit of marriage will not suffer such prejudice. It is a fact of life that many gay men and lesbian women have partners with whom they have lived for decades and shared a close, loving relationship. These individuals will be denied the right to even claim damages for emotional distress for witnessing injury or death to their partner for no other reason than that they are not legally married, a status they cannot prevent. The closeness of two people should be judged by the quality and intimacy of the relationship, not by whether there is a blood relationship or whether a document has been filed at the court house. A segment of our population should not be denied legal redress simply because of their lifestyle.

The rule we adopted in *Hill* permits a judge to first scrutinize the claim of emotional distress to determine if the relationship is sufficiently close to create an issue of fact to present to a jury. If it is, the jury will then hear all the facts of the case, including

---

[1] Family relationships beyond the first degree of consanguinity.

the nature of the relationship existing between the plaintiff and the party injured or killed. We ask juries to make all sorts of difficult determinations and deciding the closeness of a relationship is a judgment juries are uniquely qualified to make. Leaving this factual determination to the jury would give Nevada a reasonably flexible rule that does not arbitrarily bar those who would otherwise be able to establish a close relationship. The majority of this court once saw the wisdom of this rule.

Accordingly, I dissent.

NOTES TO GROTTS v. ZAHNER

1. *Non-Relatives as Eligible Plaintiffs.* Courts that recognize bystander recovery ordinarily base that result on the idea that extreme distress upon seeing a serious injury to another human being is far more foreseeable if the immediate victim is a close relative of the bystander than if the immediate victim and the bystander are strangers. Some courts continue to treat these cases as the dissent in *Grotts* recommends. For example, cohabitants who proved a stable and significant relationship were deemed to qualify for this cause of action in Dunphy v. Gregor, 642 A.2d 372 (N.J. 1994). The California Supreme Court rejects that result. See Elden v. Sheldon, 758 P.2d 582 (Cal. 1988).

2. *Inadequacy of Foreseeability Alone.* In a notable and horrible case, a plaintiff's close friend and neighbor entrusted her son to her, and the plaintiff took the child to a circus. A leopard attacked and killed the child, and the plaintiff witnessed that event. Despite the foreseeability of her distress, recovery against the circus was denied because there was no intimate family connection between the plaintiff and the child. See Eyrich ex rel. Eyrich v. Dam, 193 N.J. Super. 244, 473 A.2d 539 (App. Div.), *cert. denied*, 97 N.J. 583, 483 A.2d 127 (1984).

RABIDEAU v. CITY OF RACINE
627 N.W.2d 795 (Wis. 2001)

BABLITCH, J.

Dakota was shot by a City of Racine police officer. He subsequently died from the injury. Dakota lived with Julie Rabideau (Rabideau), who witnessed the events leading to his death. Rabideau subsequently filed a claim for damages against the City of Racine (the City). Racine County Circuit Court Judge Allan B. Torhorst granted summary judgment to the City, and the court of appeals affirmed.

The primary question presented in this case is whether Rabideau is entitled to damages for emotional distress. Although the question of whether or not a bystander may recover damages after witnessing an accident is a legal question that this court has previously addressed, this particular case is distinguishable from others: Dakota was a dog, a companion to Rabideau. . . .

We begin our analysis by briefly reviewing the facts. Rabideau and Officer Jacobi were neighbors. On March 31, 1999, Officer Jacobi had just returned home. Across the street, Rabideau was returning home as well. Dakota jumped out of Rabideau's truck. He crossed the street to the Jacobi house where Jed, the Jacobi's Chesapeake Bay retriever, was in the yard.

There is significant disagreement between the parties concerning what subsequently occurred. The City argued that Dakota came onto the Jacobi property and attacked Jed. Officer Jacobi, it is contended, shouted at Dakota to no effect. The City argues that Officer Jacobi, fearing for the safety of Jed, and for the safety of his wife and child who were nearby, fired a number of shots with his service revolver. Dakota moved toward the street and turned his head and was snarling. Officer Jacobi, believing the dog was about to charge, fired a third time and struck Dakota.

On the other hand, Rabideau contends that Dakota was sniffing Jed, not biting or acting aggressively. She asserts that she called Dakota and was crossing the street to retrieve him when shots rang out.

Although both parties agree that three shots were fired, Rabideau maintains that Dakota was stepping off the curb toward her when he was hit by Officer Jacobi's second shot. Rabideau asserts that while Dakota was struggling to crawl away, Officer Jacobi fired again and missed.

Two days after the shooting occurred, Rabideau was informed that Dakota died. Upon hearing this news, she collapsed and was given medical treatment.

Rabideau filed a complaint in small claims court, which stated: "City of Racine Police Officer Thomas Jacobi shot and killed my dog, Dakota, and caused me to collapse and require medical attention." . . .

Rabideau argues that the tort of negligent infliction of emotional distress to a bystander should encompass the facts of this case. Our tort law recognizes a claim for damages where a bystander suffers great emotional distress after witnessing an accident or its gruesome aftermath involving death or serious injury to a close relative. The elements of the claim are: "(1) that the defendant's conduct [in the underlying accident] fell below the applicable standard of care, (2) that the plaintiff suffered an injury [severe emotional distress], and (3) that the defendant's conduct was a cause-in-fact of the plaintiff's injury." Rabideau's complaint sets forth these elements.

Nevertheless, even if a plaintiff sets forth the elements of a negligence claim, a court may determine that liability is precluded by public policy considerations. Before a court makes such a determination, it is typically the better practice to submit the case to the jury. If, however, the facts of the case are not complex and the attendant public policy issues are presented in full, then this court may determine before trial if liability is precluded by public policy. Accordingly, we turn next to a consideration of the public policy concerns presented by this issue.

[T]wo concerns have historically shaped the development of the tort of negligent infliction of emotional distress. These concerns are (1) establishing that the claim is genuine, and (2) ensuring that allowing recovery will not place an unfair burden on the tortfeasor.

Where, as in the present case, the issue presented is negligent infliction of emotional distress on a bystander, three public policy factors [are] to be applied in an effort to establish that the claim is genuine, the tortfeasor is not unfairly burdened, and that other attendant public policy considerations are not contravened. First, the victim must have been killed or suffered a serious injury. Second, the plaintiff and victim must be related as spouses, parent-child, grandparent-grandchild or siblings. Third, "the plaintiff must have observed an extraordinary event, namely the incident and injury or the scene soon after the incident with the injured victim at the scene."

We need not address each of these factors because it is plain that the victim in this case is not related to Rabideau as a spouse, parent, child, sibling, grandparent or grandchild. Accordingly, she cannot maintain a claim for negligent infliction of emotional distress.

Rabideau urges that we extend this category to include companion animals. In her words, "anyone who has owned and loved a pet would agree that in terms of emotional trauma, watching the death of a pet is akin to losing a close relative." Further, she contends that we need not engage in an analysis of whether companion animals are "family," but should instead examine the rationale supporting the limitation to certain family members. Rabideau argues that the limitation of claims to family members is a means of assuring foreseeability as well as a reasonable limitation of the liability of a negligent tortfeasor. According to Rabideau, the bond between companion animals and humans is one that is sufficiently substantial to ensure that these concerns are met.

We agree, as we must, that humans form important emotional connections that fall outside the class of spouse, parent, child, grandparent, grandchild or sibling. We recognized this in *Bowen* [v. Lumbermens Mut. Cas. Co., 183 Wis. 2d 627, 517 N.W.2d 432 (1994)], and repeat here, that emotional distress may arise as a result of witnessing the death or injury of a victim who falls outside the categories established in tort law. However, the relationships between a victim and a spouse, parent, child, grandparent, grandchild or sibling are deeply embedded in the organization of our law and society. The emotional loss experienced by a bystander who witnessed the negligent death or injury of one of these categories of individuals is more readily addressed because it is less likely to be fraudulent and is a loss that can be fairly charged to the tortfeasor. The emotional harm occurring from witnessing the death or injury of an individual who falls into one of these relationships is serious, compelling, and warrants special recognition.

We concluded in *Bowen* that for the present time these tort claims would be limited; we reach the same conclusion in this case. We note that this rule of nonrecovery applies with equal force to a plaintiff who witnesses as a bystander the negligent injury of a best friend who is human as it does to a plaintiff whose best friend is a dog.

Had Rabideau been a bystander to the negligent killing of her best human friend, our negligence analysis would be complete. However, . . . the law categorizes dogs as property. We turn, therefore, to consider whether Rabideau can maintain a claim for negligent infliction of emotional distress arising from property loss.

In Kleinke v. Farmers Cooperative Supply & Shipping, 202 Wis. 2d 138, 145, 549 N.W.2d 714 (1996), we concluded that under Wisconsin's formulation of tort law, "it is unlikely that a plaintiff could ever recover for the emotional distress caused by negligent damage to his or her property." This conclusion was founded upon public policy.

The public policy analysis in *Kleinke* drew upon the reasoning of *Bowen*. In *Bowen* this court listed six public policy factors addressed by courts when considering the authenticity and fairness of an emotional distress claim. These various public policy considerations set forth in *Bowen*, and cited in *Kleinke*, are:

> (1) Whether the injury is too remote from the negligence; (2) whether the injury is wholly out of proportion to the culpability of the negligent tortfeasor; (3) whether in retrospect it appears too extraordinary that the negligence should have brought about the harm; (4) whether allowance of recovery would place an unreasonable burden on the negligent tortfeasor; (5) whether allowance of recovery would be too likely to open

the way to fraudulent claims; or (6) whether allowance of recovery would enter a field that has no sensible or just stopping point.

In this case we need only examine one of the *Bowen-Kleinke* factors to conclude that there is no basis for recovery here. This factor concerns whether allowance of recovery would enter a field that has no sensible or just stopping point. Rabideau suggests that limiting liability to the human companion of a companion animal who is killed may satisfy this concern. We find this proposed resolution unsatisfactory. First, it is difficult to define with precision the limit of the class of individuals who fit into the human companion category. Is the particular human companion every family member? the owner of record or primary caretaker? a roommate? Second, it would be difficult to cogently identify the class of companion animals because the human capacity to form an emotional bond extends to an enormous array of living creatures. Our vast ability to form these bonds adds to the richness of life. However, in this case the public policy concerns relating to identifying genuine claims of emotional distress, as well as charging tortfeasors with financial burdens that are fair, compel the conclusion that the definition suggested by Rabideau will not definitively meet public policy concerns.

Based upon all the above, we conclude that Rabideau cannot maintain a claim for the emotional distress caused by negligent damage to her property.

NOTES TO RABIDEAU v. CITY OF RACINE

1. *Significance of Emotional Relationship.*   In its analysis, the court refers to a plaintiff's close relatives, a plaintiff's close friends, and a plaintiff's companion animal. If the jurisdiction had a different position on recovery for emotional distress resulting from seeing injury to a close friend, would that have supported the plaintiff's argument in *Rabideau*?

2. *Distinguishing Between Harm to Individuals and Harm to Property.*   Are the reasons for denying emotional distress claims related to property damages different from or the same as the reasons for denying it when the emotional distress comes from seeing a close relative suffer a serious injury?

Perspective: Contractual Basis for Negligent Infliction Claims

Tort law has traditionally recognized recovery for emotional distress suffered without any immediate physical contact or harm in certain specific circumstances related to breach of contract.

> The first category of appropriate negligent-infliction cases . . . involves contractual relationships in which the defendant has assumed a contractual duty with respect to the mental well-being of the plaintiff. Cases dealing with mishandling of corpses, mistreatment of passengers by common carriers, and negligent telegraph companies are classic examples. Strictly speaking, these cases involve breaches of contract, but courts often analyze them in the rhetoric of negligence because the contractual duty is usually vaguely implied and subordinate to the main contractual relationship. Moreover, the plaintiff's emotional suffering usually resembles tort damages more closely than the

usual economic loss associated with contract breach. . . . There probably is little harm in analyzing such a case in negligence terms, rather than in the rhetoric of breach-of-contract cases. It is important, however, not to lose sight of the contractual relationship between hospital and patient as the source of the underlying duty, and therefore of the limits that prevent the negligence concept in this context from becoming an all-purpose tort.

David Crump, *Evaluating Independent Torts Based upon "Intentional" or "Negligent" Infliction of Emotional Distress: How Can We Keep Baby from Dissolving in the Bath Water?*, 34 Ariz. L. Rev. 439 (1992).

Without the special rules for these contractually based negligent infliction cases, would any of the various modern rules for recovery of damages for emotional distress allow recovery for family members emotionally harmed by a defendant who mishandled the corpse of an immediate family member or by defendant telegraph companies who negligently informed the family of the death of a loved one?

B. "Mere Economic" Harm

Cases in which a defendant's conduct causes physical harm to a plaintiff's property always allow recovery of economic damages. Where a plaintiff claims that a defendant's negligent conduct has caused the plaintiff to suffer harms that are entirely economic and that have occurred in the absence of a physical connection between the defendant and the plaintiff, courts have usually rejected those claims. As discussed in 532 Madison Avenue Gourmet Foods, Inc. v. Finlandia Center, Inc. and People Express Airlines, Inc. v. Consolidated Rail Corp., the central concern courts identify is the possibility of unlimited liability.

532 MADISON AVENUE GOURMET FOODS, INC. v. FINLANDIA CENTER, INC.

750 N.E.2d 1097 (N.Y. 2001)

KAYE, C.J.

The novel issues raised by these appeals — arising from construction-related disasters in midtown Manhattan — concern . . . a landholder's duty in negligence where plaintiffs' sole injury is lost income. . . .

Two of the three appeals involve the same event. On December 7, 1997, a section of the south wall of 540 Madison Avenue, a 39-story office tower, partially collapsed and bricks, mortar and other material fell onto Madison Avenue at 55th Street, a prime commercial location crammed with stores and skyscrapers. The collapse occurred after a construction project, which included putting 94 holes for windows into the building's south wall, aggravated existing structural defects. New York City officials directed the closure of 15 heavily-trafficked blocks on Madison Avenue — from 42nd to 57th Street — as well as adjacent side streets between Fifth and Park Avenues. The closure lasted for approximately two weeks, but some businesses nearest to 540 Madison remained closed for a longer period.

In 532 Madison Avenue Gourmet Foods v. Finlandia Center, plaintiff operates a 24-hour delicatessen one-half block south of 540 Madison, and was closed for five weeks. The two named plaintiffs in the companion case, 5th Avenue Chocolatiere v. 540 Acquisition Co., are retailers at 510 Madison Avenue, two blocks from the building, suing on behalf of themselves and a putative class of "all other business entities in whatever form, including but not limited to corporations, partnerships and sole proprietorships, located in the Borough of Manhattan and bounded geographically on the west side by Fifth Avenue, on the east by Park Avenue, on the north by 57th Street and on the south by 42nd Street." Plaintiffs allege that shoppers and others were unable to gain access to their stores during the time Madison Avenue was closed to traffic. Defendants in both cases are Finlandia Center (the building owner), 540 Acquisition Company (the ground lessee) and Manhattan Pacific Management (the managing agent).

On defendants' motions in both cases, Supreme Court dismissed plaintiffs' negligence claims on the ground that they could not establish that defendants owed a duty of care for purely economic loss in the absence of personal injury or property damage, and dismissed the public nuisance claims on the ground that the injuries were the same in kind as those suffered by all of the businesses in the community. . . .

Goldberg, Weprin & Ustin v. Tishman Construction involves the July 21, 1998 collapse of a 48-story construction elevator tower on West 43rd Street between Sixth and Seventh Avenues—the heart of bustling Times Square. Immediately after the accident, the City prohibited all traffic in a wide area of midtown Manhattan and also evacuated nearby buildings for varying time periods. Three actions were consolidated—one by a law firm, a second by a public relations firm and a third by a clothing manufacturer, all situated within the affected area. Plaintiff law firm sought damages for economic loss on behalf of itself and a proposed class "of all persons in the vicinity of Broadway and 42nd Street, New York, New York, whose businesses were caused to be closed" as well as a subclass of area residents who were evacuated from their homes. Plaintiff alleged gross negligence. . . .

Noting the enormity of the liability sought, including recovery by putative plaintiffs as diverse as hotdog vendors, taxi drivers and Broadway productions, Supreme Court concluded that the failure to allege personal injury or property damage barred recovery in negligence. . . .

The Appellate Division affirmed dismissal of the Goldberg Weprin complaint, concluding that, absent property damage, the connection between defendants' activities and the economic losses of the purported class of plaintiffs was "too tenuous and remote to permit recovery on any tort theory." The court, however, reinstated the negligence and public nuisance claims of plaintiffs 532 Madison and 5th Avenue Chocolatiere, holding that defendants' duty to keep their premises in reasonably safe condition extended to "those businesses in such close proximity that their negligent acts could be reasonably foreseen to cause injury" (which included the named merchant plaintiffs) and that, as such, they established a special injury distinct from the general inconvenience to the community at large. Two Justices dissented, urging application of the "economic loss" rule, which bars recovery in negligence for economic damage absent personal injury or property damage. The dissenters further concluded that the public nuisance claims were properly dismissed because plaintiffs could not establish special injury.

We now reverse in *532 Madison* and *5th Avenue Chocolatiere* and affirm in *Goldberg Weprin & Ustin.*

Plaintiffs contend that defendants owe them a duty to keep their premises in reasonably safe condition, and that this duty extends to protection against economic loss even in the absence of personal injury or property damage. Defendants counter that the absence of any personal injury or property damage precludes plaintiffs' claims for economic injury. . . .

As we have many times noted, foreseeability of harm does not define duty. Absent a duty running directly to the injured person there can be no liability in damages, however careless the conduct or foreseeable the harm. This restriction is necessary to avoid exposing defendants to unlimited liability to an indeterminate class of persons conceivably injured by any negligence in a defendant's act. . . .

In Strauss v. Belle Realty Co. (65 N.Y.2d 399, 492 N.Y.S.2d 555, 482 N.E.2d 34), we considered whether a utility owed a duty to a plaintiff injured in a fall on a darkened staircase during a Citywide blackout. While the injuries were logically foreseeable, there was no contractual relationship between the plaintiff and the utility for lighting in the building's common areas. As a matter of policy, we restricted liability for damages in negligence to direct customers of the utility in order to avoid crushing exposure to the suits of millions of electricity consumers in New York City and Westchester.

Even closer to the mark is Milliken & Co. v. Consolidated Edison Co. (84 N.Y.2d 469, 619 N.Y.S.2d 686, 644 N.E.2d 268), in which an underground water main burst near 38th Street and 7th Avenue in Manhattan. The waters flooded a subbasement where Consolidated Edison maintained an electricity supply substation, and then a fire broke out, causing extensive damage that disrupted the flow of electricity to the Manhattan Garment Center and interrupting the biannual Buyers Week. Approximately 200 Garment Center businesses brought more than 50 lawsuits against Con Edison, including plaintiffs who had no contractual relationship with the utility and who sought damages solely for economic loss. Relying on *Strauss,* we again held that only those persons contracting with the utility could state a cause of action. We circumscribed the ambit of duty to avoid limitless exposure to the potential suits of every tenant in the skyscrapers embodying the urban skyline.

A landowner who engages in activities that may cause injury to persons on adjoining premises surely owes those persons a duty to take reasonable precautions to avoid injuring them. We have never held, however, that a landowner owes a duty to protect an entire urban neighborhood against purely economic losses. A comparison of Beck v. FMC Corp. (53 A.D.2d 118, 121, 385 N.Y.S.2d 956, *aff'd* 42 N.Y.2d 1027, 398 N.Y.S.2d 1011, 369 N.E.2d 10) and Dunlop Tire and Rubber Corp. v. FMC Corp. (53 A.D.2d 150, 154-155, 385 N.Y.S.2d 971) is instructive. Those cases arose out of the same incident: an explosion at defendant FMC's chemical manufacturing plant caused physical vibrations, and rained stones and debris onto plaintiff Dunlop Tire's nearby factory. The blast also caused a loss of electrical power — by destroying towers and distribution lines owned by a utility — to both Dunlop Tire and a Chevrolet plant located one and one-half miles away. Both establishments suffered temporary closure after the accident. Plaintiffs in *Beck* were employees of the Chevrolet plant who sought damages for lost wages caused by the plant closure. Plaintiff Dunlop Tire sought recovery for property damage emanating from the blast and the loss of energy, and lost profits sustained during the shutdown.

In *Dunlop Tire*, the Appellate Division observed that, although part of the damage occurred from the loss of electricity and part from direct physical contact, defendant's duty to plaintiffs was undiminished. The court permitted plaintiffs to seek damages for economic loss, subject to the general rule requiring proof of the extent of the damage and the causal relationship between the negligence and the damage. The *Beck* plaintiffs, by contrast, could not state a cause of action, because, to extend a duty to defendant FMC would, "like the rippling of the waters, [go] far beyond the zone of danger of the explosion," to everyone who suffered purely economic loss.

Plaintiffs' reliance on People Express Airlines, Inc. v. Consolidated Rail Corp. (100 N.J. 246, 495 A.2d 107) is misplaced. There, a fire started at defendant's commercial freight yard located across the street from plaintiff's airport offices. A tank containing volatile chemicals located in the yard was punctured, emitting the chemicals and requiring closure of the terminal because of fear of an explosion. Allowing the plaintiff to seek damages for purely economic loss, the New Jersey court reasoned that the extent of liability and degree of foreseeability stand in direct proportion to one another: the more particular the foreseeability that economic loss would be suffered as a result of the defendant's negligence, the more just that liability be imposed and recovery permitted. The New Jersey court acknowledged, however, that the presence of members of the public, or invitees at a particular plaintiff's business, or persons traveling nearby, while foreseeable, is nevertheless fortuitous, and the particular type of economic injury that they might suffer would be hopelessly unpredictable. Such plaintiffs, the court recognized, would present circumstances defying any appropriately circumscribed orbit of duty. We see a like danger in the urban disasters at issue here, and decline to follow *People Express.*

Policy-driven line-drawing is to an extent arbitrary because, wherever the line is drawn, invariably it cuts off liability to persons who foreseeably might be plaintiffs. The *Goldberg Weprin* class, for example, would include all persons in the vicinity of Times Square whose businesses had to be closed and a subclass of area residents evacuated from their homes; the *5th Avenue Chocolatiere* class would include all business entities between 42nd and 57th Streets and Fifth and Park Avenues. While the Appellate Division attempted to draw a careful boundary at storefront merchant-neighbors who suffered lost income, that line excludes others similarly affected by the closures — such as the law firm, public relations firm, clothing manufacturer and other displaced plaintiffs in *Goldberg Weprin*, the thousands of professional, commercial and residential tenants situated in the towers surrounding the named plaintiffs, and suppliers and service providers unable to reach the densely populated New York City blocks at issue in each case.

As is readily apparent, an indeterminate group in the affected areas thus may have provable financial losses directly traceable to the two construction-related collapses, with no satisfactory way geographically to distinguish among those who have suffered purely economic losses. In such circumstances, limiting the scope of defendants' duty to those who have, as result of these events, suffered personal injury or property damage — as historically courts have done — affords a principled basis for reasonably apportioning liability.

We therefore conclude that plaintiffs' negligence claims based on economic loss alone fall beyond the scope of the duty owed them by defendants and should be dismissed. . . .

Accordingly, in 532 Madison Avenue Gourmet Foods v. Finlandia Center, the order of the Appellate Division should be reversed with costs, the defendants' motion to dismiss the complaint granted and the certified question answered in the negative. In 5th Avenue Chocolatiere, et al. v. 540 Acquisition Co., the order of the Appellate Division should be reversed with costs, the defendants' motion to dismiss the complaint granted in its entirety and the certified question answered in the negative. In Goldberg Weprin & Ustin v. Tishman Construction, the order of the Appellate Division, insofar as appealed from, should be affirmed with costs.

NOTES TO 532 MADISON AVENUE GOURMET FOODS, INC. v. FINLANDIA CENTER, INC.

1. *Principled Basis for Decision.* The court states that making defendants liable only to those who suffer personal injury or property damage is a "principled basis" for handling economic loss claims. Does the court mean that its rule reflects some important policy factors, or does it mean that its resolution involves a doctrine that is easy to apply?

2. *Fear of Immense Damages.* Judge Irving Kaufman supported the traditional "mere economic loss" rule in Kinsman Transit Co. v. City of Buffalo, 388 F.2d 821, 825 n.8 (2d Cir. 1968), using this hypothetical example:

> A driver who negligently caused such an accident would certainly be held accountable to those physically injured in the crash. But we doubt that damages would be recoverable against the negligent driver in favor of truckers or contract carriers who suffered provable losses because of the delay or to the wage earner who was forced to "clock in" an hour late. And yet it was surely foreseeable that among the many . . . who would be delayed would be truckers and wage earners.

How extreme would the total damages award likely be if even the prospective plaintiffs in this hypothetical were held to be entitled to compensation? In Eileen Silverstein, *On Recovery in Tort for Pure Economic Loss*, 32 U. Mich. J.L. Reform 403, 422-425 (1999), the author proposes calculations leading to the conclusion that the award might be "about $1.5 million, a significant sum, but hardly pauperizing in a world of multi-million dollar awards to one or two parties seriously injured in traffic accidents."

PEOPLE EXPRESS AIRLINES, INC. v. CONSOLIDATED RAIL CORP.
100 N.J. 246, 495 A.2d 107 (1985)

HANDLER, J.

This appeal presents a question that has not previously been directly considered: whether a defendant's negligent conduct that interferes with a plaintiff's business resulting in purely economic losses, unaccompanied by property damage or personal injury, is compensable in tort. . . .

On July 22, 1981, a fire began in the Port Newark freight yard of defendant Consolidated Rail Corporation (Conrail) when ethylene oxide manufactured by defendant BASF Wyandotte Company (BASF) escaped from a tank car, punctured during a "coupling" operation with another rail car, and ignited. The tank car was owned by defendant Union Tank Car Company (Union Car) and was leased to defendant BASF.

The plaintiff asserted at oral argument that at least some of the defendants were aware from prior experiences that ethylene oxide is a highly volatile substance; further, that emergency response plans in case of an accident had been prepared. When the fire occurred that gave rise to this lawsuit, some of the defendants' consultants helped determine how much of the surrounding area to evacuate. The municipal authorities then evacuated the area within a one-mile radius surrounding the fire to lessen the risk to persons within the area should the burning tank car explode. The evacuation area included the adjacent North Terminal building of Newark International Airport, where plaintiff People Express Airlines' (People Express) business operations are based. Although the feared explosion never occurred, People Express employees were prohibited from using the North Terminal for twelve hours.

The plaintiff contends that it suffered business-interruption losses as a result of the evacuation. These losses consist of canceled scheduled flights and lost reservations because employees were unable to answer the telephones to accept bookings; also, certain fixed operating expenses allocable to the evacuation time period were incurred and paid despite the fact that plaintiff's offices were closed. No physical damage to airline property and no personal injury occurred as a result of the fire.

According to People Express' original complaint, each defendant acted negligently and these acts of negligence proximately caused the plaintiff's harm. . . .

Conrail moved for summary judgment, seeking dismissal of the complaint and cross-claims against it; the motion was opposed by plaintiff, People Express, and defendants BASF and Union Car. The trial court granted Conrail's summary judgment motion on the ground that absent property damage or personal injury economic loss was not recoverable in tort. . . .

The Appellate Division granted plaintiff's interlocutory request for leave to appeal and reversed the trial court's order granting summary judgment. . . . This Court granted defendant Union Car's petition for certification, in which Conrail and BASF joined, and denied People Express' motion to dismiss the petition for certification. . . .

The single characteristic that distinguishes parties in negligence suits whose claims for economic losses have been regularly denied by American and English courts from those who have recovered economic losses is, with respect to the successful claimants, the fortuitous occurrence of physical harm or property damage, however slight. It is well-accepted that a defendant who negligently injures a plaintiff or his property may be liable for all proximately caused harm, including economic losses. . . . Nevertheless, a virtually per se rule barring recovery for economic loss unless the negligent conduct also caused physical harm has evolved throughout this century. . . .

The reasons that have been advanced to explain the divergent results for litigants seeking economic losses are varied. Some courts have viewed the general rule against recovery as necessary to limit damages to reasonably foreseeable consequences of negligent conduct. . . . The physical harm rule also reflects certain deep-seated concerns that underlie courts' denial of recovery for purely economic losses occasioned by a defendant's negligence. These concerns include the fear of fraudulent claims, mass litigation, and limitless liability, or liability out of proportion to the defendant's fault. . .

Judicial discomfiture with the rule of nonrecovery for purely economic loss throughout the last several decades has led to numerous exceptions in the general rule. Although the rationalizations for these exceptions differ among courts and cases, two common threads run throughout the exceptions. The first is that the element of foreseeability emerges as a more appropriate analytical standard to determine the question of liability than a per se prohibitory rule. The second is that the extent to which the defendant knew or should have known the particular consequences of his negligence, including the economic loss of a particularly foreseeable plaintiff, is dispositive of the issues of duty and fault.

One group of exceptions is based on the "special relationship" between the tortfeasor and the individual or business deprived of economic expectations. Many of these cases are recognized as involving the tort of negligent misrepresentation, resulting in liability for specially foreseeable economic losses. Importantly, the cases do not involve a breach of contract claim between parties in privity; rather, they involve tort claims by innocent third parties who suffered purely economic losses at the hands of negligent defendants with whom no direct relationship existed. Courts have justified their finding of liability in these negligence cases based on notions of a special relationship between the negligent tortfeasors and the foreseeable plaintiffs who relied on the quality of defendants' work or services, to their detriment. The special relationship, in reality, is an expression of the courts' satisfaction that a duty of care existed because the plaintiffs were particularly foreseeable and the injury was proximately caused by the defendant's negligence.

The special relationship exception has been extended to auditors, see H. Rosenblum, Inc. v. Adler, . . . 93 N.J. 324, 461 A.2d 138 (independent auditor whose negligence resulted in inaccurate public financial statement held liable to plaintiff who bought stock in company for purposes of sale of business to company; stock subsequently proved to be worthless); surveyors, see Rozny v. Marnul, 43 Ill. 2d 54, 250 N.E.2d 656 (1969) (surveyor whose negligence resulted in error in depicting boundary of lot held liable to remote purchaser); termite inspectors, see Hardy v. Carmichael, 207 Cal. App. 2d 218, 24 Cal. Rptr. 475 (Cal. Ct. App. 1962) (termite inspectors whose negligence resulted in purchase of infested home liable to out-of-privity buyers); engineers, see M. Miller Co. v. Central Contra Costa Sanitary Dist., 198 Cal. App. 2d 305, 18 Cal. Rptr. 13 (Cal. Ct. App. 1961) (engineers whose negligence resulted in successful bidder's losses in performing construction contract held liable); attorneys, see Lucas v. Hamm, 56 Cal. 2d 583, 15 Cal. Rptr. 821, 364 P.2d 685 (1961), *cert. den.,* 368 U.S. 987, 82 S. Ct. 603, 7 L. Ed. 2d 525 (1962) (attorney whose negligence caused intended beneficiary to be deprived of proceeds of the will was liable to beneficiary); notaries public, see Immerman v. Ostertag, 83 N.J. Super. 364, 199 A.2d 869 (Law Div. 1964); architects, see United States v. Rogers & Rogers, 161 F. Supp. 132 (S.D. Cal. 1958) (architects whose negligence resulted in use of defective concrete liable to out-of-privity prime contractor); weighers, see Glanzer v. Shepard, 233 N.Y. 236, 135 N.E. 275 (1922) (public weigher whose negligence caused remote buyer's losses was liable for loss); and telegraph companies, see Western Union Tel. Co. v. Mathis, 215 Ala. 282, 110 So. 399 (1926) (telegraph company whose negligent transmission caused plaintiff not to obtain contract was liable). . . .

Courts have found it fair and just in all of these exceptional cases to impose liability on defendants who, by virtue of their special activities, professional training or other unique preparation for their work, had particular knowledge or reason to know that others, such as the intended beneficiaries of wills . . . or the purchasers of stock who were expected to rely on the company's financial statement in the prospectus . . . would be economically harmed by negligent conduct. In this group of cases, even though the particular plaintiff was not always foreseeable, the particular class of plaintiffs was foreseeable as was the particular type of injury.

A very solid exception allowing recovery for economic losses has also been created in cases akin to private actions for public nuisance. Where a plaintiff's business is based in part upon the exercise of a public right, the plaintiff has been able to recover purely economic losses caused by a defendant's negligence. See, e.g., Louisiana ex rel. Guste v. M/V Testbank, 752 F.2d 1019 (5th Cir. 1985) (en banc) (defendants responsible for ship collision held liable to all commercial fishermen, shrimpers, crabbers and oystermen for resulting pollution of Mississippi River). . . . The theory running throughout these cases, in which the plaintiffs depend on the exercise of the public or riparian right to clean water as a natural resource, is that the pecuniary losses suffered by those who make direct use of the resource are particularly foreseeable because they are so closely linked, through the resource, to the defendants' behavior.

Particular knowledge of the economic consequences has sufficed to establish duty and proximate cause in contexts other than those already considered. In Henry Clay v. Jersey City, 74 N.J. Super. 490, 181 A.2d 545 (Ch. Div. 1962), aff'd, 84 N.J. Super. 9, 200 A.2d 787 (App. Div. 1964), for example, a lessee-manufacturer had to vacate the building in which its business was located because of the defendant city's negligent failure to maintain its sewer line while the line was repaired. While there was some property damage, the court treated the tenant's and owner's claims separately; the tenant's claims were purely economic, stemming from the loss of use of its property right, as in the instant case. Further, the city had had notice of the leak since 1957 and should have known about it even earlier. Duty, breach and proximate cause were found to exist; the plaintiff-tenant recovered lost profits and expenses incurred during the shut-down.

These exceptions expose the hopeless artificiality of the per se rule against recovery for purely economic losses. When the plaintiffs are reasonably foreseeable, the injury is directly and proximately caused by defendant's negligence, and liability can be limited fairly, courts have endeavored to create exceptions to allow recovery. The scope and number of exceptions, while independently justified on various grounds, have nonetheless created lasting doubt as to the wisdom of the per se rule of nonrecovery for purely economic losses. Indeed, it has been fashionable for commentators to state that the rule has been giving way for nearly fifty years, although the cases have not always kept pace with the hypothesis. . . .

We hold therefore that a defendant owes a duty of care to take reasonable measures to avoid the risk of causing economic damages, aside from physical injury, to particular plaintiffs or plaintiffs comprising an identifiable class with respect to whom defendant knows or has reason to know are likely to suffer such damages from its conduct. A defendant failing to adhere to this duty of care may be found liable for such economic damages proximately caused by its breach of duty.

We stress that an identifiable class of plaintiffs is not simply a foreseeable class of plaintiffs. For example, members of the general public, or invitees such as sales and service persons at a particular plaintiff's business premises, or persons travelling on a highway near the scene of a negligently-caused accident, such as the one at bar, who are delayed in the conduct of their affairs and suffer varied economic losses, are certainly a foreseeable class of plaintiffs. Yet their presence within the area would be fortuitous, and the particular type of economic injury that could be suffered by such persons would be hopelessly unpredictable and not realistically foreseeable. Thus, the class itself would not be sufficiently ascertainable. An identifiable class of plaintiffs must be particularly foreseeable in terms of the type of persons or entities comprising the class, the certainty or predictability of their presence, the approximate numbers of those in the class, as well as the type of economic expectations disrupted. . . .

Liability depends not only on the breach of a standard of care but also on a proximate causal relationship between the breach of the duty of care and resultant losses. . . . The standard of particular foreseeability may be successfully employed to determine whether the economic injury was proximately caused, i.e., whether the particular harm that occurred is compensable, just as it informs the question whether a duty exists. . . .

We conclude therefore that a defendant who has breached his duty of care to avoid the risk of economic injury to particularly foreseeable plaintiffs may be held liable for actual economic losses that are proximately caused by its breach of duty. In this context, those economic losses are recoverable as damages when they are the natural and probable consequence of a defendant's negligence in the sense that they are reasonably to be anticipated in view of defendant's capacity to have foreseen that the particular plaintiff or identifiable class of plaintiffs . . . is demonstrably within the risk created by defendant's negligence.

We are satisfied that our holding today is fully applicable to the facts that we have considered on this appeal. . . . Among the facts that persuade us that a cause of action has been established is the close proximity of the North Terminal and People Express Airlines to the Conrail freight yard; the obvious nature of the plaintiff's operations and particular foreseeability of economic losses resulting from an accident and evacuation; the defendants' actual or constructive knowledge of the volatile properties of ethylene oxide; and the existence of an emergency response plan prepared by some of the defendants . . . which apparently called for the nearby area to be evacuated to avoid the risk of harm in case of an explosion. We do not mean to suggest by our recitation of these facts that actual knowledge of the eventual economic losses is necessary to the cause of action; rather, particular foreseeability will suffice. . . .

We appreciate that there will arise many similar cases that cannot be resolved by our decision today. The cause of action we recognize, however, is one that most appropriately should be allowed to evolve on a case-by-case basis in the context of actual adjudications. . . . We perceive no reason, however, why our decision today should be applied only prospectively. . . .

Accordingly, the judgment of the Appellate Division is modified, and, as modified, affirmed. The case is remanded for proceedings consistent with this opinion.

NOTES TO PEOPLE EXPRESS AIRLINES, INC. v. CONSOLIDATED RAIL CORP.

1. *Influence of* People Express.   The opinion in *People Express* is widely known for its adoption of the "particular foreseeability" rule to substitute for the general rule of no recovery for economic harms alone. This rule reflects the same types of considerations present in the *Dillon* rule for recovery of emotional harm unaccompanied by physical harm. While often cited by New Jersey courts, this rule has not been

generally followed elsewhere. One exception is the Supreme Court of Alaska, which followed the particular foreseeability rule in Mattingly v. Sheldon Jackson College, 743 P.2d 356 (Alaska 1987). In that case, the court held that an employer stated a claim for negligently caused economic loss of income and profits when a trench in which his employees were working collapsed on and injured the employees.

2. Exceptions to the Economic Harm Rule.   The *People Express* opinion summarizes generally recognized exceptions to the economic damages rule. These exceptions are based on special noncontractual relationships between the parties that make the plaintiffs particularly foreseeable and on private actions for public nuisance in which the plaintiffs' use of the natural resource made them particularly foreseeable. A related exception applies to groups for whom the law has traditionally shown great solicitude. In Carbone v. Ursich, 209 F.2d 128 (9th Cir. 1953), the court allowed the crew of a fishing vessel to recover economic damages from the owner of another ship when the other boat fouled the fishing boat's nets, requiring the crew to stand idle for three days while repairs were made. Are sailors and seamen "particularly foreseeable" plaintiffs under the *People Express* rule?

3. Linking Losses to Defendants' Conduct.   The nature of the plaintiff's business may have made it especially easy to claim that the defendants' conduct caused losses. Airline seats are a perishable commodity. Reservations not made during the time period that the plaintiff's reservations center was closed may well have been made on other airlines; alternatively, individuals who could not make reservations during that period may have chosen not to fly at all. Would a passenger with reservations on a canceled *People Express* flight to Chicago who missed a meeting and an opportunity to close a $1 million business deal be able to collect damages under the particular foreseeability rule?

C. "Wrongful Pregnancy," "Wrongful Birth," and "Wrongful Life"

Standard tort principles apply when a physician makes errors during a patient's sterilization procedure and the patient suffers physical injury. Similarly, traditional tort principles govern cases where a physician treats a pregnant woman or a fetus and injures the woman or the fetus. Other types of recurring cases involving pregnancy and birth have sometimes been difficult for tort law.

Applying typical tort doctrines has been problematic where a failed sterilization procedure leads to the birth of a normal child. Can the birth of a child be treated as a harm? Cases of this kind have been called *wrongful pregnancy* cases. They seek to treat the occurrence of conception as a harm.

In other cases, errors in genetic counseling or prenatal diagnoses can lead to the birth of a child with birth defects. In actions called *wrongful birth*, parents claim that they would have aborted the pregnancy if they had received accurate genetic or diagnostic information. An action brought in these circumstances by the child who was born is called a *wrongful life* claim. Wrongful birth and wrongful life claims seek to treat the birth as a harm. Greco v. United States represents the mainstream approach to many of the issues involved in wrongful pregnancy, wrongful birth, and wrongful life claims.

GRECO v. UNITED STATES
893 P.2d 345 (Nev. 1995)

SPRINGER, J.

In this case we certify to the United States District Court for the District of Maryland that a mother has a tort claim in negligent malpractice against professionals who negligently fail to make a timely diagnosis of gross and disabling fetal defects, thereby denying the mother her right to terminate the pregnancy. We further certify that the child born to this mother has no personal cause of action for what is sometimes called "wrongful life." . . .

In July 1989, appellant, Sundi A. Greco, mother of co-appellant Joshua Greco, ("Joshua") filed suit individually, and on Joshua's behalf, against respondent, the United States of America. Sundi Greco and Joshua alleged that Sundi Greco's doctors at the Nellis Air Force Base in Nevada committed several acts of negligence in connection with Sundi Greco's prenatal care and delivery and that, as a result, both Sundi and Joshua are entitled to recover money damages.[2] The United States moved to dismiss the suit on the ground that the complaint failed to state a cause of action.

On July 20, 1993, the United States District Court for the District of Maryland filed a certification order with this court pursuant to NRAP 5, requesting that this court answer certain questions relating to the negligently caused unwanted birth of a child suffering from birth defects.

The Grecos, mother and child, in this case seek to recover damages from the United States arising out of the negligence of physicians who, they claim, negligently failed to make a timely diagnosis of physical defects and anomalies afflicting the child when it was still in the mother's womb. Sundi Greco asserts that the physicians' negligence denied her the opportunity to terminate her pregnancy and thereby caused damages attendant to the avoidable birth of an unwanted and severely deformed child. On Joshua's behalf, Sundi Greco avers that the physicians' negligence and the resultant denial of Joshua's mother's right to terminate her pregnancy caused Joshua to be born into a grossly abnormal life of pain and deprivation.

These kinds of tort claims have been termed "wrongful birth" when brought by a parent and "wrongful life" when brought on behalf of the child for the harm suffered by being born deformed.

We decline to recognize any action by a child for defects claimed to have been caused to the child by negligent diagnosis or treatment of the child's mother. The Grecos' argument is conditional and narrowly put, so: if this court does not allow Sundi Greco to recover damages for Joshua's care past the age of majority, it should allow Joshua to recover those damages by recognizing claims for "wrongful life." Implicit in this argument is the assumption that the child would be better off had he never been born. These kinds of judgments are very difficult, if not impossible, to make. Indeed, most courts considering the question have denied this cause of action for precisely this reason. Recognizing this kind of claim on behalf of the child would

---

[2] According to the facts as certified by the United States District Court, Joshua "was born with congenital myelomeningocele (spina bifida), congenital macro/hydrocephaly, bilateral talipes varus deformity, and Arnold Chiari malformation, type two. Joshua required placement of a ventriculoperitoneal shunt for hydrocephalus. He has paraplegia with no sensation from the hips down and suffers permanent fine and gross motor retardation and mental retardation."

require us to weigh the harms suffered by virtue of the child's having been born with severe handicaps against "the utter void of nonexistence"; this is a calculation the courts are incapable of performing. The New York Court of Appeals framed the problem this way:

> Whether it is better never to have been born at all than to have been born with even gross deficiencies is a mystery more properly to be left to the philosophers and the theologians. Surely the law can assert no competence to resolve the issue, particularly in view of the very nearly uniform high value which the law and mankind has placed on human life, rather than its absence.

Becker v. Schwartz, 46 N.Y.2d 401, 386 N.E.2d 807, 812, 413 N.Y.S.2d 895 (N.Y. 1978). We conclude that Nevada does not recognize a claim by a child for harms the child claims to have suffered by virtue of having been born.

With regard to Sundi Greco's claim against her physician for negligent diagnosis or treatment during pregnancy, we see no reason for compounding or complicating our medical malpractice jurisprudence by according this particular form of professional negligence action some special status apart from presently recognized medical malpractice or by giving it the new name of "wrongful birth." Sundi Greco either does or does not state a claim for medical malpractice; and we conclude that she does.

Medical malpractice, like other forms of negligence, involves a breach of duty which causes injury. To be tortiously liable a physician must have departed from the accepted standard of medical care in a manner that results in injury to a patient. In the case before us, we must accept as fact that Sundi Greco's physicians negligently failed to perform prenatal medical tests or performed or interpreted those tests in a negligent fashion and that they thereby negligently failed to discover and reveal that Sundi Greco was carrying a severely deformed fetus. As a result of such negligence Sundi Greco claims that she was denied the opportunity to terminate her pregnancy and that this denial resulted in her giving birth to a severely deformed child.

It is difficult to formulate any sound reason for denying recovery to Sundi Greco in the case at hand. Sundi Greco is saying, in effect, to her doctors: "If you had done what you were supposed to do, I would have known early in my pregnancy that I was carrying a severely deformed baby. I would have then terminated the pregnancy and would not have had to go through the mental and physical agony of delivering this child, nor would I have had to bear the emotional suffering attendant to the birth and nurture of the child, nor the extraordinary expense necessary to care for a child suffering from such extreme deformity and disability."

The United States advances two reasons for denying Sundi Greco's claim: first, it argues that she has suffered no injury and that, therefore, the damage element of negligent tort liability is not fulfilled; second, the United States argues that even if Sundi Greco has sustained injury and damages, the damages were not caused by her physicians. To support its first argument, the United States points out that in Szekeres v. Robinson, 102 Nev. 93, 715 P.2d 1076 (1986), this court held that the mother of a normal, healthy child could not recover in tort from a physician who negligently performed her sterilization operation because the birth of a normal, healthy child is not a legally cognizable injury. The United States argues that no distinction can be made between a mother who gives birth to a healthy child and a mother who gives birth to a child with severe deformities and that, therefore, *Szekeres* bars recovery.

Szekeres can be distinguished from the instant case. Unlike the birth of a normal child, the birth of a severely deformed baby of the kind described here is necessarily an unpleasant and aversive event and the cause of inordinate financial burden that would not attend the birth of a normal child. The child in this case will unavoidably and necessarily require the expenditure of extraordinary medical, therapeutic and custodial care expenses by the family, not to mention the additional reserves of physical, mental and emotional strength that will be required of all concerned. Those who do not wish to undertake the many burdens associated with the birth and continued care of such a child have the legal right, under Roe v. Wade and codified by the voters of this state, to terminate their pregnancies. NRS 442.250 (codifying by referendum the conditions under which abortion is permitted in this state). Sundi Greco has certainly suffered money damages as a result of her physician's malpractice.

We also reject the United States' second argument that Sundi Greco's physicians did not cause any of the injuries that Sundi Greco might have suffered. We note that the mother is not claiming that her child's defects were caused by her physicians' negligence; rather, she claims that her physicians' negligence kept her ignorant of those defects and that it was this negligence which caused her to lose her right to choose whether to carry the child to term. The damage Sundi Greco has sustained is indeed causally related to her physicians' malpractice. . . .

The certified question requires us to decide specifically what types of damages the mother may recover if she succeeds in proving her claim. Courts in these cases have struggled with what items of damages are recoverable because, unlike the typical malpractice claim, claims such as Sundi Greco's do not involve a physical injury to the patient's person. We consider each of Sundi Greco's claimed items of damage separately.

This claim for damages relates to the medical, therapeutic and custodial costs associated with caring for a severely handicapped child. There is nothing exceptional in allowing this item of damage. It is a recognized principle of tort law to "afford compensation for injuries sustained by one person as the result of the conduct of another." Extraordinary care expenses are a foreseeable result of the negligence alleged in this case, and Sundi Greco should be allowed to recover those expenses if she can prove them. This leads us to the question of how to compensate for these kinds of injuries.

Sundi Greco correctly observes that Nevada law requires the parents of a handicapped child to support that child beyond the age of majority if the child cannot support itself. Nevada recognizes the right of a parent to recover from a tortfeasor any expenses the parent was required to pay because of the injury to his or her minor child. Accordingly, Sundi Greco claims the right to recover damages for these extraordinary costs for a period equal to Joshua's life expectancy. Other states which require parents to care for handicapped children past the age of majority allow plaintiffs to recover these types of damages for the lifetime of the child or until such time as the child is no longer dependent on her or his parents. We agree with these authorities and conclude that Sundi Greco may recover extraordinary medical and custodial expenses associated with caring for Joshua for whatever period of time it is established that Joshua will be dependent upon her to provide such care.

The United States contends that if this court allows the mother to recover such extraordinary medical and custodial expenses, then it should require the district court to offset any such award by the amount it would cost to raise a non-handicapped child. To do otherwise, argues the United States, would be to grant the mother a windfall.

The offset rule has its origins in two doctrines: the "avoidable consequences rule," which requires plaintiffs to mitigate their damages in tort cases, and the expectancy rule of damages employed in contract cases, which seeks to place the plaintiff in the position he or she would have been in had the contract been performed. We conclude that neither of these doctrines is applicable to the case at bar. To enforce the "avoidable consequences" rule in the instant case would impose unreasonable burdens upon the mother such as, perhaps, putting Joshua up for adoption or otherwise seeking to terminate her parental obligations.

With regard to the expectancy rule, it would unnecessarily complicate and limit recovery for patients in other malpractice cases if we were to begin intruding contract damage principles upon our malpractice jurisprudence. The rule for compensatory damages in negligence cases is clear and workable, and we decline to depart from it.

Sundi Greco asserts that she is suffering and will continue to suffer tremendous mental and emotional pain as a result of the birth of Joshua. Several jurisdictions allow plaintiffs such as Sundi Greco to recover such damages. In line with these cases, we agree that it is reasonably foreseeable that a mother who is denied her right to abort a severely deformed fetus will suffer emotional distress, not just when the child is delivered, but for the rest of the child's life. Consequently, we conclude that the mother in this case should have the opportunity to prove that she suffered and will continue to suffer emotional distress as a result of the birth of her child.

We reject the United States' argument that this court should follow an "offset" rule with regard to damages for emotional distress. Cf. Blake v. Cruz, 108 Idaho 253, 698 P.2d 315, 320 (Idaho 1984) (requiring damages for emotional distress to be offset by "the countervailing emotional benefits attributable to the birth of the child"). Any emotional benefits are simply too speculative to be considered by a jury in awarding emotional distress damages. As Dean Prosser observes:

> In the case of the wrongful birth of a severely impaired child, it would appear that the usual joys of parenthood would often be substantially overshadowed by the emotional trauma of caring for the child in such a condition, so that application of the benefit rule would appear inappropriate in this context.

Prosser and Keeton on the Law of Torts, supra, §55 at 371 n.48 (citations omitted). . . . Moreover, it would unduly complicate the jury's task to require it to weigh one intangible harm against another intangible benefit, not because of mental distress occasioned by an injury to Joshua.

We conclude that a mother may maintain a medical malpractice action under Nevada law based on her physicians' failure properly to perform or interpret prenatal examinations when that failure results in the mother losing the opportunity to abort a severely deformed fetus. Sundi Greco should be given the right to prove that she has suffered and will continue to suffer damages in the form of emotional or mental distress and that she has incurred and will continue to incur extraordinary medical and custodial care expenses associated with raising Joshua. We decline to recognize the tort sometimes called "wrongful life."

[Dissenting opinion omitted.]

NOTES TO GRECO v. UNITED STATES

1. *Special Care Expenses During and After Childhood.* The main impetus for "wrongful life" cases — claims brought on behalf of a child born with birth defects — has been the desire of the child's parents to obtain a supply of money that will provide care for the child throughout the child's lifetime. A claim by parents for their own expenses might be limited to expenses anticipated up to the time the child becomes an adult. In *Greco*, the court referred to Nevada law that imposes a requirement on parents to support children with disabilities even after those children reach adult age. How did the existence of that statute simplify the court's analysis? Would the court have rejected the wrongful life claim in the absence of such a statute?

2. *Wrongful Birth Damages.* Does the court distinguish this case adequately from its earlier *Szekeres* decision? Is it possible that *Szekeres* was decided wrongly? A minority view treats the birth of an unwanted child, after a negligently performed sterilization procedure, as a basis for damages, including the cost of child-rearing. See Burke v. Rivo, 551 N.E.2d 1 (Mass. 1990).

3. *Offset Rule and the Benefit Principle.* The defendant in *Greco* argued that damages for the expenses to raise the child with birth defects should be offset by the expenses necessary to raise a normal child, because those costs would have been incurred anyway. A related damage rule, the benefit principle, requires costs imposed by the defendant's act to be offset by benefits the defendant has bestowed. The benefit rule has led some courts to hold that damages should be rejected in wrongful birth cases where the child is normal. These courts reason that the benefits of having a normal child are so great that they offset any costs of child-raising, even if the mother did not want to become pregnant. A weaker form of the argument is that courts should avoid comparing the benefits and costs of raising a normal child.

Statute: WRONGFUL BIRTH CLAIMS, WRONGFUL LIFE

Mich. Stat. Ann. §600.2971 (2017)

(1) A person shall not bring a civil action on a wrongful birth claim that, but for an act or omission of the defendant, a child or children would not or should not have been born.

(2) A person shall not bring a civil action for damages on a wrongful life claim that, but for the negligent act or omission of the defendant, the person bringing the action would not or should not have been born.

(3) A person shall not bring a civil action for damages for daily living, medical, educational, or other expenses necessary to raise a child to the age of majority, on a wrongful pregnancy or wrongful conception claim that, but for an act or omission of the defendant, the child would not or should not have been conceived.

(4) The prohibition stated in subsection (1), (2), or (3) applies regardless of whether the child is born healthy or with a birth defect or other adverse medical condition. The prohibition stated in subsection (1), (2), or (3) does not apply to a civil action for damages for an intentional or grossly negligent act or omission, including, but not limited to, an act or omission that violates the Michigan penal code.

Statute: WRONGFUL BIRTH; WRONGFUL LIFE
24 Me. Rev. Stat. Ann. §2931(1)-(3) (2017)

1. Intent. It is the intent of the Legislature that the birth of a normal, healthy child does not constitute a legally recognizable injury and that it is contrary to public policy to award damages for the birth or rearing of a healthy child.

2. Birth of healthy child; claim for damages prohibited. No person may maintain a claim for relief or receive an award for damages based on the claim that the birth and rearing of a healthy child resulted in damages to him. A person may maintain a claim for relief based on a failed sterilization procedure resulting in the birth of a healthy child and receive an award of damages for the hospital and medical expenses incurred for the sterilization procedures and pregnancy, the pain and suffering connected with the pregnancy and the loss of earnings by the mother during pregnancy.

3. Birth of unhealthy child; damages limited. Damages for the birth of an unhealthy child born as the result of professional negligence shall be limited to damages associated with the disease, defect or handicap suffered by the child.

NOTE TO STATUTES

Statutory Approaches. State statutes dealing with recovery for wrongful birth, life, and pregnancy take different approaches to the standard of care applicable and to whether recovery is permitted at all. The damages for which compensation may be obtained also differ.

Problem
Wrongful Pregnancy, Life, and Birth

For personal and socioeconomic reasons, Mr. and Mrs. Coleman arranged for Mrs. Coleman to receive a sterilization procedure called a bilateral tubal ligation after giving birth to their fourth child. Subsequent to the operation, Mrs. Coleman became pregnant and gave birth to a fifth child. The Colemans sued the doctors, claiming negligence in performing the procedure and claiming as damages: (1) pain, suffering, and discomfort of Mrs. Coleman as a result of the last pregnancy, (2) the cost of the tubal ligation, (3) the loss to Mr. Coleman of the comfort, companionship, services, and consortium of Mrs. Coleman, (4) the deprivation to the other four children of the care and support they would have received had the fifth child not been born, (5) medical expenses incurred by the Colemans as a result of the fifth pregnancy, and (6) care and maintenance for the fifth child. Under the two statutes above, which of these claims would be allowed? If the child had been born with birth defects, would the additional costs of raising a child with those defects have been recoverable? See Coleman v. Garrison, 327 A.2d 757 (Del. Super. Ct. 1974).

Perspective: Wrongful Life and Birth and Defensive Medicine

Potential liability for wrongful life and wrongful birth compounds the complaints of physicians concerned with the threat of lawsuits.

[T]he wrongful birth cause of action imposes liability on physicians not previously existing at common law. . . . This, in turn, creates a financial incentive for physicians to recommend amniocentesis and genetic screening in borderline cases, and in possibly most or all cases for the particularly cautious physician. The incentive is simply to avoid liability and, where there may be no liability, to avoid the costs of frivolous litigation. For example, when New York recognized the wrongful birth action, a prediction was made that legal implications would lead to the use of amniocentesis in all pregnancies. A year later, doctors were reporting use of amniocentesis on women below the age of thirty-five even though amniocentesis was not medically indicated. Fear of legal liability was a major factor cited for promoting the procedure.

The financial incentive is not only to recommend prenatal screening, but also to recommend abortion where diagnostic results are borderline, or where the physician is "cautious." Similarly, the financial incentive would lead to recommendations to abort where genetic screening has not been performed, and possibly not even medically indicated, when the physician becomes concerned that his failure to conduct such testing or recommend such procedures could expose him to eventual liability.

James Bopp, Jr., Barry A. Bostrom & Donald A. McKinney, *The "Rights" and "Wrongs" of Wrongful Birth and Wrongful Life: A Jurisprudential Analysis of Birth Related Torts*, 27 Duq. L. Rev. 461, 486-487 (1989).

How should consideration of the possibility of overdeterrence affect tort policy? Is this concern limited to physicians alone?

IV. Primary Assumption of Risk

The *primary assumption of risk* doctrine protects defendants from liability in some circumstances where risks either cannot be eliminated or would be too costly to eliminate and where those risks are typically obvious to the people who encounter them. Clover v. Snowbird Ski Resort interprets a statute that incorporates that doctrine in the context of a skiing accident. Edward C. v. City of Albuquerque analyzes the care owed by the operator of a baseball stadium with respect to the risk that patrons may be hit by batted balls.

CLOVER v. SNOWBIRD SKI RESORT
808 P.2d 1037 (Utah 1991)

HALL, C.J.

Plaintiff Margaret Clover sought to recover damages for injuries sustained as the result of a ski accident in which Chris Zulliger, an employee of defendant Snowbird Corporation ("Snowbird"), collided with her. From the entry of summary judgment in favor of defendants, Clover appeals.

Many of the facts underlying Clover's claims are in dispute. Review of an order granting summary judgment requires that the facts be viewed in a light most favorable to the party opposing summary judgment. At the time of the accident, Chris Zulliger was employed by Snowbird as a chef at the Plaza Restaurant. . . .

[After inspecting a restaurant, Zulliger skied four runs prior to beginning work at another restaurant on the mountain. He] took a route that was often taken by Snowbird employees to travel from the top of the mountain to the Plaza. About mid-way down the mountain, at a point above the Mid-Gad, Zulliger decided to take a jump off a crest on the side of an intermediate run. He had taken this jump many times before. A skier moving relatively quickly is able to become airborne at that point because of the steep drop off on the downhill side of the crest. Due to this drop off, it is impossible for skiers above the crest to see skiers below the crest. The jump was well known to Snowbird. In fact, the Snowbird ski patrol often instructed people not to jump off the crest. There was also a sign instructing skiers to ski slowly at this point in the run. Zulliger, however, ignored the sign and skied over the crest at a significant speed. Clover, who had just entered the same ski run from a point below the crest, either had stopped or was traveling slowly below the crest. When Zulliger went over the jump, he collided with Clover, who was hit in the head and severely injured.

Clover brought claims against Zulliger and Snowbird, alleging [among other claims that] Snowbird negligently designed and maintained its ski runs. . . . Zulliger settled separately with Clover. Under two separate motions for summary judgment, the trial judge dismissed Clover's claims against Snowbird [holding that] Utah's Inherent Risk of Skiing Statute, Utah Code Ann. §§78-27-51 to -54 (Supp. 1986), bars plaintiff's claim of negligent design and maintenance. . . .

. . . This ruling was based on the trial court's findings that "Clover was injured as a result of a collision with another skier, and/or the variation of steepness in terrain." Apparently, the trial court reasoned that regardless of a ski resort's culpability, the resort is not liable for an injury occasioned by one or more of the dangers listed in section 78-27-52(1). This reasoning, however, is based on an incorrect interpretation of sections 78-27-51 to -54.

Utah Code Ann. §§78-27-51 and -52(1) read in part:

INHERENT RISKS OF SKIING — PUBLIC POLICY

The Legislature finds that the sport of skiing is practiced by a large number of residents of Utah and attracts a large number of nonresidents, significantly contributing to the economy of this state.

. . . It is the purpose of this act, therefore, to clarify the law in relation to skiing injuries and the risks inherent in that sport, and to establish as a matter of law that certain risks are inherent in that sport, and to provide that, as a matter of public policy, no person engaged in that sport shall recover from a ski operator for injuries resulting from those inherent risks.

INHERENT RISK OF SKIING — DEFINITIONS

As used in this act:

(1) "Inherent risk of skiing" means those dangers or conditions which are an integral part of the sport of skiing, including, but not limited to: changing weather conditions, variations or steepness in terrain; snow or ice conditions; surface or subsurface conditions such as bare spots, forest growth, rocks, stumps, impact with lift towers and

other structures and their components; collisions with other skiers; and a skier's failure to ski within his own ability.

Section 78-27-53 states that notwithstanding anything to the contrary in Utah's comparative fault statute, a skier cannot recover from a ski area operator for an injury caused by an inherent risk of skiing. Section 78-27-54 requires ski area operators to "post trail boards at one or more prominent locations within each ski area which shall include a list of the inherent risks of skiing and the limitations on liability of ski area operators as defined in this act."

It is clear that sections 78-27-51 to -54 protect ski area operators from suits initiated by their patrons who seek recovery for injuries caused by an inherent risk of skiing. The statute, however, does not purport to grant ski area operators complete immunity from all negligence claims initiated by skiers. While the general parameters of the act are clear, application of the statute to specific circumstances is less certain. In the instant case, both parties urge different interpretations of the act. Snowbird claims that any injury occasioned by one or more of the dangers listed in section 78-27-52(1) is barred by the statute because, as a matter of law, such an accident is caused by an inherent risk of skiing. Clover, on the other hand, argues that a ski area operator's negligence is not an inherent risk of skiing and that if the resort's negligence causes a collision between skiers, a suit arising from that collision is not barred by sections 78-27-51 to -54.

Although the trial court apparently agreed with Snowbird, we decline to adopt such an interpretation. The basis of Snowbird's argument is that the language of section 78-27-52(1) stating that "'[i]nherent risk of skiing' means those dangers or conditions which are an integral part of the sport of skiing, including but not limited to: . . . collision with other skiers" must be read as defining all collisions between skiers as inherent risks. The wording of the statute does not compel such a reading. To the contrary, the dangers listed in section 78-27-52(1) are modified by the term "integral part of the sport of skiing." Therefore, ski area operators are protected from suits to recover for injuries caused by one or more of the dangers listed in section 78-27-52(1) only to the extent that those dangers, under the facts of each case, are integral aspects of the sport of skiing. Indeed, the list of dangers in section 78-27-52(1) is expressly nonexclusive. The statute, therefore, contemplates that the determination of whether a risk is inherent be made on a case-by-case basis, using the entire statute, not solely the list provided in section 78-27-52(1).

Furthermore, when the act is read in its entirety, no portion thereof is rendered meaningless. When reading section 78-27-52(1) in connection with section 78-27-54, it becomes clear that the relevance of section 78-27-52(1) is in insuring that ski area operators provide skiers with sufficient notice of the risks they face when participating in the sport of skiing, as well as ski area operators' liability in connection with these risks. It should also be noted that the interpretation urged by Snowbird would result in a wide range of absurd consequences. For example, if a skier loses control and falls by reason of the negligence of an operator, recovery for injury would depend on whether, in the fall, the skier collides with a danger listed in section 78-27-52(1). Such a result is entirely arbitrary. . . .

In construing the statute . . . a helpful first step is to note that sections 78-27-51 to -54 limit the liability of ski area operators by defining the duty they owe to their patrons. The express purpose of the statute, codified in section 78-27-51, is "to clarify the law in relation to skiing injuries and the risk inherent in the sport . . . and to establish [that] . . . no person shall recover from a ski operator for injuries resulting from those inherent risks." Inasmuch as the purpose of the statute is to "clarify the law," not to radically alter ski resort liability, it is necessary to briefly examine the relevant law at the time the statute was enacted. Although there is limited Utah case law on point, when the statute was enacted the majority of jurisdictions employed the doctrine of primary assumption of risk in limiting ski resorts' liability for injuries their patrons received while skiing. Terms utilized in the statute such as "inherent risk of skiing" and "assumes the risk" are the same terms relied upon in such cases. This language suggests that the statute is meant to achieve the same results achieved under the doctrine of primary assumption of risk. In fact, commentators suggest that the statute was passed in reaction to a perceived erosion in the protection ski area operators traditionally enjoyed under the common law doctrine of primary assumption of risk.

As we have noted in the past, the single term "assumption of risk" has been used to refer to several different, and occasionally overlapping, concepts. One concept, primary assumption of risk, is simply "an alternative expression for the proposition that the defendant was not negligent, that is, there was no duty owed or there was no breach of an existing duty." This suggests that the statute, in clarifying the "confusion as to whether a skier assumes the risks inherent in the sport of skiing," operates to define the duty ski resorts owe to their patrons.

Section 78-27-53 also supports the notion that the ski statute operates to define the duty of a ski resort. This section exempts injuries caused by the inherent risks of skiing from the operation of Utah's comparative fault statute, which was enacted to avoid the harsh results of the all-or-nothing nature of the former law by limiting a party's liability by the degree of that party's fault. Comparative principles have been applied in cases dealing with contributory negligence, secondary assumption of risk, and strict liability. Exempting suits concerning injuries caused by an inherent risk of skiing from the comparative fault statute is consistent with the assertion that the ski area operators are not at fault in such situations — that is, ski area operators have no duty to protect a skier from the inherent risks of skiing.

Finally, it is to be noted that without a duty, there can be no negligence. Such an interpretation, therefore, harmonizes the express purpose of the statute, protecting ski area operators from suits arising out of injuries caused by the inherent risks of skiing, with the fact that the statute does not purport to abrogate a skier's traditional right to recover for injuries caused by ski area operators' negligence.

A similar analysis leads to the conclusion that the duties sections 78-27-51 to -54 impose on ski resorts are the duty to use reasonable care for the protection of its patrons and, under section 78-27-54, the duty to warn its patrons of the inherent risks of skiing. Beyond the general warning prescribed by section 78-27-54, however, a ski area operator is under no duty to protect its patrons from the inherent risks of skiing. The inherent risks of skiing are those dangers that skiers wish to confront as essential characteristics of the sport of skiing or hazards that cannot be eliminated by the exercise of ordinary care on the part of the ski area operator.

As noted above, the purpose of the statute is to prohibit suits seeking recovery for injuries caused by an inherent risk of skiing. The term "inherent risk of skiing," using the ordinary and accepted meaning of the term "inherent," refers to those risks that are essential characteristics of skiing — risks that are so integrally related to skiing that the sport cannot be undertaken without confronting these risks. Generally, these risks can be divided into two categories. The first category of risks consists of those risks, such as steep grades, powder, and mogul runs, which skiers wish to confront as an essential characteristic of skiing. Under sections 78-27-51 to -54, a ski area operator is under no duty to make all of its runs as safe as possible by eliminating the type of dangers that skiers wish to confront as an integral part of skiing.

The second category of risks consists of those hazards which no one wishes to confront but cannot be alleviated by the use of reasonable care on the part of a ski resort. It is without question that skiing is a dangerous activity. Hazards may exist in locations where they are not readily discoverable. Weather and snow conditions can suddenly change and, without warning, create new hazards where no hazard previously existed. Hence, it is clearly foreseeable that a skier, without skiing recklessly, may momentarily lose control or fall in an unexpected manner. Ski area operators cannot alleviate these risks, and under sections 78-27-51 to -54, they are not liable for injuries caused by such risks. The only duty ski area operators have in regard to these risks is the requirement set out in section 78-27-54 that they warn their patrons, in the manner prescribed in the statute, of the general dangers patrons must confront when participating in the sport of skiing. This does not mean, however, that a ski area operator is under no duty to use ordinary care to protect its patrons. In fact, if an injury was caused by an unnecessary hazard that could have been eliminated by the use of ordinary care, such a hazard is not, in the ordinary sense of the term, an inherent risk of skiing and would fall outside of sections 78-27-51 to -54. . . .

Having established the proper interpretation of sections 78-27-51 to -54, the next step is to determine whether, given this interpretation, there is a genuine issue of material fact in regard to Clover's claim. First, the existence of a blind jump with a landing area located at a point where skiers enter the run is not an essential characteristic of an intermediate run. Therefore, Clover may recover if she can prove that Snowbird could have prevented the accident through the use of ordinary care. It is to be noted that Clover's negligent design and maintenance claim is not based solely on the allegation that Snowbird allowed conditions to exist on an intermediate hill which caused blind spots and allowed skiers to jump. Rather, Clover presents evidence that Snowbird was aware that its patrons regularly took the jump, that the jump created an unreasonable hazard to skiers below the jump, and that Snowbird did not take reasonable measures to eliminate the hazard. This evidence is sufficient to raise a genuine issue of material fact in regard to Clover's negligent design and maintenance claim. . . .

In light of the genuine issues of material fact . . . summary judgment was inappropriate.

Reversed and remanded for further proceedings.

NOTES TO CLOVER v. SNOWBIRD SKI RESORT

1. *Terminology.* "Primary assumption of risk," as the *Clover* court states, is usually used to mean that a defendant either owed no duty or did not breach any duty. The doctrine of *primary assumption of risk* is simply a name for a type of argument a defendant may use to rebut a plaintiff's claim or evidence of duty or breach. A court may find there is *no duty* because the harm is unforeseeable (because the plaintiff can avoid obvious dangers, perhaps by choosing not to engage in the activity) or no duty because public policy favors protecting suppliers of athletic facilities (such as ski areas that bring tourist revenues to the state). A court may find *no breach of duty* on the ground that the inherent risks are "necessary" to the sport — that is, cannot be avoided without sacrificing valuable characteristics of the sport. The *Clover* court says there is no duty with respect to inherent risks.

2. *Inherent Risks in Other Sports.* The *Clover* court identifies particular risks of skiing as "inherent." Some of these are risks skiers wish to confront, and some are risks no one would wish to confront if skiing could reasonably be conducted without them. The common features of inherent risks are that people generally know about them, and the risks cannot be eliminated by using reasonable care. As a matter of common law, should the doctrine of primary assumption of risk lead to a conclusion that there is no duty of the operator of the following sports facilities to protect the participant from the accident that occurs?

A. A bobsled run ends in an "exit chute" that is designed with an opening so that sleds can be moved out of it quickly during competitions. A competitor's sled slides out of that exit at a high rate of speed and the competitor is injured.

B. A karate student injures his back while attempting to perform a tumbling technique known as a "jump roll" over an obstacle.

C. A tennis player snags his foot in a torn vinyl hem at the bottom of a net dividing two indoor tennis courts.

See Morgan v. State, 685 N.E.2d 202 (N.Y. 1997).

Problem
Primary Assumption of Risk

The plaintiff was skiing on a sunny day. He skied roughly 30 feet on a moderately steep slope toward a natural ridge. As he came over the ridge, he noticed a trail that cut directly across the run he was on. He had been unable to see the trail earlier because it fell within a blind spot created by the ridge. The last thing he remembers about this incident is attempting to make an evasive maneuver to his left, apparently to avoid the trail.

The trail that he saw as he came over the ridge had been formed earlier in the season by novice skiers traversing the slope to negotiate an easier route down the mountain. To prevent it from becoming too rough, the operator of the ski area occasionally smoothed the trail with its snow-grooming equipment. Such trails are commonly called "cat tracks."

A witness was skiing on the cat track as the plaintiff came down on his trail. She testified that she heard someone on the trail above her and, as she looked up, saw the plaintiff in the air roughly 10 to 15 feet ahead of her. She stated that he was upright and seemed to be in control as he passed over the cat track but gradually rotated backward as he flew through the air. He landed on his neck and upper back approximately 50 feet below the cat track. He was severely injured.

The plaintiff sued the operator of the ski area, claiming that the defendant negligently designed and maintained the cat track and claiming that the area should have warned skiers about the cat track or relocated it. The ski area's experts stated that warning signs are not needed because cat tracks are common. The ski area moved for summary judgment on the grounds that cat tracks are an inherent risk of skiing. If you represent the plaintiff, how would you respond? How should the court rule? See White v. Deseelhorst, 879 P.2d 1371 (Utah 1994).

Statute: ACCEPTANCE OF INHERENT RISKS
12 Vt. Stat. §1037 (2017)

§1037. Notwithstanding the provisions of section 1036 of this title [referring to comparative negligence as a defense], a person who takes part in any sport accepts as a matter of law the dangers that inhere therein insofar as they are obvious and necessary.

Statute: SKIERS' AND TRAMWAY PASSENGERS' RESPONSIBILITIES
32 Me. Stat. §15217(1)(A) (2017)

A. "Inherent risks of skiing" means those dangers or conditions that are an integral part of the sport of skiing, including, but not limited to: existing and changing weather conditions; existing and changing snow conditions, such as ice, hardpack, powder, packed powder, slush and granular, corn, crust, cut-up and machine-made snow; surface or subsurface conditions, such as dirt, grass, bare spots, forest growth, rocks, stumps, trees and other natural objects and collisions with or falls resulting from such natural objects; lift towers, lights, signs, posts, fences, mazes or enclosures, hydrants, water or air pipes, snowmaking and snow-grooming equipment, marked or lit trail maintenance vehicles and snowmobiles, and other man-made structures or objects and their components, and collisions with or falls resulting from such man-made objects; variations in steepness or terrain, whether natural or as a result of slope design; snowmaking or snow-grooming operations, including, but not limited to, freestyle terrain, jumps, roads and catwalks or other terrain modifications; the presence of and collisions with other skiers; and the failure of skiers to ski safely, in control or within their own abilities.

Statute: DUTIES AND RESPONSIBILITIES OF EACH SKIER
Ga. Code §43-43A-7(1) (2017)

Any other provision of law to the contrary notwithstanding:
(1) Each individual skier has the responsibility for knowing the range of his or her own ability to negotiate any ski slope or trail or any portion thereof and must ski within the limits of his or her ability. Each skier expressly accepts and assumes the risk of any injury or death or damage to property resulting from any of the inherent dangers and risks of skiing, as set forth in this chapter; provided, however, that injuries sustained in a collision with another skier are not an inherent risk of the sport for purposes of this Code section.

Statute: LEGISLATIVE PURPOSE
Idaho Code §6-1101 (2017)

The legislature finds that the sport of skiing is practiced by a large number of citizens of this state and also attracts a large number of nonresidents, significantly contributing to the economy of Idaho. Since it is recognized that there are inherent risks in the sport of skiing which should be understood by each skier and which are essentially impossible to eliminate by the ski area operation, it is the purpose of this chapter to define those areas of responsibility and affirmative acts for which ski area operators shall be liable for loss, damage or injury, and to define those risks which the skier expressly assumes and for which there can be no recovery.

Statute: SPORT SHOOTING PARTICIPANTS, ACCEPTANCE OF OBVIOUS AND INHERENT RISKS

Mich. Stat. §691.1544(4) (2017)

Each person who participates in sport shooting at a sport shooting range that conforms to generally accepted operation practices accepts the risks associated with the sport to the extent the risks are obvious and inherent. Those risks include, but are not limited to, injuries that may result from noise, discharge of a projectile or shot, malfunction of sport shooting equipment not owned by the shooting range, natural variations in terrain, surface or subsurface snow or ice conditions, bare spots, rocks, trees, and other forms of natural growth or debris.

NOTES TO STATUTES

1. *Objective Test for "Obvious" and "Necessary."* These primary assumption of risk statutes illustrate different approaches to defining inherent risks. All are consistent with the common law in treating the test for the obviousness of a risk as an objective test. Rather than referring to the specific knowledge of the plaintiff, the skiing statutes either describe the risks in great detail (see the Maine statute), hold the plaintiff responsible for the risks the plaintiffs "should" understand (see the Idaho statute), or simply state that plaintiffs accept obvious and necessary risks as a matter of law (see the Vermont statute).

2. *Inherent Risks.* Where inherent risks are enumerated, there are differences among the states. Observe that Maine's treatment of collisions between skiers differs from Utah's common law interpretation in *Clover* and Georgia's statutory enumeration. States have similar statutes for a few other sports (see, for instance, Michigan's shooting statute). Do the statutorily enumerated risks all fit within the common law test for whether the risk is obvious and necessary?

EDWARD C. v. CITY OF ALBUQUERQUE

241 P.3d 1086 (N.M. 2010)

CHÁVEZ, Justice.

In this case, it is alleged that a child was struck in the head by a baseball during pregame batting practice at Isotopes stadium. The child was seated in the picnic area beyond the left field wall in fair ball territory with his family for a pre-game Little League party. The child had just begun to eat his food when, without warning, pre-game batting practice began and a baseball struck him, fracturing his skull. Plaintiffs sued the Albuquerque Baseball Club, LLC d/b/a Albuquerque Isotopes (Isotopes), the

City of Albuquerque (City), Houston McLane Co. d/b/a Houston Astros (Astros), and Dave Matranga, the player who batted the ball that struck the child (collectively "Defendants").

The question we must answer is what duty do owner/occupants of commercial baseball stadiums have to protect spectators from projectiles leaving the field of play. The district court applied the most limited duty, which is followed in a minority of jurisdictions, commonly referred to as the "baseball rule." The district court held that the duty was limited to providing screening for the area of the field behind home plate for as many spectators as may reasonably be expected to desire such protection. Because Isotopes stadium has such screening, the district court granted summary judgment to Defendants.

On appeal, the Court of Appeals reversed summary judgment regarding the City and the Isotopes "on the ground that, under the particular circumstances alleged, there are issues of material fact precluding summary judgment" and rejected application of a limited-duty baseball rule, holding instead that these Defendants owed a duty to exercise ordinary care. We granted certiorari to decide whether New Mexico should recognize a limited duty for owner/occupants of commercial baseball stadiums. . . .

What duty should owner/occupants of a baseball stadium in New Mexico have to protect spectators from projectiles that leave the field of play? The question of the existence and scope of a defendant's duty of care is a legal question that depends on the nature of the sport or activity in question, the parties' general relationship to the activity, and public policy considerations. Policy is the principal factor in determining whether a duty is owed and the scope of that duty. *Torres v. State,* 894 P.2d 386, 389 (N.M. 1995) ("Policy determines duty."); *Calkins v. Cox Estates,* 792 P.2d 36, 39 (N.M. 1990) ("The existence of a duty is a question of policy to be determined with reference to legal precedent, statutes, and other principles comprising the law."). . . .

"As a general rule, an individual has no duty to protect another from harm." *Grover v. Stechel,* 45 P.3d 80 (N.M. 2002). Certain relationships, such as a possessor of land and a visitor, however, give rise to such a duty. The special relationship between Defendants, as owners and occupants of Isotopes stadium, and Plaintiffs, as visitors, places Defendants' duty within the first category. Indeed, Defendants do not dispute that a duty is owed; they simply argue that the scope of that duty should be limited.

New Mexico generally applies a "single standard of reasonable care under the circumstances" to landowners or occupants. . . . Accordingly, our jury instructions provide that "[a]n [owner] [occupant] owes a visitor the duty to use ordinary care to keep the premises safe for use by the visitor[, whether or not a dangerous condition is obvious]." UJI 13-1309 NMRA. . . .

The approach we take [to determine whether New Mexico's duty of ordinary care for owners/occupants is appropriate in the context of commercial baseball] is consistent with the approach suggested by the American Law Institute. The Restatement notes that modification of duty is appropriate in situations when "reasonable minds could differ about the application of the negligence standard to a particular category of recurring facts." Restatement (Third) of Torts: Liability for Physical and Emotional Harm §7 cmt. i. The American Law Institute notes that courts can "render a judgment about that category of cases" under "the rubric of duty" taking "into account factors that might escape the jury's attention in a particular case, such as the overall social impact of imposing a significant precautionary obligation on a class of actors." *Id.* "Such a categorical determination . . . has the benefit of providing clearer rules of behavior for actors who may be subject to tort liability and who structure their behavior in response to that potential liability." *Id.*

. . . It was not until 1879 that the first professional team, the Providence Grays, installed a screen behind home plate for the express purpose of protecting spectators. . . .

The limited protective screening behind home plate, however, failed to eliminate spectator injuries and did not curtail burgeoning plaintiffs' claims. As a result, more baseball spectator injury cases came under appellate review . . . and courts responded by developing a baseball-specific jurisprudence. Courts almost universally adopted some form of what is known as the "baseball rule," creating on the part of ball park owners and occupants only a limited duty of care toward baseball spectators. In its most limited form, the baseball rule holds

> that where a proprietor of a ball park furnishes screening for the area of the field behind home plate where the danger of being struck by a ball is the greatest and that screening is of sufficient extent to provide adequate protection for as many spectators as may reasonably be expected to desire such seating in the course of an ordinary game, the proprietor fulfills the duty of care imposed by law and, therefore, cannot be liable in negligence.

Akins v. Glens Falls City Sch. Dist., 424 N.E.2d 531, 534 (N.Y. 1981). . . .

From the earliest cases, the legal theories underlying the baseball rule precluding recovery have been the doctrines of assumption of risk and contributory negligence. *See Quinn v. Recreation Park Ass'n,* 46 P.2d 144, 147 (Cal. 1935) (per curiam) ("[I]n accepting the unscreened seat, even temporarily, with full knowledge of the danger attached to so doing, [plaintiff] assumed the risk of injury, which precluded recovery of damages."); *Crane v. Kan. City Baseball & Exhibition Co.,* 153 S.W. 1076, 1078 (Mo. 1913) ("And if it could not be said that [plaintiff] assumed the risk, still he should not be allowed to recover, since his own contributory negligence [for choosing an unprotected seat] is apparent and indisputable.").

Nearly from the outset, courts recognized a baseball rule as a necessary divergence from the prevailing "high degree of care for . . . safety" that is owed to business invitees, given the nature of the game and the relationship between the spectator and the stadium owner or occupant. *Wells v. Minneapolis Baseball & Athletic Ass'n,* 142 N.W. 306, 707-08 (Minn. 1913).

> [T]his [business invitee] rule must be modified when applied to an exhibition or game which is necessarily accompanied with some risk to the spectators. Baseball is not free from danger to those witnessing the game. But the perils are not so imminent that due care on the part of the management requires all the spectators to be screened in.

In limiting the duty, the courts also reasoned that "a large part of those who attend prefer to sit where no screen obscures the view" and owners or occupants have "a right to cater to their desires."

While the *Akins* baseball rule arguably once represented a majority approach across jurisdictions to baseball spectator injury claims, a wide variation in the formulation of the baseball rule now exists, making the *Akins* rule the minority approach. Some jurisdictions impose duties on stadium owners greater than those pronounced in

Akins, yet less onerous than a general duty of ordinary care. *See, e.g., Lowe v. Cal. League of Prof'l Baseball,* 65 Cal. Rptr. 2d 105, 106 (1997) ("[D]efendants had a duty *not to increase* the inherent risks to which spectators at professional baseball games are regularly exposed and which they assume."); *Jones v. Three Rivers Mgmt. Corp.,* 394 A.2d 546, 550-51 (Pa. 1978) (holding that recovery is barred to those "exposed in the stands of a baseball stadium to the predictable risks of batted balls," but not to those who show that their injury was not the result of a "common, frequent and expected part of the game" (internal quotation marks and citation omitted)). . . .

This shift has been attributed, in part, to a move away from the absolute defenses of contributory negligence and assumption of risk, which functioned as complete bars to plaintiff recovery, to comparative fault tort systems. Aside from shifts in tort law, advances in the game and the business of baseball have also been significant factors contributing to court modification of the traditional baseball rule. The common theme among contemporary cases modifying the traditional baseball rule is that spectators injured by baseballs are generally allowed to advance their claim when the injury is the result of some circumstance, design, or conduct neither necessary nor inherent in the game. . . .

From [our review of] seminal and contemporary baseball spectator injury cases, it is clear that the baseball rule, rigid as it may be for injuries arising from necessary and inherent aspects of the game, historically has not been applied to preclude recovery for spectators injured in extraordinary circumstances, where conduct or situations — even stadium design flaws — leading to injury were beyond the norm. Therefore, when a stadium owner or occupant has done something to increase the risks beyond those necessary or inherent to the game, or to impede a fan's ability to protect himself or herself, the courts have generally, and we believe correctly, allowed claims to proceed for a jury to determine whether the duty was breached.

After reviewing the history of baseball spectator injury cases and the rationale and policy choices motivating those decisions, we believe that commercial baseball stadium owners/occupants owe a duty to their fans that is justifiably limited given the unique nature of their relationship, as well as the policy concerns implicated by this relationship. Accordingly, New Mexico's traditional common-law framework for land owners and occupants that would otherwise prescribe a standard duty of ordinary care is inapposite in the limited circumstance of spectator injuries resulting from the play of commercial baseball. At the same time, we reject the baseball rule pronounced in *Akins* because of its extreme and unyielding results. Instead, we modify the duty owed by commercial baseball stadium owners/occupants.

We hold, therefore, that an owner/occupant of a commercial baseball stadium owes a duty that is symmetrical to the duty of the spectator. Spectators must exercise ordinary care to protect themselves from the inherent risk of being hit by a projectile that leaves the field of play and the owner/occupant must exercise ordinary care not to increase that inherent risk. This approach recognizes the impossibility of playing the sport of baseball without projectiles leaving the field of play. This approach also balances the competing interests of spectators who want full protection by requiring screening behind home plate consistent with the *Akins* approach and allowing other spectators to participate in the game by catching souvenirs that leave the field of play. In addition, it balances the practical interest of watching a sport that encourages players to strike a ball beyond the field of play in fair ball territory to score runs with the safety and entertainment interests of the spectators in catching such balls. As long as the owner/occupant exercises ordinary care not to increase the inherent risk of being hit by a projectile leaving the field, he or she need not be concerned about adverse social and economic impacts on the citizens of New Mexico. While not of paramount concern, this approach will bring New Mexico in line with the vast majority of jurisdictions that have considered the issue. . . .

Defendants did not make a prima facie case for their entitlement to a summary judgment under the limited duty we announce today, and therefore this matter is remanded to the district court for further proceedings consistent with this Opinion.

NOTES TO EDWARD C. v. CITY OF ALBUQUERQUE

1. *Increased Risk Rule.* Even though the court in *Edward C.* never mentions the *primary assumption of risk* doctrine, its approach limits liability based on spectators' general familiarity with risks of the activity that cannot be eliminated using reasonable care. The limited risk rule adopted by court in *Edward C.* begins with the same factual questions as in *Clover.* What are the inherent risks, those risks that are essential to skiing or enjoying baseball? What risks do skiers or baseball fans wish to confront? What risks are common, frequent, and expected? And which of those risks cannot be alleviated by the use of reasonable care on the part of the operator of the ski area or ball park? Which risks can the participant or spectators take into account when deciding how to conduct themselves? Against this background, the increased risk rule then asks whether the defendant used reasonable care not to increase those risks.

2. *Limited and No-Duty Rules.* Rather than characterizing the question as the proper application of the no-duty rule, as in *Clover,* the court in *Edward C.* creates a limited-duty rule. The *Edward C.* court's approach is consistent with the Restatement (Third)'s approach to duty, which recognizes a general duty of reasonable care as well as courts' ability to modify that duty for certain categories of cases for policy reasons. The policy reasons cited include the nature of the relationship between the fan and the game (including the desire to be exposed to fly balls), as well as the policy concerns implicated by this relationship (the risks presented to spectators). To accommodate those reasons, the court defines the standard of care differently in professional baseball stadium cases than in other cases involving business invitees (where the standard is reasonable care). Would the limited-duty rule in *Edward C.* and the no-duty rule in *Clover* lead to different results in the following cases?

A. Patron of baseball stadium injured by swinging gate at entry to grandstand seats.

B. Patron injured by tripping over a beam at the top of a grandstand stairway.

C. Patron injured by falling into a hole in a walkway, under a grandstand, used to reach refreshment stands,

D. Patron injured when batted ball comes through large cutout opening on covered walkway behind seating leading to concession area in ballpark.

See Jones v. Three Rivers Management Corp., 394 A.2d 546 (Pa. 1978).

3. *Primary Versus Secondary Assumption of Risk.* With the widespread adoption of comparative negligence, which takes into account the plaintiff's awareness and voluntary confrontation of risk associated with an activity, use of assumption of risk language has waned in many courts. That should not obscure the differences between the factual situations in which those doctrines arose. Secondary qualified assumption of risk arose in situations where a particular plaintiff knowingly, voluntarily, and unreasonably confronted a risk created by a negligent or reckless defendant. Primary assumption of risk arose in situations where participants and spectators generally know about and voluntarily and reasonably confront a risk created by a careful defendant. Because secondary qualified assumption of risk involves two parties who are both at fault, it is a defense. Because primary assumption of risk involves two parties neither of whom is at fault, it involves elements of the plaintiff's case, specifically duty and/or breach.

Statute: COLORADO BASEBALL SPECTATOR SAFETY ACT

Colo. Rev. Stat. §13-21-120(1), (2), (4), (5)(a), (b) (2017)

(1) This section shall be known and may be cited as the "Colorado Baseball Spectator Safety Act of 1993."

(2) The general assembly recognizes that persons who attend professional baseball games may incur injuries as a result of the risks involved in being a spectator at such baseball games. However, the general assembly also finds that attendance at such professional baseball games provides a wholesome and healthy family activity which should be encouraged. The general assembly further finds that the state will derive economic benefit from spectators attending professional baseball games. It is therefore the intent of the general assembly to encourage attendance at professional baseball games. Limiting the civil liability of those who own professional baseball teams and those who own stadiums where professional baseball games are played will help contain costs, keeping ticket prices more affordable. . . .

(4)(a) Spectators of professional baseball games are presumed to have knowledge of and to assume the inherent risks of observing professional baseball games, insofar as those risks are obvious and necessary. These risks include, but are not limited to, injuries which result from being struck by a baseball or a baseball bat.

(b) Except as provided in subsection (5) of this section, the assumption of risk set forth in this subsection (4) shall be a complete bar to suit and shall serve as a complete defense to a suit against an owner by a spectator for injuries resulting from the assumed risks, notwithstanding the provisions of sections 13-21-111 and 13-21-111.5 [explaining how comparative negligence applies in Colorado]. Except as provided in subsection (5) of this section, an owner shall not be liable for an injury to a spectator resulting from the inherent risks of attending a professional baseball game, and, except as provided in subsection (5) of this section, no spectator nor spectator's representative shall make any claim against, maintain an action against, or recover from an owner for injury, loss, or damage to the spectator resulting from any of the inherent risks of attending a professional baseball game.

(c) Nothing in this section shall preclude a spectator from suing another spectator for any injury to person or property resulting from such other spectator's acts or omissions.

(5) Nothing in subsection (4) of this section shall prevent or limit the liability of an owner who:

(a) Fails to make a reasonable and prudent effort to design, alter, and maintain the premises of the stadium in reasonably safe condition relative to the nature of the game of baseball; [or]

(b) Intentionally injures a spectator. . . .

Statute: LIMITED LIABILITY FOR BASEBALL FACILITIES
Ariz. Rev. Stat. §12-554(A), (B) (2017)

A. An owner is not liable for injuries to spectators who are struck by baseballs, baseball bats or other equipment used by players during a baseball game unless the owner either:

1. Does not provide protective seating that is reasonably sufficient to satisfy expected requests.

2. Intentionally injures a spectator.

B. This section does not prevent or limit the liability of an owner who fails to maintain the premises of the baseball stadium in a reasonably safe condition.

NOTES TO STATUTES

1. *Limitations on Coverage.* Although the Colorado statute states that a spectator is barred from recovering damages suffered by being hit by a bat or a ball, it also states that this prohibition is subject to the owner's obligation to make a reasonable effort to maintain the premises in reasonably safe condition. Do those reasonableness obligations weaken the protections the statute offers to owners? How would it apply to the facts of Edward C. v. City of Albuquerque?

2. *Limitations on Liability.* The Colorado statute includes among its purposes "limiting the civil liability of those who own professional baseball teams" with the aim of "keeping ticket prices more affordable." The other policy justifications in that same section may support the idea of injured patrons subsidizing ticket purchasers and team owners, but does the statute provide more protection than the common law doctrine of primary assumption of risk would do? Given that the existence of a duty is a question of law for the judge, does the statute keep more cases from the jury than the common law doctrine does?

Problem
Assumption of Risk and Effect of Statutes

Suppose a plaintiff is injured by a batted ball at a baseball field. Suppose also that the plaintiff claims that the operator of the field had been negligent because, even though there was screening behind home plate, many people had previously been hit by batted balls in an area that was not protected and the operator had not taken any measures to protect additional areas. How would this claim be affected by the Colorado and Arizona statutes?

> ### *Perspective: Utility of Primary Assumption of Risk Doctrine*
>
> Because primary assumption of risk is not a defense (in contrast to secondary assumption of risk), even when a state ceases to recognize it as a formal doctrine, its underlying logic for proving duty and breach survives.
>
> > In its primary sense, implied assumption of risk focuses not on the plaintiff's conduct in assuming the risk, but on the defendant's general duty of care. The doctrine of primary implied assumption of risk "technically is not a defense, but rather a legal theory which relieves a defendant of the duty which he might otherwise owe to the plaintiff with respect to particular risks." Clearly, primary implied assumption of risk is but another way of stating the conclusion that a plaintiff has failed to establish a prima facie case by failing to establish that a duty exists. . . .
> >
> > We agree with those states that have abandoned all categories of implied assumption of risk, as well as the traditional assumption of risk terminology, in the wake of judicial or statutory adoption of a scheme of comparative fault. The types of issues raised by implied assumption of risk are readily susceptible to analysis in terms of the common-law concept of duty and the principles of comparative negligence law.
>
> Perez v. McConkey, 872 S.W.2d 897, 902, 905 (Tenn. 1994).
>
> Would abolishing the doctrine of primary assumption of risk change the jury's verdict in any case if they properly understood the concepts of duty and reasonable care?

CHAPTER 12

DAMAGES

I. Introduction

The goal of most plaintiffs is to win a judgment ordering the defendant to pay money to the plaintiff. In a small number of cases, plaintiffs seek other remedies, but money damages are the main focus of tort law. In analyzing monetary damages, courts generally refer to three categories: compensatory, punitive, and nominal damages.

Compensatory damages are meant to equal the value of actual harm caused by the defendant. They are available under all legal theories. Punitive damages serve to punish or provide extra deterrence to a defendant. They are recoverable if the defendant acted with a bad motive, such as ill will or a desire to harm, typically in intentional or recklessness cases. Their value varies according to the gravity of the defendant's conduct and the amount of money thought necessary to have the intended effect on the defendant. Nominal damages are token amounts signifying that the defendant committed an intentional tort.

This chapter covers compensatory and punitive damages, and explores how these types of damages are measured and many of the doctrines that control their use. Nominal damages, those associated with intentional torts, are discussed in Chapter 2.

II. Compensatory Damages

A. Introduction

Because damages are so important in litigation, detailed doctrines control them. Compensatory damages can be either "general" or "special." They can be based on past or anticipated future harm. In cases where a victim has died, they can be "survival" or "wrongful death" damages.

General damages, also called "noneconomic" damages, are for consequences like pain and suffering that are difficult to quantify in terms of money. Special damages, also known as "economic" damages, are for readily calculable types of expenses that are idiosyncratic to a particular plaintiff, such as medical expenses, funeral expenses, or lost earnings.

A defendant may be liable for past damages, which are for harms that have occurred up to the time of the verdict. A defendant may also be liable for future damages, which are for harms that are predicted (by a preponderance of the evidence) to occur after the verdict.

When a defendant has caused a plaintiff's death, two important types of statutes govern damages. "Survival" statutes allow a plaintiff's estate to sue on his or her behalf, as if the plaintiff had survived, to assert the plaintiff's rights. "Wrongful death" statutes allow people who have suffered losses as a result of another's tortiously caused death to recover damages. These statutes allow the children and spouse of the decedent, for instance, to recover for the loss of financial and emotional support the decedent would have provided. Plaintiffs are entitled to survival damages and wrongful death damages only under statutes, not because of common law precedents.

Cases in this section introduce the types of compensatory damages and the rules governing their recovery. Gunn v. Robertson illustrates the various types of damages and shows how a court might adjust jury awards in each category. Jordon v. Baptist Three Rivers Hospital involves the interpretation of a statute that combines typical survival and wrongful death provisions. *Jordan* also discusses damages for *loss of consortium.*

GUNN v. ROBERTSON

801 So. 2d 555 (La. Ct. App. 2001)

GOTHARD, J.

On October 19, 1998, Randall Gunn, individually and on behalf of his minor children, and his wife Tammy Gunn, filed suit for damages arising out of an automobile accident on April 1, 1998. Gunn sought general damages plus past and future medicals and wages, and loss of earning capacity. His wife and children sought loss of consortium. Named as defendants were James Robertson and State Farm Mutual Automobile Ins. Co., Robertson's automobile liability insurance carrier. . . .

Trial by jury was held on May 15-19, 2000. At its conclusion, the jury rendered a verdict in favor of the plaintiffs, finding that James Robertson was 70% at fault in the cause of the accident. The jury assessed damages as follows: $1,000.00 physical pain and suffering, $1,700.00 past medical expenses and $5,400.00 in past lost wages. . . .

In this appeal, plaintiffs present eleven allegations of error in three categories. Plaintiffs allege that the jury committed manifest error in its findings of comparative fault, in its award of general and special damages . . . .

Our jurisprudence has consistently held that in the assessment of damages, much discretion is left to the judge or jury, and upon appellate review such awards will be disturbed only when there has been a clear abuse of that discretion, And, "[i]t is only after articulated analysis of the facts discloses an abuse of discretion, that the award may on appellate review be considered either excessive or insufficient," Reck v. Stevens, 373 So. 2d 498, 501 (La. 1979). Appellate courts review the evidence in the light which most favorably supports the judgment to determine whether the trier of fact was clearly wrong in its conclusions. Before an appellate court can disturb the quantum of an award, the record must clearly reveal that the jury abused its discretion. In order to make this determination, the reviewing court looks first to the individual circumstances of the injured plaintiff. Only after analysis of the facts and circumstances peculiar to the particular case and plaintiff may an appellate court conclude that the award is inadequate.

> Prior awards under similar circumstances serve only as a general guide. If the appellate court determines that an abuse of discretion has been committed, it is then appropriate to resort to a review of prior awards, to determine the appropriate modification of the award. In such review, the test is whether the present award is greatly disproportionate to the mass of past awards for truly similar injuries. In instances where the appellate court is compelled to modify awards, the award will only be disturbed to the extent of lowering or raising an award to the highest or lowest point which is reasonably within the discretion afforded the trial court.

Theriot v. Allstate Ins. Co., 625 So. 2d 1337, 1340 (La. 1993).

We have reviewed the record in this case, and we find that the award for pain and suffering is below that which a reasonable trier of fact could assess. The testimony at trial showed that Mr. Gunn was a thirty-two year old self-employed metal worker. He had a pre-existing spinal defect, which was asymptomatic prior to the accident. Since the accident, plaintiff has been in pain, and his treating physician has testified that he will not have relief until he undergoes surgery. Defendants argue that the award of $1,000.00 [for] past pain and suffering is adequate because the jury could have found that Mr. Gunn suffered no injury as a result of the automobile accident, and that his back pain and need for surgery was caused, not by the accident, but by his pre-existing spondylolisthesis.

It is a well settled rule of law that a defendant takes his victim as he finds him and is responsible for all natural and probable consequences of his tortious conduct. When the tortfeasor's conduct aggravates a pre-existing condition, the tortfeasor must compensate the victim for the full extent of the aggravation. . . .

We have conducted a review of prior awards for past pain and suffering to determine the appropriate modification of this award, and have found the following cases.

In Manuel v. St. John the Baptist School Bd., 98-1265 (La. App. 5 Cir. 3/30/99), 734 So. 2d 766, *writ denied*, 99-1193 (La. 6/4/99) 744 So. 2d 632, this court affirmed a general damage award of $52,000.00. Plaintiff had a pre-existing disc herniation, which was exacerbated by an automobile accident, and caused the severe pain necessitating surgery.

In Lapeyrouse v. Wal-Mart Stores, Inc., 98-547 (La. App. 5 Cir. 12/16/98), 725 So. 2d 61, *writ denied*, 99-0140 (La. 3/12/99) 739 So. 2d 209, this court affirmed a general damage award of $45,000.00 to a plaintiff with a pre-existing cervical condition who suffered two herniated discs which will eventually require surgery as a result of a slip and fall.

In Alfonso v. Piccadilly Cafeteria, 95-279 (La. App. 5 Cir. 11/28/95), 665 So. 2d 589, *writ denied*, 95-3119 (La. 2/16/96) 667 So. 2d 1060, this court raised a general damages award from $11,000.00 to $25,000.00 where plaintiff suffered from pre-existing spondylolisthesis, where plaintiff was engaged in heavy manual labor and had been involved in one accident prior and one subsequent to the accident at issue, and plaintiff underwent spinal fusion surgery with "fair" results.

In this case, plaintiff was an iron worker, engaged in heavy manual labor who had a pre-existing spondylolisthesis prior to the automobile accident, and who suffers a herniated disc requiring surgery. We find that the lowest point which is reasonable within the discretion of the trier of fact is $25,000.00. Accordingly, we amend the judgment of the trial court to award to plaintiffs $25,000.00 in general damages.

Plaintiffs next challenge the award for past and future medical expenses. Plaintiffs allege that the jury erred in failing to award past medical expenses of $13,942.19 and in failing to award future medical expenses.

> A tortfeasor is required to pay for medical treatment of his victim, even over treatment or unnecessary treatment, unless such treatment was incurred by the victim in bad faith. A trier of fact is in error for failing to award the full amount of medical expenses proven by the victim. A jury errs by not awarding the full amount of medical expenses incurred as a result of injuries caused by the accident when the record demonstrates that the victim has proven them by a preponderance of the evidence.

Lombas v. Southern Foods, Inc., 00-26 (La. App. 5 Cir. 5/30/00), 760 So. 2d 1232, 1289-1290.

In this case, plaintiffs introduced evidence to support past medical expenses of $13,942.19. The defendants do not dispute the amount of medical expenses claimed. Accordingly, we amend the award for past medical expenses to award the total medical expenses of $13,942.19 awarded at trial.

Plaintiffs also allege that the jury erred in failing to award any amount for future medical expenses.

> In order to recover future medical benefits, the plaintiff must prove that these expenses will be necessary and inevitable. Future medical expenses must be established with some degree of certainty and must be supported with medical testimony and estimation of probable costs.

Hopstetter v. Nichols, 98-185 (La. App. 5 Cir. 7/28/98), 716 So. 2d 458, 462, writ denied, 98-2288 (La. 11/13/98) 731 So. 2d 263.

Here, the plaintiff established the need for surgery at a cost of $59,915.00. Again, defendant does not dispute the amount claimed, but only that the accident created the need for the surgery. Accordingly, we amend the judgment to award future medical expenses of $59,915.00.

Plaintiff next contends that the jury erred in failing to award the full amount of past lost wages, and in failing to award damages for future lost wages and for loss of earning capacity.

> To recover for actual wage loss, a plaintiff must prove the length of time missed from work due to the tort and must prove past lost earnings. Past lost earnings are susceptible of mathematical calculation from evidence offered at trial. An award for past lost earnings requires evidence as reasonably establishes the claim, which may consist of the plaintiff's own testimony. An award for past lost earnings is not subject to the much-discretion rule when it is susceptible of mathematical calculation from documentary proof. The plaintiff's uncorroborated, self-serving testimony will not be sufficient to support an award if it is shown that corroborative evidence was available and was not produced. To obtain an award for future loss of earning capacity, a plaintiff must present medical evidence that indicates with reasonable certainty that a residual disability causally related to the accident exists. Future loss of earnings, which are inherently speculative, must be proven with a reasonable degree of certainty, and purely conjectural or uncertain future loss of earnings will not be allowed.

Wehbe v. Waguespack, 98-475 (La. App. 5 Cir. 10/28/98), 720 So. 2d 1267, 1276, writ denied, 98-2907, 98-2970 (La. 1/15/99), 736 So. 2d 211, 213; citing Mathews v. Dousay 96-858 (La. App. 3 Cir. 1/15/97), 689 So. 2d 503, 720 So. 2d 1267.

In this case, the jury awarded past lost wages of $7,500.00 [sic: $5,400.00?] and failed to award any amount for future lost wages. We cannot say the jury was manifestly erroneous in this regard. While Mr. Gunn presented evidence to show that he had placed a bid on a construction job shortly after the accident, there is no evidence to show that the bid would have been accepted. Accordingly, plaintiff did not prove by a preponderance of the evidence his claim for past lost wages.

In addition, plaintiff failed to prove his claim for future lost wages. While plaintiffs' vocational expert testified that Mr. Gunn was incapable of gainful employment, defendant's vocational expert testified that Mr. Gunn had no cognitive defects and was employable at a variety of light and medium duty jobs. He further testified that Mr. Gunn was capable of upward mobility and that his potential earning capability would increase. Accordingly we find that the trier of fact did not err in failing to award further loss of earnings. . . .

For the above discussed reasons, the judgment of the district court is amended to award to plaintiff general damages of $25,000.00, along with special damages of $13,942.19 for past medical expenses, $59,915.00 for future medical expenses and $7,500.00 for past lost wages, subject to a 30% reduction for plaintiff's fault. The assessment of costs against plaintiffs is reversed and we find that defendants are liable for all costs of trial and for those incurred in this appeal.

NOTES TO GUNN v. ROBERTSON

1. *Types of Compensatory Damages.*   The court in *Gunn* considered the adequacy of the jury's award of the three types of compensatory damages that are most common: general damages (pain and suffering), past and future medical expenses, and past and future lost wages. The court increased the jury award for all but the last type. What were the court's justifications for each modification? On what evidence did the court rely?

2. *Procedural Note: Additur and Remittitur.*   When the court increases a jury award for any type of damages, the process is called *additur*. Federal judges and some states' judges do not have the power to use additur. All judges, however, have the power to reduce excessive jury verdicts, the power of *remittitur*.

Increases in jury awards are usually a response to a plaintiff's request for a new trial on the grounds that the award was too low. The defendant is given a choice to accept the increase or face a new trial. Decreases are handled the same way. They usually result from a defendant's motion for a new trial on the grounds that the award was too high. If the court agrees, the plaintiff is given a choice to accept a decrease or face a new trial.

Statute: REMITTITUR OR ADDITUR AS ALTERNATIVE
TO NEW TRIAL; REFORMATION OF VERDICT

La. Rev. Stat. 38:383 (2017)

If the trial court is of the opinion that the verdict is so excessive or inadequate that a new trial should be granted for that reason only, it may indicate to the party or his attorney within what time he may enter a remittitur or additur. This remittitur or additur is to be entered only with the consent of the plaintiff or the defendant as the case may be, as an alternative to a new trial, and is to be entered only if the issue of amount of the excess or inadequacy of the verdict or judgment can be separately and fairly ascertained. If a remittitur or additur is entered, then the court shall reform the jury verdict or judgment in accordance therewith.

NOTE TO STATUTE

Reformation of Verdicts by Appellate and Trial Courts.   The Louisiana statute applies to trial courts. In Louisiana, the jurisdiction in which *Gunn* was decided, appellate courts may also review the award to determine whether the jury has acted unreasonably in its award of damages:

> The trier of fact is given much discretion in awarding damages. The appellate court in reviewing an award to determine if there has been an abuse of this "much discretion" must look first to the facts and circumstances surrounding the particular case. If it is determined that the award is either excessive or inadequate, the court may then use prior awards to aid it in fixing an appropriate award. The reviewing court may then amend the award such that it is lowered to the highest or raised to the lowest point which is reasonable within the discretion afforded the trier of fact.

See Prevost v. Cowan, 431 So. 2d 1063, 1067 (La. Ct. App. 1983).

Perspective: Contract and Tort Damages

The underlying damage principle for breaches of tort or contractual duties is *full compensation*. But many assert that what "full" means is different in contracts and torts. One principle in contracts, the *reliance principle*, is to return the injured party to her *pre-contractual state* by awarding damages equal to the costs she has incurred. An alternative principle in contracts, the *expectation principle*, is to award enough damages so the injured party will be just as well off as if the other had performed. This second principle usually results in a greater damage award because the injured person gets damages equal to the costs she has incurred plus any profit she would have earned from the breaching person's performance.

Some claim that full compensation in torts is similar to the first contract principle, the reliance principle, because tort law awards compensation sufficient to return the injured party to the position she would have been in if there had been no accident. Tort awards that include compensation for medical expenses, for pain and suffering, and for repairs to damaged property are just like the contract damages for costs incurred. But tort law also compensates for lost future earnings — similar to the award of lost profits under the expectation measure. By allowing recovery for past and future losses, full compensation under tort is really based on the same idea as contract law — ensure that the injured person realizes all of the benefits she would have realized if there had been no breach of tort or contractual duties. See Michael B. Kelly, *The Phantom Reliance Interest in Tort Damages*, 38 San Diego L. Rev. 169 (2001).

JORDAN v. BAPTIST THREE RIVERS HOSPITAL
984 S.W.2d 593 (Tenn. 1999)

HOLDER, J. . . .

This cause of action arises out of the death of Mary Sue Douglas ("decedent"). The plaintiff, Martha P. Jordan, is a surviving child of the decedent and the administratrix of the decedent's estate. The plaintiff, on behalf of the decedent's estate, filed a medical malpractice action against the defendants, Baptist Three Rivers Hospital, Mark W. Anderson, M.D., Noel Dominguez, M.D., and Patrick Murphy, M.D. The plaintiff has alleged that the defendants' negligence caused the decedent's death.

The plaintiff's complaint sought damages for loss of consortium. . . . The defendants filed a motion to strike and a motion for judgment on the pleadings asserting that Tennessee law does not permit recovery for loss of parental consortium. . . .

The trial court granted the defendants' motion to strike. . . . We granted appeal to determine whether claims for loss of spousal and parental consortium in wrongful death cases are viable in Tennessee. . . .

A wrongful death cause of action did not exist at common law. Pursuant to the common law, actions for personal injuries that resulted in death terminated at the victim's death because "in a civil court the death of a human being could not be complained of as an injury." W. Page Keeton et al., Prosser and Keeton on the Law of Torts §127, at 945 (5th ed. 1984) ("Prosser"). "The [legal] result was that it was cheaper for the defendant to kill the plaintiff than to injure him, and that the most grievous of all injuries left the bereaved family of the victim . . . without a remedy." Id. This rule of non-liability for wrongful death was previously the prevailing view in both England and in the United States. . . .

The majority of states have enacted "survival statutes." These statutes permit the victim's cause of action to survive the death, so that the victim, through the victim's estate, recovers damages that would have been recovered *by the victim* had the victim survived. Survival statutes do not create a new cause of action; rather, the cause of action vested in the victim at the time of death is transferred to the person designated in the statutory scheme to pursue it, and the action is enlarged to include damages for the death itself. Prosser, §126, at 942-43. "[T]he recovery is the same one the decedent would have been entitled to at death, and thus included such items as wages lost after injury and before death, medical expenses incurred, and pain and suffering," and other appropriate compensatory damages suffered by the victim from the time of injury to the time of death. Id. at 943.

In contrast to survival statutes, "pure wrongful death statutes" create a *new* cause of action in favor of the survivors of the victim for *their* loss occasioned by the death. These statutes proceed "on the theory of compensating the individual beneficiaries for the loss of the economic benefit which they might reasonably have expected to receive from the decedent in the form of support, services or contributions during the remainder of [the decedent's] lifetime if [the decedent] had not been killed." Prosser, §127, at 949. Hence, most wrongful death jurisdictions have adopted a "pecuniary loss" standard of recovery, allowing damages for economic contributions the deceased would have made to the survivors had death not occurred and for the economic value of the services the deceased would have rendered to the survivors but for the death. . . .

The plain language of Tenn. Code Ann. §20-5-113 reveals that it may be classified as a survival statute because it preserves whatever cause of action was vested in the victim at the time of death. The survival character of the statute is evidenced by the language "the party suing shall have the right to recover [damages] resulting to the deceased from the personal injuries." Tennessee courts have declared that the purpose of this language is to provide "for the continued existence and passing of the right of action of the deceased, and not for any new, independent cause of action in [survivors]." Whaley v. Catlett, 103 Tenn. 347, 53 S.W. 131, 133 (Tenn. 1899). Accordingly, Tenn. Code Ann. §20-5-113 "in theory, preserve[s] the right of action which the deceased himself would have had, and . . . [has] basically been construed as falling within the survival type of . . . statutes for over a century" because it continues that cause of action by permitting recovery of damages for the death itself.

Notwithstanding the accurate, technical characterization of Tenn. Code Ann. §20-5-113 as survival legislation, the statute also creates a cause of action that compensates survivors for their losses. The statute provides that damages may be recovered *"resulting to the parties for whose use and benefit the right of action survives from the death."* Id. (emphasis added). Hence, survivors of the deceased may recover damages for *their* losses suffered as a result of the death as well as damages sustained by the deceased from the time of injury to the time of death. Our inquiry shall focus on whether survivors should be permitted to recover consortium losses. . . .

Damages under our wrongful death statute can be delineated into two distinct classifications. The first classification permits recovery for injuries sustained by the deceased from the time of injury to the time of death. Damages under the first classification include medical expenses, physical and mental pain and suffering, funeral expenses, lost wages, and loss of earning capacity.

The second classification of damages permits recovery of incidental damages suffered by the decedent's next of kin. Incidental damages have been judicially defined to *include* the pecuniary value of the decedent's life. Spencer v. A-1 Crane Serv., Inc., 880 S.W.2d 938, 943 (Tenn. 1994). Pecuniary value has been judicially defined to include "the expectancy of life, the age, condition of health and strength, capacity for labor and earning money through skill, any art, trade, profession and occupation or business, and personal habits as to sobriety and industry." Id. Pecuniary value also takes into account the decedent's probable living expenses had the decedent lived.

The wrongful death statute neither explicitly precludes consortium damages nor reflects an intention to preclude consortium damages. The statute's language does not limit recovery to purely economic losses. To the contrary, the statute's plain language appears to encompass consortium damages. Indeed, this Court has recognized that pecuniary value cannot be defined to a mathematical certainty as such a definition "would overlook the value of the [spouse's] personal interest in the affairs of the home and the economy incident to [the spouse's] services." *Thrailkill*, 879 S.W.2d at 841. We further believe that the pecuniary value of a human life is a compound of many elements. An individual family member has value to others as part of a functioning social and economic unit. This value necessarily includes the value of mutual society and protection, i.e., human companionship. Human companionship has a definite, substantial and ascertainable pecuniary value, and its loss forms a part of the value of the life we seek to ascertain. While uncertainties may arise in proof when defining the value of human companionship, the one committing the wrongful act causing the death of a human being should not be permitted to seek protection behind the uncertainties inherent in the very situation his wrongful act has created. Moreover, it seems illogical and absurd to believe that the legislature would intend the anomaly of permitting recovery of consortium losses when a spouse is injured and survives but not when the very same act causes a spouse's death. . . .

A basis for placing an economic value on parental consortium is that the education and training which a child may reasonably expect to receive from a parent are of actual and commercial value to the child. Accordingly, a child sustains a pecuniary injury for the loss of parental education and training when a defendant tortiously causes the death of the child's parent. Moreover, we recognize that:

> normal home life for a child consists of complex incidences in which the sums constitute a nurturing environment. When the vitally important parent-child relationship is impaired and the child loses the love, guidance and close companionship of a parent, the child is deprived of something that is indeed valuable and precious. No one could seriously contend otherwise.

Still by Erlandson v. Baptist Hosp., 755 S.W.2d 807, 812 (Tenn. App. 1988).

The additional considerations employed for spousal consortium may be applicable to parental consortium claims. We agree with the observation of one court that "companionship, comfort, society, guidance, solace, and protection . . . go into the vase of family happiness [and] are the things for which a wrongdoer must pay when he shatters the vase." Spangler v. Helm's New York-Pittsburgh Motor Exp., 153 A.2d 490 (Penn. 1959).

Adult children may be too attenuated from their parents in some cases to proffer sufficient evidence of consortium losses. Similarly, if the deceased did not have a close relationship with any of the statutory beneficiaries, the statutory beneficiaries will not likely sustain compensable consortium losses or their consortium losses will be nominal. The age of the child does not, in and of itself, preclude consideration of parental consortium damages. The adult child inquiry shall take into consideration factors such as closeness of the relationship and dependence (i.e., of a handicapped adult child, assistance with day care, etc.).

We hold that consortium-type damages may be considered when calculating the pecuniary value of a deceased's life. This holding does not create a new cause of action but merely refines the term "pecuniary value." Consortium losses are not limited to spousal claims but also necessarily encompass a child's loss, whether minor or adult. Loss of consortium consists of several elements, encompassing not only tangible services provided by a family member, but also intangible benefits each family member receives from the continued existence of other family members. Such benefits include attention, guidance, care, protection, training, companionship, cooperation, affection, love, and in the case of a spouse, sexual relations. Our holding conforms with the plain language of the wrongful death statutes, the trend of modern authority, and the social and economic reality of modern society. . . .

NOTES TO JORDAN v. BAPTIST THREE RIVERS HOSPITAL

1. *Wrongful Death and Survival Statutes.*   Under the common law, a person's right to sue in tort died when the person died. The person's estate could not seek damages on the deceased's behalf, and the person's dependents could not recover for their losses. As the opinion in *Jordan* indicates, wrongful death and survival statutes

changed that common law rule. Survival and wrongful death actions (1) arise at different times, (2) permit recovery by different plaintiffs, and (3) apply to different harms. A survival action arises at the time of the negligence for the benefit of the deceased person's estate (which may not be deceased's dependents) for harms caused to the deceased. The wrongful death action arises at the time of that death for the benefit of statutorily enumerated dependents for harms caused to those dependents.

To determine which of these types of statutes is relevant in a particular case, one must identify whether the person bringing suit is suing on behalf of the estate of the decedent or on his or her own behalf. Statutes describe, with a greatly varying degree of detail, the types of losses for which damages are recoverable. Were the plaintiffs in *Jordan* seeking survival damages or wrongful death damages? Why do the damages they seek fit into that category?

2. Loss of Consortium. The plaintiffs in *Jordan* sought loss of consortium damages. Such damages are also allowed in tort cases not involving death. Why was there any issue about whether loss of consortium damages were recoverable in this death case?

Statute: WRONGFUL DEATH; DAMAGES
Tenn. Code §20-5-113 (2017)

Where a person's death is caused by the wrongful act, fault, or omission of another, and suit is brought for damages [by a surviving spouse or child or personal representative], the party suing shall, if entitled to damages, have the right to recover for the mental and physical suffering, loss of time, and necessary expenses resulting to the deceased from the personal injuries, and also the damages resulting to the parties for whose use and benefit the right of action survives from the death consequent upon the injuries received.

Statute: SURVIVAL OF ACTIONS; DEATH OF PARTY
Tenn. Code §20-5-102 (2017)

No civil action commenced, whether founded on wrongs or contracts, except actions for wrongs affecting the character of the plaintiff, shall abate by the death of either party, but may be revived; nor shall any right of action arising hereafter based on the wrongful act or omission of another, except actions for wrongs affecting the character, be abated by the death of the party wronged; but the right of action shall pass in like manner as the right of action described in §20-5-106 [describing who may pursue such actions on the decedent's behalf and who will benefit from damages recovered].

Statute: ACTION FOR WRONGFUL DEATH
Alaska Stat. §09.55.580(a)-(c) (2017)

(a) Except as provided under (f) of this section [prohibiting a person who has previously killed another person from recovering damages for that person's death] and

AS 09.65.145 [limiting recovery for injury or death from livestock activity], when the death of a person is caused by the wrongful act or omission of another, the personal representatives of the former may maintain an action therefor against the latter, if the former might have maintained an action, had the person lived, against the latter for an injury done by the same act or omission. . . .

(b) The damages recoverable under this section shall be limited to those which are the natural and proximate consequence of the negligent or wrongful act or omission of another.

(c) In fixing the amount of damages to be awarded under this section, the court or jury shall consider all the facts and circumstances and from them fix the award at a sum which will fairly compensate for the injury resulting from the death. In determining the amount of the award, the court or jury shall consider but is not limited to the following:

(1) deprivation of the expectation of pecuniary benefits to the beneficiary or beneficiaries, without regard to age thereof, that would have resulted from the continued life of the deceased and without regard to probable accumulations or what the deceased may have saved during the lifetime of the deceased;

(2) loss of contributions for support;

(3) loss of assistance or services irrespective of age or relationship of decedent to the beneficiary or beneficiaries;

(4) loss of consortium;

(5) loss of prospective training and education;

(6) medical and funeral expenses.

NOTES TO STATUTES

1. *Wrongful Death and Survival Statutes Compared.* The court in *Jordan* refers to Tennessee Code §20-5-113, reproduced above. How does the language in this paragraph include both wrongful death and survival rights? Tennessee Code §20-5-102 describes the nature of the survival rights.

2. *Damages Recoverable for Wrongful Death.* A comparison of the Tennessee and Alaska wrongful death statutes illustrates the varying degrees of specificity with which recoverable damages are described and why the court in *Jordan* found the Tennessee statute silent on the recoverability of consortium damages. Are the types of damages enumerated in the Alaska statute losses suffered by the deceased or losses suffered by the family of the deceased?

B. General Damages

1. In General

Consequences of an injury that are real but cannot be evaluated in terms of typical monetary transactions are called *general damages*. These damages, sometimes called *non-economic damages*, typically result from any injury. General damages may include such subjective, non-monetary losses as pain, suffering, inconvenience, mental anguish, disability, or disfigurement incurred by the injured party, emotional distress, loss of society and companionship, loss of consortium, injury to reputation and humiliation, and destruction of the parent-child relationship.

2. Pain and Suffering

Some courts use two categories for analyzing claims for pain and suffering: some *objective injuries* are likely to cause pain and suffering for anyone who sustains them. Other "subjective" situations are cases where a plaintiff claims to have pain and suffering but it is not generally understood that anyone who had incurred the underlying injury would also feel that type of pain. The majority opinion in Rael v. F & S Co. applies this distinction to a plaintiff who complains of headaches following his injury due to the sudden explosion of a firework. The dissenting opinion describes how pain and suffering can be proved and measured.

The nebulous and nonquantifiable nature of pain and suffering leads lawyers to adopt various strategies when arguing about how much money should be awarded for it. Giant Food Inc. v. Satterfield discusses *per diem arguments*, one method plaintiffs' lawyers use to help juries quantify general damages.

RAEL v. F & S CO.

612 P.2d 1318 (N.M. Ct. App. 1979)

ANDREWS, J.

. . . Twelve year old Everett Rael was injured by a sudden explosion of a firework. His father filed this action against the fireworks supplier, Onda Enterprises, Ltd. (Onda), and the seller, F & S Company, Inc. (F & S). After the court dismissed cross-claims filed by both defendants in which each sought indemnity from the other, the jury returned a verdict for $7,000 for Everett and $339 for his father against both defendants jointly and severally. [F & S appealed.]

The Supreme Court of South Dakota, in Klein v. W. Hodgman and Sons, Inc., 77 S.D. 64, 85 N.W.2d 289 (1957), adopted the following two-pronged approach for proof of future pain and suffering:

> There are two rules by which the question of future pain and suffering may be submitted to the jury: If the injury is objective, and it is plainly apparent, from the very nature of the injury, that the injured person must of necessity undergo pain and suffering in the future then most certainly the Plaintiff would not be required to prove a fact so plainly evident, and upon making proof of such an objective injury, the jury may infer pain and suffering in the future. . . . Where the injury is subjective, and of such a nature that laymen cannot, with reasonable certainty know whether or not there will be future pain and suffering, then, in order to warrant an instruction on that point, and to authorize the jury to return a verdict for future pain and suffering, there must be offered evidence by expert witnesses, learned in human anatomy, who can testify, either from a personal examination or knowledge of the history of the case, or from a hypothetical question based on the facts, that the plaintiff, with reasonable certainty, may be expected to experience future pain and suffering, as a result of the injury proved.

We find such reasoning to be persuasive. In the instant case, the only conceivable inference of ongoing pain suffered by Everett was his claim of headaches in the back of his head. By the above standard, this would be characterized a "subjective" complaint of the plaintiff. It certainly cannot be deemed to be a matter of common knowledge that one who suffers an eye injury will also suffer headaches in the back of his head. Therefore, to justify an instruction for future pain and suffering it was necessary for the plaintiff to present evidence by a medical expert that these headaches were caused by the accident and that they would continue into the future, and for the expert to present some reasonably certain proof as to the severity and duration with which they would occur. No such testimony was presented. The record is clear that the trial court, over the objection of F & S, instructed the jury that they could award damages for future pain and suffering. This instruction is reversible error since there was no evidence to support it.

Since it is impossible to look behind the general verdict of the jury to determine how much, if any, of the award was intended to be compensation for future pain and suffering, the case is reversed and remanded for a new trial on the issue of damages alone.

SUTIN, J. (concurs in part and dissents in part). [Judge Sutin dissents with respect to the part of the ruling related to the award of damages for pain and suffering.]

The meaning of "pain and suffering" and the rules of law applicable thereto are matters of first impression.

> Perhaps one of the most nebulous yet oft-employed concepts in modern law is that of "pain and suffering." Consequently, it is rather remarkable to note that one will search in vain for any extensive judicial analysis of its essential components. While most courts, like our own, recognize that pain and suffering constitute a legitimate element of damages in certain cases, they are seemingly unanimous in silently adhering to the view that the concept is a self-evident one, neither requiring, nor capable of, precise definition or analysis. (p.93)
>
> [T]he courts apparently seek to compensate the individual for any unwarranted invasion of, or interference with, his ordinary, peaceful mental process and pursuits. Pain and suffering are, after all, but two sides of the same coin. Pain, as such, arises from some direct injury to the body which jangles the nerves into transmitting coded signals to the brain, stimulating it into an awareness of consciousness of serious bodily hurt. Mental suffering, on the other hand, seemingly refers to the individual's worry or apprehension concerning the extent of the injury, for example, the fear of resulting death. Mental suffering would also appear broad enough to include anxiety, shock, fright, humiliation, and other forms of emotional disturbance and mental distress whether or not accompanied by direct physical injury. Both pain and suffering, then, can be resolved in terms of abnormal, unpleasant mental reactions. . . . (pp.93-94)
>
> . . . Pain and suffering are mental processes which obviously cannot be seen, heard, weighed, or measured. Proving their existence in a particular case is essentially a question of proving other facts from which the trier may logically conclude that they do in fact exist in the case before him. . . . (p.95)
>
> [S]uch damages are incapable of any exact mathematical computation, and that the amount to be awarded is peculiarly within the discretion of the trier. The only standard or guide, so-called, which the trier may use in the assessment of damages is his own common sense that is, whatever he reasonably determines is fair compensation. . . . The only time the decision as to damages will be reversed is when the appellate court finds that the award is grossly divergent from what it deems to be fair compensation. . . . [T]he appeal court employs the self-same "standard" or "guide" utilized by the trial court — that of common sense. . . . "[T]he

only trouble with common-sense is that it is none too common." Be that as it may, it does seem rather harsh, nonetheless, to criticize jurors expressly or implicitly, for misusing rules and tools which were never given to them. (pp.97-98) McLoughlin, *Pain and Suffering Under Connecticut Law,* 33 Conn. Bar. J. 93 (1959).

The *McLoughlin* definition and analysis is supported by and added to by analysis in Herb v. Hollowell, 304 Pa. 128, 154 A. 582, 584-5 (1931), in which the court said:

> The nature of pain and suffering is such that no legal yardstick can be fashioned to measure accurately reasonable compensation for it. No one can measure another's pain and suffering; only the person suffering knows how much he is suffering, and even he could not accurately say what would be reasonable pecuniary compensation for it. Earning power and dollars are interchangeable; suffering and dollars are not. Two persons apparently suffering the same pain from the same kind of injury might in fact be suffering respectively pains differing much in acuteness, depending on the nervous sensibility of the sufferer. Two persons suffering exactly the same pain would doubtless differ as to what reasonable compensation for that pain would be. This being true, it follows that jurors would probably differ widely as to what is reasonable compensation for another's pain and suffering, no matter how specific the court's instructions might be. All this is merely suggestive of the practical difficulties confronting a trial judge who is about to instruct the jury as to the measure of damages for pain and suffering. It is, of course, the duty of the trial judge to make it clear to the jury that, in awarding damages for pain and suffering, the award must be limited "to compensation and compensation alone." . . . Jurors may differ widely in their conception of the word "compensation." One juror might hold that no amount of money could justly compensate one for acute pain and suffering; another might hold that even a small sum of money would be just compensation in such a case. . . .

In the case before us, the trial judge said: "There is no fixed standard as to any amount to allow for pain and suffering. That is to be guided by your judgment." This was in effect an instruction that there was no infallible objective standard with which to measure damages for these subjective elements but that they were to use good common sense in assessing damages for them. . . .

In New Mexico, the measure of damages "is the enlightened conscience of impartial jurors." Braddock v. Seaboard Air Line Railroad Company, 80 So. 2d 662 (Fla. 1955). This guide is the equivalent of "common sense and good judgment." Pain and suffering has no market price. Even the most experienced and learned physician finds no method of measuring it.

As a result, a verdict of the jury will not be disturbed unless it appears that it was influenced by partiality, prejudice, corruption of the jury, shocking in amount, or by some mistaken view of the evidence. . . .

In the instant case, the jury awarded Everett $7,000 in damages for "the nature, extent and duration of the injury," and for "the pain and suffering experienced and reasonably certain to be experienced in the future as a result of the injury."

Everett suffered forms of emotional disturbance and mental stress when a firecracker exploded in his face. Shock, fright, anxiety and trauma followed. He worried that he might be permanently blind. For four years thereafter, from time to time, up to the date of trial, he suffered headaches. We cannot, by the exercise of "common sense" say that the verdict was not the result of "the enlightened conscience of impartial jurors."

GIANT FOOD INC. v. SATTERFIELD
603 A.2d 877 (Md. App. 1992)

FISCHER, J.

Giant Food, Incorporated (Giant) appeals an adverse ruling entered in the Circuit Court for Baltimore County. Regina E. Satterfield cross-appeals the court's decision. This dispute stems from Ms. Satterfield's slip and fall which occurred in Giant Store Number 77 on July 6, 1987. Ms. Satterfield filed a complaint against Giant alleging that she sustained injuries as a result of the accident. . . . The case proceeded, and the jury found Giant negligent and awarded Ms. Satterfield $2,500 for past medical expenses and $40,000 in non-economic compensatory damages. . . .

Giant avers that the trial court committed reversible error by denying Giant's request for a particular jury instruction. Giant's request followed a statement made by Ms. Satterfield's counsel during closing argument. Ms. Satterfield's counsel suggested that the jury use a per diem calculation to award pain and suffering damages:

> I suggest that for your consideration — is fair compensation to be in pain, to suffer, to have permanent injuries, to have lost your right to enjoyment of life and have lost your ability to participate in the things that you enjoyed so much? Seven dollars and fifty cents a day is two thousand seven hundred dollars a year. You multiply that by 43 and you will have a significant number that is about one hundred and thirteen thousand dollars. And it is a large gross number. But I want you to think about each and every day that is involved in those 43 years and see if that is a reasonable number. I suggest that to you for your consideration. Obviously you are free to make whatever decision that you deem appropriate. . . .

Giant contends that the use of a specific dollar amount per unit of time and reference to a predicted life expectancy constitutes a per diem damages argument. Most states have deemed the use of a mathematical formula in determining an award for pain and suffering to be a per diem argument. They have distinguished, however, arguments which only include a lump sum payment that is not derived from multiplication of a unit of time and a dollar amount. . . . Ms. Satterfield's counsel broke down Ms. Satterfield's predicted life expectancy from years into days and arbitrarily assigned a dollar amount to be associated with her daily pain and suffering. Her counsel even went so far as to multiply the days and the dollar amount and then suggested to the jury that this product should equal the amount awarded. Clearly, this formula meets the definition of a per diem argument.

There are numerous arguments both in favor and against the use of per diem arguments. The reasons against allowing the use of per diem argument include: the lack of an evidentiary basis for converting pain and suffering into monetary terms; suggestion of monetary equivalents for pain and suffering amounts to the giving of testimony or to the expression of opinions not disclosed by the evidence; juries are frequently misled into making larger awards; admonitions of the trial court that the argument is not evidence do not erase the prejudice; the defendant is disadvantaged by being required to rebut an argument that has no basis in evidence. The arguments in support of a per diem argument include: the jury should be guided by some reasonable and practical considerations; the trier of fact should not be led to make a guess; the absence of any evidentiary yardstick makes it unlikely that counsel's argument will mislead the jury; the argument only suggests one method for the trier of fact to employ in its estimation of damages; the argument is merely suggestive and is not meant as evidence particularly when accompanied by a jury instruction to that effect; when counsel for one side has made such an argument, the opposing counsel is equally free to suggest his own amounts.

The propriety and legality of the per diem argument has been greatly debated in the courts. Many states support the view that it is wholly improper for counsel to suggest a per diem argument to the jury and that such an argument will not be allowed as a matter of law. [Citing cases from Connecticut, Delaware, Illinois, New Hampshire, New Jersey, New York, and West Virginia.] To the contrary, other states have decided that the argument is wholly appropriate and may be used by counsel at any time. [Citing cases from California, Kentucky, Louisiana, Minnesota, and New Mexico.] Still other states have decided that the use of the per diem argument by counsel is within the sole discretion of the trial court judge. [Citing cases from Arkansas, Montana, and Nevada.] . . .

[I]t is clear that per diem arguments are permissible in this State. It is also apparent that, upon request or when the trial judge sua sponte deems it appropriate, the jury must be instructed that the per diem argument made by counsel is not evidence but is merely a method suggested by a party for the purposes of calculating damages. The jury must further be instructed that an award for pain and suffering is to be based upon the jurors' independent judgment. . . .

NOTES TO RAEL v. F & S CO. AND GIANT FOOD INC. v. SATTERFIELD

1. Objective and Subjective Complaints of Pain and Suffering.   The opinions in *Rael* described when supporting evidence is needed to establish a case for future pain and suffering damages. The majority distinguishes between objective and subjective pain and suffering, requiring supporting evidence only for the latter. The dissent takes a more general approach, saying only that a plaintiff must present facts from which the factfinder may logically infer the existence of pain and suffering. This may result in plaintiff's offering the same evidence, because subjective pain and suffering requires more proof of facts than objective pain and suffering, which is "plainly apparent, from the very nature of the injury." But *Rael* illustrates how the choice of approaches makes a difference on appeal.

2. Per Diem Arguments.   *Giant Foods* provides a classic example of a *per diem* argument, where the plaintiff's attorney suggests a unit of time and a dollar value for each unit. An alternative is to allow the attorney to suggest a time-unit calculation without suggesting a specific monetary value. This was suggested in King v. Railway Express Agency, 107 N.W.2d 509, 517 (N.D. 1961) and adopted by rule in New Jersey Rule 1:7-1(b), New Jersey Rules of Court.

Lawyers have also used "per hour" arguments:

> If it were just a little bitty job to assess for non-economic damages, we'll just pick an hour. Now, it's going to be an hour when he's at work, or it's going to be an hour when he's in the courtroom, or it's going to be in the middle of the night, maybe he's asleep and maybe he's rolling around in pain. Whatever hour it is, folks, you on the jury just have to assess damages for an hour.
>
> If someone said $3.00. Oh, my, that's outrageous. I don't think so. But in this case, you see, you have to assess it for a lifetime. And there will be some hours in his life when he's relatively comfortable. And there will be some hours in his life when he's

extremely uncomfortable. But his life expectancy, as I calculate it, is 325,872 hours. And we believe that a fair sum for that amount of time is $950,000.00. We think if you award that sum for thirty-seven years and two months, 325,872 hours, it should be a no greater than awarding Marty $3.00 just for an hour.

See Meyers v. Southern Builders, Inc., 7 S.W.3d 507 (Mo. Ct. App. 1999).

3. *Per Diem and Golden Rule Arguments.* As the opinion in *Giant Foods* indicates, courts are split on whether per diem arguments for pain and suffering amounts are permissible and whether they need to be accompanied by proper instructions to the jury from the judge. Another method for attempting to quantify pain and suffering damages is the *Golden Rule argument.* Golden Rule arguments are those in which counsel asks the jurors to place themselves in the plaintiff's shoes and to award such damages as they would "charge to undergo equivalent pain and suffering." Considering the court's arguments in favor of and against per diem arguments, would the court in *Giant Foods* allow Golden Rule arguments? See Beagle v. Vasold, 417 P.2d 673 (Cal. 1966) (saying per diem arguments are permissible but not Golden Rule arguments). An objection to Golden Rule arguments is that they ask the jury to deviate from neutrality and to decide the case on the basis of personal interest, rather than on the basis of evidence about the plaintiff's circumstances.

4. *Community Safety Approaches: The Reptile Strategy.* Another approach used by plaintiff's attorneys is the so-called "reptile strategy." The strategy consists of focusing on dangers to the community and the jurors themselves that arise from the defendant's conduct. The underlying idea is to appeal to a "reptilian" portion of the brain that instinctively goes into self-protective mode and to overpower the cognitive part of the brain. An attorney might emphasize to the jury that, by finding the defendant liable for significant damages, they are able to improve their own safety and that of their family members and their community. Community safety is a legitimate concern for tort law and particularly relevant to questions of legal duty and breach of that duty. Some courts have allowed reptile arguments on that basis. See Bostick v. State Farm Mutual Automobile Insurance Co., 2017 WL 3123636 (July 21, 2017). Community safety is of less direct concern to the issue of damages, which is supposed to be based on the harm to the particular plaintiff, although it is easy to understand why plaintiffs' lawyers might want to appeal to jurors' emotions and fears.

Problem
Pain and Suffering Damages

If you practice in a jurisdiction following the approach of the majority in *Rael* and represent the plaintiff in the following cases, for which would you be obliged to present expert testimony to establish the pain and suffering in order to recover corresponding damages?

    A. Slip and fall in dining room causes shoulder injury with resulting demonstrable, permanent limited range of shoulder movement. See Paul v. Imperial Palace, Inc., 908 P.2d 226, 229 (Nev. 1995).

    B. Fall from ladder results in broken ankle with implanted plate and screws. See Krause Inc. v. Little, 34 P.3d 566 (Nev. 2001).

C. After a car accident, the plaintiff complains of continuing pain in both arms, a tingling sensation, problems with concentration, and hair loss. See Hyler v. Boyter, 823 S.W.2d 425, 426-427 (Tex. Ct. App. 1992).

D. Plaintiff has ten stitches in his head from a construction accident and complains about headaches, backaches, and sexual dysfunction. See Thompson v. Port Authority of New York, 728 N.Y.S.2d 15, 16 (N.Y. App. Div. 2001).

Problem
Per Diem Arguments

Plaintiff's counsel presented the following argument to the jury:

What award will it take to tell Grand Union what accountability means and that this is what the people in Bennington County think a human life and human suffering is worth[?] Now, let's just take one element. We have talked about pain and suffering. What would be fair compensation for pain and suffering? *Entirely up to you.*

I have a suggestion. If you think about what it is like for Susanne to go through one day with the pain that she has and think about what would be fair compensation for that one day, what do you think it would be? Would it be $100 to go through that in a day? Would it be $75? Would it be $50, $40?

Ladies and gentlemen, we want to be scrupulously fair about our request to you. So I am going to suggest to you that you award Susanne $30 a day for the loss of those three elements: pain and suffering, mental anguish, and loss of enjoyment of life. That is $10 a day for each one. *I put it to you for your consideration to follow that through.*

You would do it this way, there are 365 days a year. I am just going to put here pain and suffering, mental anguish, loss of enjoyment of life. Now there are 365 days in a year. And Susanne's six years she has already suffered in these ways and 29 more, that is 35 years total that she should be compensated for. And if you multiply 35 times 365, there are 12,775 days. And if you multiply that figure by the $30 per day I just suggested, it comes out to $383,250.

Now, another way of thinking of that is if you divide 35 years into this figure of $383,250 it comes out to slightly under $11,000 a year. Maybe that would be a help to think for you $11,000 a year to live the way she lives, to lose what she has lost. *Perhaps that would be a help for you; I don't know.*

If you represent the defendant, you may object on the ground that the counsel's reminders, italicized above, are not enough to enable the jury to avoid the difficulties associated with the per diem argument. Is this argument likely to be successful? See Debus v. Grand Union Stores of Vermont, 621 A.2d 1288 (Vt. 1993).

3. Hedonic Damages

The term *hedonic damages* describes a second type of general damage, loss of enjoyment of life's pleasures. Plaintiffs sometimes try to distinguish this loss from pain and suffering. Some courts treat hedonic damages as included in the damage award for pain and suffering. Other courts characterize hedonic losses differently from pain and suffering. They treat pain and suffering as losses that the plaintiff actually experiences, while hedonic losses are pleasures that the plaintiff never gets to experience because of injuries. Regardless of whether pain and suffering and hedonic losses are separate injuries, the appropriate amount of compensatory damages is difficult to quantify. For both types of harm, however, the amount must be calibrated to the detriment the particular plaintiff in the case is likely to have suffered. Loth v. Truck-A-Way Corp. describes what evidence will be admissible to establish the harm the particular plaintiff suffered. It analyzes three methods economists offer to quantify hedonic damages. Consider what evidence in *Loth* is admissible and what is not.

LOTH v. TRUCK-A-WAY CORP.
70 Cal. Rptr. 2d 571 (Cal. Ct. App. 1998)

ORTEGA, Acting Presiding Justice. . . .

On June 29, 1994, plaintiff Shereen Loth was on a business trip driving north on Interstate 5. Plaintiff's small car was struck by a 24-wheel tractor-trailer rig owned by defendant Truck-A-Way. The collision occurred as plaintiff's car, which was in the slow lane, was passing on the truck's right. The truck made an unsafe lane change into plaintiff's lane, and its front end hit plaintiff's car's left rear. Plaintiff's car spun in front of the truck and was pushed sideways across three lanes of traffic. Plaintiff's car eventually separated from the truck, but was struck by another vehicle before it stopped on the shoulder, facing the wrong way. . . .

Plaintiff sued Truck-A-Way and its employee driver for personal injuries, property damage, and lost earnings. Defendants conceded liability at trial, and the only issue for the jury was damages.

Plaintiff asked the jury for $208,479 in special damages, comprised of medical damages (past and future) of $27,635, temporary lost earnings of $147,675, and property damage and miscellaneous expenses of $3,507. (Those figures do not total $208,479, but that is what the jury was told both orally and in writing.)

As for pain and suffering, plaintiff asked for an unspecified amount of damages, including compensation for loss of enjoyment of life. Plaintiff, who was 27 when the accident occurred, was a star high school varsity athlete in volleyball, softball, and basketball. Before the accident, she worked 10 to 11-hour days (including a night shift as a cocktail waitress), played softball and volleyball three nights a week, and exercised at the gym every day. After the accident, she could not sit at a sewing machine for longer than an hour without pain, could not function as a cocktail waitress, could not play organized sports, and could no longer water or snow ski, jog, or golf. Her social life, which had previously revolved around her athletic activities, was severely impaired. Driving a car now causes her jaw to hurt. To prevent her jaw from clenching, she must drive with her mouth agape. She has constant lower back pain that increases with activity and sometimes shoots down her leg. She had hoped to get married and have children, but her condition has made her fearful of having children and her "sexual spontaneity is gone."

Over defendants' objection, plaintiff's expert economist Stanley V. Smith testified he had computed the basic economic value of life (apart from one's earnings from employment). Smith relied upon three types of studies of: (1) the amount society is willing to pay per capita on protective devices such as seat belts, smoke detectors, etc., (2) the risk premiums employers pay to induce workers to perform hazardous jobs, and (3) the cost/benefit analyses of federally mandated safety projects and programs. Based on those studies, Smith calculated the value of an average person's remaining 44-year life expectancy at $2.3 million, which he described as a baseline figure. Smith adjusted the baseline figure to account for plaintiff's longer than average remaining life expectancy of 53 years. He multiplied the adjusted baseline figure by various percentages reflecting plaintiff's possible degrees of disability to calculate various possible hedonic damage awards. For example, Smith told the jury that in plaintiff's case, a 33 percent loss of enjoyment would be worth $1,684,000, a 10 percent loss of enjoyment would be worth $510,000, and a 5 percent loss of enjoyment would be worth $255,000. Smith gave the jury a table to assist it in making its mathematical calculations. . . .

The jury returned a general verdict for plaintiff for $890,000. After the trial court denied defendants' motion for new trial or remittitur, defendants appealed from the judgment.

Defendants contend Smith's testimony on hedonic damages was inadmissible and the amount of the judgment was unsupported by the record.

In California, a pain and suffering award may include compensation for the plaintiff's loss of enjoyment of life. Loss of enjoyment of life, however, is only one component of a general damage award for pain and suffering. It is not calculated as a separate award.

"California case law recognizes, as one component of general damage, physical impairment which limits the plaintiff's capacity to share in the amenities of life. The California decisions rarely employ the 'enjoyment of life' rubric, yet achieve a result consistent with it. No California rule restricts a plaintiff's attorney from arguing this element to a jury. Damage for mental suffering supplies an analogue. A majority of American jurisdictions recognize the compensability of loss of enjoyment of life, some as a component of the pain and suffering award, others as a distinct item of damage." (Huff v. Tracy, 57 Cal. App. 3d at [939], 943, 129 Cal. Rptr. 551.)[6]

There is "[n]o definite standard or method of calculation . . . prescribed by law by which to fix reasonable compensation for pain and suffering." (BAJI No. 14.13 (8th ed. 1994), original brackets omitted.) As our Supreme Court stated, "One of the most difficult tasks imposed upon a jury in deciding a case involving personal injuries is to determine the amount of money the plaintiff is to be awarded as compensation for pain and suffering. No method is available to the jury by which it can objectively evaluate such damages, and no witness may express his subjective opinion on the matter. In a very real sense, the jury is asked to evaluate in terms of money a detriment for which monetary compensation cannot be ascertained with any demonstrable accuracy. As one writer on the subject has said, 'Translating pain and anguish into dollars can, at best, be only an arbitrary allowance, and not a process of measurement, and consequently the judge can, in his instructions, give the jury no standard to go by; he can only tell them to allow such amount as in their discretion they may consider reasonable. . . . The

---

[6] "There are four views as to the recovery of damages for loss of enjoyment of life (hedonic damages): (1) such damages are not recoverable; (2) such damages are recoverable as a part of the damages for pain and suffering; (3) such damages are recoverable as an element of the permanency of injury; and (4) such damages are recoverable as a separate element of damages." (3 J. Stein, Stein on Personal Injury Damages (1992) Mental Anguish, §3:18:1, p.283, fn. omitted.) Much of the debate has focused on whether the plaintiff must have been conscious or aware of the injury to recover hedonic damages. The Supreme Court of Ohio held that hedonic damages are not available to a plaintiff who was injured either in utero or at birth. In New York, the highest state court held that hedonic damages are not recoverable independently of pain and suffering damages and reversed an award of hedonic damages to a comatose plaintiff. But a New Jersey court held in Eyoma v. Falco (A.D. 1991) 589 A.2d 653, that pain and suffering damages may be awarded where the patient was comatose.

chief reliance for reaching reasonable results in attempting to value suffering in terms of money must be the restraint and common sense of the jury. . . .' (McCormick on Damages, §88, pp. 318-319.)"

The jury must impartially determine pain and suffering damages based upon evidence specific to the plaintiff, as opposed to statistical data concerning the public at large. The only person whose pain and suffering is relevant in calculating a general damage award is the plaintiff. How others would feel if placed in the plaintiff's position is irrelevant. It is improper, for example, for an attorney to ask jurors how much "they would 'charge' to undergo equivalent pain and suffering." "This so-called 'golden rule' argument is impermissible." (Brokopp v. Ford Motor Co. (1977) 71 Cal. App. 3d 841, 860, 139 Cal. Rptr. 888.) . . .

In this case, plaintiff did not make an impermissible "golden rule" argument, but she did something similar. She asked the jury to accept $2.3 million as the baseline value of life and to give her a percentage of that figure (adjusted for her age) as hedonic damages. The baseline figure, however, is not based upon an analysis of any particular individual's life. It is based upon benchmark figures such as the amount society spends per capita on selected safety devices, or the amount employers pay to induce workers to perform high risk jobs. We perceive no meaningful relationship between those arbitrarily selected benchmark spending figures and the value of an individual person's life. Moreover, our Supreme Court has rejected the notion that pain and suffering damages may be computed by some mathematical formula. Smith's hedonic damages formula, however, purports to do just that.

Defendants objected to Smith's testimony on several grounds. One objection was based on the prohibition against separately instructing the jury on general damages for pain and suffering and damages for loss of enjoyment of life. Separate instructions on pain and suffering and loss of enjoyment of life are prohibited because they could mislead a jury to award double damages for the same injury. Defendants argued below that Smith's testimony was inadmissible as a matter of law because of its potential for misleading the jury to award double damages. We find the objection was valid and we conclude, as a matter of law, Smith's testimony should have been excluded on that ground.

Our conclusion is consistent with that of other courts. "'One of the strongest arguments that has been advanced as a reason for not recognizing loss of enjoyment of life as a separate category of damages is that it duplicates or overlaps other categories of damages, such as permanent disability or pain and suffering.' Leiker v. Gafford (1989) 245 Kan. 325, 339, 778 P.2d 823, 834. . . ."

In addition, Smith's testimony should have been excluded for another reason. . . . A plaintiff's loss of enjoyment of life is not "a subject that is sufficiently beyond common experience that the opinion of an expert would assist the trier of fact[.]" (Evid. Code, §801, subd. (a).) No amount of expert testimony on the value of life could possibly help a jury decide that difficult question. A life is not a stock, car, home, or other such item bought and sold in some marketplace.

Smith's impersonal method of valuing life assumes that for the most part, all lives have the same basic value. That has democratic appeal, but Smith used no democratic processes in reaching that conclusion or selecting which benchmark figures to consider in setting the baseline figure. There is no statute Smith could have turned to for guidance. Our Legislature has not decreed that all injured plaintiffs of the same age and with the same degree of disability should recover the same hedonic damages; nor has it assigned set values in tort cases for the loss of an eye, ear, limb, or life. Moreover, our judicial law prohibits trial counsel from referring to the amounts of jury verdicts in other cases. Because counsel may not ask the jury to give the same amount of damages as in another case, it would be inconsistent to permit an expert witness to do so.

The figures Smith included in his baseline calculation have nothing to do with this particular plaintiff's injuries, condition, hobbies, skills, or other factors relevant to her loss of enjoyment of life. The studies Smith used may help explain how much consumers will pay for safer products, or how much society should pay for government-mandated safety programs, but they shed no light on how to value this particular plaintiff's pain and suffering following the automobile accident. It is speculative, at best, to say the amount society is willing to spend on seat belts or air bags has any relationship to the intrinsic value of a person's life or the value of an injured plaintiff's pain and suffering. By urging the jury to rely upon a baseline value supported by factors having nothing to do with this plaintiff's individual condition, Smith's testimony created the possibility of a runaway jury verdict.

Our present system of requiring the jury to determine, without the benefit of a mathematical formula, the amount of a general damages award is not without its faults. But unless and until the Legislature devises a method for computing pain and suffering damages, a plaintiff may not supply, through expert testimony or otherwise, her own formula for computing such damages. Just as no judge may give the jury a standard for determining pain and suffering damages, no expert may supply a formula for computing the value of life and, by extrapolation, the value of the loss of enjoyment of life. That calculation, at present, must be left to the sound discretion of the jury. . . .

While the judge correctly instructed the jury there is no single mathematical formula for computing pain and suffering damages, the instruction was insufficient to cure the error of admitting Smith's testimony. Plaintiff's counsel's argument that Smith's testimony was unrefuted rendered the instruction a mere wink and a nod. It is reasonably probable and almost a certainty the jury awarded a double recovery. Accordingly, the admission of Smith's testimony was prejudicial.

We reverse the judgment and remand for a new trial on damages. Defendants are awarded costs on appeal.

NOTES TO LOTH v. TRUCK-A-WAY CORP.

1. *Valuing the Joy of Living.* The three economic models on which expert testimony about the value of life in *Loth* was based are often subject to criticism. The first is based on consumer purchases of safety devices:

> "From the price differential between a safer product and one less safe, and the reduction of risk of dying supposedly consequent therefrom, an extrapolation is made to arrive at the hedonic value of life." Hein v. Merck & Co., Inc., 868 F. Supp. at 234. However, such reasoning is flawed because it fails to take into consideration the numerous factors that go into a consumer purchase and whether a consumer actually and accurately perceives the risk in making a purchase of one product rather than another.

See Anderson v. Nebraska Dept. of Social Services, 538 N.W.2d 732 (Neb. 1995). Spending on safety items may be greatly influenced by advertising and marketing and government-mandated safety requirements as well as people's preferences for accepting and avoiding risk.

A second economic approach is based on wage differentials for high risk and low risk jobs. Three questionable assumptions underlie this model: that workers have free choice in choosing jobs, that workers are aware of the risks, and that workers accurately evaluate the risks. Workers may accept jobs because they are the only ones available where they live (e.g., coal mines) or for which they are trained.

A third approach is based on the cost-benefit analysis conducted by government agencies in deciding whether to adopt a regulation. The criticisms of this approach reflect the political reality of government decision-making:

> [G]overnment calculations about how much to spend (or force others to spend) on health and safety regulations are motivated by a host of considerations other than the value of life: is it an election year? how large is the budget deficit? on which constituents will the burden of the regulations fall? what influence and pressure have lobbyists brought to bear? what is the view of interested constituents? And so on.

See Mercado v. Ahmed, 974 F.2d 863, 871 (7th Cir. 1992). See also Ayers v. Robinson, 887 F. Supp. 1049, 1061 n.4 (N.D. Ill. 1995):

> "The Occupational Safety and Health Administration's (OSHA's) use of risk reduction values in regulatory analysis led the agency into a major conflict with the Office of Management and Budget (OMB) in 1985. OSHA initially attempted to use a value of $3,000,000 per anonymous life saved. The OMB decided that this value was too high and suggested that OSHA use a value of $1,000,000. Eventually, OMB and OSHA reached a compromise of $2,000,000 per life saved." . . . "Although they do not always reveal their methodologies, federal agencies have set life values as low as $70,000 and as high as $132 million per life."

2. *Day-in-the-Life Videos.*   Another approach lawyers use to show the plaintiff's pain and suffering and loss of enjoyment of life's pleasures is to show the jury a "day in the life" videotape. The court in Jones v. City of Los Angeles, 24 Cal. Rptr. 2d 528, 534 (Cal. App. 1993), viewed this approach with favor:

> The videotape best describes the problems Ms. Jones encounters on a daily basis in a way mere oral testimony may not convey to the jurors. The videotape also best demonstrates the everyday problems a person with paraplegia encounters as a result of an injury of this kind. Moreover, the videotape is the most effective way to explain to the jury the extent of the assistance and medical attention required as a result of being rendered a paraplegic.

3. *Property Damage and Miscellaneous Expenses.*   The court awarded Loth $3,507 for property damage and miscellaneous expenses. We are not told what the miscellaneous expenses are in Loth v. Truck-A-Way Corp., but the property damages are quite likely to have been damages to the plaintiff's car. These damages are recoverable as special damages. Generally, the formula for recovery of property damage is the *difference in fair market value* of the property before and after the traumatic event. One alternative formulation is the *cost of repair*, which is the cost to restore the property to its pre-accident condition. Cost of repair is generally recoverable as an alternative only if it is less than the difference in fair market value. A combination of these two approaches is used where the property is repaired but is not as good as new. In addition to one of these alternatives, the plaintiff is entitled to recover the value of the loss of use of the property. See Restatement (Second) of Torts §928.

Problem
Fair Market Value or Cost of Repair

Wiese owned and operated an automobile dealership in Kokomo, Indiana. On August 22, 1989, Wells was driving his automobile and collided with a van owned by Wiese that was parked on Wiese's lot. The van had a fair market value of $29,000. Wiese had purchased the van in October 1988 for $15,000 from the General Motors Corporation and converted the van to a luxury camper vehicle for an additional cost of $12,000. General Motors paid Wiese a $1,000 rebate on the purchase price as part of a special promotion. An expert testified that the converted camper was totally useless after the accident and it would cost an additional $6,000 to restore the van to the condition in which it was received from General Motors. After the accident, without making repairs, Wiese sold the van to Al Meyer, a wholesale car dealer, for $16,000. What is the appropriate damage recovery for Wiese? Would the damage amount be different if Wiese had been in the business of renting his vans and lost $1,000 in rentals before he could replace the damaged vehicle? See Wiese-GMC, Inc. v. Wells, 626 N.E.2d 595 (Ind. Ct. App. 1993).

Perspective: Hedonic Damages

People do not live solely to earn money. They live to enjoy life. We can be confident that this is generally true because people do not typically choose to spend all their waking hours at work. Many people earn less money than they could because, after they work a 40-hour week, they find that they gain more utility (more "hedonic" pleasure) from using their time for leisure activities instead of working. Others choose lower-paying jobs they enjoy over higher-paid positions that are more unpleasant or stressful. Does the amount of income an individual forgoes in order to have leisure time provide an accurate individualized measure of that individual's enjoyment of life's pleasures? Does this correctly measure the relative enjoyment of life by highly and poorly paid people?

C. Special Damages

Objectively verifiable monetary losses caused by the defendant's conduct are called *special damages* or *economic damages*. Special damages may include medical expenses, loss of earnings, burial costs, loss of use of property, cost of replacement or repair, cost of obtaining substitute domestic services, loss of employment, and loss of business or employment opportunities. Special damages must be tailored to the circumstances of the plaintiff, and must be supported with evidence showing their type and amount.

This contrasts with the requirements for general damages. General damages must also be related to the plaintiff's circumstances, but some courts do not require detailed evidence about them.

Receipts or canceled checks may enable a plaintiff to prove some special damages, such as past medical expenses, repairs made to property, or funeral expenses. For other special damages, such as past and future wage loss and future medical expenses, the factfinder must extrapolate from evidence about the plaintiff's particular circumstances.

The plaintiff in Moody v. Blanchard Place Apartments sought damages equal to past medical expenses and past and future wage loss. The focus of the opinion is on the conflicting evidence of expert witnesses calculating the plaintiff's wage losses. Many factors go into projecting lost earning capacity, and experts may use varied methodologies. The experts in *Moody* both took inflation into account when projecting lost wages, because wages tend to rise even within the same job and even if the worker does not become more skilled. They also *discounted* the projected future wages to their *present value. Discounting* is a mathematical process by which the law adjusts damage awards for future losses. Discounting adjusts for the fact that damages are often paid as a *lump sum,* which the plaintiff receives after the judgment in his or her favor. Had there been no accident, the plaintiff would not have received those amounts, for lost future wages, for instance, until some time in the future. Getting the payment of damages now, the plaintiff can put the money in the bank or some other investment and earn interest on the money. After earning interest, the plaintiff will have more money at that future time than he or she would have had if there had been no accident. Discounting adjusts for this potential inaccuracy in damage awards.

Both the potential for future wage inflation and for earning interest on damage awards must be considered in devising rules governing awards for future damages. Kaczkowski v. Bolubasz discusses the three dominant approaches to discounting future losses to the present value. This case also systematically identifies factors that influence future wage increases.

MOODY v. BLANCHARD PLACE APARTMENTS
793 So. 2d 281 (La. Ct. App. 2001)

PEATROSS, J.

This appeal arises from a personal injury suit filed by Robert E. Moody, individually and as tutor on behalf of his two minor daughters, Leah Nicole Moody and Lacy Brooke Moody, against Defendants, Blanchard Place Apartments; its manager, Calhoun Property Management, Inc.; and their insurance carrier, Clarendon National Insurance Company; for injuries he sustained when he suffered an electric shock from a stove in an apartment he rented from Blanchard Place Apartments. . . . After trial on the merits, judgment was cast against Defendants. . . .

"Special damages" are those which either must be specially pled or have a ready market value, that is, the amount of the damages supposedly can be determined with relative certainty, such as the plaintiff's medical expenses incurred as a result of the tort.

In regard to Mr. Moody's past medical expenses, having found that his neck injury was related to the electric shock which he suffered from the Stove [sic], any related medical expenses are recoverable as well as those expenses specifically associated with treatment he received in relation to the electric shock. We, therefore, will not disturb the $32,611 which the jury awarded for his past medical expenses.

As to Mr. Moody's lost past and future wages, Dr. Luvonia Casperson, an economist, testified on behalf of Plaintiffs; and Dr. Kenneth Boudreaux, an economist, testified on behalf of Defendants. Awards for past lost wages are not susceptible to the great discretion given the factfinder, because past lost income is susceptible to mathematical calculation. Past lost income can be computed on an amount the plaintiff would, in all probability, have been earning at the time of trial; and damages for loss of past income are not necessarily limited to a multiplier of the amount earned at the time of injury.

Despite the relative certainty of mathematical calculations, however, we are faced with differing sums from each economist. The jury has awarded Mr. Moody a sum which is between the two economists' calculations, but closer to Dr. Casperson's.

Dr. Casperson has a Ph.D. in economics with a minor in accounting and finance. She has taught at Louisiana State University–Shreveport for 24 years, chairing the economics department for 7 or 8 years. Dr. Casperson testified that past lost wages are those wages, inclusive of fringe benefits, from the date of injury to the date of trial. This figure is then subjected to a discount rate which takes into consideration inflation and other economic factors. A person's previous earning capacity is also taken into consideration.

Dr. Casperson stated that, in calculating Mr. Moody's past lost income, she used 3.96 years, the amount of time from the date of injury to the date of trial. Dr. Casperson determined that Mr. Moody was receiving approximately 21.4 percent of his salary in additional fringe benefits at the time he was injured. She lowered this figure, however, to 12 percent because she determined that the fringe benefits Mr. Moody was receiving while at ResourceNet were well above average in the industry in which Mr. Moody was employed. She, therefore, used the more conservative figure of 12 percent.

Dr. Casperson used $12 per hour to calculate Mr. Moody's actual lost wages and took into account those wages Mr. Moody earned from the time of injury to trial. Mr. Moody continued working at ResourceNet for a few months following the incident, returned to iron working for a few months and, after a year of not working, found jobs in the restaurant industry as a dishwasher, busboy and counterman. Mr. Moody's wage was $8.50 per hour when he left ResourceNet in August 1997 and $12 per hour at JJ Erectors, where he did iron work until January 1998. Dr. Casperson included these wages, using earnings by Mr. Moody as reflected in his tax returns. Dr. Casperson also increased Mr. Moody's expected wage by three percent per annum after 1997 to reflect inflation. Using these sums and averages, Dr. Casperson calculated Mr. Moody's lost wages to be $60,283 and his lost fringe benefits to be $7,234.

Dr. Boudreaux, who also holds a Ph.D. in economics, and has been a professor of economics at Tulane University for over 30 years, based his calculations on Mr. Moody's wages at ResourceNet of $8.50 per hour. Dr. Boudreaux increased this amount by an inflation rate of three percent per annum, arriving at a post tax figure of $61,877 in lost wages from May 30, 1996, to the date of trial, exclusive of any actual wages earned. Dr. Boudreaux then subtracted from this figure the income which Mr. Moody earned during that period of time according to his W2s, arriving at an amount of $35,242. Dr. Boudreaux did not include loss of past fringe benefits in his calculations.

When asked if the figure would be different if he had considered Mr. Moody's last wage of $12 per hour as an iron worker, Dr. Boudreaux stated that, in his opinion, it would not be significantly different. In explaining his opinion, he stated that he figured the $8.50 wage in terms of a 40 hour week, 52 week per year job. He further stated, however, that in the construction industry, that is rarely the case since work is generally found to be per job and is dependent on weather conditions. Since iron working is a construction related occupation, Dr. Boudreaux opined that, using $12 per hour in calculating the earnings of a job which is active only about three fourths of a year, would not change the overall economic outcome.

The jury awarded a sum of $60,000 in past lost wages. This sum is between the figures given by each economist. Although the jury is not afforded as much deference when a sum is susceptible to a mathematical calculation, we cannot say that the jury was incorrect in arriving at this sum. Each economist presented plausible calculations, neither of which can be said to be wrong. We, therefore, will not disturb the jury's award of lost past wages.

Awards for loss of future income or future earning capacity, however, are inherently speculative and insusceptible of calculation with mathematical certainty. We conclude, therefore, that a greater deference is to be afforded a jury's conclusion. The factors to be considered in determining future lost income include the plaintiff's physical condition before and after his injury, his past work record and the consistency thereof, the amount the plaintiff probably would have earned absent the injury complained of and the probability that he would have continued to earn wages over the balance of his working life. A loss of future income award is not really predicated upon the difference between the plaintiff's earnings before and after a disabling injury. Such an award is predicated, more strictly considered, upon the difference between the plaintiff's earning capacity before and after a disabling injury.

In calculating Mr. Moody's lost future wages, Dr. Casperson estimated his life expectancy to be 35.1 years from the date of injury, or 75.99 years of age using the Statistical Abstract of the United States, a commonly accepted statistical source. In accordance with the Bureau of Labor Statistics, Mr. Moody's work life expectancy would be 61.09 years of age, 20.2 years from the date of injury or 16.24 years from the date of trial. She further determined that, if Mr. Moody were to work to the full Social Security retirement age of 66.17, he would work 21.32 years from the date of trial.

Dr. Casperson determined Mr. Moody's earning capacity to be $12 per hour based on his work as an iron worker, both before his injury and for a brief time following his injury. Dr. Casperson also called local steel erectors to determine the current wage and availability of work. The three percent annual increase was added to this $12 figure. Finally, Dr. Casperson calculated Mr. Moody's future wages for both 61.09 years of age and 66.17 years of age.

Including the 12 percent lost fringe benefits and a discount rate of 1.5 percent, Dr. Casperson estimated Mr. Moody's lost future earnings to age 60.9 [sic — 61.09?] to be $437,382. Using the same figures, Mr. Moody's earning capacity to age 66.17 would be $553,858. These figures were then offset by the minimum wage which totaled $265,607 for age 61.09 and $336,341 for age 66.17. Dr. Casperson testified that she felt Mr. Moody would retire from the work force at some time between the ages of 61.09 and 66.17. She stated an average of $300,974 would be reasonable.

Dr. Boudreaux, instead, determined that Mr. Moody's work life expectancy was 17.64 years from trial based on the Legal Economics tables which are derived from the census and the U.S. Bureau of Labor. He further determined that Mr. Moody's average annual income would be approximately $19,000. This amount was calculated out for an additional 17.64 years, increased at three percent per annum and discounted by approximately six percent for present value. Dr. Boudreaux explained that this figure of $181,579, which was after taxes, was the amount which Mr. Moody would have to currently place in a safe investment in order to receive about $19,000 per annum if he were totally disabled.

Assuming Mr. Moody could earn at least minimum wage in a 40 hour a week, 52 week job for that period of time, Mr. Moody would need $79,072 after taxes to supplement his income to reach $19,000 per year. Finally, Dr. Boudreaux considered the opinion of Dr. Lenora Maatouk, a vocational rehabilitation specialist, that Mr. Moody was capable of, and [had] expressed desire to become a journeyman. He would require 21-24 months of training and, upon completion, could earn an estimated $25,000 per year. Based on these figures, Dr. Boudreaux calculated Mr. Moody would only need to be compensated for the time he was being trained, which Dr. Boudreaux assumed for his calculations as 24 months. His calculations derived a sum of $27,012.

These calculations were all post-tax and did not include any loss of fringe benefits. Dr. Boudreaux explained that, because lump sum recoveries are not taxable, he was asked to include taxes. He also stated that, if Mr. Moody were able to work steadily at a full time job, even earning only minimum wage, he would likely be provided at least with group health insurance, which is the largest percentage of the cost of fringe benefits. He, therefore, did not use any such figures in his calculations.

Again, we are faced with an award by the jury which is between Dr. Casperson's figures and above Dr. Boudreaux's lowest figure. Since we do not have the benefit of the motivation which powered the jury's decision-making process and the final award in between the given figures, we cannot say that the jury erred in awarding Mr. Moody $100,000 in lost future wages. Neither of the mathematical equations can be said to be unreasonable. Further, since we are to give great deference to the jury in awarding future lost income, we will not disturb this award. . . .

NOTE TO MOODY v. BLANCHARD PLACE APARTMENTS

Lost Earning Capacity. Because damages are based on lost future earning capacity, as opposed to lost wages, a plaintiff not currently in the workforce may recover such damages. In Richmond v. Zimbrick Logging, Inc., 863 P.2d 520 (Or. Ct. App. 1993), for instance, the plaintiff was a homemaker and minister's wife. When she was injured by a logging truck, the jury awarded her $30,000 for impaired earning capacity. The appellate court affirmed the verdict:

[P]laintiff is not required to prove that she has worked in the past or intended to do so in the future. Oregon, like most jurisdictions, recognizes that the impairment of a person's earning capacity is an injury distinct from a loss of earnings.

"In determining past and future loss of earning capacity the question is not whether plaintiff would have worked, by choice. A person is entitled to compensation for the lost *capacity* to earn, whether he would have chosen to exercise it or not." Harper, James and Gray, *The Law of Torts* 549, §25.8 (2d ed. 1986).

That point was held to have particular relevance for lost earning capacity claims by homemakers in Earl v. Bouchard Transp. Co., Inc., 735 F. Supp. 1167, 1172 (E.D.N.Y. 1990):

"Regardless of whether or not a plaintiff would have exercised the choice to work as long as he could have, he or she is entitled to damages 'measured by the extent to which [plaintiff's] capacity for earnings has been reduced.' Restatement (Second) of Torts §924, comment c. In effect, the 'economic horizon of the [plaintiff] has been shortened because of the injuries.' Burke v. United States, 605 F. Supp. 981, 999 (D. Md. 1985)."

KACZKOWSKI v. BOLUBASZ
421 A.2d 1027 (Pa. 1980)

Nix, J.

Appellant instituted a complaint in trespass in Allegheny County Court of Common Pleas. The suit arose from an automobile accident in which the decedent, Eric K. Kaczkowski, was riding as a passenger in a vehicle operated by appellee. At the original trial of this matter, the jury established the liability of the appellee. Upon appellant's Motion For a New Trial, the case was returned to the trial court for a retrial on the issue of damages.

... [T]he plaintiff relied upon the trial court's charge of impairment of future earning power for the guidance of the jury. The lower court charged the jury to consider the decedent's personal characteristics to: calculate the potential gross earnings of the decedent for the period of decedent's work life expectancy; to determine the maintenance costs of the decedent for the period of decedent's work life expectancy; to deduct the personal maintenance costs from the gross earnings to produce net earnings; and to discount the net earnings to present value by six percent (6%) simple interest. Based upon the judge's instructions, the jury returned a verdict of $30,000 on behalf of the estate of Eric K. Kaczowski. ...

The issue raised by appellant is whether the trial court erred in excluding reliable economic testimony showing the impact of inflation[4] and increased productivity[5] on decedent's future earning power. ...

In this Commonwealth, we have consistently held that damages are to be compensatory to the full extent of the injury sustained. The rule "is to give actual compensation, by graduating the amount of damages exactly to the extent of the loss."

---

[4] Inflation is "the increase in the volume of money and credit relative to available goods resulting in a substantial and continuing rise in the general price level." Webster's, Third International Dictionary (1965). Inflation gains are measured in terms of what the average person refers to as "cost of living increases." An example of inflation evidencing an increase in prices unrelated to an increase in intrinsic value is that the juice content of oranges has not increased in years, but their price continues to rise.

The presence of inflation plays two distinct roles in an award for prospective damages. The first role is determining the impact of inflation on the future earnings of the victim. The second place in which inflation plays a part is in determining the appropriate interest rate to discount the future damage award to its present value.

[5] Economists recognize that there are at least four major elements which influence the rate of increase of an employee's income. These factors are: (1) the educational attainment of the participant prior to his entry into the labor market; (2) the influence of age upon the earnings of participants over their life cycle; (3) the significance of productivity and growth; and (4) the impact of inflation. Henderson, *The Consideration of Increased Productivity and Discounting of Future Earnings to Present Value,* 20 S.D. L. Rev. 307 (1976). In our analysis, we will isolate the inflation element from the other three factors, collectively called "merit" increases, which are consumed in productivity. We recognize that merit increases are controlled by different variables than the inflationary factor, and deserve separate consideration.

Forsyth v. Palmer, 14 Pa. 96, 97 (1850). Loss of future earnings is a distinct item of damages, which if properly proved, may result in recovery for the plaintiff.[7]

Inflation and productivity increasingly demand judicial attention, particularly with respect to personal injury action damages for lost future earnings. Traditionally, evidence of future inflation and productivity increases have been deemed too speculative to be included in calculating future damages even though inflation and productivity increases may drastically reduce an initially generous award. However, today, in light of clear scientific evidence of the fact that inflation and productivity have become an established part of our economy, it becomes necessary that these factors be considered in such awards.

The "law does not require that proof in support of claims for damages or in support of compensation must conform to the standard of mathematical exactness." Lach v. Fleth, 64 A.2d 821 (1949). All that the law requires is that "(a) claim for damages must be supported by a reasonable basis for calculation; mere guess or speculation is not enough." Stevenson v. Economy Bank of Ambridge, 197 A.2d 721, 727 (1964).

Personal injury awards are usually lump-sum payments, and are not paid in weekly or monthly installments. Thus, all damages for personal injuries, including damages expected to accrue in the future, must be proved and calculated at trial. The loss of future wages is discounted to its present value by using the six percent (6%) simple interest figure.[10] . . .

There are three significant approaches, traditional, middle ground, and evidentiary which the judiciary has adopted in considering the impact of future inflation and productivity on lost future earning capacity. The traditional approach ignores altogether the effects of future productivity and future inflation as being "too speculative." This view was previously adhered to by this Commonwealth. . . .

The middle ground approach is anomalous in that it permits the factfinder to consider the effects of productivity and inflation on lost future earning capacity, but prohibits expert testimony on either of these issues. The proponents of this approach argue that expert testimony on future economic trends is "speculative," yet acknowledge that such facts are within the "common experience" of all jurors and, therefore, jurors should not be prohibited from applying their common knowledge in reaching a verdict. However, it has been consistently demonstrated that expert evidence is essential to accurate economic forecasting. Since it is apparent that the middle-ground approach contributes little to the accuracy or predictability of lost future earnings,

---

[7] When an injury is a permanent one, one which will cause a loss or lessening of future earning power, a recovery may be had for the probable loss of future earnings. McCormick, Damages, 299 (20th reprint 1975). If the injured party survives, he should receive undiminished, his total estimated future earnings, but if he dies, the proper measure of damages includes a deduction based upon decedent's cost of personal maintenance. Today's opinion does not disturb our requirement for personal maintenance deductions.

[10] The rationale for reducing a lump-sum award to its present value is that:

> it is assumed that the plaintiff will invest the sum awarded and receive interest thereon. That interest accumulated over the number of relevant years will be available, in addition to the capital, to provide the plaintiff with his future support until the total is exhausted at the end of the period. The projected interest must therefore be allowed in reduction of capital lest it be claimed that the plaintiff is overcompensated.

Fleming, *Inflation and Tort Compensation,* 26 Am. J. Comp. L. 51, 66 (1977). . . .

and paradoxically allows a judge or jury to determine what an acknowledged expert cannot, we decline to adopt it.

The evidentiary approach in its several variants allows the factfinder to consider productivity and inflation in awarding damages. Since we believe that there is a reasonable basis in fact to consider the impact of inflation and productivity on lost future earnings, we conclude that the evidentiary concept is the most valid method to compute lost future earnings. However, courts employing the evidentiary method differ on the factors to be considered in assessing lost productivity on the one hand and the method to calculate the inflation component in the final lost future earning award on the other. Recognizing that there are myriad of ways to incorporate such economic data we find that there are two versions appropriate for our consideration.

The first of these two variants of the evidentiary approach was developed by the court in Feldman v. Allegheny Airlines, 382 F. Supp. 1271 (D. Conn. 1974), aff'd, 524 F.2d 384 (1st Cir. 1975). In *Feldman*, a surviving husband brought a wrongful death action as the administrator of his wife's estate. The defendant airline stipulated as to its liability and the trial was confined to the issue of damages. The court assumed that recovery for lost future earnings included the victim's lost earning capacity. In order to demonstrate the bases for the court's conclusions relative to what course the deceased's life probably would have taken, the court extrapolated the evolving pattern of Mrs. Feldman's life. The court detailed the deceased's college grades, her employment history, the opinion of the deceased held by her fellow workers, the expressed employment goals of the deceased and the potential jobs for which the deceased was qualified. The court also examined the employment history of another individual who had remarkably similar credentials as the deceased. The defendant produced one witness who testified as to the decedent's employment prospects. Based upon the above factors, the court predicted the incremental salary (productivity) increases of the decedent over her work-life expectancy.

The court was then faced with the inflation component and the task of discounting the award to its present value. The court developed a formula known as the "offset present value method" in which it subtracted the estimated inflation rate from the discount rate to calculate the inflation adjusted or "real" rate of interest. Each year's earnings were then discounted to present value by this "real" discount rate. The "real" discount rate employed by the court was 1.5%. . . .

The second variant of the evidentiary method was adopted by the Alaska Supreme Court in Beaulieu v. Elliott, 434 P.2d 665 (1967), and refined in State v. Guinn, 555 P.2d 530 (1976). Pursuant to this formula, the Alaska courts first calculate lost future earning capacity of the victim over his or her work-life expectancy. As to productivity, the Alaska court has stated: "Automatic step increases keyed to the length of service are by their very nature certain and predictable at the time of trial" and the court takes them into account when estimating the lost future earnings. State v. Guinn, 555 P.2d at 546. However, the court excluded as speculative evidence the "non-scheduled salary increases and bonuses that are granted as one progresses in his chosen occupation in terms of skill, experience and value to the employer." Id.

In order to account for the inflationary component's impact on lost future earnings and the effect of future interest rates on lump-sum payment, the Alaska court applied that "total offset method." Under the total offset method, a court does not discount the award to its present value but assumes that the effect of the future inflation rate will completely offset the interest rate, thereby eliminating any need to discount the award to its present value.

Mindful of our goal that a damage award formula should strive to be efficient, predictable as well as accurate, in computing lost future earning capacity this Commonwealth adopts the *Feldman* court's approach to calculating lost productivity and the Alaska court's total offset approach to inflation and discounting to present value. We believe that this eclectic method best computes a damage award which will fairly compensate a victim to the full extent of his or her injuries and avoids unnecessary complexities likely to produce confusion although in reality contributing little to the degree of accuracy to be obtained. Although judges and juries are not fortune tellers equipped with crystal balls, the *Feldman* approach to determining productivity as a factor in awarding future lost earnings best approximates the soothsayers by presenting the triers of fact with all relevant evidence. After laying a proper foundation, expert and lay witnesses are called upon to testify as to the victim's past and future employment possibilities. The defense may cross-examine the plaintiff's witnesses and present evidence on their own behalf. Upon a thorough evaluation of all the evidence presented, the factfinder makes an informed estimation of the victim's lost earning capacity. Although this approach may be time consuming, and like all estimations of future events may be subject to a degree of speculation, it is exceedingly more accurate to assume that the future will not remain stagnant with the past. . . .

In support of our adoption of the "total offset method" in allowing for the inflationary factor, we note that it is no longer legitimate to assume the availability of future interest rates by discounting to present value without also assuming the necessary concomitant of future inflation. We recognize that inflation has been and probably always will be an inherent part of our economy. Although the specific rate of inflation during any given period may vary, we accept the fact that inflation plays an integral part in effectuating increases in an employee's salary, and we choose to adopt a damage formula which will allow for that factor without actually requiring the factfinder to consider it as an independent element of the award. . . .

Since over the long run interest rates, and, therefore, the discount rates, will rise and fall with inflation, we shall exploit this natural adjustment by offsetting the two factors in computing lost future earning capacity. We are satisfied that the total offset method provides at least as much, if not greater, accuracy than an attempt to assign a factor that would reflect the varying changes in the rate of inflation over the years. Our experiences with the use of the six percent discount rate suggest the difficulties inherent in such an approach. As to the concomitant goals of efficiency and predictability, the desirability of the total offset method is obvious. There is no method that can assure absolute accuracy. An additional feature of the total offset method is that where there is a variance, it will be in favor of the innocent victim and not the tortfeasor who caused the loss. . . .

An additional virtue of the total offset method is its contribution to judicial efficiency. Litigators are freed from introducing and verifying complex economic data. Judge and juries are not burdened with complicated, time consuming economic testimony. Finally, by eliminating the variables of inflation and future interest rates from the damage calculation, the ultimate award is more predictable.

Henceforth, in this Commonwealth, damages will be awarded for lost future earnings that compensate the victim to the full extent of the injury sustained. Upon proper foundation, the court shall consider the victim's lost future productivity. Moreover, we find as a matter of law that future inflation shall be presumed equal to future interest rates with these factors offsetting. Thus, the courts of this Commonwealth are instructed to abandon the practice of discounting lost future earnings. By this method, we are able to reflect the impact of inflation in these cases without specifically submitting this question to the jury.

In view of the trial court's refusal to permit appellant to introduce evidence relating to a future productivity factor and our formulation of a new standard to be used for accommodating inflation in these cases, we reverse the judgment below and remand the cause for a new trial as to the damage question.

NOTES TO KACZKOWSKI v. BOLUBASZ

1. *Comparing Discounting Methods.* The implications of the choice of discounting methods for future earnings may be illustrated by a case where the plaintiff is injured and as a result takes another position at reduced pay. The following table assumes that the plaintiff's $100,000 annual income is reduced to $65,000 in the years following the accident and that the plaintiff would normally retire five years after the trial. It assumes that interest rates on risk-free investments are 5 percent and inflation is running at 3 percent per year. It ignores raises for improvements in productivity.

The first of the three methods illustrated in the table is the Offset Present Value Method described in *Kaczkowski* as the first evidentiary approach. This approach ignores inflation when considering salaries (no 3 percent cost of living raises) and the discount rate. For the illustration that follows, the discount rate is 2 percent, which is the current interest rate prevalent in the economy minus the projected future inflation rate. In *Kaczkowski, the court referred to a case using a 1 1/2 percent rate.* As the label for these approaches suggests, the proper discount rate depends on the evidence presented in a trial. As the Table below illustrates, the Offset Present Value Method may give an award that is slightly lower than either of the other methods. This method has the virtue of ignoring speculative projections of future wage growth and inflation.

The second evidentiary approach is the Inflation Adjusted Method. It is not discussed in *Kaczkowski,* but is a common alternative to the Offset Present Value Method. The Inflation Adjusted Method, as the name suggests, includes inflation in both projected salaries (3 percent raises, for instance) and discount rates. For this illustration, the discount rate is equal to the interest rate of 5 percent (2 percent, the "real" rate of interest, plus the 3 percent cost-of-living increase). It gives an award that is slightly larger than the Offset Present Value Method in this hypothetical. The difference between these awards depends on a variety of factors, including the size of the income loss and the amount of predicted inflation. This method has the virtue of attempting to reflect an image of what will happen in the real world where there often are cost of living raises.

The third method illustrated is the Total Offset Method, adopted in *Kaczkowski*. It ignores both inflation and discounting. This method results in greater awards to plaintiffs as the time period during which there is an income loss extends further into the future. The court in *Kaczkowski* identifies its advantages, the most obvious of which is its mathematical simplicity.

Very often these somewhat daunting calculations are performed by expert witnesses. Courts sometimes allow the jury to decide which of the experts was most convincing about the proper amount of the award for future losses, regardless of the method used.

Year in Which Plaintiff Would Have Received Earnings (Year 1 Is Year of Trial)	Offset Present Value Method $D = I \div (1 + DR)^{(t-1)}$	Inflation Adjusted Method $D = I(1 + i)^{(t-1)} \div (1 + DR)^{(t-1)}$	Total Offset Method $D = I$
Year 1	$35,000.00	$35,000.00	$35,000.00
Year 2	34,313.73	34,333.33	35,000.00
Year 3	33,640.91	33,679.37	35,000.00
Year 4	32,981.28	33,037.85	35,000.00
Year 5	32,334.59	32,408.56	35,000.00
Totals	**$168,270.51**	**$168,459.11**	**$175,000.00**

D = Damages, I = Lost income, i = Inflation rate, DR = Discount rate, t = Year number.
E.g., Year 3, Inflation Adjusted Method: $D = 35,000(1 + .03)^{(3-1)} \div (1 + .05)^{(3-1)} = \$33,679.37$.

2. *Discounting and Structured Settlements.* The vast majority of tort cases settle before going to trial. Payments for future losses are often paid by the defendant over a period of time, for instance, $10,000 per year for five years. The structure of this settlement may be designed to match times at which the plaintiff is likely to incur future medical expenses or when future wages would have been earned.

A well-informed lawyer must enter into settlement negotiations knowing the rules governing damages that will be awarded if the case goes to trial in order to know the amount of damages to demand or expect in settlement. A lawyer must also know *how to value structured settlements*. If a defendant offers $925,000 now or $1,000,000 paid over five years, for instance, which offer is the more attractive to the plaintiff? Unless the plaintiff has some special need to have the money now or some special reason to avoid spending all of the money now, the lawyer will want to know how to value these offers.

A *present value table* makes it easy to compare offers of present and future payment. The key decision is what interest rate the plaintiff can earn on invested payments. The portion of the table reproduced below considers just two possible interest rates, 2 percent and 5 percent. The decimal fractions in a table are called *discount factors*.

How Many Years from Now Will the Payment Be Made?	*What Interest Rate Can the Plaintiff Earn on Invested Money?*	
	2%	*5%*
0	1.000	1.000
1	.980	.952
2	.961	.907
3	.942	.864
4	.924	.823
5	.906	.784
6	.888	.746
7	.871	.711
8	.853	.677
9	.837	.645
10	.820	.614

The present value of the $925,000 offer is $925,000, because it is all paid now. The present value of $1,000,000 paid in equal installments over five years depends on when the first payment is made and the interest or *discount* rate. Assume that the first payment of $200,000 is made immediately. The present value of that payment is $200,000. The next four payments are made one, two, three, and four years in the future. To determine the present value of a future payment, multiply the amount of that payment by the discount factor for the appropriate year and interest rate.

Payment Year	*Discount Rate = 2%*	*Discount Rate = 5%*
0 (now)		1.000 × $200,000 = $200,000
1		.952 × $200,000 = $190,400
2		.907 × $200,000 = $181,400
3		.864 × $200,000 = $172,800
4		.823 × $200,000 = $164,600
Total Value	?	$909,200

For our example, each of the four future payments is equal to $200,000. If the plaintiff can earn interest of 5 percent, the present value of the payment one year from now is $200,000 times the discount factor of .952 or $190,400. The present value of the payment two years from now is .907 × $200,000 or $181,400. The present value of the entire structured settlement is $909,200, as shown above. Which settlement offer, $925,000 in cash now or $1,000,000 paid over five years, has the higher present value?

Problem
Discounting and Structured Settlements

Using the information presented above, determine which settlement offer has the higher present value if the plaintiff can only earn 2 percent on his or her investments? The difference is even more dramatic if future payments occur in the distant future. What result if the $1,000,000 were to be paid in years 6 through 10 at each interest rate?

III. Punitive Damages

As described in a leading treatise, *punitive*, or as they are often called, *exemplary* damages may be awarded when the defendant is malicious, or "oppressive, evil, wicked, guilty of wanton or morally culpable conduct, or shows flagrant indifference to the safety of others." See Dan B. Dobbs, *Law of Remedies* §3.11(2) p.319 (2d ed. 1993). Punitive damages are intended to punish defendants or to deter defendants from engaging in similar conduct rather than to compensate the plaintiff.

To recover punitive damages, the plaintiff must prove the elements of an intentional tort or recklessness of the sort that includes a conscious disregard of the high risk of serious harm to others. Peete v. Blackwell and Shugar v. Guill take slightly different approaches to the additional proof required to show particularly outrageous conduct.

The permissible amount of punitive damages is governed by both common law and constitutional law. Two questions arise: (1) Is the punitive damage award in the particular case excessive given the facts of that case? (2) Is the punitive damage award in the particular case excessive given punitive damages previously awarded to other plaintiffs in other cases arising out of the same conduct by the same defendant? State Farm Mutual Automobile Insurance Co. v. Campbell examines how the Due Process Clause limits state court awards of punitive damages.

PEETE v. BLACKWELL

504 So. 2d 222 (Ala. 1986)

TORBERT, C.J.

This is an assault and battery case. The defendant, Dr. Robert W. Peete, appeals from a judgment based on a jury verdict assessing punitive damages against him. Peete contends that punitive damages were improperly awarded in this case. For the reasons set forth below, we reject Dr. Peete's arguments and affirm the judgment of the trial court.

In late December 1983, the defendant, Dr. Robert W. Peete, hospitalized one of his patients for a severe nosebleed. As part of this patient's treatment, Dr. Peete applied anterior and posterior nasal packs to control the bleeding. On December 26, Dr. Peete was recalled to the hospital, because this patient was again experiencing difficulties. When he arrived there, he found that the string securing the posterior pack had been cut and that his patient was bleeding profusely. Because his patient was in danger of suffocation, Dr. Peete immediately sought to retrieve the pack and to control the bleeding. In order to retrieve the posterior pack, Peete required the use of a suction machine to remove the blood from his patient's throat. Unless this blood was removed, he could not see well enough to remove the pack.

He was assisted in these efforts by the plaintiff, Beverly S. Blackwell, the nurse in charge of the floor on which the patient had been hospitalized. Blackwell testified that at one point Peete struck her on the forearm and demanded that she "turn on the [goddamn] suction." She also testified that no physical injury of any kind resulted from this striking. It is from this incident that this case arose.

In a trial before a jury, Blackwell alleged that Peete had committed an assault and battery against her. She demanded $1.00 in compensatory damages and $100,000 in punitive damages. The jury returned a verdict against Peete in the amount of $10,001, indicating that the jury found for the plaintiff on her assault and battery claim and that they assessed $10,000 in punitive damages against Peete. The trial court entered judgment on this verdict and did not rule within 90 days on Peete's motion for judgment notwithstanding the verdict, his motion for new trial, or his motion to alter or amend the judgment. These motions were thus denied pursuant to A.R. Civ. P. 59.1.

Although Peete testified at trial that he did not strike the plaintiff, he does not challenge the finding that he committed an assault and battery. Rather, he argues on this appeal that the punitive damages awarded in this case were excessive or that they were improperly awarded in light of the evidence presented, and he asserts that the trial court therefore erred in denying his various post-trial motions.

Our rules regarding the award of punitive damages for assault and battery are relatively clear and well-established. While one of our recent cases stated that punitive damages are available for assault and battery where the "acts complained of were committed with malice, willfulness, or wanton and reckless disregard of the rights of others," Surrency v. Harbison, 489 So. 2d 1097, 1105 (Ala. 1986), our previous cases have typically held that assault and battery will support an award of punitive damages "whenever there is averment and proof tending to show that the act charged was wrongful and attended with an insult or other circumstances of aggravation." John R. Thompson & Co. v. Vildibill, 100 So. 139, 141 (1924). In short, the longstanding rule of this jurisdiction requires that particularized circumstances of aggravation or insult appear in cases of assault and battery if punitive damages are to be properly awarded.

Although Peete's specific challenges to the award of punitive damages are somewhat unclear, we discern two basic grounds for his objections. First, he asserts error on wholly *evidentiary* grounds. He argues that the evidence presented was insufficient to show the requisite "insult or other aggravating circumstances" required for an award of punitive damages, and he therefore asserts error in the trial court's refusal to grant his motion for judgment notwithstanding the verdict. Alternatively, he contends that, even if sufficient evidence of aggravating circumstances was presented, the actual assessment of punitive damages was against the weight and preponderance of that evidence, and he therefore asserts error in the trial court's refusal to grant his motion for new trial. . . .

Viewing this evidence in a light most favorable to the non-moving party, we find that the jury could have found that the doctor had insulted the hospital staff prior to the time the incident took place. In addition, the jury could have found that Dr. Peete cursed frequently throughout the events leading up to the incident, that he had been "yelling and hollering" earlier in the morning, and that he threw or slammed a patient's chart across a desk some time prior to the striking. Finally, the evidence is uncontradicted that Dr. Peete cursed at nurse Blackwell at the time the alleged striking occurred. While telling Blackwell to "turn on the goddamn suction" is arguably not an "insult" to Blackwell, this statement does present at least a scintilla of evidence that "aggravating circumstances" in the form of angry or intimidating behavior accompanied the assault and battery, especially when considered in light of the evidence reflecting on Peete's earlier actions. Given this evidentiary showing, the trial court properly denied Peete's motion for judgment notwithstanding the verdict.

Likewise, we do not believe that the trial court erred in failing to grant a new trial on the basis of the weight and preponderance of the evidence. Admittedly, both plaintiff and defendant testified that this incident arose in the midst of a medical emergency in which a human life was threatened. In view of this fact, which tends to indicate that this was not an "aggravated" assault and battery, reasonable minds might well differ on the question of whether a strong case was actually made for an award of punitive damages. We cannot say, however, that the evidence in this case "plainly and palpably" shows that the trial court erred in failing to grant a new trial. We find no "abuse of discretion" in the trial court's decision to allow some award of punitive damages, in view of the evidence tending to show that the required circumstances of aggravation or insult accompanied this assault and battery. Therefore, on the basis of the evidence presented, we cannot say that an award of punitive damages in some amount was improper in this case. . . .

SHUGAR v. GUILL

283 S.E.2d 507 (N.C. 1981)

Plaintiff's evidence tended to show that on 19 October 1978 around 9:25 a.m. he entered the defendant's restaurant in Tarboro known as "Cotton's Grill" for the purpose of joining several regular customers for coffee. After serving himself a cup of coffee, he joined the group. Plaintiff moved toward the table where the men sat without paying for his cup of coffee. Defendant was seated at the table, and as plaintiff took a seat at the table, he said to defendant, "This cup of coffee is on the house." Plaintiff then told defendant to "charge it against the formica that you owe me for" [referring to a continuing dispute over whether the defendant owed the plaintiff $6.25 for a piece of construction material].

Following plaintiff's comment regarding the charging of the coffee against the formica cost, defendant commented on plaintiff's cheapness and demanded that plaintiff leave the restaurant immediately. Plaintiff responded by saying, "Make me." Defendant then picked plaintiff up in a "bear hug" and started toward the door. Plaintiff managed to free himself and blows were exchanged. Plaintiff was struck about the eyes twice, and defendant's glasses were broken when he was hit in the face during the scuffle. A bystander attempted to intervene, and plaintiff, apparently thinking the melee over, dropped his hands to his side at which point defendant struck plaintiff squarely in the face breaking his nose and causing it to bleed profusely. [The plaintiff's nose was treated by a painful medical process of straightening, packing, and bandaging costing $234.]

The jury answered the issue of liability in plaintiff's favor and awarded him $2,000 in compensatory damages and $2,500 in punitive damages.

BRANCH, C.J. . . .

The rationale permitting recovery of punitive damages is that such damages may be awarded in addition to compensatory damages to punish a defendant for his wrongful acts and to deter others from committing similar acts. A civil action may not be maintained solely for the purpose of collecting punitive damages but may only be awarded when a cause of action otherwise exists in which at least nominal damages are recoverable by the plaintiff.

It is well established in this jurisdiction that punitive damages may be recovered for an assault and battery but are allowable *only* when the assault and battery is accompanied by an element of aggravation such as malice, or oppression, or gross and wilful wrong, or a wanton and reckless disregard of plaintiff's rights. . . .

Some jurisdictions permit the recovery of punitive damages on the theory of *implied* or *imputed* malice when a person intentionally does an act which naturally tends to be injurious. These jurisdictions thus infer the malice necessary to support recovery of punitive damages from *any* assault and battery. We do not adhere to this rule. To justify the awarding of punitive damages in North Carolina, there must be a showing of *actual* or *express* malice, that is, a showing of a sense of personal ill will toward the plaintiff which activated or incited a defendant to commit the alleged assault and battery.

In jury trials the usual rules governing motions for a directed verdict apply when there is such a motion as to a claim for punitive damages on the grounds of insufficiency of evidence, and the trial judge must determine as a matter of law whether the evidence when considered in the light most favorable to the plaintiff is sufficient to carry the issue of punitive damages to the jury. Application of this rule is difficult under the particular facts of the case *sub judice*, and we therefore find it helpful to review the *types* of cases in which punitive damages have been allowed. Punitive damages were recovered in cases where a clergyman while peacefully walking down a street was attacked by the defendant and severely injured; where the plaintiff while eating in a hotel dining room was compelled to sign a retraction by a show of violence, accompanied with offensive and threatening language; where defendant assaulted a weak and old person with a stick loaded with lead for the reason that defendant *thought* plaintiff was a trespasser; where a twelve year old boy was assaulted in public in the presence of others without justification or excuse. We note that all of these cases contain a thread of unprovoked, humiliating assaults, assaults on children, assaults on weaker persons, or assaults where a deadly weapon was callously used. Such is not the case before us. . . .

Applying the above-stated principles of law to the facts presented by this appeal, we conclude that the evidence presented was not sufficient to permit the jury reasonably to infer that defendant's actions were activated by personal ill will toward plaintiff or that his acts were aggravated by oppression, insult, rudeness, or a wanton and reckless disregard of plaintiff's rights. To the contrary, the evidence shows that two adults acting as adolescents engaged in an affray which was precipitated by plaintiff's "baiting" of defendant and plaintiff's invitation that he be ejected from defendant's premises. Thus, the trial court erred by denying defendant's motions to dismiss on the ground that there was not sufficient evidence to carry the issue of punitive damages to the jury. We affirm the Court of Appeals' action in vacating for the reasons set forth herein. . . .

NOTE TO PEETE v. BLACKWELL AND SHUGAR v. GUILL

When Punitive Damages Are Appropriate.   The courts in *Peete* and *Shugar* both require proof of some element of aggravation in addition to proof that the defendant's conduct was reckless or constituted an intentional tort. The court in *Shugar* notes, however, that some jurisdictions infer the additional element from the proof of recklessness or intent. These two opinions describe their standards somewhat differently for when punitive damages are appropriate. Would applying the *Shugar* standard in *Peete* or applying the *Peete* standard in *Shugar* have changed the results in those cases?

Problem
Appropriateness of Punitive Damages

A vehicle owned and operated by Dennis Rhoads was parked on a side road. Eric Heberling, while wearing a camouflage suit, aimed and shot his rifle into Rhoads's automobile and continued shooting as the automobile was driven down the road. At this time, Rhoads's automobile was occupied by three other individuals, Sandra Helm, Jacob Lopp, and Tamar Dombach. Tamar Dombach was struck six times with fragments of a shattering bullet. Pieces of the metal still remain in her body. Sandra Helm suffered a slight scratch across her lower back but received no medical attention. Would punitive damages be proper? See Rhoads v. Heberling, 451 A.2d 1378 (Pa. Super. Ct. 1982).

STATE FARM MUTUAL AUTOMOBILE INSURANCE CO. v. CAMPBELL
538 U.S. 408 (2003)

Justice KENNEDY delivered the opinion of the Court.

We address once again the measure of punishment, by means of punitive damages, a State may impose upon a defendant in a civil case. The question is whether, in the circumstances we shall recount, an award of $145 million in punitive damages, where full compensatory damages are $1 million, is excessive and in violation of the Due Process Clause of the Fourteenth Amendment to the Constitution of the United States.

I

In 1981, Curtis Campbell (Campbell) was driving with his wife, Inez Preece Campbell, in Cache County, Utah. He decided to pass six vans traveling ahead of them on a two-lane highway. Todd Ospital was driving a small car approaching from the opposite direction. To avoid a head-on collision with Campbell, who by then was driving on the wrong side of the highway and toward oncoming traffic, Ospital swerved onto the shoulder, lost control of his automobile, and collided with a vehicle driven by Robert G. Slusher. Ospital was killed, and Slusher was rendered permanently disabled. The Campbells escaped unscathed.

In the ensuing wrongful death and tort action, Campbell insisted he was not at fault. Early investigations did support differing conclusions as to who caused the accident, but "a consensus was reached early on by the investigators and witnesses that Mr. Campbell's unsafe pass had indeed caused the crash." Campbell's insurance company, petitioner State Farm Mutual Automobile Insurance Company (State Farm), nonetheless decided to contest liability and declined offers by Slusher and Ospital's estate (Ospital) to settle the claims for the policy limit of $50,000 ($25,000 per claimant). State Farm also ignored the advice of one of its own investigators and took the case to trial, assuring the Campbells that "their assets were safe, that they had no liability for the accident, that [State Farm] would represent their interests, and that they did not need to procure separate counsel." To the contrary, a jury determined that Campbell was 100 percent at fault, and a judgment was returned for $185,849, far more than the amount offered in settlement.

At first State Farm refused to cover the $135,849 in excess liability. Its counsel made this clear to the Campbells: "You may want to put for-sale signs on your property to get things moving." Nor was State Farm willing to post a supersedeas bond to allow Campbell to appeal the judgment against him. Campbell obtained his own counsel to appeal the verdict. During the pendency of the appeal, in late 1984, Slusher, Ospital, and the Campbells reached an agreement whereby Slusher and Ospital agreed not to seek satisfaction of their claims against the Campbells. In exchange the Campbells agreed to pursue a bad faith action against State Farm and to be represented by Slusher's and Ospital's attorneys. The Campbells also agreed that Slusher and Ospital would have a right to play a part in all major decisions concerning the bad faith action. No settlement could be concluded without Slusher's and Ospital's approval, and Slusher and Ospital would receive 90 percent of any verdict against State Farm.

In 1989, the Utah Supreme Court denied Campbell's appeal in the wrongful death and tort actions. State Farm then paid the entire judgment, including the amounts in excess of the policy limits. The Campbells nonetheless filed a complaint against State Farm alleging bad faith, fraud, and intentional infliction of emotional distress. The trial court initially granted State Farm's motion for summary judgment because State Farm had paid the excess verdict, but that ruling was reversed on appeal. On remand State Farm moved *in limine* to exclude evidence of alleged conduct that occurred in unrelated cases outside of Utah, but the trial court denied the motion. At State Farm's request the trial court bifurcated the trial into two phases conducted before different juries. In the first phase the jury determined that State Farm's decision not to settle was unreasonable because there was a substantial likelihood of an excess verdict.

Before the second phase of the action against State Farm we decided *BMW of North America, Inc. v. Gore,* 517 U.S. 559 (1996), and refused to sustain a $2 million punitive damages award which accompanied a verdict of only $4,000 in compensatory damages. Based on that decision, State Farm again moved for the exclusion of evidence of dissimilar out-of-state conduct. The trial court denied State Farm's motion.

The second phase addressed State Farm's liability for fraud and intentional infliction of emotional distress, as well as compensatory and punitive damages. The Utah Supreme Court aptly characterized this phase of the trial:

"State Farm argued during phase II that its decision to take the case to trial was an 'honest mistake' that did not warrant punitive damages. In contrast, the Campbells introduced evidence that State Farm's decision to take the case to trial was a result of a national scheme to meet corporate fiscal goals by capping payouts on claims company wide. This scheme was referred to as State Farm's 'Performance, Planning and Review,' or PP&R, policy. To prove the existence of this scheme, the trial court allowed the Campbells to introduce extensive expert testimony regarding fraudulent practices by State Farm in its nation-wide operations. Although State Farm moved prior to phase II of the trial for the exclusion of such evidence and continued to object to it at trial, the trial court ruled that such evidence was admissible to determine whether State Farm's conduct in the Campbell case was indeed intentional and sufficiently egregious to warrant punitive damages."

Evidence pertaining to the PP&R policy concerned State Farm's business practices for over 20 years in numerous States. Most of these practices bore no relation to third-party automobile insurance claims, the type of claim underlying the Campbells' complaint against the company. The jury awarded the Campbells $2.6 million in compensatory damages and $145 million in punitive damages, which the trial court reduced to $1 million and $25 million respectively. Both parties appealed.

The Utah Supreme Court sought to apply the three guideposts we identified in *Gore*, and it reinstated the $145 million punitive damages award. . . .

II

We recognized in *Cooper Industries, Inc. v. Leatherman Tool Group, Inc.*, 532 U.S. 424 (2001), that in our judicial system compensatory and punitive damages, although usually awarded at the same time by the same decisionmaker, serve different purposes. Compensatory damages "are intended to redress the concrete loss that the plaintiff has suffered by reason of the defendant's wrongful conduct." *Ibid.* [*See also*] *Pacific Mut. Life Ins. Co. v. Haslip*, 499 U.S. 1 (1991) ("Punitive damages are imposed for purposes of retribution and deterrence.").

While States possess discretion over the imposition of punitive damages, it is well established that there are procedural and substantive constitutional limitations on these awards. The Due Process Clause of the Fourteenth Amendment prohibits the imposition of grossly excessive or arbitrary punishments on a tortfeasor. To the extent an award is grossly excessive, it furthers no legitimate purpose and constitutes an arbitrary deprivation of property. . . .

In . . . *Gore*, we instructed courts reviewing punitive damages to consider three guideposts: (1) the degree of reprehensibility of the defendant's misconduct; (2) the disparity between the actual or potential harm suffered by the plaintiff and the punitive damages award; and (3) the difference between the punitive damages awarded by the jury and the civil penalties authorized or imposed in comparable cases. We reiterated the importance of these three guideposts in *Cooper Industries* and mandated appellate courts to conduct *de novo* review of a trial court's application of them to the jury's award. . . .

III

Under the principles outlined in *BMW of North America, Inc. v. Gore*, this case is neither close nor difficult. It was error to reinstate the jury's $145 million punitive damages award. We address each guidepost of *Gore* in some detail.

A

"The most important indicium of the reasonableness of a punitive damages award is the degree of reprehensibility of the defendant's conduct." *Gore, supra,* at 575. We have instructed courts to determine the reprehensibility of a defendant by considering whether: the harm caused was physical as opposed to economic; the tortious conduct evinced an indifference to or a reckless disregard of the health or safety of others; the target of the conduct had financial vulnerability; the conduct involved repeated actions or was an isolated incident; and the harm was the result of intentional malice, trickery, or deceit, or mere accident. The existence of any one of these factors weighing in favor of a plaintiff may not be sufficient to sustain a punitive damages award; and the absence of all of them renders any award suspect. It should be presumed a plaintiff has been made whole for his injuries by compensatory damages, so punitive damages should only be awarded if the defendant's culpability, after having paid compensatory damages, is so reprehensible as to warrant the imposition of further sanctions to achieve punishment or deterrence.

Applying these factors in the instant case, we must acknowledge that State Farm's handling of the claims against the Campbells merits no praise. The trial court found that State Farm's employees altered the company's records to make Campbell appear less culpable. State Farm disregarded the overwhelming likelihood of liability and the near-certain probability that, by taking the case to trial, a judgment in excess of the policy limits would be awarded. State Farm amplified the harm by at first assuring the Campbells their assets would be safe from any verdict and by later telling them, post-judgment, to put a for-sale sign on their house. While we do not suggest there was error in awarding punitive damages based upon State Farm's conduct toward the Campbells, a more modest punishment for this reprehensible conduct could have satisfied the State's legitimate objectives, and the Utah courts should have gone no further.

This case, instead, was used as a platform to expose, and punish, the perceived deficiencies of State Farm's operations throughout the country. The Utah Supreme Court's opinion makes explicit that State Farm was being condemned for its nationwide policies rather than for the conduct directed toward the Campbells. This was, as well, an explicit rationale of the trial court's decision in approving the award, though reduced from $145 million to $25 million. . . .

Here, the Campbells do not dispute that much of the out-of-state conduct was lawful where it occurred. They argue, however, that such evidence was not the primary basis for the punitive damages award and was relevant to the extent it demonstrated, in a general sense, State Farm's motive against its insured. This argument misses the mark. Lawful out-of-state conduct may be probative when it demonstrates the deliberateness and culpability of the defendant's action in the State where it is tortious, but that conduct must have a nexus to the specific harm suffered by the plaintiff. . . .

For a more fundamental reason, however, the Utah courts erred in relying upon this and other evidence: The courts awarded punitive damages to punish and deter conduct that bore no relation to the Campbells' harm. A defendant's dissimilar acts, independent from the acts upon which liability was premised, may not serve as the basis for punitive damages. A defendant should be punished for the conduct that harmed the plaintiff, not for being an unsavory individual or business.

The same reasons lead us to conclude the Utah Supreme Court's decision cannot be justified on the grounds that State Farm was a recidivist. Although "our holdings that a recidivist may be punished more severely than a first offender recognize that repeated misconduct is more reprehensible than an individual instance of malfeasance," *Gore*, in the context of civil actions courts must ensure the conduct in question replicates the prior transgressions.

The Campbells have identified scant evidence of repeated misconduct of the sort that injured them. Nor does our review of the Utah courts' decisions convince us that State Farm was only punished for its actions toward the Campbells. Although evidence of other acts need not be identical to have relevance in the calculation of punitive damages, the Utah court erred here because evidence pertaining to claims that had nothing to do with a third-party lawsuit was introduced at length. . . . The reprehensibility guidepost does not permit courts to expand the scope of the case so that a defendant may be punished for any malfeasance, which in this case extended for a 20-year period. In this case, because the Campbells have shown no conduct by State Farm similar to that which harmed them, the conduct that harmed them is the only conduct relevant to the reprehensibility analysis.

B

Turning to the second *Gore* guidepost, we have been reluctant to identify concrete constitutional limits on the ratio between harm, or potential harm, to the plaintiff and the punitive damages award. We decline again to impose a bright-line ratio which a punitive damages award cannot exceed. Our jurisprudence and the principles it has now established demonstrate, however, that, in practice, few awards exceeding a single-digit ratio between punitive and compensatory damages, to a significant degree, will satisfy due process. In *Haslip*, in upholding a punitive damages award, we concluded that an award of more than four times the amount of compensatory damages might be close to the line of constitutional impropriety. We cited that 4-to-1 ratio again in *Gore*. The Court further referenced a long legislative history, dating back over 700 years and going forward to today, providing for sanctions of double, treble, or quadruple damages to deter and punish. While these ratios are not binding, they are instructive. They demonstrate what should be obvious: Single-digit multipliers are more likely to comport with due process, while still achieving the State's goals of deterrence and retribution, than awards with ratios in range of 500 to 1, *id.*, or, in this case, of 145 to 1. . . .

. . . In the context of this case, we have no doubt that there is a presumption against an award that has a 145-to-1 ratio. The compensatory award in this case was substantial; the Campbells were awarded $1 million for a year and a half of emotional distress. This was complete compensation. The harm arose from a transaction in the economic realm, not from some physical assault or trauma; there were no physical injuries; and State Farm paid the excess verdict before the complaint was filed, so the Campbells suffered only minor economic injuries for the 18-month period in which State Farm refused to resolve the claim against them. The compensatory damages for the injury suffered here, moreover, likely were based on a component which was duplicated in the punitive award. Much of the distress was caused by the outrage and humiliation the Campbells suffered at the actions of their insurer; and it is a major role of punitive damages to condemn such conduct. Compensatory damages, however, already contain this punitive element. . . .

... While States enjoy considerable discretion in deducing when punitive damages are warranted, each award must comport with the principles set forth in *Gore*. Here the argument that State Farm will be punished in only the rare case, coupled with reference to its assets (which, of course, are what other insured parties in Utah and other States must rely upon for payment of claims) had little to do with the actual harm sustained by the Campbells. The wealth of a defendant cannot justify an otherwise unconstitutional punitive damages award. ... The principles set forth in *Gore* must be implemented with care, to ensure both reasonableness and proportionality.

C

The third guidepost in *Gore* is the disparity between the punitive damages award and the "civil penalties authorized or imposed in comparable cases." ...

Here, we need not dwell long on this guidepost. The most relevant civil sanction under Utah state law for the wrong done to the Campbells appears to be a $10,000 fine for an act of fraud, an amount dwarfed by the $145 million punitive damages award. The Supreme Court of Utah speculated about the loss of State Farm's business license, the disgorgement of profits, and possible imprisonment, but here again its references were to the broad fraudulent scheme drawn from evidence of out-of-state and dissimilar conduct. This analysis was insufficient to justify the award.

IV

An application of the *Gore* guideposts to the facts of this case, especially in light of the substantial compensatory damages awarded (a portion of which contained a punitive element), likely would justify a punitive damages award at or near the amount of compensatory damages. The punitive award of $145 million, therefore, was neither reasonable nor proportionate to the wrong committed, and it was an irrational and arbitrary deprivation of the property of the defendant. The proper calculation of punitive damages under the principles we have discussed should be resolved, in the first instance, by the Utah courts.

The judgment of the Utah Supreme Court is reversed, and the case is remanded for proceedings not inconsistent with this opinion.

It is so ordered.

Justice GINSBURG, dissenting.

... The large size of the award upheld by the Utah Supreme Court in this case indicates why damage-capping legislation may be altogether fitting and proper. Neither the amount of the award nor the trial record, however, justifies this Court's substitution of its judgment for that of Utah's competent decisionmakers. ...

When the Court first ventured to override state-court punitive damages awards, it did so moderately. The Court recalled that "in our federal system, States necessarily have considerable flexibility in determining the level of punitive damages that they will allow in different classes of cases and in any particular case." *Gore*, 517 U.S., at 568. Today's decision exhibits no such respect and restraint. No longer content to accord state-court judgments "a strong presumption of validity," the Court announces that "few awards exceeding a single-digit ratio between punitive and compensatory damages, to a significant degree, will satisfy due process."[2] Moreover, the Court adds, when compensatory damages are substantial, doubling those damages "can reach the outermost limit of the due process guarantee." In a legislative scheme or a state high court's design to cap punitive damages, the handiwork in setting single-digit and 1-to-1 benchmarks could hardly be questioned; in a judicial decree imposed on the States by this Court under the banner of substantive due process, the numerical controls today's decision installs seem to me boldly out of order.

I remain of the view that this Court has no warrant to reform state law governing awards of punitive damages. Even if I were prepared to accept the flexible guides prescribed in *Gore*, I would not join the Court's swift conversion of those guides into instructions that begin to resemble marching orders. For the reasons stated, I would leave the judgment of the Utah Supreme Court undisturbed.

NOTES TO STATE FARM MUTUAL AUTOMOBILE INSURANCE CO. v. CAMPBELL

1. *Common Law and Constitutional Restrictions on Punitive Damages.* The Restatement (Second) of Torts §908 comment e deals with the size of punitive damage awards. How does its test, developed decades before the *BMW of North America* decision, compare with current constitutional requirements?

> **e. Amount of damages.** In determining the amount of punitive damages, as well as in deciding whether they should be given at all, the trier of fact can properly consider not merely the act itself but all the circumstances including the motives of the wrongdoer, the relations between the parties and the provocation or want of provocation for the act. In addition, the extent of harm to the injured person can be considered by analogy to the doctrine of the criminal law by which the seriousness of a crime may depend upon the harm done, as when a battery with intent to kill results in mayhem or murder. Included in the harm to the plaintiff may be considered the fact that the plaintiff has been put to trouble and expense in the protection of his interests, as by legal proceedings in this or in other suits. The wealth of the defendant is also relevant, since the purposes of exemplary damages are to punish for a past event and to prevent future offenses, and the degree of punishment or deterrence resulting from a judgment is to some extent in proportion to the means of the guilty person.

2. *Valuing Principles?* After the Utah Supreme Court had reinstated the jury verdicts for compensatory damages and $145,000,000 in punitive damages, but before State Farm filed its Petition for Certiorari in the United States Supreme Court, State Farm offered to settle the case for $150,000,000 on the condition that the parties request the Utah Supreme Court to vacate its decision. The offer was rejected. After the Supreme Court rendered its opinion, the judgment was reduced to approximately $9,000,000. See Christensen & Jensen, P.C. v. Barrett & Daines, 194 P.3d 931 (Utah 2008) (suit among attorneys who had represented parties in litigation against State Farm, seeking a declaratory judgment regarding apportionment of attorney fees and raising issues of legal malpractice).

---

[2] *TXO Production Corp.* v. *Alliance Resources Corp.*, 509 U.S. 443, 462, n. 8, (1993), noted that "under well-settled law," a defendant's "wrongdoing in other parts of the country" and its "impressive net worth" are factors "typically considered in assessing punitive damages." It remains to be seen whether, or the extent to which, today's decision will unsettle that law.

3. *Punitive Damages.* In BMW of North America, Inc. v. Gore, 517 U.S. 559 (1996), followed in State Farm Mutual Automobile Insurance Co. v. Campbell, Justice Ginsburg and Chief Justice Rehnquist dissented. They believed that state tort reform measures were sufficient to curtail excessive punitive damages awards. The following list from Justice Ginsburg's opinion outlines some of those tort reform measures then being considered or that had been adopted by states. Observing that states were actively considering the limits on punitive damages, the opinion concluded that the majority had unnecessarily and unwisely ventured into this issue. Following are the statutes Justice Ginsburg cited:

Colorado — Colo. Rev. Stat. §§13-21-102(1)(a) and (3) (1987) (as a main rule, caps punitive damages at amount of actual damages).

Connecticut — Conn. Gen. Stat. §52-240b (1995) (caps punitive damages at twice compensatory damages in products liability cases).

Delaware — H.R. 237, 138th Gen. Ass. (introduced May 17, 1995) (would cap punitive damages at greater of three times compensatory damages, or $250,000).

Florida — Fla. Stat. §§768.73(1)(a) and (b) (Supp. 1992) (in general, caps punitive damages at three times compensatory damages).

Georgia — Ga. Code Ann. §51-12-5.1 (Supp. 1995) (caps punitive damages at $250,000 in some tort actions; prohibits multiple awards stemming from the same predicate conduct in products liability actions).

Illinois — H. 20, 89th Gen. Ass. 1995-1996 Reg. Sess. (enacted Mar. 9, 1995) (caps punitive damages at three times economic damages).

Indiana — H. 1741, 109th Reg. Sess. (enacted Apr. 26, 1995) (caps punitive damages at greater of three times compensatory damages, or $50,000).

Kansas — Kan. Stat. Ann. §§60-3701(e) and (f) (1994) (in general, caps punitive damages at lesser of defendant's annual gross income, or $5 million).

Maryland — S. 187, 1995 Leg. Sess. (introduced Jan. 27, 1995) (in general, would cap punitive damages at four times compensatory damages).

Minnesota — S. 489, 79th Leg. Sess., 1995 Reg. Sess. (introduced Feb. 16, 1995) (would require reasonable relationship between compensatory and punitive damages).

Nevada — Nev. Rev. Stat. §42.005(1) (1993) (caps punitive damages at three times compensatory damages if compensatory damages equal $100,000 or more, and at $300,000 if the compensatory damages are less than $100,000).

New Jersey — S. 1496, 206th Leg., 2d Ann. Sess. (1995) (caps punitive damages at greater of five times compensatory damages, or $350,000 in certain tort cases).

North Dakota — N.D. Cent. Code §32-03.2-11(4) (Supp. 1995) (caps punitive damages at greater of two times compensatory damages, or $250,000).

Oklahoma — Okla. Stat. tit. 23, §9.1(B)-(D) (Supp. 1996) (caps punitive damages at greater of $100,000, or actual damages, if jury finds defendant guilty of reckless disregard; and at greatest of $500,000, twice actual damages, or the benefit accruing to defendant from the injury-causing conduct, if jury finds that defendant has acted intentionally and maliciously).

Texas — S. 25, 74th Reg. Sess. (enacted Apr. 20, 1995) (caps punitive damages at twice economic damages, plus up to $750,000 additional non-economic damages).

Virginia — Va. Code Ann. §8.01-38.1 (1992) (caps punitive damages at $350,000).

Problem
Excessiveness of Punitive Damages

Applying the rules governing the amount of single and cumulative punitive damage awards, was the punitive damage award of $150 million excessive in the following case?

Ira Weinstein, a United States citizen, was killed in the terrorist bombing of the Number 18 Egged passenger bus in Jerusalem, Israel on February 25, 1996. He brought suit against the Iranian Ministry of Information and Security under the Foreign Sovereign Immunities Act of 1976, which created a federal cause of action for personal injury or wrongful death resulting from acts of state-sponsored terrorism. The defendant provided material support in the form of training and money to HAMAS so that the organization could carry out terrorist attacks such as the one on February 25, 1996.

The Iranian Ministry of Information and Security has approximately 30,000 employees and is the largest intelligence agency in the Middle East, with an estimated annual budget between $100-$400 million. The Islamic Republic of Iran gave the HAMAS organization at least $25-$50 million in 1995 and 1996, and also provided other groups with tens of millions of dollars to engage in terrorist activities. In total, Iran gave terrorist organizations, such as HAMAS, between $100 and $200 million per year during this period. The money, among other things, supported HAMAS' terrorist activities by, for example, bringing HAMAS into contact with potential terrorist recruits and by providing legitimate front activities behind which HAMAS could hide its terrorist activities. Punitive damages of $420,000,000 were awarded in two other cases in lawsuits brought by two other victims of this same bombing.

See Weinstein v. The Islamic Republic of Iran, 184 F. Supp. 2d 13 (D.D.C. 2002).

Perspective: Punitive Damages

The proper amount for an award of punitive damages inevitably depends on the goals the law is pursuing by allowing such rewards. The Restatement (Second) of Torts §908(2) allows recovery of punitive damages for "conduct that is outrageous, because of the defendant's evil motive or his reckless indifference to the rights of others." According to that section, "the trier of fact can properly consider the character of the defendant's act, the nature and extent of the harm to the plaintiff that the defendant caused or intended to cause and the wealth of the defendant." Compare a test adopted in Reynolds Metals Co. v. Lampert, 316 F.2d 272, 275 (9th Cir. 1963):

> To justify an award of punitive damages, it is not necessary that the act have been done maliciously or with bad motive. Where it has become apparent, as it has here, that compensatory damages alone, while they might compensate the

injured party, will not deter the actor from committing similar trespasses in the future, there is ample justification for an award of punitive damages.

What are the underlying goals of these alternative approaches? How does the underlying goal affect policy choices on maximum allowable punitive damage awards?

IV. Adjustments to Damages: Collateral Sources and Statutory Ceilings

Limiting the amount of damages owed by a defendant found to have committed a tortious act has been a dominant goal in the tort reform movement. Chapter 8 highlighted some states' abrogation of joint and several liability. Also, a number of states have modified a doctrine known as the *collateral source rule*. Many states have adopted statutes that impose ceilings on the amounts of damages that may be awarded either in any tort action or in particular types of tort actions such as medical malpractice cases. Perreira v. Rediger interprets a state statute that abolished the collateral source rule. Etheridge v. Medical Center Hospitals and Knowles v. United States present differing treatments of claims that statutory limits on damages deprive plaintiffs of constitutional rights.

PERREIRA v. REDIGER

778 A.2d 429 (N.J. 2001)

Long, J. . . .

[The first of these consolidated appeals, the] *Beninato* case arose when Takako Beninato, a professional dog groomer, was seriously injured during a grooming session involving a dog owned by Lenore and Leonard Achor. Beninato's health insurer, Oxford Health Plans, Inc. ("Oxford"), paid $7,357 for her medical expenses. Beninato then sued the Achors, whose homeowner's insurance carrier, Preferred Mutual Insurance Company ("Preferred"), defended the suit. . . .

The *Perreira* case arose when Maria Perreira fell on the premises of the Columbia Savings Bank ("Columbia"). She sued Columbia along with its liability carrier Atlantic Mutual Insurance Company ("Atlantic"), Michael Rediger, the bank's snow removal contractor, and Rediger's liability carrier, the Preserver Insurance Company ("Preserver"). In that case, Oxford, Perreira's health insurer, had paid about $13,000 for her medical expenses.

[The insurance companies claim that, under the collateral source rule embodied in N.J.S.A. 2A:15-97, health insurers who expend funds on behalf of an insured are allowed to recoup those payments through common law or contractual subrogation when an insured recovers a judgment against a tortfeasor. Contractual subrogation is also referred to as *contractual reimbursement*.]

The collateral source rule, with deep roots in English common law, is firmly embedded in American common law as well. It was first cited in an American judicial decision in 1854 and has had continued currency in the centuries to follow. Michael F. Flynn, *Private Medical Insurance and the Collateral Source Rule: A Good Bet?*, 22 U. Tol. L. Rev. 39, 40 (1990) (citing The Propeller Monticello v. Mollison, 58 U.S. (17 How.) 152, 15 L. Ed. 68 (1854)). The common law collateral source rule "allows an injured party to recover the value of medical treatment from a culpable party, irrespective of payment of actual medical expenses by the injured party's insurance carrier. The purpose of the collateral source rule is to preserve an injured party's right to seek tort recovery from a tortfeasor without jeopardizing his or her right to receive insurance payments for medical care." Ibid. The rule "prohibits the tortfeasor from reducing payment of a tort judgment by the amount of money received by an injured party from other sources" and "bars the submission of evidence that the injured plaintiff received payment for any part of his damages, including medical expenses, from other sources." Id. at 42. It is thus a rule of damages as well as a rule of evidence. Ibid.

According to the Restatement (Second) of Torts §920A(2) (1977), under the collateral source rule, payments made to an injured party by a source other than the tortfeasor are "not credited against the tortfeasor's liability, although they cover all or a part of the harm for which the tortfeasor is liable." The policy advanced by the rule is that "a benefit that is directed to the injured party should not be shifted so as to become a windfall for the tortfeasor." Id. §920A comment b. Thus, if an injured party has the foresight to provide that his or her medical expenses will be paid by maintaining an insurance policy, the common law collateral source rule allows him or her to benefit from that foresight by recovering not only the insurance proceeds but also the full tort judgment. Ibid.

However, in the early to mid-1980's, state legislatures began to revisit the collateral source rule based on the notion, advanced by insurance industry analysts, that the rule contributed "to the liability insurance availability and affordability crisis in this country. . . ." Christian D. Saine, *Note, Preserving the Collateral Source Rule: Modern Theories of Tort Law and a Proposal for Practical Application*, 47 Case W. Res. L. Rev. 1075, 1080 (1997). . . .

In response, many state legislatures passed comprehensive tort reform legislation in the latter half of the 1980's. Statutory modification of the collateral source rule in one form or another was a common factor among those different legislative initiatives. No universal approach was adopted in all jurisdictions.

One common legislative reform to avoid double recovery to plaintiffs requires a tort judgment to be reduced by the amount of collateral source payments but specifies that such reduction will not occur if a subrogation or reimbursement right exists.[1] A second approach permits a plaintiff [sic?] to introduce evidence at trial of collateral source benefits received, presumably to reduce the amount of the tort judgment and benefit liability carriers. Within that category, contractual reimbursement is allowed

---

[1] Subrogation substitutes the health insurer in place of the plaintiff insured "to whose rights he or she succeeds in relation to the debt and gives to the substitute all the rights, priorities, remedies, liens, and securities of the person for whom he or she is substituted." Lee R. Russ & Thomas F. Segalla, *Couch on Insurance* §222:5 (3d ed. 2000). Reimbursement, a contractual undertaking, allows the insurer to recover payments directly from its own insured upon its insured's recovery of the loss from a third party. *Couch on Insurance* 3d §222:81.

and subrogation denied to the health insurers in some states. In other states, contract reimbursement and subrogation are specifically prohibited.

A third approach does not purport to tinker with the common-law collateral source rule at all, but simply creates a statutory right to subrogation for health insurers, thus eliminating double recovery to plaintiffs and benefitting the health insurance industry.

Each of the aforementioned initiatives has the effect of avoiding double recovery to plaintiffs and thus altering the effect of the common-law collateral source rule. However, they differ dramatically regarding which segment of the insurance community will benefit from the change. Where subrogation or contract reimbursement rights are granted to health insurers, that industry is the beneficiary of the legislative modification. Where subrogation and reimbursement are prohibited, the liability carriers benefit.

Like other jurisdictions, New Jersey responded to the call for modification of the collateral source rule by enacting N.J.S.A. 2A:15-97 in 1987. Although, like the modifications enacted in other jurisdictions, its primary effect was to eliminate double recovery to plaintiffs, it was not modeled exactly on any of the other statutes. It provides:

> In any civil action brought for personal injury or death, . . . if a plaintiff receives or is entitled to receive benefits for the injuries allegedly incurred from any other source other than a joint tortfeasor, the benefits, other than workers' compensation benefits or the proceeds from a life insurance policy, shall be disclosed to the court and the amount thereof which duplicates any benefit contained in the award shall be deducted from any award recovered by the plaintiff, less any premium paid to an insurer directly by the plaintiff or by any member of the plaintiff's family on behalf of the plaintiff of the policy period during which the benefits are payable. Any party to the action shall be permitted to introduce evidence regarding any of the matters described in this act.

On its face, N.J.S.A. 2A:15-97 eliminates double recovery by directing the court to deduct from any tort judgment the amount received by plaintiff from collateral sources (other than workers' compensation and life insurance) less any insurance premiums plaintiff has paid.[2] Unlike the out-of-state enactments, the statute is silent regarding any right to subrogation or reimbursement on the part of the health insurers. . . .

As the legislative history reveals, the choice was made to favor liability carriers. . . . That legislative determination took the form of a reduction from the tort judgment of the amount received from collateral sources. By that action, the Legislature eliminated double recovery to plaintiffs, reduced the burden on the tortfeasors' liability carriers and left health insurers in the same position as they were prior to the enactment of N.J.S.A. 2A:15-97.

One of Oxford's core claims is that health insurers had a common-law equitable right to subrogation that pre-dated N.J.S.A. 2A:15-97 and that that right has to be taken into account in interpreting the collateral source statute. . . .

The rationale behind the rule against finding equitable subrogation in personal insurance contracts is set forth in one treatise as follows:

> Subrogation rights are common under policies of property or casualty insurance, wherein the insured sustains a fixed financial loss, and the purpose is to place that

---

[2] The insurance premium is essentially charged to the liability carrier because the liability carrier, not the plaintiff, has received the benefit of the insurance.

loss ultimately on the wrongdoer. To permit the insured in such instances to recover from both the insurer and the wrongdoer would permit him to profit unduly thereby.

In personal insurance contracts, however, the exact loss is never capable of ascertainment. Life and death, health, physical well being, and such matters are incapable of exact financial estimation. There are, accordingly, not the same reasons militating against a double recovery. The general rule is, therefore, that the insurer is not subrogated to the insured's rights or to the beneficiary's rights under contracts of personal insurance, at least in the absence of a policy provision so providing. Nor would a settlement by the insured with the wrongdoer bar his cause of action against the insurer. However, if a subrogation provision were expressly contained in such contracts, it probably would be enforced quite uniformly. Such a provision cannot be read into a policy by calling it an indemnity contract, however.

[3 J.A. Appleman & J. Appleman, *Insurance Law & Practice*, §1675 at 495-497.]

Thus, courts typically have not implied a non-contractual or non-statutory right to subrogation in health insurance. . . .

We turn next to contract reimbursement. Oxford's policies contained a reimbursement provision allowing it to recover expended health care costs "when payment is made directly to the member in third-party settlements or satisfied judgments." That contract provision was not authorized by law at the time the collateral source rule was amended in 1987. . . .

. . . Later, the Commissioner promulgated regulations that for the first time permitted such provisions in large group health insurance policies. . . .

The Commissioner's authorization of subrogation and reimbursement provisions in health insurance contracts must be tested against N.J.S.A. 2A:15-97. As we have indicated, in that statute the legislature eliminated double recovery to plaintiffs and allocated the benefit of what had previously been double recovery to the liability insurance industry. The Commissioner was not free to alter that scheme. [Under the New Jersey collateral source statute, benefits paid by health insurers, less associated premiums, are to be deducted from a tortfeasor's liability to a plaintiff. Heath insurers cannot invoke either the common law or a contractual right of subrogation in order to seek reimbursement for their expenses.] . . .

NOTES TO PERREIRA v. REDIGER

1. *Policy Choices and the Collateral Source Rule.* Statutory modifications of the collateral source rule involve legislative choices favoring defendants over plaintiffs and some defendants over other defendants. Who is favored and who is harmed by the New Jersey statute's changes to the traditional collateral source rule?

2. *Double Recovery, Deterrence, and Compensation.* The wisdom of a particular type of tort reform depends on what goals a legislature is pursuing:

[The collateral source rule] presents policymakers with a choice between allowing a "windfall" to the plaintiff or to the defendant in a tort case. To illustrate, consider an automobile accident case in which the victim loses his foot in the accident. The plaintiff arguably receives a "double" recovery if he gets both the proceeds of his insurance policy and tort damages for the loss of his foot. On the other hand, the negligent driver will receive a windfall if she finds she must pay less because she had the foresight to injure an insured individual.

Courts and commentators advance two major justifications for the collateral source rule: tortfeasors must pay the full costs of their actions (either to promote deterrence or for punitive reasons) and injured parties should receive the benefits of their contracts. The rule has recently come under attack, both in courts and in legislatures. Criticisms of the rule center on the costs to insurers of providing "double" recoveries for plaintiffs who are also compensated through the tort system and on rejection of the deterrence rationale for the tort system. Additionally, a leading treatise suggests that the real function of the rule is to assist plaintiffs' attorneys in financing lawsuits, since deducting insurance proceeds or government benefits from damages would reduce the size of the contingency fees available.

The theoretical efficiency rationale for allowing "double" recovery seems relatively airtight. A victim's purchase of insurance or receipt of government benefits is logically unrelated to a potential tortfeasor's conduct. Encouraging efficient behavior by potential tortfeasors therefore requires that they pay the full cost of their behavior.

See John C. Moorhouse, Andrew P. Morriss & Robert Whaples, *Law & Economics and Tort Law: A Survey of Scholarly Opinion*, 62 Alb. L. Rev. 667, 687-688 (1998). How would support for modifying the collateral source rule depend on whether the primary purpose of tort law is to deter tortious conduct or, alternatively, to compensate injured parties?

Statute: MODIFIED COLLATERAL SOURCE RULE
Colo. Rev. Stat. §13-21-111.6 (2017)

In any action by any person or his legal representative to recover damages for a tort resulting in death or injury to person or property, the court, after the finder of fact has returned its verdict stating the amount of damages to be awarded, shall reduce the amount of the verdict by the amount by which such person, his estate, or his personal representative has been or will be wholly or partially indemnified or compensated for his loss by any other person, corporation, insurance company, or fund in relation to the injury, damage, or death sustained; except that the verdict shall not be reduced by the amount by which such person, his estate, or his personal representative has been or will be wholly or partially indemnified or compensated by a benefit paid as a result of a contract entered into and paid for by or on behalf of such person. The court shall enter judgment on such reduced amount.

NOTE TO STATUTE

How does this provision differ from the traditional collateral source rule and from the statute analyzed in *Perreira*? Who benefits and who is harmed under the Colorado statute?

ETHERIDGE v. MEDICAL CENTER HOSPITALS
376 S.E.2d 525 (Va. 1989)

STEPHENSON, J.

The principal issue in this appeal is whether Code §8.01-581.15, which limits the amount of recoverable damages in a medical malpractice action, violates either the Federal or Virginia Constitution. . . .

Louise Etheridge and Larry Dodd, co-committees of the estate of Richie Lee Wilson (Wilson), sued Medical Center Hospitals (the hospital) and Donald Bedell Gordon, executor of the estate of Clarence B. Trower, Jr., deceased (Trower), alleging that the hospital and Trower were liable, jointly and severally, for damages Wilson sustained as a result of their medical malpractice. Evidence at trial revealed that, prior to her injuries, Wilson, a 35-year-old mother of three children, was a normal, healthy woman. On May 6, 1980, however, Wilson underwent surgery at the hospital to restore a deteriorating jaw bone. The surgery consisted of the removal of five-inch-long portions of two ribs by Trower, a general surgeon, and the grafting of the reshaped rib bone to Wilson's jaw by an oral surgeon. The jury found that both Trower and the hospital were negligent and that their negligence proximately caused Wilson's injuries.

Wilson's injuries are severe and permanent. She is brain damaged with limited memory and intelligence. She is paralyzed on her left side, confined to a wheelchair, and unable to care for herself or her children.

At the time of trial, Wilson had expended more than $300,000 for care and treatment. She will incur expenses for her care the remainder of her life. Her life expectancy is 39.9 years. Wilson, a licensed practical nurse, earned almost $10,000 in 1979, the last full year she worked. She contends that she proved an economic loss "in excess of $1.9 million."

The jury returned a verdict for $2,750,000 against both defendants. The trial court, applying the recovery limit prescribed in Code §8.01-581.15 (1977 Repl. Vol.), reduced the verdict to $750,000 and entered judgment in that amount. Wilson appeals.

At all times pertinent to this case, Code §8.01-581.15 provided that in an action for malpractice against a health care provider, "the total amount recoverable for any injury . . . shall not exceed seven hundred fifty thousand dollars." Wilson challenges the validity of this legislation on multiple grounds [including claims that the statute violated her right under the Virginia Constitution to a trial by jury and her rights to procedural and substantive due process under the Virginia and United States Constitutions].

On February 6, 1975, the General Assembly adopted House Joint Resolution No. 174, authorizing a study and report on malpractice insurance premiums for physicians. H.R. Res. 174, Va. Gen. Assem. (1975). The study was conducted by the State Corporation Commission's Bureau of Insurance.

Upon completion of its study in November 1975, the Bureau of Insurance submitted its report to the General Assembly. The report showed that since 1960 medical malpractice insurance rates had increased nationwide more than 1000 percent.

> The increase resulted from the number and severity of medical malpractice claims. Significantly, the report stated that 90 percent of all medical malpractice claims ever pursued originated after 1965. Bureau of Insurance, State Corporation Commission, Medical Malpractice Insurance in Virginia, the Scope and Severity of the Problem and Alternative Solutions.

Based upon its study, the General Assembly found that the increase in medical malpractice claims was directly affecting the premium cost for, and the availability of, medical malpractice insurance. Without such insurance, health care providers could not be expected to continue providing medical care for the Commonwealth's citizens.

Because of this threat to medical care services, the General Assembly, in 1976, enacted the Virginia Medical Malpractice Act (the Act). Acts 1976, c. 611.

The need and reasons for the legislation are stated in the Preamble to the Act:

> Whereas, the General Assembly has determined that it is becoming increasingly difficult for health care providers of the Commonwealth to obtain medical malpractice insurance with limits at affordable rates in excess of $750,000; and
>
> Whereas, the difficulty, cost and potential unavailability of such insurance has caused health care providers to cease providing services or to retire prematurely and has become a substantial impairment to health care providers entering into practice in the Commonwealth and reduces or will tend to reduce the number of young people interested in or willing to enter health care careers; and
>
> Whereas, these factors constitute a significant problem adversely affecting the public health, safety and welfare which necessitates the imposition of a limitation on the liability of health care providers in tort actions commonly referred to as medical malpractice cases[.] . . .

One of Wilson's primary contentions is that Code §8.01-581.15 violates her right under the Virginia Constitution to a trial by jury. She asserts that "legislation may not override the findings of a jury by prescribing an absolute limit upon the amount of damages, irrespective of the facts and the jury verdict."

Article I, §11, of the Constitution of Virginia provides, inter alia, "[t]hat in controversies respecting property, and in suits between man and man, trial by jury is preferable to any other, and ought to be held sacred." It is "well settled that . . . the State . . . Constitution [neither] guarantees [nor] preserves the right of trial by jury except in those cases where it existed when" the Constitution was adopted. . . .

The resolution of disputed facts continues to be a jury's sole function. "The province of the jury is to settle questions of fact, and when the facts are ascertained the law determines the rights of the parties." Forbes & Co. v. So. Cotton Oil Co., 108 S.E. 15, 20 (Va. 1921). Thus, the Virginia Constitution guarantees only that a jury will resolve disputed facts.

Without question, the jury's fact-finding function extends to the assessment of damages. Once the jury has ascertained the facts and assessed the damages, however, the constitutional mandate is satisfied. Thereafter, it is the duty of the court to apply the law to the facts.

The limitation on medical malpractice recoveries contained in Code §8.01-581.15 does nothing more than establish the outer limits of a remedy provided by the General Assembly. A remedy is a matter of law, not a matter of fact. A trial court applies the remedy's limitation only *after* the jury has fulfilled its fact-finding function. Thus, Code §8.01-581.15 does not infringe upon the right to a jury trial because the section does not apply until after a jury has completed its assigned function in the judicial process.

More importantly, as previously stated, the jury trial guarantee secures no rights other than those that existed at common law. Significantly, the common law never recognized a right to a full recovery in tort. Thus, although a party has the right to have a jury assess his damages, he has no right to have a jury dictate through an award the legal consequences of its assessment. For this reason, too, the limited recovery set forth in Code §8.01-581.15 effects no impingement upon the right to a jury trial.

In the present case, the jury resolved the disputed facts and assessed the damages. Wilson, therefore, was accorded a jury trial as guaranteed by the Virginia Constitution. Once the jury had determined the facts, the trial court applied the law and reduced the verdict in compliance with the cap prescribed by the General Assembly in Code §8.01-581.15. By merely applying the law to the facts, the court fulfilled its obligation. Accordingly, the remedy prescribed by the General Assembly did not infringe upon Wilson's right to a jury.

Wilson also contends that Code §8.01-581.15 violates the constitutional guarantee of due process. The due process clauses of the Federal and Virginia Constitutions provide that no person shall be deprived of life, liberty, or property without due process of law. U.S. Const. amend. XIV, §1; Va. Const. art. I, §11. Both procedural and substantive rights are protected by the due process clauses.

Procedural due process guarantees a litigant the right to reasonable notice and a meaningful opportunity to be heard. The procedural due process guarantee does not create constitutionally-protected interests; the purpose of the guarantee is to provide procedural safeguards against a government's arbitrary deprivation of certain interests.

By comparison, substantive due process tests the reasonableness of a statute vis-à-vis the legislature's power to enact the law. Ordinarily, substantive due process is satisfied if the legislation has a "reasonable relation to a proper purpose and [is] neither arbitrary nor discriminatory." *Duke v. County of Pulaski*, 247 S.E.2d 824, 829 (1978). If legislation withstands this so-called "rational basis" test, due process is not violated.

When, on the other hand, legislation affects a "fundamental right," the constitutionality of the enactment will be judged according to the "strict scrutiny" test, i.e., the law must be necessary to promote a compelling or overriding governmental interest. Those interests that have been recognized as "fundamental" include the right to free speech; the right to vote; the right to interstate travel; the right to fairness in the criminal process; the right to marry; and the right to fairness in procedures concerning governmental deprivation of life, liberty, or property. . . .

In the present case, Wilson has not been denied reasonable notice and a meaningful opportunity to be heard. Code §8.01-581.15 has no effect upon Wilson's right to have a jury or court render an individual decision based upon the merits of her case. Thus, . . . Code §8.01-581.15 creates no presumptions whatsoever regarding the individual merits of Wilson's medical malpractice claim. The section merely affects the parameters of the remedy available to Wilson after the merits of her claim have been decided. We hold, therefore, that Wilson's constitutional guarantee of procedural due process has not been violated.

The effect of Code §8.01-581.15 on the remedy available to Wilson likewise is not violative of any substantive due process right. As discussed [above], a party has no fundamental right to a particular remedy or a full recovery in tort. A statutory limitation on recovery is simply an economic regulation, which is entitled to wide judicial deference. *Duke Power Co.*, 438 U.S. at 83. Because Code §8.01-581.15 is such a regulation and infringes upon no fundamental right, the section must be upheld if it is reasonably related to a legitimate governmental purpose.

. . . The purpose of Code §8.01-581.15 — to maintain adequate health care services in this Commonwealth — bears a reasonable relation to the legislative cap — ensuring that health care providers can obtain affordable medical malpractice insurance. We hold, therefore, that substantive due process has not been violated. . . .

KNOWLES v. UNITED STATES

544 N.W.2d 183 (S.D. 1996)

SABERS, J.

Parents brought suit for severe injuries suffered by minor son while under care of Air Force hospital. The United States admitted liability and invoked the $1 million cap on medical malpractice damages. The federal district court held the cap was constitutional under the South Dakota and United States Constitutions. On appeal to the Eighth Circuit Court of Appeals, four certified questions were presented and accepted by the South Dakota Supreme Court. For the reasons set forth herein, we hold that the damages cap of SDCL 21-3-11 is unconstitutional. . . .

Kris Knowles was twelve days old when he was admitted for treatment of a fever at the Ellsworth Air Force Base Hospital, near Rapid City, South Dakota. Medical Service Specialists, the Air Force's equivalent to nurses' aides, recorded Kris' temperature. On the night before his discharge, the specialists failed to report to nurses or physicians that Kris' temperature had been dropping throughout that night. Kris developed hypoglycemia and suffered respiratory arrest resulting in severe, permanent brain damage.

William and Jane Knowles brought suit on their own behalf and for Kris for medical malpractice, emotional distress, and loss of consortium. The United States admitted liability for medical malpractice and filed a motion for entry of judgment of $1 million based on SDCL 21-3-11, which limits damages in medical malpractice actions to $1 million. . . . Knowles appealed. . . .

Initially, we note that many courts have invalidated limitations on damages based on their respective state constitutions. [Citing cases from Alabama, Illinois, New Hampshire, North Dakota, Ohio, Texas, Utah, and Washington State.]

Other jurisdictions have upheld a damages cap. [Citing cases from California, Indiana, Kansas, and Virginia.]

However, the questions presented herein generally turn on the particular constitutional provisions of the state and the case law precedent interpreting those provisions. Because the provisions of the South Dakota Constitution guaranteeing the right to jury trial . . . and due process are dispositive, we do not reach the other constitutional questions.

South Dakota Constitution article VI, §6 guarantees the right of trial by jury:

> The right of trial by jury shall remain *inviolate* and shall extend to all cases at law without regard to the amount in controversy[.]

(Emphasis added.) "Inviolate" has been defined as "free from change or blemish: pure, unbroken . . . free from assault or trespass: untouched, intact[.]" Sofie v. Fibreboard Corp., 771 P.2d 711, at 721-22 (Wash. 1989) (citing Webster's New Third International Dictionary, 1190 (1976) (amended by 780 P.2d 260). In discussing the role of the jury, the United States Supreme Court has stated:

> Maintenance of the jury as a fact-finding body is of such importance and occupies so firm a place in our history and jurisprudence that any seeming curtailment of the right to a jury trial should be scrutinized with the utmost care.

Dimick v. Schiedt, 293 U.S. 474, 486 (1935) (assessment of damages is a "matter so peculiarly within the province of the jury[.]").

"A jury is the tribunal provided by law to determine the facts and to fix the amount of damages." Schaffer v. Edward D. Jones & Co., 521 N.W.2d 921, 927 n.9 (S.D. 1994) (citation omitted). "[T]he amount of damages to be awarded is a factual issue to be determined by the trier of fact[.]" Sander v. Geib, Elston, Frost Professional Ass'n, 506 N.W.2d 107, 119 (S.D. 1993). With any jury award for personal injuries, we "have allowed [the jury] 'wide latitude'" in making its award. Id.

> We are unwilling to allow the trial court authority to limit a damages award as a matter of law. . . . *A jury determination of the amount of damages is the essence of the right to trial by jury*—to go beyond the procedural mechanisms now in place [remittitur] for reduction of a verdict and to bind the jury's discretion is to deny this constitutional right.

Moore v. Mobile Infirmary Ass'n, 592 So. 2d 156, 161 (citing Smith v. Dep't of Ins., 507 So. 2d 1080 (Fla. 1987) (invalidating a damages cap on personal injury awards) (emphasis in original). The damages cap is unconstitutional because it limits the jury verdict "automatically and absolutely" which makes the jury's function "less than an advisory status." Id. at 164 (emphasis in original).

SDCL 21-3-11 arbitrarily and without a hearing imposes a limitation of one million dollars on all damages in all medical malpractice actions. It does so without provisions for determining the extent of the injuries or resulting illness, or whether these injuries or illness resulted in death. It purports to cover even those cases where the medical costs occasioned by the malpractice alone exceed one million dollars. In other words, the damages recovered in these cases could actually be payable *to* the wrongdoers for medical expenses, not to the victims. It does so in all cases, even when a judicial determination of damages above one million dollars results from an adversarial hearing after notice. . . .

For these reasons, we hold that the damages cap violates the right to a jury trial under South Dakota Constitution article VI, §6. . . .

Under South Dakota Constitution article VI, §2, "[n]o person shall be deprived of life, liberty or property without due process of law." People have a right to be free from injury. We apply a more stringent test than the federal courts' rational basis test. The statute must "bear a real and substantial relation to the objects sought to be attained." Katz v. Bd. of Med. & Osteopathic Examiners, 432 N.W.2d 274, 278 n.6 (S.D. 1988).

Ohio uses the same test. In Morris v. Savoy, 576 N.E.2d 765, 770-71 (Ohio 1991), the Supreme Court of Ohio held that a medical malpractice damages cap was a violation of due process. A 1987 study by the Insurance Service Organization, which sets the rates of the insurance industry, found that the savings from various tort reforms including a damages cap were "marginal to nonexistent." Id. 576 N.E.2d at 771. The court concluded that the cap was irrational and arbitrary and that it did "not bear a real and substantial relation to public health or welfare[.]" Id.

In Arneson v. Olsen, 270 N.W.2d 125, 136 (N.D. 1978), the North Dakota Supreme Court examined whether a medical malpractice damages cap violated equal protection and due process under the North Dakota constitution:

> Defendants argue that there is a societal quid pro quo in that the loss of recovery potential to some malpractice victims is offset by "lower insurance premiums and lower medical care costs for all recipients of medical care." This quid pro quo does not extend to the seriously injured medical malpractice victim and does not serve to bring the limited recovery provision within the rationale of the cases upholding the constitutionality of the Workmen's Compensation Act.

Id. (quoting Wright v. Central DuPage Hosp. Ass'n, 347 N.E.2d 736, 742 (Ill. 1976). The North Dakota Supreme Court held that the damages cap violated equal protection and due process. *Arneson,* 270 N.W.2d at 135-36.

In Lyons v. Lederle Laboratories, 440 N.W.2d 769, 771 (S.D. 1989), we discussed equal protection rather than due process and stated: "We fail to perceive any rational basis for assuming that medical malpractice claims will diminish simply by requiring that suits be instituted at an earlier date." The statute of limitations in *Lyons,* which carved out an exception for minors which did not allow tolling, created an arbitrary classification of those minors with medical malpractice claims versus other tort claims. Id. Likewise, SDCL 21-3-11 creates arbitrary classifications of medical malpractice claimants and of those claimants who sustain damages over $1 million and those who do not. Those who suffer less than $1 million in damages may be compensated fully while those who suffer more shall have their damages capped.

The arbitrary classification of malpractice claimants based on the amount of damages is not rationally related to the stated purpose of curbing medical malpractice claims. See *Lyons,* 440 N.W.2d at 773 (Sabers, J. concurring specially). The legislation was adopted as a result of "some perceived malpractice crisis." Id. at 771. Many courts and commentators have argued that there was no "crisis" at all.[6]

---

[6] SDCL 21-3-11 was adopted as a result of recommendations by the 1975 South Dakota Legislature's Special Committee on Medical Malpractice. As noted by one commentator:

> Statements made by insurance representatives before the [Committee], referring to the low number of medical malpractice claims brought in the state, can only create significant doubt that South Dakota was experiencing a genuine insurance crisis at that time. Startling data on medical malpractice claims in South Dakota, North Dakota, and Minnesota, collected by the Minnesota Department of Commerce from 1982-1987 [the Hatch Study], also tends to call into question the basis for cries of *any* insurance crisis; if claim frequency and severity did not change significantly in those years, and if in those same six years only one-half of one percent of all medical malpractice plaintiffs were awarded any damages, why then did physicians' insurance premiums *triple* in that same time period?

Gail Eiesland, Note, Miller v. Gilmore: *The Constitutionality of South Dakota's Medical Malpractice Statute of Limitations,* 38 S.D. L. Rev. 672, 703 (1993) (emphasis in original).

The Hatch Study concluded that "[d]espite unchanging claim frequency and declining loss payments and loss expense, on average, physicians paid approximately triple the amount of premiums for malpractice insurance in 1987 than in 1982." Hatch Study, at 31. During that time period, there were three files where a company paid $1 million or more, and 15 files where a company paid equal to or greater than $500,000. Hatch Study, at 15-16. The Hatch Study was a study of the two major medical malpractice insurers for Minnesota, North Dakota, and South Dakota during 1982-1987.

Evidence presented to the 1975 Committee indicated that only two jury verdicts in the last few years had been obtained against doctors in South Dakota. One verdict was for $1 and the other was for $10,000.

In *Arneson,* 270 N.W.2d at 136, the North Dakota Supreme Court upheld the trial court's finding that no medical malpractice insurance availability or cost crisis existed:

> The Legislature was advised that malpractice insurance rates were determined on a national basis, and did not take into account the state-wide experience of smaller States such as North Dakota. Thus, premiums were unjustifiably high for States such as North Dakota with fewer claims and smaller settlements and judgments.

Id. Similar evidence on how rates are calculated was presented to the 1975 South Dakota Committee.

In addition, a 1986 report by the National Association of Attorneys General concluded that "insurance premium increases were not related to any purported liability crisis, but 'result[ed] largely from the insurance industry's own mismanagement.'" [Gail Eiesland, Note, Miller v. Gilmore: *The*

As noted by the court in Hoem v. State, 756 P.2d 780 (Wyo. 1988):

> It cannot seriously be contended that the extension of special benefits to the medical profession and the imposition of an additional hurdle in the path of medical malpractice victims relate to the protection of the public health.

756 P.2d at 783.

In *Moore*, 592 So. 2d at 167-169, the court examined several studies to conclude that the connection between recovery caps and decreased malpractice insurance rates was "at best, indirect and remote." Id. at 168. The court balanced this remote connection against the "direct and concrete" burden on severely injured claimants. Id. at 169; see Carson, 424 A.2d at 837 (It is "unfair and unreasonable to impose the burden of supporting the medical care industry solely upon those persons who are most severely injured and therefore most in need of compensation."). "[T]he statute operates to the advantage not only of negligent health care providers over other tortfeasors, but of those health care providers who are *most irresponsible.*" *Moore*, 592 So. 2d at 169 (emphasis in original). . . .

SDCL 21-3-11 does not treat each medical malpractice claimant uniformly. It divides claimants into two classes: those whose damages are less than $1 million and those whose damages exceed $1 million. Those who have awards below the statutory cap shall be fully compensated for their injury while those exceeding the cap are not.

Therefore, SDCL 21-3-11 does not bear a "real and substantial relation to the objects sought to be obtained" and we hold that the damages cap violates due process guaranteed by South Dakota Constitution article VI, §2.

In this instance, if we assume that the economic damages are $2 million and the noneconomic damages are $1 million, it becomes clear that the statute is neither reasonable nor constitutional. The reasons are many, but the most basic is that the statute impermissibly gives all the benefits to the wrongdoer (his liability is limited to $1 million) while it places all the corresponding detriment on the negligently injured victim (his recovery, economic & noneconomic, is limited to $1 million). There is no quid pro quo or "commensurate benefit" here. Despite a claimed medical malpractice crisis in the *rural* areas of this state, this legislation wholly failed to differentiate between rural and urban problems and solutions. It purported to cover *all* practitioners of the healing arts, including chiropractors and dentists. There is no showing of a shortage of chiropractors or dentists. The statutes purported to cover the entire state even though there was no medical malpractice crisis in the urban areas such as Minnehaha and Pennington Counties, as opposed to the rural areas.

Even in this case, we are dealing with a United States Air Force hospital situated in Pennington County. There is no showing that any United States Air Force hospital had any difficulty obtaining and keeping practitioners of the healing arts. This legislation does not bear a *real* and *substantial* relation to the objects sought to be attained and it violates many rights in the process. The fact that certain fringe benefits may result to the public in general is insufficient to save this statute. The same rationale applies to

---

Constitutionality of South Dakota's Medical Malpractice Statute of Limitations, 38 S.D. L. Rev. 672,] 685 n. 121 (quoting W. John Thomas, *The Medical Malpractice "Crisis": A Critical Examination of a Public Debate,* 65 Temp. L. Rev. 459, 473 (1992) (quoting National Association of Attorneys General, *An Analysis of the Causes of the Current Crisis of Unavailability and Unaffordability of Liability Insurance* (1986))).

prior versions of the statute. Therefore, they violate the constitutional provisions stated herein.

We are not saying that the state cannot subsidize health practitioners or even the health insurance industry. We are simply saying that it cannot be done in this manner to the sole detriment of the injured. Obviously, fewer constitutional objections would exist if the state would pay the difference to the injured; or, before the fact, to the insurer or health care provider; or, in all personal injury actions, all damages, economic and noneconomic, were limited in reasonable proportions for all those wrongfully injured for the benefit of all wrongdoers. We decline to comment on the wisdom, as opposed to the constitutionality of such approach. . . .

NOTES TO ETHERIDGE v. MEDICAL CENTER HOSPITALS AND KNOWLES v. UNITED STATES

1. *Right to a Jury Trial.* The Virginia Constitution states that "trial by jury is preferable to any other, and ought to be held *sacred.*" The South Dakota Constitution states that "The right of trial by jury shall remain *inviolate.*" Does the difference between *sacred* and *inviolate* explain the courts' different outcomes? If not, what is the key difference in their analyses?

2. *Due Process Rights.* Virginia and South Dakota use different tests for when constitutional due process rights have been violated. What are the differences? If each had used the other's test, would the outcomes have been different?

3. *The "Insurance Crisis."* In footnote 6 and in the conclusion of its opinion in Knowles v. United States, the South Dakota court questioned whether there was any need for tort reform. Would knowing whether in fact a crisis did exist affect an analysis of who benefits and who suffers from the adoption of a ceiling on damages?

13

TRADITIONAL STRICT LIABILITY

I. Introduction

For injuries caused by some kinds of activities, tort law imposes liability without regard to the actor's fault. This type of liability is usually called *strict liability*. From the point of view of a plaintiff, characterizing an activity as subject to strict liability provides a great benefit. The plaintiff does not have to show that the defendant was at fault or engaged in tortious conduct, or intended the injury, or acted negligently. A problem for contemporary tort law is determining when strict liability doctrines should apply. This chapter examines strict liability in traditional contexts of injuries caused by animals and by particularly dangerous activities. The cases in these traditional areas of strict liability describe underlying criteria for deciding whether strict liability should apply.

II. Injuries Caused by Animals

Animals can injure people, for example by biting or kicking them. Common law doctrines impose strict liability for these types of injuries when inflicted by wild animals. For injuries caused by a domesticated animal, a negligence-based cause of action is always available, but the animal's owner can also be subject to strict liability if the owner knew that the particular animal was vicious. In some states, statutes apply to injuries by domesticated animals, typically imposing strict liability regardless of the owner's knowledge of the animal's propensities.

Animals can also damage property, for example by knocking over structures, by colliding with vehicles, or by eating crops. At common law, property damage by all types of trespassing animals was governed by strict liability. Some state statutes modify the common law by allowing a strict liability action for destruction of property only if the plaintiff had maintained a fence to attempt to protect the plaintiff's property.

Clark v. Brings, involving injuries caused by a Siamese cat, introduces the common law and statutory approaches to personal injuries caused by animals. Byram v. Main, involving property damage by a trespassing donkey, reviews Maine's 1857 doctrines on the subject and applies them in a contemporary setting.

CLARK v. BRINGS

169 N.W.2d 407 (Minn. 1969)

PETERSON, J.

While working as a babysitter for respondents' three young children, appellant was without warning attacked and bitten by their pet Siamese cat. She brought this action to recover for the extensive injuries which allegedly resulted, and she appeals from an order denying a new trial after the court below directed a verdict for respondents and from the judgment entered pursuant to that verdict. These alternative contentions are argued: (1) That the common-law cause of action for injuries by animals should be changed, or the statute covering injuries by dogs judicially extended, to hold owners of cats strictly liable for the acts of their pets; (2) that the evidence in this case should be held sufficient to prove a cause of action under the common law as it now stands, that is, to show that respondents' cat was dangerous and that they were aware of the fact. . . .

Most of the problems in this appeal fall within the ambit of the common-law's system of distributing the costs of misbehavior by animals. The relevant cause of action in tort, sometimes called "the scienter action,"[1] which is not, at least in this jurisdiction, based on negligence, divides animals held as property into two classes: Domesticated animals, or those *mansuetae* or *domitae naturae*, and wild beasts, or those *ferae naturae*. In the case of injury by one of the first class, the plaintiff must prove that the particular animal was abnormal and dangerous, and that its owner or harborer let it run unfettered though he actually or constructively had knowledge of its harmful propensities — knowledge usually found to have been gleaned from specific acts of the animal prior to the injury sued upon. The possessor of an animal within the second class, on the other hand, is conclusively presumed to know of the danger, so a person injured need not prove such knowledge before he can recover.

This judicial distinction between classes of animals was clearly announced, at least by dicta, as early as 1730. The scienter action as it has come down to us is not without its modern critics, who would apply the simpler rules of liability for negligence to some or all of the situations it covers, but the ancient doctrine has long been given continuous approval and application in Minnesota.

Appellant first contends that this distinction is based on comparative economic utility, the owners of "useful" animals being somewhat protected as an encouragement to maintaining them and the owners of "useless" animals receiving no protection whatever. Although the cat may once have served rural society as a "mouser," it is argued, in modern cities it is merely a dispensable pet, the owner of which ought to be held, as would the owner of a tiger, liable for any damage it causes.

So far as this argument may be based on the relative productivity of animals, it is not well founded. It is true that the economic contribution made by certain animals has been considered by the courts in the difficult cases of animals whose tameness has

---

[1] Williams, Liability for Animals, Part Five. The name derives from a phrase in the ancient writ, "scienter retinuit," or "knowingly he has kept" a dangerous animal. Id. p.273.

seemed in doubt. Thus, holding bees to be domesticated, the court in Earl v. Van Alstine, 8 Barb. (N.Y.) 630, 636, said that "the law looks with more favor upon the keeping of animals that are useful to man, than such as are purely noxious and useless." It is also true that many of the animals which have been held to be of a harmless nature, such as milch cows, are obviously more economically productive and, in that narrow sense, more useful to society than are cats. . . .

A close examination of the authorities shows that the law's division of animals into those domesticated and those dangerous is based rather on "[e]xperience as interpreted by the English law." Holmes, The Common Law, p.157. Horses, cows, and other animals have been regarded by the courts as *domitae naturae* because "years ago, and continuously to the present time, the progeny of these classes has been found by experience to be harmless, and so the law assumes the result of this experience to be correct without further proof." Filburn v. People's Palace and Aquarium Co. L.R. 25 Q.B. 258, 260. In cases where there is doubt as to the propensities of a species, rather than looking to economic utility, . . . the courts may instead admit expert testimony on the question, as in Spring Co. v. Edgar, 99 U.S. (9 Otto) 645, 25 L. Ed. 487, involving deer kept in a park. More often, however, courts simply take judicial notice of an animal's characteristics, as in one of the earliest cases, Mason v. Keeling, 12 Mod. 332, 335, 88 Eng. Reprint 1359, 1361, where the court remarked that "the law takes notice, that a dog is not of a fierce nature, but rather the contrary." . . .

We should be most reluctant, therefore, to be the first to observe judicially in this little house pet, the cat, the "fearful symmetry" which the poet, William Blake, saw in the tiger. If the law has erred in interpreting mankind's experience with cats, or if this animal's value to society strikes an inadequate balance against whatever damage and injury it might cause, then it is for the legislature, which can best assess the total dimension of the problem, to change the common law by statute.

This change, appellant asserts alternatively, has in fact been accomplished by the legislature. She argues that Minn. St. 347.22, which makes the owner of a dog liable for the bites which it might without provocation inflict on those rightfully coming near it, by necessary implication includes cats — that is, if the owner of one pet is thus to be held liable, then the same statutory policy should be applied to the owner of another.

Minn. St. 347.22 (L. 1951, c. 315, §1) was the first statute on this subject and provides:

> If a dog, without provocation, attacks or injures any person who is peaceably conducting himself in any place where he may lawfully be in any urban area, the owner of the dog is liable in damages to the person so attacked or injured to the full amount of the injury sustained. The term "owner" includes any person harboring or keeping a dog. The term "dog" includes both male and female of the canine species.

Before 1951, a person bitten by a dog in Minnesota could recover only through the scienter action.

Whatever the theory on which this statute was enacted, its close wording would seem to preclude any extension of its severe provisions to the owners of other animals, even those others of the "leisured classes" of pets. This court has not so extended this statute in other cases, for since its enactment we have continued to apply the common law in cases involving all other beasts, including both farm animals, such as [a] bull, and animals kept for pleasure, such as [a] riding horse. . . .

If the Minnesota Legislature had in 1951 intended to revise the common law as to cats in the same manner as it abolished it as to dogs, there would have been no difficulty in doing so expressly, and there would be no apparent barrier to amending the statute now. Absent legislative action, we decline to hold that Minn. St. 347.22 applies to the owners of cats.

We must consider, then, whether appellant made out a jury issue as to her scienter action. To prove that respondents' cat had committed prior acts of viciousness, known to them, appellant's evidence was threefold: First, the cat had once before bitten a babysitter; second, the cat had scratched several members of the household; and third, the cat was usually confined to the basement.

The biting incident, although not without significance, is less significant than appellant would acknowledge. The babysitter who had been bitten testified that the incident occurred when she and the children were playing with the cat by pulling a spool across the basement floor on a string. The cat became excited from chasing it, she related, and inflicted a "superficial" bite on her ankle. The respondents, moreover, were not informed of this "attack" incident. . . .

It is true that a pet's owner need not "have notice that the animal has frequently 'broken through the tameness of his nature' into acts of aggression," and that the notice is sufficient should the animal just once "throw off the habits of domesticity and tameness, and . . . put on a savage nature." Kittredge v. Elliott, 16 N.H. 77, 81. "It is not true, as has often been stated, that 'the law allows a dog his first bite,' for if the owner has good reason to apprehend, from his knowledge of the nature and propensity of the animal, that he has become evilly inclined, the duty of care and restraint attaches." Cuney v. Campbell, 76 Minn. 59, 62, 78 N.W. 878, 879. Here, however, the testimony shows that the cat was provoked and excited by play when it inflicted the first injury, and the authorities universally hold that "[s]uch an attack is no evidence of viciousness in the animal . . . and is insufficient to render the owner liable. . . ." Erickson v. Bronson, 81 Minn. 258, 259, 83 N.W. 988. At best, to say that this bite "was vicious is merely conjecture," and the testimony thus cannot withstand a motion for a directed verdict. Eastman v. Scott, 182 Mass. 192, 194, 64 N.E. 968, 969.

The evidence that the cat had several times scratched respondents themselves, their children, and their other babysitters is scarcely more significant. The cat usually scratched them on their hands, it appears, when they were picking it up or playfully handling it. . . . [I]njuries of so slight a nature as those shown, unaccompanied by any indications of a propensity of the cat to cause greater harm, are inadequate to prove that it was dangerous and ought to have been caged or destroyed.

Appellant relies upon evidence that respondents kept their cat confined in their basement to establish knowledge and acknowledgment by respondents that their cat was dangerous. There is indeed authority to the effect that such restraint of a pet may be proof that the animal was, as its owner knew, vicious. . . . The sort of confinement shown in the case at bar, however, could hardly support an inference that respondents knew of any danger from their cat. It was kept in the basement, they testified, simply to prevent its scratching their living room furniture, not to protect against attack upon people. Respondents' three children, the youngest only about 3 years old, shared with the cat a furnished basement recreation room, where many of their toys were kept and where they often played. The precautions taken to keep the cat downstairs were minimal, consisting largely of a catch on the basement door, and the restraint was not continuously effective. The trial court, in our opinion, rightly considered the whole of this evidence far too tenuous for submission to the jury. . . .

Affirmed.

NOTES TO CLARK v. BRINGS

1. *Negligence Theory for Animal Injuries.* The *Clark* opinion shows that when a person is injured by an animal, recovery against the keeper of the animal may be based on strict liability (with no required showing of fault) or may require a showing of negligence, depending on what kind of animal is involved. In what cases must plaintiffs prove fault? Based on the facts provided in the opinion, what difficulties would the plaintiff have faced in attempting to establish negligence?

2. *Strict Liability for Animal Injuries.* The common law doctrine exposes the owner of a wild animal to strict liability for harms caused by that animal. The Restatement (Second) of Torts §506 defines "wild animal" as an animal that "is not by custom devoted to the service of mankind at the time and place at which it is kept." A cow in New York City or an elephant in New Delhi may be classified differently than a cow in rural Vermont or an elephant in rural India. This approach is consistent with both the reciprocal risk and best cost-avoider approaches. The Restatement (Third) of Torts: Liability for Physical and Emotional Harm §22 defines "wild animal" as "an animal that belongs to a category which has not been generally domesticated and which is likely, unless restrained, to cause personal injury." Would judicial treatment of a cow be different under the Second and Third Restatements? Animals that have been classified as wild include a tiger named Stubby, in Franken v. Sioux Center, 272 N.W.2d 422 (Iowa 1978); a zebra, in Smith v. Jalbert, 221 N.E.2d 744 (Mass. 1966); and a coyote, in Collins v. Otto, 369 P.2d 564 (Colo. 1962).

The common law also imposed strict liability for injuries inflicted by domesticated animals where the animal's owner knew or had reason to know that the animal had dangerous tendencies abnormal to its breed. This is sometimes called the "one bite" rule of strict liability, but that description of the rule is too simplistic. In Clark v. Brings, the court concluded that the cat's previous bites were insufficient to create strict liability. Moreover, the court observed that conduct other than a bite could put an animal's owner on notice that the animal had an aggressive nature. If non-bite conduct had given the owner a basis for knowing that a domesticated animal was vicious, then the owner would be subject to strict liability for any bite injury the animal later inflicted.

3. *Statutory Liability for Animal Injuries* Many states have enacted statutes similar to the Minnesota statute quoted by the court in *Clark.* The plaintiff argued that the statute governed this case. Note that while the statute can be described as imposing strict liability, it would not support recovery even for every person bitten by a dog. What reasoning did the court use to say that this statute should not apply to injuries cats inflict?

4. *Defenses* The Restatement (Second) of Torts §515 treats assumption of risk as a complete defense in a case of strict liability for harm caused by an animal, but does not allow a defense of contributory negligence. The Restatement (Third) of Torts: Liability for Physical and Emotional Harm §25 and comment e, reflecting the shift of most jurisdictions to a comparative negligence system, permits a reduction in the plaintiff's recovery of damages that reflects all forms of the plaintiff's contributory negligence, including unreasonable assumption of risk.

Problem
Negligence Versus Strict Liability

Bullu was an old tamed elephant kept by a circus for the purpose of entertaining circus patrons by performing tricks in the center ring of the show. Bullu also participated in parades used by the circus to attract patrons to its performances. During one parade, Bullu was scared by a dog, escaped from the handler, and ran through the circus grounds trampling a girl who was attending the parade. If the girl sues the circus, must she prove negligence on the part of the circus or may she rely on strict liability? See Behrens v. Bertram Mills Circus, Ltd., 2 Q.B. 1 (1957).

Statute: HARBORING A DOG

S.D. Codified Laws §40-34-2 (2017)

Any person owning, keeping, or harboring a dog that chases, worries, injures or kills any poultry or domestic animal is guilty of a Class 2 misdemeanor and is liable for damages to the owner thereof for any injury caused by the dog to any such poultry or animal. . . .

NOTE TO STATUTE

Statutory Recognition of Particular Harms.   The South Dakota statute provides a specific definition of the harms it seeks to remedy. If a defendant's dog entered a farmyard and bit both a farmer and a chicken, what effect would the statute have on potential recovery for harms caused by those bites?

Perspective: Rationale for Strict Liability

The court in *Clark* considers and rejects *comparative economic utility* as the basis for imposing strict liability only on wild animals. Other arguments for imposing strict liability in selected cases include the *reciprocal risk* theory and *best cost-avoider* theory. Consider how each of these theories coincides with the Restatement definitions of what animals are wild.

The reciprocal risk theory suggests that strict liability is reserved for those whose conduct imposes risks on others unlike the risk others impose on them. For instance, we all impose similar (reciprocal) risks on one another by our conduct in driving automobiles. Because the risks are reciprocal, the negligence standard is applied. A person keeping a grizzly bear or blasting with dynamite, however, imposes risks on others that are not reciprocal. The people who might be harmed by the bear or the blasting do not typically expose others to the risks of attack by a bear or harm from blasting.

The best cost-avoider theory suggests that for some categories of activities one of the parties almost always has superior knowledge of the risks presented by the conduct and how they may be avoided. This superior knowledge puts that party in the best position to avoid the costs associated with the activity. For activities in which many engage — automobile driving, for instance — generalizing about which party is the best cost-avoider is difficult, and the negligence standard is appropriate. For conduct that is not customary at a particular place at a particular time, the person engaging in the conduct is quite likely to be the best cost-avoider, and court time is saved by making that person strictly liable.

<hr>

BYRAM v. MAIN
523 A.2d 1387 (Me. 1987)

McKusick, C.J.

Defendant Peter Main appeals from a judgment entered on August 22, 1986, by the Superior Court (Penobscot County) in the amount of $27,483.52 for plaintiff Ray Byram. After a jury-waived trial the court found Main strictly liable for damages to Byram's tractor-trailer rig caused in the early morning hours of July 22, 1981, when Byram's rig struck Meadow, the pet donkey of Main's daughter, which had escaped from its enclosure and wandered onto Interstate 95 in Orono. The judgment here on review was entered following a second trial in this case, on remand from plaintiff Byram's earlier appeal to this court. . . . Before the second trial Byram amended his complaint to add a strict liability count, and by stipulation of the parties the original negligence count was dismissed with prejudice.

The sole issue presented by this second appeal is whether the owner of a domestic animal that has escaped and wandered onto a high-speed public highway is strictly liable for harm resulting from a motor vehicle's collision with that animal. Main urges us that the Superior Court erred in relying upon Decker v. Gammon, 44 Me. 322 (1857), as authority for imposing strict liability upon him and that there is no basis in common law for finding strict liability on the facts of this case. We agree, and therefore vacate the judgment for Byram. In doing so we adopt for application to the present facts the rule of liability set forth in the Restatement (Second) of Torts §518 (1977).

Decker defines three classes of cases in which the owners of animals are liable for harm done by them to others:

1. The owner of wild beasts, or beasts that are in their nature vicious, is, *under all circumstances*, liable for injuries done by them. . . .
2. If domestic animals, such as oxen and horses, injure any one, . . . *if they are rightfully in the place where they do the mischief,* the owner of such animals is not liable for such injury, unless he knew that they were accustomed to do mischief. . . .
3. The owner of domestic animals, *if they are wrongfully in the place where they do any mischief,* is liable for it, though he had no notice that they had been accustomed to do so before.

. . . Id. at 327-29 (emphasis in original). The Superior Court found that the case at bar fell within the third class.

The Superior Court misinterpreted the *Decker* court's use of the word "wrongfully" when it included in that term the donkey's extremely inappropriate presence on the interstate. Viewing *Decker* against the backdrop of the common law, we read that opinion to say that cases involving trespass by domestic animals are the only cases imposing strict liability encompassed in the third class. Under common law both in 1857 and today, an owner of a domestic animal not known to be abnormally dangerous is strictly liable only for harms caused by that animal while trespassing; if the animal causes harm in a public place, no liability is imposed upon the owner without a finding that the owner was at fault. Restatement (Second) of Torts §§504, 509, 518 (1977). The *Decker* court, in defining three classes of cases, set forth the whole common law of animal owner liability so as to fit the particular case before it into that general framework. The holding of the *Decker* case was limited to its facts. The *Decker* court decided only that strict liability applies in a fact situation that supports a trespass action. . . .

We realize that since 1857 radical changes have occurred in the nature and use of public highways, particularly those with limited access and high-speed motor traffic. Despite those changes, however, we do not read *Decker*'s words "wrongfully in the place" to apply to the facts of the case at bar. The general development of the law has not been in that direction. In fact *Decker*, when its third class is correctly interpreted to include animal trespass cases but not cases where the animal is in a merely inappropriate place when it causes harm, is still a remarkably good statement of the common law as it remains today, as reflected by the Restatement.

Furthermore, the considerations that support the strict liability rules in animal trespass and wild animal cases do not apply to the present facts. The liability imposed by courts in cases described by the third *Decker* category and by section 504 of the Restatement and the comments following[5] developed as an extension of liability for trespass by persons; the possessor of a domestic animal was identified with the animal, so that when it trespassed the owner trespassed. The imposition of strict liability for trespass protects the crucial right of the possessor of land to its exclusive use and control. Strict liability could not serve that same purpose in the case at bar because no individual has the right to the exclusive use and control of a public highway.

The first *Decker* rule, now set forth in Restatement (Second) of Torts §507,[6] imposes strict liability for the consequences of keeping a wild animal, an activity

---

[5] Restatement (Second) of Torts §504 (1977) provides in pertinent part:

> (1) . . . [A] possessor of livestock intruding upon the land of another is subject to liability for the intrusion although he has exercised the utmost care to prevent them from intruding.
> (2) The liability stated in Subsection (1) extends to any harm to the land or to its possessor or a member of his household, or their chattels, which might reasonably be expected to result from the intrusion of livestock.

"Livestock" is defined in comment (b) thereto as "those kinds of domestic animals and fowls normally susceptible of confinement within boundaries without seriously impairing their utility and the intrusion of which upon the land of others normally causes harm to the land or to crops thereon."

[6] Restatement (Second) of Torts §507 (1977) provides:

> (1) A possessor of a wild animal is subject to liability to another for harm done by the animal to the other, his person, land or chattels, although the possessor has exercised the utmost care to confine the animal, or otherwise prevent it from doing harm.
> (2) This liability is limited to harm that results from a dangerous propensity that is characteristic of wild animals of the particular class, or of which the possessor knows or has reason to know.

that, while not wrongful, exposes the community to an obvious abnormal danger.[7] The keeper of a wild animal "takes the risk that at any moment the animal may revert to and exhibit" "the dangerous propensities normal to the class to which it belongs." Restatement (Second) of Torts §507 comment c, at 11-12. Nonetheless, strict liability is not applied to all damages caused by wild animals. Even a wild animal that goes astray and causes damage to a highway traveler in circumstances similar to those of the case at bar would not at common law bring strict liability down upon its keeper.

> [The possessor of a wild animal] is liable for only such harm as the propensities of the animal's class or its known abnormal tendencies make it likely that it will inflict. Thus . . . if [a tame] bear, having escaped, goes to sleep in the highway and is run into by a carefully driven motor car on a dark night, the possessor of the bear is not liable for harm to the motorist in the absence of negligence in its custody.

Id. comment e, at 12. The rationale for imposing strict liability upon the owners of wild animals thus does not support applying anything beyond a negligence rule on the facts presented to us here.

For the purposes of this decision, therefore, we adopt the approach of Restatement (Second) of Torts §518, which is supported by the case law in Maine and elsewhere:

> Except for animal trespass, one who possesses or harbors a domestic animal that he does not know or have reason to know to be abnormally dangerous, is subject to liability for harm done . . . if, but only if,
> (a) he intentionally causes the animal to do the harm, or
> (b) he is negligent in failing to prevent the harm.

We, as does the Restatement, leave the highway traveler who is injured by colliding with a stray domestic animal solely to his remedy in negligence. The degree of care required of the animal owner is of course commensurate with the propensities of the particular domestic animal and with the location, including proximity to high-speed highways, of the place where the animal is kept by its owner. Whether the owners of large domestic pets should be required to bear more stringent responsibilities for those animals than are imposed by common law is a question the public policy makers of the other branches of state government may well wish to address.

The entry is: Judgment vacated. Remanded with directions to enter judgment for defendant.

NOTES TO BYRAM v. MAIN

1. *Limits on Strict Liability for Wild Animal Injuries.* The court in *Byram* discussed a limitation on the strict liability applied to the owner of a wild animal for injuries caused by that animal, stating that the liability will be applied only for injuries caused by its "abnormal danger," by "the dangerous propensities normal to the class to which it belongs," and by dangers "of which the possessor knows or has reason to know." What significance did these limitations have for the court's resolution of the case?

2. *Strict Liability for Trespassing Animals.* Byram v. Main focused on whether it matters where the animal was when it caused harm, not on the classification of the

---

[7] The keeping of wild animals is categorized with such dangerous activities as blasting, pile driving, storing inflammable liquids, and accumulating sewage. Prosser and Keeton on Torts §76, at 541, §78, at 547.

animal as wild or domesticated. The location of the collision between the plaintiff's vehicle and the defendant's donkey was an interstate highway. How did that fact affect the court's resolution of the case? If the collision had occurred in the plaintiff's drive-way, would the result have been the same?

Statute: TRESPASS ON CULTIVATED LAND

Nev. Rev. Stat. Ann. §569.450 (2017)

No person is entitled to collect damages, and no court in this state may award damages, for any trespass of livestock on cultivated land in this state if the land, at the time of the trespass was not enclosed by a legal fence.

Statute: RECOVERY FOR DAMAGE TO
UNFENCED LANDS; EXCEPTION

Ariz. Rev. Stat. §3-1427 (2017)

An owner or occupant of land is not entitled to recover for damage resulting from the trespass of animals unless the land is enclosed within a lawful fence, but this section shall not apply to owners or occupants of land in no-fence districts.

Statute: [NO-FENCE DISTRICT] FORMATION

Ariz. Rev. Stat. §3-1421 (2017)

A. A majority of all taxpayers [of localities meeting certain definitions] may petition the board of supervisors of the county in which such district or land is situated that a no-fence district be formed and that no fence be required around the land in the no-fence district designated in the petition.

B. Upon filing the petition, the board shall immediately enter the contents upon its records and order that the no-fence district be formed.

NOTE TO STATUTES

The common law favors those who cultivate land over those who raise cattle by requiring keepers of animals to fence them in or be liable for their trespasses. This tension between farmers and ranchers has been resolved in some states in favor of ranchers, with statutes that prohibit a strict liability action unless the plaintiff has attempted to protect his or her land (and crops) with a fence. The Nevada statute is an example of a "fencing out" statute. The Arizona statutes offer options to be selected by local areas.

III. Selected Dangerous Activities

An 1868 English case, Rylands v. Fletcher, imposed strict liability on a landowner for harm caused to a neighbor when water collected on the defendant's land escaped onto the plaintiff's land. Relying on that famous case about the "activity" of collecting water in a holding pond, American courts have considered what other activities should be subject to strict liability.

Clark-Aiken Co. v. Cromwell-Wright Co. examines the significance of Rylands v. Fletcher and applies the criteria set out in the Restatement (Second) of Torts to harm caused by water that escaped from a dam maintained by the defendant. Klein v. Pyrodyne Corp. decides whether damages from an injury associated with the display of fireworks on the Fourth of July in a public park should be available on a strict liability theory. Ely v. Cabot Oil & Gas Corp. applies the Restatement (Second) of Torts factors to determine whether strict liability should apply to hydraulic fracturing.

CLARK-AIKEN CO. v. CROMWELL-WRIGHT CO.
323 N.E.2d 876 (Mass. 1975)

TAURO, J.

This case is before us pursuant to G.L.c. 231, §111, on a report by a judge of the Superior Court. The question submitted on report is as follows: "Does Count II of the plaintiff's declaration set forth a cause of action known to the law of the Commonwealth of Massachusetts?"

The plaintiff brought an action in tort in two counts; the first alleging negligence, the second in strict liability. It seeks to recover for damage caused when water allegedly stored behind a dam on the defendant's property was released and flowed onto its property. A Superior Court judge sustained the defendant's demurrer on the ground that "Count II . . . does not allege a cause of action under the law of this Commonwealth." He held that, "in order to recover for damage caused by the water which escaped from the dam owned by the Defendants, the Plaintiffs must allege and prove that the escape was caused by intentional or negligent fault of some person or entity." The sole issue before us is whether a cause of action in strict liability exists in this Commonwealth regardless of considerations of fault on the part of the defendant. After careful consideration, we conclude that strict liability as enunciated in the case of Rylands v. Fletcher, [1868] L.R. 3 H.L. 330, is, and has been, the law of the Commonwealth. . . .

The doctrine known as strict liability, or absolute liability without fault, was first enunciated in the English case of Rylands v. Fletcher, supra. In that case, the defendants had a reservoir built on land located above a number of vacant mine shafts. When the reservoir was partially filled it burst through one of the underlying shafts, causing water to flow into the plaintiff's coal workings. The actual construction of the reservoir was undertaken by contractors of the defendants, who were found to have been negligent. The defendants themselves were unaware of the shafts, and were found not to have been negligent. The trial court found for the defendants. Fletcher v. Rylands, [1865] 3 H. & C. 774, 799.

On appeal, this decision was reversed in Fletcher v. Rylands, [1866] L.R. 1 Ex. 265. The lower appellate court considered two possible courses in the case: it could be decided on the basis of negligence, in which case the court would be required to face the issue of whether a defendant would be liable for the acts of its contractors,[3] or it could be viewed as a strict liability case, thereby obviating the need for making such a determination.

The court concluded, "[T]he true rule of law is, that the person who for his own purposes brings on his lands and collects and keeps there anything likely to do mischief if it escapes must keep it in at his peril, and, if he does not do so, is prima facie answerable for all the damage which is the natural consequence of its escape." [1866] L.R. 1 Ex. at 279. After reaching this conclusion, Mr. Justice Blackburn stated, "The view which we take of the first point *renders it unnecessary to consider* whether the defendants would or would not be responsible for the want of care and skill in the persons employed by them" (emphasis added). Id. at 287. It is clear that negligence was not a factor in the appellate court's decision of the case. Were it otherwise, the court would have been required to reach an issue on which it specifically reserved decision. In imposing strict liability, it also ruled that where only the contractors were found to have been negligent, and considering the then state of English law, negligence could not be imputed to the defendants. Thus, negligence was clearly irrelevant to the decision in that case.

On appeal to the House of Lords, Mr. Justice Blackburn's decision was upheld, although the doctrine of strict liability was narrowed somewhat. Speaking for the House, Lord Cairns stated: "[I]f the Defendants . . . had desired to use . . . [their land] for any purpose which I may term a non-natural use . . . and if in consequence of their doing so, *or* in consequence of any imperfection in the mode of their doing so, the water came to escape . . . that which the Defendants were doing they were doing at their own peril; and, if in the course of their doing it, the evil arose . . . [escape and resulting injury] then for the consequence of that, in my opinion, the Defendants would be liable" (emphasis added). Rylands v. Fletcher, [1868] L.R. 3 H.L. at 339. Although Lord Cairns limited the doctrine to include liability only for "non-natural" uses of one's land, he indicated that he "entirely concur[red]" with Mr. Justice Blackburn's analysis. Id. at 340. Further, in using the disjunctive "or" in the quotation above, he made clear that conduct of the activity itself is sufficient for imposition of liability, and that imperfection in the mode of doing so, or negligence, is merely an alternative basis therefor. . . .

Rylands v. Fletcher, supra, has been cited with approval by this court on many subsequent occasions, but liability has not been imposed in reliance thereon for a variety of reasons. These include findings that the activity in question was neither ultrahazardous nor extraordinary, Fibre Leather Mfg. Corp. v. Ramsay Mills, Inc., 329 Mass. 575, 577 (1952) ("[T]he rule of Rylands v. Fletcher 'applies to unusual and extraordinary uses [of land] which are so fraught with peril to others that the owner should not be permitted to adopt them for his own purposes without absolutely protecting his neighbors from injury or loss by reason of the use.' Where, however, the injury complained of is caused by a use that is 'ordinary and usual and in a sense natural, as incident to the ownership of the land,' liability is imposed only for negligence. . . . The installation and use of the tank in the circumstances disclosed here were not extraordinary or unusual and involved no great threat of harm to others."), and findings that one of the exceptions to the general rule was applicable . . . Cohen v. Brockton Sav. Bank, 320 Mass. 690 (1947) (act of third persons). In none of

---

[3] At that time, such liability did not exist in England. In fact, liability for the acts of contractors was not established until ten years later in Bower v. Peate, [1876] 1 Q.B.D. 321. See Prosser, Torts, §78, p.505, fn. 45 (4th ed. 1971).

these cases, however, was the validity and vitality of the doctrine challenged, and in all, it was affirmed.

Strict liability without regard to negligence or fault exists in this Commonwealth in other contexts. Notable among these are the blasting cases, where there has never been any dispute that "one carrying on blasting operations is liable without proof of negligence for all *direct* injuries to the property of another" (emphasis added). Coughlan v. Grande & Son, Inc., 332 Mass. 464, 467 (1955). Likewise, strict liability is often imposed for the keeping of wild animals. "The owner or keeper of a wild animal is strictly liable to another for damage done to his person or property. And this liability does not depend on proof of previous acts showing a vicious disposition; nor can the owner or keeper escape liability by showing that he has exercised the utmost care to confine the animal or otherwise prevent it from doing harm." Smith v. Jalbert, 351 Mass. 432, 435 (1966). The policy underlying Rylands v. Fletcher, supra, that one who for his own benefit keeps a dangerous instrumentality should be liable per se for its escape, is equally applicable to these cases. . . .

In light of what we have said, it becomes necessary to examine the parameters of the strict liability doctrine to determine whether it is applicable to the facts as pleaded in count 2 of the declaration in this case. As previously stated, Lord Cairns in Rylands v. Fletcher, supra, narrowed the applicability of strict liability to those uses of one's property which could be termed "non-natural." This limitation subsequently developed into the requirement that, in order to subject a landowner to strict liability, he must be using his property in an "unusual and extraordinary" way. Ainsworth v. Lakin, 180 Mass. 397, 400 (1902).

In United Elec. Light Co. v. Deliso Constr. Co., Inc., 315 Mass. 313, 322 (1943), this court characterized a proper subject for imposition of strict liability as "an unusual undertaking or one of such an extremely dangerous nature that it must be performed at the sole risk of the one therein engaged." Thus, while upholding the strict liability doctrine, we held nonetheless that a mixture of cement and water used in underground tunnelling which escaped onto the plaintiff's property, was not a proper subject for imposition of strict liability, on the ground that "[t]hey were ordinary materials widely used in construction work." Ibid. To the same effect is a water tank or pressing system in a commercial building, Fibre Leather Mfg. Corp. v. Ramsay Mills, Inc., 329 Mass. 575 (1952); Brian v. B. Sopkin & Sons, Inc., 314 Mass. 180 (1943), and a chemical widely used in cleaning, Kaufman v. Boston Dye House, Inc., 280 Mass. 161 (1932). Conversely, we found the useless wall of a burned out structure left standing to be an appropriate subject for strict liability, Ainsworth v. Lakin, supra, and the same is true of dams and dikes in certain circumstances. Bratton v. Rudnick, 283 Mass. 556 (1933).

This formulation of strict liability is in accord with the proposed revision of Restatement 2d: Torts (Tent. Draft No. 10, April 20, 1964), §519, which provides that "[o]ne who carries on an abnormally dangerous activity is subject to liability for harm . . . resulting from the activity, although he has exercised the utmost care to prevent such harm." Section 520 then sets out the factors to be considered in determining whether the activity in question is to be considered "abnormally dangerous." These are: "[a] Whether the activity involves a high degree of risk of harm to the person, land or chattels of others; (b) Whether the gravity of the harm which may result from it is likely to be great; (c) Whether the risk cannot be eliminated by the exercise of reasonable care; (d) Whether the activity is not a matter of common usage; (e) Whether the activity is inappropriate to the place where it is carried on; and

(f) The value of the activity to the community." Comment f to §520 states in part, "In general, abnormal dangers arise from activities which are in themselves unusual or from unusual risks created by more usual activities under particular circumstances. . . . The essential question is whether the risk created is so unusual, either because of its magnitude or because of the circumstances surrounding it, as to justify the imposition of strict liability for the harm which results from it, even though it is carried on with all reasonable care."

The tentative draft cautions against defining a type of activity as "abnormally dangerous" in and of itself, however, and advocates considering the activity in light of surrounding circumstances on the facts of each case. This, in essence, shifts consideration from the nature of the activity to the nature and extent of the risk. As an example, it distinguishes cases where large quantities of water are stored "in dangerous location in a city" from those in which "water is collected in a rural area, with no particularly valuable property near," imposing strict liability in the former but not the latter case. §520(3). We believe this approach is sound and comports well with the basic theory underlying the strict liability rule. Additionally, it finds support in our prior case law, and accordingly we choose to follow it. . . .

It is not for this court, at this juncture, to decide whether the ultimate facts established at the trial will make out a case for imposition of strict liability. "Whether the activity is an abnormally dangerous one is to be determined by the [trial] court, upon consideration of all the factors listed . . . and the weight given to each which it merits upon the facts in evidence." Restatement 2d: Torts (Tent. Draft No. 10, April 20, 1964), §520, comment, p.68. [Note that the court was citing a tentative draft of the Restatement (Second) of Torts. The final version of the Restatement contains nearly identical language, but with "that" instead of "which," in Comment l to §520. — EDS.] Moreover, the real issue is not the *sufficiency of the pleadings* but rather one of substantive law, namely the existence of strict liability as the law of Massachusetts. We decide merely that the plaintiff's declaration is sufficient to set forth a cause of action under Massachusetts law. Accordingly, (a) we answer the reported question in the affirmative and (b) we reverse the order below sustaining the defendant's demurrer.

NOTE TO CLARK-AIKEN CO. v. CROMWELL-WRIGHT CO.

Strict Liability for Abnormally Dangerous Activities. The draft Restatement provisions discussed in *Clark-Aiken* were adopted in the Restatement (Second) of Torts. The following cases, Klein v. Pyrodyne Corp., and Ely v. Cabot Oil & Gas Corp., provide additional examples of their application. The plaintiff in *Clark-Aiken* sought damages on theories of negligence and strict liability. To support a strict liability claim, the plaintiff must show that the defendant's activity should be classified as abnormally dangerous. How would the evidence required to support a negligence claim differ from the evidence required to establish strict liability?

Problem
Strict Liability for Dangerous Activities

Plaintiff Spano is the owner of a garage in Brooklyn, which was wrecked by a blast occurring on November 27, 1962. Spano sued Perini, who was engaged in constructing a tunnel in the vicinity pursuant to a contract with the City of New York. The blaster had set off a total of 194 sticks of dynamite at a construction site that was only 125 feet away from the damaged premises. Although the plaintiff alleged negligence in his complaints, he made no attempt to show that the defendant had failed to exercise reasonable care or to take necessary precautions when he was blasting. Instead, the plaintiff chose to rely solely on the principle of strict liability. Do the policies supporting strict liability apply to this case? See Spano v. Perini Corp., 250 N.E.2d 31 (N.Y. 1969).

Statute: STRICT LIABILITY FOR [OIL] CONTAINMENT, CLEANUP AND REMOVAL COSTS

N.H. Rev. Stat. Ann. §146-A:3-a, I. (2017)

I. Any person who, without regard to fault, directly or indirectly causes or suffers the discharge of oil into or onto any surface water or groundwater of this state, or in a land area where oil will ultimately seep into any surface water or groundwater of the state in violation of this chapter, or rules adopted under this chapter, shall be strictly liable for costs directly or indirectly resulting from the violation relating to:

(a) Containment of the discharged oil;

(b) Cleanup and restoration of the site and surrounding environment, and corrective measures as defined under RSA 146-A:11-a, III(a) and (b); and

(c) Removal of the oil.

NOTES TO STATUTE

1. Coverage.   Numerous state statutes similar to New Hampshire's impose strict liability for a variety of environmental harms. This statute covers pollution of both surface water and ground water and covers direct and indirect costs for containment and restoration.

2. Federal Provisions.   A complex body of federal statutes treats environmental harms. See 42 U.S.C. §9607 (2009) for treatment of pollutants other than petroleum-related pollutants, and 33 U.S.C. §2702 (2009) for treatment of petroleum-related pollutants.

Perspective: Strict Liability for Non-Reciprocal Risks

There were three levels of appellate review in Rylands v. Fletcher and numerous opinions. The following excerpt confronts the question of why there should be a strict liability duty placed on "him who brings on his land water, filth, or stenches, or any other thing which will, if it escape, naturally do damage, to prevent their escaping and injuring his neighbor."

But it was further said . . . that when damage is done to personal property, or even to the person by collision, either upon land or at sea, there must be negligence in the party doing the damage to render him legally responsible. This is no doubt true . . . but we think these cases distinguishable from the present. Traffic on the highways, whether by land or sea, cannot be conducted without exposing those whose persons or property are near it to some inevitable risk; and, that being so, those who go on the highway, or have their property adjacent to it, may well be held to do so subject to their taking upon themselves the risk of injury from that inevitable danger. . . . But there is no ground for saying that the plaintiff here took upon himself any risk arising from the uses to which the defendants should choose to apply their land. He neither knew what there might be, nor could he in any way control the defendants. . . .

Blackburn, J. Exchequer Chamber: L.R. 1 Exch. 265 (1866).

This excerpt seeks to justify denying the benefits of a strict liability action to those who use or are adjacent to a highway. One possible explanation could be that strict liability is allowed for those activities where one person imposes a "non-reciprocal risk" on others. Activities involving bringing "dangerous instrumentalities" onto the land that are "non-natural" and "unusual and extraordinary," may fairly be characterized as creating nonreciprocal risks. While automobiles may be dangerous instrumentalities, they present customary and ordinary risks, and all users of the highways impose the risks, on one another. Strict liability would therefore not be justified under the nonreciprocal risk analysis.

The best cost-avoider theory is a second explanation for denying strict liability for injuries associated with roads. Most people are aware of the risks imposed by use of the highways. That knowledge may give them some opportunity to avoid the risks, by staying away from the roads, for example. By contrast, the risks presented by dangerous instrumentalities that are non-natural, unusual, and extraordinary are hard to avoid, either because those at risk are unaware of the activity or unappreciative of the associated risks. In these cases, strict liability is appropriate. As Justice Blackburn observed: "there is no ground for saying that the plaintiff here took upon himself any risk arising from the uses to which the defendants should choose to apply their land. He neither knew what there might be, nor could he in any way control the defendants."

KLEIN v. PYRODYNE CORP.

117 Wash. 2d 1, 810 P.2d 917 (1991)

GUY, Justice.

The plaintiffs in this case are persons injured when an aerial shell at a public fireworks exhibition went astray and exploded near them. The defendant is the pyrotechnic company hired to set up and discharge the fireworks. The issue before this court is whether pyrotechnicians are strictly liable for damages caused by fireworks displays. We hold that they are.

Defendant Pyrodyne Corporation (Pyrodyne) is a general contractor for aerial fireworks at public fireworks displays. Pyrodyne contracted to procure fireworks, to provide pyrotechnic operators, and to display the fireworks at the Western Washington State Fairgrounds in Puyallup, Washington on July 4, 1987. All operators of the fireworks display were Pyrodyne employees acting within the scope of their employment duties. . . .

During the fireworks display, one of the 5-inch mortars was knocked into a horizontal position. From this position a shell inside was ignited and discharged. The shell flew 500 feet in a trajectory parallel to the earth and exploded near the crowd of onlookers. Plaintiffs Danny and Marion Klein were injured by the explosion. Mr. Klein's clothing was set on fire, and he suffered facial burns and serious injury to his eyes. . . .

The Kleins brought suit against Pyrodyne under theories of products liability and strict liability. Pyrodyne filed a motion for summary judgment, which the trial court granted as to the products liability claim. The trial court denied Pyrodyne's summary judgment motion regarding the Kleins' strict liability claim, holding that Pyrodyne was strictly liable without fault and ordering summary judgment in favor of the Kleins on the issue of liability. Pyrodyne appealed the order of partial summary judgment to the Court of Appeals, which certified the case to this court. Pyrodyne is appealing solely as to the trial court's holding that strict liability is the appropriate standard of liability for pyrotechnicians. A strict liability claim against pyrotechnicians for damages caused by fireworks displays presents a case of first impression in Washington.

The Kleins contend that strict liability is the appropriate standard to determine the culpability of Pyrodyne because Pyrodyne was participating in an abnormally dangerous activity. . . .

The modern doctrine of strict liability for abnormally dangerous activities derives from Fletcher v. Rylands, 159 Eng. Rep. 737 (1865), *rev'd*, 1 L.R.-Ex. 265, [1866] All E.R. 1, 6, *aff'd sub nom.* Rylands v. Fletcher, 3 L.R.-H.L. 330, [1868] All E.R. 1, 12, in which the defendant's reservoir flooded mine shafts on the plaintiff's adjoining land. Rylands v. Fletcher has come to stand for the rule that "the defendant will be liable when he damages another by a thing or activity unduly dangerous and inappropriate to the place where it is maintained, in the light of the character of that place and its surroundings." W. Keeton, D. Dobbs, R. Keeton & D. Owen, Prosser and Keeton on Torts §78, at 547-48 (5th ed. 1984).

The basic principle of Rylands v. Fletcher has been accepted by the Restatement (Second) of Torts (1977). . . . Section 519 of the Restatement provides that any party carrying on an "abnormally dangerous activity" is strictly liable for ensuing damages. The test for what constitutes such an activity is stated in section 520 of the Restatement. Both Restatement sections have been adopted by this court, and determination of whether an activity is an "abnormally dangerous activity" is a question of law. . . .

Section 520 of the Restatement lists six factors that are to be considered in determining whether an activity is "abnormally dangerous." The factors are as follows:

   a. existence of a high degree of risk of some harm to the person, land or chattels of others;

   b. likelihood that the harm that results from it will be great;

   c. inability to eliminate the risk by the exercise of reasonable care;

   d. extent to which the activity is not a matter of common usage;

   e. inappropriateness of the activity to the place where it is carried on; and

   f. extent to which its value to the community is outweighed by its dangerous attributes.

Restatement (Second) of Torts §520 (1977). As we previously recognized in Langan v. Valicopters, Inc., 88 Wash. 2d 855, 861-62, 567 P.2d 218 (Wash. 1977) (citing Tent. Draft No. 10, 1964, of comment (f) to section 520), the comments to section 520 explain how these factors should be evaluated:

> Any one of them is not necessarily sufficient of itself in a particular case, and ordinarily several of them will be required for strict liability. On the other hand, it is not necessary that each of them be present, especially if others weigh heavily. Because of the interplay of these various factors, it is not possible to reduce abnormally dangerous activities to any definition. The essential question is whether the risk created is so unusual, either because of its magnitude or because of the circumstances surrounding it, as to justify the imposition of strict liability for the harm that results from it, even though it is carried on with all reasonable care.

Restatement (Second) of Torts §520, comment f (1977). Examination of these factors persuades us that fireworks displays are abnormally dangerous activities justifying the imposition of strict liability.

We find that the factors stated in clauses (a), (b), and (c) are all present in the case of fireworks displays. Any time a person ignites aerial shells or rockets with the intention of sending them aloft to explode in the presence of large crowds of people, a high risk of serious personal injury or property damage is created. That risk arises because of the possibility that a shell or rocket will malfunction or be misdirected. Furthermore, no matter how much care pyrotechnicians exercise, they cannot entirely eliminate the high risk inherent in setting off powerful explosives such as fireworks near crowds. . . .

The factors stated in clauses (a), (b), and (c) together, and sometimes one of them alone, express what is commonly meant by saying an activity is ultrahazardous. Restatement (Second) of Torts §520, comment h (1977). As the Restatement explains, however, "[l]iability for abnormally dangerous activities is not . . . a matter of these three factors alone, and those stated in Clauses (d), (e), and (f) must still be taken into account." Restatement (Second) of Torts §520, comment h (1977). . . .

The factor expressed in clause (d) concerns the extent to which the activity is not a matter "of common usage." The Restatement explains that "[a]n activity is a matter of common usage if it is customarily carried on by the great mass of mankind or by many people in the community." Restatement (Second) of Torts §520, comment i (1977). As examples of activities that are not matters of common usage, the Restatement comments offer driving a tank, blasting, the manufacture, storage, transportation, and use of high explosives, and drilling for oil. The deciding characteristic is that few persons engage in these activities. Likewise, relatively few persons conduct public fireworks displays. Therefore, presenting public fireworks displays is not a matter of common usage.

Pyrodyne argues that the factor stated in clause (d) is not met because fireworks are a common way to celebrate the 4th of July. We reject this argument. Although fireworks are frequently and regularly enjoyed by the public, few persons set off special fireworks displays. Indeed, the general public is prohibited by statute from making public fireworks displays insofar as anyone wishing to do so must first obtain a license. . . .

The factor stated in clause (e) requires analysis of the appropriateness of the activity to the place where it was carried on. In this case, the fireworks display was conducted at the Puyallup Fairgrounds. Although some locations—such as over water — may be safer, the Puyallup Fairgrounds is an appropriate place for a fireworks show because the audience can be seated at a reasonable distance from the display. Therefore, the clause (e) factor is not present in this case.

The factor stated in clause (f) requires analysis of the extent to which the value of fireworks to the community outweighs its dangerous attributes. We do not find that this factor is present here. This country has a long-standing tradition of fireworks on the 4th of July. That tradition suggests that we as a society have decided that the value of fireworks on the day celebrating our national independence and unity outweighs the risks of injuries and damage.

In sum, we find that setting off public fireworks displays satisfies four of the six conditions under the Restatement test; that is, it is an activity that is not "of common usage" and that presents an ineliminably high risk of serious bodily injury or property damage. We therefore hold that conducting public fireworks displays is an abnormally dangerous activity justifying the imposition of strict liability.

This conclusion is consistent with the results reached in cases involving damages caused by detonating dynamite. This court has recognized that parties detonating dynamite are strictly liable for the damages caused by such blasting. . . . Because detonating dynamite is subject to strict liability, and because of the similarities between fireworks and dynamite, strict liability is also an appropriate standard for determining the standard of liability for pyrotechnicians for any damages caused by their fireworks displays.

Policy considerations also support imposing strict liability on pyrotechnicians for damages caused by their public fireworks displays, although such considerations are not alone sufficient to justify that conclusion. Most basic is the question as to who should bear the loss when an innocent person suffers injury through the nonculpable but abnormally dangerous activities of another. In the case of public fireworks displays, fairness weighs in favor of requiring the pyrotechnicians who present the displays to bear the loss rather than the unfortunate spectators who suffer the injuries. In addition, . . . [i]n the present case, all evidence was destroyed as to what caused the misfire of the shell that injured the Kleins. Therefore, the problem of proof this case presents for the plaintiffs also supports imposing strict liability on Pyrodyne. . . .

We hold that Pyrodyne Corporation is strictly liable for all damages suffered as a result of the July 1987 fireworks display. Detonating fireworks displays constitutes an abnormally dangerous activity warranting strict liability. Public policy also supports this conclusion. . . . Therefore, we affirm the decision of the trial court.

[Concurring opinion omitted.]

ELY v. CABOT OIL & GAS CORP.

38 F. Supp. 3d 518 (M.D. Pa. 2014)

JOHN E. JONES, District Judge

. . . In this case we are invited to take a step which no court in the United States has chosen to take, and declare hydraulic fracturing to be an ultra-hazardous activity that gives rise to strict tort liability. This lawsuit was initiated on November 19, 2009, by a group of 44 plaintiffs who collectively filed suit to recover damages for injuries and property damage allegedly suffered as the result of the defendants' natural gas drilling operations in Dimock Township, Susquehanna County, Pennsylvania . . . .

In the motion currently before the Court, the Defendants have moved for summary judgment on the Plaintiffs' claims that natural gas drilling operations and hydraulic fracturing, commonly referred to as "fracking", constitute abnormally dangerous activities under Pennsylvania law, and therefore should be subject to strict liability. The motion has been fully briefed and is ripe for disposition.

. . .

The Plaintiffs have offered limited evidence to help substantiate their claims that the Defendants' drilling operations in connection with the construction or operation of the . . . gas wells caused contamination of the Plaintiffs' water supplies. Notably, the plaintiffs have not submitted substantial evidence to support their claim that natural gas drilling operations, and hydraulic fracturing in particular, constitute ultra hazardous or abnormally dangerous activities. Instead, the Plaintiffs proffer the expert report from Anthony Ingraffea, who simply describes possible negligence and opines that fluid migration from the wells, to the extent it occurred, was "likely" due to a lack of due care relating to "faulty well design and/or construction." However, Ingraffea's report does not include expert testimony explaining that even proper drilling operations in the construction of natural gas wells, including the use of hydraulic fracturing, causes or is likely to cause contamination in water supplies, or other harm. In this regard, although Ingraffea's report focuses on *improper* well completion and faulty casing, or other negligent failings, it does not contain any explanation of, or identify any examples where a gas well was *properly constructed* and completed, and nevertheless fluid migration or water contamination occurred. Similarly, the Plaintiffs have not submitted evidence showing that the risks associated with natural gas drilling cannot be eliminated with the exercise of due care, and the Plaintiffs have not provided expert testimony to support their claim that the drilling operation of hydraulic fracturing has either affected the plaintiffs' water or property.

In contrast, the record contains a surplus of evidence not only attesting to the relative safety of natural gas drilling operations, but also to the fact that such operations are a common, growing, and important part of a modern, highly industrial society; that such operations have not been shown to have major adverse influences on water chemistry and rural drinking water supplies; that economic benefits realized from natural gas drilling operations are significant and have widespread impact on individuals and communities; and that to the extent there are environmental costs associated with natural gas drilling, they will continue to become progressively smaller as newer technology further mitigates the effect of drilling on the environment . . . .

Section 519 of the Restatement states, in pertinent part, that "[o]ne who carries on an abnormally dangerous activity is subject to liability for harm . . . of another resulting from the activity, although he exercised the utmost care to prevent the harm." Restatement (Second) of Torts §519(1) (1977); Section 520 enumerates a list of factors the court should consider in determining whether an activity is abnormally dangerous. These factors are as follows:

(a) existence of a high degree of risk of some harm to the person, land or chattels of others;
(b) likelihood that the harm that results from it will be great;
(c) inability to eliminate the risk by the exercise of reasonable care;
(d) extent to which the activity is not a matter of common usage;
(e) inappropriateness of the activity to the place where it is carried on; and

(f)   extent to which its value to the community is outweighed by its dangerous attributes.

Restatement (Second) of Torts §520 (1977).

Applying the Restatement's multi-faceted test, courts agree that the question of whether a specific activity is abnormally dangerous and, thus, gives rise to strict tort liability, is a question of law for the court to resolve . . . . In accordance with the foregoing, we will consider this competing evidence, guided by the six factors identified in the Restatement, and assessing the state of the law on this issue in Pennsylvania.

A. Whether Natural Gas Drilling Operations Present a High Degree of Risk of Harm

With respect to the first factor to be considered, we agree with the Defendants that the law in this field emphasizes that whether an activity presents a high degree of risk should not focus on whether the Defendants acted negligently, but instead should remain focused on whether the activity itself is abnormally dangerous . . . .

Viewed in this way, the Plaintiffs have not carried their burden of showing that natural gas drilling activities are abnormally dangerous . . . . [T]he evidence in the record developed by the parties contains numerous citations to governmental reports, data analysis, and expert commentary attesting to the Defendants' position that the risks from a properly drilled, cased and hydraulically fractured gas well are minimal. This evidence includes a report from the Pennsylvania General Assembly that referred to a study examining more than 200 water samples taken before and after drilling and hydraulic fracturing that revealed no major influences from gas well drilling or fracking. The evidence also indicates that Pennsylvania's Department of Environmental Protection [DEP] concluded that problems associated with natural gas drilling, to the extent they exist, "can be mitigated by proper construction of gas wells." Other evidence from within Pennsylvania and other states in which natural gas drilling occurs further supports the view that hydraulically fractured wells create, at most, relatively low risk to water supplies, and the Director of the DEP's Office of Oil and Gas Management attested that following a "million experiments" from across the country, he had not found any instances of fracking interfering with groundwater resources.

The foregoing evidence does not, we submit, entirely close the door as to whether natural gas drilling activities may present significant environmental risks when they are negligently undertaken. Indeed, instead of focusing on the inherent dangers that they claim are presented by natural gas drilling, the Plaintiffs endeavor to support their strict liability claim by pointing to opinions of their experts and mere argument in support of their view that hydraulic fracturing is unusually dangerous . . . .

The Plaintiffs also observe that courts have yet to answer the question of whether modern fracking techniques are abnormally dangerous, but in doing so that [sic] Plaintiffs do not effectively support their contention that properly conducted hydraulic fracturing and other natural gas drilling activities at issue in this case are abnormally dangerous, and we do not find that there is sufficient evidence in the Plaintiffs' favor on this point. Again, the Plaintiffs and their purported experts concentrate their arguments on the alleged results of the activity in this case, and not on the activity itself. This misplaced focus, coupled with a lack of evidence and case law to support the Plaintiffs' position causes us to find that this first factor favors the Defendants' in this case.

B. Whether the Plaintiffs Have Shown a Sufficient Likelihood that Harm Resulting from the Defendants' Gas Drilling Operations Will Be Great

The Plaintiffs also focus on the manner in which the Defendants conducted their drilling operations in an effort to establish the second relevant factor identified by the Restatement, namely, that any resulting harm from gas drilling operations will be great. We have already noted that such a focus is improper and inadequate to support the Plaintiffs' burden, since the focus of our inquiry is limited to whether the risk of harm from properly conducted drilling operations will be great. On this relevant factor, which courts have declared "pales in comparison to the others" in cases where the activity at issue is common and the use of due care can reduce risk of harm, Smith v. Weaver, 665 A.2d 1218, 1220 (Pa. Super. Ct. 1995), the evidence does not support the Plaintiffs' position. None of the Plaintiffs' experts offer an opinion that speaks to whether the likelihood of harm from Defendants' properly conducted gas drilling operations will be significant. In contrast, as discussed at length above, there is substantial evidence offered in support of the Defendants' view that proper gas drilling techniques mitigate risks, and such risks while already low will continue to be mitigated as the industry develops further safety precautions.

The only support the Plaintiffs have identified for their view that the hydraulic fracturing presents a likelihood that resulting harm will be great comes from a case involving surface blasting, which the Pennsylvania Supreme Court has held to be an ultra hazardous activity. Federoff et ux. v. Harrison Constr. Co., 66 A.2d 817 (Pa. 1949). But the Plaintiffs do not persuasively explain why the holding of that case, which involves activity involving the use of explosives on the surface that are by definition intended to cause destruction of property, is analogous to modern fracking techniques that occur thousands of feet below the surface. We do not find this distinguishable authority, decided in a quite different industrial context, is sufficient to support the Plaintiffs' argument on this second prong of the Court's analysis.

C. Whether the Exercise of Due Care Can Eliminate Risks Posed by Drilling Operations

With respect to this next factor, although we do not read the evidence in the record to conclude that all risk of harm is absolutely foreclosed by the exercise of due care, the great weight of the evidence that the parties have submitted indicates that such risks are substantially mitigated when due care is exercised. The Plaintiffs have concentrated their argument by offering a report from Anthony Ingraffea, their Rock Engineering Expert, but even this expert acknowledges that the fluid migration that the Plaintiffs have alleged interfered with their water supply was "likely" owing to negligence on the Defendants' part through "faulty well design and/or construction." This focus on negligent conduct undermines the Plaintiffs' assertion that Ingraffea's report supports their view that even the exercise of due care cannot eliminate risks. . . .

In contrast, the Defendants have pointed to evidence in the form of reports by the Manhattan Institute showing that proper drilling techniques have substantially mitigated the risks that drilling might have presented, and that these risks will become further diminished as new technologies are used. Although there appears to be some indication in the record that risks may exist, and it is undisputed that the DEP has identified instances where drilling operations caused harm, the weight of the evidence indicates that such risks may be substantially reduced through the exercise of due care in this field.

D. Whether Gas Drilling Operations Are Common in Dimock Township, Susquehanna County, Pennsylvania

The Plaintiffs maintain that hydraulic fracturing of the type at issue in this case was "novel" in Dimock Township until around the time it was introduced within the past 10 years. This spare assertion does not acknowledge that since 2000, more than 170 gas wells were permitted in the 29 square miles that comprise the Township, and that over 1,100 such wells have been permitted in Susquehanna County during the same period. Significantly, since 2009, 99.5% of these wells have been hydraulically fractured. During this time, the Commonwealth has permitted more than 9,800 wells throughout Pennsylvania. In the face of this widespread and growing area of industrial activity and natural resource development, it is difficult to credit the Plaintiffs' suggestion that natural gas drilling, and hydraulic fracturing, is a "novel" activity. Pennsylvania has had a long history with the commercial exploitation of oil and natural gas resources, and since 1859 more than 350,000 wells have been drilled in the Commonwealth. The evidence indicates that this longstanding, prevalent activity is now common, and becoming increasingly part of the economic fabric of rural communities such as those found in Susquehanna County . . . . [T]his fourth factor weighs against a finding that strict liability is appropriate in this case.

E. Whether the Defendants' Gas Drilling Operations Are Conducted in Appropriate Areas

Despite entering into leases with the Defendants authorizing them to engage in natural gas exploration on their respective properties, the Plaintiffs argue in this case that the Defendants have conducted their drilling operations in inappropriate areas. Specifically, the Plaintiffs assert that the Defendants have conducted their drilling activities in too close proximity to the Plaintiffs' water resources.

Notably, the parties are in agreement that the Pennsylvania General Assembly has issued a report in which that legislative body concluded that the current standards for the placement of gas wells in relation to other structures and environmental areas, including a requirement that wells be located at least 200 feet away from water supplies, are appropriate. That study concluded that there was insufficient evidence to support a change in this setback requirement. The General Assembly's conclusion in this regard dovetails with judicial decisions and expert commentary that gas drilling operations in rural areas area appropriate when they are subject to setback requirements. *See* Robinson Twp. v. Commonwealth of Pennsylvania, 52 A.3d 463, 487 (Pa. Commw. Ct. 2012); Restatement (Second) of Torts §520, cmt. k (1977).

The parties also are in agreement that Defendants' drilling operations conformed to setback requirements for their wells, all of which the DEP permitted. We thus cannot embrace the Plaintiffs' assertion that wells drilled in accordance with valid leases, and which were permitted by the Commonwealth's environmental regulatory body, and which otherwise complied with legal requirements with respect to setback limits, were nevertheless placed inappropriately.

F. Whether the Economic Value to the Community Outweighs Any Dangers Posed by Gas Drilling Operations

Lastly, we are directed to consider the economic value of gas drilling operations, and to weight any such value against the potential dangers that may result from the activity.

Albig v. Municipal Authority of Westmoreland County, 502 A.2d 658, 663 (Pa. Super. Ct. 1985). In *Albig,* the Superior Court indicated that this factor is particularly important in an assessment of whether an activity is subject to strict liability, observing that even if the activity "involves a serious risk of harm that cannot be eliminated with reasonable care and it is not a matter of common usage, its value to the community may be such that the danger will not be regarded as an abnormal one." *Id.* This observation is echoed in the Restatement, which notes that when the challenged activity is central to a community's economic well-being, its value is a particularly important factor in the analysis. Restatement (Second) of Torts §520, cmt. k (1977). In this case, the evidence marshaled by the parties is decidedly in the Defendants' favor, as they have highlighted benefits to Dimock Township and Susquehanna County stemming directly from natural gas drilling, and they have identified statistics showing that this industrial activity has benefits that extend throughout the Commonwealth, affecting individuals, businesses, local communities, and government. We acknowledge the Plaintiffs' argument that natural gas drilling is frequently attended by "booms and busts," and that "the jury is out on who benefits economically" from this activity. Nevertheless, review of the evidence submitted by the parties tilts this factor in Defendants' favor.[1]

. . . [W]hile we find that the Plaintiffs have failed to support their assertion under Pennsylvania law that the Defendants' gas drilling operations represent abnormally dangerous activities, we note that this conclusion does not mean that parties are wholly foreclosed from addressing concerns in this field through the courts. Rather, the Plaintiffs' claims for property damage and personal injury should be considered under traditional and longstanding negligence principles, and not under a strict liability standard.

NOTES TO KLEIN v. PYRODYNE CORP. AND ELY v. CABOT OIL & GAS CORP.

1. *Abnormally Dangerous Activities Test.* Many states have adopted the Restatement (Second)'s six-factor test for determining whether there will be strict liability for engaging in a particular activity. Courts vary widely both in what factors they think are particularly important and in how much weight they give to any particular factor in a given case. The Restatement (Third) of Torts: Liability for Physical and Emotional Harm §20 consolidates the six factors into a two-part test:

> 20. Abnormally Dangerous Activities
>   (a) A defendant who carries on an abnormally dangerous activity is subject to strict liability for physical harm resulting from the activity.
>   (b) An activity is abnormally dangerous if:
>   (1) the activity creates a foreseeable and highly significant risk of physical harm even when reasonable care is exercised by all actors; and
>   (2) the activity is not a matter of common usage.

---

[1] We do not reject out of hand the Plaintiffs' argument that the economic benefits of natural gas drilling should be considered against the costs that such activity imposes on local communities, and the strains that may be felt by local infrastructure, emergency services, law enforcement, and pressure on property values. While these social considerations are properly being debated in the media and numerous public fora, and although a thorough assessment of the benefits and burdens of drilling activity should no doubt be balanced and critical, we emphasize that the actual evidentiary record on this point, as presented by the parties, provides more support for the Defendants' assertion that the economic benefits from drilling are substantial and widespread.

The importance of factor (c) in Restatement (Second) §520, "inability to eliminate the risk by the exercise of reasonable care," is apparent from *Ely*, where the court discusses the evidence of negligence in fracking even before going through the factors, and in the Restatement (Third) §20(b)'s first element. Section 20(b)(1) incorporates the Restatement (Second)'s factors (a), (b), and (c) while (b)(2) incorporates the Restatement (Second)'s factor (d). What happened to the concerns reflected in the Restatement (Second)'s factors (e) and (f)? The location where the activity takes place may affect the magnitude of the risk or the likelihood that the harm will be great (factors (a) and (b)). For example, blasting with dynamite near a city school is more likely to cause great harm than blasting in a remote locale. The Restatement (Third) concludes that the location does not determine whether the activity is abnormally dangerous independent of factors (a) and (b).

The Restatement (Third) also concludes that the value of the activity to the community (factor (f)) is irrelevant. Engaging in an activity may be negligent if the value is small compared to the risk or not negligent if the value is great enough. But strict liability for abnormally dangerous activities is based on the idea that even though the decision to engage in the activity may be reasonable and the actor may have used reasonable care while engaged in the activity, there should be liability because of the serious risk that remains. Would the holdings in *Klein* or *Ely* be different under the Restatement (Third) test?

2. *Abnormally Dangerous Activities: Value to the Community.* The different weights given to various factors by different courts may be illustrated by considering the sixth factor, value to the community. Under the Restatement's formulation, a very dangerous activity might be subject to strict liability in one community and not in another, depending on the value of that activity in the particular community. In Koos v. Roth, 652 P.2d 1255 (Or. 1982), the court considered whether to apply strict liability to "field burning as an agricultural technique" when that burning caused damage to property belonging to a neighbor of the person burning a field. The court refused to consider the economic value of the activity, observing first that value is a subjective and controversial measure judged differently by those profiting from and endangered by the activity. Value, the court believed, can never be a conclusion of law. Second, a finding that an activity has a high economic value suggests that society would be willing to pay enough for the activity that the person engaged in the activity could afford to by insurance. If so, a high value activity should be held strictly liable because it will continue even if forced to bear all of its costs, rather than being excluded from strict liability. The *Koos* court concluded that "Society has other ways to lighten the burdens of costly but unavoidable accidents on a valued industry than to let them fall haphazardly on the industry's neighbors."

3. *Strict Liability for Common Activities.* The *Klein* court acknowledged that many members of the public enjoy fireworks displays, but it held that public fireworks displays are not a matter of common usage because most members of the community do not take part in administering public fireworks displays. How did the *Ely* court's analysis of common usage differ from that of the *Klein* court?

The Restatement (Third) of Torts asserts that, in addition to activities carried on by a large fraction of the population, activities conducted by only a few actors should also be considered matters of common usage when they are pervasive. Thus, according to the Restatement (Third), transmission of electricity through wires and natural gas through mains are matters of common usage even though only one party generally engages in the activity. These activities are pervasive, and most people's homes are connected to the activities through mains and wires. Restatement (Third) of Torts §20, comment j. Courts have generally adopted this perspective, though some courts have endorsed the application of strict liability to transportation of gasoline or propane on the highway or storage of these explosive materials in large quantities. The Restatement (Third) also declares that the idea of common usage may extend to activities in which few members of the community engage and that are not pervasive when an activity "has moved beyond its initial stages and has become common and normal." How do these ideas apply to the activities in *Klein* and *Ely*?

Plaintiffs have sought to apply strict liability to numerous fairly common activities where a negligence theory was unlikely to be successful. For example, courts have rejected strict liability in claims against: sellers of lead batteries to a recycling facility, in Thompson v. Zero Bullet Co., 692 So. 2d 805 (Ala. 1997); firearms manufacturers, in Hammond v. Colt Indus. Oper. Corp., 565 A.2d 558 (Del. Super. 1989); and beer sellers, in Maguire v. Pabst Brewing Co., 387 N.W.2d 565 (Iowa 1986).

4. *Categories of Abnormally Dangerous Activity* Because characterization of an activity as abnormally dangerous depends on evaluation of surrounding circumstances, in addition to the inherent characteristics of the activity, it is difficult to generalize about the kinds of activities to which strict liability attaches. Nonetheless, the quintessential abnormally dangerous activity is blasting, which was the subject of early cases imposing strict liability and which modern courts have recognized as a paradigm for evaluating the doctrine. Most jurisdictions recognize strict liability for blasting, and, in fact, some jurisdictions have not extended strict liability for abnormally dangerous activities beyond blasting. In addition to the activities mentioned in the material above, some courts have applied strict liability for abnormally dangerous activities to fumigation, crop dusting, ground damage from aviation, and the use and storage of some toxic materials. Outside of Washington, courts that have considered the applicability of strict liability to a public fireworks display have rejected the *Klein* court's conclusion that strict liability should apply.

As the *Ely* court acknowledged, the question of whether those who engage in modern fracking techniques should be subject to strict liability is a developing area of the law, and most jurisdictions have not yet ruled on the matter. Several recent cases in which plaintiffs filed lawsuits asserting strict liability claims for fracking-induced earthquakes have settled. Other litigation is ongoing. In *Ely* itself, after the court granted summary judgment to the defendant on the strict liability claim, the case proceeded to trial on theories of negligence and private nuisance.

Ely illustrates the difficulty of bringing multiple claims. To prove its negligence claim, for instance, the plaintiffs want to show that the fracking company failed to use ordinary care. But that evidence is in tension with its assertion in the strict liability claim that harm cannot be avoided using ordinary care. After the *Ely* jury awarded the plaintiffs more than $4 million on the negligence and nuisance claims, the court vacated the award because of "the substantial and varied weaknesses in the plaintiffs' case together with the myriad examples of inappropriate conduct." The court ordered the parties to engage in settlement proceedings before scheduling a new trial. *See* Ely v. Cabot Oil & Gas Corp., 2017 WL 1196510 (M.D. Pa. 2017).

5. *Defenses to Strict Liability for Abnormally Dangerous Activities.* The Restatement (Second) of Torts §523 treats assumption of risk as a complete defense in a case of strict liability for harm caused by abnormally dangerous activities, but the Restatement (Second) does not allow a defense of contributory negligence. Under the Restatement (Third) of Torts, §25, reflecting the shift of most jurisdictions to a comparative negligence system, unreasonable assumption of risk and contributory negligence both can reduce but not necessarily bar a plaintiff's recovery in these strict liability actions

Problem
Abnormally Dangerous Activities

Taylor suffered an eye injury when he was shot in the eye after removing his safety goggles during a paintball game at Dodge City Paint Ball. Taylor and his friend Wisley had gone to Dodge City to play paintball. Paintball games involve players on opposing teams shooting each other with paint pellets. The game was played on an open field with a creek bed, trees, and brush. Paintball game players try to capture a flag without being shot.

After arriving at Dodge City, Taylor participated in an orientation meeting in which the rules of the game were explained. At the orientation meeting, the players, including Taylor, were informed that the rules required them to keep their safety goggles on at all times while on the field of play. In the orientation, it was explained that if a player's safety goggles were to become fogged, the player must call for a referee either to help him off the field or to shield the player's face while he cleaned his goggles.

Taylor played two games of paintball without incident. In the third game, Taylor's safety goggles became fogged, so Taylor called "timeout" three or four times, assuming he was supposed to wait for the referee. Taylor lay down while he called timeout. No one gave him permission to raise his goggles, but he raised them because, as he said, "I had been there long enough. I mean, I waited for a while. No one showed up." Taylor raised his goggles and wiped them out. As he was lowering them, he was shot in the eye. Taylor could have walked off the field in the direction he came from without cleaning his goggles, but he would probably have gotten shot if he did that and would then have been out of the game.

Taylor sued the operator of the facility alleging negligence and strict liability based on operation of a paintball facility being an abnormally dangerous activity. The trial court granted summary judgment on behalf of the operator on the abnormally dangerous activity claim. Your senior partner, who represents Taylor, asks you to write a memo analyzing whether appealing that grant of summary judgment is likely to be successful. Present that analysis and your conclusion. See Taylor v. Hesser, 991 P.2d 35 (Okla. Ct. App. 1998).

Perspective: Strict Liability Where Negligence Theories Fail

One court has taken the approach that strict liability should be applied only when the negligence system fails adequately to control risks. In Indiana Harbor Belt R. Co. v. American Cyanamid Co., 916 F.2d 1174 (7th Cir. 1990), Judge Posner considered whether the shipper of a hazardous chemical, acrylonitrile, through the metropolitan area of Chicago should be strictly liable for the consequences of a chemical spill.

> By making the actor strictly liable — by denying him in other words an excuse based on his inability to avoid accidents by being more careful — we give him an incentive, missing in a negligence regime, to experiment with methods of preventing accidents that involve not greater exertions of care, assumed to be futile, but instead relocating, changing, or reducing (perhaps to the vanishing point) the activity giving rise to the accident. The greater the risk of an accident (a) and the costs of an accident if one occurs (b), the more we want the actor to consider the possibility of making accident-reducing activity changes; the stronger, therefore, is the case for strict liability.

Finding "no reason for believing that a negligence regime is not perfectly adequate to remedy and deter, at reasonable cost, the accidental spillage of acrylonitrile from rail cars," id. at 1179, Judge Posner held that the shipper was not strictly liable.

14

PRODUCTS LIABILITY

I. Introduction

Product manufacturers are among the most frequent defendants in tort suits, because products are involved in lots of injuries, and product manufacturers are usually both identifiable and solvent. Tort law's treatment of product-related injuries has been marked by drastic changes in the range of plaintiffs to whom a manufacturer may be liable and the standards that a product must meet. At common law, only the direct customer of a manufacturer could recover from that manufacturer for product-related injuries. To recover, the customer was required to show that the manufacturer had been negligent or that the product's attributes were worse than a warranty had promised they would be.

The first pro-plaintiff development in products liability law allowed people who lacked contractual connections to the manufacturer to seek damages for injuries caused by a product. The second major pro-plaintiff development supplemented the negligence cause of action with strict liability theories. Courts usually supported these new rules imposing greater liability on manufacturers with economic arguments about bearing the costs of accidents and about how the United States has changed from a society with many small local producers of goods to a society with fewer but much larger companies producing vast quantities of items.

In the 1960s and 1970s, courts in almost all states developed strict liability theories for products liability cases. Since then, judicial and legislative attention has focused on whether strict liability is really different from negligence-based liability and on the more general question of when manufacturers rather than victims of injury should pay for losses caused by products.

II. Allowing "Strangers" to Recover for Negligence: Abrogation of the Privity Requirement

Prior to the famous decision in MacPherson v. Buick Motor Co., if a manufacturer was negligent in producing a product and the product injured someone, the manufacturer would be responsible only if the victim had bought the item from the manufacturer. If the victim was not the purchaser or had purchased the item from someone else in the chain of distribution, such as a retailer, the manufacturer would be free from responsibility. *MacPherson* changed that fundamental aspect of products liability law.

MacPHERSON v. BUICK MOTOR CO.
217 N.Y. 382, 111 N.E. 1050 (1916)

CARDOZO, J.

The defendant is a manufacturer of automobiles. It sold an automobile to a retail dealer. The retail dealer resold to the plaintiff. While the plaintiff was in the car, it suddenly collapsed. He was thrown out and injured. One of the wheels was made of defective wood, and its spokes crumbled into fragments. The wheel was not made by the defendant; it was bought from another manufacturer. There is evidence, however, that its defects could have been discovered by reasonable inspection, and that inspection was omitted. There is no claim that the defendant knew of the defect and willfully concealed it. . . . The charge is one, not of fraud, but of negligence. The question to be determined is whether the defendant owed a duty of care and vigilance to any one but the immediate purchaser.

The foundations of this branch of the law, at least in this state, were laid in Thomas v. Winchester (6 N.Y. 397). A poison was falsely labeled. The sale was made to a druggist, who in turn sold to a customer. The customer recovered damages from the seller who affixed the label. "The defendant's negligence," it was said, "put human life in imminent danger." A poison falsely labeled is likely to injure any one who gets it. Because the danger is to be foreseen, there is a duty to avoid the injury. Cases were cited by way of illustration in which manufacturers were not subject to any duty irrespective of contract. The distinction was said to be that their conduct, though negligent, was not likely to result in injury to anyone except the purchaser. We are not required to say whether the chance of injury was always as remote as the distinction assumes. Some of the illustrations might be rejected to-day. The principle of the distinction is for present purposes the important thing.

Thomas v. Winchester became quickly a landmark of the law. In the application of its principle there may at times have been uncertainty or even error. There has never in this state been doubt or disavowal of the principle itself. The chief cases are well known, yet to recall some of them will be helpful. Loop v. Litchfield (42 N.Y. 351) is the earliest. It was the case of a defect in a small balance wheel used on a circular saw. The manufacturer pointed out the defect to the buyer, who wished a cheap article and was ready to assume the risk. The risk can hardly have been an imminent one, for the wheel lasted five years before it broke. In the meanwhile the buyer had made a lease of the machinery. It was held that the manufacturer was not answerable to the lessee. Loop v. Litchfield was followed in Losee v. Clute (51 N.Y. 494), the case of the explosion of a steam boiler. That decision has been criticised . . . but it must be confined to its special facts. It was put upon the ground that the risk of injury was too remote. The buyer in that case had not only accepted the boiler, but had tested it. The manufacturer knew that his own test was not the final one. The finality of the test has a bearing on the measure of diligence owing to persons other than the purchaser. . . .

These early cases suggest a narrow construction of the rule. Later cases, however, evince a more liberal spirit. First in importance is Devlin v. Smith (89 N.Y. 470). The defendant, a contractor, built a scaffold for a painter. The painter's servants were injured. The contractor was held liable. He knew that the scaffold, if improperly constructed, was a most dangerous trap. He knew that it was to be used by the workmen. He was building it for that very purpose. Building it for their use, he owed them a duty, irrespective of his contract with their master, to build it with care.

From Devlin v. Smith we pass over intermediate cases and turn to the latest case in this court in which Thomas v. Winchester was followed. That case is Statler v. Ray Mfg. Co. (195 N.Y. 478, 480). The defendant manufactured a large coffee urn. It was installed in a restaurant. When heated, the urn exploded and injured the plaintiff. We held that the manufacturer was liable. We said that the urn "was of such a character inherently that, when applied to the purposes for which it was designed, it was liable to become a source of great danger to many people if not carefully and properly constructed." It may be that Devlin v. Smith and Statler v. Ray Mfg. Co. have extended the rule of Thomas v. Winchester. If so, this court is committed to the extension. The defendant argues that things imminently dangerous to life are poisons, explosives, deadly weapons — things whose normal function it is to injure or destroy. But whatever the rule in Thomas v. Winchester may once have been, it has no longer that restricted meaning. A large coffee urn may have within itself, if negligently made, the potency of danger, yet no one thinks of it as an implement whose normal function is destruction. . . .

We hold, then, that the principle of Thomas v. Winchester is not limited to poisons, explosives, and things of like nature, to things which in their normal operation are implements of destruction. If the nature of a thing is such that it is reasonably certain to place life and limb in peril when negligently made, it is then a thing of danger. Its nature gives warning of the consequences to be expected. If to the element of danger there is added knowledge that the thing will be used by persons other than the purchaser, and used without new tests then, irrespective of contract, the manufacturer of this thing of danger is under a duty to make it carefully. That is as far as we are required to go for the decision of this case. There must be knowledge of a danger, not merely possible, but probable. It is possible to use almost anything in a way that will make it dangerous if defective. That is not enough to charge the manufacturer with a duty independent of his contract. Whether a given thing is dangerous may be sometimes a question for the court and sometimes a question for the jury. There must also be knowledge that in the usual course of events the danger will be shared by others than the buyer. Such knowledge may often be inferred from the nature of the transaction. But it is possible that even knowledge of the danger and of the use will not always be enough. The proximity or remoteness of the relation is a factor to be considered. We are dealing now with the liability of the manufacturer of the finished product, who puts it on the market to be used without inspection by his customers. If he is negligent, where danger is to be foreseen, a liability will follow.

We are not required at this time to say that it is legitimate to go back of the manufacturer of the finished product and hold the manufacturers of the component parts. To make their negligence a cause of imminent danger, an independent cause must often intervene; the manufacturer of the finished product must also fail in his duty of inspection. It may be that in those circumstances the negligence of the earlier members of the series is too remote to constitute, as to the ultimate user, an actionable wrong. . . . We leave that question open to you. We shall have to deal with it when it arises. The difficulty which it suggests is not present in this case. There is here no break in the chain of cause and effect. In such circumstances, the presence of a known danger, attendant upon a known use, makes vigilance a duty. We have put aside the notion that the duty to safeguard life and limb, when the consequences of negligence may be foreseen, grows out of contract and nothing else. We have put the source of the obligation where it ought not be. We have put its source in the law.

From this survey of the decisions, there thus emerges a definition of the duty of a manufacturer which enables us to measure this defendant's liability. Beyond all question, the nature of an automobile gives warning of probable danger if its construction is defective. This automobile was designed to go fifty miles an hour. Unless its wheels were sound and strong, injury was almost certain. It was as much a thing of danger as a defective engine for a railroad. The defendant knew the danger. It knew also that the car would be used by persons other than the buyer. This was apparent from its size; there were seats for three persons. It was apparent also from the fact that the buyer was a dealer in cars, who bought to resell. The maker of this car supplied it for the use of purchasers from the dealer just as plainly as the contractor in Devlin v. Smith supplied the scaffold for use by the servants of the owner. The dealer was indeed the one person of whom it might be said with some approach to certainty that by him the car would not be used. Yet the defendant would have us say that he was the one person whom it was under a legal duty to protect. The law does not lead us to so inconsequent a conclusion. Precedents drawn from the days of travel by stage coach do not fit the conditions of travel today. The principle that the danger must be imminent does not change, but the things subject to the principle do change. They are whatever the needs of life in a developing civilization require them to be. . . .

There is nothing anomalous in a rule which imposes upon A, who has contracted with B, a duty to C and D and others according as he knows or does not know that the subject matter of the contract is intended for their use. We may find an analogy in the law which measures the liability of landlords. If A leases to B a tumbledown house he is not liable, in the absence of fraud, to B's guests who enter it and are injured. This is because B is then under the duty to repair it, the lessor has the right to suppose that he will fulfill that duty, and if he omits to do so, his guests must look to him. . . . But if A leases a building to be used by the lessee at once as a place of public entertainment, the rule is different. There injury to persons other than the lessee is to be foreseen, and foresight of the consequences involves the creation of a duty. . . .

In this view of the defendant's liability there is nothing inconsistent with the theory of liability on which the case was tried. It is true that the court told the jury that ' an automobile is not an inherently dangerous vehicle." The meaning, however, is made plain by the context. The meaning is that danger is not to be expected when the vehicle is well constructed. The court left it to the jury to say whether the defendant ought to have foreseen that the car, if negligently constructed, would become "imminently dangerous." Subtle distinctions are drawn by the defendant between things inherently dangerous and things imminently dangerous, but the case does not turn upon these verbal niceties. If danger was to be expected as reasonably certain, there was a duty of vigilance, and this whether you call the danger inherent or imminent. In varying forms that thought was put before the jury. We do not say that the court would not have been justified in ruling as a matter of law that the car was a dangerous thing. If there was any error, it was none of which the defendant can complain.

We think the defendant was not absolved from a duty of inspection because it bought the wheels from a reputable manufacturer. It was not merely a dealer in automobiles. It was a manufacturer of automobiles. It was responsible for the finished product. It was not at liberty to put the finished product on the market without subjecting the component parts to ordinary and simple tests. . . . Under the charge of the trial judge nothing more was required of it. The obligation to inspect must vary with the nature of the thing to be inspected. The more probable the danger, the greater the need of caution. . . . Both by its relation to the work and by the nature of its business, [the manufacturer] is charged with a stricter duty.

Other rulings complained of have been considered, but no error has been found on them.

The judgment should be affirmed.

NOTE TO MacPHERSON v. BUICK MOTOR CO.

Doctrinal Change.   Before *MacPherson*, a person not in *contractual privity* with the manufacturer could not sue for injuries caused by the manufacturer's negligence. Considering the various cases cited by Justice Cardozo and his holding, under what circumstances will the manufacturer be liable to people other than the buyer?

Problem
Required Contact with Manufacturer

Roxanne Ramsey-Buckingham's estate sued R.J. Reynolds Tobacco Co. claiming that she died of lung cancer caused by cigarette smoke. Ms. Ramsey-Buckingham was not a smoker, but her estate claimed that she was injured by breathing "environmental tobacco smoke," smoke coming directly from the cigarette into the air or exhaled by people nearby who smoked. Does *MacPherson* suggest that a bystander such as Ms. Ramsey-Buckingham rather than a user of the product can recover from the manufacturer? Would the opinion support treating Ms. Ramsey-Buckingham as a "user" of the cigarettes? See *Buckingham v. R.J. Reynolds Tobacco Co.*, 713 A.2d 381 (N.H. 1998).

III. Allowing Recovery Without Proof of Negligence: Development of Strict Liability

A. Early Development

Two California decisions introduced strict liability concepts to modern products liability jurisprudence. They represent a strong pro-plaintiff emphasis. Escola v. Coca Cola Bottling Co. of Fresno, decided in 1944, is famous because of the concurring opinion by Justice Traynor. It influenced a wave of products liability developments in the 1960s and 1970s, including the opinion in Greenman v. Yuba Power Products, Inc., adopting and elaborating upon the ideas from the *Escola* concurrence almost 20 years after *Escola* had been decided.

A product injury might be the result of deficient manufacturing, deficient design, or some combination of deficient design and manufacturing. *Escola* and *Greenman* do not distinguish between these types of defect, perhaps because of their factual contexts or perhaps because litigants and courts had not yet become aware of that possible complexity.

ESCOLA v. COCA COLA BOTTLING CO. OF FRESNO
24 Cal. 2d 453, 150 P.2d 436 (1944)

GIBSON, C.J.

Plaintiff, a waitress in a restaurant, was injured when a bottle of Coca Cola broke in her hand. She alleged that defendant company, which had bottled and delivered the alleged defective bottle to her employer, was negligent in selling "bottles containing said beverage which on account of excessive pressure of gas or by reason of some defect in the bottle was dangerous . . . and likely to explode." This appeal is from a judgment upon a jury verdict in favor of plaintiff.

Defendant's driver delivered several cases of Coca Cola to the restaurant, placing them on the floor, one on top of the other, under and behind the counter, where they remained at least thirty-six hours. Immediately before the accident, plaintiff picked up the top case and set it upon a near-by ice cream cabinet in front of and about three feet from the refrigerator. She then proceeded to take the bottles from the case with her right hand, one at a time, and put them into the refrigerator. Plaintiff testified that after she had placed three bottles in the refrigerator and had moved the fourth bottle about 18 inches from the case "it exploded in my hand." The bottle broke into two jagged pieces and inflicted a deep five-inch cut, severing blood vessels, nerves and muscles of the thumb and palm of the hand. . . .

Although it is not clear in this case whether the explosion was caused by an excessive charge or a defect in the glass there is a sufficient showing that neither cause would ordinarily have been present if due care had been used. Further, defendant had exclusive control over both the charging and inspection of the bottles. Accordingly, all the requirements necessary to entitle plaintiff to rely on the doctrine of *res ipsa loquitur* to supply an inference of negligence are present. . . .

The judgment is affirmed.

TRAYNOR, J.

I concur in the judgment, but I believe the manufacturer's negligence should no longer be singled out as the basis of a plaintiff's right to recover in cases like the present one. In my opinion it should now be recognized that a manufacturer incurs an absolute liability when an article that he has placed on the market, knowing that it is to be used without inspection, proves to have a defect that causes injury to human beings. MacPherson v. Buick Motor Co. established the principle, recognized by this court, that irrespective of privity of contract, the manufacturer is responsible for an injury caused by such an article to any person who comes in lawful contact with it. In these cases the source of the manufacturer's liability was his negligence in the manufacturing process or in the inspection of component parts supplied by others. Even if there is no negligence, however, public policy demands that responsibility be fixed wherever it will most effectively reduce the hazards to life and health inherent in defective products that reach the market. It is evident that the manufacturer can anticipate some hazards and guard against the recurrence of others, as the public cannot. Those who suffer injury from defective products are unprepared to meet its consequences. The cost of an injury and the loss of time or health may be an overwhelming misfortune to the person injured, and a needless one, for the risk of injury can be insured by the manufacturer and distributed among the public as a cost of doing business. It is to the public interest to discourage the marketing of products having defects that are a menace to the public. If such products nevertheless find their way into the market it is to the public interest to place the responsibility for whatever injury they may cause upon the manufacturer, who, even if he is not negligent in the manufacture of the product, is responsible for its reaching the market. However intermittently such injuries may occur and however haphazardly they may strike, the risk of their occurrence is a constant risk and a general one. Against such a risk there should be general and constant protection and the manufacturer is best situated to afford such protection.

The injury from a defective product does not become a matter of indifference because the defect arises from causes other than the negligence of the manufacturer, such as negligence of a submanufacturer of a component part whose defects could not be revealed by inspection . . . or unknown causes that even by the device of *res ipsa loquitur* cannot be classified as negligence of the manufacturer. The inference of negligence may be dispelled by an affirmative showing of proper care. If the evidence against the fact inferred is "clear, positive, uncontradicted, and of such a nature that it can not rationally be disbelieved, the court must instruct the jury that the nonexistence of the fact has been established as a matter of law." An injured person, however, is not ordinarily in a position to refute such evidence or identify the cause of the defect, for he can hardly be familiar with the manufacturing process as the manufacturer himself is. In leaving it to the jury to decide whether the inference has been dispelled, regardless of the evidence against it, the negligence rule approaches the rule of strict liability. It is needlessly circuitous to make negligence the basis of recovery and impose what is in reality liability without negligence. If public policy demands that a manufacturer of goods be responsible for their quality regardless of negligence there is no reason not to fix that responsibility openly.

In the case of foodstuffs, the public policy of the state is formulated in a criminal statute. . . . Statutes of this kind result in a strict liability of the manufacturer in tort to the member of the public injured.

The statute may well be applicable to a bottle whose defects cause it to explode. In any event it is significant that the statute imposes criminal liability without fault, reflecting the public policy of protecting the public from dangerous products placed on the market, irrespective of negligence in their manufacture. While the Legislature imposes criminal liability only with regard to food products and their containers, there are many other sources of danger. It is to the public interest to prevent injury to the public from any defective goods by the imposition of civil liability generally.

The retailer, even though not equipped to test a product, is under an absolute liability to his customer, for the implied warranties of fitness for proposed use and merchantable quality include a warranty of safety of the product. This warranty is not necessarily a contractual one . . . for public policy requires that the buyer be insured at the seller's expense against injury. . . . The courts recognize, however, that the retailer cannot bear the burden of this warranty, and allow him to recoup any losses by means of the warranty of safety attending the wholesaler's or manufacturer's sale to him. . . . Such a procedure, however, is needlessly circuitous and engenders wasteful litigation. Much would be gained if the injured person could base his action directly on the manufacturer's warranty.

The liability of the manufacturer to an immediate buyer injured by a defective product follows without proof of negligence from the implied warranty of safety attending the sale. Ordinarily, however, the immediate buyer is a dealer who does not intend to use the product himself, and if the warranty of safety is to serve the purpose of protecting health and safety it must give rights to others than the dealer. In the words of Judge Cardozo in the *MacPherson* case . . . "The dealer was indeed the one person of whom it might be said with some approach to certainty that by him the car would not be used. Yet the defendant would have us say that he was the one person whom it was under a legal duty to protect. The law does not lead us to so inconsequent a conclusion." While the defendant's negligence in the *MacPherson* case made it unnecessary for the court to base liability on warranty, Judge Cardozo's reasoning recognized the injured person as the real party in interest and effectively disposed of the theory that the liability of the manufacturer incurred by his warranty should apply only to the immediate purchaser. It thus paves the way for a standard of liability that would make the manufacturer guarantee the safety of his product even when there is no negligence.

This court and many others have extended protection according to such a standard to consumers of food products, taking the view that the right of a consumer injured by unwholesome food does not depend "upon the intricacies of the law of sales" and that the warranty of the manufacturer to the consumer in absence of privity of contract rests on public policy. . . . Dangers to life and health inhere in other consumers' goods that are defective and there is no reason to differentiate them from the dangers of defective food products. . . .

In the food products cases the courts have resorted to various fictions to rationalize the extension of the manufacturer's warranty to the consumer: that a warranty runs with the chattel; that the cause of action of the dealer is assigned to the consumer; that the consumer is a third party beneficiary of the manufacturer's contract with the dealer. They have also held the manufacturer liable on a mere fiction of negligence: "Practically he must know it [the product] is fit, or take the consequences, if it proves destructive." Such fictions are not necessary to fix the manufacturer's liability under a warranty if the warranty is severed from the contract of sale between the dealer and the consumer and based on the law of torts. . . . Warranties are not necessarily rights arising under a contract. An action on a warranty "was, in its origin, a pure action of tort," and only late in the historical development of warranties was an action in assumpsit allowed. . . .

As handicrafts have been replaced by mass production with its great markets and transportation facilities, the close relationship between the producer and consumer of a product has been altered. Manufacturing processes, frequently valuable secrets, are ordinarily either inaccessible to or beyond the ken of the general public. The consumer no longer has means or skill enough to investigate for himself the soundness of a product, even when it is not contained in a sealed package, and his erstwhile vigilance has been lulled by the steady efforts of manufacturers to build up confidence by advertising and marketing devices such as trade-marks. . . . Consumers no longer approach products warily but accept them on faith, relying on the reputation of the manufacturer or the trade mark. . . . Manufacturers have sought to justify that faith by increasingly high standards of inspection and a readiness to make good on defective products by way of replacements and refunds. . . . The manufacturer's obligation to the consumer must keep pace with the changing relationship between them; it cannot be escaped because the marketing of a product has become so complicated as to require one or more intermediaries. Certainly there is greater reason to impose liability on the manufacturer than on the retailer who is but a conduit of a product that he is not himself able to test. . . .

The manufacturer's liability should, of course, be defined in terms of the safety of the product in normal and proper use, and should not extend to injuries that cannot be traced to the product as it reached the market.

NOTES TO ESCOLA v. COCA COLA BOTTLING CO. OF FRESNO

1. *Analytical Structure.* Justice Traynor's argument has four primary themes: (a) defective products cases can often be handled as applications of the doctrine of *res ipsa loquitur*, but that doctrine is essentially equivalent to strict liability in these cases; (b) manufacturers are always in a better position than consumers to prevent the harms, control the risks, and distribute the losses over society, so they should be held liable without regard to fault; (c) consumers can recover damages for defective products from retailers, and retailers can get compensation from manufacturers under the rules of indemnification; and (d) warranties provided under contract law provide for strict liability, and tort law and contract law should treat injuries from products the same way. What legal, factual, and policy ideas support each element of the opinion?

2. *Strict Liability for Breach of Contractual Warranty.* When there is a contract between a plaintiff and defendant for purchase and sale of the product that injures the plaintiff, the law of sales, part of contract law, permits the plaintiff to recover damages. That cause of action does not require any proof of negligence. Tort law's recognition of strict liability for product-related injuries is parallel to the strict liability in contract law.

The Uniform Commercial Code (UCC) Article 2, adopted by most states, provides that a seller may make a warranty that expressly provides guarantees about the quality of the goods to the buyer (express warranty). The UCC also states that there are implied warranties that accompany purchases of goods from merchants. Section 2-314 states that, unless the contract provides otherwise, sellers guarantee, among other things, that the goods will be "fit for the ordinary purposes for which such goods are used." Section 2-315 states that, unless the contract provides otherwise, goods will be fit for the buyer's particular purpose, "where the seller at the time of contracting has reason to know any particular purpose for which the goods are required and that the buyer is relying on the seller's skill or judgment to select or furnish suitable goods." Express and implied warranties are the sources of strict liability for defective products in contract law.

The UCC provides the following three options for state provisions on the topic of who besides a buyer may recover under contract-based strict liability.

§2-318. Third Party Beneficiaries of Warranties Express and Implied
Alternative A: A seller's warranty whether express or implied extends to any natural person who is in the family or household of his buyer or who is a guest in his home if it is reasonable to expect that such person may use, consume or be affected by the goods

and who is injured in person by breach of the warranty. A seller may not exclude or limit the operation of this section.

Alternative B: A seller's warranty whether express or implied extends to any natural person who may reasonably be expected to use, consume or be affected by the goods and who is injured in person by breach of the warranty. A seller may not exclude or limit the operation of this section.

Alternative C: A seller's warranty whether express or implied extends to any person who may reasonably be expected to use, consume or be affected by the goods and who is injured by breach of the warranty. A seller may not exclude or limit the operation of this section with respect to injury to the person of an individual to whom the warranty extends.

Statute: DEFINITION OF CONSUMER
Ind. Stat. §34-6-2-29 (2017)

Consumer for the purposes of IC 34-20 [describing products liability causes of action], means:

(1) a purchaser;

(2) any individual who uses or consumes the product;

(3) any person who, while acting for or on behalf of the injured party, was in possession and control of the product in question; or

(4) any bystander injured by the product who would reasonably be expected to be in the vicinity of the product during its reasonably expected use.

NOTE TO STATUTE

Observe that the range of people to whom the warranty extends increases in the UCC provisions, with the smallest range in Alternative A to the largest range in Alternative C. How does the Indiana statute relate to the three UCC choices?

GREENMAN v. YUBA POWER PRODUCTS, INC.
27 Cal. Rptr. 697, 59 Cal. 2d 57, 377 P.2d 897 (1963)

TRAYNOR, J.

Plaintiff brought this action for damages against the retailer and the manufacturer of a Shopsmith, a combination power tool that could be used as a saw, drill, and wood lathe. He saw a Shopsmith demonstrated by the retailer and studied a brochure prepared by the manufacturer. He decided he wanted a Shopsmith for his home workshop, and his wife bought and gave him one for Christmas in 1955. In 1957 he bought the necessary attachments to use the Shopsmith as a lathe for turning a large piece of wood he wished to make into a chalice. After he had worked on the piece of wood several times without difficulty, it suddenly flew out of the machine and struck him on the forehead, inflicting serious injuries. About ten and a half months later, he gave the retailer and the manufacturer written notice of claimed breaches of warranties and filed a complaint against them alleging such breaches and negligence.

After a trial before a jury, the court ruled that there was no evidence that the retailer was negligent or had breached any express warranty and that the manufacturer was not liable for the breach of any implied warranty. Accordingly, it submitted to the jury only the cause of action alleging breach of implied warranties against the retailer and the causes of action alleging negligence and breach of express warranties against the manufacturer. The jury returned a verdict for the retailer against plaintiff and for plaintiff against the manufacturer in the amount of $65,000. The trial court denied the manufacturer's motion for a new trial and entered judgment on the verdict. The manufacturer and plaintiff appeal. Plaintiff seeks a reversal of the part of the judgment in favor of the retailer, however, only in the event that the part of the judgment against the manufacturer is reversed.

Plaintiff introduced substantial evidence that his injuries were caused by defective design and construction of the Shopsmith. His expert witnesses testified that inadequate set screws were used to hold parts of the machine together so that normal vibration caused the tailstock of the lathe to move away from the piece of wood being turned permitting it to fly out of the lathe. They also testified that there were other more positive ways of fastening the parts of the machine together, the use of which would have prevented the accident. The jury could therefore reasonably have concluded that the manufacturer negligently constructed the Shopsmith. The jury could also reasonably have concluded that statements in the manufacturer's brochure were untrue, that they constituted express warranties,[1] and that plaintiff's injuries were caused by their breach.

The manufacturer contends, however, that plaintiff did not give it notice of breach of warranty within a reasonable time and that therefore his cause of action for breach of warranty is barred by section 1769 of the Civil Code. Since it cannot be determined whether the verdict against it was based on the negligence or warranty cause of action or both, the manufacturer concludes that the error in presenting the warranty cause of action to the jury was prejudicial.

Section 1769 of the Civil Code provides: "In the absence of express or implied agreement of the parties, acceptance of the goods by the buyer shall not discharge the seller from liability in damages or other legal remedy for breach of any promise or warranty in the contract to sell or the sale. But, if, after acceptance of the goods, the buyer fails to give notice to the seller of the breach of any promise or warranty within a reasonable time after the buyer knows, or ought to know of such breach, the seller shall not be liable therefor."

Like other provisions of the uniform sales act (Civ. Code, §§1721-1800), section 1769 deals with the rights of the parties to a contract of sale or a sale. It does not provide that notice must be given of the breach of a warranty that arises independently of a contract of sale between the parties. Such warranties are not imposed by the sales act, but are the product of common-law decisions that have recognized them in a variety of situations. . . . It is true that in many of these situations the court has invoked the sales act definitions of warranties . . . in defining the defendant's liability, but it has done so,

---

[1] In this respect the trial court limited the jury to a consideration of two statements in the manufacturer's brochure. (1) "When Shopsmith is in Horizontal Position — Rugged construction of frame provides rigid support from end to end. Heavy centerless-ground steel tubing insures perfect alignment of components." (2) "Shopsmith maintains its accuracy because every component has positive locks that hold adjustments through rough or precision work."

not because the statutes so required, but because they provided appropriate standards for the court to adopt under the circumstances presented. . . .

The notice requirement of section 1769, however, is not an appropriate one for the court to adopt in actions by injured consumers against manufacturers with whom they have not dealt. . . . "As between the immediate parties to the sale (the notice requirement) is a sound commercial rule, designed to protect the seller against unduly delayed claims for damages. As applied to personal injuries, and notice to a remote seller, it becomes a booby-trap for the unwary. The injured consumer is seldom 'steeped in the business practice which justifies the rule,' (James, *Product Liability*, 34 Texas L. Rev. 44, 192, 197) and at least until he has had legal advice it will not occur to him to give notice to one with whom he has had no dealings." (Prosser, *Strict Liability to the Consumer*, 69 Yale L.J. 1099, 1130, footnotes omitted.) . . . We conclude, therefore, that even if plaintiff did not give timely notice of breach of warranty to the manufacturer, his cause of action based on the representations contained in the brochure was not barred.

Moreover, to impose strict liability on the manufacturer under the circumstances of this case, it was not necessary for plaintiff to establish an express warranty as defined in section 1732 of the Civil Code. A manufacturer is strictly liable in tort when an article he places on the market, knowing that it is to be used without inspection for defects, proves to have a defect that causes injury to a human being. Recognized first in the case of unwholesome food products, such liability has now been extended to a variety of other products that create as great or greater hazards if defective.

Although in these cases strict liability has usually been based on the theory of an express or implied warranty running from the manufacturer to the plaintiff, the abandonment of the requirement of a contract between them, the recognition that the liability is not assumed by agreement but imposed by law . . . and the refusal to permit the manufacturer to define the scope of its own responsibility for defective products . . . make clear that the liability is not one governed by the law of contract warranties but by the law of strict liability in tort. Accordingly, rules defining and governing warranties that were developed to meet the needs of commercial transactions cannot properly be invoked to govern the manufacturer's liability to those injured by their defective products unless those rules also serve the purposes for which such liability is imposed.

We need not recanvass the reasons for imposing strict liability on the manufacturer. They have been fully articulated in the cases cited above. (See also . . . Escola v. Coca Cola Bottling Co., 24 Cal. 2d 453, 461, 150 P.2d 436, concurring opinion.) The purpose of such liability is to insure that the costs of injuries resulting from defective products are borne by the manufacturers that put such products on the market rather than by the injured persons who are powerless to protect themselves. Sales warranties serve this purpose fitfully at best. . . . In the present case, for example, plaintiff was able to plead and prove an express warranty only because he read and relied on the representations of the Shopsmith's ruggedness contained in the manufacturer's brochure. Implicit in the machine's presence on the market, however, was a representation that it would safely do the jobs for which it was built. Under these circumstances, it should not be controlling whether plaintiff selected the machine because of the statements in the brochure, or because of the machine's own appearance of excellence that belied the defect lurking beneath the surface, or because he merely assumed that it would safely do the jobs it was built to do. It should not be controlling whether the details of the sales from manufacturer to retailer and from retailer to plaintiff's wife were such that one or more of the implied warranties of the sales act arose. (Civ. Code, §1735.) "The remedies of injured consumers ought not to be made to depend upon the intricacies of the law of sales." (Ketterer v. Armour & Co., D.C., 200 F. 322, 323; Klein v. Duchess Sandwich Co., 14 Cal. 2d 272, 282, 93 P.2d 799.) To establish the manufacturer's liability it was sufficient that plaintiff proved that he was injured while using the Shopsmith in a way it was intended to be used as a result of a defect in design and manufacture of which plaintiff was not aware that made the Shopsmith unsafe for its intended use.

The manufacturer contends that the trial court erred in refusing to give three instructions requested by it. It appears from the record, however, that the substance of two of the requested instructions was adequately covered by the instructions given and that the third instruction was not supported by the evidence.

The judgment is affirmed.

NOTES TO GREENMAN v. YUBA POWER PRODUCTS, INC.

1. *Design and Manufacturing Defects, Compared.* The plaintiff's experts, as described in the court's opinion, testified that screws used to hold parts of the machine together were inadequate. If the design of the Shopsmith required use of screws of that type, the plaintiff's claim would be called, in current terminology, a *design defect* claim. On the other hand, if the design called for stronger screws but the particular Shopsmith that injured the plaintiff happened to be manufactured with weaker screws, the plaintiff's claim would be what is now called a *manufacturing defect* claim. Does Justice Traynor's opinion distinguish between these two types of claims?

2. *Negligence and Warranty, Compared.* A basic difference between negligence claims and warranty claims (and between negligence claims and strict liability claims) is that a negligence claim requires proof that the defendant acted unreasonably, while a warranty claim requires proof only that the defendant's product was not as good as warranties associated with the product required it to be. In the negligence framework, the jury must analyze how the defendant happened to produce an inadequate product, while in the warranty framework, the jury must analyze what the express and implied warranties guaranteed in terms of product quality and performance. In the context of *Greenman*, why would the plaintiff have made claims based on both negligence and warranty?

3. *Elements of the Claim.* Near the end of the *Greenman* opinion there is a simple sentence that explains that the plaintiff established a claim for strict liability by showing that "he was injured while using the Shopsmith in a way it was intended to be used as a result of a defect in design and manufacture of which plaintiff was not aware that made the Shopsmith unsafe for its intended use." What specific separate elements of required proof does this statement include?

Perspective: Total Occurrence of Injuries

Traditional strict liability may be imposed on parties who are in the best position to consider alternative ways to minimize risks and to implement those alternatives. Implicit in many of Justice Traynor's justifications for strict liability is an assumption that the adoption of strict liability will decrease the overall number of injuries related to products. One way this question can be analyzed is by comparing: (1) the precautions a manufacturer will take under a negligence system, and (2) the precautions a manufacturer will take under a strict liability system. Under a negligence system, an enterprise is likely to be characterized as negligent if it fails to spend money to prevent injuries that are likely to be more costly than an expenditure that would have prevented them. Under a strict liability system, an enterprise may have to pay for injuries regardless of whether preventing them would have been cheaper or more expensive than letting them occur. Will strict liability encourage an enterprise to avoid an injury where the anticipated payments to injured plaintiffs are less than the costs of avoiding the accident?

Another way to analyze this question is to consider whether the overall costs of being in business will be greater for an enterprise exposed to negligence liability or to strict liability. Even if a business takes the same precautions under either regime, there may be more suits or plaintiff victories in a strict liability system. If liability is really "strict," total payments to plaintiffs will be higher even if precautions taken are the same. The increased costs of doing business under strict liability might curtail the level of activity in that line of business. That reduced level of production would decrease the number of accidents. See generally A. Mitchell Polinsky & Steven Shavell, *Punitive Damages: An Economic Analysis*, 111 Harv. L. Rev. 869 (1998); and Steven Shavell, *Economic Analysis of Accident Law* (1987).

B. Restatements (Second) and (Third)

The Restatement (Second) of Torts, adopted by the American Law Institute in 1966, included §402A, which applied liability without fault (strict liability) to products cases. Section 402A became one of the most influential Restatement provisions adopted for any area of law. The provisions of §402A are closely related to the reasoning in *Escola* and *Greenman*. They reflect the general nature of those two decisions, including the treatment of product flaws without differentiating among types of possible flaws.

In 1998, the American Law Institute adopted Restatement (Third) of Torts: Products Liability. There was broad consensus that ambiguities in §402A had led to many common law developments and that changes in other aspects of tort law, in particular the ascendance of comparative negligence, made some parts of §402A difficult to apply. With regard to the actual provisions of Restatement (Third), however, there was considerable controversy, with strongly stated positions about whether it truly "restated" existing law and about whether its positions represent sound policy.

The role of the Restatements in products liability law at present is somewhat complex. Restatement (Second)'s §402A has been adopted in whole or in part in the vast majority of states. Subsequent decisions and, in some states, legislation, have changed or amplified its provisions. Only a small number of courts have responded to the Restatement (Third).

RESTATEMENT OF TORTS (SECOND)
§402A (1966)

§402A. SPECIAL LIABILITY OF SELLER OF PRODUCT FOR PHYSICAL
HARM TO USER OR CONSUMER

(1) One who sells any product in a defective condition unreasonably dangerous to the user or consumer or to his property is subject to liability for physical harm thereby caused to the ultimate user or consumer, or to his property, if

    (a) the seller is engaged in the business of selling such a product, and

    (b) it is expected to and does reach the user or consumer without substantial change in the condition in which it is sold.

(2) The rule stated in Subsection (1) applies although

    (a) the seller has exercised all possible care in the preparation and sale of his product, and

    (b) the user or consumer has not bought the product from or entered into any contractual relation with the seller.

RESTATEMENT OF TORTS (THIRD): PRODUCTS LIABILITY
(1998)

§1 LIABILITY OF COMMERCIAL SELLER OR DISTRIBUTOR FOR
HARM CAUSED BY DEFECTIVE PRODUCTS

One engaged in the business of selling or otherwise distributing products who sells or distributes a defective product is subject to liability for harm to persons or property caused by the defect.

§2 CATEGORIES OF PRODUCT DEFECTS

For purposes of determining liability under §1:

A product is defective when, at the time of sale or distribution, it contains a manufacturing defect, is defective in design, or is defective because of inadequate instructions or warnings. A product:

    (a) contains a manufacturing defect when the product departs from its intended design even though all possible care was exercised in the preparation and marketing of the product;

    (b) is defective in design when the foreseeable risks of harm posed by the product could have been reduced by the adoption of a reasonable alternative design by the seller or a predecessor in the commercial chain of distribution and the omission of the alternative design renders the product not reasonably safe;

    (c) is defective because of inadequate instructions or warnings when the foreseeable risks of harm posed by the product could have been reduced by the provision of reasonable instructions or warnings by the seller or a predecessor in the commercial chain of distribution and the omission of the instructions or warnings renders the product not reasonably safe.

NOTES TO RESTATEMENTS

1. *Coverage.* The Restatement (Second) applies only to commercial sales transactions. Leases and sales by individuals not in business may be outside its coverage. The Restatement (Third) extends its coverage to leases with its reference to those in the business of "otherwise distributing" products. The most notable difference between the two Restatements is the definition of types of product defects. What types of product defects does each Restatement define?

2. *Multiple Entities.* If a number of entities, such as a manufacturer, distributor, and retailer, are involved in the production and sale of an item, do the Restatement provisions expose each of those entities to potential liability?

Statute: DEFINITION OF PRODUCT SELLER

N.J. Stat. §2A:58C-8 (2017)

"Product seller" means any person who, in the course of a business conducted for that purpose: sells; distributes; leases; installs; prepares or assembles a manufacturer's product according to the manufacturer's plan, intention, design, specifications or formulations; blends; packages; labels; markets; repairs; maintains or otherwise is involved in placing a product in the line of commerce. The term "product seller" does not include:

(1) A seller of real property; or

(2) A provider of professional services in any case in which the sale or use of a product is incidental to the transaction and the essence of the transaction is the furnishing of judgment, skill or services; or

(3) Any person who acts in only a financial capacity with respect to the sale of a product.

NOTE TO STATUTE

Products Associated with Services. Commercial sales transactions must involve goods, not services. Sometimes a commercial transaction involves both a good and a service, as in a movie theatre (the popcorn and the movie), a hair salon (the shampoo and the haircut), or an auto repair garage (the oil filter and the installation). One approach is to apply strict liability when the predominant purpose of the transaction is to supply a good and not when it is to supply a service. A hospital's provision of a blood transfusion or a home builder's supply of contracting services, for instance, are predominantly services even though the buyer gets to keep the blood and the lumber. The supply of popcorn at a movie theatre, by contrast, is the sale of a good despite the fact that it is accompanied by the service of showing a movie.

The Restatement (Third) of Torts: Products Liability §20 takes an approach that might come out differently in various cases. It describes a number of situations that may arise. First, if the parties keep the product and service components separate, as when a lawn care firm bills separately for the fertilizer and for the application or when a repair shop bills separately for a component part, the transaction is treated as a sale of goods. Second, when the product component is consumed during the transaction, as hair dye is used up when hair is treated in a salon, the transaction is treated as a sale even without separate billing. Third, if the product is not consumed or used up by the consumer, such as a pair of barber's scissors that injures the customer because it is defective, the transaction is not considered a sale of goods by the provider to the customer. The sale of the scissors by the manufacturer to the barber, however, would be covered by strict liability, so an injured customer might have to sue the manufacturer rather than the barber.

C. Manufacturing Defects

Products liability cases are usually categorized as involving "manufacturing," "design," or "warning" defects. Manufacturing defect cases are usually straightforward. The disputes in manufacturing defect cases often concern only whether a particular unit made by the defendant conformed to the defendant's own design choices. The individual unit that injured the plaintiff may be compared to others produced by the manufacturer or to the manufacturer's design. In re Coordinated Latex Glove Litigation demonstrates this comparison. The case was the first to go to trial in a group of coordinated cases involving allegations against defendants who manufactured latex gloves.

Sometimes a manufacturing defect can be shown by testimony from people who have examined the product and compared how it was constructed to the manufacturer's specifications for it. Where examining the item is not possible, courts sometimes permit juries to infer from circumstantial evidence that the product as delivered differed in some dangerous way from the way the manufacturer intended it to be. In Myrlak v. Port Authority of New York and New Jersey, the court compares the inferences allowed in a strict liability case with the inferences represented by the *res ipsa loquitur* doctrine in negligence cases.

IN RE COORDINATED LATEX GLOVE LITIGATION
121 Cal. Rptr. 2d 301 (Cal. App. 2002)

HUFFMAN, J. . . .

On review of this order granting JNOV, we state the facts in the light most favorable to the jury's verdict. . . . [T]he plaintiffs in these coordinated cases pursue a theory of product liability that the latex gloves supplied to them caused a serious, disabling, and potentially life-threatening allergy to all forms of natural rubber latex (referred to as NRL) to develop, even though they did not have this condition prior to their extensive use of latex gloves. They accordingly claim improperly designed and manufactured NRL gloves caused this allergy by allowing excessive levels of allergenic agents, latex proteins, to remain present on the surface of the gloves during manufacture. It is not disputed that such agents may be greatly reduced or eliminated through washing and chlorinating procedures in the design and manufacture of these gloves. The issue is whether, as plaintiff complains here in the context of her manufacturing defect claim, Baxter "took too long" to make that its standard practice, in light of its knowledge and research.

McGinnis (sometimes referred to as Plaintiff) was employed as a respiratory technician by various hospitals and care facilities for a number of years between 1982 and 1996, and used thousands of pairs of Baxter NRL gloves during her career. The brands she used over 93 percent of the time, Flexam powdered exam gloves and Triflex powdered surgical gloves, were manufactured at Baxter plants in the United States and Malaysia. . . .

Both through her own use of NRL products and the use of others around her, McGinnis became sensitized to that substance to the point of developing a serious Type I latex allergy, which caused her in 1995 to experience symptoms going beyond mild symptoms of itching and skin irritation, to a life-threatening anaphylactic reaction (respiratory distress, hives and other symptoms). She was forced to leave health care work, has undergone emergency medical treatment for such reactions, and must carry medication to treat them at all times, as her allergy is a lifelong condition.

McGinnis sued Baxter and other defendants (who were no longer involved in the case by the time of trial and this appeal) on various products liability and negligence theories. The matter went to jury trial on strict liability theories of manufacturing defect and failure to warn of a defective product, as well as negligence through manufacture and failure to warn.

Extensive testimony and documentary evidence was presented at trial about the manufacturing process of NRL gloves. The critical qualities provided by rubber gloves to the health care profession include barrier protection and tactile sensitivity. The market for gloves grew tenfold from 1983 to 1990 after the FDA recommended and then in 1987 adopted universal precautions for health care workers to prevent the spread of AIDS and hepatitis, requiring expanded use of gloves and other barrier protection equipment. By 1990, Baxter was manufacturing and distributing approximately four billion gloves per year, which represented approximately half of the American medical glove market. Most of these gloves were made of NRL.

The multistep manufacturing process begins with the tapping of rubber trees and centrifuging and mixing of raw rubber, the preparation of glove molds to be positioned on a continuous conveyor line, the dipping of the mold in coagulant and rubber compounds, the leaching in water of the molds, curing, rinsing, powdering, chlorination and sterilization, and packaging of the gloves. Plaintiff presented evidence that additional washing and chlorination of the gloves would reduce allergenic protein levels, while Baxter presented evidence that these steps might lead to defects in barrier protection such as pinholes, tearing, or a change in texture. . . .

Plaintiff's counsel presented closing argument that focused upon the instruction about the manufacturing defect claim, BAJI No. 9.00.3: "A defect exists if the product differs from the intended result." He argued that the Baxter witnesses testified they had the intent, starting in 1990, to produce a low protein glove, but that although "their intentions were good, their execution was bad. And that creates a defect. They didn't execute their intent." Also, Plaintiff's counsel argued that the product could also be defective under the test "if the product differs from apparently identical products from the same manufacturer." . . .

In contrast, Baxter argued that the protein level evidence offered by Plaintiff had not been placed in context with any applicable government requirements, and that at the time Dr. Truscott was investigating the problem, complaints had been received about both high protein and low protein gloves, which made analysis at that point inconclusive. Before and after 1992, Baxter was constantly tinkering with the system to get the best protein testing system in place. This protein testing system had to be implemented while keeping production up, due to the health care profession's need for universal precautions equipment. Baxter's position was that its personnel were at the top of the heap in the production field, and although they were not perfect, they acted reasonably.

The jury returned a verdict finding that a manufacturing defect had been proven and awarded McGinnis net compensatory damages of $886,921.20. The jury also found Baxter had been negligent but there had been no causation of her injuries through negligence. A comparative fault finding was made assessing 70 percent of the negligence to Baxter, 15 percent to McGinnis, and 15 percent to her previous hospital employer (not a party to the action). The jury also rejected McGinnis's claim that a warning defect was present. . . .

After briefing and argument, the trial court granted the Baxter motion for JNOV on the single cause of action on which McGinnis had prevailed, manufacturing defect under a strict products liability theory. . . .

McGinnis's appeal . . . argues the trial court incorrectly applied both the alternative tests for a manufacturing defect as set forth in Barker v. Lull Engineering Co., 573 P.2d 443 (Cal. 1978). There, the Supreme Court opined (optimistically, in hindsight) that defining the concept of a product defect "raises considerably more difficulties in the design defect context than it does in the manufacturing or production defect context. In general, a manufacturing or production defect is readily identifiable because *a defective product is one that differs from the manufacturer's intended result or from other ostensibly identical units of the same product line.*" These concepts form the basis of BAJI 9.00.3, defining a manufacturing defect, which was given to the jury here. . . .

As explained by the Supreme Court in Brown v. Superior Court, 751 P.2d 470 (Cal. 1988) (*Brown*), under *Barker*'s strict products liability analysis, there are three types of product defects: "First, there may be a flaw in the manufacturing process, resulting in a product that differs from the manufacturer's intended result. . . . Second, there are products which are 'perfectly' manufactured but are unsafe because of the absence of a safety device, i.e., a defect in design. . . ." The third type of defect "is a product that is dangerous because it lacks adequate warnings or instructions." . . .

Here, McGinnis's case relied on the first and third types of product defects . . . and the jury rejected the third (failure to warn of a defect). Only the first type, manufacturing defect, is squarely presented as an issue in this appeal. Hence, our task is to see if, as McGinnis contends, substantial evidence was presented to support a manufacturing defect theory under either of the *Barker* formulations. . . .

In Morson v. Superior Court (2002) 90 Cal. App. 4th 775, 109 Cal. Rptr. 2d 343, this court relied on Dierks v. Mitsubishi Motors Corp. (1989) 208 Cal. App. 3d 352, 354-355, 256 Cal. Rptr. 230 as a statement of the difference between a defect in manufacture and a defect in design: "'The latter focuses upon whether the product was designed to perform as safely as an ordinary consumer would expect or whether the risk of danger inherent in the design outweighed the benefits of the design. [Citations.] The former focuses on whether the particular product involved in the accident was manufactured in conformity with the manufacturer's design. [Citations.]'" . . .

McGinnis first claims the trial court mistakenly evaluated the evidentiary record only in light of the "intended result test," by finding she failed to produce essential evidence that the high protein gloves that Baxter produced departed from its own design, specifications, or prototypes. She contends she showed, through the evidence of the research and data collection that Baxter was doing to reduce protein levels, that

Baxter had internal standards that it was developing that constituted such evidence of "formal product design, prototype, or specifications." . . .

As stated in Baxter's respondent's briefs, it was uncontested at trial "that Baxter intended to, and did, produce and sell gloves with a wide range of protein levels." These gloves met Baxter's design specifications as they existed at all the relevant times. There was no set standard for protein levels under either Baxter's corporate policies or the government regulations. Plaintiff cannot convert these undisputed facts into an adequate showing of a manufacturing defect under the *Barker* tests.

We also evaluate the evidence in light of the Baxter argument that McGinnis actually tried this case under a design defect approach, and did not change her arguments into a manufacturing defect format until she realized the design defect approach was fatally flawed. Both the traditional definitions of manufacturing defect presuppose that a suitable design is in place, but that the manufacturing process has in some way deviated from that design. Focus is on whether the particular product involved in the incident was manufactured in conformity with the manufacturer's design. Here, we are unable to separate out the raw material, NRL, from the forming and processing of it, nor does Plaintiff argue we should. The NRL gloves in this case were processed exactly as Baxter intended that they should be, in light of the state of its scientific and manufacturing knowledge at the time. This was true of all the various lines of production, even though testing was ongoing at some and not others at times. That later developments showed the product was subject to immense improvement does not necessarily show the products processed earlier were defective, under either formulation of the *Barker* test. The fact that simultaneously manufactured gloves were subject to different standards at different production lines, due to the status of the manufacturer's research and development, where scientific knowledge was as inconclusive as is shown by this record, does not require that some items must be deemed defective under a manufacturing defect approach. Rather, such arguments actually deal with design defect evidence, and the jury properly did not receive those instructions in this case. Allowing the Plaintiff's verdict to stand here would be inconsistent with the applicable public policies as stated above, for lack of any supporting evidentiary showing.

In conclusion, we believe that Plaintiff's efforts are ineffective to show that the various NRL gloves that were manufactured precisely as intended, that complied with applicable governmental standards, and that fulfilled their primary barrier function, nevertheless have manufacturing defects due to the existence of evidence of the testing, improvement, research and development efforts, targets and goals of the manufacturer, at different times and locations, reflective of the state of scientific knowledge regarding latex protein levels of exposure available to the relevant participants in this health care product context. The products did not differ from the manufacturer's intended result, nor did they have materially significant differences among identical units from the same product line. The motion for JNOV was properly granted. . .

NOTES TO IN RE COORDINATED LATEX GLOVE LITIGATION

1. *Definition of "Manufacturing Defect."* An individual unit of a manufacturer's product has a manufacturing defect if it varies from other units in an unintended way, or if it varies from the manufacturer's intended design for the product. How did the plaintiff's evidence fail to satisfy either of these definitions?

2. *Origin of Manufacturing Defect.* The plaintiff is obligated to prove only that a product fell short of the manufacturer's own specifications. The strict liability definition of "manufacturing defect" ignores questions that would be relevant in a negligence context, such as evaluating the conduct involved in the creation, inspection, and distribution of the flawed product.

MYRLAK v. PORT AUTHORITY OF NEW YORK AND NEW JERSEY
157 N.J. 84, 723 A.2d 45 (1999)

COLEMAN, J.

In this strict products liability case involving one defendant, the primary issue is whether the doctrine of *res ipsa loquitur* should be applied when liability is based upon an alleged manufacturing defect. The trial court declined to instruct the jury regarding *res ipsa loquitur.* The Appellate Division held that the trial court should have given such an instruction. We disagree and reverse. We hold that the traditional negligence doctrine of *res ipsa loquitur* generally is not applicable in a strict products liability case. We adopt, however, the "indeterminate product defect test" established in Section 3 of the Restatement (Third) of Torts: Products Liability as the more appropriate jury instruction in cases that do not involve a shifting of the burden of persuasion.

On July 6, 1991, plaintiff, John Myrlak, was injured when his chair collapsed while he was at work. At that time, plaintiff was forty-three years old, six feet six inches tall, and weighed approximately 325 pounds.

At the time of the accident, plaintiff had been seated in the chair performing his duties for approximately one hour and forty-five minutes. He suddenly heard a loud noise, and the back of his chair cracked and gave way. Plaintiff and the chair fell backwards, causing both to land parallel to the floor. Plaintiff grabbed the arms of the chair and pulled himself forward as he was falling. He injured his lower back and was hospitalized.

Plaintiff . . . filed products liability claims against the manufacturer of the chair [Girsberger] alleging both a manufacturing and a warning defect theory of liability. Plaintiff's expert was unable to . . . identify a specific defect in the chair; nor could he state that a defect caused the accident.

At the close of all of the evidence, plaintiff requested the court to charge the jury on *res ipsa loquitur* regarding the manufacturing defect claim. In denying the requested charge, the trial court stated that it wanted to avoid that phrase even though plaintiff relied on circumstantial evidence to infer that there was a manufacturing defect. The jury . . . found that plaintiff failed to establish a manufacturing defect in the chair.

The [Appellate Division] reversed the verdict in favor of the manufacturer, concluding that the trial court should have instructed the jury on *res ipsa loquitur.* We granted defendant Girsberger's petition for certification, limited to the issue whether *res ipsa loquitur* should apply to this strict products liability case.

Res ipsa loquitur permits an inference of defendant's want of due care when the following three conditions have been met: "(a) the occurrence itself ordinarily bespeaks negligence; (b) the instrumentality was within the defendant's exclusive control; and (c) there is no indication in the circumstances that the injury was the result of the plaintiff's own voluntary act or neglect."

Whether an occurrence ordinarily bespeaks negligence is based on the probabilities in favor of negligence. Hence, *res ipsa* is available if it is more probable than not that the defendant has been negligent.

In a products liability case in which the plaintiff alleges a manufacturing defect under the Act, the plaintiff has the burden to prove "the product causing the harm was not reasonably fit, suitable or safe for its intended purpose." N.J.S.A. 2A:58C-2. In the typical manufacturing defect case, a plaintiff is not required to establish negligence. In other words, a plaintiff must impugn the product but not the conduct of the manufacturer of the product.

The Act defines a manufacturing defect as a deviation "from the design specifications, formulae, or performance standards of the manufacturer or from otherwise identical units manufactured to the same manufacturing specifications or formulae." N.J.S.A. 2A:58C-2a.

Simply because a plaintiff is not required to prove fault in a strict liability case does not mean that absolute liability will be imposed upon a manufacturer. Based on our well-established case law in this area, a plaintiff must prove that the product was defective, that the defect existed when the product left the manufacturer's control, and that the defect proximately caused injuries to the plaintiff, a reasonably foreseeable or intended user.

To prove both the existence of a defect and that the defect existed while the product was in the control of the manufacturer, a plaintiff may resort to direct evidence, such as the testimony of an expert who has examined the product, or, in the absence of such evidence, to circumstantial proof. Scanlon v. General Motors Corp., 65 N.J. 582, 591 (1974).

We agree with the majority of jurisdictions that, ordinarily, the traditional *res ipsa loquitur* jury charge should not be used in strict products liability actions. As noted previously, *res ipsa loquitur* is a negligence doctrine; it is a circumstantial means of proving a defendant's lack of due care. Strict liability, on the other hand, is a theory of liability based on allocating responsibility regardless of a defendant's unreasonableness, negligence or fault. Thus, while *res ipsa* might demonstrate a manufacturer's negligence in failing to inspect or appropriately assemble a particular product, strict liability merely questions whether there is a defect in that product that existed before it left the manufacturer's control.

We recognize that as an alternative to a traditional *res ipsa loquitur* instruction, various states and commentators have advocated an intermediate-type approach for circumstantially proving the existence of a product defect. That approach appears to best serve the interest of all parties and is not inconsistent with the Act.

The *Scanlon* rule regarding circumstantial proof of a defect in a strict products liability case was adopted recently in the Restatement (Third) of Torts: Products Liability. [Section 3] provides:

> It may be inferred that the harm sustained by the plaintiff was caused by a product defect existing at the time of sale or distribution, without proof of a specific defect, when the incident that harmed the plaintiff:
>   (a) was of a kind that ordinarily occurs as a result of a product defect; and
>   (b) was not, in the particular case, solely the result of causes other than product defect existing at the time of sale or distribution.

Although Section 3 of the Restatement is based on a *res ipsa* model, it permits the jury to draw two inferences: that the harmful incident was caused by a product defect, and that the defect was present when the product left the manufacturer's control. The *res ipsa loquitur* doctrine, on the other hand, creates the single inference of negligence. Nevertheless, Section 3 of the Restatement parallels the elements of our *res ipsa loquitur* doctrine.

Section 3 of the Restatement has been referred to as the "indeterminate product test" because its use is limited to those product liability cases in which the plaintiff cannot prove a specific defect. A plaintiff can satisfy the requirements of Section 3 of the Restatement the same way as in the case of *res ipsa loquitur*, by direct and circumstantial evidence as well as evidence that negates causes other than product defect.

Other jurisdictions have adopted similar circumstantial methods for establishing an inference of a product defect in strict products liability cases. We agree with those states that in some cases, "common experience indicates that certain accidents do not occur absent some defect," and therefore an inference of a defect under specific circumstances should be permitted. Fifteen other states have adopted the principles incorporated into Section 3 of the Restatement. See Reporters' Notes to Section 3, at 115-18. We also adopt the indeterminate product defect test announced in Section 3 of the Restatement.

Because we have adopted Section 3 of the Restatement, upon retrial, plaintiff need not prove a specific defect in the chair if he can establish that the incident that harmed him is of the kind that ordinarily occurs as a result of a product defect, and that the incident was not solely the result of causes other than product defect existing at the time the chair left Girsberger's control. Restatement (Third) of Torts §3(a) and (b). If plaintiff cannot satisfy those requirements, he is not entitled to have the jury charged regarding an inference of a product defect, and plaintiff would be obligated to establish one or more manufacturing defects required by the Act, N.J.S.A. 2A:58C-2a.

That part of the Appellate Division's judgment requiring a *res ipsa loquitur* charge on the manufacturing defect claim is reversed. The matter is remanded to the Law Division for further proceedings as otherwise directed by the Appellate Division.

NOTES TO MYRLAK v. PORT AUTHORITY OF NEW YORK AND NEW JERSEY

1. *Circumstantial Evidence.* "*Res ipsa loquitur*" and the "indeterminate product defect test" used in strict liability for manufacturing defect cases are both labels for circumstantial evidence. Applying the *res ipsa* doctrine in negligence cases has three characteristics that are analogous to the indeterminate product defect test. First, *res ipsa loquitur* is limited to situations where the plaintiff is unable to identify what conduct of the defendant caused the harm. Second, to protect the defendant from liability caused by others, *res ipsa loquitur* requires that the instrumentality causing the harm has been in the defendant's control at the time of the negligence. Third, *res ipsa loquitur* permits two inferences — that negligence caused the harm and that the defendant was the negligent party. The indeterminate product defect test is analogous to *res ipsa loquitur* in each of these characteristics. To what kinds of manufacturing defect cases is this test limited? Does any part of the test protect defendants from strict liability? What inferences does the indeterminate product defect test permit?

2. *Variation in Definitions.* New Jersey is one of many states that have adopted statutes to govern various aspects of products liability actions. How does the New

Jersey statute's definition of "manufacturing defect," discussed in *Myrlak,* compare with the definition in the Restatement (Third)?

Problem
Unspecified Defect

John Whitted crashed his 1987 Chevrolet Nova into two trees in 1993 and sued the manufacturer, General Motors. The court described Mr. Whitted as six feet tall, weighing 265 pounds. He was driving home on slick roads wearing his seat belt, which included both a shoulder harness and lap belt. To avoid an oncoming car, Whitted moved the car closer to the shoulder. He moved too far, and the car slid off the road and hit the trees. The webbing of the seat belt separated, while the clasp remained connected to the buckle. Whitted remained inside the car, but he was thrust against the steering wheel. He sustained fractures to two bones in his lower left arm and cuts to his forehead. He argued that the seat belt was defective in some way but did not identify the specific defect. Would the indeterminate product defect test aid his case? See Whitted v. General Motors Corp., 58 F.3d 1200 (7th Cir. 1995).

D. Design Defects

1. Consumer Expectation and Risk-Utility Tests

The Restatement (Second) of Torts §402A recognized strict liability for products with a "defective condition unreasonably dangerous to the user or consumer or to his property." Where plaintiffs have challenged the design of products, courts have used "consumer expectation" and "risk-utility" tests to give meaning to that definition of defectiveness. In Malcolm v. Evenflo Co., Inc., the court applies and justifies a test that compares how dangerous the product actually was to how dangerous an ordinary user expected it to be. The court followed this "consumer expectation" test believing that it creates stronger incentives for safe designs than negligence doctrines create. Morton v. Owens-Corning Fiberglas Corp. provides formal statements of the consumer expectation and risk-benefit tests, describes when each test should apply, and considers what evidence is relevant to determining consumer expectations. While the consumer expectation test ignores the reasonableness of a design, the risk-utility test balances a design's costs and benefits. Warner Fruehauf Trailer Co. v. Boston applies the risk-utility test to the design of a truck's liftgate. Denny v. Ford Motor Co. involves a claim that a sports utility vehicle was defectively designed because it rolled over when the driver slammed on the brakes. It illustrates how the consumer expectation and risk-utility tests may produce different results.

MALCOLM v. EVENFLO CO.
217 P.3d 514 (Mont. 2009)

BRIAN MORRIS, J.

Chad and Jessica Malcolm (collectively Malcolms) sued Evenflo Company, Inc. (Evenflo) after their four-month-old son Tyler suffered fatal brain injuries in a rollover

Con. Exp. v. Risk Ut. Test.

car accident. The Malcolms alleged that the Evenflo "On My Way" (OMW) child safety seat contained a design defect that caused Tyler's death. The Malcolms asserted strict liability in tort. Evenflo appeals from a judgment in the Sixth Judicial District, Park County, following a jury trial. . . .

The Malcolms lived south of Livingston, Montana, on a ranch near Emigrant. Chad Malcolm was the fourth generation of the family to ranch in the area. A friend gave Jessica Malcolm the OMW while Jessica was pregnant with Tyler. Jessica called Evenflo to ask if the OMW model 207 was safe to use. Evenflo assured her that the OMW was not subject to any of their recalls and that the OMW was safe to use. . . .

Jessica Malcolm drove to Emigrant on the evening of July 16, 2000, in her 1996 Suburban to pick up pizza and a movie with her sister and her son Tyler. She then drove back south on Highway 89 toward the ranch. Malcolm's sister rode in the passenger seat and Tyler rode in the back in the OMW model 207 child seat. A northbound motorist swerved into Malcolm's lane and forced Malcolm off the road. The Suburban rolled three times, traveled down a steep incline, and stopped in a ditch. The accident occurred within sight of the Malcolms' ranch.

Jessica Malcolm did not suffer serious injury. Her sister sustained a severe head injury. The left belt hook of the OMW broke off during the rollover. The seat belt slipped out from the open-ended belt hook on the opposite side of the seat. The forces of the accident ejected the OMW from the Suburban. The OMW came to rest approximately 60 feet from the Suburban. Tyler remained strapped in the OMW. Tyler suffered brain injuries that resulted in his death.

The Malcolms' case sounded exclusively in strict liability in tort, design defect theory. The Malcolms claimed that the Evenflo OMW model 207 infant child safety seat constituted a defectively designed product that failed catastrophically even though they had used the seat in a reasonably anticipated manner. The Malcolms pointed to the OMW's open-ended belt hook design and the lack of expanded polystyrene (EPS) padding. The Malcolms contended that Evenflo could have manufactured the OMW using a feasible superior alternative design. . . .

Evenflo contended that the OMW model 207 was not defective in any way. . . . Evenflo emphasized that the production model 207 passed each of the [Federal Motor Vehicle Safety Standard (FMVSS)] tests conducted on the seat. . . .

The District Court granted the Malcolms' motion in limine to exclude arguments by Evenflo that the OMW . . . complied with FMVSS. . . . The District Court reasoned that evidence of compliance . . . "does not appear to be relevant to the issues or facts in this case." . . .

Section 27-1-719, MCA, governs design defect liability in Montana. A person who sells a product in a defective condition is liable for the physical harm caused by the defective product. A product is defective if it is dangerous to an extent beyond that anticipated by the ordinary user.

Strict liability recognizes that the seller is in the best position to insure product safety. Design defect liability therefore places the risk of loss on the manufacturer. This imposition of risk provides "an incentive to design and produce fail-safe products which exceed reasonable standards of safety." Design defect strict liability may be imposed even if the seller has "exercised all possible care," and even though the product was faultlessly manufactured. . . .

Evenflo urges this Court to adopt the *Restatement (Third) of Torts: Products Liability* §4 (1998). Section 4 provides that compliance with an applicable regulation is admissible in connection with liability for defective design. Evenflo contends that . . . this Court has adopted the *Restatement (Third)* approach in the negligence context. Evenflo argues that "[t]here is no reason why such highly relevant evidence should be admissible in negligence, but not products liability cases." . . .

The District Court correctly recognized, however, that Montana draws "a bright line" between cases asserting strict liability in tort and those grounded in negligence theory. . . .

We likewise reject Evenflo's efforts to inject negligence principles into the strict liability setting. We decline to adopt the *Restatement (Third) of Torts: Products Liability*, §4. Section 4 conflicts with the core principles of Montana's strict products liability law. To recognize Section 4 improperly would inject into strict products liability analysis the manufacturer's reasonableness and level of care — concepts that are fundamental to negligence law, but irrelevant on the issue of design defect liability. The District Court correctly relied upon Montana precedent that emphasizes the fundamental difference between strict liability and negligence law. . . .

[Affirmed with regard to the exclusion of FMVSS evidence, reversed in part, and remanded in connection with other issues.]

NOTES TO MALCOLM v. EVENFLO CO.

1. *Simplicity and Effect of the Consumer Expectation Test.* The *Malcolm* court applied the consumer expectation test, using a legislatively adopted concise definition: "A product is defective if it is dangerous to an extent beyond that anticipated by the ordinary user." The simplicity of that test — its reference only to what a user would anticipate — justified the court's conclusion that information about safety tests the product passed could properly be kept out of the trial.

2. *Origin of the Consumer Expectation Test.* The Restatement (Second) §402A provided comments that led some courts to adopt the consumer expectation test. A comment on "Defective Condition" states:

> *g. Defective Condition.* The rule stated in this Section applies only where the product is, at the time it leaves the seller's hands, in a condition not contemplated *by the ultimate consumer*, which will be unreasonably dangerous to him. . . . (emphasis added).

A comment on the "unreasonably dangerous" term also supported development of the consumer expectation test. Comment i states:

> *i. Unreasonably Dangerous.* The rule stated in this Section applies only where the defective condition of the product makes it unreasonably dangerous to the user or consumer. Many products cannot possibly be made entirely safe for all consumption, and any food or drug necessarily involves some risk of harm, if only from over-consumption. Ordinary sugar is a deadly poison to diabetics, and castor oil found use under Mussolini as an instrument of torture. That is not what is meant by "unreasonably dangerous" in this Section. The article sold must be dangerous to an extent beyond that which would be contemplated *by the ordinary consumer* who purchases it, with the ordinary knowledge common to the community as to its characteristic. Good whiskey is not unreasonably dangerous merely because it will make some people drunk, and is especially dangerous to alcoholics; but bad whiskey, containing a dangerous amount of fusel oil, is unreasonably dangerous. Good tobacco is not

unreasonably dangerous merely because the effects of smoking may be harmful; but tobacco containing something like marijuana may be unreasonably dangerous. Good butter is not unreasonably dangerous merely because, if such be the case, it deposits cholesterol in the arteries and leads to heart attacks; but bad butter, contaminated with poisonous fish oil, is unreasonably dangerous. (Emphasis added.)

3. *Distinguishing Negligence and Strict Liability.* In many states, negligence and strict liability theories have considerable overlap for design defect cases. The *Malcolm* court describes a jurisprudential view that maintains a distinction between the two theories. What reasons does the court give for imposing liability on an actor whose conduct has been reasonable?

4. *Compliance with Regulations.* In some states, compliance with regulations may be a full defense or a relevant consideration in design defect cases. Montana has not adopted either of those doctrines. The possibility that compliance with a federal regulation could preclude state-based tort liability did not arise in this case because of particular language in the governing federal statute stating that a person may not use compliance with a motor vehicle safety standard as a defense at common law and that compliance does not exempt a person from liability at common law. Compliance with regulations and the possible preemptive effect of federal regulations is discussed further in section H.

MORTON v. OWENS-CORNING FIBERGLAS CORP.
33 Cal. App. 4th 1529, 40 Cal. Rptr. 2d 22 (1995)

HAERLE, A.J.

Robert and Pamela Morton brought this strict products liability action against Owens-Corning Fiberglas Corporation (OCF) and others for damages arising from Mr. Morton's exposure to asbestos containing products and his consequent development of mesothelioma, an asbestos-caused form of cancer. . . .

From December 1959 to February 1961, Mr. Morton worked at the New York Shipbuilding Yard in Camden, New Jersey (the Shipyard). He worked as a wireman, installing cable on board ships. The majority of his time at the Shipyard was spent working on a ship called the Kitty Hawk. . . . Mr. Morton was in good health until October 1991, when he developed flu symptoms and chest pains. During the following months, Mr. Morton underwent various tests and, in May 1992, was diagnosed with mesothelioma.

The trial court ordered that the trial be bifurcated. The damages phase was tried first, to the judge, who made separate findings for each type of damages plaintiffs suffered. The liability phase was tried to a jury [that] found OCF liable to plaintiffs and responsible for 12% of their damages. . . .

[On appeal,] OCF objects to the method by which plaintiffs proved OCF's product was defective, i.e., the "consumer expectations" test. OCF contends the trial court should have granted its motion for nonsuit because the consumer expectations test does not apply to this case as a matter of law. Alternatively, OCF argues that, if the consumer expectations theory did apply, the court erred by excluding "state of the art" evidence offered to disprove plaintiffs' theory.

"[T]he term defect as utilized in the strict liability context is neither self-defining nor susceptible to a single definition applicable in all contexts." (Barker v. Lull Engineering Co. (1978) 20 Cal. 3d 413, 427, 143 Cal. Rptr. 225, 573 P.2d 443.) Our Supreme Court has identified two alternative criteria for ascertaining whether a product has a design defect.

First, the consumer expectations test provides that "a product may be found defective in design if the plaintiff demonstrates that the product failed to perform as safely as an ordinary consumer would expect when used in an intended or reasonably foreseeable manner." This test derives from the warranty heritage upon which our product liability doctrine partially rests and recognizes that "implicit in a product's presence on the market is a representation that it will safely do the job for which it was built."

The second "risk-benefit" test evolved in response to situations in which the consumer would not know what to expect because, for example, he would have no idea how safe the product could be made. Under this test, "a product may be found defective in design, even if it satisfies ordinary consumer expectations, if through hindsight the jury determines that the product's design embodies 'excessive preventable danger,' or, in other words, if the jury finds that the risk of danger inherent in the challenged design outweighs the benefits of such design."

Our Supreme Court recently clarified that the consumer expectations test is not suitable in all design defect cases because "in many instances it is simply impossible to eliminate the balancing or weighing of competing considerations in determining whether a product is defectively designed or not." (Soule v. General Motors Corp. (1994) 8 Cal. 4th 548, 562-563, 34 Cal. Rptr. 2d 607, 882 P.2d 298.) OCF contends that *Soule* establishes that the consumer expectations test does not apply to strict liability actions involving asbestos products. However, we recently rejected this precise contention in Sparks v. Owens-Illinois, Inc. (1995) 32 Cal. App. 4th 461, 472-476, 38 Cal. Rptr. 2d 739 (hereafter *Sparks*).

In *Sparks*, this court affirmed a judgment against Owens-Illinois in a case in which plaintiffs established that Owens-Illinois' asbestos-containing insulation product was defective under the consumer expectations test. Our analysis included a thorough discussion of the limited scope of the consumer expectations test as set forth by the Supreme Court in *Soule*. We applied the *Soule* analysis to the asbestos context, focusing on the "crucial question" as to "whether the circumstances of the product's failure permit an inference that the product's design performed below the legitimate, commonly accepted minimum safety assumptions of its ordinary consumers." Ultimately, we concluded that *Soule* did not preclude plaintiffs from relying on a consumer expectations theory because, among other things, "[t]here were neither 'complicated design considerations,' nor 'obscure components,' nor 'esoteric circumstances' surrounding the 'accident'" and because the product failure was "beyond the 'legitimate, commonly accepted minimum safety assumptions of its ordinary consumers.'"

. . . As in *Sparks*, the situation in the present case is one in which the everyday experiences of the consumers of OCF's product would permit a conclusion that the product's design violated minimum safety assumptions. The injury Mr. Morton incurred was not the result of esoteric circumstances or an alleged mechanical malfunction. OCF's product was not itself a complex or technical device. Further, the individuals who worked with and around this product were capable of formulating minimum expectations as to its safety. Thus, as we did in *Sparks*, we reject the contention that the consumer expectations theory does not apply to this case as a matter of law.

Further, we find sufficient evidence in the record to satisfy the consumer expectations test in the present case. Plaintiffs presented several percipient witnesses, including Mr. Morton, who testified they believed the insulation products used on the Kitty Hawk were safe and that they had no expectation that exposure to such products would make them ill.[8] OCF presented no evidence that consumers of its product knew, expected, or even suspected that product was unsafe.

OCF contends the trial court erred by precluding it from offering "state of the art" evidence which it defines as "evidence that a particular risk was neither known nor knowable by the application of scientific knowledge available at the time of manufacture and/or distribution." OCF's theory of relevance was "that Mr. Morton would not have an expectation of the product that it could be safer than the medical and scientific knowledge at the time indicated it was." The trial court ruled OCF's state of the art evidence was not relevant under the consumer expectations test.

We agree with the trial court that evidence as to what the scientific community knew about the dangers of asbestos and when they knew it is not relevant to show what the ordinary consumer of OCF's product reasonably expected in terms of safety at the time of Mr. Morton's exposure. It is the knowledge and reasonable expectations of the consumer, not the scientific community, that is relevant under the consumer expectations test. The fact that the scientific community was unaware of the dangers of asbestos, if that is a fact, would not make it any less reasonable for Mr. Morton or other consumers of OCF's products to expect that they could work with or near OCF's product without getting cancer. . . .

Finally, OCF contends that courts have admitted, in consumer expectations cases, expert evidence designed to educate the jury about the nature of the allegedly defective product. Under certain circumstances, expert testimony may be admissible to prove what ordinary consumers of the product actually expect when those expectations are beyond the lay experience common to all jurors. Our point is that evidence as to the knowledge of the scientific community is nevertheless irrelevant to prove the reasonable expectations of the consumers of OCF's product. OCF's authority does not hold to the contrary. . . .

[Judgment against the defendant was affirmed, modified as to the amount of damages awarded.]

---

[8] Mr. Morton testified there were no warnings about the dangers of asbestos dust, and nobody used masks. He believed the materials being used at the yard were safe, and did not know about the hazardous nature of asbestos dust until the early 1980's.

William Kimley worked as an electrician's assistant on the Kitty Hawk, and knew Mr. Morton. Kimley specifically remembered that OCF asbestos insulation was used on the Kitty Hawk. Kimley testified he believed the asbestos insulation used on the Kitty Hawk was safe and never expected that asbestos dust would cause cancer or other diseases.

John Murphy also worked at the New York shipyard during the time Mr. Morton was there. He specifically recalled that OCF "Kaylo" insulation was used on the Kitty Hawk. Murphy testified that, at the time he worked in the shipyard, he did not expect that dust from the insulation materials was harmful.

NOTES TO MORTON v. OWENS-CORNING FIBERGLAS CORP.

1. *Whose Expectation?*   The consumer expectation test might refer either to the expectations of a particular injured consumer, the plaintiff, or to the expectations of an "ordinary" consumer. While some courts originally took a subjective approach, the objective approach is generally accepted now. It is consistent with the language of comments g and i, discussed in the notes following the Malcolm v. Evenflo Co. opinion. This approach avoids testimony by self-interested plaintiffs about whether they expected products to have dangers that cause injuries.

2. *Choosing Between Consumer Expectation and Risk-Utility Tests.*   As described in *Morton*, California's courts apply practical criteria for deciding which test should be used to determine whether a product is defectively designed. The criteria emphasize consumers' ability to form legitimate assumptions about the dangers presented by a product. An alternative approach, adopted in Illinois, applies whichever test is dictated by the evidence the parties have offered to show that the product is defective:

> Although we have declined to adopt section 2 of the Products Liability Restatement as a statement of substantive law, we do find its formulation of the risk-utility test to be instructive. Under section 2(b), the risk-utility balance is to be determined based on consideration of a "broad range of factors," including "the magnitude and probability of the foreseeable risks of harm, the instructions and warnings accompanying the product, and the nature and strength of *consumer expectations* regarding the product, including expectations arising from product portrayal and marketing," as well as "the likely effects of the alternative design on production costs; the effects of the alternative design on product longevity, maintenance, repair, and esthetics; and the range of consumer choice among products." (Emphasis added.) Restatement (Third) of Torts: Products Liability §2, Comment f, at 23 (1998).
>
> . . . Under this formulation, consumer expectations are included within the scope of the broader risk-utility test. In addition, the test refines the consumer-expectation factor by specifically allowing for advertising and marketing messages to be used to assess consumer expectations.
>
> We adopt this formulation of the risk-utility test and hold that when the evidence presented by either or both parties supports the application of this integrated test, an appropriate instruction is to be given at the request of either party. If, however, both parties' theories of the case are framed entirely in terms of consumer expectations, including those based on advertising and marketing messages, and/or whether the product was being put to a reasonably foreseeable use at the time of the injury, the jury should be instructed only on the consumer-expectation test.

Mikolajczyk v. Ford Motor Co., 901 N.E.2d 329, 352-353 (Ill. 2008). Under this approach, if a defendant believed that the risk-utility approach would be more favorable than the consumer expectation test, how could the defendant make sure that the risk-utility test will be used rather than the consumer expectation test?

3. *Open and Obvious Dangers.*   A rigorous application of the consumer expectation test would protect many very dangerous products from being characterized as defective so long as their dangers were apparent. This result might encourage manufacturers to design products with obvious and prominent hazards. Courts have avoided this result by focusing on the "excessive preventable risk" language quoted

in *Morton* and applying the risk-utility test. For example, in Linegar v. Armour of America, 909 F.2d 1150 (8th Cir. 1990), the design of a bullet-resistant vest was called into question by the estate of a police officer who was fatally wounded while wearing it. The vest's design left parts of a wearer's sides unprotected. Because this feature was obvious, the consumer expectation test might have been a full defense. The court noted that possibility but also analyzed the risks and utility inherent in the defendant's design choices and refused to treat the obviousness of the product's shortcoming as a full defense.

Perspective: Expectations About What?

The consumer expectation test traditionally considers expectations about anticipated physical harms to product users. A different understanding of the range of people's beliefs and expectations about products would take into account people's beliefs about a wider range of product attributes. It could recognize aspects such as the distributive impact of a product's risks (such as whether risks are imposed more on people of one gender than another) and qualitative aspects of those risks (such as the manner in which a death occurs rather than just its occurrence). See Douglas A. Kysar, *The Expectations of Consumers*, 103 Colum. L. Rev. 1700 (2003).

WARNER FRUEHAUF TRAILER CO. v. BOSTON
654 A.2d 1272 (D.C. 1995)

BELSON, J. . . .

Appellee William Boston, a supervising mechanic for the Potomac Electric Power Company ("PEPCO"), was injured on the job due to the malfunction of an Anthony A-146 single cylinder liftgate attached to the back of a PEPCO truck. Boston had responded early on a Sunday morning to an emergency call to obtain a material truck and a work crew to respond to a power outage. He obtained a truck, one he had never used before, and with the help of one of his crew members began to unload it so that he could load it with equipment needed to remedy the outage. After they had used the liftgate to remove some heavy objects from the truck, and Boston's crew member had returned the liftgate platform to, or at least near, the vertical "closed" position at the back of the truck, Boston approached the liftgate to attach the safety chains. The liftgate suddenly malfunctioned, and the 1050 pound metal platform fell free, striking Boston and injuring his hip.

Boston and his wife filed a complaint against the liftgate manufacturers and the liftgate distributor, appellant Warner Fruehauf. Appellees proceeded to trial only against Warner Fruehauf, seeking damages for personal injury and loss of consortium on a theory of strict liability in tort based on the defective design of the liftgate. . . .

Most of the Bostons' evidence was directed toward establishing that the one-cylinder hydraulically-controlled liftgate was defectively designed and unreasonably dangerous in that it had no backup system to prevent a free-fall of the heavy tailgate in the event of a mechanical failure. At the close of all the evidence . . . the judge concluded that, as a matter of law, the liftgate was defectively designed and unreasonably dangerous and that no reasonable juror could find that Boston had assumed the risk of being injured by it. He therefore directed a verdict in favor of the Bostons as to liability.

The case was submitted to the jury on damages only. The jury awarded the Bostons a total of $550,000.00. Warner Fruehauf noted this appeal. . . .

To establish strict liability in tort, a plaintiff must establish that the defendant sold the product in question in a defective and unreasonably dangerous condition. In design defect cases, most jurisdictions decide this issue by applying some form of a risk-utility balancing test. We follow that approach.

In general, the plaintiff must "show the risks, costs and benefits of the product in question and alternative designs," and "that the magnitude of the danger from the product outweighed the costs of avoiding the danger." Hull v. Eaton Corp., 263 U.S. App. D.C. 311, 317, 825 F.2d 448, 453 (D.C. Cir. 1987) (design defect case, looking to Maryland law in the absence of D.C. case law "clearly setting out the necessary elements of a D.C. strict liability claim"). There are many different factors that may be considered by the jury in applying a risk-utility analysis.[12] In order to weigh properly the interests of manufacturers (or distributors), consumers, and the public, the risk-utility analysis must be applied in a flexible manner that is necessarily case specific.

In the context of this case, the risk side of the equation is comprised of the danger of death or serious injury presented by the use of a single-cylinder liftgate with no safety backup, less the extent to which that danger might have been reduced by the warning decals routinely placed on the liftgates. On the other side of the balance is the availability of commercially feasible design alternatives, a factor which indicates the utility or benefit derived from marketing the product with the design at issue in this case.

The risk of bodily injury presented by the design of the single-cylinder liftgate was serious. The evidence presented by the Bostons reveals that: (1) over half of the Anthony single-cylinder liftgates in PEPCO's fleet had reportedly experienced identical free falls; (2) tests observed by PEPCO's Safety Committee Chairman comparing Anthony single-cylinder liftgates to similar liftgates with two cylinders showed that single-cylinder liftgates would fall free in the event of a mechanical failure, but that

---

[12] For example, under New Jersey case law, some of the factors relevant to a risk-utility analysis are:

(1) The usefulness and desirability of the product — its utility to the user and to the public as a whole.

(2) The safety aspects of the product — the likelihood that it will cause injury, and the probable seriousness of the injury.

(3) The availability of a substitute product which would meet the same need and not be as unsafe.

(4) The manufacturer's ability to eliminate the unsafe character of the product without impairing its usefulness or making it too expensive to maintain its utility.

(5) The user's ability to avoid danger by the exercise of care in the use of the product.

(6) The user's anticipated awareness of the dangers inherent in the product and their avoidability, because of general public knowledge of the obvious condition of the product, or of the existence of suitable warnings or instructions.

(7) The feasibility, on the part of the manufacturer, of spreading the loss by setting the price of the product or carrying liability insurance.

O'Brien v. Muskin Corp., 94 N.J. 169, 463 A.2d 298, 304-05 (N.J. 1983) (citation omitted) (claim of defective design brought against swimming pool manufacturer).

dual-cylinder liftgates would not; (3) tests conducted after Boston's injury by PEPCO's Maintenance Superintendent showed upon a mechanical failure the liftgate involved in Boston's accident fell several times while being operated normally; and (4) the liftgate's warning decal and instructions manual — both stating that "the lift is not equipped with a back-up system to prevent falling in the event of a failure" — indicate the serious risks presented by the design of the Anthony single-cylinder liftgate.

Under a risk-utility analysis, "[a] manufacturer [or distributor] is entitled to defend a strict liability claim based on defective design by showing that a warning accompanied the product that reduced its dangers." However, while the adequacy of a warning is relevant and may even tip the balance in the decision whether a product is or is not defectively designed, it is not the sole consideration: "A warning is only one of a product's many design attributes that weigh in the balance of dangers against utility . . . but could be a pivotal design attribute in a particular case."

There is some inconsistency among the authorities concerning the effectiveness of warnings in various factual scenarios. However, we do not have to resolve the issues those authorities raise, because the warning decals in this case were inadequate as a matter of law. [O]ne of the warning decals was inadequate because the jury would have had to engage in conjecture to have concluded that it was in a location where Boston could have seen it, and because it consisted of 189 words only the last few of which contained the vague warning of possible danger quoted above. The other decal — "stand clear while lowering and raising the gate" — did not provide any warning of the specific defect alleged or of the danger created by it.

Turning to the other side of the scale, we must determine, based upon the record before us, whether the utility or benefit realized from marketing the liftgate with the design at issue outweighed any risks presented by that particular design. In order to determine whether a safer design that would have prevented the injury should have been used, the trier of fact ordinarily must consider whether any safer alternative designs were commercially feasible. . . .

The Bostons presented uncontradicted expert testimony that the liftgate, as designed, was "unreasonably dangerous." Both the Bostons' mechanical engineering expert, James Kita, and Warner Fruehauf's mechanical engineering expert, Roger Link, testified that alternative designs that would have prevented the metal platform from a free fall were available when the Anthony A-146 single-cylinder liftgate was manufactured in the mid-1970s. These alternative designs included dual-cylinder and multi-cylinder configurations, as well as the inclusion of a limit switch on the latching mechanism of the liftgate.

The Chairman of PEPCO's Safety Committee, Fred Lawless, testified that the committee had investigated six incidents in which Anthony single-cylinder liftgates "[fell] from a near-vertical folded position to the ground creating a hazard." He explained that he had observed tests demonstrating that, in the event of the failure of the locking or hooking mechanism, a single-cylinder liftgate would fall "in a split second with no warning." In the case of a similar failure, however, a dual-cylinder liftgate would "creep [down] very slowly." According to Mr. Kita's cost-benefit analysis, any one of the above alternatives was available at nominal additional cost to appellant, would have caused no reduction in the liftgate's overall utility, and would have prevented the metal platform from falling free. Principally on the basis of these factors, Mr. Kita ultimately opined within a reasonable degree of engineering certainty that the liftgate as designed was defective and unreasonably dangerous.

By contrast, Warner Fruehauf failed to offer any expert or even lay testimony to substantiate its general assertion that the liftgate as designed was safe for its intended use and was therefore neither defective nor unreasonably dangerous. Moreover, Warner Fruehauf failed to impeach or contradict any of the statements or opinions expressed by either Mr. Link or Mr. Kita. . . . Moreover, Warner Fruehauf failed to offer any evidence showing any benefit gained by marketing a single-cylinder liftgate that out-weighed the risk of death or serious bodily harm inherent in this particular design.

Although directed verdicts are granted sparingly in favor of the party who has the burden of proof, we recognize that "to the extent that the party with the burden of proof has established his case by testimony that the jury is not at liberty to disbelieve, a verdict may be directed for him. . . ." See 9 C. Wright & A. Miller, Federal Practice and Procedure §2534, at 590-91 (1971). . . .

In this case, the evidence overwhelmingly supported the Bostons, even on issues as to which they bore the burden of persuasion. Given the danger presented by the design of the liftgate, the ineffectiveness of the warning of that danger, and the uncontradicted expert testimony that safer alternative designs providing the same utility were both economically and technologically feasible, we find no error in the trial judge's conclusion that, as a matter of law, the liftgate was defectively designed and unreasonably dangerous. Warner Fruehauf . . . failed to refute the Bostons' expert testimony or to neutralize it by cross-examination. Under the circumstances, appellees' expert testimony establishing that the liftgate was defectively designed and unreasonably dangerous "must be taken as true." Therefore . . . the Bostons were entitled to a directed verdict on the issue of liability. Accordingly, the judgment is affirmed.

NOTES TO WARNER FRUEHAUF TRAILER CO. v. BOSTON

1. *Identifying Risk-Utility Factors.*   The factors set out in the court's footnote are typical of factors used by courts in a risk-utility analysis of product defect. They are derived from a classic article: Wade, *On the Nature of Strict Tort Liability for Products,* 44 Miss. L.J. 825 (1973).

2. *Risk-Utility and Reasonableness.*   A reasonable person who designs a product will likely take into account most of the elements of the risk-utility test. For this reason, a standard negligence analysis might often produce the same results as would a strict liability risk-utility test. Some distinctions, however, are possible. First, the seventh factor, feasibility of spreading the loss through insurance or raising the product's price, is excluded from a negligence analysis. Another difference is that in strict liability cases courts state that they are analyzing characteristics of the product rather than the character of the manufacturer's conduct.

3. *State of the Art and Time of Trial Knowledge.*   In a negligence case, a manufacturer is obliged to conduct itself as a reasonable person with the knowledge it has or should have regarding risks and alternatives. A reasonable person is not obliged to have all available knowledge or to acquire all available knowledge. When evaluating a product in a strict liability claim using a risk-utility test, however, many courts consider the state of the art. The state of the art includes all knowledge of risks and alternatives that is available at the time the manufacturer markets and distributes the product, *regardless of whether a reasonable manufacturer would have known about those risks and alternatives.* This assigns constructive knowledge of risks and alternatives to a manufacturer.

An approach that is more favorable to a plaintiff evaluates the safety of the product according to risks and alternatives known at the time of trial. One court held, in a case involving asbestos, that manufacturers were to be treated as if they had all knowledge of risks that was available at the time of trial, regardless of whether that knowledge had been known or discoverable at the time of marketing and distribution. See Beshada v. Johns-Manville Products Corp., 447 A.2d 539 (N.J. 1982). That court later limited its holding to the precise facts of that case (see Feldman v. Lederle Laboratories, 97 N.J. 429 (1984)) and the state's legislature subsequently adopted legislation contrary to the *Beshada* holding.

4. *Consumer Expectation Versus Risk-Utility.* The consumer expectation test and the risk-utility test need not be mutually exclusive. In evaluating these doctrines, most states have chosen among the following approaches:

a) permitting plaintiffs to choose between the consumer expectations and risk-utility tests;
b) permitting plaintiffs to show a defect using the consumer expectations test, then allowing defendants to rebut this showing using a risk-utility test;
c) permitting the consumer expectations test only in appropriate cases and otherwise requiring the risk-utility test; or
d) rejecting the consumer expectations test completely and permitting only the risk-utility approach to proving product defects.

Problem
Applying Consumer Expectation and Risk-Utility Tests

Many people have been caught in the turning augers of combines used for harvesting wheat. Combines are commonly designed with two augers, which look like huge horizontal screws that, when turning, move the wheat from one end of the grain tank to the other (the discharge auger) and disperse the grain throughout the tank (the leveling auger). The augers are in plain view to users of the combine but are extremely dangerous nevertheless. If loose clothing gets caught in the leveling auger, a user of the machine can be pulled into the tank and suffer severe injuries from the turning screw. A lawyer representing an injured user, suing on a tort theory of strict products liability for defective design, would have to appreciate the difference between the evidence required by the consumer expectation test compared to the evidence required by the risk-utility test. What obstacles to recovery would be presented by the consumer expectation test that would not be presented by the risk-utility test? See, e.g., Sperry-New Holland v. Prestage, 617 So. 2d 248 (Miss. 1993).

Perspective: Risk Spreading

Imposing liability on manufacturers may be sensible public policy for two reasons. The first is the *deep pocket theory.* This theory holds that it makes sense to place liability on the wealthier party, who has less need for the money at stake or who gives less value to each dollar and so suffers a lesser subjective loss than the poorer plaintiff. The second is the *risk spreading theory,* which holds that it makes sense to distribute the loss as widely as possible, so that many individuals suffer a small loss rather than one victim suffering a large loss.

A problem with the deep pocket theory is that manufacturers are not always wealthy. The accumulation of judgments against manufacturers can drive them into bankruptcy. In addition, it is not clear whether a company gives any particular "value" to money. A corporation is made up of its officers, employees, and stockholders. Any loss to the corporation must be a loss to them as well, and the deep pocket theory says nothing about their level of wealth compared to the victim's. Moreover, we do not know how the loss will be distributed among these constituent groups. These problems make the deep pocket theory the less favored of these two theories.

Under the risk spreading theory, manufacturers can raise prices so that accidental losses are spread over a larger group. Judge Mentz relied on this argument in Richman v. Charter Arms Corp., 571 F. Supp. 192, 203-204 (E.D. La. 1983), which involved strict liability under the theory of abnormally dangerous activities for damages to a woman who was kidnapped, robbed, raped, and murdered by a man using a handgun manufactured by the defendant:

> Perhaps the most significant fact the defendant ignores is that increased insurance costs can be passed on to consumers in the form of higher prices for handguns. The people who benefit most from marketing practices like the defendant's are handgun manufacturers and handgun purchasers. Innocent victims rarely, if ever, are beneficiaries. Consequently, it hardly seems unfair to require manufacturers and purchasers, rather than innocent victims, to pay for the risks those practices entail. Furthermore, economic efficiency seems to require the same result. In an important article on ultrahazardous activities and risk allocation, Professor Clarence Morris makes just this point. Morris, *Hazardous Enterprises and Risk Bearing Capacity*, 61 Yale L.J. 1172 (1952). In his view, "the avowed goal of the absolute liability approach is allocation of loss to the party better equipped to pass it on to the public: the superior risk bearer." Professor Morris discusses a variety of examples to show that the defendant is not always the superior risk bearer in an ultrahazardous activity case. Here is what he says, however, about bodily injury and risk-bearing capacity:
>
> > The financial burden of disabling personal injury overwhelms most people. While many can bear the cost of minor injury, prolonged infirmity and extended medical expense often exceed the financial competence of common men. Unless [common man] happens to be rich or covered by one of the more generous workmen's compensation plans, he will probably bear the risk less easily than Enterpriser. The preponderant likelihood is that Enterpriser is the better risk bearer of the two.
> >
> > . . . Thus, both fairness and economic efficiency suggest that the community would be better off if the defendant's marketing practices were classified as ultrahazardous. . . .

The manufacturer may be able to ensure against losses either by charging higher prices and holding a reserve against future liability or by buying a liability insurance policy. On the other hand, the consumer might also be able to obtain insurance.

DENNY v. FORD MOTOR CO.
639 N.Y.S.2d 250 (N.Y. 1995)

TITONE, J. . . .

As stated by the Second Circuit, this action arises out of a June 9, 1986 accident in which plaintiff Nancy Denny was severely injured when the Ford Bronco II that she was driving rolled over. The rollover accident occurred when Denny slammed on her brakes in an effort to avoid a deer that had walked directly into her motor vehicle's path. Denny and her spouse sued Ford Motor Co., the vehicle's manufacturer, asserting claims for negligence, strict products liability and breach of implied warranty of merchantability (see, UCC 2-314[2][c]; 2-318). The case went to trial in the District Court for the Northern District of New York in October of 1992.

The trial evidence centered on the particular characteristics of utility vehicles, which are generally made for off-road use on unpaved and often rugged terrain. Such use sometimes necessitates climbing over obstacles such as fallen logs and rocks. While utility vehicles are traditionally considerably larger than passenger cars, some manufacturers have created a category of down-sized "small" utility vehicles, which are designed to be lighter, to achieve better fuel economy and, presumably, to appeal to a wider consumer market. The Bronco II in which Denny was injured falls into this category.

Plaintiffs introduced evidence at trial to show that small utility vehicles in general, and the Bronco II in particular, present a significantly higher risk of rollover accidents than do ordinary passenger automobiles. Plaintiffs' evidence also showed that the Bronco II had a low stability index attributable to its high center of gravity and relatively narrow track width. The vehicle's shorter wheel base and suspension system were additional factors contributing to its instability. Ford had made minor design changes in an effort to achieve a higher stability index, but, according to plaintiffs' proof, none of the changes produced a significant improvement in the vehicle's stability.

Ford argued at trial that the design features of which plaintiffs complained were necessary to the vehicle's off-road capabilities. According to Ford, the vehicle had been intended to be used as an off-road vehicle and had not been designed to be sold as a conventional passenger automobile. Ford's own engineer stated that he would not recommend the Bronco II to someone whose primary interest was to use it as a passenger car, since the features of a four-wheel-drive utility vehicle were not helpful for that purpose and the vehicle's design made it inherently less stable.

Despite the engineer's testimony, plaintiffs introduced a Ford marketing manual which predicted that many buyers would be attracted to the Bronco II because utility vehicles were "suitable to contemporary life styles" and were "considered fashionable" in some suburban areas. According to this manual, the sales presentation of the Bronco II should take into account the vehicle's "suitab[ility] for commuting and for suburban and city driving." Additionally, the vehicle's ability to switch between two-wheel and four-wheel drive would "be particularly appealing to women who may be concerned about driving in snow and ice with their children." Plaintiffs both testified that the perceived safety benefits of its four-wheel-drive capacity were what attracted them to the Bronco II. They were not at all interested in its off-road use.

At the close of the evidence, the District Court Judge submitted both the strict products liability claim and the breach of implied warranty claim, despite Ford's objection that the two causes of action were identical. With respect to the strict products liability claim the court told the jury that "[a] manufacturer who places a product on the market in a defective condition is liable for injury which results from use of the product when the product is used for its intended or reasonably foreseeable purpose." Further, the court stated:

> A product is defective if it is not reasonably safe. . . . It is not necessary for the plaintiffs to prove that the defendant knew or should have known of the product[']s potential for causing injury to establish that the product was not reasonably safe. Rather, the plaintiffs must prove by a preponderance of the evidence that a reasonable person . . . who knew of the product's potential for causing injury and the existence of available alternative designs . . . would have concluded that such a product should not have been marketed in that condition. Such a conclusion should be reached after balancing the risks involved in using the product against the product[']s usefulness and its costs against the risks, usefulness and costs of the alternative design as compared to the product defendant did market.

With respect to the breach of implied warranty claim, the court told the jury

> The law implies a warranty by a manufacturer which places its product on the market that the product is reasonably fit for the ordinary purpose for which it was intended. If it is, in fact, defective and not reasonably fit to be used for its intended purpose, the warranty is breached.
>
> The plaintiffs claim that the Bronco II was not fit for its ordinary purpose because of its alleged propensity to roll over and lack of warnings to the consumer of this propensity.

Neither party objected to the content of these charges.

In response to interrogatories, the jury found that the Bronco II was not "defective" and that defendant was therefore not liable under plaintiffs' strict products liability cause of action. However, the jury also found that defendant had breached its implied warranty of merchantability and that the breach was the proximate cause of Nancy Denny's injuries. Following apportionment of damages, plaintiff was awarded judgment in the amount of $1.2 million.

Ford subsequently moved for a new trial under rule 59(a) of the Federal Rules of Civil Procedure, arguing that the jury's finding on the breach of implied warranty cause of action was irreconcilable with its finding on the strict products liability claim. The trial court rejected this argument, holding that it had been waived and that, in any event, the verdict was not inconsistent. [The Second Circuit Court of Appeals certified to this court the question of whether the implied warranty cause and strict products liability actions are identical.] . . .

Although the products liability theory sounding in tort and the breach of implied warranty theory authorized by the UCC coexist and are often invoked in tandem, the core element of "defect" is subtly different in the two causes of action. Under New York law, a design defect may be actionable under a strict products liability theory if the product is not reasonably safe. Since this Court's decision in Voss v. Black & Decker Mfg. Co., 59 N.Y.2d 102, 108, 463 N.Y.S.2d 398, 450 N.E.2d 204, the New

York standard for determining the existence of a design defect has required an assessment of whether "if the design defect were known at the time of manufacture, a reasonable person would conclude that the utility of the product did not outweigh the risk inherent in marketing a product designed in that manner." This standard demands an inquiry into such factors as (1) the product's utility to the public as a whole, (2) its utility to the individual user, (3) the likelihood that the product will cause injury, (4) the availability of a safer design, (5) the possibility of designing and manufacturing the product so that it is safer but remains functional and reasonably priced, (6) the degree of awareness of the product's potential danger that can reasonably be attributed to the injured user, and (7) the manufacturer's ability to spread the cost of any safety-related design changes. The above-described analysis is rooted in a recognition that there are both risks and benefits associated with many products and that there are instances in which a product's inherent dangers cannot be eliminated without simultaneously compromising or completely nullifying its benefits. In such circumstances, a weighing of the product's benefits against its risks is an appropriate and necessary component of the liability assessment under the policy-based principles associated with tort law.

The adoption of this risk/utility balance as a component of the "defectiveness" element has brought the inquiry in design defect cases closer to that used in traditional negligence cases, where the reasonableness of an actor's conduct is considered in light of a number of situational and policy-driven factors. While efforts have been made to steer away from the fault-oriented negligence principles by characterizing the design defect cause of action in terms of a product-based rather than a conduct-based analysis, the reality is that the risk/utility balancing test is a "negligence-inspired" approach, since it invites the parties to adduce proof about the manufacturer's choices and ultimately requires the fact finder to make "a judgment about [the manufacturer's] judgment" (Birnbaum, *Unmasking the Test for Design Defect: From Negligence [to Warranty] to Strict Liability to Negligence*, 33 Vand. L. Rev. 593, 610, 648). In other words, an assessment of the manufacturer's conduct is virtually inevitable, and, as one commentator observed, "[i]n general, . . . the strict liability concept of 'defective design' [is] functionally synonymous with the earlier negligence concept of unreasonable designing." (Schwartz, *New Products, Old Products, Evolving Law, Retroactive Law*, 58 N.Y.U. L. Rev. 796, 803, citing United States v. Carroll Towing Co., 159 F.2d 169, 173 [Hand, J.].)

It is this negligence-like risk/benefit component of the defect element that differentiates strict products liability claims from UCC-based breach of implied warranty claims in cases involving design defects. While the strict products concept of a product that is "not reasonably safe" requires a weighing of the product's dangers against its over-all advantages, the UCC's concept of a "defective" product requires an inquiry only into whether the product in question was "fit for the ordinary purposes for which such goods are used" (UCC 2-314[2][c]). The latter inquiry focuses on the expectations for the performance of the product when used in the customary, usual and reasonably foreseeable manners. The cause of action is one involving true "strict" liability, since recovery may be had upon a showing that the product was not minimally safe for its expected purpose—without regard to the feasibility of alternative designs or the manufacturer's "reasonableness" in marketing it in that unsafe condition.

This distinction between the "defect" analysis in breach of implied warranty actions and the "defect" analysis in strict products liability actions is explained by the differing etiology and doctrinal underpinnings of the two distinct theories. The former class of actions originates in contract law, which directs its attention to the purchaser's disappointed expectations; the latter originates in tort law, which traditionally has concerned itself with social policy and risk allocation by means other than those dictated by the marketplace. . . .

In any event, while the critics and commentators may debate the relative merits of the consumer-expectation and risk/utility tests, there is no existing authority for the proposition that the risk/utility analysis is appropriate when the plaintiff's claim rests on a claimed breach of implied warranty under UCC 2-314(2)(c) and 2-318. . . .

As a practical matter, the distinction between the defect concepts in tort law and in implied warranty theory may have little or no effect in most cases. In this case, however, the nature of the proof and the way in which the fact issues were litigated demonstrates how the two causes of action can diverge. In the trial court, Ford took the position that the design features of which plaintiffs complain, i.e., the Bronco II's high center of gravity, narrow track width, short wheel base and specially tailored suspension system, were important to preserving the vehicle's ability to drive over the highly irregular terrain that typifies off-road travel. Ford's proof in this regard was relevant to the strict products liability risk/utility equation, which required the fact finder to determine whether the Bronco II's value as an off-road vehicle outweighed the risk of the rollover accidents that could occur when the vehicle was used for other driving tasks.

On the other hand, plaintiffs' proof focused, in part, on the sale of the Bronco II for suburban driving and everyday road travel. Plaintiffs also adduced proof that the Bronco II's design characteristics made it unusually susceptible to rollover accidents when used on paved roads. All of this evidence was useful in showing that routine highway and street driving was the "ordinary purpose" for which the Bronco II was sold and that it was not "fit" — or safe — for that purpose.

Thus, under the evidence in this case, a rational fact finder could have simultaneously concluded that the Bronco II's utility as an off-road vehicle outweighed the risk of injury resulting from rollover accidents and that the vehicle was not safe for the "ordinary purpose" of daily driving for which it was marketed and sold. Under the law of this State such a set of factual judgments would lead to the concomitant legal conclusion that plaintiffs' strict products liability cause of action was not viable but that defendant should nevertheless be held liable for breach of its implied promise that the Bronco II was "merchantable" or "fit" for its "ordinary purpose." Importantly, what makes this case distinctive is that the "ordinary purpose" for which the product was marketed and sold to the plaintiff was *not* the same as the utility against which the risk was to be weighed. It is these unusual circumstances that give practical significance to the ordinarily theoretical difference between the defect concepts in tort and statutory breach of implied warranty causes of action.

From the foregoing it is apparent that the causes of action for strict products liability and breach of implied warranty of merchantability are not identical in New

York and that the latter is not necessarily subsumed by the former. It follows that, under the circumstances presented, a verdict such as the one occurring here — in which the manufacturer was found liable under an implied warranty cause of action and not liable under a strict products cause of action — is theoretically reconcilable under New York law. . . .

NOTES TO DENNY v. FORD MOTOR CO.

1. *Contrast Between Consumer Expectation and Risk-Utility Tests.* New York applies a consumer expectation test to warranty claims, and a risk-utility test to strict liability design defect claims. *Denny* illustrates the theoretical possibility that the two tests can produce different results in connection with a single product.

2. *Multiple Theories.* In some situations, warranty claims and design defect claims should obviously produce different results, as where a plaintiff contends that a product's durability was inadequate. Where safety is not an issue, it is understandable that warranty and strict liability design defect claims would yield different results. Many states have rejected, however, the possibility of differing conclusions on product safety when confronted with plaintiffs' efforts to use both warranty and strict liability claims. The Restatement (Third) of Torts: Products Liability calls for a single submission to the jury:

> Two or more factually identical defective design claims . . . should not be submitted to the trier of fact in the same case under different doctrinal labels. Regardless of the doctrinal label attached to a particular claim, design . . . claims rest on a risk-utility assessment. To allow two or more factually identical risk-utility claims to go to a jury under different labels, whether "strict liability," "negligence," or "implied warranty of merchantability," would generate confusion and may well result in inconsistent verdicts.

§2 comment n.

Problem
Comparing Product Liability Approaches

The plaintiff's decedent was killed when someone accelerated a motorboat in an area where the decedent was swimming. The outboard motor's propeller wounded the victim severely. The plaintiff sought damages from the motor manufacturer, claiming that had a guard been installed around the propeller blades, the injury would have been avoided. How would this claim be analyzed under warranty, consumer expectation, and risk-utility approaches? See Fitzpatrick v. Madonna, 623 A.2d 322 (Pa. Super. 1993).

2. Mandatory Proof of a Feasible Alternative Design

Proof of a *feasible alternative* to a defendant's design is a factor recognized in the risk-utility test used by many states. A particularly controversial element in Restatement (Third) §2(b) *requires* that a plaintiff introduce proof of a feasible alternative instead of merely permitting that type of proof. In General Motors Corp. v. Sanchez, the court analyzes the degree of detail that should be required in a state where evidence of a feasible alternative design is a mandatory component of the plaintiff's case.

GENERAL MOTORS CORP. v. SANCHEZ
997 S.W.2d 584 (Tex. 1999)

GONZALES, J.

Because there were no witnesses, relatively little is known first hand about the circumstances of the accident that is the basis of this litigation. Lee Sanchez, Jr. left his home to feed a pen of heifers in March 1993. The ranch foreman found his lifeless body the next morning and immediately called Sanchez's father. Apparently, Sanchez's 1990 Chevy pickup had rolled backward with the driver's side door open, pinning Sanchez to the open corral gate in the angle between the open door and the cab of the truck. Sanchez suffered a broken right arm and damaged right knee where the gate crushed him against the door pillar, the vertical metal column to which the door is hinged. He bled to death from a deep laceration in his right upper arm.

The Sanchez family, his estate, and his wife sued General Motors Corporation and the dealership that sold the pickup for negligence, products liability, and gross negligence based on a defect in the truck's transmission and transmission-control linkage. The plaintiffs presented circumstantial evidence to support the following theory of how the accident happened. Sanchez drove his truck into the corral and stopped to close the gate. He mis-shifted into what he thought was Park, but what was actually an intermediate, "perched" position between Park and Reverse where the transmission was in "hydraulic neutral." Expert witnesses explained that hydraulic neutral exists at the intermediate positions between the denominated gears, Park, Reverse, Neutral, Drive, and Low, where no gear is actually engaged. Under this scenario, as Sanchez walked toward the gate, the gear shift slipped from the perched position of hydraulic neutral into Reverse and the truck started to roll backwards. It caught Sanchez at or near the gate and slammed him up against it, trapping his right arm and knee. He was pinned between the gate and the door pillar by the pressure the truck exerted while idling in Reverse. Struggling to free himself, Sanchez severed an artery in his right arm and bled to death after 45 to 75 minutes.

In the trial court, G.M. offered alternative theories explaining the cause of the accident, all of which directed blame at Sanchez.

The jury rejected G.M.'s theories and found that G.M. was negligent, the transmission was defectively designed, and G.M.'s warning was so inadequate as to constitute a marketing defect. The trial court rendered judgment for actual and punitive damages of $8.5 million for the plaintiffs. A panel of the court of appeals affirmed the trial court's judgment with one justice dissenting.

Here, G.M. does not dispute that Sanchez's fatal injury was caused when he mis-shifted the truck's transmission into hydraulic neutral, which then migrated into Reverse. The parties agree that all transmissions made today can mis-shift, that no design eliminates the possibility of a mis-shift, and that a mis-shifted car is dangerous. As G.M. puts it, a "mis-shift is just physics." G.M. contends that it has no liability, even if its product is defective, because the plaintiffs failed to present evidence of a safer alternative design.

We consider first the evidence of strict liability. We will sustain G.M.'s no evidence point only if there is no more than a scintilla of evidence to prove the existence of a product defect.

A design defect renders a product unreasonably dangerous as designed, taking into consideration the utility of the product and the risk involved in its use. A plaintiff must prove that there is a safer alternative design in order to recover under a design defect theory.[9] An alternative design must substantially reduce the risk of injury and be both economically and technologically feasible.[10] We first examine the evidence concerning the operation of the transmission in Sanchez's truck and then determine whether the plaintiffs have proven a safer alternative design.

Most of the plaintiff's design evidence came in through the testimony of the plaintiffs' expert, Simon Tamny, who testified about the operation of the 700R4 transmission in Sanchez's truck. He opined that the G.M. transmission and transmission-control linkage presented a particular risk. All transmissions have an intermediate position between Reverse and Park. It is impossible, under federal standardization guidelines, to design a gear shift without an intermediate position between Reverse and Park. However, Tamny testified that G.M.'s transmission has the added danger that internal forces tend to move the gear selector toward Reverse rather than Park when the driver inadvertently leaves the lever in this intermediate position. Tamny explained how G.M. could alter the design to make the operation of the 700R4 safer.

It is possible for the gear shift to be moved to a position between Reverse and Park, called hydraulic neutral by the parties. In hydraulic neutral, the roller is perched at the peak between the two gears. At this point, Reverse is hydraulically disengaged, and the ratchet spring is forcing the parking pawl against the output shaft. Tamny performed an experiment in which he moved the gear selector of Sanchez's truck to this position six times. He disturbed the friction of the linkage four times by slapping the steering wheel; once by revving the engine, and once he took no action. In each case, the gear shift slipped into Reverse.

Tamny offered a few alterations to G.M.'s design that he contended would reduce the risk of injury. First, he suggested moving (1) the peak between Park and Reverse from its current position 5.7 degrees from Park to a position 7.5 degrees from Park and (2) the "ratchet" point (where the parking pawl contacts the output shaft) nearer to Park, from 10.9 degrees to 7.0 degrees. Second, he proposed sharpening the peak to .0010 of an inch to reduce the likelihood that the roller could perch. Third, he proposed using a stronger roller spring to increase the force pushing the rooster comb into a gear position, also reducing the likelihood that the roller would perch.

Tamny admitted that his design change would not totally eliminate the possibility of leaving the gearshift in the intermediate position of hydraulic neutral. However, according to Tamny, his design change would totally eliminate the possibility of slipping into Reverse from hydraulic neutral. Tamny described his design change as a "99% solution" to the mis-shift problem. While his design change would not eliminate the risk that the car might roll in hydraulic neutral, it would eliminate

---

[9] See Caterpillar, Inc. v. Shears, 911 S.W.2d 379, 384 (Tex. 1995).
[10] See Tex. Civ. Prac. & Rem. Code §82.005(b)(1) & (2).

the most dangerous risk of migration to Reverse and powered movement without a driver.

G.M. does not challenge that Tamny's design was technically and economically feasible. Instead, G.M. argues that, as a matter of law, Tamny's design is inadequate to prove a substantial reduction in the risk of injury because: (1) the design was not proved safer by testing; (2) the design was not published and therefore not subjected to peer review; and (3) G.M.'s statistical evidence proved that other manufacturers, whose designs incorporated some of Tamny's suggestions, had the same accident rate as G.M. These arguments however, go to the reliability and therefore the admissibility of expert evidence rather than the legal sufficiency of the evidence of a product defect.

G.M. argues that the substance of Tamny's testimony does not amount to evidence of a safer alternative design. G.M. contends that Tamny's testimony was based on "speculation and conjecture." . . . We disagree. [H]ere there is more to the evidence than an expert's bald assertion that his design would be safer. Tamny described the current operation of the 700R4 transmission at length, and explained in some detail how his proposed design would make the transmission safer by eliminating the risk that the vehicle could move in a powered gear due to an inadvertent mis-shift. "It will take you from a 90% solution to a 99% solution," he said. Tamny's testimony about the engineering principles underlying his proposed design support his conclusion that his design features would be safer than those in the 700R4.

G.M. mis-characterizes Tamny's testimony by considering whether each individual feature of Tamny's design makes the design safer, instead of considering the design as a whole, and by considering the plaintiffs' testimony in light of its statistical evidence instead of considering the plaintiffs' evidence alone. G.M. argues that none of the other manufacturers' designs incorporating different aspects of Tamny's design have proven safer than G.M.'s and that Tamny offered no testing evidence or engineering principles to show his design was safer. Without this evidence, G.M. concludes, Tamny's opinion is mere speculation.

However, the plaintiffs did not have to build and test an automobile transmission to prove a safer alternative design. A design need only prove "capable of being developed."[25] The Restatement (Third) of Torts: Products Liability takes the position that "qualified expert testimony on the issue suffices, even though the expert has produced no prototype, if it reasonably supports the conclusion that a reasonable alternative design could have been practically adopted at the time of sale." Furthermore, assuming we could consider evidence contrary to the verdict, no manufacturer has incorporated Tamny's design into an existing transmission. For that reason alone, G.M.'s statistical evidence comparing the safety of different existing designs could not conclusively establish the safety of Tamny's design.

The evidence supporting Tamny's conclusion that his design is safer raises a fact question that the jury resolved in favor of the plaintiffs. We conclude that the plaintiffs have presented more than a scintilla of evidence that Tamny's alternative design substantially reduced the risk of injury.

[Judgment for plaintiff affirmed.]

---

[25] See Boatland of Houston, Inc. v. Bailey, 609 S.W.2d 743, 748 (Tex. 1980).

NOTES TO GENERAL MOTORS CORP. v. SANCHEZ

1. *Required Proof of Feasible Alternative Design.*   The requirement that a plaintiff prove feasibility of an alternative design is adopted in §2(b) of the Restatement (Third) of Torts: Products Liability. In Potter v. Chicago Pneumatic Tool Co., 694 A.2d 1319 (Conn. 1997), the Connecticut Supreme Court declined to adopt the requirement, stating that a review of past cases failed to support the conclusion that the requirement had wide support in American case law, and suggesting that the requirement would impose too heavy an evidentiary burden on litigants because it might require costly expert testimony in situations where without that evidence a jury could easily draw an inference of improper design.

Proof of a feasible alternative design might readily be available to a plaintiff in a case where a defendant manufacturer has adopted a new and safer design after injury to a plaintiff. In many states and in federal court, that evidence is forbidden to be introduced, under a rule that is justified as providing an incentive for remedial measures. See, for example, Federal Rules of Evidence 407.

2. *Generically Unsafe Products.*   In O'Brien v. Muskin Corp., 94 N.J. 169, 184, 463 A.2d 298 (1983), the New Jersey Supreme Court evaluated an above-ground swimming pool with a very slippery plastic liner. Its low friction contributed to a serious injury suffered by someone who attempted to dive in and protect his head and neck by keeping his hands in front of them. Despite the unavailability of alternative designs, the court stated that a product for which no alternative exists can be so dangerous and of such little use that a manufacturer should bear the costs of injuries such products may cause.

In McCarthy v. Olin Corp., 119 F.3d 148 (2d Cir. 1997), plaintiffs claimed that the defendant's product, hollowpoint bullets, were defective because they were designed to inflict unusually severe harm upon impact, and because they were sold to the general population. How might the New Jersey and Texas courts respond to an argument that the manufacturer's product could not be made safe without destroying its utility?

3. *Expert Testimony.*   Expert testimony is crucial in most design defect cases. In *Sanchez,* the defendant claimed that the expert's conclusions were not sufficient to support a verdict for the plaintiff. Another common attack on expert testimony is to challenge its initial admissibility. In federal courts and in most state courts, an expert's conclusions are admissible evidence only if they are based on scientifically legitimate research or analysis. See Daubert v. Merrell Dow Pharmaceuticals, Inc., 509 U.S. 579 (1993).

Statute: PRODUCT LIABILITY ACTIONS
Mich. Comp. Laws §600.2946 (2017)

Sec. 2946. (2) In a product liability action brought against a manufacturer or seller for harm allegedly caused by a production defect, the manufacturer or seller is not liable unless the plaintiff establishes that the product was not reasonably safe at the time the specific unit of the product left the control of the manufacturer or seller and that, according to generally accepted production practices at the time the specific unit of the product left the control of the manufacturer or seller, a practical and technically feasible alternative production practice was available that would have prevented the harm without significantly impairing the usefulness or desirability of the product to users and without creating equal or greater risk of harm to others. An alternative production practice is practical and feasible only if the technical, medical, or scientific knowledge relating to production of the product, at the time the specific unit of the product left the control of the manufacturer or seller, was developed, available, and capable of use in the production of the product and was economically feasible for use by the manufacturer. Technical, medical, or scientific knowledge is not economically feasible for use by the manufacturer if use of that knowledge in production of the product would significantly compromise the product's usefulness or desirability.

Statute: STATE OF THE ART
Colo. Rev. Stat. §13-21-403(1)(a) (2017)

(1) In any product liability action, it shall be rebuttably presumed that the product which caused the injury, death, or property damage was not defective and that the manufacturer or seller thereof was not negligent if the product:

(a) Prior to sale by the manufacturer, conformed to the state of the art, as distinguished from industry standards, applicable to such product in existence at the time of sale. . . .

NOTES TO STATUTES

1. *Modern Codification of Strict Product Liability Rules.* The Michigan statute was adopted in 1995, decades after the drafting of the Restatement (Second) of Torts. What details regarding the application of strict liability to products does the Michigan statute answer that Restatement (Second) §402A does not address?

2. *State of the Art.* The power of the "state of the art" defense depends on the precise wording of applicable statutes. Under the Colorado statute, would a plaintiff have to abandon both negligence and strict product liability claims if, prior to sale of the product in question, no manufacturer had ever produced a product safer than the defendant's product?

Perspective: Choosing Among Tests for Product Defect

The Restatement (Third) rejects the consumer expectation test for design defects. As the following article excerpts show, that decision has been highly controversial. Jerry S. Phillips, *Consumer Expectations*, 53 S.C. L. Rev. 1047 (2002), states:

> Mark Twain cabled the Associated Press from London in 1897 stating: "The reports of my death are greatly exaggerated." Similarly, the reports of the death of the consumer expectations test as a standard for determining products liability are also greatly exaggerated. . . .
>
> The drafters of the Products Liability Restatement were probably largely motivated to jettison consumer expectations as the central test for determining product defectiveness because of their desire to establish reasonable alternative design under 2(b) as the essential basis for determining design defect. Section

2(b) was the cornerstone of the Products Liability Restatement from its inception.

A number of prominent courts have expressly rejected 2(b) as a basis for determining design defect. Others reject it either by using consumer expectations alone or in conjunction with risk-benefit analysis to determine consumer expectations, without making proof of a reasonable alternative design a sine qua non for determining such expectations. Risk-benefit analysis fits neatly within the definition of consumer expectations. Courts widely recognize that expert testimony may be used to establish consumer expectations. . . .

Courts reject the reasonable-alternative-design standard as the test for determining liability in design defect cases not so much because the standard often places a very heavy burden of proof on the plaintiff—although it does do that. Rather, courts, being practical, common-sense institutions, are aware that design defectiveness cannot be so easily cabined by the alternative-design test. Tort law is a many-splendored thing. It evolves in response to changing times and circumstances. Products liability for the last half century has been the crown jewel of tort law. No temporary, conservative backlash is likely to stem the creative evolution of tort law and products liability.

In contrast, Victor E. Schwartz, *The American Law Institute's Process of Democracy and Deliberation*, 26 Hofstra L. Rev. 743 (1998), states:

[W]hy have plaintiffs' lawyers claimed that the Restatement (Third) is pro-defense? . . .

The plaintiffs' advocates . . . objected vehemently to the fact that in a design defect case, the Restatement (Third) requires a plaintiff to show that a reasonable alternative design could have provided overall better safety than the original design. . . . As a practical matter, plaintiffs' lawyers in virtually every major products liability design case, from allegedly defective automobiles to medical devices, have shown the jury a reasonable alternative design. They have helped the jury visualize what was wrong with the product and how it could have been made so as to have avoided causing the plaintiff harm. Winning plaintiffs' lawyers know that this is the only practical way to litigate a design case.

E. Warnings and Instructions

Inadequate warnings accompanying products may be characterized as defects that present unreasonable dangers to users or consumers. Restatement (Second) §402A comment j says, "In order to prevent the product from being unreasonably dangerous, the seller may be required to give directions or warnings, on the container, as to its use." The Restatement (Third) §2(c) says that a product "is defective because of inadequate instructions or warnings when the *foreseeable risks* of harm posed by the product could have been reduced by the provision of *reasonable instructions or warnings*" (emphasis added). Richter v. Limax International focuses on when a manufacturer must give warnings and how much information about the risks associated with a product a manufacturer is presumed to have.

RICHTER v. LIMAX INTERNATIONAL

45 F.3d 1464 (10th Cir. 1995)

LAY, J.

Dearmedia Richter appeals from the district court's grant of judgment as a matter of law to Limax International, Inc. and LMX-Manufactures Consultants, Inc. (collectively Limax). Richter claimed that repetitive use of a mini-trampoline manufactured by Limax caused stress fractures in her ankles. In March 1991, Richter sued Limax alleging the mini-trampoline was defectively designed and came with an inadequate warning. The jury found, in a special verdict, that the mini-trampoline was not defectively designed. However, it nonetheless found Limax was liable under theories of strict liability and negligence for its failure to warn and determined damages to be $472,712 reduced by Richter's percentage of fault of thirty-eight percent.

Limax then moved for judgment as a matter of law, which the court granted. The court concluded the defendant had no duty to warn because the plaintiff had failed to prove that Limax had knowledge of the danger of stress fractures or that the danger was known in the state of the art. The court further concluded that under these circumstances Kansas law does not impose a duty on manufacturers to warn about dangers they might have discovered by conducting reasonable tests. Richter appealed. We reverse and remand to the district court with instructions to reinstate the jury's verdict and enter a judgment on the verdict.

Richter purchased a mini-trampoline from Limax on February 1, 1989. There were no instructions in or on the box containing the mini-trampoline, although the trampoline did have sticker on it stating: "This product was designed to be used only as an exercise device. It is not designed to be used for acrobatics, trampolining or any springboard type activities." Richter stated she only used the trampoline for jogging. She began by jogging for short periods of time but eventually increased her time up to sixty minutes per day. She used the product until March 10, 1989. The next day she experienced severe pain in her ankles while walking. A doctor diagnosed her as having stress fractures in her ankles. Richter testified the pain forced her to discontinue her work as a sales representative for a furniture manufacturer.

The plaintiff produced expert testimony which established relatively simple tests would have revealed that because the surface of a mini-trampoline depresses furthest in the center and decreasingly towards the edges, as a jogger's feet strike the trampoline's surface and it gives way, the inside of each foot drop further than the outside. This rotation of the foot, which is termed "eversion," occurs to a lesser degree in normal jogging, but rebound jogging markedly accentuates the degree of rotation.

Further testimony established it has long been known that lateral pulling on a bone by ligaments or muscles can cause microscopic fractures. If the bone is not allowed time to heal and the stress on the bone continues, these tiny fractures can coalesce into a stress fracture. The eversion of the feet caused by the mini-trampoline results in certain tissues pulling laterally on particular ankle bones. Richter's expert witnesses testified that long-term use of the trampoline could cause stress fractures in the affected ankle bones.

Limax admitted it conducted no tests relating to the long-term effects of jogging on the mini-trampoline and did not systematically review published studies of mini-trampolines by sports medicine and exercise specialists. The CEO of Limax testified the company had sold approximately two million mini-trampolines world-wide and Richter's complaint about stress fractures was the first Limax had received. Further, although mini-trampolines had been in use since 1975, by the time of Richter's purchase no one had yet suggested their use entailed a risk of stress fractures. No expert testifying at trial could identify any study or article on rebound jogging or mini-trampolines that reported ankle stress fractures or pointed out the risk joggers faced of incurring such an injury.

Richter, however, produced testimony by experts that observations from very simple tests, interpreted in light of well-established knowledge about the structure of the foot and the causes of stress fractures, would have made it apparent that the repetitive use of the mini-trampoline for jogging could cause stress fractures. Two experts testified the danger was well within the state of society's knowledge about such matters. . . . Although the mini-trampoline was found by the jury not to have a defective design, Richter's expert witness testimony established that the marked accentuation of eversion caused by the design of the mini-trampoline could result in her kind of injury developing from her repetitive jogging.

Richter contends Kansas law imposes a duty on manufacturers to test their products and warn consumers appropriately. In Wooderson v. Ortho Pharmaceutical Corp., the Kansas Supreme Court held an ethical drug company had a duty to warn the medical profession about what "it knows, has reason to know, or should know, based upon its position as an expert in the field, upon its research, upon cases reported to it, and upon scientific development, research, and publications in the field." 681 P.2d 1038, 1057 (Kan.), *cert. denied*, 469 U.S. 965, 105 S. Ct. 365, 83 L. Ed. 2d 301 (1984). Richter interprets the language "upon its research," to require manufacturers to test their products for their potential to injure consumers.

The district court held, "though not without misgivings," that Kansas law does not require a manufacturer to test its products for dangers not otherwise known in the state of the art. . . .

Appellate review of a district court's determination of state law is de novo. We find the district court's restrictive interpretation . . . is contrary to Kansas law on the duty of a manufacturer to warn consumers of foreseeable dangers. An earlier district court decision summed up Kansas law relating to the duty to warn consumers:

> Ordinarily, a manufacturer has a duty under Kansas law to warn consumers and users of its products when it knows or has reason to know that its product is or is likely to be dangerous during normal use. The duty to warn is a continuous one, requiring the manufacturer to keep abreast of the current state of knowledge of its products as acquired through research, adverse reaction reports, scientific literature, and other available methods. A manufacturer's failure to adequately warn of its product's reasonably foreseeable dangers renders that product defective under the doctrine of strict liability.

Pfeiffer v. Eagle Mfg. Co., 771 F. Supp. 1133, 1139 (D. Kan. 1991) (O'Connor, J., citations and footnote omitted).

Kansas applies the same test to whether a manufacturer met his duty to warn under negligence as it does under strict liability.[5]

---

[5] In determining warning issues, the test is reasonableness. . . . "[I]n all warning cases [either negligence or strict liability] — even if the plaintiff or the court claims to analyze failure to warn or inadequacy of

Kansas law makes clear this general duty to warn consumers of foreseeable dangers is not limited to ethical drug companies. In 1976, Kansas adopted the rule set out in the Restatement (Second) of Torts §402A (1965) in Brooks v. Dietz, 545 P.2d 1104, 1108 (1976), an adoption that has been repeatedly affirmed. Section 402A establishes strict liability for a seller of a product whose defective condition makes the product unreasonably dangerous. Comment h to section 402A states that where a seller "has reason to anticipate that danger may result from a particular use, . . . he may be required to give adequate warning of the danger (see Comment j), and a product sold without such warning is in a defective condition." Kansas courts have relied on both comments j and k to section 402A in concretizing the duty to warn announced in comment h.[7] These comments make clear that a product may not be defectively designed, but may nonetheless be defective because the manufacturer failed to adequately warn the users of the product of a reasonably foreseeable hazard. The Kansas Supreme Court in Savina v. Sterling Drug, Inc., 247 Kan. 105, 795 P.2d 915 (Kan. 1990), stated this proposition as follows:

> Under the strict liability theory, a plaintiff is not required to establish misconduct by the maker or seller but, instead, is required to impugn the product. The plaintiff must show the product is in "a defective condition unreasonably dangerous," which means that it must be defective in a way that subjects persons or tangible property to an unreasonable risk of harm. Prosser and Keeton, Law of Torts §99, p.695 (5th ed. 1984). A product can be defective in one of the following three ways: (1) a flaw is present in the product at the time it is sold; (2) *the producer or assembler of the product fails to adequately warn of a risk or hazard related to the way the product was designed;* or (3) the product, although perfectly manufactured, contains a defect that makes it unsafe. Prosser, §99, pp.695-98.

795 P.2d at 923 (emphasis added).

The district court's restriction of the general duty to warn to specific design defects overlooks that under Kansas law of strict liability, even if a product does not have a

---

warning in the context of a strict products liability claim — the tests actually applied condition imposition of liability on the defendant's having actually or constructively known of the risk that triggers the warning." Johnson v. American Cyanamid Co., 239 Kan. 279, 718 P.2d 1318, 1324 (1986), *aff'd*, Kan. 291, 758 P.2d 206 (1988) (quoting Kearl v. Lederle Lab., 172 Cal. App. 3d 812, 218 Cal. Rptr. 453, 465-66 (1985)).

[7] Comment j reads, in pertinent part:

> Directions or warning. In order to prevent the product from being unreasonably dangerous, the seller may be required to give directions or warning, on the container, as to its use. . . .

Where warning is given, the seller may reasonably assume that it will be read and heeded; and a product bearing such a warning, which is safe for use if it is followed, is not in defective condition, nor is it unreasonably dangerous.

Comment k reads:

> Unavoidably unsafe products. There are some products which, in the present state of human knowledge, are quite incapable of being made safe for their intended and ordinary use. . . . Such a product, properly prepared, and accompanied by proper directions and warning, is not defective, nor is it unreasonably dangerous. . . . The seller of such products, again with the qualification that they are properly prepared and marketed, and proper warning is given, where the situation calls for it, is not to be held to strict liability for unfortunate consequences attending their use, merely because he has undertaken to supply the public with an apparently useful and desirable product, attended with a known but apparently reasonable risk.

design defect, failure to warn of a foreseeable danger arising from the product's normal use makes the product defective.

The mini-trampoline was specifically intended for exercise, and in particular, for jogging. When used for this purpose, however, the mini-trampoline's design results in the foot turning in a way that places stress on the ankle bones. That the design is not defective, within the state of the known art, does not detract from the manufacturer's duty to warn the consumer of foreseeable dangers that can arise from normal use. . . .

Given that repetitive jogging on the mini-trampoline could cause stress fractures, the question becomes whether Richter presented sufficient evidence that a jury could permissibly conclude reasonable tests would have been effective in bringing this danger to light. Richter presented a substantial amount of expert testimony to the effect that visual observation of a person jogging on the mini-trampoline by someone with expertise in biomechanics, would reveal eversion and further that relatively simple tests could measure the degree of eversion. A comparison of that measurement with a measurement of the eversion caused by jogging on a flat surface would have revealed mini-trampolines cause users' feet to evert to a markedly greater degree. Testimony established that it is well known that such stresses, experienced on a repetitive basis, could cause fractures. We hold the jury could have reasonably found Richter's injury was causally related to repetitive jogging on the mini-trampoline, the use for which Limax's product was intended. The jury could also reasonably have concluded Limax should have warned users of this danger because the danger was eminently knowable given the state of the art and Limax should have known of it. . . .

Under Kansas law, both strict liability and negligence require warnings only for dangers which are reasonably foreseeable in light of the intended use of a product. The jury could reasonably have concluded that a simple consultation with a biomechanics expert would have given Limax sufficient information to arrange for appropriate testing of the mini-trampoline. No expert witness for either side expressed any doubt that the mini-trampoline accentuates eversion of the ankles or that eversion could cause stress fractures. It is true that no one appears to have considered the problem until Richter's injury occurred, but it is also true that plaintiff's evidence demonstrated that the danger was patently obvious to any expert who had a reason to look for it. The jury could permissibly conclude Limax should reasonably have foreseen that design of the mini-trampoline could result in the harm produced. Limax conceded that it did no testing or research to consider foreseeable harm arising out of the uses to which the mini-trampoline would be put. . . .

We find that the district court erred in granting a judgment as a matter of law and we therefore hold that the verdict and judgment in favor of the plaintiff should be reinstated.

NOTES TO RICHTER v. LIMAX INTERNATIONAL

1. Knowledge of Danger. *Richter* involves the issues of when and about what risks a manufacturer must warn. In the risk-utility balancing test for design defects, states treat manufacturers as if they had constructive knowledge of all risks and alternatives available to manufacturers at the time of marketing and distribution. As in Kansas, most states apply the same test to whether a manufacturer met a duty to warn under negligence as under strict liability. The Kansas court said, "In warning cases, the test is reasonableness." Compared to the constructive knowledge imposed in defective design cases, what knowledge is imputed in defective warning cases?

2. The "Read and Heed" Rule. The Restatement (Second) §402A comment j, quoted in *Richter*, stated the "read and heed" rule, which says that a seller is entitled to assume that if it has provided adequate warnings, those warnings would be read and heeded by product users. This rule is relevant to deciding whether a product was defectively designed. Consumers' expectations are informed by what they are presumed to have read. The risks presented by a product design depend on the users' awareness of the risks and ability to avoid the risks.

After a plaintiff has shown that lack of a warning has made a product defective, the plaintiff must show that "but for" the defective warning, the injury would not have occurred. The "read and heed" rule arises again in this element of the plaintiff's proof. The plaintiff must prove that he or she would have followed a warning if the defendant had provided one. A number of states allow plaintiffs the benefit of a "heeding presumption," allowing the jury to assume that the plaintiff would have obeyed a warning if it had been given. See James v. Bessemer Processing Co., 155 N.J. 279, 714 A.2d 898 (1998).

3. Defective with Adequate Warning? The Restatement (Second) §402A comment j also says that a product with an adequate warning is neither defective nor unreasonably dangerous. Many states do not follow this rule. States following the consumer expectation test have rejected this rule, saying that the warning is a factor to be considered in determining whether the product was defective and dangerous beyond a reasonable consumer's expectation. See Delaney v. Deere and Co., 999 P.2d 930 (Kan. 2000). The Restatement (Third) §2 applies the risk-utility test and, in comment l, rejects the "no defect" rule of the Restatement (Second):

> 1. Relationship between design and instruction or warning. Reasonable designs and instructions or warnings both play important roles in the production and distribution of reasonably safe products. In general, when a safer design can reasonably be implemented and risks can reasonably be designed out of a product, adoption of the safer design is required over a warning that leaves a significant residuum of such risks. For example, instructions and warnings may be ineffective because users of the product may not be adequately reached, may be likely to be inattentive, or may be insufficiently motivated to follow the instructions or heed the warnings. However, when an alternative design to avoid risks cannot reasonably be implemented, adequate instructions and warnings will normally be sufficient to render the product reasonably safe. . . . Warnings are not, however, a substitute for the provision of a reasonably safe design.
>
> The fact that a risk is obvious or generally known often serves the same function as a warning. See Comment j. However, obviousness of risk does not necessarily obviate a duty to provide a safer design. Just as warnings may be ignored, so may obvious or generally known risks be ignored, leaving a residuum of risk great enough to require adopting a safer design. See Comment d.

Illustration:

14. Jeremy's foot was severed when caught between the blade and compaction chamber of a garbage truck on which he was working. The injury occurred when he lost his balance while jumping on the back step of the garbage truck as it was moving from one stop to the next. The garbage truck, manufactured by XYZ

Motor Co., has a warning in large red letters on both the left and right rear panels that reads "DANGER — DO NOT INSERT ANY OBJECT WHILE COMPACTION CHAMBER IS WORKING — KEEP HANDS AND FEET AWAY." The fact that adequate warning was given does not preclude Jeremy from seeking to establish a design defect under Subsection (b). The possibility that an employee might lose his balance and thus encounter the shear point was a risk that a warning could not eliminate and that might require a safety guard. Whether a design defect can be established is governed by Subsection (b).

F. The "Comment k" Exception for Drugs

During the early development of strict liability for products, drugs presented a unique problem. In connection with the consumer expectation test, it was likely that a drug would be deemed defective if it caused harm to a patient, because a plausible consumer expectation for drugs is that they will be helpful, not harmful. Freeman v. Hoffman-La Roche, Inc., describes comment k to §402A — the Restatement (Second) approach to this problem — and compares it with the approach taken by Restatement (Third). The opinion decides whether a case-by-case method or a blanket rule works best.

FREEMAN v. HOFFMAN-LA ROCHE, INC.
260 Neb. 552, 618 N.W.2d 827 (2000)

CONNOLLY, J.

In this appeal, we reconsider our approach to products liability for defects in prescription drugs in light of changes in the law and the release of Restatement (Third) of Torts: Products Liability §§1 to 21 (1997) (Third Restatement). The appellant, Aimee Freeman, . . . seeks damages for injuries she sustained following her use of the prescription drug Accutane. Hoffman demurred on the basis that the petition failed to state a cause of action. Based on our decision in McDaniel v. McNeil Laboratories, Inc., 196 Neb. 190, 241 N.W.2d 822 (1976), the . . . action was dismissed with prejudice.

Freeman's operative petition alleged the following facts: On or about September 23, 1995, Freeman presented herself to her physician for treatment of chronic acne. After examination, her physician prescribed 20 milligrams daily of Accutane. Hoffman is the designer, manufacturer, wholesaler, retailer, fabricator, and supplier of Accutane.

Freeman took the Accutane daily from September 27 through October 2, 1995, and from October 4 through November 20, 1995. Hoffman alleged that as a result of taking the Accutane, she developed multiple health problems. These problems included ulcerative colitis, inflammatory polyarthritis, nodular episcleritis OS, and optic nerve head drusen. As a result, Freeman alleged that she sustained various damages. Freeman alleged that the Accutane she took was defective. . . .

In dealing with products other than prescription drugs, this court has recognized a manufacturer's liability in tort for design defects. Liability arises when an article a manufacturer has placed in the market, knowing that it is to be used without inspection for defects, proves to have a defect which causes an injury to a human being rightfully using the product. We have also adopted and applied the test set out in the Second Restatement §402A.

Under the Second Restatement, prescription drugs are treated specially under §402A, comment k. Comment k. at 353-54 provides an exception from strict liability when a product is deemed to be "unavoidably unsafe" and states:

> There are some products which, in the present state of human knowledge, are quite incapable of being made safe for their intended and ordinary use. These are especially common in the field of drugs. An outstanding example is the vaccine for the Pasteur treatment of rabies, which not uncommonly leads to very serious and damaging consequences when it is injected. Since the disease itself invariably leads to a dreadful death, both the marketing and the use of the vaccine are fully justified, notwithstanding the unavoidable high degree of risk which they involve. Such a product, properly prepared, and accompanied by proper directions and warning, is not defective, nor is it unreasonably dangerous. The same is true of many other drugs, vaccines, and the like, many of which for this very reason cannot legally be sold except to physicians, or under the prescription of a physician. It is also true in particular of many new or experimental drugs as to which, because of lack of time and opportunity for sufficient medical experience, there can be no assurance of safety, or perhaps even of purity of ingredients, but such experience as there is justifies the marketing and use of the drug notwithstanding a medically recognizable risk. The seller of such products, again with the qualification that they are properly prepared and marketed, and proper warning is given, where the situation calls for it, is not to be held to strict liability for unfortunate consequences attending their use, merely because he has undertaken to supply the public with an apparently useful and desirable product, attended with a known but apparently reasonable risk.

Application of comment k. has been justified under the law in some jurisdictions as a way to strike a balance between a manufacturer's responsibility and the encouragement of research and development of new products. Under certain instances, it is in the public interest to allow products to be marketed which are unsafe, because the benefits of the product justify its risks.

[A] few jurisdictions have interpreted comment k. in a manner that strictly excepts all prescription drugs from strict liability. Under the minority view, a drug that is properly manufactured and accompanied by an adequate warning of the risks known to the manufacturer at the time of sale is not defectively designed as a matter of law. These jurisdictions are commonly described by legal commentators as providing manufacturers with a "blanket immunity" from strict liability for design defects in prescription drugs. Our decision in *McDaniel*, supra, generally falls under this category of interpretation of comment k.

An application of comment k. to provide a blanket immunity from strict liability is widely criticized. Comment k. has proved to be difficult to interpret and apply, thus, supporting the argument that it should not be applied so strictly. Further, it is said that an approach that entirely excepts manufacturers from immunity [sic: liability] limits the discretionary powers of the courts. Also, it is argued that a blanket immunity leads to patently unjust results.

The majority of jurisdictions that have adopted comment k. apply it on a case-by-case basis, believing that societal interests in ensuring the marketing and development of prescription drugs will be adequately served without the need to resort to a rule of blanket immunity. A few courts have not specifically adopted comment k. and have instead either fashioned their own rules or treated prescription drugs in the same manner as that of all other products.

Although a variety of tests are employed among jurisdictions that apply comment k. on a case-by-case basis, the majority apply the comment as an affirmative defense, with the trend toward the use of a risk-utility test in order to determine whether the defense applies. When a risk utility test is applied, the existence of a reasonable alternative design is generally the central factor. Because the application of comment k. is traditionally viewed as an exception and a defense to strict liability, courts generally place the initial burden of proving the various risk utility factors on the defendant. Thus, under these cases, the plaintiff's burden of proof for his or her prima facie case remains the same as it is in any products liability case in the given jurisdiction.

. . . We now believe that societal interests in ensuring the marketing and development of prescription drugs can be served without resorting to a rule which in effect amounts to a blanket immunity from strict liability for manufacturers. Accordingly, we overrule *McDaniel* to the extent it applies comment k. to provide a blanket immunity from strict liability for prescription drugs. Accordingly, we must address how, or if, comment k. should be applied, or whether we should consider adopting provisions of the Third Restatement. We next address those provisions in considering what test should be applied. . . .

Section 6 of the Third Restatement pertains specifically to prescription drugs, with §6(c) applying to design defects. Section 6 at 144-45 states in part:

> (a) A manufacturer of a prescription drug or medical device who sells or otherwise distributes a defective drug or medical device is subject to liability for harm to persons caused by the defect. A prescription drug or medical device is one that may be legally sold or otherwise distributed only pursuant to a health-care provider's prescription.
>
> (b) For purposes of liability under Subsection (a), a prescription drug or medical device is defective if at the time of sale or other distribution the drug or medical device:
>
>> (1) contains a manufacturing defect as defined in §2(a); or
>>
>> (2) is not reasonably safe due to defective design as defined in Subsection (c); or
>>
>> (3) is not reasonably safe due to inadequate instructions or warnings as defined in Subsection (d).
>
> (c) A prescription drug or medical device is not reasonably safe due to defective design if the foreseeable risks of harm posed by the drug or medical device are sufficiently great in relation to its foreseeable therapeutic benefits that reasonable health-care providers, knowing of such foreseeable risks and therapeutic benefits, would not prescribe the drug or medical device for any class of patients.

There are several criticisms of §6(c), which will be briefly summarized. First, it does not accurately restate the law. . . .

Second, the reasonable physician test is criticized as being artificial and difficult to apply. The test requires fact finders to presume that physicians have as much or more of an awareness about a prescription drug product as the manufacturer. The test also ignores concerns of commentators that physicians tend to prescribe drugs they are familiar with or for which they have received advertising material, even when studies indicate that better alternatives are available.

A third criticism of particular applicability to Freeman's case is that the test lacks flexibility and treats drugs of unequal utility equally. For example, a drug used for cosmetic purposes but which causes serious side effects has less utility than a drug which treats a deadly disease, yet also has serious side effects. In each case, the drugs would likely be useful to a class of patients under the reasonable physician standard for some class of persons. Consequently, each would be exempted from design defect liability. . . .

Fourth, the test allows a consumer's claim to be defeated simply by a statement from the defense's expert witness that the drug at issue had some benefit for any single class of people. Thus, it is argued that application of §6(c) will likely shield pharmaceutical companies from a wide variety of suits that could have been brought under comment k. of the Second Restatement. As the Third Restatement, §6(c), comment f. at 149, states in part: "Given this very demanding objective standard, liability is likely to be imposed only under unusual circumstances." Thus, even though the rule is reformulated, any application of §6(c) will essentially provide the same blanket immunity from liability for design defects in prescription drugs as did the application of comment k. in the few states that interpreted it as such.

We conclude that §6(c) has no basis in the case law. We view §6(c) as too strict of a rule, under which recovery would be nearly impossible. Accordingly, we do not adopt §6(c) of the Third Restatement.

We conclude that §402A, comment k., of the Second Restatement should be applied on a case-by-case basis and as an affirmative defense in cases involving prescription drug products. Under this rule, an application of the comment does not provide a blanket immunity from strict liability for prescription drugs. Rather, the plaintiff is required to plead the consumer expectations test, as he or she would be required to do in any products liability case. The defendant may then raise comment k. as an affirmative defense. The comment will apply to except the prescription drug product from strict liability when it is shown that (1) the product is properly manufactured and contains adequate warnings, (2) its benefits justify its risks, and (3) the product was at the time of manufacture and distribution incapable of being made more safe.

. . . Freeman alleged facts that the Accutane was dangerous to an extent beyond that which would be contemplated by the ordinary consumer who purchases it, with the ordinary knowledge common to the community as to its characteristics. Accordingly, we conclude that Freeman has stated a theory of recovery based on a design defect.

NOTES TO FREEMAN v. HOFFMAN-LA ROCHE, INC.

1. *Breadth of Comment k Protection.* The *Freeman* opinion outlines the minority and majority treatment of strict liability for defectively designed drugs. The "blanket" test of the Restatement (Second) §402A, comment k, did not mean drug companies always escaped liability. Reviewing comment k, reproduced in the opinion, reveals the various grounds on which plaintiffs may bring claims.

2. *Significance of Warnings Under Restatement (Third).* The court in *Freeman* also characterizes the Restatement (Third) §6 as a blanket rule. When will a drug manufacturer be liable for a defectively designed drug under the Restatement (Second)

test and under the Restatement (Third) test? Does the Nebraska court adopt a consumer expectations test for drugs? A risk-utility test? Or both?

G. *The Learned Intermediary Doctrine*

The *learned intermediary* doctrine limits the duty of product sellers to provide warnings to the ultimate users of their products. Centocor, Inc. v. Bullen considers the policy of limiting the duty to provide warnings to patients when a medical professional is in a position to evaluate the patients' needs and convey appropriate warnings.

CENTOCOR, INC. v. BULLEN
372 S.W.3d 140 (Tex. 2012)

Justice GREEN delivered the Opinion of the Court.

. . . In March 2003, Patricia and Thomas Hamilton sued Centocor, Inc., a prescription drug manufacturer and subsidiary of Johnson & Johnson, claiming that Centocor provided "inadequate and inappropriate warnings and instruction for use" of its prescription drug Remicade, which made Remicade "defective and unreasonably dangerous," and seeking damages for injuries that Patricia allegedly incurred from using the drug. . . . The Hamiltons claimed that Remicade caused Patricia to suffer a serious drug-induced side effect called lupus-like syndrome. . . .

The jury found in favor of the Hamiltons, and the trial court entered judgment for approximately $4.6 million. The court of appeals reversed the award of future pain and mental anguish damages but affirmed the remainder of the trial court's judgment. . . .

Centocor timely petitioned this Court for review. . . .

LEARNED INTERMEDIARY DOCTRINE

Generally, a manufacturer is required to provide an adequate warning to the end users of its product if it knows or should know of any potential harm that may result from the use of its product. In certain contexts, however, the manufacturer's or supplier's duty to warn end users of the dangerous propensities of its product is limited to providing an adequate warning to an intermediary, who then assumes the duty to pass the necessary warnings on to the end users. It is firmly established in Texas that whether a duty exists is ordinarily a legal matter for the court to decide. Within the context of prescription drug manufacturers, the underlying premise for the learned intermediary doctrine is that prescription drugs are complex and vary in effect, depending on the unique circumstances of an individual user, and for this reason, patients can obtain them only through a prescribing physician.

Centocor argues that the learned intermediary doctrine applies and therefore it had no duty to warn Patricia directly of the risks and potential side effects associated with Remicade. . . .

The learned intermediary doctrine has been part of Texas jurisprudence for many years. See, e.g., Gravis v. Parke-Davis & Co., 502 S.W.2d 863, 870 (Tex. Civ. App. Corpus Christi 1973, writ ref'd n.r.e.). In *Gravis*, the court of appeals held that it was unreasonable for the law to impose a duty on prescription drug manufacturers to "specifically warn each and every patient that receives drugs prescribed by the physician or other authorized persons" and outlined the underlying rationale for the doctrine:

> The entire system of drug distribution in America is set up so as to place the responsibility of distribution and use upon professional people. The laws and regulations prevent prescription type drugs from being purchased by individuals without the advice, guidance and consent of licensed physicians and pharmacists. These professionals are in the best position to evaluate the warnings put out by the drug industry. Our holding in no way relieves the drug company in their duty to warn or to provide a product free of defects. . . .

Our decision to apply the learned intermediary doctrine in the context of prescription drugs, prescribed through a physician-patient relationship, not only comports with our prior references to the doctrine and many years of Texas case law, but it places us alongside the vast majority of other jurisdictions that have considered the issue. Our sister states have overwhelmingly adopted the learned intermediary doctrine in this context and, to date, only one state has rejected the doctrine altogether. See State ex rel. Johnson & Johnson Corp. v. Karl, 220 W.Va. 463, 647 S.E.2d 899, 913-14 (2007). The underlying rationale for the validity of the learned intermediary doctrine remains just as viable today as stated by Judge Wisdom in 1974:

> Prescription drugs are likely to be complex medicines, esoteric in formula and varied in effect. As a medical expert, the prescribing physician can take into account the propensities of the drug, as well as the susceptibilities of his patient. His is the task of weighing the benefits of any medication against its potential dangers. The choice he makes is an informed one, an individualized medical judgment bottomed on a knowledge of both patient and palliative. Pharmaceutical companies then, who must warn ultimate purchasers of dangers inherent in patent drugs sold over the counter, in selling prescription drugs are required to warn only the prescribing physician, who acts as a "learned intermediary" between manufacturer and consumer.

Reyes v. Wyeth Laboratories, 498 F.2d 1264, 1276 (Tex. Ct. App. 1974). Because patients can obtain prescription drugs only through their prescribing physician or another authorized intermediary and because the "learned intermediary" is best suited to weigh the patient's individual needs in conjunction with the risks and benefits of the prescription drug, we are in agreement with the overwhelming majority of other courts that have considered the learned intermediary doctrine and hold that, within the physician-patient relationship, the learned intermediary doctrine applies and generally limits the drug manufacturer's duty to warn to the prescribing physician.

Having concluded that the learned intermediary doctrine generally applies in the prescription drug context, we next consider whether some exception to the doctrine is warranted here, so that, despite the doctrine, Centocor retained a duty to warn the patient directly. In the more than forty-five years since courts first adopted the learned intermediary doctrine in the prescription drug context, the healthcare industry has experienced substantial changes, especially surrounding the marketing of prescription drugs. In light of these changes, some courts and commentators, including the Restatement, have recognized limited exceptions to the learned intermediary doctrine. See, e.g., Restatement (Third) of Torts: Products Liability §6 (1998)).

The most recent exception to merit significant national attention is the [direct-to-consumer (DTC)] advertising or "mass marketing" exception. Despite the significant academic literature on the topic, only a few courts have recognized a DTC advertising exception to the learned intermediary doctrine when a drug manufacturer directly markets to the consumer. [T]he New Jersey Supreme Court adopted a sweeping DTC advertising exception to the learned intermediary doctrine in Perez v. Wyeth Laboratories Inc., 734 A.2d 1245, 1246-47 (1999). *Perez* involved a prescription contraceptive called Norplant — a "hybrid" medical device that consists of a drug capsule that is surgically implanted in the patient's arm. The plaintiffs alleged that Wyeth Laboratories had conducted a massive advertising campaign, "which it directed at women rather than at their doctors," and sought damages because the DTC warnings failed to mention serious side effects including pain and permanent scarring attendant to the removal of the drug capsule. Id. at 1248. The New Jersey Supreme Court examined the theoretical underpinnings for the learned intermediary doctrine within the context of the dramatic changes associated with DTC advertising and determined that "[c]onsumer-directed advertising of pharmaceuticals thus belies each of the premises on which the learned intermediary doctrine rests." Id. at 1256. As a result, the court held that the learned intermediary doctrine no longer provided complete protection to pharmaceutical manufacturers that provided adequate warnings to physicians on the risks and benefits of a drug when that company chose to market directly to consumers. . . .

To date, West Virginia is the only state whose highest court has followed the New Jersey Supreme Court's holding in *Perez*. In State ex rel. Johnson & Johnson Corp. v. Karl, 647 S.E.2d 899 (W. Va. 2007), the West Virginia Supreme Court relied on the Perez court's reasoning to reject the learned intermediary doctrine entirely: "Given the plethora of exceptions to the learned intermediary doctrine, we ascertain no benefit in adopting a doctrine that would require the simultaneous adoption of numerous exceptions in order to be justly utilized." Id. at 910-11, 913. While *Karl* is the only instance where the highest court of another state has followed *Perez*, at least five other jurisdictions have expressly declined to adopt a DTC advertising exception to the learned intermediary doctrine.

. . . We acknowledge that some situations may require exceptions to the learned intermediary doctrine, but without deciding whether Texas law should recognize a DTC advertising exception when a prescription drug manufacturer distributes intentionally misleading information directly to patients or prospective patients, we hold that, based on the facts of this case, no exception applies.

Here, the alleged harm was not caused by Centocor's direct advertising to Patricia. At trial, the Hamiltons admitted that the first time they heard of Remicade was when Patricia's husband, Thomas, saw a textual banner displayed on the bottom ticker of the CNN news channel, which stated that the FDA had approved Remicade for the treatment of Crohn's disease. This innocuous news report is a far cry from the basis for the *Perez* court's adoption of a DTC advertising exception where the pharmaceutical company "ma[de] direct claims to consumers for the efficacy of its product" through prescription drug advertisements. . . .

The court of appeals' opinion relied heavily on evidence of Centocor's marketing strategy. While the Hamiltons introduced evidence that Centocor engaged in a multi-pronged marketing strategy meant to increase sales, including efforts to educate doctors of the financial benefits of the drug, dilute the effect of a negative peer review article, and encourage patients to "demand Remicade," its general marketing strategy has no bearing on Patricia's case because she admitted that her discussions about

Remicade and the information she received all came through her physicians who were fully aware of the risk of lupus-like syndrome.

Even so, we must believe that patients who seek prescription drugs based solely on DTC advertising will obtain them only when the prescribing physician has evaluated the potential risks and benefits for the particular patient. To safeguard the public from harmful products and misleading advertising, both the federal government and Texas law regulate the design, marketing, and distribution of prescription drugs. Although pharmaceutical companies have increased DTC advertising since courts first adopted the learned intermediary doctrine, the fundamental rationale for the doctrine remains the same: prescriptions drugs require a doctor's prescription and, therefore, doctors are best suited to communicate the risks and benefits of prescription medications for particular patients through their face-to-face interactions with those patients.

Without deciding whether Texas law should recognize any of the other exceptions to the learned intermediary doctrine, we find no reason to adopt an exception where the physician-patient relationship existed, the pharmaceutical company provided a warning to the patient's prescribing doctors that included the side effect of which the patient complains, and the patient had already visited with her prescribing physician and decided to take the drug before she saw the informational video at issue. Accordingly, we hold that it was error for the court of appeals to create a DTC or fraudulent advertising exception to the learned intermediary doctrine based on the facts of this case.

CONCLUSION

[The court also held that, assuming the warning was inadequate, Patricia had failed to prove that the failure was a legal cause of her injuries. There was no evidence that a different warning would have changed either her doctors' conduct or her own conduct.] [B]ecause there is no causation evidence to support the Hamiltons' claims, all of which are premised on Centocor's alleged failure to warn, the Hamiltons' claims must fail. We therefore need not address Centocor's remaining issues. . . . Accordingly, we reverse the portions of the court of appeals' judgment that are inconsistent with this opinion and render judgment that the Hamiltons take nothing.

NOTES TO CENTOCOR, INC. v. BULLEN

1. *The Learned Intermediary Doctrine.* When the learned intermediary doctrine applies, a manufacturer has no duty to give a warning to the plaintiff, but the manufacturer still has a duty to warn the intermediary. To recover, a plaintiff must prove that the manufacturer breached that duty and that the breach was a legal cause of the plaintiff's harm.

2. *The Learned Intermediary Doctrine and Approaches to Duty.* Modern courts interpret duty in two ways. Traditionally, duty was primarily based on the foreseeability of causing harm to a particular plaintiff. Under that view, the failure to warn a particular plaintiff will not cause harm because the learned intermediary takes on the task of providing the warning. The Restatement (Third) assumes that there generally is a duty, but courts may find classes of cases where policy reasons support only a limited duty. Under that view, manufacturers have a duty to warn intermediaries only when they can reasonably expect those intermediaries to transmit the warning. In both cases, the question of whether there is a duty is a question for the court.

3. *Duty as an Element of the Plaintiff's Case.* Proof that the defendant had a duty to the plaintiff and breached that duty is typically part of the plaintiff's prima facie case. Regardless of which approach to duty a court takes, if the learned intermediary doctrine is treated as a question of duty, it is not an affirmative defense. Affirmative defenses absolve (or limit the extent of recovery from) the defendant. If the doctrine applies and the plaintiff fails to prove that the manufacturer improperly warned the physician, the plaintiff's case fails.

Despite the fact that duty is ordinarily part of the plaintiff's prima facie case, some courts in workplace cases have held that the burden of showing that a warning from the manufacturer would have been ineffectual should be on the manufacturer. These courts shift the burden from the plaintiff (a worker using a dangerous product) to the manufacturer because the manufacturer is more likely than the worker to have information about the industry. The information would include the likelihood that workers would receive any warning the manufacturer provided.

4. *Applying the Learned Intermediary Doctrine in Non-Drug Cases.* Courts have applied the learned intermediary doctrine to manufacturers of a wide variety of goods other than drugs, such as medical devices, asbestos, bottle capping machines, propane, benzene, polyurethane roofing products, and flint used as an abrasive sanding agent. *Centocor* provides the specific rationale for applying the doctrine when there is a doctor/patient relationship. If facts show that employers or others who buy goods in bulk quantities, for instance, do not pass on the warnings, the learned intermediary doctrine will not apply. According to the Restatement (Third) Products Liability §2 comment i:

> There is no general rule as to whether one supplying a product for the use of others through an intermediary has a duty to warn the ultimate product user directly or may rely on the intermediary to relay warnings. The standard is one of reasonableness in the circumstances. Among the factors to be considered are the gravity of the risks posed by the product, the likelihood that the intermediary will convey the information to the ultimate user, and the feasibility and effectiveness of giving a warning directly to the user. Thus, when the purchaser of machinery is the owner of a workplace who provides the machinery to employees for their use, and there is reason to doubt that the employer will pass warnings on to employees, the seller is required to reach the employees directly with necessary instructions and warnings if doing so is reasonably feasible.

Just as manufacturers other than drug makers may rely on the doctrine, people other than health care professionals may be learned intermediaries.

5. *Exceptions to the Learned Intermediary Doctrine.* Two widely accepted exceptions to the learned intermediary doctrine are the mass inoculation exception and the federal regulation exceptions. The first reflects consideration of whether the manufacturer reasonably relied on an intermediary to give effective warnings. The Restatement (Third) of Torts Products Liability §6(d) provides:

> (d) A prescription drug or medical device is not reasonably safe due to inadequate instructions or warnings if reasonable instructions or warnings regarding foreseeable risks of harm are not provided to:
>
> (1) prescribing and other health-care providers who are in a position to reduce the risks of harm in accordance with the instructions or warnings; or

(2) the patient when the manufacturer knows or has reason to know that health-care providers will not be in a position to reduce the risks of harm in accordance with the instructions or warnings.

Courts have applied the rule in §6(d)(2) to situations such as mass inoculations where drugs such as vaccines are administered to patients without the personal intervention or evaluation of a health-care provider. Where patients are unlikely to receive the attention of a physician that is normally assumed when the learned intermediary doctrine is applied, drug manufacturers are often required to give direct warnings to the patients if warning is likely to be feasible and effective. The other exception applies when federal law requires direct warnings, such as the Food and Drug Administration requirement that birth control pills be sold with a package insert containing a warning. As *Centocor* reveals, only a few courts apply a third exception that rejects the learned intermediary doctrine when prescription drugs are advertised directly to consumers without adequate warnings.

Problem
Applying the Learned Intermediary Doctrine

Mr. Gomez was employed by Spincote and worked in and around abrasive blasting (also known as sandblasting). Flint for this blasting was delivered to Spincote by the manufacturer, Humble Sand and Gravel, both in bulk and in bags. There is no question that inhalation of flint caused Mr. Gomez to suffer from silicosis, a very serious injury. The dangers were well known to Spincote, but no warnings were given to employees. Federal regulations require use of air-fed hoods by workers in Mr. Gomez's position, but such workers did not regularly use them and their employers did not enforce the regulations. Although it would have been inexpensive to print warnings on the bags, it is unclear whether working conditions would have enabled employees to read those warnings. If Mr. Gomez seeks damages from Humble Sand and Flint on a failure to warn theory, should the learned intermediary doctrine apply? See Humble Sand & Gravel, Inc. v. Gomez, 146 S.W.3d 170 (Tex. 2004).

H. Plaintiff's Carelessness or Misuse of Product

When Restatement (Second) articulated what became a national trend toward adoption of strict liability for products cases, contributory negligence was still the typical system used to account for a plaintiff's own contribution to an injury. It completely barred recovery. Restatement §402A and its associated comments took the position that contributory negligence would *not* bar recovery in a strict liability products case. Nevertheless, §402A also stated that assumption of the risk would continue to operate as a complete bar to recovery and that there could be no recovery if an injury was caused by "abnormal" use of a product.

The limitations §402A placed on a defendant's ability to avoid liability because of a plaintiff's conduct were understandable, given the general motivating force behind adoption of strict liability—a belief that the legal system should be adjusted to allow plaintiffs to recover damages in most product-related injury cases. The development of comparative negligence has led almost all states to reconsider the effect of plaintiff's conduct in strict products liability cases. Smith v. Ingersoll-Rand Co. illustrates the history of these developments in a state that treats a plaintiff's conduct as a type of fault to be balanced in a comparative negligence fashion. *Smith* also illustrates the interplay between common law and statutory enactments. Daniell v. Ford Motor Co. takes a slightly different approach to types of plaintiff conduct that can be characterized as misuse, ignoring an obvious danger, and assumption of risk.

Early in the history of strict products liability, courts focused on whether the product in question was used for its intended purpose. This issue is currently considered under the label "misuse" of a product. Manufacturers formulate "misuse" arguments in a variety of ways. Daniell v. Ford Motor Company is one example. In Trull v. Volkswagen of America, Inc., the manufacturer argues that it should not be strictly liable because colliding with an automobile is not an intended use. In Hernandez v. Tokai Corp., the manufacturer argues that it should not be strictly liable for the design of its cigarette lighter because the user, a child, was not an intended user. Both of these cases focus attention on how the law evaluates misuses when considering the defectiveness of a design.

SMITH v. INGERSOLL-RAND CO.
14 P.3d 990 (Alaska 2000)

MATTHEWS, C.J.

Dan Smith suffered permanent injuries after an air compressor door fell on his head. He brought a strict products liability lawsuit in federal district court against Ingersoll-Rand Company, the manufacturer of the air compressor. Following three jury trials and a remand from the Ninth Circuit, the United States District Court for the District of Alaska, Singleton, J., certified the following [question] to this court:

> Did the 1986 Tort Reform Act change the existing law on comparative fault in products liability cases such that a plaintiff's failure to exercise ordinary care is now sufficient to raise a jury question on comparative fault?

Because the 1986 Tort Reform Act modified the definition of comparative fault in strict liability cases to include ordinary negligence, we answer the . . . question in the affirmative. On August 12, 1987, Dan Smith was injured at Prudhoe Bay while attempting to start the diesel engine of an Ingersoll-Rand portable air compressor. Smith, a light duty mechanic, was not wearing a hard hat when he was dispatched by his supervisor to start the air compressor's engine.

The air compressor was an older model that required the mechanic to open its door in order to start the engine. There was no latch on the door to hold it open. Instead, the mechanic had to prop the door open in one of three ways: (1) the fully-open position; (2) the up-and-folded position; or (3) the wedged position. The first two positions safely hold the door in place; the third position is unsafe.

The exact details of Smith's accident are unknown. Smith does not remember how he propped the door open. All that he remembers is that he opened the door, started the engine, and the "next thing [he] knew, [he] was picking the door[] up off the top of [his] head." Somehow — whether from wind, vibration, or improper placement — the door had fallen from its open position and hit Smith's head. Initially, despite some blood and swelling, Smith did not think that he was seriously injured.

However, eleven days after the accident, Smith suffered a generalized motor seizure. He had no history of seizures in his adult life. On the medevac plane out of Prudhoe Bay, he suffered another seizure. He was later diagnosed with traumatic epilepsy, presumably caused by the compressor door hitting his head.

Since the accident, Smith has continued to suffer from repeated seizures, fatigue, difficulty concentrating, lapses in memory, and other related medical problems. He lost his job because of these medical problems and remains unemployed.

In 1975 this court judicially adopted the doctrine of comparative negligence for fault-based tort actions and abolished the older, harsher doctrine of contributory negligence, which completely barred a plaintiff's recovery if he was to some degree at fault for his injuries. Under the "pure" system of comparative fault adopted by the court, a plaintiff would still be able to recover if he was comparatively at fault for his injuries, but his recovery would be reduced in proportion to his percentage of fault.

Less than a year later, in Butaud v. Suburban Marine & Sporting Goods, Inc., 555 P.2d 42, 46 (Alaska 1976), we held that comparative negligence principles also apply to products liability actions based on strict liability. But we held that comparative negligence in strict products liability cases was limited to two specific situations: (1) when the plaintiff knows that the product is defective and unreasonably and voluntarily proceeds to use it; and (2) when the plaintiff misuses the product and the misuse is a proximate cause of the injuries.

In 1986 the Alaska Legislature passed the Tort Reform Act. Modeled after the Uniform Comparative Fault Act, the Tort Reform Act was intended "to create a more equitable distribution of the cost and risk of injury and increase the availability and affordability of insurance." The legislature hoped to reduce the costs of the tort system while still ensuring "that adequate and appropriate compensation for persons injured through the fault of others" remained available.

As part of the Act, the legislature enacted a rule of comparative fault similar to the doctrine of comparative negligence which this court had adopted a decade earlier:

> In an action based on fault seeking to recover damages for injury or death to a person or harm to property, contributory fault chargeable to the claimant diminishes proportionally the amount awarded as compensatory damages for the injury attributable to the claimant's contributory fault, but does not bar recovery. [Alaska Stat. §09.17.060.]

The Act defined "fault" as acts or omissions that are in any measure negligent, reckless, or intentional toward the person or property of the actor or others, or that subject a person to strict tort liability. The term also includes breach of warranty, unreasonable assumption of risk not constituting an enforceable express consent, misuse of product for which the defendant otherwise would be liable, and unreasonable failure to avoid injury or to mitigate damages. Legal requirements of causal relation apply both to fault as the basis for liability and to contributory fault. The question before us is whether these two provisions modified the existing case law on comparative negligence in products liability cases. We conclude that they did.

The Act clearly applies to strict products liability cases. The Act applies to tort actions "based on fault." Fault is defined to include, counter-intuitively, "acts or omissions . . . that subject a person to strict liability." Products liability cases in Alaska are typically based on a strict liability theory. Thus the Act applies to strict products liability actions.

The Act's definition of comparative fault is broader than the comparative fault recognized in pre-1986 strict products liability cases. Our pre-1986 products liability cases limit comparative fault to instances of product misuse and unreasonable assumption of risk. But, in addition to "misuse of product" and "unreasonable assumption" of risk, the Act also defines "fault" as including "acts or omissions that are in any measure negligent [or] reckless. . . ." Thus, the Act modifies the pre-1986 products liability case law by expanding the type of conduct that will trigger a proportional reduction of damages to include ordinary negligence — "acts or omissions that are in any measure negligent."

The Act's modification of comparative negligence in strict products liability cases reflects a general trend occurring across the nation.[36] The recently published Third Restatement of Torts, Products Liability, observes that a "strong majority" of courts now apply comparative negligence principles in strict products liability cases. Moreover, most of these courts do not limit comparative negligence to instances of product misuse or unreasonable and voluntary assumption of risk. Instead, they allow a plaintiff's ordinary negligence to constitute comparative fault.

In addition, legislatures in other states have enacted tort reform statutes similar to the one here, incorporating a universal definition of "contributory fault" for all tort cases, including strict products liability cases. Courts in other jurisdictions have generally interpreted these statutes as incorporating an ordinary negligence framework into the comparative fault analysis in strict liability cases.

We conclude that the [1986 Tort Reform] Act changed the law. Prior to the Act, comparative negligence in products liability cases was limited to product misuse and unreasonable assumption of risk. The Act expands that definition to include other types of comparative fault, including a plaintiff's ordinary negligence.

We therefore answer the . . . certified question in the affirmative.

NOTE TO SMITH v. INGERSOLL-RAND CO.

Evolving Treatment of Plaintiffs' Fault.   Alaska's treatment of a plaintiff's blameworthy conduct in products liability cases developed according to a pattern that has been seen in many states. Strict liability for products cases was introduced at a time when contributory negligence typically barred a plaintiff's tort recovery. As part of the pro-plaintiff orientation of the strict liability action, the contributory negligence defense was withdrawn, except in circumstances involving unreasonable assumption of risk or product misuse. When the contributory negligence doctrine was replaced throughout the state's tort law with comparative negligence, a plaintiff's ordinary negligence continued to be ignored in strict liability products cases, but comparative treatment was applied to assumption of risk and misuse. Finally, a statute applied comparative principles to all kinds of fault by plaintiffs in strict liability cases.

---

[36] See Daly v. General Motors Corp., 20 Cal. 3d 725, 575 P.2d 1162, 1170, 144 Cal. Rptr. 380 (Cal. 1978) (noting that more than 30 states have extended comparative negligence principles to strict products liability). Most legal commentators view this trend with favor. See, e.g., William Keeton, et al., Prosser and Keeton on the Law of Torts §102, at 712 (5th ed. 1984) (declaring the comparative fault system to be the fairest way to allocate costs of accidents in products liability cases).

Problem
Causal Effect of Plaintiff's Conduct

A grinding wheel shattered because of a manufacturing defect while the plaintiff was using it. Instructions provided with the wheel stated that the user should wear protective clothing, including safety goggles, when using the tool and that the user should operate the tool only while standing in front of it, never to the side. The plaintiff disregarded all of these instructions. Bearing in mind that legal requirements of causal relation apply to fault when it is a basis for liability and when it is a basis for a finding of a plaintiff's comparative fault, what defenses are available to the manufacturer under the rules described in Smith v. Ingersoll-Rand Co.? See Jimenez v. Sears, Roebuck and Co., 183 Ariz. 399, 904 P.2d 861 (1994).

DANIELL v. FORD MOTOR CO.
581 F. Supp. 728 (D.N.M. 1984)

BALDOCK, D.J. . . .

In 1980, the plaintiff became locked inside the trunk of a 1973 Ford LTD automobile, where she remained for some nine days. Plaintiff now seeks to recover for psychological and physical injuries arising from that occurrence. She contends that the automobile had a design defect in that the trunk lock or latch did not have an internal release or opening mechanism. She also maintains that the manufacturer is liable based on a failure to warn of this condition. Plaintiff advances several theories for recovery: (1) strict products liability under §402A of the Restatement 2d of Torts (1965), (2) negligence, and (3) breach of express warranty and implied warranties of merchantability and fitness for a particular purpose.

Three uncontroverted facts bar recovery under any of these theories. First, the plaintiff ended up in the trunk compartment of the automobile because she felt "over-burdened" and was attempting to commit suicide. Second, the purposes of an automobile trunk are to transport, stow and secure the automobile spare tire, luggage and other goods and to protect those items from elements of the weather. Third, the plaintiff never considered the possibility of exit from the inside of the trunk when the automobile was purchased. Plaintiff has not set forth evidence indicating that these facts are controverted.

The overriding factor barring plaintiff's recovery is that she intentionally sought to end her life by crawling into an automobile trunk from which she could not escape. This is not a case where a person inadvertently became trapped inside an automobile trunk. The plaintiff was aware of the natural and probable consequences of her perilous conduct. Not only that, the plaintiff, at least initially, sought those dreadful consequences. Plaintiff, not the manufacturer of the vehicle, is responsible for this unfortunate occurrence.

Recovery under strict products liability and negligence will be discussed first because the concept of duty owed by the manufacturer to the consumer or user is the same under both theories in this case. As a general principle, a design defect is actionable only where the condition of the product is unreasonably dangerous to the user or consumer. Under strict products liability or negligence, a manufacturer has a duty to consider only those risks of injury which are foreseeable. A risk is not foreseeable by a manufacturer where a product is used in a manner which could not reasonably be anticipated by the manufacturer and that use is the cause of the plaintiff's injury. The plaintiff's injury would not be foreseeable by the manufacturer.

The purposes of an automobile trunk are to transport, stow and secure the automobile spare tire, luggage and other goods and to protect those items from elements of the weather. The design features of an automobile trunk make it well near impossible that an adult intentionally would enter the trunk and close the lid. The dimensions of a trunk, the height of its sill and its load floor and the efforts to first lower the trunk lid and then to engage its latch, are among the design features which encourage closing and latching the trunk lid while standing outside the vehicle. The court holds that the plaintiff's use of the trunk compartment as a means to attempt suicide was an unforeseeable use as a matter of law. Therefore, the manufacturer had no duty to design an internal release or opening mechanism that might have prevented this occurrence.

Nor did the manufacturer have a duty to warn the plaintiff of the danger of her conduct, given the plaintiff's unforeseeable use of the product. Another reason why the manufacturer had no duty to warn the plaintiff of the risk inherent in crawling into an automobile trunk and closing the trunk lid is because such a risk is obvious. There is no duty to warn of known dangers in strict products liability or tort. Moreover, the potential efficacy of any warning, given the plaintiff's use of the automobile trunk compartment for a deliberate suicide attempt, is questionable.

The court notes that the automobile trunk was not defective under these circumstances. The automobile trunk was not unreasonably dangerous within the contemplation of the ordinary consumer or user of such a trunk when used in the ordinary ways and for the ordinary purposes for which such a trunk is used.

Having held that the plaintiff's conception of the manufacturer's duty is in error, the court need not reach the issues of the effect of comparative negligence or other defenses such as assumption of the risk on the products liability claim. See Scott v. Rizzo, 96 N.M. 682 at 688-89, 634 P.2d 1234 at 1240-41 (1981) (In adopting comparative negligence, the New Mexico Supreme Court indicated that in strict products liability a plaintiff's "misconduct" would be a defense, but not a complete bar to recovery). The court also does not reach the comparative negligence defense on the negligence claim.

Having considered the products liability and negligence claims, plaintiff's contract claims for breach of warranty are now analyzed. Plaintiff has come forward with no evidence of any express warranty regarding exit from the inside of the trunk. In accordance with Rule 56(e) of the Federal Rules of Civil Procedure and Local Rule 9(j) (D.N.M. October 25, 1983, as amended), summary judgment on the express warranty claim is appropriate.

Any implied warranty of merchantability in this case requires that the product must be fit for the ordinary purposes for which such goods are used. The implied warranty of merchantability does not require that the buyer must prove reliance on the skill and judgment of the manufacturer. Still, the usual and ordinary purpose of an automobile trunk is to transport and store goods, including the automobile's spare tire. Plaintiff's use of the trunk was highly extraordinary, and there is no evidence that that trunk was not fit for the ordinary purpose for which it was intended.

Lastly, plaintiff's claim for a breach of implied warranty of fitness for a particular purpose cannot withstand summary judgment because the plaintiff has admitted that, at the time she purchased the automobile neither she nor her husband gave any particular thought to the trunk mechanism. Plaintiff has admitted that she did not even think about getting out from inside of the trunk when purchasing the vehicle. Plaintiff did not rely on the seller's skill or judgment to select or furnish an automobile suitable for the unfortunate purpose for which the plaintiff used it.

Wherefore, it is ordered that defendant's Motion for Summary Judgment is granted.

NOTE TO DANIELL v. FORD MOTOR CO.

Plaintiff's Conduct Outside of Comparative Fault Analysis.   Some states that have substituted comparative for contributory negligence and apply comparative negligence principles to strict products liability do not treat all types of plaintiffs' conduct as "fault," to be balanced as "comparative fault." Daniell v. Ford Motor Co. illustrates alternative ways of analyzing (a) the plaintiff's *unforeseeable* misuse of a product, (b) the plaintiff's ignoring of an open and obvious danger, (c) the plaintiff's use of a product for a purpose other than that for which it was intended, and (d) the plaintiff's assumption of known risks. If the court finds that the defendant owed no duty to the plaintiff to prevent the harm that occurred or finds that the product was not defective or finds that the defendant's design was not causally related to the harm the plaintiff suffered, the question of comparative fault never arises. The defendant needs no defense because the plaintiff has failed to present a prima facie case. How would the *Daniell* case have been decided under the rule described in Smith v. Ingersoll-Rand Co.?

Perspective: Best Risk Avoiders

One basis for imposing strict liability in some types of cases is that in those cases we can be confident that a particular class of defendants are generally in the best position to evaluate risks and take justifiable precautions. Owners of wild animals, people engaged in blasting with dynamite and other abnormally dangerous activities, and manufacturers of products generally fit this description. There are, however, cases in which that confidence is misplaced. When a consumer using a product knows of a defect, for instance, but knowingly and voluntarily uses the product because he or she is in an especially good position to avoid the associated risk, the consumer may be the best risk avoider. Also, where the risk associated with a product results only from an unforeseeable misuse, the manufacturer may not be in a good position to avoid the risk. Each of the defenses discussed in these cases may be evaluated from the perspective of whether the party in the best position to avoid the risk has an incentive, created by the imposition of liability or denial of recovery, to minimize the risk. We might ask, for instance, whether, with respect to products, misuse cases or assumption of risk cases are systematically different in this way from ordinary negligence cases.

TRULL v. VOLKSWAGEN OF AMERICA, INC.

761 A.2d 477 (N.H. 2000)

NADEAU, J. . . .

In February 1991, the plaintiffs, David and Elizabeth Trull, and their two sons, Nathaniel and Benjamin, were traveling in New Hampshire when their Volkswagen Vanagon slid on black ice and collided with an oncoming car. Both parties agree that Nathaniel and Benjamin were seated in the rear middle bench seat of the Vanagon, which was equipped with lap-only seatbelts, and were wearing the available lap belts. Benjamin died in the accident, and both Elizabeth and Nathaniel suffered severe brain injuries.

In this diversity products liability action, the plaintiffs sought damages from the defendants "on the ground that defects in the design of the Vanagon made their injuries more severe than they otherwise would have been." "Plaintiffs had two primary theories of recovery: (1) the Vanagon was defective because it was a forward control vehicle constructed in such a way that it lacked sufficient protection against a frontal impact, and (2) the Vanagon was defective because the rear bench seats, on which Nathaniel and Benjamin were seated, did not have shoulder safety belts as well as lap belts." The plaintiffs contend that the defendants are liable in, inter alia, negligence and strict liability because the automobile was not crashworthy.

[The trial court entered judgment on a jury verdict for the defendant.] The plaintiffs appealed to the United States Court of Appeals for the First Circuit, arguing, among other things, that the district court "improperly imposed on plaintiffs the burden of proving the nature and extent of the enhanced injuries attributable to the Vanagon's design." Recognizing that the question "of who, under New Hampshire law, should bear the burden in a so-called 'crashworthiness' case, poses sophisticated questions of burden allocation involving not only a choice of appropriate precedent but also an important policy choice," the court of appeals granted the plaintiffs' motion to certify the question to this court.

The plaintiffs' theory of liability for defective design is commonly referred to as the "crashworthiness," "second collision," or "enhanced injury" doctrine. See Caiazzo v. Volkswagenwerk A.G., 647 F.2d 241, 243 n.2 (2d Cir. 1981) (defining "crashworthiness" as "the protection that a passenger motor vehicle affords its passengers against personal injury or death as a result of a motor vehicle accident"); Larsen v. General Motors Corporation, 391 F.2d 495, 502 (8th Cir. 1968) (defining "second collision" as that occurring between the passenger and the interior of the vehicle).

The crashworthiness doctrine "extends the scope of liability of a manufacturer to the situations in which the construction or design of its product has caused separate or enhanced injuries in the course of an initial accident brought about by an independent cause." . . .

Two divergent approaches have been developed to analyze whether a manufacturer may be held liable for enhanced injuries arising from a defective design. The first concludes that a product's intended purpose does not include its involvement in collisions with other objects, and thus refuses to hold a manufacturer liable for enhanced injuries due to defective design resulting from such collision. See, e.g., Evans v. General Motors Corporation, 359 F.2d 822, 825 (7th Cir.), cert. denied, 385 U.S. 836, 87 S. Ct. 83, 17 L. Ed. 2d 70 (1966), overruled by Huff v. White Motor

Corp., 565 F.2d 104 (7th Cir. 1977). While the continued vitality of *Evans* is questioned, subsequent decisions continue to recognize it as a possible approach to this issue. The second approach [adopted in *Larsen*] concludes that enhanced injuries arising from collisions are foreseeable in the normal use of automobiles and imposes liability on manufacturers for such injuries. Although *Larsen* was a negligence case, courts have applied its interpretation of "intended use" to the strict liability area.

Under New Hampshire law, the duty of a manufacturer "is limited to foreseeing the probable results of the normal use of the product or a use that can reasonably be anticipated." We do not, however, restrict this rule to the "intended" purpose of the product. "Manufacturer liability may . . . attach even if the user employs the product in an unintended but foreseeable manner." . . .

We conclude, therefore, that our case law supports the *Larsen* approach. While we do not hold that manufacturers are "insurers" for defectively designed vehicles, we do hold that in a crashworthiness case, a "manufacturer should be liable for that portion of the damage or injury caused by the defective design over and above the damage or injury that probably would have occurred as a result of the impact or collision absent the defective design." . . .

When . . . plaintiffs receive injuries that are indivisible, courts are split as to whether the plaintiffs or the defendants bear the burden of segregating the injuries caused by the automobile's defect. . . .

The defendants urge us to adopt the minority approach referred to as the "Huddell-Caiazzo" approach, which places the burden on the plaintiffs to prove the nature and extent of their enhanced injuries. See Huddell v. Levin, 537 F.2d 726, 737-38 (3d Cir. 1976) (applying New Jersey law); *Caiazzo*, 647 F.2d at 250 (applying New York law).

Under the Huddell-Caiazzo approach,

> first, in establishing that the design in question was defective, the plaintiffs must offer proof of an alternative safer design, practicable under the circumstances. Second, the plaintiffs must offer proof of what injuries, if any, would have resulted had the alternative, safer design been used. Third, the plaintiffs must offer some method of establishing the extent of enhanced injuries attributable to the defective design.

The plaintiffs, conversely, urge us to adopt the majority approach referred to as the "Fox-Mitchell" approach, derived from Fox v. Ford Motor Co., 575 F.2d 774, 786-88 (10th Cir. 1978) (applying Wyoming law), and *Mitchell* [v. Volkswagenwerk, AG, 669 F.2d 1199 (8th Cir. 1982)] (applying Minnesota law).

Under the Fox-Mitchell approach, the plaintiffs must "prove only that the design defect was a substantial factor in producing damages over and above those which were probably caused as a result of the original impact or collision." This approach provides that once the plaintiffs carry the burden of proving that the defective design of the car was a substantial factor in causing the enhanced injury, the burden of proof shifts to the tortfeasors to apportion the damages between them.

The principles that guide our answer to the question of which approach New Hampshire should adopt are derived from products liability law grounded in both negligence and strict liability. . . .

In crashworthiness cases involving indivisible injuries, we conclude that the plaintiffs must prove that a "design defect was a substantial factor in producing damages over and above those which were probably caused as a result of the original impact or collision. Once the plaintiffs make that showing, the burden shifts to the defendants to show which injuries were attributable to the initial collision and which to the defect."

This answer is supported by our treatment of products liability actions, where we have, based upon a "compelling reason of policy," abandoned the higher burden of proof of negligence actions in lieu of adopting the less stringent burden of proof of strict liability. Our rationale has been that the plaintiff's burden "had proven to be, and would continue to be, a practically impossible burden." Similar policy reasons compel us to allocate the burden of apportionment to the defendants once the plaintiffs prove causation. . . .

Remanded.

NOTES TO TRULL v. VOLKSWAGEN OF AMERICA, INC.

1. *Foreseeable Non-intended Uses.* *Trull* shows that foreseeable misuses are treated differently from unforeseeable uses. In *Daniell*, the court found that it was not foreseeable that someone would use the trunk of a car to commit suicide. The common occurrence of traffic accidents makes it difficult to argue that collisions are unforeseeable, even if it is not intended that a car will be use for that "purpose." The majority view on crashworthiness reflects the belief that collisions are foreseeable in the normal use of cars. How does the foreseeability of the collision "use" of a car affect the court's analysis of whether there is a duty, whether the car was defectively designed, and for what injuries the design was a proximate cause of the plaintiff's injuries?

2. *Burden Shift.* If no one can tell what part of a vehicle occupant's injury was caused by the vehicle's defective design, why is it fair to have the defendant pay for the entire injury? Would it be worse for a plaintiff to bear some costs that he or she would not have had to bear if more information had been available than it would be for a defendant to bear some costs that it would not have had to bear if more information had been available?

HERNANDEZ v. TOKAI CORP.
2 S.W.3d 251 (Tex. 1999)

HECHT, J.

The United States Court of Appeals for the Fifth Circuit has certified to us the following question:

> Under the Texas Products Liability Act of 1993 . . . whether a disposable butane lighter, intended only for adult use, can be found to be defectively designed if it does not have a child-resistant mechanism that would have prevented or substantially reduced the risk of injury from a child's foreseeable misuse of the lighter.

The factual circumstances in which the certified question comes to us are these.

Rita Emeterio bought disposable butane lighters for use at her bar. Her daughter, Gloria Hernandez, took lighters from the bar from time to time for her personal use. Emeterio and Hernandez both knew that it was dangerous for children to play with lighters. They also knew that some lighters were made with child-resistant mechanisms, but Emeterio chose not to buy them. On April 4, 1995, Hernandez's five-year-old daughter, Daphne, took a lighter from her mother's purse on the top shelf of a closet in a bedroom in her grandparents' home and started a fire in the room that severely burned her two-year-old brother, Ruben.

Hernandez, on Ruben's behalf, sued the manufacturers and distributors of the lighter, Tokai Corporation and Scripto-Tokai Corporation (collectively, "Tokai"), in the United States District Court for the Western District of Texas, San Antonio Division. Asserting strict liability and negligence claims, Hernandez alleged that the lighter was defectively designed and unreasonably dangerous because it did not have a child-resistant safety mechanism that would have prevented or substantially reduced the likelihood that a child could have used it to start a fire. Tokai does not dispute that mechanisms for making disposable lighters child-resistant were available when the lighter Daphne used was designed and marketed, or that such mechanisms can be incorporated into lighters at nominal cost.

Tokai moved for summary judgment on the grounds that a disposable lighter is a simple household tool intended for adult use only, and a manufacturer has no duty to incorporate child-resistant features into a lighter's design to protect unintended users — children — from obvious and inherent dangers. Tokai also noted that adequate warnings against access by children were provided with its lighters, even though that danger was obvious and commonly known. In response to Tokai's motion, Hernandez argued that, because an alternative design existed at the time the lighter at issue was manufactured and distributed that would have made the lighter safer in the hands of children, it remained for the jury to decide whether the lighter was defective under Texas' common-law risk-utility test.

The federal district court granted summary judgment for Tokai, and Hernandez appealed. . . .

[The statute] does not attempt to state all the elements of a product liability action for design defect. It does not, for example, define design defect or negate the common law requirement that such a defect render the product unreasonably dangerous. Additionally, the statute was not intended to, and does not, supplant the risk-utility analysis Texas has for years employed in determining whether a defectively designed product is unreasonably dangerous. . . .

A product's utility and risk under the common-law test must both be measured with reference to the product's intended users. A product intended for adults need not be designed to be safe for children solely because it is possible for the product to come into a child's hands. . . .

A child may hurt himself or others with a hammer, a knife, an electrical appliance, a power tool, or a ladder; he may fall into a pool, or start a car. The manufacturers and sellers of such products need not make them childproof merely because it is possible for children to cause harm with them and certain that some children will do so. The risk that adults, for whose use the products were intended, will allow children access to them, resulting in harm, must be balanced against the products' utility to their intended users. . . .

A disposable lighter without a child-resistant mechanism is safe as long as its use is restricted to adults, as its manufacturer and users intend. Tokai makes lighters with and without child-resistant devices. Adults who want to minimize the possibility that their lighter may be misused by a child may purchase the child-resistant models. Adults who prefer the other model, as Hernandez and Emeterio did, may purchase it (although we note that the federal Consumer Product Safety Commission has adopted a safety standard banning the manufacture and importation of non-child-resistant disposable lighters after July 12, 1994). Whether adult users of lighters should be deprived of this choice of product design because of the risk that some children will obtain lighters that are not child-resistant and cause harm is the proper focus of the common-law risk-utility test.

The utility of disposable lighters must be measured with reference to the intended adult users. Consumer preference — that is, that users like Hernandez and Emeterio simply prefer lighters without child-resistant features — is one consideration. Tokai also argues that adults whose dexterity is impaired, such as by age or disease, cannot operate child-resistant lighters, but Hernandez disputes this. If Tokai were shown to be correct, then that would be an additional consideration in assessing the utility of non-child-resistant lighters.

The relevant risk includes consideration of both the likelihood that adults will allow children access to lighters and the gravity of the resulting harm. The risk is not that a child who plays with a lighter may harm himself. We assume that that risk is substantial. As Hernandez and Emeterio both acknowledged in this case, they would not allow a child to have a lighter and would discipline a child caught playing with one. Rather, the risk is that a lighter will come into a child's hands. The record before us suggests that children will almost certainly obtain access to lighters, that this will not happen often in comparison with the number of lighters sold, but that when it does happen the harm caused can be extreme. Each of these considerations is relevant in assessing the risk of non-child-resistant lighters. . . .

Tokai argues that the weight of authority in other jurisdictions is to reject disposable lighter design-defect claims as a matter of law. This is true, but there is more to it. Courts in jurisdictions that employ a consumer-expectation test for determining defect have mostly held that disposable lighters without childproof features are not defectively designed because they function in the manner expected by the intended adult consumers. But courts in jurisdictions employing a risk-utility analysis have mostly concluded that the determinative considerations are usually matters for the jury. Courts in risk-utility jurisdictions that have rejected disposable lighter design-defect claims as a matter of law have reasoned that the test for liability should apply differently to "simple tools" like disposable lighters.

In sum: a claimant can maintain a defective-design claim in the circumstances posited by the certified question if, but only if, with reference to the product's intended users, the design defect makes the product unreasonably dangerous, a "safer alternative design" as defined by statute is available, and the defect is the producing cause of the injury.

NOTE TO HERNANDEZ v. TOKAI CORP.

Unintended User. *Hernandez* involves an unintended but foreseeable product *user* (unlike the unintended but foreseeable *use* in *Trull*). *Hernandez* further illustrates the close connection between the user's conduct and the analysis of whether the product is defectively designed. How is the use of a butane lighter that is safe for adults but dangerous for children analyzed under the risk-utility test or the consumer expectation test?

Problem
Crashworthiness Doctrine

An eight-year-old child was playing with friends near his home when he found a bottle of Miller High Life beer that someone had discarded. According to the child, the bottle "came in contact with a telephone pole" while he was playing with it. The child later indicated that he had thrown the bottle against the pole. Following the impact of the glass container with the telephone pole the bottle shattered, and particles of glass entered the plaintiff's eye, causing severe injury. The plaintiff's basic premise is that Miller and the bottle manufacturers should have been aware of the dangers inherent in their bottles and should have accordingly designed and marketed a product better able to safely withstand such foreseeable misuse as breakage in the course of improper handling by children. Would the crashworthiness doctrine apply to this case in determining whether the design was defective? How would the *Trull* court's approach to the causation question apply in this case? See Venezia v. Miller Brewing Co., 626 F.2d 188 (1st Cir. 1980).

I. Compliance with Statutes and Regulations

A defendant's compliance with a federal statute or regulation is sometimes a complete defense to a state-based tort action. The *preemption doctrine* prohibits state claims that are expressly prohibited in federal legislation or that are impliedly prohibited. In situations where a federal statute does not have preemptive effect, states are entitled to treat proof of compliance as either a full defense or as evidence that is relevant but not conclusive regarding the issue of defectiveness.

Pliva, Inc. v. Mensing offers an introduction to preemption issues. Cases involving preemption issues may focus on interpretation of a statute's specific language about preemption or on a broader question about the possible incompatibility between the federal statutory scheme and state-based remedies.

A number of states have enacted statutes specifying how proof of compliance with a statute should be treated in products liability cases. Examples of statutes from Arkansas, Florida, and Tennessee are provided. They differ in terms of the weight they give to particular types of proof of compliance and the detail with which they specify the circumstances where such proof shall be permitted.

PLIVA, INC. v. MENSING
131 S. Ct. 2567 (2011)

Justice THOMAS.

These consolidated lawsuits involve state tort-law claims based on certain drug manufacturers' alleged failure to provide adequate warning labels for generic metoclopramide. The question presented is whether federal drug regulations applicable to generic drug manufacturers directly conflict with, and thus pre-empt, these state-law claims. We hold that they do.

I

Metoclopramide is a drug designed to speed the movement of food through the digestive system. The Food and Drug Administration (FDA) first approved metoclopramide tablets, under the brand name Reglan, in 1980. Five years later, generic manufacturers also began producing metoclopramide. The drug is commonly used to treat digestive tract problems such as diabetic gastroparesis and gastroesophageal reflux disorder. . . .

[W]arning labels for the drug have been strengthened and clarified several times. In 1985, the label was modified to warn that "tardive dyskinesia . . . may develop in patients treated with metoclopramide," and the drug's package insert added that "[t]herapy longer than 12 weeks has not been evaluated and cannot be recommended." Physician's Desk Reference 1635-1636 (41st ed. 1987)). In 2004, the brand-name Reglan manufacturer requested, and the FDA approved, a label change to add that "[t]herapy should not exceed 12 weeks in duration." And in 2009, the FDA ordered a black box warning — its strongest — which states: "Treatment with metoclopramide can cause tardive dyskinesia, a serious movement disorder that is often irreversible. . . . Treatment with metoclopramide for longer than 12 weeks should be avoided in all but rare cases."

Gladys Mensing and Julie Demahy, the plaintiffs in these consolidated cases, were prescribed Reglan in 2001 and 2002, respectively. Both received generic metoclopramide from their pharmacists. After taking the drug as prescribed for several years, both women developed tardive dyskinesia.

In separate suits, Mensing and Demahy sued the generic drug manufacturers that produced the metoclopramide they took (Manufacturers). Each alleged, as relevant here, that long-term metoclopramide use caused her tardive dyskinesia and that the Manufacturers were liable under state tort law (specifically, that of Minnesota and Louisiana) for failing to provide adequate warning labels. They claimed that "despite mounting evidence that long term metoclopramide use carries a risk of tardive dyskinesia far greater than that indicated on the label," none of the Manufacturers had changed their labels to adequately warn of that danger.

In both suits, the Manufacturers urged that federal law pre-empted the state tort claims. According to the Manufacturers, federal statutes and FDA regulations required them to use the same safety and efficacy labeling as their brand-name counterparts. This means, they argued, that it was impossible to simultaneously comply with both federal law and any state tort-law duty that required them to use a different label.

The Courts of Appeals for the Fifth and Eighth Circuits rejected the Manufacturers' arguments and held that Mensing and Demahy's claims were not pre-empted. We granted certiorari, consolidated the cases, and now reverse each.

Pre-emption analysis requires us to compare federal and state law. We therefore begin by identifying the state tort duties and federal labeling requirements applicable to the Manufacturers.

It is undisputed that Minnesota and Louisiana tort law require a drug manufacturer that is or should be aware of its product's danger to label that product in a way that renders it reasonably safe. Under Minnesota law, which applies to Mensing's lawsuit, "where the manufacturer . . . of a product has actual or constructive knowledge of danger to users, the . . . manufacturer has a duty to give warning of such dangers." Frey v. Montgomery Ward & Co., 258 N.W.2d 782, 788 (Minn. 1977). Similarly, under Louisiana law applicable to Demahy's lawsuit, "a manufacturer's duty to warn includes a duty to provide adequate instructions for safe use of a product." Stahl v. Novartis Pharmaceuticals Corp., 283 F.3d 254, 269-270 (C.A.5 2002); see also La. Rev. Stat. Ann. §9:2800.57 (West 2009). In both States, a duty to warn falls specifically on the manufacturer.

Mensing and Demahy have pleaded that the Manufacturers knew or should have known of the high risk of tardive dyskinesia inherent in the long-term use of their product. They have also pleaded that the Manufacturers knew or should have known that their labels did not adequately warn of that risk. The parties do not dispute that, if these allegations are true, state law required the Manufacturers to use a different, safer label.

Federal law imposes far more complex drug labeling requirements. We begin with what is not in dispute. Under the 1962 Drug Amendments to the Federal Food, Drug, and Cosmetic Act, 76 Stat. 780, 21 U.S.C. §301 *et seq.*, a manufacturer seeking federal approval to market a new drug must prove that it is safe and effective and that the proposed label is accurate and adequate. Meeting those requirements involves costly and lengthy clinical testing.

Originally, the same rules applied to all drugs. In 1984, however, Congress passed the Drug Price Competition and Patent Term Restoration Act, 98 Stat. 1585, commonly called the Hatch-Waxman Amendments. Under this law, "generic drugs" can gain FDA approval simply by showing equivalence to a reference listed drug that has already been approved by the FDA. This allows manufacturers to develop generic drugs inexpensively, without duplicating the clinical trials already performed on the equivalent brand-name drug. A generic drug application must also "show that the [safety and efficacy] labeling proposed . . . is the same as the labeling approved for the [brand-name] drug." §355(j)(2)(A)(v).

As a result, brand-name and generic drug manufacturers have different federal drug labeling duties. A brand-name manufacturer seeking new drug approval is responsible for the accuracy and adequacy of its label. A manufacturer seeking generic drug approval, on the other hand, is responsible for ensuring that its warning label is the same as the brand name's.

The parties do not disagree. What is in dispute is whether, and to what extent, generic manufacturers may change their labels *after* initial FDA approval. Mensing and Demahy contend that federal law provided several avenues through which the Manufacturers could have altered their metoclopramide labels in time to prevent the injuries here. The FDA, however, tells us that it interprets its regulations to require that the warning labels of a brand-name drug and its generic copy must always be the same — thus, generic drug manufacturers have an ongoing federal duty of "sameness." U.S. Brief 16. The FDA's views are "controlling unless plainly erroneous or inconsistent with the regulation[s]" or there is any other reason to doubt that they reflect the FDA's fair and considered judgment. Auer v. Robbins, 519 U.S. 542, 461 (1997).

Mensing and Demahy urge that the FDA's "changes-being-effected" (CBE) process allowed the Manufacturers to change their labels when necessary. The CBE process permits drug manufacturers to "add or strengthen a contraindication, warning, [or] precaution," 21 CFR §314.70(c)(6)(iii)(A) (2006), or to "add or strengthen an instruction about dosage and administration that is intended to increase the safe use of the drug product," §314.70(c)(6)(iii)(C). When making labeling changes using the CBE process, drug manufacturers need not wait for preapproval by the FDA, which ordinarily is necessary to change a label. They need only simultaneously file a supplemental application with the FDA.

The FDA denies that the Manufacturers could have used the CBE process to unilaterally strengthen their warning labels. The agency interprets the CBE regulation to allow changes to generic drug labels only when a generic drug manufacturer changes its label to match an updated brand-name label or to follow the FDA's instructions. The FDA argues that CBE changes unilaterally made to strengthen a generic drug's warning label would violate the statutes and regulations requiring a generic drug's label to match its brand-name counterpart's.

We defer to the FDA's interpretation of its CBE and generic labeling regulations. Although Mensing and Demahy offer other ways to interpret the regulations, we do not find the agency's interpretation "plainly erroneous or inconsistent with the regulation." Nor do Mensing and Demahy suggest there is any other reason to doubt the agency's reading. We therefore conclude that the CBE process was not open to the Manufacturers for the sort of change required by state law. . . .

The Supremacy Clause establishes that federal law "shall be the supreme Law of the Land . . . any Thing in the Constitution or Laws of any State to the Contrary notwithstanding." U.S. Const., Art. VI, cl. 2. Where state and federal law "directly conflict," state law must give way. We have held that state and federal law conflict where it is "impossible for a private party to comply with both state and federal requirements." Freightliner Corp. v. Myrick, 514 U.S. 280, 287 (1995).

We find impossibility here. It was not lawful under federal law for the Manufacturers to do what state law required of them. And even if they had fulfilled their federal duty to ask for FDA assistance, they would not have satisfied the requirements of state law.

If the Manufacturers had independently changed their labels to satisfy their state-law duty, they would have violated federal law. Taking Mensing and Demahy's allegations as true, state law imposed on the Manufacturers a duty to attach a safer label to their generic metoclopramide. Federal law, however, demanded that generic drug labels be the same at all times as the corresponding brand-name drug labels. Thus, it was impossible for the Manufacturers to comply with both their state-law duty to change the label and their federal law duty to keep the label the same. . . .

Wyeth is not to the contrary. In that case, as here, the plaintiff contended that a drug manufacturer had breached a state tort-law duty to provide an adequate warning label. 555 U.S., at 559-560. The Court held that the lawsuit was not pre-empted because it was possible for Wyeth, a brand-name drug manufacturer, to comply with both state and federal law. Specifically, the CBE regulation permitted a brand-name drug manufacturer like Wyeth "to unilaterally strengthen its warning" without prior FDA approval. 555 U.S., at 573. Thus, the federal regulations applicable to Wyeth allowed the company, of its own volition, to strengthen its label in compliance with its state tort duty.

We recognize that from the perspective of Mensing and Demahy, finding preemption here but not in *Wyeth* makes little sense. Had Mensing and Demahy taken Reglan, the brand-name drug prescribed by their doctors, *Wyeth* would control and their lawsuits would not be pre-empted. But because pharmacists, acting in full accord with state law, substituted generic metoclopramide instead, federal law pre-empts these lawsuits. We acknowledge the unfortunate hand that federal drug regulation has dealt Mensing, Demahy, and others similarly situated.

But "it is not this Court's task to decide whether the statutory scheme established by Congress is unusual or even bizarre." Cuomo v. Clearing House Assn., L.L.C., 557 U.S. 519 (2009). It is beyond dispute that the federal statutes and regulations that apply to brand-name drug manufacturers are meaningfully different than those that apply to generic drug manufacturers. Indeed, it is the special, and different, regulation of generic drugs that allowed the generic drug market to expand, bringing more drugs more quickly and cheaply to the public. But different federal statutes and regulations may, as here, lead to different pre-emption results. We will not distort the Supremacy Clause in order to create similar pre-emption across a dissimilar statutory scheme. As always, Congress and the FDA retain the authority to change the law and regulations if they so desire.

The judgments of the Fifth and Eighth Circuits are reversed, and the cases are remanded for further proceedings consistent with this opinion.

It is so ordered.

NOTES TO PLIVA, INC. v. MENSING

1. *Effect of Preemption.* When state law is preempted by federal law, state statutes, regulations, and court rulings may not be inconsistent with federal law. If a preemptive federal law (or regulation) requires that generic drug manufacturers provide certain warnings on their labels, neither a state statute nor state common law may require different warnings. In *Pliva*, the Federal Food, Drug, and Cosmetic Act, as amended, required warning labels on drugs that were different from what Minnesota and Louisiana state common law required. Preemption rules apply not only to drug warnings but also to other conduct. If a preemptive federal law (or regulation) requires that trucks weighing between six and ten tons have six wheels, a state statute may not allow only four or five wheels. Nor may a state court rule that a truck with six wheels is defective because it should have had seven or eight wheels. Careful statutory analysis indicates the extent of the preemption for each federal statute or regulation.

2. *Changing a "Bizarre" Result.* The Food and Drug Administration has proposed amendments to its regulations that would allow generic drug manufacturers to add warnings to their product labels without prior FDA approval. If the amendments become effective, future plaintiffs would likely contend that the result in *Pliva* would no longer be required. See Proposed Rule on Supplemental Applications Proposing Labeling Changes for Approved Drugs and Biological Products, 78 Fed. Reg. 67985 (2013).

Perspective: Uniformity Versus Variety and Innovation

Preemptive federal regulations impose uniform national standards with which manufacturers must comply. Whether federal regulation yields better standards than state regulations or court decisions is debatable. A benefit to applying federal standards to design defect litigation might be that the standards are likely to have been developed with some degree of impartiality and to have been developed by experts. Whether federal regulatory standards lead to better safety rules depends on how the quality of regulatory decision making compares to the quality of decision making in trials. The amount of data available and the expertise of the decision maker may be relevant factors in deciding this question. A shortcoming of applying federal standards to design defect litigation might be that they are static. While knowledge of both risks and safety precautions may grow, regulations may lag behind and be slow to respond to new information. These considerations may help the U.S. Congress decide the appropriate extent of preemption for a particular type of federal regulation.

Statute: COMPLIANCE AS EVIDENCE
Ark. Code §16-116-105(a) (2017)

(a) Compliance by a manufacturer or supplier with any federal or state statute or administrative regulation existing at the time a product was manufactured and prescribing standards of design, inspection, testing, manufacture, labeling, warning, or instructions for use of a product shall be considered as evidence that the product is not in an unreasonably dangerous condition in regard to matters covered by these standards.

Statute: GOVERNMENT RULES DEFENSE
Fla. Stat. §768.1256(1), (2) (2017)

(1) In a product liability action brought against a manufacturer or seller for harm allegedly caused by a product, there is a rebuttable presumption that the product is not defective or unreasonably dangerous and the manufacturer or seller is not liable if, at the time the specific unit of the product was sold or delivered to the initial purchaser or user, the aspect of the product that allegedly caused the harm:

    (a) Complied with federal or state codes, statutes, rules, regulations, or standards relevant to the event causing the death or injury;

    (b) The codes, statutes, rules, regulations, or standards are designed to prevent the type of harm that allegedly occurred; and

    (c) Compliance with the codes, statutes, rules, regulations, or standards is required as a condition for selling or distributing the product.

(2) In a product liability action as described in subsection (1), there is a rebuttable presumption that the product is defective or unreasonably dangerous and the manufacturer or seller is liable if the manufacturer or seller did not comply with the federal or state codes, statutes, rules, regulations, or standards which:

    (a) Were relevant to the event causing the death or injury;

    (b) Are designed to prevent the type of harm that allegedly occurred; and

    (c) Require compliance as a condition for selling or distributing the product.

Statute: PRESUMPTION FOR COMPLIANCE
Tenn. Code §29-28-104 (2017)

§29-28-104 COMPLIANCE WITH GOVERNMENT STANDARDS — REBUTTABLE PRESUMPTION

Compliance by a manufacturer or seller with any federal or state statute or administrative regulation existing at the time a product was manufactured and prescribing standards for design, inspection, testing, manufacture, labeling, warning or instructions for use of a product, shall raise a rebuttable presumption that the product is not in an unreasonably dangerous condition in regard to matters covered by these standards.

NOTE TO STATUTES

A manufacturer's compliance with a statute does not necessarily mean that the product was not defective. These statutes specify the evidentiary weight to be given to a defendant's claim that it complied with a statute or regulation. The Florida statute is more detailed than the other two examples with regard to the type of enactments to which it applies. How might that difference affect the operation of the Florida statute compared with the operation of the others?

15

TRESPASS AND NUISANCE

I. Trespass

A. Trespass to Land

The intentional tort of trespass protects people's interest in the "exclusive possession" of their land. The interest in exclusive possession is analogous to the interests in bodily integrity protected by the tort of battery and in freedom from apprehension of imminent harmful or offensive contact protected by the tort of assault.

A typical trespass-to-land case involves a defendant who, without permission, walks onto another's land. The conduct leading to the entry must be voluntary, because the *act requirement* applies to the tort of trespass, as it does to all torts. An early English case established that if a person is thrown against his will onto another's land by thugs, the thugs are the trespassers, not the person. See Smith v. Stone, 82 Eng. Rep. 533 (1647). In addition to the conduct being voluntary, the actor must intend that the act lead to an entry. A trespass may result if an actor acts intending to personally enter the land of another or to cause an object to enter or remain on the land without permission. The act is the behavior, the conduct. *Intent* is the mental state that accompanies the act — the desire or substantial certainty that an entry will result from the act.

Thomas v. Harrah's Vicksburg Corp. explores the meaning of "intent" in the trespass context. The defendant argued that trespassing on the plaintiff's land was necessary to construct a casino. The court considered the evidence of intent, the defendant's argument that they took precautions to avoid entry, and whether there was actually an unpermitted entry.

In addition to its inclusion of the act and intent requirements, the tort of trespass is similar to other intentional torts in two other ways. First, the trespass plaintiff does not need to prove actual or compensatory damages. The plaintiff may be awarded *nominal damages*, which signify that the defendant interfered with the plaintiff's rights even if the defendant caused no harm. Second, the trespass defendant may be liable for harms he or she could not have foreseen. Baker v. Shymkiv considers whether a trespasser may be liable for the death of the landowner resulting from their secretive nocturnal efforts to build a trench on the landowner's property.

THOMAS v. HARRAH'S VICKSBURG CORP.

734 So. 2d 312 (Miss. Ct. App. 1999)

PAYNE, J. . . .

This litigation stems from the development of Harrah's gambling facility in Vicksburg, Mississippi, beginning over five years ago and acts of trespass admittedly committed by Harrah's and Yates[, the contractor building the facility,] for an approximate six month period beginning in July 1993 and continuing through December 1993. The property in question is a vacant lot adjoining Surplus, which is a closely held corporation wholly owned by Thomas. [Harrah's offered evidence to establish that they took reasonable precautions to avoid entering the Thomas/Surplus land while building their facility but that the close proximity of the building and wall to the adjacent land made trespass inevitable. Following a judgment for the plaintiffs, Harrah's argued on appeal that a negligence standard should apply in this trespass case. Thomas/Surplus argued that proof of negligence is not necessary in a trespass case.]

We think it instructive to briefly look at the historical basis for the trespass to land action. Professors Prosser and Keeton note that "[h]istorically, the requirements for trespass to land under the common law action of trespass were an invasion (a) which interfered with the right of exclusive possession of the land, and (b) which was the direct result of some act committed by the defendant." W. Page Keeton et al., Prosser and Keeton on Torts, §13 at 67 (5th ed. 1984). Further, the tort of trespass to land can be committed by other than simply entering on the land; trespass occurs by placing objects on the property, by causing a third party to go onto the property, or by remaining on property after the expiration of a right of entry. Keeton §13 at 72-73.

With regard to the requisite intent for trespass to land, the Restatement (Second) of Torts §163 comment (b) addresses this issue:

> *b. Intention.* If the actor intends to be upon the particular piece of land, it is not necessary that he intend to invade the other's interest in the exclusive possession of his land. The intention which is required to make the actor liable under the rule stated in this Section is *an intention to enter upon the particular piece of land in question,* irrespective of whether the actor knows or should know that he is not entitled to enter. It is, therefore, immaterial whether or not he honestly and reasonably believes that the land is his own, or that he has the consent of the possessor or of a third person having power to give consent on his behalf, or that he has a mistaken belief that he has some other privilege to enter. [Emphasis added.]

Thus, as Professors Prosser and Keeton point out, "the intent required as a basis for liability as a trespasser is simply an intent to be at the place on the land where the trespass occurred." Keeton §13 at 73. . . .

The Thomas and Surplus position is correct in asserting that negligence is not necessary for common law trespass liability. Furthermore, while there is an intent requirement, it is very broad in definition as demonstrated in the Restatement (Second) §163 above. Common law trespass is an intrusion upon the land of another without a license or other right for one's own purpose. The testimony establishes that is exactly the case here.

Two key witnesses, Charles Wells, Harrah's construction manager for this project, and Jim Smith, the construction superintendent for Yates, admitted that there were trespasses that occurred on Thomas' property. First, Wells testified that he worked on the project from July 1993 until July 1994, and that he understood that there was a continuing dispute with Thomas over the property lines. Further, Wells admitted that he, as well as Yates, were involved in the decision to move the north wall because it encroached on Thomas' property. The plans for the facility, according to Wells, called for the building to extend "right up to the property line. . . ." Questioning by appellants' counsel also established that the trespass was inevitable:

> By Mr. Lotterhos [counsel for appellants]: Now, as a practical matter, if you were going to construct that [building] absolutely on the property line, it would have been necessary to get on the adjacent property to work on the exterior. Isn't that true?
>
> By Mr. Wells: On that ten foot face, yes, sir.
>
> By Mr. Lotterhos: Alright and that happened, didn't it?
>
> By Mr. Wells: Yes, sir.

Wells later testified that Harrah's Vice-President of Design and Construction, Pat Monson, approved of moving the encroaching wall. Second, Jim Smith, the construction superintendent for Yates on Harrah's Vicksburg project, testified for the appellees. On direct examination, Smith took great pains to detail how careful Yates was in constructing special scaffolding to avoid trespassing on the Thomas/Surplus property and emphasized the fact that he had personally fired three employees of Yates for trespassing. Additionally, Smith, in a strained and futile effort, attempted to disassociate Yates from the various subcontractors employed by Yates, while admitting that Yates had control over the subcontractors. Yet, on cross-examination, Smith admitted that scaffolding erected by Yates in conjunction with the construction of the facility was indeed on the Thomas/Surplus property and that they received permission from Thomas to enter the property for the *specific* purpose of removing the scaffolding to halt the trespass. Further, Smith admitted to repeated airspace violations on the Thomas/Surplus property with the boom swinging over the property. As did Wells, Smith also admitted that the trespass on the Thomas/Surplus property was unavoidable after the construction reached a certain point and when the wall was ultimately moved:

> By Mr. Lotterhos: And you were aware that . . . it was to be — a portion of that north wall was to be right on the Thomas property line, isn't that true?
>
> By Mr. Smith: Yes, sir.
>
> By Mr. Lotterhos: Now, you have been involved in construction a lot of years, haven't you?
>
> By Mr. Smith: Yes, sir. . . .
>
> By Mr. Lotterhos: . . . based on your experience, when you build right upon the line or wall, it is necessary to get on the outside of the wall to work on it, isn't that true?
>
> By Mr. Smith: Yes, sir, it is. . . .
>
> By Mr. Lotterhos: In order to break out that wall, you had to get on Mr. Thomas' property, didn't you?
>
> By Mr. Smith: Yes, sir, we did.

This *uncontroverted* testimony established that there were trespasses on the Thomas/Surplus property. . . .

BAKER v. SHYMKIV

451 N.E.2d 811 (Ohio 1983)

Syllabus by the Court . . .

The parties, on appeal, agreed to the following statement of facts:

1. On March 22, 1978, at 8:00 p.m. . . . [Mr. Baker] and his wife were returning home and turned into the driveway leading to their home.

2. They observed a car was parked in the driveway blocking their access, and they observed Mr. and Mrs. Shymkiv throwing tools and other equipment in the trunk of their car, close the trunk lid and jump into their car.

3. Mr. and Mrs. Baker got out of their car and observed a trench with dimensions of approximately 1 foot in width and 1½ feet in depth and more than 10 feet in length had been dug across their driveway and that a drain tile had been placed in the trench so that water from the Shymkiv property could drain through the trench and onto the property of an adjoining landowner.

4. Mr. Baker was angry and visibly upset over the actions of the Shymkivs and approached the Shymkiv automobile.

5. Mr. Shymkiv got out of the car and an argument concerning the trench followed. Mary Baker interceded and pushed herself between Homer Baker and John Shymkiv and told her husband to calm down.

6. Mary Baker indicated that she had never seen her husband so upset or angry in all the years they had been married.

7. Mrs. Baker then left the scene to call the police.

8. When Mrs. Baker returned approximately 3 minutes later she found her husband laying face-down in the mud puddle while the Shymkivs were driving away.

9. Emergency squad arrived approximately 10-15 minutes later, worked on Homer Baker and transported him to Grant Hospital where he was pronounced dead at 9:20 p.m.

10. Mary Baker has described her husband as a very easygoing person, very friendly, and not easily prone to argue or get upset.

11. Mary Baker has indicated that Homer Baker took great pride in the maintenance and upkeep of the driveway, home and yard.

In the court of common pleas, Mrs. Baker filed several claims against the Shymkivs: (1) as administratrix, for the wrongful death of Mr. Baker, and for her own pecuniary loss; and (2) for trespass seeking both compensatory and punitive damages. . . .

The trial court instructed the jury, in part:

Now, the test then [of proximate cause] is whether in the light of all the circumstances a reasonably prudent person would have *anticipated* that injury was likely to result to someone from the preponderance of the evidence or performance of the evidence or act. In other words, before liability attaches to the defendants in this case, the damages claimed by Mrs. Baker must have been *foreseen or reasonably anticipated* by the wrongdoer as likely to follow the trespass and the digging of the trench or the digging of the hole or whatever. (Emphasis added.) . . .

Locher, Judge.

This case presents one issue: whether the trial court erred by instructing the jury that only foreseeable damages could result in liability. Appellants, the Shymkivs, contend that the trial court properly charged the jury on foreseeability. We disagree. . . .

Intentional trespassers are within that class of less-favored wrongdoers. For example, under the Restatement of Torts 2d, intentional conduct is an element of trespass: "One is subject to liability to another for trespass, irrespective of whether he thereby causes harm to any legally protected interest of the other, if he *intentionally* (a) enters land in the possession of the other or causes a thing or a third person to do so. . . ." (Emphasis added.) Restatement of Torts 2d 277, Section 158. The Restatement also articulates the scope of liability for a trespass in Section 162, which states: "A trespass on land subjects the trespasser to liability for physical harm to the possessor of the land at the time of the trespass, or to the land or to his things, or to members of his household or to their things, caused by any act done, activity carried on, or condition created by the trespasser, irrespective of whether his conduct is such as would subject him to liability were he not a trespasser." Id., at pages 291-292. Comment f to Section 162 of the Restatement explains the intended effect of that provision:

> *f. Peculiar position of trespasser.* This Section states the peculiar liability to which a trespasser is subject for bodily harm caused to the possessor of land or the members of his family by the conduct of a trespasser while upon the land, irrespective of whether his conduct if it occurred elsewhere would subject him to liability to them. . . . Thus, one who trespasses upon the land of another incurs the risk of becoming liable for any bodily harm which is cause [sic] to the possessor of the land or to members of his household by any conduct of the trespasser during the continuance of his trespass, no matter how otherwise innocent such conduct may be.

Id., at page 293.

Accordingly, we hold that damages caused by an intentional trespasser need not be foreseeable to be compensable.

We affirm the judgment of the court of appeals [which had also found error in the trial court's instruction].

NOTES TO THOMAS v. HARRAH'S VICKSBURG CORP. AND BAKER v. SHYMKIV

1. *Proof of Intent.* The Restatement (Second) of Torts §8A explains that intent may be proved either by demonstrating that the defendant desired to enter or the defendant was substantially certain that his or her act would lead to an entry. On which of these alternatives did the plaintiff rely in *Thomas*?

2. *Distinguishing "Act" and "Intent."* There may be an act without any intent to enter, as when a person drives a car and, to the driver's surprise, it spins out of control on ice and ends up on another person's lawn. The driver has acted by driving the car, but neither desired nor was substantially certain that the driving would result in an entry onto the lawn. A recent case illustrates the difference between the act requirement and the intent to enter requirement. An oil company undoubtedly intended to refine oil where its refinery was, and the refining process caused the oil to leak under the plaintiffs' land. But intending to refine oil, the voluntary conduct, is not enough to make a trespass. The court held that the company must intend for the refining to cause the oil to migrate under the plaintiffs' land. See Martin v. Amoco Oil Company, 679 N.E.2d 139 (Ind. Ct. App. 1997).

3. _Negligent and Reckless Entries to Land._   Negligence is not an element of the trespass actions discussed in this chapter. Negligent and reckless entries onto land are sometimes referred to as trespasses, but such claims are analyzed using the traditional elements of duty, breach, cause, damages, as developed in Chapters 3 and 4. Actual damages must be proved to recover for entries caused by negligent or reckless conduct, while damages are available for intentional trespass without proof of actual damages.

4. _Trespass and Mistake._   The court in _Thomas_ cited Restatement (Second) of Torts §163 comment b, which states that the intent requirement is met even if the trespasser mistakenly believes that land is his own, that he has permission to be on the land. All that is required is that the defendant desired or was substantially certain that he would be on that land. Section 163 comment a emphasizes that the risk of error is on the person entering the land:

> . . . If the actor is and intends to be upon the particular piece of land in question, it is immaterial that he honestly and reasonably believes that he has the consent of the lawful possessor to enter, or, indeed, that he himself is its possessor. Unless the actor's mistake was induced by the conduct of the possessor, it is immaterial that the mistake is one such as a reasonable man knowing all the circumstances which the actor knows or could have discovered by the most careful of investigations would have made. One who enters any piece of land takes the risk of the existence of such facts as would give him a right or privilege to enter. So too, the actor cannot escape liability by showing that his mistaken belief in the validity of his title is due to the advice of the most eminent of counsel. Indeed, even though a statute expressly confers title upon him, he takes the risk that the statute may thereafter be declared unconstitutional.

The protection given to the interests of the lawful possessors of land is enhanced by the broad definition of the extent of their rights. Recall that in _Thomas_, the court referred to evidence that the contractors violated Thomas's airspace by swinging a boom over Thomas's land. Traditionally, a landowner's rights extend from "the center of the earth to the top of the sky." Intentionally extending the boom arm of a crane over the land of another qualifies as a trespassory entry even if it does not touch the plaintiff's earth. An exception has developed over the years to permit the flight path of airplanes to enter private property.

5. _Scope of Liability of Trespasser._   The doctrine of transferred intent broadens the scope of liability for actors who commit an assault or battery by making tortfeasors liable to people for types of harm they could not foresee. The Restatement (Second) of Torts §162 similarly broadens the scope of liability of an intentional trespasser, the issue raised in Baker v. Shymkiv. Section 162 states that an intentional trespasser is liable for physical harm he or she causes "irrespective of whether his conduct is such as would subject him to liability were he not a trespasser," suggesting that foreseeability of the plaintiff or harm, as traditionally required for negligence claims, would not be a limitation in claims against an intentional trespasser.

The Restatement (Third) of Torts: Liability for Physical and Emotional Harm abandons the language of foreseeability, stating in §29 that "[a]n actor's liability is limited to those harms that result from the risks that made the actor's conduct tortious." The Restatement addresses the expanded liability of intentional tortfeasors in §33, where it cites _Shymkiv_ in comment (e). It similarly states that the scope of liability for an intentional trespasser will be greater than for a person who is negligent:

§33 Scope of Liability for Intentional and Reckless Tortfeasors

(a) An actor who intentionally causes harm is subject to liability for that harm even if it was unlikely to occur.

(b) An actor who intentionally or recklessly causes harm is subject to liability for a broader range of harms than the harms for which that actor would be liable if only acting negligently. In general, the important factors in determining the scope of liability are the moral culpability of the actor, as reflected in the reasons for and intent in committing the tortious acts, the seriousness of harm intended and threatened by those acts, and the degree to which the actor's conduct deviated from appropriate care.

(c) Notwithstanding Subsections (a) and (b), an actor who intentionally or recklessly causes harm is not subject to liability for harm the risk of which was not increased by the actor's intentional or reckless conduct.

Section 33(b), however, indicates that, under the Restatement (Third) approach, the scope of liability might be limited by considering the culpability of the tortfeasor's conduct. The Restatement (Third) of Torts: Liability for Physical and Emotional Harm generally limits liability, however, to harms the risk of which made an actor's conduct tortious, as reflected in §33(c). Applying the Restatement (Third) rule may result in a narrower scope of liability than suggested in *Shymkiv*, though no courts have applied it yet to trespassers.

6. *Trespass of Invisible Particles and Intangibles.* Entry to land may be by a person or an object and a person who acts intending to cause the unpermitted entry of the object onto the land of another is also a trespasser. In trespass cases involving entry by the by-products of industrial activity, the objects entering the plaintiff's land are often very small particles such as dust or even intangible items such as radio waves, noise, or vibrations.

Jurisdictions take different approaches to whether the invasion of land by invisible particles and intangibles constitutes a trespass. Recent California cases have held that a fire that spread to the plaintiff's land from the neighbor's could be considered a trespass, see Elton v. Anheuser-Busch Beverage Group, Inc., 58 Cal. Rptr. 2d 303, 306 (Cal. App. 1996), and that electronic signals sent by a computer hacker could be trespassory, see Thrifty-Tel, Inc. v. Bezenek, 54 Cal. Rptr. 2d 468 (Cal. App. 1996). On the other hand, in a case of first impression, a Michigan court in Adams v. Cleveland-Cliffs Iron Co., 602 N.W.2d 215 (Mich. Ct. App. 1999), held that the invasion of neither airborne particles (dust from an iron ore mine) nor noise nor vibrations could be the basis for a trespass claim. A Maryland court held that low-level radioactive emission from a plant manufacturing nuclear and radioactive pharmaceuticals could qualify as a trespass, see Maryland Heights Leasing, Inc. v. Mallinckrodt, Inc., 706 S.W.2d 218 (Md. App. 1985), but a Colorado court held that electromagnetic fields and radiation waves emanating from power lines and encroaching on the plaintiffs' properties could not constitute a trespass, at least without proof of actual damages, see Public Service Co. of Colorado v. Van Wyk, 27 P.3d 377 (Colo. 2001). Several states have adopted this requirement of proof of actual damages, which is not normally a requirement for trespass, for trespasses by forces rather than physical objects. Proof of actual damages was required, for instance, in Wilson v. Interlake Steel Co., 185 Cal. Rptr. 280 (Cal. 1982) (noise from a steel factory), and Staples v. Hoefke, 235 Cal. Rptr. 165 (Cal. App. 1983) (vibrations from punch press at a leather factory).

Problem
The Act Requirement and Intent to Enter

Farmland owned and operated a fertilizer plant in which, prior to June 1982, it began using hexavalent chromium as a corrosion inhibitor in its water coolant system. Sometime prior to June 1982, the chemical leaked from the cooling system or a storage system designed to contain the chemical into the ground under Farmland's plant. The chemical traveled underground and contaminated the groundwater underneath the adjacent land, which, at the time of the suit, was owned and operated by United Proteins, Inc. (UPI), a producer of pet food. In June 1982, Farmland notified the Department of Health and Environment of the leak and began to remove the chemical from its own and UPI's land. Despite Farmland's efforts, the chemical continued to seep into the groundwater under UPI's land. UPI sued Farmland for trespass. You represent Farmland. What argument can you make to support a motion for judgment as a matter of law on these facts? See United Proteins, Inc. v. Farmland Inc., 915 P.2d 80 (Kan. 1996).

Perspective: Historical Foundation for Trespass

The importance of private property in the United States derives from its significance in English common law. In a 1765 action for trespass, Entick v. Carrington and Three Other King's Messengers, quoted in Boyd v. United States, 116 U.S. 616 (1886), Lord Camden stressed the sanctity of private property:

> The great end for which men entered into society was to secure their property. That right is preserved sacred and incommunicable in all instances where it has not been taken away or abridged by some public law for the good of the whole. . . . By the laws of England, every invasion of private property, be it ever so minute, is a trespass. No man can set his foot upon my ground without my license, but he is liable to an action, though the damage be nothing, which is proved by every declaration in trespass where the defendant is called upon to answer for bruising the grass and even treading upon the soil.

B. Trespass to Chattel and Conversion

The intentional torts of trespass to chattel and conversion extend the rules protecting possession of real property, land, to protection of chattel, which is personal property. The cases in this section illustrate that the difference between trespass to chattel and conversion is one of degree. The tort of conversion applies to more serious interferences with the lawful possessor's interest in exclusive possession of personal property. Koepnick v. Sears Roebuck & Co. is a trespass to chattel claim involving the relatively minor interference caused by Sears's security guard searching Koepnick's truck for stolen property. Note how the court identifies interferences that are not substantial enough to be characterized as actionable trespasses to chattel. United States v. Arora involves a government researcher who intentionally destroyed cells created by other researchers. This interference with possessory rights was so severe that the court characterized it as a conversion rather than a trespass to chattel. These two cases also illustrate the circumstances under which nominal, compensatory, and punitive damages are available remedies for the torts of trespass and conversion.

KOEPNICK v. SEARS ROEBUCK & CO.
762 P.2d 609 (Ariz. Ct. App. 1988)

FROEB, Presiding Judge. . . .

Koepnick was stopped in the Fiesta Mall parking lot by Sears security guards Lessard and Pollack on December 6, 1982, at approximately 6:15 p.m. Lessard and Pollack suspected Koepnick of shoplifting a wrench and therefore detained him for approximately 15 minutes until the Mesa police arrived. Upon arrival of the police, Koepnick and a police officer became involved in an altercation in which Koepnick was injured. The police officer handcuffed Koepnick, placed a call for a backup, and began investigating the shoplifting allegations. Upon investigation it was discovered that Koepnick had receipts for the wrench and for all the Sears merchandise he had been carrying. Additionally, the store clerk who sold the wrench to Koepnick was located. He verified the sale and informed Lessard that he had put the wrench in a small bag, stapled it shut, and then placed that bag into a large bag containing Koepnick's other purchases. The small bag was not among the items in Koepnick's possession in the security room. To determine whether a second wrench was involved, the police and Lessard searched Koepnick's truck which was in the mall parking lot. No stolen items were found. Having completed their investigation, the police cited Koepnick for disorderly conduct and released him. The entire detention lasted approximately 45 minutes.

Koepnick sued Sears for [inter alia] trespass to chattel. . . . After a trial on these claims, a jury awarded Koepnick . . . $100 compensatory damages and $25,000 punitive damages for trespass to chattel. . . . The court granted Sears' motion for judgment n.o.v. on the trespass to chattel charge. This appeal and cross-appeal followed.

TRESPASS TO CHATTEL

Arizona courts follow the Restatement (Second) of Torts absent authority to the contrary. The Restatement provides that the tort of trespass to a chattel may be committed by intentionally dispossessing another of the chattel or using or intermeddling with a chattel in the possession of another. Restatement (Second) of Torts §217 (1965).

The Restatement (Second) of Torts §221 (1965) defines dispossession as follows:

> A dispossession may be committed by intentionally
> (a) taking a chattel from the possession of another without the other's consent, or
> [(b) obtaining possession of a chattel from another by fraud or duress, or]
> (c) barring the possessor's access to a chattel [or
> (d) destroying a chattel while it is in another's possession, or
> (e) taking the chattel into the custody of the law].

Comment b to §221 provides that dispossession may occur when someone intentionally assumes physical control over the chattel and deals with the chattel in a way which will be destructive of the possessory interest of the other person. Comment b further provides that "on the other hand, an intermeddling with the chattel is not a dispossession unless the actor intends to exercise a dominion and control over it inconsistent with a possession in any other person other than himself."

The Restatement (Second) of Torts §218 (1965) provides:

> One who commits a trespass to a chattel is subject to liability to the possessor of the chattel if, but only if,
>
> (a) he dispossesses the other of the chattel, or
> (b) the chattel is impaired as to its condition, quality, or value, or
> (c) the possessor is deprived of the use of the chattel for a substantial time, or
> (d) bodily harm is caused to the possessor, or harm is caused to some person or thing in which the possessor has a legally protected interest.

Koepnick argued at trial that Lessard's participation in searching his truck constituted an actionable trespass to the truck. He was awarded $100 damages by the jury which he characterizes as damages for a dispossession pursuant to subsection (a) or deprivation of use pursuant to subsection (c) of §218.

The Restatement recognizes that an award of nominal damages may be made, even in the absence of proof of actual damages, if a trespass to chattel involves a dispossession. See §218, comment d. However, both parties have agreed that the $100 compensatory award is not nominal.

Sears' actions with respect to the trespass consisted of Steve Lessard accompanying a Mesa police officer out to the parking lot and looking in the truck. There is no evidence in the record of an intent on the part of Sears' employee to claim a possessory interest in the truck contrary to Koepnick's interest. No lien or ownership interest claim of any kind was made. Further, there is no evidence that Sears intentionally denied Koepnick access to his truck.

Koepnick was in the City of Mesa's custody at the time of the search and Sears had no control over how the police department conducted its investigation or the disposition of Koepnick during that investigation. There is no evidence that Sears' employees objected to any request by Koepnick to accompany them down to the vehicle.

Comment e to the Restatement §218 discusses the requirement of proof of actual damage for an actionable trespass to chattel claim.

> The interest of a possessor of chattel in its inviolability, unlike the similar interest of a possessor of land, is not given legal protection by an action for nominal damages for harmless intermeddlings with the chattel. In order that an actor who interferes with another's chattel may be liable, his conduct must affect some other and more important interest of the possessor. Therefore, one who intentionally intermeddles with another's chattel is subject to liability only if his intermeddling is harmful to the possessor's materially valuable interest in the physical condition, quality, or value of the chattel, or if the possessor is deprived of the use of the chattel for a substantial time, or some other legally protected interest of the possessor is affected as stated in Clause (c). Sufficient legal protection of the possessor's interest in the mere inviolability of his chattel is afforded by his privilege to use reasonable force to protect his possession against even harmless interference.

The search in question took approximately two minutes. Neither the truck nor its contents were damaged in any manner by the police or Sears' employee. As a matter of law, Sears' action did not constitute an actionable trespass under §218(c).

In arguing that Sears should not have been given a directed verdict in its favor on the trespass to chattel claim, Koepnick asserts that the search of his truck caused him to remain in custody longer than he would otherwise have been detained. While this may be true, there was no evidence showing any connection between $100 and the few minutes that Koepnick was detained as a result of waiting for that search to be completed — apparently 15 minutes. For a deprivation of use caused by a trespass to chattel to be actionable, the time must be so substantial that it is possible to estimate the loss that is caused. The record in the present case lacks any evidence to permit a jury to estimate any loss caused to Koepnick. It is well settled that conjecture and speculation cannot provide the basis for an award of damages. The evidence must make an approximately accurate estimate possible.

Even if a verdict on the claim of trespass could be affirmed on the basis that a dispossession occurred, the award on the verdict would necessarily be limited to nominal damages. As discussed above, both parties agree that the $100 award was not nominal. Furthermore, punitive damages were erroneously awarded because punitive damages cannot be awarded absent evidence of actual damages.

We conclude that there was no dispossession of the vehicle as contemplated under §218 of the Restatement nor was Koepnick deprived of its use for a substantial period of time. Any increase in the length of detention caused by the search is not the kind of interest protected by the tort of trespass to chattel. Accordingly, we affirm the trial court's directed verdict in favor of Sears on this issue.

The judgment of the trial court is affirmed and this matter is remanded to the trial court for proceedings in accordance with this opinion.

UNITED STATES v. ARORA
860 F. Supp. 1091 (D. Md. 1994)

MESSITTE, J.

In this civil suit for conversion and trespass, the United States contends that Doctor Prince Kumar Arora intentionally tampered with and destroyed cells in a research project at the National Institutes of Health in Bethesda, Maryland. [The cell line, dubbed Alpha 1-4, was being developed by Drs. Wong and Sei. If successful, the cell line would have significant implications for studies of alcohol, Alzheimer's disease, and neurotoxicity. While initially cordial, the relationship between Dr. Arora and Dr. Sei was straining by disagreements over who deserved credit for certain research and by allegations of harassment brought by a female graduate student that resulted in her reassignment from Dr. Arora's supervision to Dr. Sei's.] Dr. Arora denies tampering and in any case responds that the Government sustained no damages by reason of the cell deaths. . . .

. . . The Court concludes, in this most unhappy affair, that Dr. Arora did in fact tamper with and cause the death of the Alpha 1-4 cells at the NIH laboratory in Bethesda in the Spring of 1992.

WAS THERE A CONVERSION OR TRESPASS?

A) It is not necessary to recount here the historical development of the torts of trespass and conversion, a matter more than adequately explored in Prosser and Keeton on The Law of Torts, §§14-15 (5th ed. 1984). For present purposes, it suffices to observe that the difference between the two torts is fundamentally one of degree, trespass constituting a lesser interference with another's chattel, conversion a more serious exercise of dominion or control over it. See Restatement (Second) of Torts, §222A, Comment (1965).

Thus a trespass has been defined as an intentional use or intermeddling with the chattel in possession of another, Restatement (Second) of Torts, §217(b), such intermeddling occurring, inter alia, when "the chattel is impaired as to its condition, quality, or value." Restatement (Second) of Torts, §218(b). See also Walser v. Resthaven Memorial Gardens, Inc., 98 Md. App. 371, 395, 633 A.2d 466 (1993).

A "conversion," on the other hand, has been defined as:

> [a]n intentional exercise of dominion or control over a chattel which so seriously interferes with the right of another to control it that the actor may justly be required to pay the other the full value of the chattel.

Restatement (Second) of Torts, §222A(1). Whereas impairing the condition, quality or value of a chattel upon brief interference can constitute a trespass, intentional destruction or material alteration of a chattel will subject the actor to liability for conversion. Restatement (Second) of Torts, §226.

A number of factors are considered in determining whether interference with a chattel is serious enough to constitute a conversion as opposed to a trespass. These include:

a) the extent and duration of the actor's exercise of dominion or control;
b) the actor's intent to assert a right in fact inconsistent with the other's right of control;
c) the actor's good faith;
d) the extent and duration of the resulting interference with the other's right of control;
e) the harm done to the chattel;
f) the inconvenience and expense caused to the other.

Staub v. Staub, 37 Md. App. 141, at 143-144, 376 A.2d 1129 (1977), quoting Restatement (Second) of Torts, §222A(2).

Assuming for the moment that a cell line is a chattel capable of being converted or trespassed upon, it is clear that the United States owned the Alpha 1-4 cell line, and that Dr. Arora's dominion or control over it, while brief, was total. He intended to act inconsistently with Dr. Sei's right to control the cells, he did not act in good faith, and he committed the ultimate harm — he destroyed the cells. While certain easily identifiable expense was caused by Dr. Arora's inappropriate acts, it is also apparent that he caused serious inconvenience to what was a critically important research project. By this analysis, if any tort was committed, it was unquestionably a conversion, not a mere trespass.

B) But what exactly did Dr. Arora convert? It is undoubtedly fair to conclude that by his wrongful act he caused the loss of the flasks, pipets and other materials used to culture the cells, a total value of $176.68.

But did he convert the cell line? . . .

The fact is that the United States Supreme Court has recognized that a living cell line is a property interest capable of protection. Other courts have likewise acknowledged the cell line's status as property. The Court thus sees no reason why a cell line should not be considered a chattel capable of being converted. Indeed, if such a cause of action is not recognized, it is hard to conceive what civil remedy would ever lie to recover a cell line that might be stolen or destroyed, including one with immense potential commercial value, as this one apparently had and has. The Court is satisfied, therefore, under the circumstances of this case, that the Alpha 1-4 cell line was capable of being converted and that in fact Dr. Arora converted it. The more difficult question, perhaps, is how to assess damages, the next question before the Court.

WHAT COMPENSATORY DAMAGES, IF ANY, SHOULD BE ASSESSED?

A) The Government claims a broad array of damages by reason of Defendant's acts, including the costs of the flasks, materials and supplies used to create the cells, the reasonable value of the wages paid to the laboratory assistant who cultured the cells, and a sizeable amount for the delay in the research project occasioned by the conversion. Defendant, in sharp contrast, maintains that the Government has sustained no damage at all; indeed he has sought throughout to dismiss these proceedings by reason of that alleged fact.

The conventional rule in cases of conversion, it is true, fixes damages for a totally destroyed chattel at the market value as of the date of the conversion, plus interest to the date of judgment. To the extent that the chattel is a discrete tangible item of discernible market value, the calculation is fairly straightforward and presents little problem. The matter becomes more difficult when property of limited extrinsic or uncertain market value is involved.

But mere difficulty in ascertaining damages is not a basis for denying them. While the market value measure is the traditional rule in conversion cases, it is also the case, as stated by the Maryland Court of Appeals in Staub v. Staub that:

> [a]s in other tort actions, additional damages adequate to compensate an owner for other injurious consequences which result in a loss greater than the diminished or market value of the chattel at the time of the trespass or conversion may be allowed unless such claimed damages are so speculative as to create a danger of injustice to the opposite party.

37 Md. App. at 145-146, 376 A.2d 1129.

As observed by the United States District Court for the Eastern District of Pennsylvania in America East India Corp. v. Ideal Shoe Co., 400 F. Supp. 141 (E.D. Pa. 1975):

> [t]he general purpose of damages in conversion is to provide indemnity for all actual losses or injuries sustained as a natural and proximate result of the converter's wrong. The measure of damages, generally employed, is the value of the property, with interest from the time of conversion, at the time and place of the conversion. However, it is appropriate to use whatever measure of damages accomplishes the general objective of indemnity under the particular circumstances. (Citations omitted.)

400 F. Supp. at 169.

For this reason, in a number of cases involving chattels of limited extrinsic or market value, courts have allowed as damages the original or replacement cost or cost of repair of the chattel. See generally Dobbs at §5.13(1); see also Lakewood Engineering and Manufacturing Co. v. Quinn, 91 Md. App. 375, 604 A.2d 535 (1992) (allowing replacement value of household items lost in fire). And, where, as here, the converted chattel is essentially a product of creative effort as to which no original or replacement cost can fairly be assigned — for example, manuscripts or professional drawings — courts have also fixed damages based upon the value of the time that it took or would take to create the chattel. See e.g., Wood v. Cunard, 192 F. 293 (2d Cir. 1911) (taking into account the value of two years of intermittent labor required to reproduce lost manuscript); Rajkovich v. Alfred Mossner Co., 199 Ill. App. 3d 655, 145 Ill. Dec. 726, 557 N.E.2d 496 (1990) (compensating for 172 hours of architectural time at specified rate necessary to redo damaged architectural drawings); see also Redwine v. Fitzhugh, 78 Wyo. 407, 329 P.2d 257, 72 A.L.R.2d 664, *reh. den.*, 78 Wyo. 407, 330 P.2d 112 (1958) (allowing recovery for value of seed and for labor expended in sowing and cultivating seed where seed destroyed in the ground).

B) These principles find relatively easy application in the present case. The tangible chattels converted consist of the Alpha 1-4 cells and the flasks and related materials which contained them. The latter have a market value of some $176.68, while the value of the former is essentially unascertainable. But the evidence in the record also establishes the cost of creating or recreating the Alpha 1-4 cells at $273.52, the amount attributable to the services of a laboratory assistant necessary to culture the cells. The total of these two sums, $450.20, while modest, is nevertheless nontrivial. It is an amount properly awardable in this case and the Court has determined to award it.

On the other hand, the Court acknowledges the caveat of *Staub* that consequential damages may not be "so speculative as to create a danger of injustice." 37 Md. App. at 146, 376 A.2d 1129. The Court, therefore, is inclined to agree with Defendant that any effort to quantify with precision damages for delay in the research project would run counter to that principle. . . .

NOTES TO KOEPNICK v. SEARS ROEBUCK & CO. AND UNITED STATES v. ARORA

1. *Trespass to Chattels and Conversion Compared.*   The court in United States v. Arora classified the intentional killing of the cells as a conversion despite the fact that the conduct also fits within the language of a trespass to chattel: "the chattel is impaired as to its condition, quality, or value" or "the possessor is deprived of the use of the chattel." See Restatement (Second) of Torts §218. Which of the factors described by the *Arora* court led it to conclude that the interference was serious enough to be considered a conversion? Why was the security guard's interference with Koepnick's use of his truck not serious enough even to be considered a trespass?

2. *Remedies for Trespass.*   Nominal and compensatory damages are available for trespasses to land and chattel and for conversions. Damages for more serious interferences with possessory rights are naturally greater than for minor transgressions. Note the variety of approaches to calculating the full loss suffered by the plaintiff in *Arora*. Trespass plaintiffs may also sue to enjoin a defendant from continuing to trespass.

Punitive damages are available for trespass plaintiffs, as they are for victims of other intentional torts. In an omitted portion of the opinion in *Arora*, the Federal District Court, applying Maryland law, awarded $5,000 in punitive damages:

> Maryland law holds that punitive damages are awardable only if there is clear and convincing evidence of actual malice. The Court is satisfied to that degree that Dr.

Arora did act with an evil and rancorous intent against Dr. Sei. His intentional actions, moreover, not only delayed a vitally important research project; they were obviously calculated to diminish the reputation of the entire laboratory involved with the project. Beyond that, Dr. Arora had to know that his actions might deprive the scientific community of the benefits of the research involving the Alpha 1-4 cell line for some period of time, possibly forever. Finally—and here perhaps the deterrent effect of a punitive award comes most into play—his actions undermined the honor system that exists among the community of scientists, a system which is ultimately based on "truthfulness, both as a moral imperative and as a fundamental operational principle in the scientific research process." Taking all these considerations into account, the Court has determined that a punitive damage award in the amount of $5,000.00 would be fair and just.

Problem
Trespass to Chattels and Conversion

CompuServe is an online computer service linking its subscribers to the Internet and providing e-mail services. Cyber Promotions sent unsolicited e-mail advertisements on behalf of its clients to Internet users, including CompuServe subscribers. Despite CompuServe's complaints, Cyber Promotions continued to send such advertisements, which used up a considerable amount of CompuServe computer storage and processing capacity. CompuServe's subscribers complained, and some terminated the service because they paid for e-mail access on an hourly basis and deleting the e-mails cost the subscribers money. After unsuccessfully trying to prevent these e-mails by technological means, CompuServe sought to enjoin Cyber Promotions, claiming that Cyber Promotions was trespassing on CompuServe's personal property. Is this a trespass? A conversion? Neither? See CompuServe Inc. v. Cyber Promotions, Inc., 962 F. Supp. 1015 (D. Ohio 1997).

C. Privileges: Private and Public Necessity

Defenses to the tort of trespass are analogous to defenses to assault and battery. Because trespass is an unprivileged entry onto land, permission of the owner (like consent) or a public policy-based privilege (like self-defense) will affect the entrant's status and liability. Vincent v. Lake Erie Transportation Co. is a classic case exploring the liability of a private person who interferes with another's right to exclusive possession to protect her own person and property. Marty v. State of Idaho considers the liability of those who cause an unpermitted entry onto the property of another for a public rather than private purpose.

VINCENT v. LAKE ERIE TRANSPORTATION CO.
124 N.W. 221 (Minn. 1910)

O'BRIEN, J.

The steamship Reynolds, owned by the defendant, was for the purpose of discharging her cargo on November 27, 1905, moored to plaintiff's dock in Duluth. While the unloading of the boat was taking place a storm from the northeast developed, which at about 10 o'clock p.m., when the unloading was completed, had so grown in violence that the wind was then moving at 50 miles per hour and continued to increase during the night. There is some evidence that one, and perhaps two, boats were able to enter the harbor that night, but it is plain that navigation was practically suspended from the hour mentioned until the morning of the 29th, when the storm abated, and during that time no master would have been justified in attempting to navigate his vessel, if he could avoid doing so. After the discharge of the cargo the Reynolds signaled for a tug to tow her from the dock, but none could be obtained because of the severity of the storm. If the lines holding the ship to the dock had been cast off, she would doubtless have drifted away; but, instead, the lines were kept fast, and as soon as one parted or chafed it was replaced, sometimes with a larger one. The vessel lay upon the outside of the dock, her bow to the east, the wind and waves striking her starboard quarter with such force that she was constantly being lifted and thrown against the dock, resulting in its damage, as found by the jury, to the amount of $500.

We are satisfied that the character of the storm was such that it would have been highly imprudent for the master of the Reynolds to have attempted to leave the dock or to have permitted his vessel to drift away from it. One witness testified upon the trial that the vessel could have been warped into a slip, and that, if the attempt to bring the ship into the slip had failed, the worst that could have happened would be that the vessel would have been blown ashore upon a soft and muddy bank. The witness was not present in Duluth at the time of the storm, and, while he may have been right in his conclusions, those in charge of the dock and the vessel at the time of the storm were not required to use the highest human intelligence, nor were they required to resort to every possible experiment which could be suggested for the preservation of their property. Nothing more was demanded of them than ordinary prudence and care, and the record in this case fully sustains the contention of the appellant that, in holding the vessel fast to the dock, those in charge of her exercised good judgment and prudent seamanship.

It is claimed by the respondent that it was negligence to moor the boat at an exposed part of the wharf, and to continue in that position after it became apparent that the storm was to be more than usually severe. We do not agree with this position. The part of the wharf where the vessel was moored appears to have been commonly used for that purpose. It was situated within the harbor at Duluth, and must, we think, be considered a proper and safe place, and would undoubtedly have been such during what would be considered a very severe storm. The storm which made it unsafe was one which surpassed in violence any which might have reasonably been anticipated.

The appellant contends by ample assignments of error that, because its conduct during the storm was rendered necessary by prudence and good seamanship under conditions over which it had no control, it cannot be held liable for any injury resulting to the property of others, and claims that the jury should have been so instructed. An analysis of the charge given by the trial court is not necessary, as in our opinion the only question for the jury was the amount of damages which the plaintiffs were entitled to recover, and no complaint is made upon that score.

The situation was one in which the ordinary rules regulating property rights were suspended by forces beyond human control, and if, without the direct intervention of some act by the one sought to be held liable, the property of another was injured, such injury must be attributed to the act of God, and not to the wrongful act of the person sought to be charged. If during the storm the Reynolds had entered the harbor, and while there had become disabled and been thrown against the plaintiffs' dock, the plaintiffs could not have recovered. Again, if while attempting to hold fast to the dock the lines had parted, without any negligence, and the vessel carried against some other boat or dock in the harbor, there would be no liability upon her owner. But here those in charge of the vessel deliberately and by their direct efforts held her in such a position that the damage to the dock resulted, and, having thus preserved the ship at the expense of the dock, it seems to us that her owners are responsible to the dock owners to the extent of the injury inflicted.

In Depue v. Flatau, 111 N.W. 1 (Minn.), this court held that where the plaintiff, while lawfully in the defendants' house, became so ill that he was incapable of traveling with safety, the defendants were responsible to him in damages for compelling him to leave the premises. If, however, the owner of the premises had furnished the traveler with proper accommodations and medical attendance, would he have been able to defeat an action brought against him for their reasonable worth?

In Ploof v. Putnam, 71 Atl. 188, the Supreme Court of Vermont held that where, under stress of weather, a vessel was without permission moored to a private dock at an island in Lake Champlain owned by the defendant, the plaintiff was not guilty of trespass, and that the defendant was responsible in damages because his representative upon the island unmoored the vessel, permitting it to drift upon the shore, with resultant injuries to it. If, in that case, the vessel had been permitted to remain, and the dock had suffered an injury, we believe the shipowner would have been held liable for the injury done.

Theologians hold that a starving man may, without moral guilt, take what is necessary to sustain life; but it could hardly be said that the obligation would not be upon such person to pay the value of the property so taken when he became able to do so. And so public necessity, in times of war or peace, may require the taking of private property for public purposes; but under our system of jurisprudence compensation must be made.

Let us imagine in this case that for the better mooring of the vessel those in charge of her had appropriated a valuable cable lying upon the dock. No matter how justifiable such appropriation might have been, it would not be claimed that, because of the overwhelming necessity of the situation, the owner of the cable could not recover its value.

This is not a case where life or property was menaced by any object or thing belonging to the plaintiff, the destruction of which became necessary to prevent the threatened disaster. Nor is it a case where, because of the act of God, or unavoidable accident, the infliction of the injury was beyond the control of the defendant, but is one where the defendant prudently and advisedly availed itself of the plaintiffs' property for the purpose of preserving its own more valuable property, and the plaintiffs are entitled to compensation for the injury done.

Order affirmed.

LEWIS, J.

I dissent. It was assumed on the trial before the lower court that appellant's liability depended on whether the master of the ship might, in the exercise of reasonable care, have sought a place of safety before the storm made it impossible to leave the dock. The majority opinion assumes that the evidence is conclusive that appellant moored its boat at respondent's dock pursuant to contract, and that the vessel was lawfully in position at the time the additional cables were fastened to the dock, and the reasoning of the opinion is that, because appellant made use of the stronger cables to hold the boat in position, it became liable under the rule that it had voluntarily made use of the property of another for the purpose of saving its own.

In my judgment, if the boat was lawfully in position at the time the storm broke, and the master could not, in the exercise of due care, have left that position without subjecting his vessel to the hazards of the storm, then the damage to the dock, caused by the pounding of the boat, was the result of an inevitable accident. If the master was in the exercise of due care, he was not at fault. The reasoning of the opinion admits that if the ropes, or cables, first attached to the dock had not parted, or if, in the first instance, the master had used the stronger cables, there would be no liability. If the master could not, in the exercise of reasonable care, have anticipated the severity of the storm and sought a place of safety before it became impossible, why should he be required to anticipate the severity of the storm, and, in the first instance, use the stronger cables?

I am of the opinion that one who constructs a dock to the navigable line of waters, and enters into contractual relations with the owner of a vessel to moor at the same, takes the risk of damage to his dock by a boat caught there by a storm, which event could not have been avoided in the exercise of due care, and further, that the legal status of the parties in such a case is not changed by renewal of cables to keep the boat from being cast adrift at the mercy of the tempest.

MARTY v. STATE OF IDAHO
786 P.2d 524 (Idaho 1989)

JOHNSON, J.

This is a flood liability case. It involves the flooding of farmland near Mud Lake in 1984 and 1985. The owners of this farmland (the landowners) sued various governmental agencies, officers and employees (the governmental agencies) and local canal companies (the canal companies) and water users (the water users) seeking damages and injunctive relief. . . .

The Mud Lake area is a terminal basin without a natural drainage outlet, comprised of the presently diked area of Mud Lake and adjacent low-lying farmlands. In the 1920's the early settlers began diking the lake in order to reclaim productive agricultural lands from the marshes and to provide storage for irrigation. Prior to the diking of Mud Lake, the lands now owned by the landowners had been subjected to periodic flooding because they were located in a 100-year flood plain. . . .

On June 3, 1983, the board of commissioners of Jefferson County declared the area surrounding Mud Lake to be a flood emergency area and requested assistance from the governor of the State of Idaho. On June 6, 1983, the governor declared the existence of a state of extreme emergency because "excessive runoff and spring rains have seriously weakened the Mud Lake dikes" and the failure of these dikes would result in "serious flooding to approximately forty residents and several thousand acres of land" and "endanger the lives and property of the citizens of Terreton." All agencies of state government were required by the proclamation "to take action . . . to arrest or alleviate the conditions perpetuating the state of extreme emergency."

Unusually heavy rainfall in the spring of 1984 combined with the already saturated water table from 1983 to create a flow into the Mud Lake water system that had not occurred since 1923.

In a combined effort the governmental agencies, the Army Corps of Engineers, the canal companies, the water users and numerous volunteers responded to the impending flood. The Idaho Department of Water Resources (IDWR) coordinated this effort [by strengthening and increasing the height of the Mud Lake dike, which encloses the lake on the south, southeast and southwest and other efforts that resulted in the flooding of the landowners' property].

In late 1985 the landowners filed suit seeking damages and injunctive relief against the governmental agencies, the canal companies and the water users. The landowners based their claims for damages on theories of [inter alia] trespass. They alleged that their farmland had been flooded as a result of the actions and decisions of the governmental agencies, the canal companies and the water users, including the failure to construct a spillway to prevent the flooding of the landowners' farmland.

The governmental agencies, the canal companies and the water users moved for summary judgment, denying that there was any basis for liability under the theories advanced by the landowners and that their actions and decisions were immunized under several Idaho statutes. The trial court granted summary judgment dismissing all of the claims of the landowners. The landowners appealed. . . .

. . . The governmental agencies invoke the doctrine of public necessity contained in Restatement (Second) of Torts §196 (1965). The thrust of this doctrine is that "[o]ne is privileged to enter land in the possession of another if it is, or if the actor reasonably believes it to be, necessary for the purpose of averting an imminent public disaster." Id. The governmental agencies point out that a comment to the Restatement states that the privilege carries with it the privilege to do "any other acts on the premises reasonably necessary to effectuate the purpose for which the privilege exists." Id. at comment (f).

The governmental agencies acknowledge that this Court has not previously adopted the doctrine of public necessity. They cite decisions from our sister states of Washington and Colorado as demonstrating the application of the doctrine. Short v. Pierce County, 194 Wash. 421, 78 P.2d 610 (1938); Srb v. Board of County Commissioners, 43 Colo. App. 14, 601 P.2d 1082 (1979), *cert. denied,* 199 Colo. 496, 618 P.2d 1105 (1980). In *Srb* the court held that "when property is taken by the state or one of its political subdivisions under circumstances of imminent necessity, the failure justly to compensate the owner does not violate" the just compensation provision of the Colorado constitution. 601 P.2d at 1085.

Since 1864 the statutes of Idaho, first as a territory and then as a state, have declared:

> The common law of England, so far as it is not repugnant to, or inconsistent with, the constitution or laws of the United States, in all cases not provided for in these compiled laws, is the rule of decision in all courts of this state.

I.C. §73-116.

The doctrine of public necessity was the common law of England. 2 Kent's Commentaries (14th ed. 1896) 339, n.(a). In 1853 the Supreme Court of California recognized the existence of the doctrine:

> The right to destroy property, to prevent the spread of a conflagration, has been traced to the highest law of necessity, and the natural rights of man, independent of society or civil government. "It is referred by moralists and jurists to the same great principle which justifies the exclusive appropriation of a plank in a shipwreck, though the life of another be sacrificed; with the throwing overboard goods in a tempest, for the safety of a vessel; with the trespassing upon the lands of another, to escape death by an enemy. It rests upon the maxim, *Necessitas inducit privilegium quod jura privata*."

The common law adopts the principles of the natural law, and places the justification of an act otherwise tortious precisely on the same ground of necessity.

> This principle has been familiarly recognized by the books from the time of the salt-petre case, and the instances of tearing down houses to prevent a conflagration, or to raise bulwarks for the defence of a city, are made use of as illustrations, rather than as abstract cases, in which its exercise is permitted. At such times, the individual rights of property give way to the higher laws of impending necessity.

Surocco v. Geary, 3 Cal. 69, 73 (1853).

The United States Supreme Court also has stated:

> [T]he common law had long recognized that in times of imminent peril — such as when fire threatened a whole community — the sovereign could, with immunity, destroy the property of a few that the property of many and the lives of many more could be saved.

United States v. Caltex, Inc., 344 U.S. 149, 154 (1952).

These authorities convince us that although this Court has never before had the occasion to recognize the existence of the doctrine of public necessity, it was part of the common law of England. As we said in 1922 regarding another common law doctrine — the right of distress *damage feasant* — the doctrine "is applicable to this state in so far as it is not repugnant to or inconsistent with our constitution and laws." Kelly v. Easton, 35 Idaho 340, 343, 207 P. 129 (1922).

Recently, the United States District Court for the District of Idaho acknowledged the doctrine of public necessity, but stated that Idaho has abrogated the doctrine by adopting the State Disaster Preparedness Act, I.C. §46-1001, et seq. Union Pac. R.R. v. State of Idaho, 654 F. Supp. 1236, 1243, modified on other grounds, 663 F. Supp. 75 (D. Idaho 1987). In reaching this conclusion the federal district court relied on comment (g) to Restatement (Second) of Torts §196 (1965). This comment states:

> g. In many States statutes have been enacted designating certain public officials as authorized to determine the necessity for and to order the destruction of buildings in the path of a conflagration. Usually these statutes merely prescribe a condition upon which the statutory right to recover compensation from the organized community is dependent. A statute may, however, confer on specified public officials the exclusive authority to act in such matters. By such a statute, the privilege stated in this Subsection is abrogated.

We agree with the federal court that by enacting the State Disaster Preparedness Act (the Act), the legislature abrogated the common law doctrine of public necessity. The Act defines "disaster" to mean occurrence or imminent threat of widespread or severe damage, injury, or loss of life or property resulting from any natural or man made cause, including but not limited to fire, flood, earthquake, windstorm, wave action, volcanic activity, explosion, riot, or hostile military or paramilitary action.

I.C. §46-1002(3). The Act grants to the governor and to mayors and chairpersons of county commissions the authority to declare emergencies. I.C. §46-1011(1). I.C. §46-1017 also grants immunity from liability for death, injury or damage resulting from activity conducted pursuant to the Act. This statute indicates to us that the legislature intended to codify a version of the doctrine of public necessity. It is then the Act and not the doctrine of public necessity that must be considered to determine whether the landowners are entitled to pursue their claim.

Whether the landowners are entitled to compensation for inverse condemnation will first depend on whether their property was permanently damaged. What is permanent damage for recovery for inverse condemnation under our state constitution may depend on the probability of future flooding. Under the fifth and fourteenth amendments to the United States Constitution whether the damage is permanent may depend on proof of frequent and inevitably recurring inundation due to governmental action.

In the event permanent damage is shown by the landowners, the immunity provisions of I.C. §46-1017 must be applied. This immunity exists only when the state, its political subdivisions or other agencies were "acting under a declaration by proper authority." Here, the board of county commissioners did not declare an emergency until June 12, 1984. The governor declared an emergency on June 14, 1984. The emergency declared by the county commissioners was for a period of seven days. I.C. §46-1011(1). The emergency declared by the governor was for thirty days, unless extended by further declaration. I.C. §46-1008(2). Whether the actions of the governmental agencies were immunized by I.C. §46-1017 will depend on whether they were taken during these periods.

These questions should be resolved by the trial court. We reverse and remand for this purpose. . . .

NOTES TO VINCENT v. LAKE ERIE TRANSPORTATION CO. AND MARTY v. STATE OF IDAHO

1. *Obligations of Persons Who Interfere with the Possessory Rights of Others.* For policy reasons, a private person or the public may, in times of necessity, interfere with another's right to exclusive possession of real or personal property without permission. This policy prevents a trespass defendant from being liable for nominal or punitive damages. Is a private person still liable for compensatory damages? Is the public?

2. *Rights of Persons to Interfere with the Possessory Rights of Others.* The privilege of necessity affects both liability to possessors of property and liability of possessors of property. On this topic, the court in *Vincent* cites to Ploof v. Putnam, in which a boater taking refuge from a storm at another's dock was held not to be a trespasser. Moreover, because the boater was on the dock as a matter of necessity, the landowner was liable for any damages resulting from casting the boater off from the dock. See also Depue v. Flatau, also cited by the court in *Vincent*, where the landowner is held liable for damages caused to a sick person compelled to leave the premises. The privilege of necessity reflects the law's preference for human life over property rights.

The Restatement (Second) of Torts §345 describes the nature of the duty owned by a possessor of land to a person who enters the land under conditions of necessity

> **Section 345. Persons Entering in the Exercise of a Privilege**
>
> (1) Except as stated in Subsection (2), the liability of a possessor of land to one who enters the land only in the exercise of a privilege, for either a public or a private purpose, and irrespective of the possessor's consent, is the same as the liability to a licensee.
>
> (2) The liability of a possessor of land to a public officer or employee who enters the land in the performance of his public duty, and suffers harm because of a condition of a part of the land held open to the public, is the same as the liability to an invitee.

Problem
Private Necessity

Eight-year-old Patricia and her third-grade classmate Ida were walking home from their school in Methuen, Massachusetts when they saw a dog, a German Weimaraner, coming toward them on the street. They turned and ran and the dog followed them. Being frightened, the girls ran along a path behind the defendant's property, where they saw, for the first time, a black Great Dane. The Great Dane belonged to the defendant, who kept it to protect equipment he kept on the back of his property. It jumped on Patricia and knocked her down. Patricia screamed for help. Her father, who found her under the dogs on her knees with her hands on her face, took her to the hospital.

Massachusetts had a statute stating:

> If any dog shall do any damage to either the body or property of any person, the owner or keeper, or if the owner or keeper be a minor, the parent or guardian of such minor, shall be liable for such damage, unless such damage shall have been occasioned to the body or property of a person who, at the time such damage was sustained, was committing a trespass or other tort, or was teasing, tormenting or abusing such dog.

Following this statute, will the defendant (owner of the Great Dane) be liable to Patricia? See Rossi v. DelDuca, 181 N.E.2d 591 (Mass. 1962).

Perspective: Property and Liability Rules

The customary rule governing the use of private property is that an actor must negotiate with the rightful possessor for permission to use the property. This is often described as a "property rule" or "bargaining rule." The privilege of necessity substitutes a "liability rule," which allows the actor to use the property first and then pay damages, an amount determined by the court rather than by negotiations, after the fact. Torts scholars have suggested that liability rules are appropriate where it would be difficult for parties to bargain. The necessity cases seems to fit that category, though whether the facts of *Vincent*, where the parties have a preexisting contractual relationship, do so is another question.

Torts scholars have also suggested that liability for damages should be placed on the best avoider of costs, on that person who can best evaluate risks and take precautions to avoid them. A private person who would otherwise be a trespasser is relieved of some of the burdens of that categorization (nominal and punitive damages) under circumstances of necessity. Potential liability for actual damages, however, maintains an incentive for such a person to weigh the costs and benefits of his interference with the other's possession. See Guido Calabresi & A. Douglas Melamed, *Property Rules, Liability Rules, and Inalienability: One View of the Cathedral,* 85 Harv. L. Rev. 1089 (1972).

Perspective: Moral View of the Necessity Defense

Professor George C. Christie, *The Defense of Necessity Considered from the Legal and Moral Points of View,* 48 Duke L.J. 975, 995 (1999), argued that there is no moral justification for the rule in *Vincent*:

> In many states — including, for example, California, New York, and Washington, the owners and operators of aircraft are not strictly liable for ground damage that is not occasioned by their fault. In these states, requiring someone to pay for property destroyed to save lives would encourage an airline pilot who is obliged by an act of God to make a forced landing to place his life and those of his passengers in greater jeopardy because the safest alternative landing place has very valuable flower beds on it, while nearby less valuable vacant land is rockier and less flat. Surely the possible value of the property that might be destroyed should not enter into the pilot's consideration at all. The situation becomes even more ludicrous when the actor is in no danger himself but destroys property to save the life of a third party. The Restatement (Second) clearly makes the actor liable for the property he has destroyed. One would be hard put to create a doctrine more calculated to discourage people from coming to the aid of imperiled human beings.
>
> Assuming that the destruction of property is morally as well as legally permissible when necessary in order to save human lives, is there nevertheless a moral obligation to pay for the harm done? . . . After all, it is not necessary that one should have a legal obligation to do something in order for it to be true that one has a moral obligation to do that something.
>
> A moral universe in which the options are between no compensation at all or compensation for full replacement value strikes me as an overly legalistic universe and not a moral universe.

---

4. Best Cost Avoider and Necessity Doctrine. Consider the choice faced by the captain of the *Reynolds.* He could let the boat drift and face possible damage to the boat, its crew, and other boats. Or he could secure the boat to the defendant's dock and risk damage to the dock. If he will be liable for all the damages in either case, the rational choice will be to choose the option that will present the least cost. A rational, self-interested person who could use another's property with impunity would always sacrifice another's property for the sake of his own. From this perspective, the privilege created by necessity retains the desirable incentives created by potential liability. It assumes that, in necessity cases, the person faced with an emergency is the best cost avoider. Would that assumption be warranted in the *Vincent* case? Was the captain or the dock owner the best cost avoider? Should the captain be morally and legally obligated to pay for these damages?

II. Nuisance

Tort law recognizes two kinds of nuisance claims: private and public. The private nuisance cause of action protects a possessor's interest in use and enjoyment of his or her land. The public nuisance cause of action protects interests common to the public, such as the public's health, safety, comfort, and convenience.

There are important distinctions between trespass and nuisance. Unlike trespass, which is an intentional tort, nuisance claims may be based on conduct that is intentional, negligent, reckless, or violative of a statute. And unlike trespass, the tort of nuisance generally requires proof that the interference with the land possessor's interest was unreasonable. While any intentional, unpermitted entry would be a trespass, only an unreasonable interference with a land possessor's use and enjoyment would be a private or public nuisance.

Pestey v. Cushman discusses the elements of private nuisance and considers whether a dairy farm's production of odors was reasonable in light of the interests of the farmer, the neighbor, and the community. Armory Park Neighborhood Association v. Episcopal Community Services in Arizona distinguishes private from public nuisances, evaluates the reasonableness of a charitable organization's program for providing meals for the indigent in light of the interests of neighbors and the community, and discusses the special rules regulating who can bring public nuisance actions.

PESTEY v. CUSHMAN
788 A.2d 496 (Conn. 2002)

VERTEFEUILLE, J.

The issues in this common-law private nuisance action arise out of the defendants' operation of a dairy farm near the plaintiffs' home. The principal issues in this appeal are whether: (1) the trial court properly instructed the jury with respect to the unreasonableness element of the common-law private nuisance claim. . . .

The plaintiffs, James Pestey and Joan Pestey, brought this action against the defendants, Nathan R. Cushman, Nathan P. Cushman and Cushman Farms Limited Partnership, seeking money damages and injunctive and declaratory relief. After a lengthy trial, the jury returned a partial verdict for the plaintiffs for $100,000 in damages. . . .

The jury reasonably could have found the following facts. The plaintiffs' home is situated on property they own located along the west side of Route 87 in North Franklin. The defendants own and conduct farming operations on a large tract of land on the opposite side of Route 87, approximately one third of one mile north of the plaintiffs' property. In 1990, the defendants constructed a 42,000 square foot free stall barn and milking parlor on their land to house a herd of dairy cows and a pit in which to store the manure generated by the herd.

The plaintiffs first noticed objectionable odors emanating from the defendants' farm in early 1991, after the construction of the new barn. The odors were, at first, nothing more than the typical stercoraceous odors generated by a farm containing livestock. Over time, however, the odors became substantially more pungent and their character changed as they took on a sharp, burnt smell. In 1997, the defendants installed an anaerobic digestion system on their farm to process the manure generated by the dairy herd. The system was designed to mimic in a controlled manner the anaerobic process that occurs in nature. Under this process, manure is fed into the digester, which, through the use of high temperature and bacteria, breaks the organic compound into its constituent parts. The end result of a properly functioning anaerobic digestion process is the production of a low odor biosolid and a gaseous mixture that can be used as an energy source to power the digester's generators. Following the installation of the digester, the character of the odors affecting the plaintiffs' property changed again, becoming more acrid and evincing the smells of sulphur and sewage. This change was caused by the digester being either undersized or overloaded, which resulted in partially digested, higher odor manure being released at the end of the anaerobic digestion process. At times, the odors emanating from the defendants' farm were so strong that the smell would awaken the plaintiffs during the night, forcing them to close the windows of their home. Further facts will be set forth where relevant. . . .

"A private nuisance is a nontrespassory invasion of another's interest in the private use and enjoyment of land." 4 Restatement (Second), Torts §821D (1979). The law of private nuisance springs from the general principle that "[i]t is the duty of every person to make a reasonable use of his own property so as to occasion no unnecessary damage or annoyance to his neighbor." Nailor v. C.W. Blakeslee & Sons, Inc., 167 A. 548 (1933). "The essence of a private nuisance is an interference with the use and enjoyment of land." W. Prosser & W. Keeton, Torts (5th ed. 1984) §87, p.619.

The defendants' claim is based on the principle of private nuisance law that, in determining unreasonableness, "[c]onsideration must be given not only to the interests of the person harmed but also [to] the interests of the actor and to the interests of the community as a whole." 4 Restatement (Second), supra, §826, comment (c). "Determining unreasonableness is essentially a weighing process, involving a comparative evaluation of conflicting interests. . . ." 4 Restatement (Second), supra, §826, comment (c). Unreasonableness cannot be determined in the abstract, but, rather, must be judged under the circumstances of the particular case.

In the present case, the trial court instructed the jury with respect to the unreasonableness element of the nuisance claim in the following manner: "You must also ask yourselves whether the defendants' use of their property [was] reasonable. A use which is permitted or even required by law and which does not violate local land use restrictions may nonetheless be unreasonable and create a common-law nuisance. You must . . . consider and weigh . . . the location of the defendants' dairy farm, the size of the farm, the manner in which they operate the farm, including their handling and maintenance of the manure, the free stall barn, the milking parlors and the anaerobic manure digester and associated equipment and any other circumstance which you find proven which indicates whether the defendants [were] making a reasonable use of their property." The court stated further: "The question is not whether the plaintiffs or the defendants would regard the condition as unreasonable, but whether reasonable persons generally looking at the whole situation impartially and objectively would consider it [to] be reasonable."

As the charge indicates, the trial court instructed the jury to consider a multiplicity of factors in determining the unreasonableness element. The defendants' argument that the instruction did not adequately instruct the jury to consider the defendants' interests assumes that the factors set forth by the trial court only regard the plaintiffs' interests. Such an assumption is unwarranted. The jury, for instance, was instructed to consider the location of the farm in making its finding regarding reasonableness. The location of the farm as a factor inherently includes the interests of both the plaintiffs and the defendants, and the jury was just as entitled to find that the location of the farm tended to show that the defendants' use was reasonable as it was to find that the location tended to show that the defendants' use was unreasonable. In addition, the trial court explicitly instructed the jury to consider any other circumstances that it found proven that would indicate "whether the defendants [were] making a reasonable use of their property." This instruction underscored the trial court's previous instruction that the jury was to consider various factors in reaching its decision, including factors relating to the interests of both the plaintiffs and the defendants. . . .

In prescribing the [elements that a plaintiff must prove to prevail on a claim for damages in a common law private nuisance action], we look to the leading authorities in the field of common-law private nuisance for guidance. According to the Restatement (Second) of Torts, a plaintiff must prove that: (1) there was an invasion of the plaintiff's use and enjoyment of his or her property; (2) the defendant's conduct was the proximate cause of the invasion; and (3) the invasion was either intentional and unreasonable, or unintentional and the defendant's conduct was negligent or reckless. 4 Restatement (Second), supra, §822. Although the language used in this third element does not make the point clearly, under this test, showing unreasonableness is an essential element of a private nuisance cause of action based on negligence or recklessness. See id., §822, comment (k). . . .

. . . Whether the interference is unreasonable depends upon a balancing of the interests involved under the circumstances of each individual case. In balancing the interests, the fact finder must take into consideration all relevant factors, including the nature of both the interfering use and the use and enjoyment invaded, the nature, extent and duration of the interference, the suitability for the locality of both the interfering conduct and the particular use and enjoyment invaded, whether the defendant is taking all feasible precautions to avoid any unnecessary interference with the plaintiff's use and enjoyment of his or her property, and any other factors that the fact finder deems relevant to the question of whether the interference is unreasonable. No one factor should dominate this balancing of interests; all relevant factors must be considered in determining whether the interference is unreasonable.

The determination of whether the interference is unreasonable should be made in light of the fact that some level of interference is inherent in modern society. There are few, if any, places remaining where an individual may rest assured that he will be able to use and enjoy his property free from all interference. Accordingly, the interference must be substantial to be unreasonable.

Ultimately, the question of reasonableness is whether the interference is beyond that which the plaintiff should bear, under all of the circumstances of the particular case, without being compensated. With these standards in mind, we turn to the present case.

In reaching its verdict, the jury completed a set of interrogatories provided by the trial court. Each interrogatory asked the jury whether the plaintiffs had proven a specific element of the private nuisance claim, and the jury answered each interrogatory affirmatively. The first interrogatory asked: "Did the plaintiffs prove [that] the defendants' dairy farm produced odors which unreasonably interfered with [the] plaintiffs' enjoyment of their property?" This interrogatory correctly captured the crux of a common-law private nuisance cause of action for damages, i.e., whether the defendants' conduct unreasonably interfered with the plaintiffs' use and enjoyment of their property. It correctly stated that the focus in such a cause of action is on the reasonableness of the interference and not on the use that is causing the interference. In light of this conclusion, the fourth interrogatory, which involved the unreasonable use element that is at issue in this case, was superfluous. . . . We conclude that the jury interrogatories and the jury charge, considered together, properly informed the jury of the necessary elements of a common-law private nuisance cause of action for damages and provided the jury with adequate guidance with which to reach its verdict. Accordingly, the trial court's jury charge was proper under the law as clarified herein. . . .

<hr>

ARMORY PARK NEIGHBORHOOD ASSOCIATION v. EPISCOPAL COMMUNITY SERVICES IN ARIZONA

712 P.2d 914 (Ariz. 1985)

FELDMAN, J.

On December 11, 1982, defendant Episcopal Community Services in Arizona (ECS) opened the St. Martin's Center (Center) in Tucson. The Center's only purpose is to provide one free meal a day to indigent persons. Plaintiff Armory Park Neighborhood Association (APNA) is a non-profit corporation organized for the purpose of "improving, maintaining and insuring the quality of the neighborhood known as Armory Park Historical Residential District." The Center is located on Arizona Avenue, the western boundary of the Armory Park district. On January 10, 1984, APNA filed a complaint in Pima County Superior Court, seeking to enjoin ECS from operating its free food distribution program. The complaint alleged that the Center's activities constituted a public nuisance and that the Armory Park residents had sustained injuries from transient persons attracted to their neighborhood by the Center.

The superior court held a hearing on APNA's application for preliminary injunction on March 6 and 7, 1984. At the commencement of the hearing, the parties stipulated that

> . . . there is no issue concerning any State, County, or Municipal zoning ordinance, or health provision, before the Court. And, the Court may find that defendants are in compliance with the same.

The residents then testified about the changes the Center had brought to their neighborhood. Before the Center opened, the area had been primarily residential with a few small businesses. When the Center began operating in December 1982, many transients crossed the area daily on their way to and from the Center. Although the

Center was only open from 5:00 to 6:00 p.m., patrons lined up well before this hour and often lingered in the neighborhood long after finishing their meal. The Center rented an adjacent fenced lot for a waiting area and organized neighborhood cleaning projects, but the trial judge apparently felt these efforts were inadequate to control the activity stemming from the Center. Transients frequently trespassed onto residents' yards, sometimes urinating, defecating, drinking and littering on the residents' property. A few broke into storage areas and unoccupied homes, and some asked residents for handouts. The number of arrests in the area increased dramatically. Many residents were frightened or annoyed by the transients and altered their lifestyles to avoid them. . . .

A private nuisance is strictly limited to an interference with a person's interest in the enjoyment of real property. The Restatement defines a private nuisance as "a nontrespassory invasion of another's interest in the private use and enjoyment of land." Restatement (Second) of Torts §821D. A public nuisance, to the contrary is not limited to an interference with the use and enjoyment of the plaintiff's land. It encompasses any unreasonable interference with a right common to the general public.

We have previously distinguished public and private nuisances. In City of Phoenix v. Johnson, 51 Ariz. 115, 75 P.2d 30 (1938), we noted that a nuisance is public where it affects rights of "citizens as a part of the public, while a private nuisance is one which affects a single individual or a definite number of persons in the enjoyment of some private right which is not common to the public." Id. at 123, 75 P.2d 34. A public nuisance must also affect a considerable number of people. The legislature has adopted a similar requirement for its criminal code, defining a public nuisance as an interference "with the comfortable enjoyment of life or property by an entire community or neighborhood, or by a considerable number of persons. . . ." A.R.S. §13-2917.

The defendant contends that the trial court erred in finding both public and private nuisances when the plaintiff had not asserted a private nuisance claim. The defendant has read the trial court's minute entry too strictly. While we acknowledge that public and private nuisances implicate different interests, we recognize also that the same facts may support claims of both public and private nuisance. As Dean Prosser explained:

> When a public nuisance substantially interferes with the use or enjoyment of the plaintiff's rights in land, it never has been disputed that there is a particular kind of damage for which the private action will lie. Not only is every plot of land traditionally unique in the eyes of the law, but in the ordinary case the class of landowners in the vicinity of the alleged nuisance will necessarily be a limited one, with an interest obviously different from that of the general public. The interference itself is of course a private nuisance; but is none the less particular damage from a public one, and the action can be maintained upon either basis, or upon both. (Citations omitted.)

Prosser, *Private Action for Public Nuisance*, 52 Va. L. Rev. 997, 1018 (1966).

Thus, a nuisance may be simultaneously public and private when a considerable number of people suffer an interference with their use and enjoyment of land. See *Spur Industries*, 108 Ariz. at 184, 494 P.2d at 706. The torts are not mutually exclusive. Some of plaintiff's members in this case have suffered an injury to the use and enjoyment of their land. Any reference to both a public and a private nuisance by the trial court was, we believe, merely a recognition of this well-accepted rule and not error. However, both because plaintiff did not seek relief under the theory of private nuisance and because that theory might raise standing issues not addressed by the parties, we believe plaintiff's claim must stand or fall on the public nuisance theory alone.

Do the residents have standing?

Defendant argues that the Association has no standing to sue and that, therefore, the action should be dismissed. The trial court disagreed and defendant claims it erred in so doing. Two standing questions are before us. The first pertains to the right of a private person, as distinguished from a public official, to bring a suit to enjoin the maintenance of a public nuisance. The original rule at common law was that a citizen had no standing to sue for abatement or suppression of a public nuisance since

> such inconvenient or troublesome offences [sic], as annoy the whole community in general, and not merely some particular persons; and therefore are indictable only, and not actionable; as it would be unreasonable to multiply suits, by giving every man a separate right of action, by what damnifies him in common only with the rest of his fellow subjects.

IV Blackstone Commentaries 167 (1966). It was later held that a private individual might have a tort action to recover personal damages arising from the invasion of the public right. However, the individual bringing the action was required to show that his damage was different in kind or quality from that suffered by the public in common.

The rationale behind this limitation was two-fold. First, it was meant to relieve defendants and the courts of the multiple actions that might follow if every member of the public were allowed to sue for a common wrong. Second, it was believed that a harm which affected all members of the public equally should be handled by public officials. Considerable disagreement remains over the type of injury which the plaintiff must suffer in order to have standing to bring an action to enjoin a public nuisance. However, we have intimated in the past that an injury to plaintiff's interest in land is sufficient to distinguish plaintiff's injuries from those experienced by the general public and to give the plaintiff-landowner standing to bring the action. This seems also to be the general rule accepted in the United States.

We hold, therefore, that because the acts allegedly committed by the patrons of the neighborhood center affected the residents' use and enjoyment of their real property, a damage special in nature and different in kind from that experienced by the residents of the city in general, the residents of the neighborhood could bring an action to recover damages for or enjoin the maintenance of a public nuisance.

[The second standing issue was whether the association could bring the action on behalf of its members. The court held that because the purpose of the association was to "promote and preserve the use and enjoyment of the neighborhood by its residents," the association had a legitimate interest in the controversy and, for purposes of judicial economy, it was sensible to allow all the residents to bring their actions at once.]

Since the rules of a civilized society require us to tolerate our neighbors, the law requires our neighbors to keep their activities within the limits of what is tolerable by a reasonable person. However, what is reasonably tolerable must be tolerated; not all interferences with public rights are public nuisances. As Dean Prosser explains, "[t]he law does not concern itself with trifles, or seek to remedy all of the petty annoyances and disturbances of everyday life in a civilized community even from conduct committed with knowledge that annoyance and inconvenience will result." Prosser, supra, §88, at 626. Thus, to constitute a nuisance, the complained-of interference must be substantial, intentional and unreasonable under the circumstances. Our courts have generally used a balancing test in deciding the reasonableness of an interference. The trial court should look at the utility and reasonableness of the conduct and balance these factors against the extent of harm inflicted and the nature of the affected neighborhood. We noted in the early case of MacDonald v. Perry:

> What might amount to a serious nuisance in one locality by reason of the density of the population, or character of the neighborhood affected, may in another place and under different surroundings be deemed proper and unobjectionable. What amount of annoyance or inconvenience caused by others in the lawful use of their property will constitute a nuisance depends upon varying circumstances and cannot be precisely defined.

32 Ariz. 39, 50, 255 P. 494 (1927).

The trial judge did not ignore the balancing test and was well aware of the social utility of defendant's operation. His words are illuminating:

> It is distressing to this Court that an activity such as defendants [sic] should be restrained. Providing for the poor and the homeless is certainly a worthwhile, praisworthy [sic] activity. It is particularly distressing to this Court because it [defendant] has no control over those who are attracted to the kitchen while they are either coming or leaving the premises. However, the right to the comfortable enjoyment of one's property is something that another's activities should not affect, the harm being suffered by the Armory Park Neighborhood and the residents therein is irreparable and substantial, for which they have no adequate legal remedy.

Minute Entry, 6/8/84, at 8. We believe that a determination made by weighing and balancing conflicting interests or principles is truly one which lies within the discretion of the trial judge. We defer to that discretion here. The evidence of the multiple trespasses upon and defacement of the residents' property supports the trial court's conclusion that the interference caused by defendant's operation was unreasonable despite its charitable cause.

The common law has long recognized that the usefulness of a particular activity may outweigh the inconveniences, discomforts and changes it causes some persons to suffer. We, too, acknowledge the social value of the Center. Its charitable purpose, that of feeding the hungry, is entitled to greater deference than pursuits of lesser intrinsic value. It appears from the record that ECS purposes in operating the Center were entirely admirable. However, even admirable ventures may cause unreasonable interferences. We do not believe that the law allows the costs of a charitable enterprise to be visited in their entirety upon the residents of a single neighborhood. The problems of dealing with the unemployed, the homeless and the mentally ill are also matters of community or governmental responsibility.

. . . We are squarely faced, therefore, with the issue of whether a public nuisance may be found in the absence of a statute making specific conduct a crime.

In MacDonald v. Perry, supra, we indicated that the inquiry in a nuisance claim is not whether the activity allegedly constituting the nuisance is lawful but whether it is reasonable under the circumstances. The Restatement states that a criminal violation is only one factor among others to be used in determining reasonableness. That section reads:

(1) A public nuisance is an unreasonable interference with a right common to the general public.

(2) Circumstances that may sustain a holding that an interference with a public right is unreasonable include the following:

(a) Whether the conduct involves a significant interference with the public health, the public safety, the public peace, the public comfort or the public convenience, *or*

(b) whether the conduct is proscribed by a statute, ordinance or administrative regulation, *or*

(c) whether the conduct is of a continuing nature or has produced a permanent or long-lasting effect, and, as the actor knows or has reason to know, has a significant effect upon the public right.

Restatement, supra, §821B. Comment d to that section explains:

It has been stated with some frequency that a public nuisance is always a criminal offense. This statement is susceptible of two interpretations. The first is that in order to be treated as a public nuisance, conduct must have been already proscribed by the state as criminal. This is too restrictive. . . . [T]here is clear recognition that a defendant need not be subject to criminal responsibility.

Restatement, supra, §821B comment d, at 89.

Our earlier decisions indicate that a business which is lawful may nevertheless be a public nuisance. For example, in *Spur Industries,* supra, we enjoined the defendant's lawful business. We explained that "Spur is required to move not because of any wrongdoing on the part of Spur, but because of a proper and legitimate regard of the courts for the rights and interests of the public." 108 Ariz. at 186, 494 P.2d at 708. This rule is widely accepted.

We hold, therefore, that conduct which unreasonably and significantly interferes with the public health, safety, peace, comfort or convenience is a public nuisance within the concept of tort law, even if that conduct is not specifically prohibited by the criminal law. . . .

The trial court's order granting the preliminary injunction is affirmed. By affirming the trial court's preliminary orders, we do not require that he close the center permanently. It is, of course, within the equitable discretion of the trial court to fashion a less severe remedy, if possible. The opinion of the court of appeals is vacated. The case is remanded for further proceedings.

NOTES TO PESTEY v. CUSHMAN AND ARMORY PARK NEIGHBORHOOD ASSOCIATION v. EPISCOPAL COMMUNITY SERVICES IN ARIZONA

1. *Private and Public Nuisance.* The tort of private nuisance is designed to protect the interest of lawful possessors of land to the use and enjoyment of that land. The tort of public nuisance is designed to protect rights common to the public, which, according to the Restatement (Second) of Torts §821B, include the public's rights to health, safety, peace, comfort, and convenience. The torts share the common element that the interference must be unreasonable. What evidence related to reasonableness did the court consider in each case? What other elements must a private and public nuisance plaintiff prove to prevail?

2. *Derivative Responsibility.* In *Armory Park Neighborhood Association*, Episcopal Community Services was enjoined even though it was the people they were trying to help who caused the problems for the neighborhood residents. As a general rule, an actor who sets in motion the forces that eventually cause the tortious act may be liable for the damages caused by the chain of events resulting from a nuisance. See Restatement (Second) of Torts §824. Thus, operation of a bar may be enjoined where its patrons are often noisy and intoxicated and use the neighboring properties for toilet purposes and sexual misconduct (see Reid v. Brodsky, 156 A.2d 334 (Pa. 1959)) and music concerts at a mall that were designed to attract customers could be enjoined because of the increased crowds and noise in a residential neighborhood (see McQuade v. Tucson Tiller Apartments, 543 P.2d 150 (1975)). In Mark v. State Department of Fish and Wildlife, 974 P.2d 716 (Or. App. 1999), the court held that allowing users "to parade naked throughout the year all over the wildlife area" was a public and private nuisance for which the Department could be held liable if it was not otherwise immune.

3. *Trespass, Nuisance, or Both* Often an intentional, unpermitted entry onto land results in both an interference with the landowner's interest in exclusive possession of the land and the landowner's interest in use and enjoyment of the land. In such cases, the landowner has claims for both trespass and nuisance. The two legal theories are compatible with one another, but one may wonder why they are separate theories.

Historically, the tort of trespass applied only to direct and immediate entries, walking on another's land, or throwing stones or water onto it. Nuisance applied to indirect or consequential entries, such as that caused by the seepage of water or chemicals onto the land. The directness requirement for trespass still appears in some states but is diminishing in importance. Some states have eliminated it as a requirement, and others interpret the requirement broadly. In the modern law of trespass and nuisance, the distinction between the two torts is based on the nature of the interest affected by the tortfeasor's conduct.

There are other differences between the legal theories of trespass and nuisance. For instance, the entry of some kind of object or at least a force of energy is necessary for a trespass but not for a nuisance. How small or intangible the object may be or whether energy rather than an object will suffice varies by jurisdiction. See Note 4 following Baker v. Shymkiv, above. Unlike trespass, nuisance requires consideration of the substantiality and unreasonableness of the invasion of the other's interest. Trespass allows for nominal damages while nuisance does not. Trespass and nuisance may also have different statutes of limitations, giving the choice between these legal theories procedural significance.

Problem
Public and Private Nuisance

The Jamesville Federated Church plays its bells over amplified sound speakers in various musical arrangements three times a day and four times on Sundays at regular hours for a period of approximately four minutes each time. The Impellizerris sought to enjoin the church from playing its bells, complaining that the bells affect their son, who has a neurological disease and is kept awake; affect the wife, who claims to have migraine headaches and muscle spasms as a result of an accident that are aggravated by the bells;

and generally affect the Impellizerris' ability to hold conversations in their home. They claim that the sound causes severe anxiety and emotional stress. Does playing the bells interfere with the rights protected by private nuisance? By public nuisance? Are the elements of private nuisance met? Public nuisance? See Impellizerri v. Jamesville Federated Church, 428 N.Y.S.2d 550 (1979).

Statute: NUISANCE DEFINED; ACTION FOR ABATEMENT AND DAMAGES; EXCEPTIONS

Nev. Rev. Stat. §40-140(1)-(3)(2017)

1. Except as otherwise provided in this section:

(a) anything which is injurious to health, or indecent and offensive to the senses, or an obstruction to the free use of property, so as to interfere with the comfortable enjoyment of life or property;

(b) a building or place used for the purpose of unlawfully selling, serving, storing, keeping, manufacturing, using or giving away a controlled substance, . . . is a nuisance, and the subject of an action. The action may be brought by any person whose property is injuriously affected, or whose personal enjoyment is lessened by the nuisance, and by the judgment the nuisance may be enjoined or abated, as well as damages recovered.

2. It is presumed:

(a) That an agricultural activity conducted on farmland, consistent with good agricultural practice and established before surrounding nonagricultural activities is reasonable. Such activity does not constitute a nuisance unless the activity has a substantial adverse effect on the public health or safety.

(b) That an agricultural activity which does not violate a federal, state or local law, ordinance or regulation constitutes good agricultural practice.

3. A shooting range does not constitute a nuisance with respect to any noise attributable to the shooting range if the shooting range is in compliance with the provisions of all applicable statutes, ordinances and regulations concerning noise. . . .

Statute: PROSTITUTION HOUSES DEEMED PUBLIC NUISANCES

Mo. Rev. Stat. §567.080(1) (2017)

Any room, building or other structure regularly used for any prostitution activity prohibited by this chapter is a public nuisance.

Statute: SMOKING PROHIBITED IN MUNICIPAL BUILDINGS

R.I. Gen. Laws §45-2-42(a) (2017)

(a) Smoking tobacco in any form is a public nuisance and dangerous to public health and is not permitted in any municipal building within the town of East Greenwich.

Statute: DRUG PARAPHERNALIA CONTROL ACT
720 Ill. Comp. Stat. 600/3(c) (2017)

(c) Any store, place, or premises from which or in which any item of drug paraphernalia is kept for sale, offered for sale, sold, or delivered for any commercial consideration is declared to be a public nuisance.

NOTES TO STATUTES

1. *Public Policy and Private Nuisance.* Statutory definitions of "nuisance" reflect states' particular public policy concerns. Many states accord special statutory protection to those who use agricultural activities, as the Nevada statute illustrates. Perhaps more surprising is the large number of states providing some exemption for shooting ranges. Observe, however, there are limits to the immunity from nuisance suits.

2. *Nuisance Per Se.* In many cases, proving that conduct is a public nuisance is simplified by a statute, which defines the conduct as a nuisance *per se*, distinguishing it from nuisances in fact, which required a more detailed balancing to determine unreasonableness. The Nevada and Rhode Island statutes are illustrative of the many activities and uses of land defined as nuisances per se. Others include "engaging in debt management service" without a valid license (Ill. Comp. Stat. 205 §665/17 (2009)); gambling houses (La. Rev. Stat. §13:4721 (2009)); rooms, buildings, and structures used by criminal street gangs (Mo. Rev. Stat. §578.430 (2009)); and owning a vicious dog (S.D. Codified Laws §40-34-13 (2009)).

III. Remedies

A plaintiff suing for trespass or nuisance may seek an injunction or damages. The court's choice between these alternative remedies depends on a balancing of the equities favoring each party as well as larger public policy issues. Boomer v. Atlantic Cement Co. is a classic case involving a cement company that created a nuisance (and perhaps also a trespass) by causing airborne particulates to fall on the land of seven neighboring property owners. While traditional doctrine would allow the plaintiffs to win an injunction against further pollution, the court was reluctant to shut down a $45 million cement plant that caused only $185,000 in damages.

Spur Industries v. Del E. Webb Development Co. is another classic case. The plaintiff developer of land for residential real estate complained that, as he built homes closer to a preexisting feedlot for cattle, those homes were less appealing to buyers because of the flies and stench. In *Spur*, the court considers the equity of enjoining the existing feedlot when the developer deliberately chose to build in that neighborhood. Taken together, the cases illustrate the variety of difficult remedial choices facing courts.

BOOMER v. ATLANTIC CEMENT CO.
309 N.Y.S.2d 312 (N.Y. 1970)

BERGAN, J.

Defendant operates a large cement plant near Albany. These are actions for injunction and damages by neighboring land owners alleging injury to property from dirt, smoke and vibration emanating from the plant. A nuisance has been found after trial, temporary damages have been allowed; but an injunction has been denied. . . .

The cement making operations of defendant have been found by the court of Special Term to have damaged the nearby properties of plaintiffs in these two actions. That court, as it has been noted, accordingly found defendant maintained a nuisance and this has been affirmed at the Appellate Division. The total damage to plaintiffs' properties is, however, relatively small in comparison with the value of defendant's operation and with the consequences of the injunction which plaintiffs seek.

The ground for the denial of injunction, notwithstanding the finding both that there is a nuisance and that plaintiffs have been damaged substantially, is the large disparity in economic consequences of the nuisance and of the injunction. This theory cannot, however, be sustained without overruling a doctrine which has been consistently reaffirmed in several leading cases in this court and which has never been disavowed here, namely that where a nuisance has been found and where there has been any substantial damage shown by the party complaining an injunction will be granted.

The rule in New York has been that such a nuisance will be enjoined although marked disparity be shown in economic consequence between the effect of the injunction and the effect of the nuisance.

The problem of disparity in economic consequence was sharply in focus in Whalen v. Union Bag & Paper Co., 208 N.Y. 1, 101 N.E. 805. A pulp mill entailing an investment of more than a million dollars polluted a stream in which plaintiff, who owned a farm, was "a lower riparian owner." The economic loss to plaintiff from this pollution was small. This court, reversing the Appellate Division, reinstated the injunction granted by the Special Term against the argument of the mill owner that in view of "the slight advantage to plaintiff and the great loss that will be inflicted on defendant" an injunction should not be granted (p.2, 101 N.E. p.805). "Such a balancing of injuries cannot be justified by the circumstances of this case," Judge Werner noted (p.4, 101 N.E. p.805). He continued: "Although the damage to the plaintiff may be slight as compared with the defendant's expense of abating the condition, that is not a good reason for refusing an injunction" (p.5, 101 N.E. p.806).

Thus the unconditional injunction granted at Special Term was reinstated. The rule laid down in that case, then, is that whenever the damage resulting from a nuisance is found not "unsubstantial," viz., $100 a year, injunction would follow. This states a rule that had been followed in this court with marked consistency. . . .

Although the court at Special Term and the Appellate Division held that injunction should be denied, it was found that plaintiffs had been damaged in various specific amounts up to the time of the trial and damages to the respective plaintiffs were awarded for those amounts. The effect of this was, injunction having been denied, plaintiffs could maintain successive actions at law for damages thereafter as further damage was incurred.

The court at Special Term also found the amount of permanent damage attrib-utable to each plaintiff, for the guidance of the parties in the event both sides stipulated to the payment and acceptance of such permanent damage as a settlement of all the controversies among the parties. The total of permanent damages to all plaintiffs thus found was $185,000. This basis of adjustment has not resulted in any stipulation by the parties.

This result at Special Term and at the Appellate Division is a departure from a rule that has become settled; but to follow the rule literally in these cases would be to close down the plant at once. This court is fully agreed to avoid that immediately drastic remedy; the difference in view is how best to avoid it.*

One alternative is to grant the injunction but postpone its effect to a specified future date to give opportunity for technical advances to permit defendant to eliminate the nuisance; another is to grant the injunction conditioned on the payment of permanent damages to plaintiffs which would compensate them for the total economic loss to their property present and future caused by defendant's operations. For reasons which will be developed the court chooses the latter alternative.

If the injunction were to be granted unless within a short period — e.g., 18 months — the nuisance be abated by improved methods, there would be no assurance that any significant technical improvement would occur.

The parties could settle this private litigation at any time if defendant paid enough money and the imminent threat of closing the plant would build up the pressure on defendant. If there were no improved techniques found, there would inevitably be applications to the court at Special Term for extensions of time to perform on showing of good faith efforts to find such techniques.

Moreover, techniques to eliminate dust and other annoying by-products of cement making are unlikely to be developed by any research the defendant can under-take within any short period, but will depend on the total resources of the cement industry nationwide and throughout the world. The problem is universal wherever cement is made.

For obvious reasons the rate of the research is beyond control of defendant. If at the end of 18 months the whole industry has not found a technical solution a court would be hard put to close down this one cement plant if due regard be given to equitable principles.

On the other hand, to grant the injunction unless defendant pays plaintiffs such permanent damages as may be fixed by the court seems to do justice between the contending parties. All of the attributions of economic loss to the properties on which plaintiffs' complaints are based will have been redressed.

The nuisance complained of by these plaintiffs may have other public or private consequences, but these particular parties are the only ones who have sought remedies and the judgment proposed will fully redress them. The limitation of relief granted is a limitation only within the four corners of these actions and does not foreclose public health or other public agencies from seeking proper relief in a proper court.

It seems reasonable to think that the risk of being required to pay permanent damages to injured property owners by cement plant owners would itself be a reasonable, effective spur to research for improved techniques to minimize nuisance.

---

*Respondent's investment in the plant is in excess of $45,000,000. There are over 300 people employed there.

The power of the court to condition on equitable grounds the continuance of an injunction on the payment of permanent damages seems undoubted.

The damage base here suggested is consistent with the general rule in those nuisance cases where damages are allowed. "Where a nuisance is of such a permanent and unabatable character that a single recovery can be had, including the whole damage past and future resulting therefrom, there can be but one recovery" (66 C.J.S. Nuisances §140, p.947). It has been said that permanent damages are allowed where the loss recoverable would obviously be small as compared with the cost of removal of the nuisance. . . .

Thus it seems fair to both sides to grant permanent damages to plaintiffs which will terminate this private litigation. The theory of damage is the "servitude on land" of plaintiffs imposed by defendant's nuisance.

The judgment, by allowance of permanent damages imposing a servitude on land, which is the basis of the actions, would preclude future recovery by plaintiffs or their grantees.

This should be placed beyond debate by a provision of the judgment that the payment by defendant and the acceptance by plaintiffs of permanent damages found by the court shall be in compensation for a servitude on the land.

Although the Trial Term has found permanent damages as a possible basis of settlement of the litigation, on remission the court should be entirely free to re-examine this subject. It may again find the permanent damage already found; or make new findings.

The orders should be reversed, without costs, and the cases remitted to Supreme Court, Albany County to grant an injunction which shall be vacated upon payment by defendant of such amounts of permanent damage to the respective plaintiffs as shall for this purpose be determined by the court.

JASEN, Judge (dissenting).

I agree with the majority that a reversal is required here, but I do not subscribe to the newly enunciated doctrine of assessment of permanent damages, in lieu of an injunction, where substantial property rights have been impaired by the creation of a nuisance.

It has long been the rule in this State, as the majority acknowledges, that a nuisance which results in substantial continuing damage to neighbors must be enjoined. To now change the rule to permit the cement company to continue polluting the air indefinitely upon the payment of permanent damages is, in my opinion, compounding the magnitude of a very serious problem in our State and Nation today.

In recognition of this problem, the Legislature of this State has enacted the Air Pollution Control Act (Public Health Law, Consol. Laws, c. 45, §§1264 to 1299-m) declaring that it is the State policy to require the use of all available and reasonable methods to prevent and control air pollution.

The harmful nature and widespread occurrence of air pollution have been extensively documented. Congressional hearings have revealed that air pollution causes substantial property damage, as well as being a contributing factor to a rising incidence of lung cancer, emphysema, bronchitis and asthma.

The specific problem faced here is known as particulate contamination because of the fine dust particles emanating from defendant's cement plant. The particular type of nuisance is not new, having appeared in many cases for at least the past 60 years. It is interesting to note that cement production has recently been identified as a significant source of particulate contamination in the Hudson Valley. This type of pollution, wherein very small particles escape and stay in the atmosphere, has been denominated as the type of air pollution which produces the greatest hazard to human health. We have thus a nuisance which not only is damaging to the plaintiffs, but also is decidedly harmful to the general public.

I see grave dangers in overruling our long-established rule of granting an injunction where a nuisance results in substantial continuing damage. In permitting the injunction to become inoperative upon the payment of permanent damages, the majority is, in effect, licensing a continuing wrong. It is the same as saying to the cement company, you may continue to do harm to your neighbors so long as you pay a fee for it. Furthermore, once such permanent damages are assessed and paid, the incentive to alleviate the wrong would be eliminated, thereby continuing air pollution of an area without abatement.

It is true that some courts have sanctioned the remedy here proposed by the majority in a number of cases, but none of the authorities relied upon by the majority are analogous to the situation before us. In those cases, the courts, in denying an injunction and awarding money damages, grounded their decision on a showing that the use to which the property was intended to be put was primarily for the public benefit. Here, on the other hand, it is clearly established that the cement company is creating a continuing air pollution nuisance primarily for its own private interest with no public benefit.

This kind of inverse condemnation may not be invoked by a private person or corporation for private gain or advantage. Inverse condemnation should only be permitted when the public is primarily served in the taking or impairment of property. The promotion of the interests of the polluting cement company has, in my opinion, no public use or benefit.

Nor is it constitutionally permissible to impose servitude on land, without consent of the owner, by payment of permanent damages where the continuing impairment of the land is for a private use. This is made clear by the State Constitution (art. I, §7, subd. (a)) which provides that "(p)rivate property shall not be taken for *public use* without just compensation" (emphasis added). It is, of course, significant that the section makes no mention of taking for a *private* use.

In sum, then, by constitutional mandate as well as by judicial pronouncement, the permanent impairment of private property for private purposes is not authorized in the absence of clearly demonstrated public benefit and use.

I would enjoin the defendant cement company from continuing the discharge of dust particles upon its neighbors' properties unless, within 18 months, the cement company abated this nuisance.

It is not my intention to cause the removal of the cement plant from the Albany area, but to recognize the urgency of the problem stemming from this stationary source of air pollution, and to allow the company a specified period of time to develop a means to alleviate this nuisance.

I am aware that the trial court found that the most modern dust control devices available have been installed in defendant's plant, but, I submit, this does not mean that better and more effective dust control devices could not be developed within the time allowed to abate the pollution.

Moreover, I believe it is incumbent upon the defendant to develop such devices, since the cement company, at the time the plant commenced production (1962), was well aware of the plaintiffs' presence in the area, as well as the probable consequences of its contemplated operation. Yet, it still chose to build and operate the plant at this site.

In a day when there is a growing concern for clean air, highly developed industry should not expect acquiescence by the courts, but should, instead, plan its operations to eliminate contamination of our air and damage to its neighbors.

Accordingly, the orders of the Appellate Division, insofar as they denied the injunction, should be reversed, and the actions remitted to Supreme Court, Albany County to grant an injunction to take effect 18 months hence, unless the nuisance is abated by improved techniques prior to said date.

SPUR INDUSTRIES v. DEL E. WEBB DEVELOPMENT CO.
494 P.2d 700 (Ariz. 1972)

CAMERON, V.C.J.

From a judgment permanently enjoining the defendant, Spur Industries, Inc., from operating a cattle feedlot near the plaintiff Del E. Webb Development Company's Sun City, Spur appeals. Webb cross-appeals. Although numerous issues are raised, we feel that it is necessary to answer only two questions. They are:

> 1. Where the operation of a business, such as a cattle feedlot is lawful in the first instance, but becomes a nuisance by reason of a nearby residential area, may the feedlot operation be enjoined in an action brought by the developer of the residential area?
>
> 2. Assuming that the nuisance may be enjoined, may the developer of a completely new town or urban area in a previously agricultural area be required to indemnify the operator of the feedlot who must move or cease operation because of the presence of the residential area created by the developer?

The facts necessary for a determination of this matter on appeal are as follows. The area in question is located in Maricopa County, Arizona, some 14 to 15 miles west of the urban area of Phoenix, on the Phoenix-Wickenburg Highway, also known as Grand Avenue. About two miles south of Grand Avenue is Olive Avenue which runs east and west. 111th Avenue runs north and south as does the Agua Fria River immediately to the west.

Farming started in this area about 1911. In 1929, with the completion of the Carl Pleasant Dam, gravity flow water became available to the property located to the west of the Agua Fria River, though land to the east remained dependant upon well water for irrigation. By 1950, the only urban areas in the vicinity were the agriculturally related communities of Peoria, El Mirage, and Surprise located along Grand Avenue and 1½ miles north of Olive Avenue, the community of Youngtown was commenced in 1954. Youngtown is a retirement community appealing primarily to senior citizens.

In 1956, Spur's predecessors in interest, H. Marion Welborn and the Northside Hay Mill and Trading Company, developed feed-lots, about ½ mile south of Olive Avenue, in an area between the confluence of the usually dry Agua Fria and New Rivers. The area is well suited for cattle feeding and in 1959, there were 25 cattle feeding pens or dairy operations within a 7 mile radius of the location developed by Spur's predecessors. In April and May of 1959, the Northside Hay Mill was feeding between 6,000 and 7,000 head of cattle and Welborn approximately 1,500 head on a combined area of 35 acres.

In May of 1959, Del Webb began to plan the development of an urban area to be known as Sun City. For this purpose, the Marinette and the Santa Fe Ranches, some 20,000 acres of farmland, were purchased for $15,000,000 or $750.00 per acre. This price was considerably less than the price of land located near the urban area of Phoenix, and along with the success of Youngtown was a factor influencing the decision to purchase the property in question.

By September 1959, Del Webb had started construction of a golf course south of Grand Avenue and Spur's predecessors had started to level ground for more feedlot area. In 1960, Spur purchased the property in question and began a rebuilding and expansion program extending both to the north and south of the original facilities. By 1962, Spur's expansion program was completed and had expanded from approximately 35 acres to 114 acres.

Accompanied by an extensive advertising campaign, homes were first offered by Del Webb in January 1960 and the first unit to be completed was south of Grand Avenue and approximately 2½ miles north of Spur. By 2 May 1960, there were 450 to 500 houses completed or under construction. At this time, Del Webb did not consider odors from the Spur feed pens a problem and Del Webb continued to develop in a southerly direction, until sales resistance became so great that the parcels were difficult if not impossible to sell. . . .

By December 1967, Del Webb's property had extended south to Olive Avenue and Spur was within 500 feet of Olive Avenue to the north. Del Webb filed its original complaint alleging that in excess of 1,300 lots in the southwest portion were unfit for development for sale as residential lots because of the operation of the Spur feedlot.

Del Webb's suit complained that the Spur feeding operation was a public nuisance because of the flies and the odor which were drifting or being blown by the prevailing south to north wind over the southern portion of Sun City. At the time of the suit, Spur was feeding between 20,000 and 30,000 head of cattle, and the facts amply support the finding of the trial court that the feed pens had become a nuisance to the people who resided in the southern part of Del Webb's development. The testimony indicated that cattle in a commercial feedlot will produce 35 to 40 pounds of wet manure per day, per head, or over a million pounds of wet manure per day for 30,000 head of cattle, and that despite the admittedly good feedlot management and good housekeeping practices by Spur, the resulting odor and flies produced an annoying if not unhealthy situation as far as the senior citizens of southern Sun City were concerned. There is no doubt that some of the citizens of Sun City were unable to enjoy the outdoor living which Del Webb had advertised and that Del Webb was faced with sales resistance from prospective purchasers as well as strong and persistent complaints from the people who had purchased homes in that area. . . .

May Spur Be Enjoined?

The difference between a private nuisance and a public nuisance is generally one of degree. A private nuisance is one affecting a single individual or a definite small number of persons in the enjoyment of private rights not common to the public, while a public nuisance is one affecting the rights enjoyed by citizens as a part of the public. To constitute a public nuisance, the nuisance must affect a considerable number of people or an entire community or neighborhood.

Where the injury is slight, the remedy for minor inconveniences lies in an action for damages rather than in one for an injunction. Moreover, some courts have held, in the "balancing of conveniences" cases, that damages may be the sole remedy.

Thus, it would appear from the admittedly incomplete record as developed in the trial court, that, at most, residents of Youngtown would be entitled to damages rather than injunctive relief.

We have no difficulty, however, in agreeing with the conclusion of the trial court that Spur's operation was an enjoinable public nuisance as far as the people in the southern portion of Del Webb's Sun City were concerned.

§36 — 601, subsec. A reads as follows:

§36 — 601. Public Nuisances Dangerous to Public Health

A. The following conditions are specifically declared public nuisances dangerous to the public health:

1. Any condition or place in populous areas which constitutes a breeding place for flies, rodents, mosquitoes and other insects which are capable of carrying and transmitting disease-causing organisms to any person or persons.

By this statute, before an otherwise lawful (and necessary) business may be declared a public nuisance, there must be a "populous" area in which people are injured:

... (I)t hardly admits a doubt that, in determining the question as to whether a lawful occupation is so conducted as to constitute a nuisance as a matter of fact, the locality and surroundings are of the first importance. (Citations omitted.) A business which is not per se a public nuisance may become such by being carried on at a place where the health, comfort, or convenience of a populous neighborhood is affected. ... What might amount to a serious nuisance in one locality by reason of the density of the population, or character of the neighborhood affected, may in another place and under different surroundings be deemed proper and unobjectionable. ...

MacDonald v. Perry, 32 Ariz. 39, 49-50, 255 P. 494, 497 (1927).

It is clear that as to the citizens of Sun City, the operation of Spur's feedlot was both a public and a private nuisance. They could have successfully maintained an action to abate the nuisance. Del Webb, having shown a special injury in the loss of sales, had a standing to bring suit to enjoin the nuisance. The judgment of the trial court permanently enjoining the operation of the feedlot is affirmed.

Must Del Webb Indemnify Spur?

A suit to enjoin a nuisance sounds in equity and the courts have long recognized a special responsibility to the public when acting as a court of equity:

§104. Where public interest is involved.

Courts of equity may, and frequently do, go much further both to give and withhold relief in furtherance of the public interest than they are accustomed to go when only private interests are involved. Accordingly, the granting or withholding of relief may properly be dependent upon considerations of public interest. ...

27 Am. Jur. 2d, Equity, page 626.

In addition to protecting the public interest, however, courts of equity are concerned with protecting the operator of a lawfully, albeit noxious, business from the result of a knowing and willful encroachment by others near his business.

In the so-called "coming to the nuisance" cases, the courts have held that the residential landowner may not have relief if he knowingly came into a neighborhood reserved for industrial or agricultural endeavors and has been damaged thereby:

> Plaintiffs chose to live in an area uncontrolled by zoning laws or restrictive covenants and remote from urban development. In such an area plaintiffs cannot complain that legitimate agricultural pursuits are being carried on in the vicinity, nor can plaintiffs, having chosen to build in an agricultural area, complain that the agricultural pursuits carried on in the area depreciate the value of their homes. The area being primarily agricultural, and opinion reflecting the value of such property must take this factor into account. The standards affecting the value of residence property in an urban setting, subject to zoning controls and controlled planning techniques, cannot be the standards by which agricultural properties are judged.
>
> People employed in a city who build their homes in suburban areas of the county beyond the limits of a city and zoning regulations do so for a reason. Some do so to avoid the high taxation rate imposed by cities, or to avoid special assessments for street, sewer and water projects. They usually build on improved or hard surface highways, which have been built either at state or county expense and thereby avoid special assessments for these improvements. It may be that they desire to get away from the congestion of traffic, smoke, noise, foul air and the many other annoyances of city life. But with all these advantages in going beyond the area which is zoned and restricted to protect them in their homes, they must be prepared to take the disadvantages.

Dill v. Excel Packing Company, 183 Kan. 513, 525, 526, 331 P.2d 539, 548, 549 (1958).

And:

> . . . a party cannot justly call upon the law to make that place suitable for his residence which was not so when he selected it. . . .

Gilbert v. Showerman, 23 Mich. 448, 455, 2 Brown 158 (1871).

Were Webb the only party injured, we would feel justified in holding that the doctrine of "coming to the nuisance" would have been a bar to the relief asked by Webb, and, on the other hand, had Spur located the feedlot near the outskirts of a city and had the city grown toward the feedlot, Spur would have to suffer the cost of abating the nuisance as to those people locating within the growth pattern of the expanding city:

> The case affords, perhaps, an example where a business established at a place remote from population is gradually surrounded and becomes part of a populous center, so that a business which formerly was not an interference with the rights of others has become so by the encroachment of the population. . . .

City of Ft. Smith v. Western Hide & Fur Co., 153 Ark. 99, 103, 239 S.W. 724, 726 (1922).

We agree, however, with the Massachusetts court that:

> The law of nuisance affords no rigid rule to be applied in all instances. It is elastic. It undertakes to require only that which is fair and reasonable under all the circumstances. In a commonwealth like this, which depends for its material prosperity so largely on the continued growth and enlargement of manufacturing of diverse varieties, "extreme rights" cannot be enforced. . . .

Stevens v. Rockport Granite Co., 216 Mass. 486, 488, 104 N.E. 371, 373 (1914).

There was no indication in the instant case at the time Spur and its predecessors located in western Maricopa County that a new city would spring up, full-blown, alongside the feeding operation and that the developer of that city would ask the court to order Spur to move because of the new city. Spur is required to move not because of any wrongdoing on the part of Spur, but because of a proper and legitimate regard of the courts for the rights and interests of the public.

Del Webb, on the other hand, is entitled to the relief prayed for (a permanent injunction), not because Webb is blameless, but because of the damage to the people who have been encouraged to purchase homes in Sun City. It does not equitably or legally follow, however, that Webb, being entitled to the injunction, is then free of any liability to Spur if Webb has in fact been the cause of the damage Spur has sustained. It does not seem harsh to require a developer, who has taken advantage of the lesser land values in a rural area as well as the availability of large tracts of land on which to build and develop a new town or city in the area, to indemnify those who are forced to leave as a result.

Having brought people to the nuisance to the foreseeable detriment of Spur, Webb must indemnify Spur for a reasonable amount of the cost of moving or shutting down. It should be noted that this relief to Spur is limited to a case wherein a developer has, with foreseeability, brought into a previously agricultural or industrial area the population which makes necessary the granting of an injunction against a lawful business and for which the business has no adequate relief.

It is therefore the decision of this court that the matter be remanded to the trial court for a hearing upon the damages sustained by the defendant Spur as a reasonable and direct result of the granting of the permanent injunction. Since the result of the appeal may appear novel and both sides have obtained a measure of relief, it is ordered that each side will bear its own costs.

Affirmed in part, reversed in part, and remanded for further proceedings consistent with this opinion.

NOTES TO BOOMER v. ATLANTIC CEMENT CO. AND SPUR INDUSTRIES v. DEL E. WEBB DEVELOPMENT CO.

1. *Remedial Choices in* Boomer. The *Boomer* court considered four alternative remedial measures: past damages, permanent (past, present, and future) damages, delayed injunction, and immediate injunction. What were the practical and policy considerations raised by the majority and dissent in evaluating these options?

2. *Remedial Choices in* Spur. The *Spur* court presents an additional remedial option, granting the plaintiff an injunction, but requiring the plaintiff to pay for damages the defendant suffers from the injunction. What policy justifications does the court offer to support this result?

3. *Coming to the Nuisance.* It is not unusual for courts to consider the "coming to the nuisance" doctrine when balancing the equities in search of an appropriate remedy. The majority rule, however, is that the fact that the plaintiff chose to move to the location of the nuisance is not a defense to a nuisance claim. See Restatement (Second) of Torts §840D. In Lawrence v. Eastern Airlines, Inc., 81 So. 2d 632, 634 (Fla. 1955), the Supreme Court of Florida explained the reasoning:

The majority view rejects the doctrine of coming to the nuisance as an absolute defense to a nuisance action. Support for the majority view is found in the argument that the doctrine is out of place in modern society where people often have no real choices as to whether or not they will reside in an area adulterated by air pollution. In addition, the doctrine is contrary to public policy in the sense that it permits a defendant to condemn surrounding land to endure a perpetual nuisance simply because he was in the area first. Another reason given for rejecting the doctrine is that the owner of land subject to a nuisance will either have to bring suit before selling his land in order to attempt to receive the full value of the land or reconcile himself to accepting a depreciated price for the land since no purchaser would be willing to pay full value for land subject to a nuisance against which he is barred from bringing an action.

Perspective: Encouraging Valuable Land Use

By granting or denying an injunction, the court is establishing property rights, saying which one of conflicting uses may prevail. In effect, however, an injunction is only a piece of paper, one the plaintiff can sell to the defendant for the right price. Thus, if the defendant's use of the land is the more valuable, the defendant may buy the plaintiff's right to stop the defendant's use. Bargaining between the parties may ensure that the more valuable use of the land continues. Awarding permanent damages, such as in *Boomer*, is another way of testing to see which use is more valuable. If the defendant is unwilling to continue its activity in the face of making a large payment, it may be that the plaintiff's use is more valuable. Stopping the activity might, in some cases, eliminate future harm and minimize permanent damages.

Commentators have suggested that there are two questions involved in nuisance remedies. The first is to decide whether an injunction or an award of damages is more appropriate. Injunctions are appropriate remedies when negotiations between the parties are feasible and damages are appropriate when there are obstacles to bargaining. The second issue is having to decide who should get the award. That decision may be made by contemplating the equities and by considering whether the plaintiff's damages or the defendant's damages are easier to calculate. See Guido Calabresi & A. Douglas Melamed, *Property Rules, Liability Rules, and Inalienability: One View of the Cathedral*, 85 Harv. L. Rev. 1089 (1972).

DEFAMATION

I. Introduction

The tort of defamation protects a plaintiff's interest in his or her reputation. In the traditional common law of defamation, all that a plaintiff was required to prove in order to recover damages was that the defendant had communicated a defamatory statement about the plaintiff to a third party. Although the plaintiff was not required to prove that the statement was false, proof by the defendant that the statement was true was a complete defense. Defamation was a strict liability tort because there was no requirement that the defendant intended to harm the plaintiff or created an unreasonable risk of harming the plaintiff.

In some circumstances, privileges protect people from liability even if they communicate false statements. Among the beneficiaries of these privileges are judges and legislators acting in their official capacities and people speaking in certain contexts, such as testifying in court, reporting news, and giving letters of recommendation. These privileges are either *qualified* (*conditional*) or *absolute*. The privileges protect even people who publish false, defamatory statements in such contexts. Qualified privileges can be lost, or *defeated*, if the privilege is abused. An absolute privilege provides complete protection from a defamation claim. Cases in this chapter illustrate the application of frequently asserted qualified and absolute privileges.

Since the 1960s, constitutional law decisions by the U.S. Supreme Court have changed the traditional strict liability character of defamation law. To protect people's free speech rights, the law requires plaintiffs to prove that the defendant was at fault with respect to the truth or falsity of the statement. A second change is the requirement that many plaintiffs prove falsity. These changes require attention to the type of damages the plaintiff seeks and the status of the plaintiff. The last section of this chapter considers in detail the modern constitutional law of defamation.

Henderson v. Henderson introduces the elements of a modern defamation claim. Pay particular attention to the elements of the plaintiff's case.

HENDERSON v. HENDERSON

1996 WL 936966 (R.I. Super. 1996)

WILLIAMS, J. . . .

The plaintiff [Susan R. Henderson] is the ex-wife of the defendant [Brian R. Henderson]. The parties were married in 1967 and had two children, Jill Henderson (daughter) and Brett Henderson (son), both of whom are now adults. The parties subsequently separated on October 28, 1989, and were officially divorced on May 15, 1991.

After the parties were separated in October 1989, the defendant began to send a steady stream of correspondences to the plaintiff at her sister Sarah Mancini's residence, where she was living at the time, and later to a home she shared with their daughter. These correspondences were addressed to the plaintiff, referring to her as "wacco" and "Sue T. Whore" on the envelope. The defendant also wrote numerous letters and correspondences to the parties' daughter referring to the plaintiff as "wacco" and "the whore." Additionally, the defendant sent copies of a letter to the plaintiff's father and her sister referring to the plaintiff as "Sue the whore," and copies of other letters to the plaintiff's father and stepmother claiming the plaintiff had mental problems. Moreover, the defendant initialized checks that were sent to the plaintiff that allegedly had obscene connotations.

On September 22, 1992, the plaintiff filed suit against the defendant accusing him of defamation. On June 5, 1996, the plaintiff made a motion for an order permitting discovery on the issue of punitive damages. The defendant responded on June 20, 1996, by moving to strike the plaintiff's claim for punitive damages. An evidentiary hearing was held before this court on July 3, 1996 and July 5, 1996, on the motion to strike. . . .

In Rhode Island, an action for defamation requires proof of "(a) a false and defamatory statement concerning another; (b) an unprivileged communication to a third party; (c) fault amounting at least to negligence on the part of the publisher; and (d) damages." Lyons v. R.I. Public Employees Council 94, 516 A.2d 1339, 1342 (R.I. 1986). Restatement (Second) Torts 558 (1977). "Any words, if false and malicious, imputing conduct which injuriously affects a man's reputation, or which tends to degrade him in society or bring him into public hatred and contempt are in their nature defamatory." Elias v. Youngken, 493 A.2d 158, 161 (R.I. 1985).

On the evidence before it, this Court concludes that the plaintiff has made a prima facie showing that defendant's statements are defamatory. The plaintiff has shown that the defendant's numerous references to the plaintiff as being mentally unstable and a "whore" are false and defamatory statements. There is no competent evidence in the record that these statements are true. This Court is also of the opinion that the initials the defendant placed on checks made out to the defendant [sic, plaintiff?], would be found not only to be false and defamatory but possibly obscene. These statements and terms were published on envelopes, letters, checks and postcards that were communicated to third parties, including the parties' daughter and the plaintiff's sister, who testified to this at the hearing. Additionally, the evidence indicates that there was fault amounting at least to negligence on the part of the defendant, and that the plaintiff suffered damages. The statements made about the plaintiff clearly impute the kind of conduct which injuriously affects a person's reputation.

The plaintiff argues that the weight of the testimonial evidence of the plaintiff, the parties' daughter and the plaintiff's sister, as well as the exhibits introduced, answers by the defendant to requests for admissions, and the portions of the deposition transcript read into the record, more than demonstrate facts sufficient to establish a prima facie showing of egregious conduct to warrant the imposition of punitive damages. This Court agrees.

This Court believes that a prima facie showing has been made that defendant's actions arose from spite or ill will, with willful and wanton disregard of the rights and interest of the plaintiff. This Court is also of the opinion that the competent evidence of record could support a finding that the defendant's statements were published with such malice and wickedness that they rise to the level of requiring punishment over and above that provided in an award of compensatory damages.

The defendant refers this Court to Johnson v. Johnson, 654 A.2d 1212 (R.I. 1995), a Rhode Island case in which punitive damages were denied when an ex-husband called his ex-wife a "whore." However, in this Court's opinion, the *Johnson* case is entirely different from the present matter. In *Johnson*, unlike here, the trial justice found that the ex-husband's statements were essentially truthful. . . . Furthermore, the defamatory statements in *Johnson* consisted of one incident, while here the defamatory statements occurred continuously over a period of almost three years, even after the plaintiff had initially brought this defamation suit.

This Court concludes that there are adequate facts to support an award of punitive damages in this case. This Court holds that the plaintiff established in the evidentiary hearing that a prima facie case for punitive damages exists. Accordingly, the defendant's motion to strike is denied, and the plaintiff may conduct discovery on the issue of punitive damages. . . .

NOTES TO HENDERSON v. HENDERSON

1. *The Publication Requirement.* The plaintiff must prove that the defendant published a communication regarding the plaintiff. The word "publication" is a term of art referring to any kind of communication from the defendant to someone other than the plaintiff. The communication must be *about the plaintiff* and defamatory, which means it is injurious to the plaintiff's reputation.

Illustration: You might write statements in a diary that are harmful to someone's reputation. If you keep the diary locked and hidden and show it to no one, there is no publication. Just making the statement in a diary is not enough to be a basis for a defamation action. If you show the diary to someone else, however, that act would be an intentional publication of the defamatory statement, whether or not you intended to harm the person to whom it referred. If a thief stole your *carefully hidden* diary and read its contents, you would *not* be treated as having published the statement.

As the example illustrates, *publication* does not have to take place in a newspaper or some other public medium. Many defamatory publications are in written form, whether in newspapers or books or private letters. Others have been memorialized in some other tangible form, such as film, videotape, or audiotape. These publications are referred to as *libel*. More transitory forms of defamation, such as spoken words, are defined as *slander*. Other communications, such as a silent gesture, may qualify as a slanderous rather than libelous publication; for example, pointing a finger at someone to indicate that the person is the thief.

How was the defamatory statement published in *Henderson*? Was it a libel or a slander?

The plaintiff is required to prove that the defamatory statement is "about him or her." This is no problem where the defendant publishes specific injurious statements naming the plaintiff. Vague references to the plaintiff's identity or defamatory statements about a group of which the plaintiff is a member are more troublesome. The key is that the statement can reasonably be understood as applying personally to the plaintiff.

2. *Defamation Damages and Fault.* The fault element in *Henderson* appeared in two parts of the analysis. First, the court cited a rule requiring proof of "fault amounting at least to negligence on the part of the publisher." This fault requirement refers to the care the publisher took in ascertaining whether the allegedly defamatory statement was true or false. This fault requirement is the result of constitutional modifications of the common law of defamation, which are discussed in detail later in this chapter. Second, the court referred to a requirement that the plaintiff prove malice and wickedness. This fault requirement refers to the publisher's motive in publishing the statement. To recover punitive damages in this jurisdiction, the plaintiff must prove ill will, spite, willful and wanton disregard of the rights and interests of the plaintiff. Later in this chapter, the requirement of proof of malice is discussed both in the context of privileges and of constitutional developments.

Statute: LIBEL AND SLANDER — SELF-PUBLICATION
Colo. Rev. Stat. §13-25-125.5 (2017)

No action for libel or slander may be brought or maintained unless the party charged with such defamation has published, either orally or in writing, the defamatory statement to a person other than the person making the allegation of libel or slander. Self-publication, either orally or in writing, of the defamatory statement to a third person by the person making such allegation shall not give rise to a claim for libel or slander against the person who originally communicated the defamatory statement.

Statute: ONE CAUSE OF ACTION; RECOVERY
Cal. Civ. Code §3425.3 (2017)

No person shall have more than one cause of action for damages for libel or slander or invasion of privacy or any other tort founded upon any single publication or exhibition or utterance, such as any one issue of a newspaper or book or magazine or any one presentation to an audience or any one broadcast over radio or television or any one exhibition of a motion picture. Recovery in any action shall include all damages for any such tort suffered by the plaintiff in any jurisdiction.

NOTES TO STATUTES

1. *Self-Publication.* A plaintiff who spreads the harm of a defamation by repeating it to others is prohibited from basing a claim on that retelling of the defamation. The Colorado statute codifies this rule. Does this discourage a defamed person from repeating the defamation to an attorney in the course of seeking advice? Does it discourage someone who has been defamed from discussing the defamation with a friend?

2. *Single Publication Rule.* Many states have adopted the single publication rule described in the California statute. It avoids multiple lawsuits over a single defamatory publication, even if that publication reaches many people. This protects both courts and potential defendants. Only one suit may arise from a single broadcast or publication of an edition of a book or newspaper, or a single exhibition of a movie. This rule also helps the plaintiff by allowing recovery of all damages suffered in all jurisdictions in one action. It helps the defendant by barring any defamation action between the parties for damages based on that publication in all other jurisdictions. See Restatement (Second) of Torts §577A. A new suit arises from the defendant's repetition of the defamation, however, in a new edition of a book or newspaper (in a paperback or evening edition, for instance, designed to reach a new audience) or a second showing of a movie. What incentives does this create for those who publish defamatory speech?

Perspective: Internet Publication

The increased importance of the Internet gives rise to the question of whether a defamatory statement published on the Internet is a single publication, even though many individuals may view a Web site. Commentators have taken opposing views. Odelia Braun has observed,

> The size of the audience on the Internet each day is up to a thousand times larger than any single publication of print media. Information is assembled purposefully to reach wider and wider audiences so that exposure potentially increases over time, in contrast to the diminishing impact of the print media due to its decentralization after publication. . . . By failing to remove defamatory material, an Internet publisher theoretically makes a conscious decision to leave that material on the website daily. If the publisher has sustained his maximum liability when he first publishes, he has no motivation to limit the harm.

Internet Publications and Defamation: Why the Single Publication Rule Should Not Apply, 32 Golden Gate U. L. Rev. 325, 332-333 (2002). By contrast, Lori A. Wood, *Cyber-Defamation and the Single Publication Rule*, 81 B.U. L. Rev. 895, 913 (2001) has concluded that

> [p]ublications on general access sites pose the very problems the single publication rule seeks to prevent—multiplicity of actions, undue harassment of defendants, possible excess recoveries for plaintiffs through multiple suits, unnecessary depletion of judicial resources, and unnecessary exposure of the court system to stale claims in which the evidence may have been lost, and witnesses may have died, disappeared, or suffered a loss of memory.

Which argument is most compelling?

II. Defamatory Statements

Because the tort of defamation is designed to protect a person's reputation in the community, a major focus of the cases is determining which statements actually do cause harm to reputation. Some statements are obviously injurious to a person's reputation while others are not. A statement may refer to a plaintiff directly or only obliquely. It may not be obvious why the statement would injure the person's reputation. A statement of opinion may be less injurious than a statement of fact. The cases that follow describe the classifications traditionally used to identify and distinguish types of slanderous and libelous statements.

A. Libel and Slander Per Se and Per Quod

When injury to reputation obviously will flow from a statement, the statement is described as *defamatory per se*. A statement that is libelous per se or slanderous per se can reasonably be understood from the context to be harmful to the plaintiff's reputation by itself, standing alone. When the likely injury is not apparent, the statement is said to be *defamatory per quod*. A statement that is libelous or slanderous per quod can be understood to be defamatory only by reference to additional, extrinsic facts not contained in the statement and/or damages the plaintiff suffered because of the statement.

Context is often relevant to determining whether a statement contains a factual assertion people are likely to believe is defamatory. The context of a statement may show that a person misstated something to be humorous and that no one would take the statement seriously, or it may show that a person exaggerated and overstated to emphasize a point and that no one would believe the assertion to be literally true. Context may show that a statement was just an expression of opinion, even though it might have sounded like a statement of fact. Statements understood in these ways are rarely defamatory.

Gifford v. National Enquirer explains what "defamatory" means and the different proof requirements for libel per se and libel per quod. The case focuses on the need for extrinsic evidence to prove the defamatory nature of statements that are not harmful standing alone. Agriss v. Roadway Express, Inc. also explains what "defamatory" means and the variety of approaches jurisdictions have taken to establishing the defamatory character of libels and slanders.

GIFFORD v. NATIONAL ENQUIRER

23 Media L. Rep. 1016, 1993 WL 767192 (D. Cal. 1993)

BAIRD, J. . . .

On June 22, 1993 Plaintiffs, Kathie Lee Gifford and Frank Gifford, filed the instant action against the *National Enquirer* [claiming that the *National Enquirer* had defamed them]. Plaintiffs are husband and wife, and are celebrities in the television industry. Kathie Lee Gifford is the co-host of the television talk show "Live with Regis and Kathie Lee," and Frank Gifford is a sports broadcaster and is currently a co-host of "Monday

Night Football" on the ABC Television Network. Defendant is the publisher of the *National Enquirer,* a national news tabloid.

The causes of action arise out of an article published by the *National Enquirer* on May 17, 1993, concerning the circumstances surrounding Mrs. Gifford's then pending pregnancy. In their complaint, Plaintiffs allege that the article, entitled *Kathie Lee's Baby Secret: The High-Tech, No-Sex Way She Got Pregnant,* contains statements that are false, deliberately defamatory, and totally contrived. . . .

Plaintiffs further allege that by publishing the article, Defendant has intentionally and maliciously misled the public, including Plaintiffs' fans, into believing, among other things:

> (a) that the Giffords are a "desperate pair" who resorted to artificial insemination in connection with the conception of their most recent child, (b) that the Giffords used a "shocking" and "controversial" laboratory technique of "sperm spinning" in an effort to avoid having another male child, (c) that the Giffords have abandoned one or more of their publicly-stated religious beliefs, and (d) that the Giffords are hypocrites who say one thing in the public, while doing the opposite in private.

(Complaint ¶2.) . . .

Plaintiffs seek damages for injury that has allegedly occurred to their personal and professional reputations, their careers, and for emotional distress. . . .

In order to state a cause of action for libel, a plaintiff must allege, among other things, that the defendant published a written statement about the plaintiff, and that the statement was "defamatory." There are two types of libel: libel per se and libel per quod. Words that are defamatory on their face are libelous per se, while words that are innocuous on their face, but defamatory in light of extrinsic circumstances are libelous per quod. A significant distinction between the two types of libel is that libel per quod requires the plaintiff to allege the extrinsic circumstances imparting a defamatory meaning to the words, and, just as significantly, to allege special damages.

Whether a statement is defamatory is an issue to be decided by the Court as a matter of law. Robinson v. Bantam Books Inc., 339 F. Supp. 150, 157 (D.C. N.Y. 1972). As the *Robinson* court stated, "[i]n libel actions the trial court must first determine whether a publication is libelous per se and, if not, the court must determine as a matter of law whether the writing is susceptible of a defamatory meaning derivable from extrinsic facts and circumstances which must be specifically pleaded and which must be supported by proof of special damages, that is, libelous per quod." *Robinson,* 339 F. Supp. at 157.

A statement is defamatory "if it tends to expose a person to hatred, contempt or aversion, or to induce an evil or unsavory opinion of him in the minds of a substantial number of the community, even though it may impute no moral turpitude to him." Mencher v. Chelsey, 297 N.Y. 94, 100 (1947). Furthermore, "[w]ether language has that tendency depends, among other factors, upon the temper of the times, the current of contemporary public opinion, with the result that words, harmless in one age, in one community, may be highly damaging to reputation at another time or in a different place." *Chelsey,* 297 N.Y. at 100.

In making this inquiry, the New York Court of Appeals has developed various standards to guide the decision. First, the court shall not "pick out and isolate particular phrases but will consider the publication as a whole." James v. Gannet Co., Inc., 40 N.Y.2d 415, 419 (N.Y. 1976). Second, "[t]he publication will be tested by its effect upon the average reader." Id. Third, "[t]he language will be given a fair reading and the court will not strain to place a particular interpretation on the published words." Id. at 420. Finally, "it is the duty of the court . . . to understand the publication in the same manner that others would naturally do." Id.

Applying these principles to the facts alleged in Plaintiffs' Complaint, this Court finds that Plaintiffs have failed to state a claim for libel per se. When condensed to their essence, the statements made in the article at issue here merely, on their face, state that Plaintiffs conceived their second child by means of artificial insemination, and that they employed the procedure of "sperm spinning" to increase the probability that this child would be a girl. Such medical practices are common enough in contemporary society that one could hardly claim that engaging in such a practice subjects one to "hatred, contempt or aversion," or induces "an evil or unsavory opinion of him [or her] in the minds of a substantial number of the community."

Although the article allegedly calls Plaintiffs' practices "shocking," "controversial," and "high-tech extremes," such sensationalization is no doubt immediately discounted by readers. This Court can take judicial notice of the fact that one who picks up a *National Enquirer* does so with the immediate caution that what they read is in large part rhetorical hyperbole. Such speech is not the type that libel law seeks to inhibit, nor is it the type that the First Amendment would see inhibited. See Greenbelt Coop. Publishing Assoc. v. Brestler, 398 U.S. 6, 13 (1970) (finding that "even the most careless reader must have perceived that the word [blackmail] was no more than rhetorical hyperbole").

Plaintiffs also allege that the article calls Plaintiffs a "desperate pair." However, such a statement is merely an opinion issued by the *Enquirer*, and opinions are not actionable under libel law in that readers are free to reject them and make their own.

In that Plaintiffs have failed to sufficiently allege libel per se, this Court must now determine whether they have adequately alleged libel per quod. In addition to the allegations discussed above, Plaintiffs have also alleged that the article misled the public into believing that Plaintiffs have abandoned one or more of their publicly-stated religious and moral beliefs, and that Plaintiffs are hypocrites who say one thing in public, while doing the opposite in private. As Plaintiffs have not alleged that the article directly makes such statements, but only makes the statements impliedly in light of other circumstances, Plaintiffs are essentially alleging libel per quod.

However, in order to sufficiently state a claim for libel per quod, Plaintiffs must *specifically* allege the extrinsic circumstances imparting a defamatory meaning to the words actually uttered. As to Plaintiffs' claim that Defendant has implied that Plaintiffs have abandoned one or more of their publicly-stated religious and moral beliefs, Plaintiffs have alleged no extrinsic evidence to support this. For example, Plaintiffs have failed to allege what their religious and moral beliefs are, and that they have made such beliefs public.

As to Plaintiffs' claim that Defendant implied that Plaintiffs are hypocrites who say one thing in public, while doing the opposite in private, Plaintiffs have alleged that Plaintiffs "do not believe in artificial insemination, and they have stated publicly that they would not use such a procedure." (Complaint ¶10.) However, even assuming that this allegation is true, this Court finds as a matter of law that Defendant's statement that Plaintiffs did use artificial insemination does not give rise to such a strong implication of hypocrisy that it would "tend to expose [Plaintiffs] to hatred, contempt or aversion, or to induce an evil or unsavory opinion of [them] in the minds of a substantial number of the community."

Therefore, Plaintiffs have failed to state a claim for libel per quod, and this Court hereby orders that Plaintiffs' libel claim is dismissed without prejudice. . . .

AGRISS v. ROADWAY EXPRESS, INC.
483 A.2d 456 (Pa. Super. Ct. 1984)

CIRILLO, J.

> The security of his reputation or good name from the arts of detraction and slander, are rights to which every man is entitled by reason and natural justice; since without these, it is impossible to have the perfect enjoyment of any other advantage or right.

1 W. Blackstone, Commentaries 134.

Appellant William Agriss sued his employer, Roadway Express, Inc., for what he considered a slight to his good name. A jury trial was held in the Monroe County Court of Common Pleas. After appellant had presented his evidence the court entered a nonsuit. This appeal followed. . . .

Appellant had been employed by Roadway Express since 1976 as a truck driver. In February 1979 he was elected as a shop steward for Teamsters Local 229, the union representing Roadway employees based at Roadway's facility in Tannersville, Pennsylvania.

On December 21, 1979, Agriss returned from a round trip to Hartford, Connecticut, and entered the Tannersville terminal. He was scheduled to begin his vacation that day, and went to the dispatcher's window to collect his vacation paycheck. The dispatcher told Agriss to see the driver foreman, Steve Versuk, before leaving. Versuk handed Agriss a company "warning letter," signed by Versuk and initialed by Roadway relay manager Joe Moran. The letter read:

> By reason of your conduct as described below, it is necessary to issue this notice of warning. On 12/21/79 at Tannersville, Pennsylvania you violated our policy (or contract) by opening company mail. Subsequent violations of any company policy or contract will result in your receiving more severe disciplinary action up to and including discharge in accordance with Article 44 of the Central Pa. Over-the-Road and Local Cartage Supplemental Agreement.

The accusation in the letter was false, as Agriss had never, on that or any other day, opened company mail. . . .

Shortly thereafter, Agriss flew with his girlfriend to Hawaii to spend the holidays. While Agriss was in Hawaii, Roadway driver Joseph Verdier heard stories about the warning circulating in the drivers' room at the Tannersville terminal. He heard other drivers and a Roadway dispatcher saying that Agriss was going to be fired for looking into company mail. . . .

Over the next year Agriss continued to receive comments and questions about the warning letter from Roadway workers and union officials. Agriss instituted this suit, claiming that Roadway had defamed him. Trial began on January 23, 1981. After the plaintiff rested his case, the court granted the defendant's motion for compulsory nonsuit, ruling that the plaintiff's evidence failed to prove a cause of action for defamation. The court en banc denied the plaintiff's petition to remove the nonsuit. . . .

Appellant proved, for purposes of overcoming a motion for nonsuit, that when he returned from his vacation speculation was rampant among his fellow employees and union men about what exactly he had done and whether he would be discharged for it. Obviously the charge of "opening company mail" implied more to some people than that he had received a benign reprimand. For a Roadway employee to be charged with opening company mail was highly uncommon. Appellant testified that in all his time as a union steward, during which he had dealt with "thousands" of grievances, he had never heard of an employee's being warned or cited for opening company mail. More-over, the specific misconduct alleged — opening mail he had no right to open — reasonably could be interpreted to call in question appellant's general character for honesty, integrity, or trustworthiness. In fact, appellant testified that the accusation prompted people to ask him what he was accused of stealing. Giving appellant the benefit of inferences to which he is entitled, the charge "opening company mail" was capable of impugning appellant's good name or reputation in the popular sense, and these are the interests that defamation law seeks to protect. [The court also concluded that the jury could reasonably have found that people under the control of Roadway published the defamatory statements contained in the letter by revealing its contents to third parties. The warning letter was distributed to three managerial employees of Roadway and to a union representative. Somehow the contents were spread to fellow employees. The court concluded that the question of whether it was the Roadway managers who spread the word should have gone to the jury.] . . .

[In addition, the] trial court held that the charge "opening company mail" was not "libel per se," and that because it was not, the plaintiff was obliged to prove special damages in order to recover. Appellant proved no special damages; thus the court's . . . ground for entering nonsuit.

Appellant quarrels mainly with the trial court's holding that the words "opening company mail" were not "libel per se." However, we are concerned also with what the court meant by "libel per se," and with the rule it applied upon determining that the words complained of in this case were not "libel per se." Implicit in the court's decision to grant nonsuit is a distinction between "libel per se" and "libel per quod," and between different burdens of proof which these two forms of libel are thought to require. We have come to the conclusion that the "per se/per quod" distinction is without validity in the modern law of libel, and should be abolished as a means of allocating the plaintiff's burden of proof in a libel case. We also conclude that the trial court erred in nonsuiting appellant on the grounds of a rule based on the "libel per se" concept. However, our task of correcting the error is difficult because the very meaning of "libel per se," let alone its legal significance, is an enigma in this jurisdiction.

The import of "per se" in a defamation case is a problem that has kept Pennsylvania courts going in circles for generations. Originally the term meant one thing when attached to slander, and something entirely different when attached to libel. In the courts these separate meanings and the separate rules they entailed gradually drifted toward, into, and among one another, until nowadays "per se" is used so inconsistently and incoherently in the defamation context that any lawyer or judge about to use it should pause and replace it with the English words it is intended to stand for. . . .

The difficulty the courts have had with "per se" springs directly from the historical distinction between libel and slander. Before going further, we should make that distinction. Libel may be defined conveniently as "A method of defamation expressed by print, writing, pictures, or signs." Black's Law Dictionary 824 (5th ed. 1979). Slander, broadly, is usually understood to mean oral defamation. Id. at 1244.

"Per se" first cropped up in defamation law in connection with slander. At early common law a person generally could not recover for slanderous utterances unless they caused him "special harm," meaning

> harm of a material and generally of a pecuniary nature . . . result[ing] from conduct of a person other than the defamer or the one defamed which conduct is itself the result of the publication or repetition of the slander. Loss of reputation to the person defamed is not sufficient to make the defamer liable under the rule . . . unless it is reflected in material harm.

Restatement of Torts §575, Comment b (1938). The common law courts' insistence that a plaintiff in slander prove "material harm" in turn "goes back to the ancient conflict of jurisdiction between the royal and ecclesiastical courts, in which the former acquired jurisdiction over some kinds of defamation only because they could be found to have resulted in 'temporal' rather than 'spiritual' damage." Restatement (Second) of Torts §575, Comment b (1977).

Early exceptions to the requirement of proving special harm were carved for slanders imputing crime, loathsome disease, shortcomings affecting the plaintiff in his business, trade, profession, or calling, or (later) unchastity to a woman. W. Prosser, Law of Torts §112 at 754 (4th ed. 1971). These "per se" slanders were supposed to be so naturally injurious that the law allowed recovery of general or presumed damages for loss of reputation, even without proof of actual injury.

"Per se" and its counterpart "per quod" were common law pleading devices used to indicate whether the plaintiff's cause of action depended on general or special damages. Francis Murnaghan, in *From Figment to Fiction to Philosophy — The Requirement of Proof of Damages in Libel Actions*, 22 Cath. U. L. Rev. 1, 13 (1972), explains:

> In common law pleading, the right to recover general damages meant that the portion of the writ employed for institution of the suit devoted to specification of damage, and introduced by the words "per quod," became inapplicable whenever damages were presumed. To fill the void, and to signify that something had not been overlooked, the draftsmen in such cases would simply insert "per se" where the allegations of damages, headed by the phrase "per quod" otherwise would be expected.

These archaic pleading terms stuck so hardily to slander actions that today "slander per quod" and "slander per se" retain their original meanings as, respectively, slander actionable only on a showing of special harm to the plaintiff, and slander actionable even without special harm. The substantive law of defamation continues to recognize the original four categories of slander "actionable per se," see Restatement (Second), supra, §570, with all other slanders actionable only on a showing of special harm, see id., §575.

The per se/per quod distinction in libel originated differently. It was used to distinguish libel defamatory on its face ("libel per se") from libel not defamatory on its face ("libel per quod"). "Libel per quod" required a showing of facts and circumstances imparting a defamatory meaning to otherwise innocent or neutral words.[7] The plaintiff in libel per quod had to plead and prove the extrinsic facts

---

[7] Prosser's "classic case" of libel per quod is Morrison v. Ritchie & Co., [1902] 4 Fr. 645, 39 Scot. L. Rep. 432. Defendant's newspaper published a report that the plaintiff had given birth to twins. There were readers who knew she had been married only one month. Prosser, supra, at 763 n.30.

(the "inducement") imparting defamatory meaning, and the defamatory meaning (the "innuendo") imparted.

Originally, the per se/per quod distinction in slander, by which some slanders were actionable without proof of special damages while others were not, had no parallel application to libel. Any libel, whether libelous on its face or libelous only upon proof of extrinsic circumstances, was actionable with or without proof of special damages. The willingness of the law to presume damages for all libels as opposed to all slanders arose partly from the greater permanency, dissemination, and credence, and hence the greater harm, supposed naturally to attend defamations in printed or written form.

Inevitably, use of the identical per se/per quod terminology in two torts so similar in nature led to the distinct rules for libel and slander being blurred and melded together in the courts. The rule of slander per quod, requiring proof of special damages for any slander not coming under one of the four time-honored exceptions, came to be applied to "libel per quod" (i.e., libel not defamatory on its face). Under this "hybrid" rule of libel per quod, a libel not defamatory on its face was not actionable without proof of special harm. As a further twist to the hybrid scheme, a libelous imputation of crime, loathsome disease, unfitness for business or calling, or unchastity (the four imputations actionable without proof of special harm in slander) was held to be actionable without proof of special harm in libel, even if the libel were "per quod" (proven libelous through extrinsic facts).

The trial court *en banc* evidently applied this hybrid rule of libel per quod. It found appellant's evidence deficient for failure to show either "libel per se" or special harm. We agree that appellant's case did not establish that he suffered any economic or material loss amounting to "special harm." On the other hand, we believe that the words "opening company mail" did not require such proof of special damages under the hybrid rule because the charge imputed to appellant unfitness for business or calling and, arguably, criminal activity. We would, therefore, find that the trial court erroneously applied the hybrid rule to the facts of this case. However, we would be shirking our responsibility as an appellate court if we did not decide also whether the hybrid rule was the correct one to apply in the first place.

Although Prosser believed the hybrid rule of libel per quod to be the majority rule in America, see Prosser, Torts, supra, at 762-63, the American Law Institute, in both the First and Second Restatements of Torts, consistently has adhered to the traditional rule that all libels are actionable "per se," irrespective of special harm. Restatement of Torts §569; Restatement (Second) of Torts §569. The Institute views Prosser's hybrid rule as the "minority position." See Restatement (Second) of Torts §569, Comment b. Laurence Eldredge, for many years Court Reporter for the Pennsylvania Supreme Court, championed the ALI position and disputed Prosser's. See Eldredge, *The Spurious Rule of Libel Per Quod*, 79 Harv. L. Rev. 733 (1966). Eldredge listed Pennsylvania among those states holding that all libels, whether defamatory on their face or through extrinsic facts, were actionable without the need to prove special harm. Upon surveying Pennsylvania cases, we are unable either to confirm or disconfirm Eldredge's view. Instead, our survey demonstrates that Pennsylvania law on the subject remains fundamentally unsettled. We have also found that there are indeed cases to support the court *en banc*'s position that "libel per quod" is not actionable in Pennsylvania without special damages. However, searching analysis and contrary authority cast grave doubt on these cases' validity. . . .

. . . [T]here are sound policy reasons for allowing a plaintiff to recover for any libel even where he cannot prove special harm in the form of direct economic or pecuniary injury. As Justice Eagen said in Gaetano v. Sharon Herald Co., 231 A.2d 753, at 755 (Pa. 1967),

> The most important function of an action for defamation is to give the innocent and injured plaintiff a public vindication of his good name. Its primary purpose is to restore his unjustly tarnished reputation, and "reputation is the estimation in which one's character is held by his neighbors or associates." Restatement, Torts §577, comment b (1938).

By its very nature, injury to reputation does not work its greatest mischief in the form of monetary loss. Where an individual is made the victim of a false, malicious, and defamatory libel published to third persons, it is unfair to hold that vindication of his good name in the courts depends upon proof that the injury to his reputation has injured him economically as well. Once reputational damage alone is proven, the plaintiff in libel has proven his entitlement to recovery, and to make that recovery contingent on whether the damage was done by words "defamatory on their face" merely adds another irrelevant factor to the equation.

The perceived requirement of "special damages" has been narrowly interpreted by trial courts in Pennsylvania. It is seen as a complete bar to relief in defamation if the plaintiff fails to prove that reputational injury has caused concrete economic loss computable in dollars. These cases are disapproved to the extent they conflict with the rule we announce today: a plaintiff in libel in Pennsylvania need not prove special damages or harm in order to recover; he may recover for any injury done his reputation and for any other injury of which the libel is the legal cause. Courts in libel cases should be guided by the same general rules regarding damages that govern other types of tort recovery.

The order of the court *en banc* refusing to take off nonsuit is reversed; appellant to receive a new trial in accordance with this opinion; jurisdiction relinquished.

NOTES TO GIFFORD v. NATIONAL ENQUIRER AND AGRISS v. ROADWAY EXPRESS, INC.

1. *Per Se and Per Quod Defamation.* Reading *Gifford* and *Agriss* together reveals the differences among jurisdictions in the treatment of libel and slander. What are the options? To understand the law in a particular jurisdiction, you must be able to answer the following questions: (a) Do libel and slander both have per se and per quod categories? (b) What makes a libel a per se libel and what makes a slander a per se slander? (c) What additional elements must a plaintiff prove if the libel is characterized as per quod and if the slander is characterized as per quod?

How would the *Gifford* and *Agriss* courts answer each of these questions?

Would the outcome in *Agriss* have been different if the court had adopted what it calls the "hybrid" rule?

2. *Employers' Privileged Communications.* An employer is entitled to send a warning letter to an employee without fear of a defamation claim because there is no publication to a third party. The employer is also entitled to communicate the contents to others with a legitimate need to know the information in the course of business, which, in *Agriss*, included two Roadway managers, the human relations manager in the company, and the employee's union representative. These *privileged* communications would protect the employer unless the privilege was exceeded by communication to others who do not have a legitimate reason to know. In *Agriss*, the court held that it was a jury question whether this privilege was exceeded. (Privileges are discussed in greater detail later in this section of the chapter.)

3. *The Fault Requirement.*   Neither the *Gifford* nor the *Agriss* court discussed any requirement that a plaintiff prove that the defendant was at fault in ascertaining the truth or falsity of the statement. In *Gifford*, the issue never arose because the court found the plaintiffs had failed to prove that the statements were defamatory, either per se or per quod. Similarly, in *Agriss*, the excerpt of the opinion is focused more on what statements are defamatory than on any underlying fault requirement. If a statement is not defamatory, it does not matter whether there was fault.

Problem
The Defamatory Content of Statements

The court in *Gifford* describes the generally agreed upon rules for when a statement is defamatory. Which of the following statements are defamatory?

A. The defendant characterized the architect's homes as "chicken coops." See Scott-Taylor, Inc. v. Stokes, 229 A.2d 733 (Pa. 1967).

B. The defendant characterized the politician as favoring "a little Communism." See McAndrew v. Scranton Republican Publishing Co., 72 A.2d 780 (Pa. 1950).

C. The defendant accused the township supervisor, who was considering purchasing for the township lands that he partly owned, of conflict of interest "and perhaps much more." See Redding v. Carlton, 296 A.2d 880 (Pa. 1972).

Problem
Per Se or Per Quod Defamatory Statements

The plaintiffs are a husband, wife, and 14-year-old son whose house was shown on television. A KCTV-5 newscaster reported, "Others told TV-5 News most of the trouble has been traced to just two drug-dealing juveniles and about a dozen suspected drug houses in the area." Then, as a picture of the plaintiff's house was shown for approximately four seconds, he said, "And we have slides of homes that these boys are occupying; we are not revealing the names, we have given these names to the police." The plaintiffs have no connections to drug dealing. Is this statement defamatory? Per se or per quod? See Pennington v. Meredith Corp., 763 F. Supp. 415 (D. Mo. 1991).

Statute: LIBEL

Cal. Civ. Code §45 (2017)

Libel is a false and unprivileged publication by writing, printing, picture, effigy, or other fixed representation to the eye, which exposes any person to hatred, contempt, ridicule, or obloquy, or which causes him to be shunned or avoided, or which has a tendency to injure him in his occupation.

Statute: SLANDER, FALSE AND UNPRIVILEGED PUBLICATIONS WHICH CONSTITUTE

Cal. Civ. Code §46 (2017)

Slander is a false and unprivileged publication, orally uttered, and also communications by radio or any mechanical or other means which:

1. Charges any person with crime, or with having been indicted, convicted, or punished for crime;

2. Imputes in him the present existence of an infectious, contagious, or loathsome disease;

3. Tends directly to injure him in respect to his office, profession, trade or business, either by imputing to him general disqualification in those respects which the office or other occupation peculiarly requires, or by imputing something with reference to his office, profession, trade, or business that has a natural tendency to lessen its profits;

4. Imputes to him impotence or want of chastity; or

5. Which, by natural consequence, causes actual damages.

Statute: LIBEL ON ITS FACE; OTHER ACTIONABLE DEFAMATORY LANGUAGE

Cal. Civ. Code §45a (2017)

A libel which is defamatory of the plaintiff without the necessity of explanatory matter, such as an inducement, innuendo or other extrinsic fact, is said to be a libel on its face. Defamatory language not libelous on its face is not actionable unless the plaintiff alleges and proves that he has suffered special damage as a proximate result thereof. Special damage is defined in Section 48a of this code.

Statute: SPECIAL DAMAGES

Cal. Civ. Code §48a(d)(1)-(2) (2017)

(4)(a) "General damages" means damages for loss of reputation, shame, mortification, and hurt feelings.

(b) "Special damages" means all damages which plaintiff alleges and proves that he has suffered in respect to his property, business, trade, profession, or occupation, including the amounts of money the plaintiff alleges and proves he or she has expended as a result of the alleged liable, and no other.

NOTES TO STATUTES

1. *Per Se and Per Quod Defamation.* The preceding opinions in *Gifford* and *Agriss* outlined the differences among jurisdictions in the treatment of libel and slander. The California statutes do not mention the phrases "per se" or "per quod," but the three California statute sections set out above suggest different treatments of the two types of defamation in that state. According to these statutes, what distinguishes a per se libel from a per quod libel in that state? What distinguishes a per se slander from a per quod slander? What different elements must a plaintiff prove to recover damages for per se and per quod defamations according to the statutes?

2. *Libel and Slander Compared.*   The statutes distinguish between statements classified as libel and those classified as slander. What justifies different proof requirements for statements a person hears and statements a person reads?

Perspective: Defamation by Radio and Television

The common law distinctions between libel and slander developed before television and radio were invented, requiring courts or legislatures to decide into which category publications on those media fell. Michael B. Farber, *"Actual Malice" and the Standard of Proof in Defamation Cases in California: A Proposal for a Single Constitutional Standard,* 16 Sw. U. L. Rev. 577, 582-583 (1986), argued that publications by such means should be considered libel:

> In California, defamation that is accomplished by means of electronic broadcast media, either radio or television, is slander, not libel. This runs contrary to the definition of the Restatement (Second) of Torts and to the recent trend of other state courts, which have increasingly held that defamation by electronic media is libel, not slander. If the distinction between libel and slander should be based on the greater ability of the printed or broadcast word to influence opinions than the merely spoken word, as has been suggested, then defamation by radio, television, tape recording, and other media of similar permanence and ease of transmission should be classified as libel, and the California statute should be amended.

In this classification debate, others have referred to the historical reasons for distinguishing between the two types of defamation. Libel was viewed as having a greater potential for damages because statements in a written form are more permanent and may therefore do harm repeatedly. Spoken words, as required for slander, are evanescent and transitory, and their effect not likely to be so severe. Comparing this reasoning to Mr. Farber's reasoning, should live radio and TV broadcasts be treated differently from pre-recorded broadcasts? What if live programming is being taped as it is being broadcast?

B. Opinions

In general, opinions are treated as nondefamatory. Cook v. Winfrey and Milkovich v. Lorain Journal Co. illustrate the protections defamation law offers to statements of opinion. Cook v. Winfrey provides an example of a test for whether a statement alleged to be defamatory is not defamatory because it is an opinion — a conclusion about which the hearer or reader is entitled to make up his or her own mind. In Milkovich v. Lorain Journal Co., the defendant asked the U.S. Supreme Court to create a special constitutional protection for statements of opinions. The Court evaluated the protections already given to nonfactual statements by the common law.

COOK v. WINFREY

975 F. Supp. 1045 (N.D. Ill. 1997)

KOCORAS, J. . . .

This matter is before the court on the defendant's motion to dismiss the plaintiff's amended complaint for failure to state a claim upon which relief can be granted. For the reasons set forth below, this motion is granted, and the complaint is dismissed.

The following factual allegations are contained in the plaintiff's amended complaint. We are obligated to assume the truth of these allegations for purposes of deciding the motion to dismiss, without regard to whether they are in fact true or false. Plaintiff Randolph Cook ("Cook") is a resident of Columbus, Ohio. Defendant Oprah Winfrey ("Winfrey") is a television talk-show host living in Chicago. Cook and Winfrey had a relationship in the past, during which time Cook asserts that he and Winfrey used cocaine on a regular basis. In January, 1995, Cook was in contact with several media organizations with regard to publishing articles pertaining to his relationship with Winfrey. While he was entertaining offers from these organizations, Winfrey made statements both publicly and privately to third persons concerning their relationship and drug use. Cook asserts that Winfrey made statements indicating that he was a liar, that he could not be trusted or believed, that he would be sorry if he told anybody else his story, and that they had never had a prior relationship. Winfrey allegedly made similar statements in the *National Enquirer* of February 18, 1997. Cook also was attempting to seek compensation for the publication of his experiences with Winfrey in early 1995. Due to the statements made by Winfrey (discussed above), Cook's opportunity to market his story was interfered with and he was prevented from entering into an agreement with any outlet to sell his story.

As a result of the statements allegedly made by Winfrey, Cook filed a complaint against her on January 16, 1997. . . .

Cook alleges that he suffered slander . . . when Winfrey was quoted in the *National Enquirer* of February 18, 1997 as saying that "I will fight this suit until I am bankrupt before I give even a penny to this liar" and that "it's [this suit] all a pack of lies." See Complaint ¶21. . . .

In Ohio, statements of opinion are "absolutely privileged" and cannot be the basis for a defamation suit. Whether a statement is an opinion or a factual assertion is a matter of law, to be decided by the court. In determining whether a statement is fact or opinion, Ohio courts look to the "totality of the circumstances," Vail v. The Plain Dealer Publishing Co., 649 N.E.2d 182, 185 (1995), citing Scott v. News-Herald, 496 N.E.2d 699 (1986). As such, a court must analyze the allegedly defamatory statement utilizing the following considerations: 1) the specific language used; 2) whether the statement is verifiable; 3) the general context of the statement; and 4) the broader context in which the statement appeared. An analysis of these factors shows that Winfrey's statements that this suit is a "pack of lies" and that Cook is a "liar" are merely opinion, and Cook cannot maintain an action for slander based on them.

With regard to the first factor, the specific language used by Winfrey indicates that her statements were her opinions and not statements of fact. A statement such as "I will fight this suit until I am bankrupt before I give even a penny to this liar" is generally not taken seriously and does not convey to a listener that the speaker is making a factual assertion. Rather, a reasonable listener would take such a comment as an indication that the speaker had a negative opinion of the subject of the comment. This factor ties in with factor 2, since statements such as "he is a liar" are not necessarily concretely verifiable or subject to factual scrutiny. Most people, when saying someone is a liar or something is a pack of lies, are expressing their dislike for that person or the information they heard, not setting forth a factual assertion. Thus, the first two factors indicate that Winfrey's statements were opinion and not factual assertions.

Considering the third and fourth factors together, the context in which these statements were allegedly made shows that Winfrey, if she even spoke these words, was not making factual assertions. The statements were contained in the *National Enquirer*, a paper known for its sensational stories about celebrities. In addition, the story itself clearly shows that Winfrey is not being quoted directly by the reporter, but rather is having comments she allegedly made to a "friend" passed on to the paper. The tone of the story is also an important consideration, since it attempts to show how outraged Winfrey was at the commencement of this suit and the comments purportedly made by Winfrey match the article's general mood. A consideration of all of these factors indicates that an average person would not have taken the comments allegedly uttered by Winfrey as statements of fact but rather as statements of opinion. We find, therefore, that the statements made by Winfrey were her opinion, and as such she is entitled to privilege in this case. Since she is entitled to privilege, the comments cannot serve as the basis of a slander suit under Ohio law, and Cook's allegations fail to state a cognizable claim. . . .

MILKOVICH v. LORAIN JOURNAL CO.
497 U.S. 1 (1990)

CHIEF JUSTICE REHNQUIST.

Respondent J. Theodore Diadiun authored an article in an Ohio newspaper implying that petitioner Michael Milkovich, a local high school wrestling coach, lied under oath in a judicial proceeding about an incident involving petitioner and his team which occurred at a wrestling match. Petitioner sued Diadiun and the newspaper for libel, and the Ohio Court of Appeals affirmed a lower court entry of summary judgment against petitioner. This judgment was based in part on the grounds that the article constituted an "opinion" protected from the reach of state defamation law by the First Amendment to the United States Constitution. We hold that the First Amendment does not prohibit the application of Ohio's libel laws to the alleged defamations contained in the article. . . .

Since the latter half of the 16th century, the common law has afforded a cause of action for damage to a person's reputation by the publication of false and defamatory statements. . . .

However, due to concerns that unduly burdensome defamation laws could stifle valuable public debate, the privilege of "fair comment" was incorporated into the common law as an affirmative defense to an action for defamation. "The principle of 'fair comment' afford[ed] legal immunity for the honest expression of opinion on matters of legitimate public interest when based upon a true or privileged statement of fact." 1 F. Harper & F. James, Law of Torts §5.28, p.456 (1956) (footnote omitted). As this statement implies, comment was generally privileged when it concerned a matter of public concern, was upon true or privileged facts, represented the actual opinion of the speaker, and was not made solely for the purpose of causing harm. See Restatement of Torts, supra, §606. "According to the majority rule, the privilege of fair comment applied only to an expression of opinion and not to a false statement of fact, whether it was expressly stated or implied from an expression of opinion." Restatement (Second) of Torts, supra, §566, Comment a. Thus under the common law, the privilege of "fair comment" was the device employed to strike the appropriate balance between the need for vigorous public discourse and the need to redress injury to citizens wrought by invidious or irresponsible speech. . . .

Respondents would have us recognize, in addition to the established safeguards discussed above, still another First-Amendment-based protection for defamatory statements which are categorized as "opinion" as opposed to "fact." For this proposition they rely principally on the following dictum from our opinion in Gertz v. Robert Welch, Inc., 418 U.S. 323 (1974):

> Under the First Amendment there is no such thing as a false idea. However pernicious an opinion may seem, we depend for its correction not on the conscience of judges and juries but on the competition of other ideas. But there is no constitutional value in false statements of fact. 418 U.S., at 339-340.

Judge Friendly appropriately observed that this passage "has become the opening salvo in all arguments for protection from defamation actions on the ground of opinion, even though the case did not remotely concern the question." Cianci v. New Times Publishing Co., 639 F.2d 54, 61 (CA2 1980). Read in context, though, the fair meaning of the passage is to equate the word "opinion" in the second sentence with the word "idea" in the first sentence. Under this view, the language was merely a reiteration of Justice Holmes' classic "marketplace of ideas" concept. See Abrams v. United States, 250 U.S. 616, 630 (1919) (dissenting opinion) ("[T]he ultimate good desired is better reached by free trade in ideas —. . . the best test of truth is the power of the thought to get itself accepted in the competition of the market").

Thus, we do not think this passage from *Gertz* was intended to create a wholesale defamation exemption for anything that might be labeled "opinion." See *Cianci*, supra, at 62, n.10 (The "marketplace of ideas" origin of this passage "points strongly to the view that the 'opinions' held to be constitutionally protected were the sort of thing that could be corrected by discussion"). Not only would such an interpretation be contrary to the tenor and context of the passage, but it would also ignore the fact that expressions of "opinion" may often imply an assertion of objective fact.

If a speaker says, "In my opinion John Jones is a liar," he implies a knowledge of facts which lead to the conclusion that Jones told an untruth. Even if the speaker states the facts upon which he bases his opinion, if those facts are either incorrect or incomplete, or if his assessment of them is erroneous, the statement may still imply a false assertion of fact. Simply couching such statements in terms of opinion does not dispel these implications; and the statement, "In my opinion Jones is a liar," can cause as much damage to reputation as the statement, "Jones is a liar." As Judge Friendly aptly stated: "[It] would be destructive of the law of libel if a writer could escape liability for accusations of [defamatory conduct] simply by using, explicitly or implicitly, the words 'I think.'" See *Cianci, supra,* at 64. It is worthy of note that at common law, even the privilege of fair comment did not extend to "a false statement of fact, whether it was expressly stated or implied from an expression of opinion." Restatement (Second) of Torts, §566, Comment *a* (1977).

Apart from their reliance on the *Gertz* dictum, respondents do not really contend that a statement such as, "In my opinion John Jones is a liar," should be protected by a separate privilege for "opinion" under the First Amendment. But they do contend that in every defamation case the First Amendment mandates an inquiry into whether a statement is "opinion" or "fact," and that only the latter statements may be actionable. They propose that a number of factors developed by the lower courts (in what we hold was a mistaken reliance on the *Gertz* dictum) be considered in deciding which is which. But we think the "breathing space" which "[f]reedoms of expression require in order to survive," Philadelphia Newspapers, Inc. v. Hepps, 475 U.S. 767, 772 (1986) (quoting New York Times Co. v. Sullivan, 376 U.S. 254, at 272 (1964)), is adequately secured by existing constitutional doctrine without the creation of an artificial dichotomy between "opinion" and fact.

Foremost, we think *Hepps* stands for the proposition that a statement on matters of public concern must be provable as false before there can be liability under state defamation law, at least in situations, like the present, where a media defendant is involved. Thus, unlike the statement, "In my opinion Mayor Jones is a liar," the statement, "In my opinion Mayor Jones shows his abysmal ignorance by accepting the teachings of Marx and Lenin," would not be actionable. *Hepps* ensures that a statement of opinion relating to matters of public concern which does not contain a provably false factual connotation will receive full constitutional protection.

Next, the *Bresler-Letter Carriers-Falwell* line of cases provides protection for statements that cannot "reasonably [be] interpreted as stating actual facts" about an individual. Hustler Magazine, Inc. v. Falwell, 485 U.S. 46, 50 (1988). [See also Greenbelt Coop. Publishing Assoc. v. Bresler, 398 U.S. 6, 13 (1970); Letter Carriers v. Austin, 418 U.S. 264 (1974).] This provides assurance that public debate will not suffer for lack of "imaginative expression" or the "rhetorical hyperbole" which has traditionally added much to the discourse of our Nation. See id., at 53-55. . . .

We are not persuaded that, in addition to these protections, an additional separate constitutional privilege for "opinion" is required to ensure the freedom of expression guaranteed by the First Amendment. The dispositive question in the present case then becomes whether a reasonable factfinder could conclude that the statements in the Diadiun column imply an assertion that petitioner Milkovich perjured himself in a judicial proceeding. We think this question must be answered in the affirmative. As the Ohio Supreme Court itself observed: "[T]he clear impact in some nine sentences and a caption is that [Milkovich] 'lied at the hearing after . . . having given his solemn oath to tell the truth.'" *Scott,* 496 N.E.2d, at 707. This is not the sort of loose, figurative, or hyperbolic language which would negate the impression that the writer was seriously maintaining that petitioner committed the crime of perjury. Nor does the general tenor of the article negate this impression.

We also think the connotation that petitioner committed perjury is sufficiently factual to be susceptible of being proved true or false. A determination whether petitioner lied in this instance can be made on a core of objective evidence by comparing, inter alia, petitioner's testimony before the OHSAA [Ohio High School Athletic Association] board with his subsequent testimony before the trial court. As the *Scott* court noted regarding the plaintiff in that case: "[W]hether or not H. Don Scott did indeed perjure himself is certainly verifiable by a perjury action with evidence adduced from the transcripts and witnesses present at the hearing. Unlike a subjective assertion the averred defamatory language is an articulation of an objectively verifiable event." Id., at 252, 496 N.E.2d, at 707. So too with petitioner Milkovich.

The numerous decisions discussed above establishing First Amendment protection for defendants in defamation actions surely demonstrate the Court's recognition of the Amendment's vital guarantee of free and uninhibited discussion of public issues. But there is also another side to the equation; we have regularly acknowledged the "important social values which underlie the law of defamation," and recognized that "[s]ociety has a pervasive and strong interest in preventing and redressing attacks upon reputation." Rosenblatt v. Baer, 383 U.S. 75, 86 (1966). Justice Stewart in that case put it with his customary clarity:

> The right of a man to the protection of his own reputation from unjustified invasion and wrongful hurt reflects no more than our basic concept of the essential dignity and worth of every human being — a concept at the root of any decent system of ordered liberty. . . .
>
> The destruction that defamatory falsehood can bring is, to be sure, often beyond the capacity of the law to redeem. Yet, imperfect though it is, an action for damages is the only hope for vindication or redress the law gives to a man whose reputation has been falsely dishonored. Id., at 92-93 (concurring opinion).

We believe our decision in the present case holds the balance true. The judgment of the Ohio Court of Appeals is reversed, and the case is remanded for further proceedings not inconsistent with this opinion.

Reversed.

NOTES TO COOK v. WINFREY AND MILKOVICH v. LORAIN JOURNAL CO.

1. *Factual and Nonfactual Statements.* Compare the tests used in *Cook* and *Milkovich* to determine which statements are actionable defamation and which are protected nonfactual assertions. The *Cook* "totality of the circumstances" test has four specific factors. The *Milkovich* test must be inferred from the Court's discussion of the facts of that case. How do the tests differ?

2. *The Importance of Context.* Both cases involved a statement that the plaintiff had lied. Why is only one statement actionably defamatory? If the court in *Cook* had applied the test from *Milkovich*, would the outcome have been different? If the Court in *Milkovich* had applied the test from *Cook* would the result have been different?

3. *"Opinion" as a Matter of Law.* While Judge Kocoras's reasoning in Cook v. Winfrey seems quite reasonable, the United States Court of Appeals for the Seventh Circuit reversed the grant of summary judgment motion on appeal:

> Although it is certainly correct that the Ohio constitution affords an absolute privilege to expressions of opinion, the conclusion that the privilege applied to the allegedly defamatory statements in this case required the district court to resolve factual issues that should not be reached on a motion to dismiss under Rule 12(b)(c). The Ohio Supreme Court has held that a court assessing whether speech is protected opinion "must consider the totality of the circumstances" [listing the factors applied by Judge Kocoras in the district court]. Bearing these factors in mind, it is not possible to say as a

matter of law that Cook could prove no set of facts consistent with the amended complaint that would remove the alleged statements from the realm of protected opinion. In addition, Cook points to one Ohio opinion that observes that the statement "In my opinion Jones is a liar" is really a factual assertion masked as opinion, and is therefore not privileged. This is enough to reinforce the point that determining whether or not Winfrey's alleged statements were, in all the circumstances, opinions or assertions of fact requires an inquiry that goes beyond the allegations of the complaint into a consideration of the context in which the statements were uttered. It was therefore error for the district court to grant Winfrey's motion to dismiss . . . and we reverse.

Cook v. Winfrey, 141 F.3d 322, 330 (8th Cir. 1998). There are two lessons from this reversal. First, although one may disguise a factual statement as an opinion, courts may look past the disguise. Second, although judges may reasonably disagree on the application of summary judgment standards, the higher court's view prevails.

Problem
Fact Versus Opinion

Which of the following statements is/are actionably defamatory?

A. While Bloch's suit against Hoffman was pending, Hoffman made statements to Bloch's friend saying: "Bloch was a scumbag [who] doesn't pay his bills"; "Bloch was an incompetent attorney with no integrity"; that "representing Bloch was like representing a Nuremberg war criminal"; and that "Bloch was going to be very sorry he had brought an action against Hoffman and that he (Hoffman) was going to own Bloch's practice, 'the only thing of worth that [Bloch] had.'" See Schwartz v. Bloch, 2002 WL 374149 (Cal. App. 2002) (unpublished opinion) (comparing the above to statements from other cases including descriptions of another as a "creepazoid attorney" and a "loser wannabe lawyer").

B. Defending the university's punitive actions against a student against whom criminal charges were dismissed, Woodruff, a university employee, stated, "The information generated by the (university) police definitely met the definition of sexual battery, and certainly was a violation of the student code of conduct. It's not like some people want to make out, that this was two drunk people having a good time, and one of them felt bad about it the next day. For them to say (Mallory) was treated unfairly just seems kind of ridiculous, from my perspective. He definitely committed a sexual battery, from the information that was gathered." See Mallory v. Ohio University, 2001 WL 1631329 (Ohio Ct. App. 2001) (unreported opinion).

C. In a letter to the editor that appeared in the newspaper, the author accused the landlord of forcing a tenant, a grocery store, out of business by charging "exorbitant rent" and describing the landlord as a "ruthless speculator." See Wampler v. Higgins, 752 N.E.2d 962 (Ohio 2001).

III. Qualified and Absolute Privileges

Qualified and *absolute privileges* protect people who publish statements in situations where free expression is particularly important. The traditional common law of defamation did not require the plaintiff to prove that the defendant was at fault or even that the defamatory statement was false. Easy recovery created a fear that liability for defamation might *chill* (discourage) socially important speech. The common law's response to this fear was the development of privileges that protect a variety of types of speech necessary to the effective functioning of businesses and the government. These rules apply to both libel and slander.

An *absolute privilege* is the highest level of protection for socially important speech. Almost all absolute privileges involve speech by participants in governmental operations. A person defaming another in such a context is totally protected from liability. For instance, judges, attorneys, parties, witnesses, judicial personnel, and jurors publishing defamatory statements related to and part of a judicial proceeding have an absolute privilege. Similarly, participants in legislative proceedings and some federal and state executive and administrative officials are protected by absolute privilege for statements made in the course of carrying out their official duties. A significant nongovernmental communication that is absolutely privileged is a husband or wife's absolute privilege to make defamatory statements about a third party to the other spouse.

A *qualified privilege* (sometimes called a "conditional privilege") protects communications involving legitimate interests of speakers and recipients. The privilege to speak when defending one's rights, such as when responding to another's defamatory statements in order to protect one's own reputation, is similar to a "self-defense" privilege. An analogous privilege is given to speakers acting to protect the legitimate rights of others — the right of a person to know that his or her fiancé is a convicted murderer, of a prospective employer to know the qualifications of a job applicant, or of the public to receive reports on the functioning of the government.

Qualified privileges provide less than total protection because they may be *defeated*. Because these privileges protect speech within a particular social context to promote particular social interests, a plaintiff's proof of *excessive publication*, which is communication beyond the group of people who have a legitimate interest in the statement, or *express malice*, which is a bad motive, would overcome the privilege in traditional common law defamation. Additionally, in the modern law of defamation, *proof of fault* may overcome the privilege.

The following two cases explore the application and boundaries of absolute and qualified privileges. In Johnson v. Queenan, the defendant told a number of people that the plaintiff had raped her. The court considers which of these publications were privileged. Statements to some were absolutely privileged. Statements to the others were qualifiedly privileged. Shaw v. R.J. Reynolds Tobacco Co. is concerned with qualified privileges and how to defeat them. The court describes the elements of qualified privilege. The person asserting the privilege establishes that he had a legitimate interest to be protected, while the person seeking to defeat the privilege must establish that the other criteria are not met. The factual analysis in *Shaw* focuses on proof of express malice, which, if proved by the plaintiff, would defeat the privilege.

JOHNSON v. QUEENAN

12 Mass. L. Rptr. 461 (Mass. Super. Ct. 2000)

GRABAU, J. . . .

The undisputed material facts as established by the summary judgment record are as follows. Johnson alleges that Queenan raped and assaulted her in a bedroom at a private party that both Johnson and Queenan attended on November 29, 1996 in Westford, Massachusetts. Johnson acknowledges being in the bedroom and kissing Queenan. Johnson, however, contends that although she repeatedly told Queenan that she did not want to have intercourse, he held her down on the bed and raped her. Queenan denies raping Johnson, but acknowledges that Johnson was crying when he left the bedroom.

Upon leaving the bedroom, Johnson located her friend Ryan Dadmun (Dadmun) who was also at the party and told him that Queenan had just raped her. Johnson asked Dadmun to drive her home. She did not report the rape to anyone else that evening.

The next morning, Johnson telephoned Dadmun and asked him to help her make arrangements to see a doctor. After several telephone calls to various health care providers, Johnson realized that her only treatment option was the emergency room. Reluctant to go to the emergency room, Johnson asked Dadmun to bring her to her friend, Staci Scolovino's (Scolovino) home. After Johnson explained to Scolovino that Queenan raped her, Scolovino brought her to the Emerson Hospital emergency room. Johnson was not treated immediately and left the emergency room with Scolovino because the rape specialist at the emergency room was not on duty and Johnson was scheduled to work later that afternoon.

Later that evening, Dadmun again drove Johnson to Emerson Hospital's emergency room. Dr. Ingrid Balcolm and Nurse Heidi Crim (Nurse Crim) examined and treated Johnson in accordance with Massachusetts sexual assault protocol. Pursuant to G.L. c. 112 §121/2, Nurse Crim reported the alleged incident to the Westford Police Department, however, at Johnson's request Nurse Crim did not provide the police with Johnson's name. Nurse Crim encouraged Johnson to discuss the incident with her parents or a close family friend.

Based on Nurse Crim's report, the Westford Police Department began a criminal investigation of the alleged incident. On December 5, 1996, as part of this investigation, Detective Michael Perron (Detective Perron) met with the Dean of Students, Carla Scuzzarella (Scuzzarella) at Johnson's school and told her that he needed to speak with Johnson. Scuzzarella arranged to have Johnson meet privately with Detective Perron. During the meeting, Johnson gave Detective Perron her account of the events of November 29, 1996. Detective Perron also encouraged Johnson to talk to her parents and accompanied her home, where Johnson told her mother about the incident involving Queenan.

As a result of the investigation, the Westford Police charged Queenan with rape and assault and battery. . . . The Grand Jury, however, did not issue an indictment to Queenan.

. . . The plaintiff bears the initial burden of proving prima facie elements of a slander claim — "the publication of a false and defamatory statement by spoken words of and concerning the plaintiff." Ellis v. Safety Ins. Co., 41 Mass. App. Ct. 630, 635 (1996), citing Restatement (Second) of Torts §§558 and 568 (1977). . . .

STATEMENTS MADE TO DETECTIVE PERRON, ASSISTANT DISTRICT ATTORNEY BEDROSIAN, AND THE MIDDLESEX GRAND JURY

Johnson asserts that various statements made to Detective Perron, ADA Bedrosian and the Middlesex Grand Jury are privileged under Massachusetts law. Once the plaintiff meets its initial burden, the defendant has the burden to show that a privilege applies. "An absolute privilege provides a defendant with complete defense to a defamation suit even if the defamatory statement is uttered maliciously or in bad faith. A qualified or conditional privilege, on the other hand, immunizes a defendant from liability unless he or she acted with actual malice, or unless there is 'unnecessary, unreasonable or excessive publication,' and the plaintiff establishes that the defendant published the defamatory information recklessly." Mulgrew v. Taunton, 410 Mass. 631, 634 (1991). Johnson contends that her statements to Detective Perron, ADA Bedrosian and the Middlesex Grand Jury fall under an absolute privilege, thus immunizing her from any claim of defamation.

Statements made in the course of judicial proceedings which pertain to the proceeding are absolutely privileged and cannot support a claim of defamation, even if communicated with malice or in bad faith. Therefore, I find that all statements Johnson made to Detective Perron, ADA Bedrosian, and the Middlesex Grand Jury are protected under an absolute privilege because they pertain to the judicial proceeding and were made in the course of that proceeding.

STATEMENTS MADE TO NURSE CRIM, DADMUN, SCOLOVINO, AND JOHNSON'S MOTHER

Johnson also contends that her statements to Nurse Crim, Dadmun, Scolovino and her mother are conditionally privileged and thus protected against Queenan's defamation claim. Massachusetts recognizes certain privileges that are conditioned upon the manner in which they are exercised. See Sheehan v. Tobin, 326 Mass. 185, 190 (1950). One type of conditional privilege protects statements "where the publisher and the recipient have a common interest, and the communication is of a kind reasonably calculated to protect or further it." *Sheehan*, 326 Mass. at 190-91 (citations omitted). Where there is no dispute about the existence of the facts surrounding the publication, a judge must determine whether or not the privilege applies.

Here, after Johnson told Dadmun that she had been raped, he immediately brought her home. The next morning, Dadmun and Scolovino assisted Johnson in seeking medical care. Johnson told Nurse Crim about the alleged rape in order to receive the appropriate medical treatment. Johnson later confided in her mother after both Nurse Crim and Detective Perron encouraged her to do so, presumably to enable her to get proper emotional support. Thus, Johnson's publication to her two close friends Dadmun and Scolovino, Nurse Crim, and her mother are protected by a qualified privilege because the communications were reasonably calculated to further a common interest, namely Johnson's physical and emotional well-being.

Once a defendant asserts a claim of privilege, it is plaintiff's burden to prove abuse of the privilege or actual malice. In order to defeat a motion for summary judgment where state of mind, such as malice, is a material element, plaintiff must indicate "that he can produce the requisite quantum of evidence to enable him to reach the jury with his claim." Humphrey v. National Semiconductor Corp., 18 Mass. App. Ct. 132, 134 (1984), *rev. denied*, 394 Mass. 1102 (1985). Plaintiff provides no evidence to support a claim that Johnson abused the privilege through unnecessary, unreasonable or excessive publication, nor does he indicate that he can produce any evidence to enable him to reach the jury on the issue of malice. Based on the foregoing, Queenan has failed to provide sufficient evidence for a jury to infer that Johnson, without a privilege to do so, published a false and defamatory statement about Queenan. Thus, Johnson is entitled to summary judgment on Queenan's defamation counterclaim. . . .

SHAW v. R.J. REYNOLDS TOBACCO CO.

818 F. Supp. 1539 (D. Fla. 1993)

KOVACHEVICH, J. . . .

This cause came before the Court on Defendant's Motion for Summary Judgment . . .

Plaintiff was employed by Defendant from July 6, 1971 to December 6, 1989, and worked as a sales representative at the time of his termination. Plaintiff was terminated after Eli Witt, a customer of Defendant, alleged that the Plaintiff had stolen sixty cartons of cigarettes from the customer's warehouse facility. Prior to termination, Defendant conducted an inventory of the cartons of cigarettes in Plaintiff's vehicle. This inspection revealed that Plaintiff had an excess number of cartons in his van in violation of company policy, although the parties disagree as to why there was an overage. Plaintiff was tried and acquitted of the criminal charges filed by Eli Witt pertaining to the alleged theft. Following Plaintiff's termination, Dorothy Giantonio, a customer, asked a managerial employee of Defendant about the circumstances surrounding Plaintiff's departure from the company. This employee responded that the plaintiff had been fired for stealing cigarettes from another customer. Dorothy Giantonio was an acquaintance of Plaintiff and did not believe that he had stolen anything. She did not relay this information to any other persons. This is the only communication that has been established by Plaintiff in this defamation suit, although he contends that other unidentified persons and possibly prospective employers were also told that the Plaintiff was a thief. . . .

The elements that a Plaintiff must prove in a defamation case are that the Defendant published a false statement, that the statement was communicated to a third party, and that the Plaintiff suffered damages as a result of the publication. False statements which suggest that someone has committed a dishonest or illegal act are defamatory per se. As a general rule, there is a presumption of malice where statements are defamatory per se, but that presumption ceases to exist where the Defendant has a qualified privilege to make the statements. Instead, the plaintiff then has the burden of rebutting a presumption of good faith.

The elements of qualified privilege are: good faith, an interest to be upheld, a statement limited in scope to a specific purpose, published on a proper occasion, and published in a proper manner. The question of whether publication of a false statement on a certain occasion is subject to qualified privilege is a question of law to be resolved by the Court where there is no dispute as to the circumstances surrounding the publication.

A jury question is created, however, where there is sufficient evidence of the presence of express malice indicating that the qualified privilege has been abused. Express malice has been defined as "ill will, hostility, evil intention to defame and injure," and is a very high standard for a plaintiff to meet. Montgomery v. Knox, 3 So. 211 (1887). In Nodar v. Galbreath, 462 So. 2d 803, 811-12 (Fla. 1984), the Florida Supreme Court expanded the definition of express malice and stated:

> Where a person speaks upon a privileged occasion, but the speaker is motivated more by a desire to harm the person defamed than by a purpose to protect the person or social interest giving rise to the privilege, then it can be said that there was express malice and the privilege is destroyed. Strong, angry, or intemperate words do not alone

show express malice; rather, there must be a showing that the speaker used his privileged position "to gratify his malevolence." If the occasion of the communication is privileged because of a proper interest to be protected, and the defamer is motivated by a desire to protect that interest, he does not forfeit the privilege merely because he also in fact feels hostility or ill will toward the plaintiff. The incidental gratification of personal feelings of indignation is not sufficient to defeat the privilege where the primary motivation is within the scope of privilege. (Citations omitted.)

In the instant case, Plaintiff has specifically identified only one person to whom Defendant has published information relating to the Plaintiff's dismissal. The deposition testimony of Mrs. Giantonio and the employee who published the information to her are consistent with respect to material issues, and Plaintiff has failed to allege any material fact with respect to this publication which would prevent this Court from resolving this matter on summary judgment. . . .

The single publication by Defendant's employee established by Plaintiff is qualifiedly privileged, and the privilege was not abused in this particular instance. The Defendant's statements were made in good faith in response to an inquiry from a customer, its publication was limited in scope, and the information was not disclosed to additional persons. Furthermore, the parties to the conversation shared corresponding business interests: the customer had an interest in learning what happened to a sales representative with whom she had a longstanding personal and business relationship, and the Defendant had the primary motive of responding adequately to a customer's inquiry. Plaintiff has failed to offer evidence that Defendant acted with the "ill will, hostility, and evil intent to defame" required to establish express malice, or that Defendant's primary motive in publishing the information was to harm Plaintiff. In fact, the Plaintiff's only allegations relating to the presence of express malice are contained in his Affidavit which states: "I am at a total loss to discern any factual basis by which Mr. McMahon could conclude that I was a thief. Although we tolerated each other in the business relationship, we were not friends on a personal basis." Clearly, the lack of a personal friendship does not equate to express malice as defined by the Florida Supreme Court in *Nodar*.

Plaintiff further contends in his Affidavit that he believes that Defendant had been planning to fire him for some time, and that he had received a final warning a few weeks before his termination. This allegation is irrelevant to whether the Defendant acted with express malice on a later occasion when publication occurred. Florida's status as a right-to-work state prohibits Plaintiff from recovering for the loss of his employment, despite his claims for damages for lost wages in his pleadings, and accordingly, the factors surrounding his termination are only relevant to the issue of whether the Defendant knew that the allegations were false when its employee published the allegedly defamatory statements. However since Plaintiff has failed to provide this Court with any evidence of express malice, it is unnecessary to address whether the allegations of theft were true, and more importantly, whether Plaintiff has suffered any compensable injury as a result of the publication. Accordingly, it is ordered that the Defendant's Motion for Summary Judgment . . . be granted.

NOTES TO JOHNSON v. QUEENAN AND SHAW v. R.J. REYNOLDS TOBACCO CO.

1. *Absolute and Qualified Privileges.* The various third parties to whom Ms. Johnson published her allegedly defamatory statements about Mr. Queenan were

divided into two groups. Statements to one group were absolutely privileged, while statements to the other were given only a qualified privilege. What justifies the difference in treatment of the two groups?

2. *Express Malice.* The court in *Shaw* considers whether the offered proof of express malice was sufficient to defeat the qualified privilege on which the employer relied. What is that evidence? The court in *Johnson* held that Queenan had not produced any evidence to enable him to reach the jury on the issue of malice. What evidence might Queenan have produced? If he could prove that the plaintiff was angry with him because she thought he had raped her, would that testimony be useful in establishing her express malice? Would it be sufficient to overcome a qualified privilege? Consider carefully the quotation from the Florida Supreme Court's opinion in Nodar v. Galbreath.

3. *"Defamation-Proof" Defendants.* A defendant may claim that a plaintiff's reputation in the community was so tarnished that no harm could have occurred. If accepted, this claim may result in the award of only nominal damages because no damages could reasonably be presumed and no actual damages could be proved. In Wynberg v. National Enquirer, Inc., 564 F. Supp. 924, 927-928 (D. Cal. 1982), the court held that the plaintiff, who had a brief but highly publicized romance with actress Elizabeth Taylor, was libel-proof. Wynberg had been convicted of criminal conduct on five separate occasions, including a conviction for contributing to the delinquency of minors. The court concluded,

> When, for example, an individual engages in conspicuously anti-social or even criminal behavior, which is widely reported to the public, his reputation diminishes proportionately. Depending upon the nature of the conduct, the number of offenses, and the degree and range of publicity received, there comes a time when the individual's reputation for specific conduct, or his general reputation for honesty and fair dealing is sufficiently low in the public's estimation that he can recover only nominal damages for subsequent defamatory statements.

Even if a plaintiff is not completely defamation-proof, evidence of a tarnished reputation will diminish the amount of damages recoverable. See Marcone v. Penthouse International Magazine for Men, 754 F.2d 1072, 1079 (3d Cir. 1985), in which the defamation claim was brought by an attorney who had been prominently linked to a motorcycle gang, indicted in connection with drug trafficking, tried for criminal income tax evasion, and fined for punching a police officer. The court instructed the jury that it could consider this evidence in determining the appropriate amount of compensatory damages.

Problem
Qualified and Absolute Privileges

In an omitted portion of the opinion in *Johnson*, the court discussed Queenan's allegation that after the grand jury failed to indict him, Johnson told Scuzzarella, the dean of students at Johnson's school, "the bastard got off." Queenan does not allege that Johnson told Scuzzarella that he raped her. Is this statement actionable slander? Consider first whether it is slander per se or per quod. Queenan made no allegations of special damages. If this statement is otherwise actionable, is this publication absolutely or qualifiedly privileged?

Statute: EMPLOYER IMMUNITY FROM LIABILITY; DISCLOSURE OF INFORMATION REGARDING FORMER OR CURRENT EMPLOYEES

Fla. Stat. §768.095 (2017)

An employer who discloses information about a former or current employee to a prospective employer of the former or current employee upon request of the prospective employer or of the former or current employee is immune from civil liability for such disclosure or its consequences unless it is shown *by clear and convincing evidence* that the information disclosed by the former or current employer was *knowingly false* or violated any civil right of the former or current employee protected under chapter 760. (Emphasis added.)

Statute: ACTUAL MALICE

Cal. Civ. Code §48a(d)(4) (2017)

"Actual malice" means that state of mind arising from hatred or ill will toward the plaintiff; provided, however, that such a state of mind occasioned by a good faith belief on the part of the defendant in the truth of the libelous publication or broadcast at the time it is published or broadcast shall not constitute actual malice.

Statute: QUALIFIED PRIVILEGE

14 La. Rev. Stat. §49 (2017)

A qualified privilege exists and actual malice must be proved, regardless of whether the publication is true or false, in the following situations:

(1) Where the publication or expression is a fair and true report of any judicial, legislative, or other public or official proceeding, or of any statement, speech, argument, or debate in the course of the same.

(2) Where the publication or expression is a comment made in the reasonable belief of its truth, upon, (a) The conduct of a person in respect to public affairs; or (b) A thing which the proprietor thereof offers or explains to the public.

(3) Where the publication or expression is made to a person interested in the communication, by one who is also interested or who stands in such a relation to the former as to afford a reasonable ground for supposing his motive innocent.

(4) Where the publication or expression is made by an attorney or party in a judicial proceeding.

Statute: ABSOLUTE PRIVILEGE

14 La. Rev. Stat. §50 (2017)

There shall be no prosecution for defamation in the following situations:

(1) When a statement is made by a legislator or judge in the course of his official duties.

(2) When a statement is made by a witness in a judicial proceeding, or in any other legal proceeding where testimony may be required by law, and such statement is reasonably believed by the witness to be relevant to the matter in controversy.

(3) Against the owner, licensee or other operator of a visual or sound broadcasting station or network of stations or the agents or employees thereof, when a statement is made or uttered over such station or network of stations by one other than such owner, licensee, operator, agents, or employees.

NOTES TO STATUTES

1. *The Meaning of "Actual Malice."*   The California definition of "actual malice" starts off with a phrase that sounds very much like common law express malice — "that state of mind arising from hatred or ill will." This language refers to the defendant's attitudes toward the plaintiff. But the remainder of the definition refers to the defendant's attitude toward the truth of the statement — "a good faith belief on the part of the defendant in the truth of the libelous publication." If the defendant has the proper attitude toward the truth, his attitude toward the plaintiff does not matter. This definition reflects modern constitutional law developments in defamation law.

2. *Moving from Express to Actual Malice.*   Constitutional law developments have shifted some states away from requiring proof of *express malice*, a hostile attitude toward the plaintiff, for defeating qualified privileges to requiring proof of *actual malice*, a disregard of the truth. Shaw v. R.J. Reynolds, decided by the Federal District Court in Florida in 1993, referred to "express malice." As the Florida statute illustrates, the Florida legislature has since changed the nature of the qualified privilege given to employers, referring instead to whether the defendant knew the statement was false.

3. *Qualified and Absolute Privileges.*   As the Louisiana statutes illustrate, proof of actual malice is required to defeat a qualified privilege. For actions brought as a result of speech covered by an absolute privilege, it appears that no action may be brought. Observe, however, how each absolute privilege is hedged with some condition. The judge's speech must, for instance, occur "in the course of his official duties." The Louisiana statutes are from the Louisiana Criminal Code, but the Reporter's Comment (1997 Main Volume) cites examples of each of these privileges in Louisiana civil torts cases. Compare the difference in treatment of attorneys and parties to litigation on the one hand and judges and witnesses on the other. What might justify this difference?

IV. Constitutionally Required Proof of Fault

A. Introduction

Outside of the context of privileges, the common law of defamation did not require any plaintiff to prove that the allegedly defamatory statement was false or that the defendant carelessly or intentionally defamed the plaintiff. The U.S. Supreme Court's seminal decision in New York Times Co. v. Sullivan, 376 U.S. 254 (1964), changed defamation law dramatically by describing situations in which a plaintiff must prove falsity, and by adding an element of fault called *actual malice* or, sometimes, *"New York Times actual malice."* Actual malice is different from express malice of the sort described as "improper motive," or "hatred, ill will, or spite." The following excerpt from a New Mexico case, State v. Powell, summarizes the development of *constitutional defamation law* as it applies to suits by public officials and public figures.

STATE v. POWELL
839 P.2d 139 (N.M. App. 1992)

Hartz, J. . . .

In [New York Times v. Sullivan, 376 U.S. 254 (1964),] the Supreme Court created a qualified privilege to make defamatory statements relating to the official conduct of a public official. The Court ruled that the Constitution "prohibits a public official from recovering damages for a defamatory falsehood relating to his official conduct unless he proves that the statement was made with 'actual malice' — that is, with knowledge that it was false or with reckless disregard of whether it was false or not." Id. at 279-80; see Bose Corp. v. Consumers Union of United States, Inc., 466 U.S. 485, 511 n.30 (1984) (Plaintiff must demonstrate "that the defendant realized that his statement was false or that he subjectively entertained serious doubt as to the truth of his statement."). Three years after *New York Times* the qualified privilege was extended to defamatory criticism of "public figures." Curtis Publishing Co. v. Butts, 388 U.S. 130 (1967).

In adopting the qualified privilege, the Supreme Court recognized "a profound national commitment to the principle that debate on public issues should be uninhibited, robust, and wide-open, and that it may well include vehement, caustic, and sometimes unpleasantly sharp attacks on government and public officials." *New York Times,* 376 U.S. at 270. Hustler Magazine v. Falwell, 485 U.S. 46, 52 (1988), explains:

> [E]ven though falsehoods have little value in and of themselves, they are "nevertheless inevitable in free debate," Gertz v. Robert Welch, Inc., 418 U.S. 323, 340 (1974), and a rule that would impose strict liability on a publisher for false factual assertions would have an undoubted "chilling" effect on speech relating to public figures that does have constitutional value. "Freedoms of expression require 'breathing space.'" (quoting *New York Times,* supra, at 272). This breathing space is provided by a constitutional rule that allows public figures to recover for libel or defamation only when they can prove *both* that the statement was false and that the statement was made with the requisite level of culpability.

On the other hand, defamation that does not come within the *New York Times* privilege is hardly entitled to protection. As the Supreme Court stated in Garrison v. Louisiana, 379 U.S. 64, 75 (1964):

> Although honest utterance, even if inaccurate, may further the fruitful exercise of the right of free speech, it does not follow that the lie, knowingly and deliberately

published about a public official, should enjoy a like immunity. . . . [T]he use of the known lie as a tool is at once at odds with the premises of democratic government and with the orderly manner in which economic, social, or political change is to be effected. Calculated falsehood falls into that class of utterances which "are no essential part of any exposition of ideas, and are of such slight social value as a step to truth that any benefit that may be derived from them is clearly outweighed by the social interest in order and morality. . . ."

Chaplinsky v. New Hampshire, 315 U.S. 568, 572. Hence the knowingly false statement and the false statement made with reckless disregard of the truth, do not enjoy constitutional protection.

B. Defining "Actual Malice," "Public Figures," and "Matters of Public Concern"

The cases that follow describe what actual malice means, how to characterize plaintiffs as public or private figures, and how to characterize defendants' statements as being about matters of public concern or not. They also illustrate the fault rules adopted by the Supreme Court.

Fault requirements adopted by the Supreme Court for defamation law vary depending on whether the case involves a plaintiff who is: (1) a general-purpose public official or public figure; (2) a limited-purpose public official or public figure; (3) a private figure involved in a matter of public concern; or (4) a private figure involved only in matters of private concern. For each of these types of plaintiffs, courts must determine what fault rules apply for recovery of each of three types of damages: presumed, actual, and punitive. It might be helpful to construct a chart with three columns (one for the one for each type of damage) and four rows (one for each type of plaintiff) and fill it in with the fault requirements for each situation as you read each case.

1. Public Officials

The fault requirements imposed on defamation plaintiffs who are public officials arises out of the Supreme Court's interpretation of the U.S. Constitution's First Amendment right to freedom of expression. Defamation plaintiffs in these categories must prove *actual malice* in addition to whatever proof requirements imposed by the common law, including those required to defeat applicable privileges.

These relatively new rules of *constitutional defamation law* gave rise immediately to two issues: Who qualifies as a public official? What does "actual malice" mean? In Rosenblatt v. Baer, the plaintiff, Frank Baer, was supervisor of a county recreation area. The Court discusses how far down the hierarchy of government employees to extend the classification of public official. In St. Amant v. Thompson, the Supreme Court defines and applies the term "actual malice." These cases are based on the Supreme Court's interpretation of the First Amendment to the U.S. Constitution, which restricts the federal government and (because of the Fourteenth Amendment) state governments.

AMENDMENT I: FREEDOM OF RELIGION, FREEDOM OF SPEECH
AND PRESS, PEACEFUL ASSEMBLAGE, PETITION
OF GRIEVANCES

U.S. Const. amend. I

Congress shall make no law respecting an establishment of religion, or prohibiting the free exercise thereof; or abridging the freedom of speech, or of the press; or the right of the people peaceably to assemble, and to petition the government for a redress of grievances.

ROSENBLATT v. BAER
383 U.S. 75 (1966)

Mr. Justice BRENNAN delivered the opinion of the Court.

A jury in New Hampshire Superior Court awarded respondent damages in this civil libel action based on one of petitioner's columns in the *Laconia Evening Citizen.* Respondent alleged that the column contained defamatory falsehoods concerning his performance as Supervisor of the Belknap County Recreation Area, a facility owned and operated by Belknap County. In the interval between the trial and the decision of petitioner's appeal by the New Hampshire Supreme Court, we decided New York Times Co. v. Sullivan, 376 U.S. 254. We there held that consistent with the First and Fourteenth Amendments a State cannot award damages to a public official for defamatory falsehood relating to his official conduct unless the official proves actual malice — that the falsehood was published with knowledge of its falsity or with reckless disregard of whether it was true or false. The New Hampshire Supreme Court affirmed the award, finding *New York Times* no bar. We granted certiorari and requested the parties to brief and argue, in addition to the questions presented in the petition for certiorari, the question whether respondent was a "public official" under *New York Times* and under our decision in Garrison v. State of Louisiana, 379 U.S. 64; 380 U.S. 941. . . .

We remarked in *New York Times* that we had no occasion "to determine how far down into the lower ranks of government employees the 'public official' designation would extend for purposes of this rule, or otherwise to specify categories of persons who would or would not be included." 376 U.S., at 283, n.23. No precise lines need be drawn for the purposes of this case. The motivating force for the decision in *New York Times* was twofold. We expressed "a profound national commitment to the principle that debate on public issues should be uninhibited, robust, and wide-open, and that (such debate) may well include vehement, caustic, and sometimes unpleasantly sharp attacks on government and public officials." 376 U.S., at 270. There is, first, a strong interest in debate on public issues, and, second, a strong interest in debate about those persons who are in a position significantly to influence the resolution of those issues. Criticism of government is at the very center of the constitutionally protected area of free discussion. Criticism of those responsible for government operations must be free, lest criticism of government itself be penalized. It is clear, therefore, that the "public official" designation applies at the very least to those among the hierarchy of government employees who have, or appear to the public to have, substantial responsibility for or control over the conduct of governmental affairs.

This conclusion does not ignore the important social values which underlie the law of defamation. Society has a pervasive and strong interest in preventing and redressing attacks upon reputation. But in cases like the present, there is tension between this interest and the values nurtured by the First and Fourteenth Amendments. The thrust of *New York Times* is that when interests in public discussion are particularly strong as they were in that case, the Constitution limits the protections afforded by the law of defamation. Where a position in government has such apparent importance that the public has an independent interest in the qualifications and performance of the person who holds it, beyond the general public interest in the qualifications and performance of all government employees, both elements we identified in *New York Times* are present and the *New York Times* malice standards apply.[13]

As respondent framed his case, he may have held such a position. Since *New York Times* had not been decided when his case went to trial, his presentation was not shaped to the "public official" issue. He did, however, seek to show that the article referred particularly to him. His theory was that his role in the management of the Area was so prominent and important that the public regarded him as the man responsible for its operations, chargeable with its failures and to be credited with its successes. Thus, to prove the article referred to him, he showed the importance of his role; the same showing, at the least, raises a substantial argument that he was a "public official."[14]

The record here, however, leaves open the possibility that respondent could have adduced proofs to bring his claim outside the *New York Times* rule. Moreover, even if the claim falls within *New York Times*, the record suggests respondent may be able to present a jury question of malice as there defined. Because the trial here was had before *New York Times*, we have concluded that we should not foreclose him from attempting retrial of his action. We remark only that, as is the case with questions of privilege generally, it is for the trial judge in the first instance to determine whether the proofs show respondent to be a "public official."

The judgment is reversed and the case remanded to the New Hampshire Supreme Court for further proceedings not inconsistent with this opinion.

---

[13] It is suggested that this test might apply to a night watchman accused of stealing state secrets. But a conclusion that the *New York Times* malice standards apply could not be reached merely because a statement defamatory of some person in government employ catches the public's interest; that conclusion would virtually disregard society's interest in protecting reputation. The employee's position must be one which would invite public scrutiny and discussion of the person holding it, entirely apart from the scrutiny and discussion occasioned by the particular charges in controversy.

[14] It is not seriously contended, and could not be, that the fact respondent no longer supervised the Area when the column appeared has decisional significance here. To be sure, there may be cases where a person is so far removed from a former position of authority that comment on the manner in which he performed his responsibilities no longer has the interest necessary to justify the *New York Times* rule. But here the management of the Area was still a matter of lively public interest; propositions for further change were abroad, and public interest in the way in which the prior administration had done its task continued strong. The comment, if it referred to respondent, referred to his performance of duty as a county employee.

ST. AMANT v. THOMPSON
390 U.S. 727 (1968)

Mr. Justice WHITE delivered the opinion of the Court.

The question presented by this case is whether the Louisiana Supreme Court, in sustaining a judgment for damages in a public official's defamation action, correctly interpreted and applied the rule of New York Times Co. v. Sullivan, 376 U.S. 254 (1964), that the plaintiff in such an action must prove that the defamatory publication "was made with 'actual malice' — that is, with knowledge that it was false or with reckless disregard of whether it was false or not." 376 U.S., at 279-280.

On June 27, 1962, petitioner St. Amant, a candidate for public office, made a televised speech in Baton Rouge, Louisiana. In the course of this speech, St. Amant read a series of questions which he had put to J.D. Albin, a member of a Teamsters Union local, and Albin's answers to those questions. The exchange concerned the allegedly nefarious activities of E.G. Partin, the president of the local, and the alleged relationship between Partin and St. Amant's political opponent. One of Albin's answers concerned his efforts to prevent Partin from secreting union records; in this answer Albin referred to Herman A. Thompson, an East Baton Rouge Parish deputy sheriff and respondent here:

> Now, we knew that this safe was gonna be moved that night, but imagine our predicament, knowing of Ed's connections with the Sheriff's office through Herman Thompson, who made recent visits to the Hall to see Ed. We also knew of money that had passed hands between Ed and Herman Thompson . . . from Ed to Herman. We also knew of his connections with State Trooper Lieutenant Joe Green. We knew we couldn't get any help from there and we didn't know how far that he was involved in the Sheriff's office or the State Police office through that, and it was out of the jurisdiction of the City Police.

Thompson promptly brought suit for defamation, claiming that the publication had "impute[d] . . . gross misconduct" and "infer[red] conduct of the most nefarious nature." The case was tried prior to the decision in New York Times Co. v. Sullivan, supra. The trial judge ruled in Thompson's favor and awarded $5,000 in damages. Thereafter, in the course of entertaining and denying a motion for a new trial, the Court considered the ruling in *New York Times*, finding that rule no barrier to the judgment already entered. The Louisiana Court of Appeal reversed because the record failed to show that St. Amant had acted with actual malice, as required by *New York Times*. The Supreme Court of Louisiana reversed the intermediate appellate court. In its view, there was sufficient evidence that St. Amant recklessly disregarded whether the statements about Thompson were true or false. We granted a writ of certiorari.

For purposes of this case we accept the determinations of the Louisiana courts that the material published by St. Amant charged Thompson with criminal conduct, that the charge was false, and that Thompson was a public official and so had the burden of proving that the false statements about Thompson were made with actual malice as defined in New York Times Co. v. Sullivan and later cases. We cannot, however, agree with either the Supreme Court of Louisiana or the trial court that Thompson sustained this burden.

Purporting to apply the *New York Times* malice standard, the Louisiana Supreme Court ruled that St. Amant had broadcast false information about Thompson recklessly, though not knowingly. Several reasons were given for this conclusion. St. Amant had no personal knowledge of Thompson's activities; he relied solely on Albin's affidavit although the record was silent as to Albin's reputation for veracity; he failed to verify the information with those in the union office who might have known the facts; he gave no consideration to whether or not the statements defamed Thompson and went ahead heedless of the consequences; and he mistakenly believed he had no responsibility for the broadcast because he was merely quoting Albin's words.

These considerations fall short of proving St. Amant's reckless disregard for the accuracy of his statements about Thompson. "Reckless disregard," it is true, cannot be fully encompassed in one infallible definition. Inevitably its outer limits will be marked out through case-by-case adjudication, as is true with so many legal standards for judging concrete cases, whether the standard is provided by the Constitution, statutes, or case law. Our cases, however, have furnished meaningful guidance for the further definition of a reckless publication. In *New York Times,* supra, the plaintiff did not satisfy his burden because the record failed to show that the publisher was aware of the likelihood that he was circulating false information. In Garrison v. State of Louisiana, 379 U.S. 64 (1964), also decided before the decision of the Louisiana Supreme Court in this case, the opinion emphasized the necessity for a showing that a false publication was made with a "high degree of awareness of . . . probable falsity." 379 U.S., at 74. Mr. Justice Harlan's opinion in Curtis Publishing Co. v. Butts, 388 U.S. 130, 153 (1967), stated that evidence of either deliberate falsification or reckless publication "despite the publisher's awareness of probable falsity" was essential to recovery by public officials in defamation actions. These cases are clear that reckless conduct is not measured by whether a reasonably prudent man would have published, or would have investigated before publishing. There must be sufficient evidence to permit the conclusion that the defendant in fact entertained serious doubts as to the truth of his publication. Publishing with such doubts shows reckless disregard for truth or falsity and demonstrates actual malice.

It may be said that such a test puts a premium on ignorance, encourages the irresponsible publisher not to inquire, and permits the issue to be determined by the defendants' testimony that he published the statement in good faith and unaware of its probable falsity. Concededly the reckless disregard standard may permit recovery in fewer situations than would a rule that publishers must satisfy the standard of the reasonable man or the prudent publisher. But *New York Times* and succeeding cases have emphasized that the stake of the people in public business and the conduct of public officials is so great that neither the defense of truth nor the standard of ordinary care would protect against self-censorship and thus adequately implement First Amendment policies. Neither lies nor false communications serve the ends of the First Amendment, and no one suggests their desirability or further proliferation. But to insure the ascertainment and publication of the truth about public affairs, it is essential that the First Amendment protect some erroneous publications as well as true ones. We adhere to this view and to the line which our cases have drawn between false communications which are protected and those which are not.

The defendant in a defamation action brought by a public official cannot, however, automatically insure a favorable verdict by testifying that he published with a belief that the statements were true. The finder of fact must determine whether the publication was indeed made in good faith. Professions of good faith will be unlikely to prove persuasive, for example, where a story is fabricated by the defendant, is the product of his imagination, or is based wholly on an unverified anonymous telephone call. Nor will they be likely to prevail when the publisher's allegations are so inherently improbable that only a reckless man would have put them in circulation. Likewise, recklessness may be found where there are obvious reasons to doubt the veracity of the informant or the accuracy of his reports.

By no proper test of reckless disregard was St. Amant's broadcast a reckless publication about a public officer. Nothing referred to by the Louisiana courts indicates an awareness by St. Amant of the probable falsity of Albin's statement about Thompson. Failure to investigate does not in itself establish bad faith. St. Amant's mistake about his probable legal liability does not evidence a doubtful mind on his part. That he failed to realize the import of what he broadcast — and was thus "heedless" of the consequences for Thompson — is similarly colorless. Closer to the mark are considerations of Albin's reliability. However, the most the state court could say was that there was no evidence in the record of Albin's reputation for veracity, and this fact merely underlines the failure of Thompson's evidence to demonstrate a low community assessment of Albin's trustworthiness or unsatisfactory experience with him by St. Amant.

Other facts in this record support our view. St. Amant made his broadcast in June 1962. He had known Albin since October 1961, when he first met with members of the dissident Teamsters faction. St. Amant testified that he had verified other aspects of Albin's information and that he had affidavits from others. Moreover Albin swore to his answers, first in writing and later in the presence of newsmen. According to Albin, he was prepared to substantiate his charges. St. Amant knew that Albin was engaged in an internal struggle in the union; Albin seemed to St. Amant to be placing himself in personal danger by publicly airing the details of the dispute.

Because the state court misunderstood and misapplied the actual malice standard which must be observed in a public official's defamation action, the judgment is reversed and the case remanded for further proceedings not inconsistent with this opinion.

Reversed and remanded.

NOTES TO ROSENBLATT v. BAER AND ST. AMANT v. THOMPSON

1. *Test for Public Officials.* *Rosenblatt* considers what degree of fault a plaintiff must prove in a defamation case. A plaintiff who is a public official must prove, in addition to the other elements of a defamation claim, that the falsehood was published with actual malice, knowledge of its falsity or reckless disregard of whether it was true or false. What is the test from *Rosenblatt* for who qualifies as a public official? What is the likely result of applying that rule to Mr. Baer, the supervisor?

2. *Clear and Convincing Evidence of Actual Malice.* When proof of actual malice, as described in St. Amant v. Thompson, is required, the evidence must be clear and convincing, a higher standard than a simple preponderance of the evidence. Thus, the common law of defamation is altered by adding a fault requirement and requiring proof of that fault by a higher standard.

3. *Criticizing the Government.* Defamatory statements about the government or the governmental unit to which an official belongs are absolutely privileged. The *New York Times* actual malice standard applies only to defamatory statements directed at the official personally. See Rodney A. Smolla, *Law of Defamation* 22-136, §2:112 (2d ed. 2001 and 12/2001 update).

4. *Public Figures.* Speech concerning public figures is also protected by the *New York Times* actual malice standard. Because public figures may not be public employees, as public officials typically are, a test focusing on the independent importance of their qualifications for and performance in their jobs is inappropriate. Nor do public figures necessarily have "substantial responsibility for or control over the conduct of governmental affairs." Public figure status has been given to entertainers, sports figures, mobsters, authors, *Playboy* centerfold photo subjects, Nobel Prize winners, corporate leaders, and priests, among others, but some people in these categories may not qualify. A public official with sufficient notoriety, such as the President of the United States, may be classified as both a public official and a public figure. In Gray v. St. Martin's Press, the court discusses how someone gets to be classified as a public figure and the distinction between *general-purpose public figures* and *limited public figures*. As you read the following cases on public and private figures, determine what requirements would be appropriate for public officials about whom someone has made a defamatory statement unrelated to the official's office or his or her qualifications for or performance in that office.

Problems
Public Officials

Which of the following individuals is a public official and must therefore prove actual malice in order to recover in a defamation claim? Assume that each plaintiff was defamed by a statement relating to his or her official capacity.

A. An undercover informant for the Department of Inspections who is not paid a salary by the city of Baltimore but whose expenses are sometimes paid? See Jenoff v. Hearst Corp., 644 F.2d 1004 (4th Cir. 1981).

B. A court-appointed attorney for a murder defendant who is not a permanent employee of the government but who was paid for his services in this case out of public funds? See Steere v. Cupp, 602 P.2d 1267 (Kan. 1979).

C. State university print shop director called "congenital liar" by defendant? See Madison v. Yunker, 589 P.2d 126 (Mont. 1978).

D. Discharged firefighter in news broadcast about his firing? See Jones v. Palmer Communications, Inc., 440 N.W.2d 884 (Iowa 1989).

E. Student member of university senate accused of being "campus demagogue"? See Klahr v. Winterble, 418 P.2d 404 (Ariz. Ct. App. 1966).

F. License officer in vehicle licensing bureau whose duties included collecting and accounting for fees collected for licenses? See Hodges v. Oklahoma Journal Publishing Co., 617 P.2d 191 (Okla. 1980).

Problems
Clear and Convincing Evidence of Actual Malice

When proof of actual malice, as described in St. Amant v. Thompson, is required, the evidence must be *clear and convincing*, a higher standard than a simple *preponderance of the evidence*.

A. In Varanese v. Gall, 518 N.E.2d 1177 (Ohio 1988), the former county treasurer brought suit against a newspaper for publication of an election advertisement that was allegedly libelous. The ad charged various acts of misfeasance and nonfeasance in office and characterized the former treasurer as advocating the elimination of various services, including those supporting veterans, the aged, and conservation, as well as the termination of support for 4-H programs. The ad provided footnotes to the allegations, several of which cited the newspaper itself as a source thereof. The plaintiff lost the election. The following evidence was offered by the plaintiff in support of her position that the newspaper had acted with actual malice:

1. The plaintiff alleged that the newspaper could easily have checked the accuracy of the ad by reference to documents either in its possession or readily accessible to it.
2. The plaintiff alleged that a reporter employed by the newspaper attended certain public meetings at which the plaintiff spoke. The reporter would have known from the plaintiff's remarks that the plaintiff had never advocated the positions attributed to her in the ad, such as the elimination of veterans' services.
3. The plaintiff offered portions of a deposition taken of Herbert Thompson, who was the newspaper's general manager at the time the ad in question was published. These excerpts contained statements by Thompson that he did not investigate the accuracy of the ad, did not research the footnotes, and did not discuss the ad with the person responsible for advertising.
4. The plaintiff offered excerpts from the deposition of Robert Curran, the newspaper's editor at the time the ad was published. The plaintiff particularly emphasized Curran's testimony that he saw the ad several days before it was published and remarked to Thompson, the general manager, that the ad was "bullshit." Curran explained that his statement that the ad was "bullshit" was an expression of his concern that if the ad were false, the newspaper would be included in any subsequent lawsuit. He stated that his concern was the newspaper's potential exposure to suit in the event that the ad's charges proved to be untrue.

Does a *former* county treasurer qualify as a public official? Check the footnotes in *Rosenblatt*. Does this collection of evidence demonstrate by clear and convincing evidence that the newspaper acted with actual malice?

B. In Elder v. Gaffney Ledger, 533 S.E.2d 899 (S.C. 2000), a former police chief sued a newspaper for libel. A newspaper *editorial* suggested that the police chief was being paid off by drug dealers. The police chief offered the following evidence in support of his claim that the editor acted with actual malice:

1. The editor failed to investigate or verify information left by an anonymous caller and admitted that he did not have enough information to publish the information as a story.
2. The editor failed to introduce the tape recording made of the anonymous call.
3. The editor had a 1991 conviction for manufacturing marijuana and may have been motivated by his own problems with law enforcement to discredit the plaintiff.
4. The police chief's wife testified that the editor had spoken to her in a "very smart, rude" manner on one occasion and disliked her.

Does this evidence demonstrate by clear and convincing evidence that the newspaper editor acted with actual malice?

GRAY v. ST. MARTIN'S PRESS, INC.
1999 WL 813909 (D.N.H. 1999)

McAULIFFE, J.

Robert Gray brings this action seeking damages for five allegedly defamatory statements contained in *The Power House, Robert Keith Gray and the Selling of*

Access and Influence in Washington ("*The Power House*"), a book authored by Susan Trento and published by St. Martin's Press. The book discusses how members of lobbying and public relations firms influence federal government operations and focuses on Gray as one of the most powerful and well-connected members of that group.

Pending before the court are two motions for summary judgment filed by defendants. In the first, defendants assert that plaintiff is a public figure and must, therefore, demonstrate that they acted with "actual malice" in order to prevail on his defamation claims. . . .

Plaintiff is, at least in Washington, D.C., and nationally in governmental and lobbying circles, both successful and well-known. See, e.g., Affidavit of Robert K. Gray submitted in support of motion for enlargement of time for discovery (dated September 27, 1995), at para. 3 ("I have a national reputation in the area of public relations."). Defendants point out that he has also been the subject of a television documentary and the topic of (or, at a minimum, discussed in) several hundred newspaper and magazine articles. Thus, the only real question before the court concerning plaintiff's status is whether he is a "general purpose public figure" or a "limited public figure."

In Gertz v. Robert Welch, Inc., 418 U.S. 323 (1974), the Supreme Court recognized a distinction between these two types of public figures:

> Some [plaintiffs] occupy positions of such persuasive power and influence that they are deemed public figures for all purposes. More commonly, those classed as public figures have thrust themselves to the forefront of particular public controversies in order to influence the resolution of the issues involved.

Id., at 345. More recently, this court (Devine, J.) addressed the legal concepts of "general purpose public figures" and "limited public figures," observing that:

> The designation "public figure" may rest on two alternative bases. First, in some instances, an individual may achieve such pervasive fame or notoriety that he becomes a public figure for all purposes and in all contexts. Second, persons of lesser fame may nonetheless qualify as limited public figures if they "thrust themselves to the forefront of particular public controversies." Such limited public figures are subject to the "actual malice" standard only for defamation arising out of the public controversy into which they have thrust themselves.

Fagin v. Kelly, 978 F. Supp. 420, 426 (D.N.H. 1997).

In the wake of the Supreme Court's opinion in *Gertz*, supra, the Court of Appeals for the District of Columbia Circuit summarized the factors that ought to be considered when determining whether a particular person is a general purpose public figure.

> A court must first ask whether the plaintiff is a public figure for all purposes. *Gertz*, as noted above, held that a plaintiff could be found to be a general public figure only after a clear showing "of general fame or notoriety in the community, and pervasive involvement in the affairs of society. . . ." 418 U.S. at 352. He must have assumed a "role of especial prominence in the affairs of society. . . ." Time, Inc. v. Firestone, 424 U.S. 448, 453 (1976). In other words, a general public figure is a well-known "celebrity," his name a "household word." The public recognizes him and follows his words and deeds, either because it regards his ideas, conduct, or judgment as worthy of its attention or because he actively pursues that consideration.

Waldbaum v. Fairchild Publications, Inc., 627 F.2d 1287, 1294 (D.C. Cir. 1980).

On the record presently before it, the court cannot conclude that defendants have shown, as a matter of law, that plaintiff is a general purpose public figure. The record does not support the conclusion that plaintiff was a "celebrity" or that his name was a "household word." To the contrary, as plaintiff notes, several editors and other employees at St. Martin's Press who actually worked on the publication of *The Power House* admitted at their depositions that, prior to their involvement with the book, they had never heard of Robert Keith Gray. Nothing presented suggests that the public — in the District of Columbia or nationally — was better informed or more aware of Mr. Gray's general involvement in the affairs of society. Thus, while plaintiff may be extraordinarily well known in certain Washington, D.C., circles, particularly with regard to his ability to influence public opinion and provide his clients with coveted access to powerful men and women in American politics, defendants have failed to establish that he attained that degree of notoriety or celebrity usually associated with a "general purpose public figure."

It is, however, equally clear that plaintiff has attained the status of "limited public figure." As the Court of Appeals for the Eleventh Circuit has recognized:

The proper standards for determining whether plaintiffs are limited public figures are best set forth in Waldbaum v. Fairchild Publications, Inc., 627 F.2d 1287 (D.C. Cir. 1980). . . . Under the *Waldbaum* analysis, the court must (1) isolate the public controversy, (2) examine the plaintiffs' involvement in the controversy, and (3) determine whether "the alleged defamation [was] germane to the plaintiffs' participation in the controversy." *Id.*, at 1297.

Silvester v. American Broadcasting Companies, Inc., 839 F.2d 1491, 1494 (11th Cir. 1988). Here, the "public controversy" relates to familiar and often discussed public issues — the influence of, and access provided to political figures by, powerful Washington, D.C., lobbyists. And, there can be little doubt that plaintiff, one of the more powerful, influential, and successful lobbyists in Washington, qualifies as a central figure in that controversy. Finally, notwithstanding plaintiff's efforts to narrowly circumscribe the scope of the "public controversy" into which he thrust himself, each of the alleged defamatory statements set forth in *The Power House* relates directly to plaintiff's lobbying activities, his access to powerful and influential Washington "insiders," and his demonstrated ability to shape public opinion on various issues of public concern. Accordingly, the court concludes that plaintiff is a limited purpose public figure as to each of the statements at issue in this case. . . .

NOTE TO GRAY v. ST. MARTIN'S PRESS, INC.

General-Purpose Versus Limited Public Figures. The distinction between general-purpose and limited public figures is important because the general-purpose public figure must prove actual malice in any defamation case. The limited public figure status only requires proof of actual malice when the defamatory statement is connected to the matter of public concern from which that status arose. Outside that context, the limited public figure is a private figure.

Problems
General- and Limited-Purpose Public Figures

Apply the test from Gray v. St. Martin's Press, Inc. to the following facts.

A. Jack Kevorkian is the best known and most controversial proponent of assisted suicide. Dr. Kevorkian sued the American Medical Association for publishing a letter to the Michigan Attorney General stating that the plaintiff "perverts the idea of the caring and committed physician," "serves merely as a reckless instrument of death," "poses a great threat to the public," and engages in "criminal practice." The AMA also, through its officers, issued a press release alleging "continued killings" and "criminal activities" by the plaintiff. Is Jack Kevorkian a general-purpose or limited-purpose public figure? See Kevorkian v. American Medical Association, 602 N.W.2d 233 (Mich. Ct. App. 1999).

B. The real estate speculation and business practices of Gary Waicker had been the subject of newspaper articles and editorials in Baltimore from the late 1970s to the 1990s. You represent *Scranton Times*, a newspaper Waicker sues for defamation after it published an article stating that he bought property cheap by exploiting racial bigotry. Will either of the following pieces of evidence available to you be useful in establishing that Waiker is a limited purpose public figure?

1. Waicker had aggressively advertised saying, "WE PAY CASH FOR HOUSES — FAST CASH" and "NEIGHBORS — IS THERE A RUNDOWN HOUSE ON YOUR BLOCK WHICH DECREASES YOUR PROPERTY VALUE? CALL U.S." Waicker was known in the community as the owner of the businesses that had the sign.
2. Waiker had complained about the tactics of non-profit organizations that attempted to improve neighborhoods by buying, renovating, and reselling houses. He also complained to the Maryland Real Estate Commission in 1980 that the activities of a community housing developer were dangerous to the real estate industry and that it had not worked with him while working with other realtors.

See Waicker v. Scranton Times Ltd. Partnership, 688 A.2d 535 (Md. Ct. Spec. App. 1997).

3. Private Figures

In the 1974 case Gertz v. Robert Welch, Inc., the U.S. Supreme Court considered whether the constitutional protection of speech about public officials and public figures should extend to private figures. To protect and thereby encourage speech about public officials and figures, the Court required defamation plaintiffs in these categories to prove a high level of fault on the part of the defendant — actual malice — to recover any type of damages. When a private figure becomes embroiled in a public controversy, there may also be a societal interest in speech about that person. Even when there is no public controversy, the First Amendment might still be interpreted as providing some level of protection to freedom of expression. The issue for the following cases is how much constitutional protection to give to speech about private figures.

Following the *New York Times* actual malice approach, constitutional protection for private plaintiffs is provided by adding a fault requirement. Courts have considered how much fault private defamation plaintiffs must prove to recover damages. Recall that under traditional common law, plaintiffs never had to prove either fault or falsity unless a qualified privilege applied. Consistent with the constitutional interest in protecting speech about matters of public concern, the Supreme Court adopted different fault requirements for private figures involved in matters of public concern and those involved in private matters.

In addition, the Court adopted different fault standards depending on whether the private figure seeks presumed, punitive, or actual damages. Under the traditional common law, a defamation plaintiff may recover presumed damages without proof of any actual harm in a per se defamation action. A plaintiff may recover actual damages in either a per se or per quod defamation action subject to the normal rules of proof applying to general and special damages discussed in Chapter 12. Punitive damages are awarded not to compensate the plaintiff but to deter or punish the defendant for particularly egregious conduct. Concerned that awarding presumed damages without proof of actual damages or awarding punitive damages might unduly chill freedom of expression, the Supreme Court has held that proof of a higher level of fault is required for a private figure to recover these types of damages in some cases.

When organizing your understanding of the fault rules applying to different combinations of figures and contexts, you may have noticed that the Supreme Court has not yet decided what rules apply in some combinations. Lawyers and courts working on defamation cases must extend the principles derived from what the Court has said to project what rules apply for the undecided combinations. Moreover, rather than say what level of fault is required, the Supreme Court has sometimes said what is *not* required. This further complicates understanding of this topic.

a. Private Figure Involved in an Issue of Public Concern

Khawar v. Globe International, Inc. involves a photojournalist who was defamed in a book about the assassination of presidential candidate Robert F. Kennedy. The court first considers whether the photojournalist was a public or private figure and then applies the constitutional defamation law requirements for the various types of damages. This long case is included not because it is groundbreaking or creates new law. Rather, it offers particularly clear presentations and applications of the rules of constitutional defamation.

KHAWAR v. GLOBE INTERNATIONAL, INC.

965 P.2d 696 (Cal. 1998)

KENNARD, J.

We granted review to decide certain issues concerning the federal Constitution's guarantees of freedom of speech and of the press insofar as they restrict a state's ability to impose tort liability for the publication of defamatory falsehoods. More specifically, we address the definition of a "public figure" for purposes of tort and First Amendment law . . . and the showings required to support awards of compensatory and punitive damages for the republication of a defamatory falsehood. . . .

I. FACTS

In November 1988, Roundtable Publishing, Inc., (Roundtable) published a book written by Robert Morrow (Morrow) and entitled *The Senator Must Die: The Murder of*

Robert Kennedy (the Morrow book). The Morrow book alleged that the Iranian Shah's secret police (SAVAK), working together with the Mafia, carried out the 1968 assassination of United States Senator Robert F. Kennedy (Kennedy) in California and that Kennedy's assassin was not Sirhan Sirhan, who had been convicted of Kennedy's murder, but a man named Ali Ahmand, whom the Morrow book described as a young Pakistani who, on the evening of the Kennedy assassination, wore a gold-colored sweater and carried what appeared to be a camera but was actually the gun with which Ahmand killed Kennedy. The Morrow book contained four photographs of a young man the book identified as Ali Ahmand standing in a group of people around Kennedy at the Ambassador Hotel in Los Angeles shortly before Kennedy was assassinated.

Globe International, Inc., (Globe) publishes a weekly tabloid newspaper called Globe. Its issue of April 4, 1989, contained an article on page 9 under the headline: *Former CIA Agent Claims: IRANIANS KILLED BOBBY KENNEDY FOR THE MAFIA* (the Globe article). Another headline, appearing on the front page of the same issue, stated: *Iranian secret police killed Bobby Kennedy.* The Globe article, written by John Blackburn (a freelance reporter and former Globe staff reporter), gave an abbreviated, uncritical summary of the Morrow book's allegations. The Globe article included a photograph from the Morrow book showing a group of men standing near Kennedy; Globe enlarged the image of these individuals and added an arrow pointing to one of these men and identifying him as the assassin Ali Ahmand.

In August 1989, Khalid Iqbal Khawar (Khawar) brought this action against Globe, Roundtable, and Morrow, alleging that he was the person depicted in the photographs and identified in the Morrow book as Ali Ahmand, and that the book's accusation, repeated in the Globe article, that he had assassinated Kennedy was false and defamatory and had caused him substantial injury. . . .

The evidence at trial showed that in June 1968, when Kennedy was assassinated, Khawar was a Pakistani citizen and a free-lance photojournalist working on assignment for a Pakistani periodical. At the Ambassador Hotel's Embassy Room, he stood on the podium near Kennedy so that a friend could photograph him with Kennedy, and so that he could photograph Kennedy. He was aware that television cameras and the cameras of other journalists were focused on the podium and that his image would be publicized. When Kennedy left the Embassy Room, Khawar did not follow him; Khawar was still in the Embassy Room when Kennedy was shot in the hotel pantry area. Both the Federal Bureau of Investigation (FBI) and the Los Angeles Police Department questioned Khawar about the assassination, but neither agency ever regarded him as a suspect.

. . . The jury awarded Khawar $100,000 for injury to his reputation, $400,000 for emotional distress, $175,000 in presumed damages, and, after a separate punitive damages phase, $500,000 in punitive damages. . . .

II. Public Figure

We consider first Globe's contention that the trial court and the Court of Appeal erred in concluding that Khawar is a private rather than a public figure for purposes of this defamation action.

A. Background . . .

In Gertz v. Robert Welch, Inc. (1974) 418 U.S. 323 (*Gertz*), the court explained that it had imposed the actual malice requirement on defamation actions by both public officials and public figures because such persons "usually enjoy significantly greater access to the channels of effective communication and hence have a more realistic opportunity to counteract false statements than private individuals normally enjoy" (id. at p.344) and because they "have voluntarily exposed themselves to increased risk of injury from defamatory falsehood concerning them" (id. at p.345). Concerning the latter justification, the court stated: "Hypothetically, it may be possible for someone to become a public figure through no purposeful action of his own, but the instances of truly involuntary public figures must be exceedingly rare." (Ibid.)

The court then explained that there are two types of public figures: "Some occupy positions of such persuasive power and influence that they are deemed public figures for all purposes. More commonly, those classed as public figures have thrust themselves to the forefront of particular public controversies in order to influence the resolution of the issues involved. In either event, they invite attention and comment." (*Gertz*, supra, 418 U.S. 323, 345.) The court reiterated the distinction in these words: "[The public figure] designation may rest on either of two alternative bases. In some instances an individual may achieve such pervasive fame or notoriety that he becomes a public figure for all purposes and in all contexts. More commonly, an individual voluntarily injects himself or is drawn into a particular public controversy and thereby becomes a public figure for a limited range of issues. In either case such persons assume special prominence in the resolution of public questions." (Id. at p.351.)

The court contrasted these two types of public figures — the all purpose public figure and the limited purpose public figure — with an ordinary private individual: "He [the private individual] has not accepted public office or assumed an 'influential role in ordering society.' [Citation.] He has relinquished no part of his interest in the protection of his own good name, and consequently he has a more compelling call on the courts for redress of injury inflicted by defamatory falsehood. Thus, private individuals are not only more vulnerable to injury than public officials and public figures; they are also more deserving of recovery." (*Gertz*, supra, 418 U.S. 323, 345.) The court declined to impose the actual malice requirement on the recovery of damages for actual injury caused to a private figure by the publication of a defamatory falsehood.

In three later decisions, the United States Supreme Court has applied this form of analysis, similarly concluding in each that a plaintiff in a libel action was a private rather than a public figure.

B. Analysis . . .

Applying the standard here, we note, first, that Globe does not contend that Khawar is a public figure for all purposes but merely that he is a public figure for limited purposes relating to particular public controversies. Globe's main argument appears to be that publication of the Morrow book drew Khawar into public controversies surrounding Kennedy's assassination and that Khawar is therefore an involuntary public figure for the limited purpose of a report on that book. In making this argument, Globe relies on the language in *Gertz*, supra, 418 U.S. 323, 94 S. Ct. 2997, 41

L. Ed. 2d 789, that it is possible for a person "to become a public figure through no purposeful action of his own" (id. at p.345, 94 S. Ct. 2997) and that a person can become a public figure by being "drawn into a particular public controversy" (id. at p.351, 94 S. Ct. 2997). Thus, Globe concedes, at least for purposes of this one argument, that Khawar did not intentionally thrust himself into the vortex of any public controversy.

We find Globe's argument unpersuasive because characterizing Khawar as an involuntary public figure would be inconsistent with the reasons that the United States Supreme Court has given for requiring public figures to prove actual malice in defamation actions. As we have explained, the high court imposed the actual malice requirement on defamation actions by public figures and public officials for two reasons: They have media access enabling them to effectively defend their reputations in the public arena; and, by injecting themselves into public controversies, they may fairly be said to have voluntarily invited comment and criticism. (*Gertz*, supra, 418 U.S. 323, 344-345.) By stating that it is theoretically possible to become a public figure without purposeful action inviting criticism (id. at p.345), the high court has indicated that purposeful activity may not be essential for public figure characterization. But the high court has never stated or implied that it would be proper for a court to characterize an individual as a public figure in the face of proof that the individual had neither engaged in purposeful activity inviting criticism nor acquired substantial media access in relation to the controversy at issue. We read the court's decisions as precluding courts from affixing the public figure label when neither of the reasons for applying that label has been demonstrated. Thus, assuming a person may ever be accurately characterized as an involuntary public figure, we infer from the logic of *Gertz* that the high court would reserve this characterization for an individual who, despite never having voluntarily engaged the public's attention in an attempt to influence the outcome of a public controversy, nonetheless has acquired such public prominence in relation to the controversy as to permit media access sufficient to effectively counter media-published defamatory statements.

We find in the record no substantial evidence that Khawar acquired sufficient media access in relation to the controversy surrounding the Kennedy assassination or the Morrow book to effectively counter the defamatory falsehoods in the Globe article. After the assassination and before publication of the Morrow book, no reporter contacted Khawar to request an interview about the assassination. Nor was there any reason for a reporter to do so: Khawar was not a suspect in the investigation, he did not testify at the trial of the perpetrator of the assassination, and, so far as the record shows, his own views about the assassination were never publicized.

Nothing in the record demonstrates that Khawar acquired any significant media access as a result of publication of either the Morrow book or the other book, *RFK Must Die* (1970) by Robert Blair Kaiser, in which, according to Globe, questions were raised about Khawar's activities in relation to the assassination. There is no evidence that either book enjoyed substantial sales or was reviewed in widely circulated publications. . . .

The interview by the Bakersfield television station, which was the only interview in which Khawar ever participated that related in any way to the Kennedy assassination, the Morrow book, or the Globe article, occurred after and in response to the publication of the Globe article. Although this single interview demonstrates that Khawar enjoyed some media access, it is only the media access that would likely be available to any private individual who found himself the subject of sensational and defamatory accusations in a publication with a substantial nationwide circulation. (Globe distributed more than 2.7 million copies of the issue containing the Globe article.) If such access were sufficient to support a public figure characterization, any member of the media — any newspaper, magazine, television or radio network or local station — could confer public figure status simply by publishing sensational defamatory accusations against any private individual. This the United States Supreme Court has consistently declined to permit. As the court has repeatedly said, "those charged with defamation cannot, by their own conduct, create their own defense by making the claimant a public figure." (Hutchinson v. Proxmire, 443 U.S. 111, 135 (1979).)

Although Globe's primary argument is that publication of the Morrow book made Khawar an involuntary public figure, Globe may be understood to argue further that Khawar's involvement with the Kennedy assassination controversies was not entirely involuntary because, immediately before the assassination, Khawar sought and obtained a position close to Kennedy on the podium knowing that there would be substantial media coverage of the event. For a variety of reasons, this conduct does not demonstrate that Khawar voluntarily elected to encounter an increased risk of injury from defamatory falsehoods in publications like the Globe article.

First, Khawar's conduct occurred before any relevant controversy arose. The controversies discussed in the Globe article related to Kennedy's assassination and the particular theory concerning it that was proposed in the Morrow book. Khawar's conduct in standing near Kennedy at the hotel was not a voluntary association with either of those controversies because the conduct occurred before the assassination and before the Morrow book's publication. Khawar did not know, nor should he have known, that Kennedy would be assassinated moments later, much less that a book would be published 20 years thereafter containing the theory proposed in the Morrow book. We do not disagree with Globe that Kennedy's campaign for his party's nomination to the presidency may be described as a public issue or controversy, nor do we disagree that Khawar voluntarily associated himself with this public issue or controversy by allowing himself to be photographed with Kennedy at a campaign press conference. But these facts have no legal significance for purposes of this libel action. The subject of the Globe article was not Kennedy's candidacy as such, but rather Kennedy's assassination and the theory put forward in the Morrow book.

Second, even as to the public issues or controversies relating to Kennedy's candidacy, the role in these controversies that Khawar voluntarily assumed by standing near Kennedy on the podium was trivial at best. As the United States Supreme Court has stressed, "[a] private individual is not automatically transformed into a public figure just by becoming involved in or associated with a matter that attracts public attention." (Wolston v. Reader's Digest Ass'n, Inc., 443 U.W. 157, 167 (1979).) Khawar's conduct in standing near Kennedy foreseeably resulted in his being photographed with Kennedy, but a journalist who is photographed with other journalists crowded around a political candidate does not thereby assume any special prominence in relation to the political campaign issues.

Third, appearing on the podium was not conduct by which Khawar "engaged the attention of the public in an attempt to influence the resolution of the issues involved." (*Wolston*, supra, 443 U.S. 157, 168.) Khawar, who was an admirer of Kennedy, wanted to be photographed with Kennedy because the resulting photographs would have a strictly personal value as souvenirs. Khawar did not anticipate, nor did he have reason to anticipate, that inclusion of his image would make the photographs more newsworthy or would in any way affect the resolution of any public issue related to Kennedy's run for the presidency. In brief, by appearing in close proximity to Kennedy, Khawar did not engage in conduct that was "calculated to draw attention to himself in order to invite public comment or influence the public with respect to any issue." (Ibid.)

Having concluded that Khawar did not voluntarily elect to encounter an increased risk of media defamation and that before publication of the Globe article he did not enjoy media access sufficient to prevent resulting injury to his reputation, we agree with the trial court and the Court of Appeal that, for purposes of this defamation action, Khawar is a private rather than a public figure. . . .

IV.

A. Actual Malice

The First Amendment to the federal Constitution, as authoritatively construed by the United States Supreme Court, does not require a private figure plaintiff to prove actual malice to recover damages for actual injury caused by publication of a defamatory falsehood. (*Gertz*, supra, 418 U.S. 323, 347.) Rather, in this situation, the individual states may define the appropriate standard of liability for defamation, provided they do not impose liability without fault. In California, this court has adopted a negligence standard for private figure plaintiffs seeking compensatory damages in defamation actions.

There is a different rule, however, for recovery of either punitive damages or damages for presumed injury. The United States Supreme Court has held that to recover such damages, even a private figure plaintiff must prove actual malice if the defamatory statement involves matters of public concern. We agree with Globe that the Kennedy assassination is a matter of public concern.

Because in this defamation action Khawar is a private figure plaintiff, he was required to prove only negligence, and not actual malice, to recover damages for actual injury to his reputation. But Khawar was required to prove actual malice to recover punitive or presumed damages for defamation involving the Kennedy assassination. Because Khawar sought punitive and presumed damages as well as damages for actual injury, the issues of both actual malice and negligence were submitted to the jury. The jury found that in publishing the Globe article Globe acted both negligently and with actual malice. Globe challenged both findings on appeal. In this court, Globe contends that the Court of Appeal erred in rejecting its challenges to these two findings. . . .

In this context, actual malice means that the defamatory statement was made "with knowledge that it was false or with reckless disregard of whether it was false or not." (New York Times Co. v. Sullivan, supra, 376 U.S. 254, 280.) Reckless disregard, in turn, means that the publisher "in fact entertained serious doubts as to the truth of his publication." (St. Amant v. Thompson, 390 U.S. 727, 731 (1968).) To prove actual malice, therefore, a plaintiff must "demonstrate with clear and convincing evidence that the defendant realized that his statement was false or that he subjectively entertained serious doubts as to the truth of his statement." (Bose Corp. v. Consumers Union of U.S., Inc., 466 U.S. 485, 511, fn.30. (1984).)

Actual malice is judged by a subjective standard; otherwise stated, "there must be sufficient evidence to permit the conclusion that the defendant . . . had a 'high degree of awareness of . . . probable falsity.'" (Harte-Hanks Communications v. Connaughton, 491 U.S. 657, 688 (1989).) To prove this culpable mental state, the plaintiff may rely on circumstantial evidence, including evidence of motive and failure to adhere to professional standards. When, as in this case, a finding of actual malice is based on the republication of a third party's defamatory falsehoods, "failure to investigate before publishing, even when a reasonably prudent person would have done so, is not sufficient." (Harte-Hanks Communications v. Connaughton, supra, 491 U.S. 657, 688.) Nonetheless, the actual malice finding may be upheld "where there are obvious reasons to doubt the veracity of the informant or the accuracy of his reports" (ibid.), and the republisher failed to interview obvious witnesses who could have confirmed or disproved the allegations (id. at p.682) or to consult relevant documentary sources.

There were, to say the least, obvious reasons to doubt the accuracy of the Morrow book's accusation that Khawar killed Kennedy. The assassination of a nationally prominent politician, in the midst of his campaign for his party's nomination for the presidency, had been painstakingly and exhaustively investigated by both the FBI and state prosecutorial agencies. During this massive investigation, these agencies accumulated a vast quantity of evidence pointing to the guilt of Sirhan as the lone assassin. As a result, Sirhan alone was charged with Kennedy's murder. At Sirhan's trial, "it was undisputed that [Sirhan] fired the shot that killed Senator Kennedy" and "[t]he evidence also established conclusively that he shot the victims of the assault counts." (People v. Sirhan, 7 Cal. 3d 710, 717 (Cal. 1972).) The jury returned a verdict finding beyond a reasonable doubt that Sirhan was guilty of first degree murder. On Sirhan's appeal from the resulting judgment of death, this court carefully reviewed the evidence and found it sufficient to sustain the first degree murder conviction. (Id. at pp.717-728.) In asserting that Khawar, and not Sirhan, had killed Kennedy, the Morrow book was making the highly improbable claim that results of the official investigation, Sirhan's trial, and this court's decision on Sirhan's appeal, were all fundamentally mistaken.

Because there were obvious reasons to doubt the accuracy of the Morrow book's central claim, and because that claim was an inherently defamatory accusation against Khawar, the jury could properly conclude that Globe acted with actual malice in republishing that claim if it found also, as it impliedly did, that Globe failed to use readily available means to verify the accuracy of the claim by interviewing obvious witnesses who could have confirmed or disproved the allegations or by inspecting relevant documents or other evidence. The evidence at trial supports the jury's implied finding that neither Blackburn (who wrote the Globe article) nor Globe's editors made any such effort.

Preliminarily, we note that this was not a situation in which time pressures made it impossible or impractical to investigate the truth of the accusation. Kennedy had been assassinated in 1968. In November 1988, when Roundtable published the Morrow book, and in April 1989, when Globe published its article, the Kennedy assassination had long ceased to be an issue that urgently engaged the public's attention. Before publishing an article accusing a private figure of a sensational murder, Globe could well have afforded to take the time necessary to investigate the matter with sufficient thoroughness to form an independent judgment before republishing an accusation likely to have a devastating effect on the reputation of the person accused. But Globe did not do so.

Neither Blackburn nor Globe's editors contacted any of the eyewitnesses to the assassination, some of whom were prominent individuals who could easily have been located. At the trial, for example, Roosevelt Grier, a well-known former professional football player and volunteer Kennedy security aide who was present in the pantry area where Kennedy was shot, testified that after the assassination he had remained active in public life and was not "real difficult to find," but that no one from Globe had contacted him. Frank Mankiewicz, Kennedy's press secretary and a witness to the assassination, testified that in 1989, when the Globe article was published, he was vice-chairman of a public relations firm in Washington, D.C., and was listed in the telephone directory for that city, yet no one from Globe had contacted him. Nor is there any evidence that anyone working for Globe reviewed the voluminous public records of the government investigation of the Kennedy assassination or the Sirhan trial. Indeed, Globe's managing editor, Robert Taylor, conceded during his testimony that Globe made no attempt to independently investigate the truth of any of the statements in the Morrow book. In short, phrasing our conclusion in the language of the United States Supreme Court, "Accepting the jury's determination that [Globe]'s explanations for these omissions were not credible, it is likely that [Globe]'s inaction was a product of a deliberate decision not to acquire knowledge of facts that might confirm the probable falsity of [the Morrow book]'s charges." (Harte-Hanks Communications v. Connaughton, supra, 491 U.S. 657, 692.) As the United States Supreme Court added, "Although failure to investigate will not alone support a finding of actual malice, [citation], the purposeful avoidance of the truth is in a different category." (Ibid.) . . .

Having independently reviewed the record, we agree with the Court of Appeal that the evidence at trial strongly supports an inference that Globe purposefully avoided the truth and published the Globe article despite serious doubts regarding the truth of the accusation against Khawar. In short, we conclude that clear and convincing evidence supports the jury's finding that in republishing the Morrow book's false accusation against Khawar, Globe acted with actual malice — that is, with reckless disregard of whether the accusation was false or not.

B. Negligence

Globe's challenge to the sufficiency of the evidence to support the finding of negligence merits little consideration.

Because actual malice is a higher fault standard than negligence, a finding of actual malice generally includes a finding of negligence, and evidence that is sufficient to support a finding of actual malice is usually, and perhaps invariably, sufficient also to support a finding of negligence. In any event, we are satisfied that the evidence we previously reviewed, and which we have concluded clearly and convincingly establishes actual malice in the form of reckless disregard, is sufficient also to sustain the finding of negligence. . . .

The judgment of the Court of Appeal is affirmed.

NOTES TO KHAWAR v. GLOBE INTERNATIONAL, INC.

1. *Levels of Fault.* The court in *Khawar* applies both a negligence test and an actual malice test. For what types of damages must a private figure in a matter of public concern prove actual malice? What choices did the U.S. Supreme Court give to states regarding the level of fault for the other type of damages?

2. *Proof of Falsity.* Gertz v. Robert Welch, relied upon by the court in *Khawar*, is the key U.S. Supreme Court opinion on private figures involved in matters of public concern. A more recent Supreme Court case, Philadelphia Newspapers, Inc. v. Hepps,

475 U.S. 767 (1986), added to that rule, holding that in those cases, the plaintiff cannot recover damages without also showing that the statements at issue were false. This reversed the common law rule that falsity was presumed and truth was a defense to be established by the defendant. In public official and public figure cases, is there a requirement that a defamation plaintiff prove falsity?   ,

Problem
Classifying Public and Private Figures

A newspaper published an article with an erroneous headline, though the body of the story was true:

THREE PLEAD GUILTY IN CATTLE THEFTS

Oxford — Three Mississippi men have pleaded guilty to federal charges of illegally transferring cattle from Alabama to Alcorn and Tippah. Officers said Wilbur Gregory, George L. Whitten and W.L. Tatum, all of Alcorn County, were charged with moving the 112 head of cattle from Red Bay, Alabama, to Mississippi without having the animals tested for brucellosis, a bacterial disease. The three face sentencing November 30, for the misdemeanor crime.

Whitten sued the newspaper for defamation. Is the statement in the headline false? Is Whitten a public or private figure? See Whitten v. Commercial Dispatch Publishing Co., Inc., 487 So. 2d 843 (Miss. 1986).

Perspective: Constitutional Treatment of Media Defendants

While the print and broadcast media are frequently defendants in defamation actions, the U.S. Supreme Court has not decided whether special treatment of the press is appropriate, leaving scholars to debate whether speech by the media deserves special treatment. Professor Arlen W. Langvardt, *Media Defendants, Public Concerns, and Public Plaintiffs: Toward Fashioning Order from Confusion in Defamation Law*, 49 U. of Pitt. L. Rev. 91, 120-123 (1987), argued that there should be no special treatment:

The freedom of speech clause must be regarded as having been premised on the principle that nonmedia speakers and media speakers serve an educative, opinion-shaping function. Otherwise, there would have been no need in the first amendment to include both the freedom of speech and freedom of press clauses. As the Court has observed, the function of providing useful, significant, and desired information cannot be regarded as the exclusive province of the press.

There are other considerations that cut against a media-nonmedia distinction in the constitutional aspects of defamation. If the constitutional fault rules were not regarded as applicable in a nonmedia defendant case, liability without fault would apply. The imposition of such liability on a nonmedia defendant would run contrary to the risk shifting concept underlying strict liability, because nonmedia defendants generally would be less able to pay and shift the costs of judgments entered against them than would media defendants. Yet nonmedia defendants would be held liable more readily than would media defendants because of the natural effects of the enhanced burden imposed on plaintiffs when the fault requirements are made part of the elements that must be proved. Further, a false and defamatory statement published by a media defendant has a greater potential for doing widespread harm to the plaintiff's reputation than does the typical false and defamatory statement by the nonmedia defendant because of the broader circulation the media defendant's statement would get. Nevertheless, if a media-nonmedia distinction were part of the constitutional law of defamation, the nonmedia defendant would be held liable much more readily than would the media defendant. Consequently, a media-nonmedia distinction is fundamentally unsound.

Professor Langvardt also argued that it would be hard to define who was the "media." He feared that the court would use suspect factors to classify specialized publications designed to reach narrow audiences, such as "company newsletters, trade union publications, credit reports, handbills and brochures distributed by a group, and pamphlets handed out by the proverbial 'lonely pamphleteer.'"

b. Private Figure Not Involved in an Issue of Public Concern

A defendant who published a statement about a private person not involving a matter of public concern receives the lowest level of constitutional protection. In Dun & Bradstreet, Inc. v. Greenmoss Builders, the Supreme Court distinguishes between issues that are and are not of public concern and discusses the fault requirement applying to the latter type of cases. When reading *Dun & Bradstreet*, identify the levels of fault from which a state is free to choose when modifying its law to conform to constitutional requirements. The Supreme Court does not say what state courts must do in cases involving private figures not involved in matters of public concern. Rather, the Supreme Court indicates what state courts are permitted to do only by saying what is not required. Consider also the categories of damages that are not discussed by the Court.

DUN & BRADSTREET, INC. v. GREENMOSS BUILDERS
472 U.S. 749 (1985)

Justice POWELL.

In Gertz v. Robert Welch, Inc., 418 U.S. 323 (1974), we held that the First Amendment restricted the damages that a private individual could obtain from a publisher for a libel that involved a matter of public concern. More specifically, we held that in these circumstances the First Amendment prohibited awards of presumed and punitive damages for false and defamatory statements unless the plaintiff shows "actual malice" that is, knowledge of falsity or reckless disregard for the truth. The question presented in this case is whether this rule of *Gertz* applies when the false and defamatory statements do not involve matters of public concern.

Petitioner Dun & Bradstreet, a credit reporting agency, provides subscribers with financial and related information about businesses. All the information is confidential; under the terms of the subscription agreement the subscribers may not reveal it to anyone else. On July 26, 1976, petitioner sent a report to five subscribers indicating that respondent, a construction contractor, had filed a voluntary petition for bankruptcy. This report was false and grossly misrepresented respondent's assets and liabilities. That same day, while discussing the possibility of future financing with its bank, respondent's president was told that the bank had received the defamatory report. He immediately called petitioner's regional office, explained the error, and asked for a correction. In addition, he requested the names of the firms that had received the false report in order to assure them that the company was solvent. Petitioner promised to look into the matter but refused to divulge the names of those who had received the report.

After determining that its report was indeed false, petitioner issued a corrective notice on or about August 3, 1976, to the five subscribers who had received the initial report. The notice stated that one of respondent's former employees, not respondent itself, had filed for bankruptcy and that respondent "continued in business as usual." Respondent told petitioner that it was dissatisfied with the notice, and it again asked for a list of subscribers who had seen the initial report. Again petitioner refused to divulge their names.

Respondent then brought this defamation action in Vermont state court. It alleged that the false report had injured its reputation and sought both compensatory and punitive damages. The trial established that the error in petitioner's report had been caused when one of its employees, a 17-year-old high school student paid to review Vermont bankruptcy pleadings, had inadvertently attributed to respondent a bankruptcy petition filed by one of respondent's former employees. Although petitioner's representative testified that it was routine practice to check the accuracy of such reports with the businesses themselves, it did not try to verify the information about respondent before reporting it.

After trial, the jury returned a verdict in favor of respondent and awarded $50,000 in compensatory or presumed damages and $300,000 in punitive damages. [After the trial court granted Dun & Bradstreet's motion for a new trial, and the Vermont Supreme Court reversed, the U.S. Supreme Court granted certiorari to outline the extent of constitutional protections to be given to the defendant's speech.] . . .

In New York Times Co. v. Sullivan, 376 U.S. 254 (1964), the Court for the first time held that the First Amendment limits the reach of state defamation laws. That case concerned a public official's recovery of damages for the publication of an advertisement criticizing police conduct in a civil rights demonstration. As the Court noted, the advertisement concerned "one of the major public issues of our time." Id., 376 U.S., at 271. Noting that "freedom of expression *upon public questions* is secured by the First Amendment," id., at 269 (emphasis added), and that "debate *on public issues* should be uninhibited, robust, and wide-open," id., at 270 (emphasis added), the Court held that a public official cannot recover damages for defamatory falsehood unless he proves that the false statement was made with "'actual malice' — that is, with knowledge that it was false or with reckless disregard of whether it was false or not," id., at 280. In later cases, all involving public issues, the Court extended this same constitutional protection to libels of public figures, and in one case suggested in a plurality opinion that this constitutional rule should extend to libels of any individual so long as the defamatory statements involved a "matter of public or general interest," Rosenbloom v. Metromedia, Inc., 403 U.S. 29, 44 (1971) (opinion of Brennan, J.).

In Gertz v. Robert Welch, Inc., 418 U.S. 323 (1974), we held that the protections of *New York Times* did not extend as far as *Rosenbloom* suggested. *Gertz* concerned a libelous article appearing in a magazine called *American Opinion,* the monthly outlet of the John Birch Society. The article in question discussed whether the prosecution of a policeman in Chicago was part of a Communist campaign to discredit local law enforcement agencies. The plaintiff, Gertz, neither a public official nor a public figure, was a lawyer tangentially involved in the prosecution. The magazine alleged that he was the chief architect of the "frame-up" of the police officer and linked him to Communist activity. Like every other case in which this Court has found constitutional limits to state defamation laws, *Gertz* involved expression on a matter of undoubted public concern.

In *Gertz,* we held that the fact that expression concerned a public issue did not by itself entitle the libel defendant to the constitutional protections of *New York Times.* These protections, we found, were not "justified solely by reference to the interest of the press and broadcast media in immunity from liability." 418 U.S., at 343. Rather, they represented "an accommodation between [First Amendment] concern[s] and the limited state interest present in the context of libel actions brought by public persons." Ibid. In libel actions brought by private persons we found the competing interests different. Largely because private persons have not voluntarily exposed themselves to increased risk of injury from defamatory statements and because they generally lack effective opportunities for rebutting such statements, we found that the State possessed a "strong and legitimate . . . interest in compensating private individuals for injury to reputation." Id., at 348-349. Balancing this stronger state interest against the same First Amendment interest at stake in *New York Times,* we held that a State could not allow recovery of presumed and punitive damages absent a showing of "actual malice." Nothing in our opinion, however, indicated that this same balance would be struck regardless of the type of speech involved.

We have never considered whether the *Gertz* balance obtains when the defamatory statements involve no issue of public concern. To make this determination, we must employ the approach approved in *Gertz* and balance the State's interest in compensating private individuals for injury to their reputation against the First Amendment interest in protecting this type of expression. This state interest is identical to the one weighed in *Gertz.* There we found that it was "strong and legitimate." 418 U.S., at 348. A State should not lightly be required to abandon it,

> for, as Mr. Justice Stewart has reminded us, the individual's right to the protection of his own good name "reflects no more than our basic concept of the essential dignity and worth of every human being — a concept at the root of any decent system of ordered liberty. The protection of private personality, like the protection of life itself, is left primarily to the individual States under the Ninth and Tenth Amendments. . . ." Rosenblatt v. Baer, 383 U.S. 75 (1966) (concurring opinion).

Id., at 341.

The First Amendment interest, on the other hand, is less important than the one weighed in *Gertz.* We have long recognized that not all speech is of equal First Amendment importance. It is speech on "matters of public concern" that is "at the heart of the First Amendment's protection." First National Bank of Boston v. Bellotti, 435 U.S. 765, 776 (1978), citing Thornhill v. Alabama, 310 U.S. 88, 101 (1940). As we stated in

Connick v. Myers, 461 U.S. 138, 145 (1983), this "special concern [for speech on public issues] is no mystery":

> The First Amendment "was fashioned to assure unfettered interchange of ideas for the bringing about of political and social changes desired by the people." Roth v. United States, 354 U.S. 476, 484 (1957). "[S]peech concerning public affairs is more than self-expression; it is the essence of self-government." Garrison v. Louisiana, 379 U.S. 64, 74-75 (1964). Accordingly, the Court has frequently reaffirmed that speech on public issues occupies the "highest rung of the hierarchy of First Amendment values," and is entitled to special protection. NAACP v. Claiborne Hardware Co., 458 U.S. 886, 913 (1982).

In contrast, speech on matters of purely private concern is of less First Amendment concern. Id., at 146-147. As a number of state courts, including the court below, have recognized, the role of the Constitution in regulating state libel law is far more limited when the concerns that activated *New York Times* and *Gertz* are absent. In such a case,

> [t]here is no threat to the free and robust debate of public issues; there is no potential interference with a meaningful dialogue of ideas concerning self-government; and there is no threat of liability causing a reaction of self-censorship by the press. The facts of the present case are wholly without the First Amendment concerns with which the Supreme Court of the United States has been struggling.

Harley-Davidson Motorsports, Inc. v. Markley, 568 P.2d 1359, 1363 (1977).

While such speech is not totally unprotected by the First Amendment, its protections are less stringent. In *Gertz*, we found that the state interest in awarding presumed and punitive damages was not "substantial" in view of their effect on speech at the core of First Amendment concern. 418 U.S., at 349. This interest, however, *is* "substantial" relative to the incidental effect these remedies may have on speech of significantly less constitutional interest. The rationale of the common-law rules has been the experience and judgment of history that "proof of actual damage will be impossible in a great many cases where, from the character of the defamatory words and the circumstances of publication, it is all but certain that serious harm has resulted in fact." W. Prosser, Law of Torts §112, p.765 (4th ed. 1971). As a result, courts for centuries have allowed juries to presume that some damage occurred from many defamatory utterances and publications. This rule furthers the state interest in providing remedies for defamation by ensuring that those remedies are effective. In light of the reduced constitutional value of speech involving no matters of public concern, we hold that the state interest adequately supports awards of presumed and punitive damages — even absent a showing of "actual malice."

The only remaining issue is whether petitioner's credit report involved a matter of public concern. In a related context, we have held that "[w]hether . . . speech addresses a matter of public concern must be determined by [the expression's] content, form, and context . . . as revealed by the whole record." Connick v. Myers, supra, 461 U.S., at 147-148. These factors indicate that petitioner's credit report concerns no public issue. It was speech solely in the individual interest of the speaker and its specific business audience. This particular interest warrants no special protection when — as in this case — the speech is wholly false and clearly damaging to the victim's business reputation. Moreover, since the credit report was made available to only five subscribers, who, under the terms of the subscription agreement, could not disseminate it further, it cannot be said that the report involves any "strong interest in the free flow of commercial information." Id., at 764. There is simply no credible argument that this type of credit reporting requires special protection to ensure that "debate on public issues [will] be uninhibited, robust, and wide-open." New York Times Co. v. Sullivan, 376 U.S., at 270.

In addition, the speech here, like advertising, is hardy and unlikely to be deterred by incidental state regulation. It is solely motivated by the desire for profit, which, we have noted, is a force less likely to be deterred than others. Arguably, the reporting here was also more objectively verifiable than speech deserving of greater protection. In any case, the market provides a powerful incentive to a credit reporting agency to be accurate, since false credit reporting is of no use to creditors. Thus, any incremental "chilling" effect of libel suits would be of decreased significance.

We conclude that permitting recovery of presumed and punitive damages in defamation cases absent a showing of "actual malice" does not violate the First Amendment when the defamatory statements do not involve matters of public concern. Accordingly, we affirm the judgment of the Vermont Supreme Court.

NOTES TO DUN & BRADSTREET, INC. v. GREENMOSS BUILDERS

1. *Private Plaintiff in Matters Not of Public Concern.* Having been given their freedom to choose a level of fault for presumed and punitive damages, states have taken different approaches in cases involving private plaintiffs in matters not of public concern. The vast majority of states have adopted a negligence standard, while a few have adopted an actual malice standard. New York has adopted a "gross irresponsibility standard" in which the defamation plaintiff must

> establish by a preponderance of the evidence that the publisher acted in a grossly irresponsible manner without due consideration for the standards of information gathering and dissemination ordinarily followed by responsible parties.

See Chapadeau v. Utica Observer Dispatch, Inc., 341 N.E.2d 569 (N.Y. 1975). See Rodney A. Smolla, *Law of Defamation* §§3.30-3.31, 3.41-3.48 (listing the states n each category).

2. *Matters of Public Concern.* To infer what issues the Supreme Court would put in the category of *matters of public concern*, one must focus on the underlying policies to which the Court refers when deciding this question. To what policies does the opinion in *Dun & Bradstreet* refer? How did those policies affect the outcome in *Dun & Bradstreet*?

3. *Statutory Treatment of Media Defendants.* Although newspapers, magazines, and broadcasters are frequently defendants in defamation actions, the Supreme Court has not decided whether media defendants are entitled to any special constitutional protection. Media defendants nevertheless receive individual attention in state statutes. A California statute applying to libel by a newspaper and slanders by radio, for instance, limits recovery to special damages where the plaintiff has demanded and received a correction from the defendant. When correction was demanded and not given, the plaintiff may seek general, special, and punitive damages. All plaintiffs must prove actual malice to recover punitive damages, with "actual malice" defined as something closer to "express malice" than constitutional "actual malice." See Cal. Civ. Code §48a(1), (2), and (4)(d).

Problem
Matters of Public and Private Concern

Which of the following contexts in which a private figure was allegedly defamed involves an issue of private concern?

A. Gail Davis alleged that nationally known singer and actress Diana Ross defamed her by saying in a letter, "If I let an employee go, it's because either their work or their personal habits are not acceptable to me." See Davis v. Ross, 107 F.R.D. 326 (S.D.N.Y. 1985).

B. The *Sun* newspaper published a fictitious story about a woman named "Audrey Wiles," living in Australia, who quit her paper route at the age of 101 because an extramarital affair with a millionaire client on her route had left her pregnant. Next to the story was a photograph of the plaintiff, 97-year-old Nellie Mitchell, who had operated a newsstand and delivered newspapers in her community for over 50 years. Nellie Mitchell was not the person on whom the fictitious "Audrey Wiles" was based and had no connection to the fictitious story other than being old and a former newspaper delivery person. See Peoples Bank and Trust Co. of Mountain Home v. Globe International Publishing, Inc., 978 F.2d 1065 (8th Cir. 1992).

C. A man alleged that he was defamed by a woman claiming he was the father of her child. See King v. Tanner, 539 N.Y.S.2d 617 (N.Y. Sup. Ct. 1987)

Statute: LIBEL OR SLANDER
Mich. Stat. Ann. §600.2911(2)(b), (6), (7) (2017)

---

(2)(b) Exemplary and punitive damages shall not be recovered in actions for libel unless the plaintiff, before instituting his or her action, gives notice to the defendant to publish a retraction and allows a reasonable time to do so, and proof of the publication or correction shall be admissible in evidence under a denial on the question of the good faith of the defendant, and in mitigation and reduction of exemplary or punitive damages. For libel based on a radio or television broadcast, the retraction shall be made in the same manner and at the same time of the day as the original libel; for libel based on a publication, the retraction shall be published in the same size type, in the same editions and as far as practical, in substantially the same position as the original libel; and for other libel, the retraction shall be published or communicated in substantially the same manner as the original libel.

(6) An action for libel or slander shall not be brought based upon a communication involving public officials or public figures unless the claim is sustained by clear and convincing proof that the defamatory falsehood was published with knowledge that it was false or with reckless disregard of whether or not it was false.

(7) An action for libel or slander shall not be brought based upon a communication involving a private individual unless the defamatory falsehood concerns the private individual and was published negligently. Recovery under this provision shall be limited to economic damages including attorney fees.

Statute: PREREQUISITES TO RECOVERY OF VINDICTIVE OR PUNITIVE
DAMAGES IN ACTION FOR LIBEL

Ala. Code §6-5-186 (2017)

Vindictive or punitive damages shall not be recovered in any action for libel on
account of any publication unless (1) it shall be proved that the publication was made
by the defendant with knowledge that the matter published was false, or with reckless
disregard of whether it was false or not, and (2) it shall be proved that five days before
the commencement of the action the plaintiff shall have made written demand upon
the defendant for a public retraction of the charge or matter published; and the
defendant shall have failed or refused to publish within five days, in as prominent
and public a place or manner as the charge or matter published occupied, a full and fair
retraction of such charge or matter.

NOTES TO STATUTES

1. *Statutory Treatment of Public and Private Figures.* The Michigan statute
reflects the Supreme Court's classification scheme that first identifies the type of person
(public or private) and, if private, the type of matter or concern (public or private). Are
the fault requirements in the Michigan statute sufficient to meet the requirements of
the U.S. Constitution? Are the Michigan requirements more rigorous than required?

2. *Statutory Treatment of Punitive Damages.* Some statutory limitations on punitive damages may be more stringent than required by the U.S. Supreme Court's interpretation of the First Amendment. Which barriers to recovery of punitive damages by a
private plaintiff in a matter of private concern created by the Michigan and Alabama
statutes are mandated by the First Amendment?

CHAPTER 17

ALTERNATIVES TO LITIGATION

I. Introduction

The problems tort litigation addresses are complex. The cost of litigation is sometimes high, and its results are unpredictable. For these reasons, among others, it is understandable that both plaintiffs and defendants have often sought either to replace it or to change it. This chapter examines the main approaches to providing alternatives to litigation. They typically involve eliminating the need to adjudicate fault and are usually intended to reduce the overall costs of administration.

II. Replacing Litigation with Insurance Systems

A. In General

Workers' compensation statutes are the oldest and most widespread substitute for litigation. While litigation still occurs with respect to claims that workers make under this system, it does provide no-fault compensation for very large numbers of workplace injuries. The main idea of the system, to avoid litigation over fault and to provide swift compensation, has been applied in other fields as well, such as automobile-related injuries and injuries suffered from the use of vaccines or from terrorist attacks.

B. Workers' Compensation

About a century ago, a movement to create what were then called workmen's compensation laws became successful across the United States. In 1979, the Sixth Circuit described this history:

> The dominant purpose of the movement to adopt workmen's compensation laws . . . was to provide social insurance to compensate victims of industrial accidents

because it was widely believed that the limited rights of recovery available under the common law at the turn of the [twentieth] century were inadequate to protect them.

The so-called "unholy trinity" of judicially-created employer defenses, assumption of the risk, contributory negligence and the fellow servant rule, were developed and strictly enforced as legal rules in the last half of the nineteenth century. The result, according to Deans Prosser and Wade, was recovery in less than a quarter of work-related accidents, as injured workmen subsidized economic growth.

Employers generally opposed the movement for "reform"; labor generally favored it. Workmen's compensation laws were adopted as a compromise between these contending forces. Workmen were willing to exchange a set of common-law remedies of dubious value for modest workmen's compensation benefits schedules designed to keep the injured workman and his family from destitution.

Boggs v. Blue Diamond Coal Co., 590 F.2d 655, 658-659 (6th Cir. 1979).

All states now have statutes that require most employers to obtain insurance that will provide benefits to workers who suffer workplace injuries. An injured worker receives benefits regardless of whether the employer was at fault and regardless of whether the worker was at fault. The amount of benefits is usually controlled by statutes or administrative rules that specify how much will be awarded for a particular injury. This benefit to workers is balanced by a very important benefit to employers: the statutes immunize the employers from tort liability. Where there are disputes about eligibility or the size of an award, administrative agencies, rather than courts, are the initial decision makers.

Contemporary issues in workers' compensation often involve whether or not an injury is covered by the system. Fryer v. Kranz involves an attempt to withdraw a workplace injury from the workers' compensation system so that the defendant employer would be subject to a typical tort lawsuit. In contrast, Cunningham v. Shelton Security Service, Inc. represents an effort to obtain workers' compensation coverage for a worker's fatal heart attack.

FRYER v. KRANZ

616 N.W.2d 102 (S.D. 2000)

MILLER, C.J.

In this intermediate appeal, because the employee has shown there is no genuine issue of material fact as to whether employer's conduct was intentional in order to except it from workers' compensation coverage, we hold that the circuit court improperly denied the employer's motion for summary judgment.

In 1996, Clint Kranz was remodeling a building in Watertown, South Dakota, to convert it into a casino. He employed workers, including Kathy Fryer, to help with the project. As part of the cleanup, he wanted to remove grout and other residue from the ceramic tile floors. Cleaning the tile proved difficult, so he purchased muriatic acid for the job. Muriatic acid, also called hydrochloric acid, is a strong, highly corrosive chemical. The product label warned that for proper use, the acid should be diluted, the vapors are harmful when the acid is used improperly, and the product is for exterior use only. These warnings were not readable when Fryer used the chemical because the label was covered with "cement stuff."

To show Fryer how to clean the tile, Kranz poured the undiluted muriatic acid on the floor, saying "This is how we use it." Kranz said he had used the product several times. He did not warn Fryer about any dangers, although he did say the acid is "corrosive and smells really bad," and "try not to breathe it." Fryer was told to wear protective gloves. Also, a small oscillating fan was positioned nearby to circulate the air, with more fans set up in the doorways to ventilate the building.

Over the course of three to four weeks, Fryer regularly cleaned with the acid. It produced a "green cloud" when poured on the floor. The vapor made her feel nauseated, lightheaded, and she coughed when she breathed it. She thought, nonetheless, that the fumes were no more toxic than those from products like fingernail polish remover or "white-out." Yet she "complained a lot about it." She told Kranz, "It makes me feel weird. It makes me light-headed. I hate this shit." Kranz responded, "Well, when that happens, then you need to take a break and you need to go get some air." He had her continue to use the product.

On November 12, 1996, Fryer used the muriatic acid to clean a very small room where there was no ventilation. The fumes overcame her. Lightheaded and nauseated, she could not continue. She ran across the alley to a bathroom in another building and vomited. When Kranz knocked on the door, Fryer assured him that she "was fine." She did not immediately seek medical attention, but as the day progressed, she suffered chest pains, breathing problems, and her skin "hurt real bad." Later in the day, she was admitted to the hospital where she remained for four days. She continues to suffer health problems.

Fryer brought a personal injury action against Kranz in circuit court. . . . Kranz moved for summary judgment. The court denied the motion, concluding that there were material issues of fact on whether [Kranz] committed an intentional tort. We granted intermediate appeal. . . .

Workers' compensation covers employment-related accidental injury of every nature. No matter what form employer conduct takes, be it careless, grossly negligent, reckless, or wanton, if it is not a "conscious and deliberate intent directed to the purpose of inflicting an injury," workers' compensation remains the exclusive remedy. 6 Larson's Workers' Compensation Law (MB) §103.03 at 103-6 (November 1999). Even when an employer's acts entail "knowingly permitting a hazardous work condition to exist, knowingly ordering a claimant to perform an extremely dangerous job, [or] wilfully failing to furnish a safe place to work," still they come within the ambit of workers' compensation. Id. at 103-6 (November 1999) & 103-7 (May 2000).

In the workers' compensation scheme, exclusivity serves two important values: (1) it maintains "the balance of sacrifices between employer and employee in the substitution of no-fault liability for tort liability," and (2) it minimizes "litigation, even litigation of undoubted merit." Larson, supra, §103.05[6] at 103-44 (May 2000). Exclusiveness imparts efficiency to the workers' compensation system. "Every presumption is on the side of avoiding superimposing the complexities and uncertainties of tort litigation on the compensation process." Id.

When an employer intends to commit injury, as opposed to negligently or recklessly committing it, then the rationale for embracing workers' compensation disappears. Accordingly, when an employer intentionally causes a work-related injury, workers' compensation law allows an exception to the exclusive remedies for employee work-related injuries:

> The rights and remedies herein granted to an employee subject to this title, on account of personal injury or death arising out of and in the course of employment, shall exclude all other rights and remedies of such employee, his personal representatives, dependents, or next of kin, on account of such injury or death against his employer or any employee, partner, officer or director of such employer, except rights and remedies arising from intentional tort.

SDCL 62-3-2.

Only injuries "intentionally inflicted by the employer" take the matter outside the exclusivity of workers' compensation coverage. Harn v. Continental Lumber Co., 506 N.W.2d 91, 95 (S.D. 1993). "The worker must also allege facts that plausibly demonstrate an actual intent by the employer to injure or a substantial certainty that injury will be the inevitable outcome of employer's conduct." Jensen v. Sport Bowl, Inc., 469 N.W.2d 370, 372 (S.D. 1991) (citations omitted). Even when an "injury is a probable . . . result, [workers'] compensation is still the exclusive remedy." Id. The intentional tort exception is narrowly construed.

The statement of our law regarding the substantial certainty standard was summarized in *Harn*:

> The substantial certainty standard requires that the employer had actual knowledge of the dangerous condition and that the employer still required the employee to perform. Substantial certainty of injury to the employee should be equated with virtual certainty to be considered an intentional tort. . . . If an employee worked under such conditions where the employer actually knew of the danger and that injury was substantially certain (virtually certain) to occur, and such injury did occur, the employer should not escape civil liability for placing the employee in such a dangerous position. That is the type of conduct the intentional tort exception deters.

506 N.W.2d at 100.

Fryer asserts that Kranz knew she would be injured. When she complained to him about the fumes making her feel lightheaded, he replied: "Well, when that happens, then you need to take a break and you need to go get some air." Fryer stresses that Kranz used the word "when" rather than "if." To Fryer, it is notable that, although Kranz had joined Fryer in working with the acid before she complained, he sent her back to the small room alone. This, she argues, shows that her adverse reaction was inevitable and that Kranz knew it. She claims Kranz knew because she had been harmed previously, though not as seriously, by the fumes when they made her light-headed and nauseated.

"The intentional tort exception to workmen's compensation is fact specific." *Harn*, 506 N.W.2d at 99. A comparison of the present facts to the factual bases of our prior cases is necessary to appreciate the allegations proffered by Fryer. Our cases thus far have described actions that do not constitute an intentional tort. This fact results from our narrow construction of the intentional tort exception.

Most recently, in *Harn*, work was being done in an old sawmill because a new sawmill was having technical difficulties. During this work transfer, no one bothered to check whether the anti-kickback device was in place, and Harn was injured when a piece of lumber flew back out of the machine and struck him. There we held that disengaging the safety device may have made the injury probable or highly probable, but that was still not deemed to be substantially certain. . . .

Comparing the facts in prior cases to the instant action, Kranz's conduct was no more egregious than the other employers'. His supervision of Fryer may have been negligent, reckless, or even wanton, but there is simply no showing that he intended to injure her.

Even when viewed in a light most favorable to Fryer, the evidence at most proves that Kranz knew the acid vapor irritated her. Fryer contends that muriatic acid, "when used in a small, unventilated space, . . . simply can not be used without causing illness." But this was the first time the acid had been used by Kranz or any of his employees in a small, unventilated space; she has not shown in any manner that Kranz knew her injuries were virtually certain to occur.

Based on Fryer's prior experiences with the acid, Kranz knew that it caused her to become light-headed and nauseous. However, that information alone does not automatically make it virtually certain that she would be overcome by the fumes on this occasion. Indeed, the fact that she suffered no severe adverse effects on prior occasions lends credence to Kranz's position that he was not certain it would cause injury.

Moreover, the notation that Kranz personally suffered ill effects from the acid supports the opposite idea that he did not know how injurious the fumes could be. Had he purposely intended to injure his employees by exposing them to the noxious fumes, it is simply not rational to believe that he would have also knowingly and deliberately exposed himself to the fumes by helping his employees clean the grout. Nor is it any more rational to assume that he knowingly and deliberately inflicted upon himself the medical claims, damages, time setbacks, and lawsuits that his employees' exposure to the acid would entail. Larson, supra, §103.05[6] at 103-41 (May 2000).

Under these circumstances, perhaps Kranz should have known that the fumes might cause injury, or even that they would probably or likely cause injury. However, that level of knowledge was still insufficient to show intent to injure under our standard. Kranz showed that no genuine issue of material fact existed as to his intent. To overcome Kranz's motion for summary judgment, Fryer needed to show that Kranz knew with virtual certainty that such exposure would cause illness, yet still required her to work. This she failed to do. . . .

To decide this case differently would blur the line between cases involving only negligent or reckless conduct and those involving true intent to injure. In *VerBouwens* [*v. Hamm Wood Prod.*, 334 N.W.2d 874, 876 (S.D. 1983)], Justice Wollman foresaw the dire results of such an outcome:

> If the "intentional tort" exception was expanded as plaintiffs request, the focus would be upon the degree of risk of injury and the state of knowledge of the employer and the employee regarding the dangerous conduct or condition which caused the injury. This result undermines the balance of interests maintained by the worker's compensation system. First, it would thwart the goal of the system to provide employers relative immunity from liability at law. Second, it would deny many employees the swift and certain compensation they now receive under the system. The system originally required employees to surrender their right to a potentially larger recovery in a common law action for the wilful or reckless misconduct of employers, in return for expeditious recovery under worker's compensation. Employees disappointed with worker's compensation recovery would be encouraged to seek additional compensation in a common law action, increasing the role of the courts in resolving . . . accident disputes.

334 N.W.2d at 877 (Wollman, J., concurring specially) (quoting Shearer v. Homestake Mining Co., 557 F. Supp. 549, 555 (D.S.D. 1983)). . . .

Although Kranz's conduct was clearly negligent, probably reckless and possibly wanton, it does not amount to an intentional act. Therefore, the denial of Kranz's motion for summary judgment is reversed, and the case is remanded with directions that the trial court enter summary judgment in his favor.

NOTE TO FRYER v. KRANZ

Rationale for Workers' Compensation Schemes. Without explicitly making the connection between the policy and the rule, the court in Fryer v. Kranz concluded that the rationale for the workers' compensation system disappears when an employer intentionally injures an employee. Given the stated rationale, should a case with facts like those in Fryer v. Kranz be covered by workers' compensation, or should the employee be allowed to sue?

Problem
Intentional Tort Exclusion from Workers' Compensation

Would the intentional tort exception to workers' compensation exclusivity be available to the injured worker in the following situation? Alan Zimmerman was injured while employed at Valdak Car Wash, when his right arm was torn from his body. The injury occurred while he was using an industrial centrifuge extractor, a laundry machine that uses centrifugal force to spin dry towels. He was not assigned to work in the area where the machine was located and there was a clear warning on the machine to "keep your hands out of the machine." Under normal conditions, a person operating the extractor would wait until the towels were dry, pull the brake to stop the internal drum, open the lid, and remove the towels. The extractor had an interlock system to prevent the lid from opening before the drum stopped spinning. When Zimmerman was injured, the interlock system had been inoperative for months. Employees were opening the lid and reaching in for the towels while the drum was still spinning.

Valdak's management knew the interlock was inoperative but failed to repair it. Valdak's manager did not have it repaired because it would have shut down the machine and the car wash for approximately an hour and a half. According to an affidavit of Steven Akerlind, an owner of an equipment company that had serviced the extractor, he had told Valdak's manager that the extractor was substantially certain to injure someone. Some Valdak personnel had warned other employees that if they put their arm in the machine, they could lose it. See Zimmerman v. Valdak Corp., 570 N.W.2d 204 (N.D. 1997).

CUNNINGHAM v. SHELTON SECURITY SERVICE, INC.
46 S.W.3d 131 (Tenn. 2001)

ANDERSON, C.J.

In this workers' compensation case, the estate of the employee, Robert W. Cunningham, Sr., has appealed from a chancery court judgment dismissing a claim for death benefits filed against the employer, Shelton Security Service, Inc. The employee, who worked as a security guard for the employer, died of heart failure while performing his duties at a store. At the close of the employee's proof, the trial court granted the employer's motion to dismiss on the basis that the emotional stress experienced by the employee the night of his death was not extraordinary or unusual for a security guard. The Special Workers' Compensation Appeals Panel, upon reference for findings of fact and conclusions of law, found that there was sufficient evidence of causation to warrant a trial and, thus, reversed the trial court's dismissal. Thereafter, the employer filed a motion for full Court review of the Panel's decision. We granted the motion for review to consider whether the trial court erred in dismissing the employee's claim on the basis that his heart failure did not arise out of the employment because it was not caused by a mental or emotional stimulus of an unusual or abnormal nature, beyond what is typically encountered by one in his occupation. After carefully examining the record and considering the relevant authorities, we agree with the Panel and reverse the trial court's judgment.

Robert W. Cunningham, Sr. ("employee") was employed by Shelton Security Service, Inc. ("employer") as a security guard. On May 9, 1991, the employee began working as a guard assigned to the Little Barn Deli and Market on Clarksville Highway in Nashville. He died of heart failure on March 5, 1992, while performing his duties at the store.

At trial, Mishie Lynn Taylor, a night clerk at the store, testified that in the early morning hours of March 5, 1992, three young men entered the store. The employee, Robert Cunningham, Sr., who was performing his duties as a security guard, asked the young men to leave because they were attempting to shoplift. Taylor stated that the suspected shoplifters "talked back" to the employee and cursed at him. She described the verbal confrontation inside the store as "very loud" and said that the employee shouted at the individuals to leave the premises. . . . Taylor testified that the young men threatened to come back and kill the employee. According to Taylor, the employee had similar verbal confrontations with people at the store once or twice a week. She said it was common for him to "go out and yell at these people."

Taylor recounted that although the employee was upset when he returned to the store, he did not act overly concerned about the incident. A short time later, however, the employee began to complain that he did not feel well. He began rubbing his arm. Then, he said that he felt "funny and weird"; that he "had never felt like that before"; and that he could not be still. Taylor told the employee to stay where she could observe him at the front of the store, but he went outside. A few minutes later, Taylor found the employee unconscious in his car. Although Taylor promptly called an ambulance, the employee died before he reached the hospital.

Dr. Melvin Lightford, an internist and emergency room physician, testified that the employee died from "sudden cardiac death." . . . In response to a hypothetical question setting out the facts of the employee's death, Dr. Lightford testified that there was a "relationship" between the confrontation with the young men and the employee's death. Dr. Lightford opined that "the events, as hypothesized to me, did indeed precipitate what is called sudden cardiac death. . . ."

The employee's death certificate stated the cause of death as arteriosclerotic cardiovascular disease. . . .

At the close of the employee's proof, the trial court granted the employer's motion to dismiss because the emotional stress experienced by the employee the night of his death was "not extraordinary nor was it unusual in comparison to the stress he ordinarily experienced in that type of job." The Special Workers' Compensation Appeals Panel, upon reference for findings of fact and conclusions of law pursuant to Tenn. Code Ann. §50-6-225(e)(3), reversed the trial court's dismissal on the basis that there was sufficient evidence of causation to warrant a complete trial. Thereafter, the employer filed a motion for full Court review of the Panel's decision. We granted the motion to consider whether the trial court erred in dismissing the employee's claim on the basis that his heart failure did not arise out of the employment because it was not caused by a mental or emotional stimulus of an unusual or abnormal nature, beyond what is typically encountered by one in his occupation. . . .

In order to be eligible for workers' compensation benefits, an employee must suffer an "injury by accident arising out of and in the course of employment which causes either disablement or death. . . ." Tenn. Code Ann. §50-6-102(12) (1999). The statutory requirements that the injury "arise out of" and occur "in the course of" the employment are not synonymous. An injury occurs "in the course of" employment if it takes place while the employee was performing a duty he or she was employed to perform. Put another way, "the injury must have substantially originated from the 'time and space' of work, resulting in an injury directly linked to the work environment or work-related activities." Harman v. Moore's Quality Snack Foods, 815 S.W.2d 519, 527 (Tenn. Ct. App. 1991) (citation omitted). Thus, the course of employment requirement focuses on the time, place and circumstances of the injury.

In contrast, "arising out of" employment refers to "cause or origin." Id. An injury arises out of employment "when there is apparent to the rational mind, upon consideration of all the circumstances, a causal connection between the conditions under which the work is required to be performed and the resulting injury." The mere presence of the employee at the place of injury because of the employment is not sufficient, as the injury must result from a danger or hazard peculiar to the work or be caused by a risk inherent in the nature of the work. See Jackson v. Clark & Fay, Inc., 197 Tenn. 135, 270 S.W.2d 389, 390 (1954). As one court has put it, the "danger must be peculiar to the work. . . . [A]n injury purely coincidental, or contemporaneous, or collateral, with the employment . . . will not cause the injury . . . to be considered as arising out of the employment." Jackson v. Clark & Fay, Inc., 270 S.W.2d at 390.

In the present case, there is no dispute that the employee's death occurred in the course of his employment. Instead, the dispute focuses on whether the employee's death arose out of the employment. The employer argues that the employee's death did not arise out of the employment because the confrontation with the suspected shoplifters was not an abnormal or unusual occurrence for a person in the employee's occupation. The employee's estate responds that the employee's death arose out of his employment as that requirement has been applied in this Court's heart attack cases. The estate therefore urges us to reverse the trial court's dismissal of the case.

We agree with the parties that this case is controlled largely by our decisions addressing the compensability of heart attacks. The heart attack cases in this jurisdiction can be categorized into two groups: (1) those that are precipitated by physical exertion or strain, and (2) those resulting from mental stress, tension, or some type of emotional upheaval. If the heart attack results from physical exertion or strain, it is unnecessary that there be extraordinary exertion or unusual physical strain. Thus, it makes no difference that the employee, prior to the attack, suffered from preexisting heart disease or that the attack was caused by ordinary physical exertion or the usual physical strain of the employee's work.

The rule is different, however, when the heart attack is caused by a mental or emotional stimulus rather than physical exertion or strain. In such cases, "it is obvious that in order to recover when there is no physical exertion, but there is emotional stress, worry, shock, or tension, the heart attack must be immediately precipitated by a specific acute or sudden stressful event[] rather than generalized employment conditions." Thus, if the heart attack is caused by a mental or emotional stimulus rather than physical exertion or strain, there must be a "climatic event or series of incidents of an unusual or abnormal nature" if a recovery is to be permitted. Although "excessive and unexpected mental anxiety, stress, tension or worry attributable to the employment can cause injury sufficient to justify an award of benefits," Reeser v. Yellow Freight Sys., Inc., 938 S.W.2d 690, 692 (Tenn. 1997), the ordinary stress of one's occupation does not because "[e]motional stress, to some degree, accompanies the performance of any contract of employment." Allied Chem. Corp. v. Wells, 578 S.W.2d 369, 373 (Tenn. 1979). In other words, "[n]ormal ups and downs are part of any employment relationship, and as we have said on many previous occasions, do not justify finding an 'accidental injury' for purposes of worker[s'] compensation law." Bacon v. Sevier County, 808 S.W.2d at 53 (citations omitted). Accordingly, the rule is settled in this jurisdiction that physical or mental injuries caused by worry, anxiety, or emotional stress of a general nature or ordinary stress associated with the worker's occupation are not compensable. The injury must have resulted from an incident of abnormal and unusual stressful proportions, rather than the day-to-day mental stresses and tensions which workers in that field are occasionally subjected.

With these principles in mind, we review the record in the present case to determine whether the employee's death arose out of his employment. We note first that there was no physical exertion or strain involved in precipitating his heart failure. Instead, the mental stress or tension associated with confronting the suspected shoplifters caused the heart failure, at least according to some of the medical proof. Applying the law as just described, the trial court concluded the employee's death was not compensable because he was not confronted with circumstances of an unusual or abnormal nature given his work as a security guard. As the record reflects, verbal confrontations occurred at least once a week at the store, and it was common for the employee to "go out and yell at these people." However, the record also reflects that the individuals chased off by the employee threatened to return and kill him. We believe that this additional circumstance makes a difference and is sufficient to warrant the conclusion that the employee's death did not result from generalized employment conditions, but from something beyond the norm, even for a security guard. Accordingly, we find that the evidence preponderates against the trial court's finding that the employee's death did not arise out of his employment.

The reason, simply put, is that the employee has met the burden of establishing that his heart failure was caused by a mental or emotional stimulus of an unusual or abnormal nature, beyond what is typically encountered by one in the employee's position. We thus reiterate the rule again in this case that if the cause or stimulus of the heart attack is mental or emotional in nature, such as stress, fright, tension, shock, anxiety, or worry, there must be a specific, climatic event or series of incidents of an unusual or abnormal nature if the claimant is to be permitted a recovery, but no recovery is permitted for the ordinary mental stresses and tensions of one's occupation because "[e]motional stress, to some degree, accompanies the performance of any contract of employment." Allied Chem. Corp. v. Wells, 578 S.W.2d at 373. If the rule were otherwise, workers' compensation coverage would become as broad as general health and accident insurance, which it is not. . . .

In view of the foregoing discussion, we hold that the evidence preponderates against the trial court's finding that the employee's death did not arise out of his employment. Therefore, the trial court's dismissal of the case is reversed and the case remanded for further proceedings consistent with this opinion. . . .

NOTES TO CUNNINGHAM v. SHELTON SECURITY SERVICE, INC.

1. *Scope of Coverage by Workers' Compensation Systems.*   To prevent workers' compensation systems from becoming as broad as general health and accident insurance, the Tennessee statute limits benefits to injuries by accidents (a) arising out of and (b) in the course of employment. How does the court distinguish between the two phrases? How does that distinction help the court in *Cunningham* distinguish between the employee's yelling at the suspected shoplifters and their threats to kill him?

Another approach to limiting the scope of workers' compensation permits recovery for a physical injury caused by mental stress only if the claimant shows that his or her working conditions involved risks greater than those facing the general public. See Baggett v. Industrial Commission, 775 N.E.2d 908 (Ill. 2002). Would that test have given a different result in *Cunningham*?

2. *Evidentiary Rules in Administrative Proceedings.*   Agencies that administer the workers' compensation system are typically excused from following common law and statutory rules of evidence. For this reason, scientific evidence that links a worker's harm to a condition in the workplace that would not be adequate in an ordinary tort case may provide a basis for an award of compensation. In Sheridan v. Catering Management, Inc., 566 N.W.2d 110 (Neb. 1997), a bartender's claim that an injury was caused by residue from chemicals used to exterminate cockroaches was held to have been adequately supported even though the scientific evidence the claimant offered would not have been admissible in a trial.

Problem
Injury Arising Out of Employment

An editorial writer at a newspaper suffered a fatal heart attack during a meeting at which editorial board members and other staff members were arguing about what position the paper should take on an important international affairs crisis. The meeting had begun at six o'clock p.m. in a hot and crowded room. Shortly before nine o'clock, the decedent began to speak, became excited, and collapsed. If you represent the estate of the editorial writer, you may consider whether it would be fruitful to attempt to recover compensation under the workers' compensation system. Would this employee's estate be likely to receive workers' compensation under either the rule in *Cunningham* or the *Baggett* rule discussed in Note 1? See Strauss v. Freiheit, 331 N.Y.S.2d 520 (3d Dept. 1972).

Statute: SCHEDULE IN CASE OF DISABILITY

N.Y. Workers' Comp. Law §15(1), (2), and (3)(a-l) (2017)

The following schedule of compensation is hereby established:

    1. Permanent total disability. In case of total disability adjudged to be permanent sixty-six and two-thirds per centum of the average weekly wages shall be paid to the employee during the continuance of such total disability. Loss of both hands, or both arms, or both feet, or both legs, or both eyes, or of any two thereof shall, in the absence of conclusive proof to the contrary, constitute permanent total disability. . . .

    2. Temporary total disability. In case of temporary total disability, sixty-six and two-thirds per centum of the average weekly wages shall be paid to the employee during the continuance thereof, except as otherwise provided in this chapter.

    3. Permanent partial disability. In case of disability partial in character but permanent in quality the compensation shall be sixty-six and two-thirds per centum of the average weekly wages and shall be paid to the employee for the period named in this subdivision, as follows:

Member Lost	Number of Weeks' Compensation
a. Arm	312
b. Leg	288
c. Hand	244
d. Foot	205
e. Eye	160
f. Thumb	75
g. First finger	46
h. Great toe	38
i. Second finger	30
j. Third finger	25
k. Toe other than great toe	16
l. Fourth finger	15

NOTES TO STATUTE

    1. _Amounts of Awards._ These awards are set by the New York legislature, keyed to the injured workers' average weekly wages. Using the example of a worker whose annual wages were $30,000, the compensation payment for loss of a leg would be 288 multiplied by two-thirds of that worker's average weekly wages. The payment would be about $111,000. Does that seem like the right amount of compensation for the loss of a leg? Does it seem to be an amount that might be awarded by a jury in a case that was treated in the ordinary litigation system rather than in the administrative workers' compensation system?

2. *Standardization of Awards.* Injuries have different effects on different people, but the workers' compensation system ignores those variations. For example, loss of a leg might change the life of an individual who enjoyed playing sports and participating in outdoor recreation more than it would change the life of a typically sedentary person.

The award structure ignores the age of the victim, so that benefits do not vary even though a young claimant might experience 50 years of hardship due to loss of a limb while an older claimant might suffer that disability only for five or ten years.

Relating the size of award to the worker's wages simplifies the administration of the system. Does it seem sensible to treat injuries as worth more or less because of the earning power of the injured individual?

Perspective: Reforming Workers' Compensation

In its original conception, workers' compensation gave workers access to reliable compensation and denied them the opportunity to seek redress in the tort system. A recent critique of the system suggests that the "exclusive remedy doctrine is riddled with judicially-created exceptions that give injured workers the ability to circumvent the workers' compensation system," that the Americans with Disabilities Act and the Family Medical Leave Act "provide new federal protection to injured workers and leave employers tripping over conflicting obligations," and that "most workers have a multitude of insurance options available, including group health and both short and long-term disability." The authors suggest evaluating four responses: "(1) restoring the exclusive remedy doctrine; (2) creating a federal workers' compensation system; (3) establishing a choice/no fault system; and (4) eliminating the exclusive remedy doctrine." Discussing total elimination of the workers' compensation system, they suggest:

> Employees would protect themselves against an on-the-job injury just as they protect themselves against a non-workplace accident. If a third party, including his or her employer, is at fault, the employee could sue in tort. If the employee is responsible for his or her own injury, he or she could rely on individual or group health insurance to cover medical expenses and short-term or long-term disability insurance to minimize income loss. The system would no longer be a no-fault system, but instead a pure tort system where the tortfeasor bears the costs of injury. A tort system for injured workers has the same advantages as the tort system for any party seeking redress. . . .
>
> The traditional workers' compensation approach, by contrast, provided an artificially low level of compensation so as to provide an incentive to return to work. Eliminating the exclusive remedy doctrine would also eliminate this issue of insufficient compensation. . . . While

the level of recovery an injured plaintiff receives in a tort suit is also highly criticized, the formula for awarding that recovery is at least intended to fully compensate the injury. Along with increased recovery would presumably come increased deterrence against employer wrongdoing, another central tenet of tort theory.

Joan T.A. Gabel, Nancy R. Mansfield & Robert W. Klein, The *New Relationship Between Injured Worker and Employer: An Opportunity for Restructuring the System*, 35 Am. Bus. L.J. 403 (1998).

C. No-Fault Automobile Insurance

Under standard tort doctrines, a person who was injured in an automobile accident would bear the costs of those injuries personally, unless he or she could prove that the accident had been the result of another person's tortious conduct. Early forms of automobile insurance reflected this concept and protected policy holders from liability. Since insurance companies would pay damages only if their policy holders had been at fault, many cases required determinations about who caused an accident and the quality of that person's conduct.

Most states now require automobile owners to purchase insurance that provides first-party coverage in addition to liability coverage. First-party coverage means that the policy holder's own insurance company will pay for injuries suffered by the policy holder and members of the policy holder's family without regard to fault. When an injury is covered by this type of compensation, the victim is prohibited from seeking additional recovery against anyone whose conduct might have caused the injury.

The New Jersey Supreme Court described the history of its state's automobile no-fault legislation:

The No-Fault Law's goal was "compensating a larger class of citizens than the traditional tort-based system and doing so with greater efficiency and at a lower cost." Oswin v. Shaw, 129 N.J. 290, 295, 609 A.2d 415, 417 (1992) (quoting Emmer v. Merin, 233 N.J. Super. 568, 572, 559 A.2d 845, 846 (App. Div.), *cert. denied,* 118 N.J. 181, 570 A.2d 950 (1989)). That "new approach" to automobile insurance was to result

in the motoring public's securing protection at lesser cost, expediting the relief of the accident victim and his family from a frequently staggering and intolerable economic burden, and yet preserving that victim's right to full and adequate compensation in cases which *involve more serious and disabling injury.*

In addition to bringing about an intended reduction in insurance premiums, *another major benefit of the proposed system would be a reduction of the present court backlog.* A substantial percentage of civil court actions are automobile accident cases. Under the proposed plan, it is expected that *many of these cases would be settled outside the court, thereby permitting other more serious and meritorious causes to be heard with more dispatch.*

[Governor's Second Annual Message (January 11, 1972) (emphasis added).]

Although the movement to adopt no-fault legislation was the "result of ever-increasing automobile-insurance premiums," *Oswin,* supra, 129 N.J. at 295, 609 A.2d at 417, it also arose from the recognition that the necessity of determining fault in a lawsuit before recovery of medical expenses resulted in great hardship for many injured parties. See Governor's First Annual Message (January 12, 1971) (stating, "Too many injured persons must wait too long for an uncertain remedy while enduring physical and financial injury."). Thus, the proponents of the legislation anticipated that the elimination of minor personal-injury claims from the court system not only would reduce insurance premiums but also would provide prompt payment of medical expenses to injured parties.

To achieve those purposes the Legislature created the no-fault statutory scheme. Under that scheme every automobile liability-insurance policy issued in New Jersey had to provide PIP [personal injury protection] coverage, including medical-expense benefits, "without regard to negligence, liability or fault of any kind, to the named insured and members of his family residing in his household who sustained bodily injury as a result of an automobile accident." N.J.S.A. 39:6A-4. A person's no-fault insurance was to be an injured person's exclusive remedy for medical-expense claims arising out of an automobile accident.

As a trade-off for the payment of medical expenses, regardless of fault, no-fault systems provided for "either a limitation on or the elimination of conventional tort-based personal-injury lawsuits." *Oswin,* supra, 129 N.J. at 295, 609 A.2d at 417. N.J.S.A. 39:6A-8 (section 8) provided such a limitation by holding that an injured person could file a lawsuit *only* if medical expenses exceeded a $200 threshold.

Roig v. Kelsey, 641 A.2d 248 (N.J. 1994).

The relationship between standard tort law and no-fault doctrines is examined in State Farm Mutual Automobile Insurance Co. v. Peiffer, which involved a dispute between an insurance company and its policy holder. Other recurring no-fault issues involve individuals who seek to avoid the prohibition on access to the tort system or who seek to obtain the benefits of no-fault coverage in circumstances where that coverage is likely the only source from which compensation could be obtained. In Oberly v. Bangs Ambulance, Inc., New York's highest court interprets a provision of that state's no-fault statute to determine whether the plaintiff would be limited to no-fault recovery or would be permitted to bring a tort suit for damages related to his injury. In Weber v. State Farm Mutual Automobile Insurance Co., the court considers whether the no-fault benefits required by statute to be provided in automobile insurance should cover an injury caused by a hunter's discharge of a rifle as he was leaving a vehicle.

STATE FARM MUTUAL AUTOMOBILE INSURANCE CO. v. PEIFFER

955 P.2d 1008 (Colo. 1998)

BENDER, J.

This case involves an action for breach of an automobile insurance contract brought against the petitioner, State Farm, by its insured, respondent Donna Peiffer ("Peiffer"), concerning State Farm's refusal to pay personal injury protection ("PIP") benefits under Peiffer's automobile insurance policy in accordance with the Colorado Auto Accident Reparations Act, section 10-4-701 to 10-4-723, 3 C.R.S (1997) ("No-

Fault Act"). We hold that in appropriate circumstances, a trial court may provide a "thin skull" jury instruction in an action for breach of contract for PIP benefits, and we affirm the decision of the court of appeals. We return this case to the court of appeals to remand to the district court for further proceedings.

On December 24, 1990, Peiffer was injured in an automobile accident when her car was struck by another vehicle. Peiffer was insured under an automobile insurance policy issued by State Farm that included coverage for PIP benefits in accordance with the No-Fault Act. Under the policy, State Farm was responsible for payment of up to $50,000 for medical and rehabilitation treatments that were reasonable, necessary, and causally related to the automobile accident.[2]

After the accident, Peiffer began receiving extensive treatment from multiple health care providers. Although these providers believed that the treatment was necessary, State Farm instructed Peiffer to submit to several independent medical examinations ("IMEs"). In 1991, Peiffer underwent an IME by a chiropractor who indicated that Peiffer should be weaned from chiropractic treatment and massage therapy because they were unnecessary. In 1992, Peiffer underwent an IME by a psychiatrist/neurologist who stated that Peiffer's psychiatric therapy was no longer reasonably related to the accident. Also in 1992, Peiffer submitted to an IME by an orthopedic spine surgeon who found that Peiffer had reached maximum medical improvement. Based on these determinations, State Farm refused to pay for further treatment other than pool therapy.

On June 24, 1993, Peiffer sued State Farm for breach of contract for failure to pay PIP benefits, and for the tort of bad faith breach of an insurance contract. At trial, State Farm called Peiffer as a hostile witness and elicited testimony that during the IMEs, Peiffer failed to inform the examining physicians that she received substantial chiropractic treatment before the accident. . . . During closing argument, State Farm argued that Peiffer's continued treatment was not necessary because Peiffer's assertions regarding her symptoms were not credible.

Upon Peiffer's request, and over State Farm's objection, the district court gave the jury the following "thin skull" instruction:

---

[2] Section 10-4-706(1), 3 C.R.S. (1997), provides in pertinent part:

Subject to the limitations and exclusions authorized by this part 7, the minimum coverages required for compliance with this part 7 are as follows:

   . . . (b)(I) Compensation without regard to fault, up to a limit of fifty thousand dollars per person for any one accident, for payment of all reasonable and necessary expenses for medical, chiropractic, optometric, podiatric, hospital, nursing, x-ray, dental, surgical, ambulance, and prosthetic services, and nonmedical remedial care and treatment rendered in accordance with a recognized religious method of healing, performed within five years after the accident for bodily injury arising out of the use or operation of a motor vehicle. . . .

   . . . (c)(I) Compensation without regard to fault up to a limit of fifty thousand dollars per person for any one accident within ten years after such accident for payment of the cost of rehabilitation procedures or treatment and rehabilitative occupational training necessary because of bodily injury arising out of the use or operation of a motor vehicle. . . .

In determining the amount of benefits for which the Defendant, State Farm Mutual Automobile Insurance Company, is responsible to pay, you cannot reduce the amount of or refuse to award any such payments because of any physical frailties or mental condition of the Plaintiff that may have made her more susceptible to injury, disability, or impairment.

The instruction was not limited to Peiffer's tort claim. The jury awarded Peiffer $10,068 for breach of contract and $10,000 for bad faith breach of an insurance contract.

State Farm appealed, arguing that the district court erred by giving the "thin skull" instruction because the "thin skull" doctrine is a tort concept that has no application to claims of breach of contract. The court of appeals rejected State Farm's argument and affirmed the holding of the district court. State Farm then petitioned this court for certiorari review.

The "thin skull" doctrine provides that a negligent defendant is liable for harm resulting from negligent conduct even though the harm was increased by the particular plaintiff's condition at the time of the negligent conduct. In Colorado, it is fundamental that a tortfeasor must accept the victim as the victim is found. . . .

We have held that a "thin skull" instruction is appropriate in tort cases when the defendant seeks to avoid or reduce liability by employing a technique known as "spotlighting," in which the defendant calls attention to the plaintiff's preexisting conditions or predisposition to injury and asserts that the plaintiff's injuries would have been less severe had the plaintiff been an average person. However, the applicability of the "thin skull" instruction in a contract case for breach of an automobile insurance agreement for no-fault PIP benefits is an issue of first impression for this court. This issue requires us to consider the policies underlying the No-Fault Act.

The No-Fault Act governs compensation, including medical and rehabilitation benefits, for personal injuries resulting from automobile accidents regardless of fault. This scheme requires automobile owners to acquire an automobile insurance policy that complies with the minimum amount of coverage mandated by the No-Fault Act. Insurers, in turn, must pay all of the reasonable and necessary medical expenses incurred by the insured in an accident arising out of the use of an automobile, up to the limits of the policy, even if the insured was to blame for the accident. The legislature articulated the public policy of the No-Fault Act in section 10-4-702, 3 C.R.S. (1997), as follows:

> The general assembly declares that its purpose in enacting this part 7 is to avoid inadequate compensation to victims of automobile accidents; to require registrants of motor vehicles in this state to procure insurance covering legal liability arising out of ownership or use of such vehicles and also providing benefits to persons occupying such vehicles and to persons injured in accidents involving such vehicles.

In addition, this court has recognized that one of the primary purposes of the No-Fault Act was to decrease the volume of tort litigation arising out of automobile accidents.

The No-Fault Act precludes a person injured in a motor vehicle accident from bringing a traditional tort action against another person involved in the accident except under limited statutorily enumerated circumstances. However, the No-Fault

Act is not a precise substitute for a traditional tort action. For example, the Act provides benefits for injured tortfeasors, who would not be eligible to recover damages as a plaintiff in a traditional tort action. In addition, the Act allows a victim who sustains economic losses in excess of a no-fault insurance policy to recover against the tortfeasor by filing a civil lawsuit. The Act serves to maximize, not minimize, insurance coverage. The No-Fault Act "is to be liberally construed to further its remedial and beneficent purposes." Regional Transp. Dist. v. Voss, 890 P.2d 663, 669 (Colo. 1995) (quoting Travelers Indem. Co. v. Barnes, 191 Colo. 278, 283, 552 P.2d 300, 304 (1976)).

Applying these principles to the facts of this case, we agree with State Farm that the "thin skull" doctrine is a tort concept that generally does not apply to an action for breach of contract. . . .

However, damages for a breach of contract for PIP benefits are analogous to damages arising from the commission of a tort because an insurance contract for PIP benefits always involves an unforeseeable amount of money. Although the limits of the policy are within the contemplation of the parties, neither the insured nor the insurer can anticipate the precise amount of benefits to which the insured might be entitled were an automobile accident to occur. In addition, unlike a policy for life insurance or health insurance, a policy for PIP benefits due to injury arising out of an automobile accident does not contain exclusions for pre-existing conditions.

When an insurer attempts to avoid or reduce liability by "spotlighting" the insured's pre-existing conditions, a thin-skull instruction furthers the No-Fault Act's policy of fully compensating the victim. Thus, in breach of contract cases for PIP benefits, when the trial court finds that the insurer "spotlighted" the victim's pre-existing mental or physical conditions, a "thin skull" instruction may be given. . . . We affirm the decision of the court of appeals, and we return this case to the court of appeals to remand to the district court for further proceedings.

OBERLY v. BANGS AMBULANCE, INC.
751 N.E.2d 457 (N.Y. 2001)

SMITH, J.

The No-Fault Law provides a plan for compensating victims of automobile accidents for their economic losses without regard to fault or negligence. An injured party may bring a plenary action in tort, however, to recover for non-economic loss, pain and suffering, but must show that he or she has suffered a serious injury within the meaning of the No-Fault Law. The issue before this Court is whether a party bringing a claim under the no-fault serious injury category of "permanent loss of use of a body organ, member, function or system" is required to prove that the loss of use is significant or consequential.

We conclude that only a total loss of use is compensable under the "permanent loss of use" exception to the no-fault remedy. Insofar as plaintiffs have not established total "loss of use" and have abandoned any claim concerning a "permanent consequential limitation" or "significant limitation of use of a body function or system," they have failed to establish a "serious injury" within the meaning of the No-Fault Law.

Plaintiff Richard Oberly, a dentist, was injured while being transported in an ambulance owned by defendant Bangs Ambulance. Plaintiff was positioned face-up on a stretcher with an IV needle in his arm, and a five-pound IV pump was set on a shelf above him. While in transit, the ambulance struck a curb, and the IV pump toppled from the shelf and fell on his right forearm. Plaintiff suffered bruising and continues to complain of pain and cramping in that arm, which pain allegedly limits his ability to practice as a dentist.

Plaintiff and his wife commenced this personal injury action for negligence, alleging a serious injury under the No-Fault Law, Insurance Law §5102(d),[1] in Supreme Court against defendant, asserting that plaintiff had suffered a serious injury. In response to defendant's demand that they particularize the serious injury, plaintiffs identified four of the plausible injury standards under Insurance Law §5102(d): "significant disfigurement," "permanent loss of use of a body organ, member, function or system," "permanent consequential limitation of use of a body organ or member" and "significant limitation of use of a body function or system." Following joinder of issue, defendant moved for summary judgment. In opposing summary judgment, plaintiffs abandoned all of the cited serious injury standards except for the "permanent loss of use of a body organ, member, function or system" standard.

Supreme Court dismissed plaintiffs' action for lack of evidence that he had suffered a serious injury. The Appellate Division affirmed, ruling that the statute requires a party claiming a partial loss of use of a body "organ or member" to show that the limitation is "consequential or significant," and that plaintiff had not met that threshold. The two dissenting Justices concluded that the nerve damage to plaintiff's arm could constitute a partial loss of use of a body "function or system," for which no proof of significance was required.

On this appeal, plaintiffs argue that the statute does not require proof that a "permanent loss of use" of a body member is significant even if the loss is only partial. They also contend that the limitation of the use of plaintiff's arm itself qualifies as "permanent loss of use of body member, body function and body system." We disagree.

The No-Fault Law was adopted by the Legislature in 1973 to assure prompt and full compensation for economic loss and to provide for non-economic loss in the case of serious injury. As originally enacted, it contained two categories of "serious injury": first, claims for death, dismemberment, significant disfigurement, certain types of fractures and permanent loss of use of a body organ, member, function or system and second, claims for medical charges as a result of an injury that exceeded $500. In 1977 this section was replaced with the present section, which defines a serious injury as

> a personal injury which results in death; dismemberment; significant disfigurement; a fracture; loss of fetus; permanent loss of use of a body organ, member, function or system; permanent consequential limitation of use of a body organ or member; significant limitation of use of a body function or system; or a medically determined injury or impairment of a non-permanent nature which prevents the injured person from performing substantially all of the material acts which constitute such person's usual and customary daily activities for not less than ninety days during the one

---

[1] Chapter 13 of the Laws of 1973 is formally known as The Comprehensive Motor Vehicle Insurance Reparations Act. . . .

hundred eighty days immediately following the occurrence of the injury or impairment (Insurance Law §5102[d]).

The serious injury category at issue, "permanent loss of use," has been in place since 1973 without legislative change. Until today, however, the question of how this statutory section should be construed has never been squarely before this Court. We hold that to qualify as a serious injury within the meaning of the statute, "permanent loss of use" must be total.

Our holding today proceeds from both the statutory text and from the conclusion that the Legislature, in amending the definition of "serious injury" in 1977, meant to create a consistent framework. First, the statute speaks in terms of the loss of a body member, without qualification. Thus, the legislative intent is shown in the actual wording of the statute. Second, requiring a total loss is consistent with the statutory addition, in 1977, of the categories "permanent consequential limitation of use of a body organ or member" and "significant limitation of use of a body function or system." Had the Legislature considered partial losses already covered under "permanent loss of use," there would have been no need to enact the two new provisions.

While the Appellate Division properly affirmed the dismissal of plaintiffs' claim, it improperly engrafted the term "partial" to the "loss of use" standard. Because both the "permanent consequential limitation of use" standard and the "loss of use" standard require a permanent injury, and because there is no qualitative difference between a partial "loss of use" and a "limitation of use," engrafting the term "partial" creates a redundancy.

Accordingly, the order of the Appellate Division should be affirmed, with costs. . . .

WEBER v. STATE FARM MUTUAL AUTOMOBILE INSURANCE CO.
284 N.W.2d 299 (N.D. 1979)

Paulson, J.

The appellant, State Farm Mutual Automobile Insurance Company [State Farm], brought this appeal from a judgment of the district court of Ward County. The issue presented is whether or not the North Dakota Auto Accident Reparations Act [commonly known as the No-Fault Insurance Act], applies to the facts of this case. We hold that it does and affirm the judgment of the district court.

The facts are simple and undisputed. Robert Weber was the owner of a 1963 Chevrolet 4-door, 1/2 ton pickup truck insured by State Farm pursuant to the provisions of Chapter 26-41, N.D.C.C. Robert, his wife, Virginia A. Weber, Brian Bradberry, and John Gabby were hunting deer on November 12, 1977. Robert was seated in the driver's seat and Virginia was seated beside him on the right side of the front seat. Bradberry was seated in the rear seat directly behind Robert and Gabby was seated behind Virginia.

Upon spotting some deer crossing the road, Weber drove his vehicle into the ditch on the north side of North Dakota Highway 5, west of Mohall. As the pickup slowed to a halt, Gabby jumped out the right rear door. As Gabby was moving out of the door, he was feeding shells into his 270-calibre bolt action rifle. Gabby testified that he was loading the rifle and exiting from the vehicle at the same time. As he closed the bolt of the gun it discharged. The bullet from the rifle went through the open right rear door, through the back of the front seat, and struck Robert in the back while Robert was still seated behind the steering wheel. Robert was pronounced dead on arrival at Mohall Hospital.

Virginia A. Weber, as surviving spouse of Robert, made a demand on State Farm for death benefits under State Farm Policy Number 533-285-D17-34B, which policy was issued pursuant to the provisions of the North Dakota Auto Accident Reparations Act, Chapter 26-41, N.D.C.C. State Farm denied coverage and the district court action ensued.

The district court, in a bench trial, found that Robert Weber was occupying the vehicle within the meaning of §26-41-07, N.D.C.C., and that Virginia was entitled to no-fault benefits as his survivor. Judgment was entered in Virginia's favor for the policy amount of $15,000; $1,000 for funeral expenses; and $14,000 as survivor's income loss.

State Farm contends that the trial court erred because the North Dakota Auto Accident Reparations Act does not provide for coverage for this type of an accident. Counsel for State Farm argues that there was no "causal connection" between the operation of the motor vehicle and the accident which resulted. This causal connection test is one which was commonly used in interpreting the scope of coverage of insurance *policies* prior to the adoption of no-fault statutes such as Chapter 26-41, N.D.C.C.

In Norgaard v. Nodak Mutual Insurance Company, 201 N.W.2d 871 (N.D. 1972), this court adopted the causal connection test. The facts in *Norgaard* are distinguishable from those in the instant case but somewhat similar in certain respects. On August 20, 1967, Richard Norgaard and Stanley Baldock, along with two other companions, went hunting in Norgaard's 1959 Chevrolet sedan. Norgaard spotted some birds and stopped the automobile. Using the roof of the automobile as a gun rest, Norgaard discharged his rifle in the direction of the birds. At that instant, Baldock was alighting from the automobile and was struck in the back of the head by a bullet from the rifle. He died some thirteen days later.

The issue in *Norgaard* was whether the injury and subsequent death of Baldock resulted from the operation, maintenance, or use of the automobile. This court discussed the causal connection between the accident and the scope of coverage under the policy. We held that "the use of the rifle, notwithstanding it rested upon the automobile at the time of its discharge, constituted an independent and intervening cause of the injury and death of Stanley Baldock." *Norgaard*, supra, 201 N.W.2d at 876.

Norgaard is distinguishable from the instant case in several ways. *Norgaard* was decided prior to January 1, 1976, the date of adoption of the North Dakota no-fault insurance law. Therefore, it was decided at a time when fault determinations were essential to the establishment of liability. The "causal connection" test was rooted in traditional negligence principles. One of the purposes of the no-fault insurance law is to avoid protracted litigation over issues of fault or causation. *Norgaard* is also distinguishable on its facts. In the instant case, Weber was seated in his car at the steering wheel. In *Norgaard*, the victim of the accident was outside of the car. . . . The major difference between the two cases, however, is that *Norgaard* was a case involving interpretation of the scope of coverage under the insurance policy, whereas in this case we are interpreting a statute. . . .

We now turn to an interpretation of the North Dakota no-fault statute, Chapter 26-41, N.D.C.C. The trial court found that coverage existed as a result of the fact that

Weber was a person occupying the vehicle, pursuant to §26-41-07, N.D.C.C. Section 26-41-07(1), N.D.C.C., provides, in pertinent part:

> *Persons entitled to basic no-fault benefits.* — Each basic no-fault insurer of a secured motor vehicle shall pay basic no-fault benefits without regard to fault for economic loss resulting from:
>
> 1. Accidental bodily injury sustained within the United States of America, its territories or possessions, or Canada by the owner of the motor vehicle or any relative of the owner:
>
> a. *While occupying any motor vehicle,*
>
> or
>
> b. . . . . [Emphasis added.]

In interpreting a statute words are to be given their plain, ordinary, and commonly understood meaning. Consideration should be given to the ordinary sense of statutory words, the context in which they are used, and the purpose which prompted their enactment. The purpose for the Act is embodied in §26-41-02, N.D.C.C., which states:

> Legislative declaration. — The legislative assembly declares that its purpose in enacting this chapter is to avoid inadequate compensation to victims of motor vehicle accidents, to require registrants of motor vehicles in this state to procure insurance covering legal liability arising out of ownership or operation of such motor vehicles and also providing benefits to persons occupying such motor vehicles and to persons injured in accidents involving such motor vehicles; to limit the right to claim damages for noneconomic loss in certain cases; and to organize and maintain an assigned claims plan. [Emphasis added.]

Subsection 10 of §26-41-03, N.D.C.C., defines the term "occupying" as follows:

> *26-41-03. Definitions.* — As used in this chapter, the following definitions shall apply: . . . .
>
> 10. "Occupying" means to be in or upon a motor vehicle or engaged in the immediate act of entering into or alighting from the motor vehicle.

Although the legislature may not have contemplated this particular type of accident, a fair reading of the terms used would indicate that they would have provided for coverage had they considered it. This position is supported by §26-41-03(11), N.D.C.C., which defines the operation of a motor vehicle as follows:

> 11. "Operation of a motor vehicle" means operation, maintenance, or use of a motor vehicle as a vehicle. Operation of a motor vehicle does not include conduct within the course of a business of repairing, servicing, or otherwise maintaining motor vehicles unless the injury occurs off the business premises, or conduct in the course of loading and unloading the vehicle unless the injury occurs *while occupying it.* [Emphasis added.]

Section 26-41-03 excludes from coverage persons servicing or repairing a vehicle when in the course of business. The obvious reason for that exclusion is that a person injured in the course of the business of servicing a vehicle would be protected by the workmen's compensation laws. This is consistent with the purpose in making no-fault insurance mandatory: namely, expanding the umbrella of insurance coverage to protect a wider group of people. . . .

The legislature expressly excluded certain persons from coverage in §26-41-08, N.D.C.C., which provides:

> *Persons not entitled to benefits.* — Basic or optional excess no-fault benefits shall not be payable to or on behalf of any person while:
>
>   1. Occupying any motor vehicle without the expressed or implied consent of the owner or while not in lawful possession of the motor vehicle.
>
>   2. Occupying a motor vehicle owned by such person which is not insured for the benefits required by this chapter unless uninsured solely because the insurance company of such owner has not filed a form pursuant to subsection 2 of section 26-41-05 to provide the basic no-fault benefits required by this chapter.
>
>   3. In the course of a racing or speed contest, or in practice or preparation thereof.
>
>   4. Intentionally causing or attempting to cause injury to himself or another person.

Nothing in §26-41-08, N.D.C.C., indicates a legislative intent to exclude from coverage a person occupying his own car who is injured in a hunting accident.

In Paragraph XI of the findings of fact, the trial court noted that the State of North Dakota issues in excess of 102,000 general hunting licenses yearly, and in excess of 40,000 deer licenses on an annual basis. Section 20.1-01-05, N.D.C.C., makes it unlawful to carry any firearm with a cartridge in its chamber while in or on a motor vehicle. Because it is required by law and also constitutes safe hunting procedure, the acts of loading a gun when alighting from a car and unloading a gun before entering a car are common practices in North Dakota. It is foreseeable that accidents like the one in the instant case will happen and the Auto Accident Reparations Act should provide coverage absent an expressed legislative declaration to the contrary. It appears that the legislature took special care in using the term "occupying a motor vehicle" in enacting Chapter 26-41, N.D.C.C., and the plain meaning of that term indicates that coverage exists in this case.

Judgment affirmed.

NOTES TO STATE FARM MUTUAL AUTOMOBILE INSURANCE CO. v. PEIFFER, OBERLY v. BANGS AMBULANCE, INC., AND WEBER v. STATE FARM MUTUAL AUTOMOBILE INSURANCE CO.

1. *Goals and Purposes of Automobile No-Fault Insurance System.* Workers' compensation systems and automobile no-fault systems provide benefits without regard to fault and preclude access to the ordinary tort system. The cases in this chapter all refer to the legislative purposes for the two systems. Are the legislative goals the same? Do differences in the purposes explain any differences in the operation of the systems?

2. *Limits on the No-Fault System.* The New York statute discussed in Oberly v. Bangs Ambulance, Inc. allows a victim access to the traditional tort system if the victim suffers: (1) "significant disfigurement," (2) "permanent loss of use of a body organ, member, function or system," (3) "permanent consequential limitation of use of a body organ or member," or (4) "significant limitation of use of a body function or system." Prior to *Oberly*, New York decisions had made it clear that an injury had to cause a significant harm to be characterized as significant disfigurement, permanent consequential limitation of use, or significant limitation of use of a body function or system. That background would explain why the plaintiff, who suffered only bruising, cramping, and pain, responded to the defendant's summary judgment motion by abandoning all of the serious injury standards except for the "permanent loss of use of a body organ, member, function or system" standard.

How does narrowing the application of clauses like the one interpreted in *Oberly* further or thwart the primary purposes of establishing a no-fault system for automobile-related injuries?

3. *Scope of the No-Fault System.* The causal connection test described in Weber v. State Farm Mutual Automobile Insurance Co. limits the range of accidents to which the automobile no-fault system applies. The North Dakota statute supplies language defining what accidents will be included. What statutory language and what evidence supported the court's conclusion that the injury should be covered by the no-fault system? If the plaintiff had injured himself with a knife while trying to have a snack in the passenger seat of the automobile, would the no-fault system provide for compensation?

4. *Attention to Statutory Language.* Defining the scope of no-fault coverage requires careful attention to the statutes requiring that coverage. For example, Colorado's statute requires insurance companies to cover certain relatives of the insured when they are "injured in an accident involving any motor vehicle" but does not require coverage for motorcycles. In a case where the plaintiff was injured when he rode a motorcycle and collided with a truck, the Colorado Supreme Court held that because the accident involved a motor vehicle (the truck), provisions of an insurance policy that purported to deny coverage violated the statute. See DeHerrera v. Sentry Insurance Co., 30 P.3d 167 (Colo. 2001).

Perspective: Applying No-Fault Concepts to Medical Injuries

Proposals to treat medical injuries in a no-fault framework are necessarily complex. Responding to a study that showed most medical injuries in hospitals are related to failures to observe and learn from errors and to emphasis on individual conduct rather than systemic causes of error, David M. Studdert and Troyen A. Brennan have made the following suggestions in *Toward a Workable Model of "No-Fault" Compensation for Medical Injury in the United States*, 27 Am. J.L. & Med. 225 (2001):

> To be successful in the current environment . . . the push to gather more detailed information on errors and their causes must contend with practitioners' wariness of reporting events that may leave them open to accusations of negligence. Both anecdotal and empirical evidence suggest that providers are less willing to disclose information about errors they make or see when a punitive atmosphere prevails. Fear of blame among those individuals closest to errors thus poses a major obstacle to design and implementation of patient safety initiatives. This cost, together with ongoing concerns about the

performance of the medical malpractice system, underscore the need to consider alternative systems that are better able to compensate injured patients and promote high quality healthcare. . . .

The major alternative to the current tort system is the no-fault model. . . . In the medical arena, various forms of no-fault are firmly established in health care systems abroad: New Zealand and Sweden have operated no-fault systems for compensating medical injury for more than 25 years, and Finland, Denmark and Norway for more than a decade. Several small medical no-fault schemes have also been implemented in the United States to compensate specific injury types, including the Florida and Virginia schemes for birth-related neurological injury and the National Vaccine Injury Compensation Program. . . .

Workable compensation criteria are fundamental to any no-fault scheme. Adverse events occur in approximately three to five percent of hospitalizations; the budget for compensating every one would be prohibitive. In any system some uninsured costs will inevitably rebound to the injured patient. But whereas tort systems seek to confine compensation to events in which negligence caused injury, no-fault schemes offer compensation to a wider class of events. In the considerable terrain of medical injury types that lies between all adverse events and only negligent ones, the threshold for compensation in foreign no-fault systems varies.

We believe that the Swedish example of basing eligibility for compensation on the avoidability of the event is the most rational basis to compensate, and also the one that best facilitates quality improvement in medicine. While "avoidability" is a subjective determination like negligence, the Swedish experience suggests that their decision-making processes have been successful in applying it to separate eligible claims from ineligible ones. With the benefit of many years of experience, the Swedes are able to identify many types of claims that should reasonably be compensated on the strength of basic information about the circumstances of the incident and the nature of the disability suffered.

D. Statutory Responses to Specific Rare Injuries

A federal statute provides compensation to victims of injuries caused by certain vaccines. Money for the compensation comes from a tax on vaccines, and the statute establishes methods that are intended to allow for quick and easy adjudication of claims. A person who accepts an award under this statute is barred from seeking damages in the ordinary tort system. Another federal statute provides compensation to victims of the September 11, 2001 terrorist attacks. Awards under that statute are funded by general revenues rather than a specific tax. Schafer v. American Cyanamid Co. describes many of the important aspects of the vaccine statute in the context of a dispute about whether a loss of consortium suit may be brought under ordinary tort principles when the primary victim of a vaccine-related injury has accepted compensation under the act. The September 11th Victim Compensation Fund of 2001 statute shows how principles related to those applied in the vaccine statute and also in workers' compensation cases were adapted to the context of providing compensation to victims of terrorism.

SCHAFER v. AMERICAN CYANAMID CO.
20 F.3d 1 (1st Cir. 1994)

BREYER, C.J.

The National Childhood Vaccine Injury Act, 42 U.S.C. §§300aa-1 to 300aa-34, provides a special procedure to compensate those who are injured by certain vaccines. The Act bars those who accept an award under that procedure from later bringing a tort suit to obtain additional compensation. The question before us in this appeal . . . is whether the Act also bars the family of such a person from bringing a tort suit to obtain compensation for their own, related, injuries, in particular, for loss of companionship or consortium. Assuming that state law permits such suits, we find nothing in the Act that explicitly or implicitly bars them. And, we affirm the similar determination of the district court.

The National Childhood Vaccine Injury Act represents an effort to provide compensation to those harmed by childhood vaccines outside the framework of traditional tort law. Congress passed the law after hearing testimony 1) describing the critical need for vaccines to protect children from disease, 2) pointing out that vaccines inevitably harm a very small number of the many millions of people who are vaccinated, and 3) expressing dissatisfaction with traditional tort law as a way of compensating those few victims. Injured persons (potential tort plaintiffs) complained about the tort law system's uncertain recoveries, the high cost of litigation, and delays in obtaining compensation. They argued that government had, for all practical purposes, made vaccination obligatory, and thus it had a responsibility to ensure that those injured by vaccines were compensated. Vaccine manufacturers (potential tort defendants) complained about litigation expenses and occasional large recoveries, which caused insurance premiums and vaccine prices to rise, and which ultimately threatened the stability of the vaccine supply.

The Vaccine Act responds to these complaints by creating a remedial system that tries more quickly to deliver compensation to victims, while also reducing insurance and litigation costs for manufacturers. The Act establishes a special claims procedure involving the Court of Federal Claims and special masters (a system that we shall call the "Vaccine Court"). A person injured by a vaccine may file a petition with the Vaccine Court to obtain compensation (from a fund financed by a tax on vaccines). He need not prove fault. Nor, to prove causation, need he show more than that he received the vaccine and then suffered certain symptoms within a defined period of time. The Act specifies amounts of compensation for certain kinds of harm (e.g., $250,000 for death, up to $250,000 for pain and suffering). And, it specifies other types of harm for which compensation may be awarded (e.g., medical expenses, loss of earnings).

At the same time, the Act modifies, but does not eliminate, the traditional tort system, which Congress understood to provide important incentives for the safe manufacture and distribution of vaccines. The Act requires that a person injured directly by a vaccine first bring a Vaccine Court proceeding. Then, it gives that person the choice either to accept the Court's award and abandon his tort rights (which the Act transfers to the federal government), or to reject the judgment and retain his tort rights. He can also keep his tort rights by withdrawing his Vaccine Court petition if the Court moves too slowly.

The Act additionally helps manufacturers by providing certain federal modifica-tions of state tort law. For example, it forbids the award of compensation for injuries that flow from "unavoidable side effects"; it frees the manufacturer from liability for not providing direct warnings to an injured person (or his representative); it imposes a presumption that compliance with Food and Drug Administration requirements means the manufacturer provided proper directions and warnings; it limits punitive damage awards; and it requires that the trial of any tort suit take place in three phases (liability; general damages; punitive damages).

The upshot is a new remedial system that interacts in a complicated way with traditional tort lawsuits.

For present purposes, the relevant facts are simple. Lenita Schafer's small child, Melissa Schafer, received an oral polio vaccine distributed by American Cyanamid in October 1988. Lenita subsequently contracted polio (she and her family think) from Melissa's vaccine. About one year later, in December 1989, all three members of the Schafer family (Lenita, Melissa, and Lenita's husband, Mark) petitioned the Vaccine Court for compensation. In April 1990, Mark and Melissa withdrew their petitions (with permission of the Vaccine Court) and began this lawsuit against American Cyanamid, seeking damages under Massachusetts tort law for loss of Lenita's com-panionship and consortium. Lenita, who did not withdraw her petition, eventually accepted a $750,000 award from the Vaccine Court for her own injuries, thereby giving up her right to bring a tort action. At that point, American Cyanamid asked the district court to dismiss Mark's and Melissa's suit on the ground that Lenita's acceptance of the Vaccine Court award barred not only a later tort action for her own injuries, but also a later tort action by family members for related injuries. The district court denied the motion. We review that denial. . . .

Cyanamid concedes that this case focuses upon Mark's and Melissa's damages, not Lenita's; that Lenita received Vaccine Court compensation for her own damages, not Mark's or Melissa's; and that the Act's language explicitly bars Lenita, but not Mark or Melissa, from bringing a tort action to recover their own damages (which, we specify, will not duplicate Lenita's). Nonetheless, it argues that to permit Mark or Melissa to bring their own tort action (for related damages) would so seriously interfere with the Act's basic purposes that we must read the Act as implicitly barring those actions, just as it explicitly bars Lenita's. [The argument] has two essential elements—an impor-tant federal purpose and a significant state interference. And, we shall try to set forth these two elements of Cyanamid's argument in light of the Act's legislative history, and as persuasively as possible.

First, an important federal purpose of the Act is to free manufacturers from the specter of large, uncertain tort liability, and thereby keep vaccine prices fairly low and keep manufacturers in the market. . . .

Evidence in the hearing record indicated that compensation-related price increases or manufacturer withdrawal would cause serious harm. Vaccines benefit those who are vaccinated, and they have public benefits as well—when parents vac-cinate their own children, they also help stop the spread of a disease that can injure others. And, even though vaccines themselves cause a small number of serious injuries or deaths, their widespread use dramatically reduces fatalities. . . .

The upshot is that, because vaccines benefit so many (and harm so few), even small vaccine price increases, if followed by even a small decline in vaccinations, can cause more public harm through added disease than the sum-total of all the harm vaccines themselves cause through side-effects. For this kind of reason, the argument goes, Congress was importantly motivated not only by the desire effectively to compensate side-effect victims, but also by the desire to keep vaccine prices fairly low by reducing compensation costs.

Second, the availability of a state tort remedy for relatives of a victim interferes with the Act's efforts to lower manufacturers' costs. The Act seeks to achieve its cost-reducing purpose, not by denying compensation to victims (indeed, it imposes a tax upon vaccines in order to fund compensation), but by reducing the litigation and insurance costs related to lengthy, complex tort procedures and random large tort awards. . . .

But, Cyanamid points out, almost every victim has a family. And, almost every vaccine-related injury to a child will adversely affect the life of that family. In Cyanamid's view, if family members can bring a tort suit for loss of say, a child's companionship, even after the child accepts a Vaccine Court award, they will do so.

Cyanamid then says (and this is the most difficult part of Cyanamid's argument) that to permit a victim's family to bring a tort law case — even where the victim obtains a Vaccine Court award — threatens seriously to undermine the Act's "cost-related" advantages. The result will be a system in which manufacturers must pay both the Vaccine Court's easily-obtained compensation awards (through a tax) and also face large tort claims from family members. The latter means the very kind of large occasional tort awards and the kind of litigation costs that Congress hoped to diminish. Cyanamid concludes that the Act implicitly must hold family members to the election of the physically-injured victim. If that victim receives an award and can no longer pursue a court claim, then neither can the victim's family.

Cyanamid's argument is not without force, but ultimately it does not persuade us, either as a matter of statutory interpretation or in terms of pre-emption law. First, one cannot easily interpret the statute as Cyanamid wishes, for the Act has no language at all that one might read as creating a bar to the type of suit before us. To the contrary, the Act subsection that creates the tort action bar says that it does not apply to this kind of lawsuit. The language that creates the bar, §300aa-11(a), says: "no person may bring a civil action for damages" (except in accordance with the Act's Vaccine-Court-related rules) until a Vaccine Court petition "has been filed." It then states specifically that "this subsection" (i.e. the subsection with the tort action bar):

> applies only to a person who has sustained a vaccine-related injury or death and who is qualified to file a petition for compensation under the Program.

42 U.S.C. §300aa-11(a)(9). . . .

Second, the Act's legislative history does not point directly toward the "policy" conclusion that Cyanamid wishes us to draw. The legislative history says nothing at all about family members' tort suits. Its discussion of general purposes, as we have pointed out above . . . indicates two major purposes, namely, providing compensation for victims and maintaining low vaccine costs. How does Cyanamid's argument take account of the "victim compensation" objective? Because the Vaccine Court does not provide a remedy for family members, to accept Cyanamid's argument would require us to conclude that Congress, without anyone saying a word about it, intended to deprive family members of all compensatory remedies. At the same time, the second leg of Cyanamid's argument — the claim that permitting this kind of suit would significantly interfere with Congress's cost control objective — has no specific empirical support in the legislative record; and, the claim does not prove itself. . . .

Third, to accept Cyanamid's argument — that the Schafer family cannot collect both a Vaccine Court award and loss of consortium tort damages — would create judicial inconsistency. The Vaccine Court has held that a parent can both obtain a loss of consortium "award" from a state court (or the settlement of a state law claim) and also obtain compensation for her vaccinated (and injured) child from the Vaccine Court. The Vaccine Court cases all involve families that brought the tort suit first, before the child accepted Vaccine Court compensation. But, it is difficult to find any policy that would justify permitting a family to bring a suit before the Vaccine Court awards compensation to a direct victim, but not after.

. . . Cyanamid's arguments are better made to Congress than to this court. We agree with the district court that the Act, as currently written, does not bar the suit before us. . . . And, its order refusing to dismiss the case, therefore, is Affirmed.

NOTES TO SCHAFER v. AMERICAN CYANAMID CO.

1. *Limitations on Tort Suits.* The Vaccine Injury Act discourages use of the traditional tort system in two main ways: by offering compensation in exchange for a victim's right to bring a suit and by changing the rules that would apply in a suit if a victim did decide to litigate. What limitations on tort suits does the act impose, and how do the limitations alter typical state rules for products liability cases?

2. *Causation.* The statute establishes two methods for showing that a victim's injury was caused by a vaccine. Causation is treated as established if the facts of a victim's case fit the parameters in a Vaccine Injury Table adopted as part of the statute and supplemented later by administrative regulations. The Table lists types of vaccines, types of reactions, and time periods within which those reactions must occur in order for causation to be established. The other method allowed under the statute is the "non-Table" method, under which a victim may introduce evidence to show that a vaccine did cause an injury even though the injury was not manifested within the time periods specified in the Table.

In a case where a victim's death was shown to have been caused both by a vaccine and by a different medical condition unrelated to the vaccine, a court has held that a vaccination is a legal cause of a harm if it is a substantial factor in bringing about the harm and is also a but-for cause of the harm. The court adopted causation principles from the Restatement (Second) of Torts. See Shyface v. Secretary of Health & Human Services, 165 F.3d 1344 (4th Cir. 1999).

SEPTEMBER 11TH VICTIM COMPENSATION FUND OF 2001
Pub. L. No. 107-42 (Sept. 22, 2001)

SEC. 403. PURPOSE

It is the purpose of this title to provide compensation to any individual (or relatives of a deceased individual) who was physically injured or killed as a result of the terrorist-related aircraft crashes of September 11, 2001.

SEC. 404. ADMINISTRATION

(a) In general.— The Attorney General, acting through a Special Master appointed by the Attorney General, shall—

(1) administer the compensation program established under this title[.]

SEC. 405. DETERMINATION OF ELIGIBILITY FOR COMPENSATION

(a) Filing of claim.—

(1) In general.— A claimant may file a claim for compensation under this title with the Special Master. The claim shall be on the form developed under paragraph (2) and shall state the factual basis for eligibility for compensation and the amount of compensation sought.

(b) Review and Determination[.]

(1) Review.— The Special Master shall review a claim submitted under subsection (a) and determine—

(A) whether the claimant is an eligible individual under subsection (c);

(B) With respect to a claimant determined to be an eligible individual—

(i) the extent of the harm to the claimant, including any economic and noneconomic losses; and

(ii) the amount of compensation to which the claimant is entitled based on the harm to the claimant, the facts of the claim, and the individual circumstances of the claimant.

(2) Negligence.— With respect to a claimant, the Special Master shall not consider negligence or any other theory of liability.

(c) Eligibility.—

(1) In general.— A claimant shall be determined to be an eligible individual for purposes of this subsection if the Special Master determines that such claimant—

(A) is an individual described in paragraph (2); and

(B) meets the requirements of paragraph (3).

(2) Individuals.— A claimant is an individual described in this paragraph if the claimant is—

(A) An individual who—

(i) was present at the World Trade Center, (New York, New York), the Pentagon (Arlington, Virginia), or the site of the aircraft crash at Shanksville, Pennsylvania at the time, or in the immediate aftermath, of the terrorist-related aircraft crashes of September 11, 2001; and

(ii) suffered physical harm or death as a result of such an air crash;

(B) an individual who was a member of the flight crew or a passenger on American Airlines flight 11 or 77 or United Airlines flight 93 or 175, except that an individual identified by the Attorney General to have been a participant or conspirator in the terrorist-related aircraft crashes of September 11, 2001, or a representative of such individual shall not be eligible to receive compensation under this title; or

(C) in the case of a decedent who is an individual described in subparagraph (A) or (B), the personal representative of the decedent who files a claim on behalf of the decedent. . . .

(3) Requirements. —
    (A) Single claim. — Not more than one claim may be submitted under this title by an individual or on behalf of a deceased individual.
    (B) Limitation on civil action. —
        (i) In general. — Upon the submission of a claim under this title, the claimant waives the right to file a civil action (or to be a party to an action) in any Federal or State court for damages sustained as a result of the terrorist-related aircraft crashes of September 11, 2001. The preceding sentence does not apply to a civil action to recover collateral source obligations, or to a civil action against any person who is a knowing participant in any conspiracy to hijack any aircraft or commit any terrorist act.
        (ii) Pending actions. — In the case of an individual who is a party to a civil action described in clause (i), such individual may not submit a claim under this title unless such individual withdraws from such action by the date that is 90 days after the date on which regulations are promulgated under section 407.

NOTES TO SEPTEMBER 11TH VICTIM COMPENSATION FUND STATUTE

1. *Elements of Compensation Fund Statutes.* Compensation fund statutes define those eligible for compensation, typically require recipients to forgo compensation that might otherwise have been available, and establish procedures for making awards. How does the September 11th Victim Compensation Fund Statute treat each of these elements?

2. *Findings of Fact.* The statute requires determinations of (1) whether an individual was injured in one of the terrorist-related air crashes, and (2) what economic and non-economic losses that injury caused. The first of these determinations is likely to be straightforward. What complications might be related to the second determination?

TABLE OF CASES

Principal cases are indicated by italics.

TABLE OF STATUTES AND OTHER AUTHORITIES

UNIFORM ACTS

Uniform Commercial Code

RESTATEMENT (THIRD) OF TORTS: PRODUCTS LIABILITY

Uniform Comparative Fault Act

Uniform Contribution Among Tortfeasors Act

INDEX